THE
LEXINGTON
READER

THE LEXINGTON READER

LYNN Z. BLOOM

Virginia Commonwealth University

D. C. HEATH AND COMPANY

Lexington, Massachusetts

Toronto

Credits

Cover: "The Midnight Ride of Paul Revere" (1931) by Grant Wood. Estate of Grant Wood/ V.A.G.A., New York/The Metropolitan Museum of Art, Arthur Hoppock Hearn Fund, 1950. *Title-page illustration:* Minuteman statue in Lexington, Massachusetts, drawn by Dorothea Sierra, copyright © 1987 by D. C. Heath and Company. *Photos,* pages 6–15: Stan Grossfeld/*The Boston Globe.*

Published simultaneously in Canada.

Printed in the United States of America.

International Standard Book Number: 0-669-09558-3

Library of Congress Catalog Card Number: 86-80488

ACKNOWLEDGMENTS

James Agee, "Comedy's Greatest Era." Reprinted by permission of Grosset & Dunlap from *Agee on Film*, Volume One, by James Agee, Copyright © 1958 by The James Agee Trust.

Woody Allen, "Selections from the Allen Notebooks" and "The Whore of Mensa." Copyright © 1973 by Woody Allen. Reprinted from *Without Feathers*, by Woody Allen, by permission of Random House, Inc. and Woody Allen.

Judith Appelbaum and Nancy Evans, "Procedures, or How to Submit Your Manuscript," abridged from *How to Get Happily Published*. Copyright © 1978 by Judith Appelbaum and Nancy Evans. Reprinted by permission of Harper & Row, Publishers, Inc.

Philippe Aries, "The Reversal of Death: Changes in Attitude Toward Death in Western Societies," from *Death in America*, David E. Stannard, ed., University of Pennsylvania Press, 1974. Copyright 1974, American Studies Association.

Russell Baker, "Universal Military Motion," from *The New York Times*, April 4, 1981. Copyright © 1981 by The New York Times Company. Reprinted by permission.

James Baldwin, "Faulkner and Desegregation," copyright © 1956 by James Baldwin, from *Nobody Knows My Name*. Reprinted by permission of Doubleday & Company, Inc.

Charles L. Barber, "The Origin of Language," from *The Story of Speech and Language*. Originally published by Thomas Y. Crowell. Copyright © 1964 by Charles Barber. Reprinted by permission of Harper & Row, Publishers, Inc., and Pan Books, Ltd.

Carl Bernstein and Bob Woodward, "Uncovering Deception: How Investigative Reporters Work," from *All The President's Men*. Copyright © 1974 by Carl Bernstein and Bob Woodward. Reprinted by permission of Simon & Schuster, Inc.

Henry Beston, "The Headlong Wave," from *The Outermost House*. Copyright 1928, 1949, © 1956 by Henry Beston. Copyright © 1977 by Elizabeth C. Beston. Reprinted by permission of Henry Holt and Company, Inc.

Laird Bloom, "Methods of Pest Control Using Insect Pheromones." Reprinted by permission.

Lynn Z. Bloom, "How to Submit Writing for Publication," from *Fact and Artifact*. Copyright © 1985 by Harcourt Brace Jovanovich, Inc. Reprinted by permission of the publisher.

Sissela Bok, "Placebos," from *Lying: Moral Choice in Public and Private Life*. Copyright © 1978 by Sissela Bok. Reprinted by permission of Pantheon Books, a division of Random House, Inc.

Jane Brody, "Stress: Some Good, Some Bad," from *The New York Times*, August 26, 1981. Copyright © 1981 by The New York Times Company. Reprinted by permission.

Phyllis C. Richman, "Richman on Restaurants: Hunan Dynasty," from *The Washington Post*, January 6, 1985. Reprinted by permission of *The Washington Post*.

Robert Christgau, "Beth Ann and Macrobioticism," from the New York *Herald Tribune*, 1966. Copyright © 1966 I. H. T. Corporation. Reprinted by permission.

Robert Coles, "Two Languages, One Soul," from *The Old Ones of New Mexico*. Copyright © 1973 by Robert Coles. Published by the University of New Mexico Press.

Bob Considine, "Louis Knocks Out Schmeling," from *Press Box: Red Smith's Favorite Sports*

Stories, 1976, W. W. Norton. Reprinted with special permission of King Features Syndicate, Inc.

Norman Cousins, "The Right to Die," from *Saturday Review,* June 14, 1975. Copyright © 1975 *Saturday Review* magazine. Reprinted by permission.

Gwyneth Cravens, "The M & J Sanitary Tortilla Factory." Reprinted by permission; © 1984 by Gwyneth Cravens. Originally published in *The New Yorker* magazine.

Joan Didion, "Marrying Absurd," from *Slouching Towards Bethlehem* by Joan Didion. Copyright © 1966, 1967, 1968 by Joan Didion. Reprinted by permission of Farrar, Straus and Giroux, Inc. "Why I Write" copyright © 1976 by Joan Didion. First appeared in *The New York Times* Book Review. Reprinted by permission of Wallace & Sheil Agency, Inc.

William Faulkner, "The American Dream." Copyright © 1955 by William Faulkner. Reprinted from *Essays, Speeches and Public Letters by William Faulkner,* edited by James B. Meriwether, by permission of Random House, Inc.

M. F. K. Fisher, "Bar Cookies," from *With Bold Knife and Fork.* Copyright © 1968, 1969 by M. F. K. Fisher. Reprinted with permission of The Putnam Publishing Group.

Colin Fletcher, "Fires," from *The Complete Walker: The Joys and Techniques of Hiking and Backpacking,* by Colin Fletcher, illustrated by Vanna Franks. Copyright © 1968 by Colin Fletcher. Reprinted by permission of Alfred A. Knopf, Inc.

Paul Fussell, text from *The Boy Scout Handbook and Other Observations.* Copyright © 1982 by Paul Fussell. Reprinted by permission of Oxford University Press, Inc.

John Kenneth Galbraith, "Writing and Typing," ("Writing, Typing and Economics") from *Annals of an Abiding Liberal.* Copyright © 1979 by John Kenneth Galbraith. Reprinted by permission of Houghton Mifflin Company.

Joan K. Galway, "Monumental Work with Thanks to No One," from *The Washington Post,* Nov. 10, 1985. Reprinted by permission of Joan K. Galway.

Euell Gibbons, "Dandelions, The Official Remedy for Disorders," from *Stalking the Wild Asparagus.* Copyright © 1962. Reprinted by permission of David McKay Company, Inc.

Ellen Goodman, "Mother Teresa and Her Endless Fight," from *At Large.* Copyright © 1981 by The Washington Post Company. Reprinted by permission of Summit Books, a division of Simon & Schuster, Inc.

Stephen Jay Gould, "Racism and Recapitulation," from *Ever Since Darwin, Reflections in Natural History,* by permission of W. W. Norton & Company, Inc. Copyright © 1977 by Stephen Jay Gould. Copyright © 1973, 1974, 1975, 1976, 1977 by The American Museum of Natural History.

J. B. S. Haldane, from "On Being the Right Size" in *Possible Worlds & Other Essays.* Copyright 1928 by Harper & Row, Publishers, Inc. Renewed by J. B. S. Haldane. Reprinted by permission of Harper & Row, Publishers, Inc. and Chatto & Windus, Ltd.

Dianne and Robert Hales, "Exercising the Psyche," from *American Health Magazine,* June 5, 1985. Reprinted by permission of Dianne and Robert Hales, M. D.

Robert Half, "Coming Out on Top in the Job Interview," from *The Robert Half Way to Get Hired in Today's Job Market.* Copyright © 1981 by Robert Half. Reprinted with the permission of Rawson Associates.

Edward T. Hall, "Time Talks," from *The Silent Language.* Copyright © 1959 by Edward T. Hall. Reprinted by permission of Doubleday & Company, Inc.

Maida Heatter, "Brownies," from *Maida Heatter's Book of Great Chocolate Desserts.* Copyright © 1980 by Maida Heatter. Reprinted by permission of Alfred A. Knopf, Inc.

Jerome Holtzman, "I'd Like to Be Called a Good Reporter," from *The Red Smith Reader,* Dave Anderson, editor. Random House, 1982. Reprinted by permission of Jerome Holtzman.

Alfred Kazin, "Brownsville: The Kitchen" from *A Walker in the City,* copyright 1951, 1979 by Alfred Kazin. Reprinted by permission of Harcourt Brace Jovanovich, Inc.

Evelyn Fox Keller, "Barbara McClintock: A Feeling for the Organism," from *A Feeling for the Organism: The Life and Work of Barbara McClintock.* W. H. Freeman Company. Copyright © 1983.

Acknowledgments

Michael Kernan, "Bard Times at the Folger Theater," from *The Washington Post,* April 24, 1980. Reprinted by permission of *The Washington Post.*

Dave Kindred, "Smile, Rosie, and Give Them a Run for the Money," from "This Morning: The Challenges," from *The Washington Post,* April 24, 1980. Reprinted by permission of *The Washington Post.*

Martin Luther King, Jr., "Letter from Birmingham Jail—April 16, 1963" from *Why We Can't Wait.* Copyright © 1963 by Martin Luther King, Jr. Reprinted by permission of Harper & Row, Publishers, Inc.

Maxine Hong Kingston, "Uneasy Status: From Renter to Homeowner" ("Hers"), copyright © 1978 by Maxine Hong Kingston. Reprinted by permission of John Schaffner Associates, Inc.

Philip Kopper, "The Stark Simplicity of the Delmarva Coast," from *The Washington Post,* Jan. 6, 1985. Reprinted by permission of Philip Kopper.

Thomas S. Kuhn, "The Route to Normal Science," from *The Structure of Scientific Revolutions.* Copyright © 1962, 1970 by the University of Chicago Press. Reprinted by permission of the publisher.

Stanley Kunitz, "Swimming in Lake Chauggogagogmanchauggagogchabunagungamaugg," from *A Kind of Order, a Kind of Folly: Essays and Conversations.* Copyright © 1966 by Stanley Kunitz. By permission of Little, Brown and Company, in association with The Atlantic Monthly Press.

Robin Lakoff, "You Are What You Say." Originally in *Ms.* magazine. Reprinted with permission of Robin Lakoff.

Mary B. Langenberg, "Interview with Alfred Everett" and "East St. Louis, from Blues to Dirge." Reprinted by permission.

Susanne K. Langer, "Signs and Symbols," from "The Lord of Creation" in *Fortune,* January 1944. Courtesy of *Fortune* Magazine; © 1944 Time, Inc.

Margaret Laurence, from "Where the World Began," from *Heart of a Stranger.* Used by permission of the Canadian publishers, McClelland and Stewart Limited, Toronto.

D. H. Lawrence, "Benjamin Franklin," from *Studies in Classic American Literature.* Copyright © by Thomas Seltzer, Inc., renewed 1950 by Frieda Lawrence. Copyright © 1961 by The Estate of the late Frieda Lawrence. Reprinted by permission of Viking Penguin, Inc.

John Leonard, "The Only Child" and "My Son, the Roman," from *Private Lives in the Imperial City* by John Leonard. Published by Alfred A. Knopf, 1976, 1979.

Barry Lopez, "My Horse." Reprinted with permission from *The North American Review.* Copyright © 1975 by the University of Northern Iowa.

Alison Lurie, "Clothing as a Sign System" from *The Language of Clothes.* Copyright © 1981 by Alison Lurie. Reprinted by permission of Alfred A. Knopf, Inc.

Gerald Mast, "Comic Plots and Comic Climate," from *The Comic Mind: Comedy and the Movies.* Copyright © 1973. Reprinted by permission of The University of Chicago Press.

Mary McCarthy, "Uncle Myers" (from "The Tin Butterfly"), from *Memories of a Catholic Girlhood.* Copyright 1951, 1979 by Mary McCarthy. Reprinted by permission of Harcourt Brace Jovanovich, Inc. First published in *The New Yorker.*

John McPhee, "Family Doctors," from *Heirs of General Practice.* Copyright © 1984 by John McPhee. "The Pine Barrens" from "The Woods from Hog Wallow" from *The Pine Barrens.* Copyright © 1967, 1968 by John McPhee. Reprinted by permission of Farrar, Straus and Giroux, Inc.

Peter A McWilliams, "Word Processing for Writers," from *The Word Processing Book: A Short Course in Computer Literacy.* Prelude Press, 1983. Reprinted by permission of the author.

Eugene L. Meyer, "Mr. L. G. Broadmoore and the Way It Was," from *The Washington Post,* August 9, 1974. Reprinted by permission of *The Washington Post.*

Henry Mitchell, "Eudora Welty: Storyteller of the South," from *The Washington Post,* August 13, 1972. Reprinted by permission of *The Washington Post.*

Jessica Mitford, "Let Us Now Appraise Famous Writers" (abridged), from *Atlantic Monthly,* July 1970. Reprinted by permission of the author and the author's agents, Scott Meredith Literary Agency, Inc., 845 Third Avenue, New York, New York 10022.

James Morris, "The Venetian Way," from *The World of Venice,* Copyright © 1960, 1974 by James Morris. Reprinted by permission of Harcourt Brace Jovanovich, Inc., and Faber and Faber Ltd.

Jan Morris, "Manhattan: The Islanders," from *Destinations: Essays from Rolling Stone.* Copyright © 1980 by Rolling Stone Press and Jan Morris. Reprinted by permission of Oxford University Press, Inc.

Donald M. Murray, "The Maker's Eye: Revising Your Own Manuscripts." Copyright © 1973 by Donald M. Murray. Reprinted by permission of Roberta Pryor, Inc.

George Orwell, "Shooting an Elephant" and "Politics and the English Language," from *Shooting an Elephant and Other Essays.*" Copyright 1950 by Sonia Brownell Orwell; renewed 1978 by Sonia Pitt-Rivers. "Marrakech" and "Why I Write," from *Such, Such Were the Joys.* Copyright 1953 by Sonia Brownell Orwell; renewed 1981 by Mrs. George K. Perutz, Mrs. Miriam Gross, Dr. Michael Dickson, Executors of the Estate of Sonia Brownell Orwell. Reprinted by permission of Harcourt Brace Jovanovich, Inc., A. M. Heath & Company Ltd. and the estate of the late Sonia Brownell Orwell and Martin Secker & Warburg Ltd.

Dorothy Parker, "The Grandmother of the Aunt of the Gardener," from *The Portable Dorothy Parker.* Copyright © 1970 by The Viking Press, Inc. Originally published in *The New Yorker.* Copyright 1931, renewed © 1959 by The New Yorker Magazine, Inc.

Tim Payne, "On the Beach at Bar Harbor" and "A Personal Note on Tone." Reprinted by permission.

S. J. Perelman, "The Machismo Mystique," from *Vinegar Puss,* 1942, 1975, published by Simon & Schuster. Reprinted by permission of Abby and Adam Perelman, heirs of S. J. Perelman.

Noel Perrin, "Buying a Pickup Truck," from *First Person Plural: Essays of a Sometime Farmer.* Copyright © 1978 by Noel Perrin. Reprinted by permission of David R. Godine, Publisher, Inc.

Sylvia Porter, "Rules for Writing and Endorsing Checks," from *Sylvia Porter's New Money Book for the 80's.* Copyright © 1975, 1979 by Sylvia Porter. Reprinted by permission of Doubleday & Company, Inc.

Sally Quinn, "Alice Roosevelt Longworth at 90," from *The Washington Post,* February 12, 1974. Reprinted by permission of *The Washington Post.*

Richard Rodriguez, "Affirmative Action and Minority Status," from *Hunger of Memory.* Copyright © 1981 by Richard Rodriguez. Reprinted by permission of David R. Godine, Publisher, Inc.

Irma Rombauer (with Marion Rombauer-Becker), "Brownies Cockaigne," from *The Joy of Cooking.* Copyright © 1931, 1936, 1941, 1942, 1943, 1946, 1951, 1952, 1953, 1962, 1963, 1964, 1975 by Macmillan Publishing Company. Reprinted by permission of Macmillan Publishing Company.

Lillian Ross, "The Yellow Bus," from *Reporting* (Simon & Schuster). © 1960 Lillian Ross. Originally published in *The New Yorker* magazine.

Berton Roueché, "Annals of Medicine: A Contemporary Touch," from *The Medical Detectives,* Vol. II. Reprinted by permission of Harold Ober Associates. Copyright © 1982 by Berton Roueché. Originally published in *The New Yorker* magazine.

Mary Ruffin, "Mama's Smoke." Reprinted by permission.

Bertrand Russell, "What Is Matter?" from *The ABC of Relativity.* Reprinted by permission of Allen & Unwin (Publishers) Ltd.

Carl Sagan, "The Nuclear Winter." Reprinted by permission from a report from the Council for a Livable World.

Harold Schonberg, "Why a Critic Follows the Score," from *Facing the Music.* Copyright © 1981 by Harold C. Schonberg. Reprinted by permission of Summit Books, a division of Simon & Schuster, Inc.

Acknowledgments

Thomas Sebeok (with Jean Umiker-Sebeok), "Performing Animals: Secrets of the Trade." Reprinted with permission from *Psychology Today* magazine. Copyright © 1979 American Psychological Association.

Kelly Shea, "Acid Rain." Reprinted by permission.

John Simon, "Hamlet." Copyright © 1963 by John Simon. Reprinted from *Uneasy Stages: A Chronicle of New York Theater, 1963–1973,* by John Simon, by permission of Random House, Inc.

Kate Simon, "New York Luncheonettes," from *New York Places and Pleasures,* 4th edition. Copyright © 1971 by Kate Simon. Reprinted by permission of Harper & Row, Publishers, Inc.

Red Smith, "Good Ol' Boy Woody Hayes." Copyright © 1979 by Walter W. Smith. "I'd Like to Be Called a Good Reporter." Copyright © 1982 by Walter W. Smith. Reprinted from *The Red Smith Reader,* edited by Dave Anderson, by permission of Random House, Inc.

Craig Swanson, "It's the Only Video Game My Mom Lets Me Chew." Reprinted by permission.

Frank Sullivan, "The Cliché Expert Testifies as a Literary Critic," from *Sullivan at Bay* by Frank Sullivan. Originally published by J. H. Dent, London; reprinted in *Well, There's No Harm in Laughing,* published by Doubleday, 1972.

Studs Terkel, "Miss U.S.A., Emma Knight," from *American Dreams: Lost and Found.* Copyright © 1980 by Studs Terkel. Reprinted by permission of Pantheon Books, a division of Random House, Inc.

Paul Theroux, "The Journey, not the Arrival, Matters," from *The Old Patagonian Express.* Copyright © 1979 by Cape Cod Scriveners Company. Reprinted by permission of Houghton Mifflin Company.

Lewis Thomas, "A Fear of Pheromones" and "The Long Habit," from *The Lives of a Cell.* Copyright © 1971, 1972 by the Massachusetts Medical Society. Originally published in *The New England Journal of Medicine.* Reprinted by permission of Viking Penguin, Inc.

Bob Thompson, "California: An Overview," from *The American Express Pocket Guide to California.* Copyright © 1983 by Mitchell Beazley Publishers. Reprinted by permission of the publisher Simon and Schuster Inc., New York, N.Y.

James Thurber, "The Night the Bed Fell," from *My Life and Hard Times* published by Harper & Row. Copyright © 1933, 1961 James Thurber. "The Unicorn in the Garden," from *Fables For Our Time* published by Harper & Row. Copyright © 1940 James Thurber. Copyright © 1968 Helen W. Thurber. Both published by permission of Helen W. Thurber.

Calvin Trillin, "Eating in Cincinnati," from *American Fried.* Copyright © 1974 by Calvin Trillin, first appeared in *The New Yorker* magazine. Reprinted by permission of Doubleday & Company, Inc.

John R. Trimble, "Write to Be Read," from *Writing with Style: Conversations on the Art of Writing,* © 1975. Reprinted by permission of Prentice-Hall, Englewood Cliffs, New Jersey.

Mark Twain, "Uncle John's Farm," abridged from pp. 95–113 in *Mark Twain's Autobiography,* Volume I. Copyright 1924, 1952 by Clara Clemens Samosoud. Reprinted by permission of Harper & Row, Publishers, Inc.

John Updike, "Hub Fans Bid Kid Adieu." Copyright © 1960 by John Updike. Reprinted from *Assorted Prose* by permission of Alfred A. Knopf, Inc. Originally appeared in *The New Yorker* magazine.

William W. Warner, "Beautiful Swimmers," from *Beautiful Swimmers: Watermen, Crabs and the Chesapeake Bay* by William W. Warner. Copyright © 1976 by William W. Warner. Reprinted by permission of Little, Brown and Company in association with The Atlantic Monthly Press.

Eudora Welty, "E. B. White's *Charlotte's Web,*" as published in *The New York Times.* Copyright © 1952, renewed 1980 by Eudora Welty. Reprinted by permission of Russell & Volkening, Inc. as agents for the author.

Acknowledgments

PREFACE

E. B. White, essayist *par excellence,* says of his art: "The essayist is a self-liberated man, sustained by the childish belief that everything he thinks about, everything that happens to him, is of general interest. He is a fellow who thoroughly enjoys his work, just as people who take bird walks enjoy theirs. Each new excursion of the essayist, each new 'attempt,' differs from the last and takes him into new country. This delights him. Only a person who is congenitally self-centered has the effrontery and the stamina to write essays." White has captured the essence of the writers in *The Lexington Reader*—its title a reinforcement of the self-liberating activities initiated by the Minutemen's "shot heard 'round the world" at Lexington and Concord, Massachusetts, in 1776. They delight in their work; they believe, rightly or wrongly, that whatever they experience or think about is of course of consuming interest to others; they expect to make a memorable impression on their readers. Joan Didion reinforces White's views from a more assertive stance: "In many ways writing is the act of saying *I,* of imposing oneself upon other people, of saying *listen to me, see it my way, change your mind.*"

White continues, "There are as many kinds of essays as there are human attitudes or poses, as many essay flavors as there are Howard Johnson ice creams. The essayist arises in the morning and . . . selects his garb from an unusually extensive wardrobe: he can pull on any sort of shirt, be any sort of person, according to his mood or his subject matter—philosopher, scold, jester, raconteur, confidant, pundit, devil's advocate, enthusiast." The essays in *The Lexington Reader* have been chosen to reveal writers of essays in their many voices, many modes—shirts of many colors and fashions. It is my hope that the texts of the essays themselves, and the related material about the author's life, as well as about the particular work, the study questions, and strategies and suggestions for writing will enable students and their teachers to recognize in published essays elements and processes they can use in writing essays of their own.

The 122 essays in *The Lexington Reader* are drawn from many sources, particularly the most distinguished and distinctive contemporary writing about people, places, humanities and the arts, controversy, science and the social sciences, how-to, humor, and the phenomenon of writing itself. There is a leavening of classics by such authors as Swift, Franklin, and Thoreau, whose ideas and style remain as fresh and provocative today as when they were written. Of particular importance are a dozen essays by undergraduate college students, which provide not only discussions of interesting subjects (the numbing effect of video games, East St. Louis in the Roaring Twenties, the causes and cures of acid rain, the use of pheromones to control insect pests) but also models of style and particular types of writing that other students can emulate. This blend of essays by professional writers and people in other disciplines—scientists, physicians, social analysts, film and drama critics, business executives, humorists, travelers, cooks (and eaters), among others—majority and minority authors, men and women, provides a realistic representation of engaging, witty, and elegant writing of current interest.

It's unfortunate that a word more compelling than *nonfiction* has yet to be coined to convey the excitement, variety, and distinction of works that one critic has called "the literature of fact"—writing based on truth and verifiable evidence. Indeed, one of the major aims of *The Lexington Reader* is to demonstrate the versatility and stylistic finesse of which nonfiction writers are capable. Like writers of fiction, nonfiction writers shape their material into many forms that follow particular literary conventions, presenting reviews, how-to writings, investigative reporting, parodies, and other modes with great imagination and flexibility.

Like writers of fiction, nonfiction writers present characters, but these characters are real flesh and blood. Who could forget Henry Mitchell's talented but down-to-earth Eudora Welty, Sally Quinn's feisty Alice Roosevelt Longworth at 90, or Eugene Meyer's principled but anachronistic L. G. Broadmoore—all very real and extraordinarily memorable people? Like writers of fiction, nonfiction writers transport us to distinctive settings, whether John McPhee's sparsely beautiful New Jersey Pine Barrens, Tim Payne's foreboding beach at Bar Harbor, or glimpses of New York as seen by tourist Jan Morris, luncheonette habitué Kate Simon, or ghetto native Alfred Kazin.

Nonfiction writers, like writers of fiction, thrive on the cadences of people talking, whether in the brisk dialogue of sculptor Louise Nevelson, the cynical overtones of a former Miss U.S.A., or the deadpan narration of James Thurber as a calm obligato to his family's pandemonium. Nonfiction writers, too, set scenes: Mark Twain as a child, basking in the abundance of Uncle John's nurturing farm; Thoreau as an independent young man, philosophizing at provocative Walden; Maxine Hong Kingston as an established writer, proud but uneasy in her new home. Nonfiction writers provide action, and interaction, to make their points in the form of structured vignettes or more sustained activity. Joan Didion offers candid snapshots of Las Vegas weddings; George Orwell presents "Marrakech," with glimpses of hungry, forgotten, and oppressed natives, ignored by their white rulers; E. B. White unwinds a slow motion movie of the long, sweet sighs and sights of summertime, "oh summertime," at an immortal lake in Maine.

A distinctive style, as individual as a fingerprint, is as characteristic of the writer of nonfiction as it is of the fiction writer. We know Woody Allen by his neurotic but hilarious non sequiturs: "While taking my noon walk today, I had more morbid thoughts. What *is* it about death that bothers me so much? Probably the hours." We experience, in the hard-hitting style of Bob Considine, the sportswriter's ringside punch: "Listen to this, buddy, for it comes from a guy whose palms are still wet, whose throat is still dry, and whose jaw is still agape from the utter shock of watching Joe Louis knock out Max Schmeling. It was a shocking thing, that knockout—short, sharp, merciless, complete." We acknowledge the measured elegance of Virginia Woolf, with her revealing, female metaphors: "But who, then, is the desirable man—the patron who will cajole the best out of the writer's brain and bring to birth the most varied and vigorous progeny of which he is capable?" And we recognize in the rhetoric of Martin Luther King, Jr., the rhetoric of the pulpit, in which he was nurtured: "Was not Jesus an extremist for love: 'Love your enemies, bless them that curse you. . . .' Was not Amos an extremist for justice: 'Let justice roll down like waters.' . . .' Was not Paul an extremist for the Christian gospel: 'I bear in my body the marks of the Lord Jesus.' "

Nonfiction is an art, for nonfiction writers construct artifacts of the facts and figures that form the basis of their work. The writers of nonfiction, then, are artists, as justifiably proud of their craft and as troubled by the problems in "getting the words right" as Hemingway ever was when he rewrote the ending of *A Farewell to Arms,* he claimed, "thirty-nine times." It is to provide an understanding of that art, and of its manifestation in writing, that these distinctive selections have been included in *The Lexington Reader.* The essays vary in length from one to twenty pages, though most are between three and seven pages. They range in difficulty from easily accessible to rather complicated. They have been arranged to demonstrate various ways of writing about familiar topics—people, places, performances, controversy, science, how-to, and humor; the alternative Rhetorical Table of Contents indicates rhetorical groupings, and the Index is arranged alphabetically by author. Chapter One, "Writing About Writing," deals with matters crucial to the writing process—why and how writers write, how they develop a style (and how readers can develop styles of their own), and how they revise, including three versions of Richard Wright's revised (and re-revised) "Interview Comments on *Black Boy,*" and two student papers—Teresa Whitlock's original and revised versions of her essay, "My 'Professional' Hairstyle," and Mary Langenberg's "Interview with Alfred Everett" and the resulting essay, "East St. Louis, from Blues to Dirge."

The introductions to each of the chapters define the particular type of writing under discussion by identifying its conspicuous characteristics, its purposes and uses, its characteristic forms and subjects. The consistent focus of *The Lexington Reader* on writing processes includes discussions of the rhetorical strategies an author can use to effect the purposes of each type, illustrated with references to the selections that follow. These rhetorical strategies are summarized at the end of each chapter in a checklist of questions to guide student writers as they try to create their own versions of a particular type of essay. The checklists are followed by suggested writing topics especially appropriate for each type. For example, Chapter Four, "Writing About Controversy," offers strategies for writing direct and implied arguments, narratives with arguments, and articles based on investigative reporting. Among the essay topics suggested is a paper arguing against discrimination, modeled after one or another of the essays by James Baldwin, Martin Luther King, Jr., George Orwell, or Richard Rodriguez, that is included in that chapter.

The introduction and study questions for each individual essay are designed to help students focus on several salient aspects of the writing situation. The introduction to each essay provides a brief biography of the author, and identifies his or her major professional and literary works, examined from the perspective of what in the author's life or work contributed to the writing of this essay. It also indicates the principal features and distinctive characteristics of the essay in question, and—when the information is available—the author's statement on why and how he or she wrote it. The commentary on the essay itself (reinforced by study questions for selected essays) focuses on the type of essay it is and the audience for which it is intended. This introductory commentary also considers the rhetorical strategies and techniques (such as organization, emphasis, level and type of language, tone, choice of illustrations) the author uses to accomplish his or her aims. The Glossary on 807–24 explains basic terminology to aid in analyzing the essays, by oneself or in class discussion. All footnotes are by the essay authors.

The Lexington Reader also includes a remarkable collection of photographs by Pulitzer Prize–winning photographer Stan Grossfeld. These pictures, no matter what their subject—news, human interest, or scenes of everyday life—demonstrate not only Grossfeld's artistry but his great respect for his subject, medium, and audience. His accompanying philosophy of composition explains the interrelation of assignment, medium, technique, and artistry—a process in the visual medium analogous to the writing process.

The Lexington Reader has, in various ways, been in progress for the past quarter-century. I am particularly indebted to the candid commentaries of multitudes of writing students over the years, whose preferences and perplexities have so significantly influenced both the shape and emphasis of this volume, particularly its process-oriented approach to the subject. I am likewise grateful for the thoughtful suggestions of writing teachers throughout the country who have commented on various versions of *The Lexington Reader:* Jay Balderson, Western Illinois University; Don Cox, University of Tennessee; Lisa Ede, Oregon State University; Carol Hartzog, University of California—Los Angeles; Michael Johnson, University of Kansas; Nan Johnson, University of British Columbia; Linda Peterson, Yale University; and Barbara Stout, Montgomery County Community College.

Special thanks are due to the students who contributed to this volume not only their essays but comments on how they wrote them: Mary Langenberg, Washington University; Tim Payne, University of Virginia; Kelly Shea, Ken Wunderlich, Raymond Williams, and Jennifer M. Young, the College of William and Mary; Mary Ruffin, Craig Swanson, and Teresa Whitlock, Virginia Commonwealth University; and Laird Bloom, Cambridge University and Massachusetts Institute of Technology. J. Reynolds Kinzey, of Virginia Commonwealth University, himself an experienced college writing teacher, was a capable research assistant, abetted by Susan Orton, Harvard University, and Barbara Orton, Washington University. The editorial process has been conducted under the thoughtful and cheerful care of Paul Smith, Holt Johnson, and Bryan Woodhouse. My husband, Martin Bloom, has remained my best critic and best friend during the many trial runs—and occasional trials— of *The Lexington Reader*. To him I am grateful not only for his good sense and sensibility during this as during all of our writing endeavors but also for the many invaluable suggestions offered during the lap swimming that punctuates the writing of our books (he writes as much as I do). He always makes them better.

L.Z.B.

CONTENTS

Contents

Style and Language

Revising

CHAPTER TWO
Writing About People   107

Interviews

CHAPTER THREE
Writing About Places 197
Description

Narration

CHAPTER FOUR
Writing About Controversy   291
Direct Argument

Contents

Narrative with Argument, Implied and Direct

Contents

CHAPTER SIX
Humorous Writing   493
Social Criticism

Contents

Contents

CHAPTER SEVEN
How-To-Do-It Writing 571
The Right Stuff: Choosing and Using Equipment

Contents

Food/Cooking

CHAPTER EIGHT
Writing About the Social and Physical Sciences   663
Scientific Frameworks

Styles of Scientific Investigation

Contents

Contents

Ethical and Social Issues in Science

RHETORICAL
TABLE OF CONTENTS

Determining Ideas in a Sequence

Narration

Process Analysis

Analysis (including considerations of Cause and Effect)

Clarifying Ideas

Description

Definition

Division and Classification

Illustration and Example

Comparison and Contrast

Arguments and Explanations, Direct and Indirect

Appeals to Reason: Deductive Arguments

Appeals to Reason: Inductive Arguments and Explanations

Appeals to Emotion and Ethics

Literary Forms

Autobiography

Biography, Portrait, Character Sketch

Interview

Letters

Reviews

THE
LEXINGTON
READER

STAN GROSSFELD

An Interview and
Photo Essay

Grossfeld, Director of Photography for The Boston Globe, *has received numerous awards for his photography since joining the* Globe *in 1975. Among the most recent are Pulitzer Prizes in 1984 and 1985 for his work in Ethiopia, Lebanon, and at the United States-Mexican border, examples of which are included on pages 10, 11, 12, and 14. In addition to being chosen as New England Photographer of the Year five different times, and as a finalist in NASA's Journalist in Space program, Grossfeld won two Overseas Press Club Awards, for best photographic reporting from abroad, and for "human compassion" for his Ethiopian photographs.*

Grossfeld earned an M.S. in 1980 from Boston University's School of Public Communication. He is the author of Nantucket: The Other Season *(1982) and editor of* The Eyes of the Globe *(1985). Although his photographs speak for themselves, he recently discussed his art with Paul Smith, College English Editor at D. C. Heath, in the interview recorded here.*

SMITH: *Can you talk about what you have to consider when you're given a specific assignment, in contrast to how you go about freelancing, or doing what you want?*
GROSSFELD: Sure. Photography's not as easy as it looks. It's not just the moment of taking the picture. A lot of research, a lot of planning go on before you even leave the office, and that's very important. Photographers, like reporters, have to be familiar with their subject. For example, in news you'd better know who's who, so that you won't get manipulated or otherwise get yourself in trouble. I use library sources and pull the [newspaper] clips to see what's already been written on the subject. If it's an interview of a famous person, I like to be familiar with their work so I can talk to them. This will make better pictures because they'll be able to relax. If it's a big news event, I'd better know what's going on, because it might save my life. Generally I'm not dealing with a studio but with the real world where sometimes my preconceived ideas don't work. I have to be able to accept that and adapt quickly to something else.
SMITH: *Can you give an example?*
GROSSFELD: Suppose you think there's going to be a great angle, say, of marchers—I.R.A. people carrying Bobby Sands's coffin down a hill, the hill

I

being a good angle because it lets you get a large mass of people in one frame. The police may not let you go down, or you may have to get off of whatever you're standing on to shoot the scene, or the marchers may change course. So you need to have alternate plans, and an open mind.

SMITH: *Where do you get your ideas? How do you work to develop them, since you may have to do so on the spur of the moment?*

GROSSFELD: On the wild art—sometimes people call it wild art, sometimes they call it features—you roam around and try to get something interesting. That's a lot of fun, but it's also a roll of the dice. There are some days when great things happen in front of you. They're gifts. Then there are other days when you can ride or walk around for hours and have trouble finding anything that's really different. That's what we look for, something different, not things that have been done and overdone. I take the gift when it comes, but when it doesn't—well, I carry a basketball in my car, and if I'm riding around and I can't find any pictures, I'll go out and shoot baskets for ten minutes, and then I'll go back and try again.

SMITH: *Say you find something that you think is a potentially good picture, but even after you've shot baskets it isn't coming through the way you want it. What do you do?*

GROSSFELD: It's hard to get all the elements for making a good picture into a still photograph, something that will communicate some sort of emotion or feeling or elicit some response from a viewer. That takes patience, because there are so many things you can't control. People are walking in front of you and ruining some pictures because their arms and legs block the scene. Or the light or a shadow may be in the wrong spot. You really have to concentrate, to constantly keep thinking, be patient, and follow the "KISS" theory of composition—"Keep It Simple, Stupid."

SMITH: *Do you have a particular audience in mind?*

GROSSFELD: I picture readers getting up, just like I do, putting on the coffee, and then reaching outside and getting the papers, and opening them up, and I think, "That's who I'm doing it for."

SMITH: *What do they need to know?*

GROSSFELD: They need to know that you did the very best you could on every single assignment. They need to know you were trying to get something a little different for them. And they need to know that they can trust you in news situations, that you're not going to be manipulated by heads of state or public relations people or beautiful women or any of the other whores of our society. You've got to be objective, but you still need to have a point of view, and you've got to make sure that your point of view is fair.

SMITH: *Is a balanced perspective required because you work for a newspaper?*

GROSSFELD: Yes. People are depending on you to show them what's going on, especially in a news situation, and that's a lot of responsibility. If I've been to Beirut and I've taken pictures there, I'd like to think that I've shown the people here in New England what it's really like over there. That's what they want to know—"What's it like in Beirut?" And not just the terrible side. The good side, too, if I can find it.

SMITH: *How do you compose a shot?*

GROSSFELD: There are certain little tricks. The composition has to be clean and able to reproduce well in a newspaper, where it won't be nearly as clear because when it's printed the ink spreads—it's just a series of dots. Keeping that in mind helps you keep the composition clean. You can follow the Old Masters' rules of composition—you know, dividing things into thirds or—this sounds like Rembrandt—using focused lighting. Or you can look at your photographs upside down. That's an old art-school trick. If it looks good in composition upside down, it's probably going to look good right side up.

SMITH: *What about light?*

GROSSFELD: Light is what it's all about in photography. You've got to know what to do with it. The film can't take in as much contrast, as much range, as your eye can, so you have to know what the film will do and respond to that.

SMITH: *What about the placement of various elements in the picture—the central focus, the background, matters of balance or symmetry?*

GROSSFELD: The main rule is that the picture has to look good. You shouldn't be in love with your own work, so that you think everything you do is good. The main problem for students and amateurs is that they don't fill the frame, so everything's too far away. You've got to fill the frame. You've got a piece of film to work on, and it should be like a canvas. You don't see a painter using just one-quarter of the canvas. He uses the whole thing, and photographers, too, have to fill the frame. Another problem is that students are shy, so they're afraid of getting close to people. You have to get over that, too, even if you have to use a long lens.

SMITH: *Are there any major differences in shooting people, places, or events?*

GROSSFELD: It's important to be able to do it all if you want to get a job. If you're coming out of journalism school, you need to have a personal portfolio of, say, twenty 11 × 14 prints if you can afford it, or 8 × 10 if you can't, to show how versatile you are. You need to show that you can do news, you can do features, you can do sports, you can do portraits, pretty pictures. Newspaper and magazine editors are looking for versatility. It can't hurt you to be able to do it all.

SMITH: *What about the tone of the picture? Some of your shots convey an attitude toward the subject, such as familiarity, or humor, or warmth, or horror—like the shot of Arafat through the broken windshield [on page 12].*

GROSSFELD: I don't consider myself a great artist, but I know that people just look at the picture for a second and a half and then they're on to the next thing. So I have to hit them over the head with it; the pictures have to have impact. Then again, the world is such a complex and troubling place that I never pass up the opportunity to counteract that by getting a little humor into the photographs, when I can. People love to laugh.

SMITH: *What about irony?*

GROSSFELD: Some things are so bizarre or shocking that you say, "Hey, look at that!" When you find yourself saying that, as an American might about something strange in a foreign country, you'd better bring the camera to your eye and push the button, because you're seeing something different.

SMITH: *What do you do when you get to the darkroom and you're selecting the best or most appropriate shot to print?*

GROSSFELD: You have to be your own best friend in the darkroom. You have to develop your film. We skip the contact-sheet stage; we don't make contact sheets. We just look at the film through a magnifying loupe and decide which is the best frame—the frame that best tells the story. Or several frames, depending on what the story is. Then we make prints. We crop them in the darkroom. A lot of people print full frame. I don't believe in that. I don't think the reader cares if the print is $7/8$ of the frame or $8/8$ of the frame or what. You just have to get the most impact out of it.

SMITH: *Can you do various tricks after the fact that will allow certain details to leap out?*

GROSSFELD: I wouldn't call them "tricks." That's a dangerous word. You don't want anyone to think you're moving things around or changing the elements in the photo, because you're not. What you can do is to [adapt your printing to the subject and the shot]. For instance, you can print some pictures on a higher-contrast paper, to bring out the blacks and the whites.

SMITH: *When you have a range of shots of essentially the same event or the same person, taken at different angles and different exposures, how do you know which is the most effective?*

GROSSFELD: I choose what will be the best picture. Although sometimes, in tight-deadline situations, layout is dummying a space for your photograph and you have to fit that hole. But that's an extreme circumstance. I have to remember that I'm not working for an art gallery; I'm working for a newspaper. What I choose depends on what the story is, and it's very important to know that story. You don't want a picture of somebody laughing who's just been told that their son has been killed in Lebanon. You don't want them laughing, although maybe they did laugh, maybe they cried for twenty minutes and then just smiled for a second. You've got to use what portrays the person's essence. Print the very best picture, and spend a lot of time printing it so it's good, rather than making 30 half-assed prints and having the paper use one that doesn't have the quality. Your name is going underneath that picture; you have to put the quality in.

SMITH: *How would you rate these various characteristics on a scale of one to ten, ten being the highest? Content?*

GROSSFELD: Ten.

SMITH: *Accuracy?*

GROSSFELD: Ten. They're both important. Everything's important. You can't cut corners. You've got to put your heart and soul into it.

4

SMITH: *Would you find any other kind of photography attractive, other than news, with its deadlines and its focus on events?*

GROSSFELD: More and more, newspapers are using studio work in the food sections and the fashion sections. That's a completely different ballgame—there's more time, and the process is very meticulous. You're likely to be working with a food or fashion stylist, or a couple of models. You have total control of the environment, the lights, the settings. It doesn't hurt to learn that game, too.

SMITH: *From your own perspective, which is more interesting—that kind of technically correct photography, or a more immediate kind of photography that may be more flawed because you don't have time [to be deliberate] or you're getting jostled by a crowd?*

GROSSFELD: Some extremely talented, creative people do fashion and food in highly respectable ways. But for me there's nothing better than real life, what's out there on the streets. That's more fun because not only might you make a good picture, but you might learn a lot about a situation, a person, or a place in the process.

SMITH: *What's the best frame of mind for someone going into this profession?*

GROSSFELD: You've got to realize that even though you're going to be paid to have fun, and get in free to things, and have a front-row view, the payback is that you've always got to be ready to roll, to perform under pressure, to meet deadlines, to get yourself into—and out of—tight situations. You have to fasten your seatbelt for the roller-coaster ride.

7

CHAPTER ONE

Writing About Writing

To expect some people to learn to write by showing them a published essay or book is like expecting novice bakers to learn to make a wedding cake from looking at the completed confection, resplendent with icing and decorations. Indeed, the completed product in each case offers a model of what the finished work of art should look like—in concept, organization, shape, and style. Careful examination of the text (or the texture) exposes the intricacies of the finished sentences, paragraphs, logic, illustrative examples, and nuances of style. But no matter how hard you look, it's almost impossible to detect in a completed, professionally polished work much about the process by which it was composed—the numerous visions and revisions of ideas and expression, the effort, frustration, even exhilaration. Blood, sweat, and tears don't belong on the printed page any more than they belong to the gymnast's flawless, public performance on the balance beam. The audience doesn't want to agonize over the production, but to enjoy the result.

How Writers Work

It is helpful, however, for writers at any stage, whether beginning, more advanced, or publishing professionals, to understand how other writers work at their often solitary craft. Sometimes we can learn about how to do it ourselves as we see the efforts of people "whose most absorbed and passionate hours," Joan Didion explains, "are spent arranging words on paper." We can learn what has been effective or ineffective for others in their own process of creation. No matter how articulate writers are, they rarely examine their creative process while they're engaged in it; like scrutinizing one's own breathing, to do so would be ineffectively self-conscious.

Thus only after the fact do the following writers explain why and how they write: George Orwell in "Why I Write" (23–28), Joan Didion in "Why I Write" (29–34) (her title admittedly stolen from Orwell), John Kenneth Galbraith, in "Writing and Typing" (35–41), E. B. White in "Mostly About Writing: Selected Letters" (42–45), and Red Smith in "I'd Like to Be Called a Good Reporter" (46–49). For these writers, indeed for all writers, writing is an evolutionary process—the gradual development of mind, beliefs, values, and technical skill over a lifetime. As White observed in a characteristically wry letter in 1954,

> I have been writing since 1906 and it is high time I got over it. A writer, however, writes as long as he lives. It is the same as breathing except that it is bad for one's health.

As Didion explains her writing process and as White's letters reveal, a given piece of writing may be years in the making—the germ of an idea, image, character or scene may gestate for months, occasionally surfacing to conscious thought, and finally becoming the subject of intense focus as the writer develops and molds it into the finished work. Didion concentrates on "images that shimmer around the edges":

> You can't think too much about these pictures that shimmer. You just lie low and let them develop. You stay quiet. You don't talk to many people and you keep your nervous system from shorting out and you try to locate the [image] in the shimmer, the grammar in the picture.

The scene and summer pastimes at Belgrade Lakes, Maine, that White described in a letter in 1936 were familiar to him from childhood, thirty years before; the refrain, "Things don't change much," reinforces the timelessness of the subject that, as revised and interpreted by the artist, was published in 1941 as "Once More to the Lake" (232–37). In "Selections from the Allen Notebooks" (61–63), Woody Allen parodies, among other things, the narcissism of the notebooks of neurotic writers:

> Today I saw a red-and-yellow sunset and thought, How insignificant I am! Of course, I thought that yesterday, too, and it rained. I was overcome with self-loathing and contemplated suicide again—this time by inhaling next to an insurance salesman.

Woolf and Galbraith discuss the best climate for a writer. In "A Room of One's Own: Shakespeare's Sister" (50–60), Woolf invents a hypothetical sister for Shakespeare and through this ignominious example argues for creating conditions that enable everyone, women as well as men, to write: education, encouragement, stimulation, reinforcement of one's literary ability rather than suppressing women in gender-related role expectations—the maintenance of a figurative room of one's own. Galbraith advises prospective writers on ways to keep in writing trim: "One had better go to his or her typewriter every morning and stay there regardless of the result. . . . Don't wait for the golden moment." Revise: "the first draft may be a very primitive thing." Edit for brevity. Avoid alcohol: "Nothing so impairs the product." Keep your knowledge current.

Red Smith, the sportswriter's sportswriter, reinforces Galbraith's views:

> Over the years people have said to me, "Isn't it dull covering baseball every day?" My answer used to be "It becomes dull only to dull minds." Today's game is always different from yesterday's game. If you have the perception and the interest to see it, and the wit to express it, your story is always different from yesterday's story. . . . My enthusiasm is self-generating, self-renewing.

Indeed, a writer's prime asset is enthusiasm, the inspiring "god within."

Writers and Style

Writing, says Didion, "is the act of saying *I,* of imposing oneself upon other people, of saying *listen to me, see it my way, change your mind.*" As Didion implies, writings—like their authors—have individual personalities. As the essays in *The Lexington Reader* reveal, these can range from casual to controlled, flippant to dignified. Even allowing for variations in mood and subject, your style will be recognizably yours, as distinctive as a signature, as individual as a fingerprint. Style is not just fancy words and flowery images pasted onto ideas, like an ill-fitting toupee; your style will be as integral to your writing as your hand.

Crucial aspects of style include: presentation of your authorial self (persona), voice (how you sound—loud and clear, soft and true), tone (mood—sweet or sarcastic, angry or assertive, direct or evasive), level of language (formal, middle level, informal), and various matters of usage (whether or not you use the first person, contractions, repetition. . . .). In "Swimming in Lake Chauggogagogmanchauggagogchabunagungamaugg" (64–67) poet Stanley Kunitz explains why he is moved by this "fantastic porridge of syllables . . . . [the] ideal lyric in my head whose words flow together to form a single word-sentence, an unremitting stream of sound" whose style appeals to him in a way that Lake Webster, the lake's prosaic alternative name, never could. (Hint: to get a sense of the style of the lake's Indian name, recite the syllables aloud and note the rhythm, the alliteration, the echo and the promise of meaning.)

No matter how independent-minded you are, as a writer and as a human being you're bound to be influenced by contemporary taste, and to that extent your style will reflect the times as well as your own preferences. In our fitness-conscious age, lean, muscular prose is considered the essence of good writing, and the commentators on style are the leaders of Word Watchers, exhorting writers to take off flabby phrases in order to maintain a taut, well-shaped body of prose. John Trimble in "Write to Be Read" (67–71) and

George Orwell in "Politics and the English Language" (72–82) show how such style can be attained. Trimble's overarching precepts are:

1. Write with the assumption that your reader is a companionable friend with a warm sense of humor and an appreciation of simple straightforwardness.
2. Write as if you were actually talking to that friend, but talking with enough leisure to frame your thoughts concisely and interestingly.

These govern the rest of Trimble's advice, designed to create a style that is pleasant, interesting, and easy to read. For instance, he recommends using "occasional contractions"—*I'm, you're, he's, won't*—to "help you achieve a more natural, conversational rhythm." Use the first person, *I,* when you mean "I", to talk personally with your readers, rather than to distance yourself from them. Trimble emphasizes, "Use the fewest words possible and the simplest words possible" for the greatest clarity, the least obfuscation—a reiteration of Orwell's "Never use a long word where a short one will do" and "If it is possible to cut a word out, always cut it out."

In "Politics and the English Language" Orwell is particularly concerned with the disastrous consequences—for communication and for telling the truth—of violating his precepts. Slovenly English, Orwell demonstrates, is insincere, unclear, vague, and meaningless. The resulting "lifeless, imitative style" dulls the consciousness of writers and readers alike, inhibits their critical thinking and their honest expression. They become more susceptible to political conformity, bureaucratic manipulation, and lies told by government officials, prime users of such language. Orwell illustrates what he means with a number of surprisingly contemporary examples, such as "People are imprisoned for years without trial, or shot in the back of the neck or sent to die of scurvy in Arctic lumber camps: this is called *elimination of unreliable elements.*"

Linguist Robin Lakoff, in "You Are What You Say" (83–88), addresses another political aspect of language by claiming there is a women's language that, unlike forceful, emphatic men's language is "fuzzy-headed, unassertive." Women who use it, she says, will be "ridiculed for being unable to think clearly, unable to take part in a serious discussion, and therefore unfit to hold positions of power." She contends that women use euphemisms (the condescending *lady* instead of *woman*), tag questions ("The situation in Southeast Asia is terrible, isn't it?"), and phrase commands as requests ("Will you close the door?") to avoid commitment and "conflict with the addressee"; her implied argument for unisex language is an argument for equality between men and women.

Revising

Revision means literally "to see again." When you take a second, careful look at what you've written casually or as a first draft, chances are you'll decide to change it. As Donald Murray, himself a Pulitzer Prize–winning journalist, observes in "The Maker's Eye: Revising Your Own Manuscripts" (89–93):

> Rewriting isn't virtuous. It isn't something that ought to be done. It is
> simply something that most writers find they have to do to discover what
> they have to say and how to say it. It is a condition of the writer's life.

Many people think that revision means correcting the spelling and punctuation of a first—and only—draft. Writers who care about their work know that such changes, though necessary, are editorial matters remote from the heart of real revising. For to revise is to rewrite. And rewrite. The way in which you wrote the original draft may help you to identify aspects of your writing to focus on in revision. If you used the first draft to generate ideas, in revising you'll want to shape them to achieve a precise focus, organized to reinforce your emphasis. Thus, even in making a grocery list, if your original version identified the items in the order they occurred to you, as lists often do, in revision you could regroup them by categories of similar items, easier to shop for: produce, staples, meat, dairy products—with extra details for the most important items—"a pound of Milagro super-hot green chiles," and "a half gallon of double chocolate extra fudge ice cream."

If your customary first draft is a sketchy statement of basic ideas, in revision you'll need to elaborate on the essentials, supplying illustrations and additional information. Teresa Whitlock does this in revising "My Professional Hairstyle" (102–105), a humorous account of her first college haircut; as a result, she accommodates her audience, which she had largely ignored in the first draft. For instance, the readers of her first draft don't learn what her hair looked like before it was cut, yet without that information they can't assess the ultimate damage. Nor are they told what went on during the cutting process, or what kind of a person Teresa herself is—important in determining whether she is foolish, vain, or a sadder-but-wiser victim. In the revision Teresa added information about *who* was present; *what* they were saying and doing; *what* her hair looked like before, during, and after the massacre; *why* Chantay kept on cutting her hair shorter and shorter. In the process, the author reveals herself more fully as a likable person, the optimistic victim of her own shortcomings.

On the other hand, if your early drafts include a great deal more than you need to capture the peripheral as well as the central ideas, your revision may consist of deleting irrelevant ideas and redundant illustrations. Sometimes writers incorporate numerous background thoughts that occurred to them as they were finding a focus. A comparison of the first, third, and last (of six) versions of Richard Wright's "Interview Comments on *Black Boy*" (93–102) reveals how, in the course of cutting the manuscript by half (from slightly over a thousand words to slightly over five hundred), Wright made major changes. In the revision, for instance, he worked out a clear structure that reflected his new emphasis—on "how it was possible for me to feel that my life had a meaning which my Jim Crow, southern environment denied." In revision his focus changed from a writer-oriented narrative to audience-conscious exposition as he deleted numerous reminiscences about his personal discoveries and life history and shifted to an emphasis on the events—the publication of *Black Boy* and the effects of "living in the South." Moreover, in the revisions Wright developed a new conception of his audience; although his first draft was largely for himself, he knew he would ultimately have to address an audience of outside readers, whom (as other interviews reveal) he had first envisioned as incredulous whites and fearful blacks. As he rewrote, he grew to see his readers as allies, rather than as antagonists, people who understood his struggle for freedom, so central to American history and familiar to anyone who "came hopefully from the Old World" to the New. This shared "hunger for freedom" enables Wright's readers, white and black alike, to identify with the struggle represented in *Black Boy*.

Wright and Whitlock, like other writers, demonstrate in the various versions of their revised essays significant changes in content, form, voice, tone, word choice, sentence structure, and mechanics—the essence of the revising process that Murray describes in "The Maker's Eye." Even though as Murray says, "the words on the page are never finished," the later versions illustrate the truth of Neil Simon's optimistic observation: "Rewriting is when writing really gets to be fun. . . . In baseball you only get three swings and you're out. In rewriting, you get almost as many swings as you want and you know, sooner or later, you'll hit the ball."

The Writing Process

GEORGE ORWELL

Why I Write

Through his novels of political protest, Animal Farm *(1945) and* Nineteen Eighty-Four *(1949), Orwell's name has become synonymous with resistance to political totalitarianism. Born in Bengal while his English father was in the Bengal civil service, Orwell (1903–1950)—the pseudonym for Eric Blair—was educated at Eton College but left before graduating to serve with the Indian imperial police in Burma 1922–1927. Disillusioned with the service (see "Shooting an Elephant," 335–40), he decided to become a writer and returned to Europe. His first book,* Down and Out in Paris and London *(1933), based on his experiences as a dishwasher in Paris and a pickup laborer in England, is a plea for greater understanding of the economically and socially downtrodden.*

In 1936 Orwell left England to fight in the Spanish Civil War, and later became a war correspondent for the B.B.C. and the Observer. *In "Why I Write" he identifies the main reasons why people write—"sheer egoism," "esthetic enthusiasm," "historical impulse,"—and his main reason for writing that became apparent in Spain—"political purpose, the desire to push the world in a certain direction, to alter people's idea of the kind of society that they should strive after." He continues, "Every line of serious work that I have written since 1936 has been written directly or indirectly against totalitarianism and for democratic socialism, as I understand it." Yet, unlike many political polemicists, Orwell has raised political writing to an art; it must speak clearly, directly, to the heart as well as to the head, to the eye as well as to the mind.*

From a very early age, perhaps the age of five or six, I knew that when I grew up I should be a writer. Between the ages of about seventeen and twenty-four I tried to abandon this idea, but I did so with the consciousness that I was outraging my true nature and that sooner or later I should have to settle down and write books.

I was the middle child of three, but there was a gap of five years on either side, and I barely saw my father before I was eight. For this and other reasons I was somewhat lonely, and I soon developed disagreeable mannerisms which made me unpopular throughout my schooldays. I had the lonely child's habit of making up stories and holding conversations with imaginary persons, and I think from the very start my literary ambitions were mixed up with the feeling of being isolated and undervalued. I knew that I had a facility with words and a power of facing unpleasant facts, and I felt that this created a sort of private world in which I could get my own back for my failure in everyday life. Nevertheless the volume of serious—*i.e.* seriously intended—writing which I produced all through my childhood and boyhood would not amount to half a dozen pages. I wrote my first poem at the age of four or five, my mother taking it down to dictation. I cannot remember anything about it except that it was about a tiger and the tiger had "chair-like teeth"—a good enough phrase, but I fancy the poem was a plagiarism of Blake's "Tiger, Tiger." At eleven, when the war of 1914–18 broke out, I wrote a patriotic poem which was printed in the local newspaper, as was another, two years later, on the death of Kitchener. From time to time, when I was a bit older, I wrote bad and usually unfinished "nature poems" in the Georgian style. I also, about twice, attempted a short story which was a ghastly failure. That was the total of the would-be serious work that I actually set down on paper during all those years.

3   However, throughout this time I did in a sense engage in literary activities. To begin with there was the made-to-order stuff which I produced quickly, easily and without much pleasure to myself. Apart from school work, I wrote *vers d'occasion,* semi-comic poems which I could turn out at what now seems to me astonishing speed—at fourteen I wrote a whole rhyming play, in imitation of Aristophanes, in about a week—and helped to edit school magazines, both printed and in manuscript. These magazines were the most pitiful burlesque stuff that you could imagine, and I took far less trouble with them than I now would with the cheapest journalism. But side by side with all this, for fifteen years or more, I was carrying out a literary exercise of a quite different kind: this was the making up of a continuous "story" about myself, a sort of diary existing only in the mind. I believe this is a common habit of children and adolescents. As a very small child I used to imagine that I was, say, Robin Hood, and picture myself as the hero of thrilling adventures, but quite soon my "story" ceased to be narcissistic in a crude way and became more and more a mere description of what I was doing and the things I saw. For minutes at a time this kind of thing would be running through my head: "He pushed the door open and entered the room. A yellow beam of sunlight, filtering through the muslin curtains, slanted on to the table, where a matchbox, half open, lay beside the inkpot. With his right hand in his pocket he moved across to the window. Down in the street a tortoiseshell cat was chasing a dead leaf," etc., etc. This habit continued till I was about twenty-five, right through my non-literary years. Although I had to search, and did search, for the right words, I seemed to be making this descriptive effort almost against my will, under a kind of compulsion from outside. The "story" must, I suppose, have reflected the styles of the various writers I admired at different ages, but so far as I remember it always had the same meticulous descriptive quality.

4   When I was about sixteen I suddenly discovered the joy of mere words, *i.e.* the sounds and associations of words. The lines from *Paradise Lost*—

> So hee with difficulty and labour hard
> Moved on: with difficulty and labour hee,

24

which do not now seem to me so very wonderful, sent shivers down my backbone; and the spelling "hee" for "he" was an added pleasure. As for the need to describe things, I knew all about it already. So it is clear what kind of books I wanted to write, in so far as I could be said to want to write books at that time. I wanted to write enormous naturalistic novels with unhappy endings, full of detailed descriptions and arresting similes, and also full of purple passages in which words were used partly for the sake of their sound. And in fact my first completed novel, *Burmese Days,* which I wrote when I was thirty but projected much earlier, is rather that kind of book.

I give all this background information because I do not think one can assess a writer's motives without knowing something of his early development. His subject matter will be determined by the age he lives in—at least this is true in tumultuous, revolutionary ages like our own—but before he ever begins to write he will have acquired an emotional attitude from which he will never completely escape. It is his job, no doubt, to discipline his temperament and avoid getting stuck at some immature stage, or in some perverse mood: but if he escapes from his early influences altogether, he will have killed his impulse to write. Putting aside the need to earn a living, I think there are four great motives for writing, at any rate for writing prose. They exist in different degrees in every writer, and in any one writer the proportions will vary from time to time, according to the atmosphere in which he is living. They are:

1. Sheer egoism. Desire to seem clever, to be talked about, to be remembered after death, to get your own back on grownups who snubbed you in childhood, etc., etc. It is humbug to pretend that this is not a motive, and a strong one. Writers share this characteristic with scientists, artists, politicians, lawyers, soldiers, successful businessmen—in short, with the whole top crust of humanity. The great mass of human beings are not acutely selfish. After the age of about thirty they abandon individual ambition—in many cases, indeed, they almost abandon the sense of being individuals at all—and live chiefly for others, or are simply smothered under drudgery. But there is also the minority of gifted, wilful people who are determined to live their own lives to the end, and writers belong in this class. Serious writers, I should say, are on the whole more vain and self-centred than journalists, though less interested in money.

2. Esthetic enthusiasm. Perception of beauty in the external world, or, on the other hand, in words and their right arrangement. Pleasure in the impact of one sound on another, in the firmness of good prose or the rhythm of a good story. Desire to share an experience which one feels is valuable and ought not to be missed. The esthetic motive is very feeble in a lot of writers, but even a pamphleteer or a writer of textbooks will have pet words and phrases which appeal to him for non-utilitarian reasons;

5

or he may feel strongly about typography, width of margins, etc. Above the level of a railway guide, no book is quite free from esthetic considerations.

3. Historical impulse. Desire to see things as they are, to find out true facts and store them up for the use of posterity.

4. Political purpose—using the word "political" in the widest possible sense. Desire to push the world in a certain direction, to alter other people's idea of the kind of society that they should strive after. Once again, no book is genuinely free from political bias. The opinion that art should have nothing to do with politics is itself a political attitude.

6   It can be seen how these various impulses must war against one another, and how they must fluctuate from person to person and from time to time. By nature—taking your "nature" to be the state you have attained when you are first adult—I am a person in whom the first three motives would outweigh the fourth. In a peaceful age I might have written ornate or merely descriptive books, and might have remained almost unaware of my political loyalties. As it is I have been forced into becoming a sort of pamphleteer. First I spent five years in an unsuitable profession (the Indian Imperial Police, in Burma), and then I underwent poverty and the sense of failure. This increased my natural hatred of authority and made me for the first time fully aware of the existence of the working classes, and the job in Burma had given me some understanding of the nature of imperialism: but these experiences were not enough to give me an accurate political orientation. Then came Hitler, the Spanish civil war, etc. By the end of 1935 I had still failed to reach a firm decision. I remember a little poem that I wrote at that date, expressing my dilemma:

> A happy vicar I might have been
> Two hundred years ago,
> To preach upon eternal doom
> And watch my walnuts grow;
>
> But born, alas, in an evil time,
> I missed that pleasant haven,
> For the hair has grown on my upper lip
> And the clergy are all clean-shaven.
>
> And later still the times were good,
> We were so easy to please,
> We rocked our troubled thoughts to sleep
> On the bosoms of the trees.
>
> All ignorant we dared to own
> The joys we now dissemble;
> The greenfinch on the apple bough
> Could make my enemies tremble.

26

But girls' bellies and apricots,
Roach in a shaded stream,
Horses, ducks in flight at dawn,
All these are a dream.

It is forbidden to dream again;
We maim our joys or hide them;
Horses are made of chromium steel
And little fat men shall ride them.

I am the worm who never turned,
The eunuch without a harem;
Between the priest and the commissar
I walk like Eugene Aram;

And the commissar is telling my fortune
While the radio plays,
But the priest has promised an Austin Seven,
For Duggie always pays.

I dreamed I dwelt in marble halls,
And woke to find it true;
I wasn't born for an age like this;
Was Smith? Was Jones? Were you?

The Spanish war and other events in 1936–7 turned the scale and thereafter I knew where I stood. Every line of serious work that I have written since 1936 has been written, directly or indirectly, *against* totalitarianism and *for* democratic socialism, as I understand it. It seems to me nonsense, in a period like our own, to think that one can avoid writing of such subjects. Everyone writes of them in one guise or another. It is simply a question of which side one takes and what approach one follows. And the more one is conscious of one's political bias, the more chance one has of acting politically without sacrificing one's esthetic and intellectual integrity.

What I have most wanted to do throughout the past ten years is to make political writing into an art. My starting point is always a feeling of partisanship, a sense of injustice. When I sit down to write a book, I do not say to myself, "I am going to produce a work of art." I write it because there is some lie that I want to expose, some fact to which I want to draw attention, and my initial concern is to get a hearing. But I could not do the work of writing a book, or even a long magazine article, if it were not also an esthetic experience. Anyone who cares to examine my work will see that even when it is downright propaganda it contains much that a full-time politician would consider irrelevant. I am not able, and I do not want, completely to abandon the world-view that I acquired in childhood. So long as I remain alive and well I shall continue to feel strongly about prose style, to love the surface of the earth, and to take a pleasure in solid objects and scraps of useless information. It is no use trying to suppress that side of myself. The job is to reconcile

7

my ingrained likes and dislikes with the essentially public, non-individual activities that this age forces on all of us.

8   It is not easy. It raises problems of construction and of language, and it raises in a new way the problem of truthfulness. Let me give just one example of the cruder kind of difficulty that arises. My book about the Spanish civil war, *Homage to Catalonia,* is, of course, a frankly political book, but in the main it is written with a certain detachment and regard for form. I did try very hard in it to tell the whole truth without violating my literary instincts. But among other things it contains a long chapter, full of newspaper quotations and the like, defending the Trotskyists who were accused of plotting with Franco. Clearly such a chapter, which after a year or two would lose its interest for any ordinary reader, must ruin the book. A critic whom I respect read me a lecture about it. "Why did you put in all that stuff?" he said. "You've turned what might have been a good book into journalism." What he said was true, but I could not have done otherwise. I happened to know, what very few people in England had been allowed to know, that innocent men were being falsely accused. If I had not been angry about that I should never have written the book.

9   In one form or another this problem comes up again. The problem of language is subtler and would take too long to discuss. I will only say that of late years I have tried to write less picturesquely and more exactly. In any case I find that by the time you have perfected any style of writing, you have always outgrown it. *Animal Farm* was the first book in which I tried, with full consciousness of what I was doing, to fuse political purpose and artistic purpose into one whole. I have not written a novel for seven years, but I hope to write another fairly soon. It is bound to be a failure, every book is a failure, but I do know with some clarity what kind of book I want to write.

10   Looking back through the last page or two, I see that I have made it appear as though my motives in writing were wholly public-spirited. I don't want to leave that as the final impression. All writers are vain, selfish and lazy, and at the very bottom of their motives there lies a mystery. Writing a book is a horrible, exhausting struggle, like a long bout of some painful illness. One would never undertake such a thing if one were not driven on by some demon whom one can neither resist nor understand. For all one knows that demon is simply the same instinct that makes a baby squall for attention. And yet it is also true that one can write nothing readable unless one constantly struggles to efface one's own personality. Good prose is like a window pane. I cannot say with certainty which of my motives are the strongest, but I know which of them deserve to be followed. And looking back through my work, I see that it is invariably where I lacked a *political* purpose that I wrote lifeless books and was betrayed into purple passages, sentences without meaning, decorative adjectives and humbug generally.

Questions

1. Orwell says people write for four main reasons (paragraph 5). Identify and explain these. Do you write for any of these reasons, or for others? What does Orwell mean by saying that throughout the past ten years he has "most wanted to make political writing into an art" (paragraph 7)?

2. Why does Orwell spend the first third (paragraphs 1–4) of his essay giving an account of his "early development" as a writer? What is the logic of beginning *The Lexington Reader* with this essay?

3. If "good prose is like a window pane," as Orwell says (paragraph 10), and the writer has truly effaced his personality, as Orwell recommends, how is it possible to differentiate one writer's style from another's? What are the distinctive features of Orwell's own style?

4. Orwell says that "When I was about sixteen I suddenly discovered the joy of . . . the sounds and associations of words" (paragraph 4). Can you find any such memorable words in this essay? in your own reading or writing?

JOAN DIDION

Why I Write

Novelist and essayist Didion was born in Sacramento, California, in 1934, educated at the University of California in Berkeley, and won Vogue's *Prix de Paris contest, which led to a job with that magazine. In 1964 she married writer John Gregory Dunne, "in lieu of seeing a psychiatrist," and the couple moved back to Los Angeles to collaborate on screenplays (*Panic in Needle Park *(1971),* A Star Is Born *(1976)), and to try to forge a family and community "in the face of what many people believe to be a moral vacuum." Indeed, in her novels,* Run River *(1963),* Play It as It Lays *(1971),* A Book of Common Prayer *(1977), and* Democracy *(1984), and in two collections of essays,* Slouching Towards Bethlehem *(1968) and* The White Album *(1979), Didion consistently focuses on people who are estranged from the traditional values of religion, family, and society, but who are unwilling—or unable—to completely accept the loss of those values.*

In "Why I Write" Didion defines a writer as "a person whose most absorbed and passionate hours are spent arranging words on pieces of paper." She speaks with pleasure of the aesthetic and auditory satisfaction, the "infinite power" of shifting sentences around as she tries to convey "the pictures in my mind." Even though she "stole the title" from Orwell, Didion's mission as a writer is indeed far more aesthetic than political. She explained in an interview in 1977,

> *I never had faith that the answers to human problems lay in anything that could be called political. I thought the answers, if there were answers, lay someplace in man's soul. I have an aversion to social action because it usually meant social regulation . . . interference, rules . . . The ethic I was raised in was specifically a*

Western frontier ethic. That means being left alone and leaving others alone . . . the highest form of human endeavor.

But make no mistake. As writers say "listen to me, see it my way, change your mind," *they're committing an "aggressive, even hostile act." Didion has observed that*

I am so physically small, so temperamentally unobtrusive, and so neurotically inarticulate that people tend to forget that my presence runs counter to their best interests. And it always does. That is one last thing to remember: writers are always selling somebody out.

1   Of course I stole the title for this talk, from George Orwell. One reason I stole it was that I like the sound of the words: *Why I Write.* There you have three short unambiguous words that share a sound, and the sound they share is this:

I

I

I

2   In many ways writing is the act of saying *I,* of imposing oneself upon other people, of saying *listen to me, see it my way, change your mind.* It's an aggressive, even a hostile act. You can disguise its aggressiveness all you want with veils of subordinate clauses and qualifiers and tentative subjunctives, with ellipses and evasions—with the whole manner of intimating rather than claiming, of alluding rather than stating—but there's no getting around the fact that setting words on paper is the tactic of a secret bully, an invasion, an imposition of the writer's sensibility on the reader's most private space.

3   I stole the title not only because the words sounded right but because they seemed to sum up, in a no-nonsense way, all I have to tell you. Like many writers I have only this one "subject," this one "area": the act of writing. I can bring you no reports from any other front. I may have other interests: I am "interested," for example, in marine biology, but I don't flatter myself that you would come out to hear me talk about it. I am not a scholar. I am not in the least an intellectual, which is not to say that when I hear the word "intellectual" I reach for my gun, but only to say that I do not think in abstracts. During the years when I was an undergraduate at Berkeley I tried, with a kind of hopeless late-adolescent energy, to buy some temporary visa into the world of ideas, to forge for myself a mind that could deal with the abstract.

4   In short I tried to think. I failed. My attention veered inexorably back to the specific, to the tangible, to what was generally considered, by everyone I knew then and for that matter have known since, the peripheral. I would try to contemplate the Hegelian dialectic and would find myself concentrating

instead on a flowering pear tree outside my window and the particular way the petals fell on my floor. I would try to read linguistic theory and would find myself wondering instead if the lights were on in the bevatron up the hill. When I say that I was wondering if the lights were on in the bevatron you might immediately suspect, if you deal in ideas at all, that I was registering the bevatron as a political symbol, thinking in shorthand about the military-industrial complex and its role in the university community, but you would be wrong. I was only wondering if the lights were on in the bevatron, and how they looked. A physical fact.

I had trouble graduating from Berkeley, not because of this inability to deal with ideas—I was majoring in English, and I could locate the house-and-garden imagery in "The Portrait of a Lady" as well as the next person, "imagery" being by definition the kind of specific that got my attention—but simply because I had neglected to take a course in Milton. For reasons which now sound baroque I needed a degree by the end of that summer, and the English department finally agreed, if I would come down from Sacramento every Friday and talk about the cosmology of "Paradise Lost," to certify me proficient in Milton. I did this. Some Fridays I took the Greyhound bus, other Fridays I caught the Southern Pacific's City of San Francisco on the last leg of its transcontinental trip. I can no longer tell you whether Milton put the sun or the earth at the center of his universe in "Paradise Lost," the central question of at least one century and a topic about which I wrote 10,000 words that summer, but I can still recall the exact rancidity of the butter in the City of San Francisco's dining car, and the way the tinted windows on the Greyhound bus cast the oil refineries around Carquinez Straits into a grayed and obscurely sinister light. In short my attention was always on the periphery, on what I could see and taste and touch, on the butter, and the Greyhound bus. During those years I was traveling on what I knew to be a very shaky passport, forged papers: I knew that I was no legitimate resident in any world of ideas. I knew I couldn't think. All I knew then was what I couldn't do. All I knew then was what I wasn't, and it took me some years to discover what I was.

Which was a writer.

By which I mean not a "good" writer or a "bad" writer but simply a writer, a person whose most absorbed and passionate hours are spent arranging words on pieces of paper. Had my credentials been in order I would never have become a writer. Had I been blessed with even limited access to my own mind there would have been no reason to write. I write entirely to find out what I'm thinking, what I'm looking at, what I see and what it means. What I want and what I fear. Why did the oil refineries around Carquinez Straits seem sinister to me in the summer of 1956? Why have the night lights in the bevatron burned in my mind for twenty years? *What is going on in these pictures in my mind?*

When I talk about pictures in my mind I am talking, quite specifically, about images that shimmer around the edges. There used to be an illustration in every elementary psychology book showing a cat drawn by a patient in varying stages of schizophrenia. This cat had a shimmer around it. You could see the molecular structure breaking down at the very edges of the cat: the cat became the background and the background the cat, everything interacting, exchanging ions. People on hallucinogens describe the same perception of objects. I'm not a schizophrenic, nor do I take hallucinogens, but certain images do shimmer for me. Look hard enough, and you can't miss the shimmer. It's there. You can't think too much about these pictures that shimmer. You just lie low and let them develop. You stay quiet. You don't talk to many people and you keep your nervous system from shorting out and you try to locate the cat in the shimmer, the grammar in the picture.

9   Just as I meant "shimmer" literally I mean "grammar" literally. Grammar is a piano I play by ear, since I seem to have been out of school the year the rules were mentioned. All I know about grammar is its infinite power. To shift the structure of a sentence alters the meaning of that sentence, as definitely and inflexibly as the position of a camera alters the meaning of the object photographed. Many people know about camera angles now, but not so many know about sentences. The arrangement of the words matters, and the arrangement you want can be found in the picture in your mind. The picture dictates the arrangement. The picture dictates whether this will be a sentence with or without clauses, a sentence that ends hard or a dying-fall sentence, long or short, active or passive. The picture tells you how to arrange the words and the arrangement of the words tells you, or tells me, what's going on in the picture. *Nota bene:*

10   It tells you.

11   You don't tell it.

12   Let me show you what I mean by pictures in the mind. I began "Play It As It Lays" just as I have begun each of my novels, with no notion of "character" or "plot" or even "incident." I had only two pictures in my mind, more about which later, and a technical intention, which was to write a novel so elliptical and fast that it would be over before you noticed it, a novel so fast that it would scarcely exist on the page at all. About the pictures: the first was of white space. Empty space. This was clearly the picture that dictated the narrative intention of the book—a book in which anything that happened would happen off the page, a "white" book to which the reader would have to bring his or her own bad dreams—and yet this picture told me no "story," suggested no situation. The second picture did. This second picture was of something actually witnessed. A young woman with long hair and a short white halter dress walks through the casino at the Riviera in Las Vegas at one in the morning. She crosses the casino alone and picks up a house telephone. I watch her because I have heard her paged, and recognize her name: she is a minor actress I see around Los Angeles from time to time, in places like Jax and once in a gynecologist's office in the Beverly Hills Clinic, but have never

met. I know nothing about her. Who is paging her? Why is she here to be paged? How exactly did she come to this? It was precisely this moment in Las Vegas that made "Play It As It Lays" begin to tell itself to me, but the moment appears in the novel only obliquely, in a chapter which begins:

"Maria made a list of things she would never do. She would never: walk   13
through the Sands or Caesar's alone after midnight. She would never: ball at a party, do S-M unless she wanted to, borrow furs from Abe Lipsey, deal. She would never: carry a Yorkshire in Beverly Hills."

That is the beginning of the chapter and that is also the end of the   14
chapter, which may suggest what I meant by "white space."

I recall having a number of pictures in my mind when I began the novel I   15
just finished, "A Book of Common Prayer." As a matter of fact one of these pictures was of that bevatron I mentioned, although I would be hard put to tell you a story in which nuclear energy figured. Another was a newspaper photograph of a hijacked 707 burning on the desert in the Middle East. Another was the night view from a room in which I once spent a week with paratyphoid, a hotel room on the Colombian coast. My husband and I seemed to be on the Colombian coast representing the United States of America at a film festival (I recall invoking the name "Jack Valenti" a lot, as if its reiteration could make me well), and it was a bad place to have fever, not only because my indisposition offended our hosts but because every night in this hotel the generator failed. The lights went out. The elevator stopped. My husband would go to the event of the evening and make excuses for me and I would stay alone in this hotel room, in the dark. I remember standing at the window trying to call Bogotá (the telephone seemed to work on the same principle as the generator) and watching the night wind come up and wondering what I was doing eleven degrees off the equator with a fever of 103. The view from that window definitely figures in "A Book of Common Prayer," as does the burning 707, and yet none of these pictures told me the story I needed.

The picture that did, the picture that shimmered and made these other   16
images coalesce, was the Panama airport at 6 A.M. I was in this airport only once, on a plane to Bogotá that stopped for an hour to refuel, but the way it looked that morning remained superimposed on everything I saw until the day I finished "A Book of Common Prayer." I lived in that airport for several years. I can still feel the hot air when I step off the plane, can see the heat already rising off the tarmac at 6 A.M. I can feel my skirt damp and wrinkled on my legs. I can feel the asphalt stick to my sandals. I remember the big tail of a Pan American plane floating motionless down at the end of the tarmac. I remember the sound of a slot machine in the waiting room. I could tell you that I remember a particular woman in the airport, an American woman, a *norteamericana*, a thin *norteamericana* about 40 who bore a big square emerald in lieu of a wedding ring, but there was no such woman there.

I put this woman in the airport later. I made this woman up, just as I later   17 made up a country to put the airport in, and a family to run the country. This woman in the airport is neither catching a plane nor meeting one. She is ordering tea in the airport coffee shop. In fact she is not simply "ordering" tea but insisting that the water be boiled, in front of her, for twenty minutes. Why is this woman in this airport? Why is she going nowhere, where has she been? Where did she get that big emerald? What derangement, or disassociation, makes her believe that her will to see the water boiled can possibly prevail?

18   "She had been going to one airport or another for four months, one could see it, looking at the visas on her passport. All those airports where Charlotte Douglas's passport had been stamped would have looked alike. Sometimes the sign on the tower would say 'Bienvenidos' and sometimes the sign on the tower would say 'Bienvenue,' some places were wet and hot and others dry and hot, but at each of these airports the pastel concrete walls would rust and stain and the swamp off the runway would be littered with the fuselages of cannibalized Fairchild F-227's and the water would need boiling.

19   "I knew why Charlotte went to the airport even if Victor did not.

20   "I knew about airports."

21   These lines appear about halfway through "A Book of Common Prayer," but I wrote them during the second week I worked on the book, long before I had any idea where Charlotte Douglas had been or why she went to airports. Until I wrote these lines I had no character called "Victor" in mind: the necessity for mentioning a name, and the name "Victor," occurred to me as I wrote the sentence. *I knew why Charlotte went to the airport* sounded incomplete. *I knew why Charlotte went to the airport even if Victor did not* carried a little more narrative drive. Most important of all, until I wrote these lines I did not know who "I" was, who was telling the story. I had intended until that moment that the "I" be no more than the voice of the author, a 19th-century omniscient narrator. But there it was:

22   "I knew why Charlotte went to the airport even if Victor did not.

23   "I knew about airports."

24   This "I" was the voice of no author in my house. This "I" was someone who not only knew why Charlotte went to the airport but also knew someone called "Victor." Who was Victor? Who was this narrator? Why was this narrator telling me this story? Let me tell you one thing about why writers write: had I known the answer to any of these questions I would never have needed to write a novel.

Questions

1. Didion defines writing as "The act of saying *I*, of imposing oneself upon other people, of saying *listen to me, see it my way, change your mind*" (paragraph 2). What does she mean? How do her reasons for writing compare with Orwell's? with yours?

2. For Didion, novelist and essayist, her writing is dictated by "the pictures in my mind . . . images that shimmer around the edges" (paragraph 8). To what extent is your writing influenced by images? sounds? motions? other nonverbal stimuli? Or is your writing primarily inspired by words—your own or others'? How do you know when you get a good idea?

3. In some places Didion appears to be talking to herself, in other places to an audience she addresses as "you." Is she writing to you personally? to readers of her novels? to aspiring writers? to anyone else? How can you tell?

4. Is it possible for someone to learn how to write well by reading how others, such as Orwell and Didion, do it?

JOHN KENNETH GALBRAITH
Writing and Typing

Galbraith is an emeritus professor of economics at Harvard whose numerous writings illustrate his claim that "there is no mystery in the science of economics that cannot be phrased in good English prose." He was born in 1908 at Iona Station, Ontario, Canada, earned a B.S. at the University of Toronto and an M.S. and a Ph.D. in economics at the University of California, Berkeley. He taught at Princeton as well as at Harvard; was deputy head of the Office of Price Administration and economic adviser to the National Defense Advisory Committee during World War II; was an editor of Fortune *magazine; and served as ambassador to India, 1961–1963. His many books include classic works on economics:* The Great Crash *(1955),* The Affluent Society *(1958),* The New Industrial State *(1967), and* The Nature of Mass Poverty *(1979); a novel; books on China, on the Scottish, and on Indian painting; and, most recently, an autobiography,* A Life in Our Times *(1981).*

"Writing and Typing" is a graceful, witty account of Galbraith's views on the art of writing, including his own. His advice is sound: "go to [the] typewriter every morning and stay there"; revise ("the first draft is a very primitive thing"); edit for brevity; "nothing so impairs the product" as alcohol. With tongue in cheek he criticizes the obscurity and vagueness of academic writers: "The man who makes things clear is a scab. He is criticized less for his clarity than for his treachery." All of this implies an important distinction between "writing and typing."

Nine or ten years ago, when I was spending a couple of terms at Trinity College, Cambridge, I received a proposal of more than usual interest from the University of California. It was that I take a leave from Harvard and accept a visiting chair in rhetoric at Berkeley. They assured me that rhetoric was a traditional and not, as one would naturally suppose, a pejorative title. My task would be to hold seminars with the young on what I had learned about writing in general and on technical matters in particular. 1

I was attracted by the idea. I had spent decades attempting to teach the 2 young about economics, and the practical consequences were not reassuring. When I entered the field in the early nineteen-thirties, it was generally known that the modern economy could suffer a serious depression and that it could have a serious inflation. In the ensuing forty years my teaching had principally advanced to the point of telling that it was possible to have both at the same time. This was soon to be associated with the belief of William Simon and Alan Greenspan, the guiding hands of Richard Nixon and Gerald Ford, that progress in this field is measured by the speed of the return to the ideas of the eighteenth century. A subject in which it can be believed that you go ahead by going back has many problems for a teacher. Things are better now. Mr. Carter's economists do not believe in going back. But, as I've elsewhere urged, they are caught in a delicate balance between their fear of inflation and unemployment and their fear of doing anything about them. It is hard to conclude that economics is a productive intellectual and pedagogical investment.

3   Then I began to consider what I could tell about writing. My experience was certainly ample. I had been initiated by two inspired professors in Canada, O. J. Stevenson and E. C. McLean. They were men who deeply loved their craft and who were willing to spend endless hours with a student, however obscure his talent. I had been an editor of *Fortune,* which in my day meant mostly being a writer. Editor was thought a more distinguished title, and it justified more pay. Both as an editor proper and as a writer, I had had the close attention of Henry Robinson Luce. Harry Luce is in danger of being remembered only for his political judgment, which left much to be desired; he found unblemished merit in John Foster Dulles, Robert A. Taft and Chiang Kai-shek. But more important, he was an acute businessman and a truly brilliant editor. One proof is that while Time, Inc. publications have become politically more predictable since he departed, they have become infinitely less amusing.

4   Finally, as I reflected on my qualifications, there was the amount of my life that I have spent at a typewriter. Nominally I have been a teacher. In practice I have been a writer—as generations of Harvard students have suspected. Faced with the choice of spending time on the unpublished scholarship of a graduate student or the unpublished work of Galbraith, I have rarely hesitated. Superficially at least, I was well qualified for that California chair.

5   There was, however, a major difficulty. It was that I could tell everything I knew about writing in approximately half an hour. For the rest of the term I would have nothing to say except as I could invite discussion, this being the last resort of the distraught academic mind. I could use up a few hours telling how a writer should deal with publishers. This is a field of study in which I especially rejoice. All authors should seek to establish a relationship of warmth, affection and mutual mistrust with their publishers in the hope that the uncertainty will add, however marginally, to compensation.

But instruction on how to deal with publishers and how to bear up under the inevitable defeat would be for a very advanced course. It is not the sort of thing that the average beginning writer at Berkeley would find immediately practical.

So I returned to the few things that I could teach. The first lesson would have had to do with the all-important issue of inspiration. All writers know that on some golden mornings they are touched by the wand; they are on intimate terms with poetry and cosmic truth. I have experienced those moments myself. Their lesson is simple; they are a total illusion. And the danger in the illusion is that you will wait for them. Such is the horror of having to face the typewriter that you will spend all your time waiting. I am persuaded that, hangovers apart, most writers, like most other artisans, are about as good one day as the next (a point that Trollope made). The seeming difference is the result of euphoria, alcohol or imagination. All this means that one had better go to his or her typewriter every morning and stay there regardless of the result. It will be much the same. 6

All professions have their own way of justifying laziness. Harvard professors are deeply impressed by the jeweled fragility of their minds. Like the thinnest metal, these are subject terribly to fatigue. More than six hours of teaching a week is fatal—and an impairment of academic freedom. So, at any given moment, the average professor is resting his mind in preparation for the next orgiastic act of insight or revelation. Writers, by the same token, do nothing because they are waiting for inspiration. 7

In my own case there are days when the result is so bad that no fewer than five revisions are required. However, when I'm greatly inspired, only four are needed before, as I've often said, I put in that note of spontaneity which even my meanest critics concede. My advice to those eager students in California would have been, "Don't wait for the golden moment. Things may well be worse." 8

I would also have warned against the flocking tendency of writers and its use as a cover for idleness. It helps greatly in the avoidance of work to be in the company of others who are also waiting for the golden moment. The best place to write is by yourself because writing then becomes an escape from the terrible boredom of your own personality. It's the reason that for years I've favored Switzerland, where I look at the telephone and yearn to hear it ring. 9

The question of revision is closely allied with that of inspiration. There may be inspired writers for whom the first draft is just right. But anyone who is not certifiably a Milton had better assume that the first draft is a very primitive thing. The reason is simple: writing is difficult work. Ralph D. Paine, who managed *Fortune* in my time, used to say that anyone who said 10 writing was easy was either a bad writer or an unregenerate liar. Thinking, as Voltaire avowed, is also a very tedious process which men or women will do anything to avoid. So all first drafts are deeply flawed by the need to combine composition with thought. Each later one is less demanding in this regard; hence the writing can be better. There does come a time when revision is for the sake of change—when one has become so bored with the words that anything that is different looks better. But even then it may *be* better.

11   For months when I was working on *The Affluent Society,* my title was "The Opulent Society." Eventually I could stand it no longer; the word opulent had a nasty, greasy sound. One day, before starting work, I looked up the synonyms in the dictionary. First to meet my eye was the word "affluent." I had only one worry; that was whether I could possibly sell it to my publisher. All publishers wish to have books called *The Crisis in American Democracy.* The title, to my surprise, was acceptable. Mark Twain once said that the difference between the right word and almost the right word is the difference between lightning and a lightning bug.

12   Next, I would have stressed a rather old-fashioned idea—brevity—to those students. It was, above all, the lesson of Harry Luce. No one who worked for him ever again escaped the feeling that he was there looking over one's shoulder. In his hand was a pencil; down on each page one could expect, at any moment, a long swishing wiggle accompanied by the comment: "This can go." Invariably it could. It was written to please the author and not the reader. Or to fill in the space. The gains from brevity are obvious; in most efforts to achieve it, the worst and the dullest go. And it is the worst and the dullest that spoil the rest.

13   I know that brevity is now out of favor. The *New York Review of Books* prides itself on giving its authors as much space as they want and sometimes twice as much as they need. Writing for television, on the other hand, as I've learned in the last few years, is an exercise in relentless condensation. It has left me with the feeling that even brevity can be carried to extremes. But the danger, as I look at some of the newer fashions in writing, is not great.

14   The next of my injunctions, which I would have imparted with even less hope of success, would have concerned alcohol. Nothing is so pleasant. Nothing is so important for giving the writer a sense of confidence in himself. And nothing so impairs the product. Again there are exceptions: I remember a brilliant writer at *Fortune* for whom I was responsible who could work only with his hat on and after consuming a bottle of Scotch. There were major crises for him in the years immediately after World War II when Scotch was difficult to find. But it is, quite literally, very sobering to reflect on how many good American writers have been destroyed by this solace—by the sauce. Scott Fitzgerald, Sinclair Lewis, Thomas Wolfe, Ernest Hemingway, William Faulkner—the list goes on and on. Hamish Hamilton, once my English

publisher, put the question to James Thurber: "Jim, why is it so many of your great writers have ruined themselves with drink?" Thurber thought long and carefully and finally replied, "It's this way, Jamie. They wrote those novels, which sold very well. They made a lot of money and so they could buy whisky by the case."

Their reputation was universal. A few years before his death, John Steinbeck, an appreciative but not a compulsive drinker, went to Moscow. It was a triumphal tour, and in a letter that he sent me about his hosts, he said: "I found I enjoyed the Soviet hustlers pretty much. There was a kind of youthful honesty about their illicit intentions that was not without charm." I later heard that one night, after a particularly effusive celebration, he decided to return to the hotel on foot. On the way he was overcome by fatigue and the hospitality he had received and sat down on a bench in a small park to rest. A policeman, called a militiaman in Moscow, came along and informed John, who was now asleep, and his companion, who spoke Russian, that the benches could not be occupied at that hour. His companion explained, rightly, that John was a very great American writer and that an exception should be made. The militiaman insisted. The companion explained again and insisted more strongly. Presently a transcendental light came over the policeman's face. He looked at Steinbeck asleep on the bench, inspected his condition more closely, recoiled slightly from the fumes and said, "Oh, oh, Gemingway." Then he took off his cap and tiptoed carefully away. 15

We are all desperately afraid of sounding like Carrie Nation. I must take the risk. Any writer who wants to do his best against a deadline should stick to Coca-Cola. 16

Next, I would have wanted to tell my students of a point strongly pressed, if my memory serves, by George Bernard Shaw. He once said that as he grew older, he became less and less interested in theory, more and more interested in information. The temptation in writing is just the reverse. Nothing is so hard to come by as a new and interesting fact. Nothing is so easy on the feet as a generalization. I now pick up magazines and leaf through them looking for articles that are rich with facts; I don't much care what they are. Evocative and deeply percipient theory I avoid. It leaves me cold unless I am the author of it myself. My advice to all young writers would be to stick to research and reporting with only a minimum of interpretation. And even more this would be my advice to all older writers, particularly to columnists. As one's feet give out, one seeks to have the mind take their place. 17

Reluctantly, but from a long and terrible experience, I would have urged my class to recognize the grave risks in a resort to humor. It does greatly lighten one's task. I've often wondered who made it impolite to laugh at one's own jokes, for it is one of the major enjoyments in life. And that is the point. 18

Humor is an intensely personal, largely internal thing. What pleases some, including the source, does not please others. One laughs; another says, "Well, I certainly see nothing funny about that." And the second opinion has just as much validity as the first, maybe more. Where humor is concerned, there are no standards—no one can say what is good or bad, although you can be sure that everyone will. Only a very foolish man will use a form of language that is wholly uncertain in its effect. And that is the nature of humor.

19 There are other reasons for avoiding humor. In our society the solemn person inspires far more trust than the one who laughs. The politician allows himself one joke at the beginning of his speech. A ritual. Then he changes his expression and affects an aspect of morbid solemnity signaling that, after all, he is a totally serious man. Nothing so undermines a point as its association with a wisecrack; the very word is pejorative.

20 Also, as Art Buchwald has pointed out, we live in an age when it is hard to invent anything that is as funny as everyday life; how could one improve, for example, on the efforts of the great men of television to attribute cosmic significance to the offhand and hilarious way Bert Lance combined professed fiscal conservatism with an unparalleled personal commitment to the deficit financing of John Maynard Keynes? And because the real world is so funny, there is almost nothing you can do, short of labeling a joke a joke, to keep people from taking it seriously. A number of years ago in *Harper's* I invented the theory that socialism in our time was the result of our dangerous addiction to team sports. The ethic of the team is all wrong for free enterprise. Its basic themes are cooperation; team spirit; acceptance of leadership; the belief that the coach is always right. Authoritarianism is sanctified; the individualist is a poor team player, a menace. All this our vulnerable adolescents learn. I announced the formation of an organization to combat this deadly trend and to promote boxing and track instead. I called it the CAI—Crusade for Athletic Individualism. Scores wrote in to *Harper's* asking to join. Or demanding that baseball be exempted. A batter is, after all, on his own. I presented the letters to the Kennedy Library.

21 Finally, I would have come to a matter of much personal interest, one that is intensely self-serving. It concerns the peculiar pitfalls for the writer who is dealing with presumptively difficult or technical matters. Economics is an example, and within the field of economics the subject of money, with the history of which I have been much concerned, is an especially good case. Any specialist who ventures to write on money with a view to making himself intelligible works under a grave moral hazard. He will be accused of oversimplification. The charge will be made by his fellow professionals, however obtuse or incompetent, and it will have a sympathetic hearing from the layman. That is because no layman really expects to understand about money, inflation or the International Monetary Fund. If he does, he suspects that he is being fooled. Only someone who is decently confusing can be respected.

In the case of economics there are no important propositions that can- 22
not, in fact, be stated in plain language. Qualifications and refinements are
numerous and of great technical complexity. These are important for separating the good students from the dolts. But in economics the refinements rarely,
if ever, modify the essential and practical point. The writer who seeks to be
intelligible needs to be right; he must be challenged if his argument leads to
an erroneous conclusion and especially if it leads to the wrong action. But he
can safely dismiss the charge that he has made the subject too easy. The truth
is not difficult.

Complexity and obscurity, on the other hand, have professional value; 23
they are the academic equivalents of apprenticeship rules in the building
trades. They exclude the outsiders, keep down the competition, preserve the
image of a privileged or priestly class. The man who makes things clear is a
scab. He is criticized less for his clarity than for his treachery.

Additionally, and especially in the social sciences, much unclear writing is 24
based on unclear or incomplete thought. It is possible with safety to be
technically obscure about something you haven't thought out. It is impossible to be wholly clear on something you don't understand; clarity exposes
flaws in the thought. The person who undertakes to make difficult matters
clear is infringing on the sovereign right of numerous economists, sociologists and political scientists to make bad writing the disguise for sloppy,
imprecise or incomplete thought. One can understand the resulting anger.
Adam Smith, John Stuart Mill and John Maynard Keynes were writers of
crystalline clarity most of the time. Marx had great moments, as in *The
Communist Manifesto*. Economics owes very little, if anything, to the practitioners of scholarly obscurity. However, if any of my California students
had come to me from the learned professions, I would have counseled them
that if they wanted to keep the confidence of their colleagues, they should do
so by always being complex, obscure and even a trifle vague.

You might say that all this constitutes a meager yield for a lifetime of 25
writing. Or perhaps, as someone once said of Jack Kerouac's prose, not
writing but typing.

E. B. WHITE

Mostly About Writing:
Selected Letters

"The essayist," writes White in the Foreword to The Essays of E. B. White *(1977),*

> *is a self-liberated man, sustained by the childish belief that everything he thinks about, everything that happens to him, is of general interest. He is the fellow who thoroughly enjoys his work, just as people who take bird walks enjoy theirs. Each new excursion of the essayist, each new "attempt," differs from the last and takes him into new country. This delights him. Only a person who is congenitally self-centered has the effrontery and the stamina to write essays.*

In the process of defining the essayist White has, of course, characterized himself, though his writing is of such superb quality, despite its apparent casualness, that even the minutiae of his daily life and thoughts do in fact become "of general interest."

Born in peaceful Mount Vernon, New York, in 1899, White was editor of the Cornell Daily Sun *during his senior year in college, 1920–21. In 1927, after several years of writing advertising, he joined the staff of the year-old* New Yorker, *writing "Talk of the Town" and "Notes and Comments" columns. Over the next thirty years he also wrote an estimated thirty thousand witty rejoinders to "newsbreaks," mangled sentences and misprints that filled out* New Yorker *columns and appeared under headings that White invented, such as "Letters We Never Finished Reading." In 1957 the Whites (Katherine was a beloved fiction editor at the* New Yorker*) moved permanently to Allen Cove, Maine, where White continued to inform and delight until his death in 1985. His distinguished, classic works include the essays collected in* One Man's Meat *(1944),* The Second Tree from the Corner *(1954), and* The Points of the Compass *(1962); landmark advice on how to write clear, plain prose in* The Elements of Style *(rev. 1973), an elaboration of the advice of his Cornell professor, William Strunk; and children's books,* Stuart Little *(1945),* Charlotte's Web *(1952), and* The Trumpet of the Swan *(1970). His works reflect White's lifelong sympathy for creatures great and small, adults and children, birds, animals, and insects—including pigs and spiders, as the following letters reveal.*

To STANLEY HART WHITE

Thursday
Bert Mosher's.
Belgrade Lakes, Maine
[1936?]

Dear Stan:

I returned to Belgrade. Things haven't changed much. There's a train called the Bar Harbor Express, and Portland is foggy early in the morning, and the Pullman blankets are brown and thin and cold. But when you look out of the window in the diner, steam is rising from pastures and the sun is

out, and pretty soon the train is skirting a blue lake called Messalonski.
Things don't change much. Even the names, you still hear them: names like
Caswell, Bartlett, names like Bickford, Walter Gleason, Damren. Gram lives
alone in the chowder house, down by the lake, brooding on days before the
farm burnt, hanging draperies the Count sends her from abroad. The lake
hangs clear and still at dawn, and the sound of a cowbell comes softly from a
faraway woodlot. In the shallows along shore the pebbles and driftwood
show clear and smooth on bottom, and black water bugs dart, spreading a
wake and a shadow. A fish rises quickly in the lily pads with a little plop, and a
broad ring widens to eternity. The water in the basin is icy before breakfast,
and cuts sharply into your nose and ears and makes your face blue as you
wash. But the boards of the dock are already hot in the sun, and there are
doughnuts for breakfast and the smell is there, the faintly rancid smell that
hangs around Maine kitchens. Sometimes there is little wind all day, and on
still hot afternoons the sound of a motorboat comes drifting five miles from
the other shore, and the droning lake becomes articulate, like a hot field. A
crow calls, fearfully and far. If a night breeze springs up, you are aware of a
restless noise along the shore, and for a few minutes before you fall asleep you
hear the intimate talk between fresh-water waves and rocks that lie below
bending birches. The insides of your camp are hung with pictures cut from
magazines, and the camp smells of lumber and damp. Things don't change
much. Meadow stream has a beginning in the pickerel weeds. If you push
along quietly, a blue heron will rise with a heavy squawk and a flap. The ends
of logs that jut out are covered with the dung of little animals that come there
to eat fresh mussels and wash their paws at the stream-side. Over at the Mills
there's a frog box, sunk half in the water. People come there in boats and buy
bait. You buy a drink of Birch Beer at Bean's tackle store. Big bass swim lazily
in the deep water at the end of the wharf, well fed. Long lean guide boats kick
white water in the stern till they suck under. There are still one cylinder
engines that don't go. Maybe it's the needle valve. At twilight, cows come
hesitantly down the little woods roads behind the camps to steal a drink in
the cove. They belong to a man named Withers. Withers' cows. Pasture bars
are cedar, stripped of bark, weathered grey. On rainy days swallows come and
dip water, and the camps are cold. When the wind swings into the north, the
blow comes. It comes suddenly, and you know a change has come over
things, instinctively. Next day you will see a little maple, flaming red, all alone
in a bog. It's cold and fearsome by the lake. The wind still holds strong into
the second morning, and white caps are as thick as whiskers. When you get
back on the road, away from the lake, the road lies warm and yellow, and you
hear the wind fussing in the treetops behind you and you don't care. The
rocks in the stream behind the Salmon Lake House are colored red and
colored green, where the boats have scraped them under water. The clothesline behind Walter Gleason's house is flapping with white wash. . . . There's a

house on a hill where a lady lived that used to keep cats. Along the road the apples are little and yellow and sweet. Puddles dry in the sun, and the mud cakes, and yellow butterflies diddle in the new mud. Cow trails lead up slopes through juniper beds and thistles and grey rocks, and below you the lake hangs blue and clear, and you see the islands plain. Sometimes a farm dog barks. Yes, sir, I returned to Belgrade, and things don't change much. I thought somebody ought to know.

En

TO SHIRLEY WILEY

[New York]
March 30, 1954

Dear Miss Wiley:

My wife is helpful to me in my writing, but she does not write. She is an editor. An editor is a person who knows more about writing than writers do but who has escaped the terrible desire to write. I have been writing since 1906 and it is high time I got over it. A writer, however, writes as long as he lives. It is the same as breathing except that it is bad for one's health. Some of my writings have won prizes but awards of that sort are not very much fun or satisfaction and I would rather have a nice drink of ginger ale, usually. Writing does have its rewards but they do not come in packages.

Hope I've answered all your questions.

Sincerely,
E. B. White

TO J. DONALD ADAMS

[New York]
September 28th, 1956

Dear Mr. Adams:

Thanks for your letter inviting me to join the Committee of the Arts and Sciences for Eisenhower.

I must decline, for secret reasons.

Sincerely,
E. B. White

TO JOHN DETMOLD

25 West 43rd Street
February 10, 1953

Dear John:

I shall of course sign the book for your mother, and will deliver it to Peter for presentation on February 20.

As to your notion of an allegory, there is none. "Charlotte's Web" is a tale of the animals in my barn, not of the people in my life. When you read it, just relax. Any attempt to find allegorical meanings is bound to end disastrously, for no meanings are in there. I ought to know.

Sincerely,
Andy White

To MRS. B. J. KASTON

[New York]
April 10, 1953

Dear Mrs. Kaston:

Thanks for the letter and the picture of Charlotte's cousin, which is very pretty.

The idea of the writing in Charlotte's Web came to me one day when I was on my way down through the orchard carrying a pail of slops to my pig. I had made up my mind to write a children's book about animals, and I needed a way to save a pig's life, and I had been watching a large spider in the backhouse, and what with one thing and another, the idea came to me.

Sincerely,
E. B. White

To MRS. N. J. SHOPLAND

[New York]
September 28, 1961

Dear Mrs. Shopland:

. . . The characters in "Charlotte's Web" were not presented as hicks; today's farmer is anything but. Neither were they presented as intellectuals who use the language with precision. Very few people in any walk of life speak and write precisely and correctly, and I don't myself. Your two letters, for example, contained mistakes—in the first letter you spelled grammar "grammer," and in the second letter you used the word "forbearers" when you meant "forebears."

I know the Zuckermans and the Arables quite well, and although I am not a farmer, many of my good friends are. I agree with you that the modern farmer is often a man of considerable education. But I think you are under a misapprehension about the nature of writing and the duties of a writer. I do not write books to raise any group's cultural level, I simply put down on paper the things I see and hear. I report speech as I hear it, not as it appears in books of rhetoric. If you ever take up writing, I advise you to keep your ears open, and never mind about culture.

Sincerely,
E. B. White

RED SMITH

I'd Like to Be Called a Good Reporter

"People go to spectator sports to have fun and then they grab the paper to read about it and have fun again," is the credo of master sports columnist Red Smith, who believed that "sports isn't Armageddon," it's entertainment. Smith was born in Green Bay, Wisconsin, in 1905 (before the Packers' time) and graduated from Notre Dame in 1927, in the middle of the Rockne years. His career as a sportswriter began with the St. Louis Star, *1928–1936; he then spent a decade with the* Philadelphia Recorder, *as he says, following a baseball team for whom the pennant race was only a rumor. He wrote for* The New York Times *from 1971 until his death in 1982.*

In the following interview, Smith reflects on his career as a reporter, its mixture of hard work and enjoyment, for "today's game is always different from yesterday's game . . . and your story is always different from yesterday's story." He defends the validity of sports writing against charges of triviality, because "sports constitute a valid part of our culture, our civilization." Smith identifies his need, like any writer's, to maintain enthusiasm for a job he's done, season after season, for over fifty years: "My enthusiasm is self-generating, self-renewing." It keeps him writing "painstakingly," rewriting, striving for E. B. White's clear and captivating prose in an attempt to make every piece a home run.

1   NEW CANAAN, CONNECTICUT, 1973. I never felt that I was a bug-eyed fan as such. I wasn't one of those who dreamed of being a sportswriter and going around the country traveling with ballplayers and getting into the games free and, oh, dear diary, what a break. I'm not pretending that I haven't enjoyed this hugely. I have. I've loved it. But I never had any soaring ambition to be a sportswriter, per se. I wanted to be a newspaperman, and came to realize I didn't really care which side of the paper I worked on.

2   I'm too lazy to change over now, to start something new at this stage: I just got so comfortable in so many years in sports. But otherwise I still feel that way. I never cared. When I went to Philadelphia I didn't know what side of the paper I'd be on. I had done three or four years of rewrite and general reporting in St. Louis when I accepted the offer in Philadelphia. I knew how many dollars a week I was going to get. That was the essential thing. I never asked what they wanted me to do.

3   The guy I admire most in the world is a good reporter. I respect a good reporter, and I'd like to be called that. I'd like to be considered good and honest and reasonably accurate. The reporter has one of the toughest jobs in the world—getting as near the truth as possible is a terribly tough job. I was a local side reporter in St. Louis and Milwaukee. I wasn't as good as some. I wasn't one of those who could go out and find the kidnapper and the child. But I got my facts straight and did a thorough job.

4   I like to report on the scene around me, on the little piece of the world as

46

I see it, as it is in my time. And I like to do it in a way that gives the reader a little pleasure, a little entertainment. I've always had the notion that people go to spectator sports to have fun and then they grab the paper to read about it and have fun again.

I've always tried to remember—and this is an old line—that sports isn't   5
Armageddon. These are just little games that little boys can play, and it really isn't important to the future of civilization whether the Athletics or the Browns win. If you can accept it as entertainment, and write it as entertainment, then I think that's what spectator sports are meant to be.

I've been having fun doing this seminar at Yale, once a week. They call it   6
Sports in American Society. I don't know what that name means, but obviously it's a big, broad topic and I have got guys up to help me. It's a round-table discussion, eighteen students, but usually there are a couple missing so it's about fifteen. We bat around everything from the reserve system to amateurism and professionalism, and yesterday they wanted to talk about sports journalism, a subject I have been avoiding because I wanted them to do the talking. As a rule, I fire out a subject and say, "What do you think about this?" and they kick it around. I like that better. I knew that if I was alone I'd do all the talking, so I got Leonard Koppett of the *Times* up there to help. And Koppett said that generally speaking sportswriters aren't the most brilliant people in the world because really smart people do something else besides traveling with a ball club for twenty-five years. I don't know. Did you ever feel discontented, feel the need to do something that other people would say was more important?

During the war, World War II, I was of draft age. By that I mean I hadn't   7
yet gotten to be thirty-eight. I was registered for the draft, but I had a family and didn't think I could afford to be a private in the army and I didn't want to go looking for one of those phony public relations commissions. So I just kept traveling with the last-place Philadelphia Athletics and, oh boy, more than once I thought, What the hell am I doing here? But that was during the war. Outside of that I never felt any prodding need to solve the problems of the world. You can help a little by writing about games, especially if you're writing a column.

Oh, I don't know if I've ever helped, but I have tried to stay aware of the   8
world outside, beyond the fences, outside the playing field, and to let that awareness creep into the column sometimes. Occasionally, I've thrown a line about a Spiro Agnew or a Richard Nixon into a piece. I wouldn't imagine I had any effect, excepting to make an occasional reader write and say, "Stick to sports, you bum. What do you know about politics?"

Sure, I respect the Tom Wickers. He's certainly more effective. But   9
somehow I have felt that my time wasn't altogether wasted. I haven't been ashamed of what I've done. I seem to be making apologies for it. I don't mean to, because I feel keeping the public informed in any area is a perfectly worthwhile way to spend your life. I think sports constitute a valid part of

our culture, our civilization, and keeping the public informed and, if possible, a little entertained about sports is not an entirely useless thing.

10   I did get a kick out of covering an occasional political convention, but even then my approach to it was as a sportswriter viewing a very popular spectator sport, and I tried to have fun with it. I did the presidential conventions in '56 and again in '68. The 1956 Democratic convention in Chicago was a pretty good one. Happy Chandler was a candidate for the presidential nomination. They finally nominated Adlai Stevenson and almost nominated John Kennedy for Vice President. Kennedy was in the Stockyard Inn writing his acceptance speech when they decided to go for Coonskin Cap—Kefauver. Anyway, there was Happy Chandler. He was a good, soft touch for one column. There was Governor Clements of Tennessee. He made one of the great cornball keynote addresses of our time, and he was good for another column. Let me see, what else? Oh, yes, Truman came on. He looked like the old champ, trying to make a comeback, like Dempsey. Truman wasn't running for reelection, but he showed up at the convention and made for lively copy. On the whole I just felt loose and easy and free to write what I pleased, and it seemed to come off well.

11   Over the years people have said to me, "Isn't it dull covering baseball every day?" My answer used to be "It becomes dull only to dull minds." Today's game is always different from yesterday's game. If you have the perception and the interest to see it, and the wit to express it, your story is always different from yesterday's story. I thoroughly enjoyed covering baseball daily.

12   I still think every game is different, not that some of them aren't dull, but it's a rare person who lives his life without encountering dull spots. It's up to the writer to take a lively interest and see the difference. Of course most of my years I was with a club to which a pennant race was only a rumor—the Philadelphia Athletics. I did ten years with them. They were always last.

13   I don't agree with him, but yesterday, at Yale, Leonard Koppett said one of the great untrue clichés in sports is that the legs go first. He said that's not true. He insists that the enthusiasm, the desire go first. And he said this is generally true of the athlete and, of course, when the athlete gets above thirty-five or forty he just can't go on. He's physically unable to. The writer can go on, he is able to physically, but Leonard believes writers lose their enthusiasm, too. He thinks very few writers of forty-five have had the enthusiasm of their youth for the job. He said he didn't know how writers of sixty-five felt, and I said, "Neither do I, but I don't think I've lost my enthusiasm." If I did, I'd want to quit.

14   My enthusiasm is self-generating, self-renewing. My life, the way it's been going now, I see very few baseball games in the summer. I'll start with the opening of the season. I'll see the games then, but things like the Kentucky Derby and Preakness get in the way, and lately we've had a home up in Martha's Vineyard, where I like to spend as much of the summer as I can,

48

working from there. By the time the World Series comes along I may feel that I've had very little baseball for the year. But I find that old enthusiasm renewing itself when I sit there at the playoffs.

I don't enjoy the actual labor of writing. I love my job, but I find one of the disadvantages is the several hours at the typewriter each day. That's how I pay for this nice job. And I pay pretty dearly. I sweat. I bleed. I'm a slow writer. Once, through necessity, I was a fast rewrite man, when I had to be. I had no choice.

But when I began doing a column, which is a much more personal thing, I found it wasn't something that I could rip off the top of my head. I had to do it painstakingly. I'm always unhappy, very unhappy, at anything that takes less than two hours. I can do it in two hours, if I must. But my usual answer to the question "How long does it take to write a column?" is "How much time do I have?" If I have six hours, I take it. I wish I could say that the ones that take six hours turn out better. Not necessarily. But I will say this: I do think that, over three hundred days, effort pays off. If you do the best you can every day, taking as much time as necessary, or as much time as you have, then it's going to be better than if you brushed it off.

It's not very often that I feel gratified with a piece I've just written. Very often I feel, "Well, this one is okay." Or "This one will get by." The next day when I read it in print, clean and in two-column measure, it often looks better. But sometimes I'm disappointed. If I think I've written a clinker, I'm terribly depressed for twenty-four hours. But when you write a good one, you feel set up, the adrenaline is flowing.

Arthur Daley once told me that Paul Gallico asked him, "How many good columns do you strive for?"

Arthur said, "One every day."

And Gallico said, "I'll settle for two a week."

In my later years I have sought to become simpler, straighter, and purer in my handling of the language. I've had many writing heroes, writers who have influenced me. Of the ones still alive, I can think of E. B. White. I certainly admire the pure, crystal stream of his prose. When I was very young as a sportswriter I knowingly and unashamedly imitated others. I had a series of heroes who would delight me for a while and I'd imitate them—Damon Runyon, Westbrook Pegler, Joe Williams. This may surprise you, but at the top of his game I thought Joe Williams was pretty good.

I think you pick up something from this guy and something from that. I know that I deliberately imitated those three guys, one by one, never together. I'd read one daily, faithfully, and be delighted by him and imitate him. Then someone else would catch my fancy. That's a shameful admission. But slowly, by what process I have no idea, your own writing tends to crystallize, to take shape. Yet you have learned some moves from all these guys and they are somehow incorporated into your own style. Pretty soon you're not imitating any longer.

Questions

1. What is a "good reporter," according to Smith? Do you agree with Smith's assertion that to write well one needs "enthusiasm" for the job (paragraphs 13–14)?

2. "I'd Like to Be Called a Good Reporter" was originally a newspaper column. How does the fact that newspaper paragraphing is determined as much by sight (a break at every column inch) as by sense affect Smith's division of his subject matter?

3. In what ways does Smith's informal, sometimes slangy language ("grab the paper," "guys") fit his subject? How does he convey a conversational tone? create an authorial personality (persona)?

4. Does Smith's discussion of writing apply exclusively to sportswriting? Why or why not?

VIRGINIA WOOLF

A Room of One's Own: Shakespeare's Sister

Woolf, an extraordinarily talented novelist, is recognized particularly for her innovations in point of view and stream-of-consciousness technique and for her psychologically penetrating characterizations of women. Now, nearly fifty years after her suicide by drowning in 1941 at age 59, interest remains high in both her works and in her life, as reflected in the recent publication of five hefty volumes of her Diary—*a thoughtful, sometimes satiric, often anguished, commentary on the writer's life and work.*

In 1912 Virginia, daughter of esteemed biographer Sir Leslie Stephen, and member of the creative, bohemian "Bloomsbury Group," married socialist writer Leonard Woolf—"the wisest decision of my life." Leonard subordinated his own career to sustain his wife's work and her fragile psychological health; together they founded the innovative Hogarth Press, and she wrote the novels which established her reputation: Jacob's Room *(1922),* Mrs. Dalloway *(1925),* To the Lighthouse *(1927), and* The Waves *(1931). Woolf's many distinguished essays demonstrate how the novelist's skills serve the essayist well. In "Shakespeare's Sister," for example, she creates a compelling cautionary tale of the frustration and ruin of Shakespeare's talented imaginary sister, and uses this to dramatically illustrate what creative people, women as well as men, need to accomplish their work. Indeed, "a room of one's own," from which this selection is excerpted, has become a modern metaphor for mental—as well as physical—space to think and create and work without interruption from the clutter of everyday life.*

1   It was disappointing not to have brought back in the evening some important statement, some authentic fact. Women are poorer than men because—this or that. Perhaps now it would be better to give up seeking for the truth, and receiving on one's head an avalanche of opinion hot as lava, discoloured as dish-water. It would be better to draw the curtains; to shut out distractions;

to light the lamp; to narrow the enquiry and to ask the historian, who records not opinions but facts, to describe under what conditions women lived, not throughout the ages, but in England, say in the time of Elizabeth.

For it is a perennial puzzle why no woman wrote a word of that extraor- **2** dinary literature when every other man, it seemed, was capable of song or sonnet. What were the conditions in which women lived, I asked myself; for fiction, imaginative work that is, is not dropped like a pebble upon the ground, as science may be; fiction is like a spider's web, attached ever so lightly perhaps, but still attached to life at all four corners. Often the attachment is scarcely perceptible; Shakespeare's plays, for instance, seem to hang there complete by themselves. But when the web is pulled askew, hooked up at the edge, torn in the middle, one remembers that these webs are not spun in midair by incorporeal creatures, but are the work of suffering human beings, and are attached to grossly material things, like health and money and the houses we live in.

I went, therefore, to the shelf where the histories stand and took down **3** one of the latest, Professor Trevelyan's *History of England*. Once more I looked up Women, found "position of," and turned to the pages indicated. "Wife-beating," I read, "was a recognised right of man, and was practised without shame by high as well as low. . . . Similarly," the historian goes on, "the daughter who refused to marry the gentleman of her parents' choice was liable to be locked up, beaten and flung about the room, without any shock being inflicted on public opinion. Marriage was not an affair of personal affection, but of family avarice, particularly in the 'chivalrous' upper classes. . . . Betrothal often took place while one or both of the parties was in the cradle, and marriage when they were scarcely out of the nurses' charge." That was about 1470, soon after Chaucer's time. The next reference to the position of women is some two hundred years later, in the time of the Stuarts. "It was still the exception for women of the upper and middle class to choose their own husbands, and when the husband had been assigned, he was lord and master, so far at least as law and custom could make him. Yet even so," Professor Trevelyan concludes, "neither Shakespeare's women nor those of authentic seventeenth-century memoirs, like the Verneys and the Hutchinsons, seem wanting in personality and character." Certainly, if we consider it, Cleopatra must have had a way with her; Lady Macbeth, one would suppose, had a will of her own; Rosalind, one might conclude, was an attractive girl. Professor Trevelyan is speaking no more than the truth when he remarks that Shakespeare's women do not seem wanting in personality and character. Not being a historian, one might go even further and say that women have burnt like beacons in all the works of all the poets from the beginning of time— Clytemnestra, Antigone, Cleopatra, Lady Macbeth, Phèdre, Cressida, Rosalind, Desdemona, the Duchess of Malfi, among the dramatists; then among the prose writers: Millamant, Clarissa, Becky Sharp, Anna Karenina, Emma Bovary, Madame de Guermantes—the names flock to mind, nor do they recall women "lacking in personality and character." Indeed, if woman had no existence save in the fiction written by men, one would imagine her a person of the utmost importance; very various; heroic and mean; splendid and sordid; infinitely beautiful and hideous in the extreme; as great as a man, some think even greater.[1] But this is woman in fiction. In fact, as Professor Trevelyan points out, she was locked up, beaten and flung about the room.

4   A very queer, composite being thus emerges. Imaginatively she is of the highest importance; practically she is completely insignificant. She pervades poetry from cover to cover; she is all but absent from history. She dominates the lives of kings and conquerors in fiction; in fact she was the slave of any boy whose parents forced a ring upon her finger. Some of the most inspired words, some of the most profound thoughts in literature fall from her lips; in real life she could hardly read, could scarcely spell, and was the property of her husband.

5   It was certainly an odd monster that one made up by reading the historians first and the poets afterwards—a worm winged like an eagle; the spirit of life and beauty in a kitchen chopping up suet. But these monsters, however amusing to the imagination, have no existence in fact. What one must do to bring her to life was to think poetically and prosaically at one and the same moment, thus keeping in touch with fact—that she is Mrs. Martin, aged thirty-six, dressed in blue, wearing a black hat and brown shoes; but not losing sight of fiction either—that she is a vessel in which all sorts of spirits and forces are coursing and flashing perpetually. The moment, however, that one tries this method with the Elizabethan woman, one branch of illumination fails; one is held up by the scarcity of facts. One knows nothing detailed, nothing perfectly true and substantial about her. History scarcely mentions her. And I turned to Professor Trevelyan again to see what history meant to him. I found by looking at his chapter headings that it meant—

6   "The Manor Court and the Methods of Open-field Agriculture . . . The Cistercians and Sheep-farming . . . The Crusades . . . The University . . . The House of Commons . . . The Hundred Years' War . . . The Wars of the Roses

---

[1] "It remains a strange and almost inexplicable fact that in Athena's city, where women were kept in almost Oriental suppression as odalisques or drudges, the stage should yet have produced figures like Clytemnestra and Cassandra, Atossa and Antigone, Phèdre and Medea, and all the other heroines who dominate play after play of the 'misogynist' Euripides. But the paradox of this world where in real life a respectable woman could hardly show her face alone in the street, and yet on the stage woman equals or surpasses man, has never been satisfactorily explained. In modern tragedy the same predominance exists. At all events, a very cursory survey of Shakespeare's work (similarly with Webster, though not with Marlowe or Jonson) suffices to reveal how this dominance, this initiative of women, persists from Rosalind to Lady Macbeth. So too in Racine; six of his tragedies bear their heroines' names; and what male characters of his shall we set against Hermione and Andromaque, Bérénice and Roxane, Phèdre and Athalie? So again with Ibsen; what men shall we match with Solveig and Nora, Hedda and Hilda Wangel and Rebecca West?"—F. L. Lucas, *Tragedy*, pp. 114–15.

. . . The Renaissance Scholars . . . The Dissolution of the Monasteries . . . Agrarian and Religious Strife . . . The Origin of English Sea-power . . . The Armada . . ." and so on. Occasionally an individual woman is mentioned, an Elizabeth, or a Mary; a queen or a great lady. But by no possible means could middle-class women with nothing but brains and character at their command have taken part in any one of the great movements which, brought together, constitute the historian's view of the past. Nor shall we find her in any collection of anecdotes. Aubrey hardly mentions her. She never writes her own life and scarcely keeps a diary; there are only a handful of her letters in existence. She left no plays or poems by which we can judge her. What one wants, I thought—and why does not some brilliant student at Newnham or Girton supply it?—is a mass of information; at what age did she marry; how many children had she as a rule; what was her house like; had she a room to herself; did she do the cooking; would she be likely to have a servant? All these facts lie somewhere, presumably, in parish registers and account books; the life of the average Elizabethan woman must be scattered about somewhere, could one collect it and make a book of it. It would be ambitious beyond my daring, I thought, looking about the shelves for books that were not there, to suggest to the students of those famous colleges that they should re-write history, though I own that it often seems a little queer as it is, unreal, lop-sided; but why should they not add a supplement to history? calling it, of course, by some inconspicuous name so that women might figure there without impropriety? For one often catches a glimpse of them in the lives of the great, whisking away into the background, concealing, I sometimes think, a wink, a laugh, perhaps a tear. And, after all, we have lives enough of Jane Austen; it scarcely seems necessary to consider again the influence of the tragedies of Joanna Baillie upon the poetry of Edgar Allan Poe; as for myself, I should not mind if the homes and haunts of Mary Russell Mitford were closed to the public for a century at least. But what I find deplorable, I continued, looking about the bookshelves again, is that nothing is known about women before the eighteenth century. I have no model in my mind to turn about this way and that. Here I am asking why women did not write poetry in the Elizabethan age, and I am not sure how they were educated; whether they were taught to write; whether they had sitting-rooms to themselves; how many women had children before they were twenty-one; what, in short, they did from eight in the morning till eight at night. They had no money evidently; according to Professor Trevelyan they were married whether they liked it or not before they were out of the nursery, at fifteen or sixteen very likely. It would have been extremely odd, even upon this showing, had one of them suddenly written the plays of Shakespeare, I concluded, and I thought of that old gentleman, who is dead now, but was a bishop, I think, who declared that it was impossible for any woman, past, present, or to come, to have the genius of Shakespeare. He wrote to the papers about it. He also told a lady who applied to him for information that cats do not as a matter of fact go to heaven, though they have, he added, souls of a sort. How much thinking those old gentlemen used to save one! How the borders of ignorance shrank back at their approach! Cats do not go to heaven. Women cannot write the plays of Shakespeare.

7   Be that as it may, I could not help thinking, as I looked at the works of Shakespeare on the shelf, that the bishop was right at least in this; it would have been impossible, completely and entirely, for any woman to have written the plays of Shakespeare in the age of Shakespeare. Let me imagine, since facts are so hard to come by, what would have happened had Shakespeare had a wonderfully gifted sister, called Judith, let us say. Shakespeare himself went, very probably—his mother was an heiress—to the grammar school, where he may have learnt Latin—Ovid, Virgil and Horace—and the elements of grammar and logic. He was, it is well known, a wild boy who poached rabbits, perhaps shot a deer, and had, rather sooner than he should have done, to marry a woman in the neighbourhood, who bore him a child rather quicker than was right. That escapade sent him to seek his fortune in London. He had, it seemed, a taste for the theatre; he began by holding horses at the stage door. Very soon he got work in the theatre, became a successful actor, and lived at the hub of the universe, meeting everybody, knowing everybody, practising his art on the boards, exercising his wits in the streets, and even getting access to the palace of the queen. Meanwhile his extraordinarily gifted sister, let us suppose, remained at home. She was as adventurous, as imaginative, as agog to see the world as he was. But she was not sent to school. She had no chance of learning grammar and logic, let alone of reading Horace and Virgil. She picked up a book now and then, one of her brother's perhaps, and read a few pages. But then her parents came in and told her to mend the stockings or mind the stew and not moon about with books and papers. They would have spoken sharply but kindly, for they were substantial people who knew the conditions of life for a woman and loved their daughter—indeed, more likely than not she was the apple of her father's eye. Perhaps she scribbled some pages up in an apple loft on the sly, but was careful to hide them or set fire to them. Soon, however, before she was out of her teens, she was to be betrothed to the son of a neighbouring wool-stapler. She cried out that marriage was hateful to her, and for that she was severely beaten by her father. Then he ceased to scold her. He begged her instead not to hurt him, not to shame him in this matter of her marriage. He would give her a chain of beads or a fine petticoat, he said; and there were tears in his eyes. How could she disobey him? How could she break his heart? The force of her own gift alone drove her to it. She made up a small parcel of her belongings, let herself down by a rope one summer's night and took the road to London. She was not seventeen. The birds that sang in the hedge were not more musical than she was. She had the quickest fancy, a gift like her brother's, for the tune of words. Like him, she had a taste for the theatre. She stood at the stage door; she wanted to act, she said. Men laughed in her

face. The manager—a fat, loose-lipped man—guffawed. He bellowed something about poodles dancing and women acting—no woman, he said, could possibly be an actress. He hinted—you can imagine what. She could get no training in her craft. Could she even seek her dinner in a tavern or roam the streets at midnight? Yet her genius was for fiction and lusted to feed abundantly upon the lives of men and women and the study of their ways. At last—for she was very young, oddly like Shakespeare the poet in her face, with the same grey eyes and rounded brows—at last Nick Greene the actor-manager took pity on her; she found herself with child by that gentleman and so—who shall measure the heat and violence of the poet's heart when caught and tangled in a woman's body?—killed herself one winter's night and lies buried at some cross-roads where the omnibuses now stop outside the Elephant and Castle.

That, more or less, is how the story would run, I think, if a woman in Shakespeare's day had had Shakespeare's genius. But for my part, I agree with the deceased bishop, if such he was—it is unthinkable that any woman in Shakespeare's day should have had Shakespeare's genius. For genius like Shakespeare's is not born among labouring, uneducated, servile people. It was not born in England among the Saxons and the Britons. It is not born today among the working classes. How, then, could it have been born among women whose work began, according to Professor Trevelyan, almost before they were out of the nursery, who were forced to it by their parents and held to it by all the power of law and custom? Yet genius of a sort must have existed among women as it must have existed among the working classes. Now and again an Emily Brontë or a Robert Burns blazes out and proves its presence. But certainly it never got itself on to paper. When, however, one reads of a witch being ducked, of a woman possessed by devils, of a wise woman selling herbs, or even of a very remarkable man who had a mother, then I think we are on the track of a lost novelist, a suppressed poet, of some mute and inglorious Jane Austen, some Emily Brontë who dashed her brains out on the moor or mopped and mowed about the highways crazed with the torture that her gift had put her to. Indeed, I would venture to guess that Anon, who wrote so many poems without signing them, was often a woman. It was a woman Edward Fitzgerald, I think, suggested who made the ballads and the folk-songs, crooning them to her children, beguiling her spinning with them, or the length of the winter's night.

This may be true or it may be false—who can say?—but what is true in it, so it seemed to me, reviewing the story of Shakespeare's sister as I had made it, is that any woman born with a great gift in the sixteenth century would certainly have gone crazed, shot herself, or ended her days in some lonely cottage outside the village, half witch, half wizard, feared and mocked at. For it needs little skill in psychology to be sure that a highly gifted girl who had tried to use her gift for poetry would have been so thwarted and hindered by other people, so tortured and pulled asunder by her own contrary instincts, that she must have lost her health and sanity to a certainty. No girl could have walked to London and stood at a stage door and forced her way into the presence of actor-managers without doing herself a violence and suffering an anguish which may have been irrational—for chastity may be a fetish invented by certain societies for unknown reasons—but were none the less inevitable. Chastity had then, it has even now, a religious importance in a woman's life, and has so wrapped itself round with nerves and instincts that to cut it free and bring it to the light of day demands courage of the rarest. To have lived a free life in London in the sixteenth century would have meant for a woman who was poet and playwright a nervous stress and dilemma which might well have killed her. Had she survived, whatever she had written would have been twisted and deformed, issuing from a strained and morbid imagination. And undoubtedly, I thought, looking at the shelf where there are no plays by women, her work would have gone unsigned. That refuge she would have sought certainly. It was the relic of the sense of chastity that dictated anonymity to women even so late as the nineteenth century. Currer Bell, George Eliot, George Sand, all the victims of inner strife as their writings prove, sought ineffectively to veil themselves by using the name of a man. Thus they did homage to the convention, which if not implanted by the other sex was liberally encouraged by them (the chief glory of a woman is not to be talked of, said Pericles, himself a much-talked-of man), that publicity in women is detestable. Anonymity runs in their blood. The desire to be veiled still possesses them. They are not even now as concerned about the health of their fame as men are, and, speaking generally, will pass a tombstone or a signpost without feeling an irresistible desire to cut their names on it, as Alf, Bert or Chas. must do in obedience to their instinct, which murmurs if it sees a fine woman go by, or even a dog, Ce chien est à moi. And, of course, it may not be a dog, I thought, remembering Parliament Square, the Sieges Allee and other avenues; it may be a piece of land or a man with curly black hair. It is one of the great advantages of being a woman that one can pass even a very fine negress without wishing to make an Englishwoman of her.

10   That woman, then, who was born with a gift of poetry in the sixteenth century, was an unhappy woman, a woman at strife against herself. All the conditions of her life, all her own instincts, were hostile to the state of mind which is needed to set free whatever is in the brain. But what is the state of mind that is most propitious to the act of creation, I asked. Can one come by any notion of the state that furthers and makes possible that strange activity? Here I opened the volume containing the Tragedies of Shakespeare. What was Shakespeare's state of mind, for instance, when he wrote *Lear* and *Antony and Cleopatra*? It was certainly the state of mind most favourable to poetry that there has ever existed. But Shakespeare himself said nothing about it. We only know casually and by chance that he "never blotted a line." Nothing indeed was ever said by the artist himself about his state of mind until the eighteenth century perhaps. Rousseau perhaps began it. At any rate, by the

nineteenth century self-consciousness had developed so far that it was the habit for men of letters to describe their minds in confessions and autobiographies. Their lives also were written, and their letters were printed after their deaths. Thus, though we do not know what Shakespeare went through when he wrote *Lear,* we do know what Carlyle went through when he wrote the *French Revolution;* what Flaubert went through when he wrote *Madame Bovary;* what Keats was going through when he tried to write poetry against the coming of death and the indifference of the world.

And one gathers from this enormous modern literature of confession and self-analysis that to write a work of genius is almost always a feat of prodigious difficulty. Everything is against the likelihood that it will come from the writer's mind whole and entire. Generally material circumstances are against it. Dogs will bark; people will interrupt; money must be made; health will break down. Further, accentuating all these difficulties and making them harder to bear is the world's notorious indifference. It does not ask people to write poems and novels and histories; it does not need them. It does not care whether Flaubert finds the right word or whether Carlyle scrupulously verifies this or that fact. Naturally, it will not pay for what it does not want. And so the writer, Keats, Flaubert, Carlyle, suffers, especially in the creative years of youth, every form of distraction and discouragement. A curse, a cry of agony, rises from those books of analysis and confession. "Mighty poets in their misery dead"—that is the burden of their song. If anything comes through in spite of all this, it is a miracle, and probably no book is born entire and uncrippled as it was conceived. 11

But for women, I thought, looking at the empty shelves, these difficulties were infinitely more formidable. In the first place, to have a room of her own, let alone a quiet room or a sound-proof room, was out of the question, unless her parents were exceptionally rich or very noble, even up to the beginning of the nineteenth century. Since her pin money, which depended on the good will of her father, was only enough to keep her clothed, she was debarred from such alleviations as came even to Keats or Tennyson or Carlyle, all poor men, from a walking tour, a little journey to France, from the separate lodging which, even if it were miserable enough, sheltered them from the claims and tyrannies of their families. Such material difficulties were formidable; but much worse were the immaterial. The indifference of the world which Keats and Flaubert and other men of genius have found so hard to bear was in her case not indifference but hostility. The world did not say to her as it said to them, Write if you choose; it makes no difference to me. The world said with a guffaw, Write? What's the good of your writing? Here the psychologists of Newnham and Girton might come to our help, I thought, looking again at the blank spaces on the shelves. For surely it is time that the effect of discouragement upon the mind of the artist should be measured, as I have seen a dairy company measure the effect of ordinary milk and Grade A milk upon the body of the rat. They set two rats in cages side by side, and of 12 the two one was furtive, timid and small, and the other was glossy, bold and big. Now what food do we feed women as artists upon? I asked, remembering, I suppose, that dinner of prunes and custard. To answer that question I had only to open the evening paper and to read that Lord Birkenhead is of opinion—but really I am not going to trouble to copy out Lord Birkenhead's opinion upon the writing of women. What Dean Inge says I will leave in peace. The Harley Street specialist may be allowed to rouse the echoes of Harley Street with his vociferations without raising a hair on my head. I will quote, however, Mr. Oscar Browning, because Mr. Oscar Browning was a great figure in Cambridge at one time, and used to examine the students at Girton and Newnham. Mr. Oscar Browning was wont to declare "that the impression left on his mind, after looking over any set of examination papers, was that, irrespective of the marks he might give, the best woman was intellectually the inferior of the worst man." After saying that Mr. Browning went back to his rooms—and it is this sequel that endears him and makes him a human figure of some bulk and majesty—he went back to his rooms and found a stable-boy lying on the sofa—"a mere skeleton, his cheeks were cavernous and sallow, his teeth were black, and he did not appear to have the full use of his limbs. . . . 'That's Arthur' [said Mr. Browning]. 'He's a dear boy really and most high-minded.' " The two pictures always seem to me to complete each other. And happily in this age of biography the two pictures often do complete each other, so that we are able to interpret the opinions of great men not only by what they say, but by what they do.

13   But though this is possible now, such opinions coming from the lips of important people must have been formidable enough even fifty years ago. Let us suppose that a father from the highest motives did not wish his daughter to leave home and become a writer, painter or scholar. "See what Mr. Oscar Browning says," he would say; and there was not only Mr. Oscar Browning; there was the *Saturday Review;* there was Mr. Greg—the "essentials of a woman's being," said Mr. Greg emphatically, "are that *they are supported by, and they minister to, men*"—there was an enormous body of masculine opinion to the effect that nothing could be expected of women intellectually. Even if her father did not read out loud these opinions, any girl could read them for herself; and the reading, even in the nineteenth century, must have lowered her vitality, and told profoundly upon her work. There would always have been that assertion—you cannot do this, you are incapable of doing that—to protest against, to overcome. Probably for a novelist this germ is no longer of much effect; for there have been women novelists of merit. But for painters it must still have some sting in it; and for musicians, I imagine, is even now active and poisonous in the extreme. The woman composer stands where the actress stood in the time of Shakespeare. Nick Greene, I thought, remembering the story I had made about Shakespeare's sister, said that a woman acting put him in mind of a dog dancing. Johnson repeated the phrase two hundred years later of women preaching. And here, I said, opening a book about

music, we have the very words used again in this year of grace, 1928, of women who try to write music. "Of Mlle. Germaine Tailleferre one can only repeat Dr. Johnson's dictum concerning a woman preacher, transposed into terms of music. 'Sir, a woman's composing is like a dog's walking on his hind legs. It is not done well, but you are surprised to find it done at all.' "[2] So accurately does history repeat itself.

Thus, I concluded, shutting Mr. Oscar Browning's life and pushing away the rest, it is fairly evident that even in the nineteenth century a woman was not encouraged to be an artist. On the contrary, she was snubbed, slapped, lectured and exhorted. Her mind must have been strained and her vitality lowered by the need of opposing this, of disproving that. For here again we come within range of that very interesting and obscure masculine complex which has had so much influence upon the woman's movement; that deep-seated desire, not so much that *she* shall be inferior as that *he* shall be superior, which plants him wherever one looks, not only in front of the arts, but barring the way to politics too, even when the risk to himself seems infinitesimal and the suppliant humble and devoted. Even Lady Bess-borough, I remembered, with all her passion for politics, must humbly bow herself and write to Lord Granville Leveson-Gower: ". . . notwithstanding all my violence in politics and talking so much on that subject, I perfectly agree with you that no woman has any business to meddle with that or any other serious business, farther than giving her opinion (if she is ask'd)." And so she goes on to spend her enthusiasm where it meets with no obstacle whatsoever upon that immensely important subject, Lord Granville's maiden speech in the House of Commons. The spectacle is certainly a strange one, I thought. The history of men's opposition to women's emancipation is more inter-esting perhaps than the story of that emancipation itself. An amusing book might be made of it if some young student at Girton or Newnham would collect examples and deduce a theory—but she would need thick gloves on her hands, and bars to protect her of solid gold.

But what is amusing now, I recollected, shutting Lady Bessborough, had to be taken in desperate earnest once. Opinions that one now pastes in a book labelled cock-a-doodle-dum and keeps for reading to select audiences on summer nights once drew tears, I can assure you. Among your grandmothers and great-grandmothers there were many that wept their eyes out. Florence Nightingale shrieked aloud in her agony.[3] Moreover, it is all very well for you, who have got yourselves to college and enjoy sitting-rooms—or is it only bed-sitting-rooms?—of your own to say that genius should disregard such opinions; that genius should be above caring what is said of it. Unfortu-nately, it is precisely the men or women of genius who mind most what is

14

15

---

[2] *A Survey of Contemporary Music,* Cecil Gray, p. 246.
[3] See *Cassandra,* by Florence Nightingale, printed in *The Cause,* by R. Strachey.

said of them. Remember Keats. Remember the words he had cut on his tombstone. Think of Tennyson; think—but I need hardly multiply instances of the undeniable, if very unfortunate, fact that it is the nature of the artist to mind excessively what is said about him. Literature is strewn with the wreckage of men who have minded beyond reason the opinions of others.

16   And this susceptibility of theirs is doubly unfortunate, I thought, returning again to my original enquiry into what state of mind is most propitious for creative work, because the mind of an artist, in order to achieve the prodigious effort of freeing whole and entire the work that is in him, must be incandescent, like Shakespeare's mind, I conjectured, looking at the book which lay open at *Antony and Cleopatra*. There must be no obstacle in it, no foreign matter unconsumed.

17   For though we say that we know nothing about Shakespeare's state of mind, even as we say that, we are saying something about Shakespeare's state of mind. The reason perhaps why we know so little of Shakespeare—compared with Donne or Ben Jonson or Milton—is that his grudges and spites and antipathies are hidden from us. We are not held up by some "revelation" which reminds us of the writer. All desire to protest, to preach, to proclaim an injury, to pay off a score, to make the world the witness of some hardship or grievance was fired out of him and consumed. Therefore his poetry flows from him free and unimpeded. If ever a human being got his work expressed completely, it was Shakespeare. If ever a mind was incandescent, unimpeded, I thought, turning again to the bookcase, it was Shakespeare's mind.

WOODY ALLEN

Selections from the Allen Notebooks

Woody Allen, a contemporary version of Buster Keaton (with a hint of Charlie Chaplin), was born in Brooklyn in 1935 and educated at "a school for emotionally disturbed teachers." After a succession of television writing jobs, and stints as a nightclub comedian, Allen shifted to a career in films, as screenwriter, actor, and director. Among his dozen films are Bananas *(1970),* Play It Again, Sam *(1972),* Annie Hall *(1975), for which he won Academy Awards for directing and screenwriting,* Manhattan *(1979) and* Hannah and Her Sisters *(1986). Collections of his parodies and other* New Yorker *pieces include* Getting Even *(1971),* Without Feathers *(1975), and* Side Effects *(1980).*

Allen's most familiar comic figure in both his films and his writings is said to closely resemble himself—a well-intentioned, intellectual New Yorker, inept and highly neurotic, unsuccessful in love and business. With the aid of psychoanalysis, he is continually searching for love, stability, and security, but never attains these for long. Such a persona emerges in "Selections from the Allen Notebooks," a complete work (not "selections") in which even the title parodies the conventional format of writers' notebooks. Here, as in Allen's other writing, much of the humor emerges from a careful mixing of voices and styles—the silly with the serious; the slapstick with the intellectual; the commonplace with the bizarre; with hints of Kafka, Dostoevsky, Freud, and Emily Dickinson—a blend that encourages us to laugh ourselves out of the solemn self-absorption that keeping a notebook can produce.

Following are excerpts from the hitherto secret private journal of Woody Allen, which will be published posthumously or after his death, whichever comes first.

Getting through the night is becoming harder and harder. Last evening, I had the uneasy feeling that some men were trying to break into my room to shampoo me. But why? I kept imagining I saw shadowy forms, and at 3 A.M. the underwear I had draped over a chair resembled the Kaiser on roller skates. When I finally did fall asleep, I had that same hideous nightmare in which a woodchuck is trying to claim my prize at a raffle. Despair.

      1

I believe my consumption has grown worse. Also my asthma. The wheezing comes and goes, and I get dizzy more and more frequently. I have taken to violent choking and fainting. My room is damp and I have perpetual chills and palpitations of the heart. I noticed, too, that I am out of napkins. Will it never stop?

      2

Idea for a story: A man awakens to find his parrot has been made Secretary of Agriculture. He is consumed with jealousy and shoots himself, but unfortunately the gun is the type with a little flag that pops out, with the word "Bang" on it. The flag pokes his eye out, and he lives—a chastened human being who, for the first time, enjoys the simple pleasures of life, like farming or sitting on an air hose.

      3

Thought: Why does man kill? He kills for food. And not only food: frequently there must be a beverage.

      4

Should I marry W.? Not if she won't tell me the other letters in her name. And what about her career? How can I ask a woman of her beauty to give up the Roller Derby? Decisions . . .

      5

Once again I tried committing suicide—this time by wetting my nose and inserting it into the light socket. Unfortunately, there was a short in the wiring, and I merely caromed off the icebox. Still obsessed by thoughts of death, I brood constantly. I keep wondering if there is an afterlife, and if there is will they be able to break a twenty?

      6

I ran into my brother today at a funeral. We had not seen one another for fifteen years, but as usual he produced a pig bladder from his pocket and

      7

began hitting me on the head with it. Time has helped me understand him better. I finally realize his remark that I am "some loathsome vermin fit only for extermination" was said more out of compassion than anger. Let's face it: he was always much brighter than me—wittier, more cultured, better educated. Why he is still working at McDonald's is a mystery.

8   Idea for story: Some beavers take over Carnegie Hall and perform *Wozzeck*. (Strong theme. What will be the structure?)

9   Good Lord, why am I so guilty? Is it because I hated my father? Probably it was the veal-parmigian' incident. Well, what *was* it doing in his wallet? If I had listened to him, I would be blocking hats for a living. I can hear him now: "To block hats—that is everything." I remember his reaction when I told him I wanted to write. "The only writing you'll do is in collaboration with an owl." I still have no idea what he meant. What a sad man! When my first play, *A Cyst for Gus,* was produced at the Lyceum, he attended opening night in tails and a gas mask.

10   Today I saw a red-and-yellow sunset and thought, How insignificant I am! Of course, I thought that yesterday, too, and it rained. I was overcome with self-loathing and contemplated suicide again—this time by inhaling next to an insurance salesman.

11   Short story: A man awakens in the morning and finds himself transformed into his own arch supports. (This idea can work on many levels. Psychologically, it is the quintessence of Kruger, Freud's disciple who discovered sexuality in bacon.)

12   How wrong Emily Dickinson was! Hope is not "the thing with feathers." The thing with feathers has turned out to be my nephew. I must take him to a specialist in Zurich.

13   I have decided to break off my engagement with W. She doesn't understand my writing, and said last night that my *Critique of Metaphysical Reality* reminded her of *Airport*. We quarreled, and she brought up the subject of children again, but I convinced her they would be too young.

14   Do I believe in God? I did until Mother's accident. She fell on some meat loaf, and it penetrated her spleen. She lay in a coma for months, unable to do anything but sing "Granada" to an imaginary herring. Why was this woman in the prime of life so afflicted—because in her youth she dared to defy convention and got married with a brown paper bag on her head? And how can I believe in God when just last week I got my tongue caught in the roller of an electric typewriter? I am plagued by doubts. What if everything is an

illusion and nothing exists? In that case, I definitely overpaid for my carpet. If only God would give me some clear sign! Like making a large deposit in my name at a Swiss bank.

Had coffee with Melnick today. He talked to me about his idea of having all government officials dress like hens.   15

Play idea: A character based on my father, but without quite so promi-   16
nent a big toe. He is sent to the Sorbonne to study the harmonica. In the end, he dies, never realizing his one dream—to sit up to his waist in gravy. (I see a brilliant second-act curtain, where two midgets come upon a severed head in a shipment of volleyballs.)

While taking my noon walk today, I had more morbid thoughts. What *is*   17
it about death that bothers me so much? Probably the hours. Melnick says the soul is immortal and lives on after the body drops away, but if my soul exists without my body I am convinced all my clothes will be too loose-fitting. Oh, well . . .

Did not have to break off with W. after all, for as luck would have it, she   18
ran off to Finland with a professional circus geek. All for the best, I suppose, although I had another of those attacks where I start coughing out of my ears.

Last night, I burned all my plays and poetry. Ironically, as I was burning   19
my masterpiece, *Dark Penguin,* the room caught fire, and I am now the object of a lawsuit by some men named Pinchunk and Schlosser. Kierkegaard was right.

Style and Language

STANLEY KUNITZ

Swimming in Lake Chauggogagogmanchauggagog- chabunagungamaugg

The essay title is a metaphor for how Kunitz relates to language—total immersion in an "elaborate series of sounds" that contain "a whole complex of thought, emotion and feeling." This is appropriate for Kunitz, a poet, editor, and teacher who was born in Worcester, Massachusetts, in 1905, not far from Lake Chauggog. . . . Kunitz earned a B.A. from Harvard in 1926, Phi Beta Kappa, and an M.A. in 1929, and since then has taught at Yale, Princeton, Columbia, Vassar, and elsewhere. His first book of poetry was Intellectual Things *(1930), his most recent,* The Poems of Stanley Kunitz, 1928–1978 *(1978); his poetry was awarded a Pulitzer Prize in 1959. Kunitz also edited the Yale Series of Younger Poets 1969–1977, and was Poetry Consultant for the Library of Congress.*

Here Kunitz tries to explain how poets write—a somewhat mystical process that involves, in addition to immersion in language primitive and potent, stamina, imagination, energy, insight, the ability to hear and see a subject from multiple perspectives, the intuitive good judgment to know when to revise. As other authors in this book reveal, prose writers often work this way, too.

1   When I was a boy in Massachusetts one of my favorite haunts was Lake Webster, named from the town of its location. It was a lovely lake, in a then relatively unspoiled countryside, but no lovelier, I suppose, than several other lakes and ponds that I could have frequented nearer my home in Worcester. The reason for my preference was that I had made a thrilling discovery while browsing among the books of local history in the Worcester Public Library. There I learned that the Indians who once lived on the shores of Lake Webster had a word of their own for it: *Chauggogagogmanchauggagogchabunagungamaugg.* To think that this was reputed to be the longest lake-name in the world! To know, moreover, that this fantastic porridge of syllables made sense, and what delicious sense, signifying: "I-fish-on-my-side, you-fish-on-your-side, nobody-fishes-in-the-middle!" I practiced how to say it, priding myself on talking Indian . . . nor to this very day have I forgotten the combination.

2   To utter that mouthful, to give the lake its secret name, was somehow to possess it, to assert my power over the spot, as by an act of magic. Years later, when I became interested in philology, I read, with a sense of *déjà vu*, the theory that in the beginning of the human adventure a word consisted of a

long and elaborate sound or series of sounds associated with the ritual of the tribe and expressed in a chant with appropriate gestures; that into each word-sentence, as in extant primitive languages, a whole complex of thought, emotion and feeling was packed.

One of the familiar grievances of the modern poet is that language gets more and more shabby and debased in everyday usage, until even the great words that men must live by lose their lustre. How to make words potent and magical again, how to restore their lost vitality? A poet is a man who yearns to swim in Lake Chauggogagogmanchauggagogchabunagungamaugg, not in Lake Webster. He loves a language that reaches all the way back to its primitive condition. So it is that the words of a poem are full of subterranean electric feelings, pent-up music, sleeping gestures. A poem trembles on the verge of lapsing into music, of breaking into dance: but its virtue lies in resisting the temptation—in remaining language. There is an ideal lyric in my head whose words flow together to form a single word-sentence, an unremitting stream of sound, as in the Indian lake-name; I am not reconciled to the knowledge that I shall never be able to write it.

A good deal of craft goes into the making of a poem, much more than most readers and some writers suspect. Poems are not produced by the will; and craft alone, though it may assure the manufacture of a reasonably competent set of verses, is insufficient for the creation of a poem. How many times have I heard my poet-friends, in the doldrums between poems, despair of the possibility of writing another! Solitude and a fierce attentiveness precede insight, which other ages could call "vision" without embarrassment. "The man wipes his breath from the window pane," wrote Yeats, "and laughs in his delight at all the varied scene." Or as Blake phrased it earlier: "If the doors of perception were cleansed, everything would appear to man as it is, infinite."

The poets whom I most admire look on life with a watchful and affectionate eye, unfogged by sentimentality. They study the things of the world, but not from the world's view. One of their disciplines is to resist the temptation to skim poems off the top of their minds. Poets need stamina as much as they need imagination. Indeed, when we speak of the imagination, we imply an activity of surplus energy . . . energy beyond what is required for mere survival. An interviewer once asked me a rather brash question: "What do you consider to be your chief asset as a poet?"—to which I gave the reply that I thought he deserved: "My ability to stay awake after midnight." Perhaps I was more serious than I intended. Certainly the poems of mine that I am most committed to are those that I recall fighting for hardest, through the anxious hours, until I managed to come out on the other side of fatigue, where I could begin to breathe again, as though the air had changed and I had found my second wind.

6   One such poem that I can offer, not without trepidation, for comment is "End of Summer":*

>   An agitation of the air
>   A perturbation of the light
>   Admonished me the unloved year
>   Would turn on its hinge that night.
>
>   I stood in the disenchanted field
>   Amid the stubble and the stones,
>   Amazed, while a small worm lisped to me
>   The song of my marrow-bones.
>
>   Blue poured into summer blue,
>   A hawk broke from his cloudless tower,
>   The roof of the silo blazed, and I knew
>   That part of my life was over.
>
>   Already the iron door of the north
>   Clangs open: birds, leaves, snows
>   Order their populations forth,
>   And a cruel wind blows.

7   I can remember how and where that poem began more than a decade ago. It was an afternoon in late September. I was chopping weeds in the field behind my house in Bucks County, Pennsylvania. Toward sunset I heard a commotion in the sky and looked up, startled to observe wedge after wedge of wild geese honking downriver, with their long necks pointing south. I watched until the sun sank and the air turned chill. Then I put away my garden tools and walked back to the house, shivering with a curious premonition. After dinner I went upstairs to my study and tried until dawn to get the words down on paper. Nothing came that seemed right to me. Five days later I had hundreds of lines, but they still added up to nothing. In the middle of the fifth night I experienced a revelation: what was wrong with my enterprise was that I was attempting to compose a descriptive piece about the migration of the birds, whereas it was the disturbance of the heart that really concerned me and that insisted on a language. At this point I opened the window, as it were, and let the geese fly out. Then the poem came with a rush.

8   In my first draft the opening lines read:

>   The agitation of the air,
>   The perturbation of the light. . . .

I write my poems by speaking them—they are meant to be heard. What I heard displeased my ear because the plethora of "the's" made too thick a

---

* *Selected Poems*, p. 48.

sound. The indefinite articles that I introduced in my revision serve to open up the lines and to accelerate the tempo.

In the second stanza the words that interest me most are "amazed" and "lisped." Both of them were afterthoughts. Originally my posture was "surprised," while the invertebrate redundantly "sang" its song. "Amazed" is much more open-mouthed and suspended than "surprised"; moreover, it hooks on to "admonished" and "amid" before it, to "marrow" in the next line, and to "blazed" in the next stanza. At the same time it relieves the passage of a frightful excess of sibilants. As for "lisped," I consider it the perfectly right and proper thing for a small worm to do.

The image of the roof of the silo flashing back the sunlight suggests an epiphany to me, the precise moment of illumination. Actually, I had no silo on my place in the Delaware Valley: it forced itself into my poem, to erupt as the climax of a progression, out of another landscape that had once been dear to me, and I recognized instantaneously that it came with the imprimatur of psychological truth.

In the final stanza the opening of "the iron door of the north" releases the arctic blast before which, in sequence, are driven "birds, leaves, snows," three variants of migration. After the fact I am aware that here the sounds become harsher, as the rhythm is sprung and the strong stressing hammered out. In my own reading of the poem I give the concluding syllable an almost painful protraction, as though the wind would never stop blowing.

Earlier I said that I had let the geese fly out of the poem. Was I mistaken? It occurs to me now that their ghosts are present, their wings keep beating, from the first word to the last in "End of Summer."

JOHN TRIMBLE
Write to Be Read

Trimble, a professor of English at the University of Texas, Austin, since 1970, was born in Niagara Falls, Ontario, in 1940, graduated from Princeton in 1962, and earned a doctorate in English from the University of California, Berkeley, in 1971. "Write to Be Read," from Trimble's enjoyable Writing with Style: Conversations on the Art of Writing *(1975) offers, in the manner of Strunk and White's classic* Elements of Style, *twenty-six precepts for attaining an "authentic and readable style." His first two precepts epitomize his own style exactly:*

> *Write with the assumption that your reader is a companionable friend with a warm sense of humor and an appreciation of simple straightforwardness. Write as if you were actually talking to that friend, but talking with enough leisure to frame your thoughts concisely and interestingly.*

The two best ways I know of promoting an authentic and readable style are these:

1 Write with the assumption that your reader is a companionable friend with a warm sense of humor and an appreciation of simple straightforwardness.
2 Write as if you were actually talking to that friend, but talking with enough leisure to frame your thoughts concisely and interestingly.

If you tack these two tips on the wall in front of your writing desk and make a habit of continually glancing at them, I predict that the readability quotient of your prose style will take a dramatic leap upwards. Here are some additional tips:

3 Substitute the pronoun *that* for *which* wherever possible. The one is conversational, the other bookish. Reserve *which* for those places where a comma would normally precede it. Example: "The shortage, which has now reached critical proportions, is likely to remain a problem." Here the *which* clause merely adds some nonessential information and thus functions as a parenthesis. Contrast to: "The shortage that he spoke of is likely to remain a problem." Here the *that* clause serves to specify the particular shortage being referred to; hence it defines or restricts the subject, "shortage," and mustn't be separated from it by commas. The rule is: if you can remove the clause without damaging the sense of the sentence, use *which* and a comma before it.

4 Use occasional contractions. They'll keep you from taking yourself too seriously, tell your reader that you're not a prude, and help you achieve a more natural, conversational rhythm in your style. The most popular contractions are those involving *am, are, is,* and *not.* Among that group the following are especially natural to the ear:

I'm
you're, we're, they're
he's, she's, here's
won't, wouldn't, don't, doesn't, can't

Contractions, though, are like kisses: when bestowed indiscriminately, they lose their effect, in fact seem cheap. Hold them in reserve. Save them for when you want to civilize an otherwise barbarous-sounding sentence like "Let us start now because I will not be in town tomorrow" or "Would you not think a stuffed shirt wrote this sentence?"

5 If you mean "I," *say* "I." Don't wrap your identity in such pomposities as "the writer" or "one" or "this author" or "we." Reserve "we" and "our" for those situations where you're referring to both your reader and yourself—i.e., where there really is more than one of you involved. Reserve "one" for when you mean "a person," as in "One would have to be a lawyer to understand that." When referring to the reader alone, address him as "you," not

"the reader." The printed page already puts enough distance between the two of you. Why add to it?

6 Use dashes to isolate concluding phrases for emphasis or humorous effect. . . .

7 Use dialogue wherever your context warrants it—it's intrinsically dramatic. Also use imagined thoughts. Example:

> Events inexorably force Enobarbus to a decision—an impossible one. It would seem that he's thinking here something like this: "My mind tells me to leave Antony for Rome. My heart tells me to leave Rome for Antony. Both courses of action are right, and both are wrong. To go either way is to deny a central fact of my existence. I am a Roman, but I am also a man. There seems to be only one solution: death. It will eliminate the need to choose."

8 As a general rule of thumb, if you have written three long sentences in a row, make your fourth a short one. And don't be afraid of the very short sentence. Sometimes even a single word works beautifully, as this example from humorist Gregg Hopkins shows:

> Many American parents have voiced the opinion that today's colleges are veritable breeding grounds for premarital sex. Nonsense. Each year, literally tens of students graduate with their virtue still intact.

9 The more abstract your argument, the more you should lace it with graphic illustrations, analogies, apt quotations, and concrete details. These are aids not only to your reader's understanding but also to his memory. In fact, he'll probably remember the illustration or analogy far longer than he will the abstract idea itself. If the illustration is a good one, though, he'll often be able to reconstruct the thought with a little effort, so it will have served its purpose twice over.

10 Keep your adjectives to a minimum. Let strong nouns do the work of adjectives. You'll find that this will simplify your style *and* give it more point. I think that Voltaire overstated the case a bit, though, when he observed, "The adjective is the enemy of the noun." A more sensible maxim is Twain's: "As to the Adjective: when in doubt, strike it out."

11 Avoid weak (trite) adverbs like *very, extremely, really,* and *terribly.* Instead of saying, "She was very upset by the news," say "She was shattered by the news." The use of *very* and its cognates usually betrays a distrust of the power of the word that follows it. If it's not as strong as you want it, find another word. There always is one.

12 Use the fewest words possible and the simplest words possible. Occasionally, to be sure, the longer word will be the only right word: it may express the idea concisely, or contribute just the rhythm and texture wanted, or gratify your reader with the joy of surprise. . . . But be warned: the more you surrender to the temptation to use big words—"gigundas," I call them—

the further you are apt to stray from your true feelings and the more you will tend to write a style designed to impress rather than to serve the reader. Also, fancy prose can give a writer the delusion that he's really saying something significant, when it may be that he's using rhetoric defensively to conceal from himself how little he actually has to say. Oratory should never be asked to substitute for accuracy and truth. So, follow Henry Thoreau's famous advice, for your own protection: "Simplify, simplify." This may sound easy. It isn't. "To write simply is as difficult as to be good," sighed Somerset Maugham. Hemingway agreed: "Writing plain English is hard work."

13 Make sure that each sentence you write is manifestly connected to the ones immediately preceding and following it. There's no other way to achieve smooth continuity.

14 In a long essay or report, periodically summarize your argument so that your reader will be able to keep his bearings. It's often effective to cast these summaries in the form of brief transitional paragraphs, perhaps only three or four sentences in length. They make a welcome change of pace and serve to graphically separate the stages in your argument.

15 If you enjoy putting questions to your reader, it's prudent to pose them at the beginning of a paper and answer them. If you put them at the tail end and leave your reader the job of answering them, you may achieve only confusion, not resolution.

16 Use semicolons to reduce choppiness, particularly when you have several related sentences in parallel structure. Also use them for a change of pace. . . .

17 Read your prose aloud. *Always* read your prose aloud. If it sounds as if it's come out of a machine or a social scientist's report (which is approximately the same thing), spare your reader and rewrite it.

18 Instead of always saying "first" and "second," occasionally use the numerals themselves in parentheses. It's a superstition that numerals have no place in serious writing. For proof of this, browse through any major anthology of expository prose—*The Norton Reader,* for example.

19 Written-out numbers such as *twenty-eight* are unwieldy. Most authorities recommend that you use the numerals themselves over 20 and the written form for all numbers under 20. But why write *eighteen* when it's so much simpler to write *18?* What can possibly be objectionable about *18?* The purist would probably answer: "It lacks the dignity of *eighteen.*" Such a person doubtless undresses with the lights out. I recommend that you use the numerals themselves from 10 on and congratulate yourself on your common sense.

20 If you begin a sentence with *and* or *but* (and you should occasionally), don't put a comma after it. You want to speed up your prose with those words, and the comma would simply cancel out any gain. The comma is necessary only if a parenthetical clause immediately follows that first word— e.g., "But, from all the evidence, that proves to be a sound conclusion."

21 Give free rein to your sense of humor wherever possible. What's called "serious writing" need not be solemn writing. F. L. Lucas, in his excellent book *Style,* observed with characteristic good sense: "No manual of style that I know has a word to say of good humour; and yet, for me, a lack of it can sometimes blemish all the literary beauties and blandishments ever taught."

22 There's as much psychology in paragraphing properly as in any other aspect of writing. Long paragraphs send off alarms in most readers' minds; very short paragraphs suggest insubstantiality and flightiness; a long succession of medium-length paragraphs indicates no imagination and proves monotonous. Moral: vary your pacing to keep your piece alive and vital, as Dr. Seuss advised.

23 Choose your title with care. Make it accurately descriptive (leave the "teasing" title to cute writers) and try to give it zing. Remember, it's your reader's introduction to your paper. A pedestrian title is about as welcoming as a burned-out motel sign.

24 Avoid exclamation points, which have been cheapened by comic-strip cartoonists (who haven't yet discovered the period) and by advertising copywriters. . . .

25 If you've written a paragraph that sounds heavy and tortured, put down your pencil and ask yourself: "If I were actually speaking these thoughts to a friend, how would I probably say them?" Then go ahead and talk them *out loud,* and when you're finished, write down as nearly as you can recall what you said. The chances are good that many of your talked-out sentences will be an improvement over the earlier, labored version of them.

26 Another tip for the same crisis is this: Take a 10-minute break and read a few paragraphs of a writer whose style you relish. Try to *soak in* that style; try to feel yourself actually writing those paragraphs as you read them. Then say to yourself, "OK, now, how would Blank rewrite my paragraph?" and let yourself go. This usually works. And even when it doesn't, it will at least enable you to gain a fresh perspective on what you've written. That's half the battle right there.

Questions

1. Trimble's propositions for writing stem from his overriding precepts, given at the beginning of his essay, that to attain an "authentic and readable style" a writer should write as if talking straightforwardly to a "companionable friend with a warm sense of humor." Do you have such an audience, either for actual conversation or for writing? If so, how does this audience influence your style? If not, what would you imagine the effect of such listeners or readers to be?

2. Trimble's advice ("Use occasional contractions." "If you mean 'I', *say* 'I'.") contradicts the "rules" of some others, who warn against contractions and writing in the first person. Who's right? How do you as a writer decide which alternative to use?

3. What determines the order of Trimble's 26-item list? Does it seem like a list to you? Why or why not?

4. Does Trimble practice what he preaches? What features of word choice, sentence length and variation, person, punctuation, and other matters, characterize Trimble's style? If your style shares these characteristics, does your writing sound like Trimble's? Why or why not?

GEORGE ORWELL

Politics and the English Language

Many contemporary writers, including E. B. White, Red Smith, and others who appear in The Lexington Reader *agree with John Trimble's view that "we're witnessing in this country a revolution in the notion of what constitutes a good style for serious writing—a movement towards greater clarity, naturalness, vigor, informality, and individuality." Indeed, in some states the law requires contracts, wills, terms of credit, and comparable documents to be written in terms average readers can understand. The first phase of the revolution in English writing began in Shakespeare's time, with a resounding shot being fired by Lord Bacon.*

The Patrick Henry of the contemporary revolution is George Orwell; in 1946 he outlined his attack in the essay that has become a classic, "Politics and the English Language." Although some of the examples he cites may be dated, their generic equivalent still survives, in bureaucracies, in committee reports, insurance policies, academic and technical jargon, political speeches. Despite the efforts of latter-day Orwells to scour the language bright, murk, double-talk, and obfuscation remain wherever people write dishonestly, pretentiously, or simply without the thinking and ruthless editing that result in crystalline meaning and sparkling style.

1   Most people who bother with the matter at all would admit that the English language is in a bad way, but it is generally assumed that we cannot by conscious action do anything about it. Our civilization is decadent and our language—so the argument runs—must inevitably share in the general collapse. It follows that any struggle against the abuse of language is a sentimental archaism, like preferring candles to electric light or hansom cabs to aeroplanes. Underneath this lies the half-conscious belief that language is a natural growth and not an instrument which we shape for our own purposes.

2   Now, it is clear that the decline of a language must ultimately have political and economic causes: it is not due simply to the bad influence of this or that individual writer. But an effect can become a cause, reinforcing the original cause and producing the same effect in an intensified form, and so on indefinitely. A man may take to drink because he feels himself to be a failure, and then fail all the more completely because he drinks. It is rather the same thing that is happening to the English language. It becomes ugly and inaccu-

rate because our thoughts are foolish, but the slovenliness of our language makes it easier for us to have foolish thoughts. The point is that the process is reversible. Modern English, especially written English, is full of bad habits which spread by imitation and which can be avoided if one is willing to take the necessary trouble. If one gets rid of these habits one can think more clearly, and to think clearly is a necessary first step towards political regeneration: so that the fight against bad English is not frivolous and is not the exclusive concern of professional writers. I will come back to this presently, and I hope that by that time the meaning of what I have said here will have become clearer. Meanwhile, here are five specimens of the English language as it is now habitually written.

These five passages have not been picked out because they are especially   3
bad—I could have quoted far worse if I had chosen—but because they illustrate various of the mental vices from which we now suffer. They are a little below the average, but are fairly representative samples. I number them so that I can refer back to them when necessary:

1.   I am not, indeed, sure whether it is not true to say that the Milton who once seemed not unlike a seventeenth-century Shelley had not become, out of an experience even more bitter in each year, more alien [*sic*] to the founder of that Jesuit sect which nothing could induce him to tolerate.

Professor Harold Laski
(Essay in *Freedom of Expression*)

2.   Above all, we cannot play ducks and drakes with a native battery of idioms which prescribes such egregious collocations of vocables as the Basic *put up with* for *tolerate* or *put at a loss* for *bewilder*.

Professor Lancelot Hogben (*Interglossa*)

3.   On the one side we have the free personality: by definition it is not neurotic, for it has neither conflict nor dream. Its desires, such as they are, are transparent, for they are just what institutional approval keeps in the forefront of consciousness; another institutional pattern would alter their number and intensity; there is little in them that is natural, irreducible, or culturally dangerous. But *on the other side,* the social bond itself is nothing but the mutual reflection of these self-secure integrities. Recall the definition of love. Is not this the very picture of a small academic? Where is there a place in this hall of mirrors for either personality or fraternity?

Essay on psychology in *Politics* (New York)

4.   All the "best people" from the gentlemen's clubs, and all the frantic fascist captains, united in common hatred of Socialism and bestial horror of the rising tide of the mass revolutionary movement, have turned to acts of provocation, to foul incendiarism, to medieval legends of poisoned wells, to legalize their own destruction of proletarian organizations, and rouse the agitated petty-bourgeoisie to chauvinistic fervor on behalf of the fight against the revolutionary way out of the crisis.

Communist pamphlet

5. If a new spirit is to be infused into this old country, there is one thorny and contentious reform which must be tackled, and that is the humanization and galvanization of the B.B.C. Timidity here will bespeak canker and atrophy of the soul. The heart of Britain may be sound and of strong beat, for instance, but the British lion's roar at present is like that of Bottom in Shakespeare's *Midsummer Night's Dream*—as gentle as any sucking dove. A virile new Britain cannot continue indefinitely to be traduced in the eyes, or rather ears, of the world by the effete languors of Langham Place, brazenly masquerading as "standard English." When the Voice of Britain is heard at nine o'clock, better far and infinitely less ludicrous to hear aitches honestly dropped than the present priggish, inflated, inhibited, school-ma'amish arch braying of blameless bashful mewing maidens!

Letter in *Tribune*

4   Each of these passages has faults of its own, but, quite apart from avoidable ugliness, two qualities are common to all of them. The first is staleness of imagery; the other is lack of precision. The writer either has a meaning and cannot express it, or he inadvertently says something else, or he is almost indifferent as to whether his words mean anything or not. This mixture of vagueness and sheer incompetence is the most marked characteristic of modern English prose, and especially of any kind of political writing. As soon as certain topics are raised, the concrete melts into the abstract and no one seems able to think of turns of speech that are not hackneyed: prose consists less and less of *words* chosen for the sake of their meaning, and more and more of *phrases* tacked together like the sections of a prefabricated henhouse. I list below, with notes and examples, various of the tricks by means of which the work of prose-construction is habitually dodged:

5   *Dying metaphors.* A newly invented metaphor assists thought by evoking a visual image, while on the other hand a metaphor which is technically "dead" (e.g. *iron resolution*) has in effect reverted to being an ordinary word and can generally be used without loss of vividness. But in between these two classes there is a huge dump of worn-out metaphors which have lost all evocative power and are merely used because they save people the trouble of inventing phrases for themselves. Examples are: *Ring the changes on, take up the cudgels for, toe the line, ride roughshod over, stand shoulder to shoulder with, play into the hands of, no axe to grind, grist to the mill, fishing in troubled waters, on the order of the day, Achilles' heel, swan song, hotbed.* Many of these are used without knowledge of their meaning (what is a "rift," for instance?), and incompatible metaphors are frequently mixed, a sure sign that the writer is not interested in what he is saying. Some metaphors now current have been twisted out of their original meaning without those who use them even being aware of the fact. For example, *toe the line* is sometimes written *tow the line*. Another example is *the hammer and the anvil,* now always used with the implication that the anvil gets the worst of it. In real life it is always the anvil that breaks the hammer, never the other way about: a writer who stopped to

think what he was saying would be aware of this, and would avoid perverting the original phrase.

Operators or *verbal false limbs*. These save the trouble of picking out appropriate verbs and nouns, and at the same time pad each sentence with extra syllables which give it an appearance of symmetry. Characteristic phrases are *render inoperative, militate against, make contact with, be subjected to, give rise to, give grounds for, have the effect of, play a leading part (role) in, make itself felt, take effect, exhibit a tendency to, serve the purpose of, etc., etc.* The keynote is the elimination of simple verbs. Instead of being a single word, such as *break, stop, spoil, mend, kill*, a verb becomes a *phrase*, made up of a noun or adjective tacked on to some general-purposes verb such as *prove, serve, form, play, render*. In addition, the passive voice is wherever possible used in preference to the active, and noun constructions are used instead of gerunds (*by examination of* instead of *by examining*). The range of verbs is further cut down by means of the *-ize* and *de-* formations, and the banal statements are given an appearance of profundity by means of the *not un-* formation. Simple conjunctions and prepositions are replaced by such phrases as *with respect to, having regard to, the fact that, by dint of, in view of, in the interests of, on the hypothesis that;* and the ends of sentences are saved by anticlimax by such resounding common-places as *greatly to be desired, cannot be left out of account, a development to be expected in the near future, deserving of serious consideration, brought to a satisfactory conclusion*, and so on and so forth.

Pretentious diction. Words like *phenomenon, element, individual* (as noun), *objective, categorical, effective, virtual, basic, primary, promote, constitute, exhibit, exploit, utilize, eliminate, liquidate*, are used to dress up simple statement and give an air of scientific impartiality to biased judgments. Adjectives like *epoch-making, epic, historic, unforgettable, triumphant, age-old, inevitable, inexorable, veritable*, are used to dignify the sordid processes of international politics, while writing that aims at glorifying war usually takes on an archaic color, its characteristic words being: *realm, throne, chariot, mailed fist, trident, sword, shield, buckler, banner, jackboot, clarion*. Foreign words and expressions such as *cul de sac, ancien régime, deus ex machina, mutatis mutandis, status quo, gleichschaltung, weltanschauung*, are used to give an air of culture and elegance. Except for the useful abbreviations *i.e., e.g.,* and *etc.,* there is no real need for any of the hundreds of foreign phrases now current in English. Bad writers, and especially scientific, political and sociological writers, are nearly always haunted by the notion that Latin or Greek words are grander than Saxon ones, and unnecessary words like *expedite, ameliorate, predict, extraneous, deracinated, clandestine, subaqueous* and hundreds of others constantly gain ground from their Anglo-Saxon opposite numbers.[1] The jargon peculiar

---

[1] An interesting illustration of this is the way in which the English flower names which were in use till very recently are being ousted by Greek ones, *snapdragon* becoming *antirrhinum, forget-*

to Marxist writing (*hyena, hangman, cannibal, petty bourgeois, these gentry, lacquey, flunkey, mad dog, White Guard,* etc.) consists largely of words and phrases translated from Russian, German or French; but the normal way of coining a new word is to use a Latin or Greek root with the appropriate affix and, where necessary, the size formation. It is often easier to make up words of this kind (*deregionalize, impermissible, extramarital, nonfragmentary* and so forth) than to think up the English words that will cover one's meaning. The result, in general, is an increase in slovenliness and vagueness.

8   *Meaningless words.* In certain kinds of writing, particularly in art criticism and literary criticism, it is normal to come across long passages which are almost completely lacking in meaning.[2] Words like *romantic, plastic, values, human, dead, sentimental, natural, vitality,* as used in art criticism, are strictly meaningless, in the sense that they not only do not point to any discoverable object, but are hardly ever expected to do so by the reader. When one critic writes, "The outstanding feature of Mr. X's work is its living quality," while another writes, "The immediately striking thing about Mr. X's work is its peculiar deadness," the reader accepts this as a simple difference of opinion. If words like *black* and *white* were involved, instead of the jargon words *dead* and *living,* he would see at once that language was being used in an improper way. Many political words are similarly abused. The word *Fascism* has now no meaning except in so far as it signifies "something not desirable." The words *democracy, socialism, freedom, patriotic, realistic, justice,* have each of them several different meanings which cannot be reconciled with one another. In the case of a word like *democracy,* not only is there no agreed definition, but the attempt to make one is resisted from all sides. It is almost universally felt that when we call a country democratic we are praising it: consequently the defenders of every kind of régime claim that it is a democracy, and fear that they might have to stop using the word if it were tied down to any one meaning. Words of this kind are often used in a consciously dishonest way. That is, the person who uses them has his own private definition, but allows his hearer to think he means something quite different. Statements like *Marshal Pétain was a true patriot, The Soviet Press is the freest in the world, The Catholic Church is opposed to persecution,* are almost always made with intent to deceive. Other words used in variable meanings, in most cases

---

me-not becoming *myosotis,* etc. It is hard to see any practical reason for this change of fashion: it is probably due to an instinctive turning-away from the more homely word and a vague feeling that the Greek word is scientific.

[2] Example: "Comfort's catholicity of perception and image, strangely Whitmanesque in range, almost the exact opposite in aesthetic compulsion, continues to evoke that trembling atmospheric accumulative hinting at a cruel, an inexorably serene timelessness. . . . Wrey Gardiner scores by aiming at simple bull's-eyes with precision. Only they are not so simple, and through this contented sadness runs more than the surface bitter-sweet of resignation." (Poetry Quarterly.)

more or less dishonestly, are: *class, totalitarian, science, progressive, reactionary, bourgeois, equality.*

Now that I have made this catalogue of swindles and perversions, let me give another example of the kind of writing that they lead to. This time it must of its nature be an imaginary one. I am going to translate a passage of good English into modern English of the worst sort. Here is a well-known verse from *Ecclesiastes:* **9**

"I returned and saw under the sun, that the race is not to the swift, nor the battle to the strong, neither yet bread to the wise, nor yet riches to men of understanding, nor yet favour to men of skill; but time and chance happeneth to them all." **10**

Here it is in modern English: **11**

"Objective consideration of contemporary phenomena compels the conclusion that success or failure in competitive activities exhibits no tendency to be commensurate with innate capacity, but that a considerable element of the unpredictable must invariably be taken into account."

This is a parody, but not a very gross one. Exhibit (3), above, for instance, contains several patches of the same kind of English. It will be seen that I have not made a full translation. The beginning and ending of the sentence follow the original meaning fairly closely, but in the middle the concrete illustrations—race, battle, bread—dissolve into the vague phrase "success or failure in competitive activities." This had to be so, because no modern writer of the kind I am discussing—no one capable of using phrases like "objective consideration of contemporary phenomena"—would ever tabulate his thoughts in that precise and detailed way. The whole tendency of modern prose is away from concreteness. Now analyse these two sentences a little more closely. The first contains forty-nine words but only sixty syllables, and all its words are those of everyday life. The second contains thirty-eight words of ninety syllables: eighteen of its words are from Latin roots, and one from Greek. The first sentence contains six vivid images, and only one phrase ("time and chance") that could be called vague. The second contains not a single fresh, arresting phrase, and in spite of its ninety syllables it gives only a shortened version of the meaning contained in the first. Yet without a doubt it is the second kind of sentence that is gaining ground in modern English. I do not want to exaggerate. This kind of writing is not yet universal, and outcrops of simplicity will occur here and there in the worst-written page. Still, if you or I were told to write a few lines on the uncertainty of human fortunes, we should probably come much nearer to my imaginary sentence than to the one from *Ecclesiastes.* **12**

As I have tried to show, modern writing at its worst does not consist in picking out words for the sake of their meaning and inventing images in order to make the meaning clearer. It consists in gumming together long strips of words which have already been set in order by someone else, and making the results presentable by sheer humbug. The attraction of this way **13** of writing is that it is easy. It is easier—even quicker, once you have the habit—to say *In my opinion it is not an unjustifiable assumption that* than to say *I think*. If you use ready-made phrases, you not only don't have to hunt about for words; you also don't have to bother with the rhythms of your sentences, since these phrases are generally so arranged as to be more or less euphonious. When you are composing in a hurry—when you are dictating to a stenographer, for instance, or making a public speech—it is natural to fall into a pretentious, Latinized style. Tags like *a consideration which we should do well to bear in mind* or *a conclusion to which all of us would readily assent* will save many a sentence from coming down with a bump. By using stale metaphors, similes and idioms, you save much mental effort, at the cost of leaving your meaning vague, not only for your reader but for yourself. This is the significance of mixed metaphors. The sole aim of a metaphor is to call up a visual image. When these images clash—as in *The Fascist octopus has sung its swan song, the jackboot is thrown into the melting pot*—it can be taken as certain that the writer is not seeing a mental image of the objects he is naming; in other words he is not really thinking. Look again at the examples I gave at the beginning of this essay. Professor Laski (1) uses five negatives in fifty-three words. One of these is superfluous, making nonsense of the whole passage, and in addition there is the slip *alien* for akin, making further nonsense, and several avoidable pieces of clumsiness which increase the general vagueness. Professor Hogben (2) plays ducks and drakes with a battery which is able to write prescriptions, and, while disapproving of the everyday phrase *put up with,* is unwilling to look *egregious* up in the dictionary and see what it means; (3), if one takes an uncharitable attitude towards it, is simply meaningless: probably one could work out its intended meaning by reading the whole of the article in which it occurs. In (4), the writer knows more or less what he wants to say, but an accumulation of stale phrases chokes him like tea leaves blocking a sink. In (5), words and meaning have almost parted company. People who write in this manner usually have a general emotional meaning—they dislike one thing and want to express solidarity with another—but they are not interested in the detail of what they are saying. A scrupulous writer, in every sentence that he writes, will ask himself at least four questions, thus: What am I trying to say? What words will express it? What image or idiom will make it clearer? Is this image fresh enough to have an effect? And he will probably ask himself two more: Could I put it more shortly? Have I said anything that is avoidably ugly? But you are not obliged to go to all this trouble. You can shirk it by simply throwing your mind open and letting the ready-made phrases come crowding in. They will construct your sentences for you—even think your thoughts for you, to a certain extent—and at need they will perform the important service of partially concealing your meaning even from yourself. It is at this point that the special connections between politics and the debasement of language becomes clear.

14 In our time it is broadly true that political writing is bad writing. Where

it is not true, it will generally be found that the writer is some kind of rebel, expressing his private opinions and not a "party line." Orthodoxy, of whatever color, seems to demand a lifeless, imitative style. The political dialects to be found in pamphlets, leading articles, manifestos, White Papers and the speeches of under-secretaries do, of course, vary from party to party, but they are all alike in that one almost never finds in them a fresh, vivid, home-made turn of speech. When one watches some tired hack on the platform mechanically repeating the familiar phrases—*bestial atrocities, iron heel, bloodstained tyranny, free peoples of the world, stand shoulder to shoulder*—one often has a curious feeling that one is not watching a live human being but some kind of dummy: a feeling which suddenly becomes stronger at moments when the light catches the speaker's spectacles and turns them into blank discs which seem to have no eyes behind them. And this is not altogether fanciful. A speaker who uses that kind of phraseology has gone some distance towards turning himself into a machine. The appropriate noises are coming out of his larynx, but his brain is not involved as it would be if he were choosing his words for himself. If the speech he is making is one that he is accustomed to make over and over again, he may be almost unconscious of what he is saying, as one is when one utters the responses in church. And this reduced state of consciousness, if not indispensable, is at any rate favorable to political conformity.

In our time, political speech and writing are largely the defence of the indefensible. Things like the continuance of British rule in India, the Russian purges and deportations, the dropping of the atom bombs on Japan, can indeed be defended, but only by arguments which are too brutal for most people to face, and which do not square with the professed aims of political parties. Thus political language has to consist largely of euphemism, question-begging and sheer cloudy vagueness. Defenceless villages are bombarded from the air, the inhabitants driven out into the countryside, the cattle machine-gunned, the huts set on fire with incendiary bullets: this is called *pacification*. Millions of peasants are robbed of their farms and sent trudging along the roads with no more than they can carry: this is called *transfer of population* or *rectification of frontiers*. People are imprisoned for years without trial, or shot in the back of the neck or sent to die of scurvy in Arctic lumber camps: this is called *elimination of unreliable elements*. Such phraseology is needed if one wants to name things without calling up mental pictures of them. Consider for instance some comfortable English professor defending Russian totalitarianism. He cannot say outright, "I believe in killing off your opponents when you can get good results by doing so." Probably, therefore, he will say something like this:

"While freely conceding that the Soviet régime exhibits certain features which the humanitarian may be inclined to deplore, we must, I think, agree that a certain curtailment of the right to political opposition is an unavoidable concomitant of transitional periods, and that the rigors which the Russian people have been called upon to undergo have been amply justified in the sphere of concrete achievement."

17   The inflated style is itself a kind of euphemism. A mass of Latin words falls upon the facts like soft snow, blurring the outlines and covering up all the details. The great enemy of clear language is insincerity. When there is a gap between one's real and one's declared aims, one turns as it were instinctively to long words and exhausted idioms, like a cuttlefish squirting out ink. In our age there is no such thing as "keeping out of politics." All issues are political issues, and politics itself is a mass of lies, evasions, folly, hatred and schizophrenia. When the general atmosphere is bad, language must suffer. I should expect to find—this is a guess which I have not sufficient knowledge to verify—that the German, Russian and Italian languages have all deteriorated in the last ten or fifteen years, as a result of dictatorship.

18   But if thought corrupts language, language can also corrupt thought. A bad usage can spread by tradition and imitation, even among people who should and do know better. The debased language that I have been discussing is in some ways very convenient. Phrases like *a not unjustifiable assumption, leaves much to be desired, would serve no good purpose, a consideration which we should do well to bear in mind,* are a continuous temptation, a packet of aspirins always at one's elbow. Look back through this essay, and for certain you will find that I have again and again committed the very faults I am protesting against. By this morning's post I have received a pamphlet dealing with conditions in Germany. The author tells me that he "felt impelled" to write it. I open it at random, and here is almost the first sentence that I see: "[The Allies] have an opportunity not only of achieving a radical transformation of Germany's social and political structure in such a way as to avoid a nationalistic reaction in Germany itself, but at the same time of laying the foundations of a co-operative and unified Europe." You see, he "feels impelled" to write—feels, presumably, that he has something new to say—and yet his words, like cavalry horses answering the bugle, group themselves automatically into the familiar dreary pattern. This invasion of one's mind by ready-made phrases (*lay the foundations, achieve a radical transformation*) can only be prevented if one is constantly on guard against them, and every such phrase anaesthetizes a portion of one's brain.

19   I said earlier that the decadence of our language is probably curable. Those who deny this would argue, if they produced an argument at all, that language merely reflects existing social conditions, and that we cannot influence its development by any direct tinkering with words and constructions. So far as the general tone or spirit of a language goes, this may be true, but it is not true in detail. Silly words and expressions have often disappeared, not through any evolutionary process but owing to the conscious action of a minority. Two recent examples were *explore every avenue* and *leave no stone unturned,* which were killed by the jeers of a few journalists. There is a long list of flyblown metaphors which could similarly be got rid of if enough people would interest themselves in the job; and it should also be possible to

laugh the *not un-* formation out of existence,[3] to reduce the amount of Latin and Greek in the average sentence, to drive out foreign phrases and strayed scientific words, and, in general, to make pretentiousness unfashionable. But all these are minor points. The defence of the English language implies more than this, and perhaps it is best to start by saying what it does *not* imply.

To begin with it has nothing to do with archaism, with the salvaging of obsolete words and turns of speech, or with the setting up of a "standard English" which must never be departed from. On the contrary, it is especially concerned with the scrapping of every word or idiom which has outworn its usefulness. It has nothing to do with correct grammar and syntax, which are of no importance so long as one makes one's meaning clear, or with the avoidance of Americanisms, or with having what is called a "good prose style." On the other hand it is not concerned with fake simplicity and the attempt to make written English colloquial. Nor does it even imply in every case preferring the Saxon word to the Latin one, though it does imply using the fewest and shortest words that will cover one's meaning. What is above all needed is to let the meaning choose the word, and not the other way about. In prose, the worst thing one can do with words is to surrender to them. When you think of a concrete object, you think wordlessly, and then, if you want to describe the thing you have been visualizing you probably hunt about till you find the exact words that seem to fit it. When you think of something abstract you are more inclined to use words from the start, and unless you make a conscious effort to prevent it, the existing dialect will come rushing in and do the job for you, at the expense of blurring or even changing your meaning. Probably it is better to put off using words as long as possible and get one's meaning as clear as one can through pictures or sensations. Afterwards one can choose—not simply *accept*—the phrases that will best cover the meaning, and then switch round and decide what impression one's words are likely to make on another person. This last effort of the mind cuts out all stale or mixed images, all prefabricated phrases, needless repetitions, and humbug and vagueness generally. But one can often be in doubt about the effect of a word or a phrase, and one needs rules that one can rely on when instinct fails. I think the following rules will cover most cases:

(i) Never use a metaphor, simile or other figure of speech which you are used to seeing in print.

(ii) Never use a long word where a short one will do.

(iii) If it is possible to cut a word out, always cut it out.

(iv) Never use the passive where you can use the active.

(v) Never use a foreign phrase, a scientific word or a jargon word if you can think of an everyday English equivalent.

(vi) Break any of these rules sooner than say anything outright barbarous.

---

[3] One can cure oneself of the *not un-* formation by memorizing this sentence: *A not unblack dog was chasing a not unsmall rabbit across a not ungreen field.*

These rules sound elementary, and so they are, but they demand a deep change of attitude in anyone who has grown used to writing in the style now fashionable. One could keep all of them and still write bad English, but one could not write the kind of stuff that I quoted in those five specimens at the beginning of this article.

21   I have not here been considering the literary use of language, but merely language as an instrument for expressing and not for concealing or preventing thought. Stuart Chase and others have come near to claiming that all abstract words are meaningless, and have used this as a pretext for advocating a kind of political quietism. Since you don't know what Fascism is, how can you struggle against Fascism? One need not swallow such absurdities as this, but one ought to recognize that the present political chaos is connected with the decay of language, and that one can probably bring about some improvement by starting at the verbal end. If you simplify your English, you are freed from the worst follies of orthodoxy. You cannot speak any of the necessary dialects, and when you make a stupid remark its stupidity will be obvious, even to yourself. Political language—and with variations this is true of all political parties, from Conservatives to Anarchists—is designed to make lies sound truthful and murder respectable, and to give an appearance of solidity to pure wind. One cannot change this all in a moment, but one can at least change one's own habits, and from time to time one can even, if one jeers loudly enough, send some worn-out and useless phrase—some *jackboot, Achilles' heel, hotbed, melting pot, acid test, veritable inferno* or other lump of verbal refuse—into the dustbin where it belongs.

Questions

1. Orwell wrote this essay in 1946 to reverse the decline and "abuse of language." Over forty years later, do the features of "staleness of imagery" and "lack of precision" that he identified (paragraph 4, p. 74) still appear in writing, or has Orwell's campaign been successful?

2. Examine a piece of inflated or murky writing to see whether it exhibits any or most of the characteristics to which Orwell particularly objects: dying metaphors (paragraph 4), operators or verbal false limbs (paragraph 4), pretentious diction (paragraph 4), meaningless words (paragraph 4), long strips of other people's words gummed together (paragraph 10). Do these features invariably result in bad writing?

3. How does bad writing spread, according to Orwell (see paragraphs 11–15)? Is it possible to eradicate bad writing? If so, how?

4. Do Orwell's six rules for good writing (paragraph 17) address all the problems of bad writing that he has identified? What kind of style would ultimately result from a rigid application of rules ii ("Never use a long word where a short one will do.") and iii ("Omit excess words.")? Does he beg the question with rule vi ("Break any of these rules sooner than say anything outright barbarous.")?

5. How congruent is Orwell's advice with Trimble's? Do they agree on an ideal prose style? Can you find examples of good writing that violate their rules?

ROBIN LAKOFF

You Are What You Say

Lakoff (b. 1942) earned her B.A. and Ph.D. at Radcliffe College and Harvard University, and is currently a linguistics professor at the University of California, Berkeley. Her research in women's language has resulted in "You Are What You Say," first published in Ms. magazine in 1974; in Language and Women's Place, *1975; and in considerable controversy.* Ms. *itself is a form of address for women that, like Mr., does not connote marital status as* Miss *and* Mrs. *do. Although intended as a nonprejudicial term,* Ms. *itself continues to arouse various prejudices, pro and con—just ask someone.*

Lakoff asserts that there is a "women's language" that, unlike forceful, emphatic "men's language," is "fuzzy-headed, unassertive," and that women who use it will be "ridiculed for being unable to think clearly, unable to take part in a serious discussion, and therefore unfit to hold a position of power." She says, for instance, that women—but not men—use tag questions ("The situation in Southeast Asia is terrible, isn't it?") and phrase commands as requests ("Will you please close the door?") as a way of avoiding commitment and "conflict with the addressee." She also points out the double standard of speech used by both men and women: lady, *for instance, has frivolous and derogatory connotations that* woman *does not. Lakoff's assertions become an argument, don't they?*

"Women's language" is that pleasant (dainty?), euphemistic never-aggressive way of talking we learned as little girls. Cultural bias was built into the language we were allowed to speak, the subjects we were allowed to speak about, and the ways we were spoken of. Having learned our linguistic lesson well, we go out in the world, only to discover that we are communicative cripples—damned if we do, and damned if we don't.

If we refuse to talk "like a lady," we are ridiculed and criticized for being unfeminine. ("She thinks like a man" is, at best, a left-handed compliment.) If we do learn all the fuzzy-headed, unassertive language of our sex, we are ridiculed for being unable to think clearly, unable to take part in a serious discussion, and therefore unfit to hold a position of power.

It doesn't take much of this for a woman to begin feeling she deserves such treatment because of inadequacies in her own intelligence and education.

"Women's language" shows up in all levels of English. For example, women are encouraged and allowed to make far more precise discriminations in naming colors than men do. Words like *mauve, beige, ecru, aquamarine, lavender,* and so on, are unremarkable in a woman's active vocabulary, but largely absent from that of most men. I know of no evidence suggesting that women actually *see* a wider range of colors than men do. It is simply that fine discriminations of this sort are relevant to women's vocabularies, but not to men's; to men, who control most of the interesting affairs of the world, such distinctions are trivial—irrelevant.

5   In the area of syntax, we find similar gender-related peculiarities of speech. There is one construction, in particular, that women use conversationally far more than men: the tag question. A tag is midway between an outright statement and a yes-no question; it is less assertive than the former, but more confident than the latter.

6   A *flat statement* indicates confidence in the speaker's knowledge and is fairly certain to be believed; a *question* indicates a lack of knowledge on some point and implies that the gap in the speaker's knowledge can and will be remedied by an answer. For example, if, at a Little League game, I have had my glasses off, I can legitimately ask someone else: "Was the player out at third?" A *tag question,* being intermediate between statement and question, is used when the speaker is stating a claim, but lacks full confidence in the truth of that claim. So if I say, "Is Joan here?" I will probably not be surprised if my respondent answers "no"; but if I say, "Joan is here, isn't she?" instead, chances are I am already biased in favor of a positive answer, wanting only confirmation. I still want a response, but I have enough knowledge (or think I have) to predict that response. A tag question, then, might be thought of as a statement that doesn't demand to be believed by anyone but the speaker, a way of giving leeway, of not forcing the addressee to go along with the views of the speaker.

7   Another common use of the tag question is in small talk when the speaker is trying to elicit conversation: "Sure is hot here, isn't it?"

8   But in discussing personal feelings or opinions, only the speaker normally has any way of knowing the correct answer. Sentences such as "I have a headache, don't I?" are clearly ridiculous. But there are other examples where it is the speaker's opinions, rather than perceptions, for which corroboration is sought, as in "The situation in Southeast Asia is terrible, isn't it?"

9   While there are, of course, other possible interpretations of a sentence like this, one possibility is that the speaker has a particular answer in mind—"yes" or "no"—but is reluctant to state it baldly. This sort of tag question is much more apt to be used by women than by men in conversation. Why is this the case?

10   The tag question allows a speaker to avoid commitment, and thereby avoid conflict with the addressee. The problem is that, by so doing, speakers may also give the impression of not really being sure of themselves, or looking to the addressee for confirmation of their views. This uncertainty is reinforced in more subliminal ways, too. There is a peculiar sentence-intonation pattern, used almost exclusively by women, as far as I know, which changes a declarative answer into a question. The effect of using the rising inflection typical of a yes-no question is to imply that the speaker is seeking confirmation, even though the speaker is clearly the only one who has the requisite information, which is why the question was put to her in the first place:

(Q) When will dinner be ready?
(A) Oh . . . around six o'clock . . . ?

It is as though the second speaker were saying, "Six o'clock—if that's okay with you, if you agree." The person being addressed is put in the position of having to provide confirmation. One likely consequence of this sort of speech pattern in a woman is that, often unbeknownst to herself, the speaker builds a reputation of tentativeness, and others will refrain from taking her seriously or trusting her with any real responsibilities, since she "can't make up her mind," and "isn't sure of herself."

Such idiosyncrasies may explain why women's language sounds much more "polite" than men's. It is polite to leave a decision open, not impose your mind, or views, or claims, on anyone else. So a tag question is a kind of polite statement, in that it does not force agreement or belief on the addressee. In the same way a request is a polite command, in that it does not force obedience on the addressee, but rather suggests something be done as a favor to the speaker. A clearly stated order implies a threat of certain consequences if it is not followed, and—even more impolite—implies that the speaker is in a superior position and able to enforce the order. By couching wishes in the form of a request, on the other hand, a speaker implies that if the request is not carried out, only the speaker will suffer; noncompliance cannot harm the addressee. So the decision is really left up to the addressee. The distinction becomes clear in these examples: 11

Close the door.
Please close the door.
Will you close the door?
Will you please close the door?
Won't you close the door?

In the same way as words and speech patterns used *by* women undermine her image, those used *to describe* women make matters even worse. Often a word may be used of both men and women (and perhaps of things as well); but when it is applied to women, it assumes a special meaning that, by implication rather than outright assertion, is derogatory to women as a group. 12

The use of euphemisms has this effect. A euphemism is a substitute for a word that has acquired a bad connotation by association with something unpleasant or embarrassing. But almost as soon as the new word comes into common usage, it takes on the same old bad connotations, since feelings about the things or people referred to are not altered by a change of name; thus new euphemisms must be constantly found. 13

There is one euphemism for *woman* still very much alive. The word, of course, is *lady*. *Lady* has a masculine counterpart, namely *gentleman*, occasionally shortened to *gent*. But for some reason *lady* is very much commoner than *gent(leman)*. 14

15　　The decision to use *lady* rather than *woman,* or vice versa, may considerably alter the sense of a sentence, as the following examples show:

> (a) A woman (lady) I know is a dean at Berkeley.
> (b) A woman (lady) I know makes amazing things
> 　　out of shoelaces and old boxes.

16　　The use of *lady* in (a) imparts a frivolous, or nonserious, tone to the sentence: the matter under discussion is not one of great moment. Similarly, in (b), using *lady* here would suggest that the speaker considered the "amazing things" not to be serious art, but merely a hobby or aberration. If *woman* is used, she might be a serious sculptor. To say *lady doctor* is very condescending, since no one ever says *gentleman doctor* or even *man doctor.* For example, mention in the San Francisco *Chronicle* of January 31, 1972, of Madalyn Murray O'Hair as the *lady atheist* reduces her position to that of scatterbrained eccentric. Even *woman atheist* is scarcely defensible: sex is irrelevant to her philosophical position.

17　　Many women argue that, on the other hand, *lady* carries with it overtones recalling the age of chivalry: conferring exalted stature on the person so referred to. This makes the term seem polite at first, but we must also remember that these implications are perilous: they suggest that a "lady" is helpless, and cannot do things by herself.

18　　*Lady* can also be used to infer frivolousness, as in titles of organizations. Those that have a serious purpose (not merely that of enabling "the ladies" to spend time with one another) cannot use the word *lady* in their titles, but less serious ones may. Compare the *Ladies' Auxiliary* of a men's group, or the *Thursday Evening Ladies' Browning and Garden Society* with *Ladies' Liberation* or *Ladies' Strike for Peace.*

19　　What is curious about this split is that *lady* is in origin a euphemism—a substitute that puts a better face on something people find uncomfortable—for *woman.* What kind of euphemism is it that subtly denigrates the people to whom it refers? Perhaps *lady* functions as a euphemism for *woman* because it does not contain the sexual implications present in *woman:* it is not "embarrassing" in that way. If this is so, we may expect that, in the future, *lady* will replace woman as the primary word for the human female, since *woman* will have become too blatantly sexual. That this distinction is already made in some contexts at least is shown in the following examples, where you can try replacing *woman* with *lady*:

> (a) She's only twelve, but she's already a woman.
> (b) After ten years in jail, Harry wanted to find a woman.
> (c) She's my woman, see, so don't mess around with her.

20　　Another common substitute for *woman* is *girl.* One seldom hears a man past the age of adolescence referred to as a boy, save in expressions like "going out with the boys," which are meant to suggest an air of adolescent frivolity and irresponsibility. But women of all ages are "girls": one can have a man—not a boy—Friday, but only a girl—never a woman or even a lady—Friday; women have girlfriends, but men do not—in a nonsexual sense—have boyfriends. It may be that this use of *girl* is euphemistic in the same way the use of *lady* is: in stressing the idea of immaturity, it removes the sexual connotations lurking in *woman*. *Girl* brings to mind irresponsibility: you don't send a girl to do a woman's errand (or even, for that matter, a boy's errand). She is a person who is both too immature and too far from real life to be entrusted with responsibilities or with decisions of any serious or important nature.

Now let's take a pair of words which, in terms of the possible relationships in an earlier society, were simple male-female equivalents, analogous to *bull: cow*. Suppose we find that, for independent reasons, society has changed in such a way that the original meanings now are irrelevant. Yet the words have not been discarded, but have acquired new meanings, metaphorically related to their original senses. But suppose these new metaphorical uses are no longer parallel to each other. By seeing where the parallelism breaks down, we discover something about the different roles played by men and women in this culture. One good example of such a divergence through time is found in the pair, *master: mistress*. Once used with reference to one's power over servants, these words have become unusable today in their original master-servant sense as the relationship has become less prevalent in our society. But the words are still common.

Unless used with reference to animals, *master* now generally refers to a man who has acquired consummate ability in some field, normally nonsexual. But its feminine counterpart cannot be used this way. It is practically restricted to its sexual sense of "paramour." We start out with two terms, both roughly paraphrasable as "one who has power over another." But the masculine form, once one person is no longer able to have absolute power over another, becomes usable metaphorically in the sense of "having power over *something*." *Master* requires as its object only the name of some activity, something inanimate and abstract. But *mistress* requires a masculine noun in the possessive to precede it. One cannot say: "Rhonda is a mistress." One must be *someone's* mistress. A man is defined by what he does, a woman by her sexuality, that is, in terms of one particular aspect of her relationship to men. It is one thing to be an *old master* like Hans Holbein, and another to be an *old mistress*.

The same is true of the words *spinster* and *bachelor*—gender words for "one who is not married." The resemblance ends with the definition. While *bachelor* is a neuter term, often used as a compliment, *spinster* normally is used pejoratively, with connotations of prissiness, fussiness, and so on. To be a bachelor implies that one has a choice of marrying or not, and this is what makes the idea of a bachelor existence attractive, in the popular literature. He has been pursued and has successfully eluded his pursuers. But a spinster is one who has not been pursued, or at least not seriously. She is old, unwanted goods. The metaphorical connotations of *bachelor* generally suggest sexual freedom; of *spinster,* puritanism or celibacy.

24　　　These examples could be multiplied. It is generally considered a *faux pas,* in society, to congratulate a woman on her engagement, while it is correct to congratulate her fiancé. Why is this? The reason seems to be that it is impolite to remind people of things that may be uncomfortable to them. To congratulate a woman on her engagement is really to say, "Thank goodness! You had a close call!" For the man, on the other hand, there was no such danger. His choosing to marry is viewed as a good thing, but not something essential.

25　　　The linguistic double standard holds throughout the life of the relationship. After marriage, bachelor and spinster become man and wife, not man and woman. The woman whose husband dies remains "John's widow;" John, however, is never "Mary's widower."

26　　　Finally, why is it that salesclerks and others are so quick to call women customers "dear," "honey," and other terms of endearment they really have no business using? A male customer would never put up with it. But women, like children, are supposed to enjoy these endearments, rather than being offended by them.

27　　　In more ways than one, it's time to speak up.

Revising

DONALD M. MURRAY

The Maker's Eye:
Revising Your Own Manuscripts

Murray was a successful writer long before he began teaching others to write. Born in Boston in 1924, he was educated at the University of New Hampshire (B.A., 1948) and Boston University. He wrote editorials for the Boston Herald, *1948–54, for which he won a Pulitzer Prize in 1954, and then became a contributing editor of* Time. *Murray has taught English at the University of New Hampshire since 1963, and has written numerous essays, books of short stories, poetry, and a novel,* The Man Who Had Everything *(1964). A* Writer Teaches Writing *(1964, rev. 1985), an explanation of how people really write, has been highly influential in persuading writing teachers to encourage their students to focus on the process of writing, rather than on the finished product.*

In Murray's view, shared by many professional writers as well as writing teachers, revision is central to the composing process. To dispel doubts, Murray offers not only the example of his own essay but the experiences of a number of other professional writers: " 'Good writing is essentially rewriting.' " After spending two pages to convince skeptical readers that rewriting is "a condition of the writer's life," Murray offers a straightforward account of just how writers move through the process of revising, by making changes—in content, in form and in proportion, and finally in voice and word choice—that will substantially improve their work, even though "the words on a page are never finished."

When students complete a first draft, they consider the job of writing done—and their teachers too often agree. When professional writers complete a first draft, they usually feel that they are at the start of the writing process. When a draft is completed, the job of writing can begin.

That difference in attitude is the difference between amateur and professional, inexperience and experience, journeyman and craftsman. Peter F. Drucker, the prolific business writer, calls his first draft "the zero draft"—after that he can start counting. Most writers share the feeling that the first draft, and all of those which follow, are opportunities to discover what they have to say and how best they can say it.

To produce a progression of drafts, each of which says more and says it more clearly, the writer has to develop a special kind of reading skill. In school we are taught to decode what appears on the page as finished writing. Writers, however, face a different category of possibility and responsibility when they read their own drafts. To them the words on the page are never finished. Each can be changed and rearranged, can set off a chain reaction of confusion or clarified meaning. This is a different kind of reading which is possibly more difficult and certainly more exciting.

4   Writers must learn to be their own best enemy. They must accept the criticism of others and be suspicious of it; they must accept the praise of others and be even more suspicious of it. Writers cannot depend on others. They must detach themselves from their own pages so that they can apply both their caring and their craft to their own work.

5   Such detachment is not easy. Science fiction writer Ray Bradbury supposedly puts each manuscript away for a year to the day and then rereads it as a stranger. Not many writers have the discipline or the time to do this. We must read when our judgment may be at its worst, when we are close to the euphoric moment of creation.

6   Then the writer, counsels novelist Nancy Hale, "should be critical of everything that seems to him most delightful in his style. He should excise what he most admires, because he wouldn't thus admire it if he weren't . . . in a sense protecting it from criticism." John Ciardi, the poet, adds, "The last act of the writing must be to become one's own reader. It is, I suppose, a schizophrenic process, to begin passionately and to end critically, to begin hot and to end cold; and, more important, to be passion-hot and critic-cold at the same time."

7   Most people think that the principal problem is that writers are too proud of what they have written. Actually, a greater problem for most professional writers is one shared by the majority of students. They are overly critical, think everything is dreadful, tear up page after page, never complete a draft, see the task as hopeless.

8   The writer must learn to read critically but constructively, to cut what is bad, to reveal what is good. Eleanor Estes, the children's book author, explains: "The writer must survey his work critically, cooly, as though he were a stranger to it. He must be willing to prune, expertly and hard-heartedly. At the end of each revision, a manuscript may look . . . worked over, torn apart, pinned together, added to, deleted from, words changed and words changed back. Yet the book must maintain its original freshness and spontaneity."

9   Most readers underestimate the amount of rewriting it usually takes to produce spontaneous reading. This is a great disadvantage to the student writer, who sees only a finished product and never watches the craftsman who takes the necessary step back, studies the work carefully, returns to the task, steps back, returns, steps back, again and again. Anthony Burgess, one of the most prolific writers in the English-speaking world, admits, "I might revise a page twenty times." Roald Dahl, the popular children's writer, states, "By the time I'm nearing the end of a story, the first part will have been reread and altered and corrected at least 150 times. . . . Good writing is essentially rewriting. I am positive of this."

10   Rewriting isn't virtuous. It isn't something that ought to be done. It is simply something that most writers find they have to do to discover what they have to say and how to say it. It is a condition of the writer's life.

11   There are, however, a few writers who do little formal rewriting, primar-

ily because they have the capacity and experience to create and review a large number of invisible drafts in their minds before they approach the page. And some writers slowly produce finished pages, performing all the tasks of revision simultaneously, page by page, rather than draft by draft. But it is still possible to see the sequence followed by most writers most of the time in rereading their own work.

Most writers scan their drafts first, reading as quickly as possible to catch the larger problems of subject and form, then move in closer and closer as they read and write, reread and rewrite. 12

The first thing writers look for in their drafts is *information*. They know that a good piece of writing is built from specific, accurate, and interesting information. The writer must have an abundance of information from which to construct a readable piece of writing. 13

Next writers look for *meaning* in the information. The specifics must build to a pattern of significance. Each piece of specific information must carry the reader toward meaning. 14

Writers reading their own drafts are aware of *audience*. They put themselves in the reader's situation and make sure that they deliver information which a reader wants to know or needs to know in a manner which is easily digested. Writers try to be sure that they anticipate and answer the questions a critical reader will ask when reading the piece of writing. 15

Writers make sure that the *form* is appropriate to the subject and the audience. Form, or genre, is the vehicle which carries meaning to the reader, but form cannot be selected until the writer has adequate information to discover its significance and an audience which needs or wants that meaning. 16

Once writers are sure the form is appropriate, they must then look at the *structure*, the order of what they have written. Good writing is built on a solid framework of logic, argument, narrative, or motivation which runs through the entire piece of writing and holds it together. This is the time when many writers find it most effective to outline as a way of visualizing the hidden spine by which the piece of writing is supported. 17

The element on which writers may spend a majority of their time is *development*. Each section of a piece of writing must be adequately developed. It must give readers enough information so that they are satisfied. How much information is enough? That's as difficult as asking how much garlic belongs in a salad. It must be done to taste, but most beginning writers underdevelop, underestimating the reader's hunger for information. 18

As writers solve development problems, they often have to consider questions of *dimension*. There must be a pleasing and effective proportion among all the parts of the piece of writing. There is a continual process of subtracting and adding to keep the piece of writing in balance. 19

Finally, writers have to listen to their own voices. *Voice* is the force which drives a piece of writing forward. It is an expression of the writer's authority and concern. It is what is between the words on the page, what glues the 20 piece of writing together. A good piece of writing is always marked by a consistent, individual voice.

21   As writers read and reread, write and rewrite, they move closer and closer to the page until they are doing line-by-line editing. Writers read their own pages with infinite care. Each sentence, each line, each clause, each phrase, each word, each mark of punctuation, each section of white space between the type has to contribute to the clarification of meaning.

22   Slowly the writer moves from word to word, looking through language to see the subject. As a word is changed, cut, or added, as a construction is rearranged, all the words used before that moment and all those that follow that moment must be considered and reconsidered.

23   Writers often read aloud at this stage of the editing process, muttering or whispering to themselves, calling on the ear's experience with language. Does this sound right—or that? Writers edit, shifting back and forth from eye to page to ear to page. I find I must do this careful editing in short runs, no more than fifteen or twenty minutes at a stretch, or I become too kind with myself. I begin to see what I hope is on the page, not what actually is on the page.

24   This sounds tedious if you haven't done it, but actually it is fun. Making something right is immensely satisfying, for writers begin to learn what they are writing about by writing. Language leads them to meaning, and there is the joy of discovery, of understanding, of making meaning clear as the writer employs the technical skills of language.

25   Words have double meanings, even triple and quadruple meanings. Each word has its own potential for connotation and denotation. And when writers rub one word against the other, they are often rewarded with a sudden insight, an unexpected clarification.

26   The maker's eye moves back and forth from word to phrase to sentence to paragraph to sentence to phrase to word. The maker's eye sees the need for variety and balance, for a firmer structure, for a more appropriate form. It peers into the interior of the paragraph, looking for coherence, unity, and emphasis, which make meaning clear.

27   I learned something about this process when my first bifocals were prescribed. I had ordered a larger section of the reading portion of the glass because of my work, but even so, I could not contain my eyes within this new limit of vision. And I still find myself taking off my glasses and bending my nose towards the page, for my eyes unconsciously flick back and forth across the page, back to another page, forward to still another, as I try to see each evolving line in relation to every other line.

28   When does this process end? Most writers agree with the great Russian writer Tolstoy, who said, "I scarcely ever reread my published writings; if by chance I come across a page, it always strikes me: all this must be rewritten; this is how I should have written it."

29   The maker's eye is never satisfied, for each word has the potential to

ignite new meaning. This article has been twice written all the way through the writing process, and it was published four years ago. Now it is to be republished in a book. The editors made a few small suggestions, and then I read it with my maker's eye. Now it has been re-edited, re-revised, re-read, re-re-edited, for each piece of writing to the writer is full of potential and alternatives.

A piece of writing is never finished. It is delivered to a deadline, torn out 30 of the typewriter on demand, sent off with a sense of accomplishment and shame and pride and frustration. If only there were a couple more days, time for just another run at it, perhaps then. . . .

Questions

1. Why does Murray say that when a first "draft is completed, the job of writing can begin" (paragraph 1)? Do you agree or disagree? If you thought before you read this that writing one draft of a given essay was enough, has Murray convinced you otherwise?

2. How does Murray explain John Ciardi's analysis of the "schizophrenic process" of becoming one's own reader, "to be passion-hot and critic-cold at the same time" (paragraph 6)? Why does he consider it so important for writers to be both?

3. What are writers looking for when they revise? Is Murray's list (paragraphs 13–20) realistic? comprehensive? appropriate for you? When do you start revising? When do you stop?

4. How can writers be sure that their "maker's eye" has in revision an accurate perception of the "need for variety and balance, for a firmer structure, for a more appropriate form . . . for coherence, unity, and emphasis" (paragraph 26)? How do you, as a writer, know whether your writing is good or not? Does Murray's essay provide enough information to enable you to be an accurate judge of your own work? Why or why not?

5. What kind of an authorial personality does Murray convey? Does this make you more or less willing to take his advice than you might from a different personality?

RICHARD WRIGHT

Interview Comments
on *Black Boy*

Wright was born in 1908 in a sharecropper's cabin on a plantation near Nachez, Missis-sippi; he died in Paris in 1960, internationally known for his autobiographical Black Boy *(1945); a collection of stories,* Uncle Tom's Children *(1938), and a novel,* Native Son *(1940). American Hunger, written as the second part of* Black Boy *but not published until 1977, delineates Wright's experiences in the North, 1927–40, especially in Chicago, where he learned to distrust nearly all whites.*

In the remarks below on how he came to write Black Boy, *Wright discusses the questions—inappropriate ones, he felt—that people raised about this account of his first seventeen years. The book, a searing indictment of racial segregation and hatred in the South, focuses on the violence, poverty, and constant hunger that plagued his growing up in a family deserted by his father, given up on by his chronically ill mother, and dominated by his fanatically religious grandmother. Wright composed six different drafts of this statement. Although he retained the original structure, proceeding from an introduction to a discussion of four books that greatly influenced Wright's perception of his youthful experiences, to the social message of* Black Boy, *to a conclusion, he condensed the original version by over 50 percent. In the process, he moved from writing primarily for himself to addressing an audience of outside readers—incredulous whites and fearful blacks (as other interviews reveal) whom he had to convince that* Black Boy's *usually harsh depiction of the black experience in America is realistic. Consequently, it is meaningful to their lives as well as to his own, because all share a common heritage, "the hunger for freedom."*

First Draft (with Second-Draft Corrections) *

1   Since my book, BLACK BOY, has been published,
I've been interviewed many times ~~by the press and
radio; but almost always I was called upon to~~ answered *a lot of*
questions ~~which I did not personally consider impor-
tant~~. *But'* And I never had a chance to say what I *really* wanted to
say.

2   And strangely enough, what I ~~do~~ have to say about
BLACK BOY does not concern the facts contained in ~~that~~ *the*
book, facts which ~~in my opinion~~ are quite obvious,
~~facts which really constitute a tremendous understate-
ment~~. What I do want to talk about is how I came to
feel that ~~the~~ *those* facts *possessed* ~~recorded in BLACK BOY had for me~~
sufficient importance to warrant my writing about
them, how it was possible for me, born and bred in a
seperate, Jim Crow culture, *and* to feel that my life possessed a meaning which my environment denied. ~~That
sense came slowly, bit by bit~~.

3   When I left the South, ~~in my 18-19th year~~, my head
and heart ~~were full of~~ *filled with* a jumble of confused impressions and memories, I wondered dimly about the meaning
of the life I had lived, the experiences I had had.

* Note that this and the following draft show typographical errors and strikeovers, just as Wright composed them at the typewriter.

Then, far away from the South, in another city and in another culture, I read Dostoeevsky's THE HOUSE OF THE DEAD, a description of the lives of political prisoners in exile in Siberia. The life depicted so toughed me that it formed an insight into the Negro life that I had seen and lived in the South. Dostoevsky described how prisoners living in close contact vented their hostility upon each other rather than upon the Czar ~~or his officers~~ who had sent them there. That strange pattern of conduct made me remember how Negroes in the South had *often* vented their hostility upon each other rather than upon the whites above them who shaped and ruled their lives. Reading, to me, was a kind of re-membering.

It was through looking at the experiences of the Negro in the South through alien eyes that those expe-riences cast themselves into meaningful forms. I knew that THE HOUSE OF THE DEAD was a true book, for I had already lived certain aspects of it in the South.

Another book that impressed me a great deal after I had left the South, *which* was George Moore's CONFESSIONS OF A YOUNG MAN / *a* ~~this book~~ delt with the struggles of an *individual* ~~young man~~ against the restricting influences of an En-glish Victorian environment. ~~I know while reading that book that it was a true book, for~~ I, *too* had grown up amidst ~~what would sound very strange to many whites,~~ a black Puritanical enviroment in the South. Once again, ~~through the eyes of George Moore~~ I was able, in look-ing back through alien eyes, to see something meaning-ful in my life, to understand and grasp it for the first time. Still another book yielded something to me, James Joyce's THE PORTRAIT OF THE ARTIST AS A YOUNG MAN. *This book* ~~here again I had a chance to to grasp the meaning of phases of my own environment by looking at them through the eyes of an alien artist, by seeing~~

~~them in the guises of another life.~~ Joyce's ~~THE POR-TRAIT OF THE ARTIST AS A YOUNG MAN~~ was particularly meaningful, ~~to me,~~ for it depicted a double revolt. Joyce's hero, *Stephen* revolted against the Catholic Church and the life of Dublin of his day; and also it must be remembered that *Stephen's* Ireland was at grips, ~~as she seems always to be,~~ with imperialistic England. *and* The Negro in the South, he *it* ~~is is to~~ live in and breathe *of* the culture of his times, must wrench himself *emotionally* free of his southern environment and while doing so he knows that that environment ~~is at war~~ is ~~warred upon~~ *dominated* by the white's ~~environment~~ above it. I'll mention one more book, D. H. Lawrence's SONS AND LOVERS, which dealt with the experiences of a son of an English mining family, *a* ~~this~~ son *who* sought to ~~claim himself and be himself against the claims and~~ *escape the* demands of his family and environment. I knew too that that book was true, for I had lived some phases of it in the South.

6   I've mentioned these books more or less at random. I did not have in mind any of these books when I wrote BLACK BOY. The point of this is simple: I do not believe that it is possible for a Negro boy growing up in the South, *today* clinging simply to the bleak, prejudice-ridden suothern environment, to develop that sense of ~~distance~~ objectivity that would enable him to see ~~it~~ *and* and understand ~~it~~ *his life.* All too often he is claimed ~~by it~~ *his environment,* completely. ~~The experiences described in BLACK BOY, nine hundred and xxxx ninty nine times out of a thousand, usually crush the people who undergo them.~~ What the southern envornment offers *to* a young Negro is utterly lacking in ~~that xxxxxxxx~~ *that* nourishment ~~to make~~ *that* ~~him live~~ *would* enable him to live and develop as a man.

7   Lynching is a terrible thing. But there are many forms of lynching. There is a lynching of men's xxxxxxx spirits as well as their bodies. Physical

lynching occurs rather infrequently. Spirutual lynching occurs every day, every hours, and every moment of the day in the South for the Negro.

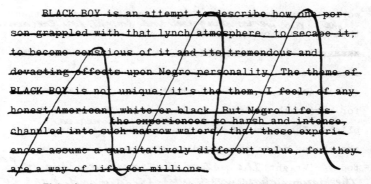

~~BLACK BOY is an attempt to describe how one person grappled with that lynch atmosphere, to secabe it, to become conscious of it and its tremendous and devasting effects upon Negro personality. The theme of BLACK BOY is not unique; it's the them, I feel, of any honest American, white or black. But Negro life is the experiences so harsh and intense, channled into such narrow waters, that these experiences assume a qualitatively different value, for they are a way of life for millions.~~

8

~~This brings me to something rather interesting.~~

9

Those of you you read BLACK BOY can know the truth of ~~what is contained in the book~~ *it* in a very simple way. Ask yourselvies as you read how often in your own lives have you had to grapple with the kind of problems depicted there. I'm not naive when I make this suggestion. I realize that ██████████ the██ ███ broad masses of the American people are not compelled to live through experiences as scalding as those described in BLACK BOY. Hence, merely because the experiences are alien to *the* sons and daughters of America*'s* middle class families, to whom ███ education is a matter of course, *to whom is* food something to be taken for granted, *to whom is* freedom a heritage, there might be some doubt ~~about the truthfulness about such~~ *astonishment about* experiences ~~as these~~ *related in such astonishment* ~~contained in~~ BLACK BOY. If there is any ~~doubt~~, then I'd suggest that they broaden██ and educate themselves by reading the literaute of other nations, ~~the books written by~~ *the* ~~men beyond the boundaries of our own country; to read the~~ literature of other people who have been compelled to meet and try to master such experiences, That ought ███ not to be a difficult task ~~today~~, for Europe is full of such people, *and* the world is full of them. The majority of men on earth today live such

lives. ~~The job of trying to be~~ *The struggle for freedom* free, is the ~~xxxx~~ fact

that fills the consciousness of mankind all over the

world ~~today.~~ Maybe ~~some of us~~ *we* in America ha~~ve~~*ve* forgotten

that. The ~~nation that remembers it will be the nation~~ *one* ~~*But we too struggled and fought for freedom*~~

~~xxxxwill whose word will be law and hope for billions~~

~~of people.~~

10   Hence, I feel that Negroes in America have a duty

for beyond themselves in reminding ˌthe nation of their

plight. The voice of the submerged Negro ˌ*in America* is but one of

the chorus of voices sounding for freedom everywhere

today. (Wright) *The nation that realizes this will be*
the nation whose word will be law and hope for
billions of common men.

Third Draft

1   Since my book, BLACK BOY, was published, I've been

(originally 1, 2) interviewed many times, but I've yet to have the chance

to say what I want to say about it. I do not want to

discuss the obvious facts in the book, but I do want to

say a word about how I cam to feel that those facts

possessed sufficient importance to warrant my writing

about them, how it was possible for me, born and bred

in the Jim Crow culture of the South, to come to feel

that my life had a meaning that my environment denied.

2   I ~~left the South~~ *came North* in my 19th year, filled with ~~won~~

(orig. 3, 4) *the hunger to know. Books became my life.* ~~dorment about the meaning of the life I had lived.~~

When I lived in the South, I was doomed
to look always at life thru the eyes which
the South had given me, and bewilderment
and fear have made me mute and afraid.
But after I left the South, luck gave me
new eyes, borrowed eyes with which to
look back and see the meaning of what
I had lived through.

I began to see thru the eyes of others.
~~Then, far away from the South, in another culture,~~ I
read Dostoevsky's THE HOUSE OF THE DEAD, an autobiographical novel describing the lives of/prisoners in
exile/in Siberia/, ~~The life depicted there gave me insight into the life I had lived and seen in the South.
Dostoevsky described~~ *and those* how prisoners, living in crowded
barracks often vented their hostility upon one an-
other/, ~~That strange conduct~~ *and it made* made me remember how Negroes in the South, crowded into their Black Belt
areas, often vented their restlessness and hostility
upon one another, forgetting that their lives were
conditioned and ruled by the whites above them. Reading, for me, was a kind of remembering.

~~After I had left the South~~ *T*here was another book
that ~~impressed me a great deal.~~ *shed a lot of light for me.* It was George Moore's
CONFESSIONS OF A YOUNG MAN. It depected how ~~a young
man~~ *an English youth* resisted the restrictions of ~~an English~~ *a* Victorian
environment; and once again I was able, in looking
back through alien eyes, to see something meaningful
in my life. Still another book had meaning for me,
James Joyce's THE PORTRAIT OF THE ARTIST AS A YOUNG
MAN. This book was particularly revealing, for it depected the double revolt of Joyce's hero, Stephen,
against the oppressive religious life of Ireland and
against the imperialism of England which sought to
strangle Irish aspirations. I was reminded that the
Negro in the South, if he is to learn to live ~~in and
breathe of the culture of his time,~~ must free himself
emotionally from his stifling environment, that same
environment that is dominated and exploited by the
whites above it. I'll mention one more book, D.H. Lawrence's SONS AND LOVERS, which dealt with the experiences of a son of an English coal mining family, a son
who sought to escape the crushing claims of his environment. ~~I know that that book was true, for I had
lived phases of it in the South.~~

3

(orig. 5)

4
(orig. 6)

I've mentioned these books at random. I had none of them in mind when I wrote BLACK BOY. I cite their influence upon me to show some of the literary sources of BLACK BOY, to show how my attitude was endlessly modified by them. Above all, I cite them to say that I do not believe that it is possible for a Negro boy growing up in the environment of the South today to develop that sense of objectivity *which* ~~that~~ will enable him to grasp and understand his life. All too often he is claimed by ~~that~~ *his* environment, blighted by it. I say it to show that the southern Negro needs help from the outside *if he is to live.*

5
(orig. 7)

Lynching is ~~a terrible thing. But there are~~ many forms ~~of lynching.~~ There is the lynching of men's spirits as well as their bodies. Physical lynching is a rather infrequent ~~thing,~~ but spiritual lynching occurs every day, ~~every hour, every moment~~ for the Negro in the South.

6
(orig. 9)

I know that ~~the masses of the American people are not compelled today to live~~ the scalding experiences described in BLACK BOY. ~~These experiences~~ are alien to the sons and daughters of America's middle class white families, to whom education is a matter of course thing, to whom food is something to be taken for granted, to whom freedom is ~~a heritage. Yet BLACK BOY~~ *Yet to those whites who recall how, in the early* ~~is an American story, and to those whites who care to~~ *days of our land, how* ~~let their minds drift back to the early days in this land when~~ their forefathers struggled for freedom, BLACK BOY cannot be a strange story~~, an astonishing story.~~ Neither can it be alien to Jews who came hopefully to this land from the Old World; ~~it cannot be alien to the~~ Irish, the Poles, the Italians ~~who came here. Surely it cannot be alient to the teeming, homeless millions who roam ravaged Europe this hour.~~

7
(orig. 9, 10)

Because the Hunger for freedom fills the hearts of men all *this war-ravaged* over the world today. ~~Hence,~~ I feel that Negroes in *a sacred obligation*

```
American have a moral duty to remind the nation con-

stantly of their plight, that they have a sacred obli-

gation to haunt this nation with their claim and their

problem. For the voice of the submerged Negro in

America is but one of the chorus of voices sounding

for freedom everywhere today.
```

Sixth and Final Version

Since my book, *Black Boy,* was published, I've been interviewed many times, but I've yet to say what I really want to say about it. I don't want to discuss the events described there, but I do want to tell how I came to feel that those events possessed enough importance to compel me to write about them; how it was possible for me to feel that my life had a meaning which my Jim Crow, southern environment denied.

Living in the South doomed me to look always through eyes which the South had given me, and bewilderment and fear made me mute and afraid. But after I had left the South, luck gave me other eyes, new eyes with which to look at the meaning of what I'd lived through.

I came North in my 19th year, filled with the hunger to know. Books were the windows through which I looked at the world. I read Dostoevsky's *The House of the Dead,* an autobiographical novel depicting the lives of exiled prisoners in Siberia, how they lived in crowded barracks and vented their hostility upon one another. It made me remember how Negroes in the South, crowded into their Black Belts, vented their hostility upon one another, forgetting that their lives were conditioned by the whites above them. To me reading was a kind of remembering.

Another book shed light for me, George Moore's *Confessions of a Young Man,* which described how an English youth resisted the restrictions of a Victorian environment; and at once I was able, in looking back through alien eyes, to see my own life. There was another book, James Joyce's *The Portrait of the Artist as a Young Man,* which depicted the double revolt of an Irish youth against the oppressive religious life of Ireland, an Ireland which England was seeking to strangle. I was reminded of the stifling Negro environment in the South, an environment that is exploited by the whites above it. I'll mention one more book, D. H. Lawrence's *Sons and Lovers,* which dealt with the experiences of a son of an English coal mining family, a son who sought to escape the demands of a bleak environment.

I had in mind none of these books I've mentioned when I wrote *Black Boy.* But books like these endlessly modified my attitude. The point is this: I do not believe that it is possible for a Negro boy growing up in the environment of the South today to develop that sense of objectivity that will enable him to grasp the meaning of his life. If he is to learn to live, he needs help from the outside. Lynching is a terror that has many forms; there is the lynching of men's spirits as well as their bodies, and spiritual lynching occurs every day for the Negro in the South.

6   I know that the scalding experiences of *Black Boy* are alien to most Americans to whom education is a matter of course thing, to whom food is something to be taken for granted, to whom freedom is a heritage. Yet to those whites who recall how, in the early days of this land, their forefathers struggled for freedom, *Black Boy* cannot be a strange story. Neither can it be a strange story to the Jews, the Poles, the Irish, and the Italians who came hopefully to this land from the Old World. Because the hunger for freedom fills the hearts of men all over this war-ravaged earth today, I feel that Negroes in America have a moral duty, a sacred obligation to remind the nation constantly of their plight, their claim, their problem. And when you hear the voice of the submerged Negro in America, remember that it is but one of the world-wide chorus of voices sounding for freedom everywhere.

TERESA WHITLOCK (Student)
My "Professional" Hairstyle

Whitlock, a native of Roanoke, Virginia (b. 1962), graduated from Virginia Commonwealth University in 1984 with a B.A. in psychology. She is currently teaching in a Virginia high school. The first version of this paper, an account of her first college haircut, was too brief to fulfill its humorous potential. For instance, Teresa erroneously counts on her readers to know what her hair looked like before it was cut, yet without this information they can't assess the ultimate damage. She also omits the details of the central action—the actual cutting of her hair; she needs to show them what happened, rather than simply to tell them about the incident. And she needs to characterize herself more fully; readers don't know whether she's foolish, vain, naive, too trusting, sadder but wiser, or all of these.

In the revision, Teresa focused on adding information about who was present; what they were saying and doing; what her hair looked like before, during, and after the massacre; why Chantay, with Teresa's encouragement, continued to cut her hair shorter and shorter. In the process, she characterized herself more fully; she's a likeable person, the optimistic victim of her own flaws, someone with whom most readers can fully sympathize. In the revision, she has eliminated the earlier repetitive wording and made a few subtle puns and allusions: "there is no free haircut" revitalizes the meaning of the cliché, "there is no free lunch." She also uses repetition effectively, in the ironic variations on "Chantay always knew what she was doing." Indeed.

Version I

1   Risks are a part of everyone's life. Since I'm usually a trusting person, I often get myself into situations that I later realize I could have avoided. After getting into one of these situations, I learned that a favor may not be a favor at all.

About two years ago just after I entered my freshman year, I decided I wanted a change. One Saturday before dinner I decided to wash my hair. Afterwards, I went to my friend's room to ask if I could use her hair dryer and mentioned that I wished I could get my hair cut into a carefree style. She said she'd do me a favor and that she'd be happy to cut my hair for me. Since her hair always looked good, I agreed to let her cut mine. Several other people were in the room also, talking and waiting around for dinner. As my friend cut my hair, I was thinking how nice it was to finally get my hair cut into a carefree style. After telling her what style I wanted, I relaxed.

After what seemed like an eternity, she finally said she was finished and let me look at the results. When I looked in the mirror, I thought I was looking at another person. My hair was so short that it stood up on my head like Woodstock's! I couldn't believe it! Gone were my long locks, replaced by short curly stubs of what was supposedly hair. Everyone in the room was laughing at my head and my friend who had committed this act just kept saying, "Oh, I'm so sorry, I didn't mean to cut it so short." Her apologies didn't calm me. I was still furious.

Finally everyone managed to control their laughter and someone suggested trying a curling iron to make the hair lie down a bit. Not knowing what else to do, I gave it a try, only to find that my hair was too short to fit around the curlers! By now I was really upset, but had to laugh at my predicament because it was somewhat funny. After trying everything we could think of to make my hair presentable, I finally came up with the perfect solution. A hat! Yes, I ended up wearing a hat to dinner and to classes for a few weeks until my hair started growing again. Lucky for me it was winter. Boy, did I learn a lesson!

Revision

I'm too trusting, and because I trust others too much I take unnecessary risks. When people tell me they know how to do something, I believe them. When they offer to help me in their supposed expertise I let them—a risk indeed, as I too often learn that their aid does more harm than good. With friends like these, who needs to talk to strangers?

Two years ago, in the fall of my freshman year, I decided to wash my shoulder-length hair before Saturday dinner. Afterwards, when borrowing my friend's hair dryer, I mentioned that I wanted to get my hair cut into a shorter style that would be easy to care for. I wanted to be able to wash it, blow it dry, and curl it just a little on the ends to make it look pretty. "I'll do you a favor," beamed Chantay. "I'll be happy to cut your hair." Since she cut and permed her own hair and it always looked good, I agreed, pleased that my wish could be executed so soon—and for free.

I should have realized that there is no free haircut. But instead, I trustingly told her to cut two or three inches off the back, and to cut the front even shorter so it would hold the curl better. Then I relaxed and joined in the conversation with our other friends in the room who were waiting to go down to dinner.

4   Chantay began to cut my hair from the back first, so I couldn't see how much she was cutting off. I could tell by the feel that she was working from the top down to create a layered look, which was fine with me as long as it curled. As the hair began to pile up on the floor, I was still pleased; after all, Chantay knew more about what she was doing than I did. Before she started to cut the front, she stopped and asked me to look at the back to see whether it was short enough. I looked in the mirror, foolishly trusting what I saw in the dim light, and told her to cut another inch off. Which she did.

5   When Chantay began to cut the front, she repeated the procedure she'd used on the back, starting at the top and working down. At first she cut only an inch off. But that made it even with the back, and I wanted the front shorter, so she obligingly cut off another inch in front. At this point I became aware of remarks from the others in the room; "You gonna cut off all her hair, or what?" "Good thing Halloween was last week!" And I began to get a little nervous, but Chantay always knew what she was doing.

6   So I said "O.K." when she told me she was going to cut off "just a little more in the back to make it curl faster on the ends." After all, that was just what I'd wanted. The remarks continued, this time with sneers: "You getting scissor happy, ain'tcha?" "Girl, you should see the back of your head!" Whether or not Chantay always knew what she was doing, I decided to see for myself.

7   When I looked in the mirror, I thought I was seeing another person. My hair was so short that it stood up on my head like Woodstock's! I couldn't believe it! Gone were my long locks, replaced by short curly stubs of what was supposedly hair. Everyone in the room was laughing at my head. "Pure punk!" "The New Wave—ain't never gonna wave again!" Chantay looked remorseful. "Oh, I'm so sorry, I didn't mean to cut it so short. I'm so sorry. And, besides, it looks kinda cute." Her apologies didn't calm me. I was so furious I couldn't speak.

8   Amidst the laughter—even Chantay was by this time beginning to smile—someone suggested trying a curling iron to make the hair lie down a bit. Not knowing what else to do, I gave it a try, only to find that my hair was too short to fit around the curlers. Even though I was horrified by the mass of wiry wisps that sprouted from my scalp, I was beginning to laugh at my predicament. After all, everyone else was. But I wasn't going to dinner until I did something with my hair.

9   So I starved that night as I tried different solutions. As my friends cut out for a good evening, Chantay gave me some tiny rollers that she had used to perm her hair. Fortunately, my hair fit around them, but they curled it so tight that my hair came out matted to my head. I thought I could solve that problem by washing my hair and using a brush to curl it while blowing it dry, . . . that only made me look scared to death. My well-fed friends gave me

some hairspray, but that was no better. And creams simply changed the wires to scraggles.

Before I missed yet another meal I came up with the perfect solution. A 10 hat! I wore a cream-colored knitted hat to meals and to classes, but when some wise-guy snatched off my hat and called me "Baldilocks," I bought a black beret to match my gloves. Chantay was the first to admit that it looked chic. After that, the smart comments ceased, and I trusted in the black beret until my hair grew long enough to look good. Lucky for me it was winter.

Writing About Writing

Strategies

1. What is my intended audience? In what ways, if any, must I accommodate the audience's level of knowledge of the subject? their biases, beliefs, backgrounds?

2. What kind of authorial persona am I presenting, intentionally or otherwise? Do I consciously play any roles (expert, innocent, or other)? Do I appear to be any or all of the following: knowledgeable, honest, original, interesting, a competent writer? Do I say anything that might undermine my credibility or sensitivity? If so, what must I change to alter the negative elements?

3. What level(s) of language (see *diction* in glossary) have I used throughout this writing? formal? middle-level? informal? some combination? What level(s) of language have I attained through what means—for instance, vocabulary, tone, sentence and paragraph organization, length? How well does this level or combination of levels suit my subject and myself as a writer?

4. Am I following any of the instructions given by the writers in this chapter, such as Galbraith, Trimble, Orwell, or Murray? Which ones? Are they working as I expected them to?

5. If asked, could I give a good reason for my use of any illustration, piece of information, word, phrase, sentence, or organizational pattern in the entire essay? (Incidentally, "It sounds better that way" is a very good reason, as Kunitz would argue in "Swimming in Lake Chauggogagog . . .") Do I like what I've written? If not, what am I willing to do to improve the writing?

Suggestions

1. Keep a writer's notebook for two weeks, a month, or even a semester, in which you write for fifteen minutes or so five times a week. Include items you might use later in other writing—notes about people you meet whose appearance, clothing, jobs, hobbies, mannerisms, or ways of speaking are interesting or unusual; places you want to remember; odd names or colorful words or figures of speech; amusing or startling incidents; reactions to your reading—newspapers and magazines, required or professional texts, pleasure reading.

2. Pick one (or more) entries from your writer's notebook and expand it into an essay.

3. If you write for reasons other than academic course requirements, write an essay on "Why I Write," in the manner of either George Orwell (23–28) or Joan Didion (29–

34). Do you like to write? Why or why not? Explain what you intend to accomplish when you write and how you work on a particular piece or type of writing. Do you usually succeed?

4. Write an essay on "How I Write," in the manner of John Kenneth Galbraith's "Writing and Typing" (35–41). Are your place (kitchen, dorm room, library), time (morning, afternoon, night, weekends), and means of writing (pencil and pad, typewriter, or computer) conducive to good writing? Why or why not? Do you plan in advance much of what you're going to say, or do you invent and develop your material as you write? How much revising do you do—and what kind?

5. Do you agree with the precepts of Trimble ("Write to Be Read," 67–71) and Orwell ("Politics and the English Language," 72–82) that encourage writers to be clear, concise, and conversational? Write an essay in which you either reinforce or take issue with their advice, using illustrative examples of what you consider bad and good writing gleaned from your own reading (and writing, if desired).

6. Pick an essay you like (from this book or elsewhere) and write a straightforward imitation of it—in subject, structure, and style. A narrative (like Orwell's "Shooting an Elephant," 335–40) or how-to essay (like many of those in Chapter 7) would be among the easiest to start with.

7. Write a brief parody of a type of writing (diary, typical newspaper sports or wedding column, a Western or Gothic novel or romance, or any other form you like) or of a particular author (Hemingway, Salinger, Faulkner, or another), or of a specific literary work. For instance, you might write a parody of a fable, as Thurber did in "The Unicorn in the Garden" (561–62), or of a detective story, as Woody Allen did in "The Whore of Mensa" (552–56).

8. Using Lakoff's "You Are What You Say" (83–88) for reference, analyze your own speech and the speech of two or three men and women you know to see whether your evidence supports Lakoff's contention that men and women speak differently. Write an essay in which you discuss whether the men and women have different vocabularies, different ways of asking questions and making assertions, and different labels for terms involving men and women. On the basis of your findings, what, if any, recommendations would you make for literary style?

9. Pick one of your own writings that needs revising, and revise it according to the process that Murray recommends in "The Maker's Eye" (89–93). If you have received any suggestions for changes from peers, teachers, or friends, take these into account as you revise, but feel free to disregard them if you have good reasons for doing so.

10. After an interval of two weeks or longer, revise the revision you wrote for # 9, or another revision.

CHAPTER TWO

Writing About People

When someone asked that crusty commentator, H.L. Mencken, why he continued to write about people, given his contempt for what he called "the booboisie," he replied, "Why do people go to zoos?" People are a favorite subject to write about—in *interviews;* in *self-portraits* or *character sketches of others;* in *personal narratives,* in which the author becomes a character (as well as a central consciousness) in his or her own story; in *vignettes,* glimpses of a personality or someone in action, embedded in other types of writing; and in full-scale *biographies* and *autobiographies.*

Significantly, in writing about ourselves or others we learn who we are and who we can be. We can discover our heritage—as individuals or as members of families or cultural, ethnic, or racial groups. We can explore what it means to grow up male or female in a particular environment: on a farm, in a tenement, in a small town, suburb, or large city. Through personal writings we can interpret our history, recent or more remote, as we try to understand the significance of the Jazz Age or the Vietnam War era, slavery or the Civil Rights movement. Written recollections can preserve the knowledge of fragile or vanishing ways of life (in the New Mexico mountains or the New Jersey Pine Barrens), or of forgotten or unusual trades or professions (repairing antique machinery, establishing a hospital in the tropics).

Personal writings can also help us understand our contemporaries and our own world. We can examine the good times—parties in high (and bourgeois and humble) society, creation and recreation, success and the appearance of success. We can come to understand the bad times, as well: orphanhood, drug abuse, brutality. Personal writings can reveal the myriad facets of multiple roles: child, parent, grandparent; friend, lover, enemy; citizen, public or private. People can tell about a way of life and what they live for simply through explaining how they live. And so our lives can touch.

Writing Interviews

Talking with people about their favorite subject, themselves, is a pleasant and relatively simple way to do original writing without extensive research. If you're the interviewer you'll listen a lot, ask key questions, and take careful notes (perhaps supplemented by a tape recorder), but may choose—as Studs Terkel does in his interview with "Miss U.S.A., Emma Knight" (113–17)— to keep yourself entirely out of the picture. In a question-and-answer format, such as in Joan Galway's interview with Louise Nevelson (118–22), you'll ask questions, either framed to elicit specific information or intended to encourage the speaker to elaborate on the topic at hand. But the interviewer won't talk much; he or she is not engaging in a dialogue but in a monologue.

In either case, when writing up an interview from notes, you'll have to edit the material you've collected in order to organize and use the salvageable 10 percent of the interview's "pure gold," as Terkel called it. There is a convention of interviews, and of portraits derived from interviews, that the writer has the freedom to reorganize the original material, which is likely to be repetitive and full of digressions, into a pattern that is logical, topical, chronological, or otherwise satisfying. Contrary to the practice when working with printed or other documentary sources, when you're writing up interviews you don't supply ellipses (. . .) each time you omit or move words (so you subject won't . . . appear . . . to be . . . stuttering), or otherwise indicate that you've reorganized the original material. The focus is always on the subject of the portrait, not on the brushstrokes of its creation.

Interviews can be primarily biographical, encompassing an entire life, as does Henry Mitchell's "Eudora Welty: Storyteller of the South" (167–75), derived from two days of interviews with Eudora Welty, as well as a careful reading of her works and reviews of them. Interviews can focus on a particular role the subject played, as Studs Terkel does with Emma Knight's performance as Miss U.S.A., 1973, or on specific aspects of that role, as Joan Galway does with Louise Nevelson's development as a sculptor. Or interviews can emphasize events or eras in which the subject participated, as in Langenberg's "Interview with Alfred Everett" (122–35), treating a decade of her subject's experiences of growing up in East St. Louis in the Roaring Twenties. Langenberg's article, "East St. Louis, from Blues to Dirge" (135–41), incorporates considerable material from the interview but shifts the focus, as is true of many writings derived from interviews. In the completed essay Langenberg supplements the original source with a great deal of additional material derived from other sources—in this case, primarily East St. Louis newspapers:

> With the ratification of the Eighteenth Amendment prohibiting the sale of intoxicating liquors, on January 18, 1920, the first seeds of change were sown on the East Side.
>
> The [East St. Louis] *Journal* devoted a large portion of its front page on January 16, 1920, to a story about the feelings of the local populace on the

new law. The newspaper reported that ". . . Saloon keepers generally take a philosophic view. They feel that the public in general did not protest against the law, but submitted to every encroachment so meekly that the fanatics were encouraged and went the limit . . . . In many homes, intoxicants will be made for home consumption and the efforts of any governmental agency to stop this will be defied and defeated . . . .

What was background in the interview becomes foreground in the completed essay, which now focuses on the mores and manners of the city, rather than on the teenage Everett coming of age there: "As *The Journal* predicted, homeowners began to make their own intoxicants . . . ."

Character Sketches and Portraits

A character sketch or portrait aims to make a person, anyone at all—rich man, poor man, beggar man, thief—come alive for an audience who may know very little about the subject. You have to know the subject well, either personally or through a great deal of documentary or other auxiliary information. You also have to convey what makes that person memorable—through a wealth of quotations from conversation or letters, through a multitude of specific details that show the person in one or more contexts relevant to the focus of the portrait—at home, at work or in play, in action (even if that action is a state of mind) and interaction with family, friends, coworkers, people in the community. Such details will reveal ways in which the subject is like others or different, unusual or commonplace, attractive or unattractive. And they'll show the subject's temperament—constant or mercurial, optimistic or pessimistic, theoretical or practical—however that person appears to you as a writer. Thus Terkel's brief but revealing quotation about Emma Knight's first minute as Miss U.S.A.:

> So I signed [the contract] and the phone rang and the guy was from a Chicago paper and said: "Tell me, is it Miss or Ms.?" I said: "It's Ms." He said: "You're kidding." I said: "No, I'm not." He wrote an article the next day saying something like it finally happened: a beauty queen, a feminist. I thought I was a feminist before I was a beauty queen, why should I stop now?

John Leonard, in "The Only Child" (142–44), and Mary Ruffin, in "Mama's Smoke" (145–47), are trying to come to terms with people who are lost to them, Leonard's brother through drug abuse, Ruffin's mother through death when Mary was thirteen. These portraits inevitably reveal the writers' intense involvement with their subjects as they try to capture the essence of personalities past and present. Thus Leonard emphasizes the contrast between his brother's present, drug-dazed schizophrenic self and the exemplary young man he had been a decade earlier:

> This is the man who introduced me to the mysteries of mathematical science, the man I could never beat at chess . . . . Now there is static in his head . . . . He has an attention span of about thirty seconds.

And Mary's mother, Peggy, drifts in and out of Mary's dreams, reveries, and everyday activities, the cigarette smoke of mother then, daughter now, blending with Peggy's wraithlike image:

> Usually she surfaces so briefly and unobtrusively that I'm not sure she has been there until after she's gone. Sometimes she appears an old haggard crone, the salt in her hair so thick that the pepper looks like dirt streaks washing away. Other times she is vital, younger than I am, the sheen of her black hair almost blinding.

Mary McCarthy in "Uncle Myers" (147–55) and Frederick Douglass in "Resurrection" (155–59) present portraits of themselves in relation to terrible but memorable people who wronged them grievously. Uncle Myers, Mary's guardian after her parents died when she was a child, "all two hundred and five pounds . . . and gross blue eyes," was stupid, insensitive, petty, mean, and brutal. McCarthy anatomizes this mass of "swollen passivity," who "did nothing for a living" and beat her "all the time, as a matter of course," especially when she won an essay contest at ten, "to teach me a lesson, he said, lest I become stuck-up." The adult writer not only arouses her readers' righteous anger, she evens the score. Douglass, typical of many writers of personal narratives, analyzes a critical event in his life, when as a sixteen-year-old slave he successfully defied Mr. Covey, the overseer, who beat him unmercifully. Here the focus is on himself; his adversary is subordinate, for this victory, says Douglass in retrospect,

> was the turning point in my career as a slave. It kindled the few expiring embers of freedom, and revived within me a sense of my own manhood. It recalled the departed self-confidence, and inspired me again with a determination to be free. . . . I did not hesitate to let it be known . . . that the white man who expected to succeed in whipping, must also succeed in killing me.

Some writings about people treat their subjects as representatives of a role, a class, an ethnic group; their names scarcely matter, for their individual identities are subordinate to their significance as members of a group. Such is the case with the old Hispanic woman of New Mexico whose eloquent monologue interview Robert Coles quotes extensively in "Two Languages, One Soul" (162–66). From her own words we learn a great deal about her powerful reverence for God, and for nature, and of her equally strong sense of family and of self:

> At midday we take our tea outside and sit on our bench, our backs against the wall of the house. Neither of us wants pillows. . . . The bench feels strong to us, not uncomfortable. The tea warms us inside, the sun on the outside. I joke with my husband; I say we are part of the house: the adobe gets baked, and so do we. For the most part we say nothing, though. It is enough to sit and be part of God's world. We hear the birds talking to each other, and are grateful they come as close to us as they do . . . .

Yet Coles never tells us the speaker's name; she is simply a quintessential representative of *The Old Ones of New Mexico,* as Coles titled the book that includes this interview.

In other portraits, the subject is intended to inspire the readers, or to serve as a positive (or sometimes negative) moral example. Some people, like Mother Teresa, winner of the 1979 Nobel Peace Prize for her work to alleviate the "poverty and hunger and distress" of India's poor, are so saintly that even to look for a flaw would seem heretical. In "Mother Teresa and Her Endless Fight" (160–62), Ellen Goodman wisely focuses on the symbolic, inspirational meaning of this distinguished humanitarian—"a woman who gets up every morning of her life to tend endless streams of victims of life's longest war of attrition"—rather than overwhelming her all-too-human readers with an extensive catalog of Mother Teresa's "absolutely awesome" good deeds.

Biographical Essays and Obituaries

Biographical essays are usually (though not always) more comprehensive than portraits or character sketches, though they employ comparable techniques. So do well-written obituaries. "Say nothing but good of the dead," a convention of nineteenth-century biographical writing, has been superseded by the twentieth-century view that biographical subjects, the dead as well as the living, should be depicted "warts and all," as long as the negative material is not libelous. Thus the obituary of "Albert Schweitzer" (175–84) by Alden Whitman, chief obituary writer for *The New York Times,* is a detailed account of Schweitzer's life and work as a "theologian, musicologist, virtuoso on the organ, physician and surgeon, missionary, lecturer, writer, and philosopher . . . besides being the builder and animating force of the famous hospital complex at Lambarene." Balanced against this astonishing list of accomplishments are such assessments as:

> For all his self-abnegation, Schweitzer had a bristly character . . . a formidable sense of his own importance to Lambarene, and a do-good paternalism toward Africans that smacked more of the nineteenth than of the twentieth century.

Likewise, Sally Quinn's "Alice Roosevelt Longworth at 90" (185–93) captures the distillation of wit, wormwood, and gall that are the essence of this self-declared exhibitionist: " 'I'm always on stage. All Roosevelts are exhibitionists . . . That, my dear, is what becomes of peasants.' "

As the writings about people in this section illustrate, there are many ways to organize the account of a life or of a personality. You can organize writings about people chronologically, to describe a particular experience or relationship, if not the entire life itself, from start to finish, as Terkel's "Miss U.S.A." does. Personal writings that focus on the process of emotional, psychological, physical, or professional maturation usually proceed from beginning to end, as do writings that emphasize the gaining of an insight over time; Douglass's "Resurrection" exemplifies this. Other writings may be structured according to a pattern of psychological dominance, proceeding from either the least compelling feature or phenomenon to the most notable one, or the reverse. Leonard's portrait of his brother is organized according to the progressively abnormal aspects of the brother's psychological deterioration, which parallel their deteriorating relationship. Other portraits are arranged like pointillist paintings, with brief, somewhat self-contained vignettes or anecdotes juxtaposed to form a coherent image of the subject.

Henry Mitchell's biographical essay "Eudora Welty: Storyteller of the South" is far more subtle in content and in organization than its casual, conversational tone implies. Mitchell constructs it like the movement of a symphony, with the major theme, Welty's stature as a major American writer, introduced at the outset:

> Some say Eudora Welty writes best of all, in all Hinds County, but she has never taken to prideful airs. Others say she's the best in all central Mississippi or all America.

This motif recurs at intervals through reviews of her works, literary history, accounts of her literary earnings, with a general assessment of her literary reputation recapitulated at the finale. Interwoven as counterpoint are vignettes of Welty and "two young men with Jesus haircuts" getting "pitched right out of a Jackson [Mississippi] restaurant," Welty cooking lunch, working in her garden and taking care of her aging mother, and other variations on these themes.

Indeed, there are as many ways to write about people as there are people to write about. Indeed, as Virginia Woolf has observed, "A biography is considered complete if it merely accounts for six or seven selves, whereas a person may have as many thousand." No single self or combination of selves, no single way to present that person, is necessarily better than another. What intrigues the writer or compels the reader emerges vividly to make not only the writing but its subject live, now and always.

Interviews

STUDS TERKEL

Miss U.S.A., Emma Knight

Terkel's memorable interviews reinforce his claim that "the so-called ordinary people are far more interesting than celebrities." Louis Terkel was born in New York City in 1912; his nickname "Studs" (after James T. Farrell's proletarian hero, Studs Lonigan) proclaims his loyalty to America's working class. Although he earned a Ph.D. (1932) and a law degree (1934) from the University of Chicago, Terkel worked as a civil servant, a stage actor, and a movie-house manager before beginning his career as a radio and television broadcaster. As the host of "Studs' Place," Terkel began the hundreds of interviews that he would later shape into distinctive collections of oral histories. These include Division Street: America *(1966)*, Hard Times: An Oral History of the Great Depression *(1970)*, Working: People Talk About What They Do All Day and How They Feel About What They Do *(1974)*, and* The Good War: An Oral History of World War II *(1984)*.

As an interviewer, Terkel is a sympathetic and encouraging listener. People reveal to him their life experiences great and small, their hopes and fears, dreams and disappointments. Then Terkel selects, cuts, and shapes; a sixty-page interview may be condensed to six pages, the "pure gold" at the heart, the essential subject speaking directly to the reader. In the interview below, from American Dreams: Lost and Found *(1980), Emma Knight, Miss U.S.A. of 1973, speaks candidly about the gulf between the illusion of the American Dream as a beauty queen and its exploitative reality. Sensitivity balances wise-cracking cynicism in this captivating portrait of a woman ordinary yet extraordinary.*

Miss U.S.A., 1973. She is twenty-nine.

I wince when I'm called a former beauty queen or Miss U.S.A. I keep thinking they're talking about someone else. There are certain images that come to mind when people talk about beauty queens. It's mostly what's known as t and a, tits and ass. No talent. For many girls who enter the contest, it's part of the American Dream. It was never mine.   1

You used to sit around the TV and watch Miss America and it was exciting, we thought, glamorous. Fun, we thought. But by the time I was eight or nine, I didn't feel comfortable. Soon I'm hitting my adolescence, like fourteen, but I'm not doing any dating and I'm feeling awkward and ugly. I'm much taller than most of the people in my class. I don't feel I can compete the way I see girls competing for guys. I was very much of a loner. I felt intimidated by the amount of competition females were supposed to go through with each other. I didn't like being told by *Seventeen* magazine: Subvert your interests if you have a crush on a guy, get interested in what he's   2 interested in. If you play cards, be sure not to beat him. I was very bad at these social games.

3   After I went to the University of Colorado for three and a half years, I had it. This was 1968 through '71. I came home for the summer. An agent met me and wanted me to audition for commercials, modeling, acting jobs. Okay. I started auditioning and winning some.

4   I did things actors do when they're starting out. You pass out literature at conventions, you do print ads, you pound the pavements, you send out your resumés. I had come to a model agency one cold day, and an agent came out and said: "I want you to enter a beauty contest." I said: "No, uh-uh, never, never, never. I'll lose, how humiliating." She said: "I want some girls to represent the agency, might do you good." So I filled out the application blank: hobbies, measurements, blah, blah, blah. I got a letter: "Congratulations. You have been accepted as an entrant into the Miss Illinois-Universe contest." Now what do I do? I'm stuck.

5   You have to have a sponsor. Or you're gonna have to pay several hundred dollars. So I called up the lady who was running it. Terribly sorry, I can't do this. I don't have the money. She calls back a couple of days later: "We found you a sponsor, it's a lumber company."

6   It was in Decatur. There were sixty-some contestants from all over the place. I went as a lumberjack: blue jeans, hiking boots, a flannel shirt, a pair of suspenders, and carrying an axe. You come out first in your costume and you introduce yourself and say your astrological sign or whatever it is they want you to say. You're wearing a banner that has the sponsor's name on it. Then you come out and do your pirouettes in your one-piece bathing suit, and the judges look at you a lot. Then you come out in your evening gown and pirouette around for a while. That's the first night.

7   The second night, they're gonna pick fifteen people. In between, you had judges' interviews. For three minutes, they ask you anything they want. Can you answer questions? How do you handle yourself? Your poise, personality, blah, blah, blah. They're called personality judges.

8   I thought: This will soon be over, get on a plane tomorrow, and no one will be the wiser. Except that my name got called as one of the fifteen. You have to go through the whole thing all over again.

9   I'm thinking: I don't have a prayer. I'd come to feel a certain kind of distance, except that they called my name. I was the winner, Miss Illinois. All I could do was laugh. I'm twenty-two, standing up there in a borrowed evening gown, thinking: What am I doing here? This is like Tom Sawyer becomes an altar boy.

10   I was considered old for a beauty queen, which is a little horrifying when you're twenty-two. That's very much part of the beauty queen syndrome: the young, untouched, unthinking human being.

11   I had to go to this room and sign the Miss Illinois-Universe contract

right away. Miss Universe, Incorporated, is the full name of the company. It's owned by Kaiser-Roth, Incorporated, which was bought out by Gulf & Western. Big business.

I'm sitting there with my glass of champagne and I'm reading over this contract. They said: "Oh, you don't have to read it." And I said: "I never sign anything that I don't read." They're all waiting to take pictures, and I'm sitting there reading this long document. So I signed it and the phone rang and the guy was from a Chicago paper and said: "Tell me, is it Miss or Ms.?" I said: "It's Ms." He said: "You're kidding." I said: "No, I'm not." He wrote an article the next day saying something like it finally happened: a beauty queen, a feminist. I thought I was a feminist before I was a beauty queen, why should I stop now?

Then I got into the publicity and training and interviews. It was a throwback to another time where crossed ankles and white gloves and tea-cups were present. I was taught how to walk around with a book on my head, how to sit daintily, how to pose in a bathing suit, and how to frizz my hair. They wanted curly hair, which I hate.

One day the trainer asked me to shake hands. I shook hands. She said: "That's wrong. When you shake hands with a man, you always shake hands ring up." I said: "Like the pope? Where my hand is up, like he's gonna kiss it?" Right. I thought: Holy mackerel! It was a very long February and March and April and May.

I won the Miss U.S.A. pageant. I started to laugh. They tell me I'm the only beauty queen in history that didn't cry when she won. It was on network television. I said to myself: "You're kidding." Bob Barker, the host, said: "No, I'm not kidding." I didn't know what else to say at that moment. In the press releases, they call it the great American Dream. There she is, Miss America, your ideal. Well, not my ideal, kid.

The minute you're crowned, you become their property and subject to whatever they tell you. They wake you up at seven o'clock next morning and make you put on a negligee and serve you breakfast in bed, so that all the New York papers can come in and take your picture sitting in bed, while you're absolutely bleary-eyed from the night before. They put on the Kaiser-Roth negligee, hand you the tray, you take three bites. The photographers leave, you whip off the negligee, they take the breakfast away, and that's it. I never did get any breakfast that day. (Laughs.)

You immediately start making personal appearances. The Jaycees or the chamber of commerce says: "I want to book Miss U.S.A. for our Christmas Day parade." They pay, whatever it is, seven hundred fifty dollars a day, first-class air fare, round trip, expenses, so forth. If the United Fund calls and wants me to give a five-minute pitch on queens at a luncheon, they still have to pay a fee. Doesn't matter that it's a charity. It's one hundred percent to Miss Universe, Incorporated. You get your salary. That's your prize money for the year. I got fifteen thousand dollars, which is all taxed in New York. Maybe out of a check of three thousand dollars, I'd get fifteen hundred dollars.

18   From the day I won Miss U.S.A. to the day I left for Universe, almost two months, I got a day and a half off. I made about two hundred fifty appearances that year. Maybe three hundred. Parades, shopping centers, and things. Snip ribbons. What else do you do at a shopping center? Model clothes. The nice thing I got to do was public speaking. They said: "You want a ghost writer?" I said: "Hell, no, I know how to talk." I wrote my own speeches. They don't trust girls to go out and talk because most of them can't.

19   One of the big execs from General Motors asked me to do a speech in Washington, D.C., on the consumer and the energy crisis. It was the fiftieth anniversary of the National Management Association. The White House, for some reason, sent me some stuff on it. I read it over, it was nonsense. So I stood up and said: "The reason we have an energy crisis is because we are, industrially and personally, pigs. We have a short-term view of the resources available to us; and unless we wake up to what we're doing to our air and our water, we'll have a dearth, not just a crisis." Oh, they weren't real pleased. (Laughs.)

20   What I resent most is that a lot of people didn't expect me to live this version of the American Dream for myself. I was supposed to live it their way.

21   When it came out in a newspaper interview that I said Nixon should resign, that he was a crook, oh dear, the fur flew. They got very upset until I got an invitation to the White House. They wanted to shut me up. The Miss Universe corporation had been trying to establish some sort of liaison with the White House for several years. I make anti-Nixon speeches and get this invitation.

22   I figured they're either gonna take me down to the basement and beat me up with a rubber hose or they're gonna offer me a cabinet post. They had a list of fifteen or so people I was supposed to meet. I've never seen such a bunch of people with raw nerve endings. I was dying to bring a tape recorder but thought if you mention the word "Sony" in the Nixon White House, you're in trouble. They'd have cardiac arrest. But I'm gonna bring along a pad and paper. They were patronizing. And when one of 'em got me in his office and talked about all the journalists and television people being liberals, I brought up blacklisting, *Red Channels,* and the TV industry. He changed the subject.

23   Miss Universe took place in Athens, Greece. The junta was still in power. I saw a heck of a lot of jeeps and troops and machine guns. The Americans were supposed to keep a low profile. I had never been a great fan of the Greek junta, but I knew darn well I was gonna have to keep my mouth shut. I was still representing the United States, for better or for worse. Miss Philippines won. I ran second.

At the end of the year, you're run absolutely ragged. That final evening, they usually have several queens from past years come back. Before they crown the new Miss U.S.A., the current one is supposed to take what they call the farewell walk. They call over the PA: Time for the old queen's walk. I'm now twenty-three and I'm an old queen. And they have this idiot farewell speech playing over the airwaves as the old queen takes the walk. And you're sitting on the throne for about thirty seconds, then you come down and they announce the name of the new one and you put the crown on her head. And then you're out.

As the new one is crowned, the reporters and photographers rush on the stage. I've seen photographers shove the girl who has just given her reign up thirty seconds before, shove her physically. I was gone by that time. I had jumped off the stage in my evening gown. It is very difficult for girls who are terrified of this ending. All of a sudden (snaps fingers), you're out. Nobody gives a damn about the old one.

Miss U.S.A. and remnants thereof is the crown stored in the attic in my parents' home. I don't even know where the banners are. It wasn't me the fans of Miss U.S.A. thought was pretty. What they think is pretty is the banner and crown. If I could put the banner and crown on that lamp, I swear to God ten men would come in and ask it for a date. I'll think about committing an axe murder if I'm not called anything but a former beauty queen. I can't stand it any more.

Several times during my year as what's-her-face I had seen the movie *The Sting*. There's a gesture the characters use which means the con is on: they rub their nose. In my last fleeting moments as Miss U.S.A., as they were playing that silly farewell speech and I walked down the aisle and stood by the throne, I looked right into the camera and rubbed my finger across my nose. The next day, the pageant people spent all their time telling people that I hadn't done it. I spent the time telling them that, of course, I had. I simply meant: the con is on. (Laughs.)

Miss U.S.A. is in the same graveyard that Emma Knight the twelve-year-old is. Where the sixteen-year-old is. All the past selves. There comes a time when you have to bury those selves because you've grown into another one. You don't keep exhuming the corpses.

If I could sit down with every young girl in America for the next fifty years, I could tell them what I liked about the pageant, I could tell them what I hated. It wouldn't make any difference. There're always gonna be girls who want to enter the beauty pageant. That's the fantasy: the American Dream.

JOAN GALWAY

Louise Nevelson:
Monumental Work with
Thanks to No One

Nevelson was born in Kiev, Russia, in 1899 and emigrated to Rockland, Maine, with her family in 1903. Predictive of her future career, "by the age of six," notes Washington Post interviewer Joan Galway, she was already "carving and assembling scraps of wood found in her father's lumber yard." In an early marriage, she soon realized that she could not conform to the life of a New York society matron; a divorce enabled her to concentrate on her art.

She went to Germany in the early 1930s to study with Hans Hofmann, and then to Mexico, where she has lived for over sixty years, to study with muralist Diego Rivera. During the 30s and 40s, she also learned from artists Picasso, Duchamp, and De Kooning, and gradually developed a style of her own. On relief by the end of the 30s, the fate of many artists, in desperation she allowed the Works Progress Administration (WPA) to subsidize her work for a time; it took until the mid-60s for her to attain the international reputation she now enjoys. A critic has said, "Her enormous walls and total environments rank high among the monumental art of the 20th century"—achievements recognized by permanent installations at the National Gallery of Art and the Hirshorn, among numerous museum collections, and the award of a National Medal of Art in 1985.

1   Q: *How did you endure the disappointment of not selling a piece of your work for 30 years?*

2   A: I don't think it was 30 years, but it was a long time. And if I did sell, it probably [was just] a little; it wasn't a sale, you see. What kept me going was there was nothing else, it was either suicide or the work.

3   Q: *Did you contemplate suicide many times in your life?*

4   A: Not many, but [for] a long period, let's put it that way.

5   Q: *You did not have the most easy life.*

6   A: I think my life has been difficult, and *is* difficult, in spite of everything.

7   Q: *Among the elements in your work that your are noted for are wit and surprise. You include found objects in your work, such as discarded chair legs found on a sidewalk, duck decoys, ten-pins, painted toilet seats.*

8   A: Anything. I don't see them as that. I see it as form. It's round and it tapers down here. It has reflection, you see.

9   Q: *In your life you have divested yourself of all material goods. You've given away your furniture, your personal collections and even your own work. Why?*

10   A: Well, I was beginning to see things from a whole different point of view and I didn't want them around. I wasn't attached to it. Second, you have an expense and rentals to take care of things. And maybe I just didn't want to have it. I just felt I just didn't want to see anything. For a long time.

11   Q: *You have even destroyed your own work. Isn't there a sense of loss?*

A: Well, not when you're as rich as I am. 12

Q: *Many artists regard their creations as their children.* 13

A: Even so. When children grow up, they go on their own, unless you're a 14
nut and keep them on a chain.

Q: *Most of your major works are monumental, you're prolific. Has anyone ever* 15
suggested that you "work like a man?"

A: A lot of people have a preconceived idea of what working like a man 16
means, but actually there's nothing that says that some women are not as
strong—even physically—as men. I have artist friends that are very well-
known and they say art is art. But I say for myself, being a woman, that my
work is feminine. And if it's big and monumental, well, so what? When you
study metaphysics, you don't make those distinctions.

As I said, I don't know what truth is. I don't care what they call it. I think 17
anyone that is going to search for truth is a nut. I don't care who they are,
because if it hasn't been found by the biggest minds on earth, I'm not going
to find it. It's a mystery and I've made my peace with that with a question
mark. It gives me peace. I'll never answer it, but the question mark is very
valid for me.

Q: *There are many different definitions of art. What is yours?* 18

A: Art is life. It's the most important thing. It's very important to me, 19
because I live it. And living it means that every second that you put another
thing together, that's an addition of awareness. Art is living, an awareness of
living. Some people get up in the morning, they have breakfast, take a
shower, get breakfast, go to work, come back and go out and see a movie. I'm
sorry to say that that wouldn't suit me.

Q: *Have the years taken a toll on your physical powers?* 20

A: I think so, but then it gave me something. It's a balance. You pay a price 21
for everything. And you're willing to. Because what I do anyway is I see a
world every moment. A world and a world and a world and a world. So it's
an addition. Within me I have it all. I've learned to dress and I've learned to
take care of things with such economy that I can claim so much of my time. I
don't go to beauty parlors. I don't do many things. They take time away from
the other more important things in my life. My work.

Q: *You've said that when you were a child, you were often frightened by the things* 22
that you said because they seemed so automatic. Could you give me an example?

A: Well, yes. I was probably about 9 or 10. There was a little girl I remember 23
in my class. Her name was Blanche. We went to the library to get books.
There was a Miss Hitchcock, I remember. The first thing older people asked
younger children [is], "And what are you going to do when you grow up?"
Miss Hitchcock asked Blanche, and I think she said "I'm going to be a
bookkeeper," or whatever. Then she turned to me. There was a plaster statue
of Joan of Arc on a table. I said, "I want to be an artist, a painter." Then I
looked and I saw this [statue] and I said, "No, I want to be a sculptor because
I don't want paint to help me." I went home scared to death, because I

thought to myself, "That object said it with me." That object was almost talking.

24 Q: *How did you feel when recognition came?*

25 A: I'll tell you bluntly. I wanted to communicate. Some people want physical love. Some want spiritual love. I wanted to communicate. As a matter of fact I wanted to communicate more then than I do now. So, when it came, I was still angry because it was late and I had struggled so, on all levels. And I'll tell you a secret, I'm *still* angry.

26 Q: *Are you a saver of memories?*

27 A: Not too much. I don't think that my memories are that exciting that I want to remember! I think I live in the present.

28 Q: *It's been reported that even though you've had and still do have enormous drive and a singleness of purpose, you still found time for dressing with a flair or drinking, swearing and having more than a few romances?*

29 A: Well, that's all true. Creative energy is found out in life.

30 Q: *You were also on America's Best Dressed list. Do you look at fashion as an art?*

31 A: Yes, I do. I have a floor upstairs full of clothes now. I like throwing them like collages.

32 Q: *Do you think you have ever created a masterpiece?*

33 A: I wasn't hunting for a masterpiece. I was hunting for life. Listen, we have the Michelangelos and this and that. Well, I think it's really a tragedy that the human mind was trapped in these concepts. They would have been just as great. I don't think they were hunting to climb a mountain or for a masterpiece. That's why I don't believe in that and I never did a thing that I didn't work in that direction.

34 You can move yourself, you can be aware, you can sing, you can dance. I studied.

35 Q: *All the arts? Dance, drama, poetry—?*

36 A: You bet your sweet life.

37 Q: *What did you get from a study of all of these?*

38 A: I never would have come to the ultimate of freedom, as I did, without them. Like a flower you unfold. As an example, in 1932 I thought of myself as a nice lady in New York. I was one of Diego Rivera's assistants. We all lived in the same place on 810 West 13th Street. It was a building for artists. In the building was a dance teacher and one of her students was John Flanagan, a noted sculptor at that time and his wife. This dance teacher invited me to her place and they wore leotards and lay on the floor and [pretended] to be frogs or birds or something. I was indignant that I would get in a leotard and lay down on the floor and begin to think I'm a frog. That didn't appeal to me. But I went again and before I knew it I was in leotards leaping around and loving it. That freed me of being a stiff matron. And, of course, your mind goes with it, your consciousness.

39 Q: *Why have there not been more great artists who also happen to be women?*

40 A: Because they were diverted. When I said I was going to leave and study

art, I left to go to Europe to study with Hans Hofmann in 1931. Now, if you said you were going to a concert to hear Beethoven or Mozart, you were quite a lady. But if you dared to say that you wanted to *be* a composer, you were no place. I didn't think like that. I really didn't think, "I'm a woman." I just thought I was an artist [and] I was goddamned sure about myself. I wasn't going to croak until I did what I did.

Q: *After an exhibit of yours in 1941, one reviewer wrote, "We found the artist was a woman and we checked our enthusiasm."*   41

A: She went up to see the show and she thought it was from some very modern, probably a French or European sculptor and took [offense] that it was a woman. It was so strong. I don't care about that. I have the energy, so why such an issue?   42

Q: *People see that size in your art and they think it's a contradiction in terms?*   43

A: Yes, but what is the use, where I sit, to give a goddamn what others do or say?   44

Q: *Where do you think your drive comes from?*   45

A: My father was that way. Now, I loved my mother. I don't think you like both parents the same way. You like one for certain things and another for certain things. My mother was my heart and soul. She was beautiful, delicate and just a lovely lady. When I hear kids fighting—. I can tell you right now I never contradicted my mother. She didn't say anything to contradict. My father weighed what I weigh now all his life, 140 pounds. One day he bought a car, a Ford, and of course he didn't learn to drive the car. He was driving it and he drove into a couple of fences. I was going home from high school, and I see him on the street jumping around, and I said, "What are you in a hurry for?" "Well," he said, "I've got to do this and do that." "Well, why don't you take the car?" I said. He said, "But I'm in a hurry."   46

Q: *What was being a Russian immigrant in Maine like?*   47

A: The tough part is you were a greenhorn. You didn't go to church. Everything was against you. You didn't live as you wished.   48

Q: *Did that early isolation, in a sense, drive you?*   49

A: I think it did a lot. It didn't drive me into art, but it made me aware of the price you pay. In early life, I understood that labor, as we understood it, was a slavery. I decided when I was a sophomore or so that I was never going to work. I saw what my father had to pay for his things, and I saw friends of mine graduate and be glad to get jobs at a lawyer's office for six dollars a week. I've made sure that my son doesn't have to work. I don't believe in it, it's slavery.   50

Q: *So what you do is not work? It's intensely physical. Some of your walls are 55 feet high.*   51

A: That doesn't matter. It's still not *labor*. I like the word labor. See the difference?   52

Q: *Do you have a feeling of gratitude toward a number of people?*   53

A: No. Where were they when I needed them? And not only that, when you   54 don't have anything, they won't give you a cup of coffee. Why should I have gratitude? When they did something for me, it was really, more or less, to their advantage as well as mine. Certainly, I think the weight was on their side. I know people that wouldn't say it the way I say it, but I'll still say it.

55 Q: *Any regrets?*

56 A: I've worked for everything that I have and then some. Every day of my life I have done the best I know how. So what can I say?

57 Q: *What's it like to be in a state of intense creativity?*

58 A: Heavenly.

MARY LANGENBERG (Student)

East St. Louis, from Blues to Dirge

Although Langenberg majored in music at Illinois Wesleyan College of Music (1943–44), and in journalism and English at Washington University (1944–45, 1974–75), her primary occupations have been in business management, most recently as founder and owner of ExecUTours, a St. Louis employee relocation service, and in community service. In St. Louis she has been an officer and board member of numerous civic and philanthrophic organizations, ranging from the United Fund to the Visiting Nurse Association to the Art Museum and the Missouri Committee for the Humanities.

Langenberg's experience of transforming an interview into a publishable essay about the subject in the appropriate contexts is typical. Although conducting the interview with "Alfred Everett" took only an evening, Langenberg spent many weeks reading primary documents (mostly newspapers) to get specific background information about the historical, geographical, and cultural characteristics of the time and place. She explains, "The interview itself was an easy task. 'Alfred' is an entertaining gent who communicates well, with a distinct element of humor. The difficulty came in attempting to capture the charm of this colorful character, to keep his persona intact, and not lose any of it in the translation. The most taxing work involved weekly trips to the public library of East St. Louis to pore over microfilm tapes of The Daily Journal, *a now-extinct newspaper published there in the twenties."*

Transcript: Interview with "Alfred Everett"

(The following is a verbatim transcript of a taped interview with Alfred B. Everett (his name and some others changed by request), senior partner of one of St. Louis's most distinguished law firms, who describes himself as a "prominent club man.")

1   Q: Alfred, the era of the 1920's has been called

the Jazz Age and you were in college about that time,

weren't you?

A: Yes. The Jazz Age or the Roaring Twenties, 2
which was, of course, a very unique time . . . and as
time passes, seems to become more unique. I was 14
years old in 1920 and I went to college in 1922 at 16,
which I do not recommend. Nevertheless, I was in college—two different schools—with an interval between
from '22 to '27. I came out to begin my practice of
law. I think it was an interesting time, as far as I am
concerned, to have been in the '20s from age 14 to 24,
in age.

Q: It was an impressionable age, right? 3

A: Very. 4

Q: Tell me about the young people of that period 5
. . . your peer group at that time. How did they dress,
for instance?

A: Well, that was the age of the Flappers. The 6
girls all had short dresses and there was lots of
swinging around . . . dancing the Charleston and the
Black Bottom were the big deals. We danced on the excursions boats (I went to high school in East St.
Louis) . . . the J. S. and St. Paul and they were the
greatest place ever for dancing. Big floor . . . fine
bands. Our proms at the East St. Louis High School was
a twelve to twelve deal. We had twelve hours of dancing. You always took a girl who was a good dancer cause
you danced every dance—about 43 or 44 dances—and you
wanted somebody you could trade!

They had some great bands. I remember particu- 7
larly Fate Marable, one of the great colored jazz band
leaders, innovators, of all times. He came from Kentucky by way of New Orleans. He had Louis Armstrong as
a youngster playing in the front row in his band and
some other fine musicians.

Q: Did you own a raccoon coat? 8

A: Dressing at college definitely included the 9

raccoon coat. But I didn't own one. Everybody had a yellow slicker that was all jazzed up decorated with paint and ink. In my high school days, we had the bell-bottomed trousers, everything was nipped in at the waist and everybody tried to slick their hair down to look like Rudolph Valentino.

10   I got to college and found that I had to get rid of all those clothes. You got into the four-button suits, the Norfolk jacket, etc. Bell-bottoms were out in college.

11   I was in college two and a half years and then went to work for Boyd's, a very nice clothing store, for two years before I went back to college in the South. College, among other things, taught you how to dress. The button-down shirt, regimental ties, and so forth were the college uniform. The button-down shirt is still a very fine shirt, fifty years later. Brooks Brothers brought it out.

12   Q: Do you want to tell me about the circumstances as to why your college career was interrupted?

13   A: Well, my college was interrupted, to put it that way, for the reason that I was expelled from college. The Dean of Men thought that maybe I, and others, at different times overdid the drinking bit, and so I was bounced out. Much to the chagrin of my parents and so on. But it was a good thing in a way, . . . I was bounced out of college when most people were entering, at 18. My father was a man of influence but he couldn't quite swing it to get my expulsion set aside and get me back in college. That was probably the best thing that ever happened to me. Then he got me a job at Boyd's and I saved up my own money and put myself through Law School at Cumberland University in Tennessee. A famous old Law School, and particularly famous, because it was a one-year law course. Still in existence, but not as a one-year term. . . .

[*section omitted on sports in the '20s*]

Q: Alfred, the '20s have been described as one of   14
the wildest decades in our country's history. Midnight, January 16, 1920, was the beginning of Prohibition, when the 18th Amendment went into effect. Did
you ever visit a Speakeasy?

A: I guess I visited about two hundred speak-   15
easies!!

Q: Would you just describe a typical Speakeasy?   16

A: Well, East St. Louis and Toledo, Ohio, were   17
known as the two most "wide-open" towns in the United
States, in the Speakeasy era. The Speakeasy was a saloon, or a flat . . . first floor, second floor, third
floor. They always had a peep-hole in the door, so
they could check you out . . . so that they'd know you.
We had a little trouble with one Speakeasy in East St.
Louis because the proprietor had a glass eye. He'd get
drunk with the customers . . . that was old Duke Davis
. . . and we'd rap on his door and then we'd wait and
wait. Finally, we'd yell to him, "Get your good eye on
the peep-hole," because he'd be looking out with his
glass eye and couldn't see anybody!

Q: How did you know where these Speakeasies were?   18

A: Oh, we just knew 'em. The Stevenson Brothers   19
were a famous pair in East St. Louis. They originated
with the booze in Cuba and they'd bring it to New Orleans. They had a fleet of trucks with license plates
for every state between New Orleans and there. They'd
bring it in . . . put it in a big storage vault . . .
and they were what you'd call "wholesalers." They had
a big speakeasy and saloon which was in the nature of a
club. When the Stevensons were there, they'd buy all
the drinks. Ray Stevenson, the older brother, was assassinated in New Orleans by some rival. He was a
strong personality and a strong fellow. His younger

brothers didn't carry on quite as well. Of course, repeal came in in '33. But in East St. Louis, they had
wide open gambling, slot machines, prostitution.

20   They had a "Valley" there that was unpaved. And
left unpaved cause there were so many ruts that you
couldn't rush through and had to slow down. You <u>had</u> to
pay attention to the people who were advertising their
wares. This was an area of two streets, about four
blocks long. Flood lights for the different houses
were provided by the city! They had a wide-open Valley
. . . colored and white . . . and all sorts of horse
parlors, or bookie joints.

21   Q: The city supported this?

22   A: The Valley commenced at the end of the block in
which the City Hall was situated. They had, I guess,
twenty speakeasies across the street from the City
Hall and in every direction. Two of the noted fellows
over there--Razz Pendleton and another fella--were the
ones who took Jack Dempsey off a locomotive (he was an
assistant fireman) and started him on his career.
Whenever Dempsey returned to East St. Louis . . . he
was that kind of fellow . . . he always visited. I was
in a speakeasy once at Doggie Farris's and Dempsey
walked in. Nobody bought a drink but him and everybody
would hear he was in town and go tearing over. He
didn't drink himself, but every saloon in East St.
Louis had a picture of Dempsey in it. He was a big
hero. He never forgot those fellows who were his
friends.

23   Q: We've heard a lot about bathtub gin? in those
days. Did you know how to make it?

24   A: Yeah. Made a lot of gin.

25   Q: How did you do it?

26   A: It was about half and half alcohol and distilled water, with some juniper berry extract and

glycerine. I'm reminded of the time we were making up
a batch in the Knights of Columbus building which was
a bachelor residence place in East St. Louis. We got
our ingredients, except for the alcohol, from the drug
store across the street. We had a pint of alcohol and
were making a quart of gin out of it, so we went over
to the drug store and got the glycerine. Stirred it up
and it became very cloudy. It looked like milk, so we
wondered what in the world had happened. So I dashed
across to the drug store and the druggist saw me coming and says, "All right, how much did you spoil?"
Well, of course, I doubled it up and told him it was a
quart of alcohol that we'd spoiled. It turned out he
had given me castor oil by mistake instead of glycerine.

In college, we weren't so particular. We kept our   27
alcohol straight and we just mixed it up with regular
hydrant water. We kept the straight alcohol because
that was it's most compact form. Sometimes a fraternity brother might steal, you know, so we could hide
it easier if we had a smaller container.

Q: I wonder how it got the name "bathtub gin." You   28
didn't make it in a bathtub, did you?

A: Well, some people probably made it in a bathtub   29
in big quantities. At the Knights of Columbus Building
. . . I'm speaking of again . . . we had a big fish
bowl which would hold as much as four or five gallons,
I guess. Almost the size of a bathtub. And we'd make it
up in that, now and then, and produce a couple gallons
of gin . . . if we had that much alcohol. (Laughter.)

Q: Now, let's talk about the women of the twen-   30
ties. We hear a lot about women's lib these days, but,
actually, weren't the ladies of the twenties and thirties sort of pioneers in this movement? The 19th
Amendment in 1920 gave Women the Vote. Was there any

discussion you can recall within your family or among
your friends about this watershed decision?

31   A: Not that I recall. Nobody at that time . . . of
course, I didn't vote until 1927 when I became 21 . . .
and most of the girls I knew were my age or perhaps a
little older. So we didn't pay much attention to the
right of women to vote.

32   Q: What about your mother? How did she feel about
it?

33   A: Well, she voted, all right . . . because my
father was in politics all the time . . . running for
this, that and the other . . . so she voted and helped
get some others out, although she was not too active,
as some women are these days.

34   Q: Do you think the ladies' votes elected Warren
Harding? Wasn't he the first president to run for office after women had the vote?

35   A: Yes, he ran in 1920. One of my father's stories
was that he (my father) was the only Democrat in the
State of Illinois who was elected in the Harding landslide. Harding, of course, was a Republican. . . .

[section omitted on Alfred having a car at college]

36   Q: Just to kind of recap about the 20s, Alfred.
Some of the big news stories which broke at that time
. . . I'd like to know if you have any recollections
about any of them.

37   A: I guess the biggest one, I'd say, was Lindbergh's flight, to Paris, in May of '27. We listened
to the account of that on the radio down in Lebanon,
Tennessee . . . just a month before I graduated. It was
particularly interesting to me because the flight was
originally financed and promoted in St. Louis. I later
became a member of the old club, the Racquet Club, and

they still have a table in the barroom where five, six
or seven citizens sat around and decided to finance
Lindbergh . . .

[*section omitted on Alfred's college roommate*]

Q: Just one other facet of the 20s that I'd like   38
to cover with you, Alfred . . . the movies. Didn't Al
Jolson make the first talking picture?

A: Yes. I think that is correct. There may have   39
been some little thing or other, but that seems to be
the first real talking picture. Warner Brothers
brought it out, "The Jazz Singer," in 1927, as I recall.

Q: I know you are a great Jolson fan.   40

A: I AM A GREAT JOLSON FAN! Jolson was born in   41
1886, so he was 41 years old when that picture was made
. . . but, of course, he'd had a big career on Broadway
up to 1920.

Q: How about some of the other movie stars of that   42
time? Did you ever see any of these really big movie
stars in person?

A: I saw Doug Fairbanks, Jr., at a Liberty Bond   43
Rally in East St. Louis . . . that would be in 1917 or
18. The Gish Girls worked at a candy store in East
Louis. Lillian and Dorothy Gish. That was before my
time. I went to the movies a lot, but serials were a
great big deal, then. Pearl White.

Q: This was the thing where you had to go back   44
every week to see what would happen next?

A: Yep. Every week for twenty weeks. They'd   45
string 'em out. Pearl White and Ruth Roland . . . William S. Hart . . . and a great star that nobody remembers now, but he was tremendous in the early 20s, but
he was my mother's favorite. This was J. Warren Kerri-

gan . . . a real good—lookin' Irishman, and he was a
great star.

46 Q: I wonder why he appealed to your mother?

47 A: 'Cause he was so good—lookin' and she was so
Irish!

48 Q: What about the Stock Market Crash? That was
right about the end of the 20s. Black Tuesday, October 29, 1929.

49 A: Right.

50 Q: Do you have any personal recollection of that
event?

51 A: I remember it occurring . . . it didn't bother
me much 'cause I didn't have a dime in it and I didn't
have a dime to have in it! So I got a free education. I
can remember a little better the Bank Holiday in 1933.
I'd been practicing for six years and I remember a law
suit that I settled after a lot of negotiations and
got a cashier's check. The lawyer on the other side
said, "Well, Alfred, a cashier's check is always all
right, except right now, you don't turn loose of that
release until the check is cleared. Well, we put the
check in on a Wednesday, it cleared on Thursday, the
bank closed on Friday and never did open up. I was sitting in a restaurant when the word came out about the
first of March, '33, that the banks were closing and I
know it was around the first because it was payday. I
dashed out of the restaurant, dashed upstairs to our
office and put in a "stop order" on checks I'd issued
. . . trying to salvage out of my paycheck maybe the
great sum of fifty or a hundred dollars. I called the
banker, whom I'd known all my life, and explained to
them and they didn't blame me . . . and I, of course,
redeemed the checks that I had issued, but I salvaged
what was left. . . .

52 . Q: You were interrupted a minute ago, in relating
a story about your friends down in Cumberland.

A: Yeah. Well that was a kind of a story about 53
booze. This was in 1926. My landlord and landlady in
this very nice private home where I lived had some
guests in one night. I could hear them carrying on
. . . and they came up and invited me down for a drink.
I came down . . . went to the kitchen, and they said,
"We're getting some supplies in." Pretty soon, some
fellow, one of the guests, came in with a paper sack
filled with little bottles which he dumped out on the
sink, so I asked, "What is it we're drinking?" They
said, "It's Jake." I said, "What's that?" They said,
"Jamaica Ginger, which is vanilla extract." Mix it
with water and it sends you right along! I had a few
that evening. I never tried it again.

Later on, it gained a lot of prominence in the 54
news and so forth. There was a lot of Jake——Jamaica
Ginger——that was put out that was pretty bad. It
killed a lot of people. It didn't last very long, but
it was a product of the times.

Q: You were one of the lucky ones? 55

A: Evidently. (laughter) 56

Q: Alfred, what is your recollection of the crime 57
picture in the 20s? Weren't the big crime syndicates
pretty much tied into prohibition? Tell me about the
criminal element that you can remember.

A: Well, they were undoubtedly tied into it. Per- 58
sonally, I didn't have much contact with that. No
question but what the gangsters and the hoodlum element, like Al Capone and all the mobsters and gangsters in Chicago, came into the picture over the bootleg profits. Now, East St. Louis, as I have related,
was wide-open with prostitution, gambling and bootlegging completely wide open. There weren't any gangsters
there as we know them.

Q: No violence? 59

A: No violence. No shooting, murdering or any of 60

131

that sort of thing. I mentioned that Ray Stevenson was
killed, but he was killed down in New Orleans. Killed
in some bootleg war down there. Later on, in 1930-31,
the Sheltons moved into East St. Louis. They were a
well-known gang, originating in Wayne County, Illinois. They were up in Peoria, then back down to East
St. Louis. I knew them . . . met them.

61   Q: How did you meet them?

62   A: At these speakeasies and saloons. It was still
before repeal. There was Carl Shelton, and Bernie and
Earl. They were, later on, pretty well killed off, but
they were gangsters.

63   Q: Were they a sophisticated type?

64   A: Not at all.

65   Q: Country-smart?

66   A: They were kinda country, and kinda tough.
Pleasant enough to talk with . . . didn't bother anybody like me . . . but they were a country outfit and
they didn't mind killing anybody. It didn't seem to
bother them. They were a tough bunch, but they didn't
last long.

67   Q: But your impression of the three of these
rather notorious people was just kind of farm boys?

68   A: Well, uh, real tough farm boys! . . .

[section omitted on free lunches]

69   Q: Tell me some more about that twelve-to-twelve
prom.

70   A: My mother got me two ten-dollar silk shirts.
Now in 1920-21, that was a big deal. I remember one was
pink and green and the other was red and blue. Very
striped. They had detachable collars. I'd take my
shirts along and wear one for six hours and then I'd
change shirts, and then I'd wear the other for another
six hours. You danced in your shirt sleeves.

Q: Did you wear a tie? 71

A: O yeah. Wore a slender, thin black tie with a 72
cameo pin.

Q: So you were always fresh. 73

A: Well, I thought I was. (laughter) 74

Q: Tell me about the time when you borrowed the 75
car down in Tennessee?

A: This was when I was at Cumberland in Lebanon, 76
Tennessee. We used to go to a grocery store on the town
square and the grocer made home brew. So we'd go in the
back room and drink home brew. He admired all of us
. . . he was a real country guy . . . and the five or
six of us who frequented there were all from cities.
So he'd call me "St. Louis," and he'd call another
fella "Baltimore" and so on. He just adored us. Well
they had a dance one night in one of these outdoor
dance pavilions. They were permanent places, but they
were open. Had a big cupola over them. We'd go out
there and they'd bring a band in . . . everybody was a
dollar a head . . . everybody would go out and dance!
Well a friend of mine and I lined up a couple of girls
to go to the dance, but the next question was how were
we going to get them out there? It was about two miles
out there. So I went over to my grocer—bootlegger
friend and he had a Ford with a kind of a pick—up truck
in the back. That was his car. So I wondered if I could
borrow it for the dance that night. Well, you'd have
thought I was going to make him a Duke, or something,
because he thought it was a great honor. He wanted me
to take it, then and there. Well, I took it. We took
our girls out there and I guess we got drunk. Well, I
KNOW, we did, as a matter of fact. We came back . . . I
remember there was a kind of chicken wire fence all
around the back of this grocery store. Well, we had a
couple of flat tires. (His tires were not in the best
of shape) We blew out a couple tires, but we got our

girls home, or did something with them. . . . Anyhow,
we were trying to get the car home. I missed the gate
at the grocery store, so I went on through another
section of the fence and left his car there . . . with
two flat tires. . . .

[*anecdotes about drunken college friend omitted*]

77 Q: Alfred, what is your recollection of your really high moment in the 20s? Your most successful moment in the 20s?

78 A: Oh . . . I don't know. I guess I must think
that the high moment in the 20s was when I graduated
from Law School, and got a position with a very nice
law firm . . . It was up to me from then on.

79 Q: Did you have a moment of decision, though . . .
when you really had to make a decision that could have
been a turning point in your life?

80 A: Yes. I would say that that was when I was working at Boyd's. I was doing pretty well at Boyd's. I was
only 19 or 20 years old, but I was on commission. I was
hustling around, making pretty fair money for a 19 or
20 year old. I decided I'd go back to school. The head
of the department, a buyer, and a very talented guy,
with whom I worked, said, "Now, here . . . I don't
blame you for wanting to go back to college . . . I
never got to go to college myself, but I don't blame
you. I won't say anything more than the fact that if
you stay right here, you'll succeed me." I might say
that the fellow working along side of me, Charlie
Wheeler, a shirt salesman, went on and became the
President of Boyd's [*a big St. Louis department store*].

81 So that was a moment of decision . . . but I must
say, I didn't take much time to decide it. I was going
back to school. It was pre-ordained that I was going

to be a <u>lawyer</u> because so many of my family were. Not
my father, but three of my uncles.

    Q: Your family, they were pleased with this deci-   82
sion, weren't they?

    A: O yes, yes.   83

    Q: While it was a momentous decision, as you look   84
back on it, at the time, you weren't conscious
of. . . .

    A: I had decided I was going to give it three   85
years. I was 21 years old when I came out of college
. . . just as young as you can be to start practicing
law. I said, "I'm going to give it three years. If I
don't like it, I'll go to something else." No question
that I made the right choice, even though I liked the
clothing business. . . .

Completed Article: East St. Louis, from Blues to Dirge

> I want to be happy,
> But I won't be happy,
> 'Til I make you happy, too. . . .
> "No, No, Nanette"—1924

The War was over. The Great Depression had not begun. Everybody   1
wanted to be happy!

In the decade of the twenties, happiness wore many faces. It was the new   2
freedom of short skirts, bobbed hair and the demise of the chaperone. It was
the stimulation of jazz bands and the Dance Cult. It was found in the forbidden Casbah of the speakeasy and the titillation of bathtub gin.

As this social revolution swept the country, every city, town and hamlet   3
was affected in some way, including the community of East St. Louis, Illinois. Just three hundred miles south of Chicago and separated from St.
Louis, Missouri, by the waters of the Mississippi River, East St. Louis, in the
twenties, became one of the most "wide-open" towns in the United States.
Bootlegging and gambling operations took place in the shadow of City Hall.
The red-light district, known as the "Valley," was located within easy walking
distance of the Court House.

In 1920, sixty-six thousand people lived in East St. Louis. There were   4
forty-four churches of various denominations within the city limits, and
thirty-four schools.

The educational system was about average for a community of this size in   5
the Middle-West. The schools were segregated . . . not an unusual practice in

Southern Illinois in those days . . . and East St. Louis was definitely "Southern-oriented." Forward-looking citizens, who cared enough to be vocal, expressed the view that the schools were too crowded. With some regularity, they urged the Board of Education to consider new school sites. The schools' health program was adequate for the times—each student was required to have a smallpox vaccination. The vaccinations were free and the text books were free. The athletic program produced teams who represented their schools in a creditable manner at various contests throughout the state.

6   Blue-collar employment, at least, was within easy reach of most East Side families because of the heavy concentration of industry there—Aluminum Ore, Monsanto, Armour, and Swift Packing Company, to name a few.

7   It was a good place to live and raise your kids. And there were plenty of kids there—good, solid families like the Everett family on Kingston Drive.

8   On a recent rainy evening, Alfred B. Everett, now a resident of St. Louis, talked about his early years in East St. Louis and his memories of the Jazz Age.

9   Alfred was fourteen years old in 1920, and lived in an area between East St. Louis and Belleville, known as The Bluffs. Alfred's father built the house in 1910 and located it on the highest spot in the city, known as "Everett's Hill." It was the first "bungalow with a breakfast room" in Southern Illinois. The handsome tile for the breakfast room floor was purchased in St. Louis. It came from one of the buildings of the Louisiana Purchase Exposition when the great St. Louis World's Fair was dismantled.

10   Alfred recalls, among the highlights of his youth, the trips on the excursion boats. Because of their proximity to the Mississippi River, East St. Louisans had easy access to the two river steamers, the *J. S.* and *St. Paul,* both owned and operated by Streckfus Steamers, Inc. There was always great excitement as the crowds scrambled out of the street cars which had carried them over to the Missouri side of the river. They hurried up the loading dock at Eads Bridge and fanned out over the double decks in search of their favorite amusement. There was something for everyone: card games, a penny arcade, and plenty of deck chairs for those who just wanted to watch the passing scene as the boat moved downstream.

11   The riverboat's ballroom was a place of special enchantment. Two large mirrored globes hung from the ceiling. As they rotated slowly in the intense beam of the spotlights, thousands of tiny diamond-like reflections spun around the ceiling, creating a shower of starlight in the darkened hall. It was heady stuff for those young dancers as they swayed and shimmied to the intoxicating syncopation of Jazz! The Charleston. The Black Bottom. Balling the Jack. Everybody knew those dance steps and vied with each other to display their expertise.

12   Alfred recalls an East St. Louis High School prom on board one of the excursion boats. "It was a twelve-to-twelve deal," he said. "We had twelve hours of dancing. You always took a girl who was a good dancer, 'cause you danced every dance . . . and you wanted somebody you could trade."

When describing the proper apparel for such affairs, he said, "You 13
danced in your shirt sleeves. My mother got me two ten-dollar silk shirts to
wear to the prom. Now, in 1920, that was a *big deal!* They were striped, with
detachable collars, and I took both shirts along. I wore one for six hours,
changed, and wore the other one for six hours. With a change of shirts, I was
always fresh. . . ."

Fate Marable, known as the "dean of riverboat jazz," was one of Alfred's 14
favorites. He played jazz piano up and down the river on the excursion boats
and led a group known as the *Jazz-E-Saz-Band.* Alfred describes Fate Marable as "one of the great, colored jazz band leaders and innovators of all
times. He came up from New Orleans, by way of Kentucky; Louis Armstrong, as a youngster, played in the front row of the band."

Alfred was not alone in his love of riverboat jazz. In the summer of 1928, 15
five thousand people boarded the steamer *St. Paul* to hear Louis Armstrong
play. The story is that the boat shook so much from the movement of the
passengers on board that it was in danger of capsizing and had to return to
port early.

As Alfred remembers, there was nothing in the early twenties to forecast 16
the conditions which exist in East St. Louis today. "When I lived there, it was
nothing like this at all," Alfred said. "It was a rather nice, industrial town,
second only to Chicago as a railroad center for the nation. It had some very
nice residential sections. In the late 'teens and early twenties, I would say the
quality of life on both sides of the river was pretty much the same."

Alfred's recollection was amplified by the East St. Louis newspaper, *The* 17
Daily Journal. On May 20, 1920, the paper stated that East St. Louis had
shown "phenomenal growth, financially and industrially, during the decade
of 1910 to 1920."

However, with the ratification of the Eighteenth Amendment prohibit- 18
ing the sale of intoxicating liquors, on January 18, 1920, the first seeds of
change were sown on the East Side.

The Journal devoted a large portion of its front page on January 16, 1920, 19
to a story about the feelings of the local populace on the new law. The
newspaper reported that ". . . Saloon keepers generally take a philosophic
view. They feel that the public in general did not protest against the law, but
submitted to every encroachment so meekly that the fanatics were encouraged and went the limit when the war gave them their opportunity . . .
There is much muttering and protest in the rank and file of the people and
many bitter expressions are heard." *The Journal* further declared that ". . . In
many homes, intoxicants will be made for home consumption and the efforts
of any governmental agency to stop this will be defied and defeated at least by
the present generation . . . accustomed to its tipple. . . ." The Volstead Act
was on the books, but in East St. Louis, hardly anybody noticed.

As *The Journal* predicted, homeowners began to make their own intoxi- 20
cants. The art of cooking "alky," making home brew and mixing bathtub gin
became national pastimes overnight. East St. Louis joined the crowd!

21 Baumeister's Drug Store, on the corner of Columbia and State Streets, advertised the popular proprietary drugs of the day—Drake's Croup Remedy, Bromo-Quinine, Pond's Vanishing Cream, and Sloan's Liniment. They did not have to advertise their most popular commodity and biggest seller—glycerine, a necessary ingredient for bathtub gin.

22 Alfred recited the recipe for this popular elixir: "You take half grain alcohol and half distilled water, some juniper berry extract and some glycerine. I remember making up a batch in the Knights of Columbus building, a bachelor residence place in East St. Louis. We had all the stuff except for the glycerine, so I went over to Baumeister's Drug Store and got the glycerine. We mixed it all up, stirred it well, and it became very cloudy. It looked like milk! We knew something was wrong, so I dashed across to the drug store and the druggist saw me coming. 'All right . . . how much did you spoil?' he asked me. He'd given me *castor oil* instead of glycerine, by mistake!"

23 There was a certain element of risk in consuming some of the concoctions made from the contraband. Wood alcohol was described as "not habit-forming" since few of the people who drank it (believing it to be grain alcohol) ever survived!

24 Another readily available intoxicant with lethal properties was Jamaica Ginger, popularly known as "jake." *The Journal* carried an account of the arrest of one Harry Brace, a member of the media employed by a St. Louis paper, who was picked up on December 30, 1920, "with two bottles of 'jake' in his pocket and an unknown quantity inside him."

25 Alfred Everett described his introduction to "jake" when his neighbors, who were having a party, asked him in for a drink. "We were all in the kitchen and one of the guests came in with a paper sack filled with little bottles which he dumped on the sink. I asked, 'What is it we're drinking?' They said, 'It's 'jake,' Jamaica Ginger, vanilla extract. You mix it with a little water and it sends you right along!' I had a few that evening, but I never tried it again.

26 "Later on, it gained a lot of publicity because it killed a lot of people. I was one of the lucky ones! It didn't last long, but it was a product of the times."

27 With the passage of the Volstead Act, saloon keepers were supposed to close their doors, or change their bars into soda fountains, but many continued to sell alcohol illegally. The speakeasy was born.

28 Alfred remembers many speakeasies on the East Side. Some were saloons and some operated in flats or apartment buildings. They always had a peephole in the front door for identification of the caller. "We had a little trouble with one speakeasy in East St. Louis," Alfred said, "because the proprietor had a glass eye . . . that was old 'Duke' Davis. He'd get drunk with the customers. We'd rap on his door and then we'd wait and wait. Finally, we'd yell at him, 'Get your good eye on the peephole, Duke!' because he'd be looking out with his glass eye and couldn't see anybody."

29 Even before speakeasies became so abundant on the East Side, prostitu-

tion was a well-established fact of life there. The activity was confined to one section of town known as the "Valley." It was an area bounded by Missouri, Ohio, Collinsville Avenues and Second Street. Alfred remembers that the streets were unpaved, by design. "It was left unpaved because there were so many ruts, you couldn't rush through in your automobile. You *had* to slow down. You *had* to pay attention to the people who were advertising their wares."

As Alfred describes the "Valley," it was not particularly attractive. "The houses were just shacks. There were no fancy places there, like the call houses in St. Louis. There were houses for both colored and white, and the city provided flood lights for the various establishments."

Prior to the twenties, John M. Chamberlain, a reform mayor, ordered the district cleaned out. *The Journal* reported that ". . . at midnight, March 31, 1915, the electric pianos played their last syncopated melody; the taxi drivers drove away with their last 'cargo' of inebriated habitues of the various places, and before dawn, the last of the harlots was claimed by oblivion. . . ."

However, this quiet did not last, and it was not long before the "Valley" was in full operation again. Later on, the "Valley" passed out of existence because of the expansion of business within the city. The First National Bank of East St. Louis decided to enlarge their building and parking lot and acquired some of the property. The houses were demolished. Alfred's recollection is that "it kind of died out as the property was encroached upon by legitimate business."

Gambling was very much a part of the East Side picture in the twenties. Horse parlors and bookie joints were easy to find and slot machines were, literally, everywhere. "You couldn't go into a grocery store," Alfred said, "without seeing a couple of slot machines. I guarantee you . . . those slot machines produced three or four thousand dollars a year for the grocery store."

When asked about the source for the slot machines, Alfred said, "The 'syndicate' put the slot machines in. They weren't gangsters, exactly. You wouldn't call them the Mafia, but they were the guys who had control of the slot machines."

By *Chicago* standards, East St. Louis did not have much violence during the twenties. The law enforcement agencies were willing to accommodate the bootleggers and prostitutes, and there didn't seem to be too much rivalry among the underworld characters whose preserve was the East Side.

Alfred did recall the Stevenson brothers, Ray and Vernon, who were famous local bootleggers. "They originated the booze in Cuba," Alfred said, "and would bring it into the States at New Orleans. They had a fleet of trucks with license plates for every state between New Orleans and East St. Louis. They were what you'd call 'wholesalers,' but they operated a speakeasy and saloon, which was in the nature of a club, right across from City Hall on Third Street."

37   Alfred remembered that Ray Stevenson, the older brother, was killed in a bootleggers' war, but did not recall the exact circumstances. They were bizarre by anybody's measure!

38   *The Daily Journal* reported that Ray Stevenson was killed January 22, 1926, at 5:00 A.M., in New Orleans, "after jumping overboard from a craft believed to have been engaged in rum-running activities." The accident occurred in a location regarded as "bootlegger territory, in the bayou of St. Bernard Parish." Stevenson was riding in a thirty-foot motor boat when a larger boat approached on a collision course. Stevenson jumped overboard and his body was mangled by the propeller of the other boat.

39   While the coroner reported that Stevenson had been duckhunting, rather than rum-running, speculation was that a rival bootlegger had put him out of business, using a propeller instead of the usual tommygun!

40   In its obituary column, captioned "Death's Calendar," Mr. Stevenson is described by *The Daily Journal* as having "entered into rest, suddenly."

41   Stevenson's family and friends gave him a first-class, gangster-style funeral with an expensive casket and tons of floral offerings. Alfred remembers that the funeral was almost the ruination of his friend, Ramey Elliot. "Ramey was in the florist business, but he was a kind of sport, and liked to associate with these hot shots. The Stevenson funeral brought in ten or fifteen thousand dollars cash in one week for Ramey's florist business, and he thought it was going to be like that every week! He got to spending money—throwing it around—and it really spoiled him."

42   In reminiscing about some of the conditions in the twenties which could have contributed to the present sad state of East St. Louis, Alfred thought "the industrial development might have had something to do with it because it brought in the cheaper labor from the South. It seemed good at the time, but contributed to the deterioration in the long run."

43   However, the chief cause of the decline of East St. Louis, according to Alfred Everett, was political corruption. "The poverty, pollution, industrialization . . . none of that really contributed as much as the political corruption," Alfred said. "As the bootlegging situation developed, and the gambling and wide-open prostitution, it tinged every city administration because there was all of this graft.

44   "From 1927 on, we didn't have anything but a corrupt, thieving administration, until the present mayor, James Williams. I believe he is an honest man."

45   Alfred continued, "There never was a breathing space. If you have a corrupt administration and then get an honest guy for eight years, you can get something done. But East St. Louis just had one crook after the other."

46   Today, it is only a two-minute drive from St. Louis across the Veterans Bridge, which terminates on the East Side at the intersection of Fifth Street and Martin Luther King Boulevard. The speakeasies are gone. The "Valley" is gone. The State of Illinois lottery has replaced the slot machines. Aban-

doned buildings, vacant lots strewn with litter, and rooming houses with sagging porches dominate the scene. A pall of smoke and human desolation drapes the landscape.

Out of the dim past, you just might hear a jazz band playing, but the   47
tempo has changed. The jubilant beat of "The Saints Go Marching In" is lost in the mournful wail of a muted trumpet, lamenting the death of a city.

Questions

1. In the interview, note how long Langenberg's questions are in relation to the length of Everett's answers. What does she say to elicit lengthy, specific answers?

2. In addition to taking down Everett's words, in her transcript of the interview what other devices does Langenberg use to convey her subject's personality and manner of speaking?

3. In transforming the interview, with its primary focus on Everett's experiences in East St. Louis during the Roaring 20s, into an essay emphasizing the character of the city during that time, Langenberg adds considerable information about its historical, geographical, and cultural characteristics. Compare the interview with the completed essay to show what Langenberg has added, where the new material is placed, and what its effect is.

4. What kind of a character does Everett appear to have been in the 20s, judging from his self-report in the interview? Is the older man recalling his experience of fifty years earlier much different from his younger self? Do either or both of these personalities appear in the completed essay? If so, where and how extensively? If not, why not?

5. In the completed essay what, if any, traces of Langenberg as an interviewer remain?

Character Sketches/Portraits

JOHN LEONARD

The Only Child

Leonard, book reviewer and analyst of contemporary life, was born in Washington, D.C., in 1939. He attended Harvard, and graduated in 1962 from the University of California at Berkeley. After beginning his writing career as a novelist—he published The Naked Martini *in 1961 and* Crybaby of the Western World *in 1969—he started reviewing books for the* New York Times, *where he has been Book Editor since 1971. His thoughtful, eloquent reviews and essays analyzing contemporary life (collected as* Private Lives in the Imperial City, *1979) have gained critical acclaim and a wide audience. Leonard often focuses on families and on the difficulties of maintaining significant relationships in a society that is increasingly urbanized, mechanized, and insecure.*

"The Only Child" demonstrates that a character sketch, unlike an interview in which the interviewer is generally unobtrusive, can reveal the writer's nature as well as his subject's. The essay unfolds gradually into deepening levels of psychological complexity. Leonard begins by describing his brother's physical appearance, and shows the disparity between the young man's early promise and what he has become. Then, through examining his brother's room, Leonard reveals the tortured mind of its occupant. In a final twist, Leonard suggests that the fires of the 1960s burned not only his brother but himself—and, by implication, many of the rest of us, as well.

1   He is big. He always has been, over six feet, with that slump of the shoulders and tuck in the neck big men in this country often affect, as if to apologize for being above the democratic norm in size. (In high school and at college he played varsity basketball. In high school he was senior class president.) And he looks healthy enough, blue-eyed behind his beard, like a trapper or a mountain man, acquainted with silences. He also grins a lot.

2   Odd, then, to have noticed earlier—at the house, when he took off his shabby coat to play Ping-Pong—that the white arms were unmuscled. The coat may have been a comment. This, after all, is southern California, where every man is an artist, an advertiser of himself; where every surface is painted and every object potted; where even the statues seem to wear socks. The entire population ambles, in polyesters, toward a Taco Bell. To wear a brown shabby cloth coat in southern California is to admit something.

3   So he hasn't been getting much exercise. Nor would the children have elected him president of any class. At the house they avoided him. Or, since he was too big to be avoided entirely, they treated his presence as a kind of odor to pass through hurriedly, to be safe on the other side. They behaved like cats. Of course, he ignored them. But I think they were up to more than

just protecting themselves from his lack of curiosity. Children are expert readers of grins.

His grin is intermittent. The dimples twitch on and off; between them, teeth are bared; above them, the blue eyes disappear in a wince. This grin isn't connected to any humor the children know about. It may be a tic. It could also be a function of some metronome made on Mars. It registers inappropriate intervals. We aren't listening to the same music.   4

This is the man who introduced me to the mysteries of mathematical science, the man I could never beat at chess, the man who wrote haiku and played with computers. Now there is static in his head, as though the mind had drifted off its signal during sleep. He has an attention span of about thirty seconds.   5

I am to take him back to where he lives, in the car I have rented in order to pretend to be a Californian. We are headed for a rooming house in one of the beach cities along a coast of off-ramps and oil wells. It is a rooming house that thinks of itself as Spanish. The ruined-hacienda look requires a patio, a palm tree and several miles of corrugated tile. He does not expect me to come up to his room, but I insist. I have brought along a six-pack of beer.   6

The room is a slum, and it stinks. It is wall-to-wall beer cans, hundreds of them, under a film of ash. He lights cigarettes and leaves them burning on the windowsill or the edge of the dresser or the lip of the sink, while he thinks of something else—Gupta sculpture, maybe, or the Sephiroth Tree of the Kabbalah. The sink is filthy, and so is the toilet. Holes have been burnt in the sheet on the bed, where he sits. He likes to crush the beer cans after he has emptied them, then toss them aside.   7

He tells me that he is making a statement, that this room is a statement, that the landlord will understand the meaning of his statement. In a week or so, according to the pattern, they will evict him, and someone will find him another room, which he will turn into another statement, with the help of the welfare checks he receives on account of his disability, which is the static in his head.   8

There are no books, no newspapers or magazines, no pictures on the wall. There is a television set, which he watches all day long while drinking beer and smoking cigarettes. I am sufficiently familiar with the literature on schizophrenia to realize that this room is a statement he is making about himself. I am also sufficiently familiar with his history to understand that, along with his contempt for himself, there is an abiding arrogance. He refuses medication. They can't make him take it, any more than they can keep him in a hospital. He has harmed no one. One night, in one of these rooms, he will set himself on fire.   9

He talks. Or blurts: scraps from Oriental philosophers—Lao-tzu, I think—puns, incantations, obscenities, names from the past. There are conspiracies; I am part of one of them. He grins, winces, slumps, is suddenly   10 tired, wants me to get out almost as much as I want to get out, seems to have lapsed in a permanent parenthesis. Anyway, I have a busy schedule.

11   Well, speed kills slowly, and he fiddled too much with the oxygen flow to his brain. He wanted ecstasy and revelation, the way we grew up wanting a bicycle, a car, a girlfriend. These belonged to us by right, as middle-class Americans. So, then, did salvation belong to us by right. I would like to thank Timothy Leary and all the other sports of the 1960's who helped make this bad trip possible. I wish R. D. Laing would explain to me, once again and slowly, how madness is a proof of grace. "The greatest magician," said Novalis, "would be the one who would cast over himself a spell so complete that he would take his own phantasmagorias as autonomous appearances."

12   One goes back to the rented car and pretending to be a Californian as, perhaps, one had been pretending to be a brother. It is odd, at my age, suddenly to have become an only child.

Questions

1. What details of his brother's appearance and behavior does Leonard use to characterize this nameless man? In what ways does showing the brother in his chosen context—a filthy room (paragraphs 6–9) and in an alien context—"at the house" (paragraphs 2, 3)—help to explain the brother's personality and illness? What determines the order in which Leonard presents this information—and at what point do we know that his brother is psychologically disturbed?

2. Leonard uses many natural symbols to characterize his brother. What does he intend to indicate by the fact that his brother "played varsity basketball" in high school and college (paragraph 1)? That his brother "grins a lot" (paragraph 1)? That his brother wore "a brown shabby cloth coat in southern California" (paragraph 2)? That Leonard could never beat him at chess (paragraph 5)? That his brother now "has an attention span of about thirty seconds" (paragraph 5)?

3. Why doesn't Leonard identify his brother by name? What is Leonard's attitude toward his brother? Does he expect his readers to share this? Why does he want readers to know about his brother?

4. Can Leonard expect readers who were little children in the 1960s to understand without further elaboration the elements of the counterculture, such as drug-taking, social nonconformity, and the influence of Timothy Leary and R. D. Laing, to which he only alludes in the essay? For this essay, published a decade later, should Leonard have provided more explanation?

MARY RUFFIN (Student)

Mama's Smoke

Ruffin was born in Richmond, Virginia, in 1963 and graduated from Virginia Common-wealth University in 1985 with a B.A. in English. She is currently enrolled there in a Master of Fine Arts program in creative writing, with a concentration in poetry. Her mother, an artist and aspiring writer, died when Ruffin was 13. "Mama's Smoke," a combination of epitaph, eulogy, and portrait, is the daughter's attempt to come to terms with the meaning of her mother's life and death, and with the complexity of their relationship, which exists after death, as in life.

I never thought I would smoke. With her it was different—she started way back when it was cool to smoke—had been the very picture of glamour. But that was before the surgeon general determined the hazardousness that is as immediate in the origins of my consciousness as once-upon-a-time. 1

Myths are absorbing. I've been told of the chains of unfiltered Camels she used to smoke, never without the legendary ivory holder between fingers with blood-red nails. By the time I was around she had switched to Merits. 2

Peggy thrived on craving. She wanted only the best for me, the best being an abstraction she pondered incessantly. When I was little I would sit on the ancient wobbly wooden stool in the corner of the kitchen, rocking and squeaking, listening to her. I liked that spot because it was right over the heat duct in the winter, and caught the breeze through the screen door in the utility room in the summer. Evenings, I asked her all kinds of questions—never afraid to broach any subject—and her answers usually took off miracu-lously, soaring. 3

"Not 'plain'! Pure and ageless, incorruptible! That's what your name is. That's why I gave it to you. I always hated mine with a passion! When people called me 'Margaret' I felt squeamish. And 'Maggie'—ugh—a literal punch in the stomach! But it's awkward to go through life with a nickname. It makes you feel always like you're not quite ever really yourself. I didn't want that for you." 4

If I didn't understand the songs she sang, I knew the syllables by heart. Sometimes I would just listen to the rhythm of her plastic-soled slippers. I creaked my stool in time as her slippers slid on the red and white tiles, moving from one end of the long counter to the other and back, to the sink, ice box, sink again, stove, counter. There was a regularity to the irregularity that soothed me. 5

As I draw deeply on my menthol Virginia Slim Light, looking through the yellowing black and white snapshots in the rusty old cookie tin she held onto for twenty-some-odd years, I wonder what happened to make me start smoking. The lid is difficult to open. Inside there are faces, one face altered over and over, with fierce green eyes flashing, despite the brittle fadedness of 6 the images. My hazel eyes have the spark, but only enough of a spark to torment me, to always make me seem not quite all me. Peggy stays away when I look at the pictures of her—maybe she doesn't identify with them anymore herself. She certainly used to.

7 But she also used to answer me when I called, and she no longer does that either. Often deep in my sleep I glimpse her and chase her through strange insidescapes, but she always refuses to recognize me. Once recently she consented to meet me in an abandoned ice rink. When I skated in late, she simply stared down my apologies. Suddenly busying herself with an old movie projector, her back to me, she became a flailing chaos of limbs in the darkness of the rink. I gave in to the oppression of futility and seated myself behind her. At first the picture jumped and lurched on the screen, out of focus, broke once, and then smoothed out. Peggy danced a vaudeville set in our old kitchen, twirling whisks and spatulas to the soundtrack of "Clementine." When the lights came on she had disappeared, and I was alone shivering, with the distorted tune ringing in my ears.

8 Usually she surfaces so briefly and unobtrusively that I'm not sure she has been there until after she's gone. Sometimes she appears an old haggard crone, the salt in her hair so thick that the pepper looks like dirt streaks washing away. Other times she is vital, younger than I am, the sheen of her black hair almost blinding. In the buttered daylight of my kitchen, as I stand blankly staring at the can of Crisco and the Pyrex measuring cup, I guess it is the sudden memory of a physics lesson that makes me think of using water to measure the solid substance. Displacement. Only later, as I gently knead the biscuit dough, careful not to bruise it, I realize that she has been there. Her smirk of disgust at the soybean powder in the open cabinet gave her away—she couldn't resist a mild "eee-gad" under her breath.

9 Peggy is steeped in colloquialism, figures of speech that barely escape the shallows of cliché. She wrote a novel once, some kind of sequel to *Gone With The Wind* and now she comes to me at the typewriter sometimes, though rarely at the notebook stage, and whispers more criticism than commentary. She burned it, burned it in a fit of rage. Justified, for they wouldn't make her known. One attempt, one refusal. The only grace is to make a clean break.

10 She is something like a sequel to herself, elliptical and confusing, out of context. She speaks in fragments, interrupting in the middle of my own sentences, giving to others the illusion that I have spoken her words. But that's not exactly accurate either. The others don't know her, don't know her words from mine. The illusion is mine.

11 The hiss of the word "fixatif" on a spray can evokes a frustrated whimper of reminiscence. The bite of turpentine and linseed oil draws her. She is a painter of portraits and has rendered a likeness of almost everyone she is close to at one time or another, I believe, with the exception of herself. When I pick up a piece of charcoal she jumps in and jerks my hand, refusing to let me catch an image clearly. I have forsaken our art and she will not let me be

forgiven so easily. But when I settle back and contemplate my own regrets, she relents. I feel her take her dry brush in hand and trace my features, a delicious tickle I revered as a child.

The legacy of paint stains on her pale turquoise smock, like the rhythm of the shuffle of her slippers on the floor, is her highest art. She denies it, of course, as obstinately as she refuses to appear when I look for her in the mirror. But she proves it as she shows up at those moments when I catch my reflection unexpectedly out of the corner of my eye. 12

The conversations we have now in black coffee cups and clouds of smoke are the closest we come to shared sustenance. They are always late, the times when it's most conspicuous to be awake. We plan the colors for the drapes and throw pillows to furnish some future studio. The studio gradually takes shape, perfect, and then shatters in a coughing fit. I hear her in another room, hacking, fading, and then she's gone. 13

Just as she never stays, she never stays away for long. She was beautiful in her day and she still preens, still believes underneath in the ultimate importance of surfaces. 14

At parties, her old acquaintances appear as her friends. They ask me if I'm in the art school and the flinching negative reply is overridden by their awe at my study of "philosophy." 15

"So like her! Right down to the hair and eyes, though not quite so dark, not quite so green. But underneath, Peggy *was* a philosopher, she was, so wise . . . ." 16

And Peggy surfaces and "eee-gads" so loudly in my ear that the friends' politenesses go under and my own return politenesses are just-not-quite-right. I sip my wine and kick Peggy in the shin. The acquaintances wander off whispering, "Almost the spitting image, except not nearly so . . . *genuine* . . . . This new generation . . . ." 17

Later, Peggy and I have pillow fights. The pillows are wet. The stains in the morning are on my face in the angry mirror. My eyes are hazel, murky. Peggy's eyes are clear, stinging green. When the lids began to droop, right before they closed for good, she cried bitterly in the mirror. Then I felt simple bewilderment, turning more complex. She still will not understand that her smock is finer than the portraits. We light up. We cough out our truce. 18

MARY McCARTHY

Uncle Myers

McCarthy graduated from Vassar in 1933, and began a career in journalism in New York. She has written several volumes of social analysis and cultural commentary, including the award-winning Occasional Prose *(1985). Among her dozen novels are* The Company She Keeps *(1942),* A Charmed Life *(1954),* Birds of America *(1971), and the bestselling*

The Group *(1954)*. *As the title of her short story collection,* Cast a Cold Eye *(1950)* *implies,* McCarthy *herself has earned "an international reputation for biting satire and uncanny perception," recognized by two Guggenheim fellowships and membership in the National Institute of Arts and Letters.*

She brings both to bear in her unsentimental autobiography, Memories of a Catholic Girlhood *(1957) from which "Uncle Myers" is reprinted below. McCarthy was an abominably treated little rich girl. Her wealthy, indulgent parents died in the influenza epidemic of 1918, when she was six, and for five years she and her younger brothers were raised in circumstances so harsh they longed for the warmth of the local orphanage. Mary's pathetic, middle-aged Aunt Margaret was a weak-willed collaborator in child rearing with Myers, her recently acquired (perhaps "bought") fat, boorish, lower-middle-class husband. As Mary narrates Myers's systematic abuse of the childrens' souls, spirits, intellects, and bodies, she avoids the melodramatic emotions that these pitiful, painful scenes could so easily create and presents instead an even more chilling—and ultimately more convincing—unemotional statement of his "capricious brutality." The resulting devastating portrait is the writer's best revenge.*

1 The man we had to call Uncle Myers was no relation to us. This was a point on which we four orphan children were very firm. He had married our great-aunt Margaret shortly before the death of our parents and so became our guardian while still a benedict—not perhaps a very nice eventuality for a fat man of forty-two who has just married an old maid with a little income to find himself summoned overnight from his home in Indiana to be the hired parent of four children, all under seven years old.

2 When Myers and Margaret got us, my three brothers and me, we were a handful; on this there were no two opinions in the McCarthy branch of the family. The famous flu epidemic of 1918, which had stricken our little household en route from Seattle to Minneapolis and carried off our parents within a day of each other, had, like all God's devices, a meritorious aspect, soon discovered by my grandmother McCarthy: a merciful end had been put to a regimen of spoiling and coddling, to Japanese houseboys, iced cakes, picnics, upset stomachs, diamond rings (imagine!), an ermine muff and neckpiece, furred hats and coats. My grandmother thanked her stars that Myers and her sister Margaret were available to step into the breach. Otherwise, we might have had to be separated, an idea that moistened her hooded grey eyes, or been taken over by "the Protestants"—thus she grimly designated my grandfather Preston, a respectable Seattle lawyer of New England antecedents who, she many times declared with awful emphasis, had refused to receive a Catholic priest in his house! But our Seattle grandparents, coming on to Minneapolis for the funeral, were too broken up, she perceived, by our young mother's death to protest the McCarthy arrangements. Weeping, my Jewish grandmother (Preston, born Morganstern), still a beauty, like her lost daughter, acquiesced in the wisdom of keeping us together in the religion my mother had espoused. In my sickbed, recovering from the flu in my grandmother McCarthy's Minneapolis house, I, the eldest and the only girl, sat up

and watched the other grandmother cry, dampening her exquisite black veil. I did not know that our parents were dead or that my sobbing grandmother—whose green Seattle terraces I remembered as delightful to roll down on Sundays—had just now, downstairs in my grandmother McCarthy's well-heated sun parlor, met the middle-aged pair who had come on from Indiana to undo her daughter's mistakes. I was only six years old and had just started school in a Sacred Heart convent on a leafy boulevard in Seattle before the fatal November trek back east, but I was sharp enough to see that Grandmother Preston did not belong here, in this dour sickroom, and vain enough to pride myself on drawing the inference that something had gone awry.

We four children and our keepers were soon installed in the yellow house at 2427 Blaisdell Avenue that had been bought for us by my grandfather McCarthy. It was situated two blocks away from his own prosperous dwelling, with its grandfather clock, tapestries, and Italian paintings, in a block that some time before had begun to "run down." Flanked by two-family houses, it was simply a crude box in which to stow furniture, and lives, like a warehouse; the rooms were small and brownish and for some reason dark, though I cannot think why, since the house was graced by no ornamental planting; a straight cement driveway ran up one side; in the back, there was an alley. Downstairs, there were a living room, a "den," a dining room, a kitchen, and a lavatory; upstairs, there were four bedrooms and a bathroom. The dingy wallpaper of the rooms in which we children slept was promptly defaced by us; bored without our usual toys, we amused ourselves by making figures on the walls with our wet tongues. This was our first crime, and I remember it because the violence of the whipping we got surprised us; we had not known we were doing wrong. The splotches on the walls remained through the years to fix this first whipping and the idea of badness in our minds; they stared at us in the evenings when, still bored but mute and tamed, we learned to make shadow figures on the wall—the swan, the rabbit with its ears wiggling—to while away the time.

It was this first crime, perhaps, that set Myers in his punitive mold. He saw that it was no sinecure he had slipped into. Childless, middle-aged, he may have felt in his slow-turning mind that his inexperience had been taken advantage of by his wife's grandiloquent sister, that the vexations outweighed the perquisites; in short, that he had been sold. This, no doubt, was how it must have really looked from where he sat—in a brown leather armchair in the den, wearing a blue work shirt, stained with sweat, open at the neck to show an undershirt and lion-blond, glinting hair on his chest. Below this were workmen's trousers of a brownish-gray material, straining at the buttons and always gaping slightly, just below the belt, to show another glimpse of underwear, of a yellowish white. On his fat head, frequently, with its crest of bronze curly hair, were the earphones of a crystal radio set, which he sometimes, briefly, in a generous mood, fitted over the grateful ears of one of my little brothers.

5   A second excuse for Myers' behavior is manifest in this description. He had to contend with Irish social snobbery, which looked upon him dispassionately from four sets of green eyes and set him down as "not a gentleman." "My father was a gentleman and you're not"—what I meant by these categorical words I no longer know precisely, except that my father had had a romantic temperament and was a spendthrift; but I suppose there was also included some notion of courtesy. Our family, like many Irish Catholic new-rich families, was filled with aristocratic delusions; we children were always being told that we were descended from the kings of Ireland and that we were related to General "Phil" Sheridan, a dream of my great-aunt's. More precisely, my great-grandfather on this side had been a streetcar conductor in Chicago.

6   But at any rate Myers (or Meyers) Shriver (or Schreiber—the name had apparently been Americanized) was felt to be beneath us socially. Another count against him in our childish score was that he was a German, or, rather, of German descent, which made us glance at him fearfully in 1918, just after the armistice. In Minneapolis at that time, there was great prejudice among the Irish Catholics, not only against the Protestant Germans, but against all the northern bloods and their hateful Lutheran heresy. Lutheranism to us children was, first of all, a religion for servant girls and, secondly, a sort of yellow corruption associated with original sin and with Martin Luther's tongue rotting in his mouth as God's punishment. Bavarian Catholics, on the other hand, were singled out for a special regard; we saw them in an Early Christian light, brunette and ringleted, like the Apostles. This was due in part to the fame of Oberammergau and the Passion Play, and in part to the fact that many of the clergy in our diocese were Bavarians; all through this period I confided my sins of disobedience to a handsome, dark, young Father Elderbush. Uncle Myers, however, was a Protestant, although, being too indolent, he did not go to church; he was not one of us. And the discovery that we could take refuge from him at school, with the nuns, at church, in the sacraments, seemed to verify the ban that was on him; he was truly outside grace. Having been impressed with the idea that our religion was a sort of logical contagion, spread by holy books and good example, I could never understand why Uncle Myers, bad as he was, had not caught it; and his obduracy in remaining at home in his den on Sundays, like a somnolent brute in its lair, seemed to me to go against nature.

7   Indeed, in the whole situation there was something unnatural and inexplicable. His marriage to Margaret, in the first place: he was younger than his wife by three years, and much was made of this difference by my grandmother McCarthy, his wealthy sister-in-law, as though it explained everything in a slightly obscene way. Aunt Margaret, née Sheridan, was a well-aged quince of forty-five, with iron-gray hair shading into black, a stiff carriage, high-necked dresses, unfashionable hats, a copy of *Our Sunday Visitor* always under her arm—folded, like a flail—a tough dry skin with soft

colorless hairs on it, like dust, and furrowed and corrugated, like the prunes we ate every day for breakfast. It could be said of her that she meant well, and she meant especially well by Myers, all two hundred and five pounds, dimpled double chin, and small, glinting, gross blue eyes of him. She called him "Honeybunch," pursued him with attentions, special foods, kisses, to which he responded with tolerance, as though his swollen passivity had the character of a male thrust or assertion. It was clear that he did not dislike her, and that poor Margaret, as her sister said, was head over heels in love with him. To us children, this honeymoon rankness was incomprehensible; we could not see it on either side for, quite apart from everything else, both parties seemed to us very old, as indeed they were, compared to our parents, who had been young and handsome. That he had married her for her money occurred to us inevitably, though it may not have been so; very likely it was his power over her that he loved, and the power he had to make her punish us was perhaps her strongest appeal to him. They slept in a bare, ugly bedroom with a tall, cheap pine chiffonier on which Myers' black wallet and his nickels and dimes lay spread out when he was at home—did he think to arouse our cupidity or did he suppose that this stronghold of his virility was impregnable to our weak desires? Yet, as it happened, we did steal from him, my brother Kevin and I—rightfully, as we felt, for we were allowed no pocket money (two pennies were given us on Sunday morning to put into the collection plate) and we guessed that the money paid by our grandfather for the household found its way into Myers' wallet.

And here was another strange thing about Myers. He not only did 8 nothing for a living but he appeared to have no history. He came from Elkhart, Indiana, but beyond this fact nobody seemed to know anything about him—not even how he had met my aunt Margaret. Reconstructed from his conversation, a picture of Elkhart emerged for us that showed it as a flat place consisting chiefly of ball parks, poolrooms, and hardware stores. Aunt Margaret came from Chicago, which consisted of the Loop, Marshall Field's, assorted priests and monsignors, and the black-and-white problem. How had these two worlds impinged? Where our family spoke freely of its relations, real and imaginary, Myers spoke of no one, not even a parent. At the very beginning, when my father's old touring car, which had been shipped on, still remained in our garage, Myers had certain seedy cronies whom he took riding in it or who simply sat in it in our driveway, as if anchored in a houseboat; but when the car went, they went or were banished. Uncle Myers and Aunt Margaret had no friends, no couples with whom they exchanged visits—only a middle-aged, black-haired, small, emaciated woman with a German name and a yellowed skin whom we were taken to see one afternoon because she was dying of cancer. This protracted death had the aspect of a public execution, which was doubtless why Myers took us to it; that is, it was a spectacle and it was free, and it inspired restlessness and depression. Myers was the perfect type of rootless municipalized man who finds his pleasures in the handouts or overflow of an industrial civilization. He enjoyed standing on a curbstone, watching parades, the more nondescript the better, the Labor Day parade being his favorite, and next to that a military parade, followed by the commercial parades with floats and girls dressed in costumes; he would even go to Lake Calhoun or Lake Harriet for doll-carriage parades and competitions of children dressed as Indians. He like bandstands, band concerts, public parks devoid of grass; skywriting attracted him; he was quick to hear of a department-store demonstration where colored bubbles were blown, advertising a soap, to the tune of "I'm Forever Blowing Bubbles," sung by a mellifluous soprano. He collected coupons and tinfoil, bundles of newspaper for the old rag-and-bone man (thus interfering seriously with our school paper drives), free samples of cheese at Donaldson's, free tickets given out by a neighborhood movie house to the first installment of a serial—in all the years we lived with him, we never saw a full-length movie but only those truncated beginnings. He was also fond of streetcar rides (could the system have been municipally owned?), soldiers' monuments, cemeteries, big, coarse flowers like cannas and cockscombs set in beds by city gardeners. Museums did not appeal to him, though we did go one night with a large crowd to see Marshal Foch on the steps of the Art Institute. He was always weighing himself on penny weighing machines. He seldom left the house except on one of these purposeless errands, or else to go to a ball game, by himself. In the winter, he spent the days at home in the den, or in the kitchen, making candy. He often had enormous tin trays of decorated fondants cooling in the cellar, which leads my brother Kevin to think today that at one time in Myers' life he must have been a pastry cook or a confectioner. He also liked to fashion those little figures made of pipe cleaners that were just then coming in as favors in the better candy shops, but Myers used *old* pipe cleaners, stained yellow and brown. The bonbons, with their pecan or almond topping, that he laid out in such perfect rows were for his own use; we were permitted to watch him set them out, but never—and my brother Kevin confirms this—did we taste a single one.

9   In the five years we spent with Myers, the only candy I ever had was bought with stolen money and then hidden in the bottom layer of my paper-doll set; the idea of stealing to buy candy and the hiding place were both lifted from Kevin. Opening my paper-doll box one day, I found it full of pink and white soft-sugar candies, which it seemed to me God or the fairies had sent me in response to my wishes and prayers, until I realized that Kevin was stealing, and using my paper-doll box for a cache; we had so few possessions that he had no place of his own to hide things in. Underneath the mattress was too chancy, as I myself found when I tried to secrete magazines of Catholic fiction there; my aunt, I learned, was always tearing up the bed and turning the mattress to find out whether you had wet it and attempted to hide your crime by turning it over. Reading was forbidden us, except for schoolbooks and, for some reason, the funny papers and magazine section of

the Sunday Hearst papers, where one read about leprosy, the affairs of Count Boni de Castellane, and a strange disease that turned people to stone creepingly from the feet up.

This prohibition against reading was a source of scandal to the nuns who taught me in the parochial school, and I think it was due to their intervention with my grandmother that finally, toward the end, I was allowed to read openly the Camp Fire Girls series, *Fabiola,* and other books I have forgotten. Myers did not read; before the days of the crystal set, he passed his evenings listening to the phonograph in the living room: Caruso, Harry Lauder, "Keep the Home Fires Burning," "There's a Sweet Little Nest," and "Listen to the Mocking Bird." It was his pleasure to make the four of us stand up in a line and sing to him the same tunes he had just heard on the phonograph, while he laughed at my performance, for I tried to reproduce the staccato phrasing of the sopranos, very loudly and off key. Also, he hated long words, or, rather, words that he regarded as long. One summer day, in the kitchen, when I had been ordered to swat flies, I said, "They disappear so strangely," a remark that he mimicked for years whenever he wished to humiliate me, and the worst of this torture was that I could not understand what was peculiar about the sentence, which seemed to me plain ordinary English, and, not understanding, I knew that I was in perpetual danger of exposing myself to him again.

So far as we knew, he had never been in any army, but he liked to keep smart military discipline. We had frequently to stand in line, facing him, and shout answers to his questions in chorus. "Forward *march!*" he barked after every order he gave us. The Fourth of July was the only holiday he threw himself into with geniality. Anything that smacked to him of affectation or being "stuck-up" was subject to the harshest reprisals from him, and I, being the oldest, and the one who remembered my parents and the old life best, was the chief sinner, sometimes on purpose, sometimes unintentionally.

When I was eight, I began writing poetry in school: "Father Gaughan is our dear parish priest/ And he is loved from west to east." And "Alas, Pope Benedict is dead,/ The sorrowing people said." Pope Benedict at that time was living, and, as far as I know, in good health; I had written this opening couplet for the rhyme and the sad idea; but then, very conveniently for me, about a year later he died, which gave me a feeling of fearsome power, stronger than a priest's power of loosing and binding. I came forward with my poem and it was beautifully copied out by our teacher and served as the school's elegy at a memorial service for the Pontiff. I dared not tell that I had had it ready in my desk. Not long afterward, when I was ten, I wrote an essay for a children's contest on "The Irish in American History," which won first the city and then the state prize. Most of my facts I had cribbed from a series on Catholics in American history that was running in *Our Sunday Visitor.* I worked on the assumption that anybody who was Catholic must be Irish, and then, for good measure, I went over the signers of the Declaration of Independence and added any name that sounded Irish to my ears. All this was clothed in rhetoric invoking "the lilies of France"—God knows why, except that I was in love with France and somehow, through Marshal MacMahon, had made Lafayette out an Irishman. I believe that even Kosciusko figured as an Irishman *de coeur*. At any rate, there was a school ceremony, at which I was presented with the city prize (twenty-five dollars, I think, or perhaps that was the state prize); my aunt was in the audience in her best mallard-feathered hat, looking, for once, proud and happy. She spoke kindly to me as we walked home, but when we came to our ugly house, my uncle silently rose from his chair, led me into the dark downstairs lavatory, which always smelled of shaving cream, and furiously beat me with the razor strop—to teach me a lesson, he said, lest I become stuck-up. Aunt Margaret did not intervene. After her first look of discomfiture, her face settled into folds of approval; she had been too soft. This was the usual tribute she paid Myers' greater discernment—she was afraid of losing his love by weakness. The money was taken, "to keep for me," and that, of course, was the end of it. Such was the fate of anything considered "much too good for her," a category that was rivaled only by its pendant, "plenty good enough."

13 We were beaten all the time, as a matter of course, with the hairbrush across the bare legs for ordinary occasions, and with the razor strop across the bare bottom for special occasions, like the prize-winning. It was as though these ignorant people, at sea with four frightened children, had taken a Dickens novel—*Oliver Twist,* perhaps, or *Nicholas Nickleby*—for a navigation chart. Sometimes our punishments were earned, sometimes not; they were administered gratuitously, often, as preventive medicine. I was whipped more frequently than my brothers, simply by virtue of seniority; that is, every time one of them was whipped, I was whipped also, for not having set a better example, and this was true for all four of us in a descending line. Kevin was whipped for Preston's misdeeds and for Sheridan's, and Preston was whipped for Sheridan's, while Sheridan, the baby and the favorite, was whipped only for his own. This naturally made us fear and distrust each other, and only between Kevin and myself was there a kind of uneasy alliance. When Kevin ran away, as he did on one famous occasion, I had a feeling of joy and defiance, mixed with the fear of punishment for myself, mixed with something worse, a vengeful anticipation of the whipping *he* would surely get. I suppose that the two times I ran away, his feelings were much the same—envy, awe, fear, admiration, and a certain evil thrill, collusive with my uncle, at the thought of the strop ahead. Yet, strange to say, nobody was beaten on these historic days. The culprit, when found, took refuge at my grandmother's, and a fearful hush lay over the house on Blaisdell Avenue at the thought of the monstrous daring and deceitfulness of the runaway; Uncle Myers, doubtless, was shaking in his boots at the prospect of explanations to the McCarthy family council. The three who remained at home were sentenced to spend the day upstairs, in strict silence. But if my uncle's impartial

application of punishment served to make us each other's enemies very often, it did nothing to establish discipline, since we had no incentive to behave well, not knowing when we might be punished for something we had not done or even for something that by ordinary standards would be considered good. We knew not when we would offend, and what I learned from this, in the main, was a policy of lying and concealment; for several years after we were finally liberated, I was a problem liar.

Despite Myers' quite justified hatred of the intellect, of reading and education (for he was right—it *was* an escape from him), my uncle, like all dictators, had one book that he enjoyed. It was *Uncle Remus,* in a red cover— a book I detested—which he read aloud to us in his den over and over again in the evenings. It seemed to me that this reduction of human life to the level of talking animals and this corruption of language to dialect gave my uncle some very personal relish. He knew I hated it and he rubbed it in, trotting my brother Sheridan on his knee as he dwelt on some exploit of Br'er Fox's with many chuckles and repetitions. In *Uncle Remus,* he had his hour, and to this day I cannot read anything in dialect or any fable without some degree of repugnance. . . .

14

FREDERICK DOUGLASS

Resurrection

Douglass (1817–1895) was born a slave in Talbot County, Maryland. Unlike many slaves, he learned to read, and the power of this accomplishment, coupled with an iron physique and a will to match, enabled him to escape to New York in 1838. For the next twenty-five years, he toured the country as a powerful spokesman for the abolitionist movement, serving as an advisor to Harriet Beecher Stowe, author of Uncle Tom's Cabin *and to President Lincoln, among others. After the war he campaigned for civil rights for blacks and women. In 1890 his political significance was acknowledged in his appointment as Minister to Haiti.*

Slave narratives, written or dictated by the hundreds in the nineteenth century, provided memorable accounts of the physical, geographical, and psychological movement from captivity to freedom, from dependence to independence. Douglass' autobiography is memorable for its forthright language and absence of stereotyping of either whites or blacks; his people are multidimensional. Crisis points, and the insights and opportunities they provide, are natural topics for personal writing. This episode, taken from the first version (of four) of The Narrative of the Life of Frederick Douglass, an American Slave *(1845), explains the incident that was "the turning point in my career as a slave," for it enabled him to make the transformation from slave to human being.*

I have already intimated that my condition was much worse, during the first six months of my stay at Mr. Covey's, than in the last six. The circumstances leading to the change in Mr. Covey's course toward me form an epoch in my

1

humble history. You have seen how a man was made a slave; you shall see how a slave was made a man. On one of the hottest days of the month of August, 1833, Bill Smith, William Hughes, a slave named Eli, and myself, were engaged in fanning wheat. Hughes was clearing the fanned wheat from before the fan. Eli was turning, Smith was feeding, and I was carrying wheat to the fan. The work was simple, requiring strength rather than intellect; yet, to one entirely unused to such work, it came very hard. About three o'clock of that day, I broke down; my strength failed me; I was seized with a violent aching of the head, attended with extreme dizziness; I trembled in every limb. Finding what was coming, I nerved myself up, feeling it would never do to stop work. I stood as long as I could stagger to the hopper with grain. When I could stand no longer, I fell, and felt as if held down by an immense weight. The fan of course stopped; every one had his own work to do; and no one could do the work of the other, and have his own go on at the same time.

2   Mr. Covey was at the house, about one hundred yards from the treading-yard where we were fanning. On hearing the fan stop, he left immediately, and came to the spot where we were. He hastily inquired what the matter was. Bill answered that I was sick, and there was no one to bring wheat to the fan. I had by this time crawled away under the side of the post and rail-fence by which the yard was enclosed, hoping to find relief by getting out of the sun. He then asked where I was. He was told by one of the hands. He came to the spot, and, after looking at me awhile, asked me what was the matter. I told him as well as I could, for I scarce had strength to speak. He then gave me a savage kick in the side, and told me to get up. I tried to do so, but fell back in the attempt. He gave me another kick, and again told me to rise. I again tried, and succeeded in gaining my feet; but, stooping to get the tub with which I was feeding the fan, I again staggered and fell. While down in this situation, Mr. Covey took up the hickory slat with which Hughes had been striking off the half-bushel measure, and with it gave me a heavy blow upon the head, making a large wound, and the blood ran freely; and with this again told me to get up. I made no effort to comply, having now made up my mind to let him do his worst. In a short time after receiving this blow, my head grew better. Mr. Covey had now left me to my fate. At this moment I resolved, for the first time, to go to my master, enter a complaint, and ask his protection. In order to do this, I must that afternoon walk seven miles; and this, under the circumstances, was truly a severe undertaking. I was exceed-ingly feeble; made so as much by the kicks and blows which I received, as by the severe fit of sickness to which I had been subjected. I, however, watched my chance, while Covey was looking in an opposite direction, and started for St. Michael's: I succeeded in getting a considerable distance on my way to the woods, when Covey discovered me, and called after me to come back, threatening what he would do if I did not come. I disregarded both his calls and his threats, and made my way to the woods as fast as my feeble state would allow; and thinking I might be overhauled by him if I kept the road, I

walked through the woods, keeping far enough from the road to avoid detection, and near enough to prevent losing my way. I had not gone far before my little strength again failed me. I could go no farther. I fell down, and lay for a considerable time. The blood was yet oozing from the wound on my head. For a time I thought I should bleed to death; and think now that I should have done so, but that the blood so matted my hair as to stop the wound. After lying there about three quarters of an hour, I nerved myself up again, and started on my way, through bogs and briers, barefooted and bareheaded, tearing my feet sometimes at nearly every step; and after a journey of about seven miles, occupying some five hours to perform it, I arrived at master's store. I then presented an appearance enough to affect any but a heart of iron. From the crown of my head to my feet, I was covered with blood. My hair was all clotted with dust and blood; my shirt was stiff with blood. My legs and feet were torn in sundry places with briers and thorns, and were also covered with blood. I suppose I looked like a man who had escaped a den of wild beasts, and barely escaped them. In this state I appeared before my master, humbly entreating him to interpose his authority for my protection. I told him all the circumstances as well as I could, and it seemed, as I spoke, at times to affect him. He would then walk the floor, and seek to justify Covey by saying he expected I deserved it. He asked me what I wanted. I told him, to let me get a new home; that as sure as I lived with Mr. Covey again, I should live with but to die with him; that Covey would surely kill me; he was in a fair way for it. Master Thomas ridiculed the idea that there was any danger of Mr. Covey's killing me, and said that he knew Mr. Covey, that he was a good man, and that he could not think of taking me from him; that, should he do so, he would lose the whole year's wages; that I belonged to Mr. Covey for one year, and that I must go back to him, come what might; and that I must not trouble him with any more stories, or that he would himself *get hold of me.* After threatening me thus, he gave me a very large dose of salts, telling me that I might remain in St. Michael's that night, (it being quite late,) but that I must be off back to Mr. Covey's early in the morning; and that if I did not, he would *get hold of me,* which meant that he would whip me. I remained all night, and, according to his orders, I started off to Covey's in the morning, (Saturday morning,) wearied in body and broken in spirit. I got no supper that night, or breakfast that morning. I reached Covey's about nine o'clock; and just as I was getting over the fence that divided Mrs. Kemp's fields from ours, out ran Covey with his cowskin, to give me another whipping. Before he could reach me, I succeeded in getting to the cornfield; and as the corn was very high, it afforded me the means of hiding. He seemed very angry, and searched for me a long time. My behavior was altogether unaccountable. He finally gave up the chase, thinking, I suppose, that I must come home for something to eat; he would give himself no further trouble in looking for me. I spent that day mostly in the woods, having the alternative before me,—to go home and be whipped to death, or stay in the woods and be starved to death. That night, I fell in with Sandy Jenkins, a slave with whom I was somewhat acquainted. Sandy had a free wife who lived about four miles from Mr. Covey's; and it being Saturday, he was on his way to see her. I told him my circumstances, and he very kindly invited me to go home with him. I went home with him, and talked this whole matter over, and got his advice as to what course it was best for me to pursue. I found Sandy an old adviser. He told me, with great solemnity, I must go back to Covey; but that before I went, I must go with him into another part of the woods, where there was a certain *root*, which, if I would take some of it with me, carrying it *always on my right side,* would render it impossible for Mr. Covey, or any other white man, to whip me. He said he had carried it for years; and since he had done so, he had never received a blow, and never expected to while he carried it. I at first rejected the idea, that the simple carrying of a root in my pocket would have any such effect as he had said, and was not disposed to take it; but Sandy impressed the necessity with much earnestness, telling me it could do no harm, if it did no good. To please him, I at length took the root, and, according to his direction, carried it upon my right side. This was Sunday morning. I immediately started for home; and upon entering the yard gate, out came Mr. Covey on his way to meeting. He spoke to me very kindly, bade me drive the pigs from a lot near by, and passed on towards the church. Now, this singular conduct of Mr. Covey really made me begin to think that there was something in the *root* which Sandy had given me; and had it been on any other day than Sunday, I could have attributed the conduct to no other cause than the influence of that root; and as it was, I was half inclined to think the *root* to be something more than I at first had taken it to be. All went well till Monday morning. On this morning, the virtue of the *root* was fully tested. Long before daylight, I was called to go and rub, curry, and feed, the horses. I obeyed, and was glad to obey. But whilst thus engaged, whilst in the act of throwing down some blades from the loft, Mr. Covey entered the stable with a long rope; and just as I was half out of the loft, he caught hold of my legs, and was about tying me. As soon as I found what he was up to, I gave a sudden spring, and as I did so, he holding to my legs, I was brought sprawling on the stable floor. Mr. Covey seemed now to think he had me, and could do what he pleased; but at this moment—from whence came the spirit I don't know—I resolved to fight; and, suiting my action to the resolution, I seized Covey hard by the throat; and as I did so, I rose. He held on to me, and I to him. My resistance was so entirely unexpected, that Covey seemed taken all aback. He trembled like a leaf. This gave me assurance, and I held him uneasy, causing the blood to run where I touched him with the ends of my fingers. Mr. Covey soon called out to Hughes for help. Hughes came, and while Covey held me, attempted to tie my right hand. While he was in the act of doing so, I watched my chance, and gave him a heavy kick close under the ribs. This kick fairly sickened Hughes, so that he left me in the hands of Mr. Covey. This kick had the effect of not only weakening Hughes, but Covey also. When he saw Hughes bending over with pain, his courage quailed. He asked me if I meant to persist in my resistance. I told him I did, come what might; that he had used me like a brute for six months, and that I was determined to be used so no longer. With that, he strove to drag me to a stick that was lying just out of the stable door. He meant to knock me down. But just as he was leaning over to get the stick, I seized him with both hands by his collar, and brought him by a sudden snatch to the ground. By this time, Bill came. Covey called upon him for assistance. Bill wanted to know what he could do. Covey said, "Take hold of him, take hold of him!" Bill said his master hired him out to work, and not to help whip me; so he left Covey and myself to fight our own battle out. We were at it for nearly two hours. Covey at length let me go, puffing and blowing at a great rate, saying that if I had not resisted, he would not have whipped me half so much. The truth was, that he had not whipped me at all. I considered him as getting entirely the worst end of the bargain; for he had drawn no blood from me, but I had from him. The whole six months afterwards, that I spent with Mr. Covey, he never laid the weight of his finger upon me in anger. He would occasionally say, he didn't want to get hold of me again. "'No,'" thought I, "you need not; for you will come off worse than you did before."

This battle with Mr. Covey was the turning-point in my career as a slave.   3
It rekindled the few expiring embers of freedom, and revived within me a sense of my own manhood. It recalled the departed self-confidence, and inspired me again with a determination to be free. The gratification afforded by the triumph was a full compensation for whatever else might follow, even death itself. He only can understand the deep satisfaction which I experienced, who has himself repelled by force the bloody arm of slavery. I felt as I never felt before. It was a glorious resurrection, from the tomb of slavery, to the heaven of freedom. My long-crushed spirit rose, cowardice departed, bold defiance took its place; and I now resolved that, however long I might remain a slave in form, the day had passed forever when I could be a slave in fact. I did not hesitate to let it be known of me, that the white man who expected to succeed in whipping, must also succeed in killing me.

Questions

1. Writers sometimes present self-portraits through showing themselves in action, characterizing their behavior (often, in contrast with that of others) in a single, memorable incident. Why did Douglass select his successful defiance of Mr. Covey as a critical event? He provides considerable detail about his appearance after his first beating by Covey (paragraph 2), but scarcely any about the appearance of either Covey or Master Thomas. Why?

2. What kind of person is Douglass as a character in his own narrative? As the writer of this incident, twelve years after the fact? How does his fairly formal and sober

diction reinforce his self-characterization? How does it enhance the significance of the event he narrates?

3. What, if anything, does Douglass expect his audience to do about slavery, as a consequence of having read his narrative and encountered his changed personality and opportunities? Would he have expected slaveowners to read it and reform? Why or why not?

4. Why is paragraph 2 so long? Should it have been divided into shorter units, or is the longer unit preferable? Justify your answer.

ELLEN GOODMAN

Mother Teresa and
Her Endless Fight

Goodman, born in Brookline, Massachusetts, in 1941, graduated from Radcliffe in 1963, and worked briefly as a reporter for Newsweek *before beginning her newspaper career with the* Detroit Free Press. *Since 1971 she has written a popular column of news commentary for the* Boston Globe, *syndicated to more than 200 newspapers, and collected in three volumes,* Close to Home *(1979),* At Large *(1981), and* Keeping in Touch *(1985). In 1980 she received the Pulitzer Prize for distinguished commentary. In her writing, from a viewpoint that combines common sense and humanitarian values, she addresses issues close to home, often matters particularly affecting families, working women, the poor, and the otherwise disadvantaged.*

These concerns are reflected in Goodman's tribute, "Mother Teresa and Her Endless Fight," written in October 1979 to commemorate Mother Teresa's award of the Nobel Peace Prize. In the process of paying tribute to a woman many regard as a living saint, Goodman wisely keeps her focus on her audience, people like us who are scarcely ready for sainthood. To identify all of Mother Teresa's activities would make the portrait too "awesome," perhaps overwhelming, so Goodman spends more time suggesting what this distinguished humanitarian might mean to us rather than in describing what she actually does. With her usual good judgment, Goodman refrains from admonishing us to "go and do likewise." We won't. We all know that. But Goodman gently and firmly reminds us, by quoting from the "odd" combination of Fidel Castro and Pope John Paul II, that if we put our ideologies and excuses aside even for a moment, we will recognize that Mother Teresa is a vision of what people could become.

1   In the photograph, she is holding an emaciated child. There have been, surely, enough of them, a ready supply of emaciated children in Mother Teresa's life. She has lived in a sea of sick, a Black Hole of Calcutta's poor.

2   Even now, if she were to distribute every dollar of her $192,000 Nobel Peace Prize, one by one, she would run out of money long before she ran out of poor in that one teeming city.

3   The portrait of this woman is absolutely awesome. She is no statesman who makes a treaty in an air-conditioned chamber and then goes home to a

ticker-tape parade. Here is a woman who gets up every morning of her life to tend endless streams of victims of life's longest war of attrition. Without an expectation of victory.

Most of us in her place could not have stood a week or a two-year tour of duty before being overwhelmed by pain and a sense of futility. There are times we all look at good work and good workers as if they were shoveling sand into the wind. But here is a woman who always sees people. 4

So, the awarding of the Nobel Prize for Peace to Mother Teresa is a pinch at our consciences—that unpopular and obsolete part of our ethical anatomy. People today don't talk about their consciences and how to appease them; they talk about guilt-trips and how to avoid them. 5

But Mother Teresa reminds us how often we think of the poor of the world as sand. Most of us live according to self-interest. The truly selfless are as rare as Nobel Prize winners. 6

But it is a question of how wide our definition of self-interest is and how much it rules our lives. 7

It is hard, at a time when many Americans feel desperate about their heating bills or their ability to buy a home of their own, to think about the emaciated child. It's hard when we haven't eliminated poverty in America to think about Calcutta. I don't fault this. It just is. 8

We can't measure one person's pain against another's. But it isn't hard to measure one person's standard of living against another. The anxiety of the couple worried about a 12 percent mortgage and the anxiety of a couple worried about food is utterly different. 9

When the Nobel committee awarded its peace prize to Mother Teresa (and I do not forget that they also awarded one to Henry Kissinger), they did so because "poverty and hunger and distress also constitute a threat to peace." 10

The gap between the rich and the poor of the world makes this country look like an egalitarian utopia. The gap between the rich and the poor of the world is a true source of insecurity and hostility. We are the rich and it is harder and harder to get away from it. 11

It's odd to quote Fidel Castro and Pope John Paul II in one breath. But in their back-to-back visits to this country, they both gave the same message: "Some countries possess abundant resources while others have nothing." 12

However dubious Castro's credentials or motivations, his words ring true and we know it. "I have come to warn that, if we do not eliminate our present injustices and inequalities peacefully and wisely, the future will be apocalyptic. Bombs may kill the hungry, the sick and the ignorant, but they cannot kill hunger, disease and ignorance. Nor can they kill the righteous rebellion of the people; and in the holocaust, the rich who are the ones who have the most to lose in this world will also die." 13

Mother Teresa said that, "The great thing about the poor is that they are not discontented. They don't hate us despite their immense suffering. It is a mystery we cannot understand." 14

Perhaps she is right. Perhaps they are too tired or too concerned with 15

161

survival for hatred. But I doubt it. When "have nots" see the "haves," they want to know why.

16   The Nobel Prize award and the words of two visitors from two different worlds suggest that each year we need a broader definition of self-interest: one that sees the world as our neighborhood, one that sees our conscience as a guide, not as a guilt-trip.

17   "I have been told I spoil the poor by my work," says Mother Teresa. "Well at least one congregation is spoiling the poor, because everyone else is spoiling the rich."

18   Few of us are or can be as selfless or dedicated as this woman. But perhaps, for a few minutes, she helped us wipe the sand from our eyes, so we could see the people.

ROBERT COLES

Two Languages, One Soul

Robert Coles's writings, particularly the Children of Crisis *series, have made him one of America's most influential psychiatrists. He was born in Boston in 1929, received an A.B. from Harvard in 1950, an M.D. from Columbia in 1954, and now holds over 25 honorary degrees. In 1958 he began teaching at Harvard, where he is currently a professor of psychiatry and medical humanities.*

Coles began the Children of Crisis *series in 1967, while he was working with black children suffering from the hostility of whites during the early days of integration; Volumes 2 and 3 of the series won a Pulitzer Prize in 1973. Most of Coles's twenty-five books are concerned with groups outside the mainstream of American society—for example,* Migrants, Sharecroppers, and Mountaineers *(1972),* Eskimos, Chicanos, and Indians *(1978), and* Women of Crisis: Lives of Struggle and Hope *(1978), written with his wife. Coles's writings reveal the pride and strength of his subjects. In the selection below, from* The Old Ones of New Mexico *(1975), Coles depicts his subject's dignity, self-respect, and love of God and her mountain existence by letting her speak in her own words, simple yet poetic.*

1   . . . Here are the words of an elderly woman who has had virtually no schooling and speaks a mixture of Spanish (which I have translated) and terse but forceful English. She lives in a small, isolated mountain community well to the north of Santa Fe and enjoys talking with her visitor: "Sometimes I have a moment to think. I look back and wonder where all the time has gone to—so many years; I cannot say I like to be reminded how many. My sister is three years older, eighty this May. She is glad to talk of her age. I don't like to mention mine. Maybe I have not her faith in God. She makes her way every day to church. I go only on Sundays. Enough is enough; besides, I don't like the priest. He points his finger too much. He likes to accuse us—each week it is a different sin he charges us with. My mother used to read me Christ's

words when I was a girl—from the old Spanish Bible her grandmother gave to her on her deathbed. I learned that Christ was a kind man; He tried to think well of people, even the lowest of the low, even those at the very bottom who are in a swamp and don't know how to get out, let alone find for themselves some high, dry land.

"But this priest of ours gives no one the benefit of the doubt. I have no right to find fault with him; I know that. Who am I to do so? I am simply an old lady, and I had better watch out: the Lord no doubt punishes those who disagree with His priests. But our old priest who died last year was so much finer, so much better to hear on a warm Sunday morning. Every once in a while he would even lead us outside to the courtyard and talk with us there, give us a second sermon. I felt so much better for listening to him. He was not in love with the sound of his own voice, as this new priest is. He did not stop and listen to the echo of his words. He did not brush away dust from his coat, or worry if the wind went through his hair. He was not always looking for a paper towel to wipe his shoes. My husband says he will buy this priest a dozen handkerchiefs and tell him they are to be used for his shoes only. Here when we get rain we are grateful, and it is not too high a price to pay, a little mud to walk through. Better mud that sticks than dust that blows away.

"Well, I should not go on so long about a vain man. We all like to catch ourselves in the mirror and find ourselves good to look at. Here I am, speaking ill of him, yet I won't let my family celebrate my birthdays any more; and when I look at myself in the mirror a feeling of sadness comes over me. I pull at my skin and try to erase the lines, but no luck. I think back: all those years when my husband and I were young, and never worried about our health, our strength, our appearance. I don't say we always do now; but there are times when we look like ghosts of ourselves. I will see my husband noticing how weak and tired I have become, how hunched over. I pretend not to see, but once the eyes have caught something, one cannot shake the picture off. And I look at him, too; he will straighten up when he feels my glance strike him, and I quickly move away. Too late, though; he has been told by me, without a word spoken, that he is old, and I am old, and that is our fate, to live through these last years.

"But it is not only pity we feel for ourselves. A few drops of rain and I feel grateful; the air is so fresh afterwards. I love to sit in the sun. We have the sun so often here, a regular visitor, a friend one can expect to see often and trust. I like to make tea for my husband and me. At midday we take our tea outside and sit on our bench, our backs against the wall of the house. Neither of us wants pillows; I tell my daughters and sons that they are soft—those beach chairs of theirs. Imagine beach chairs here in New Mexico, so far from any ocean! The bench feels strong to us, not uncomfortable. The tea warms us inside, the sun on the outside. I joke with my husband; I say we are part of the house: the adobe gets baked, and so do we. For the most part we say nothing, though. It is enough to sit and be part of God's world. We hear the birds talking to each other, and are grateful they come as close to us as they do; all the more reason to keep our tongues still and hold ourselves in one place. We listen to cars going by and wonder who is rushing off. A car to us is a mystery. The young understand a car. They cannot imagine themselves not driving. They have not the interest we had in horses. Who is to compare one lifetime with another, but a horse is alive and one loves a horse and is loved by a horse. Cars come and go so fast. One year they command all eyes. The next year they are a cause for shame. The third year they must be thrown away without the slightest regret. I may exaggerate, but not much!

5   "My moods are like the church bell on Sunday: way up, then down, then up again—and often just as fast. I make noises, too; my husband says he can hear me smiling and hear me turning sour. When I am sour I am really sour—sweet milk turned bad. Nothing pleases me. I am more selfish than my sister. She bends with the wind. I push my heels into the ground and won't budge. I know enough to frown at myself, but not enough to change. There was a time when I tried hard. I would talk to myself as if I was the priest. I would promise myself that tomorrow I would be different. I suppose only men and women can fool themselves that way; an animal knows better. Animals are themselves. We are always trying to be better—and often we end up even worse than we were to start with.

6   "But now, during the last moments of life, I think I have learned a little wisdom. I can go for days without an upset. I think I dislike our priest because he reminds me of myself. I have his long forefinger, and I can clench my fist like him and pound the table and pour vinegar on people with my remarks. It is no good to be like that. A man is lucky; it is in his nature to fight or preach. A woman should be peaceful. My mother used to say all begins the day we are born: some are born on a clear, warm day; some when it is cloudy and stormy. So, it is a consolation to find myself easy to live with these days. And I have found an answer to the few moods I still get. When I have come back from giving the horses each a cube or two of sugar, I give myself the same. I am an old horse who needs something sweet to give her more faith in life!

7   "The other day I thought I was going to say goodbye to this world. I was hanging up some clothes to dry. I love to do that, then stand back and watch and listen to the wind go through the socks or the pants or the dress, and see the sun warm them and make them smell fresh. I had dropped a few clothes-pins, and was picking them up, when suddenly I could not catch my breath, and a sharp pain seized me over my chest. I tried hard to stand up, but I couldn't. I wanted to scream but I knew there was no one nearby to hear. My husband had gone to the store. I sat down on the ground and waited. It was strong, the pain; and there was no one to tell about it. I felt as if someone had lassoed me and was pulling the rope tighter and tighter. Well here you are, an old cow, being taken in by the good Lord; that is what I thought.

"I looked at myself, sitting on the ground. For a second I was my old self again—worrying about how I must have appeared there, worrying about my dress, how dirty it would get to be. This is no place for an old lady, I thought—only for one of my little grandchildren, who love to play out here, build their castles of dirt, wetted down with water I give to them. Then more pain; I thought I had about a minute of life left. I said my prayers. I said goodbye to the house. I pictured my husband in my mind: fifty-seven years of marriage. Such a good man! I said to myself that I might not see him ever again; surely God would take him into Heaven, but as for me, I have no right to expect that outcome. Then I looked up to the sky and waited. 8

"My eye caught sight of a cloud. It was darker than the rest. It was alone. It was coming my way. The hand of God, I was sure of it! So that is how one dies. All my life, in the spare moments a person has, I wondered how I would go. Now I knew. Now I was ready. I thought I would soon be taken up to the cloud and across the sky I would go, and that would be that. But the cloud kept moving, and soon it was no longer above me, but beyond me; and I was still on my own land, so dear to me, so familiar after all these years. I can't be dead, I thought to myself, if I am here and the cloud is way over there, and getting further each second. Maybe the next cloud—but by then I had decided God had other things to do. Perhaps my name had come up, but He had decided to call others before me, and get around to me later. Who can ever know His reasons? Then I spotted my neighbor walking down the road, and I said to myself that I would shout for him. I did, and he heard. But you know, by the time he came I had sprung myself free. Yes, that is right, the pain was all gone. 9

"He helped me up, and he was ready to go find my husband and bring him back. No, I told him, no; I was all right, and I did not want to risk frightening my husband. He is excitable. He might get some kind of attack himself. I went inside and put myself down on our bed and waited. For an hour—it was that long, I am sure—my eyes stared at the ceiling, held on to it for dear life. I thought of what my life had been like: a simple life, not a very important one, maybe an unnecessary one. I am sure there are better people, men and women all over the world, who have done more for their neighbors and yet not lived as long as I have. I felt ashamed for a few minutes: all the complaints I'd made to myself and to my family, when the truth has been that my fate has been to live a long and healthy life, to have a good and loyal husband, and to bring two sons and three daughters into this world. I thought of the five children we had lost, three before they had a chance to take a breath. I wondered where in the universe they were. In the evening sometimes, when I go to close loose doors that otherwise complain loudly all night, I am likely to look at the stars and feel my long-gone infants near at hand. They are far off, I know; but in my mind they have become those stars—very small, but shining there bravely, no matter how cold it is so far 10 up. If the stars have courage, we ought to have courage; that is what I was thinking, as I so often have in the past—and just then he was there, my husband, calling my name and soon looking into my eyes with his.

11   "I'm all right, I told him. He didn't know what had happened; our neighbor had sealed his lips, as I told him to do. But my husband knows me, so he knew I looked unusually tired; and he couldn't be easily tricked by me. The more I told him I'd just worked too hard, that is all, the more he knew I was holding something back. Finally, I pulled my ace card. I pretended to be upset by his questions and by all the attention he was giving me. I accused him: why do you make me want to cry, why do you wish me ill, with those terrible thoughts of yours? I am not ill! If you cannot let me rest without thinking I am, then God have mercy on you for having such an imagination! God have mercy! with the second plea to our Lord, he was beaten and silent. He left me alone. I was about to beg him to come back, beg his forgiveness. But I did not want him to bear the burden of knowing; he would not rest easy by day or by night. This way he can say to himself: she has always been cranky, and she will always be cranky, so thank God her black moods come only now and then—a spell followed by the bright sun again.

12   "I will say what I think happened: I came near going, then there was a change of heart up there in Heaven, so I have a few more days, or weeks, or months, or years—who knows? As for a doctor, I have never seen one, so why start now? Here we are so far away from a hospital. We have no money. Anglos don't like us, anyway: we are the poor ones, the lost ones. My son tells me the Anglos look down on us—old people without education and up in the hills, trying to scrape what we can from the land, and helped only by our animals. No matter; our son is proud of us. He is proud to stay here with us. He says that if he went to the city he would beg for work and be told no, no, no: eventually he might be permitted to sweep someone's floor. Better to hold on to one's land. Better to fight it out with the weather and the animals.

13   "Again I say it: doctors are for others. My mother and my aunt delivered my children. I once went to see a nurse; she worked for the school and she told me about my children—the diseases they get. Thank you, I said. Imagine: she thought I knew nothing about bringing up children, or about the obstacles God puts in their way to test them and make them stronger for having gone through a fever, a rash, some pain. No, I will see no nurse and no doctor. They are as far from here as the stars. Oh, that is wrong; they are much farther. The stars I know and recognize and even call by name. They are my names, of course; I don't know what others call the stars. Is it wrong to do that? Perhaps I should ask the priest. Perhaps the stars are God's to name, not ours to treat like pets—by addressing them familiarly. But it is too late; my sins have been recorded, and I will soon enough pay for each and every one of them."

Lives in Review:
Biographical Essays

HENRY MITCHELL

Eudora Welty:
Storyteller of the South

Henry Mitchell (b. 1923), like Ms. Welty, is a Southerner. He grew up in Memphis and spent seven years at the University of Virginia, where he left law school without a degree. For fifteen years he was a reporter for the Memphis Commercial Appeal, *and then edited* The Delta Review. *Since 1970 he has written feature articles and garden columns for the* Washington Post, *some of which have been collected as* The Essential Earthman *(1981). Mitchell has been praised for writing about gardening the way "Melville wrote about whales. He knows the concrete and technical lore . . . and he is given to linking the homely details with intimations of the eternal."*

Mitchell uses the same techniques in his portrait of Eudora Welty, grande dame of American letters, to which he brings, as a Newspaper Guild citation says, "elegant writing, wit and knowledge to subjects too often dealt with in pedestrian style." This elegant essay is very complex and more "literary" than most newspaper articles. Mitchell begins with a defiantly "down home" characterization of his subject: "she has never taken to prideful airs." Then follows a deceptively casual, rambling, anecdotal account of a couple of days spent with a friend who happens to be an excellent cook and the best writer in Hinds County, Mississippi, and quite possibly in the entire United States. But within this fabric are woven book reviews, literary history and criticism, the financial history of Welty's publications, even a polite argument between Mitchell and Welty about which writers have influenced her the most—all the while maintaining a personal, intimate atmosphere. The essay only seems to ramble; it is integrated by themes introduced, then dropped, then reintroduced and developed a few paragraphs later—roses, wildflowers, Welty's mother, characters in her novels—which, like the roses, are worth taking risks for.

JACKSON, MISS.—Some say Eudora Welty writes best of all, in all Hinds County, but she has never taken to prideful airs. Others say she's the best in all central Mississippi or all America. 1

"Shoot!" she says, or "Foot!" when the paid or, as you might say, store-bought critics start up their steady songs of praise. 2

"Now Eudora," a friend once said to her, "how come you read those reviews. Lots of writers don't read reviews at all." 3

"I know a lot of writers that don't," she said, "but I do. I've got too much curiosity not to." 4

Which is, as the Lord knows, true. Miss Welty has more curiosity than a tiger cat. Besides, though she won't exactly say so, it's fairly nice to pick up a 5 paper or magazine and see them having consistent and urgent fits about both your last two books. She writes them for hours off and on in her bedroom right here in Jackson and they are, as some would say, a wonder to behold.

6   One fellow in the *Washington Post* (writer Reynolds Price) just flung up his arms in print and said there's no point comparing *Losing Battles* (1970) to other American novels. He suggested, for starters, you might compare it with "The Tempest" by the late W. Shakespeare, and then just took it on from there.

7   "Yes, I know he did," said Miss Welty when I had the pleasure of her company and her cooking for two days recently, "and I am really going to speak to him about it. Shakespeare is a bit much."

8   He was the worst, the *Post* reviewer, for making a decent person blush. The paper down in Houston just said the book was a "gigantic achievement" and at the *New York Times* they only spoke of their "general rejoicing" though they did add Miss Welty has the surest comic sense of any American writer alive. In Philadelphia where the cautious restraining Quaker influence is still felt they modestly called it a masterpiece and let it go at that.

9   "I do like to read blurbs," said Miss Welty. "And when I go through a book I look unconsciously for good ones."

10   "Ain't she kind of a recluse?" asked the cab driver that eventually showed up to carry me to the Welty house in the first place. He pronounced it "reckless." The idea of a reckless Eudora Welty is something to make a dog laugh. Reckless she is not. But then recluse she is not, either. It would irk the fire out of her if she knew that cab driver thought she was that.

11   It's a rare day she doesn't meet a friend (and when you're born and live 60 years in Mississippi and went to school and are still in the same not-very-big town, you have enough friends to get by on) for a small toddy or lunch or supper. Usually it's at home—theirs or hers—because Southern people are not much for wandering about in strange restaurants except in New Orleans where their origins are different.

12   Miss Welty's family had no Deep South background though she is famous for her Southern characters. Her father came to Jackson from Ohio and her mother from West Virginia. But Miss Welty has lived all her life in Jackson; she won a holiday from school once for learning to spell all 82 counties of Mississippi along with the county seats, and some of them are tricky—Oktibbeha, for instance. It is also known with certainty she used to purchase penny Tootsie Rolls and with equal certainty that even then she had a care with her writing and delighted classmates.

13   She still lives in the new Welty brick house (built scarcely 50 years ago), with spacious 1920-generous halls. Some of the walls have cracked—Miss Welty says Jackson is built on marl over shifting sands. It is somewhat like a time-lapse earthquake: You resign yourself to repairing cracked walls.

14   Miss Welty was pitched right out of a Jackson restaurant recently, though, which shows among other things she is no recluse. It was all because

she was hostess to two young men with Jesus haircuts, and long hair is something the restaurant owner has a real thing about.

"But maybe you were mistaken—maybe you misunderstood the wait- 15 ress," somebody asked Miss Welty since, after all, a restaurant is no more likely to throw Miss Welty out in Jackson than Alice Roosevelt at the Rive Gauche, it being an honor in both cases.

"I did not misunderstand the waitress," said Eudora, with just a slight 16 rise of tone, as if to say she did not go around misunderstanding anything humans are likely to do. "She said very plainly, 'You all will have to go.'" But she did say not to feel bad about it—they pitched customers out all the time for having long hair and the wonder of it is they have any customers left, barber styles being what they are.

The humor was not lost, even at the time, on Miss Welty, but there are 17 times to express anger so she fired off a letter to the *Clarion Ledger* about it. The young guests weren't drunk or disorderly or doing anything but sitting there like unshorn lambs hoping for a shrimp cocktail. Eudora won't go back.

She stated her position right there in the letter. She acted and now need 18 not dwell on it further. She has no grudges. Or if she has, it's not about restaurant owners but grand and immortal enemies like death, yellow leaves or nematodes:

"You wouldn't know it," she said, "but this garden was once beautiful. 19 My mother really kept after it." Both mother and daughter were fine garden- ers—the ones that really know, as distinct from the ones that just have masses of color. They used to read V. Sackville-West in the *Observer* and Elizabeth Lawrence and so on. And from those excellent rungs they went right on up, to a garden that really meant something.

The year the nematodes came things mainly died. Mrs. Welty was ill— 20 she died in recent years—and Miss Welty was writing *Losing Battles* at home with her and two nurses and laughing a great deal (the book is beyond grief and funny as owls in heaven) and the nurses did not approve of anything.

And right in the middle of it the nematodes did in the roses, which had 21 been packed in that garden tight as a trunk, but nothing that could be tried availed at all. Miss Welty planted a crabapple at the beginning rosebed to keep her mother from being too much aware of disasters in the main plant- ing.

Ordinarily an attack on her roses would have brought Mrs. Welty right 22 out of the kitchen, as they say, but she was past those battles then. Many treasures went. The old "Gloire de Dijon" and "Fortune's Yellow Climbers" succumbed, and so did even the great "Mermaid." But "Safrano," the old tea rose, is blooming yet, and "Silver Moon" pulled through and so did "Lady Banks."

Her characters in her stories are like the roses—some make it, some 23 don't. Her first story, "Death of a Traveling Salesman" (1936, when Miss Welty was 24), is about a man whose vehicle doesn't work, who sees nothing the way it really is and who dies without having made much sense of himself or anything else in the world.

24   Her last novel, *The Optimist's Daughter,* is also about people who are trying to figure out who they are (and who are commonly confused and mistaken) and one point of the story is that there is little difference among classes once the accents, the intonations and the other superficial marks of caste are allowed for.

25   That is why, probably, the story of Phoenix Jackson (in *The Green Curtain* decades ago) is still admired, though few of its readers have any direct experience with the heroine, a very old black woman walking to and from the doctor's to get medicine for her grandson who swallowed lye.

26   Some of her readers think *Losing Battles* is her most typical and best book, though critics seem to keep hinting it's a tour de force.

27   It is the story of a white farming family in that part of Mississippi near the Tennessee-Alabama-Mississippi border. The time is the 1930s, the characters are of the poorest sort, but proud and self-reliant and highly conscious of the claims and bonds of family.

28   The author thinks nobody would believe it, if the setting were the present, and that is why it is set 40 years ago. "I wanted the characters to be down to bedrock—no money, no education, no nothing, except themselves—the rest being all cleared away to begin with."

29   Even so, the characters are complicated, and most of them misunderstand their roles. *Losing Battles* is partly about the battles they lose, and the title is partly ironic, about the battles they win, sometimes without knowing it.

30   The hero is named Jack, scion of the family, who has been sent to Parchman Prison for no good reason and who returns in time for the annual family reunion.

31   If a comparison to Shakespeare seems extravagant, and it does, one man who objected to that extravagance found himself comparing it to "The Iliad" and *Don Quixote.*

32   "It reminds me of 'The Iliad' he said."

33   "*Everything* reminds *me* of 'The Iliad,' " Miss Welty replied.

34   The speech of the narrative, the plainness and elegance of the language, the stripped quality of the action, the intense quality of the personal relationships and the occasional heightening of the dialogue for emotional effect—even to the extent of introducing an archaic note—all reflect the general method of Homer more than Shakespeare.

35   The comic element of this and many other stories is more like Damon Runyon or Cervantes than Mark Twain.

36   But just as one critic risked seeming like a fool by comparing it to Shakespeare's "Tempest," many readers seem a trifle foolish recalling (as they read it) Cervantes and Homer. Just as the reviewers seemed generally to think in large terms and high precedents, so readers often seem to react as if Miss Welty were an oracle or a priestess rather than a good storyteller.

"I got a letter last week from a man in Taiwan," she said, "who for   37
reasons best known to himself wanted me to be 'the grandmother' for his
children. It's a warm nice letter, but how do you answer anything like that? I
don't want to be anybody's damn grandmother.

"And here's a letter from a nun—I think nuns write letters a good bit—   38
complaining some story I wrote is unfair to Campfire Girls or Girl Scouts. I
don't know how to answer that. Here's another one, from a nun in India who
has fallen in love with a priest and wants my advice. How would I know? I do
so wish these people well, but I have no idea how to write them or even how
to begin."

Another letter recently came from a nice person who wanted to know   39
why her stories had not dealt with the Jews in the Mississippi ghettos.

"We have Jews in Mississippi as you know, but they don't live in ghettos.   40
They are more likely to be mayor of the town. When I get letters that
bewilder me—well, I'm thinking of getting some letter paper that says 'You
Just Can't Get There From Here.'"

But what many of the letters have in common is an unspoken assumption   41
that Miss Welty understands all there is to understand about virtually any
human relationship.

Her last two novels, like all her work, began as short stories. *Losing*   42
Battles was meant to end when Jack returned from prison to join the family
reunion, but Miss Welty had fallen hopelessly in love with him by the time he
made his first appearance on page 71, too many characters had already built
him up as a hero.

So she allowed herself a few more pages to deal with Jack—436 pages, to   43
be exact—and the result is her novel that she still thinks of in terms of a story
rather than a grand panorama of the world.

Her last novel, issued this spring, *The Optimist's Daughter,* also began as a   44
short story that wouldn't stop.

"It's the first thing I've ever done that has direct autobiographical infor-   45
mation in it. I'm not sure that was right—the mother is based on my mother.
The boys are her brothers—I think I may have added an extra one—and the
West Virginia part is set in her own country."

The most notable thing in the book is a prolonged and lyrical coda (". . .   46
His white shirt would shine for a long time almost without moving in her
sight, like Venus in the sky of Mount Salus, while grandmother, mother and
little girl sat outlasting the light, waiting for him to climb home. . .").

Few things are riskier than "fine writing," but Miss Welty has never been   47
afraid to risk it. She spoke once in conversation of plant explorers who go to
Nepal and Sikkim, risking their lives to introduce alpine flowers to gardens.

"Now that's something—discovering new primroses—that's worth tak-   48
ing trouble with, worth risking something for," she said.

She seemed to set the plant explorers bringing garden treasures from the   49
Himalayas over against the ordinary world we all live in everyday: "Words
almost don't mean anything anymore. The meanings, anything can be a lie

now. It doesn't make any difference whether something is fair or makes sense."

50   The decline of personal courtesy, the increasing power of pressure and loudness, the reliance on shadowy image rather than substantial reality, all disturb her.

51   But nothing, apparently, disturbs her comic sense, even when she alludes to politics, and she goes no farther than an allusion: "All these people, come to think of it, so many politicians, people like Napoleon, are not much taller than short."

52   It was pointed out you couldn't say Lyndon Johnson was short.

53   "No," she said. "I guess you'd have to say he was not much taller than tall."

54   As a now-celebrated writer, Miss Welty tries to give herself time to think and feel—she has cut out lecturing since she no longer has to do it to earn money, and she does not usually see reporters, not out of snobbery, but because she is never sure what to say to them and because there is only so much time in life.

55   But if a reporter does get a chance to see her, she will talk for 12 hours and cook supper as well. She is fairly sure in the back of her mind that a visitor would rather eat a hamburger in the local Horror Room than dine at ease at home with Eudora Welty, but once she is persuaded that her visitor will make do with Eudora Welty's food as readily as the local hash house, she spreads a feast of cold consomme with avocado puree and sour cream in it and roast beef and other sliced meats and fine cheeses and a salad and tomatoes dead ripe and red as an Indian Cling (the peach of Southern childhood memories) and strong fresh coffee.

56   It tasted great—no danger of confusing it with something out of a vending machine.

57   Not only does she like to cook, and to cook without any interference or "help," she also likes to talk and refuses to let anybody help her with the dishes.

58   In her own reading, apart from garden books, cookbooks and virtually any other kind of book, she has a special enthusiasm for mystery novels or whodunits and for dictionaries. She has the great Oxford English Dictionary and wastes many delectable hours with it just for fun.

59   She likes poetry, especially Yeats, Donne and Marvell, but says, "I'm really afraid I'm not on the right wavelength for modern poetry. I'm a thoroughly visual person. I have to have a sensuous—is that right, sensuous?—yes, I always have to think—a sensuous image."

60   The fondness for visual images is constant throughout her stories. She compares such visual, if unlikely, things as fading red roses to the color of a bird dog's tongue and the locust's evening song to the sound of seed being poured into a tin bucket.

61   But always her taste for comedy breaks through. Apropos of nothing

(except the American belief in signs) she mentioned her favorite sign, once seen in a train station: "No laughing or loud talking while train is in station."

And in spite of the intense admiration of many readers—the ones that ask her advice about falling in love with a priest, for instance—she sees no sign of becoming a "cult" writer with her own set of worshipers.   62

"I'd hate to be a sort of cult figure, and I've never seen any signs of it. It would be dreadful. First you'd begin to believe it, then you'd get absurd and stupid. I've never been a big seller, not really a popular writer, and most people never heard of me."   63

It's true that only in the last two years has she been able to support herself—in her 60s—by writing. Her famous short stories at first were turned down endlessly and then published cheap. Her collection *The Green Curtain,* with such famous stories as "The Worn Path," "Why I Live at the P.O." and "The Petrified Man," has been in print since the early '40s but has sold only 6,700 copies in its first three decades and first two editions.   64

As Miss Welty's agent, Diarmuid Russell of New York, observed in *Shenandoah,* the literary quarterly, that is "not riches for author or publisher," or, for that matter, agent.   65

"I couldn't live without Diarmuid," said Miss Welty. (The name is pronounced Dermott.) He became her agent in 1940 and she's never had another. Russell is son of the writer A. E., and, incidentally, is an authority on American wild flowers.   66

"When he offered to be my agent, I didn't even know there *were* agents. I just sent my stories off to magazines and when they came back, I sent them off somewhere else. It's still the best way. It's how everybody gets started. But now with legal things—permission to reprint and overseas rights—I could never keep up with all that.   67

"Until my last two books I never could live on just my writing. I was very lucky, I was able to lecture, and schools were good at getting me to come, sometimes for a one-shot lecture, sometimes longer. So I was always able to manage, but I never made any money. There was *The New Yorker,* though. They have the idea it's the writers who should make some money from the magazine. They pay well; yes, even when they know they could get a story for less. But of course the trouble is, you never know if you can write a story. . . .   68

"You can't time that kind of work to fit in with when you need the money."   69

From one *New Yorker* story Miss Welty bought two Fords, one for a niece and one for herself.   70

Somebody once suggested that if she drove about in an amazing automobile and issued epigrams on television once a month she'd soon be thought an oracle.   71

"Oh, no, I've already tested that in a way. I had a 16-year-old Ford. It ran fine, I still don't know why I turned it in. But anyway, even when I had it, nobody thought I was an oracle."   72

73   When she sees her books newly issued she feels uneasy—"I'm never prepared for the reviews. I'm never prepared for anything, I mean I have no idea what people will think of the book. When I see my book for sale, I realize here's something I've been doing privately in Jackson, and now suddenly people anywhere can see it, what only I've seen. I feel very vulnerable."

74   Her own favorite author is Jane Austen, a writer she returns to again and again. Unlike many Southern writers she has no special taste for Milton; she took a course in Milton years ago and has barely read him since.

75   "Are you trying to say you're not a Puritan?" she was asked.

76   "No, I'm a Puritan, all right. But I am saying if you substitute Jane Austen instead of Milton, you'll come closer. Sorry."

77   No sketch of a Southern writer in the past century has ever been written, so far as I know, without the writer adoring Milton. It was suggested that maybe Milton's influence is so pervasive that she has absorbed by osmosis.

78   "Sorry. Jane Austen."

79   But then writers often are not aware of major influences, as we all know.

80   "And I've never read one word of James Fenimore Cooper. Yes, he's having a revival. I think that's sad. As if he had to be revived. I know a literary reputation is a fragile thing. Somebody told me once, watch out when a woman writer passes 50, they all turn on you. Sometimes I think they decide, 'Oh, we're so damned tired of saying she writes well.' "

81   She grinned and rose from her chair to fetch a private literary treasure somebody sent her—a student's essay question on Shakespeare. The allusion to critics made her think of Shakespeare and her somewhat saucy humor made her think not of some great scene in a play but of a Georgia boy's essay. It was clear the youth did not know Shakespeare from a sack of vanilla beans but he did understand he was supposed to say something grand, so he wound up:

82   "Some say William was a moment without a tomb, star of the poet, swan of the lake."

83   Miss Welty, reading it, laughed almost to limpness.

84   "Moment without a tomb—now there's a title for you," she said between gasps. (Henry Miller once said he loved her stories but not her titles.) She is a connoisseur of titles and names. Naming her characters is very difficult for her.

85   "There are some marvelous names right here in Mississippi. I used to take a lot of the state newspapers and in the old days I loved to read the *Oxford Eagle*. There was one woman whose name kept turning up there, but I always felt any name around Oxford was automatically the property of Mr. Faulkner. He had such perfect names. I don't know if this is true, but somebody once told me they mentioned a name to Mr. Faulkner and he said, 'Yes, I know the name well. Can hardly wait for her to die' so he could use it."

86   Miss Welty now is thinking of publishing a book of lectures, but is not sure—would there really be anything fresh and fine, would there really be any point to it?

"Well, with two sensationally received novels in a row in two years, had   87
you ever thought of writing a flop just for a change of pace?" somebody asked
her.

"What would really bother me was if I wrote a flop and it was praised—   88
just out of habit. And I think things like that can happen."

Milton, of course, would have thought so, too.   89

Questions

1. Biographical portraits often contain extensive quotations from both the subject and others, as does this portrait of Welty. What does Mitchell do to make these quotations mesh comfortably with one another and with his own writing? What does his down-home, folksy language ("she has never taken to prideful airs," paragraph 1; "making a decent person blush," paragraph 8) convey about his subject, one of America's major authors?

2. This essay covers various aspects of Welty's writing—her literary reputation, how she writes, literary history and the response of critics and scholars to her work, her earnings from writing—interspersed with discussions of Welty's childhood, her relationship with her mother and with the townspeople in Jackson, Mississippi, her cooking and gardening, and a myriad of other subjects. What is the organizational pattern of such a seemingly casual essay? How do such diverse topics contribute to a portrait of the subject?

3. For what sorts of readers is this portrait, originally published in *The Washington Post*, intended? Must one have read at least some of Welty's works to understand it? to appreciate the personality presented here? Or is this portrait self-contained?

4. What is Mitchell's attitude toward Welty as a person? toward her writing? Does this portrait compel you to share his attitude? Does it make you want to read her books? . Why or why not?

ALDEN WHITMAN

Albert Schweitzer

Whitman is best known for the elegant biographical portraits he composed as chief obituary writer at The New York Times *between 1965 and his retirement in 1978. Born in Nova Scotia in 1913, and educated at Harvard (B.A., '34), Whitman began his journalistic career in 1943 with the New York* Herald Tribune, *where he worked as a copy editor until joining the* Times *staff as a reporter in 1951. His books include* Early American Labor Parties *(1944),* Portrait: Adlai E. Stevenson *(1965),* The End of a Presidency *(1971), and two collections of* Times *obituaries,* The Obituary Book *(1971) and* Come to Judgment *(1980).*

For Schweitzer's portrait to appear in a book called Come to Judgment *is doubly meaningful. Given Schweitzer's dedication to religious values, "judgment" resounds with apocalyptic overtones, but it also reflects Whitman's secular perspective of a journalist concerned with writing an obituary that will offer some "final" judgment, balanced and public, of a man widely regarded as a saint at the time of his death. Whitman even illustrates these judgments by using numerous quotations from his subject. Indeed, he devotes the entire first half of the essay to assessing Schweitzer's achievements; only after that does Whitman, with a skillful transition at the end of paragraph 15, go back to review Schweitzer's life in chronological order. Whitman's generally favorable but candid portrait obliges us to ponder the question, How does a person, seriously flawed in some ways, achieve secular sainthood?*

1   The concept of man's redemption through beneficent activity—the theme of Part II of Goethe's *Faust,* a metaphysical poem much admired by Albert Schweitzer—threaded through his long, complex, and sometimes curious life. With Faust himself he could join in saying:

> This sphere of earthly soil
> Still gives us room for lofty doing.
> Astounding plans e'en now are brewing:
> I feel new strength for bolder toil. . . .
> The Deed is everything, the Glory naught.

"You must give some time to your fellow man," Schweitzer counseled in paraphrase. "Even if it's a little thing, do something for those who have need of a man's help, something for which you get no pay but the privilege of doing it." This was an essential of his ethical system, more formally known as Reverence for Life, which he elaborated before his death at the age of ninety. Fittingly, he died in Gabon—formerly part of French Equatorial Africa—at the jungle-compound hospital that he had established and maintained against great odds.

2   Like Goethe, on whose life and works he was an authority, Schweitzer came near to being a comprehensive man. Theologian, musicologist, virtuoso on the organ, physician and surgeon, missionary, lecturer, writer, and philosopher with his own system of ethics: he was all these things besides being the builder and animating force of the famous hospital complex at Lambaréné. He was eclectic, and to a marked degree. Franco-German in culture, yet cosmopolitan, he drew deeply from eighteenth-century sources, especially Bach in music and Kant in philosophy. At the same time he was a child of the late nineteenth century; he accepted its creature comforts, but rejected its complacent attitudes toward progress. In line with the twentieth century, he sought to put religion on a rational footing and comprehend the advances of science; yet he was a foe to materialism and to twentieth-century standards of material success.

3   As a person, Schweitzer was an equally curious mixture. Widely honored with degrees, citations, scrolls, medals, special stamps, even the Nobel Prize for Peace in 1952, he seemed oblivious to panoply. He did not preen himself or utter cosmic statements at the drop of a cause. Instead, he seemed to many observers a simple, almost rustic man who dressed in rumpled clothing, suffered fools gladly, stated fundamental verities patiently and paternally, and

worked unobtrusively. In this respect, he was undoubtedly made more of by cultists than he was willing to make of himself, although he was by no means a man with a weak ego. Some of his more ardent admirers insisted that he was a jungle saint, even a modern Christ. But Schweitzer would have none of this adulation; he was quite satisfied that his spiritual life was its own reward, that he was redeemed by works. For him the search for the good life had profound religious implications. "Anyone can rescue his human life," he once said, "who seizes every opportunity of being a man by means of personal action, however unpretending, for the good of fellow men who need the help of a fellow man." He sought to exemplify the idea that man, through good works, can be in the world and in God at one and the same time.

For all his self-abnegation, Schweitzer had a bristly character, at least in   4
his later years, a formidable sense of his own importance to Lambaréné, and a do-good paternalism toward Africans that smacked more of the nineteenth than of the twentieth century. For example, John Gunther, the American journalist, got a dressing-down from Schweitzer for writing that he re-sembled Buffalo Bill and also, perhaps, for implying that he did not know what was going on in nationalist Africa. If Schweitzer was thin-skinned to criticism from irreverent journalists, he heard little of it at Lambaréné, where his proprietorship was unquestioned. Not only did he design the station, but he helped build it with his own hands. His coworkers were quite familiar with the businesslike and sometimes grumpy and brusque Schweitzer in a solar hat, who hurried along the construction of a building by gingering up the native craftsmen with a sharp: "Allez-vous OPP! Allez-vous OPP-opp. Hupp, upp, OPP!"

When Schweitzer was in residence at Lambaréné, virtually nothing was   5
done without consulting him. Once, for instance, he all but halted the sta-tion's work when he received a letter from a Norwegian child seeking a feather from Parsifal, his pet pelican. He insisted on seeing to it personally that the youngster got a prompt and touching reply from his pen before work was permitted to resume. His autocracy, however, was more noticeable as his years advanced and as his medical assistants grew less awed by him. He regarded most Africans as children or primitives. It was said that he had scarcely ever talked with an adult African on adult terms. He had little but contempt for the nationalist movement, for his attitudes were firmly grounded in nineteenth-century benevolence. Although thousands of Afri-cans called him "le grand docteur," others plastered his village with signs, "Schweitzer, go home!"

"At this stage," Schweitzer said in 1963, "Africans have little need for   6
advanced training. They need very elementary schools run along the old missionary plan with the Africans going to school for a few hours every day and then going back to the fields. Agriculture, not science or industrializa-tion, is their greatest need." His attitude was sharply expressed in a story he liked to tell of his orange trees. "I let the Africans pick all the fruit they want,"

he said. "You see, the good Lord has protected the trees. He made the Africans too lazy to pick them bare." Although his views on Africa were sadly out of date, he did what no man had done before him—healed thousands and welded world attention to Africa's many plights. A jungle saint he may not have been; a jungle pioneer he surely was.

7   Whatever Schweitzer's personal idiosyncrasies, he constructed a profound and enduring ethical system expressed in the principle *Ehrfurcht vor dem Leben,* or Reverence for Life. It is conceivably the only philosophical concept ever to spring to life amid a herd of hippopotamuses. According to Schweitzer's account, he had been baffled in getting an answer to the question: Is it at all possible to find a real and permanent foundation in thought for a theory of the universe that shall be both ethical and affirmative of the world and life? The answer came in a flash of mystic illumination in September 1915, as he was steaming up the Ogoué River in Africa. Late in the third day of his journey he was on deck thinking and writing. "At the very moment when, at sunset, we were making our way through a herd of hippopotamuses, there flashed upon my mind, unforeseen and unsought, the phrase 'Reverence for Life.'

8   "The iron door had yielded," he went on, "the path in the thicket had become visible. Now I had my way to the idea in which world- and life-affirmation and ethics are contained side by side! Now I knew that the world-view of ethical world- and life-affirmation, together with its ideal of civilization, is founded in thought."

9   Schweitzer's ethical system, elucidated at length in *The Philosophy of Civilization,* is boundless in its domain and in its demands. He summarized it once by saying, "A man is ethical only when life, as such, is sacred to him, that of plants and animals as that of his fellow men, and when he devotes himself helpfully to all life that is in need of help." "Let me give you a definition of ethics," he wrote on another occasion. "It is good to maintain and further life; it is bad to damage and destroy life. And this ethic, profound, universal, has the significance of a religion. It *is* religion."

10   Called upon to be specific about Reverence for Life, he explained that the concept

> does not allow the scholar to live for science alone, even if he is very useful to the community in so doing. It does not permit the artist to exist only for his art, even if it gives the inspiration to many by its means. It refuses to let the businessman imagine that he fulfills all legitimate demands in the course of his business activity. It demands from all that they should sacrifice a portion of their own lives for others.

11   Schweitzer earnestly sought to live his philosophy. He was genuinely proud of his medical and missionary station at Lambaréné. He had scratched it out of the jungle beginning in 1913; and, although the station was many

times beset by adversities that would have discouraged a less dedicated man, it had grown at his death to more than 70 buildings, 350 beds, and a leper village of 200 persons.

The compound was staffed by five unpaid physicians, seven nurses, and thirteen volunteer helpers. Visitors who equated cleanliness and tidiness with medicine were horrified by the station, for every patient was encouraged to bring one or two members of his family to cook for him in the ditches beside the wards. Babies, even in the leper enclave, dropped toys into the dust of unpaved streets, then popped the playthings into their mouths. Animals wandered freely in and out of the compound, including Schweitzer's pet parrot (which was not taught to talk because that would lower its dignity) and a hippopotamus that once invaded the vegetable garden. Lambaréné resembled not so much a hospital as a native village where physicians cared for the sick. Actually, Schweitzer preferred (and planned) it in this fashion on the ground that the natives would shun an elaborate, shiny, and impersonal institution. The compound even lacked electricity, except for the operating and dental rooms, and members of the staff read by kerosene lamp. Of course it had no telephone or radio or airstrip. 12

His view that "simple people need simple healing methods," however it might have outraged medical sophisticates, won for Lambaréné a tremendous measure of native confidence. Thousands flocked there; thousands responded to Schweitzer's sermons as well as to his scalpel; for he believed that the good shepherd saves not only the animal but also his soul. Lambaréné was suffused with Reverence for Life to what some critics thought was an exaggerated degree. Mosquitoes were not swatted, nor pests and insects doused with chemicals; they were let alone, and humans put up with them. Indeed, building was often brought to a halt lest nests of ants be killed or disturbed. On the other hand, patients received splendid medical care; and few seemed to suffer greatly from the compound's lack of spit and polish. 13

Schweitzer's accomplishments are recognized even by his most caustic critics. One of them, Gerald McKnight, wrote in his book *Verdict on Schweitzer*: 14

> The temptation for Schweitzer to see Lambaréné as a place cut off from the world, in which he can preserve its original forms and so reject any theory of treatment or life other than his own, is understandable when one considers the enormous achievement he has attained in his own lifetime. He came to the Ogoué in 1913 when horses drew the buses of London and leprosy was considered an incurable scourge. Housed originally in the grounds of a mission, he chose to leave this comparative sanctuary for the unknown and forbidding regions of the jungle nearby.
>
> No doubt a wish to have absolute dominion over his hospital drove him to this course, linked with the inner purpose which had brought him to Africa, but it was none the less heroic. Today, the hospital has grown,

entirely under his hand and direction, into a sizable colony where between 500 and 600 people live in reasonable comfort. No greater tribute to his abilities as a conqueror of the jungle need be cited than the fact—regarded locally as something of a miracle—of his own survival.

15   Schweitzer came to French Equatorial Africa as a tall, handsome, broadly powerful young man with a shock of rich black hair, enormous mustaches, and a look of piercing determination in his bold eyes. The years thinned and grayed his hair (without making it less unruly); age seamed his face, shrank his frame, made him appear bandy-legged; time softened his eyes, made them less severe; but determination to make his life an "argument" for his ethical creed was as firm at ninety as it was on his thirtieth birthday, the day he decided to devote the rest of his life as a physician to the natives of Africa. Schweitzer's arrival at this decision was calculated, a step in a quest for a faith to live by. It was a search that had haunted him, driven him, since childhood.

16   Albert Schweitzer was born at Kayserberg, Haute Alsace (now Haut-Rhin), on January 14, 1875, not long after Germany had annexed the province from war-prostrate France. During that year his father, a Lutheran pastor, moved with his wife and eldest son to the neighboring village of Günsbach among the foothills of the Vosges. It was to this picture-book Franco-German village and its vineyards that Schweitzer would always return between periods of self-imposed exile in Africa. As a child he was frail and an indifferent student in everything but music, for which he showed the interest of a prodigy. He began to play the church organ at eight, when his feet barely reached the pedals. At eighteen he entered the University of Strasbourg as a student in theology, philosophy, and musical theory. By this time he had also studied the organ briefly in Paris under the legendary Charles-Marie Widor, who was so impressed with his pupil's talents that he taught him then and later without fee. He became a notable organist, especially in the works of Bach, and his recitals in Europe helped to finance his medical work in Africa.

17   Schweitzer's university life was interrupted by a year of compulsory military service in 1894, a period that proved crucial to his religious thinking and to his life's vocation. The moment of awakening came as he was reading Matthew 10 and 11 in Greek, chapters that contain Jesus' injunctions to his apostles, among them the one that commands, "Heal the sick, cleanse the lepers, raise the dead, cast out devils: freely ye have received, freely give," and the verse that urges men, "Take my yoke upon you, and learn from me; for I am meek and lowly in heart: and ye shall find rest unto your souls."

18   Schweitzer was struck not only by the application of these verses to himself, but even more by the overall content of the two chapters as expressed in Jesus' assertion that "the kingdom of heaven is at hand." These chapters started a chain of thought that resulted in *The Quest for the Historical Jesus*. Published in 1910, it at once established its author as an eminent, if controversial, theologian whose explosive ideas had a profound influence on con-

temporary religious thinking. He depicted Jesus as a man of his times who shared the eschatological ideas of late Judaism and who looked for an immediate end of the world. Jesus, Schweitzer contended, believed himself the Messiah who would rule in a new kingdom of God when the end came; at first Jesus believed that his Messianic reign would begin before his disciples returned from the teaching mission commanded of them in Matthew 10. When the world's end did not occur, according to Schweitzer's view, Jesus concluded that he must undergo an atoning sacrifice, and that the great transformation would take place on the cross. This, too, failed; hence, Schweitzer argued, the despairing cry, "My God, my God, why hast thou forsaken me?"

"The Jesus of Nazareth . . . who founded the kingdom of Heaven upon earth, and died to give his work the final consecration, never had any existence," he wrote. "He is a figure designed by rationalism, endowed with life by liberalism and clothed by modern theology in an historical garb." Schweitzer maintained, nonetheless, that Jesus' concepts are eternal. 19

> In reality, that which is eternal in the words of Jesus is due to the very fact that they are based on an eschatological world-view, and contain the expression of a mind for which the contemporary world with its historical and social circumstances no longer had any existence. They are appropriate, therefore, to any world, for in every world they raise the man who dares to meet their challenge, and does not turn them and twist them into meaninglessness, above his world and time, making him inwardly free, so that he is fitted to be, in his own world and in his own time, a simple channel of the power of Jesus.

While these beliefs were maturing in Schweitzer's mind, he continued his student life at Strasbourg and fixed with great precision the course of his future. In 1896, at the age of twenty-one, he pledged himself that he would give the following nine years to science and art and then devote himself to the service of suffering humanity. In those nine years he completed his doctoral thesis in philosophy, a study of Immanuel Kant's views on religion; studied the organ, again with Widor in Paris; won another doctorate in theology; was ordained a curate; taught theology and became principal of the faculty at Strasbourg; wrote *The Mystery of the Kingdom of God;* and, at Widor's urging, completed a study of the life and art of Johann Sebastian Bach. The English version, *J. S. Bach,* is a two-volume translation of the German text, itself an entire reworking of the first version written in French. It approaches Bach as a musician-poet and concentrates on his chorales, cantatas, and Passion music. Schweitzer presents Bach as a religious mystic, as cosmic as the forces of nature. Bach, he said, was chiefly a church composer. As such, and as a Lutheran, "it is precisely to the chorale that the work of Bach owes its greatness." 20

"The chorale not only puts in his possession the treasury of Protestant 21 music," Schweitzer wrote, "but also opens to him the riches of the Middle Ages and of the sacred Latin music from which the chorale itself came. From whatever direction he is considered Bach is, then, the last word in an artistic evolution which was prepared in the Middle Ages, freed and activated by the Reformation, and arrives at its full expression in the eighteenth century."

22   Turning to Bach's nonchurch music, Schweitzer said:

> The Brandenburg concertos are the purest product of Bach's polyphonic style. We really seem to see before us what the philosophy of all ages con- ceives as the fundamental mystery of things—that self-unfolding of the idea in which it creates its own opposite in order to overcome it, and so on and on until it finally returns to itself, having meanwhile traversed the whole of existence.

Schweitzer's probing conception of Bach created a sensation in its time. It still remains a classic study, not only for the detailed instructions it provides for the playing of Bach, but also for its challenging esthetic. As a virtuoso of the organ, Schweitzer brought to his playing a scholarship that was infused with romanticism, in which the printed note was sometimes ignored while the composer's pictorial poetry and symbolism were accentuated.

23   True to his pledge, Schweitzer turned from music and theology to service to others. On October 13, 1905, he posted letters from Paris to his parents and friends saying that at the start of the winter term he would become a medical student to prepare himself for the life of a physician in French Equatorial Africa. His friends objected vigorously, but he did not listen. This decision, like so many others in his life, was the product of religious medita- tion. He had pondered the meaning of the parable of Dives and Lazarus and its application to his times, and he had concluded that Dives represented opulent Europe, and Lazarus, with his open sores, the sick and helpless of Africa. Explaining his decision later in more mundane terms, Schweitzer said: "I wanted to be a doctor that I might be able to work without having to talk. For years I had been giving myself out in words. This new form of activity I could not represent to myself as talking about the religion of love, but only as an actual putting it into practice."

24   For seven years, from 1906 until he received his M.D. degree in Febru- ary 1913, Schweitzer studied medicine, but he did not entirely cut himself off from his other worlds. Attending the University of Strasbourg, he still served as curate at St. Nicholas, played concerts on the organ, conducted a heavy correspondence, and examined Pauline ideas, especially that of dying and being born again "in Jesus Christ." This last resulted in a book, *Paul and His Interpreters,* published in English in 1912. That same year he resigned his curateship and his posts at the university and married Hélène Bresslau, the daughter of a well-known Strasbourg historian. A scholar herself, she became a trained nurse in order to share her husband's life in Africa.

25   On Good Friday 1913, the couple set sail from Bordeaux for Africa,

where Schweitzer established a hospital on the grounds of the Lambaréné station of the Paris Missionary Society. The society, wary of Schweitzer's unorthodox religious views, had barred him from preaching at the station, but agreed to accept his medical skills. Lambaréné, on the Ogoué River a few miles from the Equator, is in the steaming jungle. Its climate is among the world's worst, with fiercely hot days, clammy nights, and seasonal torrents of rain. The natives had all the usual diseases, plus Hansen's disease (leprosy), dysentery, elephantiasis, sleeping sickness, malaria, yellow fever, and animal wounds. From the first, when the hospital was a broken-down hen coop, natives flocked to it on foot, by improvised stretcher, or by dugout canoe for medical attention.

Schweitzer had barely started to clear the jungle when World War I broke out. He and his wife, both German citizens, were interned as prisoners of war for four months, then released to continue the work of the hospital. In this time and the succeeding months he started to write the two-volume *The Philosophy of Civilization,* his masterwork in ethics, which was published in 1923. It is a historical review of ethical thought leading to his own original contribution of Reverence for Life as an effective basis for a civilized world. The book (and other of his writings) disputed the theory that human progress toward civilization was inevitable. He disagreed sharply with Aristotle that man's knowledge of right and wrong would surely lead him to make the right choices; he maintained, instead, that man must rationally formulate an ethical creed and then strive to put it into practice. In Reverence for Life, he concluded, "knowledge passes over into experience."

In 1917 the Schweitzers were returned to France and later to Alsace. To support himself and to carry on the work at Lambaréné, he joined the medical staff of the Strasbourg Hospital, preached, gave lectures and organ recitals, traveled, and wrote. He returned to Africa alone in 1925, while his wife and his daughter, Rhena, who was born in 1919, remained in Europe. In the almost eight years of his absence, the jungle had reclaimed the hospital grounds, and the buildings had to be rebuilt. This was no sooner under way than Schweitzer fell ill, an epidemic of dysentery broke out, and a famine set in. The epidemic prompted him to move his hospital to a larger site two miles up the Ogoué, where expansion was possible and where gardens and orchards could be planted. Two physicians had arrived from Europe, and he turned over all medical responsibilities to them and to two nurses for a year and a half while he supervised and helped to fell trees, clear ground, and construct buildings. The main hospital room and the dispensary were complete when he departed for Europe in midsummer, 1927. He returned to Lambaréné in 1929 and remained for two years, establishing a pattern of work in Africa and sojourns in Europe during which he lectured, wrote, and gave concerts to raise funds for his hospital. On one of these occasions, in 1949, he visited the United States and lectured on Goethe at a conference in Aspen, Colorado.

28   Hundreds flocked to hear him and to importune him. On one occasion a group of tourists pulled him away from the dinner table to get an explanation of his ethics. He responded with remarkable courtesy for about twenty minutes until one questioner prodded him for a specific application of Reverence for Life. "Reverence for Life," he replied, "means my answering your kind inquiries; it also means your reverence for my dinner hour." The tourists got the point and he returned to his meal. On his trips to Europe, he invariably made his headquarters at his home in Günsbach, which was expanded into a leave and rest center for the hospital staff. Of an afternoon he could often be glimpsed leaving his house to slip over to the church to play the organ; and sometimes he ventured afield to repair old church instruments.

29   In the closing years of his life he received many honorary degrees and other tokens of the esteem in which he was held, including honorary membership in the British Order of Merit. His choice as a Nobelist was popular, for Schweitzer was widely perceived in Europe and the United States as a person who had done much good without having wrought much harm. This perception was certainly prevalent when he celebrated his ninetieth birthday at Lambaréné in 1965 (he had lived there almost continuously since his wife's death in 1957), when hundreds of Africans, Europeans, and Americans gathered to wish him well. By this time he was virtually a secular saint, and criticisms were not welcomed. The overwhelming view was summed up in a message from the president of the United States; "In your commitment to truth and service," the cable read, "you have touched and deepened the lives of millions you have never met."

30   As an epitaph, it serves Schweitzer well. He could easily be diminished for his faults, but his accomplishments, on balance, were testimony to a singular devotion to the ideals of his youth, ideals of service that Goethean men of good will have always found ennobling.

Questions

1. A well-written obituary is really an interpretive biographical essay about the life of the subject; the subject's death is incidental. What major motifs of Schweitzer's life does Whitman identify and explain?

2. Many obituaries proceed chronologically, from the subject's birth to death. Whitman, instead, devotes the entire first half of the piece to assessing Schweitzer's achievements before beginning a chronological review of Schweitzer's life. What is the effect of this organizational pattern? Would the more conventional chronological pattern have obscured some of the important themes of Schweitzer's life? Why or why not?

3. James Boswell, Samuel Johnson's biographer *par excellence,* has said that to capture the subject's essence the portrait must not be totally flattering, but must reveal "warts and all." In what ways does Whitman convey the controversy over some of Schweitzer's activities? his difficult personality? the limitations of his work? do these negative features undermine or strengthen the portrait? Is the portrait balanced? Should it be?

4. Newspaper obituaries tend to be emotionally neutral, and nonjudgmental about the subject's activities and personality traits. Is this true of Whitman's portrait of Schweitzer? Could you learn from this obituary that Schweitzer was regarded by many as an exceptionally great man, and was mourned worldwide at his death? What is the tone of Whitman's writing here? Is it consistent throughout this unusually long obituary?

SALLY QUINN

Alice Roosevelt Longworth at 90

Quinn's style as a reporter for The Washington Post, *for which she began writing in 1969, is as feisty as the subject of the portrait below. Although Quinn was born in Georgia in 1941, as the child of a military family she lived in Japan, Mexico, and Europe, as well as many parts of the United States, before attending Smith College. Her career as a reporter was interrupted in 1973–74 for a stint as the first network anchorwoman, with CBS Morning News, but ultimately the* Post *has dominated both her professional and private life, for she married Managing Editor Ben Bradlee in 1978.*

Alice Longworth, claims Quinn, "has been revered and feared, adored and detested," but always the outrageous talk of the town. Although, as her antagonists point out, "she has never really done anything worthwhile in her life," Quinn shows through revealing details ("her phone rings endlessly"), interpretations, and scenes replete with pungent quotations, why this daughter of a President, wife of a prominent Speaker of the House, remained a snobbish wit, as sought after at ninety as when she was nineteen.

"I still," she muses, rapping her bony fingers against her graying head, "more or less have my, what they call, marbles," and she pulls her flowered shawl around her a little closer, throws her head back and laughs gleefully. 1

Alice Roosevelt Longworth is 90 years old today. 2

"I may be an old crone but I can still put on the harness and lumber down the street." 3

When Mrs. Longworth, or Mrs. L. as she prefers to be called by intimates, turned 89 last year she had only a small tea party to celebrate. "I'm saving my energy for a big bash next year," she said ". . . if I'm still kicking around." 4

This afternoon at 5 she will have her 90th birthday party. "It will be a marvelous and horrible scene," she declares. 5

She will love every minute of it. "I must say, I'm always on stage. All Roosevelts are exhibitionists," she says. "Am I? Decidedly so. That, my dear, is what becomes of peasants." 6

And she agrees to an interview a few days before the birthday, set for 5 o'clock tea. "It's irresistible," she admits later. "The delight of pouring out yourself to someone who listens with rapt attention and takes down every precious word." 7

8   Her maid, Janie McLaughlin, answers the door and leads the way through the darkened foyer, up the stairs, past the rattiest looking animal skin that you ever saw, hanging on the wall. The Siberian tiger skin belonged to her big-game hunting father, Teddy Roosevelt.

9   At the top of the stairs, one can hear a cheerful, lively voice on the floor above, chatting away on the phone. Janie picks up a large brass gong and an equally large mallet. The sound reverberates through the house. The telephone conversation upstairs ceases. When Mrs. Longworth appears a few minutes later, she remarks laughingly, "Isn't it funny how things change? I used to sound the gong for my servants. Now they sound it for me."

10   Her living room is cluttered, cozy, comfortable and dingy, done in pale faded colors, some velvets and flowered prints. The rugs and upholstery are so frayed that in some spots the threads barely hang together. Over the backs and arms of the furniture are pieces of yellowing plastic, a not very earnest attempt at preservation. One suspects that the decay might even be cultivated, a sort of scene-setter, a proper milieu for the venerable inhabitant of the old Dupont Circle mansion that she has occupied for most of her life.

11   And of course there is The Pillow—the needlepoint pillow that has been so often noticed and to which her detractors point when they deplore her mischievous nature. It, too, is wrapped in plastic and it says, "If you haven't got anything nice to say about anyone, come and sit here by me."

12   Alice Longworth is a controversial figure in Washington. Those who don't know her—the public, or "the great rancid masses" as she likes to say— see her only as a formidable, amusing, highly entertaining, iconoclastic old lady. But among those in the inner sanctum, those who frequent the Georgetown salons, those who refer to her as "Mrs. L.," there is a sharp division of opinion about her which often causes unpleasant moments.

13   There are those who think she is cruel, mean and malicious, that she uses other people as the butt of her humor, that she will hurt someone for the sake of a catchy one-liner, that she is essentially cold and insensitive to other people's feelings. She outrages some with her scorn of her cousin Eleanor Roosevelt ("I leave the good deeds to Eleanor") and they readily point out that Mrs. Longworth has never really *done* anything worthwhile in her life.

14   Alice Longworth has lived in Washington since William McKinley was assassinated and her father became President in 1901. She was 17 years old. She has known every President since Benjamin Harrison, who was in office from 1889 to 1893. Some she liked and some she didn't; over the years she has never hesitated to reveal her exact sentiments about them, or anyone else for that matter.

15   She has been a favorite of Harry Truman, John Kennedy, Lyndon Johnson and Richard Nixon, but there was no love lost between her and Warren Harding, and Woodrow Wilson. President Eisenhower bored her.

She supported her father when President Roosevelt was running in 1912   16
on the Progressive ticket and her husband, Cincinnati congressman Nicholas
Longworth, whom she married when she was 22 and he was 36, was running
for re-election on the Republican ticket. Her father was responsible for her
husband's defeat. "It was too horrible, really," she says about that period.
"Poor Nick, he stayed out, came back in two years, and then became Speaker,
so all was well."

Her total fascination with politics and the people in politics has never   17
waned, though she says now that it's far more interesting when "you've got
family in it."

At 41 she had her only child, daughter Pauline, who was widowed at 26   18
and died at 31. She left an only daughter, Joanna Sturm. Mrs. Longworth's
granddaughter is now 27 and lives with her in the Dupont Circle house.

In 1931, Nicholas Longworth, who by then had become the powerful   19
House Speaker, died. Mrs. Longworth never remarried, preferring to remain
alone, leading the independent life she seemed always to want, unhindered by
the restrictions being the daughter of a President or the wife of a Speaker of
the House must have placed upon her.

After spending several hours with Mrs. Longworth it would seem that   20
those who say she is a malicious person are unjustified. To be sure there is a
bite to her tongue, but, more often than not, statements that might be
thought mean or shocking by some have an edge of truth to them. Mrs.
Longworth is honest. "That," she says, "infuriates people."

As for alleged lack of sympathy for others' problems: She never talks   21
about her own sadnesses, "Never, I just don't want to," and she doesn't want
to hear about anybody else's.

"I don't think I am insensitive or cruel. I laugh, I have a sense of humor. I   22
like to tease. I must admit a sense of mischief does get hold of me from time
to time. I'm a hedonist. I have an appetite for being entertained. Isn't it
strange how that upsets people? And I don't mind what I do unless I'm
injuring someone in some way.

"I had a pious cousin who used to say she lived in the palace of truth and   23
she would go up to some horrible-looking creature with an ugly red nose and
say, 'You have an ugly red nose.' "

Having been a President's daughter and so often in the public eye, Mrs.   24
Longworth has had her share of criticism. But she thinks she is not as
sensitive today. "Criticism doesn't bother me. It's so lovely to be able to say
that."

"But," pipes up granddaughter Joanna, "you've been old long enough so   25
that people don't criticize you anymore. They're all so overly respectful."

"Isn't it fascinating?" Mrs. Longworth asks. "It's that dreadful desire of   26
human beings to worship."

27 Her granddaughter, Joanna Sturm, wearing pants and a sweater, has just entered the room and sinks into a chair next to the sofa as Janie brings in the tea tray: a silver kettle over a burner that Mrs. Longworth lights herself, bread and butter, cookies and a tiny fresh chocolate cake.

28 Joanna is tall with longish, light brown hair, a strong, pretty, intelligent face and an open, easy, likable manner. She is completely at home with her grandmother, who, when she is in the room, relies on her for advice.

29 Joanna will often come out with an opinion Mrs. Longworth clearly agrees with, and the older woman will gasp with mock horror and disapproval.

30 "I," says Joanna, with an engaging smile, "am the silent accomplice."

31 "I'm full of respect for the younger generation," says her grandmother, smiling sanctimoniously at Joanna.

32 Alice Longworth finds the publicity about her "absolutely fascinating. I view it from a totally detached point of view but I suppose I can sort of see why they want to interview me. I am more amusing than most President's daughters."

33 One of her most recent interviews was with another President's daughter, Julie Eisenhower, who wrote the story for *The Saturday Evening Post*.

34 "Totally inane," declares Joanna.

35 "Oh, Joanna," says Mrs. Longworth, laughing, "it wasn't either. It was lovely."

36 Later, Janie clears the tea things away and brings in Mrs. Longworth's dinner tray. Mrs. Longworth offers dinner to her guest, then peeks under the plate cover. "Oh good, spareribs, I love spareribs. No one ever serves them. They're fattening, too, and I just can't seem to put on weight. I only weigh 92 pounds."

37 As soon as she has inspected the meal and begun to dig in, Mrs. Longworth steers the conversation into the beginnings of a gossip session.

38 "I'll tell you who I think is awfully nice," she says. "Margaret Truman. I've always liked her a great deal.

39 "I haven't seen the Johnson girls at all. I always get them mixed up but they seem to like to have a good time.

40 "And Julie Eisenhower has got something. She seems rather smart. Joanna scoffed at her piece about me and I suppose it was rather scoffable, but I did it because I wanted to show that we're friends. I like Julie better than Tricia. I've never been able to get on with Tricia. She seems rather pathetic, doesn't she? I wonder what's wrong with her?"

41 Mrs. Longworth keeps on munching, venturing opinions, trying out names for reaction.

42 "I like Jackie very much. But I've always wondered what on earth made her marry Onassis. He's a repulsive character. He reminds me of Mr. Punch . . . Jack was so attractive.

43 "Ethel," says Mrs. Longworth, "is behaving very badly these days.

There's a certain brash quality about her I never liked. I liked Bobby though, a great deal."

Mrs. Longworth cannot stand pomposity or false piety and will go to great lengths to skewer someone guilty of taking himself too seriously. "I'm probably bad about people who have noble, fine and marvelous thoughts. That's so depressing. I never could stand the little pious family things that my sanctimonious cousins used to do. But they're all dead now." 44

Alice Longworth is a survivor in a town where the word is an anachronism. She has been revered and feared, adored and detested, but there has never been a time when she has not been talked about. Her outrageous utterances about people and events began when she was a child and she is still adding to the list of quotable quotes. 45

She would admit that when McKinley was assassinated and her father became President that her feeling was "utter rapture," she was "ecstatic," a line that appalled people in its directness. But she'll just as readily mock herself. When she had her second mastectomy several years ago, she remarked later that she was the "only topless octagenarian" in Georgetown Hospital. 46

Interviews are always one way of securing information. Mrs. Longworth is as curious and observant as an interviewer, taking the situation in quickly, optimistically prepared to be entertained, amused, informed; but just as braced, graciously, of course, to be bored. 47

She talks quickly, through her teeth in a rather upper-class way that she will exaggerate for effect from time to time. Often her verbal speed makes it difficult to understand. 48

Her eyes are very clear. They dart back and forth. Her hands rest in her lap but she twists her fingers as her mind leaps about. Occasionally she will leap up to point out some relic, memento or photograph across the room. 49

She roars with laughter at the irreverent suggestion that one should prostrate oneself at her feet at the sound of her gong and points her finger admiringly, "Ah," she says, "you've a wicked nature, horrid, I like that." 50

She is as ready with a topical jab about young people as she is about past generations, and just as much at home with young people as if she were in her 20s. A session with her and Joanna could almost be a woman's consciousness-raising session, but for her irreverence about anything taken too seriously. And she once said, "I've never liked people my own age." 51

Joanna works for the National Women's Political Caucus and, in fact, the treasurer of the NWPC, Lucille Flanigan, lives with them on the top floor. Joanna tells Mrs. Longworth that Lucille will not be there for tea. 52

"I'm all for the women's cause," says Mrs. Longworth. "I saw too much of the 'silly little womanizing' over the years. But I'm not violent about it. I've never been treated as an inferior by any man." 53

Mrs. Longworth is reminded of a story of a friend of hers in the old days (the turn of the century) who, after being forbidden by her father to see a 54 young man, dressed in men's clothes and cut her hair. The father remarked, "What an odd revenge."

55   Mrs. Longworth laughs heartily. "Homosexuality and lesbianism were very fashionable in those days," she says. "And it was quite acceptable. At least as far as I was concerned."

56   "Tell her about the incident in the White House garden," prompts Joanna.

57   It seems Margaret Cassini, Igor's mother and the daughter of a South American ambassador, had been a great friend of Alice Longworth's and they had taken a walk one day in the White House garden.

58   Miss Cassini proceeded to tell young Alice that a mutual friend was saying horrid things about her. Alice asked what, and the friend replied that a certain Miss Alice Barney was claiming to be in love with Alice.

59   "I don't think that's nasty, why I think that's lovely, so nice. I'm so glad to hear she is," Mrs. Longworth recalls saying with a mischievous smile.

60   Margaret Cassini apparently snorted with contempt, which pleased young Alice enormously.

61   "Still," she says, "usually I thought it better to keep away from joking about the lesbian thing since my father was President. But you know in those days people were always having love affairs with their poodles and putting tiny flowers in strange places. But they talked amusingly about their affairs. My family didn't, though. They would have gone absolutely mad with horror. Especially my younger sister Ethel. She would have fainted dead away. But I don't think I have ever been scandalized."

62   Mrs. Longworth was loving the conversation.

63   "Not in the sense of moral outrage," says Joanna. "But you're being aesthetically outraged constantly."

64   "Yes, that's true," says Mrs. Longworth. "By sexual things, by tasteless things. And then some things I think are terribly funny. Like dear old men's things hanging all around them. I think that's terribly funny."

65   What?

66   "Men's penises, my dear," she says very deliberately leaning forward, waiting for a reaction.

67   As soon as she is greeted by a howl of astonished laughter, she leans back and howls delightedly herself and Joanna joins in.

68   "Oh, I can see it in the paper now," says Mrs. Longworth. "Dear old Mrs. Longworth sitting with her granddaughter talking about men's penises."

69   The talk moves to marriage versus living together. Would she, if she were Joanna's age today, have married?

70   "No, I never would marry again. I might live with people. But not for long. I really wouldn't want to do anything pondering or noble or taking a position about someone again. But I might rather just spend a night with them, or an afternoon or something."

She pauses, then reflects for a moment: "Still," she says, "I'm afraid I do 71
believe in marriage."

"Why?" asks Joanna. "You hardly reveled in it yourself." 72

"That's true. I hardly reveled in it." · 73

"You hardly advise it for me," says Joanna. 74

"I suppose I'm just a neutral person," she muses. "But I followed my 75
father's marriages. He was always so full of guilt. I loved my father but I was
never particularly close to him. I enjoyed my stepmother. But it's mean to talk
about your parents that way. I don't want to talk about my parents."

The subject is changed. 76

Well, if Alice Longworth wouldn't have married if she were young to- 77
day, what would she do?

"I would have run for office. If I were very young I would try to get over 78
the shyness of speaking in public. I still have it. I shuddered with terror when
people tried to make me get up and speak. It was just false pride I suppose.
But I'm really very shy.

"Every once in a while it hits me. I was like a tenement child, you know, 79
deformed with my legs (she had a disease as a child that was suspected later to
have been polio), and I was always very conscious of that. My stepmother
used to stretch my legs every night."

Mrs. Longworth also feels shy, she says, because she was the only child of 80
Theodore Roosevelt and his first wife. "My brothers used to tease me about
not having the same mother. They were very cruel about it and I was terribly
sensitive."

Often accused of being vain, because of her great beauty, Alice Long- 81
worth seems unaware of her looks and says she never really thought she was
pretty, even when she was young. She jokes now about losing her hair and
not having bought a new dress since she was 80.

"I thought I was a rather pathetic creature, terribly homely and that they 82
were just saying I was pretty because I was the President's daughter. Some
times I look at pictures of myself then, trying to see what they thought was
pretty. But then I determined not to be a pathetic creature. I decided to
defeat it so I became resistant, contrary, and I tried to be conspicuous. That
feeling has lasted in some way."

The conversation moves to accents, and Mrs. Longworth says she apes 83
whomever she is with. "Except LBJ," she chortles. "And I never aped Pat and
Dick," she adds.

"Thank goodness," pipes up Joanna. 84

"Mean!" chides Mrs. Longworth. 85

What kind of people does she like, who amuses her, interests her? 86

"Oh, just the people in this very room, my dear," she coos. 87

"That's not usually true," says Joanna. 88

Does she like Gerald Ford? 89

90   "Who's Gerald Ford? Oh yes, the Vice President. Do I know Gerald Ford, Joanna?"

91   "I hope not."

92   "Oh, Joanna," she says with a grin. "You're so intolerant." She begins to warm up to the game.

93   What about the Nixons?

94   She suddenly goes serious and says a bit stiffly, "The Nixons are old friends. I've liked them for years. I've known them for a long, long time. I don't talk about them."

95   A pall comes over the conversation and for a few seconds there is grim silence.

96   "Well, that certainly put an end to that conversation," jokes Joanna. "Maybe we'd better change the subject."

97   Mrs. Longworth giggles and agrees and offers tea with honey.

98   That was not the end of that.

99   The temptation to get back to Nixon is too much. And later, in the midst of another conversation, Mrs. Longworth leans forward bursting with a less than flattering opinion about how Watergate has been handled by the President—for whom she has always, until now, had only the highest praise. She goes on a bit, then leans back and says, deliberately savoring the pleasure of her remark: "But that my dear, is just between us and not for your story."

100   As she turns 90, Mrs. Longworth is not thinking about the end. Her phone rings endlessly, she has callers to tea every day, she still reads till 3 or 4 every morning, and she still goes with friends to dinner parties, which she adores.

101   She has "plenty of money," as she will tell you, so there are no worries there.

102   "I have no problems," she will say. "It's easier to grow old if you are able to relax. I relax like mad and I'm interested in everything. Thank heavens I haven't gotten senile. I have good old gusto, that's all."

103   But in the last year Mrs. Longworth has not been terribly well. Perhaps her two bouts with cancer are taking their toll. She went to her first dinner party in six weeks the other day and was exhausted all the next day.

104   "I'm crumbling with old age," she says with a wry smile and adds, with just the tiniest trace of concern, "It's just in the last year that I have been getting obviously older."

105   Mrs. Longworth, for all her impeccable manner, is a snob. "I do believe in privilege," she says resolutely. And part of her snobbism is a kind of nose-thumbing. "*Épater* (titillate) *les bourgeois*," she will say with a nicely turned French accent.

106   Some people say she has mellowed in her old age. Does she think she has?

107   "No," she says brightly.

Alice Longworth can still laugh at herself and laughing at herself gives   108
her license to laugh at others.

"When they start comparing you to the Washington Monument," she   109
says, "you just have to open your eyes and take a good look at yourself."

Writing About People

Strategies

1. Why do I want to write about this person? to gain an understanding of the subject's motives, conflicts, or problems? to provide a character sketch or brief biography? to tell a story? to use some aspect of the person's life as a good or bad example? to explain the person's job or a memorable period of history or event he or she experienced?

2. What do I want to emphasize—personality or character, activities, abilities (or their absence)? roles, relationships? growth and maturation (social, psychological, intellectual)? membership in a group, or living in a particular place or time? What details, incidents, background information do I need to include to explain the characteristics I've chosen? What information can I exclude, and on what grounds (that it's repetitive, unrepresentative, trivial—but trivial information can often be revealing, . . .)?

3. Do I like (or dislike) my subject strongly enough to sustain my interest and that of my readers? Will my readers share my attitude toward the subject at the outset, or will I have to convince them that my interpretation is valid? How will my attitude toward the subject determine my choice of language in writing about that person?

4. If I know the subject personally, have I tried to re-create his or her manner of speaking, gesturing, or other forms of communication, verbal and nonverbal? through what means? How much background information have I supplied, and how does it relate to the material directly pertinent to this subject him- or herself? (See Mary Langenberg, "An Interview with Alfred Everett" and "East St. Louis: From Blues to Dirge," (122–41.)

5. Through what means—direct commentary, indirect commentary (through a selection of the subject's words and revealing details)—have I provided an interpretation of my subject? Is my representation fair? Should it be?

Suggestions

1. Sometimes a meaningful incident or significant relationship with someone can help us to mature, easily or painfully, as Frederick Douglass explains in "Resurrection," (155–59). Tell the story of such an incident or relationship in your own life or in the life of someone you know well. If this incident or relationship was a turning point in your life, or provided you with an important change of self-image (as did Douglass's defiance of the cruel overseer), present enough information so readers can understand the causes and effects of the change, and can recognize the before-and-after portraits.

2. Interview a person whose life, background, personality, work, or recreation interests you. Let the subject talk (and do most of the talking) for an hour or so on topics of particular interest to you; keep it focused by means of key questions. Take notes during the interview, and corroborate these (if possible) by taping the interview. If you write it up in interview format, edit it to eliminate redundancies and to group the

material either topically or chronologically; see the Joan Galway interview with Louise Nevelson (118–22) and Mary Langenberg's interview with Alfred Everett (122–35).

3. Using the material you collected during the interview, write up the interview as a portrait of your subject (see Studs Terkel, "Miss U.S.A., Emma Knight," 113–17; Henry Mitchell, "Eudora Welty: Storyteller of the South," 167–75; and Sally Quinn, "Alice Roosevelt Longworth at 90," 185–93). In addition to editing out re-dundancies and arranging the remaining material either topically or chronologically, you'll need to supply additional details that reveal the subject's characteristic setting, milieus, manner and mannerisms, even the tone of voice. If you're changing the fo-cus, as did Mary Langenberg in "East St. Louis, from Blues to Dirge," 135–41, you may need to add considerable information about what you're emphasizing—the back-ground, history, nature of the occupation or value system, for example. Where will you find the best sources of such information—the library? the subject's household or hometown? elsewhere?

4. Using the techniques explained in 2 and 3, write a portrait of an unusual, eccentric, or otherwise bizarre person whom you like, admire, or in other ways approve of, as Eugene Mayer does in "Mr. L.G. Broadmoore and the Way It Was" (546–50). To make sure you've conveyed your point of view, let someone unfamiliar with your subject read your essay, and see whether you have convinced the reader to share your opinion. If not, what information or changes of emphasis do you need to supply?

5. Explain what it's like to be a typical person in a role, typical or atypical—say, a student, or a worker on an assembly line, in a restaurant or store, in a particular trade or profession, through "A Day in the Life of . . . ." (You can use your own experience or an interview as the basis of this account.) What skills, training, and personal qualities does the job require? If you find that life stimulating, demanding, conducive to professional or personal growth, be sure to show why. If you find it to be boring or demeaning, your narrative might be an implied protest or an argument for change.

6. Write a portrait of someone, yourself or another person you know well, that emphasizes their philosophy of life or values, as does Robert Coles in "Two Lan-guages, One Soul," 162–66. Or write an imaginary autobiographical portrait of your-self as you expect to be ten (or twenty) years from now; specify which age. What major characteristics of your present personality, values, or life style will you have retained? Which do you expect to have changed, and why?

7. Tell the story of a special relationship you have (or have had) with another per-son—parent or grandparent, brother or sister, friend, spouse, teacher, mentor, em-ployer (see John Leonard's "The Only Child," 142–44, and "My Son, the Roman," 544–46; Mary Ruffin's "Mama's Smoke," 145–47; and E. B. White's "Once More to the Lake," 232–37). You may wish to convey its essence through narrating one or two typical incidents.

8. Have you ever witnessed an event important to history, sports, science, or some other field of endeavor? If so, tell the story either as an eyewitness, or from the point of view of someone looking back on it and more aware now of its true meaning. If possible, put the event into its appropriate historical, political, athletic, or other context, as John Updike does with Ted Williams's last game in "Hub Fans Bid Kid Adieu" (470–83).

9. Write an obituary of someone you know by reputation or accomplishment, if not personally (see Alden Whitman's "Albert Schweitzer," 175–84). This should focus on the main aspects of the subject's life and character, positive and negative, rather than on the phenomena of the subject's manner of dying (unless the latter is what made the person notable). You will need to assess the significance of the subject's life.

10. Pick a controversial aspect of someone's life (possibly your own), and write a portrait that presents and interprets the controversy (see Whitman's "Albert Schweitzer" and Quinn's "Alice Roosevelt Longworth at 90"). If you use contradictory sources, you'll need to assess the merits of the evidence and interpretation in each. To resolve the controversy, will you favor one interpretation over the others, or give each equal weight?

CHAPTER THREE

Writing About
Places

E very place on earth is in some ways unique, yet every place can be
understood by strangers as well as by intimates, partly because of
the features it has in common with other places, partly because
of the common elements of our encounters with it. Yet because a place is not
only a spot on the map but a gleam in the eye—and the heart—of the
beholder, there are many ways to write about any given location.

Take Washington, D.C., for instance. Its very existence could serve as a
stimulus for expressing your views on what it means to be an American
citizen—or a recent immigrant. Residents could write about its unique features as a hometown, from the perspective of where they live or work,
whereas visitors could offer impressions of Washington as the nation's capital. From an historic perspective, you could write on the capital's role in the
Civil War, or during the Depression, or as the site of civil rights marches and
antiwar protests in the 60s. From a political point of view, you could discuss
how Washington works as a political and bureaucratic city, or analyze its
political climate during a given presidential administration. Or you could
treat the city as the symbol of our country—as viewed by foreign antagonists,
by prospective immigrants, or by a group of citizens with vested interests,
such as lobbyists. You could imagine Washington as an international city, a
model of city planning, or as the repository of national treasures, from art to
archives. Or you could write a tourguide to the city, emphasizing its museums, monuments, theaters, zoo and arboretum, embassies, restaurants, shopping. . . . The possibilities are full of possibility!

The Travel Writer's Personality

The best writings about places and travel, including all of the writings here,
bear the powerful imprint of the writer's personality, individualistic, idiosyncratic, and opinionated. These writers do not offer slick Kodachrome snap-

shots of landscapes of predictably blue skies and calm waters; even when writers love the places they live or visit, their writings on the subject are neither sentimental nor sanitized. They comment on the ugly as well as the beautiful, the problems as well as the pleasures. For instance, Margaret Laurence begins her description of her "small prairie" hometown in Canada with:

> A strange place it was, that place where the world began. A place of incredible happenings, splendors and revelations, despairs like multitudinous pits of isolated hells. A place of shadow-spookiness, inhabited by the unknowable dead. A place of jubilation and of mourning, horrible and beautiful. [212]

Even E. B. White, who in "Once More to the Lake" (232–37) waxes lyrical on the joys of rural summertime, ends an account of an idyllic afternoon by anticipating "the chill of death."

To write memorably about places mundane or magnificent, you need to be extraordinarily aware of and responsive to the surroundings, alert to the subtleties as well as to the more conspicuous features of the land, the climate, the animal and plant life, the culture, and the people. Writings about places are likely to contain a high proportion of sensory details, as the writer recreates the sights, sounds, smells, tastes, and textures of a place experienced or remembered. Thus Mark Twain recalls "Uncle John's Farm" (237–42):

> I can see the blue clusters of wild grapes hanging among the foliage of the saplings, and I remember the taste of them and the smell. . . . I can feel the thumping rain, upon my head, of hickory nuts and walnuts when we were out in the frosty dawn to scramble for them with the pigs . . . . I know the stain of blackberries, and how pretty it is . . . .

Twain saves this from sentimentality, an excess of emotion in relation to the subject that is fatal to descriptions of places (or anything else), with a dose of humorous realism: ". . . and I know the stain of walnut hulls, and how little it minds soap and water, also what grudged experience it had of either of them."

Open-mindedness enhances awareness. In writing about a place as a visitor or a newcomer, you'll find more to say if you're receptive to terrain, weather, people, and customs that may be very different from your own. From curiosity then, rather than from smug chauvinism, the writer can get to know the natives as well as the territory. From human sympathy, the writer can try to understand why such people behave as they do, what they like or dislike about where they live, and why they put up with what others might find intolerable—especially if judged according to your hometown norms. Of course, you can still see a place negatively; in "Marrying Absurd" (514–17) Joan Didion finds Las Vegas an unreal city of lost souls for whom "marriage, like craps, is a game to be played when the table seems hot."

But if given a chance, and a fresh perspective, even mundane places can become surprisingly interesting. John McPhee's analysis of New Jersey's forgotten Pine Barrens (205–10) presents a compelling and sympathetic view of the thousand-square-mile forest and its independent, idiosyncratic inhabitants. His first glimpse of the house of Fred Brown, a resident of Hog Wallow (pop. 25) reveals

> . . . the pump that stands in his yard. It was something of a wonder that I noticed the pump, because there were, among other things, eight automobiles in the yard, two of them on their sides and one of them upside down. . . . Around the cars were old refrigerators, vacuum cleaners, partly dismantled radios, cathode-ray tubes, a short wooden ski . . . mandolins, engine heads, and maybe a thousand other things.

There is no hint of big-city-sophisticate-jeering-the-hayseeds condescension here—indeed, McPhee's fascination becomes our own.

Nature Writing

You may want to reflect on the natural world for its own sake, or for your own. As your gaze ranges from the earth to the heavens to the sea and home again, you'll be observing animals and plants and how they live, with and without human interference. You'll move to the rhythm of the day and the night, the seasons and the tides, the wind and the waves, as Henry Beston reveals in "The Headlong Wave" (202–204): "Listen to ["the long wintry roaring of the sea"] for a while, and it will seem but one remote and formidable sound; listen still longer and you will discern in it a symphony of breaker thunderings, an endless, distant, elemental cannonade. There is beauty in it, and ancient terror." This kind of writing about nature differs from science writing (see Chapter 8) because it is far more personal, more impressionistic, and more idiosyncratically interpretive.

Writers often use their encounters with the natural world to try to understand themselves, to develop a philosophy of life as their understanding grows in depth and breadth. Thoreau explains in "Where I Lived and What I Lived For" (251–61) that he spent two years in the woods at Walden Pond "because I wished to live deliberately, to front only the essential facts of life, and see if I could not learn what it had to teach, and not, when I came to die, discover that I had not lived." Tim Payne, a student inspired by Thoreau, decided on a surprisingly depressing vacation trip to "The Beach at Bar Harbor" (265–67), Maine, that he'd "go force some uplifting significance out of the beach." Once Payne learned to respect the strength, stability, and power of the sea, he was able to accept the ocean on its own terms, rather than on his. In the process he developed his own self-reliance and maturity, symbolized by his unwillingness to carry away from the beach even a perfect sand dollar.

The independence, self-reliance, and resourcefulness exhibited by Thoreau and Payne are typical of nature writers. They love solitude: "I love to be alone," says Thoreau, "I have, as it were, my own sun and moon and stars, and little world all to myself." Isolation makes the nature writer ever more aware of his or her emotional and intellectual reactions to the natural world, as well as to the nuances and subtle interplay of forces in that world itself. Beston observes, in "The Headlong Wave":

> The sea has many voices. Listen to the surf, really lend it your ears, and you will hear in it a world of sounds: hollow boomings and heavy roarings, great watery tumblings and tramplings, long hissing seethes, sharp, rifle-shot reports, splashes, whispers, the grinding undertone of the stones. . . . [the sea] is also constantly changing its tempo, its pitch, its accent, and its rhythm, being now loud and thundering, now almost placid, now furious, now grave and solemn-slow, now a simple measure, now a rhythm monstrous with a sense of purpose and elemental will.

Nature writers are usually optimistic; their detailed discoveries justify their confidence that careful observation will be both revealing and rewarding.

Writing About Travels and Adventures

We are a nation of travelers, and accounts of adventures that focus on places unusual or exotic are particularly appealing to American readers, with their heritage of discovery, conquest, and settlement of new territories. Writing about the experience of travel can be even more challenging than analyzing familiar ground. You can focus on the route, the mode of transportation, traveling companions, or "the poetry of motion." Paul Theroux claims that "It's the journey, not the arrival, that matters" (261–64), and creates anew the adventures of getting there, via the Orient Express, the Old Patagonian Railway, and other memorable means of locomotion.

Adventure lies in the minds and spirits of those who encounter it. Every place we haven't seen before, every familiar place viewed from a different or unusual perspective, such as a new home (Kingston, 243–46), an old neighborhood revisited (Kazin, 246–50), the beach in winter (Kopper, 272–77), becomes a possibility to explore and to write about. Thus Morris delights in revealing new vistas of familiar cities, in personal, idiosyncratic accounts of "Venice" (216–22) and "Manhattan" (222–30). These incorporate information about the place's history, geography, economy, religion, politics, literature, and entertainment (among other features), but ultimately strive to capture the character of the citizens, for better and for worse:

> The Venetian libraries concern themselves assiduously with Venice. The pictures that hang in Venetian houses are nearly always of Venetian scenes. Venice is a shamelessly self-centered place, in a constant glow of elderly narcissism.

If the literal journey encourages self-knowledge, spiritual or psychological insight, so much the better. As Alfred Kazin reminisces about his mother's kitchen in the Brownsville (New York) Jewish ghetto in which he grew up, he realizes that

> All my memories of that kitchen are dominated by the nearness of my mother sitting all day long at her sewing machine, by the clacking of the

treadle . . . . The kitchen was her life. Year by year, as I began to take in her fantastic capacity for labor and her anxious zeal, I realized it was ourselves she kept stitched together. (248)

Advice to Travelers

As a writer you can provide practical advice for travelers by serving as expert guide and interpreter. Without being patronizing, to help the uninitiated make sense of a place, you'll need to answer the questions of *where* is the place in question? *What* are its notable features—in terms of its history, religion, politics, culture, recreation and entertainment, shopping. *How* can one get there? *Where* can travelers stay? *What's* good to eat? Bob Thompson's advice for travelers to California, in "California: An Overview" (268–71) touches on all these topics as a prelude to a more extensive discussion in *The American Express Pocket Guide to California*. Phillip Kopper's commentary on "The Stark Simplicity of the Delmarva Coast" (272–77) is a more detailed and explicit guide to food, lodging, and recreation during the off-season at the beach. Kate Simon's perspective on "New York Luncheonettes" (277–82) is even more restricted, as she offers recommendations on specific luncheonettes and advice on how to get a seat in a crowded Manhattan luncheonette at noon: "When you see a near-finished piece of pie, or a cup of coffee tilted fairly high, make your move. Take a stand behind the tilter and don't budge." On the other hand, Calvin Trillin, author of "Eating in Cincinnati" (282–87), concentrates on down-home cooking that may be more fun to read about than to eat:

> Cincinnati eaters take it for granted that the basic way to serve chili is on spaghetti, just as they take it for granted that the other ways to serve it go up to a five-way (chili, spaghetti, onions, cheese, and beans) and that the people who do the serving are Greeks.

Other types of writing about places—discussing places for the purposes of social criticism, either simply to call attention to existing problems (as Didion does in indicting Las Vegas weddings in "Marrying Absurd"), or to encourage change or reform (as William Warner does in his plea to clean up the dying Chesapeake Bay)—will be discussed in Chapters 6 and 8.

One last word: In most writing about places, less is more; as with seasonings, a hint of the sights, sounds, smells of a place is more stimulating to the reader's imagination than writing laden with adjectives, adverbs, and extensive modifiers. There's one major exception: When you want to convey the impression of abundance, superabundance, crowdedness, or other excesses, in such instances, as Mae West has observed, "Too much of a good thing is absolutely splendid." Thus Twain can itemize the vast menu of his childhood repasts, and McPhee can list fourteen specific items and "a thousand other things" in Fred Brown's crowded front yard. On a first draft you can cram in as much as you want; on revisions you'll need to edit out this self-indulgence. Travel light.

Description

HENRY BESTON

The Headlong Wave

Henry Beston (1888–1968) stands firmly in the tradition of philosophical New England nature writers. His best known book, The Outermost House: A Year of Life on the Great Beach of Cape Cod *(1928), echoes Thoreau's* Walden, or Life in the Woods. *In his books Beston, like Thoreau, reminds us that the experience of nature is essential not only for our own physical life but for our spiritual life, as well. As a nature writer, Beston faces the descriptive writer's responsibilities to use careful, accurate, specific description to make us both see the place he describes and understand its significance. Indeed, he must restore to natural objects the significance that their very familiarity often obscures.*

If you've heard one wave, haven't you heard them all? Not really, Beston suggests. In his friendly, casual, down-to-earth manner, Beston gains our trust by admitting that he, too, doesn't always hear the waves that are constantly crashing about his house. Then he teaches us to listen for the triple rhythms, to count the sets of waves, to distinguish between the pattern of sounds on fair days and the "mechanically same" but different sound of storm surf. By the end of the section, in recounting his own quasi-mystical experience with the One Wave, the father of all waves, Beston enables us, too, to recognize the root meaning of the word "awesome"—that sense of wonder and terror a human should feel when confronting the sacred. If Beston's simple magic has worked, we should experience this feeling by the end of the essay.

1   This morning I am going to try my hand at something that I do not recall ever having encountered either in a periodical or in a book, namely, a chapter on the ways, the forms, and the sounds of ocean near a beach. Friends are forever asking me about the surf on the great beach and if I am not sometimes troubled or haunted by its sound. To this I reply that I have grown unconscious of the roar, and though it sounds all day long in my waking ears, and all night long in my sleeping ones, my ears seldom send on the long tumult to the mind. I hear the roar the instant I wake in the morning and return to consciousness, I listen to it a while consciously, and then accept and forget it; I hear it during the day only when I stop again to listen, or when some change in the nature of the sound breaks through my acceptance of it to my curiosity.

2   They say here that great waves reach this coast in threes. Three great waves, then an indeterminate run of lesser rhythms, then three great waves again. On Celtic coasts it is the seventh wave that is seen coming like a king out of the grey, cold sea. The Cape tradition, however, is no half-real, half-mystical fancy, but the truth itself. Great waves do indeed approach this beach by threes. Again and again have I watched three giants roll in one after

the other out of the Atlantic, cross the outer bar, break, form again, and follow each other in to fulfilment and destruction on this solitary beach. Coast guard crews are all well aware of this triple rhythm and take advantage of the lull that follows the last wave to launch their boats.

It is true that there are single giants as well. I have been roused by them in the night. Waked by their tremendous and unexpected crash, I have sometimes heard the last of the heavy overspill, sometimes only the loud, withdrawing roar. After the roar came a briefest pause, and after the pause the return of ocean to the night's long cadences. Such solitary titans, flinging their green tons down upon a quiet world, shake beach and dune. Late one September night, as I sat reading, the very father of all waves must have flung himself down before the house, for the quiet of the night was suddenly overturned by a gigantic, tumbling crash and an earthquake rumbling; the beach trembled beneath the avalanche, the dune shook, and my house so shook in its dune that the flame of a lamp quivered and pictures jarred on the wall.

The three great elemental sounds in nature are the sound of rain, the sound of wind in a primeval wood, and the sound of outer ocean on a beach. I have heard them all, and of the three elemental voices, that of ocean is the most awesome, beautiful, and varied. For it is a mistake to talk of the monotone of ocean or of the monotonous nature of its sound. The sea has many voices. Listen to the surf, really lend it your ears, and you will hear in it a world of sounds: hollow boomings and heavy roarings, great watery tumblings and tramplings, long hissing seethes, sharp, rifle-shot reports, splashes, whispers, the grinding undertone of stones, and sometimes vocal sounds that might be the half-heard talk of people in the sea. And not only is the great sound varied in the manner of its making, it is also constantly changing its tempo, its pitch, its accent, and its rhythm, being now loud and thundering, now almost placid, now furious, now grave and solemn-slow, now a simple measure, now a rhythm monstrous with a sense of purpose and elemental will.

Every mood of the wind, every change in the day's weather, every phase of the tide—all these have subtle sea musics all their own. Surf of the ebb, for instance, is one music, surf of the flood another, the change in the two musics being most clearly marked during the first hour of a rising tide. With the renewal of the tidal energy, the sound of the surf grows louder, the fury of battle returns to it as it turns again on the land, and beat and sound change with the renewal of the war.

Sound of surf in these autumnal dunes—the continuousness of it, sound of endless charging, endless incoming and gathering, endless fulfilment and dissolution, endless fecundity, and endless death. I have been trying to study out the mechanics of that mighty resonance. The dominant note is the great spilling crash made by each arriving wave. It may be hollow and booming, it may be heavy and churning, it may be a tumbling roar. The second fundamental sound is the wild seething cataract roar of the wave's dissolution and the rush of its foaming waters up the beach—this second sound *diminuendo*. The third fundamental sound is the endless dissolving hiss of the inmost slides of foam. The first two sounds reach the ear as a unisonance—the booming impact of the tons of water and the wild roar of the up-rush blending—and this mingled sound dissolves into the foam-bubble hissing of the third. Above the tumult, like birds, fly wisps of watery noise, splashes and counter splashes, whispers, seethings, slaps, and chucklings. An overtone sound of other breakers, mingled with a general rumbling, fells earth and sea and air.

7   Here do I pause to warn my reader that although I have recounted the history of a breaker—an ideal breaker—the surf process must be understood as mingled and continuous, waves hurrying after waves, interrupting waves, washing back on waves, overwhelming waves. Moreover, I have described the sound of a high surf in fair weather. A storm surf is mechanically the same thing, but it *grinds,* and this same long, sepulchral grinding—sound of utter terror to all mariners—is a development of the second fundamental sound; it is the cry of the breaker water roaring its way ashore and dragging at the sand. A strange underbody of sound when heard through the high, wild screaming of a gale.

8   Breaking waves that have to run up a steep tilt of the beach are often followed by a dragging, grinding sound—the note of the baffled water running downhill again to the sea. It is loudest when the tide is low and breakers are rolling beach stones up and down a slope of the lower beach.

9   I am, perhaps, most conscious of the sound of surf just after I have gone to bed. Even here I read myself to drowsiness, and, reading, I hear the cadenced trampling roar filling all the dark. So close is the Fo'castle to the ocean's edge that the rhythm of sound I hear oftenest in fair weather is not so much a general tumult as an endless arrival, overspill, and dissolution of separate great seas. Through the dark, mathematic square of the screened half window, I listen to the rushes and the bursts, the tramplings, and the long, intermingled thunderings, never wearying of the sonorous and universal sound.

10   Away from the beach, the various sounds of the surf melt into one great thundering symphonic roar. Autumnal nights in Eastham village are full of this ocean sound. The "summer people" have gone, the village rests and prepares for winter, lamps shine from kitchen windows, and from across the moors, the great levels of the marsh, and the bulwark of the dunes resounds the long wintry roaring of the sea. Listen to it a while, and it will seem but one remote and formidable sound; listen still longer and you will discern in it a symphony of breaker thunderings, an endless, distant, elemental cannonade. There is beauty in it, and ancient terror. I heard it last as I walked through the village on a starry October night; there was no wind, the leafless trees were still, all the village was abed, and the whole sombre world was awesome with the sound.

JOHN McPHEE

The Pine Barrens

John McPhee was born in Princeton, New Jersey, in 1931, graduated from Princeton University, and still lives, writes, and teaches in his home town, although most of his work appears in The New Yorker, *for which he has written regularly since 1964. McPhee's first book,* A Sense of Where You Are *(1965) concerns Princeton, but his other books have taken him farther away from home than Hog Wallow (pop. 25), described below. He traveled to Florida to write* Oranges *(1967), to Maine for* The Survival of the Bark Canoe *(1975), and Alaska for* Coming into the Country *(1978). His most recent books,* Basin and Range *(1981) and* In Suspect Terrain *(1983) are about geology.*

Since 1975, McPhee has taught a writing seminar at Princeton in "The Literature of Fact," which focuses on "the application of creative writing techniques to journalism and other forms of nonfiction." In the selection below, from The Pine Barrens *(1967), McPhee lets his point and his point of view emerge through thousands of specific, concrete details, which do not overwhelm us because of his graceful, though unobtrusive, style. If he can make us see it his way, he can make us feel about it as he does. In the first paragraphs, McPhee provides facts about geography, highways, the sparse population of the Pine Barrens in contrast to New Jersey's teeming transportation corridor. Instead of editorializing about the beauty and value of this fragile, forgotten place, McPhee presents two of those population statistics, Pine Barrens inhabitants Fred Brown and Bill Wasovwich, in the pungent context of Brown's crowded yard and house, and lets them raise the question of what could happen to their corner of the Garden State in a mechanized future.*

From the fire tower on Bear Swamp Hill, in Washington Township, Burling-   1
ton County, New Jersey, the view usually extends about twelve miles. To the
north, forest land reaches to the horizon. The trees are mainly oaks and pines,
and the pines predominate. Occasionally, there are long, dark, serrated stands
of Atlantic white cedars, so tall and so closely set that they seem to be spread
against the sky on the ridges of hills, when in fact they grow along streams
that flow through the forest. To the east, the view is similar, and few people
who are not native to the region can discern essential differences from the
high cabin of the fire tower, even though one difference is that huge areas out
in this direction are covered with dwarf forests, where a man can stand
among the trees and see for miles over their uppermost branches. To the
south, the view is twice broken slightly—by a lake and by a cranberry bog—
but otherwise it, too, goes to the horizon in forest. To the west, pines, oaks,
and cedars continue all the way, and the western horizon includes the summit
of another hill—Apple Pie Hill—and the outline of another fire tower, from
which the view three hundred and sixty degrees around is virtually the same
as the view from Bear Swamp Hill, where, in a moment's sweeping glance, a
person can see hundreds of square miles of wilderness. The picture of New
Jersey that most people hold in their minds is so different from this one that,
considered beside it, the Pine Barrens, as they are called, become as incongruous as they are beautiful. West and north of the Pine Barrens is New Jersey's

central transportation corridor, where traffic of freight and people is more concentrated than it is anywhere else in the world. The corridor is one great compression of industrial shapes, industrial sounds, industrial air, and thousands and thousands of houses webbing over the spaces between the factories. Railroads and magnificent highways traverse this crowded scene, and by 1985 New Jersey hopes to have added so many additional high-speed roads that the present New Jersey Turnpike will be quite closely neighbored by the equivalent of at least six other turnpikes, all going in the same direction. In and around the New Jersey corridor, towns indistinguishably abut one another. Of the great unbroken city that will one day reach at least from Boston to Richmond, this section is already built. New Jersey has nearly a thousand people per square mile—the greatest population density of any state in the Union. In parts of northern New Jersey, there are as many as forty thousand people per square mile. In the central area of the Pine Barrens—the forest land that is still so undeveloped that it can be called wilderness—there are only fifteen people per square mile. This area, which includes about six hundred and fifty thousand acres, is nearly as large as Yosemite National Park. It is almost identical in size with Grand Canyon National Park, and it is much larger than Sequoia National Park, Great Smoky Mountains National Park, or, for that matter, most of the national parks in the United States. The people who live in the Pine Barrens are concentrated mainly in small forest towns, so the region's uninhabited sections are quite large—twenty thousand acres here, thirty thousand acres there—and in one section of well over a hundred thousand acres there are only twenty-one people. The Pine Barrens are so close to New York that on a very clear night a bright light in the pines would be visible from the Empire State Building. A line ruled on a map from Boston to Richmond goes straight through the middle of the Pine Barrens. The halfway point between Boston and Richmond—the geographical epicenter of the developing megalopolis—is in the northern part of the woods, about twenty miles from Bear Swamp Hill.

2   Technically, the Pine Barrens are much larger than the thousand or so square miles of them that remain wild, and their original outline is formed by the boundaries of a thick layer of sand soils that covers much of central and southern New Jersey—down the coast from the outskirts of Asbury Park to the Cape May Peninsula, and inland more than halfway across the state. Settlers in the seventeenth and eighteenth centuries found these soils unpromising for farms, left the land uncleared, and began to refer to the region as the Pine Barrens. People in New Jersey still use the term, with variants such as "the pine belt," "the pinelands," and, most frequently, "the pines." Gradually, development of one kind or another has moved in over the edges of the forest, reducing the circumference of the wild land and creating a manmade boundary in place of the natural one. This transition line is often so abrupt that in many places on the periphery of the pines it is possible to be at one moment in farmland, or even in a residential development or an indus-

trial zone, and in the next moment to be in the silence of a bewildering green country, where a journey of forty or fifty miles is necessary to get to the farms and factories on the other side. I don't know where the exact center of the pines may be, but in recent years I have spent considerable time there and have made outlines of the integral woodland on topographic maps and road maps, and from them I would judge that the heart of the pine country is in or near a place called Hog Wallow. There are twenty-five people in Hog Wallow. Some of them describe it, without any apparent intention to be clever, as a suburb of Jenkins, a town three miles away, which has forty-five people. One resident of Hog Wallow is Frederick Chambers Brown. I met him one summer morning when I stopped at his house to ask for water.

Fred Brown's house is on an unpaved road that curves along the edge of a wide cranberry bog. What attracted me to it was the pump that stands in his yard. It was something of a wonder that I noticed the pump, because there were, among other things, eight automobiles in the yard, two of them on their sides and one of them upside down, all ten years old or older. Around the cars were old refrigerators, vacuum cleaners, partly dismantled radios, cathode-ray tubes, a short wooden ski, a large wooden mallet, dozens of cranberry pickers' boxes, many tires, an orange crate dated 1946, a cord or so of firewood, mandolins, engine heads, and maybe a thousand other things. The house itself, two stories high, was covered with tarpaper that was peeling away in some places, revealing its original shingles, made of Atlantic white cedar from the stream courses of the surrounding forest. I called out to ask if anyone was home, and a voice called back, "Come in. Come in. Come on the hell in."

I walked through a vestibule that had a dirt floor, stepped up into a kitchen, and went on into another room that had several overstuffed chairs in it and a porcelain-topped table, where Fred Brown was seated, eating a pork chop. He was dressed in a white sleeveless shirt, ankle-top shoes, and undershorts. He gave me a cheerful greeting and, without asking why I had come or what I wanted, picked up a pair of khaki trousers that had been tossed onto one of the overstuffed chairs and asked me to sit down. He set the trousers on another chair, and he apologized for being in the middle of his breakfast, explaining that he seldom drank much but the night before he had had a few drinks and this had caused his day to start slowly. "I don't know what's the matter with me, but there's got to be something the matter with me, because drink don't agree with me anymore," he said. He had a raw onion in one hand, and while he talked he shaved slices from the onion and ate them between bites of the chop. He was a muscular and well-built man, with short, bristly white hair, and he had bright, fast-moving eyes in a wide-open face. His legs were trim and strong, with large muscles in the calves. I guessed that he was about sixty, and for a man of sixty he seemed to be in remarkably good shape. He was actually seventy-nine. "My rule is: Never eat except when you're hungry," he said, and he ate another slice of the onion.

5   In a straight-backed chair near the doorway to the kitchen sat a young man with long black hair, who wore a visored red leather cap that had darkened with age. His shirt was coarse-woven and had eyelets down a V neck that was laced with a thong. His trousers were made of canvas, and he was wearing gum boots. His arms were folded, his legs were stretched out, he had one ankle over the other, and as he sat there he appeared to be sighting carefully past his feet, as if his toes were the outer frame of a gunsight and he could see some sort of target in the floor. When I had entered, I had said hello to him, and he had nodded without looking up. He had a long, straight nose and high cheekbones, in a deeply tanned face that was, somehow, gaunt. I had no idea whether he was shy or hostile. Eventually, when I came to know him, I found him to be as shy a person as I have ever had a chance to know. His name is Bill Wasovwich, and he lives alone in a cabin about half a mile from Fred. First his father, then his mother left him when he was a young boy, and he grew up depending on the help of various people in the pines. One of them, a cranberry grower, employs him and has given him some acreage, in which Bill is building a small cranberry bog of his own, "turfing it out" by hand. When he is not working in the bogs, he goes roaming, as he puts it, setting out cross-country on long, looping journeys, hiking about thirty miles in a typical day, in search of what he calls "events"— surprising a buck, or a gray fox, or perhaps a poacher or a man with a still. Almost no one who is not native to the pines could do this, for the woods have an undulating sameness, and the understory—huckleberries, sheep laurel, sweet fern, high-bush blueberry—is often so dense that a wanderer can walk in a fairly tight circle and think that he is moving in a straight line. State forest rangers spend a good part of their time finding hikers and hunters, some of whom have vanished for days. In his long, pathless journeys, Bill always emerges from the woods near his cabin—and about when he plans to. In the fall, when thousands of hunters come into the pines, he sometimes works as a guide. In the evenings, or in the daytime when he is not working or roaming, he goes to Fred Brown's house and sits there for hours. The old man is a widower whose seven children are long since gone from Hog Wallow, and he is as expansively talkative and worldly as the young one is withdrawn and wild. Although there are fifty-three years between their ages, it is obviously fortunate for each of them to be the other's neighbor.

6   That first morning, while Bill went on looking at his outstretched toes, Fred got up from the table, put on his pants, and said he was going to cook me a pork chop, because I looked hungry and ought to eat something. It was about noon, and I was even hungrier than I may have looked, so I gratefully accepted his offer, which was a considerable one. There are two or three small general stores in the pines, but for anything as fragile as a fresh pork chop it is necessary to make a round trip from Fred's place of about fifty miles. Fred went into the kitchen and dropped a chop into a frying pan that was crackling with hot grease. He has a fairly new four-burner stove that uses bottled gas.

He keeps water in a large bowl on a table in the kitchen and ladles some when he wants it. While he cooked the meat, he looked out a window through a stand of pitch pines and into the cranberry bog. "I saw a big buck out here last night with velvet on his horns," he said. "Them horns is soft when they're in velvet." On a nail high on one wall of the room that Bill and I were sitting in was a large meat cleaver. Next to it was a billy club. The wall itself was papered in a flower pattern, and the wallpaper continued out across the ceiling and down the three other walls, lending the room something of the appearance of the inside of a gift box. In some parts of the ceiling, the paper had come loose. "I didn't paper this year." Fred said. "For the last couple months, I've had sinus." The floor was covered with old rugs. They had been put down in random pieces, and in some places as many as six layers were stacked up. In winter, when the temperature approaches zero, the worst cold comes through the floor. The only source of heat in the house is a wood-burning stove in the main room. There were seven calendars on the walls, all current and none with pictures of nudes. Fading into pastel on one wall was a rotogravure photograph of President and Mrs. Eisenhower. A framed poem read:

> God hath not promised
> Sun without rain
> Joy without sorrow
> Peace without pain.

Noticing my interest in all this, Fred reached into a drawer and showed me what appeared to be a postcard. On it was a photograph of a woman, and Fred said with a straight face that she was his present girl, adding that he meets her regularly under a juniper tree on a road farther south in the pines. The woman, whose appearance suggested strongly that she had never been within a great many miles of the Pine Barrens, was wearing nothing at all. 7

I asked Fred what all those cars were doing in his yard, and he said that one of them was in running condition and the rest were its predecessors. The working vehicle was a 1956 Mercury. Each of the seven others had at one time or another been his best car, and each, in turn, had lain down like a sick animal and had died right there in the yard, unless it had been towed home after a mishap elsewhere in the pines. Fred recited, with affection, the history of each car. Of one old Ford, for example, he said, "I upset that up to Speedwell in the creek." And of an even older car, a station wagon, he said, "I busted that one up in the snow. I met a car on a little hill, and hit the brake, and hit a tree." One of the cars had met its end at a narrow bridge about four miles from Hog Wallow, where Fred had hit a state trooper, head on. 8

The pork was delicious and almost crisp. Fred gave me a potato with it, and a pitcher of melted grease from the frying pan to pour over the potato. He also handed me a loaf of bread and a dish of margarine, saying, "Here's your bread. You can have one piece or two. Whatever you want." 9

10   Fred apologized for not having a phone, after I asked where I would have to go to make a call, later on. He said, "I don't have no phone because I don't have no electric. If I had electric, I would have had a phone in here a long time ago." He uses a kerosene lamp, a propane lamp, and two flashlights.

11   He asked where I was going, and I said that I had no particular destination, explaining that I was in the pines because I found it hard to believe that so much unbroken forest could still exist so near the big Eastern cities, and I wanted to see it while it was still there. "Is that so?" he said, three times. Like many people in the pines, he often says things three times. "Is that so? Is *that* so?"

12   I asked him what he thought of a plan that has been developed by Burlington and Ocean counties to create a supersonic jetport in the pines, connected by a spur of the Garden State Parkway to a new city of two hundred and fifty thousand people, also in the pines.

13   "They've been talking about that for three years, and they've never give up," Fred said.

14   "It'd be the end of these woods," Bill said. This was the first time I heard Bill speak. I had been there for an hour, and he had not said a word. Without looking up, he said again, "It'd be the end of these woods, I can tell you that."

15   Fred said, "They could build ten jetports around me. I wouldn't give a damn."

16   "You ain't going to be around very long," Bill said to him. "It would be the end of these woods."

17   Fred took that as a fact, and not as an insult. "Yes, it would be the end of these woods," he said. "But there'd be people here you could do business with."

18   Bill said, "There ain't no place like this left in the country, I don't believe—and I travelled around a little bit, too."

19   Eventually, I made the request I had intended to make when I walked in the door. "Could I have some water?" I said to Fred. "I have a jerry can and I'd like to fill it at the pump."

20   "Hell, yes," he said. "That isn't my water. That's God's water. That's God's water. That right, Bill?"

21   "I *guess* so," Bill said, without looking up. "It's good water, I can tell you that."

22   "That's God's water," Fred said again. "Take all you want."

Questions

1. Writers often focus on the inhabitants of a place in attempting to describe it, as McPhee does here. What is his attitude toward the inhabitants of the Pine Barrens, as represented by Fred Brown and Bill Wasovwich? Does his attitude toward the people

reinforce his attitude toward the place? How does McPhee want his readers to feel about the Pine Barrens?

2. Descriptions of places often begin with a broad vista and gradually move toward a closeup of a small area. Here, McPhee's description begins by looking at the Pine Barrens from a fire tower; the vista extends as far as the eye can see, "about twelve miles." How much narrower has this view become by the middle of paragraph 1? What is the perspective by the end of the paragraph? In paragraph 2 the focus becomes still narrower—as a transition to what in paragraphs 3 and 4?

3. What governs the organization of McPhee's description of Fred Brown's yard and house (paragraphs 3, 4)? What determines the organization of details in his description of Brown's kitchen (paragraph 6)? Argue for or against including descriptions of the photograph of the woman "wearing nothing at all" (paragraph 7) and of the old cars in Brown's yard (paragraph 8).

4. McPhee's description of the Pine Barrens moves with the natural rhythms of speech from silence to sound, from conversation to phrases repeated three times. What is the effect of concluding with the triple repetition of " 'That's God's water' "?

MARGARET LAURENCE
Where the World Began

Laurence was born in Manitoba, Canada, in 1926, earned a B.A. from the University of Manitoba in 1946, and found, in Canada where, as she says, "my world began," "a world which gave me my own lifework to do, because it was here that I learned the sight of my own particular eyes." That lifework was to be a writer, but to see Canada clearly enough to be able to write about it Laurence first had to leave the country. She and her husband lived in Somaliland for two years, where she edited for the Somali government A Tree of Poverty *(1954), an anthology of Somali poetry and prose. Her first novel,* The Prophet's Camel Bell *(1963), about the hardships of the Haud Desert, likewise had an African setting, as did some of the stories in* The Tomorrow Tamer and Other Stories *(1964). Since then her work has focused on her native Canada:* The Stone Angel *(1964),* A Jest of God *(1966) (published in the United States as* Rachel, Rachel *and made into a movie of the same name), and, most recently,* Heart of a Stranger *(1977), in which the following selection appears.*

In determining who we are it's important to know where we are, where our world began. Like it or not, we're identified by our contexts: American or Canadian, urban or suburban, small town or rural. To be a perpetual wanderer, a person without a country, is to be incredibly lonesome; to be without a place is to be devoid of an identity. Yet the place of one's origin can be legion; Laurence identifies her hometown only as "a small prairie town" and therefore typical of its kind. Such towns, stereotyped by outsiders as "bleak, flat, uninteresting," offer manifold attractions, some beautiful or engaging, some "bizarre, agonizingly repressive or cruel at times" to the insiders nurtured and formed there. Through a series of specific scenes Laurence presents a portrait of the girl she was as she describes the town: the winter sleighrides and snowshoeing, summer droughts, river life, and small town society, conventional and eccentric, living and dead. She concludes on a more general note; wherever she may live, her "true roots" are Canadian, and she is a Canadian for life.

1   A strange place it was, that place where the world began. A place of incredible happenings, splendors and revelations, despairs like multitudinous pits of isolated hells. A place of shadow-spookiness, inhabited by the unknowable dead. A place of jubilation and of mourning, horrible and beautiful.

2   It was, in fact, a small prairie town.

3   Because that settlement and that land were my first and for many years my only real knowledge of this planet, in some profound way they remain my world, my way of viewing. My eyes were formed there. Towns like ours, set in a sea of land, have been described thousands of times as dull, bleak, flat, uninteresting. I have had it said to me that the railway trip across Canada is spectacular, except for the prairies, when it would be desirable to go to sleep for several days, until the ordeal is over. I am always unable to argue this point effectively. All I can say is—well, you really have to live there to know that country. The town of my childhood could be called bizarre, agonizingly repressive or cruel at times, and the land in which it grew could be called harsh in the violence of its seasonal changes. But never merely flat or uninteresting. Never dull.

4   In winter, we used to hitch rides on the back of the milk sleigh, our moccasins squeaking and slithering on the hard rutted snow of the roads, our hands in ice-bubbled mitts hanging onto the box edge of the sleigh for dear life, while Bert grinned at us through his great frosted mustache and shouted the horse into speed, daring us to stay put. Those mornings, rising, there would be the perpetual fascination of the frost feathers on windows, the ferns and flowers and eerie faces traced there during the night by unseen artists of the wind. Evenings, coming back from skating, the sky would be black but not dark, for you could see a gold glitter of stars from one side of the earth's rim to the other. And then the sometime astonishment when you saw the Northern Lights flaring across the sky, like the scrawled signature of God. After a blizzard, when the snowplow hadn't yet got through, school would be closed for the day, the assumption being that the town's young could not possibly flounder through five feet of snow in the pursuit of education. We would then gaily don snowshoes and flounder for miles out into the white dazzling deserts, in pursuit of a different kind of knowing. If you came back too close to night, through the woods at the foot of the town hill, the thin black branches of poplar and chokecherry now meringued with frost, sometimes you heard coyotes. Or maybe the banshee wolf-voices were really only inside your head.

5   Summers were scorching, and when no rain came and the wheat became bleached and dried before it headed, the faces of farmers and townsfolk

would not smile much, and you took for granted, because it never seemed to have been any different, the frequent knocking at the back door and the young men standing there, mumbling or thrusting defiantly their requests for a drink of water and a sandwich if you could spare it. They were riding the freights, and you never knew where they had come from, or where they might end up, if anywhere. The Drought and Depression were like evil deities which had been there always. You understood and did not understand.

Yet the outside world had its continuing marvels. The poplar bluffs and the small river were filled and surrounded with a zillion different grasses, stones, and weed flowers. The meadowlarks sang undaunted from the twanging telephone wires along the gravel highway. Once we found an old flat-bottomed scow, and launched her, poling along the shallow brown waters, mending her with wodges of hastily chewed Spearmint, grounding her among the tangles of yellow marsh marigolds that grew succulently along the banks of the shrunken river, while the sun made our skins smell dusty-warm. 6

My best friend lived in an apartment above some stores on Main Street (its real name was Mountain Avenue, goodness knows why), an elegant apartment with royal-blue velvet curtains. The back roof, scarcely sloping at all, was corrugated tin, of a furnace-like warmth on a July afternoon, and we would sit there drinking lemonade and looking across the back lane at the Fire Hall. Sometimes our vigil would be rewarded. Oh joy! Somebody's house burning down! We had an almost-perfect callousness in some ways. Then the wooden tower's bronze bell would clonk and toll like a thousand speeded funerals in a time of plague, and in a few minutes the team of giant black horses would cannon forth, pulling the fire wagon like some scarlet chariot of the Goths, while the firemen clung with one hand, adjusting their helmets as they went. 7

The oddities of the place were endless. An elderly lady used to serve, as her afternoon tea offering to other ladies, soda biscuits spread with peanut butter and topped with a whole marshmallow. Some considered this slightly eccentric, when compared with chopped egg sandwiches, and admittedly talked about her behind her back, but no one ever refused these delicacies or indicated to her that they thought she had slipped a cog. Another lady dyed her hair a bright and cheery orange, by strangers often mistaken at twenty paces for a feather hat. My own beloved stepmother wore a silver fox neckpiece, a whole pelt, *with the embalmed (?) head still on*. My Ontario Irish grandfather said, "sparrow grass," a more interesting term than asparagus. The town dump was known as "the nuisance grounds," a phrase fraught with weird connotations, as though the effluvia of our lives was beneath contempt but at the same time was subtly threatening to the determined and sometimes hysterical propriety of our ways. 8

Some oddities were, as idiom had it, "funny ha ha"; others were "funny peculiar." Some were not so very funny at all. An old man lived, deranged, in 9 a shack in the valley. Perhaps he wasn't even all that old, but to us he seemed a wild Methuselah figure, shambling among the underbrush and the tall couchgrass, muttering indecipherable curses or blessings, a prophet who had forgotten his prophecies. Everyone in town knew him, but no one knew him. He lived among us as though only occasionally and momentarily visible. The kids called him Andy Gump, and feared him. Some sought to prove their bravery by tormenting him. They were the medieval bear baiters, and he the lumbering bewildered bear, half blind, only rarely turning to snarl. Everything is to be found in a town like mine. Belsen, writ small but with the same ink.

10   All of us cast stones in one shape or another. In grade school, among the vulnerable and violet girls we were, the feared and despised were those few older girls from what was charmingly termed "the wrong side of the tracks." Tough in talk and tougher in muscle, they were said to be whores already. And may have been, that being about the only profession readily available to them.

11   The dead lived in that place, too. Not only the grandparents who had, in local parlance, "passed on" and who gloomed, bearded or bonneted, from the sepia photographs in old albums, but also the uncles, forever eighteen or nineteen, whose names were carved on the granite family stones in the cemetery, but whose bones lay in France. My own young mother lay in that graveyard, beside other dead of our kin, and when I was ten, my father, too, only forty, left the living town for the dead dwelling on the hill.

12   When I was eighteen, I couldn't wait to get out of that town, away from the prairies. I did not know then that I would carry the land and town all my life within my skull, that they would form the mainspring and source of the writing I was to do, wherever and however far away I might live.

13   This was my territory in the time of my youth, and in a sense my life since then has been an attempt to look at it, to come to terms with it. Stultifying to the mind it certainly could be, and sometimes was, but not to the imagination. It was many things, but it was never dull.

14   The same, I now see, could be said for Canada in general. Why on earth did generations of Canadians pretend to believe this country dull? We knew perfectly well it wasn't. Yet for so long we did not proclaim what we knew. If our upsurge of so-called nationalism seems odd or irrelevant to outsiders, and even to some of our own people (*what's all the fuss about?*), they might try to understand that for many years we valued ourselves insufficiently, living as we did under the huge shadows of those two dominating figures, Uncle Sam and Britannia. We have only just begun to value ourselves, our land, our abilities. We have only just begun to recognize our legends and to give shape to our myths.

15   There are, God knows, enough aspects to deplore about this country. When I see the killing of our lakes and rivers with industrial wastes, I feel rage and despair. When I see our industries and natural resources increasingly

taken over by America, I feel an overwhelming discouragement, especially as I cannot simply say "damn Yankees." It should never be forgotten that it is we ourselves who have sold such a large amount of our birthright for a mess of plastic Progress. When I saw the War Measures Act being invoked in 1970, I lost forever the vestigial remains of the naïve wish-belief that repression could not happen here, or would not. And yet, of course, I had known all along in the deepest and often hidden caves of the heart that anything can happen anywhere, for the seeds of both man's freedom and his captivity are found everywhere, even in the microcosm of a prairie town. But in raging against our injustices, our stupidities, I do so as *family,* as I did, and still do in writing, about those aspects of my town which I hated and which are always in some ways aspects of myself.

The land still draws me more than other lands. I have lived in Africa and in England, but splendid as both can be, they do not have the power to move me in the same way as, for example, that part of southern Ontario where I spent four months last summer in a cedar cabin beside a river. "Scratch a Canadian, and you find a phony pioneer," I used to say to myself in warning. But all the same it is true, I think, that we are not yet totally alienated from physical earth, and let us only pray we do not become so. I once thought that my lifelong fear and mistrust of cities made me a kind of old-fashioned freak; now I see it differently.   16

The cabin has a long window across its front western wall, and sitting at the oak table there in the mornings, I used to look out at the river and at the tall trees beyond, green-gold in the early light. The river was bronze; the sun caught it strangely, reflecting upon its surface the near-shore sand ripples underneath. Suddenly, the crescenting of a fish, gone before the eye could clearly give image to it. The old man next door said these leaping fish were carp. Himself, he preferred muskie, for he was a real fisherman and the muskie gave him a fight. The wind most often blew from the south, and the river flowed toward the south, so when the water was wind-riffled, and the current was strong, the river seemed to be flowing both ways. I liked this, and interpreted it as an omen, a natural symbol.   17

A few years ago, when I was back in Winnipeg, I gave a talk at my old college. It was open to the public, and afterward a very old man came up to me and asked me if my maiden name had been Wemyss. I said yes, thinking he might have known my father or my grandfather. But no. "When I was a young lad," he said, "I once worked for your great-grandfather, Robert Wemyss, when he had the sheep ranch at Raeburn." I think that was a moment when I realized all over again something of great importance to me. My long-ago families came from Scotland and Ireland, but in a sense that no longer mattered so much. My true roots were here.   18

I am not very patriotic, in the usual meaning of that word. I cannot say "My country right or wrong" in any political, social or literary context. But one thing is inalterable, for better or worse, for life.   19

20   This is where my world began. A world which includes the ancestors—
both my own and other people's ancestors who become mine. A world which
formed me, and continues to do so, even while I found it in some of its
aspects, and continue to do so. A world which gave me my own lifework to
do, because it was here that I learned the sight of my own particular eyes.

JAMES MORRIS
The Venetian Way

*James Morris, later Jan Morris, was born in Somerset, England, in 1926. Between 1943
and 1947 Morris served as a lieutenant with the 9th Lancers; married in 1947, he fathered
five children. After a brief stint with the Arab News Agency in Cairo, Morris studied at
Oxford; he received a B.A. from Christ Church College in 1951 and an M.A. in 1961.
During the same decade Morris was also a foreign correspondent, first for the London* Times,
then for the Manchester Guardian. *In 1961 Morris began the career as a travel writer that
continues to this day, writing over twenty books on travel—in the Middle East, the Far East,
Africa, Europe, and the United States. The most recent are* Destinations *(1980),* Journeys
(1984), and The Mother of Waters *(1985). The exception is* Conundrum *(1974), which
with candid eloquence explains the author's process of becoming female.*

*Morris prefers "impressionistic journalism" to objective writing, which he considers too
detached. In 1961 when he published* The World of Venice *he believed that it represented
his "finest writing . . . because I had to get involved." Morris, fully engaged with the subject,
provides a thoughtful guide to this ancient, captivating city, telling us what Venetians are
like, what they think about themselves, what they think about us, and how we should think
about them. As with many personal travel accounts, we finish the essay feeling as if we have
participated in Morris's experience of the city, but because he has presented a balanced,
believable account of its flaws as well as its triumphs, we're glad to have shared his experience,
involvement, and enthusiasm.*

1   You can tell a Venetian by his face. Thousands of other Italians now live in
Venice, but the true-born Venetian is often instantly recognizable. He probably has Slav blood in him, perhaps Austrian, possibly Oriental tinctures from
the distant past, and he is very far indeed from the stock music-hall Latin.
Morose but calculating is the look in his limpid eye, and his mouth is enig-
matical. His nose is very prominent, like the nose of a Renaissance grandee,
and there is to his manner an air of home-spun guile and complacency, as of a
man who has made a large fortune out of slightly shady dealings in artichokes. He is often bow-legged (but not from too much riding) and often
pale (but not from lack of sunshine). Occasionally his glance contains a glint
of sly contempt, and his smile is distant: usually he is a man of gentle reserve,
courteous, ceremonious, his jacket neatly buttoned and his itchy palm discreetly gloved. The Venetians often remind me of Welshmen, and often of

Jews, and sometimes of Icelanders, and occasionally of Afrikaners, for they have the introspective melancholy pride of people on their own, excluded from the fold of ordinary nations. They feel at once aloof, suspicious and kind. They are seldom boisterous or swashbuckling, and when you hear a Venetian say *'Buona sera, bellissima Signorina!'* he says it without flourish or flattery, with a casual inclination of the head. The Venetian in the street can be uncompromising, and cheerfully butts you in the stomach with the tip of her loaf, or drops her laundry-basket agonizingly on your toe. The Venetian in the shop has a special muffled *politesse,* a restrained but regretful decorum that is part of the ambience of the city.

Observe a pair of Venetian housewives meeting, and you will see re- 2 flected in all their gestures the pungent character of Venice. They approach each other hard-faced and intent, for they are doing their shopping, and carry in their baskets the morning's purchases—which seem to consist so far, this being a thrifty city, of an ounce of shrimps, a gramme of sugar, two eggs and a sample-size tube of tooth-paste: but as they catch sight of each other a sudden soft gleam of commiseration crosses their faces, as though they are about to barter sympathies over some irreparable loss, or share an unusually tender confidence. Their expressions instantly relax, and they welcome each other with a protracted exchange of greetings, rather like the benign grace-notes and benedictions with which old-school Arabs encounter their friends. Their tone of voice is surprised but intimate, falling and rising with penetra-tion through the din of the market: and they sound as though they are simultaneously sympathetic about something, and mournful about some-thing, and a little peevish, and resigned, and reluctantly amused. ('Poor Venice!' the housewife sometimes sighs, leaning from her balcony window: but it is little more than a wry slogan, like a commuter's exorcism upon the weather, or one of those general complaints, common to us all, about the universal decline of everything.)

They talk for five or ten minutes, sometimes shaking their heads anx- 3 iously or shifting their weight from one foot to another, and when they part they wave good-bye to each other in a manner all their own, holding their right hands vertically beside their shoulders, and slightly wagging the tips of all five fingers. In a flash their expressions are earnestly mercantile again, and they are disputing the price of beans with a spry but knowing greengrocer.

The modern Venetians are not a stately people. They are homely, provin- 4 cial, fond, complacent. At heart this is a very *bourgeois* city. The Venetians have lost the unassertive confidence of power, and love to be thought well of. There was a time when kings and pontiffs bowed before the Doge of Venice, and Titian, the most lordly of the Venetian painters, once graciously allowed the Emperor Charles V of Spain and Austria to pick up the paint brush he had accidentally dropped. But by the end of the eighteenth century the Venetians were already becoming testy of criticism, like Americans before their time of power, or Englishmen after theirs. Parochial to a Middle-Western degree was the reply sent by Giustina Renier Michiel, the last great lady of the Republic, when Chateaubriand dared to write an article unflattering to Venice ('a city against nature—one cannot take a step without being obliged to get into a boat!'). Frigid is the disapproval of the contemporary Venetian *grande dame,* if you venture to suggest that some of the city's gardens might be the better for a pair of shears.

5   The Venetian way is the right way, and the Venetian nearly always knows best. In the church of San Salvatore there is an Annunciation by Titian which, being a little unconventional in style, so surprised its monastic sponsors that they flatly declared it to be unfinished, or perhaps not really by Titian at all; the old artist was understandably annoyed, and wrote on the bottom of the picture, where you may see it still, the irritated double inscription *Titianus Fecit. Fecit.* I have often sympathized with him, faced with the know-all Venetians, for the true son of Venice (and even more, the daughter) is convinced that the skills, arts and sciences of the world ripple outwards, in ever-weakening circles, from the Piazza of St. Mark. If you want to write a book, consult a Venetian professor. If you want to tie a knot in a rope, ask a Venetian how. If you want to know how a bridge is built, look at the Rialto. To learn how to make a cup of coffee, frame a picture, stuff a peacock, phrase a treaty, clean your shoes, sew a button on a blouse, consult the appropriate Venetian authority.

6   'The Venetian custom' is the criterion of good sense and propriety. Pitying, lofty but condescending is the smile on the Venetian face, when you suggest frying the fish in breadcrumbs, instead of in flour. Paternal is the man in the camera shop, as he demonstrates to you the only correct way to focus your Leica. 'It is our custom'—by which the Venetian means not merely that Venetian things are best, but that they are probably unique. Often and again you will be kindly told, as you step from the quayside into your boat, that Venetian seaweed is slippery: and I have even heard it said that Venetian water is inclined to be wet.

7   These are the harmless conceits of the parish pump. Foreigners who have lived in Venice for years have told me how detached they have grown to feel from the affairs of the world at large, as though they are mere onlookers: and this sense of separateness, which once contributed to the invincibility of the Republic, now bolsters Venetian complacencies. Like poor relations or provincial bigwigs, the Venetians love to ponder the glories of their pedigree, tracing their splendours ever further back, beyond the great Doges and the Tribunes to Rome herself (the Giustinian family claims descent from the Emperor Justinian) and even into the mists of pre-history, when the original Venetians are variously supposed to have come from Paphlagonia, from the Baltic, from Babylon, from Illyria, from the coast of Brittany, or directly, like nymphs, out of the morning dew. Venetians love to tell you about 'my grandfather, a man of much cultural and intellectual distinction'; or invite

you to share the assumption that the opera at the Fenice is, on the whole, the best and most cultural on earth; or point out the Venetian artist Vedova as the greatest of his generation ('But perhaps you're not, shall we say, *au fait* with the tendencies of contemporary art, such as are demonstrated here in Venice at our Biennale?'). Every Venetian is a connoisseur, with a strong bias towards the local product. The guides at the Doge's Palace rarely bother to mention the startling paintings by Hieronymus Bosch that hang near the Bridge of Sighs—he was not, after all, a Venetian. The Venetian libraries concern themselves assiduously with Venice. The pictures that hang in Venetian houses are always of Venetian scenes. Venice is a shamelessly self-centred place, in a constant glow of elderly narcissism.

There is nothing offensive to this local pride, for the Venetians are not 8 exactly boastful, only convinced. Indeed, there is sometimes real pathos to it. Modern Venice is not so preeminent, by a half, as they like to suppose. Its glitter and sparkle nearly all comes with the summer visitors, and its private intellectual life is sluggish. Its opera audiences (except in the galleries) are coarse and inattentive, and few indeed are the fairy motor boats that arrive, in the dismal winter evenings, at the once brilliant water-gate of the Fenice. There is not one genuine full-time theatre in the city. Concerts, except in the tourist season, are generally second-rate and expensive. The university is a mere appendage of Padua. The celebrated printing houses of Venice, once the finest in Europe, have nearly all gone. Venetian cooking is undistinguished, Venetian workmanship is variable. The old robust seafaring habits have long been dissipated, so that the average Venetian never goes too near the water, and makes a terrible fuss if a storm blows up. In many ways Venice is a backwater. Some people say she is dead on her feet. Memphis, Leeds and Léopoldville are all bigger, and all livelier. Genoa handles twice as much shipping. There is a better orchestra in Cincinnati, a better newspaper in Manchester, a better university in Capetown; and any week-end yachtswoman, sailing her dinghy at Chichester or Newport, will tie you as practical a knot as a gondolier.

But there, love is blind, especially if there is sadness in the family. The 9 Venetians love and admire their Venice with a curious fervency. The Republic was "a family, with the Doge as grandpapa," and Venetians still view the city possessively. Passers-by will recommend a *trattoria* to you as though they actually owned the place, and the beadle at the door of St. Mark's Basilica is at least as proud as the Patriarch. Some Venetians, especially poorer people, also see the fun of their situation, and laugh at the notion of traffic lights on a canal, or a garage for a gondola.

The Venetian, no less than the tourist, likes to walk about his city. 10 'Where are you off to?' you may ask an acquaintance. 'To the Piazza', he replies: but he can give you no reason, if you ask him why. He goes to St. Mark's for no definite purpose, to meet nobody specific, to admire no particular spectacle. He simply likes to button his coat, and sleek his hair a little, assume an air of rather portentous melancholy and stroll for an hour or two among the sumptuous trophies of his heritage. Hardly a true Venetian crosses the Grand Canal without the hint of a pause, however vestigial, to breathe its beauties. Our housekeeper grumbles sometimes about the narrowness of Venice, its cramped and difficult nature; but never was a lover more subtly devoted to her protector, or an idealist to his flaming cause. Venice is a sensual city, and there is something physiological about the devotion she inspires, as though the very fact of her presence can stimulate the bloodstream.

11   I was once in Venice on the day of the Festival of the Salute, in November, when the Venetians, to celebrate the ending of a seventeenth-century plague, erect a temporary bridge across the Grand Canal and process to the great church of Santa Maria della Salute. In the evening I posted myself at the end of the bridge, a rickety structure of barges and timber. (It was designed, so I was reassuringly told, 'according to an immemorial pattern', but one November in the 1930s it collapsed, just as Sir Osbert Sitwell was crossing it.) There, turning up my collar against the bitter sea wind, I watched the Venetians walking to evening Mass, in twos or threes or youth groups, cosily wrapped. There was a curiously proprietorial feeling to their progress: and as each little group of people turned the corner to the bridge, and saw the lights of the quay before them, and the huge dome of the Salute floodlit in the dusk, 'Ah!' they said, clicking their tongues with affection, 'how beautiful she looks tonight!'—for all the world as though some frail but favourite aunt were wearing her best lacy bed-jacket for visitors.

12   This self-esteem makes for narrow horizons and short focuses. Many poor Venetians, even in 1960, have never been to the mainland of Italy. Thousands have never visited the outer islands of the lagoon. You sometimes hear stories of people who have never crossed the Grand Canal or set eyes on the Piazza of St. Mark. Simple Venetians are often extraordinarily ignorant about geography and world affairs, and even educated people (like most islanders) are frequently poor linguists.

13   The Venetians indeed have a language of their own, a rich and original dialect, only now beginning to lose its vigour under the impact of cinema and television. It is a slurred but breezy affair, lively enough for Goldoni to write some of his best plays in it, formal enough to be the official language of the Venetian Republic. Byron called it 'a sweet bastard Latin'. Dazed are the faces of visiting linguists, confronted by this hairy hybrid, for its derivation is partly French, and partly Greek, and partly Arabic, and partly German, and probably partly Paphlagonian too—the whole given a fine extra blur by a queer helter-skelter, sing-song manner of delivery. Often the Venetian seems to be mouthing no particular words, only a buttery succession of half-enunciated consonants. The Venetian language is very fond of Xs and Zs, and as far as possible ignores the letter L altogether, so that the Italian *bello*, for

example, comes out *beo*. There are at least four Italian-Venetian dictionaries, and from these you can see that sometimes the Venetian word bears no resemblance to the Italian. A fork is *forchetta* in Italian, but *piron* in Venetian. The Venetian baker is *pistor,* not *fornaio*. A watch is *relozo,* not *orologio*. The Venetian pronouns are *mi, ti, lu, nu, vu, lori*. When we say 'thou art', and the Italians '*tu sei*', the Venetians say '*ti ti xe*'. The Venetian word *lovo* means first a wolf, and secondly a stock-fish.

This distinctive and attractive language also specializes in queer contrac-   14
tions and distortions, and the street signs of the city, still often expressed in the vernacular, can be very confusing. You may look, consulting your guide book, for the church of Santi Giovanni e Paolo; but the street sign will call it San Zanipolo. The church of Sant' Alvise was originally dedicated to St. Louis. What the Venetians call San Stae is really Sant' Eustachio. San Stin is Santo Stefano. Sant' Aponal is Sant' Apollinare. The convent of Santa Maria di Nazareth, used as a leper colony, was so long ago blurred into San Lazzaretto that it has given its corruption to almost all the languages of the earth. What holy man is commemorated by the Fondamenta Sangiantoffetti I have never been able to discover, and it took me some time to realize that the titular saint of San Zan Degola was San Giovanni Decollato, St. John the Beheaded. Most inexplicable of all, the church of the Saints Ermagora and Fortunato is known to the Venetians as San Marcuola, a usage which they toss at you with every appearance of casual logic, but never a word of explanation. It is, as they would say, their custom.

Venice itself, compact though the city is, remains criss-crossed with local   15
flavours and loyalties. Each district, each clamorous market square has its own recognizable atmosphere—here harsh, here kindly, here simple, here sophisticated. Even more than London, Venice remains a collection of villages. In one you may be sure of kindly treatment, courteous shopmen and friendly women: in another, experience will teach you to be hard-skinned, for its manners may be gruff and its prices unyielding. Even the dialect varies from quarter to quarter, though only half a mile may separate them, and there are words in use at one end of Venice that are quite unfamiliar at the other. Street names appear over and over again, so independent is each section of the city: there are a dozen lanes called *Forno* in Venice, and thirteen named for the Madonna.

Until modern times the city was divided into two implacably rival fac-   16
tions, the Nicolotti and the Castellani, based upon long-forgotten animosities in the early days of settlement; and so riotous were the brawls between the two parties that the old Rialto bridge had a drawbridge in the middle, enabling the authorities to separate the mobs, by a swift tug of a rope, leaving them glaring at each other impotently across the void. This deep-rooted hostility gradually lost its venom, and degenerated into mock combats, regattas and athletic competitions, until in 1848 the old rivals were reconciled in a secret dawn ceremony at the Salute, as a gesture of unity against Austrian

rule. Today the factions are dead and almost forgotten (though you might not think so from the more imaginative guide books); but there remains an element of prickly parochial pride, based upon a parish or a square, and sometimes boisterously expressed.

17   None of this is surprising. Venice is a maze of waterways and alleys, crooked and unpredictable, following the courses of antique channels in the mud, and unimproved by town planners. Until the last century only one bridge, the Rialto, spanned the Grand Canal. In the days before motor boats and tarred pavements it must have been a fearfully tiresome process to move about Venice, let alone take ship to the mainland: and who can wonder if the people of Santa Margherita, satisfied with their own shops and taverns, rarely bothered to trudge all the way to Santa Maria Formosa? Sometimes a Venetian housewife announces conclusively that there are no cabbages in the city today: but what she means is that the greengrocer at the corner of Campo San Barnaba, with whom her family custom has been traditionally associated since the days of the early Crusades, has sold out of the vegetable this morning.

JAN MORRIS

Manhattan: The Islanders

Here Morris, like many travel writers, conveys the essence of the slightly foreign, somewhat familiar place through impressionistic images that can be glimpsed and overheard, but her pace is so rapid that she rarely lingers long enough to provide more than an overview. She begins with the arresting symbol of a polar bear in the Central Park Zoo. This potentially magnificent and unique animal is displaced and trapped in the middle of Manhattan, "the greatest of all the zoos," whose inhabitants, like the bear, restlessly "prowl up and down, like victims of some terrific spell." Morris moves from "images of confinement" to unconventional images of the city's beauty—how it looks on a hazy hot day, on a "gray lowering day," and early in the morning at Battery Park, where the city seems "eerily isolated and exposed."

Morris then shifts (paragraph II) from solitude to crowds—an ethnic festival, invigorated by diverse languages, exotic foods, cheerfully cosmopolitan throngs. Another cut (paragraph 15) to Central Park, examined this time from the perspectives of safety (Beware!), tradition (horse-drawn barouches), irony (permanent street people, "bony and malodorous" in the shadow of ritzy Fifth Avenue apartments), vaudeville (ridiculous joggers), uneasiness (lounging street gangs). Then, more impressions, this time historical—of Manhattan's legendary peak between World Wars I and II, "the days of the American innocence, before responsibility set in," the expansive days against which Morris contrasts the more modest present, finding the New York of today mature, mellow, and charming.

1   Sometimes, from the high office windows of the *Rolling Stone* offices in Manhattan, you can make out a faint white blob in the green of Central Park far below. It is like the unresolved blur of a nebula in the night sky: and just as through a telescope the fuzz in Andromeda resolves itself into M31, so that

whitish object in the park, defined through binoculars, becomes a phenomenon hardly less spectacular. It is the polar bear in the Central Park Zoo, and even as you focus your lenses, bringing his indistinct physique into clarity, with a shaggy shake of his head he swings his great form vigorously from one extremity of his cage to the other.

The bear lives alone in his compound down there, and I am told that he 2 is a character of weird and forceful originality—sadly neurotic, some informants suggested, genuinely imaginative, others thought. He is a bear like no other, and it is not the fact of his captivity that makes him so, I am sure, but its remarkable location. Destiny has deposited that animal plumb in the middle of Manhattan: you might say he is the central New Yorker. He affects me profoundly, whenever I see him, and when I put my binoculars down, and only the suggestion of him remains, apparently inanimate among the trees, all around him in my mind's eye the marvelous and terrible island of Manhattan concentrically extends, ring after ring of cage, ditch or rampart, precinct limit and electoral boundary, Hudson, East River and Atlantic itself—the greatest of all the zoos, whose inhabitants prowl up and down, like victims of some terrific spell, for ever and ever within it.

For Manhattan really is an island, even now, separated from the main- 3 land still by a channel just wide enough for the Circle Line boats to continue their pleasure circuits, and it is this condition of enclave that gives the place its sting. Like the bear, its citizens are heightened, one way or another, by their confinement. If they are unhappier than most populaces, they are merrier too. If they are trapped in some ways, they are brilliantly liberated in others. Sometimes their endless pacing to and fro is sad to see, but when the weather is right and the sap is rising, then it assumes an exhilarating rhythm, and the people of Manhattan seem to dance along their avenues, round and round the city squares, in and out the sepulchral subway.

Images of confinement certainly haunt me in Manhattan but the first 4 thing that always strikes me, when I land once more on the island, is its fearful and mysterious beauty. Other cities have built higher now, or sprawl more boisterously over their landscapes, but there is still nothing like the looming thicket of the Manhattan skyscrapers, jumbled and overbearing. Le Corbusier hated this ill-disciplined spectacle, and conceived his own Radiant City, an antiseptic hybrid of art and ideology, in direct antithesis to it. His ideas, though, mostly bounced off this vast mass of vanity. Tempered though it has been from time to time by zoning law and social trend, Manhattan remains a mammoth mess, a stupendous clashing of light and dark and illusory perspective, splotched here and there by wastelands of slum or demolition, wanly patterned by the grid of its street system, but essentially, whatever the improvers do to it, whatever economy decrees or architectural fashion advises, the supreme monument to that elemental human instinct, Free-For-All.

But the glowering ecstasy of it! No other city, not even Venice, projects 5 for me a more orgiastic kind of allure. I do not mean the popular phallic symbolism of the place, its charged erections thrusting always into the sky. I am thinking of more veiled seductions, the shadows in its deep streets, the watchfulness, the ever-present hint of concealment or allusion. The clarity of Manhattan is what the picture postcards emphasize, but I prefer Manhattan hazed, Manhattan reticent and heavy-eyed.

6   I like it, for instance, on a very, very hot day, a day when emerging into the streets from the air conditioning is like changing continents. Then a film of chemical vapor seems to drift around the city, fudging every edge, gauzing every vista. Exhausted, half-deserted, the island seems to stand stupefied in the haze: but sometimes flashes of sunlight, piercing the humidity, are reflected momentarily off windows or metal roofs, and then I am reminded of those uncertain but resplendent cities, vaporous but diamond-twinkling, which stand in the backgrounds of all the best fairy tales.

7   Conversely on a gray lowering day it is like some darkling forest. The tops of the buildings are lost in fog, and only their massive bases, like the trunks of so many gigantic oaks, are to be seen beneath the cloud base. I feel a mushroom feeling in Manhattan then, and the huddled scurry of the people on the sidewalks, the shifting patterns of their umbrellas, the swish of cars through pothole puddles, the blinking of the traffic lights one after another through the slanting rain, the plumes of steam which, like geysers from the subterranean, spout into the streets—all this speaks fancifully to me, here in *urbanissimus,* of clearing, glade and woodland market.

8   But best of all, for this reluctant and secretive beauty of the island, I like to walk very early in the morning down to Battery Park, the southernmost tip of it, its gazebo on the world, looking out across the great bay towards the Narrows and the open sea. This is a melancholy pleasure, for the shipping which used to make this the busiest basin on earth has mostly been dispersed now. Most of the Atlantic liners sail no more, the freighters mostly berth elsewhere around the bay, and of the myriad public ferries which used to bustle like so many water insects to and from Manhattan, only the old faithful to Staten Island survives.

9   So early in the morning, the scene down at the Battery is not likely to be bustling. If it is misty, it is likely to be a little spooky, in fact. The mist lies heavy over the grayish water, muffled sirens sound, somewhere a sound-buoy intermittently hoots. Perhaps a solitary tanker treads cautiously toward Brooklyn, or a pilot boat, its crew collars-up against the dank, chugs out toward the Narrows. Early commuters emerge blearily from the ferry station; two or three layabouts are stretched on park benches, covered in rags and newspaper; a police car sometimes wanders by, its policemen slumped in their seats dispassionately, like men at the end of a shift.

10   It seems eerily isolated and exposed, and you feel as though the few of you are all alone, there at the water's edge. But as the morning draws on and the mist clears, something wonderful happens. It is like the printing of a

Polaroid picture. The wide sweep of the bay gradually reveals its outlines, the Statue of Liberty appears unforeseen upon her plinth, lesser islands show themselves, and as you turn your back upon the water, glistening now in the freshening breeze, it turns out that the tremendous presence of Manhattan itself, its serried buildings rank on rank, has been looking over your shoulder all the time. . . .

Often, when I am at large in this incomparable city, I feel myself to be among ultimates. *How're they gonna get me back on the farm?* This is, after all, The City of our times, as Rome was in classical days, as Constantinople was through centuries of Mediterranean history. This is everyone's metropolis, for there is no nation that has not contributed something to Manhattan, if only a turn of phrase or a category of bun. I went one day to the street festival which is held each May on Ninth Avenue, one of the most vividly cosmopolitan thoroughfares on the island, and realized almost too piquantly what it means to be a city of all peoples: smell clashing with smell, from a mile of sidewalk food stalls, sesame oil at odds with curry power, Arabic drifting into Ukrainian among the almost impenetrable crowds, Yiddish colliding with Portuguese, and all the way down the avenue the discordant blending of folk-music, be it from Polish flageolet, Mexican harmonica or balalaika from Sofia. 11

Nothing provincial there! And if over the past 300 years the clambering upon this huge raft of refugees, adventurers, idealists and crooks from every land has given Manhattan always a quality of paradigm or fulcrum, so when it comes to the end of the world, I think, most people can most easily imagine the cataclysm in the context of this island. The great towers crumpling and sagging into themselves, the fires raging up the ravaged boulevards, the panicked rush of the people, like rats or lemmings, desperately into the boiling water—these are 20th-century man's standard images of Doomsday: and in my own view, if God is truly going to sit one day in judgment upon the doings of mankind, he is likely to set up court on the corner of Broadway and Forty-second Street, where he can deal first (and leniently I am sure) with the purveyors of Sextacular Acts Live on Stage. . . . 12

Everything comes onto the island: nothing much goes off, even by evaporation. Once it was a gateway to a New World, now it is a portal chiefly to itself. Manhattan long ago abandoned its melting-pot function. Nobody even tries to Americanize the Lebanese or the Lithuanians now, and indeed the ethnic enclaves of the island seem to me to become more potently ethnic each time I visit the place. Nothing could be much more Italian than the Festival of St. Anthony of Padua down on Mulberry Street, when the families of Little Italy stroll here and there through their estate, pausing often to greet volatile contemporaries and sometimes munching the soft-shelled crabs which, spread-eagled on slices of bread like zoological specimens, are offered loudly for sale by street vendors. Harlem has become almost a private city in 13 itself, no longer to be slummed through by whities after dinner, while Manhattan's Chinatown is as good a place as anywhere in the world to test your skill at that universal challenge, trying to make a Chinese waiter smile.

14   So the lights blaze down fiercely upon a tumultuous arena: but its millions of gladiators (and wild beasts) are not in the least disconcerted by the glare of it, or daunted by the symbolic battles in which they are engaged, but are concerned chiefly to have swords of the fashionable length, to be seen to advantage from the more expensive seats, and preferably to face the lions at the same time as Jackie Onassis, say, or Dick Cavett if you like.

15   Back to the park. At the center of the world's present preoccupation with Manhattan, for one reason and another, stands Central Park. "Don't go walking in that Park," they will warn you from China to Peru, or "Tell me frankly," they ask, "is it true what they say about Central Park?"

16   The Park is the center of the island too, no man's land amid the surrounding conflict of masonry—on the postal map it forms a big oblong blank, the only portion of Manhattan without a zip code. To the north is Harlem, to the south is Rockefeller Center, on one flank is the opulence of the Upper East Side, to the west are the newly burgeoning streets that sprout, teeming with artists, agents, Polish grocers and music students, right and left off Columbus Avenue. It is like a big rectangular scoop in the city, shoveled out and stacked with green. It covers 840 acres, and it is almost everything, to my mind, that a park should not be.

17   This is a heretical view. Central Park is enormously admired by specialists in planning and urban design. The architectural critic of the *New York Times* calls it the city's greatest single work of architecture. It was laid out in 1856 by Frederick Law Olmsted and Calvert Vaux, and ever since everybody has been saying how marvelous it is. "One of the most beautiful parks in the world," thought Baedeker, 1904. "This great work of art," says the AIA *Guide to New York City, 1978*.

18   Not me. With its gloomy hillocks obstructing the view, with its threadbare and desolate prairies, with its consciously contrived variety of landscapes, with its baleful lake and brownish foliage, with the sickly carillon which, hourly from the gates of its appalling zoo, reminds me horribly of the memorial chimes at Hiroshima, Central Park seems to me the very antithesis of the fresh and natural open space, the slice of countryside, that a city park should ideally be.

19   Nevertheless the world is right when, invited to think of Manhattan, it is likely to think first these days of Central Park. If I deny its ethereal beauty, I do not for a moment dispute its interest. It is one of the most interesting places on earth. "It is inadvisable," warns the Michelin guide, 1968, "to wander alone through the more deserted parts of the park": but wandering alone nevertheless through this extraordinary retreat, dominated on all sides by the towering cliffs of Manhattan, is to enjoy one of the greatest of all human shows, in perpetual performance from dawn through midnight.

You want tradition? There go the lumbering barouches, their horse   20
smells hanging pungent in the air long after they have left their stands outside
the Plaza, their Dutch trade delegates, their Urological Association conven-
tioneers, or even their honeymooners from Iowa, somewhat self-consciously
sunk in their cushions, and their coachmen leaning back, as they have leant
for a century or more, whip in hand to ask their customers where they're
from.

You want irony? Consider the layabouts encouched apparently perma-   21
nently on their benches along the East Side, beyond the open-air bookstalls,
prickly and raggedy, bony and malodorous, camped there almost in the
shadow of the sumptuous Fifth Avenue apartment houses, and more tellingly
still perhaps, actually within earshot of the feebly growling lions, the cackling
birds and funereal carillon of the zoo.

You want vaudeville? Try the joggers on their daily exercise. Dogged   22
they lope in their hundreds around the ring road, generally cleared of traffic
on their behalf, like migrating animals homed in upon some inexplicable
instinct, or numbed survivors from some catastrophe out of sight. Some are
worn lean as rakes by their addiction, some drop the sweat of repentant
obesity. Some flap with huge ungainly breasts. Some tread with a predatory
menace, wolflike in the half-hour before they must present that memo about
ongoing supportive expenditures to Mr. Cawkwelt at the office. Sometimes
you may hear snatches of very Manhattan conversations, as the enthusiasts
labor by—*So you're saying* (gasp) *that since 1951* (pant) *there's been no meaningful change whatever* (puff) *in our society?* Sometimes you may observe a
jogger who has taken his dog with him on a leash, and who, obliged to pause
while the animal defecates behind a bush, compromises by maintaining a
standing run, on the spot, looking consequently for all the world as though
he is dying for a pee himself.

But no, it is the sinister you want, isn't it? *"It is inadvisable to wander*   23
alone, despite the frequent police patrols on horseback or by car. . . ." That is what
Central Park is most famous for these days, and it is not hard to find. I have
never been mugged in Central Park, never seen anyone else harmed either,
but I have had my chill moments all the same. More than once, even as the
joggers pad around their circuit, I have noticed perched distantly on the
rocky outcrops which protrude among the dusty trees, groups of three or
four youths, silently and thoughtfully watching. They wear dark glasses, as
likely as not, and big floppy hats, and they recline upon their rock in attitudes
of mocking but stealthy grace, motionless, as though they were fingering
their flick-knives.

I waved to one such group of watchers once, as I walked nervously by: 24
but they responded only by looking at each other in a bewildered way, and
shifting their long legs a trifle uneasily upon the stone.

All around the city roars. Well, no, not roars—buzzes, perhaps. The   25
energy of Manhattan is less leonine than waspish, and its concerns are, for so
tremendous a metropolis, wonderfully individual and idiosyncratic. Despite

appearances, Manhattan is an especially human city, where personal aspirations, for better or for worse, unexpectedly take priority.

26   Perhaps this is because, unlike either of the other global cities (for in my view there are only two, Paris and London)—unlike its peers, New York is not a capital. True, the headquarters of the United Nations is down by the East River, but architecturally it is the perfect reflection of its lackluster political self, and one hardly notices it. True too that the municipal affairs of this city, being on so momentous a scale, are equivalent I suppose to the entire political goings-on of many lesser republics. But it is not really a political city. Affairs of state and patriotism rarely intrude. Even the state capital is far away in Albany, and Manhattan conversations do not often turn to infighting within the Democratic party, or the prospects of Salt III.

27   There is not much industry on the island, either, in any sociological or aesthetic sense: few blue-collared workers making for home with their lunch boxes, few manufacturing plants to belch their smoke into the Manhattan sky. This is a city of more intricate concerns, a city of speculators and advisers, agents and middlemen and sorters-out and go-betweens. Many of the world's most potent corporations have their headquarters here, but their labor forces are mostly conveniently far away. Fortunes are made here, and reputations, not steel ingots or automobiles.

28   The pace of New York is legendary, but nowadays in my opinion illusory. Businessmen work no harder, no faster, than in most other great cities. But New Yorkers spend so much time contemplating their personal affairs, analyzing themselves, examining their own reactions, that the time left for business is necessarily rushed. Do not suppose, when the Vice-President of Automated Commercial leaves his office in such a hurry, that he is meeting the Overseas Sales Director of Toyuki Industries: good gracious no, he is leaving early because he simply must have it out face to face with Brian about his disgraceful behavior with that Edgar person in the disco last night.

29   More than any other place I know, to do business in New York you must understand your colleagues' circumstances. They often need worrying out. There are some telltale signs indeed, like tribal tattoos—short hair for Brian and Edgar, for example, droopy moustaches and canvas shoes for aspirant literary men, rasping voices and nasal intonations for girls who hope to get into television, hands in trouser pockets for Ivy League executives. But you should take no chances. The tangles of Manhattan marital and emotional life, which provide inexhaustible hours of instruction to the social observer, set the tone of this place far more than torts, share prices or bills of lading. . . .

30   "Give me your tired, your poor, your huddled masses yearning to breathe free. . . ." An occasional Russian dissident appears in New York these days, to endure his statutory press conference before being whisked away to CIA debriefing or associate professorship somewhere. But the loss of the grand old purpose, so stoutly declaimed by the Lady of Liberty out there in the bay, means that Manhattan is recognizably past its prime.

Every city has its heyday, the moment when its purpose is fulfilled and its   31
spirit bursts into full flower, and Manhattan's occurred I think in the years
between the Great Depression, when the indigents squatted in Central Park,
and the end of World War II, when the GIs returned in splendor as the
saviors of liberty. In those magnificent years this small island, no more than a
fantastic dream to most of the peoples of the world, stood everywhere for the
fresh start and the soaring conception. Manhattan was Fred Astaire and the
sun-topped Chrysler Building! Manhattan was the Jeep and Robert Benchley! Manhattan was rags-to-riches, free speech, Mayor La Guardia and the
Rockettes!

No wonder nostalgia booms on Broadway. Those were the days of the   32
American innocence, before responsibility set in, and every dry and racy old
song of the period, every new Art Deco furniture boutique, is an expression
of regret. European Powers pine for their lost glories with bearskin parades
or jangling cavalry: New York looks back with *Ain't Misbehavin'*, or the
refurbishing, just as it was, of that prodigy of Manhattan gusto, Radio City
Music Hall (whose designer reportedly had ozone driven through its ventilator shafts, to keep its audiences festive, and toyed with the idea of laughing gas too. . .). Fortunately the old days come quickly in a city that is not yet
300 years old, and the authentic bitter-sweetness is relatively easy to achieve.
I was touched myself by the furnishing of a restaurant equipped entirely with
the fittings of one of the old Atlantic liners, those dowagers of the Manhattan
piers, until I discovered that the ship concerned was the *Caronia,* whose
launching I remember as clear as yesterday.

The memories of that time are legendary already, and moving fast into   33
myth. Nothing in travel stirs me more than the dream of that old Manhattan,
the Titan City of my childhood, when the flamboyant skyscrapers soared one
after the other into empyrean, when John D. Rockefeller, Jr., pored over the
plans for his Center like a modern Midas, when the great liners stalked
through the bay with their complements of celebrities and shipboard reporters, and the irrepressible immigrants toiled and clawed their way up the line
of Manhattan, from Ellis Island to the Lower East Side to the Midtown
affluence of their aspirations. Its monuments are mostly there to see still,
newly fashionable as the buildings of the day-before-yesterday are apt to
become, and sometimes even now you may stumble across one of its success
stories: the waiter proudly boasting that, since arriving penniless and friend-
less from Poland, he has never been out of work for a day—the famous
publisher, in the penthouse suite of his own skyscraper, whose mother landed
in Manhattan with a placard around her neck, announcing her name, trade
and language.

Rockefeller Center is the theater of this mood. Raymond Hood, the   34
creator of its central structure, the RCA Building, was reminded one day that
he had come to Manhattan in the first place with the declared intention of

becoming the greatest architect in New York. "So I did," he responded, looking out of the window at that stupendous thing, jagged and command- ing high above, "and by God, so I am!" The magnificent brag, the revelatory vision, the ruthless opportunism, the limitless resource—these were the attri- butes of Rockefeller Center, as of Manhattan, in the heady years of its con- struction: and when at winter time they turn the sunken cafe into an ice rink, then in the easy delight of the skaters under the floodlights, some so hilari- ously inept, some so showily skillful, with the indulgent crowd leaning over the railings to watch, and the waltz music only half drowned by the city's rumble—then I sometimes seem to be, even now, back in those boundless years of certainty. . . .

35   Manhattan is no longer the fastest, the most daring or even I dare say the richest. For a symbol of its civic energies now, I recommend an inspection of the abandoned West Side Highway, the victim of seven years' municipal indecision, which staggers crumbling on its struts above a wilderness of empty lots, truck parks and shattered warehouses, the only signs of enterprise being the cyclists who cheerfully trundle along the top of it, and the railway coaches of the Ringling Bros., Barnum and Bailey Circus which park them- selves habitually underneath.

36   The falter came, I believe, in the fifties and sixties, when Manhattan began to see laissez faire, perhaps, as a less than absolute ideology. Doubts crept in. The pace slowed a bit. The sense of movement lagged. All the great ships no longer came in their grandeur to the Manhattan piers; the New York Airports were far from the island; today even the helicopters, which were for a couple of decades the lively familiars of Manhattan, are banned from their wayward and fanciful antics around the skyscrapers. Bauhaus frowned down upon Radio City Music Hall, in those after-the-glory years, and most of Manhattan's midcentury architecture was, by Hood's standards, timid and banal. The truly original buildings were few, and worse still for my taste, the swagger-buildings were not built at all.

37   When, in the early 1970s, the World Trade Center was erected in a late spasm of the old hubris—the two tallest towers on earth then, beckoning once more the world across the bay—all Manhattan groaned at the change in its familiar skyline, and to this day it is hard to find a New Yorker willing to admit to admiration for that arrogant pair of pylons. The fashionable philos- ophy of smallness strongly appealed to New Yorkers, in their new mood of restraint, and nowadays when citizens want to show you some inno- vation they are proud of, they generally take you to a dainty little curbside park with waterfalls, or Roosevelt Island, an itsy-bitsy enclave of socio- logical good taste. Suavity, discretion and even modesty are the architec- tural qualities admired in Manhattan now, and the colossal is no longer welcomed. . . .

Questions

1. It's hard for a writer to characterize one of the world's best-known major cities from an original perspective, so often has it been described, particularly when readers are looking for familiar landmarks. Why would Morris even bother to try? Has she achieved an informative mix of the novel and the familiar? Why or why not?

2. Many of the best writings about places bear the indelible stamp of the observer, the traveler, on a particular journey at a particular time. In what ways has Morris conveyed her own personality and her particular travels as well as her perspective? Compare Morris's account of Manhattan with Kate Simon's insider's interpretation of "New York Luncheonettes" (277–82).

3. Yet the traveler's views are often superficial, as viewed from the perspective of the native. Drawing on your own knowledge of New York, how deeply and accurately would you say Morris understands the city? Is her view idiosyncratic, or representative of many travelers come to the big city? She wrote this in 1979; what, if anything, would have to be added or altered to bring the essay up to date?

4. What is the effect, individually and cumulatively, of the staccato, slightly slangy beginning sentences of the middle of this essay: "Nothing provincial there!" (paragraph 12). "Back to the park" (paragraph 15). "Not me" (paragraph 18). And the triplet: "You want tradition?" (paragraph 20). "You want irony?" (paragraph 21). "You want vaudeville?" (paragraph 22). Followed by the variation, "But no, it is the sinister you want, isn't it?" (paragraph 23). Do these provide appropriate transitions from one topic to the next?

Narration

E. B. WHITE

Once More to the Lake

This narrative of father and son, timeless generations in the eternal Maine countryside (described also in the letter to Stanley Hart White quoted on pp. 42–44), conveys significant intangibles (love—parental and filial; the importance of nature; the inevitability of growth, change, and death) through memorably specific details. White leads us to the lake itself ("cool and motionless"), down the path to yesteryear, where the continuity of generations inter-mingles past, present, and future until they become almost indistinguishable: "the years were a mirage and there had been no years. . . ." Everywhere White's son does the same things White had done at the same lake as a boy—putting about in the same outboard, catching the same bass, drinking the same soda pop, enjoying the same ritualistic swim after the same summer thunderstorm. And "everywhere we went I had trouble making out which was I, the one walking at my side, the one walking in my pants." The mood of "peace and goodness and jollity" that White recreates indelibly shifts, however, as the cosmic chill of the last sentence reminds us of the inevitable passing of generations, despite the hope of the future.

1   One summer, along about 1904, my father rented a camp on a lake in Maine and took us all there for the month of August. We all got ringworm from some kittens and had to rub Pond's Extract on our arms and legs night and morning, and my father rolled over in a canoe with all his clothes on; but outside of that the vacation was a success and from then on none of us ever thought there was any place in the world like that lake in Maine. We returned summer after summer—always on August 1st for one month. I have since become a salt-water man, but sometimes in summer there are days when the restlessness of the tides and the fearful cold of the sea water and the incessant wind which blows across the afternoon and into the evening make me wish for the placidity of a lake in the woods. A few weeks ago this feeling got so strong I bought myself a couple of bass hooks and a spinner and returned to the lake where we used to go, for a week's fishing and to revisit old haunts.

2   I took along my son, who had never had any fresh water up his nose and who had seen lily pads only from train windows. On the journey over to the lake I began to wonder what it would be like. I wondered how time would have marred this unique, this holy spot—the coves and streams, the hills that the sun set behind, the camps and the paths behind the camps. I was sure the tarred road would have found it out and I wondered in what other ways it would be desolated. It is strange how much you can remember about places like that once you allow your mind to return into the grooves which lead back. You remember one thing, and that suddenly reminds you of another thing. I guess I remembered clearest of all the early mornings, when the lake

was cool and motionless, remembered how the bedroom smelled of the lumber it was made of and of the wet woods whose scent entered through the screen. The partitions in the camp were thin and did not extend clear to the top of the rooms, and as I was always the first up I would dress softly so as not to wake the others, and sneak out into the sweet outdoors and start out in the canoe, keeping close along the shore in the long shadows of the pines. I remembered being very careful never to rub my paddle against the gunwale for fear of disturbing the stillness of the cathedral.

The lake had never been what you would call a wild lake. There were   3 cottages sprinkled around the shores, and it was in farming country although the shores of the lake were quite heavily wooded. Some of the cottages were owned by nearby farmers, and you would live at the shore and eat your meals at the farmhouse. That's what our family did. But although it wasn't wild, it was a fairly large and undisturbed lake and there were places in it which, to a child at least, seemed infinitely remote and primeval.

I was right about the tar: it led to within half a mile of the shore. But   4 when I got back there, with my boy, and we settled into a camp near a farmhouse and into the kind of summertime I had known, I could tell that it was going to be pretty much the same as it had been before—I knew it, lying in bed the first morning, smelling the bedroom, and hearing the boy sneak quietly out and go off along the shore in a boat. I began to sustain the illusion that he was I, and therefore by simple transposition, that I was my father. This sensation persisted, kept cropping up all the time we were there. It was not an entirely new feeling, but in this setting it grew much stronger. I seemed to be living a dual existence. I would be in the middle of some simple act, I would be picking up a bait box or laying down a table fork, or I would be saying something, and suddenly it would be not I but my father who was saying the words or making the gesture. It gave me a creepy sensation.

We went fishing the first morning. I felt the same damp moss covering   5 the worms in the bait can, and saw the dragonfly alight on the tip of my rod as it hovered a few inches from the surface of the water. It was the arrival of this fly that convinced me beyond any doubt that everything was as it always had been, that the years were a mirage and there had been no years. The small waves were the same, chucking the rowboat under the chin as we fished at anchor, and the boat was the same boat, the same color green and the ribs broken in the same places, and under the floor-boards the same fresh-water leavings and debris—the dead helgramite, the wisps of moss, the rusty discarded fishhook, the dried blood from yesterday's catch. We stared silently at the tips of our rods, at the dragonflies that came and went. I lowered the tip of mine into the water, tentatively, pensively dislodging the fly, which darted two feet away, poised, darted two feet back, and came to rest again a little farther up the rod. There had been no years between the ducking of this dragonfly and the other one—the one that was part of memory. I looked at the boy, who was silently watching his fly, and it was my hands that held his rod, my eyes watching. I felt dizzy and didn't know which rod I was at the end of.

6   We caught two bass, hauling them in briskly as though they were mackerel, pulling them over the side of the boat in a businesslike manner without any landing net, and stunning them with a blow on the back of the head. When we got back for a swim before lunch, the lake was exactly where we had left it, the same number of inches from the dock, and there was only the merest suggestion of a breeze. This seemed an utterly enchanted sea, this lake you could leave to its own devices for a few hours and come back to, and find that it had not stirred, this constant and trustworthy body of water. In the shallows, the dark, water-soaked sticks and twigs, smooth and old, were undulating in clusters on the bottom against the clean ribbed sand, and the track of the mussel was plain. A school of minnows swam by, each minnow with its small individual shadow, doubling the attendance, so clear and sharp in the sunlight. Some of the other campers were in swimming, along the shore, one of them with a cake of soap, and the water felt thin and clear and unsubstantial. Over the years there had been this person with the cake of soap, this cultist, and here he was. There had been no years.

7   Up to the farmhouse to dinner through the teeming, dusty field, the road under our sneakers was only a two-track road. The middle track was missing, the one with the marks of the hooves and the splotches of dried, flaky manure. There had always been three tracks to choose from in choosing which track to walk in; now the choice was narrowed down to two. For a moment I missed terribly the middle alternative. But the way led past the tennis court, and something about the way it lay there in the sun reassured me; the tape had loosened along the backline, the alleys were green with plantains and other weeds, and the net (installed in June and removed in September) sagged in the dry noon, and the whole place steamed with midday heat and hunger and emptiness. There was a choice of pie for dessert, and one was blueberry and one was apple, and the waitresses were the same country girls, there having been no passage of time, only the illusion of it as in a dropped curtain—the waitresses were still fifteen; their hair had been washed, that was the only difference—they had been to the movies and seen the pretty girls with the clean hair.

8   Summertime, oh summertime, pattern of life indelible, the fade-proof lake, the woods unshatterable, the pasture with the sweetfern and the juniper forever and ever, summer without end; this was the background, and the life along the shore was the design, the cottages with their innocent tranquil design, their tiny docks with the flagpole and the American flag floating against the white clouds in the blue sky, the little paths over the roots of the trees leading from camp to camp and the paths leading back to the outhouses and the can of lime for sprinkling, and at the souvenir counters at the store the miniature birch-bark canoes and the post cards that showed things looking a little better than they looked. This was the American family at play,

escaping the city heat, wondering whether the newcomers in the camp at the head of the cove were "common" or "nice," wondering whether it was true that the people who drove up for Sunday dinner at the farmhouse were turned away because there wasn't enough chicken.

It seemed to me, as I kept remembering all this, that those times and those summers had been infinitely precious and worth saving. There had been jollity and peace and goodness. The arriving (at the beginning of August) had been so big a business in itself, at the railway station the farm wagon drawn up, the first smell of the pine-laden air, the first glimpse of the smiling farmer, and the great importance of the trunks and your father's enormous authority in such matters, and the feel of the wagon under you for the long ten-mile haul, and at the top of the last long hill catching the first view of the lake after eleven months of not seeing this cherished body of water. The shouts and cries of the other campers when they saw you, and the trunks to be unpacked, to give up their rich burden. (Arriving was less exciting nowadays, when you sneaked up in your car and parked it under a tree near the camp and took out the bags and in five minutes it was all over, no fuss, no loud wonderful fuss about trunks.) 9

Peace and goodness and jollity. The only thing that was wrong now, really, was the sound of the place, an unfamiliar nervous sound of the outboard motors. This was the note that jarred, the one thing that would sometimes break the illusion and set the years moving. In those other summertimes all motors were inboard; and when they were at a little distance, the noise they made was a sedative, an ingredient of summer sleep. They were one-cylinder and two-cylinder engines, and some were make-and-break and some were jump-spark, but they all made a sleepy sound across the lake. The one-lungers throbbed and fluttered, and the twin-cylinder ones purred and purred, and that was a quiet sound too. But now the campers all had outboards. In the daytime, in the hot mornings, these motors made a petulant, irritable sound; at night, in the still evening when the afterglow lit the water, they whined about one's ears like mosquitoes. My boy loved our rented outboard, and his great desire was to achieve singlehanded mastery over it, and authority, and he soon learned the trick of choking it a little (but not too much), and the adjustment of the needle valve. Watching him I would remember the things you could do with the old one-cylinder engine with the heavy flywheel, how you could have it eating out of your hand if you got really close to it spiritually. Motor boats in those days didn't have clutches, and you would make a landing by shutting off the motor at the proper time and coasting in with a dead rudder. But there was a way of reversing them, if you learned the trick, by cutting the switch and putting it on again exactly on the final dying revolution of the flywheel, so that it would kick back against compression and begin reversing. Approaching a dock in a strong following breeze, it was difficult to slow up sufficiently by the ordinary coasting method, and if a boy felt he had complete mastery over his motor, he was 10 tempted to keep it running beyond its time and then reverse it a few feet from the dock. It took a cool nerve, because if you threw the switch a twentieth of a second too soon you would catch the flywheel when it still had speed enough to go up past center, and the boat would leap ahead, charging bull-fashion at the dock.

11   We had a good week at the camp. The bass were biting well and the sun shone endlessly, day after day. We would be tired at night and lie down in the accumulated heat of the little bedrooms after the long hot day and the breeze would stir almost imperceptibly outside and the smell of the swamp drift in through the rusty screens. Sleep would come easily and in the morning the red squirrel would be on the roof, tapping out his gay routine. I kept remembering everything, lying in bed in the mornings—the small steamboat that had a long rounded stern like the lip of a Ubangi, and how quietly she ran on the moonlight sails, when the older boys played their mandolins and the girls sang and we ate doughnuts dipped in sugar, and how sweet the music was on the water in the shining night, and what it had felt like to think about girls then. After breakfast we would go up to the store and the things were in the same place—the minnows in a bottle, the plugs and spinners disarranged and pawed over by the youngsters from the boys' camp, the fig newtons and the Beeman's gum. Outside, the road was tarred and cars stood in front of the store. Inside, all was just as it had always been, except there was more Coca-Cola and not so much Moxie and root beer and birch beer and sarsaparilla. We would walk out with a bottle of pop apiece and sometimes the pop would backfire up our noses and hurt. We explored the streams, quietly, where the turtles slid off the sunny logs and dug their way into the soft bottom; and we lay on the town wharf and fed worms to the tame bass. Everywhere we went I had trouble making out which was I, the one walking at my side, the one walking in my pants.

12   One afternoon while we were there at that lake a thunderstorm came up. It was like the revival of an old melodrama that I had seen long ago with childish awe. The second-act climax of the drama of the electrical disturbance over a lake in America had not changed in any important respect. This was the big scene, still the big scene. The whole thing was so familiar, the first feeling of oppression and heat and a general air around camp of not wanting to go very far away. In midafternoon (it was all the same) a curious darkening of the sky, and a lull in everything that had made life tick; and then the way the boats suddenly swung the other way at their moorings with the coming of a breeze out of the new quarter, and the premonitory rumble. Then the kettle drum, then the snare, then the bass drum and cymbals, then crackling light against the dark, and the gods grinning and licking their chops in the hills. Afterward the calm, the rain steadily rustling in the calm lake, the return of light and hope and spirits, and the campers running out in joy and relief to go swimming in the rain, their bright cries perpetuating the deathless joke about how they were getting simply drenched, and the children screaming

with delight at the new sensation of bathing in the rain, and the joke about getting drenched linking the generations in a strong indestructible chain. And the comedian who waded in carrying an umbrella.

When the others went swimming my son said he was going in too. He 13 pulled his dripping trunks from the line where they had hung all through the shower, and wrung them out. Languidly, and with no thought of going in, I watched him, his hard little body, skinny and bare, saw him wince slightly as he pulled up around his vitals the small, soggy, icy garment. As he buckled the swollen belt suddenly my groin felt the chill of death.

Questions

1. Writers sometimes describe a place and recreate its ambience to reinforce the relationships among the people who live or visit there. In "Once More to the Lake," how do the ways in which the boy and his father relate to the lake environment emphasize their personal relationship? In what ways do these resemble the relationship between the narrator and his father, the boy's grandfather? Why does White refer to these people only by their family relationships, but not by their names?

2. Places are also characterized by the events, activities, incidents that predictably occur there. Identify some of these in "Once More to the Lake." Do they follow the pattern of the visitors' daily or weekly activities? What else might determine their order, concluding with the thunderstorm and its aftermath (paragraphs 12–13)?

3. This nameless lake is also timeless. Explain why. What are the effects of White's frequent repetition of time-related phrases ("there had been no years") and words ("same")?

4. Trimble (pp. 67–71) and Orwell (pp. 72–82) advise writers to be sparing of adjectives and adverbs, and to put the weight on nouns and verbs instead. Is this easy or desirable to do in describing places? Does White follow this advice? consistently? Pick a paragraph and analyze it to illustrate your answer.

MARK TWAIN

Uncle John's Farm

Samuel Clemens, born in 1835, grew up in the Mississippi River town of Hannibal, Missouri, that he immortalized in The Adventures of Tom Sawyer *(1876) and* The Adventures of Huckleberry Finn *(1885). In his* Autobiography, *published posthumously in 1924, he remarks on the difficulty of separating fact from fiction: "When I was younger I could remember anything, whether it had happened or not; but my faculties are decaying now, and soon I shall be so I cannot remember any but the things that never happened." Indeed, in the beginning stages of his literary career, as a reporter, free-lance writer, and lecturer, he drew on his experiences in the still-wild West. His first best seller was* The Innocents Abroad *(1869), a slightly fictionalized account of a pilgrimage of Americans to*

Europe and to the Holy Land, which Clemens had covered for the Alta California, *a San Francisco newspaper. With his success came a move East (to Buffalo and then Hartford), marriage into money and society, and international fame. As Clemens aged and experienced bankruptcy and the deaths of his wife and daughter, his attacks on American culture and human nature became progressively more caustic, in such works as "The Man That Corrupted Hadleyburg" (1900) and* The Mysterious Stranger, *published in 1916, after Twain's death in 1910.*

In the following extract from The Autobiography, *Twain "tells the truth mostly," but, as Huck warns, "there were things which he stretched." Indeed,* The Autobiography *presents two central characters, the boy Sam Clemens, who enjoyed every aspect of his Uncle John Quarles's Florida, Missouri, farm, as recalled by the older, wiser, and sometimes more cynical author, Mark Twain. Modern writers of nonfiction, like Twain, often use "stretchers" if the "exigencies of literature" make them seem truer to the spirit of the place, person, or event than do the actual facts. The spirit is amply reinforced by an abundance of sensory details—of sound, of smell, of touch ("I do not know any creature that is pleasanter to the touch" [than a bat], and especially of taste ("I know the taste of maple sap") and sight ("I know the look of Uncle Dan'l's kitchen as it was on the privileged nights, when I was a child, and I can see the white and black children grouped on the hearth, with the firelight playing on their faces and the shadows flickering up on the walls. . . .").*

1   For many years I believed that I remembered helping my grandfather drink his whisky toddy when I was six weeks old, but I do not tell about that any more, now; I am grown old and my memory is not as active as it used to be. When I was younger I could remember anything, whether it had happened or not; but my faculties are decaying now, and soon I shall be so I cannot remember any but the things that never happened. It is sad to go to pieces like this, but we all have to do it.

2   My uncle, John A. Quarles, was a farmer, and his place was in the country four miles from Florida. He had eight children and fifteen or twenty negroes, and was also fortunate in other ways, particularly in his character. I have not come across a better man than he was. I was his guest for two or three months every year, from the fourth year after we removed to Hannibal till I was eleven or twelve years old. I have never consciously used him or his wife in a book, but his farm has come very handy to me in literature once or twice. In *Huck Finn* and in *Tom Sawyer, Detective* I moved it down to Arkansas. It was all of six hundred miles, but it was no trouble; it was not a very large farm—five hundred acres, perhaps—but I could have done it if it had been twice as large. And as for the morality of it, I cared nothing for that; I would move a state if the exigencies of literature required it.

3   It was a heavenly place for a boy, that farm of my uncle John's. The house was a double log one, with a spacious floor (roofed in) connecting it with the kitchen. In the summer the table was set in the middle of that shady and breezy floor, and the sumptuous meals—well, it makes me cry to think of them. Fried chicken, roast pig; wild and tame turkeys, ducks, and geese; venison just killed; squirrels, rabbits, pheasants, partridges, prairie-chickens;

biscuits, hot batter cakes, hot buckwheat cakes, hot "wheat bread," hot rolls, hot corn pone; fresh corn boiled on the ear, succotash, butter-beans, string-beans, tomatoes, peas, Irish potatoes, sweet potatoes; butter-milk, sweet milk, "clabber"; watermelons, muskmelons, cantaloupes—all fresh from the garden; apple pie, peach pie, pumpkin pie, apple dumplings, peach cobbler—I can't remember the rest. . . .

The farmhouse stood in the middle of a very large yard, and the yard was fenced on three sides with rails and on the rear side with high palings; against these stood the smoke-house; beyond the palings was the orchard; beyond the orchard were the negro quarters and the tobacco fields. The front yard was entered over a stile made of sawed-off logs of graduated heights; I do not remember any gate. In a corner of the front yard were a dozen lofty hickory trees and a dozen black walnuts, and in the nutting season riches were to be gathered there.

Down a piece, abreast the house, stood a little log cabin against the rail fence; and there the woody hill fell sharply away, past the barns, the corncrib, the stables, and the tobacco-curing house, to a limpid brook which sang along over its gravelly bed and curved and frisked in and out and here and there and yonder in the deep shade of overhanging foliage and vines—a divine place for wading, and it had swimming pools, too, which were forbidden to us and therefore much frequented by us. For we were little Christian children and had early been taught the value of forbidden fruit. . . .

I can see the farm yet, with perfect clearness. I can see all its belongings, all its details; the family room of the house, with a "trundle" bed in one corner and a spinning-wheel in another—a wheel whose rising and falling wail, heard from a distance, was the mournfulest of all sounds to me, and made me homesick and low spirited, and filled my atmosphere with the wandering spirits of the dead; the vast fireplace, piled high, on winter nights, with flaming hickory logs from whose ends a sugary sap bubbled out, but did not go to waste, for we scraped it off and ate it; the lazy cat spread out on the rough hearthstones; the drowsy dogs braced against the jambs and blinking; my aunt in one chimney corner, knitting; my uncle in the other, smoking his corn-cob pipe; the slick and carpetless oak floor faintly mirroring the dancing flame tongues and freckled with black indentations where fire coals had popped out and died a leisurely death; half a dozen children romping in the background twilight; "split"-bottomed chairs here and there, some with rockers; a cradle—out of service, but waiting, with confidence; in the early cold mornings a snuggle of children, in shirts and chemises, occupying the hearthstone and procrastinating—they could not bear to leave that comfortable place and go out on the windswept floor space between the house and kitchen where the general tin basin stood, and wash.

Along outside of the front fence ran the country road, dusty in the summertime, and a good place for snakes—they liked to lie in it and sun themselves; when they were rattlesnakes or puff adders, we killed them; when

4

5

6

7

they were black snakes, or racers, or belonged to the fabled "hoop" breed, we fled, without shame; when they were "house snakes," or "garters," we carried them home and put them in Aunt Patsy's work basket for a surprise; for she was prejudiced against snakes, and always when she took the basket in her lap and they began to climb out of it it disordered her mind. She never could seem to get used to them; her opportunities went for nothing. And she was always cold toward bats, too, and could not bear them; and yet I think a bat is as friendly a bird as there is. My mother was Aunt Patsy's sister and had the same wild superstitions. A bat is beautifully soft and silky; I do not know any creature that is pleasanter to the touch or is more grateful for caressings, if offered in the right spirit. I know all about these coleoptera, because our great cave, three miles below Hannibal, was multitudinously stocked with them, and often I brought them home to amuse my mother with. It was easy to manage if it was a school day, because then I had ostensibly been to school and hadn't any bats. She was not a suspicious person, but full of trust and confidence; and when I said, "There's something in my coat pocket for you," she would put her hand in. But she always took it out again, herself; I didn't have to tell her. It was remarkable, the way she couldn't learn to like private bats. The more experience she had, the more she could not change her views.

8   Beyond the road where the snakes sunned themselves was a dense young thicket, and through it a dim-lighted path led a quarter of a mile; then out of the dimness one emerged abruptly upon a level great prairie which was covered with wild strawberry plants, vividly starred with prairie pinks, and walled in on all sides by forests. The strawberries were fragrant and fine, and in the season we were generally there in the crisp freshness of the early morning, while the dew beads still sparkled upon the grass and the woods were ringing with the first songs of the birds.

9   Down the forest slopes to the left were the swings. They were made of bark stripped from hickory saplings. When they became dry they were dangerous. They usually broke when a child was forty feet in the air, and this was why so many bones had to be mended every year. I had no ill luck myself, but none of my cousins escaped. There were eight of them, and at one time and another they broke fourteen arms among them. But it cost next to nothing, for the doctor worked by the year—twenty-five dollars for the whole family. I remember two of the Florida doctors, Chowning and Meredith. They not only tended an entire family for twenty-five dollars a year, but furnished the medicine themselves. Good measure, too. Only the largest persons could hold a whole dose. Castor oil was the principal beverage. . . .

10   The country schoolhouse was three miles from my uncle's farm. It stood in a clearing in the woods and would hold about twenty-five boys and girls. We attended the school with more or less regularity once or twice a week, in summer, walking to it in the cool of the morning by the forest paths, and back in the gloaming at the end of the day. All the pupils brought their

dinners in baskets—corn dodger, buttermilk, and other good things—and sat in the shade of the trees at noon and ate them. It is the part of my education which I look back upon with the most satisfaction. My first visit to the school was when I was seven. A strapping girl of fifteen, in the customary sunbonnet and calico dress, asked me if I "used tobacco"—meaning did I chew it. I said no. It roused her scorn. She reported me to all the crowd, and said:

"Here is a boy seven years old who can't chew tobacco." 11

By the looks and comments which this produced I realized that I was a 12 degraded object, and was cruelly ashamed of myself. I determined to reform. But I only made myself sick; I was not able to learn to chew tobacco. I learned to smoke fairly well, but that did not conciliate anybody and I remained a poor thing, and characterless. I longed to be respected, but I never was able to rise. Children have but little charity for one another's defects.

As I have said, I spent some part of every year at the farm until I was 13 twelve or thirteen years old. The life which I led there with my cousins was full of charm, and so is the memory of it yet. I can call back the solemn twilight and mystery of the deep woods, the earthy smells, the faint odors of the wild flowers, the sheen of rain-washed foliage, the rattling clatter of drops when the wind shook the trees, the far-off hammering of woodpeckers and the muffled drumming of wood pheasants in the remoteness of the forest, the snapshot glimpses of disturbed wild creatures scurrying through the grass—I can call it all back and make it as real as it ever was, and as blessed. I can call back the prairie, and its loneliness and peace, and a vast hawk hanging motionless in the sky, with his wings spread wide and the blue of the vault showing through the fringe of their end feathers. I can see the woods in their autumn dress, the oaks purple, the hickories washed with gold, the maples and the sumachs luminous with crimson fires, and I can hear the rustle made by the fallen leaves as we plowed through them. I can see the blue clusters of wild grapes hanging among the foliage of the saplings, and I remember the taste of them and the smell. I know how the wild blackberries looked, and how they tasted, and the same with the pawpaws, the hazelnuts, and the persimmons; and I can feel the thumping rain, upon my head, of hickory nuts and walnuts when we were out in the frosty dawn to scramble for them with the pigs, and the gusts of wind loosed them and sent them down. I know the stain of blackberries, and how pretty it is, and I know the stain of walnut hulls, and how little it minds soap and water, also what grudged experience it had of either of them. I know the taste of maple sap, and when to gather it, and how to arrange the troughs and the delivery tubes, and how to boil down the juice, and how to hook the sugar after it is made, also how much better hooked sugar tastes than any that is honestly come by, let bigots say what they will. I know how a prize watermelon looks when it is sunning its fat rotundity among pumpkin vines and "simblins"; I know how to tell when it is ripe without "plugging" it; I know how inviting it looks when it is cooling itself in a tub of water under the bed, waiting; I know how it looks when it lies on the table in the sheltered great floor space between house and kitchen, and the children gathered for the sacrifice and their mouths watering; I know the crackling sound it makes when the carving knife enters its end, and I can see the split fly along in front of the blade as the knife cleaves its way to the other end; I can see its halves fall apart and display the rich red meat and the black seeds, and the heart standing up, a luxury fit for the elect; I know how a boy looks behind a yard-long slice of that melon, and I know how he feels; for I have been there. I know the taste of the watermelon which has been honestly come by, and I know the taste of the watermelon which has been acquired by art. Both taste good, but the experienced know which tastes best. I know the look of green apples and peaches and pears on the trees, and I know how entertaining they are when they are inside of a person. I know how ripe ones look when they are piled in pyramids under the trees, and how pretty they are and how vivid their colors. I know how a frozen apple looks, in a barrel down cellar in the wintertime, and how hard it is to bite, and how the frost makes the teeth ache, and yet how good it is, notwithstanding. I know the disposition of elderly people to select the specked apples for the children, and I once knew ways to beat the game. I know the look of an apple that is roasting and sizzling on a hearth on a winter's evening, and I know the comfort that comes of eating it hot, along with some sugar and a drench of cream. I know the delicate art and mystery of so cracking hickory nuts and walnuts on a flatiron with a hammer that the kernels will be delivered whole, and I know how the nuts, taken in conjunction with winter apples, cider, and doughnuts, make old people's old tales and old jokes sound fresh and crisp and enchanting, and juggle an evening away before you know what went with the time. I know the look of Uncle Dan'l's kitchen as it was on the privileged nights, when I was a child, and I can see the white and black children grouped on the hearth, with the firelight playing on their faces and the shadows flickering upon the walls, clear back toward the cavernous gloom of the rear, and I can hear Uncle Dan'l telling the immortal tales which Uncle Remus Harris was to gather into his book and charm the world with, by and by; and I can feel again the creepy joy which quivered through me when the time for the ghost story was reached—and the sense of regret, too, which came over me, for it was always the last story of the evening and there was nothing between it and the unwelcome bed. . . .

Questions

1. Descriptions of places often depend heavily on sensory details, as does Twain's description of "Uncle John's Farm." Identify details that appeal to the senses of sight, sound, taste, touch, and smell. How does their abundance—at times, superabundance—affect you as a reader?

2. In places Twain's description also involves long lists or catalogues—of foods (paragraph 3), of the sights and sounds and activities of farm life (paragraph 13). How

does he vary the itemization to keep the lists and details appealing and not monotonous? Do the lists look or sound like lists? What determines the order of the items on these lists?

3. Twain, like many successful autobiographers, manages the difficult feat of using the language of an adult to recall events from his childhood. Find a typical passage in which he enables us to see the experience as a child would but to imply or offer an adult's interpretation. When he says that the farm was "a heavenly place for a boy" (paragraph 3) is he speaking from the perspective of the adult, or the child, or both?

4. In the last paragraph (13) Twain's reminiscences are identified by many sentences beginning with parallel constructions, "I can call back," "I know," "I remember." What is the effect of this much repetition?

MAXINE HONG KINGSTON

Uneasy Status:
From Renter to Homeowner

Kingston's autobiographical writings are haunted by questions of belonging: how much does she belong to China, to her family, to America, how much to herself alone? And what belongs to her? Kingston was born in Stockton, California, in 1940, the eldest American-born child of recent Chinese immigrants. At home she learned Chinese, her only language until she started first grade, and Chinese customs from stories exchanged in her parents' laundry. She graduated from the University of California at Berkeley in 1962, married an American of European descent, and has taught at high schools and universities in California and Hawaii. She publishes poetry, stories, and essays in national magazines, but is best known for her autobiography, The Woman Warrior: Memoirs of a Girlhood Among Ghosts *(1975), winner of the National Book Critics Circle Award for Nonfiction, and* China Men *(1980), winner of the American Book Award.*

At the beginning of "Uneasy Status: From Renter to Homeowner," Kingston makes us aware that the decision of whether to rent or to buy becomes particularly complicated if one is "the first and only person in the family . . . who didn't rely on being landed to belong to this planet." Kingston's characteristic style reinforces her ambivalence; there is a sense of brooding, of questioning what is myth and what is reality, of trying to connect the past (legendary or otherwise) with the present and the future. Although she expresses an Eastern acceptance of fate—she will write in her new garret, the bombs will fall—the essay ends on a Western note of discontent, imbalance, unrest. Kingston, who recently visited the Chinese village of her ancestors as part of a delegation of American writers, still belongs to two cultures ("Even now China wraps double binds around my feet."), and that tension reinforces the dynamism of her work, struggling "to connect new words in new ways."

It has been a month now since we moved into our own, bought, house. So far, we've been renters. I have liked saying, "Gotta make the rent" and "This much set aside for rent" and "Rent party." I could excuse doing scut work: "It pays the rent." 1

2   A renter can move quickly, no leases, drop the cleaning deposit and go. Plumbing, wiring, walls, roof, floors keep to their proper neutral places under the sun among the stars. If we looked at each other one day and decided that we really shouldn't have gotten married after all, we could dismantle the brick-and-plank bookshelf or leave it, no petty talk about material things. The householder is only one incarnation away from snail or turtle or kangaroo. In religions, the householder doesn't levitate like the monk. In politics, the householder doesn't say, "Burn it down to the ground." I had never become a housewife, the first and only person in the family (except for those caught in land redistribution movements) who didn't rely on being landed to belong on this planet.

3   But as soon as we drove up to this house, we liked it, its very quirks fitting ours: cascades of vines, lichen and moss on lava rock, moss-colored finches, two murky ponds thick with water hyacinth, an iridescent green toad hopping into the blue ginger, a monkeypot tree with a stone bench underneath, three trees like Van Gogh's cypresses in the front yard, pines in back, an archway like an ear or an elbow with no purpose but to be walked through, an arched New England vestibule for taking off snowy coats and boots, a dining room with glass doors, only one bedroom but two makeshifts, a bathroom like a chapel, a kitchen with a cooler, through whose slats you could look down at the earth and smell it, and—the clincher—a writer's garret, the very writer's garret of your imagination, bookshelves along an entire wall and a window overlooking trees and the ponds—the whole thing against a mountain and around the corner from the apocryphal hut where Robert Louis Stevenson wrote his Hawaii works. Somebody had built a desk into the garret wall, so all I'd need is a chair.

4   What thick novels I could brood here with no interrupting chapter breaks but one long thought from front to back cover. For the first time I'd write not on a corner of a dining table or in a sectioned-off part of the living room but in a room designated for no other purpose. This would be the place to connect words in new ways, to write what has not been written before, write what only I and no other can write.

5   We wanted to look behind the hollow walls. Right away we found two concealed cupboards, one of them with seven pigeonholes; the artist who painted in the garret must have stored brushes there, or perhaps it was where a sea captain or his widow kept their rolled-up maps. The person who once sat at the desk had written in pencil on the wall: "eros agape philos," as promising words as any.

6   But when we had talked about house-buying, both of us thought immediately about dying, as if the house-owning and the death wires, like the smell and memory wires, cross or connect in the brain. Perhaps the brain automatically adds 20 years of mortgage on to one's age. I'd be lucky to live so long.

And moving is such a frightening, primal activity. "Move" was one of the 7
first English words my parents ever used, such an early word I thought it was
Chinese—"moo-fu," a Chinese-American word that connotes "pick up your
pants and go."

Renting was beginning to feel irresponsible. Our friend who teaches 8
university classes how to calculate how many grams are gained or lost on a
protein exchange, how much alfalfa turns into how much hamburger, for
example, told us about the time when each earthling will have one square
foot of room. Our friend quit the city and bought five acres in the mountains;
he has a stream and will install solar energy and grow food, raise a goat, make
the five acres a self-sufficient system. We heard about a family that had all
their teeth pulled out, bought their own boat and sailed for an island that's
not on the maps. If we owned a vacant lot somewhere, when the world
famine comes, we can go there to sleep or sit.

Coincidentally, strange ads were appearing in the classifieds: "Ideal 9
place for you and your family in the event of war, famine, strike (strike?) or
natural disaster."

So the advantages—to have a place for meeting when the bombs fall and 10
to write in a garret—outweighed the ownership-is-death connection, and we
bought the house.

The writer's garret is a myth about cheap housing. In real life, to have a 11
garret, the writer has to own the house under the garret and the land under
the house and the trees on the land to have an inspiring green view.

On the day we moved in, I tried walking about and thinking: "This tree 12
is my tree." "This flower is mine." "This grass and dirt are mine." I was
relieved to discover that I did not believe it for a moment.

At the escrow office (new word "escrow"), I only stared at the papers. 13
Earll read them, and so found out that this land had been given to E. H.
Rogers by a Royal Hawaiian Land Grant. "We don't belong on it," he said.
But, I rationalized, isn't all land Israel? No matter what year you claim it,
what property is there that didn't belong to a former owner who has good
moral reason for a claim? We, for example, have a right to go to China and
say we own our farm, the one piece of property in the world that has belonged to our family since unrecorded history. Ridiculous, isn't it? Also,
doesn't the average American move every five years? We just keep exchanging
with one another.

The way to deal with moving in was to establish a Headquarters, which I 14
decided would be in the dining room, a small powerful spot, surprisingly not
the garret, which is secretive. The Headquarters would consist of a card table
and a lawn chair, a typewriter, papers and pencils.

It takes about 10 minutes to arrange, and I feel moved in, capable; from 15
the Headquarters, I will venture into the rest of the house. Earll assembles
and talks about a Basic Kit, by which I think he means a toothbrush and

toothpaste. "The Basic Kit is all I really need," he keeps saying, at which I take offense—as if the rest of the house and possessions were my doing. I retaliate that all I need is my Headquarters.

16   Our son's method of moving in is to decide that his bedroom will be the one in the attic, next to the writer's garret, and he spreads everything he owns over the strangeness.

17   As at every place we have ever moved to, we throw mattresses on the living-room floor and sleep there for several nights—to establish ourselves in the middle of the house, to weigh it down. The night comes black into the uncurtained windows.

18   I attack the house from my Headquarters, and again appreciate being married to a person whose geometry is not much different from mine. I don't see how people live together whose eyes can't automatically agree on how much space there should be between pictures and which magnetic pole the head of the bed points to and which the feet.

19   The final thing that makes it possible to move into the house is our promise to each other that if we cannot bear the weight of ownership, we can always sell, though we know from 15 years of marriage that this is like saying, "Well, if the marriage doesn't work out, we can always get a divorce." You don't know how you change in the interim.

ALFRED KAZIN

Brownsville: The Kitchen

Kazin was born in 1915 in Brooklyn's Brownsville district, characterized in the section of A Walker in the City *that follows. He read and studied and wrote his way out of the ghetto to become one of America's major literary critics. He earned a B.S. from the City College of New York in 1935 and an M.A. from Columbia in 1938, worked for* The New Republic *and then for* Fortune *before beginning the university teaching career generated by the acclaim for his first book of criticism,* On Native Grounds *(1942). In the course of his career as a teacher at Harvard, the University of California, Smith, Black Mountain College, the University of Minnesota, CUNY, and elsewhere, Kazin has been at the center of American literary studies and critical controversies.*

The three volumes of Kazin's autobiography, A Walker in the City *(1951),* Starting Out in the Thirties *(1962), and* New York Jew *(1978), express the motifs established in "Brownsville: The Kitchen": his "Russian immigrant-socialist background, the resurgent sense of his own Jewishness, and the 'raw power, mass, and volume' " of New York, the city to which he is bound by a mixture of love and longing, fascination and repulsion. In this excerpt, Kazin solves a basic writing problem by creating a central focal point that allows him to narrate an entire childhood in only ten paragraphs. He focuses on the kitchen, "the largest room and center of the house," repeating the word "kitchen" as the grammatical subject of five of the first six topic sentences. Of course, the kitchen, the sewing machine, the fabrics, the*

*various lights from naked bulbs, flames, candles, and the sun only serve to disclose the real
subject matter of the essay—the people who live and work, fear and hope and pray in that
kitchen. These visible symbols of Kazin's childhood bind the essay as they integrated his early
life, and they help us to see, as well as to feel, what that experience was like for him.*

In Brownsville tenements the kitchen is always the largest room and the   1
center of the household. As a child I felt that we lived in a kitchen to which
four other rooms were annexed. My mother, a "home" dressmaker, had her
workshop in the kitchen. She told me once that she had begun dressmaking
in Poland at thirteen; as far back as I can remember, she was always making
dresses for the local women. She had an innate sense of design, a quick eye for
all the subtleties in the latest fashions, even when she despised them, and
great boldness. For three or four dollars she would study the fashion magazines with a customer, go with the customer to the remnants store on Bel-
mont Avenue to pick out the material, argue the owner down—all remnants
stores, for some reason, were supposed to be shady, as if the owners dealt in
stolen goods—and then for days would patiently fit and baste and sew and fit
again. Our apartment was always full of women in their housedresses sitting
around the kitchen table waiting for a fitting. My little bedroom next to the
kitchen was the fitting room. The sewing machine, and old nut-brown Singer
with golden scrolls painted along the black arm and engraved along the two
tiers of little drawers massed with needles and thread on each side of the
treadle, stood next to the window and the great coal-black stove which up to
my last year in college was our main source of heat. By December the two
outer bedrooms were closed off, and used to chill bottles of milk and cream,
cold borscht and jellied calves' feet.

The kitchen held our lives together. My mother worked in it all day long,   2
we ate in it almost all meals except the Passover *seder,* I did my homework and
first writing at the kitchen table, and in winter I often had a bed made up for
me on three kitchen chairs near the stove. On the wall just over the table
hung a long horizontal mirror that sloped to a ship's prow at each end and
was lined in cherry wood. It took up the whole wall, and drew every object in
the kitchen to itself. The walls were a fiercely stippled whitewash, so often
rewhitened by my father in slack seasons that the paint looked as if it had
been squeezed and cracked into the walls. A large electric bulb hung down
the center of the kitchen at the end of a chain that had been hooked into the
ceiling; the old gas ring and key still jutted out of the wall like antlers. In the
corner next to the toilet was the sink at which we washed, and the square tub
in which my mother did our clothes. Above it, tacked to the shelf on which
were pleasantly ranged square, blue-bordered white sugar and spice jars,
hung calendars from the Public National Bank on Pitkin Avenue and the
Minsker Progressive Branch of the Workmen's Circle; receipts for the payment of insurance premiums, and household bills on a spindle; two little
boxes engraved with Hebrew letters. One of these was for the poor, the other

to buy back the Land of Israel. Each spring a bearded little man would suddenly appear in our kitchen, salute us with a hurried Hebrew blessing, empty the boxes (sometimes with a sidelong look of disdain if they were not full), hurriedly bless us again for remembering our less fortunate Jewish brothers and sisters, and so take his departure until the next spring, after vainly trying to persuade my mother to take still another box. We did occasionally remember to drop coins in the boxes, but this was usually only on the dreaded morning of "midterms" and final examinations, because my mother thought it would bring me luck. She was extremely superstitious, but embarrassed about it, and always laughed at herself whenever, on the morning of an examination, she counseled me to leave the house on my right foot. "I know it's silly," her smile seemed to say, "but what harm can it do? It may calm God down."

3   The kitchen gave a special character to our lives; my mother's character. All my memories of that kitchen are dominated by the nearness of my mother sitting all day long at her sewing machine, by the clacking of the treadle against the linoleum floor, by the patient twist of her right shoulder as she automatically pushed at the wheel with one hand or lifted the foot to free the needle where it had got stuck in a thick piece of material. The kitchen was her life. Year by year, as I began to take in her fantastic capacity for labor and her anxious zeal, I realized it was ourselves she kept stitched together. I can never remember a time when she was not working. She worked because the law of her life was work, work and anxiety; she worked because she would have found life meaningless without work. She read almost no English; she could read the Yiddish paper, but never felt she had time to. We were always talking of a time when I would teach her how to read, but somehow there was never time. When I awoke in the morning she was already at her machine, or in the great morning crowd of housewives at the grocery getting fresh rolls for breakfast. When I returned from school she was at her machine, or conferring over *McCall's* with some neighborhood woman who had come in pointing hopefully to an illustration—"Mrs. Kazin! Mrs. Kazin! Make me a dress like it shows here in the picture!" When my father came home from work she had somehow mysteriously interrupted herself to make supper for us, and the dishes cleared and washed, was back at her machine. When I went to bed at night, often she was still there, pounding away at the treadle, hunched over the wheel, her hands steering a piece of gauze under the needle with a finesse that always contrasted sharply with her swollen hands and broken nails. Her left hand had been pierced through when as a girl she had worked in the infamous Triangle Shirtwaist Factory on the East Side. A needle had gone straight through the palm, severing a large vein. They had sewn it up for her so clumsily that a tuft of flesh always lay folded over the palm.

4   The kitchen was the great machine that set our lives running; it whirred down a little only on Saturdays and holy days. From my mother's kitchen I gained my first picture of life as a white, overheated, starkly lit workshop

redolent with Jewish cooking, crowded with women in housedresses, strewn with fashion magazines, patterns, dress material, spools of thread and at whose center, so lashed to her machine that bolts of energy seemed to dance out of her hands and feet as she worked, my mother stamped the treadle hard against the floor, hard, hard, and silently, grimly at war, beat out the first rhythm of the world for me.

Every sound from the street roared and trembled at our windows—a mother feeding her child on the doorstep, the screech of the trolley cars on Rockaway Avenue, the eternal smash of a handball against the wall of our house, the clatter of *"der Italyéner"*'s cart packed with watermelons, the sing-song of the old-clothes men walking Chester Street, the cries *"Árbes! Árbes! Kinder! Kinder! Heyse gute árbes!"* All day long people streamed into our apartment as a matter of course—"customers," upstairs neighbors, downstairs neighbors, women who would stop in for a half-hour's talk, salesmen, relatives, insurance agents. Usually they came in without ringing the bell—everyone knew my mother was always at home. I would hear the front door opening, the wind whistling through our front hall, and then some familiar face would appear in our kitchen with the same bland, matter-of-fact inquiring look: no need to stand on ceremony: my mother and her kitchen were available to everyone all day long.

At night the kitchen contracted around the blaze of light on the cloth, the patterns, the ironing board where the iron had burned a black border around the tear in the muslin cover; the finished dresses looked so frilly as they jostled on their wire hangers after all the work my mother had put into them. And then I would get that strangely ominous smell of tension from the dress fabrics and the burn in the cover of the ironing board—as if each piece of cloth and paper crushed with light under the naked bulb might suddenly go up in flames. Whenever I pass some small tailoring shop still lit up at night and see the owner hunched over his steam press; whenever in some poorer neighborhood of the city I see through a window some small crowded kitchen naked under the harsh light glittering in the ceiling, I still smell that fiery breath, that warning of imminent fire. I was always holding my breath. What I must have felt most about ourselves, I see now, was that we ourselves were like kindling—that all the hard-pressed pieces of ourselves and all the hard-used objects in that kitchen were like so many slivers of wood that might go up in flames if we came too near the white-blazing filaments in that naked bulb. Our tension itself was fire, we ourselves were forever burning—to live, to get down the foreboding in our souls, to make good.

Twice a year, on the anniversaries of her parents' deaths, my mother placed on top of the ice-box an ordinary kitchen glass packed with wax, the *yortsayt,* and lit the candle in it. Sitting at the kitchen table over my homework, I would look across the threshold to that mourning-glass, and sense that for my mother the distance from our kitchen to *der heym,* from life to death, was only a flame's length away. Poor as we were, it was not poverty that drove my mother so hard; it was loneliness—some endless bitter brooding over all those left behind, dead or dying or soon to die; a loneliness locked up in her kitchen that dwelt every day on the hazardousness of life and the nearness of death, but still kept struggling in the lock, trying to get us through by endless labor.

8   With us, life started up again only on the last shore. There seemed to be no middle ground between despair and the fury of our ambition. Whenever my mother spoke of her hopes for us, it was with such unbelievingness that the likes of us would ever come to anything, such abashed hope and readiness for pain, that I finally came to see in the flame burning on top of the ice-box death itself burning away the bones of poor Jews, burning out in us everything but courage, the blind resolution to live. In the light of that mourning-candle, there were ranged around me how many dead and dying—how many eras of pain, of exile, of dispersion, of cringing before the powers of this world!

9   It was always at dusk that my mother's loneliness came home most to me. Painfully alert to every shift in the light at her window, she would suddenly confess her fatigue by removing her pince-nez, and then wearily pushing aside the great mound of fabrics on her machine, would stare at the street as if to warm herself in the last of the sun. "How sad it is!" I once heard her say. "It grips me! It grips me!" Twilight was the bottommost part of the day, the chillest and loneliest time for her. Always so near to her moods, I knew she was fighting some deep inner dread, struggling against the returning tide of darkness along the streets that invariably assailed her heart with the same foreboding— Where? Where now? Where is the day taking us now?

10   Yet one good look at the street would revive her. I see her now, perched against the windowsill, with her face against the glass, her eyes almost asleep in enjoyment, just as she starts up with the guilty cry—"What foolishness is this in me!"—and goes to the stove to prepare supper for us: a moment, only a moment, watching the evening crowd of women gathering at the grocery for fresh bread and milk. But between my mother's pent-up face at the window and the winter sun dying in the fabrics—"Alfred, see how beautiful!"—she has drawn for me one single line of sentience.

Place as the Context for Gaining Self-Knowledge

HENRY DAVID THOREAU

Where I Lived and What I Lived For

Thoreau (1817–1862), essayist, poet, and diarist, spent his life in his birthplace of Concord, Massachusetts, graduated from Harvard in 1837, and thereafter worked at odd jobs— teaching, manufacturing lead pencils, gardening, fence-building, surveying—while doing his real work as an original thinker. As a Transcendentalist, strongly influenced by the works of Kant, Coleridge, and Goethe, he believed that a certain kind of intuitive knowledge transcended the limits of human experience and the senses, and that ideas and the natural world were more important and more powerful than material things. These views are reflected in his major works, A Week on the Concord and Merrimack Rivers (1849), and Walden, or Life in the Woods (1854), a record of his famous two years at Walden Pond, in Concord, where he lived alone in a house he made, and became the model of self-reliance so praised by his mentor, Ralph Waldo Emerson. He grew his own food, chopped his own wood, and lived frugally while feasting on the bounty of nature and the cosmos.

Although "Where I Lived and What I Lived For" is famous as a philosophical manifesto and meditation on nature, it is, like its author, individualistic and highly unconventional. Thoreau describes and interprets his "experiment" in the woods as a way of raising his own consciousness and that of his readers; "I do not propose to write an ode to dejection, but to brag as lustily as chanticleer in the morning . . . if only to wake my neighbors up." He wrote to put heaven and earth in proper perspective, to find out what is essential to a good life well lived, and what is not. Thoreau's rustic, down to earth, back-to-the-woods persona is carefully contrived; his writing is ever informed by classical learning, wide reading, and the philosopher's sophisticated mind.

At a certain season of our life we are accustomed to consider every spot as the possible site of a house. I have thus surveyed the country on every side within a dozen miles of where I live. In imagination I have bought all the farms in succession, for all were to be bought, and I knew their price. I walked over each farmer's premises, tasted his wild apples, discoursed on husbandry with him, took his farm at his price, at any price, mortgaging it to him in my mind; even put a higher price on it,—took everything but a deed of it,—took his word for his deed, for I dearly love to talk,—cultivated it, and him too to some extent, I trust, and withdrew when I had enjoyed it long enough, leaving him to carry it on. This experience entitled me to be regarded as a sort of real-estate broker by my friends. Wherever I sat, there I might live, and the landscape radiated from me accordingly. What is a house but a *sedes*, a seat?— 1 better if a country seat. I discovered many a site for a house not likely to be soon improved, which some might have thought too far from the village, but to my eyes the village was too far from it. Well, there I might live, I said, and there I did live, for an hour, a summer and a winter life; saw how I could let the years run off, buffet the winter through, and see the spring come in. The future inhabitants of this region, wherever they may place their houses, may be sure that they have been anticipated. An afternoon sufficed to lay out the land into orchard, wood-lot, and pasture, and to decide what fine oaks or pines should be left to stand before the door, and whence each blasted tree could be seen to the best advantage; and then I let it lie, fallow perchance, for a man is rich in proportion to the number of things which he can afford to let alone.

2 My imagination carried me so far that I even had the refusal of several farms,—the refusal was all I wanted,—but I never got my fingers burned by actual possession. The nearest that I came to actual possession was when I bought the Hollowell place, and had begun to sort my seeds, and collected materials with which to make a wheelbarrow to carry it on or off with; but before the owner gave me a deed of it, his wife—every man has such a wife—changed her mind and wished to keep it, and he offered me ten dollars to release him. Now, to speak the truth, I had but ten cents in the world, and it surpassed my arithmetic to tell, if I was that man who had ten cents, or who had a farm, or ten dollars, or all together. However, I let him keep the ten dollars and the farm too, for I had carried it far enough; or rather, to be generous, I sold him the farm for just what I gave for it, and, as he was not a rich man, made him a present of ten dollars, and still had my ten cents, and seeds, and materials for a wheelbarrow left. I found thus that I had been a rich man without any damage to my poverty. But I retained the landscape, and I have since annually carried off what it yielded without a wheelbarrow. With respect to landscapes,—

> "I am monarch of all I *survey*,
> My right there is none to dispute."

3 I have frequently seen a poet withdraw, having enjoyed the most valuable part of a farm, while the crusty farmer supposed that he had got a few wild apples only. Why, the owner does not know it for many years when a poet has put his farm in rhyme, the most admirable kind of invisible fence, has fairly impounded it, milked it, skimmed it, and got all the cream, and left the farmer only the skimmed milk.

4 The real attractions of the Hollowell farm, to me, were: its complete retirement, being about two miles from the village, half a mile from the nearest neighbor, and separated from the highway by a broad field; its bounding on the river, which the owner said protected it by its fogs from frosts in the spring, though that was nothing to me; the gray color and ruinous state of the house and barn, and the dilapidated fences, which put

such an interval between me and the last occupant; the hollow and lichen-covered apple trees, gnawed by rabbits, showing what kind of neighbors I should have; but above all, the recollection I had of it from my earliest voyages up the river, when the house was concealed behind a dense grove of red maples, through which I heard the house-dog bark. I was in haste to buy it, before the proprietor finished getting out some rocks, cutting down the hollow apple trees, and grubbing up some young birches which had sprung up in the pasture, or, in short, had made any more of his improvements. To enjoy these advantages I was ready to carry it on; like Atlas, to take the world on my shoulders,—I never heard what compensation he received for that,—and do all those things which had no other motive or excuse but that I might pay for it and be unmolested in my possession of it; for I knew all the while that it would yield the most abundant crop of the kind I wanted. If I could only afford to let it alone. But it turned out as I have said.

All that I could say, then, with respect to farming on a large scale—I have always cultivated a garden—was, that I had had my seeds ready. Many think that seeds improve with age. I have no doubt that time discriminates between the good and the bad; and when at last I shall plant, I shall be less likely to be disappointed. But I would say to my fellows, once for all, As long as possible live free and uncommitted. It makes but little difference whether you are committed to a farm or the county jail. 5

Old Cato whose "De Re Rustica" is my "Cultivator," says,—and the only translation I have seen makes sheer nonsense of the passage,—"When you think of getting a farm turn it thus in your mind, not to buy greedily; nor spare your pains to look at it, and do not think it enough to go round it once. The oftener you go there the more it will please you, if it is good." I think I shall not buy greedily, but go round and round it as long as I live, and be buried in it first, that it may please me the more at last. 6

The present was my next experiment of this kind, which I purpose to describe more at length, for convenience putting the experience of two years into one. As I have said, I do not propose to write an ode to dejection, but to brag as lustily as chanticleer in the morning, standing on his roost, if only to wake my neighbors up. 7

When first I took up my abode in the woods, that is, began to spend my nights as well as days there, which, by accident, was on Independence Day, or the Fourth of July, 1845, my house was not finished for winter, but was merely a defence against the rain, without plastering or chimney, the walls being of rough, weather-stained boards, with wide chinks, which made it cool at night. The upright white hewn studs and freshly planed door and window casings gave it a clean and airy look, especially in the morning, when its timbers were saturated with dew, so that I fancied that by noon some sweet gum would exude from them. To my imagination it retained through-out the day more or less of this auroral character, reminding me of a certain 8 house on a mountain which I had visited a year before. This was an airy and unplastered cabin, fit to entertain a travelling god, and where a goddess might trail her garments. The winds which passed over my dwelling were such as sweep over the ridges of mountains, bearing the broken strains, or celestial parts only, of terrestrial music. The morning wind forever blows, the poem of creation is uninterrupted; but few are the ears that hear it. Olympus is but the outside of the earth everywhere.

9   The only house I had been the owner of before, if I except boat, was a tent, which I used occasionally when making excursions in the summer, and this is still rolled up in my garret; but the boat, after passing from hand to hand, has gone down the stream of time. With this more substantial shelter about me, I had made some progress toward settling in the world. This frame, so slightly clad, was a sort of crystallization around me, and reacted on the builder. It was suggestive somewhat as a picture in outlines. I did not need to go out of doors to take the air, for the atmosphere within had lost none of its freshness. It was not so much within doors as being a door where I sat, even in the rainiest weather. The Harivansa says, "An abode without birds is like a meat without seasoning." Such was not my abode, for I found myself suddenly neighbor to the birds; not by having imprisoned one, but having caged myself near them. I was not only nearer to some of those which commonly frequent the garden and the orchard, but to those wilder and more thrilling songsters of the forest which never, or rarely, serenade a villager,—the wood-thrush, the veery, the scarlet tanger, the field-sparrow, the whippoorwill, and many others.

10   I was seated by the shore of a small pond, about a mile and half south of the village of Concord and somewhat higher than it, in the midst of an extensive wood between that town and Lincoln, and about two miles south of that our only field known to fame, Concord Battle Ground; but I was so low in the woods that the opposite shore, half a mile off, like the rest, covered with wood, was my most distant horizon. For the first week, whenever I looked out on the pond it impressed me like a tarn high up on the side of a mountain, its bottom far above the surface of other lakes, and, as the sun arose, I saw it throwing off its nightly clothing of mist, and here and there, by degrees, its soft ripples or its smooth reflecting surface was revealed, while the mists, like ghosts, were stealthily withdrawing in every direction into the woods, as at the breaking up of some nocturnal conventicle. The very dew seemed to hang upon the trees later into the day than usual, as on the sides of mountains.

11   This small lake was of most value as a neighbor in the intervals of a gentle rain-storm in August, when, both air and water being perfectly still, but the sky overcast, mid-afternoon had all the serenity of evening, and the wood thrush sang around, and was heard from shore to shore. A lake like this is never smoother than at such a time; and the clear portion of the air above it being shallow and darkened by clouds, the water, full of light and reflections, becomes a lower heaven itself so much the more important. From a hilltop

near by, where the wood had been recently cut off, there was a pleasing vista southward across the pond, through a wide indentation in the hills which form the shore there, where their opposite sides sloping toward each other suggested a stream flowing out in that direction through a wooded valley, but stream there was none. That way I looked between and over the near green hills to some distant and higher ones in the horizon, tinged with blue. Indeed, by standing on tiptoe I could catch a glimpse of some of the peaks of the still bluer and more distant mountain ranges in the northwest, those true-blue coins from heaven's own mint, and also of some portion of the village. But in other directions, even from this point, I could not see over or beyond the woods which surrounded me. It is well to have some water in your neighborhood, to give buoyancy to and float the earth. One value even of the smallest well is, that when you look into it you see the earth is not continent but insular. This is as important as that it keeps butter cool. When I looked across the pond from this peak toward the Sudbury meadows, which in time of flood I distinguished elevated perhaps by a mirage in their seething valley, like a coin in a basin, all the earth beyond the pond appeared like a thin crust insulated and floated even by this small sheet of intervening water, and I was reminded that this on which I dwelt was but *dry land*.

Though the view from my door was still more contracted, I did not feel crowded or confined in the least. There was pasture enough for my imagination. The low shrub oak plateau to which the opposite shore arose stretched away toward the prairies of the West and the steppes of Tartary, affording ample room for all the roving families of men. "There are none happy in the world but beings who enjoy freely a vast horizon,"—said Damodara, when his herds required new and larger pastures. 12

Both place and time were changed, and I dwelt nearer to those parts of the universe and to those eras in history which had most attracted me. Where I lived was as far off as many a region viewed nightly by astronomers. We are wont to imagine rare and delectable places in some remote and more celestial corner of the system, behind the constellation of Cassiopeia's Chair, far from noise and disturbance. I discovered that my house actually had its site in such a withdrawn, but forever new and unprofaned, part of the universe. If it were worth the while to settle in those parts near to the Pleiades or the Hyades, to Aldebaran or Altair, then I was really there, or at an equal remoteness from the life which I had left behind, divided and twinkling with as fine a ray to my nearest neighbor, and to be seen only in moonless nights by him. Such was that part of creation where I had squatted;— 13

> "There was a shepherd that did live,
>   And held his thoughts as high
> As were the mounts whereon his flocks
>   Did hourly feed him by."

What should we think of the shepherd's life if his flocks always wandered to higher pastures than his thoughts?

14   Every morning was a cheerful invitation to make my life of equal simplicity, and I may say innocence, with Nature herself. I have been as sincere a
worshipper of Aurora as the Greeks. I got up early and bathed in the pond;
that was a religious exercise, and one of the best things which I did. They say
that characters were engraven on the bathing tub of King Tchingthang to
this effect—"Renew thyself completely each day; do it again, and again, and
forever again." I can understand that. Morning brings back the heroic ages. I
was as much affected by the faint hum of a mosquito making its invisible and
unimaginable tour through my apartment at earliest dawn, when I was sitting
with door and windows open, as I could be by any trumpet that ever sang of
fame. It was Homer's requiem; itself an Iliad and Odyssey in the air, singing
its own wrath and wanderings. There was something cosmical about it; a
standing advertisement, till forbidden, of the everlasting vigor and fertility of
the world. The morning, which is the most memorable season of the day, is
the awakening hour. Then there is least somnolence in us; and for an hour, at
least, some part of us awakes which slumbers all the rest of the day and night.
Little is to be expected of that day, if it can be called a day, to which we are
not awakened by our Genius, but by the mechanical nudgings of some ser-
vitor, are not awakened by our own newly acquired force and aspirations
from within, accompanied by the undulations of celestial music, instead of
factory bells, and a fragrance filling the air—to a higher life than we fell asleep
from; and thus the darkness bear its fruit, and prove itself to be good, no less
than the light. The man who does not believe that each day contains an
earlier, more sacred, and auroral hour than he has yet profaned, has despaired
of life, and is pursuing a descending and darkening way. After a partial
cessation of his sensuous life, the soul of man, or its organs rather, are
reinvigorated each day, and his Genius tries again what noble life it can make.
All memorable events, I should say, transpire in morning time and in a
morning atmosphere. The Vedas say, "All intelligences awake with the morning." Poetry and art, and the fairest and most memorable of the actions of
men, date from such an hour. All poets and heroes, like Memmon, are the
children of Aurora, and emit their music at sunrise. To him whose elastic and
vigorous thought keeps pace with the sun, the day is a perpetual morning. It
matters not what the clocks say or the attitudes and labors of men. Morning
is when I am awake and there is a dawn in me. Moral reform is the effort to
throw off sleep. Why is it that men give so poor an account of their day if
they have not been slumbering? They are not such poor calculators. If they
had not been overcome with drowsiness, they would have performed something. The millions are awake enough for physical labor; but only one in a
million is awake enough for effective intellectual exertion, only one in a
hundred millions to a poetic or divine life. To be awake is to be alive. I have
never yet met a man who was quite awake. How could I have looked him in
the face?

15   We must learn to reawaken and keep ourselves awake, not by mechanical
aids, but by an infinite expectation of the dawn, which does not forsake us in

our soundest sleep. I know of no more encouraging fact than the unquestionable ability of man to elevate his life by a conscious endeavor. It is something to be able to paint a particular picture, or to carve a statue, and so to make a few objects beautiful; but it far more glorious to carve and paint the very atmosphere and medium through which we look, which morally we can do. To affect the quality of the day, this is the highest of arts. Every man is tasked to make his life, even in its details, worthy of the contemplation of his most elevated and critical hour. If we refused, or rather used up, such paltry information as we get, the oracles would distinctly inform us how this might be done.

I went to the woods because I wished to live deliberately, to front only 16 the essential facts of life, and see if I could not learn what it had to teach, and not, when I came to die, discover that I had not lived. I did not wish to live what was not life, living is so dear, nor did I wish to practice resignation, unless it was quite necessary. I wanted to live deep and suck out all the marrow of life, to live so sturdily and Spartan-like as to put to rout all that was not life, to cut a broad swath and shave close, to drive life into a corner, and reduce it to its lowest terms, and, if it proved to be mean, why then to get the whole and genuine meanness of it, and publish its meanness to the world; or if it were sublime, to know it by experience, and be able to give a true account of it in my next excursion. For most men, it appears to me, are in a strange uncertainty about it, whether it is of the devil or of God and have *somewhat hastily* concluded that it is the chief end of man here to "glorify God and enjoy him forever."

Still we live meanly, like ants; though the fable tells us that we were long 17 ago changed into men; like pygmies we fight with cranes; it is error upon error, and clout upon clout, and our best virtue has for its occasion a superfluous and evitable wretchedness. Our life is frittered away by detail. An honest man has hardly need to count more than his ten fingers, or in extreme cases he may add his ten toes, and lump the rest. Simplicity, simplicity, simplicity! I say, let your affairs be as two or three, and not a hundred or a thousand; instead of a million count half a dozen, and keep your accounts on your thumb-nail. In the midst of this chopping sea of civilized life, such are the clouds and storms and quicksands and thousand-and-one items to be allowed for. that a man has to live, if he would not founder and go to the bottom and not make his port at all, by dead reckoning, and he must be a great calculator indeed who succeeds. Simplify, simplify. Instead of three meals a day, if it be necessary eat but one; instead of a hundred dishes, five; and reduce other things in proportion. Our life is like a German Confederacy, made up of petty states, with its boundary forever fluctuating, so that even a German cannot tell you how it is bounded at any moment. The nation itself, with all its so-called internal improvements, which, by the way, are all external and superficial, is just such an unwieldy and overgrown establishment, cluttered with furniture and tripped up by its own traps, ruined by luxury and heedless expense, by want of calculation and a worthy aim, as the million households in the land; and the only cure for it, as for them, is in a rigid economy, a stern and more than Spartan simplicity of life and elevation of purpose. It lives too fast. Men think that it is essential that the *Nation* have commerce, and export ice, and talk through a telegraph, and ride thirty miles an hour, without a doubt, whether *they* do or not; but whether we should live like baboons or like men, is a little uncertain. If we do not get out sleepers, and forge rails, and devote days and nights to the work, but go to tinkering upon our *lives* to improve *them,* who will build railroads? And if railroads are not built, how shall we get to Heaven in season? But if we stay at home and mind our business, who will want railroads? We do not ride on the railroad; it rides upon us. Did you ever think what those sleepers are that underlie the railroad? Each one is a man, an Irishman, or a Yankee man. The rails are laid on them, and they are covered with sand, and the cars run smoothly over them. They are sound sleepers, I assure you. And every few years a new lot is laid down and run over; so that, if some have the pleasure of riding on a rail, others have the misfortune to be ridden upon. And when they run over a man that is walking in his sleep, a supernumerary sleeper in the wrong position, and wake him up, they suddenly stop the cars, and make a hue and cry about it, as if this were an exception. I am glad to know that it takes a gang of men for every five miles to keep the sleepers down and level in their beds as it is, for this is a sign that they may sometime get up again.

18   Why should we live with such hurry and waste of life? We are determined to be starved before we are hungry. Men say that a stitch in time saves nine, and so they take a thousand stitches to-day to save nine tomorrow. As for *work,* we haven't any of any consequence. We have the Saint Vitus' dance, and cannot possibly keep our heads still. If I should only give a few pulls at the parish bell-rope, as for a fire, that is, without setting the bell, there is hardly a man on his farm in the outskirts of Concord, notwithstanding that press of engagements which was his excuse so many times this morning, nor a boy, nor a woman, I might almost say, but would forsake all and follow that sound, not mainly to save property from the flames, but, if we will confess the truth, much more to see it burn, since burn it must, and we, be it known, did not set it on fire,—or to see it put out, and have a hand in it, if that is done as handsomely; yes, even if it were the parish church itself. Hardly a man takes a half-hour's nap after dinner, but when he wakes he holds up his head and asks, "What's the news?" as if the rest of mankind had stood his sentinels. Some give directions to be waked every half-hour, doubtless for no other purpose; and then, to pay for it, they tell what they have dreamed. After a night's sleep the news is as indispensable as the breakfast. "Pray tell me any-thing new that has happened to a man anywhere on this globe,"—and he reads it over his coffee and rolls, that a man has had his eyes gouged out this morning on the Wachito River, never dreaming the while that he lives in the dark unfathomed mammoth cave of this world, and has but the rudiment of an eye himself.

19   For my part, I could easily do without the post-office. I think that there

are very few important communications made through it. To speak critically, I never received more than one or two letters in my life—I wrote this some years ago—that were worth the postage. The penny-post is, commonly, an institution through which you seriously offer a man that penny for his thoughts which is so often safely offered in jest. And I am sure that I never read any memorable news in a newspaper. If we read of one man robbed, or murdered, or killed by accident, or one house burned, or one vessel wrecked, or one steamboat blown up, or one cow run over on the Western Railroad, or one mad dog killed, or one lot of grasshoppers in the winter,—we never need read of another. One is enough. If you are acquainted with the principle, what do you care for a myriad instances and applications? To a philosopher all *news,* as it is called, is gossip and they who edit and read it are old women over their tea. Yet not a few are greedy after this gossip. There was such a rush, as I hear, the other day at one of the offices to learn the foreign news by the last arrival, that several large squares of plate glass belonging to the establishment were broken by the pressure,—news which I seriously think a ready wit might write a twelvemonth, or twelve years, beforehand with sufficient accuracy. As for Spain, for instance, if you know how to throw in Don Carlos and the Infanta, and Don Pedro and Seville and Granada, from time to time in the right proportions,—they may have changed the names a little since I saw the papers,—and serve up a bull-fight when other entertainments fail, it will be true to the letter, and give us as good an idea of the exact state or ruin of things in Spain as the most succinct and lucid reports under this head in the newspapers: and as for England, almost the last significant scrap of news from that quarter was the revolution of 1649, and if you have learned the history of her crops for an average year, you never need attend to that thing again, unless your speculations are of a merely pecuniary character. If one may judge who rarely looks into the newspapers, nothing new does ever happen in foreign parts, a French revolution not excepted.

What news! how much more important to know what that is which was never old! "Kieou-he-yu (great dignitary of the state of Wei) sent a man to Khoung-tseu to know his news. Khoung-tseu caused the messenger to be seated near him, and questioned him in these terms: What is your master doing? The messenger answered with respect: My master desires to diminish the number of his faults, but he cannot come to the end of them. The messenger being gone, the philosopher remarked: What a worthy messenger! What a worthy messenger!" The preacher, instead of vexing the ears of drowsy farmers on their day of rest at the end of the week,—for Sunday is the fit conclusion of an ill-spent week, and not the fresh and brave beginning of a new one,—with this one other draggle-tail of a sermon, should shout with thundering voice, "Pause! Avast! Why so seeming fast, but deadly slow?"

Shams and delusions are esteemed for soundest truths, while reality is fabulous. If men would steadily observe realities only, and not allow themselves to be deluded, life, to compare it with such things as we know, would be like a fairy tale and the Arabian Nights' Entertainments. If we respected

20

21

only what is inevitable and has a right to be, music and poetry would resound along the streets. When we are unhurried and wise, we perceive that only great and worthy things have any permanent and absolute existence, that petty fears and petty pleasures are but the shadow of the reality. This is always exhilarating and sublime. By closing the eyes and slumbering, and consenting to be deceived by shows, men establish and confirm their daily life of routine and habit everywhere, which still is built on purely illusory foundations. Children, who play life, discern its true law and relations more clearly than men, who fail to live it worthily, but who think that they are wiser by experience, that is, by failure. I have read in a Hindoo book, that "there was a king's son, who, being expelled in infancy from his native city, was brought up by a forester, and growing up to maturity in that state, imagined himself to belong to the barbarous race with which he lived. One of his father's ministers having discovered him, revealed to him what he was, and the misconception of his character was removed, and he knew himself to be a prince. So soul," continues the Hindoo philosopher, "from the circumstances in which it is placed, mistakes its own character, until the truth is revealed to it by some holy teacher, and then it knows itself to be *Brahma*." I perceive that we inhabitants of New England live this mean life that we do because our vision does not penetrate the surface of things. We think that that *is* which *appears* to be. If a man should walk through this town and see only the reality, where, think you, would the "Mill-dam" go to? If he should give us an account of the realities he beheld there, we should not recognize the place in his description. Look at a meeting-house, or a court-house, or a jail, or a shop, or a dwelling-house, and say what that thing really is before a true gaze, and they would all go to pieces in your account of them. Men esteem truth remote, in the outskirts of the system, behind the farthest star, before Adam and after the last man. In eternity there is indeed something true and sublime. But all these times and places and occasions are now and here. God himself culminates in the present moment, and will never be more divine in the lapse of all the ages. And we are enabled to apprehend at all what is sublime and noble only by the perpetual instilling and drenching of the reality that surrounds us. The universe constantly and obediently answers to our conceptions; whether we travel fast or slow, the track is laid for us. Let us spend our lives in conceiving then. The poet or the artist never yet had so fair and noble a design but some of his posterity at least could accomplish it.

22   Let us spend one day as deliberately as Nature, and not be thrown off the track by every nutshell and mosquito's wing that falls on the rails. Let us rise early and fast, or break fast, gently and without perturbation; let company come and let company go, let the bells ring and the children cry,— determined to make a day of it. Why should we knock under and go with the stream? Let us not be upset and overwhelmed in that terrible rapid and whirlpool called a dinner, situated in the meridian shallows. Weather this danger and you are safe, for the rest of the way is down hill. With unrelaxed nerves, with morning vigor, sail by it, looking another way, tied to the mast

like Ulysses. If the engine whistles, let it whistle till it is hoarse for its pains. If the bell rings, why should we run? We will consider what kind of music they are like. Let us settle ourselves, and work and wedge our feet downward through the mud and slush of opinion, and prejudice, and tradition, and delusion, and appearance, that alluvion which covers the globe, through Paris and London, through New York and Boston and Concord, through Church and State, through poetry and philosophy and religion, till we come to a hard bottom and rocks in place, which we can call *reality*, and say, This is, and no mistake; and then begin, having a *point d'appui*, below freshet and frost and fire, a place where you might found a wall or a state, or set a lamp-post safely, or perhaps a gauge, not a Nilometer, but a Realometer, that future ages might know how deep a freshet of shams and appearances had gathered from time to time. If you stand right fronting and face to face to a fact, you will see the sun glimmer on both its surfaces, as if it were a cimeter, and feel its sweet edge dividing you through the heart and marrow, and so you will happily conclude your mortal career. Be it life or death, we crave only reality. If we are really dying, let us hear the rattle in our throats and feel cold in the extremities; if we are alive, let us go about our business.

Time is but the stream I go a-fishing in. I drink at it; but while I drink I see the sandy bottom and detect how shallow it is. Its thin current slides away, but eternity remains. I would drink deeper; fish in the sky, whose bottom is pebbly with stars. I cannot count one. I know not the first letter of the alphabet. I have always been regretting that I was not as wise as the day I was born. The intellect is a cleaver; it discerns and rifts its way into the secret of things. I do not wish to be any more busy with my hands than is necessary. My head is hands and feet. I feel all my best faculties concentrated in it. My instinct tells me that my head is an organ for burrowing, as some creatures use their snout and fore paws, and with it I would mine and burrow my way through these hills. I think that the richest vein is somewhere hereabouts; so by the divining-rod and thin rising vapors I judge; and here I will begin to mine.

23

PAUL THEROUX

The Journey, not the Arrival, Matters

Theroux, a world-class travel writer is, fittingly enough, a perpetual world traveler. Claiming that he never planned to "be gone so long," he left Massachusetts, where he was born (in Medford in 1941) and earned a B.A. (at the University of Massachusetts in Amherst in 1963), and went to Africa to serve in the Peace Corps. He stayed abroad as a lecturer in English in Malawi, Uganda, and Singapore from 1963 until 1970. In recent years, home has largely been London, with summers on Cape Cod, but because Theroux travels so much he regards writing—his full-time occupation—at home as a vacation. He has written a dozen books of fiction, including Waldo *(1967),* Sinning with Annie and Other Stories *(1972),* Picture Place *(1978),* The Mosquito Coast *(1981), and, most recently,* Half Moon Street: Two Short Novels *(1984).*

Writing About Places

Although critics consider Theroux a gifted novelist, his travel books have captured the popular imagination. Indeed, he uses the novelist's techniques to set scenes, present characters (speaking in their typical, often bizarre, dialogue), and to convey the variable pace of his lengthy journeys described in The Great Railway Bazaar: By Train Through Asia *(1975),* The Old Patagonian Express: By Train Through the Americas *(1979), and in his satiric (some say unfair) look at the English on vacation,* The Kingdom by the Sea *(1983). In the following passage, which narrates the beginning of his railway journey from Boston to Patagonia, Theroux reflects, slowly and with seeming casualness, on the significance of leisurely travel (planes go too fast and can be defined in negatives, "you didn't get highjacked, you didn't crash"). He prefers to go by train, where one can "progress from the familiar to the slightly odd, to the totally foreign, and finally to the outlandish." The Chinese say that "a journey of a thousand miles begins with a single step"; in Theroux's case, such a journey begins with the simplest of events.*

1 Travel is a vanishing act, a solitary trip down a pinched line of geography to oblivion.

> What's become of Waring
> Since he gave us all the slip?

But a travel book is the opposite, the loner bouncing back bigger than life to tell the story of his experiment with space. It is the simplest sort of narrative, an explanation which is its own excuse for the gathering up and the going. It is motion given order by its repetition in words. That sort of disappearance is elemental, but few come back silent. And yet the convention is to telescope travel writing, to start—as so many novels do—in the middle of things, to beach the reader in a bizarre place without having first guided him there. "The white ants had made a meal of my hammock," the book might begin; or, "Down there, the Patagonian valley deepened to gray rock, wearing its eons' stripes and split by floods." Or, to choose actual first sentences at random from three books within arm's reach:

> "It was toward noon on March 1, 1898, that I first found myself entering the narrow and somewhat dangerous harbour of Mombasa, on the east coast of Africa."
>
> (Lt. Col. J. H. Patterson, *The Man-Eaters of Tsavo*)

> " 'Welcome!' says the big signboard by the side of the road as the car completes the corkscrew ascent from the heat of the South Indian plains into an almost alarming coolness."
>
> (Mollie Panter-Downes, *Ooty Preserved*)

> "From the balcony of my room I had a panoramic view over Accra, capital of Ghana."
>
> (Alberto Moravia, *Which Tribe Do You Belong To?*)

My usual question, unanswered by these—by most—travel books, is, How did you get there? Even without the suggestion of a motive, a prologue is welcome, since the going is often as fascinating as the arrival. Yet because curiosity implies delay, and delay is regarded as a luxury (but what's the hurry, anyway?), we have become used to life being a series of arrivals or departures, or triumphs and failures, with nothing noteworthy in between. Summits matter, but what of the lower slopes of Parnassus? We have not lost faith in journeys from home, but the texts are scarce. Departure is described as a moment of panic and ticket-checking in an airport lounge, or a fumbled kiss at a gangway; then silence until, "From the balcony of my room I had a panoramic view over Accra . . ."

Travel, truly, is otherwise. From the second you wake up you are headed   2
for the foreign place, and each step (now past the cuckoo clock, now down Fulton to the Fellsway) brings you closer. *The Man-Eaters of Tsavo* is about lions devouring Indian railway laborers in Kenya at the turn of the century. But I would bet there was a subtler and just as riveting book about the sea journey from Southampton to Mombasa. For his own reasons, Lieutenant Colonel Patterson left it unwritten.

The literature of travel has become measly; the standard opening, that   3
farcical nose-against-the-porthole view from the plane's tilted fuselage. The joke opening, that straining for effect, is now so familiar it is nearly impossible to parody. How does it go? "Below us lay the tropical green, the flooded valley, the patchwork quilt of farms, and as we emerged from the cloud I could see dirt roads threading their way into the hills, and cars so small they looked like toys. We circled the airport, and as we came in low for the landing, I saw the stately palms, the harvest, the roof tops of the shabby houses, the square fields stitched together with crude fences, the people like ants, the colorful . . ."

I have never found this sort of guesswork very convincing. When I am   4
landing in a plane, my heart is in my mouth; I wonder—doesn't everyone?— if we are going to crash. My life flashes before me, a brief selection of sordid and pathetic trivialities. Then a voice tells me to stay in my seat until the plane comes to a complete stop; and when we land, the loudspeakers break into an orchestral version of "Moon River." I suppose if I had the nerve to look around I might see a travel writer scribbling, "Below us lay the tropical green . . ."

Meanwhile, what of the journey itself? Perhaps there is nothing to say.   5
There is not much to say about most airplane journeys. Anything remarkable must be disastrous, so you define a good flight by negatives: you didn't get hijacked, you didn't crash, you didn't throw up, you weren't late, you weren't nauseated by the food. So you are grateful. The gratitude brings such relief, your mind goes blank, which is appropriate, for the airplane passenger is a time traveler. He crawls into a carpeted tube that is reeking of disinfectant; he is strapped in to go home, or away. Time is truncated or, in any case, warped: he leaves in one time zone and emerges in another. And from the moment he

steps into the tube and braces his knees on the seat in front, uncomfortably upright—from the moment he departs, his mind is focused on arrival. That is, if he has any sense at all. If he looked out the window, he would see nothing but the tundra of the cloud layer, and above it empty space. Time is brilliantly blinded: there is nothing to see. This is the reason so many people are apologetic about taking planes. They say, "What I'd really like to do is forget these plastic jumbos and get a three-masted schooner and just stand there on the poop deck with the wind in my hair."

6   But apologies are not necessary. An airplane flight may not be travel in any accepted sense, but it certainly is magic. Anyone with the price of a ticket can conjure up the castled crag of Drachenfels or the Lake Isle of Innisfree by simply using the right escalator at, say, Logan Airport in Boston. But it must be said that there is probably more to animate the mind, more of travel, in that one ascent on the escalator, than in the whole plane journey itself. The rest—the foreign country, what constitutes the arrival—is the ramp of an evil-smelling airport. If the passenger conceives of this species of transfer as travel and offers the public his book, the first foreigner the reader meets is either a clothes-grubbing customs man or a mustached demon at the immigration desk. Although it has become the way of the world, we still ought to lament the fact that airplanes have made us insensitive to space; we are encumbered, like lovers in suits of armor.

7   This is obvious. What interests me is the waking in the morning, the progress from the familiar to the slightly odd, to the rather strange, to the totally foreign, and finally to the outlandish. The journey, not the arrival, matters; the voyage, not the landing. Feeling cheated that way by other travel books, and wondering what exactly it is I have been denied, I decided to experiment by making my way to travel-book country, as far south as the trains run from Medford, Massachusetts; to end my book where travel books begin.

8   I had nothing better to do. I was at a stage I had grown to recognize in my writing life. I had just finished a novel, two years of indoor activity. Looking for something else to write, I found that instead of hitting nails on the head I was only striking a series of glancing blows. I hated cold weather. I wanted some sunshine. I had no job. What was the problem? I studied maps and discovered that there was a continuous track from my house in Medford to the Great Plateau of Patagonia in southern Argentina. There, in the town of Esquel, one ran out of railways. There was no line to Tierra del Fuego; but between Medford and Esquel, rather a lot of them.

9   In this vagrant mood I boarded that first train, the one people took to work. They got off; their train trip was already over. I stayed on; mine was just beginning.

TIM PAYNE (Student)

On the Beach at Bar Harbor

Payne was born in Hartford, Connecticut, in 1959, went to high school in Annandale, Virginia, and earned a B.A. in English, Phi Beta Kappa, from the College of William and Mary in 1982. On a Mellon Fellowship, he spent the next three years as a doctoral student at the University of Virginia, and is currently living in Charlottesville, Virginia.

Writers often use places—natural or man-made settings, the climate, the weather—as "objective correlatives" of the psychological or emotional state of the characters in those contexts, expressing intense passion, for instance, in the midst of a storm. In this manner Payne uses the rugged setting—and its natural changes—to reinforce his changing mood. He also endows with symbolic meaning the seemingly simple action of picking up shells on the beach, but leaves the reader to ponder its significance.

A year after writing the essay, Payne said, "My feelings about Bar Harbor are still the same—complex, challenging, and positive. I have pried at and forced and squeezed the experience for widely scattered significance, and I have dressed it up in quickly decaying robes of nostalgia and rhetoric. But the hard fact of the place and of my time there remains, an austere but steadfast viewing point against which I can measure my changing perspective of myself."

Bar Harbor, Maine, arrived midway in the two week camping trip which had to serve as my summer vacation—the period for recuperation. It followed an exhausting, numbing freshman year and would precede three tedious months of summer work and a horrendously disconcerting sophomore year. Two weeks to recover from one entire year and to prepare for another call for a tight and intense schedule of rest and relaxation. Although three days into the trip I had written to myself with naive confidence and optimism, "Perhaps the experience is effecting its purpose," I was depending a lot upon the Bar Harbor experience to work some magic on me.

Dan and I drove into a camping area on the north side of one finger of the harbor early Thursday afternoon. Clouds immediately began to attack the sun, allowing winter to sweep in and overpower the tentative and un-rooted spring warmth and the equally unrooted elation which I had stumbled into after a frightening and depressing Tuesday full of rain. After we set up camp, Dan went off to explore the beach and perhaps to seek some poetic inspiration for his next letter to Phyllis. I thought I would read to ward off the forces of depression which were hovering hungrily around my aloneness; but Holden Caulfield was himself depressed as hell, as I recall, and Mr. Thoreau was unsympathetically referring to his aloneness as solitude. So with my "intense rest" schedule's winged chariot perched heavily on my back, I decided I'd go force some uplifting significance out of the beach myself.

Getting *to* the beach was a little more work than I had expected, how-ever. The beach dropped off from an untapered stretch of pine trees with the

265

unsettling abruptness of a rollercoaster drop or of the editing in a home movie. As far as I could see, a teetering pile of rocks was the only way down to beach-level—certainly a far cry from the soliciting accessibility of the big-name beaches farther south.

4   I climbed down. There wasn't much sand; in its place was a forbidding carpet of bruise-colored oyster shells that crackled accusingly under my shoes. I went down closer to the water, stepping around or between the shells when I could. The waves in this secluded section of the harbor were uninspiring. No pressing sense of the powerful forces of the sea greeted me or flooded over and into me. But there *was* something unsettling and even foreboding about the boulders scattered haphazardly across the beach. They were left, I am told, by long-extinct glaciers which carved this land and have stood for centuries against the tidal push and tug of the harbor, unmoved. And yet somehow, when I first saw them, they reminded me of a child's toys, silent on the lawn, abandoned merely for the night.

5   It was growing cold again. The ice clouds had left, but now the sun was descending and evening was blowing in. I crouched down against my bare legs, and looked for shells. You always have to bring home some shells from a beach, I remembered, if there are any worth bringing. I picked up one or two small conch-like shells and a few spiral gut pieces of other such shells—perhaps because conch shells and even appreciable *pieces* of conch shells are such a rare find on populous beaches, or perhaps because these were all there were except for the mobs of oyster shells. I carried these shells around for a while, but they soon became heavy in my hand, like a fish which is too small. I threw them back down on the beach, and I felt free of something but also afraid of having gained nothing, as yet, from the beach.

6   Even so I was all right. The cold was not so oppressive now, or perhaps I was up for it, feeling myself a bit pugnacious. There was nothing inviting or accommodating about this beach, and still I was all right. I was used to beaches and cities and vacations that played for you. And you would play up to them, and they would play some more, selling themselves. This beach was unkempt and unpolished, colored by its stark boulders and the clumps of green and yellow sea plants, varnished so heavily with a lifeless brown as to look like vomit. It was indifferent, but oddly so, almost transcendingly so, like a large animal interrupted at its bath. And this indifference whetted my combative spirit, my desire to overcome and take something.

7   I walked along the beach and met Dan. We sat down on some rocks at the water's edge. The tide was coming in, and as it rose it reabsorbed and inspirited the vomited sea plants which, I could now see, were actually connected to what *had* been the beach and was *now* the harbor floor. And then I also spotted a *real* shell-find—whole sand dollars. Not too-small fish this time. I quickly collected several of the sand dollars, but then I got selective and threw back all but the few most perfect ones. As we got up from the rocks, however, to escape being overtaken by the tide, even these felt too

heavy in my hand to carry home, ~~and I threw them back in~~ as well. Again I felt free of something, and afraid.

The rising tide eventually took away all of the beach and covered the foreboding rocks, in pushing up to the foot of the steep climb that led back up to camp-level. There was a house perched on the upper level, overlooking the harbor and boldly pressing toward the edge. It too was stark, and there was a tension in its immobility, as if it were bracing itself against something, preparing for something. It seemed not to be inhabited, although it must have been, for it was well kept-up and well secured, looking out at nothing but the lapping harbor and the soft, darkening mountain on the other side. Staring out unflinchingly and intently, as the silent tide turned back out, and Dan and I turned in—I, like a certain heaviness in the hand of something. 8

Questions

1. Payne, inspired by his reading of Thoreau's *Walden* (251–61) decided to "force some uplifting significance" out of his experience on the beach at Bar Harbor (paragraph 2). Because he "was used to beaches and cities and vacations that played for you" (paragraph 6), what did he expect to get from this vacation?

2. But Bar Harbor, in contrast to Payne's expectation, is "indifferent" (paragraph 6). What effects does this unexpected, difficult setting have on him? What does he gain from the experience? Has he completely come to terms with it by the end of the essay?

3. In fulfillment of his belief that "You always have to bring home some shells from a beach . . . if there are any worth bringing" (paragraph 5), Payne first collects pieces of "conch-like shells" (paragraph 5), then whole sand dollars (paragraph 7). Why does he throw them back? Why does Payne present the image of the house, the only man-made structure in the entire essay, so near the end? How does he interpret it in the context of the natural setting (paragraph 8)?

4. The usual advice to writers is "Show, don't tell." Yet Payne tells the readers twice that he was "afraid" (paragraphs 5, 7). Does he ever *show*, through his actions or interpretation of the setting, that he is afraid? What is he afraid of?

Advice for Travelers

BOB THOMPSON

California: An Overview

Bob Thompson (b. 1934) is a free-lance writer and editor living in California. His books include Sunset Beachcomber's Guide to the Pacific Coast *(1966),* The California Wine Book, *co-authored with Hugh Johnson (1976), and* The American Express Pocket Guide to California *(1983 edition), which begins with "California: An Overview" (title supplied).*

   This selection is a good example of a brief, well-written overview intended for prospective travelers new to an area. The first part lays out the state geographically, historically, and culturally. The second part presents an overview of the major population areas, Los Angeles and San Francisco, characterizes each, and identifies some of the other population centers, ending (paragraph 11) with a note on local cuisine—always of interest to travelers. The third part, only two paragraphs long, is a quick sketch of California's "natural beauties"— mountains, Lake Tahoe, warm and cold-water oceans, redwoods, pines, and "gin-clear" air. The survey concludes with four paragraphs on California's history, inevitably intertwined with the state's economic development—in gold, oil, land, and currently, the aerospace and microelectric industries. From sunshine to Silicon Valley in eighteen concise—yet graceful— paragraphs is an efficient orientation indeed.

Introduction

1   California lives with two stereotypes: first, that the sun always shines on the beach; second, that the citizens are eccentric at best. Concerning the first, it is true the sun does shine on the beaches every day, or almost, S [south] from Santa Barbara. It is even true that persistent sunshine encourages people to be outdoors and playing as happily in winter as in summer throughout much of the state. But it is also true that San Francisco has a long, sandy beach, where, in high summer, people go around in woolen overcoats while 11° C(52°F) air carries shredded fog past at 25 mph. And it is only one of several places where a seersucker suit can be a mistake on the Fourth of July. As for eccentricity, a whole park full of adults roller-skating on a weekday morning pales next to the sight of a man driving an old Chevrolet along a freeway while playing a trumpet, or of another with dark glasses and white cane riding a bicycle along a rural highway. Such scenes, all true, do not encourage the belief that the work ethic is alive and well in California . . . . it is left to dull statistics to record that the productivity of state farmers results in a $14-billion crop each year, or to the imagination to judge how much intellectual effort underlies Silicon Valley's leadership in the invention and development of microcircuit computers.

In short, the best advice anyone can offer a visitor is to ignore the stereo- 2
types. The beaches are superb and the eccentrics enchanting, but they hide
what California does best: within its 900-mile length and among its 23½
million citizens, it sustains both natural and social contrast, even conflict, to
an astonishing degree. Hunting out the glorious differences is, above all,
what makes a stay in California most memorable.

The Sierra Nevada demonstrates what a mountain range ought to be. 3
Death Valley epitomizes deserts. In a state that is mostly grassy hills, the
redwood forests are on such a scale that one tree can be cut up to make a
decent grove by lesser standards. The Central Valley has no peer among
agricultural empires. Offset against these outdoor assets is San Francisco, the
very model of a small, old-fashioned city, and also Los Angeles, the apparent
prototype of the urban gigantism that may be our future.

Fittingly, a short range of small mountains is the most significant land- 4
mark of the greatest single contrast in this state of dramatic contrasts. Rivers
of people flow back and forth across the Tehachapis every day, but somehow
the ideas that make southern California one world and northern California
another fail to cross the pass, or get around the end. Their ridge line is the
proposed boundary in every scheme that would divide California into two
states—schemes that are continuously afoot and are deadly serious to
whichever half is getting short shrift in the State Capitol at the time, but
which are a bit of a joke to the half in control. Northern Californians,
outvoted and watching their water go southwards via a giant aqueduct, take
the serious view just now.

Although differences between northern and southern California are real, 5
they do not yield to easy explanation. According to the one currently popular
generalization, southern California sees the rules of society as still in the draft
stage, while northern California already has grown staid; in this view, the
southern types will seize an opportunity while the northerners wonder if
grandfather would have approved. According to an equally popular theory,
southern California still holds dear the grandfatherly ideas of growth, private
property and the kind of personal freedom symbolized by the automobile,
while northern California has moved to an era of questioning all of those
values when they hinder retaining or even restoring the natural environment.

Populous California. Los Angeles and San Francisco symbolize the south 6
and north, and are the two great magnets for visitors.

Los Angeles County has a population of 7½ million. The official city 7
contains less than half the total, but the distinction between county and city is
almost irrelevant. The web of freeways links the whole so neatly that locals
think nothing of driving almost 100 miles for a swim, a good doubles match
or a great dinner.

Los Angeles has been described as '49 suburbs in search of a city.' If this 8
ever was true, it no longer is. A city center is now evident in the historic

downtown, where cultural and community life is rich and getting richer. On the other hand it is also true that its overwhelming size keeps Los Angeles a bewildering collection of fragments in the eyes of many. Indeed the urban mass sprawls so far that bewildered visitors do not notice when they have left Los Angeles County for Orange County or San Bernardino, both places where the citizens think of themselves as being quite distinct from the citizens of LA.

9   San Francisco, meanwhile, sits like a thimble on the little thumb of its peninsula. Its population has declined from 725,000 to a current 674,000, making it only fourth largest among California's cities. But these figures mislead. The population of the bay area stands at almost 5 million, and, if freeway traffic jams are any indication, most of these are daily commuters to downtown San Francisco.

10   Where San Francisco differs most from Los Angeles, weather aside, is in how much variety it manages to sustain within its intimate scale. While LA keeps its distinctive communities separated by miles, in San Francisco the distance from Little Italy to Chinatown is the width of Columbus Avenue. The charm of this is indisputable and beyond reproduction.

11   Los Angeles and San Francisco are not the only cities in California, nor can all of the other urban communities properly be regarded as cities. San Diego is a major fishing and navy port and a casual beach resort. San Jose is the commercial hub for the electronics and aerospace industry in Silicon Valley. Both are larger than San Francisco but less citified. Monterey-Carmel, Palm Springs and Santa Barbara, on the other hand, are small towns by population, but are in fact elegantly polished resorts and civilized retreats. Even in the farm valleys there are cities of size and variety. Sacramento, Fresno and Bakersfield are the largest and best-known among them, but Redding, Santa Rosa, Stockton and others can be of interest for reasons ranging from good fishing to fine food.

12   Perhaps it is inevitable—certainly it is fortunate—that a state so blessed with rich land should develop an interest in gastronomy. Quality ingredients and generous portions have characterized American food; imaginative preparation has not. In California, however, imagination plays a major part in country and city kitchens alike, stimulated, no doubt, by excellent wines from the many vineyard valleys.

13   **Natural California.** In addition to its cultivated riches, California is also blessed with an astonishing diversity of natural ones. Some—oil and gold— are economic. Most are the beauties of a landform more varied than the societies that inhabit it. Among these beauties are Lake Tahoe, one of the world's great alpine lakes, the glacial sculpture of Yosemite Valley, the wind-hewn deserts of Death Valley, redwood forests and, far from least, the coast-lines S of Monterey and N of San Francisco, where gin-clear air lets the eye

wander to infinity along rocky cliffs, which often reach as high as 1,000 ft above the surf. Another quality of the coast is that it borders two altogether different oceans. A warm-water ocean, with the weather to match, makes southern California's beaches flawlessly suitable for swimming; and the slope of those beaches toward Australia gives the kind of ruler-straight waves surfers dream about. In contrast, the cold-water seas N of Santa Barbara keep people ashore where they can admire the scenery.

In a quieter way, plants also give California a great deal of its distinctive character. In addition to two species of redwoods, which grow naturally nowhere else on earth, other trees that are unique to the state: Monterey cypress, Bristlecone pine and Torrey pine, to name examples recognizable on sight. Yet in the end it is some of the commonest sights that make California unmistakable. Perhaps the one inescapable image which dominates, except on the far northern coast, is of cultivated valleys threading through ranks of grassy hills, with an occasional oak to emphasize the bareness of the slopes. 14

History. From discovery in the 16th century—first by Cabrillo then by Drake—to early colonization, nearly two-and-a-half centuries elapsed. The development of the West Coast began in earnest in the early 19th century, as Mexico gained independence from Spain and kept California as a colony, then tried unsuccessfully to keep American settlers out. In quick succession, the settlers declared their independence in the Bear Flag Revolt; the U.S. declared war on Mexico and seized California; gold was discovered and the '49 Gold Rush began. 15

The newly built transcontinental railroads that accompanied this westward migration brought the new state closer to the rest of the Union and helped establish San Francisco as the dominant city on the West Coast. Los Angeles, meanwhile, was no more than a sleepy pueblo and remained so until the century turned. Then its fortune was made by the discovery of oil in the area now known as Long Beach. 16

California's third great natural resource, its rich soil, had to await the construction of one of the world's most ambitious irrigation systems, the Central Valley Project. One measure of its effect is that Fresno County alone, sparsely farmed before the project, valued its 1980 farm income at $2 billion. 17

There is also a fourth source of wealth and power, which has come from a purely human resource, the intellects of physicists and engineers. The current era began, at least symbolically, with the development of the DC-3 airliner and has since defined California like no other era since the Gold Rush. Advanced technology in aerospace and, more recently, microelectronics, dominates California industry; furthermore, the people who make that world work also own and enjoy a great proportion of the hot tubs, racquetball clubs and handmade houses that visitors think of when they look for the California of today. 18

Questions

1. What major topics does Thompson cover in this overview of California? Why are these of particular interest to prospective tourists? Are there other topics that you as a traveler would want such a quick sketch to cover?

2. Thompson assumes that his audience is unfamiliar with California. How can you tell?

3. In writing such an overview, authors have to condense and omit a great deal of information. Yet, by the same token, they have to present a great deal of information in a concise format. How well has Thompson performed these tasks?

4. Brief though it is, this kind of an overview is designed to make the traveler want to come to the place it describes. What in Thompson's account would lure tourists to California? Does he write in a welcoming, inviting style? Identify its distinctive features.

PHILIP KOPPER

The Stark Simplicity
of the Delmarva Coast

Kopper, a naturalist and free-lance writer, lives in Washington, D.C. Born in New York City in 1937, he earned a B.A. from Yale in 1959, and after working for a year on the office staff of Look *magazine, became a reporter for the* Baltimore Sun, *1960–61, and then for* The Washington Post, *1961–66. He is an award-winning contributor to such publications as the* Encyclopedia Britannica, Smithsonian Magazine, The American Scholar, *and* The National Geographic; *his books include* The Wild Edge: Life and Lore of the Great Atlantic Beaches *(1979) and* The National Museum of Natural History *(1982).*

"The Stark Simplicity of the Delmarva Coast" combines an appreciative account of the author's trip to the Delaware-Maryland-Virginia coast at the height of the off-season with advice to travelers—either rugged types seeking a comparable adventure, or armchair voyagers who, snug by the fireside, simply like to read about the seaside in winter. Kopper makes favorable comparisons between the beach at midwinter, when wild birds and animals stalk the solitary shore, and summer when it's "hot, hectic, high priced." He discusses what to do (walk—bundled up, swim—sometimes, go to museums, eat, sleep)—at bargain prices. And how and where to do it, governed by two rules: "Take an extra of everything" (because "On a cold beach everything that can get wet probably won't dry out by morning.") and "Call ahead to book a room or a meal." Kopper's advice is sensible but not preachy, intended to help travelers anticipate and thereby avoid problems that might spoil the splendor of an off-beat weekend.

1   Along Delmarva's coast the cardboard signs on snack bar doors tell as true a tale as one devised by a fisherman who spent all night throwing bait at waves. "Closed 'til Spring" they say—but don't you believe it. Eternally welcoming, the beach stays open all winter.

Just don't expect it to be like Labor Day: hot, hectic, high priced.   2

Every boardwalk carnival and taffy stand is closed up tighter than a clam   3
with an anxiety attack. T-shirt artists have gone the way of ospreys: south or
simply elsewhere. Gone, too, are parking problems, crowds and noise. Instead you'll find bright or ghostly air, wild beauty and a sort of solitude that
can stand company if you care to take a friend or lover. It's a different shore
now.

Beachcombing is never better than after a three-day storm that brings the   4
sea swirling up the face of outer dunes, leaving driftwood high and drying for
next year's bonfires. Every tide carries its cache of curiosities: the monstrously
toothed jaws of angler fish, shells too heavy for summer waves to push
ashore, and odd artifacts that run the gamut from jet fuel tanks to bits of
wooden ships—even a tusk dropped by some litterbugging mammoth 10,000
years ago.

Quicker animals haunt the swale and ponds behind the barrier dune: 5
deer, raccoons, even otters if you care to track them down. In the hour
surrounding sundown on my latest trip, I was investigated by one muskrat,
22 sika deer, a whitetail, uncounted squirrels and one red fox (actually, she
wasn't a bit interested but trotted past my car like gymnast Mary Lou Retton
late for practice).

The winter action has little to do with strangers or new-found friends. (If   6
you want companionship, a new book or old wine, bring your own.) But the
birds abide. Sanderlings race the surf's wash up slopes of wet sand made
shorter and steeper by harsher waves than summer's. Multitudes of Canadas
and snow geese, brants and swans patrol the marshes and make the sky loud
with honking song. Sea ducks not seen here in summer bob beyond the surf
where pelicans now scout, collapse their wings and crash, to come up gulping.

There may still be fish too—sea trout, spot, flounder—and if no fish,   7
then fishermen nonetheless. Where I'd seen one solitary surfer the day before,
at dawn two thermal-clad surfcasters worked a break in the curling wave,
waiting for a school of mullet to lure big blues in over the bar.

If fauna isn't your game, go for the freshest air imaginable and the sort of   8
pace that makes clocks and calendars disappear. Why feel pressed to swim and
fish, learn to windsurf, rent a sailboat, take a guided nature walk, host a
clambake, attend an auction, write a dozen postcards, try that new seafood
house or read "Ulysses" and get a tan—all in one visit? Winter beach trips last
two or three days—not weeks—and short days at that, though memorable
ones.

For example, my wife and I have trouble remembering which New Year's   9
Eve we drank a Chateau d'Yquem in black-tie elegance and first met two of
our now dearest friends in town. And did we throw the party in '80 or go out
with the Smiths? The last nights of most years blur. Except for the year we
ended at the beach.

10   At a varnished table we dined on oysters and crab-stuffed flounder. The wine was a sort that many shoreside houses offer, something chaste of pretense.

11   Back at the motel by 9, Mary watched Pavarotti via cable (which is *de rigueur* in every coastal hamlet though we *still* can't get it in Chevy Chase) and finished making my Christmas gift, the pieced quilt now in our son's nursery. I wallowed in the luxury of a hardback thriller. We did some justice to the champagne we'd wisely brought from home and were happily asleep before Guy Lombardo oiled the night with "Auld Lang Syne." Next morning we were up at dawn, out and about in glory. Thus began a vintage year, though it's a fine way to start any week in winter.

12   Browsing the nearby coast again just weeks ago, we found the towns dark, empty and inviting. A bartender in Virginia Beach put it this way: "See the flashing yellow lights on Atlantic Avenue? They won't turn red until Easter." Caesar's Restaurant had crossed its Rubicon that Sunday evening, the Riverboat looked beached, the Aloha had waved a last hello/goodbye, the Waves had ebbed for winter. Even on McDonald's was boarded up, though a score of bright motel signs offered such freebies as "FRIG HBO."

13   Despite a dozen summer visits to this town, I'd never been inside the Maritime Historical Museum hard by the beach, a gem of an old Life Saving Station that celebrates the storm-tossed rescues of yore. (It also displays oddities, like the mammoth tusk someone found a year ago.) Somehow I'd never taken the time to stop in when the sun baked the beach until cocktail hour. But in winter, when beachfront towers cast cold shadows across the sand soon after lunch, seeing indoor sights makes sense.

14   Up in Delaware, Henlopen Park's Jack Goins brags that "our sun goes down on standard time," since there are no high-rises to block its shine. The almost pristine beach aside, a most intriguing man-made thing to ponder here is offshore: the salvage vessel bringing up a fortune in gold coins from a treasure ship sunk in 1787. (But ponder from afar; the crew doesn't welcome visitors.)

15   For an absolutely pristine beach, try the remote barrier islands of the Virginia Coast Preserve, which boasts no greater development than a long-abandoned Coast Guard station. Crossing the open water calls for a sound boat and a captain who's wise to the shifting bays. It's bound to be an uncomfortable trip (perhaps a dangerous one) for the inestimable reward of virtually virgin shores. Even the Nature Conservancy, which owns and administers the preserves, does not take people there this time of year. But who knows what you might find if you went?

16   A winter beach is full of surprises. There is unaccustomed space—on the sand and even at the curbs in towns, for parking. The crowds are gone, and with them the traffic. The high rates are gone too. Hundred-dollar summer rooms cost less than half while many decent motels advertise doubles in the

$20 range. Like the price, even the pace is different—since a day's outing simply cannot last as long. All this translates into new choices: To walk the empty shores, of course; and to test the antique shops en route, to scout summer rentals while realtors are easy to reach, to visit the local museum.

Certainly the weather is chancier than in July, but for even the mildly   17
hardy there's still time to swim if you pick a sunny day with calm air or a south wind. Within a week of Christmas for some years running, I tested the Atlantic, a three-hour drive from Washington. Older now (and unable to go at the drop of a warm front), this year I swam long enough to get wet all over within a week of Thanksgiving.

On ordinary winter days, it's enough to just explore the empty, eerie   18
strand. Gales have blown the light sand away, leaving dark layers of heavier grains and minute mesas, each one topped with a tiny crag of broken shell. Make no mistake: The bitter winds that carve these tiny mountains can take your breath away. The winter walker sometimes finds the kind of cold that freezes seas and only an hour's steaming bath can cure. But what rare luxury—to soak with cold glass of warming rum while *reading* a field guide, something one rarely finds the time to do.

All that said, there are perils as dire for the beachcomber between now   19
and April as for any blond who falls asleep under a summer sun. Most involve the amenities of food, drink and shelter, though some have to do with nature. For instance, there's a law that states, "On a cold beach everything that can get wet probably won't dry out by morning." Thus the easy corollary: "Take an extra of everything." Pack one more pair of rough shoes, socks, old wool pants, etc. than you think you'll need. Next, while you can forget sunburn as a problem—the sun's up shorter hours and lower in the sky to boot—watch out for windburn. And mind the cold; pack a hot thermos for your longer walks.

As for difficulties not involved with nature, remember the establishments   20
that stay open all winter can be as eccentric as their winter clients. Because so many places do close, the motels that stay open may be empty one weekend and full the next.

The trouble, for the traveler, is the inconsistency from place to place and   21
week to week. A sales convention in a large beach resort can almost fill the better beds. In a smaller town a few student goups on science trips can take all the rooms. I remember walking the Ocean City boardwalk an hour after dark one winter night and not seeing another soul, while the hotels cried for guests like hungry gulls. But down the road at Chincoteague, every room was full for a decoy carnival or somesuch.

Restaurants can be just as erratic. Chincoteague's Channel Bass Inn,   22
which lays a good table (at alarming prices), is closed several days a week. Blocks away Klaus Luehning, new owner/chef of the old Beachway, offers superb salt oysters, nicely broiled fish and sublime pastries every day at lower

rates. But since he opens by dawn, on quiet nights he might lock up by 8 in order to practice what he calls a newly necessary skill, "sleeping fast."

23   Thus the simple rule of the winter beach: Call ahead to book a room or a meal. You'll learn whether your favorite place of two summers ago is (a) open, (b) run by the same people, (c) operating the way it did. Chincoteague has suffered several invasions in recent years: by salad bars, for example, and liquor by the drink.

24   To our greater surprise, virtually every motel within miles now prohibits pets. Ignorant of the new rule, we were saved from eviction only when the Driftwood's desk clerk took Dickens, our mutt, home for the night. By comparison, the Sheraton Beach Inn in Virginia Beach welcomed the dog (or at least permitted him), and even enthroned him in the restaurant on a banquette with a water view. (Of course, they weren't very busy. This time of year the help often outnumbers clientele.) Better yet, the soup really was homemade, and the fresh shrimp and crab cooked with skill, if not genius.

25   (Having scorned beachfront motels in my childless past, I now admit they can be a blessing when an infant has you in tow. Tim loves playing in the sand and chasing the inconstant gulls. But he likes amenities from plastic pails to a portable crib. It's all very well to hike with him in the backpack, but the closer to the ocean one stays, the easier it is for Dad. Now I see the point of digs right on the beach.)

26   In plain places, don't expect the fancy. Don's Restaurant and Fish Market offers hearty breakfasts—if insistently simple ones—favored by Chincoteague fishermen. The three-meal menu offered omelets for breakfast and oyster dinners. Could an oyster omelet then be had? The boss answered with one loud word: "No!"

27   This all suggests a rule that might hold true half the time. Quaint establishments can be charming or irksome, depending on your mood, while chains can be counted on to keep up to their national norm; if they allow pets and kids in Oshkosh, they'll do the same in Ocean City. On the down side, a chain motel at the beach will seem the same as one inland. Choose it for midlevel quality, or gamble on a local inn for color and distinction.

28   As for food, another rule applies—or no rule at all. With fishing boats pulling up outside the door, you'd think that local eateries would offer splendid cooking. Not always. Too many shoreside cooks have been seduced by microwave salesmen with scandalous results and turn sea scallops into cloying, clinging wads of rubber. In winter more than summer—because some tonier places do close—it can be even harder to find good seafood. Let reputation be your guide. Ask several locals and hope two of them agree; if three call the same place "the best on the island" (any island), chances are it's good by city standards.

29   As for the beaches easily reached from Washington, they can be as unforgettably beautiful as anywhere. One recent morning a west wind howled

loud enough at the bayside Coast Guard station to raise a small craft warning (a huge crimson pennant, if you've never seen one). But in the island's lee the ocean was calm, unruffled. Only a rising tide and groundswell drove the waves ashore in straight ranks that rose into perfect arcs, then crested to throw wisps of spray toward Spain, beyond the pristine horizon.

By late afternoon the whole world's palette had turned to muted tones: a   30
gray ocean under an ashen sky. Even the beach grass had lost its green, while the laurel and pines became silhouettes. Then, as dusk arrived, beneath the blue-black western sky two slivers of scarlet flamed bright as blood in stunning spectacle, promising a perfect winter day.

The beach abides in winter, with moods and grandeur never seen in   31
warmer months. So hit the shore this month, before another season brings other beauty. Right now's the best time to go this time of year.

Questions

1. What are the main things travelers need to know about a place they might visit? Does Kopper cover all the essentials? What has he left out, if anything? He mentions specific prices only once, in connection with room rates (paragraph 16). Should he have discussed them more extensively?

2. Advice to travelers is hard to give without sounding overbearing or preachy. How does Kopper manage to offer his advice without pontificating?

3. In the process of describing the Delmarva coast and its pleasures during winter, Kopper depicts himself and his family (even Dickens, their dog) and their style of traveling. Does this enhance or detract from the travel information he provides? Suppose the prospective traveler's personality or way of traveling differs considerably from the author's; would Kopper then lose that reader?

4. Kopper has deliberately picked an off-beat way to treat his subject, by discussing a trip to the beach during the off-season. Is his purpose to encourage others to take such a trip at that time of year? to entertain armchair travelers, snug by the fire? any other reason? Who is likely to read this?

KATE SIMON

New York Luncheonettes

Kate Simon (b. 1913) is best known for her travel books, which include Mexico: Places and Pleasures *(third edition, 1979),* Italy: Places in Between *(rev. ed., 1984), and* Fifth Avenue: A Very Special History *(1978). She can, as a critic notes, "re-create a place, a pleasure, a human type in two or three sharp sentences," as she does in capturing the essential place of her childhood in her autobiographical* Bronx Primitive: Portraits in a Childhood *(1982) and* A Wider World: Portraits in an Adolescence *(1986). An immigrant from the Warsaw ghetto, she grew up in a tenement in the exotic world of, as she explains, "a Jewish-*

277

German-Polish-Greek-Hungarian-Rumanian," slightly Irish, Sicilian, and Italian Bronx neighborhood where no outsider, that is, anyone who spoke English without a foreign accent, was trusted. Like many writers from precarious backgrounds, her way up and out of the tenements was through education, much gained from voracious reading of public library books, which culminated in a B.A. earned during the Depression from Hunter College.

Simon's love for her adopted city mingles with a witty perception of its manners and mores. In the selection below, from New York, Places and Pleasures: An Uncommon Guidebook *(revised edition, 1971), the street-smart author provides a survival guide to enable tourists to take an enjoyable bite out of the Big Apple without getting stung in return. As with many travel guides, Simon's writing is direct and efficiently organized: "The first is . . . The second is . . . And there is a third." The danger of such lists and catalogs is that the very format that enables readers to find the essential information quickly can become predictable and boring. Simon's consummate style prevents this. With a few vivid phrases she sets the scene ("you walk to the front counter, which is barnacled by a solid wall of backs, each head bent over its trough"), introduces its major characters ("The customer . . . has the right to be sullen, taciturn, tired, disgruntled, or gay and loquacious"); and offers advice on how novices can cope with both ("Take a stand behind [someone with a "near-finished piece of pie"] and don't budge."). Only then does she recommend specific luncheonettes, grouped according to their common geographical location, each epitomized with a witty phrase, vignette, or succulent sentence.*

1   There are two sets of facts you should know about the advice given here. The first is that the price designations (without drinks) which appear with each restaurant should be translated as: *modest*—up to $5 for a dinner; *moderate*—up to $8; *expensive*—anything above. The second is that many restaurants are closed through summer weekends and for several weeks during the summer; it is advisable to phone before you go. Also, "open Sundays" often means dinners only.

2   And then there is a third, a fact of life; the rent and, consequently, the prices in a restaurant go up, the chef's wife leaves him, the headwaiter has dental trouble, the proprietor can't cope, and the pleasure promised turns sour. For such possibilities, apologies beforehand and a hope that yours is not one of those days of doom.

A Pause in the Day's Occupation

3   Dining in the sense of leisured, festive eating, garnished with decor and service, will be dealt with farther on. Here we should like to consider the luncheonette, the place for purveying lunches (which would also include the chains such as Stouffer's, Schrafft's and Childs', but these latter are too large, too anonymous, too famous and sometimes too flavorless to consider here). The New York City luncheonette, whether it is called a "Coffee House" or "Louie's," is personal, crowded and reeking of flavor.

4   Luncheonettes vary widely, from those which occupy a slice of a shop,

just large enough to contain eight stools, a counter, a coffee urn, a refrigerator and stove, to vast establishments with three or four large sets of stools-and-counter, a balcony with tables, and a monstrous growth of artificial jungle leaves trailing from the balcony railing. Informality is what they all have in common. No headwaiter will usher you in or thank you out, no waiter will hover, no waiter-in-training will refill your water glass or give you a second pat of butter. You'll have to battle your way *alone* if you sit at the counter.

We'll set the scene: It is one o'clock and you're hungry. On a side street in midtown you've spotted a luncheonette, whose undecorated window gives only its name and the day's menu. You push your way through a group just emerging, past the cashier's desk. On your left as you enter there is likely to be a glut of boys waiting to take lunch orders out to the surrounding offices. Beyond this small mob is the genie who frantically fills and seals coffee jars and wraps sandwiches delivered to him with loud announcements by a distant assistant (with speed and sureness, he also pours milk, cuts pie, mixes sodas, ladles soup—less like a man than a perspiring octopus). You move along to survey the possibilities of a seat and food. In the back, a cul-de-sac of steamy animation, there are no seats, so you walk to the front counter, which is barnacled by a solid wall of backs, each head bent over its trough. There is only one thing to do—it is rude and could be annoying if New Yorkers were not so thoroughly inured to it (also, *you* will shortly be the victim of the same act). As you make your way down the counter, examine each plate. If it contains a salad or spaghetti or soup, there's more to come, so search on. When you see a near-finished piece of pie, or a cup of coffee tilted fairly high, make your move. Take a stand behind the tilter and don't budge. You have a situation calling for some delicacy: How close can you stand without annoying your enthroned predecessor or tripping him as he slides off the stool? And yet, how politely far can you stand without running the risk of having someone, fleet and slippery, straddle the seat before you can get to it? It is a problem that requires neat judgment and sharp alertness, but it can be handled, and the triumph is worth the effort.

Once settled, you feel the breeze of a menu being waved in front of your face. Grab it before it disappears, and study—if the counterman lets you—the rather astonishing list. In the larger luncheonettes the menu reflects (more than anyplace except the subway) the really international quality of the city. You'll find Italian spaghetti, Hungarian goulash, Spanish omelet, Rumanian-Jewish pastrami, Southern fried chicken, and Chinese spareribs among the hamburgers and tuna fish salads. These more exotic menus prevail mainly in midtown, where the clientele has mixed and pampered tastes, but there are more and more dishes which have lost their stamp of origin and are becoming indispensably New York City items. For instance, Irish saloons, German *Bierstuben* and Spanish-American "greasy spoons" all display signs advertising hot pastrami; and Chinese egg rolls nest cosily near hot Italian sausages on the feast day of St. Gennaro. There is a very small candy-newspaper-lunch shop near Union Square which apparently caters to Puerto Ricans. On its windows is often chalked "Pasteles—dumplings" and "Pastelillos—knishes," bypassing the English language entirely and adopting not only the Yiddish dish, but the Yiddish word for it, just as menus in Chinese restaurants list won ton (dumpling) soup as "kreplach" soup, assuming that this would be understandable to a major portion of the clientele, and it is.

7

No matter what its size or menu, the luncheonette is almost always an unbuttoned, relaxed place. It is a refuge from the office and from home, and its intimacy has the additional charm of indifference. If an habitué tells the counterman, "You gave me last night's coffee. Whatsa matter, you can't afford fresh coffee every day?" the counterman is not inclined to fire him as his boss might, or sulk as his wife would, but casually answers, "Gowan, it's the bad taste in your mouth; you got a lousy disposition today." Each one has let off steam and no one carries off injury. The customer, it is understood, has the right to be sullen, taciturn, tired, disgruntled, or gay and loquacious. The man behind the counter has the same rights and the thick air rings with bustle, bawdry and the swift exchange of insult. It can be an enriching half hour and instructive in the speech and humor of a large segment of New York, if you have the nerve to keep your seat that long.

8

The greatest concentration of luncheonettes is, naturally, in the side streets between Lexington Avenue and Sixth, between 34th and 48th Streets. If you are a searcher for the most profound of any kind of experience, look for those whose countermen are pale and spare, with waterlogged skins and washed-out eyes, the effects of very slow drowning in coffee-urn steam and hot dishwater; these are the men with the best-oiled tongues and most free-wheeling personalities.

9

Although a good number of coffeehouses (those that designate themselves "espresso") won't shine as long as the sun does, there are some which provide short luncheon menus attached to lists of Italian, Austrian and Turkish coffee.

10

Greenwich Village, too, has some early-rising coffeehouses among its too many. (There was a time when an empty store was taken over by derelicts or Gypsies. Now someone rushes in a few tables and chairs—preferably of the old ice-cream-parlor variety, too narrow and too hard—and a can of whitewash for the walls, purple for the facade, a shuddering mobile to hang, a wornout dress mannequin to place at the door, *et voilà!* a coffeehouse.)

11

In the East Midtown area, there are: *The Isle of Capri* (1028 Third Ave., near 61st St.), which serves decent Neapolitan dishes and drinks like orzata and tamarindo, as well as Italian styles of coffee; *Serendipity* (225 E. 60th St.), which serves lunches, dinner, Sunday brunches and coffee late into the night in the back of its extravagantly chic shop; on Second Avenue, near 53rd

Street, a small, pleasant place called *Back Street,* which serves modest lunches and Italian coffee.

The best coffeehouses belong to the upper East Side, probably because they reflect the tastes of the Middle Europeans who use them seriously. There are a good number of coffee, *schlag* and strudel houses on 86th Street and several others strewn through the neighborhood. Consider seriously *Gach's,* attached to its large bakery at 314 E. 78th St. It has neat sandwiches, lovely cakes and Hungarian ladies doing what they did in old Buda or was it Pest, engulfing pastries as they babble in the odd, sloping rhythms of their unique language. 12

On the sacred principle that prices must always outstrip wages, small restaurants, cafeterias and luncheonettes have become too expensive for those who live on the edges of marginal jobs: messengers, file clerks, part-time saleswomen with sons to put through college, bargain hunters and those who would rather buy that extra pair of bluejeans rather than eat roundly. For these, standing at counters outside and inside, or sitting, or walking away with and munching on the street, there are recent establishments that center their offerings on the basic, peasant, poor-man's fillers of several countries. A chain of clean, long-countered places with the chummy name of *Zum Zum* are spreading their baroque curves of wurst, slabs of bread and hot potato salad into a number of *hausfrau*-ly sausage-hung halls in the center of the city. A place that calls itself, appallingly, the World's Wurst supplies similar fare. 13

Spinach pies, once the exotica of a few Greek restaurants and bakeries on Atlantic Avenue in Brooklyn, have made their way into the glass cases, cheek by jowl with the flat Near Eastern bread pita, used to fold around chips of lamb cut from a tall, rotating spear embedded in thousands of slices, rather like the old-fashioned pin on which neighborhood butchers impaled bills. Barbaric, phallic, antiquely suggestive, and very good accompanied by a hottish sauce and bits of onion and, importantly, filling and cheap, as these things go. The Village is full of these souvlaki places and there is a frantic dispenser—plus Italian *pasticcio,* doughnuts, meat balls, pork chops—in a small place that gives the effect of a typhoon in a funnel at lunchtime on 59th Street, immediately east of Lexington Avenue. It all adds still another trumpet blast to the brassy symphony that is the area. The customers are black ladies from Virginia, casing the big city, hippies, Greek families who use the few tables and counters at the back, adolescents from the suburbs in for a day's shopping and rubbing their nubile shoulders against Real Life, a few Chinese customers who can say only, "Same like yesterday" (and they seem to get it) and almost anyone else attracted by the miscellany and affable lunchtime frenzy. 14

Back in the Village, again, a proliferation of Indian restaurants with their mounds of rice studded with dark bits of meat and their pools of dal, an air of sadness as if *they* had lost the Empire, and occasionally special student prices 15 for the populace of New York University. And, of course, pizza covers the city almost as thoroughly as does our smog. (For the combination of pizza, hero, souvlaki, curry and a few etceteras, examine the stands and steamy windows of Sullivan, Thompson and Bleecker Streets.)

NOTE: A shrewd way of eating well and not too expensively is to have your large meal in the middle of the day when most good restaurants serve dinners (disguised as luncheons) at considerably less cost than they do at night. Keep in mind, also, that First, Second and Third Avenue "pub" types serve large, bibulous brunches all Sunday afternoon and into the evening.

CALVIN TRILLIN

Eating in Cincinnati

Calvin Trillin, called by master chef Craig Claiborne "the Homer, Dante, and Shakespeare of American food," was born in Kansas City, Missouri, in 1935, which, he claims, deadpan, has "The best restaurants in the world . . . of course." Despite the culinary attractions of his hometown, which he uses as a continual point of reference in his three books of essays on American food—American Fried *(1974)*, Alice, Let's Eat *(1978)*, and* Third Helpings *(1983)—Trillin has spent much time in the East. Following his graduation from Yale in 1957 and three years as a reporter for* Time *magazine 1960–1963, Trillin has been a writer for* The New Yorker *ever since. He has also written columns for* The Nation *since 1978;* Uncivil Liberties *(1982) is a collection of his political essays.*

"Eating in Cincinnati"—not quite as good as Kansas City, but almost—is a typical saga in which Trillin, in the guise of a staunch supporter of hearty, down-home cooking (and eating), bellies up to the table and defends his choices against all comers. This personal narrative is not a conventional restaurant guide; Trillin doesn't list the restaurants of Cincinnati and award stars, but he does provide considerable information, idiosyncratic and prejudicial, about Cincinnatians and their ways—the most startling item of which is that these midwestern All-Americans eat their chili over spaghetti and expect to have it served to them by Greeks. Trillin, who has also been called "the overeater's Woody Allen" because of his comic style, claims that the proof is in the eating—and possibly in the heartburn. Whether readers agree with his taste or not, he provides an example of how a sympathetic traveler can appreciate and enjoy the cuisine of Cincinnati, and that kind of personal involvement may be the best kind of advice a traveler can get.

1 Harry Garrison, the eater who had agreed to serve as my consultant in Cincinnati, had been recommended by my friend Marshall J. Dodge III—a fact that gave me pause, particularly after Marshall described him as a calliope-restorer by trade. I don't mean that I harbor any prejudice against calliope-restorers or that I think Marshall would make a frivolous recommendation. Marshall is a practical man. He has a practicality so pure, in fact, that it sometimes makes him appear eccentric. He is an uncompromising

bicyclist—partly because bicycling is the most practical way to get around New York—and when he travels to, say, Cincinnati, he merely removes the wheels of one of his bicycles, stuffs the parts into something that resembles a swollen Harvard bookbag, and checks the mysterious bundle along with his luggage. If the ticket agent asks what the bag contains, Marshall looks at him solemnly—Marshall can manage an awesomely solemn look when the occasion calls for one—and says that the bag contains his grandmother's wheelchair. Like New York's most photographed bicyclist, John V. Lindsay—a tall man who was once the mayor—Marshall attended Buckley and St. Paul's and Yale, and it is implicit in his appearance and manner that he takes the presence of many generations of Dodges at those institutions before him and after him as a matter of course. But if it is practical to take along a knapsack while riding his bicycle, Marshall takes along a knapsack. Then if someone happens to ask him, say, if he knows the address of a good calliope-restorer in Cincinnati, he can reach into the knapsack, pull out a small file of three-by-five cards, and thumb through it until he finds the answer.

What concerned me about depending on Marshall's recommendation for a guide to Cincinnati is that the knapsack is much more likely to produce the address of an expert on antique piano rolls or a supplier of Cajun-dialect phonograph albums than a specialist in French-fried onion rings or barbecue—a natural outgrowth of Marshall's own specialty, which is regional humor. (He has made an album of Down East stories called *Bert and I* and he has presented his monologues before groups in various parts of the country, always arriving by plane and bike.) I hinted about my concern to Marshall, but he assured me that Garrison would be the perfect guide to Cincinnati and environs. He was not certain if it had been Garrison who put him on to a small restaurant in Rabbit Hash, Kentucky, that served what Marshall remembered as the best fried chicken in the world, but he was certain that it was Garrison who had introduced him to Professor Harry L. Suter, an elderly musicologist who was able to play the piano and the violin simultaneously by means of an invention the professor called the viola-pan.

Garrison, I found out, not only restores calliopes but also restores and sells player pianos, appears professionally around the state as Uncle Sam the Magician, delivers an occasional lecture on how to detect crooked gambling devices, and in the midst of all those activities manages to spend more than the ordinary amount of time at table. He was not going to be able to meet me until a few hours after I arrived in Cincinnati, but he had suggested on the phone that for my first taste of authentic Cincinnati chili, at lunch, I might want to try the unadorned product and therefore should start with what is known locally as "a bowl of plain." He had no way of knowing, of course, that I have never eaten the unadorned version of anything in my life and that I once threatened to place a Denver counterman under citizen's arrest for leaving the mayonnaise off my California burger.

"What should I order if I don't want to start with the plain?" I asked.

5   "Try a four-way," Garrison said.

6   In Cincinnati, everyone knows that a four-way is chili on spaghetti with cheese and onions added. I never saw any numbers on menus in Cincinnati, but it is accepted that a customer can walk into any chili parlor—an Empress or a Skyline or any of the independent neighborhood parlors—and say "One three-way" and be assured of getting chili on spaghetti with cheese. Cincinnati eaters take it for granted that the basic way to serve chili is on spaghetti, just as they take it for granted that the other ways to serve it go up to a five-way (chili, spaghetti, onions, cheese, and beans) and that the people who do the serving are Greeks. When the Kiradjieff family, which introduced authentic Cincinnati chili at the Empress in 1922, was sued several years ago by a manager who alleged that he had been fired unfairly, one of his claims amounted to the contention that anyone fired under suspicious circumstances from a chili parlor with Empress's prestige was all through in the Greek community. There are probably people in Cincinnati who reach maturity without realizing that Mexicans eat anything called chili, in the same way that there are probably young men from Nevada who have to be drafted and sent to an out-of-state Army camp before they realize that all laundromats are not equipped with slot machines.

7   What is called chili in America, of course, has less similarity to the Mexican dish than American football has to the game known as football just about everywhere else in the world. Like American football, though, it long ago became the accepted version within the borders, and anyone in, say, northern New Mexico who wanted to claim that the version served there (green or red chili peppers sliced up and cooked into a kind of stew) is the only one entitled to the name would have no more chance of being listened to than a soccer enthusiast who made a claim to the television networks for equal time with the N.F.L. As American chili goes, what is served in Cincinnati is sweeter than what I used to have at Dixon's and what I still have occasionally at the Alamo—a Tex-Mex chili parlor in Manhattan that offers eight or ten combination plates, all of which taste exactly alike, and is famous for a notation on the menu that says, "All combinations above without beans 25¢ extra." (I know people who have tried to work out the economics of how much the Alamo has to pay a professional bean-extractor to come out ahead on that offer, but a definite figure has eluded them.) The chili in Cincinnati is less ferocious than Texas chili, but I wouldn't want to carry the comparison any further. I decided a long time ago that I like chili, but not enough to argue about it with people from Texas.

8   To an out-of-towner, the chili in various Cincinnati chili parlors may seem pretty much alike, but there are natives who have stayed up late at night arguing about the relative merits of Empress and Skyline or explaining that the secret of eating at the downtown Empress is to arrive when the chili is at its freshest, which happens to be at about nine in the morning. In Cincinnati, people are constantly dropping into a new neighborhood chili parlor only to

find out that it serves the best chili in the world. One chili fanatic I met was a supporter of a place across the river, in Kentucky, that he claimed serves a six-way and a seven-way.

"What could possibly be in a seven-way?" I asked.　9

"I don't know," he said. "They won't even tell you." I later learned from　10
Bert Workum, a serious eater who works for the Kentucky *Post* in Covington, just across the river from Cincinnati, that the Dixie Chili parlor in Kentucky has once served a seven-way by including eggs (fried or scrambled) and cut-up frankfurters but is now serving only a six-way, having abandoned its egg-cooking operation. Workum also told me that the chicken restaurant Marshall J. Dodge III probably had in mind was McKnight's, which is in Cynthiana, Kentucky, rather than in Rabbit Hash. I told him that Dodge was the kind of person who would never say Cynthiana if there was any excuse to say Rabbit Hash.

Garrison had turned out to be a large man who wears three-piece suits　11
and a full beard and has what used to be called an ample stomach. He appreciates good food, but even at a restaurant that he might patronize mainly beause it has a pleasant atmosphere or is open late at night or charges reasonable prices he is what one of his friends described as a Clean Plate Ranger. One of his friends, a man who runs a barbecue restaurant called the Barn and Rib Pit in downtown Cincinnati, told me, "I love to see Harry eat ribs. He just inhales those ribs. You look at him and he's just glowin'."

I spent an afternoon with Garrison riding around Cincinnati, and found　12
him to be one of those rare Americans who truly savors his city. I was still a bit concerned that he might be someone who would be more excited about finding an authentic boogie-woogie pianist or maybe a mechanical violin in perfect working order than he would about stumbling onto, say, the classic corn fritter. But he relieved my fears somewhat by describing what we were going to have for dinner at his house as "the best fried chicken in the world." At about that time, by coincidence, we passed a run-down looking restaurant whose sign actually said, WORLD'S BEST FRIED CHICKEN. Garrison glanced at it contemptuously. "I don't see any point in considering his claim at all," he said.

There was a lot of food talk among the dinner guests at Garrison's that　13
evening, and there was also some staggering acorn squash and the best apple pie I have ever tasted. The chicken was delicious, but I still think the best fried chicken I have ever eaten was at a sort of outdoor homecoming that Cherokee County, Georgia, held for Dean Rusk, a native son, shortly after he was named Secretary of State—fried chicken so good that I still nurture a hope, against long odds, that Cherokee County will someday produce another Secretary of State and throw another homecoming.

Garrison finished off the meal by handing around made-in-Cincinnati　14
cigars and treating the entire company to a display of smoke-ring blowing. Garrison's smoke-ring technique includes a remarkable motion by which he

more or less nudges the ring along by pushing at the air a few inches behind it—a variation of the assistance that curlers offer a curling stone by sweeping away at the ice in its path. Between rings, Garrison announces his performance with the kind of grandiloquence he must use on the magic stage, and he is as irritable as a matador about the threat of air movement that could mar his artistry. Just when everyone at the table expects a ring to emerge, Garrison is likely to pause, glance around sternly, and say, in a majestic voice, "I detect human breathing in this room." Even after having stopped eating for a while to watch the smoke-ring blowing, none of us felt up to the late-night visit to the Barn and Rib Pit Garrison had contemplated. The fact that I knew the proprietor was white made me less disappointed at missing the Barn and Rib Pit than I might have been. Going to a white-run barbecue is, I think, like going to a gentile internist: It might turn out all right, but you haven't made any attempt to take advantage of the percentages.

15   Garrison had promised me a special treat for my last night in Ohio—a treat to be found in a restaurant near Oxford—but even as we drove to the restaurant he insisted that precisely what the treat was would have to be a surprise. After the day I had spent, I figured it might require more than a surprise treat to induce me to take any food on my fork. At about eleven, I had stopped at the downtown Empress to see what it looked like, and, deciding that it might be rude to leave without eating (particularly so early in the freshness cycle), had polished off a three-way. For lunch, Garrison had led me to a splendid place called Stenger's Café, which he described as the last of the old-fashioned workingman's bars left in what had been the old German section of Cincinnati known as Over the Rhine. At Stenger's I cleaned a plate on which the counterman had piled mettwurst, two potato pancakes, a helping of beans, some beets, bread and butter, and, at the last minute, a piece of beef from a tray I had spotted being carried across the room. For that, I had parted with one dollar and twenty-eight cents. My appetite was returning as we drove, though, and Garrison helped it along by describing what we might have eaten at a few of the places he had considered taking me to before he decided on the restaurant in Oxford—including a place in Kentucky that specialized in farm food like ham with gravy.

16   "Red-eye gravy?" I asked.

17   "Red-eye gravy," Garrison said.

18   We drove along for a few miles while I thought that over.

19   "Is it too late to turn back toward Kentucky?" I asked.

20   "You'll love the place we're going," Garrison said. "It's going to have a fine surprise for you."

21   The place he had picked out was a restaurant outside Oxford called the Shady Nook. It turned out to be a normal-looking suburban restaurant with a sign in four or five colors of neon in the parking lot. Garrison insisted that we sit at the bar for a while to have shrimp cocktails and some wine. Behind

the bar there was a stage that went completely around the room, and in front of the stage was a covered square that looked as if it might be a small orchestra pit. I was beginning to wonder what the surprise was. I didn't see anything amazing about the shrimp except how many of them Garrison was eating. Between bites he managed to say hello to a man he identified as the owner of the Shady Nook and to explain how Professor Harry L. Suter happened to design the viola-pan as he whiled away the time on the top floor of his house in Moscow, Ohio, during the great flood of 1913. Garrison told me that he had hired Professor Suter to play a Christmas party in 1959, and had the pleasure of being able to say in the introduction that it was the Professor's first Cincinnati appearance since the summer of 1917, when he played the Bell Telephone picnic. I couldn't spot anything extraordinary on the plates of the people already eating, but somehow I got it in my mind that the surprise was going to be either The Great Cherry Cobbler or maybe even The Classic Onion Ring. Suddenly, the recorded music that I had been listening to without realizing it was turned off. From deep within what I had thought was an orchestra pit came a rumbling noise. Before my eyes there arose a gigantic gold, intricately carved, four-keyboard, three-ton Wurlitzer Theater Organ. The owner of the Shady Nook climbed up on the stool, high above the bar, and—by playing at least all four keyboards at once and flicking on and off several dozen switches at the same time—transformed the Shady Nook into Radio City Music Hall. I was indeed surprised. Harry Garrison looked at the theater organ and looked at me and beamed.

Writing About Places

Strategies

1. Why am I writing about this particular place? To present and interpret factual (for instance, geographical or historical) information about it? to re-create its essence and meaning as I have experienced it? to use the place to argue or illustrate a point? as the site of a momentous event or revelation? What mixture of objective information and subjective interpretations will best fit my purpose?

2. If my audience is completely unfamiliar with the place, how much and what kinds of basic information will I have to provide so they can understand what I'm talking about? (For example, can I assume that my readers have seen oceans, but not necessarily the Indian Ocean, the subject of my paper?) If my readers are familiar with the subject, in what ways can I treat it to depart from the hackneyed, the conventional?

3. Have I included enough specific details, vignettes, and other evidence about the inhabitants of the place and its ambience to put my readers on the scene? Have I let the details demonstrate the essence of the place and my view of it, rather than overtly belaboring my interpretation of it? Is my writing consequently understated? (If it's overstated, how can I justify the excesses?) Is my writing unsentimental, even when I love the place? Should it be that way?

4. How will I organize my writing about this place? As a narration, in chronological order? spatially, from the most remote to the closest (or vice versa)? psychologically, from the most- to the least-familiar aspects (or vice versa)? according to what an observer is likely to notice first, second . . . last? topically, by what a traveler needs to know (how to get around, what to see, where to stay, where to eat, what to buy)? or according to some other pattern?

5. What, if anything, have I demonstrated about the relation of the place to its inhabitants? Will my readers be sympathetic toward or want to go to the places I like? have I made a good case for why they should avoid or be repelled by those I dislike?

Suggestions

1. Write a description of a place you have visited that you either liked or disliked a great deal and have seen essentially as an outsider. You may include yourself as a character if you wish, but keep the focus on the place rather than on yourself. Identify some of its unusual features, and some characteristics that are typical, but don't make your description picture-postcard pretty, even if you like the place. Be realistic—you'll be more convincing. (See John McPhee, "The Pine Barrens," 205–10; James Morris, "The Venetian Way," 216–22; and Jan Morris, "Manhattan," 222–30.)

2. Write a reminiscence of a place that has had considerable significance for you (either during your childhood or more recently)—positive, negative, or both. Demonstrate its meaning through description, a series of vignettes, or an account of one or two quintessential people or events you associate with that place, to convey your understanding to readers unfamiliar with it. (See Margaret Laurence, "Where the World Began," 211–16; Mark Twain, "Uncle John's Farm," 237–42; Alfred Kazin, "Brownsville: The Kitchen," 246–50.)

3. Explain how your involvement with or experiences in a place led to greater self-knowledge. (See Henry David Thoreau, "Where I Lived and What I Lived For," 251–61; Tim Payne, "On the Beach at Bar Harbor," 265–67.)

4. Write an essay focusing on a place (town, city, region, or nation) that is the site of social, ecological, or other problems. In conveying the essence of the place, convey also the essence of the problem, and imply some of the causes and effects of that problem. (See George Orwell, "Marrakech," 341–46; Joan Didion, "Marrying Absurd," 514–17; William Warner, "The Islands of Chesapeake Bay: Looking Ahead," 788–97.)

5. Re-create the ambience of a room, building, or institution, through physical description and/or an account of its major functions or of the activities that typically occur there. (See Mark Twain, "Uncle John's Farm," 237–42; Alfred Kazin, "Brownsville: The Kitchen," 246–50; Gwyneth Cravens, "The M & J Sanitary Tortilla Factory," 461–67.)

6. Focus on a place, or a characteristic feature of a place, in close-up; describe it in minute detail, capturing its appearance, sounds, tastes, and textures. Through careful selection and arrangement of details convey not only an impression of the place but your attitude toward it, favorable or otherwise. (See Henry Beston, "The Headlong Wave," 202–204; Gwyneth Cravens, "The M & J Sanitary Tortilla Factory," 461–67; Joan Didion, "Marrying Absurd," 514–17.)

7. Write a brief travel guide to a place you know well, indicating its notable features, museums, facilities for recreation and entertainment, how to get there, where to stay, where to eat, what to buy, when to go. Or, pick one of these characteristics and expand your discussion into a thoroughly detailed essay. (See Bob Thompson, "California: An Overview," 268–71; Philip Kopper, "The Stark Simplicity of the Delmarva Coast," 272–77; Kate Simon, "New York Luncheonettes," 277–82.)

8. In the spirit of Paul Theroux's motto, "The journey, not the arrival, matters" (261–64), write an account of a memorable journey, important either because of the physical, emotional, or psychological experience of travel; or because of the phenomenon of leaving somewhere for an unknown experience.

9. Explain a change of location as a change of status. Maxine Hong Kingston's "Uneasy Status: From Renter to Homeowner" (243–46) is one example. Moving from home to a dormitory or an apartment, moving from the city to the suburbs (or vice versa), moving from an apartment to a house, or even from one room or one house to another can provide the context for the change of status, and for how the mover feels about both the move and the change.

10. Look at a familiar place from an unfamiliar perspective (the summer beach in winter; the stern beach at Bar Harbor to a visitor used to hospitable southern beaches; Manhattan as seen by a sophisticated English adult, or by high school students from Bean Blossom Township, Indiana) and convey this novel view to your readers, either as prospective travelers to it, or as people who can gain some fresh understanding from this new look. (See Philip Kopper, "The Stark Simplicity of the Delmarva Coast," 272–77; Tim Payne, "On the Beach at Bar Harbor," 265–67; Jan Morris, "Manhattan," 222–31; Lillian Ross, "The Yellow Bus," 500–14.)

CHAPTER FOUR

Writing About Controversy

The world is full of controversy, actual or potential. You can argue over the meanings of words and concepts (love or beauty or justice, for example), the truth of interpretations (When doctors prescribe placebos are they necessarily lying to the patients?), the merits and demerits of social changes (racial integration), public policies (affirmative action), or ethical concerns (the right to die). Whenever you express your attitude toward something you raise the possibility of controversy, of debate with those who may disagree with you. Indeed, as the essays throughout this volume reveal, writers of portraits, reviews, and interpretations of places, processes ("how-to"), and scientific phenomena are presenting the subject from their points of view, arguing their cases. Directly and indirectly the point of view, tone, and selection of supporting evidence and illustrations combine to make the writer's case. For instance, "when the white man turns tyrant it is his own freedom that he destroys" is the thesis of George Orwell's seemingly simple tale of "Shooting an Elephant" (335–40), which culminated in his reluctant killing of an elephant to please the hostile Burmese crowd that egged him on.

Taking a stand on a controversial matter, whether overtly or by implication, can serve a variety of purposes. You can call attention to the existence of a problem (Should college admissions be influenced by affirmative-action policies?), you can demand an investigation of it (Is our college's affirmative-action policy effective in recruiting minority students? Why or why not?), you can defend or attack the status quo (What price affirmative action?), or you can argue for reform (Start—or stop—affirmative action!). A complex writing might perform all of these functions simultaneously. Whatever your approach, in writing about controversy you will want to convince your readers that the subject itself is a problem, that the causes or effects are what you say they are, for both the short and long term, and that your solutions (if you offer any) are the right ones.

Direct Argument

An argument, as we're using the term here, does not mean a knockdown confrontation over an issue: "The South is the best place in the country to live!" "No it's not. It's full of ticks, mud, and kudzu." Nor is an argument hard-sell brainwashing that admits of no alternatives: "America—love it or leave it!" When you construct an argument, however, as a reasonable writer you'll present a reasonable proposition that states what you believe. You'll offer appeals based on logic and evidence (probably buttressed by emotion) to try to convince your readers of the merits of what you say—and of the demerits of your antagonists' views. Sometimes, but not always, you'll also argue that they should adopt a particular course of action.

Unless you're writing an implied argument (discussed below) that makes its point through satire, irony, or some other oblique means, you'll probably want to identify the issue at hand and justify its significance early in the essay, defining key terms as they occur. In her argument against "Placebos" (319– 24), philosopher Sissela Bok gets right to the point in the first sentence:

> The common practice of prescribing placebos to unwitting patients illus-
> trates the two miscalculations so common to minor forms of deceit: ignor-
> ing possible harm and failing to see how gestures assumed to be trivial build
> up into collectively undesirable practices.

Early in the argument, in the third sentence, she defines placebos, the central term in her argument: "They can be sugar pills, salt-water injections—in fact, any medical procedure which has no specific effect on a patient's condition, but which can have powerful psychological effects leading to relief from symptoms such as pain or depression."

There are a number of suitable ways to organize the body of your argu-ment. If your audience is inclined to agree with much of what you say (this is not the case with most of the direct arguments here), you might want to put your strongest point first and provide the most evidence for that, before proceeding to the lesser points, arranged in order of descending importance. For an antagonistic audience you could reverse the order, beginning with the points easiest to accept or agree with and concluding with the most difficult. Martin Luther King, Jr., uses this pattern in "Letter from Birmingham Jail" (304–18), as he argues to an ostensible audience of moderate Alabama cler-gymen but actually to the entire world, that "one has not only a legal but a moral responsibility to disobey unjust laws." Or you could work from the most familiar to the least familiar points, as William Faulkner does in his extended definition of "The American Dream" (297–99) to argue, finally, that Americans have "emasculated all meaning whatever" from the American Dream—"freedom, democracy, patriotism."

Whatever organizational pattern you choose, you'll need to provide supporting evidence. One or more of the following types are common, and they're often used in combination:

Facts and figures, sometimes including cost/benefit analyses. King says, "We have waited more than 340 years for our constitutional and Godgiven rights. The nations of Asia and Africa are moving with jetlike speed toward gaining political independence . . . ."

Specific examples, from contemporary life, history, or literature. In "The Reversal of Death" (324–31) cultural historian Philippe Aries argues that the old ways of dealing with death, as a natural process to be treated openly and with dignity, are superior to the covert, hypocritical modern denial of death. His vast evidence includes interpretations of the deaths of La Fontaine's plowman, Roland, Tristam, Tolstoy's peasants, Don Quixote, Mme. de La Ferronays, Louis XIV, amd Mme. de Montespan.

Case histories. Norman Cousins argues in "The Right to Die" (332–34) that people have the right to die, even to take their own lives, if the alternative is "to live without dignity or sensitivity." He makes his point primarily through the extended case history of the suicides of Henry P. Van Dusen, retired president of Union Theological Seminary, and his wife at a point when "they would soon become completely dependent for even the most elementary needs and functions."

Analogies. Every case history is an implied analogy; the single case is intended to represent many others like itself. So are many personal examples. King's experiences of discrimination in a segregated society are legion: "For years now I have heard the word 'Wait!' It rings in the ear of every Negro with piercing familiarity. This 'Wait' has almost always meant 'Never'."

Personal opinion, derived from professional expertise or personal experience. In "Faulkner and Desegregation" (299–304), James Baldwin presents a variety of personal opinions to rebut Faulkner's go-slow view of racial integration in the South, based on what Baldwin considers the fallaciously optimistic view that "the white Southerner, with no *coercion* from the rest of the nation, will lift himself above his *ancient, crippling bitterness* and refuse to add to his already *intolerable burden of blood guiltiness*" (italics added to indicate Baldwin's opinionated language).

Expert opinions, derived from others' expertise or experience. King supports his argument against segregation with references to Jesus ("an extremist for love, truth and goodness"), Amos, Paul, Martin Luther, John Bunyan, Abraham Lincoln, Thomas Jefferson—extremists all, in the cause of justice.

After you've written a direct argument, have someone who disagrees with you read it critically to look for loopholes. Your critic's guidelines could be the same questions you might ask yourself while writing the paper: What do I want to prove? How do I want my readers to react? What is my strongest evidence? my weakest? Is there other (and better) evidence I need? Does my organizational pattern strengthen the argument? Have I anticipated opposing points of view? If you can satisfy yourself and a critic, you can take on the world. Or is that a logical fallacy?

Implied Argument, with Emphasis on Narrative

In an implied argument you'll be making your point primarily through emotional and rhetorical techniques that reinforce (or sometimes circumvent) rational means and objective evidence. When you write from passion you expect your readers to respond with equal fervor: "I have a dream." "The only thing we have to fear is fear itself." "We shall overcome."

You can't incite your readers, either to agree with you or to take action on behalf of the cause you favor, by bleeding all over the page. The process of writing and rewriting and revising again (see Chapter One) will act to cool your red-hot emotion, and will enable you to modulate in subsequent drafts what you might have written the first time just to get it out of your system. As the essays in this section and elsewhere (particularly in humorous social criticism, 500–32) reveal, writers whose implied arguments are most effective, such as Jonathan Swift's in "A Modest Proposal," themselves exercise considerable control over both literary techniques and their evidence. Many of these techniques are commonly associated with narrative fiction—a narrative persona (possibly but not necessarily a version of the author) who may be a participant in the activities; a shifting point of view among various participants and the narrator; dialogue; character conflict; the setting of scenes; symbolic use of objects and natural phenomena; and careful attention to tone, including irony and satire. These techniques make implied arguments compelling to read, even though they may at times be more emotional than logical and thus depart from the principles of sound direct argumentation.

In "Marrakech" (341–46), for instance, George Orwell juxtaposes a series of vignettes to corroborate his claim that all colonial empires are sustained by dehumanization of the poor, nonwhite natives. A characteristic illustrative incident occurred in the public gardens when he was feeding a gazelle:

> [They are] almost the only animals that look good to eat when they are still alive; in fact, one can hardly look at their hindquarters without thinking of mint sauce. . . . It nibbled rapidly at the bread, then lowered its head and tried to butt me, then took another nibble and then butted again. . . .
>
> An Arab navvy working on the path nearby lowered his heavy hoe and sidled towards us. He looked from the gazelle to the bread and from the bread to the gazelle, with a sort of quiet amazement, as though he had never seen anything quite like this before. Finally he said shyly in French: "I could eat some of that bread."
>
> I tore off a piece and he stowed it gratefully in some secret place under his rags. This man is an employee of the Municipality.

The components of this short extract are:

The characters: Orwell-as-character, gazelle, navvy.

The setting: the Marrakech public gardens.

Theme: hunger, of beast and man.

The plot: man feeding gazelle (*action*) is approached by a laborer who himself wants to eat the gazelle's food (*conflict*). Man feeds navvy (*resolution of conflict*).

Dialogue: "I could eat some of that bread."

Orwell uses comparable techniques with a single extended example in "Shooting an Elephant" (335–40), as does Robert Christgau in "Beth Ann and Macrobioticism" (353–60), an understated indictment of the ultimately fatal extremism of Beth Ann and Charlie Simon, hippie artists of the 1960s who "had been high on hashish, cocaine, heroin, amphetamine, LSD and DMT . . . not to mention sex, food, art and the infinite reaches of the human spirit"—and their final, foolish high, a deadly macrobiotic diet.

In "None of This Is Fair" (361–65) Richard Rodriguez uses the example of his own life to attack affirmative action, and to claim that instead of giving special privileges to middle-class minority students, universities should work "to make higher education accessible to the genuinely socially disadvantaged." As a bright, high-achieving scholarship student Rodriguez, a Chicano, received financial aid and job offers not extended to equally well-qualified whites. In the essay's climactic action, he declines all the prestigious job offers, and so makes his personal statement.

John McPhee's "Family Doctors" (346–53) uses a detailed portrait of quintessential family doctor, David Jones, living on a farm in Aroostook County, Maine, to make the point that family doctors living in the areas they serve, rather than remote teams of superspecialists, are essential to the health of rural America. We follow Jones throughout a full day on the job, from early morning until late afternoon as he cares with humane sympathy for old people, babies, potato harvesters, alcoholics, heart patients. And then we follow him home to feed the pigs, turkeys, horses on his farm, "To have a place like this was always my dream. As a physician, you can go somewhere else and make more money, but you can't live like this. You walk up on that knoll, you see Mt. Katahdin."

Investigative Reporting

Investigative writers, a newly respectable label for not-always-genteel muckrakers, chip away at the status quo, looking for cracks and fault lines in the foundations of society, pens poised to split their subjects wide open. In "Uncovering Deception: How Investigative Reporters Work" (366–76), from *All the President's Men,* Carl Bernstein and Bob Woodward transform the long, painstaking, and often tedious process of searching for evidence into high drama. They explain how by following up on leads, acting on hunches, checking out cryptic information (such as "W.H." noted next to a man's name in an address book) and circumstantial evidence, they collected a mountain of evidence that, when interpreted, led directly to W.H.—the White House. The qualities they exhibit in this investigation—fascination with the subject, confidence that results will be forthcoming, enormous perseverance, pushiness (if someone won't answer a request for information, keep asking—that person or someone else), and a willingness to take risks, personal and professional—are the essence of investigative reporting.

"Let Us Now Appraise Famous Writers" (377–88) reveals that Jessica Mitford used similar techniques in her investigation of the fraudulent Famous Writers School. The School's advertising encouraged naive and generally untalented aspiring writers to enroll in an extremely costly correspondence course, in the mistaken belief that their writing would be critiqued personally by Bennet Cerf, Faith Baldwin, or other Famous Writers, and that the students would soon be publishing their own work. Mitford interviewed all the Famous Writers, School executives, and some disgruntled former students; she toured the school, where fifty-five nonfamous nonwriters composed canned paragraphs of criticism for some 50,000 manuscripts a year. She compared the School's course with the much cheaper—and considerably better—university writing courses around the country. The publication of her article (delayed because several magazines refused to print it, fearing that Famous Writers School would withdraw their lucrative ads) closed down the School.

Such is the ultimate power of writing about controversy—to promote enormous social changes (such as racial integration), to lobby for or against public policy (affirmative action) and ethical concerns (the right to die with dignity), to ferret out lies and fraud and deceit. Perhaps even to topple a Presidency. What would you like your writings about controversy to accomplish?

Direct Argument

WILLIAM FAULKNER
The American Dream

William Faulkner was born in New Albany, Mississippi, in 1897, as the Old South lay already dying. When Faulkner himself lay dying, in 1962 in Oxford, Mississippi—the lifelong home that Faulkner's novels had mythologized into the Southern Camelot—the Old South of rural communities, close family ties, and traditional values was being resurrected as the more prosperous, more materialistic, industrialized New South. Coming of age as a writer in this time of cultural transition, Faulkner came to understand not only his native South but America as well.

Faulkner dropped out of the University of Mississippi after his freshman year to travel and work at odd jobs. Although he appeared on the surface to be a loafer (he was fired from his post-office job at Ole Miss for inattentiveness) and a drifter, he was on a deeper level hard at work, writing and rewriting the novels for which he was to be awarded the Nobel Prize for Literature in 1950: The Sound and the Fury *(1929),* As I Lay Dying *(1930),* Light in August *(1934),* Absalom, Absalom *(1936), and* Go Down, Moses *(1942). His literary success came late, and with great difficulty, for Faulkner's innovative style, sympathetic stand on racial integration, bizarre characters, and sometimes sensational subject matter initially shocked the public (in 1930 one editor rejected* Sanctuary, *saying if he published it "we'd both be in jail") and repelled the critics.*

Faulkner's writing is characterized by two styles, often intermingled. His informal style employs simple vocabulary and straightforward syntax; his far more formal style, in which "The American Dream" was written, has long, complicated sentences expressing complex and sometimes seemingly contradictory ideas intended to reflect the complexity and intensity of "the human heart in conflict with itself." The first two sentences of paragraph 5, for example, seem tortured: ". . . our forefathers did not bequeath to us . . . but rather bequeathed us, their successors to the dream." Nevertheless, they reflect the anguish of a Southerner, like Faulkner, bound paradoxically to tradition and history and at the same time enamored of the American dream that tells us to shatter tradition and history and live in the complete freedom of individual liberty. Of course, this dilemma is not exclusively Southern; the American dream Faulkner describes was—and still is—betrayed in Massachusetts as well as in Mississippi. Faulkner's complex sentences reflect the hope and the despair, the celebration and the sense of failure, that any thoughtful American must experience when pondering the gap between our dream and our reality.

This was the American Dream: a sanctuary on the earth for individual man: a condition in which he could be free not only of the old established closed-corporation hierarchies of arbitrary power which had oppressed him as a mass, but free of that mass into which the hierarchies of church and state had compressed and held him individually thralled and individually impotent.

A dream simultaneous among the separate individuals of men so asunder and scattered as to have no contact to match dreams and hopes among the old nations of the Old World which existed as nations not on citizenship but subjectship, which endured only on the premise of size and docility of the subject mass; the individual men and women who said as with one simultaneous voice: "We will establish a new land where man can assume that every individual man—not the mass of men but individual men—has inalienable right to individual dignity and freedom within a fabric of individual courage and honorable work and mutual responsibility."

3   Not just an idea, but a condition: a living human condition designed to be coeval with the birth of America itself, engendered created and simultaneous with the very air and word America, which at that one stroke, one instant, should cover the whole earth with one simultaneous suspiration like air or light. And it was, it did: radiating outward to cover even the old weary repudiated still-thralled nations, until individual men everywhere, who had no more than heard the name, let alone knew where America was, could respond to it, lifting up not only their hearts but the hopes too which until now they did not know—or anyway dared not remember—that they possessed.

4   A condition in which every man would not only not be a king, he wouldn't even want to be one. He wouldn't even need to bother to need to be the equal of kings because now he was free of kings and all their similar congeries; free not only of the symbols but of the old arbitrary hierarchies themselves which the puppet-symbols represented—courts and cabinets and churches and schools—to which he had been valuable not as an individual but only as that integer, his value compounded in that immutable ratio to his sheer mindless numbers, that animal increase of his will-less and docile mass.

5   The dream, the hope, the condition which our forefathers did not bequeath to us, their heirs and assigns, but rather bequeathed us, their successors, to the dream and the hope. We were not even given the chance then to accept or decline the dream, for the reason that the dream already owned and possessed us at birth. It was not our heritage because we were its, we ourselves heired in our successive generations to the dream by the idea of the dream. And not only we, their sons born and bred in America, but men born and bred in the old alien repudiated lands, also felt that breath, that air, heard that promise, that proffer that there was such a thing as hope for individual man. And the old nations themselves, so old and so long-fixed in the old concepts of man as to have thought themselves beyond all hope of change, making oblation to that new dream of that new concept of man by gifts of monuments and devices to mark the portals of that inalienable right and hope: "There is room for you here from about the earth, for all ye individually homeless, individually oppressed, individually unindividualised.". . .

6   . . . That dream was man's aspiration in the true meaning of the word aspiration. It was not merely the blind and voiceless hope of his heart: it was the actual inbreathe of his lungs, his lights, his living and unsleeping metabo-

lism, so that we actually lived the Dream. We did not live *in* the dream: we lived the Dream itself, just as we do not merely live *in* air and climate, but we live Air and Climate; we ourselves individually representative of the Dream, the Dream itself actually audible in the strong uninhibited voices which were not afraid to speak *cliché* at the very top of them, giving to the *cliché*-avatars of "Give me liberty or give me death" or "This to be self-evident that all individual men were created equal in one mutual right to freedom" which had never lacked for truth anyway, assuming that hope and dignity are truth, a validity and immediacy absolving them even of *cliché*.

That was the Dream: not man created equal in the sense that he was created black or white or brown or yellow and hence doomed irrevocably to that for the remainder of his days—or rather, not doomed with equality but blessed with equality, himself lifting no hand but instead lying curled and drowsing in the warm and airless bath of it like the yet-wombed embryo; but liberty in which to have an equal start at equality with all other men, and freedom in which to defend and preserve that equality by means of the individual courage and the honorable work and the mutual responsibility. Then we lost it. It abandoned us, which had supported and protected and defended us while our new nation of new concepts of human existence got a firm enough foothold to stand erect among the nations of the earth, demanding nothing of us in return save to remember always that, being alive, it was therefore perishable and so must be held always in the unceasing responsibility and vigilance of courage and honor and pride and humility. It is gone now. We dozed, slept, and it abandoned us. And in that vacuum now there sound no longer the strong loud voices not merely unafraid but not even aware that fear existed, speaking in mutual unification of one mutual hope and will. Because now what we hear is a cacophony of terror and conciliation and compromise babbling only the mouthsounds; the loud and empty words which we have emasculated of all meaning whatever—freedom, democracy, patriotism—with which, awakened at last, we try in desperation to hide from ourselves that loss. . . .

7

JAMES BALDWIN

Faulkner and Desegregation

"The most difficult (and most rewarding) thing in my life has been the fact that I was born a Negro and was forced, therefore, to effect some kind of truce with this reality. (Truce, by the way, is the best one can hope for)." Sometimes this is an armed truce, as Baldwin's writings, fiction and nonfiction, anatomize what it means to be black in a largely white America—examining with a mixture of compassion, bitterness, and anger the complex social, political, and sexual fabric of that life. Baldwin was born in Harlem in 1924, the son of an unremittingly tense and hostile father, an evangelical lay preacher, "proud and ingrown,

like a toe-nail." After graduating from DeWitt Clinton High School, Baldwin supported his writing through a series of fellowships—Saxton, Rosenwald, Guggenheim, Partisan Review, Ford Foundation. For a decade he wrote his major works in Paris: the autobiographical Go Tell It on the Mountain *(1953),* Notes of a Native Son *(1955), and Giovanni's* Room *(1956). Returning to New York in the early 1960s as an activist in the civil rights movement, he published the critical* The Fire Next Time *(1963). His most recent novel is* Just Above My Head *(1979).*

"Faulkner and Desegregation," from Nobody Knows My Name *(1961), expresses the characteristic outrage of Baldwin, international spokesman for blacks, at the go-slow position of William Faulkner, spokesman for Southern whites after the Supreme Court ordered integration of the public schools in 1954. Although in "The American Dream" (1955) Faulkner argued for freedom, liberty, and equality for all, in 1956, in a "Letter to the North" printed in* Life, *he advised integrationists to*

> *Go slow now. Stop now for a time . . . . give [the white establishment Southerner] a space in which to get his breath . . . to look about and see that (1) Nobody is going to force integration on him from the outside; (2) That he himself faces an obsolescence in his own land which only he can cure. . . .*

Although Faulkner may have been, in his own estimation, well-intentioned, Baldwin's sarcasm mercilessly points out the flaws in both the logic and the morality of that position. There is no truce, no compromise, in Baldwin's righteous insistence on integration now ("the time is always now"); in his view, "salvation" is action rather than pious traditionalism.

1   Any real change implies the breakup of the world as one has always known it, the loss of all that gave one an identity, the end of safety. And at such a moment, unable to see and not daring to imagine what the future will now bring forth, one clings to what one knew, or thought one knew; to what one possessed or dreamed that one possessed. Yet, it is only when a man is able, without bitterness or self-pity, to surrender a dream he has long cherished or a privilege he has long possessed that he is set free—he has set himself free—for higher dreams, for greater privileges. All men have gone through this, go through it, each according to his degree, throughout their lives. It is one of the irreducible facts of life. And remembering this, especially since I am a Negro, affords me almost my only means of understanding what is happening in the minds and hearts of white Southerners today.

2   For the arguments with which the bulk of relatively articulate white Southerners of good will have met the necessity of desegregation have no value whatever as arguments, being almost entirely and helplessly dishonest, when not, indeed, insane. After more than two hundred years in slavery and ninety years of quasi-freedom, it is hard to think very highly of William Faulkner's advice to "go slow." "They don't mean go slow," Thurgood Marshall is reported to have said, "they mean don't go." Nor is the squire of Oxford very persuasive when he suggests that white Southerners, left to their own devices, will realize that their own social structure looks silly to the rest of the world and correct it of their own accord. It has looked silly, to use

Faulkner's rather strange adjective, for a long time; so far from trying to correct it, Southerners, who seem to be characterized by a species of defiance most perverse when it is most despairing have clung to it, at incalculable cost to themselves, as the only conceivable and as an absolutely sacrosanct way of life. They have never seriously conceded that their social structure was mad. They have insisted, on the contrary, that everyone who criticized it was mad.

Faulkner goes further. He concedes the madness and moral wrongness of the South but at the same time he raises it to the level of a mystique which makes it somehow unjust to discuss Southern society in the same terms in which one would discuss any other society. "Our position is wrong and untenable," says Faulkner, "but it is not wise to keep an emotional people off balance." This, if it means anything, can only mean that this "emotional people" have been swept "off balance" by the pressure of recent events, that is, the Supreme Court decision outlawing segregation. When the pressure is taken off—and not an instant before—this "emotional people" will presumably find themselves once again on balance and will then be able to free themselves of an "obsolescence in [their] own land" in their own way and, of course, in their own time. The question left begging is what, in their history to date, affords any evidence that they have any desire or capacity to do this. And it is, I suppose, impertinent to ask just what Negroes are supposed to do while the South works out what, in Faulkner's rhetoric, becomes something very closely resembling a high and noble tragedy.

The sad truth is that whatever modifications have been effected in the social structure of the South since the Reconstruction, and any alleviations of the Negro's lot within it, are due to great and incessant pressure, very little of it indeed from within the South. That the North has been guilty of Pharisaism in its dealing with the South does not negate the fact that much of this pressure has come from the North. That some—not nearly as many as Faulkner would like to believe—Southern Negroes prefer, or are afraid of changing, the status quo does not negate the fact that it is the Southern Negro himself who, year upon year, and generation upon generation, has kept the Southern waters troubled. As far as the Negro's life in the South is concerned, the NAACP is the only organization which has struggled, with admirable single-mindedness and skill, to raise him to the level of a citizen. For this reason alone, and quite apart from the individual heroism of many of its Southern members, it cannot be equated, as Faulkner equates it, with the pathological Citizen's Council. One organization is working within the law and the other is working against and outside it. Faulkner's threat to leave the "middle of the road" where he has, presumably, all these years, been working for the benefit of Negroes, reduces itself to a more or less up-to-date version of the Southern threat to secede from the Union.

Faulkner—among so many others!—is so plaintive concerning this "middle of the road" from which "extremist" elements of both races are driving him that it does not seem unfair to ask just what he has been doing there until now. Where is the evidence of the struggle he has been carrying on there on behalf of the Negro? Why, if he and his enlightened confreres in the South have been boring from within to destroy segregation, do they react with such panic when the walls show any signs of falling? Why—and how—does one move from the middle of the road where one was aiding Negroes into the streets—to shoot them?

6   Now it is easy enough to state flatly that Faulkner's middle of the road does not—cannot—exist and that he is guilty of great emotional and intellectual dishonesty in pretending that it does. I think this is why he clings to his fantasy. It is easy enough to accuse him of hypocrisy when he speaks of man being "indestructible because of his simple will to freedom." But he is not being hypocritical; he means it. It is only that Man is one thing—a rather unlucky abstraction in this case—and the Negroes he has always known, so fatally tied up in his mind with his grandfather's slaves, are quite another. He is at his best, and is perfectly sincere, when he declares, in *Harpers,* "To live anywhere in the world today and be against equality because of race or color is like living in Alaska and being against snow. We have already got snow. And as with the Alaskan, merely to live in armistice with it is not enough. Like the Alaskan, we had better use it." And though this seems to be flatly opposed to his statement (in an interview printed in *The Reporter*) that, if it came to a contest between the federal government and Mississippi, he would fight for Mississippi, "even if it meant going out into the streets and shooting Negroes," he means that, too. Faulkner means everything he says, means them all at once, and with very nearly the same intensity. This is why his statements demand our attention. He has perhaps never before more concretely expressed what it means to be a Southerner.

7   What seems to define the Southerner, in his own mind at any rate, is his relationship to the North, that is to the rest of the Republic, a relationship which can at the very best be described as uneasy. It is apparently very difficult to be at once a Southerner and an American; so difficult that many of the South's most independent minds are forced into the American exile; which is not, of course, without its aggravating, circular effect on the interior and public life of the South. A Bostonian, say, who leaves Boston is not regarded by the citizenry he has abandoned with the same venomous distrust as is the Southerner who leaves the South. The citizenry of Boston do not consider that they have been abandoned, much less betrayed. It is only the American Southerner who seems to be fighting, in his own entrails, a peculiar, ghastly, and perpetual war with all the rest of the country. ("Didn't you say," demanded a Southern woman of Robert Penn Warren, "that you was born down here, used to live right near here?" And when he agreed that this was so: "Yes . . . but you never said where you living now!")

8   The difficulty, perhaps, is that the Southerner clings to two entirely antithetical doctrines, two legends, two histories. Like all other Americans, he must subscribe, and is to some extent controlled by the beliefs and the principles expressed in the Constitution; at the same time, these beliefs and

principles seem determined to destroy the South. He is, on the one hand, the proud citizen of a free society and, on the other, is committed to a society which has not yet dared to free itself of the necessity of naked and brutal oppression. He is part of a country which boasts that it has never lost a war; but he is also the representative of a conquered nation. I have not seen a single statement of Faulkner's concerning desegregation which does not inform us that his family has lived in the same part of Mississippi for generations, that his greatgrandfather owned slaves, and that his ancestors fought and died in the Civil War. And so compelling is the image of ruin, gallantry and death thus evoked that it demands a positive effort of the imagination to remember that slaveholding Southerners were not the only people who perished in that war. Negroes and Northerners were also blown to bits. American history, as opposed to Southern history, proves that Southerners were not the only slaveholders, Negroes were not even the only slaves. And the segregation which Faulkner sanctifies by references to Shiloh, Chickamauga, and Gettysburg does not extend back that far, is in fact scarcely as old as the century. The "racial condition" which Faulkner will not have changed by "mere force of law or economic threat" was imposed by precisely these means. The Southern tradition, which is, after all, all that Faulkner is talking about, is not a tradition at all: when Faulkner evokes it, he is simply evoking a legend which contains an accusation. And that accusation, stated far more simply than it should be, is that the North, in winning the war, left the South only one means of asserting its identity and that means was the Negro.

"My people owned slaves," says Faulkner, "and the very obligation we have to take care of these people is morally bad." "This problem is . . . far beyond the moral one it is and still was a hundred years ago, in 1860, when many Southerners, including Robert Lee, recognized it as a moral one at the very instant they in turn elected to champion the underdog because that underdog was blood and kin and home." But the North escaped scot-free. For one thing, in freeing the slave, it established a moral superiority over the South which the South has not learned to live with until today; and this despite—or possibly because of—the fact that this moral superiority was bought, after all, rather cheaply. The North was no better prepared than the South, as it turned out, to make citizens of former slaves, but it was able, as the South was not, to wash its hands of the matter. Men who knew that slavery was wrong were forced, nevertheless, to fight to perpetuate it because they were unable to turn against "blood and kin and home." And when blood and kin and home were defeated, they found themselves, more than ever, committed: committed, in effect, to a way of life which was as unjust and crippling as it was inescapable. In sum, the North, by freeing the slaves of their masters, robbed the masters of any possibility of freeing themselves of the slaves.

When Faulkner speaks, then, of the "middle of the road," he is simply speaking of the hope—which was always unrealistic and is now all but smashed—that the white Southerner, with no coercion from the rest of the nation, will lift himself above his ancient, crippling bitterness and refuse to add to his already intolerable burden of blood-guiltiness. But this hope would seem to be absolutely dependent on a social and psychological stasis which simply does not exist. "Things have been getting better," Faulkner tells us, "for a long time. Only six Negroes were killed by whites in Mississippi last year, according to police figures." Faulkner surely knows how little consolation this offers a Negro and he also knows something about "police figures" in the Deep South. And he knows, too, that murder is not the worst thing that can happen to a man, black or white. But murder may be the worst thing a man can do. Faulkner is not trying to save Negroes, who are, in his view, already saved; who, having refused to be destroyed by terror, are far stronger than the terrified white populace; and who have, moreover, fatally, from his point of view, the weight of the federal government behind them. He is trying to save "whatever good remains in those white people." The time he pleads for is the time in which the Southerner will come to terms with himself, will cease fleeing from his conscience, and achieve, in the words of Robert Penn Warren, "moral identity." And he surely believes, with Warren, that "Then in a country where moral identity is hard to come by, the South, because it has had to deal concretely with a moral problem, may offer some leadership. And we need any we can get, if we are to break out of the national rhythm, the rhythm between complacency and panic."

II   But the time Faulkner asks for does not exist—and he is not the only Southerner who knows it. There is never time in the future in which we will work out our salvation. The challenge is in the moment, the time is always now.

MARTIN LUTHER KING, JR.

Letter from Birmingham Jail

"Letter from Birmingham Jail," recently identified by a national committee on the humanities as one of the world's greatest literary masterpieces, reveals why Martin Luther King, Jr., was the most influential leader of the American civil rights movement in the 1950s and 1960s, and, why, with Mahatma Gandhi, he was one of this century's most influential advocates for human rights. He was born in Atlanta in 1929, the son of a well-known Baptist clergyman, educated at Morehouse College, and ordained in his father's denomination.

A forceful and at times charismatic leader, Dr. King became at 26 a national spokesman for the civil rights movement when in 1955 he led a successful boycott of the segregated bus system of Montgomery, Alabama. Dr. King became president of the Southern Christian Leadership Conference and led the sit-ins and demonstrations—including the 1964 march on Washington, D.C., which climaxed with his famous "I Have a Dream" speech—that helped to ensure passage of the 1964 Civil Rights Act and the Voting Rights Act of 1965. He received the Nobel Peace Prize in 1964. Toward the end of his life, cut short by assassination in 1968, Dr. King was increasingly concerned with improving the rights and the lives of the nation's poor, irrespective of race, and with ending the war in Viet Nam. His birthday became a national holiday in 1986.

In 1963 King wrote the letter reprinted below while imprisoned for "parading without a permit." Though ostensibly replying to eight clergymen—Protestant, Catholic, and Jewish—who feared violence in the Birmingham desegregation demonstrations, King actually intended his letter for the worldwide audience his civil rights activities commanded. Warning that America had more to fear from passive moderates ("the appalling silence of good people") than from extremists, King defended his policy of "non-violent direct action" and explained why he was compelled to disobey "unjust laws"—supporting his argument with references to Protestant, Catholic, and Jewish examples ("Was not Jesus an extremist for love?"), as well as to the painful examples of segregation in his own life.

April 16, 1963

My Dear Fellow Clergymen:

While confined here in the Birmingham city jail, I came across your recent statement calling my present activities "unwise and untimely." Seldom do I pause to answer criticism of my work and ideas. If I sought to answer all the criticisms that cross my desk, my secretaries would have little time for anything other than such correspondence in the course of the day, and I would have no time for constructive work. But since I feel that you are men of genuine good will and that your criticisms are sincerely set forth, I want to try to answer your statement in what I hope will be patient and reasonable terms.

I think I should indicate why I am here in Brimingham, since you have been influenced by the view which argues against "outsiders coming in." I have the honor of serving as president of the Southern Christian Leadership Conference, an organization operating in every southern state, with head-quarters in Atlanta, Georgia. We have some eighty-five affiliated organizations across the South, and one of them is the Alabama Christian Movement for Human Rights. Frequently we share staff, educational and financial resources with our affiliates. Several months ago the affiliate here in Birmingham asked us to be on call to engage in a nonviolent direct-action program if such were deemed necessary. We readily consented, and when the hour came we lived up to our promise. So I, along with several members of my staff, am

AUTHOR'S NOTE: This response to a published statement by eight fellow clergymen from Alabama (Bishop C. C. J. Carpenter, Bishop Joseph A. Durick, Rabbi Hilton L. Grafman, Bishop Paul Hardin, Bishop Holan B. Harmon, the Reverend George M. Murray, the Reverend Edward V. Ramage and the Reverend Earl Stallings) was composed under somewhat constricting circumstances. Begun on the margins of the newspaper in which the statement appeared while I was in jail, the letter was continued on scraps of writing paper supplied by a friendly Negro trusty, and concluded on a pad my attorneys were eventually permitted to leave me. Although the text remains in substance unaltered, I have indulged in the author's prerogative of polishing it for publication.

here because I was invited here. I am here because I have organizational ties here.

3   But more basically, I am in Birmingham because injustice is here. Just as the prophets of the eighth century B.C. left their villages and carried their "thus saith the Lord" far beyond the boundaries of their home towns, and, just as the Apostle Paul left his village of Tarsus and carried the gospel of Jesus Christ to the far corners of the Greco-Roman world, so am I compelled to carry the gospel of freedom beyond my own home town. Like Paul, I must constantly respond to the Macedonian call for aid.

4   Moreover, I am cognizant of the interrelatedness of all communities and states. I cannot sit idly by in Atlanta and not be concerned about what happens in Birmingham. Injustice anywhere is a threat to justice everywhere. We are caught in an inescapable network of mutuality, tied in a single garment of destiny. Whatever affects one directly, affects all indirectly. Never again can we afford to live with the narrow, provincial "outside agitator" idea. Anyone who lives inside the United States can never be considered an outsider anywhere within its bounds.

5   You deplore the demonstrations taking place in Birmingham. But your statement, I am sorry to say, fails to express a similar concern for the conditions that brought about the demonstrations. I am sure that none of you would want to rest content with the superficial kind of social analysis that deals merely with effects and does not grapple with underlying causes. It is unfortunate that demonstrations are taking place in Birmingham, but it is even more unfortunate that the city's white power structure left the Negro community with no alternative.

6   In any nonviolent campaign there are four basic steps: collection of the facts to determine whether injustices exist; negotiation; self-purification; and direct action. We have gone through all these steps in Birmingham. There can be no gainsaying the fact that racial injustice engulfs this community. Birmingham is probably the most thoroughly segregated city in the United States. An ugly record of brutality is widely known. Negroes have experienced grossly unjust treatment in the courts. There have been more unsolved bombings of Negro homes and churches in Birmingham than in any other city in the nation. These are the hard brutal facts of the case. On the basis of these conditions, Negro leaders sought to negotiate with the city fathers. But the latter consistently refused to engage in good-faith negotiation.

7   Then, last September, came the opportunity to talk with leaders of Birmingham's economic community. In the course of the negotiations, certain promises were made by the merchants—for example, to remove the stores' humiliating racial signs. On the basis of these promises, the Reverend Fred Shuttlesworth and the leaders of the Alabama Christian Movement for Human Rights agreed to a moratorium on all demonstrations. As the weeks and months went by, we realized that we were the victims of a broken promise. A few signs, briefly removed, returned; the others remained.

As in so many past experiences, our hopes had been blasted, and the shadow of deep disappointment settled upon us. We had no alternative except to prepare for direct action, whereby we would present our very bodies as a means of laying our case before the conscience of the local and the national community. Mindful of the difficulties involved, we decided to undertake a process of self-purification. We began a series of workshops on nonviolence, and we repeatedly asked ourselves: "Are you able to accept blows without retaliating?" "Are you able to endure the ordeal of jail?" We decided to schedule our direct-action program for the Easter season, realizing that except for Christmas, this is the main shopping period of the year. Knowing that a strong economic-withdrawal program would be the by-product of direct action, we felt that this would be the best time to bring pressure to bear on the merchants for the needed change. 8

Then it occurred to us that Birmingham's mayoralty election was coming up in March, and we speedily decided to postpone action until after election day. When we discovered that the Commissioner of Public Safety, Eugene "Bull" Connor, had piled up enough votes to be in the run-off, we decided again to postpone action until the day after the run-off so that the demonstrations could not be used to cloud the issues. Like many others, we waited to see Mr. Connor defeated, and to this end we endured postponement after postponement. Having aided in this community need, we felt that our direct-action program could be delayed no longer. 9

You may well ask: "Why direct action? Why sit-ins, marches and so forth? Isn't negotiation a better path?" You are quite right in calling for negotiation. Indeed, this is the very purpose of direct action. Nonviolent direct action seeks to create such a crisis and foster such a tension that a community which has constantly refused to negotiate is forced to confront the issue. It seeks so to dramatize the issue that it can no longer be ignored. My citing the creation of tension as part of the work of the nonviolent-resister may sound rather shocking. But I must confess that I am not afraid of the word "tension." I have earnestly opposed violent tension, but there is a type of constructive nonviolent tension which is necessary for growth. Just as Socrates felt that it was necessary to create a tension in the mind so that individuals could rise from the bondage of myths and half-truths to the unfettered realm of creative analysis, and objective appraisal, so must we see the need for nonviolent gadflies to create the kind of tension in society that will help men rise from the dark depths of prejudice and racism to the majestic heights of understanding and brotherhood. 10

The purpose of our direct-action program is to create a situation so crisis-packed that it will inevitably open the door to negotiation. I therefore concur with you in your call for negotiation. Too long has our beloved Southland been bogged down in a tragic effort to live in monologue rather than dialogue. 11

One of the basic points in your statement is that the action that I and my 12 associates have taken in Birmingham is untimely. Some have asked: "Why didn't you give the new city administration time to act?" The only answer that I can give to this query is that the new Birmingham administration must be prodded about as much as the outgoing one, before it will act. We are sadly mistaken if we feel that the election of Albert Boutwell as mayor will bring the millennium to Birmingham. While Mr. Boutwell is a much more gentle person than Mr. Connor, they are both segregationists, dedicated to maintenance of the status quo. I have hope that Mr. Boutwell will be reasonable enough to see the futility of massive resistance to desegregation. But he will not see this without pressure from devotees of civil rights. My friends, I must say to you that we have not made a single gain in civil rights without determined legal and nonviolent pressure. Lamentably, it is an historical fact that privileged groups seldom give up their privileges voluntarily. Individuals may see the moral light and voluntarily give up their unjust posture; but, as Reinhold Niebuhr has reminded us, groups tend to be more immoral than individuals.

13   We know through painful experience that freedom is never voluntarily given by the oppressor; it must be demanded by the oppressed. Frankly, I have yet to engage in a direct-action campaign that was "well timed" in the view of those who have not suffered unduly from the disease of segregation. For years now I have heard the word "Wait!" It rings in the ear of every Negro with piercing familiarity. This "Wait" has almost always meant "Never." We must come to see, with one of our distinguished jurists, that "justice too long delayed is justice denied."

14   We have waited for more than 340 years for our constitutional and Godgiven rights. The nations of Asia and Africa are moving with jetlike speed toward gaining political independence, but we still creep at horse-and-buggy pace toward gaining a cup of coffee at a lunch counter. Perhaps it is easy for those who have never felt the stinging darts of segregation to say, "Wait." But when you have seen vicious mobs lynch your mothers and fathers at will and drown your sisters and brothers at whim; when you have seen hate-filled policemen curse, kick and even kill your black brothers and sisters; when you see the vast majority of your twenty million Negro brothers smothering in an airtight cage of poverty in the midst of an affluent society; when you suddenly find your tongue twisted and your speech stammering as you seek to explain to your six-year-old daughter why she can't go to the public amusement park that has just been advertised on television, and see tears welling up in her eyes when she is told that Funtown is closed to colored children, and see ominous clouds of inferiority beginning to form in her little mental sky, and see her beginning to distort her personality by developing an unconscious bitterness toward white people; when you have to concoct an answer for a five-year-old son who is asking: "Daddy, why do white people treat colored people so mean?"; when you take a cross-country drive and find it necessary to sleep night after night in the uncomfortable corners of your

automobile because no motel will accept you; when you are humiliated day in and day out by nagging signs reading "white" and "colored"; when your first name becomes "nigger," your middle name becomes "boy" (however old you are) and your last name becomes "John," and your wife and mother are never given the respected title "Mrs."; when you are harried by day and haunted by night by the fact that you are a Negro, living constantly at tiptoe stance, never quite knowing what to expect next, and are plagued with inner fears and outer resentments; when you are forever fighting a degenerating sense of "nobodiness"—then you will understand why we find it difficult to wait. There comes a time when the cup of endurance runs over, and men are no longer willing to be plunged into the abyss of despair. I hope, sirs, you can understand our legitimate and unavoidable impatience.

You express a great deal of anxiety over our willingness to break laws. 15 This is certainly a legitimate concern. Since we so diligently urge people to obey the Supreme Court's decision of 1954 outlawing segregation in the public schools, at first glance it may seem rather paradoxical for us consciously to break laws. One may well ask: "How can you advocate breaking some laws and obeying others?" The answer lies in the fact that there are two types of laws: just and unjust. I would be the first to advocate obeying just laws. One has not only a legal but a moral responsibility to obey just laws. Conversely, one has a moral responsibility to disobey unjust laws. I would agree with St. Augustine that "an unjust law is no law at all."

Now, what is the difference between the two? How does one determine 16 whether a law is just or unjust? A just law is a man-made code that squares with the moral law or the law of God. An unjust law is a code that is out of harmony with the moral law. To put it in the terms of St. Thomas Aquinas: An unjust law is a human law that is not rooted in eternal law and natural law. Any law that uplifts human personality is just. Any law that degrades human personality is unjust. All segregation statutes are unjust because segregation distorts the soul and damages the personality. It gives the segregator a false sense of superiority and the segregated a false sense of inferiority. Segregation, to use the terminology of the Jewish philosopher Martin Buber, substitutes an "I-it" relationship for an "I-thou" relationship and ends up relegating persons to the status of things. Hence segregation is not only politically, economically and sociologically unsound, it is morally wrong and sinful. Paul Tillich has said that sin is separation. Is not segregation an existential expression of man's tragic separation, his awful estrangement, his terrible sinfulness? Thus it is that I can urge men to obey the 1954 decision of the Supreme Court, for it is morally right; and I can urge them to disobey segregation ordinances, for they are morally wrong.

Let us consider a more concrete example of just and unjust laws. An 17 unjust law is a code that a numerical or power majority group compels a minority group to obey but does not make binding on itself. This is *difference* made legal. By the same token, a just law is a code that a majority compels a minority to follow and that it is willing to follow itself. This is *sameness* made legal.

18 Let me give another explanation. A law is unjust if it is inflicted on a minority that, as a result of being denied the right to vote, had no part in enacting or devising the law. Who can say that the legislature of Alabama which set up that state's segregation laws was democratically elected? Throughout Alabama all sorts of devious methods are used to prevent Negroes from becoming registered voters, and there are some counties in which even though Negroes constitute a majority of the population, not a single Negro is registered. Can any law enacted under such circumstances be considered democratically structured?

19 Sometimes a law is just on its face and unjust in its application. For instance, I have been arrested on a charge of parading without a permit. Now, there is nothing wrong in having an ordinance which requires a permit for a parade. But such an ordinance becomes unjust when it is used to maintain segregation and to deny citizens the First-Amendment privilege of peaceful assembly and protest.

20 I hope you are able to see the distinction I am trying to point out. In no sense do I advocate evading or defying the law, as would the rabid segregationist. That would lead to anarchy. One who breaks an unjust law must do so openly, lovingly, and with a willingness to accept the penalty. I submit that an individual who breaks a law that conscience tells him is unjust, and who willingly accepts the penalty of imprisonment in order to arouse the conscience of the community over its injustice, is in reality expressing the highest respect for law.

21 Of course, there is nothing new about this kind of civil disobedience. It was evidenced sublimely in the refusal of Shadrach, Meshach and Abednego to obey the laws of Nebuchadnezzar, on the ground that a higher moral law was at stake. It was practiced superbly by the early Christians, who were willing to face hungry lions and the excruciating pain of chopping blocks rather than submit to certain unjust laws of the Roman Empire. To a degree, academic freedom is a reality today because Socrates practiced civil disobedience. In our own nation, the Boston Tea Party represented a massive act of civil disobedience.

22 We should never forget that everything Adolf Hitler did in Germany was "legal" and everything the Hungarian freedom fighters did in Hungary was "illegal." It was "illegal" to aid and comfort a Jew in Hitler's Germany. Even so, I am sure that, had I lived in Germany at the time, I would have aided and comforted my Jewish brothers. If today I lived in a Communist country where certain principles dear to the Christian faith are suppressed, I would openly advocate disobeying that country's antireligious laws.

23 I must make two honest confessions to you, my Christian and Jewish brothers. First, I must confess that over the past few years I have been gravely disappointed with the white moderate. I have almost reached the regrettable

conclusion that the Negro's great stumbling block in his stride toward freedom is not the White Citizen's Counciler or the Ku Klux Klanner, but the white moderate, who is more devoted to "order" than to justice; who prefers a negative peace which is the absence of tension to a positive peace which is the presence of justice; who constantly says: "I agree with you in the goal you seek, but I cannot agree with your methods of direct action"; who paternalistically believes he can set the timetable for another man's freedom; who lives by a mythical concept of time and who constantly advises the Negro to wait for a "more convenient season." Shallow understanding from people of good will is more frustrating than absolute misunderstanding from people of ill will. Lukewarm acceptance is much more bewildering than outright rejection.

I had hoped that the white moderate would understand that law and order exist for the purpose of establishing justice and that when they fail in this purpose they become the dangerously structured dams that block the flow of social progress. I had hoped that the white moderate would understand that the present tension in the South is a necessary phase of the transition from an obnoxious negative peace, in which the Negro passively accepted his unjust plight, to a substantive and positive peace, in which all men will respect the dignity and worth of human personality. Actually, we who engage in nonviolent direct action are not the creators of tension. We merely bring to the surface the hidden tension that is already alive. We bring it out in the open, where it can be seen and dealt with. Like a boil that can never be cured so long as it is covered up but must be opened with all its ugliness to the natural medicines of air and light, injustice must be exposed, with all the tension its exposure creates, to the light of human conscience and the air of national opinion before it can be cured. 24

In your statement you assert that our actions, even though peaceful, must be condemned because they precipitate violence. But is this a logical assertion? Isn't this like condemning a robbed man because his possession of money precipitated the evil act of robbery? Isn't this like condemning Socrates because his unswerving commitment to truth and his philosophical inquiries precipitated the act by the misguided populace in which they made him drink hemlock? Isn't this like condemning Jesus because his unique God-consciousness and never-ceasing devotion to God's will precipitated the evil act of crucifixion? We must come to see that, as the federal courts have consistently affirmed, it is wrong to urge an individual to cease his efforts to gain his basic constitutional rights because the quest may precipitate violence. Society must protect the robbed and punish the robber. 25

I had also hoped that the white moderate would reject the myth concerning time in relation to the struggle for freedom. I have just received a letter from a white brother in Texas. He writes: "All Christians know that the colored people will receive equal rights eventually, but it is possible that you are in too great a religious hurry. It has taken Christianity almost two 26 thousand years to accomplish what it has. The teachings of Christ take time to come to earth." Such an attitude stems from a tragic misconception of time, from the strangely irrational notion that there is something in the very flow of time that will inevitably cure all ills. Actually, time itself is neutral; it can be used either destructively or constructively. More and more I feel that the people of ill will have used time much more effectively than have the people of good will. We will have to repent in this generation not merely for the hateful words and actions of the bad people but for the appalling silence of the good people. Human progress never rolls in on wheels of inevitability; it comes through the tireless efforts of men willing to be co-workers with God, and without this hard work, time itself becomes an ally of the forces of social stagnation. We must use time creatively, in the knowledge that the time is always ripe to do right. Now is the time to make real the promise of democracy and transform our pending national elegy into a creative psalm of brotherhood. Now is the time to lift our national policy from the quicksand of racial injustice to the solid rock of human dignity.

27   You speak of our activity in Birmingham as extreme. At first I was rather disappointed that fellow clergymen would see my nonviolent efforts as those of an extremist. I began thinking about the fact that I stand in the middle of two opposing forces in the Negro community. One is a force of complacency, made up in part of Negroes who, as a result of long years of oppression, are so drained of self-respect and a sense of "somebodiness" that they have adjusted to segregation; and in part of a few middle-class Negroes who, because of a degree of academic and economic security and because in some ways they profit by segregation, have become insensitive to the problems of the masses. The other force is one of bitterness and hatred, and it comes perilously close to advocating violence. It is expressed in the various black nationalist groups that are springing up across the nation, the largest and best-known being Elijah Muhammad's Muslim movement. Nourished by the Negro's frustration over the continued existence of racial discrimination, this movement is made up of people who have lost faith in America, who have absolutely repudiated Christianity, and who have concluded that the white man is an incorrigible "devil."

28   I have tried to stand between these two forces, saying that we need emulate neither the "do-nothingism" of the complacent nor the hatred and despair of the black nationalist. For there is the more excellent way of love and nonviolent protest. I am grateful to God that, through the influence of the Negro church, the way of nonviolence became an integral part of our struggle.

29   If this philosophy had not emerged, by now many streets of the South would, I am convinced, be flowing with blood. And I am further convinced that if our white brothers dismiss as "rabble-rousers" and "outside agitators" those of us who employ nonviolent direct action, and if they refuse to support our nonviolent efforts, millions of Negroes will, out of frustration and

despair, seek solace and security in black-nationalist ideologies—a development that would inevitably lead to a frightening racial nightmare.

Oppressed people cannot remain oppressed forever. The yearning for freedom eventually manifests itself, and that is what has happened to the American Negro. Something within has reminded him of his birthright of freedom, and something without has reminded him that it can be gained. Consciously or unconsciously, he has been caught up by the *Zeitgeist,* and with his black brothers of Africa and his brown and yellow brothers of Asia, South America and the Caribbean, the United States Negro is moving with a sense of great urgency toward the promised land of racial justice. If one recognizes this vital urge that has engulfed the Negro community, one should readily understand why public demonstrations are taking place. The Negro has many pent-up resentments and latent frustrations, and he must release them. So let him march; let him make prayer pilgrimages to the city hall; let him go on freedom rides—and try to understand why he must do so. If his repressed emotions are not released in nonviolent ways, they will seek expression through violence; this is not a threat but a fact of history. So I have not said to my people: "Get rid of your discontent." Rather, I have tried to say that this normal and healthy discontent can be channeled into the creative outlet of nonviolent direct action. And now this approach is being termed extremist.

But though I was initially disappointed at being categorized as an extremist, as I continued to think about the matter I gradually gained a measure of satisfaction from the label. Was not Jesus an extremist for love: "Love your enemies, bless them that curse you, do good to them that hate you, and pray for them which despitefully use you, and persecute you." Was not Amos an extremist for justice: "Let justice roll down like waters and righteousness like an ever-flowing stream." Was not Paul an extremist for the Christian gospel: "I bear in my body the marks of the Lord Jesus." Was not Martin Luther an extremist: "Here I stand; I cannot do otherwise, so help me God." And John Bunyan: "I will stay in jail to the end of my days before I make a butchery of my conscience." And Abraham Lincoln: "This nation cannot survive half slave and half free." And Thomas Jefferson: "We hold these truths to be self-evident, that all men are created equal. . . ." So the question is not whether we will be extremists, but what kind of extremists we will be. Will we be extremists for hate or for love? Will we be extremists for the preservation of injustice or for the extension of justice? In that dramatic scene on Calvary's hill three men were crucified. We must never forget that all three were crucified for the same crime—the crime of extremism. Two were extremists for immorality, and thus fell below their environment. The other, Jesus Christ, was an extremist for love, truth and goodness, and thereby rose above his environment. Perhaps the South, the nation and the world are in dire need of creative extremists.

I had hoped that the white moderate would see this need. Perhaps I was

30

31

32

313

too optimistic; perhaps I expected too much. I suppose I should have realized that few members of the oppressor race can understand the deep groans and passionate yearnings of the oppressed race, and still fewer have the vision to see that injustice must be rooted out by strong, persistent and determined action. I am thankful, however, that some of our white brothers in the South have grasped the meaning of this social revolution and committed themselves to it. They are still all too few in quantity, but they are big in quality. Some— such as Ralph McGill, Lillian Smith, Harry Golden, James McBride Dabbs, Ann Braden and Sarah Patton Boyle—have written about our struggle in eloquent and prophetic terms. Others have marched with us down nameless streets of the South. They have languished in filthy, roach-infested jails, suffering the abuse and brutality of policemen who view them as "dirty nigger-lovers." Unlike so many of their moderate brothers and sisters, they have recognized the urgency of the moment and sensed the need for powerful "action" antidotes to combat the disease of segregation.

33   Let me take note of my other major disappointment. I have been so greatly disappointed with the white church and its leadership. Of course, there are some notable exceptions. I am not unmindful of the fact that each of you has taken some significant stands on this issue. I commend you, Reverend Stallings, for your Christian stand on this past Sunday, in welcoming Negroes to your worship service on a nonsegregated basis. I commend the Catholic leaders of this state for integrating Spring Hill College several years ago.

34   But despite these notable exceptions, I must honestly reiterate that I have been disappointed with the church. I do not say this as one of those negative critics who can always find something wrong with the church. I say this as a minister of the gospel, who loves the church; who was nurtured in its bosom; who has been sustained by its spiritual blessings and who will remain true to it as long as the cord of life shall lengthen.

35   When I was suddenly catapulted into the leadership of the bus protest in Montgomery, Alabama, a few years ago, I felt we would be supported by the white church. I felt that the white ministers, priests and rabbis of the South would be among our strongest allies. Instead, some have been outright opponents, refusing to understand the freedom movement and misrepresenting its leaders; all too many others have been more cautious than courageous and have remained silent behind the anesthetizing security of stained-glass windows.

36   In spite of my shattered dreams, I came to Birmingham with the hope that the white religious leadership of this community would see the justice of our cause and, with deep moral concern, would serve as the channel through which our just grievances could reach the power structure. I had hoped that each of you would understand. But again I have been disappointed.

37   I have heard numerous southern religious leaders admonish their worshipers to comply with a desegregation decision because it is the law, but I

have longed to hear white ministers declare: "Follow this decree because integration is morally right and because the Negro is your brother." In the midst of blatant injustices inflicted upon the Negro, I have watched white churchmen stand on the sideline and mouth pious irrelevancies and sanctimonious trivialities. In the midst of a mighty struggle to rid our nation of racial and economic injustice, I have heard many ministers say: "Those are social issues, with which the gospel has no real concern." And I have watched many churches commit themselves to a completely other-worldly religion which makes a strange, un-Biblical distinction between body and soul, between the sacred and the secular.

I have traveled the length and breadth of Alabama, Mississippi and all the other southern states. On sweltering summer days and crisp autumn mornings I have looked at the South's beautiful churches with their lofty spires pointing heavenward. I have beheld the impressive outlines of her massive religious-education buildings. Over and over I have found myself asking: "What kind of people worship here? Who is their God? Where were their voices when the lips of Governor Barnett dripped with words of interposition and nullification? Where were they when Governor Wallace gave a clarion call for defiance and hatred? Where were their voices of support when bruised and weary Negro men and women decided to rise from the dark dungeons of complacency to the bright hills of creative protest?" 38

Yes, these questions are still in my mind. In deep disappointment I have wept over the laxity of the church. But be assured that my tears have been tears of love. There can be no deep disappointment where there is not deep love. Yes, I love the church. How could I do otherwise? I am in the rather unique position of being the son, the grandson and the great-grandson of preachers. Yes, I see the church as the body of Christ. But, oh! How we have blemished and scarred that body through social neglect and through fear of being nonconformists. 39

There was a time when the church was very powerful—in the time when the early Christians rejoiced at being deemed worthy to suffer for what they believed. In those days the church was not merely a thermometer that recorded the ideas and principles of popular opinion; it was a thermostat that transformed the mores of society. Whenever the early Christians entered a town, the people in power became disturbed and immediately sought to convict the Christians for being "disturbers of the peace" and "outside agitators." But the Christians pressed on, in the conviction that they were "a colony of heaven," called to obey God rather than man. Small in number, they were big in commitment. They were too God-intoxicated to be "astronomically intimidated." By their effort and example they brought an end to such ancient evils as infanticide and gladiatorial contests. 40

Things are different now. So often the contemporary church is a weak, ineffectual voice with an uncertain sound. So often it is an archdefender of the status quo. Far from being disturbed by the presence of the church, the 41 power structure of the average community is consoled by the church's silent—and often even vocal—sanction of things as they are.

42 But the judgment of God is upon the church as never before. If today's church does not recapture the sacrificial spirit of the early church, it will lose its authenticity, forfeit the loyalty of millions, and be dismissed as an irrelevant social club with no meaning for the twentieth century. Every day I meet young people whose disappointment with the church has turned into outright disgust.

43 Perhaps I have once again been too optimistic. Is organized religion too inextricably bound to the status quo to save our nation and the world? Perhaps I must turn my faith to the inner spiritual church, the church within the church, as the true *ekklesia* and the hope of the world. But again I am thankful to God that some noble souls from the ranks of organized religion have broken loose from the paralyzing chains of conformity and joined us as active partners in the struggle for freedom. They have left their secure congregations and walked the streets of Albany, Georgia, with us. They have gone down the highways of the South on tortuous rides for freedom. Yes, they have gone to jail with us. Some have been dismissed from their churches, have lost the support of their bishops and fellow ministers. But they have acted in the faith that right defeated is stronger than evil triumphant. Their witness has been the spiritual salt that has preserved the true meaning of the gospel in these troubled times. They have carved a tunnel of hope through the dark mountain of disappointment.

44 I hope the church as a whole will meet the challenge of this decisive hour. But even if the church does not come to the aid of justice, I have no despair about the future. I have no fear about the outcome of our struggle in Birmingham, even if our motives are at present misunderstood. We will reach the goal of freedom in Birmingham and all over the nation, because the goal of America is freedom. Abused and scorned though we may be, our destiny is tied up with America's destiny. Before the pilgrims landed at Plymouth, we were here. Before the pen of Jefferson etched the majestic words of the Declaration of Independence across the pages of history, we were here. For more than two centuries our forebears labored in this country without wages; they made cotton king; they built the homes of their masters while suffering gross injustice and shameful humiliation—and yet out of a bottomless vitality they continued to thrive and develop. If the inexpressible cruelties of slavery could not stop us, the opposition we now face will surely fail. We will win our freedom because the sacred heritage of our nation and the eternal will of God are embodied in our echoing demands.

45 Before closing I feel impelled to mention one other point in your statement that has troubled me profoundly. You warmly commended the Birmingham police force for keeping "order" and "preventing violence." I doubt that you would have so warmly commended the police force if you had seen

its dogs sinking their teeth into unarmed, nonviolent Negroes. I doubt that you would so quickly commend the policemen if you were to observe their ugly and inhumane treatment of Negroes here in the city jail; if you were to watch them push and curse old Negro women and young Negro girls; if you were to see them slap and kick old Negro men and young boys; if you were to observe them as they did on two occasions, refuse to give us food because we wanted to sing our grace together. I cannot join you in your praise of the Birmingham police department.

It is true that the police have exercised a degree of discipline in handling the demonstrators. In this sense they have conducted themselves rather "non-violently" in public. But for what purpose? To preserve the evil system of segregation. Over the past few years I have consistently preached that non-violence demands that the means we use must be as pure as the ends we seek. I have tried to make clear that it is wrong to use immoral means to attain moral ends. But now I must affirm that it is just as wrong, or perhaps even more so, to use moral means to preserve immoral ends. Perhaps Mr. Connor and his policemen have been rather nonviolent in public, as was Chief Pritchett in Albany, Georgia, but they have used the moral means of nonviolence to maintain the immoral end of racial injustice. As T. S. Eliot has said: "The last temptation is the greatest treason: To do the right deed for the wrong reason." 46

I wish you had commended the Negro sit-inners and demonstrators of Birmingham for their sublime courage, their willingness to suffer and their amazing discipline in the midst of great provocation. One day the South will recognize its real heroes. They will be the James Merediths, with the noble sense of purpose that enables them to face jeering and hostile mobs, and with the agonizing loneliness that characterizes the life of the pioneer. They will be old, oppressed, battered Negro women, symbolized in a seventy-two-year-old woman in Montgomery, Alabama, who rose up with a sense of dignity and with her people decided not to ride segregated buses, and who responded with ungrammatical profundity to one who inquired about her weariness: "My feet is tired, but my soul is at rest." They will be the young high school and college students, the young ministers of the gospel and a host of their elders, courageously and nonviolently sitting in at lunch counters and willingly going to jail for conscience' sake. One day the South will know that when these disinherited children of God sat down at lunch counters, they were in reality standing up for what is best in the American dream and for the most sacred values in our Judaeo-Christian heritage, thereby bringing our nation back to those great wells of democracy which were dug deep by the founding fathers in their formulation of the Constitution and the Declaration of Independence. 47

Never before have I written so long a letter. I'm afraid it is much too long to take your precious time. I can assure you that it would have been much 48 shorter if I had been writing from a comfortable desk, but what else can one do when he is alone in a narrow jail cell, other than write long letters, think long thoughts and pray long prayers?

49   If I have said anything in this letter that overstates the truth and indicates an unreasonable impatience, I beg you to forgive me. If I have said anything that understates the truth and indicates my having a patience that allows me to settle for anything less than brotherhood, I beg God to forgive me.

50   I hope this letter finds you strong in the faith. I also hope that circumstances will soon make it possible for me to meet each of you, not as an integrationist or a civil-rights leader but as a fellow clergyman and a Christian brother. Let us all hope that the dark clouds of racial prejudice will soon pass away and the deep fog of misunderstanding will be lifted from our fear-drenched communities, and in some not too distant tomorrow the radiant stars of love and brotherhood will shine over our great nation with all their scintillating beauty.

> Yours for the cause of Peace and Brotherhood,
> Martin Luther King, Jr.

Questions

1. When King was jailed in Birmingham in 1963 he was the world's foremost leader in the civil rights movement, and could consequently assume that anything he wrote from jail would be read worldwide, irrespective of its recipient. Is King's document a letter, conventionally considered a written communication to a particular (and usually, restricted) audience, or a manifesto, a public declaration of beliefs, opinions, objectives, policy? What clues in the text provide your answer?

2. In paragraph 4 King makes several assertions on which he bases the rest of his extensive argument. What are they? Does he ever prove them, or does he assume that readers, even his antagonists, will take them for granted? Likewise, in paragraph 5 King asserts that Birmingham's "white power structure left the Negro community with no alternative" but to commit civil disobedience. Does he ever prove this? Does he need to? Is it a debatable statement?

3. How does King deal with the argument that civil rights activists are too impatient, that they should go slow because " 'It has taken Christianity almost two thousand years to accomplish what it has' " (paragraph 26)? Compare his argument with Baldwin's rebuttal to Faulkner (299–304) in evidence, approach to the audience, and tone.

4. King uses a wide and varied array of evidence to support his argument, including the views of theologians; assertions of principle—legal, moral, and divine; analyses of America's and Georgia's history and current politics; and incidents from his own experience, as a Southern black, a clergyman, a parent, and a civil rights leader. Identify some of these types of evidence (and others, if you wish) and comment on their suitability to his argument. Is each type of evidence equally appropriate, or is some evidence more convincing than other evidence? Explain your answer.

SISSELA BOK

Placebos

Bok, a moral philosopher, was born in Stockholm, Sweden, in 1934, the daughter of economist Gunnar Myrdal. She studied at the Sorbonne before earning a B.A. from George Washington University in 1957 and a Ph.D. from Harvard in 1970. Since 1972 Bok has been affiliated with the Harvard-MIT Division of Health Sciences and Technology as a lecturer in medical ethics and as director of projects on teaching ethics and on professional ethics. Her numerous writings on the subject include an edited volume, The Dilemmas of Euthanasia *(1975), and* Secrets: On the Ethics of Concealment and Revelation *(1983), which focuses on increased secrecy in medicine, law, and government—for instance, through the use of lie-detector tests. Like other philosophers, Bok is opposed to lying, though she takes issue with some in claiming that "In special situations, lying can be justifiable—as in crises that are clear-cut and life-threatening," such as when police lie to criminals to secure the release of hostages.*

Bok's prevailing view, however, is represented in the following selection, a chapter from Lying: Moral Choices in Public and Private Life *(1978). Here she agues that whenever physicians lie to their patients by administering placebos—sugar pills or other supposedly benign substances—instead of genuine medicine, they ignore possible harm and fail "to see how gestures assumed to be trivial build up into collectively undesirable practices." Here she begins with a single, apparently minor case of a high school girl whose doctor prescribed vitamins instead of the tranquilizers she requested. Bok then widens the scope of her argument, and of the problem, by showing the potentially devastating consequences of such seemingly innocuous actions on much larger groups—indeed, on whole populations, including parents who insist on unnecessary antibiotics for their children, and unwitting control groups in experiments. Her dispassionate tone and logical organization are characteristic of moral argument, as is Bok's ultimate appeal to the common values of openness and truth that she and her readers are presumed to share.*

The common practice of prescribing placebos to unwitting patients illustrates the two miscalculations so common to minor forms of deceit: ignoring possible harm and failing to see how gestures assumed to be trivial build up into collectively undesirable practices. Placebos have been used since the beginning of medicine. They can be sugar pills, salt-water injections—in fact, any medical procedure which has no specific effect on a patient's condition, but which can have powerful psychological effects leading to relief from symptoms such as pain or depression.

Placebos are prescribed with great frequency. Exactly how often cannot be known, the less so as physicians do not ordinarily talk publicly about using them. At times, self-deception enters in on the part of physicians, so that they have unwarranted faith in the powers of what can work only as a placebo. As with salesmanship, medication often involves unjustified belief in the excellence of what is suggested to others. In the past, most remedies were of a kind that, unknown to the medical profession and their patients, could have only placebic benefits, if any.

3   The derivation of "placebo," from the Latin for "I shall please," gives the word a benevolent ring, somehow placing placebos beyond moral criticism and conjuring up images of hypochondriacs whose vague ailments are dispelled through adroit prescriptions of beneficent sugar pills. Physicians often give a humorous tinge to instructions for prescribing these substances, which helps to remove them from serious ethical concern. One authority wrote in a pharmacological journal that the placebo should be given a name previously unknown to the patient and preferably Latin and polysyllabic, and added:

> [I]t is wise if it be prescribed with some assurance and emphasis for psycho-therapeutic effect. The older physicians each had his favorite placebic prescriptions—one chose tincture of Condurango, another the Fluidextract of *Cimicifuga nigra*.

4   After all, health professionals argue, are not placebos far less dangerous than some genuine drugs? And more likely to produce a cure than if nothing at all is prescribed? Such a view was expressed in a letter to *The Lancet*:

> Whenever pain can be relieved with a ml of saline, why should we inject an opiate? Do anxieties or discomforts that are allayed with starch capsules require administration of a barbiturate, diazepam, or propoxyphene?

5   Such a simplistic view conceals the real costs of placebos, both to individuals and to the practice of medicine. First, the resort to placebos may actually prevent the treatment of an underlying, undiagnosed problem. And even if the placebo "works," the effect is often short-lived; the symptoms may recur, or crop up in other forms. Very often, the symptoms of which the patient complains are bound to go away by themselves, sometimes even from the mere contact with a health professional. In those cases, the placebo itself is unnecessary; having recourse to it merely reinforces a tendency to depend upon pills or treatments where none is needed.

6   In the aggregate, the costs of placebos are immense. Many millions of dollars are expended on drugs, diagnostic tests, and psychotherapies of a placebic nature. Even operations can be of this nature—a hysterectomy may thus be performed, not because the condition of the patient requires such surgery, but because she goes from one doctor to another seeking to have the surgery performed, or because she is judged to have a great fear of cancer which might be alleviated by the very fact of the operation.

7   Even apart from financial and emotional costs and the squandering of resources, the practice of giving placebos is wasteful of a very precious good: the trust on which so much in the medical relationship depends. The trust of those patients who find out they have been duped is lost, sometimes irretrievably. They may then lose confidence in physicians and even in bona fide

medication which they may need in the future. They may obtain for themselves more harmful drugs or attach their hopes to debilitating fad cures.

The following description of a case where a placebo was prescribed reflects a common approach: 8

A seventeen-year-old girl visited her pediatrician, who had been taking care of her since infancy. She went to his office without her parents, although her mother had made the appointment for her over the telephone. She told the pediatrician that she was very healthy, but that she thought she had some emotional problems. She stated that she was having trouble sleeping at night, that she was very nervous most of the day. She was a senior in high school and claimed she was doing quite poorly in most of her subjects. She was worried about what she was going to do next year. She was somewhat overweight. This, she felt, was part of her problem. She claimed she was not very attractive to the opposite sex and could not seem to "get boys interested in me." She had a few close friends of the same sex.

Her life at home was quite chaotic and stressful. There were frequent battles with her younger brother, who was fourteen, and with her parents. She claimed her parents were always "on my back." She described her mother as extremely rigid and her father as a disciplinarian, who was quite old-fashioned in his values.

In all, she spent about twenty minutes talking with her pediatrician. She told him that what she thought she really needed was tranquilizers, and that that was the reason she came. She felt that this was an extremely difficult year for her, and if she could have something to calm her nerves until she got over her current crises, everything would go better.

The pediatrician told her that he did not really believe in giving tranquilizers to a girl of her age. He said he thought it would be a bad precedent for her to establish. She was very insistent, however, and claimed that if he did not give her tranquilizers, she would "get them somehow." Finally, he agreed to call her pharmacy and order medication for her nerves. She accepted graciously. He suggested that she call him in a few days to let him know how things were going. He also called her parents to say that he had a talk with her and was giving her some medicine that might help her nerves.

Five days later, the girl called the pediatrician back to say that the pills were really working well. She claimed that she had calmed down a great deal, that she was working things out better with her parents, and had a new outlook on life. He suggested that she keep taking them twice a day for the rest of the school year. She agreed.

A month later, the girl ran out of pills and called her pediatrician for a refill. She found that he was away on vacation. She was quite distraught at not having any medication left, so she called her uncle who was a surgeon in the next town. He called the pharmacy to renew her pills and, in speaking to the druggist, found out that they were only vitamins. He told the girl that the pills were only vitamins and that she could get them over the counter and didn't really need him to refill them. The girl became very distraught, feeling that she had been deceived and betrayed by her pediatrician. Her parents, when they heard, commented that they thought the pediatrician was "very clever."

9   The patients who do *not* discover the deception and are left believing that a placebic remedy has worked may continue to rely on it under the wrong circumstances. This is especially true with drugs such as antibiotics, which are sometimes used as placebos and sometimes for their specific action. Many parents, for example, come to believe that they must ask for the prescription of antibiotics every time their child has a fever or a cold. The fact that so many doctors accede to such requests perpetuates the dependence of these families on medical care they do not need and weakens their ability to cope with health problems. Worst of all, those children who cannot tolerate antibiotics may have severe reactions, sometimes fatal, to such unnecessary medication.

10   Such deceptive practices, by their very nature, tend to escape the normal restraints of accountability and can therefore spread more easily than others. There are many instances in which an innocuous-seeming practice has grown to become a large-scale and more dangerous one. Although warnings against the "entering wedge" are often rhetorical devices, they can at times express justifiable caution; especially when there are great pressures to move along the undesirable path and when the safeguards are insufficient.

11   In this perspective, there is much reason for concern about placebos. The safeguards against this practice are few or nonexistent—both because it is secretive in nature and because it is condoned but rarely carefully discussed in the medical literature. And the pressures are very great, and growing stronger, from drug companies, patients eager for cures, and busy physicians, for more medication, whether it is needed or not. Given this lack of safeguards and these strong pressures, the use of placebos can spread in a number of ways.

12   The clearest danger lies in the gradual shift from pharmacologically inert placebos to more active ones. It is not always easy to distinguish completely inert substances from somewhat active ones and these in turn from more active ones. It may be hard to distinguish between a quantity of an active substance so low that it has little or no effect and quantities that have some effect. It is not always clear to doctors whether patients require an inert placebo or possibly a more active one, and there can be the temptation to resort to an active one just in case it might also have a specific effect. It is also much easier to deceive a patient with a medication that is known to be "real" and to have power. One recent textbook in medicine goes so far as to advocate the use of small doses of effective compounds as placebos rather than inert substances—because it is important for both the doctor and the patient to believe in the treatment! This shift is made easier because the dangers and side effects of active agents are not always known or considered important by the physician.

Meanwhile, the number of patients receiving placebos increases as more   13
and more people seek and receive medical care and as their desire for instant,
push-button alleviation of symptoms is stimulated by drug advertising and by
rising expectations of what science can do. The use of placebos for children
grows as well, and the temptations to manipulate the truth are less easily
resisted once such great inroads have already been made.

Deception by placebo can also spread from therapy and diagnosis to   14
experimentation. Much experimentation with placebos is honest and consented to by the experimental subjects, especially since the advent of strict
rules governing such experimentation. But grievous abuses have taken place
where placebos were given to unsuspecting subjects who believed they had
received another substance. In 1971, for example, a number of Mexican-
American women applied to a family-planning clinic for contraceptives.
Some of them were given oral contraceptives and others were given placebos,
or dummy pills that looked like the real thing. Without fully informed consent, the women were being used in an experiment to explore the side effects
of various contraceptive pills. Some of those who were given placebos experienced a predictable side effect—they became pregnant. The investigators
neither assumed financial responsibility for the babies nor indicated any concern about having bypassed the "informed consent" that is required in ethical
experiments with human beings. One contented himself with the observation
that if only the law had permitted it, he could have aborted the pregnant
women!

The failure to think about the ethical problems in such a case stems at   15
least in part from the innocent-seeming white lies so often told in giving
placebos. The spread from therapy to experimentation and from harmlessness
to its opposite often goes unnoticed in part *because* of the triviality believed to
be connected with placebos as white lies. This lack of foresight and concern is
most frequent when the subjects in the experiment are least likely to object
or defend themselves; as with the poor, the institutionalized, and the very
young.

In view of all these ways in which placebo usage can spread, it is not   16
enough to look at each incident of manipulation in isolation, no matter how
benevolent it may be. When the costs and benefits are weighed, not only the
individual consequences must be considered, but also the cumulative ones.
Reports of deceptive practices inevitably leak out, and the resulting suspicion
is heightened by the anxiety which threats to health always create. And so
even the health professionals who do not mislead their patients are injured by
those who do; the entire institution of medicine is threatened by practices
lacking in candor, however harmless the results may appear in some individual cases.

This is not to say that all placebos must be ruled out; merely that they   17
cannot be excused as innocuous. They should be prescribed but rarely, and
only after a careful diagnosis and consideration of non-deceptive alternatives;

they should be used in experimentation only after subjects have consented to their use.

Questions

1. Bok begins her argument by defining the key term *placebo* (paragraph 1) in a neutral, nonjudgmental way. At what point in her argument does her disapproval of the use of placebos become apparent?

2. From paragraph 5 on, Bok identifies and criticizes the "real costs of placebos, both to individuals and to the practice of medicine." What are these costs? What determines the order in which Bok presents these? Does Bok make any distinction among the kinds of placebos and the different circumstances under which they are administered, or does she consider every use of a placebo equally problematic?

3. Bok's tone is dispassionate and unemotional, in comparison with the impassioned tone of Baldwin and Faulkner, who are also arguing on moral grounds. Is restraint or emotion better in making moral arguments, or does the tone depend on the nature of the subject and the writer's temperament and authorial stance? Explain your answer.

4. Show how and where Bok anticipates contradictory arguments from lay or medical persons favoring placebos and incorporates rebuttals into her argument. Is it possible to argue effectively without doing this?

PHILIPPE ARIES

The Reversal of Death: Changes in Attitude Toward Death in Western Societies

Aries (1914–1984), from Maisons Lafitte, France, was trained in history at the Sorbonne, and modestly described himself as a "weekend historian"; he worked in Paris as an agronomic researcher at the Institute of Applied Research for Tropical and Subtropical Fruits. Yet during the last twenty-five years of his life he produced major books on childhood and on death that have significantly changed our understanding of how western culture has viewed these most fundamental human experiences. Centuries of Childhood: A Social History of Family Life *(1960) discusses the development of family relationships in Western Europe, as reflected in changing conceptions of childhood, whether tender or tough, innocent or depraved. Aries's most recent works,* Western Attitudes Toward Death *(1974) and* The Hour of Our Death *(1981), synthesize a thousand years of human experiences of death and mourning.*

In "The Reversal of Death" Aries not only demonstrates, through abundant examples from life and literature, that "for thousands of years man was lord and master of his death, and the circumstances surrounding it. Today this has ceased to be so." Through these same examples Aries also presents an argument, more often implied than stated explicitly, that the old ways of dealing with death are far superior to the new, for they are honest, not hypocrit-

324

ical, and maintain the dignity and control of the dying person. A major challenge of this kind of argument, which covers a vast amount of material in a few pages, is to move quickly and yet remain convincing. His comprehensive knowledge of the subject enables him to choose compelling examples; with stylistic finesse he paints vivid miniatures, quick sketches. Thus to illustrate the thesis of the first paragraph, quoted above, Aries interprets the deaths of LaFontaine's plowman, Roland, Tristam, Tolstoy's peasants, Don Quixote, Mme. de La Ferronnays, Louis XIV, and Mme. de Montespan. We follow the priest with the viaticum; *we are there. Such details establish not only Aries's argument but his credibility; any author who knows how cobblers died in the fourteenth century must understand how people die today. Thus, when we come to the crux—and most debatable part—of his argument we are likely to trust the author, for he has already won our confidence.*

For thousands of years man was lord and master of his death, and the circumstances surrounding it. Today this has ceased to be so.   1

It used to be understood and accepted that a man knew when he was dying, whether he became spontaneously aware of the fact or whether he had to be told. It seemed reasonable to our old storytellers that, as the plowman in La Fontaine says, man would feel his approaching death. In those days death was rarely sudden, even in the case of an accident or a war, and sudden death was much feared, not only because there was no time for repentance, but because it deprived a man of the experience of death. Thus death was almost always presaged, especially since even minor illnesses often turned out to be fatal. One would have had to be mad not to see the signs, and moralists and satirists made it their job to ridicule those foolish enough to deny the evidence. Roland "feels that death is taking all of him," Tristam "felt that his life was draining away, he realized that he was dying." Tolstoy's peasant replied to the goodwoman who asked him if he were all right: "Death is here"; for Tolstoy's peasants died like Tristam or like La Fontaine's plowman, having the same resigned, comfortable attitude toward it. This is not to say that the attitude toward death was the same throughout all this long period of time, but that it survived in some social strata from one generation to the next despite competition from other styles of death.   2

When the person involved was not the first to become aware of his fate, others were expected to warn him. A papal document of the Middle Ages made this a task of the doctor, a task he for a long time carried out unflinchingly. We find him at Don Quixote's bedside: "He took his pulse, and was not happy with the results. He therefore told him that whatever he did, he should think of saving his soul, as his body was in grave danger." The *artes moriendi* of the fifteenth century also charged with this task the "spiritual" friend (as opposed to "carnal" friends), who went by the name—so repugnant to our modern fastidiousness—of *nuncius mortis*.   3

As man progressed through time, the higher up the social and urban ladder he climbed, the less he himself was aware of his approaching death, and the more he had to be prepared for it; consequently, the more he had to   4 depend on those around him. The doctor renounced the role that for so long had been his, probably in the eighteenth century. In the nineteenth century he spoke only when questioned, and then somewhat reticently. Friends no longer had to intervene, as in the time of Gerson or even Cervantes, because from the seventeenth century on, it was the family that took care of this—a sign of development in family feeling. An example of this can be seen in the de La Ferronnays household in 1848. Mme. de La Ferronnays had fallen ill. The doctor announced that her condition was dangerous, and "one hour later, hopeless." Her daughter wrote: "When she came out of the bath . . . she suddenly said to me, while I was thinking of a good way to tell her what the doctor thought: 'but I can't see anything any more, I think I'm going to die.' " She immediately recited an ejaculatory prayer. " 'Oh Jesus,' " the daughter then remarked, " 'what a strange joy I felt from those calm words at such a terrible time.' " She was relieved because she had been spared the distress of making a nevertheless indispensable disclosure. The relief is a modern characteristic, the necessity to disclose the truth is ancient.

5   Not only was the dying man to be deprived of his death, he also had to preside over it. As people were born in public, so did they die in public, and not only the king, as is well known from Saint-Simon's famous pages on the death of Louis XIV, but everyone. Countless engravings and paintings depict that scene for us. As soon as someone "was helplessly sick in bed," his room filled with people—parents, children, friends, neighbors, fellow guild members. The windows and shutters were closed. Candles were lit. When passersby in the streets met a priest carrying the *viaticum*, custom and piety demanded that they follow him into the dying man's room, even if he was a stranger. The approach of death transformed the room of a dying man into a sort of public place. Pascal's remark, "man will die alone," which has lost much of its impact on us since today man almost always dies alone, can only be understood in this context. For what Pascal meant was that in spite of all the people crowded around his bed, the dying man was alone. The enlightened doctors of the end of the eighteenth century, who believed in the qualities of fresh air, complained a great deal about this bad habit of crowding into the rooms of sick people. They tried to have the windows opened, the candles snuffed, and the crowd of people turned out.

6   We should not make the mistake of thinking that to be present at these last moments was a devout custom prescribed by the Church. The enlightened or reformed priests had tried, long before the doctors, to do away with this crowd so that they could better prepare the sick person for a virtuous end. As early as the *artes moriendi* of the fifteenth century it had been recommended that the dying man be left alone with God so that he should not be distracted from the care of his soul. And again, in the nineteenth century, it sometimes happened that very pious people, after yielding to the custom, asked the numerous onlookers to leave the room, all except the priest, so that nothing would disturb their private conversation with God. But these were

rare examples of extreme devotion. Custom prescribed that death was to be marked by a ritual ceremony in which the priest would have his place, but only as one of many participants. The leading role went to the dying man himself. He presided over the affair with hardly a misstep, for he knew how to conduct himself, having previously witnessed so many similar scenes. He called to him one by one his relatives, his friends, his servants, "even down to the lowliest," Saint-Simon said, describing the death of Mme. de Montespan. He said farewell to them, asked their pardon, gave them his blessing. Invested with sovereign authority by the approach of death, especially in the eighteenth and nineteenth centuries, the dying person gave orders and advice, even when this dying person was a very young girl, almost a child.

Today nothing remains either of the sense that everyone has or should have of his impending death, or of the public solemnity surrounding the moment of death. What used to be appreciated is now hidden; what used to be solemn is now avoided.   7

It is understood that the primary duty of the family and the doctor is to conceal the seriousness of his condition from the person who is to die. The sick person must no longer ever know (except in very rare cases) that his end is near. The new custom dictates that he die in ignorance. This is not merely a habit that has innocently crept into the customs—it has become a moral requirement. Vladimir Jankélévitch confirmed this unequivocally during a recent colloquium of doctors on the subject: "Should we lie to the patient?" "The liar," he stated, "is the one who tells the truth. . . . I am against the truth, passionately against the truth. . . . For me, the most important law of all is the law of love and charity."[1] Was this quality then lacking prior to the twentieth century, since ethics made it obligatory to inform the patient? In such opposition we see the extent of this extraordinary reversal of feelings, and then of ideas. How did this come about? It would be too hasty to say that in a society of happiness and well-being there is no longer any room for suffering, sadness and death. To say this is to mistake the result for the cause.   8

It is strange that this change is linked to the development in family feelings, and to the emotional centrality of the family in our world. In fact, the cause for the change must be sought in the relationship between a sick person and his family. The family has no longer been able to tolerate the blow it had to deal to a loved one, and the blow it also had to deal to itself, in bringing death closer and making it more certain, in forbidding all deception and illusion. How many times have we heard it said of a spouse or a parent: "At least I had the satisfaction of knowing that he never felt he was dying"? *This "not feeling oneself dying" has in our everyday language replaced the "feeling one's impending death" of the seventeenth century.*   9

In point of fact, it must happen quite often—but the dead never tell— that the sick person knows quite well what is happening, and pretends not to   10

[1] *Médecine de France,* 177 (1966), 3–16, repr. in Jankélévitch, *La mort* (Paris: Flammarion, 1966).

know for the sake of those around him. For if the family has loathed to play *nuncius mortis,* a role which in the Middle Ages and at the beginning of modern times it was not asked to play, the main actor has also abdicated. Through fear of death? But death has always existed. Only it used to be laughed at—"What haste you are in, O cruel goddess!"—while society compelled the terrified dying man nevertheless to act out the great scene of farewells and departure. Some say this fear is innate, but its suppression is equally innate. The fear of death does not explain why the dying man turns his back on his own death. Again we must seek for the explanation in the history of the family.

11   The man of the late Middle Ages and the Renaissance (as opposed to the man of the early Middle Ages, like Roland, who still lives in Tolstoy's peasants) insisted on participating in his own death, because he saw in his death the moment when his individuality received its ultimate form. He was master over his life only insofar as he was master over his death. His death was his, and his alone. However, beginning with the seventeenth century he no longer had sole sovereignty over his own life and, consequently, over his death. He shared his death with his family, whereas previously his family had been isolated from the serious decisions he, and he alone, had to make regarding his death.

12   Last wills and testaments are a case in point. From the fourteenth century to the beginning of the eighteenth century, the will was one way for each person to express himself freely while at the same time it was a token of defiance—or lack of confidence—with regard to his family. Thus, when in the eighteenth century family affection triumphed over the traditional mistrust by the testator of his inheritors, the last will and testament lost its character of moral necessity and personal warm testimony. This was, on the contrary, replaced by such an absolute trust that there was no longer any need for written wills. The last spoken wishes became at long last sacred to the survivors, and they considered themselves to be committed from then on to respect these wishes to the letter. For his part, the dying man was satisfied that he could rest in peace on the word of his close ones. This trust that began in the seventeenth and eighteenth centuries and was developed in the nineteenth century, has in the twentieth century turned into alienation. As soon as serious danger threatens one member of a family, the family immediately conspires to deprive him of information and thus his freedom. The patient then becomes a minor, like a child or a mental defective, to be taken into charge and separated from the rest of the world by his spouse or parents. They know better than he what he should do and know. He is deprived of his rights, specifically the formerly essential right of knowing about his death, of preparing for it, of organizing it. And he lets this happen because he is convinced that it is for his own good. He relies on the affection of his family. If, in spite of everything, he does guess the truth, he will pretend to not know it. Death used to be a tragedy—often comic—acted out for the benefit of a

man who was about to die. Today, death is a comedy—always tragic—acted out for the benefit of a man who does not know he is about to die.

Without the progress of medicine the pressure of family feeling would probably not have been sufficient to make death disappear so quickly and so completely. Not so much because of the real conquests made by medicine as because, as a result of medicine, in the mind of the sick man death has been replaced by illness. This substitution first appeared in the second half of the nineteenth century. When the dying peasant in Tolstoy's *Three Deaths* (1859) was asked where he hurt, he replied: "I hurt all over, death is here: that's what it is." On the other hand Ivan Ilych (1886), after overhearing a conversation that could leave him in no doubt, continues to think obstinately of his floating kidney, of his infected appendix, which can be cured by the doctor or the surgeon. The illness has become the focus of illusion. His wife treats him like a child who is disobeying the doctor's orders: he is not taking his medicine properly, that is why he is not getting better.

Moreover, it is clear that, with the advancements in therapeutics and surgery, it has become increasingly more difficult to be certain that a serious illness is fatal; the chances of recovering from it have increased so much. Even with diminished capacities, one can still live. Thus, in our world where everyone acts as though medicine is the answer to everything—where even though Caesar must die one day, there is absolutely no reason for oneself to die—incurable diseases, particularly cancer, have taken on the hideous, terrifying aspects of the old representations of death. More than the skeleton or mummy of the *macabres* of the fourteenth and fifteenth centuries, more than the leper with his bell, cancer today is death. However, the disease must be incurable (or thought to be so) in order for death to be allowed to come forward and take on its name. The anguish this releases forces society to hurriedly intensify its customary demands of silence, and thus to bring this overly dramatic situation to the banal level of an afternoon walk.

People die, then, in secret—more alone than Pascal ever imagined. This secrecy results from refusing to admit the imminent death of a loved one by concealing it beneath the veil of a persistent disease. There is another aspect of this secrecy that American sociologists have succeeded in interpreting. What we have been inclined to view as avoidance, they have shown to be the empirical establishment of a style of dying in which discretion appears as the modern form of dignity. It is, with less poetry, the death of Mélisande, a death of which Jankélévitch would approve.

A study has been made by Barney G. Glaser and Anselm L. Strauss in six hospitals in the San Francisco Bay Area of the reactions toward death of the interdependent group of the patient, his family and the medical personnel (doctors and nurses).[2] What happens when it is known that the patient is nearing his end? Should the family be notified, or the patient himself, and

[2] *Awareness of Dying* (Chicago: Aldine, 1965).

when? For how long should life be prolonged by artificial means, and at what point should the individual be permitted to die? How does the medical staff behave toward a patient who does not know, or who pretends not to know, or who does know that he is dying? These problems no doubt arise in every modern family, but within the confines of a hospital, a new authority intervenes: the medical authority. Today people are dying less and less at home, more and more in hospitals; indeed, the hospital has become the modern place for dying, which is why Glaser and Strauss' observations are important. However, the scope of their book goes beyond empirical analyses of attitudes. The authors have discovered a new ideal way of dying which has replaced the theatrical ceremonies of the Romantic era and, in a more general way, of the traditional public nature of death. There is a new model for dying which they explain almost naively, comparing it with their concrete observations. Thus we see taking shape a "style of dying," or rather an "acceptable style of living while dying," an "acceptable style of facing death." The accent is placed on the word "acceptable." It is essential, indeed, that the death be such that it can be accepted or tolerated by the survivors.

17   If doctors and nurses (the nurses with more reticence) delay for as long as possible notifying the family, if they are reluctant to notify the patient himself, the reason is that they are afraid of becoming caught up in a chain of sentimental reactions that would bring about a loss of self-control, their own as much as that of the patient or the family. To dare to speak of death, to admit death into social relations, is no longer, as in former times, to leave the everyday world undisturbed; it brings about an exceptional, outrageous and always dramatic situation. Death used to be a familiar figure, and moralists had to make him hideous in order to create fear. Now the word has only to be mentioned to provoke an emotive tension incompatible with the equilibrium of everyday life. "An acceptable style of dying," then, is one that avoids "status-forcing scenes," scenes that tear the person out of his social role, that violate his social role. These scenes are patients' crises of despair, their cries, their tears, and in general, any demonstrations that are too impassioned, too noisy or even too moving, that might upset the serenity of the hospital. This would be the "embarrassingly graceless dying," the style of dying that would embarrass the survivors, the opposite of the acceptable style of dying. It is in order to avoid this that nothing is said to the patient. Basically, however, what is essential is less whether the patient does or does not know, but rather, that if he does know he should have the good taste and the courage to be discreet. He should behave in such a manner that the hospital staff can forget that he knows, and can communicate with him as though death were not hovering about them. Communication is, in fact, an equally necessary factor. It is not enough for the patient to be discreet, he must also be open and receptive to messages. His indifference might set up the same "embarrassment" among the medical personnel as would an excess of demonstration.

There are, then, two ways to die badly: one consists of seeking an exchange of emotions; the other is to refuse to communicate.

The authors very earnestly cite the case of an old woman who conducted herself very well at first, according to convention: she cooperated with the doctors and nurses, and fought bravely against her illness. Then one day she decided that she had fought enough, the time had come to give up. She closed her eyes and did not open them again: in this way she was signifying that she was withdrawing from the world, and was awaiting her end alone. Formerly this sign of introspection would have surprised no one and would have been respected. In the California hospital, it drove the doctors and nurses to despair, and they quickly sent for one of the patient's sons to come by plane, he being the only person capable of persuading her to open her eyes and not go on "hurting everybody." Patients also sometimes turn toward the wall and remain in that position. This is recognizable, not without emotion, as one of man's oldest gestures when he feels death approaching. The Jews of the Old Testament died this way and, even in the sixteenth century, the Spanish Inquisition recognized by this sign an unconverted Marrano. Tristam died in this way: "He turned toward the wall and said: 'I can hold on to my life no longer.'" Nevertheless, in our time the doctors and nurses of a California hospital saw in this ancient gesture nothing but an antisocial refusal to communicate, an unpardonable renouncement of the vital struggle. [18]

We should realize that the surrender of the patient is censured not only because it demoralizes the medical personnel, representing as it does a failure to meet a moral obligation, but also because it supposedly reduces the capacity for resistance of the patient himself. It thus becomes as much to be feared as the "status-forcing scenes." This is why, today, American and British doctors are less often hiding the seriousness of their case from terminal patients. This year British television broadcast a program on cancer patients who had been apprised very accurately of their situation; this broadcast was intended as an encouragement to tell the truth. The doctors probably think that a man who has been told, if he is stable, will be more willing to undergo treatment in the hope of living to the full his last remaining days and, when all is said and done, will die just as discreetly and with as much dignity as if he had known nothing. This is the death of the good American, as described by Jacques Maritain in a book designed for the American public: he is led by the medical personnel "to think in a sort of dream, that the act of dying amid happy smiles, amid white garments like angels' wings would be a veritable pleasure, a moment of no consequence: relax, take it easy, it's nothing." This is also, with a little less of the commercial smile and a little more music, the humanistic, dignified death of the contemporary philosopher: to disappear "*pianissimo* and, so to speak, on tiptoe" (Jankélévitch). [19]

NORMAN COUSINS
The Right to Die

Cousins, author, lecturer, and for forty years editor of The Saturday Review, *has brought to all of these roles his concern with the fundamental social, political—and simply human— problems confronting contemporary Americans. Indeed, his lifelong contributions to education, journalism, and public service have been acknowledged with a dozen honorary degrees and numerous other awards, including the United Nations Peace Medal in 1971. Cousins's many books include* The Good Inheritance: The Democratic Chance *(1942),* The Quest for Immortality *(1974), and* The Human Option *(1981).*

His best-seller, The Anatomy of An Illness as Perceived by the Patient *(1979), explains how Cousins overcame a crippling, degenerative, supposedly irreversible spinal disease and excruciating pain through undertaking his own unconventional, medically unproven treatment. He discovered the therapeutic power of laughter by watching Marx Brothers comedies: "ten minutes of genuine belly laughter had an anesthetic effect and would give me at least two hours of pain-free sleep." Cousins's independence of mind, celebration of a full life, and deep compassion for others influence his feelings about the Van Dusens' suicide. He does not try to avoid the controversial nature of their act, but his sympathy and calm tone help readers recognize that even if we disagree with the Van Dusens' decision, we can respect it as the rational, personal exercise of free will.*

1 The world of religion and philosophy was shocked recently when Henry P. Van Dusen and his wife ended their lives by their own hands. Dr. Van Dusen had been president of Union Theological Seminary; for more than a quarter-century he had been one of the luminous names in Protestant theology. He enjoyed world status as a spiritual leader. News of the self-inflicted death of the Van Dusens, therefore, was profoundly disturbing to all those who attach a moral stigma to suicide and regard it as a violation of God's laws.

2 Dr. Van Dusen had anticipated this reaction. He and his wife left behind a letter that may have historic significance. It was very brief, but the essential point it made is now being widely discussed by theologians and could represent the beginning of a reconsideration of traditional religious attitudes toward self-inflicted death. The letter raised a moral issue: does an individual have the obligation to go on living even when the beauty and meaning and power of life are gone?

3 Henry and Elizabeth Van Dusen had lived full lives. In recent years, they had become increasingly ill, requiring almost continual medical care. Their infirmities were worsening, and they realized they would soon become completely dependent for even the most elementary needs and functions. Under these circumstances, little dignity would have been left in life. They didn't like the idea of taking up space in a world with too many mouths and too little food. They believed it was a misuse of medical science to keep them technically alive.

4 They therefore believed they had the right to decide when to die. In

making that decision, they weren't turning against life as the highest value; what they were turning against was the notion that there were no circumstances under which life should be discontinued.

An important aspect of human uniqueness is the power of free will. In his books and lectures, Dr. Van Dusen frequently spoke about the exercise of this uniqueness. The fact that he used his free will to prevent life from becoming a caricature of itself was completely in character. In their letter, the Van Dusens sought to convince family and friends that they were not acting solely out of despair or pain. 5

The use of free will to put an end to one's life finds no sanction in the theology to which Pitney Van Dusen was committed. Suicide symbolizes discontinuity; religion symbolizes continuity, represented at its quintessence by the concept of the immortal soul. Human logic finds it almost impossible to come to terms with the concept of nonexistence. In religion, the human mind finds a larger dimension and is relieved of the ordeal of a confrontation with non-existence. 6

Even without respect to religion, the idea of suicide has been abhorrent throughout history. Some societies have imposed severe penalties on the families of suicides in the hope that the individual who sees no reason to continue his existence may be deterred by the stigma his self-destruction would inflict on loved ones. Other societies have enacted laws prohibiting suicide on the grounds that it is murder. The enforcement of such laws, of course, has been an exercise in futility. 7

Customs and attitudes, like individuals themselves, are largely shaped by the surrounding environment. In today's world, life can be prolonged by science far beyond meaning or sensibility. Under these circumstances, individuals who feel they have nothing more to give to life, or to receive from it, need not be applauded, but they can be spared our condemnation. 8

The general reaction to suicide is bound to change as people come to understand that it may be a denial, not an assertion, of moral or religious ethics to allow life to be extended without regard to decency or pride. What moral or religious purpose is celebrated by the annihilation of the human spirit in the triumphant act of keeping the body alive? Why are so many people more readily appalled by an unnatural form of dying than by an unnatural form of living? 9

"Nowadays," the Van Dusens wrote in their last letter, "it is difficult to die. We feel that this way we are taking will become more usual and acceptable as the years pass. 10

"Of course, the thought of our children and our grandchildren makes us sad, but we still feel that this is the best way and the right way to go. We are both increasingly weak and unwell and who would want to die in a nursing home? 11

"We are not afraid to die. . . ." 12

Pitney Van Dusen was admired and respected in life. He can be admired 13 and respected in death. "Suicide," said Goethe, "is an incident in human life which, however much disputed and discussed, demands the sympathy of every man, and in every age must be dealt with anew."

14   Death is not the greatest loss in life. The greatest loss is what dies inside us while we live. The unbearable tragedy is to live without dignity or sensitivity.

Questions

1. Cousins's opinion on "the right to die" with dignity derives from his view that a life without "beauty and meaning and power" is not worth living. In whose opinion is there a "right to die"? Is this a fundamental human right, like the rights to "life, liberty, and the pursuit of happiness" guaranteed by our Constitution?

2. Cousins argues his case largely from the single example of the suicides of a noted theologian and his wife. Is this single case sufficient to make a convincing argument for the entire human race?

3. Does Cousins give appropriate weight to opposing views? Does Cousins pay adequate attention to religious opposition to suicide (paragraph 6)? Is Cousins accurate in saying that the enforcement of laws against suicide "of course, has been an exercise in futility" (paragraph 7)? ("Of course," by the way, often signals implied disagreement, despite its apparent certainty.) Why else might societies enact laws against suicide?

4. Does the fact that Van Dusen was a theologian influence the nature and merit of Cousins's case? Could or should the argument be the same if the suicide had been a distressed teenager? a skid-row bum? an esteemed public official convicted of embezzlement? any human being at all?

Narrative with Argument, Implied and Direct

GEORGE ORWELL

Shooting an Elephant

Orwell was candid about the argumentative, political purpose of all his writing: "My starting point is always a feeling of partisanship, a sense of injustice . . . . I write because there is some lie that I want to expose, some fact to which I want to draw attention, and my initial concern is to get a hearing." Of the many possible ways to call attention to an injustice, in this case, the evils of imperialism, Orwell here tells a seemingly simple tale. As he recounts the single, extended incident that culminated in his reluctant killing of an elephant to please the hostile crowd that egged him on, he implicitly indicts the relations between white colonial governors and the natives they treat as objects rather than as people.

The effectiveness of this "single case" approach is well known to writers of fables, parables, advertising; the pathetic example of a single crippled child can be more moving than cold statistics about thousands of afflicted victims. One picture, a single memorable story, can be worth a hundred arguments, a thousand speeches.

In Moulmein, in lower Burma, I was hated by large numbers of people—the 1 only time in my life that I have been important enough for this to happen to me. I was sub-divisional police officer of the town, and in an aimless, petty kind of way anti-European feeling was very bitter. No one had the guts to raise a riot, but if a European woman went through the bazaars alone some-body would probably spit betel juice over her dress. As a police officer I was an obvious target and was baited whenever it seemed safe to do so. When a nimble Burman tripped me up on the football field and the referee (another Burman) looked the other way, the crowd yelled with hideous laughter. This happened more than once. In the end the sneering yellow faces of young men that met me everywhere, the insults hooted after me when I was at a safe distance, got badly on my nerves. The young Buddhist priests were the worst of all. There were several thousands of them in the town and none of them seemed to have anything to do except stand on street corners and jeer at Europeans.

All this was perplexing and upsetting. For at that time I had already made 2 up my mind that imperialism was an evil thing and the sooner I chucked up my job and got out of it the better. Theoretically—and secretly, of course—I was all for the Burmese and all against their oppressors, the British. As for the job I was doing, I hated it more bitterly than I can perhaps make clear. In a job like that you see the dirty work of Empire at close quarters. The wretched prisoners huddling in the stinking cages of the lock-ups, the grey, cowed faces of the long-term convicts, the scarred buttocks of the men who had been flogged with bamboos—all these oppressed me with an intolerable sense of guilt. But I could get nothing into perspective. I was young and ill-educated and I had had to think out my problems in the utter silence that is imposed on every Englishman in the East. I did not even know that the British Empire is dying, still less did I know that it is a great deal better than the younger empires that are going to supplant it. All I knew was that I was stuck between my hatred of the empire I served and my rage against the evil-spirited little beasts who tried to make my job impossible. With one part of my mind I thought of the British Raj as an unbreakable tyranny, as something clamped down, *in saecula saeculorum,* upon the will of prostrate peoples: with another part I thought that the greatest joy in the world would be to drive a bayonet into a Buddhist priest's guts. Feelings like these are the normal by-products of imperialism; ask any Anglo-Indian official, if you can catch him off duty.

3   One day something happened which in a roundabout way was enlightening. It was a tiny incident in itself, but it gave me a better glimpse than I had had before of the real nature of imperialism—the real motives for which despotic governments act. Early one morning the sub-inspector at a police station the other end of town rang me up on the 'phone and said that an elephant was ravaging the bazaar. Would I please come and do something about it? I did not know what I could do, but I wanted to see what was happening and I got on to a pony and started out. I took my rifle, an old .44 Winchester and much too small to kill an elephant, but I thought the noise might be useful *in terrorem*. Various Burmans stopped me on the way and told me about the elephant's doings. It was not, of course, a wild elephant, but a tame one which had gone "must." It had been chained up, as tame elephants always are when their attack of "must" is due, but on the previous night it had broken its chain and escaped. Its mahout, the only person who could manage it when it was in that state, had set out in pursuit, but had taken the wrong direction and was now twelve hours' journey away, and in the morning the elephant had suddenly reappeared in the town. The Burmese population had no weapons and were quite helpless against it. It had already destroyed somebody's bamboo hut, killed a cow and raided some fruit-stalls and devoured the stock; also it had met the municipal rubbish van and, when the driver jumped out and took to his heels, had turned the van over and inflicted violences upon it.

4   The Burmese sub-inspector and some Indian constables were waiting for me in the quarter where the elephant had been seen. It was a very poor quarter, a labyrinth of squalid bamboo huts, thatched with palm-leaf, winding all over a steep hillside. I remember that it was a cloudy, stuffy morning at the beginning of the rains. We began questioning the people as to where the elephant had gone and, as usual, failed to get any definite information. That is invariably the case in the East; a story always sounds clear enough at a

distance, but the nearer you get to the scene of events the vaguer it becomes. Some of the people said that the elephant had gone in one direction, some said that he had gone in another, some professed not even to have heard of any elephant. I had almost made up my mind that the whole story was a pack of lies, when we heard yells a little distance away. There was a loud, scandalized cry of "Go away, child! Go away this instant!" and an old woman with a switch in her hand came round the corner of a hut, violently shooing away a crowd of naked children. Some more women followed, clicking their tongues and exclaiming; evidently there was something that the children ought not to have seen. I rounded the hut and saw a man's dead body sprawling in the mud. He was an Indian, a black Dravidian coolie, almost naked, and he could not have been dead many minutes. The people said that the elephant had come suddenly upon him round the corner of the hut, caught him with its trunk, put its foot on his back and ground him into the earth. This was the rainy season and the ground was soft, and his face had scored a trench a foot deep and a couple of yards long. He was lying on his belly with arms crucified and head sharply twisted to one side. His face was coated with mud, the eyes wide open, the teeth bared and grinning with an expression of unendurable agony. (Never tell me, by the way, that the dead look peaceful. Most of the corpses I have seen looked devilish.) The friction of the great beast's foot had stripped the skin from his back as neatly as one skins a rabbit. As soon as I saw the dead man I sent an orderly to a friend's house nearby to borrow an elephant rifle. I had already sent back the pony, not wanting it to go mad with fright and throw me if it smelt the elephant.

The orderly came back in a few minutes with a rifle and five cartridges, 5 and meanwhile some Burmans had arrived and told us that the elephant was in the paddy fields below, only a few hundred yards away. As I started forward practically the whole population of the quarter flocked out of the houses and followed me. They had seen the rifle and were all shouting excitedly that I was going to shoot the elephant. They had not shown much interest in the elephant when he was merely ravaging their homes, but it was different now that he was going to be shot. It was a bit of fun to them, as it would be to an English crowd; besides they wanted the meat. It made me vaguely uneasy. I had no intention of shooting the elephant—I had merely sent for the rifle to defend myself if necessary—and it is always unnerving to have a crowd following you. I marched down the hill, looking and feeling a fool, with the rifle over my shoulder and an ever-growing army of people jostling at my heels. At the bottom, when you got away from the huts, there was a metalled road and beyond that a miry waste of paddy fields a thousand yards across, not yet ploughed but soggy from the first rains and dotted with coarse grass. The elephant was standing eight yards from the road, his left side towards us. He took not the slightest notice of the crowd's approach. He was tearing up bunches of grass, beating them against his knees to clean them and stuffing them into his mouth.

6   I had halted on the road. As soon as I saw the elephant I knew with perfect certainty that I ought not to shoot him. It is a serious matter to shoot a working elephant—it is comparable to destroying a huge and costly piece of machinery—and obviously one ought not to do it if it can possibly be avoided. And at that distance, peacefully eating, the elephant looked no more dangerous than a cow. I thought then and I think now that his attack of "must" was already passing off; in which case he would merely wander harmlessly about until the mahout came back and caught him. Moreover, I did not in the least want to shoot him. I decided that I would watch him for a little while to make sure that he did not turn savage again, and then go home.

7   But at that moment I glanced round at the crowd that had followed me. It was an immense crowd, two thousand at the least and growing every minute. It blocked the road for a long distance on either side. I looked at the sea of yellow faces above the garish clothes—faces all happy and excited over this bit of fun, all certain that the elephant was going to be shot. They were watching me as they would watch a conjurer about to perform a trick. They did not like me, but with the magical rifle in my hands I was momentarily worth watching. And suddenly I realized that I should have to shoot the elephant after all. The people expected it of me and I had got to do it; I could feel their two thousand wills pressing me forward, irresistibly. And it was at this moment, as I stood there with the rifle in my hands, that I first grasped the hollowness, the futility of the white man's dominion in the East. Here was I, the white man with his gun, standing in front of the unarmed native crowd—seemingly the leading actor of the piece; but in reality I was only an absurd puppet pushed to and fro by the will of those yellow faces behind. I perceived in this moment that when the white man turns tyrant it is his own freedom that he destroys. He becomes a sort of hollow, posing dummy, the conventionalized figure of a sahib. For it is the condition of his rule that he shall spend his life in trying to impress the "natives," and so in every crisis he has got to do what the "natives" expect of him. He wears a mask, and his face grows to fit it. I had got to shoot the elephant. I had committed myself to doing it when I sent for the rifle. A sahib has got to act like a sahib; he has got to appear resolute, to know his own mind and do definite things. To come all that way, rifle in hand, with two thousand people marching at my heels, and then to trail feebly away, having done nothing—no, that was impossible. The crowd would laugh at me. And my whole life, every white man's life in the East, was one long struggle not to be laughed at.

8   But I did not want to shoot the elephant. I watched him beating his bunch of grass against his knees, with that preoccupied grandmotherly air that elephants have. It seemed to me that it would be murder to shoot him. At that age I was not squeamish about killing animals, but I had never shot an elephant and never wanted to. (Somehow it always seems worse to kill a *large* animal.) Besides, there was the beast's owner to be considered. Alive, the elephant was worth at least a hundred pounds; dead, he would only be worth

the value of his tusks, five pounds, possibly. But I had got to act quickly. I turned to some experienced-looking Burmans who had been there when we arrived, and asked them how the elephant had been behaving. They all said the same thing: he took no notice of you if you left him alone, but he might charge if you went too close to him.

It was perfectly clear to me what I ought to do. I ought to walk up to   9
within, say, twenty-five yards of the elephant and test his behavior. If he charged, I could shoot; if he took no notice of me, it would be safe to leave him until the mahout came back. But also I knew that I was going to do no such thing. I was a poor shot with a rifle and the ground was soft mud into which one would sink at every step. If the elephant charged and I missed him, I should have about as much chance as a toad under a steam-roller. But even then I was not thinking particularly of my own skin, only of the watchful yellow faces behind. For at that moment, with the crowd watching me, I was not afraid in the ordinary sense, as I would have been if I had been alone. A white man mustn't be frightened in front of "natives"; and so, in general, he isn't frightened. The sole thought in my mind was that if anything went wrong those two thousand Burmans would see me pursued, caught, trampled on and reduced to a grinning corpse like that Indian up the hill. And if that happened it was quite probable that some of them would laugh. That would never do. There was only one alternative. I shoved the cartridges into the magazine and lay down on the road to get a better aim.

The crowd grew very still, and a deep, low, happy sigh, as of people who   10
see the theatre curtain go up at last, breathed from innumerable throats. They were going to have their bit of fun after all. The rifle was a beautiful German thing with cross-hair sights. I did not then know that in shooting an elephant one would shoot to cut an imaginary bar running from ear-hole to ear-hole. I ought, therefore, as the elephant was sideways on, to have aimed straight at his ear-hole; actually I aimed several inches in front of this, thinking the brain would be further forward.

When I pulled the trigger I did not hear the bang or feel the kick—one   11
never does when a shot goes home—but I heard the devilish roar of glee that went up from the crowd. In that instant, in too short a time, one would have thought, even for the bullet to get there, a mysterious, terrible change had come over the elephant. He neither stirred nor fell, but every line of his body had altered. He looked suddenly stricken, shrunken, immensely old, as though the frightful impact of the bullet had paralysed him without knocking him down. At last, after what seemed a long time—it might have been five seconds, I dare say—he sagged flabbily to his knees. His mouth slobbered. An enormous senility seemed to have settled upon him. One could have imagined him thousands of years old. I fired again into the same spot. At the second shot he did not collapse but climbed with desperate slowness to his feet and stood weakly upright, with legs sagging and head drooping. I fired a third time. That was the shot that did for him. You could see the agony of it

jolt his whole body and knock the last remnant of strength from his legs. But in falling he seemed for a moment to rise, for as his hind legs collapsed beneath him he seemed to tower upward like a huge rock toppling, his trunk reaching skywards like a tree. He trumpeted, for the first and only time. And then down he came, his belly towards me, with a crash that seemed to shake the ground even where I lay.

12 I got up. The Burmans were already racing past me across the mud. It was obvious that the elephant would never rise again, but he was not dead. He was breathing very rhythmically with long rattling gasps, his great mound of a side painfully rising and falling. His mouth was wide open—I could see far down into caverns of pale pink throat. I waited a long time for him to die, but his breathing did not weaken. Finally I fired my two remaining shots into the spot where I thought his heart must be. The thick blood welled out of him like red velvet, but still he did not die. His body did not even jerk when the shots hit him, the tortured breathing continued without a pause. He was dying, very slowly and in great agony, but in some world remote from me where not even a bullet could damage him further. I felt that I had got to put an end to that dreadful noise. It seemed dreadful to see the great beast lying there, powerless to move and yet powerless to die, and not even to be able to finish him. I sent back for my small rifle and poured shot after shot into his heart and down his throat. They seemed to make no impression. The tortured gasps continued as steadily as the ticking of a clock.

13 In the end I could not stand it any longer and went away. I heard later that it took him half an hour to die. Burmans were bringing dahs and baskets even before I left, and I was told they had stripped his body almost to the bones by the afternoon.

14 Afterwards, of course, there were endless discussions about the shooting of the elephant. The owner was furious, but he was only an Indian and could do nothing. Besides, legally I had done the right thing, for a mad elephant has to be killed, like a mad dog, if its owner fails to control it. Among the Europeans opinion was divided. The older men said I was right, the younger men said it was a damn shame to shoot an elephant for killing a coolie, because an elephant was worth more than any damn Coringhee coolie. And afterwards I was very glad that the coolie had been killed; it put me legally in the right and it gave me a sufficient pretext for shooting the elephant. I often wondered whether any of the others grasped that I had done it solely to avoid looking a fool.

Questions

1. What is the thesis of Orwell's essay? Does it appear overtly in the essay? If so, where? Whether it does or not, how much of the essay must one read before the thesis becomes apparent? Is delaying the thesis in arguing a controversial issue a good strategy for attracting potentially hostile or indifferent readers?

2. What does Orwell say he should have done with regard to the elephant (paragraph 9)? Why did he betray his own convictions (paragraph 7)? What clues do your answers provide as to why Orwell wrote "Shooting an Elephant"? Do you think he was as analytic during the actual experience as he became when in 　 rpreting it later, as he wrote the essay? Could this argument become a generalized plea against betraying one's own principles?

3. Sometimes writers build an argument around a central figure, incident, or event that can be interpreted figuratively as well as literally, as Orwell does here. Explain how the elephant itself, and the shooting of the elephant, function on both literal and symbolic levels.

4. Why does Orwell devote so much space to the preparations for shooting the elephant (paragraphs 7–9) and to the actual shooting (paragraphs 10–12)? Why is the conclusion (paragraphs 13–14) so short, in comparison with those sections? Is this proportioning a good model for most arguments—to make the case thoroughly but not to prolong it after the climactic point?

GEORGE ORWELL

Marrakech

In "Marrakech" Orwell varies the technique he uses in "Shooting an Elephant." In "Marrakech" he also indicts the mutually degrading relations between colonists and natives through juxtaposing several precision snapshots of typical Moroccan scenes: flies rushing after a corpse in a funeral procession; a cemetery full of lumps, unmarked grave sites of forgotten people; a hungry zookeeper envying a well-fed, succulent-looking gazelle; starving Jews in the ghetto; broken-down women bearing heavier burdens than broken-down animals; soldiers bearing rifles. Each individual picture is powerful because it is understated; the stark, gruesome realities depicted do not need the enhancement of color. Orwell's writing, seemingly objective, reportorial, makes his readers see, literally and metaphorically, the demoralizing, dehumanizing effects of imperialism.

As the corpse went past the flies left the restaurant table in a cloud and rushed after it, but they came back a few minutes later. 1

The little crowd of mourners—all men and boys, no women—threaded their way across the market-place between the piles of pomegranates and the taxis and the camels, wailing a short chant over and over again. What really appeals to the flies is that the corpses here are never put into coffins, they are merely wrapped in a piece of rag and carried on a rough wooden bier on the shoulders of four friends. When the friends get to the burying-ground they hack an oblong hole a foot or two deep, dump the body in it and fling over it a little of the dried-up, lumpy earth, which is like broken brick. No gravestone, no name, no identifying mark of any kind. The burying-ground is merely a huge waste of hummocky earth, like a derelict building-lot. After a month or two no one can even be certain where his own relatives are buried. 2

3   When you walk through a town like this—two hundred thousand inhabitants, of whom at least twenty thousand own literally nothing except the rags they stand up in—when you see how the people live, and still more how easily they die, it is always difficult to believe that you are walking among human beings. All colonial empires are in reality founded upon that fact. The people have brown faces—besides, there are so many of them! Are they really the same flesh as yourself? Do they even have names? Or are they merely a kind of undifferentiated brown stuff, about as individual as bees or coral insects? They rise out of the earth, they sweat and starve for a few years, and then they sink back into the nameless mounds of the graveyard and nobody notices that they are gone. And even the graves themselves soon fade back into the soil. Sometimes, out for a walk, as you break your way through the prickly pear, you notice that it is rather bumpy underfoot, and only a certain regularity in the bumps tells you that you are walking over skeletons.

4   I was feeding one of the gazelles in the public gardens.

Gazelles are almost the only animals that look good to eat when they are still alive, in fact, one can hardly look at their hindquarters without thinking of mint sauce. The gazelle I was feeding seemed to know that this thought was in my mind, for though it took the piece of bread I was holding out it obviously did not like me. It nibbled rapidly at the bread, then lowered its head and tried to butt me, then took another nibble and then butted again. Probably its idea was that if it could drive me away the bread would somehow remain hanging in mid-air.

5   An Arab navvy working on the path nearby lowered his heavy hoe and sidled toward us. He looked from the gazelle to the bread and from the bread to the gazelle, with a sort of quiet amazement, as though he had never seen anything quite like this before. Finally he said shyly in French:

6   "I could eat some of that bread."

7   I tore off a piece and he stowed it gratefully in some secret place under his rags. This man is an employee of the Municipality.

8   When you go through the Jewish quarters you gather some idea of what the medieval ghettoes were probably like. Under their Moorish rulers the Jews were only allowed to own land in certain restricted areas, and after centuries of this kind of treatment they have ceased to bother about overcrowding. Many of the streets are a good deal less than six feet wide, the houses are completely windowless, and sore-eyed children cluster everywhere in unbelievable numbers, like clouds of flies. Down the centre of the street there is generally running a little river of urine.

9   In the bazaar huge families of Jews, all dressed in the long black robe and little black skull-cap, are working in dark fly-infested booths that look like caves. A carpenter sits cross-legged at a prehistoric lathe, turning chair-legs at lightning speed. He works the lathe with a bow in his right hand and guides the chisel with his left foot, and thanks to a lifetime of sitting in this position

his left leg is warped out of shape. At his side his grandson, aged six, is already starting on the simpler parts of the job.

I was just passing the coppersmiths' booths when somebody noticed that I was lighting a cigarette. Instantly, from the dark holes all around, there was a frenzied rush of Jews, many of them old grandfathers with flowing grey beards, all clamouring for a cigarette. Even a blind man somewhere at the back of one of the booths heard a rumour of cigarettes and came crawling out, groping in the air with his hand. In about a minute I had used up the whole packet. None of these people, I suppose, works less than twelve hours a day, and every one of them looks on a cigarette as a more or less impossible luxury.

As the Jews live in self-contained communities they follow the same trades as the Arabs, except for agriculture. Fruit-sellers, potters, silversmiths, blacksmiths, butchers, leather-workers, tailors, water-carriers, beggars, porters—whichever way you look you see nothing but Jews. As a matter of fact there are thirteen thousand of them, all living in the space of a few acres. A good job Hitler isn't here. Perhaps he is on his way, however. You hear the usual dark rumours about the Jews, not only from the Arabs but from the poorer Europeans.

"Yes, *mon vieux,* they took my job away from me and gave it to a Jew. The Jews! They're the real rulers of this country, you know. They've got all the money. They control the banks, finance—everything."

"But," I said, "isn't it a fact that the average Jew is a labourer working for about a penny an hour?"

"Ah, that's only for show! They're all moneylenders really. They're cunning, the Jews."

In just the same way, a couple of hundred years ago, poor old women used to be burned for witchcraft when they could not even work enough magic to get themselves a square meal.

All people who work with their hands are partly invisible, and the more important the work they do, the less visible they are. Still, a white skin is always fairly conspicuous. In northern Europe, when you see a labourer ploughing a field, you probably give him a second glance. In a hot country, anywhere south of Gibraltar or east of Suez, the chances are that you don't even see him. I have noticed this again and again. In a tropical landscape one's eye takes in everything except the human beings. It takes in the dried-up soil, the prickly pear, the palm-tree and the distant mountain, but it always misses the peasant hoeing at his patch. He is the same colour as the earth, and a great deal less interesting to look at.

It is only because of this that the starved countries of Asia and Africa are accepted as tourist resorts. No one would think of running cheap trips to the Distressed Areas. But where the human beings have brown skins their poverty is simply not noticed. What does Morocco mean to a Frenchman? An orange-grove or a job in government service. Or to an Englishman? Camels, castles, palm-trees, Foreign Legionnaires, brass trays and bandits. One could probably live here for years without noticing that for nine-tenths of the people the reality of life is an endless, back-breaking struggle to wring a little food out of an eroded soil.

18   Most of Morocco is so desolate that no wild animal bigger than a hare can live on it. Huge areas which were once covered with forest have turned into a treeless waste where the soil is exactly like broken-up brick. Nevertheless a good deal of it is cultivated, with frightful labour. Everything is done by hand. Long lines of women, bent double like inverted capital Ls, work their way slowly across the field, tearing up the prickly weeds with their hands, and the peasant gathering lucerne for fodder pulls it up stalk by stalk instead of reaping it, thus saving an inch or two on each stalk. The plough is a wretched wooden thing, so frail that one can easily carry it on one's shoulder, and fitted underneath with a rough iron spike which stirs the soil to a depth of about four inches. This is as much as the strength of the animals is equal to. It is usual to plough with a cow and a donkey yoked together. Two donkeys would not be quite strong enough, but on the other hand two cows would cost a little more to feed. The peasants possess no harrows, they merely plough the soil several times over in different directions, finally leaving it in rough furrows, after which the whole field has to be shaped with hoes into small oblong patches, to conserve water. Except for a day or two after the rare rainstorms there is never enough water. Along the edges of the fields channels are hacked out to a depth of thirty or forty feet to get at the tiny trickles which run through the subsoil.

19   Every afternoon a file of very old women passes down the road outside my house, each carrying a load of firewood. All of them are mummified with age and the sun, and all of them are tiny. It seems to be generally the case in primitive communities that the women, when they get beyond a certain age, shrink to the size of children. One day a poor old creature who could not have been more than four feet tall crept past me under a vast load of wood. I stopped her and put a five-sou piece (a little more than a farthing) into her hand. She answered with a shrill wail, almost a scream, which was partly gratitude but mainly surprise. I suppose that from her point of view, by taking any notice of her, I seemed almost to be violating a law of nature. She accepted her status as an old woman, that is to say as a beast of burden. When a family is travelling it is quite usual to see a father and a grown-up son riding ahead on donkeys, and an old woman following on foot, carrying the baggage.

20   But what is strange about these people is their invisibility. For several weeks, always at about the same time of day, the file of old women had hobbled past the house with their firewood, and though they had registered themselves on my eyeballs I cannot truly say that I had seen them. Firewood was passing—that was how I saw it. It was only that one day I happened to be walking behind them, and the curious up-and-down motion of a load of wood drew my attention to the human being underneath it. Then for the first

time I noticed the poor old earth-coloured bodies, bodies reduced to bones and leathery skin, bent double under the crushing weight. Yet I suppose I had not been five minutes on Moroccan soil before I noticed the overloading of the donkeys and was infuriated by it. There is no question that the donkeys are damnably treated. The Moroccan donkey is hardly bigger than a St Bernard dog, it carries a load which in the British army would be considered too much for a fifteen-hands mule, and very often its pack-saddle is not taken off its back for weeks together. But what is peculiarly pitiful is that it is the most willing creature on earth, it follows its master like a dog and does not need either bridle or halter. After a dozen years of devoted work it suddenly drops dead, whereupon its master tips it into the ditch and the village dogs have torn its guts out before it is cold.

This kind of thing makes one's blood boil, whereas—on the whole—the plight of the human beings does not. I am not commenting, merely pointing to a fact. People with brown skins are next door to invisible. Anyone can be sorry for the donkey with its galled back, but it is generally owing to some kind of accident if one even notices the old woman under her load of sticks.   21

As the storks flew northward the Negroes were marching southward—a long, dusty column, infantry, screw-gun batteries and then more infantry, four or five thousand men in all, winding up the road with a clumping of boots and a clatter of iron wheels.   22

They were Senegalese, the blackest Negroes in Africa, so black that sometimes it is difficult to see whereabouts on their necks the hair begins. Their splendid bodies were hidden in reach-me-down khaki uniforms, their feet squashed into boots that looked like blocks of wood, and every tin hat seemed to be a couple of sizes too small. It was very hot and the men had marched a long way. They slumped under the weight of their packs and the curiously sensitive black faces were glistening with sweat.   23

As they went past a tall, very young Negro turned and caught my eye. But the look he gave me was not in the least the kind of look you might expect. Not hostile, not contemptuous, not sullen, not even inquisitive. It was the shy, wide-eyed Negro look, which actually is a look of profound respect. I saw how it was. This wretched boy, who is a French citizen and has therefore been dragged from the forest to scrub floors and catch syphilis in garrison towns, actually has feelings of reverence before a white skin. He has been taught that the white race are his masters, and he still believes it.   24

But there is one thought which every white man (and in this connection it doesn't matter twopence if he calls himself a Socialist) thinks when he sees a black army marching past. "How much longer can we go on kidding these people? How long before they turn their guns in the other direction?"   25

It was curious, really. Every white man there has this thought stowed somewhere or other in his mind. I had it, so had the other onlookers, so had the officers on their sweating chargers and the white NCOs marching in the ranks. It was a kind of secret which we all knew and were too clever to tell;   26 only the Negroes didn't know it. And really it was almost like watching a flock of cattle to see the long column, a mile or two miles of armed men, flowing peacefully up the road, while the great white birds drifted over them in the opposite direction, glittering like scraps of paper.

JOHN McPHEE
Family Doctors

In "Family Doctors," originally published in The New Yorker *in 1984, McPhee uses techniques similar to those in "The Pine Barrens" (205–10). In making his controversial point, that family doctors living in the areas they serve, rather than remote teams of superspecialists, are essential to the health of rural America, McPhee inundates us with a deluge of short, specific case histories of the "insane" number of patients a typical family doctor in Maine must see. Through a multitude of specific details, vignettes, even statistics, McPhee presents an overview of family medical practice and a portrait, an extended definition, of a contemporary, quintessential family doctor, David Jones.*

We meet Jones, 31, in his rustic, almost old-fashioned context, as he embarks on a house call in "his pickup, the back of which is full of farm hardware and pig feed . . . with his stethoscope on the seat beside him." Jones then goes to his office, in a remodeled firehouse still inhabited by pigeons whose cooing "serves the purpose Muzak serves in Scarsdale." McPhee subtly shows how a combination of the rustic and the modern, a blending of sophisticated medical knowledge with fundamental human values—("It's [the patients'] right to be seen at home if they really can't get out")—contributes to the holistic view of human and humane health that characterizes family doctors. Such doctors, McPhee demonstrates, are themselves whole people—a combination of physician, worker, farmer, family member, neighbor, good citizen, appreciator of nature—rather than merely technicians. Jones's final quotation sums it up: "I don't charge my neighbors. I don't feel right doing that. . . . As a physician, you can go somewhere else and make more money, but you can't live like this. You walk up on that knoll, you see Mt. Katahdin. I'd love to be a trapper in Alaska. This is my compromise."

1 David Jones' farm consists of a house, a barn, a good-sized general-utility shed, and a hundred and four acres of land, some of which is woodlot. An antique sign has been tacked up on an inside wall of the shed:

LICENSED DOCTOR
•

HEALING
•

COUNSELLING
•

HOUSE CALLS
CHEERFULLY MADE

The sign dates from the era of the horse-and-sleigh, but in each of its claims and proclamations it applies to David Jones. Cheerfully, he makes house calls—gets into his pickup, the back of which is full of farm hardware and pig feed, and, with his stethoscope on the seat beside him, goes to see a woman with severe back pain, an old man with shingles, a woman with cancer who is dying at home. These patients live in and near Washburn, Maine, a town with some false-front buildings and a street so wide it vividly recalls the frontier days of the Old East. There is a clock in the white steeple of the First Baptist Church. The hands say eleven-forty-three and are correct twice a day. Side streets shortly turn into dirt roads and become the boundaries of potato fields. Washburn has a preponderance of old and young poor. The population is two thousand, and, often, not much is stirring but Dr. Jones. His office is on the ground floor of what was once a clapboard firehouse, its bell tower still standing at one corner. Pigeons live upstairs, and even in the walls. They make their presence heard. In the examining rooms, they provide the white noise. They serve the purpose Muzak serves in Scarsdale. Dr. Jones set up his practice in 1982. In no time, word was everywhere that he would visit people's homes. "It's their right to be seen at home if they really can't get out," he says. "Besides that, I get to see the house, the family—how the people live. A house call in Washburn is a town event. The rest of the people want to know how the patient is doing. I was some sort of popular hit when I first came up here, and I got a lot of TV coverage." The television station, in Presque Isle, which is ten miles from Washburn and fifteen from Jones' farm, covered Dr. Jones not only because he was some sort of popular hit but also because he was a throwback to Eocene time. Moreover, he was a new, young, American-trained doctor in the catchment area of the Presque Isle hospital, and as such was local news. When Jones and Sanders Burstein, finishing the residency in Augusta, had shown interest in being interviewed about practicing in the Presque Isle area, the hospital offered a chartered aircraft to fetch them.

All this was happening at a time when newspapers were increasingly reporting a "doctor glut" in America, saying that too many physicians had been trained and now they were on the sidewalks looking for work. "By and large, doctors are city people" is Jones' comment. "And so are their wives. They're not willing to go out into the country. They want to eat their cake and have it, too."

In the United States, the geographic distribution of doctors is not commensurate with the spread of people generally. The ratios of doctors to various populations are, indeed, grossly atilt. By and large, doctors are city people. The percentage of doctors in big metropolitan areas is four or five times what it is in towns fifteen to twenty-five thousand—not to mention the much lesser coverage of the small, scattered hamlets of a state like Maine. The doctor glut, if there is one, is an urban situation, and Jones seems to be right. Doctors are either unwilling or—because of the requirements of their various specialties—unable to go out into the country. Whatever the reason—from free choice to economic need—few would go as far as Jones.

5   If you get into your car in New York City and drive two hundred and sixty-five miles, you reach Maine. Then drive three hundred and fifty miles more and look around for Jones. His farm, by latitude, is a hundred miles farther north than Ottawa, and it is in a county that is considerably larger than the state of Connecticut. The County, as it is simply and universally referred to in Maine, has fewer than fourteen people per square mile—a statistic that owes itself to thousands of square miles of uninhabited forest. Along the eastern edge of the forest is cleared country—potato farmland— where most of the people of Aroostook County live. When they say, as they often do, that someone is from downcountry, the person could be from Mattawamkeag, sixty miles north of Bangor.

6   "I thought I'd have to work hard to start a practice here," Jones remarked one day about a year after his arrival. "It's been the opposite. Patients just come out of the woodwork. I'm overwhelmed. I really am." He sees them not only in Washburn but in Presque Isle as well, where thirty and sometimes forty will come through his examining rooms in a day—numbers he describes as "insane" and, whatever else they may signify, are obviously not conducive to the unhurried dialogues that are meant to knit the insights in a family practice. "I go on four hours' sleep if necessary," he said, and added, with a wistful shift of tone, "I'm a hyper individual anyway. I have to keep busy. If I slow down, I crack."

7   This freshly minted doctor, aged thirty-one, has a few gray strands in his hair, which is otherwise a dark and richly shining brown, and falls symmetrically from a part in the center to cover his ears. His mustache seems medical, in that it spreads flat beyond the corners of his mouth and suggests no prognosis, positive or negative. He wears a bow tie but no white coat or any sort of jacket. In examining rooms, he has the habit of resting on his haunches while he talks to patients, one result being that he is talking up to them even if they happen to be five years old.

8   "Now, have a seat up here and we'll take a listen to your heart and lungs," he says to a jack-of-all-trades who is seventy-six years old and is suffering from angina. The patient goes away with a prescription for nitroglycerin. "Old people come here once a month for reassurance," Jones remarks as he moves out of the examining room and, riffling through a family history, prepares to go into another. "The old people up here grew up in the County, and they're tremendously proud. They want to pay. Even if I say to them 'Medicare will pay for it—you've met your deductible,' they say, 'Can't we pay you something?' You meet very proud people up here—and, with regard to health care, there is better patient compliance than you'd find in a city."

9   Barb Maynard is in for a check on herself and her first baby, who looks around with interest and without complaint. She is a big, strong-framed woman, who went into labor and with three pushes gave birth to a ten-

pound-eleven-ounce son. Jones was much impressed. Among his questions now is one that has to do with oats. The Joneses barter with the Maynards, baby care for oats.

A twenty-eight-year-old woman comes in with spasmodic pain in her lower right side. She suffers from adult-onset diabetes, evidently a result of excessive weight. She has dieted valiantly and has recently had a baby. Jones worries that she may have dieted too valiantly. Gallbladder disease tends to occur in women after pregnancy or after they have lost a good deal of weight.   10

A harvester operator comes in saying his back is killing him. Most of the year, he is a potato packer, but this is the harvest. It is the event of the Aroostook year—like June among the cherry orchards of eastern Washington. In late September, early October, schools are closed for three weeks in the County, and people from high-school age upward stand all day and into the night on the harvesters—huge crawling structures that suggest gold dredges and move about as slowly, down the long rows across the vastly cambered land at what seems like ten to the minus seven miles per hour. The people on the harvesters differentiate potatoes from glacial cobbles, to which the potatoes bear some resemblance. As the harvester operator sits on the examining table, his jeans ride up from ankle-length unlaced boots. He has a bushy beard, and his long dark-blond hair is tied behind his head. His blood pressure is a hundred and forty-four over seventy-eight. He weighs two hundred and seventy pounds.   11

"Do you smoke or drink?" Jones asks him.   12

He says, "I smoke cigarettes but mostly chew."   13

"You have a disadvantage," Jones says gently. "You're heavy. It aggravates back problems. It could cause a disk."   14

The telephone rings. The caller says, "Doc, I need an antibiotic."   15

"I'm sorry. I can't prescribe it over the phone."   16

"Doc, this is the harvest."   17

Jones capitulates, gives the prescription over the phone. "I have to admit I have bastardized some of my values," he says afterward. "Before I came here, I never did that. But then I had never lived in Aroostook County. If you took people from Boston or New Jersey and put them on the harvest, two out of three would die."   18

René Vaillancourt comes in—thirteen years old and, by law, forbidden to work on a harvester. He handpicks. Some days ago, he cut his finger on a barrel. The skin is taut and glistens with extension. The end of the finger resembles a grape. Rainy—as his name is pronounced—is a deer hunter, and this is his trigger finger. More important to him, he is a basketball player, and the season approaches. Most important, he is missing a part of the harvest. Jones tells Rainy that for him the harvest is over, and prepares the hand for office surgery. His arm covered with green cloth, his finger presented to the scalpel, the boy asks Jones, "Will I be able to help my dad cut wood?"   19

"Not for a few days," says Jones.   20

21   And Rainy says, "Good."

22   Jones began this working day, as usual, with buttered coffee cake and a stack of bacon in the cafeteria at the Presque Isle hospital, where he spent the morning first-assisting in the operating room and making his daily rounds. He used to breakfast on three sausages and a pile of hash browns at the hospital every day, but he lightened the menu after he gained weight. Over coffee with a colleague, he talked trapping—muskrat, marten, fisher, mink—and the changeable value of pelts. When the colleague said he had picked up a beautiful mink dead on the road, Jones was thoughtful for a moment and appeared envious. He said he himself had made forty dollars last year "just on road kills," and eight hundred dollars on his fall and winter trap lines. As a boy, he trapped raccoons and muskrats along the Charles River, and on a year away from college he set up a trap line and ran it from a cabin where he lived alone in Maine. During his years in the Maine-Dartmouth residency, he set up a trap line within five miles of Augusta and brought down upon himself the scorn of other residents.

23   In those years, Jones also moonlighted on weekends in the County, working sixty-hour shifts in the emergency room in Caribou for twenty-five dollars an hour. It was a two-hundred-and-fifty-mile drive between Augusta and Caribou, not infrequently at twenty below zero in whiteouts with forty-mile winds, but Jones wanted the money to help pay for his envisioned farm. "In the Caribou E.R.," he says, "a lot of it was family practice: sore throats, cuts, chest pains, asthma, earaches—mundane general care. But I learned a lot, and learned to be comfortable with what I knew." Now and again, there was a chain-saw laceration, and, one weekend in three, a Code Ninety-nine. "Essentially, someone who's dead. The heart stops. You have to do your best to get it started again. The Code Ninety-nine was the most important thing I was there for—that and to keep the other doctors from having to get up in the night."

24   Among his patients on this September morning's rounds in the Presque Isle hospital, Staff Doctor Jones looked in on a young man—scarcely out of high school—in the intensive-care unit with aortic-root dilation. The I.C.U. has a picture window that frames the jagged silhouettes of dense black spruce and balsam fir. Moving down the corridor, Jones remarked that fourteen hours of surgery seemed to be indicated and the chance of death was one in four.

25   He looked in on Elizabeth Kelso, seventy-four years old. "My heart is pounding so hard," she said. "Really, it's getting me down. And I don't like the nurses."

26   "Blast me instead of them," Jones said. "I've got broad shoulders. You had a heart attack. Did you know that?"

27   Elizabeth Kelso nodded, and said to him, "I thought that's what it was."

28   He stopped at the beds of a chronic alcoholic with cirrhosis and a woman whose face was blotched with bruises as a result of a mysterious fall. A few

hours hence, she would be given a CAT scan. Computerized axial tomography—the procedural eponym—is done by a machine that costs about a million dollars. It can discover and define tumors beyond the abilities of the X-ray. A syndicate of Aroostook doctors recently bought a CAT scanner and had it fitted into a tractor-trailer. When the truck pulls up to a hospital, it is as if a 747 were docking at a gate at Kennedy. An accordion-pleated passageway distends from the hospital wall and hooks up to the trailer. Patients are CAT-scanned in the truck.

Jones had a word with Lauretta Smith, hospitalized for acute hypertension and double vision—seventy-seven years old, with Valentine-heart earrings, silver arrows through the hearts. 29

"They won't let me have what I see on the menu," she complained. 30

And Jones said, "What do you want to eat?" 31

"Biscuits." 32

"I think at your age to put you on a special diet that makes you feel bad is not a good idea. Have your biscuits. Just don't tell anybody." 33

"I want ice cream, too." 34

"You can have the ice cream." 35

"I don't know why the blood pressure don't stay down." 36

"May I have a listen to you? I want to listen to your heart." 37

"You knew Etta, didn't you? My sister?" 38

Back in the corridor, Jones said, "When people pass a certain age, the diets you impose should not be too restrictive. Eating is important, and it's one of the few recreations some older people have. You see how much she wanted a biscuit? If it keeps her cholesterol slightly elevated, what's lost? A lot is gained. I think we get hung up sometimes, running things by the book. A doctor can get too aggressive and upset the apple cart, do a lot of damage. People can be worse off than before you started doing anything." 39

Encountering a colleague in the hall, he was soon caught up in intense consultation. "How big are they?" he asked. 40

"Small." 41

"You're not going to eat those guys until April. They get worms. Look at their stools carefully. Clear up the worms, and pigs grow." 42

Jones buys piglets for twenty-five dollars, and feeds them, among other things, day-old bread, which he buys for two dollars and fifty cents a barrel. In all, he invests about a hundred and twenty dollars in a pig, and sells it to a meat market for something like three hundred. "There's easier money in doctoring," he says. "But farm money is worth eight times as much to me as money I make doctoring. Farm money is deep-rooted inside of me." Farm money and trapping money are coin of the true realm compared with the forty-five thousand dollars he was guaranteed by the hospital if he would set himself up in its catchment area—a sum, incidentally, that his earnings have greatly exceeded. 43

And now, in Washburn, Jones looks over the replaced fingertip of a 44 carpenter. "When it granulates in like this, it grows slowly from the sides," he says. "I think it's going to be all right. You lost about a third of an inch."

45 The carpenter, Tom Dow, is a leathery man in his sixties, who seems undisturbed. "We'll get it back," he tells Jones. "I think it will stretch out."

46 Joyce Sperry, seventy-one years old, has in recent times undergone a colostomy, a hysterectomy, and a vein stripping, with the result that her problem list is reduced to hypertension. As she departs for the winter in a trailer park in Florida, Jones tells her not to worry.

47 Hazel Campbell, seventy-seven, updates Jones on her hypertension, her edema, and her skin cancer, and bids him goodbye with a wave of a three-pronged cane.

48 A thirty-five-year-old man with canker sores thinks he has cuts on his tongue. Jones explains canker sores, and discovers, without surprise, that the patient loves to eat tomatoes immersed in vinegar.

49 Cole Chandler, nine months old and screaming, is in for a well-baby check. His mother wants to know if she should get up and care for him when he yells at night.

50 "Let him cry," says Jones.

51 After two more well babies, a mammogram, an atrial fibrillation, a chronic obstructive pulmonary problem, and a thoracic-outlet syndrome, Jones completes his day. He charges twenty dollars for an office visit, ten for a recheck. A complete physical goes for thirty-five dollars, not including lab work or electrocardiogram. "If I have to put three stitches in someone's head, that's where I can charge," he says. "I get forty-five dollars for suturing a laceration, sixty if I spend a long time. The stitches come out for free." Getting into his pickup, he drives on narrow roads through fields toward home. The sun is low. He has pigs to feed, turkeys, horses—helping his wife, Sabine, run the farm. "Doctors coin money when they do procedures," he remarks en route. "Family practice doesn't have any procedures. A urologist has cystoscopies, a gastroenterologist has gastroscopies, a dermatologist has biopsies. They can do three or four of those and make five or six hundred dollars in a single day. We get nothing when we use our time to understand the lives of our patients. Technology is rewarded in medicine, it seems to me, and not thinking."

52 Jones spent two high-school summers working in the Alaska Range, among people of multiple skills. The experience increased his need to be such a person, too. "I get bored doing one thing," he explains. "I admire people with ability to do different things. Within medicine, it's nice to think that I'll be taking care of the kids I deliver." His maternal grandfather and grandmother were general practitioners. They had a joint practice in Buffalo. Growing up in suburban Boston, Jones climbed trees to earn spending money—far above the ground with safety belt and chain saw, deftly amputating limbs. He became a long-distance runner, competing in Boston Marathons, and was sometimes inconvenienced when the running gave him sub-

ungual hematoma—painful pressure under the nails of his big toes. He dealt with it by heating paper clips until they glowed red, then poking them into his toenails to relieve the pressure. His surgical techniques had nowhere to go but up.

He met Sabine when he was a medical student at the University of   53
Vermont. She was a medical-surgical technician who was born in Germany and had come to Vermont at the age of thirteen. The University of Vermont is unusual in its requirement that medical students declare a major. Jones without hesitation declared for family practice—although, by his description, "it made you a second-class citizen in some of the training."

Approaching his home, he slows down, and briefly describes his various   54
neighbors. The dairy farmers regard him as a late sleeper. They, who get up at four-thirty, frequently call him two hours later, always with the same question—sarcastically asking, "Did I wake you?"

"I don't charge my neighbors," he says. "I don't feel right doing that."   55
His driveway runs through woods, in which the eye threads its way to visible clearings. He pauses for a few moments after making the turn, and says, "To have a place like this was always my dream. As a physician, you can go somewhere else and make more money, but you can't live like this. You walk up on that knoll, you see Mt. Katahdin. I'd love to be a trapper in Alaska. This is my compromise."

ROBERT CHRISTGAU
Beth Ann and Macrobioticism

Christgau, a journalist "interested in those places where popular culture and avant-garde culture intersect," has written primarily about popular music and film, though his analysis of the hippie counterculture in the essay below is perhaps his best-known work. Christgau was born in New York in 1942, earned a B.A. from Dartmouth in 1962, and has worked primarily in New York ever since, writing for The Village Voice *since 1969; his column on "Rock & Roll" appeared there 1969–72, followed in 1974 by "Consumer Guide." Christgau has also written a column on "Secular Music" for* Esquire, *film criticism for* Cheetah *and* Fusion, *and a book,* Any Old Way You Choose It: Rock and Other Pop Music, 1967– 73 (1973).*

In "Beth Ann and Macrobioticism" Christgau uses the techniques of fiction to tell the true and tragic story of two young extremists. The extremism of Beth Ann and Charlie, which had on various occasions led them to get high "on marijuana, hashish, cocaine, heroin, amphetamine, LSD and DMT . . . not to mention sex, food, art and the infinite reaches of the human spirit," also led them to adopt macrobioticism "as a new gospel" and to adhere zealously to a "dangerously unsound" macrobiotic diet. In a series of scenes, narrated as if the writer were present as an objective but nevertheless critical eyewitness, we see Beth Ann transformed over a period of months from a strikingly beautiful, healthy woman of 23 to a "living skeleton," impervious to the pleas of her bourgeois parents to see a doctor, neglected by the very gurus she worshipped, supported to the death by her devoted but equally deluded husband. Although Christgau himself does not preach, his extended illustration presents an indirect but powerful indictment of an entire counterculture within a counterculture.

1   One afternoon last February, Charlie Simon and his wife, Beth Ann, were walking in Washington Square Park. The Simons did not get out often, but when they did, people noticed them. Charlie, lean and dark, wore a bushy beard and shoulder-length hair, striking even in the Village. Beth Ann, small in the bust and full in the hip, with shimmering black hair and wide-eyed olive-skinned face, was more than striking—she was beautiful.

2   Beth Ann and Charlie were feeling high. They were high on the weather, which was clear and mild. They were also high on marijuana, which was nothing new. They had been high on marijuana very often since returning from Mexico at the end of 1963. During that time they had also been high on hashish, cocaine, heroin, amphetamine, LSD and DMT (Di-Methyl-Tryptamine) not to mention sex, food, art and the infinite reaches of the human spirit.

3   Unfortunately, they had also been wretched on precisely the same things, and the wretchedness seemed to be taking over. The sexual freedom of their marriage was turning a little scary. They were thinking of becoming vegetarians without knowing exactly why. They produced art objects in a compulsive stream, though they suspected that art was only an ego defense, a fortification erected by the self against the self's larger possibilities. And yet it was these larger possibilities, illuminated by drugs, which made them most wretched of all, for they had discovered that the religious experience induced by hallucinogens had its diabolic side, and the Devil had been taking them on trips they didn't really want to make.

4   The Simons were in deep, and they knew it could get deeper. Physical addiction was not the problem; the addiction was psychological and social. Kicking drugs would mean kicking a whole way of life. Yet, though it seemed impossible, they were trying. They managed to give up coffee and cigarettes and dreamed of moving to the country and having the baby they had almost had two years before, when Beth Ann miscarried. It is likely that as they tasted a bit of Nature in the park, with the sun beaming down among the bare trees, they were dreaming just that dream—the two of them off on a farm, away from all the ugliness and complexity of the urban drug scene, with time to meditate, to work, to grow. The dream must have seemed almost palpable in the freshening air. Then Nature turned around and kicked Charlie in the head.

5   For the wretchedness wasn't just spiritual—it manifested itself physically. Beth Ann suffered from intermittent leg pains, Charlie from migraine headaches. The migraines had struck almost daily for years, as often as four or five times a day. A two-hour headache was not uncommon, and one siege had

lasted two days. Doctors could do nothing; psychoanalysts were helpless. Once in a while there was a respite—LSD had provided relief for almost a month—but they always came back. And so, inevitably, on that lovely day in Washington Square, a bolt of pain seared through Charlie Simon's head.

The Simons lived at 246 Grand Street, between Chrystie and the Bow- 6 ery, where they rented the two floors over a luncheonette for $100. But Charlie, Fiorinal and Cafergot pills in his pocket, decided to seek relief at the home of a friend on Bedford Street in the West Village, and when he got there, the friend had something new for him to try.

His wife had been fooling around with the macrobiotic diet, a largely 7 vegetarian regime based on organically grown whole grain and the avoidance of sugar, which is expounded in a book called *Zen Macrobiotics* by self-described philosopher-scientist Georges Ohsawa. The book contains a lengthy section in which cures for virtually every human ailment from dandruff to leprosy are prescribed, as: "MIGRAINE: Diet No. 7 with a little gomasio. You will be cured in a few days."

Charlie was skeptical. He had eaten at the macrobiotic restaurant, the 8 Paradox, about six months before, and had not been impressed with food or clientele. But he consented to a spoonful of gomasio, a mixture of sea salt and sesame seeds, which is the staple condiment of the macrobiotic diet. He swallowed. The headache vanished. It was the end of the old life for Charlie. For Beth Ann, it was the end of a lot more.

Charlie and Beth Ann—friends invariably speak of them as a unit—were 9 something special on the scene. Both 23, they lived largely on the weekly check from Charlie's father, a prosperous but by no means opulent Clifton, N.J., dentist. Although the run-of-the-mill coffee-house gabbler might pine for such an arrangement, it is rarely considered cool among working artists to live off your parents. Yet the working artists in the Simons' circle never asked questions. The mystical tenor of the Simons' involvement with drugs was also unusual. For most of their older friends, marijuana was a giggle, not a way of life, and the other stuff was to be handled with extreme caution.

But Charlie and Beth Ann were not cautious people, and it was that, 10 more than their considerable artistic and intellectual gifts, which made them charismatically attractive to a good number of serious and moderately successful young artists. Charlie and Beth Ann were the enthusiasts, the extremists, the evangelists. If there was something to be tried—be it jazz or Morgan automobiles or psychedelics (consciousness-expanding drugs) or a new recipe for meat loaf—they would try it to the limit. Their involvement was always complete. And they always came back to spread the word.

Suddenly, macrobiotics was the new gospel, as the Simons completely 11 transformed their lives in a few weeks. They cut off drugs, and politely but firmly informed the itinerant hopheads who were in the habit of dropping around that they would have to turn on somewhere else. They gave up sex, not permanently, they told themselves, but until they could readjust to the new life. Beth Ann stopped taking birth-control pills. Charlie shaved his beard and cut his hair. They sold books, records and hi-fi equipment to make a little extra money and they stopped painting. Their new-found time was spent studying, discussing and contemplating the philosophy of macro-biotics.

12   Macrobiotics has almost nothing to do with Zen. Its central concept, yin and yang, is borrowed from Taoism. Ohsawa contends that all the physical and spiritual diseases of modern man result from his consuming too much yin (basically, potassium, although there are dozens of parallels) or too much yang (sodium)—usually too much yin. Grain is the basic food because it contains the same five-to-one potassium-sodium balance which is found in healthy blood. Dieters increase their intake of (yang) salt and drink as little (yin) liquid as possible.

13   Most fruits (too yin) and all red meat (too yang) are shunned, as are chemicals (additives and drugs, almost all yin, as well as "unnatural") and Western medicine. According to Ohsawa, the diet is not merely a sure means to a perfect physical health. Adhered to in religious faith and humility, it is also the path to spiritual health and enlightenment. And significantly for the Simons, whose psychedelic journeys had turned into nightmares, the source of health is placed not in the depths of the self, but in "the absolute justice and infinite wisdom of the Order of the Universe."

14   Most nutritionists regard the diet as dangerously unsound. Even in its most liberal form it provides virtually no calcium or Vitamin C, and the version which the Simons followed, Diet No. 7, was anything but liberal, consisting entirely of grain and tea. The reason they chose No. 7, of course, was that it *wasn't* liberal; Ohsawa proclaims it as the most extreme, most direct way to health. As usual, Charlie jumped on first, but Beth Ann, after some initial skepticism, soon overtook him in enthusiasm.

15   Enthusiasm was necessary, for Diet No. 7 was difficult. The worst trial was Charlie's third day, when he went through a period of "sugar with-drawal," which he claims was every bit as violent as a previous withdrawal from heroin. After that it was just a little rigorous for a while, and then it became a way of life. Although Ohsawa places no limit on quantity, the Simons ate relatively little—it's hard to gorge yourself when you're required to chew every mouthful 50 times—and each lost 20 pounds in a month, with Beth Ann's weight settling at about 110 and Charlie's at 120. But the loss didn't bother them; in fact, they took it as a sign of health.

16   And why not? They felt better than they ever had in their lives. Not only were the migraines and leg pains gone, but all of the minor fatigues and aches, the physical annoyances that everyone lives with, seemed to have disappeared. They slept less than six hours a night. They even felt high on the

diet, with spontaneous flashes that seemed purer and more enlightening than anything they had felt on drugs. Always domestic, Beth Ann became an excellent macrobiotic cook. She and Charlie spent most of their time outdoors, together, although they were seeing their old friends occasionally and converting many of them to modified versions of the diet. One joyous day, they threw out every useless palliative in the medicine cabinet and then transfomed their empty refrigerator—a beautiful $250 Gibson Double-Door Deluxe—into a piece of pop sculpture, with sea shells in the egg compartments and art supplies and various pieces of whimsy lining the shelves.

But at least one person was totally unimpressed—Sess Wiener, Beth   17
Ann's father. A vigorous pragmatist who had fought off both poverty and tuberculosis in his youth to become a prominent Paterson lawyer, all Sess knew was that his beautiful daughter was much too skinny. Unlike the drugs, which had been more or less out of his ken, the diet ran directly contrary to his own experience, and he opposed it vehemently. It was one more false step on the road to nowhere which his daughter had been traveling ever since she had insisted on marrying one of the most conspicuous young bums in the state of New Jersey four years before. The salubrious effects of the diet he regarded as a combination of self-hypnosis and folk medicine. He certainly didn't think they had anything to do with the absolute justice and infinite wisdom of the Order of the Universe.

Charlie himself experienced similar suspicions occasionally, but Beth   18
Ann's faith in the diet was always strong. Her only doubts were about herself. She felt she was dangerously *sanpaku,* which is to say (in Japanese) that the whites of her eyes showed underneath the iris, which is to say (in Macrobiotic) that she was gravely ill and destined for a tragic end. She was ashamed of the yang-ness of her upper legs, which were still muscular (strength is male, yang) and covered with downy hair. ("If a Japanese man discovers hair on the legs of a woman," Ohsawa writes, "it makes his flesh crawl.") The yang troubles in her legs she attributed to meat, a food she had always eaten but never relished, and she assumed the complete cure for both herself and her husband would be a long, long process because of the poisonous drugs their systems had accumulated. Their sin had been deep. She did not feel ready to start sex again.

But after a few months, the Simons did feel ready for art. Before the diet,   19
they had balanced their pastoral impulse with a pop sensibility which delighted in the trivia of an affluent culture. That sensibility slowly atrophied. Beth Ann's work, in which the romantic mood had always been tempered by a hard-edge quality, became softer and vaguer. But she was happy with it— all of its "diabolic aspects," she said, had disappeared.

In the ensuing months, the Simons studied Oriental philosophy, theories   20
of reincarnation, hara, breathing exercises, astrology, alchemy, spiritualism and hermeticism, and became more and more impatient with Western

thought. They went for rides in the country, or swimming with Irma Paule, head of the Ohsawa Foundation on Second Avenue, where most macrobiotic people in New York buy their food. At Irma's request they provided lodging for a Zen monk named Oki. Beth Ann suspected he was a fraud—in a month they saw him consume nothing but tea and beer, and he laughed at macrobiotics. Early in August, they took Oki to visit Paradox Lost, a macrobiotic camp in New Jersey. The Wiener summer home was near by, so the Simons decided to drop in. It was a mistake.

21   Sess Wiener had not seen his daughter in three weeks, and what he saw now appalled him. She had begun to lose weight again. There were red spots on her skin. She was complaining of pains in her hips and back and having some difficulty walking. Charlie was troubled with what he said were kidney stones, and sometimes his kidney attacks were accompanied by migraine. The Simons took a quick swim, then looked at each other. The vibrations from Sess were very bad. They left.

22   But Beth Ann was sick, and she kept on getting sicker. Her legs began to swell, and when she took the macrobiotic specific for swelling, a third of a pint of radish drink for three successive days, nothing happened. (Later, when Charlie's legs began to swell, he followed his instincts instead of the book and took a full pint of the drink every day, a most unmacrobiotic quantity. He got better.) Irma Paule, who claims to have been cured of paralytic arthritis on macrobiotics five years ago, told Beth Ann she had been through a similar period. She could have told Beth Ann some other things. She could have told her about Monty Scheier, who had died at her side in Union City on April 18, 1961. Or she could have told the story of Rose Cohen, who died in Knickerbocker hospital early in October, 1961, of salt poisoning and malnutrition, after having gone on macrobiotics a few months before. Or she might have told Beth Ann she was showing all the symptoms of scurvy. Instead, she told Beth Ann to vary Diet No. 7 with some raw vegetables.

23   As far as it went, this was good advice. In his books in English, Ohsawa's endorsement of No. 7 is somewhat ambiguous—while he prescribes it for almost every ill, he also implies that it is not a lifetime regimen. Beth Ann's sister Wendy and her brother-in-law Paul Klein, both on a more liberal macrobiotic diet, tried to tell her this, and so did Charlie. But Beth Ann was unmoved. Irma, she said, a little self-righteously, was a coward—afraid to "encounter the deep change" which continued adherence to Diet No. 7 entailed. Instead of widening her diet, she fasted altogether—four times for a total of about fourteen days in September. During each fast she would seem to improve, then tail off when it was over. The same thing would happen in the aftermath of any especially painful period of suffering. By the end of September she was bedridden, and Charlie was doing all the cooking and housework. He never really tried to convince Beth Ann that she should get off the diet, or even that she should see a doctor, although he did broach the

subject a few times. Sometimes his will to stick with it was even stronger than hers. He was not feeling too well either. Sex had ceased to be a possibility.

On the evening of October 13, Sess and Min Wiener came to visit their daughter in New York. When Sess glimpsed her lying on a mattress in a corner, he gasped and visibly turned color. Beth Ann was a living skeleton. Her legs were no longer yang, they were skin and bones. Her eyes, still *sanpaku*, were sunken in their sockets. She could barely sit up. She could not have weighed more than 80 pounds. 24

"Beth Ann," Sess said, "You are going to die. Do you want to die?" 25

Slowly, Beth Ann explained it once again. "Daddy, I am not going to die. I am going to get well, and when I get rid of all these poisons in my body I will be well for the rest of my life." 26

For the next two hours, Sess Wiener used every iota of his hortatory power to get Beth Ann to see a doctor, but it was useless. For Beth Ann, this was just another version of the argument she and her father had been having ever since her marriage, and before. Now she could show him once and for all that it was possible to do things differently and still be right. She had never understood her father's values, grounded in the everyday world he had overcome with such difficulty. The everyday world had never been a problem for her, and now she felt herself on the verge of conquering a much greater world, the world within. She had arrived at the perfect antithesis. What better way to set yourself against materialism than to destory the very substance of your own body? As her father's vehemence grew, she became more and more immovable. It was very bad, and before it was over Min Wiener had threatened to kill Charlie if he let her daughter die, and Charlie had threatened to call the police because Min threatened to kill him, and Sess had dared Charlie to do just that, and Beth Ann had decided she never wanted to see her parents again. The vibrations were just too much. 27

But Sess Wiener could not desert his daughter. The next day he enlisted the aid of Paul Klein, who together with Charlie, convinced Beth Ann to move in with Charlie's parents in Clifton. She had two conditions: that under no circumstances would a doctor be summoned, and that under no circumstances would her parents be permitted to see her. 28

Charlie was relieved. He had felt for a long time that it would do Beth Ann good to get away from the city, and especially Grand Street, which had so many bad connotations for both of them. And although Beth Ann carped and complained for the entire ambulance ride to Clifton, she cheered up when she got there, and did some watercolors—from a prone position, for she could no longer sit up—of the garden outside her window. Her parents tried to see her after she arrived, but the Simons stuck to their promise. 29

Beth Ann was still on Diet No. 7, with extra salt to counteract what she now believed was an excess of yin. She had written to Ohsawa describing her case and asking his advice. A few days after she got to Clifton she got her reply: You are a brave girl; stay on No. 7. Charlie, meanwhile, made an 30 alarming discovery: in one of Ohsawa's innumerable books in French, he warns specifically that no one is to stay on Diet No. 7 for more than two months except under his personal care.

31   But Beth Ann stayed on No. 7. She got no better. She spoke to one of her parents on the phone almost every day, but she claimed their negative waves were making it harder for her to get well. And she could feel negative waves from Dorothy Simon all the way across the house. She wrote Ohsawa again.

32   About two weeks after the move to Clifton, Charlie got a telegram from Oki asking for a lift from Kennedy Airport. As he drove out, Charlie had a sudden premonition that Beth Ann wasn't going to make it. He had never felt that way before, but at the airport he asked Oki, who was famous as a healer, to come and take a look at Beth Ann. Oki said he'd try to find the time. He didn't.

33   Two days later, Beth Ann sat up—not by herself, but with the aid of Dorothy Simon. Charlie, too weak to assist, watched as she agonized. It was awful. There had always been something people couldn't quite get hold of in Beth Ann, and as she had advanced on the diet this ethereal side had become more prominent. Even Charlie no longer felt in complete touch. But now he looked into his wife's face and was sure of what he saw: horror, horror at the extent of her own weakness and the outpouring of will it would take to overcome it. Then the horror changed to resignation, and Charlie's premonition returned. For the next five days his temperature ranged between 102 and 104 degrees.

34   On the morning of November 9, he woke at six in a high fever. Across the room, Dr. and Mrs. Simon were sitting with Beth Ann. He could not understand what was wrong and drifted off. When he got up again, his parents were gone, but Beth Ann told him what she believed was wrong— she had poisoned herself with too much salt.

35   Despite Irma Paule's reluctance to discuss such matters, almost every macrobiotic person has heard the story of the 24-year-old macrobiotic in Boston who died with carrot juice being poured down his throat after an overdose of salt. Charlie called Paul Klein, then set about fixing his wife some carrots. Paul arrived. They decided Irma must be summoned. Paul went back to New York for Irma.

36   Charlie sat at the head of his wife's bed. In the mail that morning there had been another letter from Ohsawa, telling Beth Ann she had misunderstood the diet completely and advising her to start all over again. He advised her especially to avoid salt. But all Charlie could do now was give her carrots. He lifted her head and fed her a spoonful. An orange dribble remained on her mouth.

37   "That's good," she said. Then her head rolled back in his hands, her eyes became very *sanpaku*, and she died. Charlie was still giving mouth-to-mouth resuscitation when the police arrived half an hour later.

Questions

1. In this argument, Christgau uses the novelist's techniques to tell a cautionary tale. Identify the characters—major and minor—he presents, the contrasting values they hold and lifestyles they represent, and the conflicts that form the line of both the narrative and the argument it contains.

2. Throughout our lives we make many judgments about people based on the varied contexts in which they function—where they live, the company they keep, what material possessions they have or don't have, even the contents of their refrigerators. Identify some of these various contexts in which Charlie and Beth Ann lived and died, and explain the significance of these as ascertained from the numerous details that Christgau provides.

3. What is Christgau arguing against? How can you tell? What values does he assume his readers hold? How are these likely to influence whether or not readers will agree with his point of view?

4. This essay was written in 1966, when the counterculture and the anti–Vietnam War protests were in full swing. Does it speak essentially only to problems of that era, or has Christgau transcended that time to address more universal issues?

RICHARD RODRIGUEZ

None of This Is Fair

The extent to which Richard Rodriguez, the son of Mexican immigrants, should emphasize his ethnic heritage is the overwhelming question of his autobiographical Hunger of Memory: The Education of Richard Rodriguez *(1982). He was born in San Francisco in 1944, spoke Spanish at home, and didn't learn English until he began grammar school in Sacramento. Although for a time he refused to speak Spanish, he studied that language in high school as if it were a foreign language; today he argues vociferously and controversially against bilingual education. Nevertheless, classified as Mexican-American, he benefited from Affirmative Action programs, and on scholarships he earned a B.A. from Stanford, an M.A. from Columbia, and a Ph.D. in Renaissance literature from the University of California at Berkeley. As this article, later incorporated into* Hunger of Memory, *makes clear, Rodriguez felt uneasy about the ethics of Affirmative Action even while he was receiving the benefits of this social policy. As he explains, he finally made the moral decision to refuse teaching offers from Yale and other prestigious universities because he thought those offers were made mainly because of his ethnic ancestry. Rodriguez now lives in San Francisco, where he is a lecturer, educational consultant, and free-lance writer.*

Rodriguez's "act of contrition" raises a potentially unsettling truth about argumentative writing: the person making the argument is as important as the argument itself. Aristotle and the classical Greeks knew that, but today many educated people want to pretend that the logic and support—the content—of the argument are all that matter. This simply isn't true. Many of the sentences below could be spoken, as they have been, by white conservatives, but it is one thing when a white conservative (a bigot, perhaps?) criticizes Affirmative Action, and another when the speaker is Mexican-American (a "coconut") or black (an "oreo cookie" or "Uncle Tom"). That doesn't mean Rodriguez is necessarily right, but his argu-

ment is harder to ignore than it would be if it came from a white conservative, because we assume that Rodriguez, obviously a concerned, sensitive Mexican-American, cares about the well-being of other Mexican-Americans, an assumption we might not be so willing to make about a conservative Anglo. Whatever the truth about Affirmative Action, the truth about arguments remains unchanged since the days of classical Greece: the character of the speaker or writer, always implicit in the argument, affects the way we respond to it. We won't accept an argument from someone we don't trust.

1   My plan to become a professor of English—my ambition during long years in college at Stanford, then in graduate school at Columbia and Berkeley— was complicated by feelings of embarrassment and guilt. So many times I would see other Mexican-Americans and know we were alike only in race. And yet, simply because our race was the same, I was, during the last years of my schooling, the beneficiary of their situation. Affirmative Action programs had made it all possible. The disadvantages of others permitted my promotion; the absence of many Mexican-Americans from academic life allowed my designation as a "minority student."

2   For me opportunities had been extravagant. There were fellowships, summer research grants, and teaching assistantships. After only two years in graduate school, I was offered teaching jobs by several colleges. Invitations to Washington conferences arrived and I had the chance to travel abroad as a "Mexican-American representative." The benefits were often, however, too gaudy to please. In three published essays, in conversations with teachers, in letters to politicians and at conferences, I worried the issue of Affirmative Action. Often I proposed contradictory opinions. Though consistent was the admission that—because of an early, excellent education—I was no longer a principal victim of racism or any other social oppression. I said that but still I continued to indicate on applications for financial aid that I was a Hispanic-American. It didn't really occur to me to say anything else, or to leave the question unanswered.

3   Thus I complied with and encouraged the odd bureaucratic logic of Affirmative Action. I let government officials treat the disadvantaged condition of many Mexican-Americans with my advancement. Each fall my presence was noted by Health, Education, and Welfare department statisticians. As I pursued advanced literary studies and learned the skill of reading Spenser and Wordsworth and Empson, I would hear myself numbered among the culturally disadvantaged. Still, silent, I didn't object.

4   But the irony cut deep. And guilt would not be evaded by averting my glance when I confronted a face like my own in a crowd. By late 1975, nearing the completion of my graduate studies at Berkeley, I was so wary of the benefits of Affirmative Action that I feared my inevitable success as an applicant for a teaching position. The months of fall—traditionally that time of academic job-searching—passed without my applying to a single school. When one of my professors chanced to learn this in late November, he was astonished, then furious. He yelled at me: Did I think that because I was a

minority student jobs would just come looking for me? What was I thinking? Did I realize that he and several other faculty members had already written letters on my behalf? Was I going to start acting like some other minority students he had known? They struggled for success and then, when it was almost within reach, grew strangely afraid and let it pass. Was that it? Was I determined to fail?

I did not respond to his questions. I didn't want to admit to him, and thus to myself, the reason I delayed.

I merely agreed to write to several schools. (In my letter I wrote: "I cannot claim to represent disadvantaged Mexican-Americans. The very fact that I am in a position to apply for this job should make that clear.") After two or three days, there were telegrams and phone calls, invitations to interviews, then airplane trips. A blur of faces and the murmur of their soft questions. And, over someone's shoulder, the sight of campus buildings shadowing pictures I had seen years before when I leafed through Ivy League catalogues with great expectations. At the end of each visit, interviewers would smile and wonder if I had any questions. A few times I quietly wondered what advantage my race had given me over other applicants. But that was an impossible question for them to answer without embarrassing me. Quickly, several persons insisted that my ethnic identity had given me no more than a "foot inside the door"; at most, I had a "slight edge" over other applicants. "We just looked at your dossier with extra care and we like what we saw. There was never any question of having to alter our standards. You can be certain of that."

In the early part of January, offers arrived on stiffly elegant stationery. Most schools promised terms appropriate for any new assistant professor. A few made matters worse—and almost more tempting—by offering more: the use of university housing; an unusually large starting salary; a reduced teaching schedule. As the stack of letters mounted, my hesitation increased. I started calling department chairmen to ask for another week, then 10 more days—"more time to reach a decision"—to avoid the decision I would need to make.

At school, meantime, some students hadn't received a single job offer. One man, probably the best student in the department, did not even get a request for his dossier. He and I met outside a classroom one day and he asked about my opportunities. He seemed happy for me. Faculty members beamed. They said they had expected it. "After all, not many schools are going to pass up getting a Chicano with a Ph.D. in Renaissance literature," somebody said laughing. Friends wanted to know which of the offers I was going to accept. But I couldn't make up my mind. February came and I was running out of time and excuses. (One chairman guessed my delay was a bargaining ploy and increased his offer with each of my calls.) I had to promise a decision by the 10th; the 12th at the very latest.

On the 18th of February, late in the afternoon, I was in the office I shared with several other teaching assistants. Another graduate student was sitting across the room at his desk. When I got up to leave, he looked over to say in an uneventful voice that he had some big news. He had finally decided to accept a position at a faraway university. It was not a job he especially wanted, he admitted. But he had to take it because there hadn't been any other offers. He felt trapped, and depressed, since his job would separate him from his young daughter.

10   I tried to encourage him by remarking that he was lucky at least to have found a job. So many others hadn't been able to get anything. But before I finished speaking I realized that I had said the wrong thing. And I anticipated his next question.

11   "What are your plans?" he wanted to know. "Is it true you've gotten an offer from Yale?"

12   I said that it was. "Only, I still haven't made up my mind."

13   He stared at me as I put on my jacket. And smiling, then unsmiling, he asked if I knew that he too had written to Yale. In his case, however, no one had bothered to acknowledge his letter with even a postcard. What did I think of that?

14   He gave me no time to answer.

15   "Damn!" he said sharply and his chair rasped the floor as he pushed himself back. Suddenly, it was to *me* that he was complaining. "It's just not right, Richard. None of this is fair. You've done some good work, but so have I. I'll bet our records are just about equal. But when we look for jobs this year, it's a different story. You get all of the breaks."

16   To evade his criticism, I wanted to side with him. I was about to admit the injustice of Affirmative Action. But he went on, his voice hard with accusation. "It's all very simple this year. You're a Chicano. And I am a Jew. That's the only real difference between us."

17   His words stung me: there was nothing he was telling me that I didn't know. I had admitted everything already. But to hear someone else say these things, and in such an accusing tone, was suddenly hard to take. In a deceptively calm voice, I responded that he had simplified the whole issue. The phrases came like bubbles to the tip of my tongue: "new blood"; "the importance of cultural diversity"; "the goal of racial integration." These were all the arguments I had proposed several years ago—and had long since abandoned. Of course the offers were unjustifiable. I knew that. All I was saying amounted to a frantic self-defense. I tried to find an end to a sentence. My voice faltered to a stop.

18   "Yeah, sure," he said. "I've heard all that before. Nothing you say really changes the fact that Affirmative Action is unfair. You see that, don't you? There isn't any way for me to compete with you. Once there were quotas to keep my parents out of certain schools; now there are quotas to get you in and the effect on me is the same as it was for them."

19   I listened to every word he spoke. But my mind was really on something else. I knew at that moment that I would reject all of the offers. I stood there

silently surprised by what an easy conclusion it was. Having prepared for so many years to teach, having trained myself to do nothing else, I had hesitated out of practical fear. But now that it was made, the decision came with relief. I immediately knew I had made the right choice.

My colleague continued talking and I realized that he was simply right. 20 Affirmative Action programs *are* unfair to white students. But as I listened to him assert his rights, I thought of the seriously disadvantaged. How different they were from white, middle-class students who come armed with the testimony of their grades and aptitude scores and self-confidence to complain about the unequal treatment they now receive. I listen to them. I do not want to be careless about what they say. Their rights are important to protect. But inevitably when I hear them or their lawyers, I think about the most seriously disadvantaged, not simply Mexican-Americans, but of all those who do not ever imagine themselves going to college or becoming doctors: white, black, brown. Always poor. Silent. They are not plaintiffs before the court or against the misdirection of Affirmative Action. They lack the confidence (my confidence!) to assume their right to a good education. They lack the confidence and skills a good primary and secondary education provides and which are prerequisites for informed public life. They remain silent.

The debate drones on and surrounds them in stillness. They are distant, 21 faraway figures like the boys I have seen peering down from freeway overpasses in some other part of town.

Questions

1. What is Affirmative Action? What is reverse discrimination? What does Rodriguez's comparison of his job-seeking experience with those of his white male classmates illustrate about these terms? Does Rodriguez intend for his readers to generalize on the basis of the job-seeking experiences of himself and his two white male classmates, one Jewish?

2. Rodriguez has been attacked as an Uncle Juan (a Chicano Uncle Tom) for claiming that he and other middle-class minority students improperly benefit from Affirmative Action programs that do not aid "all those who do not ever imagine themselves going to college or becoming doctors: white, black, brown. Always poor. Silent." Does Rodriguez convince you that he is right? Why or why not? Would his case have been stronger if he had illustrated it with an example of such disadvantaged people, rather than with the privileged people he represents?

3. Does Rodriguez present himself as an attractive character in this article, a portion of his autobiography? Does he expect readers to agree with his decision—principled or quixotic—to turn down numerous offers of good jobs? How does he expect readers' reactions to his personality to affect their reactions to his argument?

4. Why does Rodriguez use indirect discourse in paragraphs 8–10, 17, and 20, and direct conversation in paragraphs 11–16 and 18? What would the effects of the argument have been if he had used indirect discourse instead of direct conversation in paragraphs 11–16 and 18?

Investigative Reporting

BOB WOODWARD AND CARL BERNSTEIN

Uncovering Deception:
How Investigative Reporters Work

It is hard to imagine a more dramatic climax to the work of investigative reporting than the conclusion to the Watergate Affair, when the discoveries made by two junior reporters of The Washington Post *ultimately brought down the presidency of Richard Nixon. As this excerpt from* All the President's Men *(1974) shows, Woodward and Bernstein are surprising collaborators, very different in background and temperament. The street smart Bernstein was born in 1944 in Washington, D.C., attended (but didn't finish) the University of Maryland, and worked his way up from copyboy to reporter for the* Washington Star *before coming to the* Post. *Woodward, born in 1943, was far more Establishment, grew up in Wheaton, Illinois; graduated from Yale in 1965, and served as a naval officer before becoming a reporter for* The Washington Post. *Since the days of glory with* All the President's Men *(1974) and* The Final Days *(1976), Bernstein has moved to ABC in New York. Woodward, now an editor of the* Post, *has written, with Scott Armstrong,* The Brethren *(1979), a critical look at the Supreme Court; and* Wired *(1984), an investigation into the drug-riddled life and death of comedian John Belushi.*

Although only one brief weekend in the continuing Watergate investigation is described here, Woodward and Bernstein manage to transform the painstaking and often tedious process of searching for evidence into high drama. They detail how through tracking down leads, acting on hunches, checking out cryptic information (such as W.H. noted by a man's name in an address book) and circumstantial evidence, they amassed a collection of mosaic fragments that, when interpreted, led directly to W.H.—the White House. Patience, pushiness (if someone won't answer your request for information, keep asking), perseverance (if you keep asking the same questions to enough people, sooner or later people—even in the White House and the Pentagon—will tell you all sorts of things they shouldn't), and a willingness to take risks are the guiding principles not only for this collaboration but for other significant investigative reporting.

1   June 17, 1972. Nine o'clock Saturday morning. Early for the telephone. Woodward fumbled for the receiver and snapped awake. The city editor of the *Washington Post* was on the line. Five men had been arrested earlier that morning in a burglary at Democratic headquarters, carrying photographic equipment and electronic gear. Could he come in?

2   Woodward had worked for the *Post* for only nine months and was always looking for a good Saturday assignment, but this didn't sound like one. A burglary at the local Democratic headquarters was too much like most of what he had been doing—investigative pieces on unsanitary restaurants and

small-time police corruption. Woodward had hoped he had broken out of that; he had just finished a series of stories on the attempted assassination of Alabama Governor George Wallace. Now, it seemed, he was back in the same old slot.

Woodward left his one-room apartment in downtown Washington and walked the six blocks to the *Post*. The newspaper's mammoth newsroom— over 150 feet square with rows of brightly colored desks set on an acre of sound-absorbing carpet—is usually quiet on Saturday morning. Saturday is a day for long lunches, catching up on work, reading the Sunday supplements. As Woodward stopped to pick up his mail and telephone messages at the front of the newsroom, he noticed unusual activity around the city desk. He checked in with the city editor and learned with surprise that the burglars had not broken into the small local Democratic Party office but the headquarters of the Democratic National Committee in the Watergate office-apartment-hotel complex.

It was an odd place to find the Democrats. The opulent Watergate, on the banks of the Potomac in downtown Washington, was as Republican as the Union League Club. Its tenants included the former Attorney General of the United States John N. Mitchell, now director of the Committee for the Re-election of the President; the former Secretary of Commerce Maurice H. Stans, finance chairman of the President's campaign; the Republican national chairman, Senator Robert Dole of Kansas; President Nixon's secretary, Rose Mary Woods; and Anna Chennault, who was the widow of Flying Tiger ace Claire Chennault and a celebrated Republican hostess; plus many other prominent figures of the Nixon administration.

The futuristic complex, with its serpent's-teeth concrete balustrades and equally menacing prices ($100,000 for many of its two-bedroom cooperative apartments), had become the symbol of the ruling class in Richard Nixon's Washington. Two years earlier, it had been the target of 1000 anti-Nixon demonstrators who had shouted "Pigs," "Fascists" and "*Sieg Heil*" as they tried to storm the citadel of Republican power. They had run into a solid wall of riot-equipped Washington policemen who had pushed them back onto the campus of George Washington University with tear gas and billy clubs. From their balconies, anxious tenants of the Watergate had watched the confrontation, and some had cheered and toasted when the protesters were driven back and the westerly winds off the Potomac chased the tear gas away from the fortress. Among those who had been knocked to the ground was *Washington Post* reporter Carl Bernstein. The policeman who had sent him sprawling had probably not seen the press cards hanging from his neck, and had perhaps focused on his longish hair.

As Woodward began making phone calls, he noticed that Bernstein, one of the paper's two Virginia political reporters, was working on the burglary story, too.

7   Oh God, not Bernstein, Woodward thought, recalling several office tales about Bernstein's ability to push his way into a good story and get his byline on it.

8   That morning, Bernstein had Xeroxed copies of notes from reporters at the scene and informed the city editor that he would make some more checks. The city editor had shrugged his acceptance, and Bernstein had begun a series of phone calls to everybody at the Watergate he could reach—desk clerks, bellmen, maids in the housekeeping department, waiters in the restaurant.

9   Bernstein looked across the newsroom. There was a pillar between his desk and Woodward's, about 25 feet away. He stepped back several paces. It appeared that Woodward was also working on the story. That figured, Bernstein thought. Bob Woodward was a prima donna who played heavily at office politics. Yale. A veteran of the Navy officer corps. Lawns, greensward, staterooms and grass tennis courts, Bernstein guessed, but probably not enough pavement for him to be good at investigative reporting. Bernstein knew that Woodward couldn't write very well. One office rumor had it that English was not Woodward's native language.

10   Bernstein was a college dropout. He had started as a copy boy at the *Washington Star* when he was 16, become a full-time reporter at 19, and had worked at the *Post* since 1966. He occasionally did investigative series, had covered the courts and city hall, and liked to do long, discursive pieces about the capital's people and neighborhoods.

11   Woodward knew that Bernstein occasionally wrote about rock music for the *Post*. That figured. When he learned that Bernstein sometimes reviewed classical music, he choked that down with difficulty. Bernstein looked like one of those counterculture journalists that Woodward despised. Bernstein thought that Woodward's rapid rise at the *Post* had less to do with his ability than his Establishment credentials.

12   They had never worked on a story together. Woodward was 29, Bernstein 28.

13   The first details of the story had been phoned from inside the Watergate by Alfred E. Lewis, a veteran of 35 years of police reporting for the *Post*. Lewis was something of a legend in Washington journalism—half cop, half reporter, a man who often dressed in a blue regulation Metropolitan Police sweater buttoned at the bottom over a brass Star-of-David buckle. In 35 years, Lewis had never really "written" a story; he phoned the details in to a rewrite man, and for years the *Washington Post* did not even have a typewriter at police headquarters.

14   The five men arrested at 2:30 A.M. had been dressed in business suits and all had worn Playtex rubber surgical gloves. Police had seized a walkie-talkie, 40 rolls of unexposed film, two 35-millimeter cameras, lock picks, pen-size tear-gas guns, and bugging devices that apparently were capable of picking up both telephone and room conversations.

15   "One of the men had $814, one $800, one $215, one $234, one $230,"

Lewis had dictated. "Most of it was in $100 bills, in sequence. . . . They seemed to know their way around; at least one of them must have been familiar with the layout. They had rooms on the second and third floors of the hotel. The men ate lobster in the restaurant there, all at the same table that night. One wore a suit bought in Raleigh's. Somebody got a look at the breast pocket."

Woodward learned from Lewis that the suspects were going to appear in 16 court that afternoon for a preliminary hearing. He decided to go.

Woodward had been to the courthouse before. The hearing procedure 17 was an institutionalized fixture of the local court's turnstile system of justice: A quick appearance before a judge who set bond for accused pimps, prostitutes, muggers—and, on this day, the five men who had been arrested at the Watergate.

A group of attorneys—known as the "Fifth Street Lawyers" because of 18 the location of the courthouse and their storefront offices—were hanging around the corridors as usual, waiting for appointments as government-paid counsel to indigent defendants. Two of the regulars—a tall, thin attorney in a · frayed sharkskin suit and an obese, middle-aged lawyer who had once been disciplined for soliciting cases in the basement cellblock—were muttering their distress. They had been tentatively appointed to represent the five accused Watergate burglars and had then been informed that the men had retained their own counsel, which is unusual.

Woodward went inside the courtroom. One person stood out. In a 19 middle row sat a young man with fashionably long hair and an expensive suit with slightly flared lapels, his chin high, his eyes searching the room as if he were in unfamiliar surroundings.

Woodward sat down next to him and asked if he was in court because of 20 the Watergate arrests.

"Perhaps," the man said. "I'm not the attorney of record. I'm acting as an 21 individual."

He said his name was Douglas Caddy and he introduced a small, anemic- 22 looking man next to him as the attorney of record, Joseph Rafferty, Jr. Rafferty appeared to have been routed out of bed; he was unshaven and squinted as if the light hurt his eyes. The two lawyers wandered in and out of the courtroom. Woodward finally cornered Rafferty in a hallway and got the names and addresses of the five suspects. Four of them were from Miami, three of them Cuban-Americans.

Caddy didn't want to talk. "Please don't take it personally," he told 23 Woodward. "It would be a mistake to do that. I just don't have anything to say."

Woodward asked Caddy about his clients. 24

"They are not my clients," he said. 25

But you are a lawyer? Woodward asked. 26

"I'm not going to talk to you." 27

28   Caddy walked back into the courtroom. Woodward followed.

29   "Please, I have nothing to say."

30   Would the five men be able to post bond? Woodward asked.

31   After politely refusing to answer several more times, Caddy replied quickly that the men were all employed and had families—factors that would be taken into consideration by the judge in setting bond. He walked back into the corridor.

32   Woodward followed: Just tell me about yourself, how you got into the case.

33   "I'm not in the case."

34   Why are you here?

35   "Look," Caddy said, "I met one of the defendants, Bernard Barker, at a social occasion."

36   Where?

37   "In D.C. It was cocktails at the Army-Navy Club. We had a sympathetic conversation . . . that's all I'm going to say."

38   How did you get into the case?

39   Caddy pivoted and walked back in. After half an hour, he went out again.

40   Woodward asked how he got into the case.

41   This time Caddy said he'd gotten a call shortly after 3:00 A.M. from Barker's wife. "She said her husband had told her to call me if he hadn't called her by three, that it might mean he was in trouble."

42   Caddy said he was probably the only attorney Barker knew in Washington, and brushed off more questions, adding that he had probably said too much.

43   At 3:30 P.M., the five suspects, still dressed in dark business suits but stripped of their belts and ties, were led into the courtroom by a marshal. They seated themselves silently in a row and stared blankly toward the bench, kneading their hands. They looked nervous, respectful and tough.

44   Earl Silbert, the government prosecutor, rose as their case was called by the clerk. Slight, intent and owlish with his horn-rimmed glasses, he was known as "Earl the Pearl" to Fifth Streeters familiar with his fondness for dramatic courtroom gestures and flowery speech. He argued that the five men should not be released on bond. They had given false names, had not cooperated with the police, possessed "$2300 in cold cash, and had a tendency to travel abroad." They had been arrested in a "professional burglary" with a "clandestine" purpose. Silbert drew out the word "clandestine."

45   Judge James A. Belsen asked the men their professions. One spoke up, answering that they were "anti-communists," and the others nodded their agreement. The Judge, accustomed to hearing unconventional job descriptions, nonetheless appeared perplexed. The tallest of the suspects, who had given his name as James W. McCord, Jr., was asked to step forward. He was balding, with a large, flat nose, a square jaw, perfect teeth and a benign expression that seemed incongruous with his hard-edged features.

The Judge asked his occupation. 46

"Security consultant," he replied. 47

The Judge asked where. 48

McCord, in a soft drawl, said that he had recently retired from govern- 49
ment service. Woodward moved to the front row and leaned forward.

"Where in government?" asked the Judge. 50

"CIA," McCord whispered. 51

The Judge flinched slightly. 52

Holy shit, Woodward said half aloud, the CIA. 53

He got a cab back to the office and reported McCord's statement. Eight 54
reporters were involved in putting together the story under the byline of
Alfred E. Lewis. As the 6:30 P.M. deadline approached, Howard Simons, the
Post's managing editor, came into the city editor's office at the south side of
the newsroom. "That's a hell of a story," he told the city editor, Barry
Sussman, and ordered it onto Sunday's front page.

The first paragraph of the story read: "Five men, one of whom said he is 55
a former employee of the Central Intelligence Agency, were arrested at 2:30
A.M. yesterday in what authorities described as an elaborate plot to bug the
offices of the Democratic National Committee here."

A federal grand jury investigation had already been announced, but even 56
so it was Simons' opinion that there still were too many unknown factors
about the break-in to make it the lead story. "It could be crazy Cubans," he
said.

Indeed, the thought that the break-in might somehow be the work of the 57
Republicans seemed implausible. On June 17, 1972, less than a month before
the Democratic convention, the President stood ahead of all announced
Democratic candidates in the polls by no less than 19 points. Richard Nixon's
vision of an emerging Republican majority that would dominate the last
quarter of the century, much as the Democrats had dominated two previous
generations, appeared possible. The Democratic Party was in disarray as a
brutal primary season approached its end. Senator George McGovern of
South Dakota, considered by the White House and Democratic Party professionals alike to be Nixon's weakest opponent, was emerging as the clear
favorite to win the Democrats' nomination for President.

The story noted: "There was no immediate explanation as to why the five 58
suspects would want to bug the Democratic National Committee offices, or
whether or not they were working for any other individuals or organizations."

Bernstein had written another story for the Sunday paper on the sus- 59
pects. Four were from Miami: Bernard L. Barker, Frank A. Sturgis, Virgilio
R. Gonzalez and Eugenio R. Martinez. He had called a *Miami Herald* reporter and obtained a long list of Cuban exile leaders. A *Post* reporter had
been sent from the President's press party in Key Biscayne to make checks in
Miami's Cuban community. All four of the Miami suspects had been in-

volved in anti-Castro activities and were also said to have CIA connections. ("I've never known if he works for the CIA or not," Mrs. Barker told Bernstein. "The men never tell the women anything about that.") Sturgis, an American soldier of fortune and the only non-Cuban among them, had been recruiting militant Cubans to demonstrate at the Democratic national convention, according to several persons. One Cuban leader told Bernstein that Sturgis and others whom he described as "former CIA types" intended to use paid provocateurs to fight anti-war demonstrators in the streets during the national political conventions.

60 Woodward left the office about eight o'clock that Saturday night. He knew he should have stayed later to track down James McCord. He had not even checked the local telephone directory to see if there was a James McCord listed in Washington or its suburbs.

61 The national staff of the *Washington Post* rarely covers police stories. So, at Sussman's request, both Bernstein and Woodward returned to the office the next morning, a bright Sunday, June 18, to follow up. An item moving on the Associated Press wire made it embarrassingly clear why McCord had deserved further checking. According to campaign spending reports filed with the government, James McCord was the security coordinator of the Committee for the Reelection of the President (CRP).

62 The two reporters stood in the middle of the newsroom and looked at each other. What the hell do you think it means? Woodward asked. Bernstein didn't know.

63 In Los Angeles, John Mitchell, the former U.S. Attorney General and the President's campaign manager, issued a statement: "The person involved is the proprietor of a private security agency who was employed by our committee months ago to assist with the installation of our security system. He has, as we understand it, a number of business clients and interests, and we have no knowledge of these relationships. We want to emphasize that this man and the other people involved were not operating on either our behalf or with our consent. There is no place in our campaign or in the electoral process for this type of activity, and we will not permit or condone it."

64 In Washington, the Democratic national chairman, Lawrence F. O'Brien, said the break-in "raised the ugliest question about the integrity of the political process that I have encountered in a quarter-century of political activity. No mere statement of innocence by Mr. Nixon's campaign manager, John Mitchell, will dispel these questions."

65 The wire services, which had carried the Mitchell and O'Brien statements, could be relied upon to gather official pronouncements from the national politicians. The reporters turned their attention to the burglars.

66 The telephone book listed the private security consulting agency run by McCord. There was no answer. They checked the local "criss-cross" directories which list phone numbers by street addresses. There was no answer at

either McCord's home or his business. The address of McCord Associates, 414 Hungerford Drive, Rockville, Maryland, is a large office building, and the cross-reference directory for Rockville lists the tenants. The reporters divided the names and began calling them at home. One attorney recalled that a teenage girl who had worked part-time for him the previous summer knew McCord, or perhaps it was the girl's father who knew him. The attorney could only remember vaguely the girl's last name—Westall or something like that. They contacted five persons with similar last names before Woodward finally reached Harlan A. Westrell, who said he knew McCord.

Westrell, who obviously had not read the papers, wondered why Woodward wanted to know about McCord. Woodward said simply that he was seeking information for a possible story. Westrell seemed flattered and provided some information about McCord, his friends and his background. He gave Woodward some other names to call. 67

Gradually, a spare profile of McCord began to emerge: a native of the Texas Panhandle; deeply religious, active in the First Baptist Church of Washington; father of an Air Force Academy cadet and a retarded daughter; ex-FBI agent; military reservist; former chief of physical security for the CIA; teacher of a security course at Montgomery Junior College; a family man; extremely conscientious; quiet; reliable. John Mitchell's description of McCord notwithstanding, those who knew him agreed that he worked full-time for the President's re-election committee. 68

Several persons referred to McCord's integrity, his "rocklike" character, but there was something else. Westrell and three others described McCord as the consummate "government man"—reluctant to act on his own initiative, respectful of the chain of command, unquestioning in following orders. 69

Woodward typed out the first three paragraphs of a story identifying one of the Watergate burglars as a salaried security coordinator of the President's re-election committee and handed it to an editor on the city desk. A minute later, Bernstein was looking over the editor's shoulder, Woodward noticed. Then Bernstein was walking back to his desk with the first page of the story; soon he was typing. Woodward finished the second page and passed it to the editor. Bernstein had soon relieved him of it and was back at his typewriter. Woodward decided to walk over and find out what was happening. 70

Bernstein was rewriting the story. Woodward read the rewritten version. It was better. 71

That night, Woodward drove to McCord's home, a large two-story brick house, classically suburban, set in a cul-de-sac not far from Route 70-S, the main highway through Rockville. The lights were on, but no one answered the door. 72

After midnight, Woodward received a call at home from Eugene Bachinski, the *Post*'s regular night police reporter. The night police beat is generally considered the worst assignment at the paper. The hours are bad— 73

from about 6:30 P.M. to 2:30 A.M. But Bachinski—tall, goateed and quiet—
seemed to like his job, or at least he seemed to like the cops. He had come to
know many of them quite well, saw a few socially and moved easily on his
nightly rounds through the various squads at police headquarters: homicide,
vice (grandly called the Morals Division), traffic, intelligence, sex, fraud,
robbery—the catalogue of city life as viewed by the policeman.

74   Bachinski had something from one of his police sources. Two address
books, belonging to two of the Miami men arrested inside the Watergate,
contained the name and phone number of a Howard E. Hunt, with the small
notations "*W. House*" and "*W.H.*" Woodward sat down in a hard chair by his
phone and checked the telephone directory. He found a listing for E. Howard Hunt, Jr., in Potomac, Maryland, the affluent horse-country suburb in
Montgomery County. No answer.

75   At the office next morning, Woodward made a list of the leads. One of
McCord's neighbors had said that he had seen McCord in an Air Force
officer's uniform, and another had said that McCord was a lieutenant colonel
in the Air Force Reserve. Half a dozen calls to the Pentagon later, a personnel
officer told him that James McCord was a lieutenant colonel in a special
Washington-based reserve unit attached to the Office of Emergency Pre-
paredness. The officer read him the unit roster, which contained only 15
names. Woodward started calling. On the fourth try, Philip Jones, an enlisted
man, mentioned casually that the unit's assignment was to draw up lists of
radicals and to help develop contingency plans for censorship of the news
media and U.S. mail in time of war.

76   Woodward placed a call to a James Grimm, whose name and Miami
telephone number Bachinski had said was in the address book of Eugenio
Martinez. Mr. Grimm identified himself as a housing officer for the University of Miami, and said that Martinez had contacted him about two weeks
earlier to ask if the university could find accommodations for about 3000
Young Republicans during the GOP national convention in August. Woodward called CRP, the Republican National Committee headquarters and
several party officials who were working on convention planning in Washington and Miami. All said they had never heard of Martinez or of plans to use
the university for housing Young Republicans.

77   But the first priority on that Monday was Hunt. The Miami suspects'
belongings were listed in a confidential police inventory that Bachinski had
obtained. There were "two pieces of yellow-lined paper, one addressed to
'Dear Friend Mr. Howard,' and another to 'Dear Mr. H.H.,'" and an unmailed envelope containing Hunt's personal check for $6.36 made out to the
Lakewood Country Club in Rockville, along with a bill for the same amount.

78   Woodward called an old friend and sometimes source who worked for
the federal government and did not like to be called at his office. His friend
said hurriedly that the break-in case was going to "heat up," but he couldn't
explain and hung up.

It was approaching 3:00 P.M., the hour when the *Post*'s editors list in a "news budget" the stories they expect for the next day's paper. Woodward, who had been assigned to write Tuesday's Watergate story, picked up the telephone and dialed 456-1414—the White House. He asked for Howard Hunt. The switchboard operator rang an extension. There was no answer. Woodward was about to hang up when the operator came back on the line. "There is one other place he might be," she said. "In Mr. Colson's office." 79

"Mr. Hunt is not here now," Colson's secretary told Woodward, and gave him the number of a Washington public-relations firm, Robert R. Mullen and Company, where she said Hunt worked as a writer. 80

Woodward walked across to the national desk at the east end of the newsroom and asked one of the assistant national editors, J. D. Alexander, who Colson was. Alexander, a heavy-set man in his mid-thirties with a thick beard, laughed. Charles W. Colson, special counsel to the President of the United States, was the White House "hatchet man," he said. 81

Woodward called the White House back and asked a clerk in the personnel office if Howard Hunt was on the payroll. She said she would check the records. A few moments later, she told Woodward that Howard Hunt was a consultant working for Colson. 82

Woodward called the Mullen public-relations firm and asked for Howard Hunt. 83

"Howard Hunt here," the voice said. 84

Woodward identified himself. 85

"Yes? What is it?" Hunt sounded impatient. 86

Woodward asked Hunt why his name and phone number were in the address books of two of the men arrested at the Watergate. 87

"Good God!" Howard Hunt said. Then he quickly added, "In view that the matter is under adjudication, I have no comment," and slammed down the phone. 88

Woodward thought he had a story. Still, anyone's name and phone number could be in an address book. The country-club bill seemed to be additional evidence of Hunt's connection with the burglars. But what connection? A story headlined "White House Consultant Linked to Bugging Suspects" could be a grievous mistake, misleading, unfair to Hunt. 89

Woodward called Ken W. Clawson, the deputy director of White House communications, who had been a *Post* reporter until the previous January. He told Clawson what was in the address books and police inventory, then asked what Hunt's duties at the White House were. Clawson said he would check. 90

An hour later, Clawson called back to say that Hunt had worked as a White House consultant on declassification of the Pentagon Papers and, more recently, on a narcotics intelligence project. Hunt had last been paid as a consultant on March 29, he said, and had not done any work for the White House since. 91

"I've looked into the matter very thoroughly, and I am convinced that 92 neither Mr. Colson nor anyone else at the White House had any knowledge of, or participation in, this deplorable incident at the Democratic National Committee," Clawson said.

93   The comment was unsolicited.

94   Woodward phoned Robert F. Bennett, president of the Mullen public-relations firm, and asked about Hunt. Bennett, the son of Republican Senator Wallace F. Bennett of Utah, said, "I guess it's no secret that Howard was with the CIA."

95   It had been a secret to Woodward. He called the CIA, where a spokesman said that Hunt had been with the agency from 1949 to 1970.

96   Woodward didn't know what to think. He placed another call to his government friend and asked for advice. His friend sounded nervous. On an off-the-record basis he told Woodward that the FBI regarded Hunt as a prime suspect in the Watergate investigation for many reasons aside from the address-book entries and the unmailed check. Woodward was bound not to use the information in a story because it was off the record. But his friend assured him that there would be nothing unfair about a story which reported the address-book and country-club connections. That assurance could not be used in print either.

97   Barry Sussman, the city editor, was intrigued. He dug into the *Post* library's clippings on Colson and found a February 1971 story in which an anonymous source described Colson as one of the "original back room boys . . . the brokers, the guys who fix things when they break down and do the dirty work when it's necessary." Woodward's story about Hunt, which identified him as a consultant who had worked in the White House for Colson, included the quotation and noted that it came from a profile written by "Ken W. Clawson, a current White House aide who until recently was a [*Washington Post*] reporter."

98   The story was headlined "White House Consultant Linked to Bugging Suspects."

99   That morning at the Florida White House in Key Biscayne, presidential press secretary Ronald L. Ziegler briefly answered a question about the break-in at the Watergate by observing: "Certain elements may try to stretch this beyond what it is." Ziegler described the incident as "a third-rate burglary attempt" not worthy of further White House comment.

100   The next day, Democratic Party chairman O'Brien filed a $1 million civil damage suit against the Committee for the Re-election of the President. Citing the "potential involvement" of Colson in the break-in, O'Brien charged that the facts were "developing a clear line to the White House" and added: "We learned of this bugging attempt only because it was bungled. How many other attempts have there been and just who was involved? I believe we are about to witness the ultimate test of this administration that so piously committed itself to a new era of law and order just four years ago."

JESSICA MITFORD

Let Us Now Appraise
Famous Writers

If your image of a muckraker—the older, less-dignified term for an investigative reporter—is of a hard-bitten, chain smoking, angry young man of the streets, the patrician demeanor and urbane wit of Jessica Mitford, grande dame of contemporary muckrakers, may come as a surprise. Although born at Batesford Mansion, England, in 1917, the daughter of Lord and Lady Redesdale, and educated at home, as explained in her autobiographical volumes, Daughters and Rebels *(1960) and* A Fine Old Madness *(1977), her lifelong radicalism belies her conservative heritage. Indeed, Mitford's sisters include Nancy, a novelist and biographer, Diana, and Unity. While they espoused Fascism during Hitler's rise, Jessica married a Communist sympathizer and fled to Loyalist Spain during the Spanish Civil War. Her desire to expose and expunge social wrongs underlies Mitford's best-selling* The American Way of Death *(1963), an investigative exposé of the funeral industry, and* Kind and Unusual Punishment: The Prison Business *(1973). Her most recent book is a meticulous memoir of a friend, Phillip Toynbee,* Faces of Phillip *(1984).*

An investigative reporter struggling to expose corruption is the writer's equivalent of St. George going out to slay the dragon, and, like St. George, the work of an investigator can be misunderstood or resented, even by those glad to see the dragon dead. The actual combat with the dragon is a glorious public event, but spectators are unaware of the months, sometimes years, of lonesome effort the private preparation takes. As Mitford makes clear in the coda to this article, she was finally able to slay the fraudulent Famous Writers School through reading, research, interviews, visits to the site of the fraud, more research, more interviews, polite—and more punchy—skirmishes with publishers, and the secret weapon of all successful dragon fighters, great good luck. As Mitford's conclusion shows, no victory over evil is ever final; dragons, like the phoenix, are reborn in the ashes of yesterday's newspapers—which is why we continue to need St. Georges.

> Beware of the scribes who like to go about in long robes, and love salutations in the market places . . . and the places of honor at feasts; who devour widows' houses . . .
>
> Luke 20:46, 47

In recent years I have become aware of fifteen Famous Faces looking me straight in the eye from the pages of innumerable magazines, newspapers, fold-out advertisements, sometimes in black-and-white, sometimes in living color, sometimes posed in a group around a table, sometimes shown singly, pipe in hand in book-lined study or strolling through a woodsy countryside: the Guiding Faculty of the Famous Writers School.*

*They are: Faith Baldwin, John Caples, Bruce Catton, Bennett Cerf, Mignon G. Eberhart, Paul Engle, Bergen Evans, Clifton Fadiman, Rudolf Flesch, Phyllis McGinley, J. D. Ratcliff, Rod Serling, Max Shulman, Red Smith, Mark Wiseman.

2   Here is Bennett Cerf, most famous of them all, his kindly, humorous face aglow with sincerity, speaking to us in the first person from a mini-billboard tucked into our Sunday newspaper:

> If you want to write, my colleagues and I would like to test your writing aptitude. We'll help you find out whether you can be trained to become a successful writer. . . .

J. D. Ratcliff, billed in the ads as "one of America's highest-paid free-lance authors," thinks it's a shame, too:

> I can't understand why more beginners don't take the short road to publication by writing articles for magazines and newspapers. It's a wonderful life.

3   The short road is attained, the ads imply, via the aptitude test which Bennett Cerf and his colleagues would like you to take so they may "grade it free of charge." If you are one of the fortunate ones who do well on the test, you may "enroll for professional training." After that, your future is virtually assured, for the ads promise that "Fifteen Famous Writers will teach you to write successfully at home."

4   These offers are motivated, the ads make clear, by a degree of altruism not often found in those at the top of the ladder. The Fifteen have never forgotten the tough times—the "sheer blood, sweat and rejection slips," as J. D. Ratcliff puts it—through which they suffered as beginning writers; and now they want to extend a helping hand to those still at the bottom rung. "When I look back, I can't help thinking of all the time and agony I would have saved if I could have found a real 'pro' to work with me," says Ratcliff.

5   How can Bennett Cerf—Chairman of the Board of Random House, columnist, television personality—and his renowned colleagues find time to grade all the thousands of aptitude tests that must come pouring in, and on top of that fulfill their pledge to "teach you to write successfully at home"? What are the standards for admission to the school? How many graduates actually find their way into the "huge market that will pay well for pieces of almost any length" which, says J. D. Ratcliff, exists for the beginning writer? What are the "secrets of success" that the Famous Fifteen say they have "poured into a set of specially created textbooks"? And how much does it cost to be initiated into these secrets?

6   My mild curiosity about these matters might never have been satisfied had I not learned, coincidentally, about two candidates for the professional training offered by the Famous Writers who passed the aptitude test with flying colors: a seventy-two-year-old foreign-born widow living on Social Security, and a fictitious character named Louella Mae Burns.

7   The adventures of these two impelled me to talk with Bennett Cerf and other members of the Guiding Faculty, to interview former students, to examine the "set of specially created textbooks" (and the annual stockholders'

reports, which proved in some ways more instructive), and eventually to visit the school's headquarters in Westport, Connecticut.

An Oakland lawyer told me about the seventy-two-year-old widow. She had come to him in some distress: a salesman had charmed his way into her home and at the end of his sales pitch had relieved her of $200 (her entire bank account) as down payment on a $900 contract, the balance of which would be paid off in monthly installments. . . . No sooner had the salesman left than she thought better of it, and when the lessons arrived she returned them unopened.

To her pleas to be released from the contract, the Famous Writers replied: "Please understand that you are involved in a legal and binding contract," and added that the school's policy requires a doctor's certificate attesting to the ill health of a student before she is permitted to withdraw.

There was a short, sharp struggle. The lawyer wrote an angry letter to the school demanding prompt return of the $200 "fraudulently taken" from the widow, and got an equally stiff refusal in reply. He then asked the old lady to write out in her own words a description of the salesman's visit. She produced a garbled, semi-literate account, which he forwarded to the school with the comment "This is the lady whom your salesman found to be 'very qualified' to take your writing course. I wonder if Mr. Cerf is aware of the cruel deceptions to which he lends his name?" At the bottom of his letter, the lawyer wrote the magic words "Carbon copies to Bennett Cerf and to Consumer Frauds Division, U.S. Attorney's Office." Presto! The school suddenly caved in and returned the money in full.

Louella Mae Burns, the other successful candidate, is the brainchild of Robert Byrne and his wife. I met her in the pages of Byrne's informative and often hilarious book *Writing Rackets* (Lyle Stuart, 1969, $3.95), which treats of the lures held out to would-be writers by high-priced correspondence schools, phony agents who demand a fee for reading manuscripts, the "vanity" presses that will publish your book for a price.

Mrs. Byrne set out to discover at how low a level of talent one might be accepted as a candidate for "professional training" by the Famous Writers. Assuming the personality of a sixty-three-year-old widow of little education, she tackled the aptitude test.

The crux of the test is the essay, in which the applicant is invited to "tell of an experience you have had at some time in your life." Here Louella Mae outdid herself: "I think I can truthfully say to the best of my knowledge that the following is truly the most arresting experience I have ever undergone. My husband, Fred, and I, had only been married but a short time. . . ." Continuing in this vein, she describes "one beautiful cloudless day in springtime" and

a flock of people who started merging along the sidewalk. . . . When out of the blue came a honking and cars and motorcycles and policemen. It was really something! Everybody started shouting and waving and we finally essayed to see the reason of all this. In a sleek black limousine we saw real close Mr. Calvin Coolidge, the President Himself! It was truly an unforgettable experience and one which I shall surely long remember.

14　　This effort drew a two-and-a-half-page typewritten letter from Donald T. Clark, registrar of Famous Writers School, which read in part: "Dear Mrs. Burns, Congratulations! The enclosed Test unquestionably qualifies you for enrollment . . . only a fraction of our students receive higher grades. . . . In our opinion, you have a basic writing aptitude which justifies professional training." And the clincher: "You couldn't consider breaking into writing at a better time than today. Everything indicates that the demand for good prose is growing much faster than the supply of trained talent. Just consider how a single article can cause a magazine's newsstand sales to soar; how a novel can bring hundreds of thousands in movie rights. . . ."

15　　There is something spooky about this exchange, for I later found out that letters to successful applicants are written not by a "registrar" but by copywriters in the Madison Avenue office of the school's advertising department. Here we have Donald T. Clark's ghost writer in earnest correspondence with ghost Louella Mae Burns.

16　　Perhaps these two applicants are not typical of the student body. What of students who show genuine promise, those capable of "mastering the basic skills" and achieving a level of professional competence? Will they, as the school suggests, find their way into "glamorous careers" and be "launched on a secure future" as writers?

17　　Robert Byrne gives a gloomy account of the true state of the market for "good prose" and "trained talent." He says that of all lines of work free-lance writing is one of the most precarious and worst paid (as who should know better than Bennett Cerf & Co.?). He cites a survey of the country's top twenty-six magazines. Of 79,812 unsolicited article manuscripts, fewer than a thousand were accepted. Unsolicited fiction manuscripts fared far worse. Of 182,505 submitted, only 560 were accepted. Furthermore, a study based on the earnings of established writers, members of the Authors League with published books to their credit, shows that the average free-lance earns just over $3,000 a year—an income which, Byrne points out, "very nearly qualifies him for emergency welfare assistance."

18　　What have the Famous Fifteen to say for themselves about all this? Precious little, it turns out. Most of those with whom I spoke were quick to disavow any responsibility for the school's day-to-day operating methods and were unable to answer the most rudimentary questions: qualifications for admission, teacher-student ratio, cost of the course. They seemed astonished, even pained, to think people might be naïve enough to take the advertising at face value.

19　　"If anyone thinks we've got time to look at the aptitude tests that come in, they're out of their mind!" said Bennett Cerf. And Phyllis McGinley: "I'm only a figurehead. I thought a person had to be qualified to take the course, but since I never see any of the applications or the lessons, I don't know. Of course, somebody with a real gift for writing wouldn't have to be taught to write."

One of the FWS brochures says, "On a short story or novel you have at hand the professional counsel of Faith Baldwin . . . all these eminent authors in effect are looking over your shoulder as you learn." Doesn't that mean in plain English, I asked Miss Baldwin, that she will personally counsel students? "Oh, that's just one of those things about advertising; most advertisements are somewhat misleading," she replied. "Anyone with common sense would know that the fifteen of us are much too busy to read the manuscripts the students send in." . . . 20

Like his colleagues on the Guiding Faculty, Mr. Cerf does no teaching, takes no hand in recruiting instructors or establishing standards for the teaching program, does not pass on advertising copy except that which purports to quote him, does not supervise the school's business practices: "I know *nothing* about the business and selling end and I care *less*. I've nothing to do with how the school is run, I can't put that too strongly to you. But it's been run extremely cleanly. I mean that from my heart, Jessica." What, then, is his guiding role? "I go up there once or twice a year to talk to the staff." The Guiding Faculty, he said, helped to write the original textbooks. His own contribution to these was a section on how to prepare a manuscript for publication: "I spent about a week talking into a tape machine about how a manuscript is turned into a book—practical advice about double-spacing the typescript, how it is turned into galleys, through every stage until publication." How many books by FWS students has Random House published? "Oh, come on, you must be pulling my leg—no person of any sophistication whose book we'd publish would have to take a mail order course to learn how to write." 21

However, the school does serve an extremely valuable purpose, he said, in teaching history professors, chemistry professors, lawyers, and businessmen to write intelligibly. I was curious to know why a professor would take a correspondence course in preference to writing classes available in the English department of his own university—who are all these professors? Mr. Cerf did not know their names, nor at which colleges they are presently teaching. 22

While Mr. Cerf is by no means uncritical of some aspects of mail order selling, he philosophically accepts them as inevitable in the cold-blooded world of big business—so different, one gathers, from his own cultured world of letters. "I think mail order selling has several built-in deficiencies," he said. "The crux of it is a very hard sales pitch, an appeal to the gullible. Of course, once somebody has signed a contract with Famous Writers he can't get out of it, but that's true with every business in the country." . . . 23

With one accord the Famous Writers urged me to seek answers to ques- 24 tions about advertising policy, enrollment figures, costs, and the like from the director of the school, Mr. John Lawrence, former president of William Morrow publishing company. Mr. Lawrence invited me to Westport so that I could see the school in operation, and meet Mr. Gordon Carroll, who is now serving as director of International Famous Writers schools.

25   The Famous Schools are housed in a row of boxlike buildings at the edge of Westport ("It's Westport's leading industry," a former resident told me), which look from the outside like a small modern factory. Inside, everything reflects expansion and progress. The spacious reception rooms are decorated with the works of Famous Artists, the parent school, and Famous Photographers, organized in 1964.

26   The success story, and something of the *modus operandi,* can be read at a glance in the annual shareholders' reports and the daily stock market quotations. (The schools have gone public and are now listed on the New York Stock Exchange as FAS International.)

27   Tuition revenue for the schools zoomed from $7,000,000 in 1960 to $48,000,000 in 1969. During this period, the price per share of common stock rose from $5 to $40. (It has fallen sharply, however, in recent months.)

    The schools' interest in selling as compared with teaching is reflected more accurately in the corporate balance sheets than in the brochures sent to prospective students. In 1966 (the last time this revealing breakdown was given), when total tuition revenue was $28,000,000, $10,800,000 was spent on "advertising and selling" compared with $4,800,000 on "cost of grading and materials." . . .

28   From Messrs. Lawrence and Carroll I learned these salient facts about Famous Writers School:

    The cost of the course . . . : $785, if the student makes a one-time payment. But only about 10 percent pay in a lump sum. The cost to the 90 percent who make time payments, including interest, is about $900, or roughly twenty times the cost of extension and correspondence courses offered by universities.

29   Current enrollment is 65,000, of which three-quarters are enrolled in the fiction course, the balance in nonfiction, advertising, business writing. Almost 2,000 veterans are taking the course at the taxpayers' expense through the GI Bill. Teaching faculty: 55, for a ratio of 1,181⁴⁄₅ students per instructor.

30   There are 800 salesmen deployed throughout the country (for a ratio of 14³⁄₅ salesmen for every instructor) working on a straight commission basis. . . .

31   If Bennett Cerf and his colleagues haven't time to grade the aptitude tests, who has? Their stand-ins are two full-timers and some forty pieceworkers, mostly housewives, who "help you find out whether you can be trained to become a successful writer" in the privacy of their homes. There are no

standards for admission to FWS, one of the full-timers explained. "It's not the same thing as a grade on a college theme. The test is designed to indicate your *potential* as a writer, not your present ability." Only about 10 percent of the applicants are advised they lack this "potential," and are rejected.

The instructors guide the students from cheerful little cubicles equipped with machines into which they dictate the "two-page letter of criticism and advice" promised in the advertising. They are, Gordon Carroll told me, former free-lance writers and people with editorial background: "We never hire professional teachers, they're too *dull!* Deadly dull. Ph.D.s are the worst of all!" (Conversely, a trained teacher accustomed to all that the classroom offers might find an unrelieved diet of FWS students' manuscripts somewhat monotonous.) . . .

As I watched the instructors at work, I detected a generous inclination to accentuate the positive in the material submitted. Given an assignment to describe a period in time, a student had chosen 1933. Her first paragraph, about the election of F.D.R. and the economic situation in the country, could have been copied out of any almanac. She had followed this with "There were breadlines everywhere." I watched the instructor underline the breadlines in red, and write in the margin: "Good work, Mrs. Smith! It's a pleasure working with you. You have recaptured the atmosphere of those days."

Although the key to the school's financial success is its huge dropout rate ("We couldn't make any money if all the students finished," Famous Writer Phyllis McGinley had told me in her candid fashion), the precise percentage of dropouts is hard to come by. . . .

However, according to my arithmetic based on figures furnished by the school, the dropout rate must be close to 90 percent. Each student is supposed to send in 24 assignments over a three-year period, an average of 8 a year. With 65,000 enrolled, this would amount to more than half a million lessons a year, and the 55 instructors would have to race along correcting these at a clip of one every few minutes. But in fact (the instructors assured me) they spend an hour or more on each lesson, and grade a total of only about 50,000 a year. What happens to the other 470,000 lessons? "That's baffling," said Mr. Carroll. "I guess you can take a horse to the water, but you can't make him drink."

These balky nags are, however, legally bound by the contract whether or not they ever crack a textbook or send in an assignment. What happens to the defaulter who refuses to pay? Are many taken to court? "None," said Mr. Lawrence. "It's against our policy to sue in court." . . .

Mrs. Virginia Knauer, the President's Assistant for Consumer Affairs, with whom I discussed this later, suspects there is another question involved. "The Famous Writers would never win in court," she said indignantly. "A lawsuit would expose them—somebody should take *them* to court. Their

32

33

34

35

36

37

advertising is reprehensible, it's very close to being misleading." Needless to say, the debtors are not informed of the school's moral scruples against lawsuits. . . .

38   On the whole, [Lawrence and Carroll] said, FWS salesmen are very carefully screened; only one applicant in ten is accepted. They receive a rigorous training in ethical salesmanship; every effort is made to see that they do not "oversell" the course or stray from the truth in their home presentation.

39   Eventually I had the opportunity to observe the presentation in the home of a neighbor who conjured up a salesman for me by sending in the aptitude test. A few days after she had mailed it in, my neighbor got a printed form letter (undated) saying that a field representative of the school would be in the area next week for a very short while and asking her to specify a convenient time when he might telephone for an appointment. There was something a little fuzzy around the edges here—for she had not yet heard from the school about her test—but she let that pass.

40   The "field representative" (. . . the Famous Writers avoid the term "salesman") when he arrived had a ready explanation: the school had telephoned to notify him that my neighbor had passed the test, and to tell him that luckily for her there were "a few openings still left in this enrollment period"—it might be months before this opportunity came again!

41   The fantasy he spun for us, which far outstripped anything in the advertising, would have done credit to the school's fiction course.

42   Pressed for facts and figures, he told us that two or three of the Famous Fifteen are in Westport at all times working with "a staff or forty or fifty experts in their specialty" evaluating and correcting student manuscripts. . . . Your Guiding Faculty member, could be Bennett Cerf, could be Rod Serling depending on your subject, will review at least one of your manuscripts, and may suggest a publisher for it. . . . There are 300 instructors for 3,000 students ("You mean, one teacher for every ten students?" I asked. "That's correct, it's a ratio unexcelled by any college in the country," said the field representative without batting an eye). . . . Hundreds of university professors are currently enrolled. . . . 75 percent of the students publish in their first year, and the majority more than pay for the course through their sales. . . . There are very few dropouts because only serious, qualified applicants (like my neighbor) are permitted to enroll. . . .

43   During his two-hour discourse, he casually mentioned three books recently published by students he personally enrolled—one is already being made into a movie! "Do tell us the names, so we can order them?" But he couldn't remember, offhand: "I get so darn many announcements of books published by our students."

44   Oh, clean-cut young man, does your mother know how you earn your living? (And, Famous Fifteen, do yours?)

45   The course itself is packaged for maximum eye-appeal in four hefty "two-

toned, buckram-bound" volumes with matching loose-leaf binders for the lessons. The textbooks contain all sorts of curious and disconnected matter: examples of advertisements that "pull"; right and wrong ways of ending business letters; paragraphs from the *Saturday Evening Post, This Week, Reader's Digest;* quotations from successful writers like William Shakespeare, Faith Baldwin, Mark Twain, Mark Wiseman, Winston Churchill, Red Smith; an elementary grammar lesson ("*Verbs* are action words. A *noun* is the name of a person, place or thing"); a glossary of commonly misspelled words; a standard list of printer's proof-marking symbols. . . .

Throughout the course the illusion is fostered that the student is, or soon   46
will be, writing for publication: "Suppose you're sitting in the office of a magazine editor discussing an assignment for next month's issue . . ." The set of books includes a volume entitled "How to Turn Your Writing Into Dollars," which winds up on a triumphal note with a sample publisher's contract and a sample agreement with a Hollywood agent.

In short, there is really nothing useful in these books that could not be   47
found in any number of writing and style manuals, grammar texts, marketing guides, free for the asking in the public library. . . .

The student sales department of the [Famous Writers] magazine is also   48
worth watching. Presumably the school puts its best foot forward here, yet the total of all success stories recorded therein each year is only about thirty-five, heavily weighted in the direction of small denominational magazines, local newspapers, pet lovers' journals, and the like. Once in a while a student strikes it rich with a sale to *Reader's Digest, Redbook, McCall's,* generally in "discovery" departments of these magazines that specifically solicit first-person anecdotes by their readers as distinct from professional writers: Most Unforgettable Character, Turning-Point, Suddenly It Happens to You.

The school gets enormous mileage out of these few student sales. The   49
same old successful students turn up time and again in the promotional literature. Thus an ad in the January 4, 1970, issue of *The New York Times* Magazine features seven testimonials: "I've just received a big, beautiful check from the *Reader's Digest*. . . ." "I've just received good news and a check from *Ellery Queen's Mystery Magazine*. . . ." "Recently, I've sold three more articles. . . ." How recently? Checking back through old copies of *Famous Writers* magazine, I found the latest of these success stories had appeared in the student sales department of a 1968 issue; the rest had been lifted from issues of 1964 and 1965.

As for the quality of individual instruction, the reactions of several for-   50
mer FWS students with whom I spoke were varied. Only one—a "success story" lady featured in FWS advertising who has published four juvenile books—expressed unqualified enthusiasm. Two other successes of yesteryear, featured in the school's 1970 ad, said they had never finished the course and had published nothing since 1965.

A FWS graduate who had completed the entire course (and has not, to   51 date, sold any of her stories) echoed the views of many: "It's tremendously overblown, there's a lot of busywork, unnecessary padding to make you think you're getting your money's worth. One peculiar thing is you get a different instructor for each assignment, so there's not much of the 'personal attention' promised in the brochures." However, she added, "I have to be fair. It did get me started, and it did make me keep writing."

52   I showed some corrected lessons that fell into my hands to an English professor. One assignment: "To inject new life and color and dimension into a simple declarative sentence." From the sentence "The cat washed its paws," the student had fashioned this: "With fastidious fussiness, the cat flicked his pink tongue over his paws, laying the fur down neatly and symmetrically." The instructor had crossed out "cat" and substituted "the burly gray tomcat." With fastidious fussiness, the lanky, tweed-suited English professor clutched at his balding, pink pate and emitted a low, agonized groan of bleak, undisguised despair: "Exactly the sort of wordy stuff we try to get students to *avoid*." . . .

53   The phenomenal success to FWS in attracting students (if not in holding them) does point to an undeniable yearning on the part of large numbers of people not only to see their work published, but also for the sort of self-improvement the school purports to offer. . . . For shut-ins, people living in remote rural areas, and others unable to get classroom instruction, correspondence courses may provide the opportunity for supervised study.

54   Recognizing the need, some fifteen state universities offer correspondence courses that seem to me superior to the Famous Writers course for a fraction of the cost. . . .

55   Unobtrusively tucked away in the *Lifelong Learning* bulletin of the University of California Extension at Berkeley are two such offerings: Magazine Article Writing, 18 assignments, fee $55; and Short Story Theory and Practice, 15 assignments, fee $35 ($5 more for out-ot-state enrollees). There are no academic requirements for these courses, anybody can enroll. Those who, in the instructor's opinion, prove to be unqualified are advised to switch to an elementary course in grammar and composition.

56   Cecilia Bartholomew, who has taught the short-story course by correspondence for the past twelve years, is herself the author of two novels and numerous short stories. She cringes at the thought of drumming up business for the course: "I'd be a terrible double-dealer to try to *sell* people on it," she said. Like the Famous Writers instructors, Mrs. Bartholomew sends her students a lengthy criticism of each assignment, but unlike them she does not cast herself in the role of editor revising stories for publication: "It's the improvement in their writing technique that's important. The aim of my course is to develop in each student a professional standard of writing. I'll tell him when a piece is good enough to submit to an editor, but I'll never tell him it will sell." Have any of her students sold their pieces? "Yes, quite a few.

Some have published in volumes of juvenile stories, some in *Hitchcock Mysteries*. But we don't stress this at all."

In contrast, Louise Boggess, who teaches Magazine Article Writing by   57
correspondence in addition to her classes in "professional writing" at the
College of San Mateo, exudes go-ahead salesmanship: she believes that most
of her students will eventually find a market for their work. The author of
several how-to-do-it books (among them *Writing Articles That Sell,* which
she uses as the text for her course), she points her students straight toward
the mass writing market. In her streamlined, practical lessons the emphasis is
unabashedly on formula writing that will sell. Her very first assignment is
how to write a "hook," meaning an arresting opening sentence. . . .

During the eighteen months she has been teaching the correspondence   58
course, several of her 102 students have already sold pieces to such magazines
as *Pageant, Parents, Ladies Circle, Family Weekly.* She has had but six dropouts, an enviable record by FWS standards.

My brief excursion into correspondence-school-land taught me little,   59
after all, that the canny consumer does not already know about the difference
between buying and being sold. As Faith Baldwin said, most advertising is
somewhat misleading; as Bennett Cerf said, the crux of mail order selling is a
hard pitch to the gullible. We know that the commission salesman will, if we
let him into our homes, dazzle and bemuse us with the beauty, durability,
unexcelled value of his product, whatever it is. As for the tens of thousands
who sign up with FWS when they could get a better and cheaper correspondence course through the universities (or, if they live in a city, Adult Education Extension courses), we know from reading Vance Packard that people
tend to prefer things that come in fancy packages and cost more.

There is probably nothing actually illegal in the FWS operation, al-   60
though the consumer watchdogs have their eye on it.

Robert Hughes, counsel for the Federal Trade Commission's Bureau of   61
Deceptive Practices, told me he has received a number of complaints about
the school, mostly relating to the high-pressure and misleading sales pitch.
"The real evil is in the solicitation and enrollment procedures," he said.
"There's a basic contradiction involved when you have profit-making organizations in the field of education. There's pressure to maximize the number of
enrollments to make more profit. Surgery is needed in the enrollment procedure."

There is also something askew with the cast of characters in the forego-   62
ing drama which would no doubt be quickly spotted by FWS instructors in
television scriptwriting ("where the greatest market lies for the beginning
writer," as the school tells us).

I can visualize the helpful comment on my paper: "Good work, Miss   63
Mitford. The Oakland widow's problem was well thought through. But
characterization is weak. You could have made your script more believable
had you chosen a group of shifty-eyed hucksters out to make a buck, one step

ahead of the sheriff, instead of these fifteen eminently successful and solidly respectable writers, who are well liked and admired by the American viewing public. For pointers on how to make your characters come to life in a way we can all identify with, I suggest you study Rod Serling's script *The Twilight Zone,* in the kit you received from us. Your grade is D −. It has been a pleasure working with you. Good luck!"

Questions

1. In "Let Us Now Appraise Famous Writers," Mitford provides a step-by-step account of her investigation of the Famous Writers School, a very expensive correspondence program for aspiring writers that flourished in the 1960s. What was there about the advertising and the school's procedures that aroused her suspicions? Were they justified?

2. In conducting her investigation, Mitford interviewed Famous Writers School executives, the "Famous Fifteen" sponsoring writers, paper graders at the school, and lawyers (including her own husband, a lawyer for one of the cheated customers). She read the school's advertising, much of their correspondence, their newsletter, and their textbooks—as well as competing textbooks and announcements for much-less-expensive college courses. Explain her investigative procedure. Does she have enough evidence to back up the very serious charges she has made? Does her evidence convince you?

3. Was Mitford conducting an unbiased investigation? Or did she begin by assuming that the Famous Writers School was guilty? What evidence leads you to your answer? Operating from her perspective as an investigative reporter, rather than as a judge, should she have tried to remain impartial during her investigation?

4. What is the prevailing tone of Mitford's writing? Does this help or hinder her credibility as an investigative reporter? Is her account of this investigation written to warn prospective customers of the Famous Writers School? to entertain general readers? to demonstrate what a clever and thorough reporter she is? any other reasons? Which purpose(s) does her tone best suit?

Writing About Controversy

Strategies

1. Do I want to convince my audience of the truth of a particular matter? Do I want essentially to raise their consciousness of an issue? Do I want to promote a belief or refute a theory? Or do I want to move my readers to action? if to action, what kind? to change their minds, attitudes or behavior? to right a wrong, alter a situation?

2. At the outset, do I expect my audience to agree with my ideas? to be neutral about the issues at hand? or to be opposed to my views? Can I build into my writing responses to my readers' anticipated reactions, such as rebuttals to their possible objections? Or illustrative examples calculated to counter their views? Do I know enough about my subject to be able to do this?

3. What is my strongest (and presumably most controversial) point, and where should I put it? (Or, if it is implied rather than stated overtly, by what place in the writing should that point be apparent?) at the beginning, if my audience agrees with my views? at the end, after a gradual build-up, for an antagonistic audience? How much development (and consequent emphasis) should each point (or illustration) have?

4. What will be my best sources of evidence? my own experience? firsthand inspection of the place(s) or situations in which the problem has occurred? the experiences or opinions of people I know personally, or have interviewed? published opinion from experts in a relevant field? scientific evidence? written records—notes, memos, letters, reports, historic documents? economic, statistical, or other numerical data?

5. How can I interpret my evidence to move my readers to accept it? Should I explain overtly, briefly or elaborately, or should I let the examples and other evidence speak for themselves? To accomplish my purpose, should I use much, if any, emotional language? Should my appeal be overt, direct? Or would indirection, understatement, be more effective? Would irony, saying the opposite of what I really mean (as Swift did in "A Modest Proposal") be more appropriate than a direct approach?

Suggestions

Write an essay that attempts to persuade one of the following audiences through a combination of appeals to reason, emotion, and ethics.

1. To an audience that is discriminating against a particular group: Stop discrimination! (See James Baldwin, "Faulkner and Desegregation," 299–304; Martin Luther King, Jr., "Letter from Birmingham Jail," 304–18; George Orwell, "Shooting an Elephant" and "Marrakech," 335–46; Richard Rodriguez, "None of This Is Fair," 361–65.)

2. To prospective buyers or users of a deceptive or otherwise fraudulent service or product: Beware! (See Sissela Bok, "Placebo," 319–24; Jessica Mitford, "Let Us Now Appraise Famous Writers," 377–88.)

3. To people engaging in behavior that threatens their lives or their health: Stop doing _____ (or, Stop doing _____ to excess)—smoking, drinking, overeating, undereating, using drugs. Or, Start doing _____—exercising regularly, using seatbelts, planning for the future through getting an education, a stable job, an investment plan, a retirement plan .... (See Robert Christgau, "Beth Ann and Macrobioticism," 353–60; Dianne and Robert Hales, "Exercising the Psyche," 622–28.)

4. To movers and shapers of social policy (perhaps your senator or representative): Push for a public policy (or law) that benefits a particular constituency—the poor, women, dependent children, runaways, a particular minority race, the aged, the terminally ill, veterans (of a particular war), recipients of Social Security, or another group of your choice. (See Philippe Aries, "The Reversal of Death," 324–31; Norman Cousins, "The Right to Die," 332–34; John McPhee, "Family Doctors," 346–53.)

5. To an athlete, or to an athletic coach: Play according to the rules, and exhibit good sportsmanship. (See Red Smith, "Good Ol' Boy Woody Hayes," 484–86; Dave Kindred, "Smile, Rosie, and Give Them a Run for the Money," 486–90.)

6. To a prospective employer: I'm the best person for the job. Hire me. (See Robert Half, "Coming Out on Top in the Job Interview," 642–50.) Or, To admissions officers of a particular college, university, or of a program within that institution (such as a medical or law school, graduate program, or a division with a special undergraduate degree): Let me in.

7. To a prospective attender of a play, concert, film, or restaurant: Try it, you'll like it! Or, Avoid this disaster! (See Shaw, Simon, and Kernan, on Shakespeare, 429–39; Young, "The Rock Fantasy," 400–403; Richman, Cravens, and Trillin on restaurants, 459–67, 282–87.)

8. To a prospective traveler: Visit this place! Or, Avoid it like the plague! (See Morris on Venice and Manhattan, 216–30; Bob Thompson, "California: An Introduction," 268–71; Philip Kopper, "The Stark Simplicity of the Delmarva Coast," 272–77.)

9. To an audience whom you want to introduce to someone special: I'd like you to meet . . . (See Studs Terkel, "Miss U.S.A.," 113–17; Henry Mitchell, "Eudora Welty," 167–75; Alden Whitman, "Albert Schweitzer," 175–84; Eugene Meyer, "Mr. L. G. Broadmoore . . ." 546–50.)

10. To despoilers of the environment: Stop, before it's all gone! (See Kelly Shea, "Acid Rain," 773–75; William Warner, "The Islands of Chesapeake Bay," 788–97; Carl Sagan, "The Nuclear Winter," 797–803.)

CHAPTER FIVE

Writing About Performance: Music, Film, Drama, Literature, Restaurants, Sports

Behind every good review, literary analysis, and sports column is a passionate reviewer, even though most of that love, like most of what the writer knows about the subject, may not show on the surface. This doesn't mean that you have to love, or even like, every concert you review, every football game you watch. Indeed, if you admire everything indiscriminately, your readers won't be able to trust your continually benign perspective. But you do have to love the medium you're writing about.

Love keeps reviewers knowledgeable. Only love will enable you to sit through the mediocre and bad films as well as the good, to watch every game of the local soccer league all season, to learn everything you need to know about the subject to satisfy other devotees as well as more casual readers. You don't have to be an expert, but in order to write well about the performance at hand you do have to understand the rules and strategies of the game, the skills of the art, and current developments in the medium. If you love the subject, learning enough to write it is fun, not work; you pick up knowledge on the field, in the concert hall, and through reading, reading, reading.

Knowledge keeps reviewers lovable, for it enables them to be convincing.

George Bernard Shaw's sheer knowledge of the subject makes a compelling case for his assertion that *Hamlet* (429–34) requires a classical actor, who

> can present a dramatic hero as a man whose passions are those which have produced the philosophy, the poetry, the art, and the statecraft of the world, and not merely those which have produced its weddings, coroners' inquests, and executions.

Shaw is credible not because he himself is a major playwright (he wasn't when he wrote the review) but because he has obviously thought deeply about the subject. Readers may not agree with him, but they will respect his opinion.

Love of the subject also keeps reviewers hopeful, eager to believe that the performance they are about to encounter will be very good, or very entertaining, or in other ways very interesting; writers and their readers can always learn from a defeat or a disaster. Red Smith, distinguished, delightful sportswriter for *The New York Times,* explains the philosophy of his daily column (46–49):

> Over the years people have said to me, "Isn't it dull covering baseball every day?" My answer used to be "It becomes dull only to dull minds." Today's game is always different from yesterday's game. If you have the perception and the interest to see it, and the wit to express it, your story is always different from yesterday's story.

A reviewer doesn't have to create an audience; the bookworms, rock fans, and tennis buffs already exist. Although you can capitalize on your readers' interest, you will also have to sustain their attention through responding to the major reasons they read reviews: for information, interpretation and evaluation, and entertainment.

Information in Reviews

Reviews and sports writings need to provide enough essential information about a performance to enable readers to decide for themselves whether to read it or attend it or comparable performances by the same group. You can skip what readers already know; none of the Shakespeare reviewers in this section provides plot summaries. But readers will need to know the name of the performing group and its principal artists; and the date, place, mode, and works performed during the performance in question. Thus Kernan's review, "Bard Times at Folger Theater" (437–39), indicates that he's discussing a performance of excerpts from Shakespeare's plays (*what*) at the Folger Library (*where*) on the Bard's birthday, April 23, 1980 (*when*), by Washington, D.C., area elementary schoolchildren (*who*).

Readers who haven't read the book or seen the play or film will need to know the plot (but don't give away the ending, especially to tell whodunit). Thus in "Comedy's Greatest Era" (404–19), James Agee summarizes the major action of *Safety Last,* a silent "comedy of thrills," at the same time analyzing the comic technique of its star, Harold Lloyd:

> In *Safety Last,* as a rank amateur, [Lloyd] is forced to substitute for a human fly and climb a medium-sized skyscraper. Dozens of awful things happen to him. He gets fouled up in a tennis net. Popcorn falls on him from a window above, and the local pigeons treat him like a cross between a lunch wagon and St. Francis of Assisi. A mouse runs up his britches-leg, and the crowd below salutes his desperate dance on the window ledge with wild applause of the daredevil. . . .

> [In the climactic gag] Lloyd is driven out to the dirty end of a flagpole by a furious dog; the pole breaks and he falls, just managing to grab the minute hand of a huge clock. His weight promptly pulls the hand down from IX to VI. . . . Now, hideously, the whole clockface pulls loose and slants from its trembling springs above the street.

Writers of reviews and especially of more extensive critical commentary often include a great deal of background information, as much as is necessary to put a particular work or performance into its historical, intellectual, artistic, social, or political contexts. Because a review is largely self-contained, you'll have to decide what background is useful in interpreting a given performance, in itself and in relation to the performer's (or others') work in general. What information is necessary to avoid misinterpretation, or to help in understanding the work at hand?

In writing with a historical or evolutionary perspective, background information is critical. Thus in "Hub Fans Bid Kid Adieu" (470–83), John Updike explains the significance of the day Ted Williams retired from baseball by reviewing what Williams had meant to the Red Sox and to Boston fans during his long, complicated, twenty-year career:

> The affair between Boston and Ted Williams has been no mere summer romance; it has been a marriage, composed of spats, mutual disappointments, and, toward the end, a mellowing hoard of shared memories. It falls into three stages, which may be termed Youth, Maturity, and Age . . . .

Likewise, Paul Fussell's analysis of *The Official Boy Scout Handbook* (1979) (451–55) examines the work as a cultural artifact, a reflection of the ability of its sponsoring organization to survive in a changing world, yet to maintain a core of significant values unchanged from the publication of the first edition in 1910. Fussell considers the "cosmetic" changes in Scouting, comparing past with present: "breeches of thirty years ago have yielded to trousers," "the handclasp is now the normal civilian one, but given with the left hand," and "there's much less emphasis on knots than formerly." However, the book's greatest strength, he says, is its "good sense,"

> psychological and ethical as well. Indeed, this handbook is among the very few remaining popular repositories of something like classical ethics,

deriving from Aristotle and Cicero . . . The constant moral theme is the inestimable benefits of looking objectively outward and losing consciousness of
self in the work to be done.

Interpretation and Evaluation in Reviews

People often read reviews or sports articles to help them decide what to see,
where to go. They use the review for an implied cost/benefit analysis to help
decide whether the subject is worth the time, money, or effort—to get to, to
understand, to appreciate, to enjoy. If not, what are the alternatives? Thus
readers of reviews are implicitly considering such matters as:

Identification: What's the specific topic? (Is *The Women's Room* a novel or a
treatise on plumbing?)

Relevance: Will it interest me?

Level of difficulty: Will I understand it? with or without a lot of effort?

Familiarity: Is it too commonplace—or too innovative—for me to cope
with?

You'll address these concerns, implicitly or explicitly, with the information and evaluation you provide. What you choose to include—and exclude—and the amount of space you devote to each item is in itself almost as
evaluative as an explicit discussion of the quality of the performance. If you
devote most of a review's space to the acting, as Shaw does in "Hamlet,"
there's little room left to discuss much else. You may comment on something
because of its national or international significance (all the films directed by
Bergman or Fellini), its regional relevance (rodeos in the West, horse shows
in the East), its local interest (the hometown soccer league), or simply because you like or dislike it. Jennifer M. Young acknowledges the last criterion
in her conclusion to "The Rock Fantasy" (400–403):

> The new breed of concert-goer seeks no message or hidden meanings in the
> lyrics as a way of justifying his musical preferences. Rock music is thus no
> great social force; what is of importance is his specific personal reaction to it.
> Perhaps this idea is best expressed in a popular song . . . in which the singer
> simply asserts that although the music is "only" rock and roll, he likes it
> simply because he likes it. For such a person, this whole analysis of the
> reasons why he likes it would be beside the point.

Your standards for evaluating a performance or technique will probably
be influenced by some or all of the following criteria, your emphasis by how
important you think they are:

Technical quality: Harold Schonberg explains "Why a Critic Follows the
Score" (397–99): "It is not to check up on the artists. Rather it is to *see*
as well as hear what they do."

Level of professionalism: You expect more from professionals than from amateurs, more from veterans than from novices, more from adults than from children—and you may be more indulgent in evaluating hometown performances than more remote ones.

Aesthetic aspects: Eudora Welty observes of E. B. White's *Charlotte's Web* (456–58): "It has the liveliness and felicity, tenderness and unexpectedness, grace and humor and praise of life, and the good backbone of succinctness that only the most highly imaginative stories possess."

What are the best and worst features of a performance? Your assessment will emphasize the extremes more than the mundane aspects. What you discuss first—and most extensively—will establish the tone of your review as positive or negative. In her review of the "Hunan Dynasty" (459–61), Phyllis C. Richman comments first on the restaurant's attractive features:

First, a dining room of "gracefulness and lavish space";

"Second, service is a strong priority";

"Third, the food is largely good if not quite wonderful" and the menu is "long and eclectic."

Not until the ninth paragraph, near the end of the review, does she note, "I have found only one dismal main dish in a fairly broad sampling: lemon chicken had no redeeming feature in its doughy, greasy, overcooked and underseasoned presentation."

How does this performance compare with others by the same and different performers? Is it the best—or the worst—of a good or bad season, of your memory, of all time? Or is it essentially mediocre? In "Good Ol' Boy Woody Hayes" (484–86), Red Smith assesses the most recent abuses of Ohio State football coach Woody Hayes in light of his whole career, and according to an ideal standard of appropriate behavior for coaches:

> People keep saying that Woody Hayes is a great football coach who overstayed his time. This implies that there was a time when slugging a member of the opposing team was proper coachly deportment.
>
> Let's face it, throwing a punch at Charlie Bauman of Clemson was only the last degrading incident in a pattern of behavior that had long distinguished the Ohio State coach. For years, Hayes had been throwing tantrums, screaming abuse and striking out at anyone within reach when his team was losing.

Does a given performer or performance fulfill its potential? Your answer implies that you've determined the potential in advance. Thus Gwyneth Cravens recounts her pilgrimage to "The M & J Sanitary Tortilla Factory" (461–67) in anticipation of its excellent Mexican food, particularly the carne adobada burrito, "a freshly made flour tortilla wrapped around . . . diced roast pork . . . simmered in a hot red chile sauce—and drowned in . . . green chile sauce flavored with whole cumin seeds, garlic, and oregano." This fiery concoction fulfills her every expectation; as she takes "the first bite of a burrito," she feels "truly blessed."

Conventions of Reviews

Reviews must be concise, self-contained, and unified. Reviewers and sports columnists are rarely allocated more than two thousand words, and sometimes fewer than five hundred. (Writers of extended interpretive articles, such as Agee in "Comedy's Greatest Era," and Gerald Mast in "Comic Plots and Comic Climate," have more latitude.) So you have to be highly selective. Yet even though your audience may be devoted to the subject, you must assume that most of them are unfamiliar with the work, performance, or game at hand—that's why they're reading your review (unless they've seen a production and want your judgment to corroborate their views!). Because most reviews are read casually, over the breakfast coffee, on the subway, before bedtime, you should assume that your readers won't look anything up—and you'll need to include enough information so they won't have to. "There should be unity to a review," says Clarence Olson, Book Editor of the *St. Louis Post-Dispatch,* "a beginning in which a theme is established, a middle in which this theme is fleshed out with details and supported by logical arguments, and an end that returns to the basic theme or offers a summary conclusion"—often reinforced by a symbol, metaphor, or other stylistic device woven throughout the review.

Many patterns of organization are appropriate for reviews, as the writings in this section indicate. Nevertheless, reviews have several common formats. Reviews often proceed chronologically or sequentially, describing the performance of a play or the narrative of a novel in the order in which the events took place. Or they provide a brief overview of the performance and then highlight the most conspicuous strengths and weaknesses. Reviews may also be organized by comparing the current performance with previous ones, either by the same or different performers. "Which is better?" they implicitly ask. Or they offer a dominant impression of the most conspicuous (best or worst) features first, and deal briefly with the lesser aspects. In any case, the lead paragraph in a review is of crucial importance, not only in engaging the readers, but in providing cues to the review's emphasis, tone, and organization.

Red Smith has observed, "People go to spectator sports to have fun and then they grab the paper to read about it and have fun again." You'll want to re-create that enjoyment for yourself, as well, when you write the review.

Music

HAROLD SCHONBERG

Why a Critic Follows the Score

Schonberg was born in New York City in 1915, memorized his father's large collection of classical records, and to this day finds that music is "always in my head, waking and, apparently, sleeping . . . . [my wife asks when I'm sleeping,] 'What are you listening to?' I mumble the name of the piece without waking up." At twelve, he says, "I resolved to be a music critic. I could always write easily and coherently, and I figured out that to get paid for doing the thing I loved best—listening to music and comparing performances—was the life for me. I had a critical mind . . . constantly asking questions, probing, reading, comparing, trying to work out a rationale." After earning a B.A. at Brooklyn College and an M.A. at New York University in music and English, Schonberg began writing reviews for music magazines, interrupted his service as an army paratrooper in World War II, and was music critic for The New York Times *1950–1980 (winning a Pulitzer Prize in 1971), when he became cultural correspondent. His eight books include collections of short biographies of pianists, conductors, composers—and chess grand masters.*

In Facing the Music *(1981), which includes the following essay, Schonberg amplifies his views on what makes a good critic:*

> *Music critics after all, are in effect telling Rudolf Serkin how to play the piano, Zubin Mehta how to conduct . . . and to do that, one must have a lifetime of background and knowledge to fall back upon. A lot of confidence and a strong ego also help. . . . As long as a critic retains his integrity, plays no favorites, works out of a love for his art, has a passionate conviction and brings to his work a background equivalent to that of the musicians he is reviewing, he can do no more. Young critics tend to enter the field full of grand visions for the betterment of the musical world. They are much tougher than the older, more experienced ones. Later all critics come to realize that they are not going to revolutionize music. . . . Critics don't make careers. Artists make careers.*

The letters one gets. On my desk for some months has been reposing a furious diatribe about the review of a pianist I wrote about in February. The writer was mad. Also scatological. Also ungrammatical. Also unoriginal ("we were not at the same concert": I wish I had a dollar for every time a letter came in with those immortal words). Also anonymous.   1

He did raise a few points worth discussion, however, including my frequent habit of bringing scores and the sheet music to concerts. "If you didn't have your nose buried in the Beethoven sonata scores, you might have been able to get involved with the playing and have had time . . . to enjoy the beauty of his playing. If you are silly enough to take the printed page   2 as the gospel truth and if you are not at this stage of your career familiar with the Beethoven sonatas then perhaps retirement is to be considered?"

3   That remark about taking the printed page as gospel really hurt. As far as I know, I was the first critic anywhere, in books and articles, to inveigh against the deadening, stultifying literalism that in my opinion was afflicting performances everywhere. Year after year I was patiently, and sometimes not so patiently, pointing out that that music was more than an architectural plan; that notation was an inexact science; that it was the artist's job to reflect his own personality as well as that of the composer. I screamed and carried on, pointing out that literalism was fake musicianship; that composers themselves, especially the nineteenth-century composers, expected performers to take liberties in phrase and tempo and even, occasionally, with the text.

4   I believed then, as I believe now, that surprisingly little is known about Romantic performance practice—and it is still nineteenth-century music that forms the bulwark of the repertory. Artists know that they have to "do" something in this music, but they do not exactly know what has to be done. The result is mannerism instead of style. Or literalism instead of spontaneity.

5   Only in recent years has there been a re-examination of Romanticism, and now musicians are beginning to come around, as well as critics and anonymous letter-writers. As one who in a way started the whole thing, I am rather pleased—and amused—to find my words fifteen years back parroted almost verbatim as though they were brand new. But to be accused of the very thing I have fought against? Go soak your head.

6   About this business of bringing scores to concerts: It is not to check up on the artists. Rather it is to *see* as well as hear what they do. I dare say I know the literature as well as my furious anonymist. But even in pieces that we have memorized at the keyboard, how many without the music in front of us remember every dotted eighth note, every tempo indication, every expression marking? The point of bringing the music is to look at what has come down to us, and then see exactly what the artist does with it.

7   For every artist, even the literalist, "does" things to music. Listen to twenty different recordings of the *Waldstein* and you are necessarily going to get twenty slightly—or in some cases not so slightly—different views of the sonata. It may be hard to tell the literalists apart, but when the score is before you, differences do spring to life.

8   Score reading, except for certain modern works, is not that difficult, especially when the piece in question is one that you know. An experienced score reader does not have his nose perpetually in the score. He turns pages more or less automatically, knowing exactly where the musician is going to be at any given point. He may not even look at the pages. But when something a bit unusual happens, there is the score to verify the point.

9   When something unusual does happen, I jot it down. My scores are full of little notations about the habits and ideas of musicians: an effective luft-pause that Bernstein may have inserted into a Mahler symphony; a fermata

that Bjoerling employed in a particular aria; a curious way of taking a phrase by this musician; a harmonic change by that; a reorchestration, an unexpected change in tempo, an accelerando—whatever the artist "does" that is away from the printed mathematics of the score. All are noted down, with the names of the perpetrators. Perhaps in future years scholars might have an interesting time going through my score collection.

And I have the habit of timing performances. I do it automatically, pressing the plunger of my wrist watch. Timings are interesting. I find it intriguing that on one occasion Isaac Stern played the Brahms Violin Concerto in 38 minutes, 15 seconds; and the next time around, 32 minutes, 27 seconds. Different conductor, different hall, different acoustics, and Stern felt differently about the concerto that day. Interesting. Proving nothing at all, but interesting. I find it interesting that Toscanini, reputedly a "fast" conductor, was slower than Rossi in the *Falstaff* recording. I find it interesting that certain artists are invariably outside the orthodox tempo parameters.

Most interesting of all, some twenty-five years of timings in my scores lead to the conclusion that there is a sort of glacial shift in the contemporary understanding of tempo. Teachers tell us time and again that because of the speed of our modern age, tempos also have speeded up. Older musicians, they say, were representatives of a calmer, more relaxed age and were nowhere near as rushed as we are. But the timings on my scores suggest otherwise. Far from being faster, we seem to be much slower than our forebears were. Perhaps it has been the crazy, skewed idea of "musicianship" operating in our time, but whatever the reason, timings today are slower than they were a generation ago.

And that is why I take scores to concerts. Not to see how closely musicians adhere to the score, but to see how they depart from it. Musicians without ideas are not very stimulating musicians. When a musician has ideas, I like to jot them down as part of a permanent record that otherwise would instantly vanish as soon as the piece was over. Performance is such an evanescent art. A painter fixes a conception forever with the tip of his brush; the writer is there for eternity; the poor performing artist's ideas in the concert hall are a brilliant bubble that explodes upon the instant. (Yes, he can make records, but those are so different from what happens when stage and audience interact in a live performance.)

Dare I also say that some musicians can be so dull that following the score is an antidote against going to sleep? There also are scores and scores. Does a conductor use a corrupt version of a Haydn symphony or is he educated enough to encompass the latest findings? What Bruckner edition is he using? And so on. Bringing scores to concerts can answer many questions. I won't apologize to my angry friend. On the contrary. One remark, though, I shall keep in mind, and try to turn pages more quietly. Scores in large format and old, crackly paper are not easy to manage.

JENNIFER M. YOUNG (Student)

The Rock Fantasy

Young (b. 1958) a native of Roanoke, Virginia, majored in English at the College of William and Mary, where she won state and national awards for a student newspaper article of investigative reporting, detailing CIA activities on campus in the late 1960s. After graduation in 1980, she worked for five years as a reporter on the Henderson (N.C.) Daily Dispatch. *She is now the education writer for the* Winston-Salem Journal.*

Here Young is analyzing not a specific performance, but the characteristics of rock stars and rock concerts, focusing on the causes and effects of the behaviors of rock stars and their audiences, and the influence each has on the other. In the process, she presents an implied criticism of their collective behavior—an implied argument that rock stars are cynical manipulators and that their gullible audiences foolishly endow them with divine characteristics they don't deserve. Although she observed in 1982, "It seems that teenagers don't idolize rock musicians as much as they once did," that was before Prince and Madonna and their ecstatic, gyrating, look-alike audiences appeared on the scene.

1   If a Mecca exists for today's youth, it must take the form of a rock concert. Such a colossal event draws people from surprisingly distant places and from oddly diverging lifestyles. The sophisticated college student may be seated next to the wide-eyed junior high cheerleader, the latter showing fright at the approach of a wild-eyed freak. How do these incompatible character types find a mutual appeal in rock concerts? What induces young people to exchange the few dollars earned through babysitting or car washing for a concert ticket?

2   To many, the answer is immediately obvious—the music is the source of appeal at a concert. The quality of the sound produced, however, frequently casts doubt on this explanation. Unquestionably, rock concerts are loud; the decibel level at some reportedly exceeds that attained by a jet plane on take-off. In addition, this aural assault is often intensified by an out-of-tune guitar, by the faltering voice of the performer, or by the bad acoustics in the concert hall. Rock groups generally correct these problems in a studio; their recordings may even boast pleasing harmonies with intelligible lyrics. So why do we battle crowds to secure choice seating at a concert? Why endure the stench of beer spilled in our lap? Somehow an evening spent at home listening to a $100 speaker system and staring wistfully at the rock star's poster on the wall constitutes an inadequate substitute for the real thing. The atmosphere is just not the same.

3   A concert creates a magical, otherworldly atmosphere, reminiscent of a childhood never-never land. An eerie darkness shrouds the hall, and then, just as in our favorite fairy tale, the supernatural being (otherwise identified by the vulgar term, "rock star") appears in a burst of light. In another context he would have been known as a "god out of the machine." Bizarre lighting

schemes and gimmicks such as mock hangings or fire-breathing contribute to the atmosphere of otherworldliness in some acts. The fans are permitted only a brief glimpse of the star before he vanishes once more in the darkness, only to materialize the following evening in a concert hall hundreds of miles away. The stage becomes the rock star's only natural habitat; for us, he can have no existence apart from it. We can scarcely conceive of our idols performing such mundane activities as going to the dentist, shopping for tuna fish, or changing the baby. Perhaps we have a need to believe in an illusory creature of the night, somehow different from ourselves. Who fits this description better than a rock star?

Many rock musicians consciously work to maintain the aura of mystery surrounding themselves. Typically, they walk on stage and proceed to sneer at or completely ignore the audience. If a star is especially articulate, he may yell, "A-a-all ri-i-ight! Gonna rock to-o- ni-i-ight!" He cannot use the vocabulary of the common man, for fear of being mistakenly identified as such. Besides, a few well-timed thrusts of the hips communicate the message just as well. The audience responds wildly to this invitation, and the concert is off to a good start. The performer has successfully gauged the mood of the spectators; now his task is to manipulate it, through his choice of material and through such actions as dancing, prancing, foot-stomping, and unearthly screaming. His movements, gestures, and often, his bizarre clothing, high heels, and make-up deliberately violate accepted standards of conduct and appearance. He can afford to take chances and to risk offending people; after all, as every good student of mythology knows, deities are not bound by the same restrictions as mere mortals. The Dionysus figure on the stage tempts us to follow him into the never-never land where inhibitions are nonexistent.

Initially, the audience may be content to allow the performer alone to defy civilized constraints. We rebel vicariously; the smashing of instruments onstage perhaps serves as a catharsis for our own destructive impulses. As the intensity and excitement of the concert mount, however, the audience is drawn into the act. People begin to sing along, clap, yell, dance, or shake their fists. This is a particularly favorable setting for the release of tensions by the timid. No one can hear their screams (the music is too loud) and no one can see the peculiar movements of their bodies (the hall is dark, and the strange smoke reduces visibility—everyone's eyes are glued to the stage anyhow). The rock god has successfully asserted his power over our bodies, and now all that remains is for him to master our minds and our imaginations.

Since inhibitions have been jarred loose by the pulsating rhythm, our thoughts can at last run free. Like children, we return to the world of fantasy (with a few adult modifications). The bright young star in front of us flashes overt sexuality and personifies D. H. Lawrence's Phallic Force. The spectators begin to wonder about his sex life, which must be infinitely more fulfilling than their own. The college girl concludes that the rock star would be a much more exciting lover than that bespectacled "preppie" in biology lab. Her younger sister can safely dream of a tender first experience with the rock star. Objectively, she knows that it will never really happen and thus, she need not even have guilt feelings about this fantasy. The males in the audience recognize the star's appeal and fancy themselves enjoying the most interesting fringe benefit of his job—obliging the "groupies."

7   Obviously, young people project their fantasies onto the rock star, endowing him with the powers, attractions, and beliefs that they wish to see in themselves or in those close to them. They can create his personality at will because in one sense, he is just a figment of their imaginations. Thus some may choose to regard him as a sex symbol; for others, he may represent nonconformity and the youthful search for individuality. Unquestionably, in the past, a major appeal of rock music was the shock effect it produced on parents. This attraction may diminish now that the early rock and roll "rebels" are parents themselves and the age of the young devotees is steadily decreasing. At present, however, many young teens still attend rock concerts, believing that they are asserting independence and maturity. Ironically, they conform perfectly—to the expectations and pressures of their peer group.

8   For young people, familiarity with rock music is a status symbol, a sign of sophistication. Everyone eagerly awaits the great rite of passage—driving the car (unescorted by adults) to a concert; such a feat elevates the teenager to the rank of homeroom hero for a day. A concert gives the teen a chance to brag about how many albums he owns or about his knowledge of the star's personal life. In this manner, he may join the ranks of the enlightened, sophisticated crowd at school. He finds security in identifying with this group, and profiteers at concerts successfully capitalize on this need to fit in. How else do we explain the fact that teenagers (and even older people) spend ten dollars for a rock star t-shirt which invariably shrinks four sizes the first time that it is washed?

9   The idealistic, socially conscious members of the audience may see the rock star as a messiah or guru, a proponent of truth, love, and peace. They project their own attitudes regarding justice, materialism, and other social issues onto the performer. Apparently, they see no inconsistency in the rock star lamenting greed in our culture; maybe they forget that he escapes from the stage into a limousine which whisks him quickly to the airport and his waiting jet.

10   This idealistic group has become smaller in recent years, with the absence of a burning social issue uniting youthful consciousnesses and with the tendency toward introspection and self-absorption. The new breed of concert-goers seeks no message or hidden meanings in the lyrics as a way of justifying his musical preferences. Rock music is thus no great social force; what is of importance is his specific personal reaction to it. Perhaps this idea is best expressed in a popular song from a few years ago in which the singer simply asserts that although the music is "only" rock and roll, he likes it simply

because he likes it. For such a person, this whole analysis of the reasons why he likes it would be beside the point.

Questions

1. Young assumes throughout that the characteristic rock audience is young—primarily high-school and college-student age. What effects does she say rock stars have on this audience? Does Young imply, or do you think, that rock stars would have the same effects on an older audience? Why or why not? Is she herself writing for an audience of rock fans?

2. In Young's opinion, to what extent is the rock star his own creation, and to what extent is he "a figment of [the audience's] imaginations" (paragraph 7)? Do you agree with her interpretation? What effect does Young intend to have on her readers by pointing out the rock star's manipulative (paragraph 4) and contradictory (paragraph 9) behavior?

3. What is the significance of the title of this essay, "The Rock Fantasy"? In how many senses can you interpret "fantasy"?

4. Young refers to the star as "the rock god" (paragraph 5). Through what figures of speech does she reinforce this image? Is the star's mystery related to this image? What are the causes and effects of this mystery?

Film

JAMES AGEE

Comedy's Greatest Era

Agee, born in Knoxville, Tennessee, in 1909, is best remembered for his lyrical A Death in the Family, *though he died in 1955 of a heart attack before finishing it. Nevertheless, the novel, published in 1957 from manuscripts his editors pieced together, won a Pulitzer Prize. Yet during his lifetime Agee was known for his journalism, such as* Let Us Now Praise Famous Men *(1941), a moving study of Alabama sharecroppers during the Depression. Also recognized for his film criticism, he was one of the first to champion film as a legitimate art form, rather than as merely entertainment, though he did warn producers never to go over the heads of their audience. (Agee himself grew up in a "fairly solidly lower middle-class" neighborhood in Knoxville.) Indeed, Agee proved his own cinematic credentials by writing a number of film scripts, including adaptations of C. S. Forester's* The African Queen *(1952) and Stephen Crane's* The Bride Comes to Yellow Sky *(1952).*

In "Comedy's Greatest Era," Agee demonstrates the two qualities essential to any critic's success—a vast love of the subject combined with an equally extensive knowledge of it. These keep the reviewer credible, just as they provide the endurance to sit through the bad as well as the good, the conventional and the experimental, the new as well as the familiar. Agee's distinctively graphic, often rhythmic prose ("All these people zipped and caromed about the pristine world of the screen as jazzily as a convention of water bugs") elevates his reviews, such as the one following, to the status of classics.

1   In the language of screen comedians four of the main grades of laugh are the titter, the yowl, the bellylaugh and the boffo. The titter is just a titter. The yowl is a runaway titter. Anyone who has ever had the pleasure knows all about a bellylaugh. The boffo is the laugh that kills. An ideally good gag, perfectly constructed and played, would bring the victim up this ladder of laughs by cruelly controlled degrees to the top rung, and would then proceed to wobble, shake, wave and brandish the ladder until he groaned for mercy. Then, after the shortest possible time out for recuperation, he would feel the first wicked tickling of the comedian's whip once more and start up a new ladder.

2   The reader can get a fair enough idea of the current state of screen comedy by asking himself how long it has been since he has had that treatment. The best of comedies these days hand out plenty of titters and once in a while it is possible to achieve a yowl without overstraining. Even those who have never seen anything better must occasionally have the feeling, as they watch the current run or, rather, trickle of screen comedy, that they are having to make a little cause for laughter go an awfully long way. And anyone who has watched screen comedy over the past ten or fifteen years is bound to

realize that it has quietly but steadily deteriorated. As for those happy atavists who remember silent comedy in its heyday and the bellylaughs and boffos that went with it, they have something close to an absolute standard by which to measure the deterioration.

When a modern comedian gets hit on the head, for example, the most he is apt to do is look sleepy. When a silent comedian got hit on the head he seldom let it go so flatly. He realized a broad license, and a ruthless discipline within that license. It was his business to be as funny as possible physically, without the help or hindrance of words. So he gave us a figure of speech, or rather of vision, for loss of consciousness. In other words he gave us a poem, a kind of poem, moreover, that everybody understands. The least he might do was to straighten up stiff as a plank and fall over backward with such skill that his whole length seemed to slap the floor at the same instant. Or he might make a cadenza of it—look vague, smile like an angel, roll up his eyes, lace his fingers, thrust his hands palms downward as far as they would go, hunch his shoulders, rise on tiptoe, prance ecstatically in narrowing circles until, with tallow knees, he sank down the vortex of his dizziness to the floor, and there signified nirvana by kicking his heels twice, like a swimming frog. 3

Startled by a cop, this same comedian might grab his hatbrim with both hands and yank it down over his ears, jump high in the air, come to earth in a split violent enough to telescope his spine, spring thence into a coattail-flattening sprint and dwindle at rocket speed to the size of a gnat along the grand, forlorn perspective of some lazy back boulevard. 4

Those are fine clichés from the language of silent comedy in its infancy. The man who could handle them properly combined several of the more difficult accomplishments of the acrobat, the dancer, the clown and the mime. Some very gifted comedians, unforgettably Ben Turpin, had an immense vocabulary of these clichés and were in part so lovable because they were deep conservative classicists and never tried to break away from them. The still more gifted men, of course, simplified and invented, finding out new and much deeper uses for the idiom. They learned to show emotion through it, and comic psychology, more eloquently than most language has ever managed to, and they discovered beauties of comic motion which are hopelessly beyond reach of words. 5

It is hard to find a theater these days where a comedy is playing; in the days of the silents it was equally hard to find a theater which was not showing one. The laughs today are pitifully few, far between, shallow, quiet and short. They almost never build, as they used to, into something combining the jabbering frequency of a machine gun with the delirious momentum of a roller coaster. Saddest of all, there are few comedians now below middle age and there are none who seem to learn much from picture to picture, or to try anything new. 6

To put it unkindly, the only thing wrong with screen comedy today is that it takes place on a screen which talks. Because it talks, the only comedians 7 who ever mastered the screen cannot work, for they cannot combine their comic style with talk. Because there is a screen, talking comedians are trapped into a continual exhibition of their inadequacy as screen comedians on a surface as big as the side of a barn.

8   At the moment, as for many years past, the chances to see silent comedy are rare. There is a smattering of it on television—too often treated as something quaintly archaic, to be laughed at, not with. Some two hundred comedies—long and short—can be rented for home projection. And a lucky minority had access to the comedies in the collection of New York's Museum of Modern Art, which is still incomplete but which is probably the best in the world. In the near future, however, something of this lost art will return to regular theaters. A thick straw in the wind is the big business now being done by a series of revivals of W. C. Fields's memorable movies, a kind of comedy more akin to the old silent variety than anything which is being made today. Mack Sennett now is preparing a sort of pot-pourri variety show called *Down Memory Lane* made up out of his old movies, featuring people like Fields and Bing Crosby when they were movie beginners, but including also interludes from silents. Harold Lloyd has re-released *Movie Crazy*, a talkie, and plans to revive four of his best silent comedies (*Grandma's Boy, Safety Last, Speedy* and *The Freshman*). Buster Keaton hopes to remake at feature length, with a minimum of dialogue, two of the funniest short comedies ever made, one about a porous homemade boat and one about a prefabricated house.

9   Awaiting these happy events we will discuss here what has gone wrong with screen comedy and what, if anything, can be done about it. But mainly we will try to suggest what it was like in its glory in the years from 1912 to 1930, as practiced by the employees of Mack Sennett, the father of American screen comedy, and by the four most eminent masters: Charlie Chaplin, Harold Lloyd, the late Harry Langdon and Buster Keaton.

10   Mack Sennett made two kinds of comedy: parody laced with slapstick, and plain slapstick. The parodies were the unceremonious burial of a century of hamming, including the new hamming in serious movies, and nobody who has missed Ben Turpin in *A Small Town Idol,* or kidding Erich von Stroheim in *Three Foolish Weeks* or as *The Shriek of Araby,* can imagine how rough parody can get and still remain subtle and roaringly funny. The plain slapstick, at its best, was even better: a profusion of hearty young women in disconcerting bathing suits, frisking around with a gaggle of insanely incompetent policemen and of equally certifiable male civilians sporting museum-piece mustaches. All these people zipped and caromed about the pristine world of the screen as jazzily as a convention of water bugs. Words can hardly suggest how energetically they collided and bounced apart, meeting in full gallop around the corner of a house; how hard and how often they fell on their backsides; or with what fantastically adroit clumsiness they got themselves fouled up in folding ladders, garden hoses, tethered animals and each other's headlong cross-purposes. The gestures were ferociously emphatic; not

a line or motion of the body was wasted or inarticulate. The reader may remember how splendidly upright wandlike old Ben Turpin could stand for a Renunciation Scene, with his lampshade mustache twittering and his sparrowy chest stuck out and his head flung back like Paderewski assaulting a climax and the long babyish back hair trying to look lionlike, while his Adam's apple, an orange in a Christmas stocking, pumped with noble emotion. Or huge Mack Swain, who looked like a hairy mushroom, rolling his eyes in a manner patented by French Romantics and gasping in some dubious ecstasy. Or Louise Fazenda, the perennial farmer's daughter and the perfect low-comedy housemaid, primping her spit curl; and how her hair tightened a good-looking face into the incarnation of rampant gullibility. Or snouty James Finlayson, gleefully foreclosing a mortgage, with his look of eternally tasting a spoiled pickle. Or Chester Conklin, a myopic and inebriated little walrus stumbling around in outsize pants. Or Fatty Arbuckle, with his cold eye and his loose, serene smile, his silky manipulation of his bulk and his satanic marksmanship with pies (he was ambidextrous and could simultaneously blind two people in opposite directions).

The intimate tastes and secret hopes of these poor ineligible dunces were ruthlessly exposed whenever a hot stove, an electric fan or a bulldog took a dislike to their outer garments: agonizingly elaborate drawers, worked up on some lonely evening out of some Godforsaken lace curtain; or men's underpants with big round black spots on them. The Sennett sets—delirious wallpaper, megalomaniacally scrolled iron beds, Grand Rapids *in extremis*—outdid even the underwear. It was their business, after all, to kid the squalid braggadocio which infested the domestic interiors of the period, and that was almost beyond parody. These comedies told their stories to the unaided eye, and by every means possible they screamed to it. That is one reason for the India-ink silhouettes of the cops, and for convicts and prison bars and their shadows in hard sunlight, and for barefooted husbands, in tigerish pajamas, reacting like dervishes to stepped-on tacks. 11

The early silent comedians never strove for or consciously thought of anything that could be called artistic "form," but they achieved it. For Sennett's rival, Hal Roach, Leo McCarey once devoted almost the whole of a Laurel and Hardy two-reeler to pie-throwing. The first pies were thrown thoughtfully, almost philosophically. Then innocent bystanders began to get caught into the vortex. At full pitch it was Armageddon. But everything was calculated so nicely that until late in the picture, when havoc took over, every pie made its special kind of point and piled on its special kind of laugh. 12

Sennett's comedies were just a shade faster and fizzier than life. According to legend (and according to Sennett) he discovered the sped tempo proper to screen comedy when a green cameraman, trying to save money, cranked too slow. . . . Realizing the tremendous drumlike power of mere motion to exhilarate, he gave inanimate objects a mischievous life of their own, broke every law of nature the tricked camera would serve him for and 13 made the screen dance like a witches' Sabbath. The thing one is surest of all to remember is how toward the end of nearly every Sennett comedy, a chase (usually called the "rally") built up such ɑ majestic trajectory of pure anarchic motion that bathing girls, cops, comics, dogs, cats, babies, automobiles, locomotives, innocent bystanders, sometimes what seemed like a whole city, an entire civilization, were hauled along head over heels in the wake of that energy like dry leaves following an express train.

14   "Nice" people, who shunned all movies in the early days, condemned the Sennett comedies as vulgar and naive. But millions of less pretentious people loved their sincerity and sweetness, their wild-animal innocence and glorious vitality. They could not put these feelings into words, but they flocked to the silents. The reader who gets back deep enough into that world will probably even remember the theater: the barefaced honky-tonk and the waltzes by Waldteufel, slammed out on a mechanical piano; the searing redolence of peanuts and demirep perfumery, tobacco and feet and sweat; the laughter of unrespectable people having a hell of a fine time, laughter as violent and steady and deafening as standing under a waterfall.

15   Sennett wheedled his first financing out of a couple of ex-bookies to whom he was already in debt. He took his comics out of music halls, burlesque, vaudeville, circuses and limbo, and through them he tapped in on that great pipeline of horsing and miming which runs back unbroken through the fairs of the Middle Ages at least to ancient Greece. He added all that he himself had learned about the large and spurious gesture, the late decadence of the Grand Manner, as a stage-struck boy in East Berlin, Connecticut and as a frustrated opera singer and actor. The only thing he claims to have invented is the pie in the face, and he insists, "Anyone who tells you he has discovered something new is a fool or a liar or both."

16   The silent-comedy studio was about the best training school the movies have ever known, and the Sennett studio was about as free and easy and as fecund of talent as they came. All the major comedians we will mention worked there, at least briefly. So did some of the major stars of the twenties and since—notably Gloria Swanson, Phyllis Haver, Wallace Beery, Marie Dressler and Carole Lombard. Directors Frank Capra, Leo McCarey and George Stevens also got their start in silent comedy; much that remains most flexible, spontaneous and visually alive in sound movies can be traced, through them and others, to this silent apprenticeship. Everybody did pretty much as he pleased on the Sennett lot, and everybody's ideas were welcome. Sennett posted no rules, and the only thing he strictly forbade was liquor. A Sennett story conference was a most informal affair. During the early years, at least, only the most important scenario might be jotted on the back of an envelope. Mainly Sennett's men thrashed out a few primary ideas and carried them in their heads, sure the better stuff would turn up while they were shooting, in the heat of physical action. This put quite a load on the prop man; he had to have the most improbable apparatus on hand—bombs, trick

telephones, what not—to implement whatever idea might suddenly turn up. All kinds of things did—and were recklessly used. Once a low-comedy auto got out of control and killed the cameraman, but he was not visible in the shot, which was thrilling and undamaged; the audience never knew the difference.

Sennett used to hire a "wild man" to sit in on his gag conferences, whose whole job was to think up "wildies." Usually he was an all but brainless, speechless man, scarcely able to communicate his idea; but he had a totally uninhibited imagination. He might say nothing for an hour; then he'd mutter "You take . . ." and all the relatively rational others would shut up and wait. "You take this cloud . . ." he would get out, sketching vague shapes in the air. Often he could get no further; but thanks to some kind of thought-transference, saner men would take this cloud and make something of it. The wild man seems in fact to have functioned as the group's subconscious mind, the source of all creative energy. His ideas were so weird and amorphous that Sennett can no longer remember a one of them, or even how it turned out after rational processing. But a fair equivalent might be one of the best comic sequences in a Laurel and Hardy picture. It is simple enough—simple and real, in fact, as a nightmare. Laurel and Hardy are trying to move a piano across a narrow suspension bridge. The bridge is slung over a sickening chasm, between a couple of Alps. Midway they meet a gorilla. 17

Had he done nothing else, Sennett would be remembered for giving a start to three of the four comedians who now began to apply their sharp individual talents to this newborn language. The one whom he did not train (he was on the lot briefly but Sennett barely remembers seeing him around) wore glasses, smiled a great deal and looked like the sort of eager young man who might have quit divinity school to hustle brushes. That was Harold Lloyd. The others were grotesque and poetic in their screen characters in degrees which appear to be impossible when the magic of silence is broken. One, who never smiled, carried a face as still and sad as a daguerreotype through some of the most preposterously ingenious and visually satisfying physical comedy ever invented. That was Buster Keaton. One looked like an elderly baby and, at times, a baby dope fiend; he could do more with less than any other comedian. That was Harry Langdon. One looked like Charlie Chaplin, and he was the first man to give the silent language a soul. 18

When Charlie Chaplin started to work for Sennett he had chiefly to reckon with Ford Sterling, the reigning comedian. Their first picture together amounted to a duel before the assembled professionals. Sterling, by no means untalented, was a big man with a florid Teutonic style which, under this special pressure, he turned on full blast. Chaplin defeated him within a few minutes with a wink of the mustache, a hitch of the trousers, a quirk of the little finger. 19

With *Tillie's Punctured Romance*, in 1914, he became a major star. Soon after, he left Sennett when Sennett refused to start a landslide among the 20 other comedians by meeting the raise Chaplin demanded. Sennett is understandably wry about it in retrospect, but he still says, "I was right at the time." Of Chaplin he says simply, "Oh well, he's just the greatest artist that ever lived." None of Chaplin's former rivals rate him much lower than that; they speak of him no more jealously than they might of God. We will try here only to suggest the essence of his supremacy. Of all comedians he worked most deeply and most shrewdly within a realization of what a human being is, and is up against. The Tramp is as centrally representative of humanity, as many-sided and as mysterious, as Hamlet, and it seems unlikely that any dancer or actor can ever have excelled him in eloquence, variety or poignancy of motion. As for pure motion, even if he had never gone on to make his magnificent feature-length comedies, Chaplin would have made his period in movies a great one singlehanded even if he had made nothing except *The Cure,* or *One A.M.* In the latter, barring one immobile taxi driver, Chaplin plays alone, as a drunk trying to get upstairs and into bed. It is a sort of inspired elaboration on a soft-shoe dance, involving an angry stuffed wildcat, small rugs on slippery floors, a Lazy Susan table, exquisite footwork on a flight of stairs, a contretemps with a huge, ferocious pendulum and the funniest and most perverse Murphy bed in movie history—and, always made physically lucid, the delicately weird mental processes of a man ethereally sozzled.

21   Before Chaplin came to pictures people were content with a couple of gags per comedy; he got some kind of laugh every second. The minute he began to work he set standards—and continually forced them higher. Anyone who saw Chaplin eating a boiled shoe like brook trout in *The Gold Rush,* or embarrassed by a swallowed whistle in *City Lights,* has seen perfection. Most of the time, however, Chaplin got his laughter less from the gags, or from milking them in any ordinary sense, than through his genius for what may be called *inflection*—the perfect, changeful shading of his physical and emotional attitudes toward the gag. Funny as his bout with the Murphy bed is, the glances of awe, expostulation and helpless, almost whimpering desire for vengeance which he darts at this infernal machine are even better.

22   A painful and frequent error among tyros is breaking the comic line with a too-big laugh, then a letdown; or with a laugh which is out of key or irrelevant. The masters could ornament the main line beautifully; they never addled it. In *A Night Out* Chaplin, passed out, is hauled along the sidewalk by the scruff of his coat by staggering Ben Turpin. His toes trail; he is as supine as a sled. Turpin himself is so drunk he can hardly drag him. Chaplin comes quietly to, realizes how well he is being served by his struggling pal, and with a royally delicate gesture plucks and savors a flower.

23   The finest pantomime, the deepest emotion, the richest and most poignant poetry were in Chaplin's work. He could probably pantomime Bryce's *The American Commonwealth* without ever blurring a syllable and make it paralyzingly funny into the bargain. At the end of *City Lights* the blind girl

who has regained her sight, thanks to the Tramp, sees him for the first time. She has imagined and anticipated him as princely, to say the least; and it has never seriously occurred to him that he is inadequate. She recognizes who he must be by his shy, confident, shining joy as he comes silently toward her. And he recognizes himself, for the first time, through the terrible changes in her face. The camera just exchanges a few quiet close-ups of the emotions which shift and intensify in each face. It is enough to shrivel the heart to see, and it is the greatest piece of acting and the highest moment in movies.

Harold Lloyd worked only a little while with Sennett. During most of 24 his career he acted for another major con edy producer, Hal Roach. He tried at first to offset Chaplin's influence and establish his own individuality by playing Chaplin's exact opposite, a character named Lonesome Luke who wore clothes much too small for him and whose gestures were likewise as unChaplinesque as possible. But he soon realized that an opposite in itself was a kind of slavishness. He discovered his own comic identity when he saw a movie about a fighting parson: a hero who wore glasses. He began to think about those glasses day and night. He decided on horn rims because they were youthful, ultravisible on the screen and on the verge of becoming fashionable (he was to make them so). Around these large lensless horn rims he began to develop a new character, nothing grotesque or eccentric, but a fresh, believable young man who could fit into a wide variety of stories.

Lloyd depended more on story and situation than any of the other major 25 comedians (he kept the best stable of gagmen in Hollywood, at one time hiring six); but unlike most "story" comedians he was also a very funny man from inside. He had, as he has written, "an unusually large comic vocabulary." More particularly he had an expertly expressive body and even more expressive teeth, and out of his thesaurus of smiles he could at a moment's notice blend prissiness, breeziness and asininity, and still remain tremendously likable. His movies were more extroverted and closer to ordinary life than any others of the best comedies: the vicissitudes of a New York taxi driver; the unaccepted college boy who, by desperate courage and inspired ineptitude, wins the Big Game. He was especially good at putting a very timid, spoiled or brassy young fellow through devastating embarrassments. He went through one of his most uproarious Gethsemanes as a shy country youth courting the nicest girl in town in *Grandma's Boy*. He arrived dressed "strictly up to date for the Spring of 1862," as a subtitle observed, and found that the ancient colored butler wore a similar flowered waistcoat and moldering cutaway. He got one wandering, nervous forefinger dreadfully stuck in a fancy little vase. The girl began cheerfully to try to identify that queer smell which dilated from him; Grandpa's best suit was rife with mothballs. A tenacious litter of kittens feasted off the goose grease on his home-shined shoes.

Lloyd was even better at the comedy of thrills. In *Safety Last*, as a rank 26 amateur, he is forced to substitute for a human fly and to climb a medium-sized skyscraper. Dozens of awful things happen to him. He gets fouled up in a tennis net. Popcorn falls on him from a window above, and the local pigeons treat him like a cross between a lunch wagon and St. Francis of Assisi. A mouse runs up his britches-leg, and the crowd below salutes his desperate dance on the window ledge with wild applause of the daredevil. A good deal of this full-length picture hangs thus by its eyelashes along the face of a building. Each new floor is like a new stanza in a poem; and the higher and more horrifying it gets, the funnier it gets.

27   In this movie Lloyd demonstrates beautifully his ability to do more than merely milk a gag, but to top it. (In an old, simple example of topping, an incredible number of tall men get, one by one, out of a small closed auto. After as many have clambered out as the joke will bear, one more steps out: a midget. That tops the gag. Then the auto collapses. That tops the topper.) In *Safety Last* Lloyd is driven out to the dirty end of a flagpole by a furious dog; the pole breaks and he falls, just managing to grab the minute hand of a huge clock. His weight promptly pulls the hand down from IX to VI. That would be more than enough for any ordinary comedian, but there is further logic in the situation. Now, hideously, the whole clockface pulls loose and slants from its trembling springs above the street. Getting out of difficulty with the clock, he makes still further use of the instrument by getting one foot caught in one of these obstinate springs.

28   A proper delaying of the ultrapredictable can of course be just as funny as a properly timed explosion of the unexpected. As Lloyd approaches the end of his horrible hegira up the side of the building in *Safety Last,* it becomes clear to the audience, but not to him, that if he raises his head another couple of inches he is going to get murderously conked by one of the four arms of a revolving wind gauge. He delays the evil moment almost interminably, with one distraction and another, and every delay is a suspense-tightening laugh; he also gets his foot nicely entangled in a rope, so that when he does get hit, the payoff of one gag sends him careening head downward through the abyss into another. Lloyd was outstanding even among the master craftsmen at setting up a gag clearly, culminating and getting out of it deftly, and linking it smoothly to the next. Harsh experience also taught him a deep and funda-mental rule: never try to get "above" the audience.

29   Lloyd tried it in *The Freshman*. He was to wear an unfinished, basted-together tuxedo to a college party, and it would gradually fall apart as he danced. Lloyd decided to skip the pants, a low-comedy cliché, and lose just the coat. His gagmen warned him. A preview proved how right they were. Lloyd had to reshoot the whole expensive sequence, build it around defective pants and climax it with the inevitable. It was one of the funniest things he ever did.

30   When Lloyd was still a very young man he lost about half his right hand (and nearly lost his sight) when a comedy bomb exploded prematurely. But in spite of his artificially built-out hand he continued to do his own dirty

work, like all of the best comedians. The side of the building he climbed in *Safety Last* did not overhang the street, as it appears to. But the nearest landing place was a roof three floors below him, as he approached the top, and he did everything, of course, the hard way, that is, the comic way, keeping his bottom stuck well out, his shoulders hunched, his hands and feet skidding over perdition.

If great comedy must involve something beyond laughter, Lloyd was not   31
a great comedian. If plain laughter is any criterion—and it is a healthy counterbalance to the other—few people have equaled him, and nobody has ever beaten him.

Chaplin and Keaton and Lloyd were all more like each other, in one   32
important way, than Harry Langdon was like any of them. Whatever else the others might be doing, they all used more or less elaborate physical comedy; Langdon showed how little of that one might use and still be a great silent-screen comedian. In his screen character he symbolized something as deeply and centrally human, though by no means as rangily so, as the Tramp. There was, of course, an immense difference in inventiveness and range of virtuosity. It seemed as if Chaplin could do literally anything on any instrument in the orchestra. Langdon had one queerly toned, unique little reed. But out of it he could get incredible melodies.

Like Chaplin, Langdon wore a coat which buttoned on his wishbone and   33
swung out wide below, but the effect was very different: he seemed like an outsized baby who had begun to outgrow his clothes. The crown of his hat was rounded and the brim was turned up all around, like a little boy's hat, and he looked as if he wore diapers under his pants. His walk was that of a child which had just gotten sure on its feet, and his body and hands fitted that age. His face was kept pale to show off, with the simplicity of a nursery-school drawing, the bright, ignorant, gentle eyes and the little twirling mouth. He had big moon cheeks, with dimples, and a Napoleonic forelock of mousy hair; the round, docile head seemed large in ratio to the cream-puff body. Twitchings of his face were signals of tiny discomforts too slowly registered by a tinier brain; quick, squirty little smiles showed his almost prehuman pleasures, his incurably premature trustfulness. He was a virtuoso of hesitations and of delicately indecisive motions, and he was particularly fine in a high wind, rounding a corner with a kind of skittering toddle, both hands nursing his hatbrim.

He was as remarkable a master as Chaplin of subtle emotional and mental   34
process and operated much more at leisure. He once got a good three hundred feet of continuously bigger laughs out of rubbing his chest, in a crowded vehicle, with Limburger cheese, under the misapprehension that it was a cold salve. In another long scene, watching a brazen showgirl change her clothes, he sat motionless, back to the camera, and registered the whole lexicon of lost innocence, shock, disapproval and disgust, with the back of his neck. His scenes with women were nearly always something special. Once a

lady spy did everything in her power (under the Hays Office) to seduce him. Harry was polite, willing, even flirtatious in his little way. The only trouble was that he couldn't imagine what in the world she was leering and pawing at him for, and that he was terribly ticklish. The Mata Hari wound up foaming at the mouth.

35   There was also a sinister flicker of depravity about the Langdon character, all the more disturbing because babies are premoral. He had an instinct for bringing his actual adulthood and figurative babyishness into frictions as crawley as a fingernail on a slate blackboard, and he wandered into areas of strangeness which were beyond the other comedians. In a nightmare in one movie he was forced to fight a large, muscular young man; the girl Harry loved was the prize. The young man was a good boxer; Harry could scarcely lift his gloves. The contest took place in a fiercely lighted prize ring, in a prodigious pitch-dark arena. The only spectator was the girl, and she was rooting against Harry. As the fight went on, her eyes glittered ever more brightly with blood lust and, with glittering teeth, she tore her big straw hat to shreds.

36   Langdon came to Sennett from a vaudeville act in which he had fought a losing battle with a recalcitrant automobile. The minute Frank Capra saw him he begged Sennett to let him work with him. Langdon was almost as childlike as the character he played. He had only a vague idea of his story or even of each scene as he played it; each time he went before the camera Capra would brief him on the general situation and then, as this finest of intuitive improvisers once tried to explain his work, "I'd go into my routine." The whole tragedy of the coming of dialogue, as far as these comedians were concerned—and one reason for the increasing rigidity of comedy ever since—can be epitomized in the mere thought of Harry Langdon confronted with a script.

37   Langdon's magic was in his innocence, and Capra took beautiful care not to meddle with it. The key to the proper use of Langdon, Capra always knew, was "the principle of the brick." "If there was a rule for writing Langdon material," he explains, "it was this: his only ally was God. Langdon might be saved by the brick falling on the cop, but it was *verboten* that he in any way motivate the brick's fall." Langdon became quickly and fantastically popular with three pictures, *Tramp, Tramp, Tramp, The Strong Man* and *Long Pants;* from then on he went downhill even faster. "The trouble was," Capra says, "that high-brow critics came around to explain his art to him. Also he developed an interest in dames. It was a pretty high life for such a little fellow." Langdon made two more pictures with high-brow writers, one of which (*Three's a Crowd*) had some wonderful passages in it, including the prize-ring nightmare; then First National canceled his contract. He was reduced to mediocre roles and two-reelers which were more rehashes of his old gags; this time around they no longer seemed funny. "He never did really understand what hit him," says Capra. "He died broke [in 1944]. And he died of a

broken heart. He was the most tragic figure I ever came across in show business."

Buster Keaton started work at the age of three and one-half with his 38 parents in one of the roughest acts in vaudeville ("The Three Keatons"); Harry Houdini gave the child the name Buster in admiration for a fall he took down a flight of stairs. In his first movies Keaton teamed with Fatty Arbuckle under Sennett. He went on to become one of Metro's biggest stars and earners; a Keaton feature cost about $200,000 to make and reliably grossed $2,000,000. Very early in his movie career friends asked him why he never smiled on the screen. He didn't realize he didn't. He had got the dead-pan habit in variety; on the screen he had merely been so hard at work it had never occurred to him there was anything to smile about. Now he tried it just once and never again. He was by his whole style and nature so much the most deeply "silent" of the silent comedians that even a smile was as deafeningly out of key as a yell. In a way his pictures are like a transcendent juggling act in which it seems that the whole universe is in exquisite flying motion and the one point of repose is the juggler's effortless, uninterested face.

Keaton's face ranked almost with Lincoln's as an early American arche- 39 type; it was haunting, handsome, almost beautiful, yet it was irreducibly funny; he improved matters by topping it off with a deadly horizontal hat, as flat and thin as a phonograph record. One can never forget Keaton wearing it, standing erect at the prow as his little boat is being launched. The boat goes grandly down the skids and, just as grandly, straight on to the bottom. Keaton never budges. The last you see of him, the water lifts the hat off the stoic head and it floats away.

No other comedian could do as much with the dead pan. He used this 40 great, sad, motionless face to suggest various related things: a one-track mind near the track's end of pure insanity; mulish imperturbability under the wildest of circumstances; how dead a human being can get and still be alive; an awe-inspiring sort of patience and power to endure, proper to granite but uncanny in flesh and blood. Everything that he was and did bore out his rigid face and played laughs against it. When he moved his eyes, it was like seeing them move in a statue. His short-legged body was all sudden, machinelike angles, governed by a daft aplomb. When he swept a semaphorelike arm to point, you could almost hear the electrical impulse in the signal block. When he ran from a cop his transitions from accelerating walk to easy jogtrot to brisk canter to headlong gallop to flogged-piston sprint—always floating, above this frenzy, the untroubled, untouchable face—were as distinct and as soberly in order as an automatic gearshift.

Keaton was a wonderfully resourceful inventor of mechanistic gags (he 41 still spends much of his time fooling with Erector sets); as he ran afoul of locomotives, steamships, prefabricated and over-electrified houses, he put himself through some of the hardest and cleverest punishment ever designed for laughs. In *Sherlock Jr.,* boiling along on the handlebars of a motorcycle quite unaware that he has lost his driver, Keaton whips through city traffic, breaks up a tug-of-war, gets a shovelful of dirt in the face from each of a long line of Rockette-timed ditch-diggers, approaches a log at high speed which is hinged open by dynamite precisely soon enough to let him through and, hitting an obstruction, leaves the handlebars like an arrow leaving a bow, whams through the window of a shack in which the heroine is about to be violated, and hits the heavy feet-first, knocking him through the opposite wall. The whole sequence is as clean in motion as the trajectory of a bullet.

42   Much of the charm and edge of Keaton's comedy, however, lay in the subtle leverages of expression he could work against his nominal dead pan. Trapped in the side-wheel of a ferryboat, saving himself from drowning only by walking, then desperately running, inside the accelerating wheel like a squirrel in a cage, his only real concern was, obviously, to keep his hat on. Confronted by Love, he was not as dead-pan as he was cracked up to be, either; there was an odd, abrupt motion of his head which suggested a horse nipping after a sugar lump.

43   Keaton worked strictly for laughs, but his work came from so far inside a curious and original spirit that he achieved a great deal besides, especially in his feature-length comedies. (For plain hard laughter his nineteen short comedies—the negatives of which have been lost—were even better.) He was the only major comedian who kept sentiment almost entirely out of his work, and he brought pure physical comedy to its greatest heights. Beneath his lack of emotion he was also uninsistently sardonic; deep below that, giving a disturbing tension and grandeur to the foolishness, for those who sensed it, there was in his comedy a freezing whisper not of pathos but of melancholia. With the humor, the craftsmanship and the action there was often, besides, a fine, still and sometimes dreamlike beauty. Much of his Civil War picture *The General* is within hailing distance of Mathew Brady. And there is a ghostly, unforgettable moment in *The Navigator* when, on a deserted, softly rolling ship, all the pale doors along a deck swing open as one behind Keaton and, as one, slam shut, in a hair-raising illusion of noise.

44   Perhaps because "dry" comedy is so much more rare and odd than "dry" wit, there are people who never much cared for Keaton. Those who do cannot care mildly.

45   As soon as the screen began to talk, silent comedy was pretty well finished. The hardy and prolific Mack Sennett made the transfer; he was the first man to put Bing Crosby and W. C. Fields on the screen. But he was essentially a silent-picture man, and by the time the Academy awarded him a special Oscar for his "lasting contribution to the comedy technique of the screen" (in 1938), he was no longer active. As for the comedians we have spoken of in particular, they were as badly off as fine dancers suddenly required to appear in plays.

46   Harold Lloyd, whose work was most nearly realistic, naturally coped least unhappily with the added realism of speech; he made several talking

comedies. But good as the best were, they were not so good as his silent work, and by the late thirties he quit acting. A few years ago he returned to play the lead (and play it beautifully) in Preston Sturges's *The Sin of Harold Diddlebock*, but this exceptional picture—which opened, brilliantly, with the closing reel of Lloyd's *The Freshman*—has not yet been generally released.

Like Chaplin, Lloyd was careful of his money; he is still rich and active. 47
Last June, in the presence of President Truman, he became Imperial Potentate of the A.A.O.N.M.S. (Shriners). Harry Langdon, as we have said, was a broken man when sound came in.

Up to the middle thirties Buster Keaton made several feature-length 48
pictures (with such players as Jimmy Durante, Wallace Beery and Robert Montgomery); he also made a couple of dozen talking shorts. Now and again he managed to get loose into motion, without having to talk, and for a moment or so the screen would start singing again. But his dark, dead voice, though it was in keeping with the visual character, tore his intensely silent style to bits and destroyed the illusion within which he worked. He gallantly and correctly refuses to regard himself as "retired." Besides occasional bits, spots and minor roles in Hollywood pictures, he has worked on summer stages, made talking comedies in France and Mexico and clowned in a French circus. This summer he has played the straw hats in *Three Men on a Horse*. He is planning a television program. He also has a working agreement with Metro. One of his jobs there is to construct comedy sequences for Red Skelton.

The only man who really survived the flood was Chaplin, the only one 49
who was rich, proud and popular enough to afford to stay silent. He brought out two of his greatest nontalking comedies, *City Lights* and *Modern Times,* in the middle of an avalanche of talk, spoke gibberish and, in the closing moments, plain English in *The Great Dictator,* and at last made an all-talking picture, *Monsieur Verdoux,* creating for that purpose an entirely new character who might properly talk a blue streak. *Verdoux* is the greatest of talking comedies though so cold and savage that it had to find its public in grimly experienced Europe.

Good comedy, and some that was better than good, outlived silence, but 50
there has been less and less of it. The talkies brought one great comedian, the late, majestically lethargic W. C. Fields, who could not possibly have worked as well in silence; he was the toughest and the most warmly human of all screen comedians, and *It's a Gift* and *The Bank Dick,* fiendishly funny and incisive white-collar comedies, rank high among the best comedies (and best movies) ever made. Laurel and Hardy, the only comedians who managed to preserve much of the large, low style of silence and who began to explore the comedy of sound, have made nothing since 1945. Walt Disney, at his best an inspired comic inventor and teller of fairy stories, lost his stride during the war and has since regained it only at moments. Preston Sturges has made brilliant, satirical comedies, but his pictures are smart, nervous comedy-

dramas merely italicized with slapstick. The Marx Brothers were sidesplitters but they made their best comedies years ago. Jimmy Durante is mainly a nightclub genius; Abbott and Costello are semiskilled laborers, at best; Bob Hope is a good radio comedian with a pleasing presence, but not much more, on the screen.

51   There is no hope that screen comedy will get much better than it is without new, gifted young comedians who really belong in movies, and without freedom for their experiments. For everyone who may appear we have one last, individious comparison to offer as a guidepost.

52   One of the most popular recent comedies is Bob Hope's *The Paleface*. We take no pleasure in blackening *The Paleface;* we single it out, rather, because it is as good as we've got. Anything that is said of it here could be said, with interest, of other comedies of our time. Most of the laughs in *The Paleface* are verbal. Bob Hope is very adroit with his lines and now and then, when the words don't get in the way, he makes a good beginning as a visual comedian. But only the beginning, never the middle or the end. He is funny, for instance, reacting to a shot of violent whisky. But he does not know how to get still funnier (*i.e.,* how to build and milk) or how to be funniest last (*i.e.,* how to top or cap his gag). The camera has to fade out on the same old face he started with.

53   One sequence is promisingly set up for visual comedy. In it, Hope and a lethal local boy stalk each other all over a cow town through streets which have been emptied in fear of their duel. The gag here is that through accident and stupidity they keep just failing to find each other. Some of it is quite funny. But the fun slackens between laughs like a weak clothesline, and by all the logic of humor (which is ruthlessly logical) the biggest laugh should come at the moment, and through the way, they finally spot each other. The sequence is so weakly thought out that at that crucial moment the camera can't afford to watch them; it switches to Jane Russell.

54   Now we turn to a masterpiece. In *The Navigator* Buster Keaton works with practically the same gag as Hope's duel. Adrift on a ship which he believes is otherwise empty, he drops a lighted cigarette. A girl finds it. She calls out and he hears her; each then tries to find the other. First each walks purposefully down the long, vacant starboard deck, the girl, then Keaton, turning the corner just in time not to see each other. Next time around each of them is trotting briskly, very much in earnest; going at the same pace, they miss each other just the same. Next time around each of them is going like a bat out of hell. Again they miss. Then the camera withdraws to a point of vantage at the stern, leans its chin in its hand and just watches the whole intricate superstructure of the ship as the protagonists stroll, steal and scuttle from level to level, up, down and sidewise, always managing to miss each other by hair's-breadths, in an enchantingly neat and elaborate piece of tim-ing. There are no subsidiary gags to get laughs in this sequence and there is little loud laughter; merely a quiet and steadily increasing kind of delight.

When Keaton has got all he can out of this fine modification of the movie chase he invents a fine device to bring the two together: the girl, thoroughly winded, sits down for a breather, indoors, on a plank which workmen have left across sawhorses. Keaton pauses on an upper deck, equally winded and puzzled. What follows happens in a couple of seconds at most: air suction whips his silk topper backward down a ventilator; grabbing frantically for it, he backs against the lip of the ventilator, jackknifes and falls in backward. Instantly the camera cuts back to the girl. A topper falls through the ceiling and lands tidily, right side up, on the plank beside her. Before she can look more than startled, its owner follows, head between his knees, crushes the topper, breaks the plank with the point of his spine and proceeds to the floor. The breaking of the plank smacks Boy and Girl together.

It is only fair to remember that the silent comedians would have as hard a   55
time playing a talking scene as Hope has playing his visual ones, and that writing and directing are as accountable for the failure as Hope himself. But not even the humblest journeymen of the silent years would have let themselves off so easily. Like the masters, they knew, and sweated to obey, the laws of their craft.

Questions

1. What are some of the major characteristics of the comic styles of the comedians Agee analyzes here: Chaplin, Lloyd, Langdon, Keaton? How do Agee's illustrations successfully explain Buster Keaton's funniness, although he "never smiled on screen"?

2. How has Agee tried to demonstrate the accuracy of the thesis implied by his title, that comedy's greatest era was during the period of silent films? Are you convinced? Agee's essay was written before the film prominence of Woody Allen, Peter Sellers, and Mel Brooks. Explain whether you think that the comic styles of these actors or others would cause Agee to change his mind.

3. To what extent, if any, does your understanding of Agee's illustrations depend on whether or not you've seen any of the actors or films he's discussing? How can a reviewer or commentator make a review as self-contained as possible, so readers won't need to have much background to understand it? Or shouldn't reviewers be concerned with this?

4. In explaining the actors' comic styles, Agee, as a careful commentator, provides definitions of various aspects of comic technique. For instance, "topping a gag" is overtly defined and illustrated in paragraph 27. Considering that "milking a gag" has been illustrated in paragraphs 21, 22, and 26, why doesn't Agee label this technique until paragraph 27? What illustration does he provide for the rule, "Never try to get 'above' the audience" (paragraph 29)? How is this single example sufficient to make his point?

GERALD MAST

Comic Plots and Comic Climate

Mast's life has focused on films practically from birth, in Los Angeles in 1940. He first performed in a Hollywood movie at eight, and continued acting well into his graduate work at the University of Chicago, from which he received three degrees, including a doctorate in 1967. Since then he has directed professional and university theater in Chicago, New York, and Provincetown, Massachusetts, while teaching at the Staten Island College of the City University of New York and at the University of Chicago. His books on film include A Short History of the Movies *(1971),* The Comic Mind: Comedy and the Movies *(1973), and an anthology of readings on* Film Theory and Criticism *(1974).*

This article is an example of clear, well-organized, informative, academic writing. Mast enumerates the eight principal comic plots and explains what makes a comedy a comedy (analogous to explaining what makes a joke a joke); analysis enables us to articulate what we already know in our hearts.

Comic Plots

1   There are eight comic film plots, eight basic structures by which film comedies have organized their human material. The film shares six of the eight with both the drama and the novel, one of the eight with only the novel, and one seems completely indigenous to the cinema.

2   1. The first is the familiar plot of New Comedy—the young lovers finally wed despite the obstacles (either within themselves or external) to their union. Boy meets girl; boy loses girl; boy gets girl. Many twists and surprises have been injected into this structure—in fact, it was full of twists and surprises in its infancy with Plautus and Terence. Shakespeare used transsexual twists in *Twelfth Night* and *As You Like It;* in *A Midsummer Night's Dream* he twists the romantic platitude that beauty is in the eye of the beholder; in *Much Ado About Nothing* the twist is the irony that the boy and girl do not know they are the boy and girl. Shaw reversed the active and passive sexes of New Comedy in *Man and Superman.* Ionesco burlesqued boy-gets-girl in *Jack, or The Submission.* This plot, with or without unexpected wrinkles, serves as the structural model for such films as *Bringing Up Baby* (the girl is the aggressive kook), *The Marriage Circle, Adam's Rib,* and *The Awful Truth* (boy and girl happen to be husband and wife), *It Happened One Night, Trouble in Paradise, Seven Chances, The Graduate* ("the other woman" is the girl's mother), and many, many more.

3   Merely concluding the action with a marriage (or an implied union of the romantic couple) is not sufficient for creating a comic plot. Many non-comic films end that way—*The Birth of a Nation, Stagecoach, The 39 Steps, Way Down East, Spellbound.* But in such films the final romantic union is parenthetic to the central action—the overcoming of a series of dangerous, murderous problems. After successfully combating terrible foes, the pro-

tagonist earns both life and love as his rewards. This is the typical plot of melodrama (in more dignified terms, "action" or "adventure" films). The adventure plot is a contemporary, totally secularized descendant of the medieval romance, and such films might be truly labeled "romances." In the comic plot, however, the amorous conclusion grows directly and exclusively from amorous complications.

The next three comic plots are all distillations of elements that were combined in Aristophanic Old Comedy.   4

2. The film's structure can be an intentional parody or burlesque of some other film or genre of films. Aristophanes parodied Euripides; Shakespeare parodied both classical heroism and courtly romance in *Troilus and Cressida;* Fielding began by parodying Richardson in *Joseph Andrews* and heroic tragedy in *The Tragedy of Tragedies* and *The Covent Garden Tragedy;* Ionesco parodies the well-made *boulevard* play in *The Bald Soprano.* In films there were specific parodies of silent hits—*The Iron Nag, The Halfback of Notre Dame.* Mack Sennett parodied melodrama and Griffith's last-minute rescues in *Barney Oldfield's Race for Life* and *Teddy at the Throttle.*   5

Parody plots flourished in the days of the one- and two-reelers. Feature-length parodies have been rarer. Keaton's *The Three Ages* is a parody of *Intolerance,* and his *Our Hospitality* parodies both the stories of the Hatfield-McCoy feuds and Griffith's last-minute rescue from the murderous falls in *Way Down East.* Many Abbott and Costello films parodied serious horror films. Woody Allen's *Take the Money and Run* is a series of parodies of film genres and styles; his *Bananas,* a series of parodies of specific films. The parodic plot is deliberately contrived and artificial; it is not an "imitation of a human action" but an imitation of an imitation. Perhaps, for this reason, it is best suited to the short form.   6

3. The *reductio ad absurdum* is a third kind of comic plot. A simple human mistake or social question is magnified, reducing the action to chaos and the social question to absurdity. The typical progression of such a plot —rhythmically—is from one to infinity. Perfect for revealing the ridiculousness of social or human attitudes, such a plot frequently serves a didactic function. After all, reduction to the absurd is a form of argument. Aristophanes used it by taking a proposition (if you want peace, if you want a utopian community, if you want to speculate abstractly) and then reducing the proposition to nonsense—thereby implying some more sensible alternative.   7

But the *reductio ad absurdum* need not serve didactic purposes exclusively. Feydeau typically takes a small human trait—jealousy, extreme moral fastidiousness—and multiplies it to infinity. Ionesco combines the farcical and intellectual potential of the *reductio ad absurdum* in plays such as *The Lesson*—which reduces the process of education to the absurd—and *The New Tenant*—which reduces man's dependence on material objects to the absurd.   8

In films, too, the *reductio ad absurdum* has served as the basis for both   9 pure farce and bitter intellectual argument. The Laurel and Hardy two-reelers are the perfect example of the *reductio ad absurdum* as pure fun—a single mistake in the opening minutes leads inexorably to final chaos. However, some of the most haunting and bitter film comedies are those which take some intellectual position and reduce it to horrifying nonsense. The reason both *Monsieur Verdoux* and *Doctor Strangelove* are comedies *structurally* (they are comedies for other reasons, too), despite their emphasis on deaths and horrors, is that they share this common comic shape. *Verdoux* reduces to the absurd the proposition that murder serves socially useful and emotionally necessary purposes; *Strangelove* deflates the proposition that man needs atomic weapons and military minds to preserve the human race. There is also an implied reduction to the absurd in Renoir's *The Rules of the Game,* although that is not its primary structural principle. Renoir's film is built on the proposition that good form is more important than sincere expressions of feeling. He reduces the proposition to death.

10   4. The structural principle of this Renoir film is more leisurely, analytical, and discursive than the taut, unidirectional, rhythmically accelerating *reductio ad absurdum*. This structure might be described as an investigation of the workings of a particular society, comparing the responses of one social group or class with those of another, contrasting people's different responses to the same stimuli and similar responses to different stimuli. Such plots are usually multileveled, containing two, three, or even more parallel lines of action. The most obvious examples of such plots are Shakespeare's comedies in which love (*A Midsummer Night's Dream*), deceptive appearances (*Much Ado About Nothing*), or the interrelation of human conduct and social environment (*As You Like It*) is examined from several social and human perspectives. Many Restoration comedies (Congreve's *Love for Love,* Wycherley's *The Country Wife*) and their descendants (Sheridan's *The Rivals*) are constructed on similar principles. In films, this multilevel social analysis serves as the basis of many Renoir films (*Boudu sauvé des eaux, The Rules of the Game, The Golden Coach*), of Clair's *À Nous la liberté,* Carné's *Bizarre, Bizarre,* and Chaplin's *The Great Dictator*. In films there is something very French about this structure.

11   5. The fifth comic-film structure is familiar in narrative fiction but very uncommon on the stage. It is unified by the central figure of the film's action. The film follows him around, examining his responses and reactions to various situations. This is the familiar journey of the picaresque hero—Don Quixote, Huck Finn, Augie March—whose function is to bounce off the people and events around him, often, in the process, revealing the superiority of his comic bouncing to the social and human walls he hits.

12   This form is probably less suited to the stage simply because it's sprawling structure requires a series of imaginative encounters for the *picaro* that could not be effectively depicted on a stage, given the theater's boundaries of time and space. But the film, completely free from such tyrannies (one of the points at which the film is closer to narrative fiction than to the drama), can

give the *picaro* as interesting and believable a series of opponents as any novelist. The most outstanding film *picaro* is, of course, Chaplin. Significantly, he begins to use the picaresque structure as he begins to mature with the Essanay films of 1915 (very few of his Keystones use it) and keeps it until *Modern Times* (1936), after which he drops it. The other major film *picaro* is Jacques Tati. But few of Chaplin's silent rivals ever used the loose, personality-centered structure: Langdon (traces of the picaresque only in *Tramp, Tramp, Tramp* and *The Strong Man*), Keaton (perhaps in a few two-reelers but not in the features), Lloyd (never the *picaro;* always up to his neck in a very clear, goal-oriented plot). The picaresque structure also shapes such bitter comedies as *Nights of Cabiria* and *A Clockwork Orange.*

6. The next comic-film plot is one that would seem to have no analogue in any other fictional form. The structure might best be described with a musical term—"riffing." But it could as easily be called "goofing," or "miscellaneous bits," or "improvised and anomalous gaggery." This was the structure of most of Chaplin's Keystones, simply because it was one of the two major Sennett structures (parody was the other). The Sennett riffing films take some initial situation—perhaps a place (a beach, a lake, a field), an event (auto races, a dance contest, a circus), an object (Tin Lizzies), an animal (lion), and then run off a series of gags that revolve around this central situation. The only sources of such a film's unity (other than the place, event, thing, or animal) are the performers' tendency to reappear from gag to gag and the film's unceasing rhythmic motion. Pace and motion become unifying principles in themselves. Perhaps the riffing film has no literary analogue because no other form (dance and music would be the closest) is so dependent on pace, motion, and physical energy. The outstanding examples of more recent riffing films are the two Richard Lester-Beatles pictures, *A Hard Day's Night* and *Help,* Louis Malle's *Zazie dans le métro,* and the Woody Allen comedies, which riff with a fairly anomalous collection of parodies and jokes. 13

Each of these six plots usually produces a comedy, though there are obvious exceptions. *King Lear* uses the multi-plot structure (4) for tragic ends, and many Elizabethan and Jacobean plays (*Doctor Faustus, The Changeling,* Beaumont and Fletcher's) interweave multiple lines of action for non-comic effects. In films, *Children of Paradise, Ship of Fools,* and *The Magnificent Ambersons* might be described as non-comic films with multilevel structures. And the amorous plot of boy-eventually-gets-girl (1) can serve as the basis of weepy melodramas as well as comedies. The difference between Lubitsch's *The Merry Widow* (1934) and von Stroheim's (1925) is the difference between a comic and non-comic use of the same structural pattern. 14

Finally, there are two other plots that have been used as frequently for non-comic ends as comic ones. 15

7. One is the kind that is also typical of melodramatic (or adventure or "romance") films. The central character either chooses to perform or is forced to accept a difficult task, often risking his life in the process. The plot then 16

traces his successful accomplishment of the task, often with his winning the battle, the girl, and the pot of gold at the end of the rainbow. Non-comic versions of his plot include *My Darling Clementine, North by Northwest, Rio Bravo, Tol'able David, the Maltese Falcon, The Thief of Bagdad* (1924), and thousands of other films—many of which contain comic elements and touches. Comic versions of the plot include *The General, The Navigator* (indeed, most of Keaton), *The Kid Brother, The Mollycoddle, The Lavender Hill Mob*, and many others. The difference between a comic and non-comic use of the plot depends entirely on whether the film creates a comic "climate" in the interest of arousing laughter or a non-comic one in the interest of arousing suspense, excitement, and expectation.

17   8. The same distinction holds true for the final plot form of comic films—the story of the central figure who eventually discovers an error he has been committing in the course of his life. This is, of course, the plot of *Oedipus Rex, Macbeth, Othello,* and any prototypic Aristotelian-Sophoclean tragedy. But it is also the plot of *Tartuffe, The Plain Dealer,* and *Major Barbara.* In films, the plot serves comically in *Mr. Smith Goes to Washington, The Freshman, Sullivan's Travels, Hail the Conquering Hero* (indeed, much of Sturges), *The Apartment* (and much of Wilder), and many others. The comic versions of the plot take place in a comic climate, which is a function of who makes the discovery, what the discovery is, and what the consequences of the discovery are.

Comic Climate

18   This term condenses the notion that an artist builds signs into a work to let us know that he considers it a comedy and wishes us to take it as such. It is functional to sidestep theory on the premise that we pretty much know what *a* comedy is even if we do not know what Comedy is. What are the signs by which we recognize that we are in the presence of a comic work?

19   Here Elder Olson's concept of "worthlessness" is useful. A worthless action is one that we do not take seriously, that we consider trivial and unimportant rather than a matter of extreme importance, of life and death.* Now, if comedy does indeed depict matters of life and death, then the reason such a depiction remains comic is because it *has not been handled as if it were* a matter of life and death. This device will, at some point, lead the audience to reflect that it has been lulled into taking the supremely serious as trivial—a reflection that is precisely the aim of much contemporary comedy. But whether a comedy asks for such reflection or not, the comic craftsman plants a series of signs that lets us know the action is taking place in a comic world, that it will be "fun" (even if at some moments it will not be), that we are to enjoy and not to worry.

---

* Olson defines comedy as "the imitation of a worthless action . . . effecting a *katastasis* of concern through the absurd."

1. When the film begins, perhaps even before it, the filmmaker transmits 20
cues to our responses. The first might be the title. It is not worth making too
much of titles, and obviously titles such as *The General, Modern Times,* and
The Marriage Circle do not tell us a lot—although Bergson notes that most
comedies bear generic titles (*The Alchemist*) rather than specific names (*Macbeth*). But titles such as *Much Ado About Nothing, Super-Hooper-Dyne Lizzies,
Three's a Crowd, Sullivan's Travels,* and *Doctor Strangelove: or How I Learned to
Stop Worrying and Love the Bomb* tell us a good deal about what to expect
from what follows.

2. The characters of the film rather quickly tell us if the climate is comic. 21
If a familiar comedian plays the central role, we can be *almost* certain that the
climate is comic (unless the filmmaker deliberately plays on our assumptions).
Keaton's presence makes *The General* take place in a comic world—despite
the fact that the film is full of adventure, suspense, war, and death. When
Chaplin dropped the picaresque journey for other plot structures, he still
used our expectations about Charlie to tell us in what light to view the action.
He first appears in *Monsieur Verdoux* trimming flowers, showing great concern for a tiny caterpillar, his familiar mustache turned up in an insane,
amputated version of Dali's. Meanwhile the remains of his last wife are going
up in smoke (literally) in an incinerator in the rearground of the frame.
Chaplin's comically finicky character informs us how to view the grisly activities in his incinerator. His familiar comic *persona* influences every reaction we
have to the film, much as the sight of Will Kemp or Robert Armin must have
done for audiences in the Theater or the Globe.

One-dimensional characters who represent comic types, either physically 22
or psychologically, also line up our responses in the intended direction.
Because of the pervasiveness of these types, critics have consistently identified
comic character with "the base," "the lowly," "the mechanical," or "the ridiculous." But such identifications are not necessarily valid. Such terms fail to fit
any of the great comic film *personae.* Many comic films deliberately use inelastic, mechanical types in the minor roles and perfectly supple, nonstereotypic
human beings in the major ones—just as Shakespeare did in his comedies.

3. The subject matter of the film's story might also inform us of a comic 23
climate. Subjects such as trying to invent doughnuts without holes or participating in a cross-country walking race are necessarily comic. But if the subject
matter is not intrinsically trivial, a comedy reduces important subject matter
to trivia. In *Doctor Strangelove* a serious subject, the destruction of the human
race, is treated as if it were no more important than inventing hole-free
doughnuts. And in *Bananas,* a political assassination (a topic horrifyingly
fresh in the American memory) is staged as if it were a televised sporting
contest.

4. The dialogue can let us know the climate is comic—because it either 24
is funny or is delivered in a funny, incongruous, mechanical, or some other
unnatural way. The opening sequence of Preston Sturges's *Sullivan's Travels* is

a breathless series of one-line jokes in which a studio chief and a young, idealistic director debate the validity of making films with a social message. The comic dialogue of this opening scene is essential to the effect of the rest of the film, which gets precariously close to the edge of bathos in its later sequences (indeed it may fall over that edge despite the opening jokes). The suave dialogue between Herbert Marshall and the waiter taking his order for supper in *Trouble in Paradise* informs us that the action and world to follow are comic, as do the subjects and manner of Cary Grant's breathlessly rapid discussion with his former wife in the opening scene of *His Girl Friday*.

25   5. Any hint of artistic self-consciousness—that the filmmaker knows he is making a film—can wrench us out of the illusion of the film and let us know that the action is not to be taken seriously. Such self-consciousness can assert itself in moments of burlesque or parody of topical issues or figures, parodies of other films or film styles, in gimmicky cinematic tricks, or in any other device that reminds the audience it is watching something artificial, "worthless." *Singin' in the Rain* self-consciously parodies the story of a star's meteoric rise from obscurity to fame and fortune; *Trouble in Paradise* parodies picture-postcard romance by juxtaposing a garbage collector and a shot of romantic Venice; *Doctor Strangelove* begins with a parody of a love scene as two planes enjoy sexual intercourse to the violinic strains of "Try a Little Tenderness." One trend in recent films is to add self-conscious, intrusive manipulation of cinematic elements to non-comic films as well. Such films, while proclaiming the film event as "not real," attempt to create an intense kinetic metaphor for the feeling of an event rather than comic detachment.

26   6. The examples above reveal that the motion picture can use distinctly cinematic tools to create its comic or non-comic climate. What the director shoots, how he shoots and edits it, and how he underscores the pictures for the ear establish the way an audience responds. A piece of comic business at the beginning of a film can color our responses for the next two hours—or until the film informs us to alter them.* Chaplin and Lubitsch are two masters at creating hilariously informative business for the beginnings of their films. In *The Gold Rush* Charlie enters the screen world unknowingly pursued by a bear; in *City Lights* he is grandiosely unveiled as he sleeps on the statute of Civic Virtue and Justice. Whatever else such shots mean in the films—and they mean plenty—they are hilariously funny surprises. Lubitsch's *So This Is Paris* begins as an apparent parody of a Valentino sheik-type movie, only to surprise us by revealing an ordinary domestic couple practicing a dance routine. *The Merry Widow* captures a gaudy military parade as

---

*Although the comic climate persists throughout a comic film, I have been concentrating on how we feel that climate at a film's beginning. Establishing the comic climate is, in effect, an element of exposition.

Maurice Chevalier sings "Girls, Girls, Girls." Then two oxen walk ploddingly down the street in the opposite direction, disrupting the order and precision of the singer and the marching band. The apparent "seriousness" of this display of European pageantry has been permanently and effectively ruptured. The manipulation of physical business, so important to an art that depends on the visual and, hence, physical, provides one of the important clues about a film's emotional climate.

So does the director's handling of camera angle, editing, lighting, and sound. Are the shots close or distant? Does he shoot from below, from above, or at eye level? Is the lighting bright and even, or somberly tonal? Is the editing invisible or obtrusive, rapid or languid with dissolves? Is the sound track cheery, tense, contrapuntal, silent? There are no formulas as to what techniques and methods will or won't inevitably produce comic effects, but that the union and combination of lighting, camera angle, decor, editing rhythm, music, etc. do shape the way we respond is undeniable.   27

In the film medium the handling of physical action, the photographing of images, the styles of camera, editing, and sound have far more importance than Aristotle accorded "melody" and "spectacle" in the drama. Whereas Aristotle relegated these two concrete physical assaults of the drama to the two least important aesthetic places, the motion picture, given its greater physical freedom, is far more dependent on them. The handling of image and sound becomes literally, a part of a film's "diction"—its method of "saying" what it has to "say." The common view that there is a grammar and rhetoric of film underscores the fact that cinematic technique is a kind of language. Whereas imagery in a literal form transmits itself verbally, imagery in the films is explicitly visual. Just as jokes, puns, wit, or comic imagery shape our reaction to a comic novel or play, a film's cinematic "diction" shapes our awareness that the action takes place in a comic or non-comic world.   28

A comic film, then, is either (*a*) one with a comic plot and comic climate or (*b*) one with a not necessarily comic plot but a pervasive enough comic climate so that the overall effect is comic. For example, the reason von Stroheim's *Merry Widow* is melodrama while Lubitsch's *Merry Widow* is comedy is that Lubitsch has created a comic climate for his film by almost all available means. Von Stroheim's subject matter is gloomy and brutal (duels, deaths, and semi-rapes); his characters are often vicious and perverted; and his manipulation of cinematic devices—camera angle, rhythms of cutting, lighting—is quiet and gloomily tonal. Lubitsch, using the same basic story and characters with the same names, fleshes out the structure with frivolous incidents; and he uses song, farcical minor characters, clever physical business, and self-conscious games with the camera and sound track.   29

An even more revealing (and more complicated) contrast is that between a comic film such as *The General* and a non-comic one such as *The 39 Steps*. Both use the same plot (the series of dangerous obstacles), the same motiva-   30 tion (both protagonists must overcome obstacles to survive), the same conclusion (both men succeed and win the lady fair). Both films are journeys. Both turn upon accidents and ironies.

31   But *The 39 Steps* is a heroic action performed by a non-heroic character; *The General* is a heroic action performed by a comic character. *The General* establishes a comic climate early and maintains it throughout the film. Gags define Buster Keaton's character as comic before he ever begins his adventure in search of a locomotive; *The General* introduces slapstick gags even at the most perilous moments. While *The 39 Steps* has wonderful comic moments—the feuding man and woman handcuffed together in a double bed; the man delivering a rousing impromptu political speech although ignorant of the views of the expected speaker—these moments of themselves do not, and are not intended to, create a comic climate.

Drama

GEORGE BERNARD SHAW
Hamlet

Shaw thoroughly enjoyed his theatrical posture as "the great man standing at odds with society"; indeed, his first major attempt at social reform was to try, through his dramatic criticism, to drag the Victorian English theater into the modern age. His early life did little to prepare Shaw for such an influential intellectual role. Born in Dublin in 1856 into an English, "vaguely Protestant" family, Shaw left school at fourteen, lived with his alcoholic father, and worked for five years "pursuing a strange passion for neat book-keeping" in a land agent's office. But in 1876, fed up with Irish provincialism, he decided to follow his mother—a Shavian "New Woman," a singing teacher—to London. He helped to found the intellectual utopian socialist Fabian Society; its principles permeate the novels and socialist tracts he wrote during this time.

From 1888 to 1894 Shaw was a music critic for The Star *and* The World, *and then wrote what has become landmark dramatic criticism for* Saturday Review, *1895–98. There he attempted, through the wit, sarcasm, and outspokenness that characterize the following review of* Hamlet, *to "create the taste by which he was to be appreciated," including lobbying for public acceptance of the controversial Ibsen. Deciding to practice what he preached, Shaw began writing his own plays, partly as a means of combating what he regarded as repressive and hypocritical Victorian morality. His most successful plays, including* Man and Superman *(1902),* Major Barbara *(1905),* Pygmalion *(1912), and* Saint Joan *(1923) present vigorous characters engaging in sprightly skirmishes, usually polemical, sometimes political. Shaw died at 94; his* Collected Plays *(1975) ultimately filled seven volumes.*

The Forbes-Robertson Hamlet at the Lyceum is, very unexpectedly at that address, really not at all unlike Shakespear's play of the same name. I am quite certain I saw Reynaldo in it for a moment; and possibly I may have seen Voltimand and Cornelius; but just as the time for their scene arrived, my eye fell on the word "Fortinbras" in the program, which so amazed me that I hardly know what I saw for the next ten minutes. Ophelia, instead of being a strenuously earnest and self-possessed young lady giving a concert and recitation for all she was worth, was mad—actually mad. The story of the play was perfectly intelligible, and quite took the attention of the audience off the principal actor at moments. What is the Lyceum coming to? Is it for this that Sir Henry Irving has invented a whole series of original romantic dramas, and given the credit of them without a murmur to the immortal bard whose profundity (as exemplified in the remark that good and evil are mingled in our natures) he has just been pointing out to the inhabitants of Cardiff, and whose works have been no more to him than the word-quarry from which he has hewn and blasted the lines and titles of masterpieces which are really all his own? And now, when he has created by these means a reputation for Shakespear, he no sooner turns his back for a moment on London than Mr Forbes-Robertson competes with him on the boards of his own theatre by actually playing off against him the authentic Swan of Avon. Now if the result had been the utter exposure and collapse of that impostor, poetic justice must have proclaimed that it served Mr Forbes-Robertson right. But alas! the wily William, by literary tricks which our simple Sir Henry has never quite understood, has played into Mr Forbes-Robertson's hands so artfully that the scheme is a prodigious success. The effect of this success, coming after that of Mr Alexander's experiment with a Shakespearean version of As You Like It, makes it almost probable that we shall presently find managers vying with each other in offering the public as much of the original Shakespearean stuff as possible, instead of, as heretofore, doing their utmost to reassure us that everything that the most modern resources can do to relieve the irreducible minimum of tedium inseparable from even the most heavily cut acting version will be lavished on their revivals. It is true that Mr Beerbohm Tree still holds to the old scepticism, and calmly proposes to insult us by offering us Garrick's puerile and horribly caddish knockabout farce of Katharine and Petruchio for Shakespear's Taming of the Shrew; but Mr Tree, like all romantic actors, is incorrigible on the subject of Shakespear.

2   Mr Forbes-Robertson is essentially a classical actor, the only one, with the exception of Mr Alexander, now established in London management. What I mean by classical is that he can present a dramatic hero as a man whose passions are those which have produced the philosophy, the poetry, the art, and the statecraft of the world, and not merely those which have produced its weddings, coroners' inquests, and executions. And that is just the sort of actor that Hamlet requires. A Hamlet who only understands his love for Ophelia, his grief for his father, his vindictive hatred of his uncle, his fear of ghosts, his impulse to snub Rosencrantz and Guildenstern, and the sportsman's excitement with which he lays the "mousetrap" for Claudius, can, with sufficient force or virtuosity of execution, get a great reputation in the part, even though the very intensity of his obsession by these sentiments (which are common not only to all men but to many animals) shews that the characteristic side of Hamlet, the side that differentiates him from Fortinbras, is absolutely outside the actor's consciousness. Such a reputation is the actor's, not Hamlet's. Hamlet is not a man in whom "common humanity" is raised by great vital energy to a heroic pitch, like Coriolanus or Othello. On the contrary, he is a man in whom the common personal passions are so superseded by wider and rarer interests, and so discouraged by a degree of critical self-consciousness which makes the practical efficiency of the instinctive man on the lower plane impossible to him, that he finds the duties dictated by conventional revenge and ambition as disagreeable a burden as commerce is to a poet. Even his instinctive sexual impulses offend his intellect; so that when he meets the woman who excites them he invites her to join

him in a bitter and scornful criticism of their joint absurdity, demanding "What should such fellows as I do crawling between heaven and earth?" "Why wouldst thou be a breeder of sinners?" and so forth, all of which is so completely beyond the poor girl that she naturally thinks him mad. And, indeed, there is a sense in which Hamlet is insane; for he trips over the mistake which lies on the threshold of intellectual self-consciousness: that of bringing life to utilitarian or Hedonistic tests, thus treating it as a means instead of an end. Because Polonius is "a foolish prating knave," because Rosencrantz and Guildenstern are snobs, he kills them as remorselessly as he might kill a flea, shewing that he has no real belief in the superstitious reason which he gives for not killing himself, and in fact anticipating exactly the whole course of the intellectual history of Western Europe until Schopenhauer found the clue that Shakespear missed. But to call Hamlet mad because he did not anticipate Schopenhauer is like calling Marcellus mad because he did not refer the Ghost to the Psychical Society. It is in fact not possible for any actor to represent Hamlet as mad. He may (and generally does) combine some notion of his own of a man who is the creature of affectionate sentiment with the figure drawn by the lines of Shakespear; but the result is not a madman, but simply one of those monsters produced by the imaginary combination of two normal species, such as sphinxes, mermaids, or centaurs. And this is the invariable resource of the instinctive, imaginative, romantic actor. You will see him weeping bucketsful of tears over Ophelia, and treating the players, the gravedigger, Horatio, Rosencrantz, and Guildenstern as if they were mutes at his own funeral. But go and watch Mr Forbes-Robertson's Hamlet seizing delightedly on every opportunity for a bit of philosophic discussion or artistic recreation to escape from the "cursed spite" of revenge and love and other common troubles; see how he brightens up when the players come; how he tries to talk philosophy with Rosencrantz and Guildenstern the moment they come into the room; how he stops on his country walk with Horatio to lean over the churchyard wall and draw out the gravedigger whom he sees singing at his trade; how even his fits of excitement find expression in declaiming scraps of poetry; how the shock of Ophelia's death relieves itself in the fiercest intellectual contempt for Laertes's ranting, whilst an hour afterwards, when Laertes stabs him, he bears no malice for that at all, but embraces him gallantly and comradely; and how he dies as we forgive everything to Charles II for dying, and makes "the rest is silence" a touchingly humorous apology for not being able to finish his business. See all that; and you have seen a true classical Hamlet. Nothing half so charming has been seen by this generation. It will bear seeing again and again.

And please observe that this is not a cold Hamlet. He is none of your logicians who reason their way through the world because they cannot feel their way through it: his intellect is the organ of his passion: his eternal self-criticism is as alive and thrilling as it can possibly be. The great soliloquy— 3 no: I do NOT mean "To be or not to be": I mean the dramatic one, "O what a rogue and peasant slave am I!"—is as passionate in its scorn of brute passion as the most bull-necked affirmation or sentimental dilution of it could be. It comes out so without violence: Mr Forbes-Robertson takes the part quite easily and spontaneously. There is none of that strange Lyceum intensity which comes from the perpetual struggle between Sir Henry Irving and Shakespear. The lines help Mr Forbes-Robertson instead of getting in his way at every turn, because he wants to play Hamlet, and not to slip into his inky cloak a changeling of quite another race. We may miss the craft, the skill double-distilled by constant peril, the subtlety, the dark rays of heat generated by intense friction, the relentless parental tenacity and cunning with which Sr. Henry nurses his own pet creations on Shakespearean food like a fox rearing its litter in the den of a lioness; but we get light, freedom, naturalness, credibility, and Shakespear. It is wonderful how easily everything comes right when you have the right man with the right mind for it— how the story tells itself, how the characters come to life, how even the failures in the cast cannot confuse you, though they may disappoint you. And Mr Forbes-Robertson has certainly not escaped such failures, even in his own family. I strongly urge him to take a hint from Claudius and make a real ghost of Mr Ian Robertson at once; for there is no sort of use in going through that scene night after night with a Ghost so solidly, comfortably, and dogmatically alive as his brother. The voice is not a bad voice; but it is the voice of a man who does not believe in ghosts. Moreover, it is a hungry voice, not that of one who is past eating. There is an indescribable little complacent drop at the end of every line which no sooner calls up the image of purgatory by its words than by its smug elocution it convinces us that this particular penitent is cosily warming his shins and toasting his muffin at the flames instead of expiating this bad acting in the midst of them. His aspect and bearing are worse than his recitations. He beckons Hamlet away like a beadle summoning a timid candidate for the post of junior footman to the presence of the Lord Mayor. If I were Mr Forbes-Robertson I would not stand that from any brother: I would cleave the general ear with horrid speech at him first. It is a pity; for the Ghost's part is one of the wonders of the play. And yet, until Mr Courtenay Thorpe divined it the other day, nobody seems to have had a glimpse of the reason why Shakespear would not trust anyone else with it, and played it himself. The weird music of that long speech which should be the spectral wail of a soul's bitter wrong crying from one world to another in the extremity of its torment, is invariably handed over to the most squaretoed member of the company, who makes it sound, not like Rossetti's Sister Helen, or even, to suggest a possible heavy treatment, like Mozart's statue-ghost, but like Chambers's Information for the People.

4   Still, I can understand Mr Ian Robertson, by sheer force of a certain quality of sententiousness in him, overbearing the management into casting him for the Ghost. What I cannot understand is why Miss Granville was cast for the Queen. It is like setting a fashionable modern mandolinist to play

Haydn's sonatas. She does her best under the circumstances; but she would have been more fortunate had she been in a position to refuse the part.

On the other hand, several of the impersonations are conspicuously successful. Mrs Patrick Campbell's Ophelia is a surprise. The part is one which has hitherto seemed incapable of progress. From generation to generation actresses have, in the mad scene, exhausted their musical skill, their ingenuity in devising fantasias in the language of flowers, and their intensest powers of portraying anxiously earnest sanity. Mrs Patrick Campbell, with that complacent audacity of hers which is so exasperating when she is doing the wrong thing, this time does the right thing by making Ophelia really mad. The resentment of the audience at this outrage is hardly to be described. They long for the strenuous mental grasp and attention coherence of Miss Lily Hanbury's conception of maiden lunacy; and this wandering, silly, vague Ophelia, who no sooner catches an emotional impulse than it drifts away from her again, emptying her voice of its tone in a way that makes one shiver, makes them horribly uncomfortable. But the effect on the play is conclusive. The shrinking discomfort of the King and Queen, the rankling grief of Laertes, are created by it at once; and the scene, instead of being a pretty interlude coming in just when a little relief from the inky cloak is welcome, touches us with a chill of the blood that gives it its right tragic power and dramatic significance. Playgoers naturally murmur when something that has always been pretty becomes painful; but the pain is good for them, good for the theatre, and good for the play. I doubt whether Mrs Patrick Campbell fully appreciates the dramatic value of her quite simple and original sketch— it is only a sketch—of the part; but in spite of the occasional triviality of its execution and the petulance with which it has been received, it seems to me to settle finally in her favor the question of her right to the very important place which Mr Forbes-Robertson has assigned to her in his enterprises.

I did not see Mr Bernard Gould play Laertes: he was indisposed when I returned to town and hastened to the Lyceum; but he was replaced very creditably by Mr Frank Dyall. Mr Martin Harvey is the best Osric I have seen: he plays Osric from Osric's own point of view, which is, that Osric is a gallant and distinguished courtier, and not, as usual, from Hamlet's, which is that Osric is "a waterfly." Mr Harrison Hunter hits off the modest, honest Horatio capitally; and Mr Willes is so good a Gravedigger that I venture to suggest to him that he should carry his work a little further, and not virtually cease to concern himself with the play when he has spoken his last line and handed Hamlet the skull. Mr Cooper Cliffe is not exactly a subtle Claudius; but he looks as if he had stepped out of a picture by Madox Brown, and plays straightforwardly on his very successful appearance. Mr Barnes makes Polonius robust and elderly instead of aged and garrulous. He is good in the scenes where Polonius appears as a man of character and experience; but the senile exhibitions of courtierly tact do not match these, and so seem forced and farcical.

Mr Forbes-Robertson's own performance has a continuous charm, interest, and variety which are the result not only of his well-known grace and accomplishment as an actor, but of a genuine delight—the rarest thing on our stage—in Shakespear's art, and a natural familiarity with the plane of his imagination. He does not superstitiously worship William: he enjoys him and understands his methods of expression. Instead of cutting every line that can possibly be spared, he retains every gem, in his own part or anyone else's, that he can make time for in a spiritedly brisk performance lasting three hours and a half with very short intervals. He does not utter half a line; then stop to act; then go on with another half line; and then stop to act again, with the clock running away with Shakespear's chances all the time. He plays as Shakespear should be played, on the line and to the line, with the utterance and acting simultaneous, inseparable and in fact identical. Not for a moment is he solemnly conscious of Shakespear's reputation or of Hamlet's momentousness in literary history: on the contrary, he delivers us from all these boredoms instead of heaping them on us. We forgive him the platitudes, so engagingly are they delivered. His novel and astonishingly effective and touching treatment of the final scene is an inspiration, from the fencing match onward. If only Fortinbras could also be inspired with sufficient force and brilliancy to rise to the warlike splendor of his helmet, and make straight for that throne like a man who intended to keep it against all comers, he would leave nothing to be desired. How many generations of Hamlets, all thirsting to outshine their competitors in effect and originality, have regarded Fortinbras, and the clue he gives to this kingly death for Hamlet, as a wildly unpresentable blunder of the poor foolish old Swan, than whom they all knew so much better! How sweetly they have died in that faith to slow music, like Little Nell in The Old Curiosity Shop! And now how completely Mr Forbes-Robertson has bowled them all out by being clever enough to be simple.

8   By the way, talking of slow music, the sooner Mr Hamilton Clark's romantic Irving music is stopped, the better. Its effect in this Shakespearean version of the play is absurd. The four Offenbachian young women in tights should also be abolished, and the part of the player-queen given to a man. The courtiers should be taught how flatteringly courtiers listen when a king shews off his wisdom in wise speeches to his nephew. And that nice wooden beach on which the ghost walks would be the better for a seaweedy looking cloth on it, with a handful of shrimps and a pennorth of silver sand.

Questions

1. Shaw's classic review of *Hamlet* assumes that his readers are familiar with the play itself, and that he can therefore concentrate on the strengths and weaknesses of the particular performance at hand. Show how this assumption governs what he includes and excludes from the review. When can reviewers in general assume that their readers know the work under consideration?

2. Shaw, later to become a major dramatist, was just beginning to write plays while he was a drama critic. How does this review reflect Shaw's knowledge of acting? of stage directing?

3. Shaw expresses definite opinions, positive and negative, not only about the actors and directors of the Forbes-Robertson *Hamlet*, but about other productions of the same play as well. Is it fair to the performers for a reviewer to be this opinionated? (Compare Shaw's review with Simon's review of *Hamlet*, which follows. Simon is equally opinionated, but far more bad-tempered.) To what extent do you as a reader feel obliged to agree with such an outspoken reviewer? Are you intimidated?

4. How much about the subject should a reviewer know in order to write a credible review? Must every reviewer be as knowledgeable as Shaw?

JOHN SIMON

Hamlet

As a critic of movies, theater, and culture, Simon has been judged "as absolute and arrogant in his judgments as any dictator of culture, a rigidity that is his great strength and weakness." He was born in Yugoslavia in 1925, came to the United States in 1941, and by 1959 had earned three degrees from Harvard, including a doctorate. In the 1950s he taught literature at M.I.T. and at Bard College. Since then he has combined an editorial career, with the Mid-Century Book Society, 1959–1961, and with Crofts Classics, 1966–75, with writing film and theater criticism for Commonweal, Theater Arts, Esquire, *and* New York *magazine. His books include* Private Screenings: Views of the Cinema of the Sixties *(1967),* Movies into Films *(1971),* and Singularities: Essays on the Theatre, 1964–1974 *(1976). He defends his opinionated, acerbic style with the vitriolic observation, "But 'personal attacks'—what are these 'personal attacks'? Does anyone really want criticism to be impersonal? written by a computer?"*

Simon's surliness stands in conspicuous contrast to Shaw's good-humored criticism. In his characteristicaly ill-tempered review of Nicol William's Hamlet *which follows (from* Uneasy Stages: A Chronicle of the New York Theatre, 1963–73 *[1976]), Simon assumes, probably correctly, that his readers are familiar with the play. He assumes, perhaps incorrectly, that he knows better than the director or the actors how* Hamlet *should best be performed. Whether readers will be convinced or repelled by the critic's harsh judgments may depend on how much they trust, or are repelled by, this savage persona—a risk the critic takes, just as any professional cast takes risks in every performance.*

The portrayals of Hamlet through the ages constitute a psychiatric nosography. There have been Oedipal Hamlets, homosexual Hamlets, transvestite Hamlets (played by actresses), Hamlets suffering from aboulia, dementia praecox, and diverse other ills the mind is heir to. But it remained for Nicol Williamson's Hamlet to suffer from an acute sinus condition. Williamson has a tendency to sound like an electric guitar twanged away at, with fearful

1

symmetry, high-low, high-low, high-low. It is a maniacal singsong, so stringently nasal that the lips seem to part only for visual effect.

2   Add to this the accent. It has been called Midlands, North Country and Cockney with a loose overlay of culture. Only Henry Higgins could correctly place it South of the Beatles or North of the Stones and identify the veneer as grammar- or council-school. But even Colonel Pickering could tell that it isn't Hamlet. I am not against modernizations, and am all for trying to find a contemporary equivalent for the Sweet Prince; but surely Jimmy Porter or Bill Maitland or some other Osbornian professional griper is no conscionable correspondence for the exacting idealist turned cosmic malcontent.

3   Then there is the appearance. The equine head with the mad Viking locks jiggling behind the nape and neck; the unweeded, piratical beard and brushwood mustache; the obstreperously lower-class features; the gangling, skulking body; the legs, not exactly spindly, but with more than a hint of octopus about them—all this is unsettling and finally disruptive. It is not tradition that I cling to, nor am I indulging my snobbery: in real life, a prince can look and behave very unlike a prince. But as our innovators are first to point out, a play is not real life but an artifact that creates its own universe and laws, and though these can be bent to accommodate certain idiosyncrasies, scant good can come of breaking them.

4   Which is not to say that the dogged Williamson doesn't have some very effective moments. The entire business with the Players, the Play Scene itself, the scenes with Rosencrantz and Guildenstern work very handily, with the real sparks flying when Hamlet rubs R. and G., those two dry sticks, together. Even in some of his weakest moments, as in the Closet Scene or in the soliloquies, Williamson will erupt from among some shabbily or indifferently read lines with one or two that possess marvelous shrewdness, animal vitality or insidiously ironic scorn. And there are times when the tenor of querulous fault-finding does rise to metaphysical exasperation, and the play becomes— not quite poetry, but a superb prose translation. Not for long, however. The good prose soon collapses into aborted poetry.

5   What about Tony Richardson's staging (if Richardson's it be, for rumor has it that with Williamson for a star, you don't need a director)? A few things work: best of all, the Play Scene (particularly the truly clever dumb show done as a cheerfully Anglicized *commedia dell' arte*); almost as good are the scenes leading up to and away from this. In other words, the production has a substantial middle and extremely rickety extremities; for rising action, it substitutes bulging action. The crowd scenes, with the noted exception, are dully staged, partly perhaps because the production was arena-style in London, and insufficient time was allowed for tucking it behind a proscenium. The courtiers are few in number and pallid of aspect; they mostly hold poses, rather like a frieze in very low relief.

6   Even bravura scenes get badly mangled. The killing of Polonius falls flatter than the old man's corpse, which never gets dragged around by Ham-

let. The near-demise of Claudius at his prayers lacks all suspense and punch. The Hamlet-Ophelia scenes substitute sexual horseplay for authentic feeling. And the final holocaust is perfunctory, with the King standing about like a fatted calf, just waiting to be slaughtered, and no one in the entire court thinking of coming to his defense. When there is directorial invention, it is likely to be of the foolish kind, as when Hamlet's letter is delivered by the sailors waylaying Horatio, one of them jumping him and sticking a dagger at his throat, while the other tauntingly holds up the missive before him—sheer nonsense. Worst of all is the Ghost, who does not even seem to be the ghost of Hamlet's father, but that of Ellis Rabb. He is heralded and accompanied by electronics that sound like Kennedy airport at peak-traffic time, and remains invisible somewhere way above our heads, presumably in a Boeing 707. His (Williamson's) voice is heard on a multiple-echoed, fadeout-ridden sound track left over from some C-grade horror movie.

The supporting performances are mostly quite insupportable. Francesca 7 Annis is lovely and charming as the sane Ophelia, but unmoving as the mad one. Patrick Wymark's Claudius is a bloated gnome who keeps chopping up, indeed garbling, his lines; Mark Dignam's competently old-hat Polonius would be equally at home in any *Hamlet* from Betterton's to Irving's; Constance Cummings' Gertrude is both wooden and inconspicuous—a bashful marionette; Gordon Jackson's Horatio might as well be his Scottish simpleton schoolmaster in *The Prime of Miss Jean Brodie;* Michael Pennington's Laertes is a brash mod lout; and Peter Gale's Osric a faggot's nightmare. Roger Livesey is a delightful actor who tragically lost his voice; to cast him here (First Player, Gravedigger) is less to help than to pillory him. Jocelyn Herbert's set is pedestrian and unadaptable; her costumes plagiarize the dawn: the whole cast seems to go about in russet mantles clad. But it's good night, sweet prince, all the same.

MICHAEL KERNAN

Bard Times
at the Folger Theater

Kernan is a Washington Post *reporter who often reviews film and theater productions. He was born in Utica, New York, in 1927 and earned a B.A.* cum laude *from Harvard in 1949. He wrote for the* Watertown (New York) Times *from 1949 until 1953, and spent over a decade with the* Redwood City (California) Tribune *before joining the* Post *in 1969. Kernan also writes articles and fiction for such magazines as* Life, The Saturday Evening Post, *and* Readers' Digest. The Violet Dots (1978) *is his account of English life during World War II.*

Reviewers adapt their criteria and their expectations to the company they keep. John Simon's severe review of Nicol Williamson's Hamlet (435–37) *makes appropriate demands of a professional company; Kernan's indulgent, tongue-in-cheek review of elementary school scenes from Shakespeare accommodates the fact that none of these amateur thespians had ever heard, seen, or read a Shakespeare play before their debut reported here. Kernan, ever diplomatic, says little about their acting (although he does refer to it once as "vehement"), notes without comment the unusually brisk pace of Romeo and Juliet ("a shade over 21 minutes"), and concentrates—safely—on their costumes (Macbeth "wore horn-rimmed glasses like a power-mad executive"). Shakespeare himself could be very harsh with the professional child actors who competed with his own Globe players—"an aerie of children, little eyases, that cry out on the top of question, and are most tyranically clapp'd for it" (Hamlet, IIii, 339–341). Kernan's benign commentary, however, illustrates that in judging amateur productions the critic's "Quality of mercy is not strained,/It droppeth as the gentle rain from heaven . . . ."*

1   You know you're immortal for sure when they celebrate your 416th birthday with a flea market.

2   William Shakespeare was born yesterday. He was a Taurus. (So were Marx, Freud, Hitler, Hearst, Barbra Streisand and Ulysses S. Grant. Good old Taurus.)

3   No, really, it was lovely party at the Folger. They sold costumes for $3 to $250 and Fiberglas shields for $75. They sold T-shirts, old playbills, stained glass and baubles.

But that was just the beginning.

4   There was an afternoon tea party by Twigs and Lady Henderson, wife of the British ambassador. There was a fashion show, a wine and cheese party where you could eat and drink all you could hold for $15 (with the famous bartender Baseball Bill Holdforth, dressed as Falstaff, holding forth at the beer keg) and a mayor's proclamation.

5   Actor Brian Corrigan roamed the scene looking just exactly (so they told me) like Shakespeare himself, and volunteers in Renaissance clothes were everywhere. Later the group heard some harp music and watched a takeoff on "Richard II."

6   But the thing you really wanted to be there for was the kids. They had a festival of excerpts from plays by the Old Boy, and they came from six schools, as far away as Vienna, Va., fourth- to sixth-graders.

7   We missed the Murch school version of "Macbeth" with six Witches (everyone always wants to be a Witch) but did catch the Haycock school's opening scenes from the play. We can report that King Duncan's voice is changing and that Lady Macbeth looked smashing in a black gown with pearls, striking sparks in her scene with Macbeth, who wore horn-rimmed glasses like a power-mad executive.

8   Carderock Springs school presented a brisk "Romeo and Juliet" in a shade over 21 minutes, cutting directly from the banishment to the tomb scene. The acting was vehement.

9   That infallibly funny play-within-a-play from "Midsummer Night's

Dream" was done with verve and pratfalls by Grace Brethren Christian day school, ending with a silent, ghostly dance of fairies.

Between plays, children wandered about in their capes and boots (plastic, with the fleece-lined tops turned down) and swords and crowns and charcoal mustaches. They made a lot of noise and skittered around like water bugs when they got the chance.   10

Parents drifted among them with anxious faces and shopping bags full of cloth.   11

The "Midsummer Night's Dream" people all wore yellow T-shirts with their names on the back: Bottom, Quince, Indian Boy and so on.   12

Someone called for a show of hands: How many had never seen a Shakespeare play before? Everyone. How many had never seen, heard or read one before? No one.   13

Child actors don't believe in wasting time with pauses in their dialogue, so the whole program went along very quickly. The morning show ran nearly an hour ahead of schedule.   14

In fact it all happened so fast that some parents missed seeing their kids in action. One of the stars of "Taming of the Shrew" was so upset that they repeated the excerpt later.   15

Nobody missed a single line all day.   16

Shakespeare would have been so touched.   17

Questions

1. Reviewers of amateur productions cannot hold the performers to professional standards, but must adapt their commentary to what can reasonably be expected. Show how Kernan has done so in this review of several excerpts of Shakespeare's plays performed by elementary schoolchildren.

2. Kernan refers only once to the acting (in a 21-minute excerpt from *Romeo and Juliet* as "vehement"). Why doesn't he say more about the acting? What does he concentrate on instead? Why?

3. What is the tone of Kernan's review? Is he laughing with or at the productions? the actors? Does he expect the production's audience, no doubt composed of the actors' parents and teachers, to share his reactions?

4. This review appeared in *The Washington Post*. Why would a major metropolitan newspaper send its principal drama critic to review such a performance? What response does he expect from the *Post* readers?

Literature

VIRGINIA WOOLF

The Patron and the Crocus

In "A Room of One's Own" (50–60) Woolf demonstrates that a novelist can use her primary gift, story telling, to create an essay. In "The Patron and the Crocus" she uses two other literary devices, personification and symbol, to integrate the essay. The "patron" personifies Woolf's concept of audience, not only a varying group of readers with diverse interests and tastes, but an audience that will support the writer financially and creatively. The "crocus" symbolizes the writer's subject, described differently for different patrons, "an imperfect crocus until it has been shared."

1   Young men and women beginning to write are generally given the plausible but utterly impracticable advice to write what they have to write as shortly as possible, as clearly as possible, and without other thought in their minds except to say exactly what is in them. Nobody ever adds on these occasions the one thing needful: "And be sure you choose your patron wisely," though that is the gist of the whole matter. For a book is always written for somebody to read, and, since the patron is not merely the paymaster, but also in a very subtle and insidious way the instigator and inspirer of what is written, it is of the utmost importance that he should be a desirable man.

2   But who, then, is the desirable man—the patron who will cajole the best out of the writer's brain and bring to birth the most varied and vigorous progeny of which he is capable? Different ages have answered the question differently. The Elizabethans, to speak roughly, chose the aristocracy to write for and the playhouse public. The eighteenth-century patron was a combination of coffee-house wit and Grub Street bookseller. In the nineteenth century the great writers wrote for the half-crown magazines and the leisured classes. And looking back and applauding the splendid results of these different alliances, it all seems enviably simple, and plain as a pikestaff compared with our own predicament—for whom should we write? For the present supply of patrons is of unexampled and bewildering variety. There is the daily Press, the weekly Press, the monthly Press; the English public and the American public; the best-seller public and the worst-seller public; the high-brow public and the red-blood public; all now organised self-conscious entities capable through their various mouthpieces of making their needs known and their approval or displeasure felt. Thus the writer who has been moved by the sight of the first crocus in Kensington Gardens has, before he sets pen to paper, to choose from a crowd of competitors the particular patron who suits

him best. It is futile to say, "Dismiss them all; think only of your crocus," because writing is a method of communication; and the crocus is an imperfect crocus until it has been shared. The first man or the last may write for himself alone, but he is an exception and an unenviable one at that, and the gulls are welcome to his works if the gulls can read them.

Granted, then, that every writer has some public or other at the end of his pen, the high-minded will say that it should be a submissive public, accepting obediently whatever he likes to give it. Plausible as the theory sounds, great risks are attached to it. For in that case the writer remains conscious of his public, yet is superior to it—an uncomfortable and unfortunate combination, as the works of Samuel Butler, George Meredith, and Henry James may be taken to prove. Each despised the public; each desired a public; each failed to attain a public; and each wreaked his failure upon the public by a succession, gradually increasing in intensity, of angularities, obscurities, and affectations which no writer whose patron was his equal and friend would have thought it necessary to inflict. Their crocuses in consequence are tortured plants, beautiful and bright, but with something wry-necked about them, malformed, shrivelled on the one side, overblown on the other. A touch of the sun would have done them a world of good. Shall we then rush to the opposite extreme and accept (if in infancy alone) the flattering proposals which the editors of the *Times* and the *Daily News* may be supposed to make us—"Twenty pounds down for your crocus in precisely fifteen hundred words, which shall blossom upon every breakfast table from John o' Groats to the Land's End before nine o'clock to-morrow morning with the writer's name attached"? 3

But will one crocus be enough, and must it not be a very brilliant yellow to shine so far, to cost so much, and to have one's name attached to it? The Press is undoubtedly a great multiplier of crocuses. But if we look at some of these plants, we shall find that they are only very distantly related to the original little yellow or purple flower which pokes up through the grass in Kensington Gardens about this time of year. The newspaper crocus is amazing but still a very different plant. It fills precisely the space allotted to it. It radiates a golden glow. It is genial, affable, warmhearted. It is beautifully finished, too, for let nobody think that the art of "our dramatic critic" of the *Times* or of Mr. Lynd of the *Daily News* is an easy one. It is no despicable feat to start a million brains running at nine o'clock in the morning, to give two million eyes something bright and brisk and amusing to look at. But the night comes and these flowers fade. So little bits of glass lose their lustre if you take them out of the sea; great prima donnas howl like hyenas if you shut them up in telephone boxes; and the most brilliant of articles when removed from its element is dust and sand and the husks of straw. Journalism embalmed in a book is unreadable. 4

The patron we want, then, is one who will help us to preserve our 5 flowers from decay. But as his qualities change from age to age, and it needs considerable integrity and conviction not to be dazzled by the pretensions or bamboozled by the persuasions of the competing crowd, this business of patron-finding is one of the tests and trials of authorship. To know whom to write for is to know how to write. Some of the modern patron's qualities are, however, fairly plain. The writer will require at this moment, it is obvious, a patron with the book-reading habit rather than the play-going habit. Nowadays, too, he must be instructed in the literature of other times and races. But there are other qualities which our special weaknesses and tendencies demand in him. There is the question of indecency, for instance, which plagues us and puzzles us much more than it did the Elizabethans. The twentieth-century patron must be immune from shock. He must distinguish infallibly between the little clod of manure which sticks to the crocus of necessity, and that which is plastered to it out of bravado. He must be a judge, too, of those social influences which inevitably play so large a part in modern literature, and able to say which matures and fortifies, which inhibits and makes sterile. Further, there is emotion for him to pronounce on, and in no department can he do more useful work than in bracing a writer against sentimentality on the one hand and a craven fear of expressing his feeling on the other. It is worse, he will say, and perhaps more common, to be afraid of feeling than to feel too much. He will add, perhaps, something about language, and point out how many words Shakespeare used and how much grammar Shakespeare violated, while we, though we keep our fingers so demurely to the black notes on the piano, have not appreciably improved upon *Antony and Cleopatra*. And if you can forget your sex altogether, he will say, so much the better; a writer has none. But all this is by the way—elementary and disputable. The patron's prime quality is something different, only to be expressed perhaps by the use of that convenient word which cloaks so much—atmosphere. It is necessary that the patron should shed and envelop the crocus in an atmosphere which makes it appear a plant of the very highest importance, so that to misrepresent it is the one outrage not to be forgiven this side of the grave. He must make us feel that a single crocus, if it be a real crocus, is enough for him; that he does not want to be lectured, elevated, instructed, or improved; that he is sorry that he bullied Carlyle into vociferation, Tennyson into idyllics, and Ruskin into insanity; that he is now ready to efface himself or assert himself as his writers require; that he is bound to them by a more than maternal tie; that they are twins indeed, one dying if the other dies, one flourishing if the other flourishes; that the fate of literature depends upon their happy alliance—all of which proves, as we began by saying, that the choice of a patron is of the highest importance. But how to choose rightly? How to write well? Those are the questions.

D. H. LAWRENCE

Benjamin Franklin

Lawrence, always physically frail, raged throughout his short life against what he believed to be the emotional deadness of the twentieth century, which he feared would turn us all into automatons, neither dead nor truly alive. He combated this potential degeneration with twenty years of frenzied writing, in which he produced over fifty books, including novels, short stories, poetry, travel accounts, and other nonfiction. T. S. Eliot epitomized the common critical opinion, that Lawrence was "a writer who had to write often badly in order to write sometimes well."

The problems of modern life mirror Lawrence's own tensions. His birthplace in 1885 in an ugly, coal-mining town in Nottinghamshire, England, was a constant reminder of the squalor of modern industrialism. The continuing conflict between his spiritual, educated, genteel mother and his physical, barely literate coal-miner father became to Lawrence a symbol of the conflicting halves of the modern mind. As a young man, Lawrence sided with his mother; he won a King's Scholarship and became a schoolmaster at Croydon, near London. But after he eloped with Frieda von Richthofen, the German wife of one of his teachers, Lawrence began to drift toward the "dark religion of the blood," the primal awareness of an instinctual life, including sexual passion, that his father had symbolized. With Frieda, Lawrence roamed the globe for some fifteen years, from Italy to Australia to Mexico and New Mexico, seeking intellectual and artistic freedom, and ultimately a cure for the tuberculosis from which he died in 1930. During this time, he wrote some of the most important and controversial novels of the twentieth century: Sons and Lovers *(1913),* Women in Love *(1920),* The Plumed Serpent *(1926), and* Lady Chatterley's Lover *(1928)—for which he was prosecuted for obscenity, as he was for* The Rainbow *(1915).*

The analysis of "Benjamin Franklin," below, from Studies in Classic American Literature *(1923) is characteristic of Lawrence's themes and style, his strengths and weaknesses. Some of his exuberant pronouncements are the insights of genius, some seem hyperbolically angry, almost mad (but which are which?). (See Franklin's "Rules," 635–37.) The essay is held together by its electricity, energy, and communication of the presence of a mind passionately at work. It offers no firm answers, for Lawrence believed that writing should be like life, "In everything the shimmer of creation and never the finality of the created."*

The Perfectibility of Man! Ah heaven, what a dreary theme! The perfectibility of the Ford car! The perfectibility of which man? I am many men. Which of them are you going to perfect? I am not a mechanical contrivance.   1

Education! Which of the various me's do you propose to educate, and which do you propose to suppress?   2

Anyhow, I defy you. I defy you, oh society, to educate me or to suppress me, according to your dummy standards.   3

The ideal man! And which is he, if you please? Benjamin Franklin or Abraham Lincoln? The ideal man! Roosevelt or Porfirio Díaz?   4

There are other men in me, besides this patient ass who sits here in a tweed jacket. What am I doing, playing the patient ass in a tweed jacket? Who am I talking to? Who are you, at the other end of this patience?   5

6   Who are you? How many selves have you? And which of these selves do you want to be?

7   Is Yale College going to educate the self that is in the dark of you, or Harvard College?

8   The ideal self! Oh, but I have a strange and fugitive self shut out and howling like a wolf or a coyote under the ideal windows. See his red eyes in the dark? This is the self who is coming into his own.

9   The perfectibility of man, dear God! When every man as long as he remains alive is in himself a multitude of conflicting men. Which of these do you choose to perfect, at the expense of every other?

10   Old Daddy Franklin will tell you. He'll rig him up for you, the pattern American. Oh, Franklin was the first downright American. He knew what he was about, the sharp little man. He set up the first dummy American.

11   At the beginning of his career this cunning little Benjamin drew up for himself a creed that should "satisfy the professors of every religion, but shock none."

12   Now wasn't that a real American thing to do?

13   *"That there is One God, who made all things."*

14   (But Benjamin made Him.)

15   *"That He governs the world by His Providence."*

16   (Benjamin knowing all about Providence.)

17   *"That He ought to be worshipped with adoration, prayer, and thanksgiving."*

18   (Which cost nothing.)

19   *"But——"* But me no buts, Benjamin, saith the Lord.

20   *"But that the most acceptable service of God is doing good to men."*

21   (God having no choice in the matter.)

22   *"That the soul is immortal."*

23   (You'll see why, in the next clause.)

24   *"And that God will certainly reward virtue and punish vice, either here or hereafter."*

25   Now if Mr. Andrew Carnegie, or any other millionaire, had wished to invent a God to suit his ends, he could not have done better. Benjamin did it for him in the eighteenth century. God is the supreme servant of men who want to get on, to *produce*. Providence. The provider. The heavenly store-keeper. The everlasting Wanamaker.

26   And this is all the God the grandsons of the Pilgrim Fathers had left. Aloft on a pillar of dollars.

27   *"That the soul is immortal."*

28   The trite way Benjamin says it!

29   But man has a soul, though you can't locate it either in his purse or his pocket-book or his heart or his stomach or his head. The *wholeness* of a man is his soul. Not merely that nice little comfortable bit which Benjamin marks out.

30   It's a queer thing is a man's soul. It is the whole of him. Which means it is

the unknown him, as well as the known. It seems to me just funny, professors and Benjamins fixing the functions of the soul. Why, the soul of man is a vast forest, and all Benjamin intended was a neat back garden. And we've all got to fit into his kitchen garden scheme of things. Hail Columbia!

The soul of man is a dark forest. The Hercynian Wood that scared the Romans so, and out of which came the white-skinned hordes of the next civilization. 31

Who knows what will come out of the soul of man? The soul of man is a dark vast forest, with wild life in it. Think of Benjamin fencing it off! 32

Oh, but Benjamin fenced a little tract that he called the soul of man, and proceeded to get it into cultivation. Providence, forsooth! And they think that bit of barbed wire is going to keep us in pound for ever? More fools they. 33

This is Benjamin's barbed wire fence. He made himself a list of virtues, which he trotted inside like a grey nag in a paddock. 34

1. TEMPERANCE. Eat not to fulness; drink not to elevation.
2. SILENCE. Speak not but what may benefit others or yourself; avoid trifling conversation.
3. ORDER. Let all your things have their places; let each part of your business have its time.
4. RESOLUTION. Resolve to perform what you ought; perform without fail what you resolve.
5. FRUGALITY. Make no expense but to do good to others or yourself—i.e., waste nothing.
6. INDUSTRY. Lose no time, be always employed in something useful; cut off all unnecessary action.
7. SINCERITY. Use no hurtful deceit; think innocently and justly, and, if you speak, speak accordingly.
8. JUSTICE. Wrong none by doing injuries, or omitting the benefits that are your duty.
9. MODERATION. Avoid extremes, forbear resenting injuries as much as you think they deserve.
10. CLEANLINESS. Tolerate no uncleanliness in body, clothes, or habitation.
11. TRANQUILLITY. Be not disturbed at trifles, or at accidents common or unavoidable.
12. CHASTITY. Rarely use venery but for health and offspring, never to dulness, weakness, or the injury of your own or another's peace or reputation.
13. HUMILITY. Imitate Jesus and Socrates.

A Quaker friend told Franklin that he, Benjamin, was generally considered proud, so Benjamin put in the Humility touch as an afterthought. The amusing part is the sort of humility it displays. "Imitate Jesus and Socrates," and mind you don't outshine either of these two. One can just imagine Socrates and Alcibiades roaring in their cups over Philadelphian Benjamin, 35 and Jesus looking at him a little puzzled, and murmuring: "Aren't you wise in your own conceit, Ben?"

36   "Henceforth be masterless," retorts Ben. "Be ye each one his own master unto himself, and don't let even the Lord put His spoke in." "Each man his own master" is but a puffing up of masterlessness.

37   Well, the first of Americans practised this enticing list with assiduity, setting a national example. He had the virtues in columns, and gave himself good and bad marks according as he thought his behaviour deserved. Pity these conduct charts are lost to us. He only remarks that Order was his stumbling block. He could not learn to be neat and tidy.

38   Isn't it nice to have nothing worse to confess?

39   He was a little model, was Benjamin. Doctor Franklin. Snuff-coloured little man! Immortal soul and all!

40   The immortal soul part was a sort of cheap insurance policy.

41   Benjamin had no concern, really, with the immortal soul. He was too busy with social man.

   1. He swept and lighted the streets of young Philadelphia.
   2. He invented electrical appliances.
   3. He was the centre of a moralizing club in Philadelphia, and he wrote the moral humorisms of Poor Richard.
   4. He was a member of all the important councils of Philadelphia, and then of the American colonies.
   5. He won the cause of American Independence at the French Court, and was the economic father of the United States.

42   Now what more can you want of a man? And yet he is *infra dig.*, even in Philadelphia.

43   I admire him. I admire his sturdy courage first of all, then his sagacity, then his glimpsing into the thunders of electricity, then his common-sense humour. All the qualities of a great man, and never more than a great citizen. Middle-sized, sturdy, snuff-coloured Doctor Franklin, one of the soundest citizens that ever trod or "used venery."

44   I do not like him.

45   And, by the way, I always thought books of Venery were about hunting deer.

46   There is a certain earnest naïveté about him. Like a child. And like a little old man. He has again become as a little child, always as wise as his grandfather, or wiser.

47   Perhaps, as I say, the most complete citizen that ever "used venery."

48   Printer, philosopher, scientist, author and patriot, impeccable husband and citizen, why isn't he an archetype?

49   Pioneer, Oh Pioneers! Benjamin was one of the greatest pioneers of the United States. Yet we just can't do with him.

50   What's wrong with him then? Or what's wrong with us?

51   I can remember, when I was a little boy, my father used to buy a scrubby

yearly almanac with the sun and moon and stars on the cover. And it used to prophesy bloodshed and famine. But also crammed in corners it had little anecdotes and humorisms, with a moral tag. And I used to have my little priggish laugh at the woman who counted her chickens before they were hatched and so forth, and I was convinced that honesty was the best policy, also a little priggishly. The author of these bits was Poor Richard, and Poor Richard was Benjamin Franklin, writing in Philadelphia well over a hundred years before.

And probably I haven't got over those poor Richard tags yet. I rankle still with them. They are thorns in young flesh. 52

Because, although I still believe that honesty is the best policy, I dislike policy altogether; though it is just as well not to count your chickens before they are hatched, it's still more hateful to count them with gloating when they *are* hatched. It has taken me many years and countless smarts to get out of that barbed wire moral enclosure that Poor Richard rigged up. Here am I now in tatters and scratched to ribbons, sitting in the middle of Benjamin's America looking at the barbed wire, and the fat sheep crawling under the fence to get fat outside, and the watch-dogs yelling at the gate lest by chance anyone should get out by the proper exit. Oh America! Oh Benjamin! And I just utter a long loud curse against Benjamin and the American corral. 53

Moral America! Most moral Benjamin. Sound, satisfied Ben! 54

He had to go to the frontiers of his State to settle some disturbance among the Indians. On this occasion he writes: 55

> We found that they had made a great bonfire in the middle of the square; they were all drunk, men and women quarrelling and fighting. Their dark-coloured bodies, half-naked, seen only by the gloomy light of the bonfire, running after and beating one another with fire-brands, accompanied by their horrid yellings, formed a scene the most resembling our ideas of hell that could well be imagined. There was no appeasing the tumult, and we retired to our lodging. At midnight a number of them came thundering at our door, demanding more rum, of which we took no notice.
>
> The next day, sensible they had misbehaved in giving us that disturbance, they sent three of their counsellors to make their apology. The orator acknowledged the fault, but laid it upon the rum, and then endeavoured to excuse the rum by saying: "The Great Spirit, who made all things, made everything for some use; and whatever he designed anything for, that use it should always be put to. Now, when he had made the rum, he said: Let this be for the Indians to get drunk with. And it must be so."
>
> And, indeed, if it be the design of Providence to extirpate these savages in order to make room for the cultivators of the earth, it seems not improbable that rum may be the appointed means. It has already annihilated all the tribes who formerly inhabited all the seacoast. . . .

This, from the good doctor with such suave complacency, is a little disenchanting. Almost too good to be true. 56

But there you are! The barbed wire fence. "Extirpate these savages in 57 order to make room for the cultivators of the earth." Oh, Benjamin Franklin! He even "used venery" as a cultivator of seed.

58 Cultivate the earth, ye gods! The Indians did that, as much as they needed. And they left off there. Who built Chicago? Who cultivated the earth until it spawned Pittsburgh, Pa.?

59 The moral issue! Just look at it! Cultivation included. If it's a mere choice of Kultur or cultivation, I give it up.

60 Which brings us right back to our question, what's wrong with Benjamin, that we can't stand him? Or else, what's wrong with us, that we find fault with such a paragon?

61 Man is a moral animal. All right. I am a moral animal. And I'm going to remain such. I'm not going to be turned into a virtuous little automaton as Benjamin would have me. "This is good, that is bad. Turn the little handle and let the good tap flow," saith Benjamin, and all America with him. "But first of all extirpate those savages who are always turning on the bad tap."

62 I am a moral animal. But I am not a moral machine. I don't work with a little set of handles or levers. The Temperance-silence-order-resolution-frugality-industry-sincerity-justice-moderation-cleanliness-tranquillity-chastity-humility keyboard is not going to get me going. I'm really not just an automatic piano with a moral Benjamin getting tunes out of me.

63 Here's my creed, against Benjamin's. This is what I believe:

> *"That I am I."*
> *"That my soul is a dark forest."*
> *"That my known self will never be more than a little clearing in the forest."*
> *"That gods, strange gods, come forth from the forest into the clearing of my known self, and then go back."*
> *"That I must have the courage to let them come and go."*
> *"That I will never let mankind put anything over me, but that I will try always to recognize and submit to the gods in me and the gods in other men and women."*

64 There is my creed. He who runs may read. He who prefers to crawl, or to go by gasoline, can call it rot.

65 Then for a "list." It is rather fun to play at Benjamin.

1. TEMPERANCE. Eat and carouse with Bacchus, or munch dry bread with Jesus, but don't sit down without one of the gods.
2. SILENCE. Be still when you have nothing to say; when genuine passion moves you, say what you've got to say, and say it hot.
3. ORDER. Know that you are responsible to the gods inside you and to the men in whom the gods are manifest. Recognize your superiors and your inferiors, according to the gods. This is the root of all order.
4. RESOLUTION. Resolve to abide by your own deepest promptings, and to sacrifice the smaller thing to the greater. Kill when you must, and be killed the same: the *must* coming from the gods inside you, or from the men in whom you recognize the Holy Ghost.

5. FRUGALITY. Demand nothing; accept what you see fit. Don't waste your pride or squander your emotion.
6. INDUSTRY. Lose no time with ideals; serve the Holy Ghost; never serve mankind.
7. SINCERITY. To be sincere is to remember that I am I, and that the other man is not me.
8. JUSTICE. The only justice is to follow the sincere intuition of the soul, angry or gentle. Anger is just, and pity is just, but judgment is never just.
9. MODERATION. Beware of absolutes. There are many gods.
10. CLEANLINESS. Don't be too clean. It impoverishes the blood.
11. TRANQUILLITY. The soul has many motions, many gods come and go. Try and find your deepest issue, in every confusion, and abide by that. Obey the man in whom you recognize the Holy Ghost; command when your honour comes to command.
12. CHASTITY. Never "use" venery at all. Follow your passional impulse, if it be answered in the other being; but never have any motive in mind, neither offspring nor health nor even pleasure, nor even service. Only know that "venery" is of the great gods. An offering-up of yourself to the very great gods, the dark ones, and nothing else.
13. HUMILITY. See all men and women according to the Holy Ghost that is within them. Never yield before the barren.

There's my list. I have been trying dimly to realize it for a long time, and only America and old Benjamin have at last goaded me into trying to formulate it.   66

And now I, at least, know why I can't stand Benjamin. He tries to take away my wholeness and my dark forest, my freedom. For how can any man be free, without an illimitable background? And Benjamin tries to shove me into a barbed wire paddock and make me grow potatoes or Chicagoes.   67

And how can I be free, without gods that come and go? But Benjamin won't let anything exist except my useful fellow men, and I'm sick of them; as for his Godhead, his Providence, He is Head of nothing except a vast heavenly store that keeps every imaginable line of goods, from victrolas to cat-o'-nine tails.   68

And how can any man be free without a soul of his own, that he believes in and won't sell at any price? But Benjamin doesn't let me have a soul of my own. He says I am nothing but a servant of mankind—galley-slave I call it—and if I don't get my wages here below—that is, if Mr. Pierpont Morgan or Mr. Nosey Hebrew or the grand United States Government, the great US, US or SOMEOFUS, manages to scoop in my bit, along with their lump—why, never mind, I shall get my wages HEREAFTER.   69

Oh Benjamin! Oh Binjum! You do NOT suck me in any longer.   70

And why, oh why should the snuff-coloured little trap have wanted to take us all in? Why did he do it?   71

Out of sheer human cussedness, in the first place. We do all like to get   72 things inside a barbed wire corral. Especially our fellow men. We love to round them up inside the barbed wire enclosure of FREEDOM, and make 'em work. *"Work, you free jewel, WORK!"* shouts the liberator, cracking his whip. Benjamin, I will not work. I do not choose to be a free democrat. I am absolutely a servant of my own Holy Ghost.

73   Sheer cussedness! But there was as well the salt of a subtler purpose. Benjamin was just in his eyeholes—to use an English vulgarism, meaning he was just delighted—when he was at Paris judiciously milking money out of the French monarchy for the overthrow of all monarchy. If you want to ride your horse to somewhere you must put a bit in his mouth. And Benjamin wanted to ride his horse so that it would upset the whole apple-cart of the old masters. He wanted the whole European apple-cart upset. So he had to put a strong bit in the mouth of his ass.

74   "Henceforth be masterless."

75   That is, he had to break-in the human ass completely, so that much more might be broken, in the long run. For the moment it was the British Government that had to have a hole knocked in it. The first real hole it ever had: the breach of the American rebellion.

76   Benjamin, in his sagacity, knew that the breaking of the old world was a long process. In the depths of his own under-consciousness he hated England, he hated Europe, he hated the whole corpus of the European being. He wanted to be American. But you can't change your nature and mode of consciousness like changing your shoes. It is a gradual shedding. Years must go by, and centuries must elapse before you have finished. Like a son escaping from the domination of his parents. The escape is not just one rupture. It is a long and half-secret process.

77   So with the American. He was a European when he first went over the Atlantic. He is in the main a recreant European still. From Benjamin Franklin to Woodrow Wilson may be a long stride, but it is a stride along the same road. There is no new road. The same old road, become dreary and futile. Theoretic and materialistic.

78   Why then did Benjamin set up this dummy of a perfect citizen as a pattern to America? Of course, he did it in perfect good faith, as far as he knew. He thought it simply was the true ideal. But what we *think* we do is not very important. We never really know what we are doing. Either we are materialistic instruments, like Benjamin, or we move in the gesture of creation, from our deepest self, usually unconscious. We are only the actors, we are never wholly the authors of our own deeds or works. IT is the author, the unknown inside us or outside us. The best we can do is to try to hold ourselves in unison with the deeps which are inside us. And the worst we can do is to try to have things our own way, when we run counter to IT, and in the long run get our knuckles rapped for our presumption.

79   So Benjamin contrived money out of the Court of France. He was contriving the first steps of the overthrow of all Europe, France included.

You can never have a new thing without breaking an old. Europe happens to be the old thing. America, unless the people in America assert themselves too much in opposition to the inner gods, should be the new thing. The new thing is the death of the old. But you can't cut the throat of an epoch. You've got to steal the life from it through several centuries.

And Benjamin worked for this both directly and indirectly. Directly, at the Court of France, making a small but very dangerous hole in the side of England, through which hole Europe has by now almost bled to death. And indirectly in Philadelphia, setting up this unlovely, snuff-coloured little ideal, or automaton, of a pattern American. The pattern American, this dry, moral, utilitarian little democrat, has done more to ruin the old Europe than any Russian nihilist. He has done it by slow attrition, like a son who has stayed at home and obeyed his parents, all the while silently hating their authority, and silently, in his soul, destroying not only their authority but their whole existence. For the American spiritually stayed at home in Europe. The spiritual home of America was, and still is, Europe. This is the galling bondage, in spite of several billions of heaped-up gold. Your heaps of gold are only so many muck-heaps, America, and will remain so till you become a reality to yourselves. 80

All this Americanizing and mechanizing has been for the purpose of overthrowing the past. And now look at America, tangled in her own barbed wire, and mastered by her own machines. Absolutely got down by her own barbed wire of shalt-nots, and shut up fast in her own "productive" machines like millions of squirrels running in millions of cages. It is just a farce. 81

Now is your chance, Europe. Now let Hell loose and get your own back, and paddle your own canoe on a new sea, while clever America lies on her muck-heaps of gold, strangled in her own barbed wire of shalt-not ideals and shalt-not moralisms. While she goes out to work like millions of squirrels in millions of cages. Production! 82

Let Hell loose, and get your own back, Europe! 83

PAUL FUSSELL
The Boy Scout Handbook

Fussell, the son of a millionaire, was born in Pasadena, California, in 1924, earned a B. A. from Pomona College, and graduate degrees from Harvard in 1949 and 1952. During World War II he served as an infantry officer and was twice wounded; he claims that his army service was "the formative experience" of his life, imbuing him with "a deep sense of irony," an appreciation of satire, and a lifelong attraction to other cultures.

Although Fussell has been a professor of English since 1955 (first at Rutgers, most recently at the University of Pennsylvania), his studies of society and literature are interdisciplinary. He explains, "I am persuaded by . . . George Orwell that literary, cultural, social, ethical, and political commentary can be virtually the same thing." Fussell's eclecticism is manifested in such diverse works as Poetic Meter and Poetic Form *(1965), and* The Great War and Modern Memory *(1975), a study of the British literary experience of World War I, which won both the National Book Critics Circle Award and the National Book Award.* Class: A Guide through the American Status System *(1983) typifies Fussell's witty, often iconoclastic, approach to his subject; he says of social class: "If the dirty little secret used to be sex, now it is the facts about social class. No subject today is more likely to offend." But no subject today is more likely to please than "The Boy Scout Handbook" (1982), a sympathetic, low-key appreciation of the virtues promoted in the 1979 edition of the classic* Boy Scout Handbook. *This essay illustrates two other principles of Fussell's criticism: it can be lively, rather than deadened by "the masquerade of solemnity," and it can be eclectic: "regardless of its social status or intellectual pretensions a thing is literature if it's worth reading more than a couple of times for illumination or pleasure."*

1   It's amazing how many interesting books humanistic criticism manages not to notice. Staring fixedly at its handful of teachable masterpieces, it seems content not to recognize that a vigorous literary-moral life constantly takes place just below (sometimes above) its vision. What a pity Lionel Trilling or Kenneth Burke never paused to examine the intersection of rhetoric and social motive among, say, the Knights of Columbus or the Elks. That these are their fellow citizens is less important than that the desires and rituals of these groups are desires and rituals, and thus of permanent social and psychological consequence. The culture of the Boy Scouts deserves this sort of look-in, especially since the right sort of people don't know much about it.

2   The right sort consists, of course, of liberal intellectuals. They have often gazed uneasily at the Boy Scout movement. After all, a general, the scourge of the Boers, invented it; Kipling admired it; the Hitlerjugend (and the Soviet Pioneers) aped it. If its insistence that there is a God has not sufficed to alienate the enlightened, its khaki uniforms, lanyards, salutes, badges, and flag-worship have seemed to argue incipient militarism, if not outright fascism. The movement has often seemed its own worst enemy. Its appropriation of Norman Rockwell as its official Apelles has not endeared it to those of exquisite taste. Nor has its cause been promoted by events like the TV appearance a couple of years ago of the Chief Pardoner, Gerald Ford, rigged out in scout neckerchief, assuring us from the teleprompter that a Scout is Reverent. Then there are the leers and giggles triggered by the very word "scoutmaster," which in knowing circles is alone sufficient to promise comic pederastic narrative. "*All* scoutmasters are homosexuals," asserted George Orwell, who also insisted that "*All* tobacconists are Fascists."

3   But anyone who imagines that the scouting movement is either sinister or stupid or funny should spend a few hours with the latest edition of *The Official Boy Scout Handbook* (1979). Social, cultural, and literary historians could attend to it profitably as well, for after *The Red Cross First Aid Manual, The World Almanac,* and the Gideon Bible, it is probably the best-known

book in this country. Since the first edition in 1910, twenty-nine million copies have been read in bed by flashlight. The first printing of this ninth edition is 600,000. We needn't take too seriously the ascription of authorship to William ("Green Bar Bill") Hillcourt, depicted on the title page as an elderly gentleman bare-kneed in scout uniform and identified as Author, Naturalist, and World Scouter. He is clearly the Ann Page or Reddy Kilowatt of the movement, and although he's doubtless contributed to this handbook (by the same author is *Baden-Powell: The Two Lives of a Hero* [1965]), it bears all the marks of composition by committee, or "task force," as it's called here. But for all that, it's admirably written. And although a complex sentence is as rare as a reference to girls, the rhetoric of this new edition has made no compromise with what we are told is the new illiteracy of the young. The book assumes an audience prepared by a very good high-school education, undaunted by terms like *biosphere, ideology,* and *ecosystem.*

The pliability and adaptability of the scout movement explains its re- 4 markable longevity, its capacity to flourish in a world dramatically different from its founder's. Like the Roman Catholic Church, the scout movement knows the difference between cosmetic and real change, and it happily embraces the one to avoid any truck with the other. Witness the new American flag patch, now worn at the top of the right sleeve. It betokens no access of jingoism or threat to a civilized internationalism. It simply conduces to dignity by imitating a similar affectation of police and fire departments in anarchic towns like New York City. The message of the flag patch is not "I am a fascist, straining to become old enough to purchase and wield guns." It is, rather, "I can be put to quasi-official use, and like a fireman or policeman I am trained in first aid and ready to help."

There are other innovations, none of them essential. The breeches of 5 thirty years ago have yielded to trousers, although shorts are still in. The wide-brimmed army field hat of the First World War is a fixture still occasionally seen, but it is now augmented by headwear deriving from succeeding mass patriotic exercises: overseas caps and berets from World War II, and visor caps of the sort worn by General Westmoreland and sunbelt retirees. The scout handclasp has been changed, perhaps because it was discovered in the context of the new internationalism that the former one, which the little finger was separated from the other three on the right hand, transmitted inappropriate suggestions in the Third World. The handclasp is now the normal civilian one, but given with the left hand. There's now much less emphasis on knots than formerly; as if to signal this change, the neckerchief is no longer religiously knotted at the tips. What used to be known as artificial respiration ("Out goes the bad air, in comes the good") has given way to "rescue breathing." The young are now being familiarized with the metric system. Some bright empiric has discovered that a paste made of meat tenderizer is the best remedy for painful insect stings. Constipation is not the bugbear it was a generation ago. And throughout there is a striking new lyricism. "Feel the wind blowing through your hair," the scout is adjured, just as he is exhorted to perceive that Being Prepared for life means learning "to live happy" and—equally important—"to die happy." There's more emphasis now on fun and less on duty; or rather, duty is validated because, properly viewed, it is a pleasure. (If that sounds like advice useful to grown-ups as well as to sprouts, you're beginning to get the point.)

6   There are only two possible causes of complaint. The term "free world" surfaces too often, although the phrase is mercifully uncapitalized. And the Deism is a bit insistent. The United States is defined as a country "whose people believe in a supreme being." The words "In God We Trust" on the coinage and currency are taken almost as a constitutional injunction. The camper is told to carry along the "Bible, Testament, or prayer book of your faith," even though, for light backpacking, he is advised to leave behind air mattress, knife and fork, and pancake turner. When the scout finds himself lost in the woods, he is to "stay put and have faith that someone will find you." In aid of this end, "Prayer will help." But the religiosity is so broad that it's harmless. The words "your church" are followed always by the phrase "or synagogue." The writers have done as well as they can considering that they're saddled with the immutable twelve points of Baden-Powell's Scout Law, stating unambiguously that "A Scout is Reverent" and "faithful to his religious duties." But if "You have the right to worship God in your own way," you must see to it that "others retain their right to worship God in their way." Likewise, if "you have the right to speak your mind without fear of prison or punishment," you must "ensure that right for others, even when you do not agree with them." If the book adheres to any politics, they can hardly be described as conservative; they are better described as slightly archaic liberal. It is broadly hinted that industrial corporations are prime threats to clean air and conservation. In every illustration depicting more than three boys, one is black. The section introducing the reader to some Great Americans pays respects not only to Franklin and Edison and John D. Rockefeller and Einstein; it also makes much of Walter Reuther and Samuel Gompers, as well as Harriet Tubman, Martin Luther King, and Whitney Young. There is a post-Watergate awareness that public officials must be watched closely. One's civic duties include the obligation to "keep up on what is going on around you" in order to "get involved" and "help change things that are not good."

7   Few books these days could be called compendia of good sense. This is one such, and its good sense is not merely about swimming safely and putting campfires "cold out." The good sense is psychological and ethical as well. Indeed, this handbook is among the very few remaining popular repositories of something like classical ethics, deriving from Aristotle and Cicero. Except for the handbooks' adhesions to the motif of scenic beauty, it reads as if the Romantic movement had never taken place. The constant moral theme is the inestimable benefits of looking objectively outward and losing consciousness of self in the work to be done. To its young audience vulnerable to invitations

to "trips" and trances and anxious self-absorption, the book calmly says: "Forget yourself." What a shame the psychobabblers of Marin County will never read it.

There is other invaluable advice, applicable to adults as well as to scouts. Some is practical, like "Never use flammable fluids to start a charcoal fire. They burn off fast, lighting only a little of the charcoal." Some is civic-moral: "Take a 2-hour walk where you live. Make a list of things that please you, another of things that should be improved." And then the kicker: "Set out to improve them." Some advice is even intellectual, and pleasantly uncompromising: "Reading trash all the time makes it impossible for anyone to be anything but a second-rate person." But the best advice is ethical: "Learn to think." "Gather knowledge." "Have initiative." "Respect the rights of others." Actually, there's hardly a better gauge for measuring the gross official misbehavior of the seventies than the ethics enshrined in this handbook. From its explicit ethics you can infer such propositions as "A scout does not tap his acquaintances' telephones," or "A scout does not bomb and invade a neutral country, and then lie about it," or "A scout does not prosecute war unless, as the Constitution provides, it has been declared by the Congress." Not to mention that because a scout is clean in thought, word, and deed, he does not, like Richard Nixon, designate his fellow citizens "shits" and then both record his filth and lie about the recordings ("A scout tells the truth").

Responding to Orwell's satiric analysis of "Boys' Weeklies" forty years ago, the boys' author Frank Richards, stigmatized by Orwell as a manufacturer of excessively optimistic and falsely wholesome stories, observed that "The writer for young people should . . . endeavor to give his young readers a sense of stability and solid security, because it is good for them, and makes for happiness and peace of mind." Even if it is true, as Orwell objects, that the happiness of youth is a cruel delusion, then, says Richards, "Let youth be happy, or as happy as possible. Happiness is the best preparation for misery, if misery must come. At least the poor kid will have had something." In the current world of Making It and Getting Away with It, there are not many books devoted to associating happiness with virtue. The shelves of the CIA and the State Department must be bare of them. "Horror swells around us like an oil spill," Terrence Des Pres said recently. "Not a day passes without more savagery and harm." He was commenting on Philip Hallie's *Lest Innocent Blood Be Shed,* an account of a whole French village's trustworthiness, loyalty, helpfulness, friendliness, courtesy, kindness, cheerfulness, and bravery in hiding scores of Jews during the Occupation. Des Pres concludes: "*Goodness.* When was the last time anyone used that word in earnest, without irony, as anything more than a doubtful cliché?" *The Official Boy Scout Handbook,* for all its focus on Axmanship, Backpacking, Cooking, First Aid, Flowers, Hiking, Map and Compass, Semaphore, Trees, and Weather, is another book about goodness. No home, and certainly no government office, should be without a copy. The generously low price of $3.50 is enticing, and so is the place on the back cover where you're invited to inscribe your name.

Questions

1. Why review the latest edition of a popular classic, fiction or nonfiction, if readers are presumably familiar with one or more of the earlier editions? Surely they are likely to know some version of *The Boy Scout Handbook,* first published in 1910.

2. Sometimes a review of a work or other performance becomes a defense of its subject. Why does Fussell begin his review, written in 1979, with a defense of the Boy Scout movement?

3. Find passages that show how Fussell treats the *Boy Scout Handbook* as the embodiment of the highest ideals of American culture. Does he as a reviewer treat his subject with the same reverence that the *Handbook* shows for the subjects it discusses? Should he do so?

4. Fussell asserts that cynics and "the psychobabblers of Marin County" would probably scoff at the *Boy Scout Handbook*. Would they also reject Fussell's interpretation of it? Why or why not?

EUDORA WELTY

E. B. White's *Charlotte's Web*

Henry Mitchell has conveyed the essence of Eudora Welty's personality, character, and career as a writer in "Eudora Welty: Storyteller of the South" (167–75).

Welty's review of E. B. White's children's classic, Charlotte's Web, *succinctly shows why the book appeals to grownups as well as to children. Although Welty assumes, as the reviewer of any new work must, that her audience is unfamiliar with the book, she does not recount the plot. Instead, she begins by identifying (in this order) its mood and tone ("It has liveliness and felicity, tenderness and unexpectedness . . ."), its time and setting, and its characters in general ("good and bad . . . talented and untalented . . . vegetarian and blood-drinking . . . the real thing"). Then she sketches the main characters: Wilbur the pig ("of a sweet nature"—perhaps a country cousin to the pig in White's "Death of a Pig," 533–39); Charlotte the spider and the heroine, in part, because of her ability to write; Templeton the rat with "no milk of rodent kindness"; and the goose who repeats everything. After only hinting at the plot ("how Charlotte sets in to save Wilbur's life"), Welty ends by identifying the book's themes ("friendship on earth, love and affection, adventure and miracle . . .") and in the last two paragraphs offers a brief assessment that makes explicit what she has already implied.*

The sophisticated concepts and straightforward language of Welty's engaging review reveal what all outstanding writers and reviewers of children's literature know—never talk down. For to speak in condescending, euphemistic, or cutesy language is to demean both the subject and the audience. Although Welty's ultimate assessment, "adorable," verges on the cute, in the main her review, like the book, appeals to adults and children alike.

1   If I had the qualifications (a set of spinnerets and the know-how), I'd put in tonight writing "Adorable" across my web, to be visible Sunday morning hung with dewdrops for my review of *Charlotte's Web*.

Mr. E. B. White has written his book for children, which is nice for us   2
older ones, as it calls for big type. It has liveliness and felicity, tenderness and
unexpectedness, grace and humor and praise of life, and the good backbone
of succinctness that only the most highly imaginative stories possess.

Most of *Charlotte's Web* takes place in the Zuckerman barn, through the   3
passing of the four seasons.

> Life in the barn was very good—night and day, winter and summer, spring
> and fall, dull days and bright days. It was the best place to be, . . . with the
> garrulous geese, the changing seasons, the heat of the sun, the passage of
> swallows, the nearness of rats, the sameness of sheep, the love of spiders, the
> smell of manure, and the glory of everything.

The characters are varied—good and bad, human and animal, talented   4
and untalented, warm and cold, ignorant and intelligent, vegetarian and
blood-drinking—varied, but not opposites; they are the real thing.

Wilbur is of a sweet nature—he is a spring pig—affectionate, responsive   5
to moods of the weather and the song of the crickets, has long eyelashes, is
hopeful, partially willing to try anything, brave, subject to faints from bash-
fulness, loyal to friends, enjoying a good appetite and a soft bed, and a little
likely to be overwhelmed by the sudden chance for freedom. He changes the
subject when the conversation gets painful, and a buttermilk bath brings out
his beauty. When he was a baby the sun shone pink through his ears, endear-
ing him to a little girl named Fern. She is his protector, and he is the hero.

Charlotte A. Cavitica ("But just call me Charlotte") is the heroine: a large   6
gray spider "about the size of a gumdrop." She has eight legs, and can wave
them in friendly greeting. On her friends' waking up in the morning, they see
what she's written for them—"Salutations!"—though it may have kept her
working all night. She tells Wilbur right away that she drinks blood, and
Wilbur on first acquaintance begs her not to say that.

"Why not? It's true, and I have to say what is true," says Charlotte. "I am   7
not entirely happy about my diet of flies and bugs, but it's the way I'm made.
A spider has to pick up a living somehow or other, and I happen to be a
trapper. I just naturally build a web and trap flies and other insects. My
mother was a trapper before me. Her mother was a trapper before her. All
our family have been trappers . . . I have to think things out, catch what I can,
take what comes. And it just so happens, my friend, that what comes is flies
and insects and bugs."

Charlotte cannot stand hysterics. ("Slowly, slowly," says Charlotte.   8
"Never hurry, and never worry.") She knows how many eggs are in her egg
sac because she got started counting one night and couldn't stop (594). She
saves Wilbur's life, because she can write—can and does. "It is not often that
someone comes along who is a true friend and a good writer. Charlotte was
both."

There is Templeton, the rat that lives under Wilbur's trough—well, he   9

457

constitutes somebody to talk to. "Talking with Templeton was not the most interesting occupation in the world, but it was better than nothing." "The rat had no morals, no conscience, no scruples, no consideration, no decency, no milk of rodent kindness, no compunction, no higher feeling, no friendliness, no anything." Templeton grudges his help to others, then brags about it, can fold his hands behind his head, and sometimes acts like a spoiled child.

10   There is the goose, who knows barnyard ways. "It's the old pail-trick, Wilbur . . . He's trying to lure you into captivity-ivity. He's appealing to your stomach." The goose always repeats everything. "It is my idio-idio-idiosyncrasy."

11   I do not intend to spoil the story for anybody by giving away the plot—how Charlotte sets in to save Wilbur's life. (Wilbur is grateful and says, "Don't fail to let me know if there's anything I can do to help, no matter how slight.") How Charlotte's own life was saved by a rotten goose egg. ("I'm delighted," gabbled the goose, "that the egg was never hatched.") How the Zuckermans take Wilbur to the Fair to enter him for the prize, and Charlotte hides in the crate ("We can't tell what may happen at the Fair Grounds. Somebody's got to go along who knows how to write") and so does Templeton, once he hears about the spoils of the midway. ("Is this appetizing yarn of yours true? I like high living, and what you say tempts me.")

12   What the book is about is friendship on earth, love and affection, adventure and miracle, life and death, trust and treachery, night and day and the seasons. As a piece of work it is just about perfect, and perfectly effortless and magical, as far as I can see, in the doing. Here is Charlotte, working through the night at her writing and talking to herself to cheer herself on: "Now for the R! Up we go! Attach! Descend! Pay out line! Whoa! Attach! Good! Up you go! Repeat! Attach! Descend! Pay out line! Whoa, girl! Steady now! Attach! Climb! Over to the right! Pay out line! Attach! Now right and down and swing that loop around and around! . . . Good girl!"

13   What the book "proves"—in the words the minister in the story hands down to his congregation on the Sunday after Charlotte writes "Some Pig" in her web—is "that human beings must always be on the watch for the coming of wonders." Dr. Dorian has this to say: "Oh, no, I don't understand it. But for that matter I don't understand how a spider learned to spin a web in the first place. When the words appeared, everyone said they were a miracle. But nobody pointed out that the web itself is a miracle." The author will only say: "Charlotte was in a class by herself."

14   "At-at-at, at the risk of repeating myself," as the goose says, I will say *Charlotte's Web* is an adorable book.

Restaurants

PHYLLIS C. RICHMAN

Richman on Restaurants:
Hunan Dynasty

Richman, a native Washingtonian, was born in 1939, earned a B.A. from Brandeis in 1961, and did graduate work at the University of Pennsylvania and at Purdue. In the early 1960s she worked as a city planner in Philadelphia, then as a free-lance writer until she became a restaurant critic and food writer for The Washington Post *in 1976. Her savory columns tempt the appetites of readers, as well as diners, and have been collected in annual editions of* Dining Out in Washington *and* Best Restaurants and Others *since 1975. She is also the co-author of* Barter: How to Get Almost Anything without Money *(1978).*

This restaurant review employs a characteristic format. The restaurant's vital statistics are stated at the beginning, separate from the actual text of the review: name, location, hours of lunch and dinner, whether or not reservations are needed, prices for lunch, dinner, and estimated cost of a complete dinner, per person. Then, after a lead paragraph that favorably compares the Hunan Dynasty with the stereotypical Chinese restaurant, Richman discusses the ambience ("attractive"—"gracefulness and lavish space"), the service ("polished"), the presentation of the food ("proudly arranged"), an overview of the menu, with typical prices ("a lot for your money"), appetizers ("few standouts"), main dishes—in general ("generally good but not often memorable"), with detailed analyses of specific outstanding dishes, good (crispy shrimp with walnuts, orange beef), and dismal (lemon chicken). Her conclusion is a summary, "a top-flight neighborhood restaurant—with good food, caring service and very fair prices." When we read reviews we look for predictable and logical formats in order to find information quickly; though restaurant reviews may discuss the service and prices last, instead of near the beginning, they nearly always comment on the meal in the order in which it is served. It would be disconcerting for readers—as well as diners—to have dessert first!

Hunan Dynasty

215 Pennsylvania Ave. SE. 546-6161.
Open daily 11 a.m. to 3 p.m. for lunch, 3 p.m. to 10 p.m. for dinner, until 11 p.m. on Friday and Saturday. AE, MC, V, DC. Reservations suggested for large parties.
Prices for lunch: appetizers $2 to $4.50, entrees $4.75 to $6.50; for dinner, appetizers $1 to $13.95 (combination platter), entrees $6.75 to $18. Complete dinner with wine or beer, tax and tip about $20 a person.

Chinese restaurants in America were once places one went just to eat. Now one goes to dine. There are now waiters in black tie, cloths on the tables and space between those tables, art on the walls and decoratively carved vegeta-

1

bles on the plate—elegance has become routine in Chinese restaurants. What's more, in Chinese restaurants the ingredients are fresh (have you ever found frozen broccoli in a Chinese kitchen?), and the cooking almost never sinks below decent. By its nature Chinese food is cooked to order, except perhaps on buffets. And it is usually moderately priced. In other words, if you're among unfamiliar restaurants and looking for good value, Chinese restaurants now are routinely better than ever.

2 The Hunan Dynasty is an example of what makes Chinese restaurants such reliable choices. A great restaurant? It is not. A good value? Definitely. A restaurant to fit nearly any diner's need? Probably.

3 First, it is attractive. There are no silk tassels, blaring red lacquer or Formica tables; instead there are white tablecloths and subtle glass etchings. It is a dining room—or dining rooms, for the vastness has been carved into smaller spaces—of gracefulness and lavish space.

4 Second, service is a strong priority. The waiters look and act polished, and serve with flourishes from the carving of a Peking duck to the portioning of dishes among the diners. I have found some glitches—a forgotten appetizer, a recommendation of two dishes that turned out nearly identical—but most often the service has been expert.

5 Third, the food is largely good if not quite wonderful, and it is proudly arranged on platters and garnished with vegetables carved into flowers, a far cry from the old stainless-steel-covered-dish Chinese restaurant style. This is the kind of Chinese restaurant sophisticated enough to have a separate wine list and to stock good Asian beers.

6 Then there is the menu, long and eclectic, with samplings from Szechuan, Peking, Canton and Hunan styles and a satisfying array of meats and seafoods even though it strays no farther than shrimp, scallops, lobster and two whole fish dishes among the seafoods. Prices are moderate, with most main dishes $6 to $10. You get a lot for your money.

7 Among the appetizers, there are few standouts, though only the spring rolls—with a filling that is nearly all cabbage under the thin, crisp wrappers—are a definite disappointment. Fried wontons are greaseless and crisp; meat dumplings tend to be bland and their dough a bit crumbly, but they are certainly acceptable; and the cold dishes and soups are just good enough, not memorable. The best of the appetizers is sweet-and-sour spareribs, small juicy pieces that are rich with the flavor of five-spice powder and sweetened soy marinade.

8 As for the main dishes, don't take the "hot and spicy" asterisks too seriously, for this kitchen is not out to offer you a test of fire. The peppers are there, but not in great number. And, like the appetizers, the main dishes are generally good but not often memorable. Fried dishes—and an inordinate number of them seem to be fried—are crunchy and not greasy. Vegetables are bright and crisp. Eggplant with hot garlic sauce is properly unctuous; Peking duck is as fat-free and crackly-skinned as you could hope (though the

pancakes were rubbery). And seafoods—shrimp, scallops, lobster—are tenderly cooked, though they are not the most full-flavored examples of those ingredients.

I have found only one dismal main dish in a fairly broad sampling: lemon chicken had no redeeming feature in its doughy, greasy, overcooked and underseasoned presentation. Otherwise, not much goes wrong. Crispy shrimp with walnuts might be preferable stir-fried rather than batter-fried, but the tomato-red sauce and crunchy walnuts made a good dish. Orange beef could use more seasoning but the coating was nicely crusty and the meat tender. Dragon and Phoenix might have been more successful if the chicken hadn't been deep-fried (and nearly identical to the General Tso's Chicken), and the lobster had little seafood taste, but both were pleasant in texture and flavor. And even better than those dishes listed as Chef's Specials were scallops and shrimp with garlic sauce, blanketed with julienned vegetables and gingered brown sauce; a fried whole fish strewn with chunky green peppers and onions in a sweet-sour sauce that avoided being cloying; and homey, gravy-drenched pan-fried noodles with plenty of mixed meats.

So with the opening of the Hunan Dynasty, Washington did not add a stellar Chinese restaurant to its repertoire, but that is not necessarily what the city needed anyway. Hunan Dynasty is a top-flight neighborhood restaurant—with good food, caring service and very fair prices—that is attractive enough to set a mood for celebration and easygoing enough for an uncomplicated dinner with the family after work.

GWYNETH CRAVENS

The M & J Sanitary Tortilla Factory

Cravens, born in Mitchell, South Dakota, was educated at the University of New Mexico and New York University. Currently the fiction editor of The New York Times, *Cravens previously served as a contributing editor of* Harper's. *Her extensive writing also includes essays in* The New Yorker *and* Transatlantic Review. *In 1976 she published (with co-author John Marr)* The Black Death, *a novel about a plague that overwhelms New York City. Her other novels include* Love and Work *(1982) and* Heart's Desire *(1986).*

Cravens's commentary on "The M & J Sanitary Tortilla Factory" is an essay of appreciation—for its proprietor, its ambience, its heritage, its classic food, all interrelated. Cravens approaches her subject in a leisurely manner, beginning with an overview that includes a glimpse of Bea Montoya; a snapshot of the neighborhood of the M & J, its delights heralded by the "delicious aroma of tortillas baking"; a closer look at Bea, seemingly relaxed but in friendly, constant motion as she waits on customers. Then Cravens visits the kitchen and tortilla factory, explaining how "two thousand dozen" tortillas are made in a day. The tortillas' inevitable fate leads to a brief history of New Mexican cuisine, interwoven with New Mexican history, and a digression on the official state vegetable, the chile pepper and its many variations. Finally, in paragraph 14, Cravens gets to the culinary climax, the menu itself, and spends the last quarter of the essay discussing the carne adobada burrito and other M & J specialties. Her personal reaction to both the food and the restaurant has overtones of a religious experience: "The delicious flavors of cumin and chile and pork and tortilla exploded on my palate. Tears came to my eyes. I felt, as I always do at this moment in the M & J, when I return after a long absence and take the first bite of a burrito, truly blessed."

1   For over three centuries, the people of the Rio Grande Valley have been grinding dried corn, mixing it with water to make dough, patting the dough into tortillas, and baking them. Today, the process continues, in a stream-lined form, a few miles from the Rio Grande—in Albuquerque, at the M & J Sanitary Tortilla Factory, home of the Five-Hongo Burrito and winner of the "PM Magazine" TV show Ultra Supremo Burrito Rating for the State of New Mexico. The chatelaine of this enterprise, which includes a small but flourishing restaurant, is Beatrice Montoya, a bustling, affectionate, youthful-looking woman everyone calls Bea. . . .

2   Whenever I'm in Albuquerque, my hometown, I lose no time in getting to the M & J Sanitary Tortilla Factory to see Bea and her crackerjack waitress, Dorothy Bustamante, to assuage my fairly constant yearning for the heart-warming Five-Hongo Burrito . . . . On a recent afternoon typical of the Duke City—windy, dusty, and blindingly sunny—I drove through the downtown area, which has been partly levelled and rebuilt over the last decade to look like any modern American city anywhere, with multi-story office buildings and wide brick malls with saplings in planters, to the M & J. Its immediate surroundings . . . have remained essentially unchanged. There is a bus depot, a church, a mortuary, a bar, a newspaper office, a few small warehouses, and some old frame houses. The tortilla factory is a white, one-story, flat-roofed building with arched windows in the front, where the restaurant is, facing a parking lot, the railroad yards, and the Sandia Mountains (*"sandía"* means "watermelon"), which rise like blue icebergs to the east of town. The minute I got out of the car, I could smell the hot, dry, delicious aroma of tortillas baking and sopaipillas and tostadas frying. Sopaipillas are puffy, hollow, pillow-shaped pastries eaten with honey; tostadas are cut-up wedges of corn tortilla that have been deep-fried and are used to scoop up hot sauce. As I went in, I noticed that a colored poster of San Martín Caballero in the window next to the door was turned around to face the street; usually, it faces inward. San Martín is on horseback holding a cloak aloft as a nearly naked beggar crouches nearby, lifting his arms in supplication. As always, next to the poster was a full glass of water.

3   Beatrice Montoya has long auburn hair, brown sloe eyes, perky eye-brows, and a ready smile. Today, she was dressed in high heels, neatly pressed jeans, a blouse with a leopard-skin print, and the necklace she always wears. It is a pendant of the Blessed Hand, or La Mano Poderosa, an open hand of gold with a cross on the palm—a gift from a customer. She called out a greeting from the counter where the cash register sits, under a big wooden

wall plaque of a greenback, hurried to a table where a retired couple had just sat down, made inquiries about their health and their children and grandchildren, took an order for burritos, filled some red plastic tumblers at another table from a big pitcher of ice water, sponged off a green vinyl tablecloth at another table, and then came up to me. "Hi, hon!" she said. "How are you doing?" She has a lilting, pleasant voice and an expressive face. We talked for a minute, and she told me that it had been a slow day—the restaurant was only two-thirds full. But then it was a Saturday, and she gets most of her customers on weekdays, from nearby office and government buildings. "I turned San Martín Caballero around anyway—to pull in those customers," she said.

"I wondered about that," I said.   4

"When business is good, I turn him back around. You know the story,   5
sugar? San Martín Caballero is the patron saint of restaurants. That nude beggar says to him, 'I'll do anything for you if you will give me a piece of your cloak,' and San Martín Caballero—*caballero* means 'horseman' or 'gentleman'—says, 'I will if you promise to give my horse some water every day.' You look in a restaurant that's doing well and you might see that the people have remembered to leave out a glass of water for San Martín Caballero's horse."

Bea told me she was shorthanded, because Dorothy Bustamante, the   6
M & J's waitress for the past decade (she is so efficient that she often writes up the orders of regular customers when she sees them coming down the street), had gone to Las Vegas for the weekend. Bea's daughter, Eileen, had to come in with her infant son, to whom Bea refers as her grandbaby, to help out.

Later, when Bea had some time, she took me into the back, into a room   7
about a third the size of a high-school gym, where the tortilla-making machinery and the kitchen are situated. The tortillas are manufactured under the supervision of Jake Montoya, Bea's husband and co-proprietor. The process begins the way it has for centuries, with dried corn kernels soaking in a solution of lime and water. At the M & J, three hundred pounds of white corn at a time are brought to a boil in a chest-high metal bin, drained and thoroughly rinsed, and then shovelled into a hopper and ground into a fine, moist paste called *masa*. (Traditionally, the corn has been ground on a *metate*, a slab of smooth stone, with a *mano*, a sort of stone rolling pin. Although some Indians still do it this way as a daily practice or on ceremonial occasions—corn, especially white and blue cornmeal, is sacred to the Pueblo Indians—people from nearby pueblos often come to the M & J to buy their *masa*.) The *masa* goes into a spreader, which rolls the dough to a thickness of about one-sixteenth of an inch and stamps it into circles about six inches across. These drop onto a conveyor belt that passes over gas flames, flips the tortillas, bakes them once again, and then sends them out onto a mesh

conveyor belt to cool. Someone at the end—Lupe Guerrero, his brother Rosolio Guerrero, or Lino Ramirez, longtime employees who double as cooks during restaurant hours—stacks them and puts them into packages.

8   I asked Bea how the M & J Sanitary Tortilla Factory got its name.

9   "M and J are the initials of some previous owners, but the original Sanitary Tortilla Factory goes back forty-five or fifty years," she said. "People had always made tortillas by hand, and so when a machine was invented to make them the owners called the new kind sanitary tortillas. The first machine could make only four tortillas a minute. Now we can make two thousand dozen a day, and that's by nine in the morning—we start early, because the restaurant is open from nine-thirty to three. We make more tortillas around Christmas, when the demand is bigger. We also make flour tortillas fresh every day, but we do those by hand." The flour tortillas are made from wheat flour, baking powder, and lard, and are rolled out with a rolling pin and baked on a greaseless griddle. Handmade flour tortillas are moister and thicker than machine-made flour tortillas, and better-tasting.

10   Bea pointed to a sign near the kitchen. It said: "Un Buen Empleado Cuida Su Trabajo." She explained, "It means that a good employee takes care of his job."

11   Most of the tortillas are distributed daily to restaurants and schools around the city or sold over the counter at the M & J. But quite a few go directly into the M & J kitchen, where they are turned into tostadas to go in baskets on the tables in the restaurant or used to make burritos, enchiladas, and tacos prepared mostly according to recipes that have been handed down in Jake's and Bea's families for many generations.

12   Bea comes from a family of ranchers in the high mountains of northern New Mexico, near Raton. Since her mother's death, she has become the matriarch of her extended family, whose members often come to her for solace or advice. Jake, a quiet man with a black mustache who stays in the background, is from Taos, where his family is active in politics. They met in Albuquerque in 1960, when they were working at a Mexican restaurant. She was a waitress and he was a cook. As Bea tells it, he refused to pay attention to her. "I was always asking if I could bring him anything—a glass of water or something—and he always said no. He would just ignore me. One day, it was real hot, and I brought him a big glass of iced tea. I don't know what all I put in it—hot sauce, chile peppers, you name it. You should have seen him come through that kitchen door!" Ten years ago, when they acquired the M & J, the restaurant had only a few tables. Jake and Bea enlarged it, adding tables, chairs, and booths they picked up here and there until it was big enough to seat a hundred and forty people—it often does—and began cooking, from their own recipes and those of their aunts and grandmothers, fresh and from scratch, the traditional food of New Mexico.

13   Native New Mexicans tend to be touchy about their cuisine. They don't like it to be confused with Mexican food, any more than they care to be

considered Mexicans. In the fifteen-forties, Spanish conquistadores crossed the desert of northern New Spain and discovered a land of vast arid plains, scrub-dotted mesas, and rugged mountain ranges. In the seventeenth and eighteenth centuries, colonists and their priests followed, making their way by oxcart up the Rio Grande Valley from New Spain to what they now called Nuevo Mexico. They built adobe houses and missions and, over the years, often intermarried with Pueblo Indians. To this day, many New Mexicans refer to themselves as "Spanish." The traditional cuisine that evolved relied strictly on what was locally available; until the coming of the railroad, in the late nineteenth century, the region was quite isolated. The recipes usually combine chiles, and sauces made from chiles, with meat, beans, and cheese in various ways. The flour or corn tortilla is a foundation for many of the dishes, and also serves sometimes as a spoon, and even as a plate. The seasonings are usually coriander, cumin, oregano, and garlic. The intensity of flavor of these herbs, grown at high altitude in a dry climate flooded with sun, is extraordinary. But the power and the glory of the cuisine flow from the chile pepper. It is hard to exaggerate the tenderness and fervor with which the majority of New Mexicans regard the chile and its products. The New Mexico Legislature has declared the chile, along with the pinto bean, the official state vegetable. The chile pepper and its sauces are not to be confused with chili—widely held to be a dubious conglomeration emanating from the large, suspiciously regarded state due east. The chile is sung about in love songs like "La Llorona" ("The Weeping Woman"): *"Soy como el chile verde, Llorona, picante pero sabroso"* ("I am like the green chile, Llorona, hot but tasty"). Its cultivation and its nutritional value (it has plenty of Vitamin C, and long before anyone had heard of vitamins the chile was considered a cure-all) are studied and enhanced at New Mexico State University, Las Cruces. Because of the depth of feeling people have about the chile, it gives rise to many violent arguments and closely held beliefs. For years, there has been a controversy about where the best chiles come from. Certainly, the flavor of New Mexican chiles is distinct and indescribable—it seems to bloom forward on the palate, and these peppers do not burn the way, for instance, jalapeño peppers, popular in the cuisine of Mexico, do—and no one would consider trying chiles from out of state. Some people are partial to the chiles from the north, from around Chimayó—a town famed for El Santuario de Chimayó, a Catholic church built over a hole in the ground from which pilgrims take sacred, healing dirt. Although Bea is from the north, she swears by the chiles grown in the south, around Hatch and Las Cruces. She is very picky about the chiles she buys for the restaurant. The dried red chiles, from which red chile sauce is made (after the seeds and veins are removed, the chiles are soaked in warm water, pureed, and simmered with spices and herbs), must be a bright red, and she searches for a particular taste and aroma. When she is selecting green chiles, she just takes a bite of one. If it's good and stinging, then she knows it's a good chile.

14   The most popular item on the menu at the M & J is the carne adobada burrito (spelled "adovada" in the menu in deference to the regional Spanish dialect, which contains many archaic usages and in which "b" is pronounced almost as "v"). It is this masterpiece that has won the M & J the "PM Magazine" Ultra Supremo Burrito Rating for the State of New Mexico. It is this masterpiece that has caused the New Mexico *Independent,* an occasionally vehement weekly published and edited for the past fourteen years by Mark Acuff and written chiefly by him in the guise of various personae (Duncan H. Gonzales writes the food column, Parnelli Gonzales the automobile column, Jean-Claude Gonzales the skiing column, and Paul Gonzales the religion column), to award the M & J the highest possible gastronomic award, five hongos ("hongo" means "mushroom," and can refer to hallucinogenic mushrooms), every year since 1978. Acuff takes his chiles seriously. In a recent column, he wrote that "the International Society of Connoisseurs of Green and Red Chile, Albuquerque Pod, has scheduled a meeting . . . for, among other things, the purpose of proposing to the legislature that a penalty be added to the State Vegetable Law making it punishable to spell chile in Texan (chili). . . . *Chile* is spelt that way in the law, and that's the way it is. The law doesn't say what *chili* is, but most of us know the word refers to that horrible red gook served in places like Texas and New York. You know—the kind you are expected to put crumbled crackers and catsup in, urrgh. . . . I've already discussed this dire problem with the governor, and although he didn't give a formal commitment, he indicated he generally agrees with the idea. The penalty, of course, will be deportation to Texas." Acuff recently moved the office of the *Independent* into a building half a block from the M & J. Lest he be accused of favoritism, he invited his readers this year to do the judging (there are many categories in which hongos are awarded or withheld—worst hamburger, ugliest building, best place to watch the sunset in New Mexico, best eatery for overhearing strange conversations, best lingerie shop), and the M & J came out the overwhelming winner in the restaurant category. There are probably many other superb dishes on the menu at the M & J: chiles rellenos (green chiles filled with longhorn cheese, dipped in batter, and deep-fried), blue-corn enchiladas (made from tortillas of ground blue corn, which are a beautiful slate blue and have a delicate texture and flavor), huevos rancheros (eggs in red or green chile sauce, with a side of refried beans, rice, and a couple of tortillas or sopaipillas), posole (hominy cooked with red chile sauce and pork), menudo (there is a sign in the window advertising menudo, and Bea says a lot of people come in for it; she calls it "the champion of breakfasts" but is a little reluctant to describe it—menudo is the lining of a cow's stomach cooked with chile).

15   I'm sure these are all good things to eat, but I can never get past the carne adobada burrito. It is a freshly made flour tortilla wrapped around a generous helping of carne adobada—diced roast pork that has been simmered in a hot red chile sauce—and drowned in red or green chile sauce flavored with whole cumin seeds, garlic, and oregano.

I took a seat in a corner booth, under a bright yellow-red-orange-and-blue painting of Our Lady of Guadalupe, who, according to Bea, watches over the M & J. Eileen, the Montoyas' daughter, a dreamy-eyed young woman with a mop of fine black curls, came over and took my order. She said that her baby, slumbering on an infant seat on a table nearby, didn't want to sleep at night. After she left, to wait on an Indian in a big black Stetson who had taken a seat at a table near white plaster statues of the Virgin and St. Francis of Assisi, I scooped up some table sauce—a mixture of chopped tomatoes, chiles, and a pepper called yellow-hot, which, even in minute amounts, has the force to take the top of your head off if you're not careful—with a tostada and basked in happy anticipation. The restaurant is a single room lit by fluorescent tubes overhead and painted white. The smells and noises from the kitchen and the factory in the back and the conversations of the customers and Bea's and Eileen's banter combined to give an impression of cozy well-being. . . .

Regulars at the M & J have told me over the years that Bea often quietly gives food to the poor and takes food to invalids in the neighborhood. She routinely prays and lights candles for customers who have to go into the hospital.

Eileen brought me a basket of hot sopaipillas and a plate with a carne adobada burrito in green chile sauce. I immediately took a bite of the burrito and then a bite of sopaipilla with honey in order to bank the fire of the chile sauce. My heart pounded. The light in the room seemed to grow brighter. The delicious flavors of cumin and chile and pork and tortilla exploded on my palate. Tears came to my eyes. I felt, as I always do at this moment in the M & J, when I return after a long absence and take the first bite of a burrito, truly blessed. I drank a big glass of ice water.

After lunch, I paid my check and collected my supplies—tortillas, blue-corn tortillas, flour tortillas, and several pints of red chile sauce, green chile sauce, and carne adobada. It was late, and Bea and Eileen were wiping off the tables and pushing the chairs up against them. Bea presented me with a bag of cherry-filled empanaditas she had made. They're little fruit-filled turnovers that ordinarily appear in New Mexican households around holiday times. I added the empanaditas to the staples that I hoped would keep body and soul together until my next visit. "Things are going well for you," I said.

"I thank God for the good *and* the bad," Bea told me. "This old lady that used to come in before she died—we called her Gramita—had a little hand grinder, and she would grind her corn for her tortillas that way. Well, Gramita used to say that God must be so tired because people are always asking him for favors, always putting requests in the basket of the Infant Jesus. She said, 'That basket doesn't go up to God with very many thank-you notes.' So I always thank God for everything, good and bad. But He's been mostly good to me. He's been *incredible* to me!"

Sports

BOB CONSIDINE

Louis Knocks Out Schmeling

Considine (1906–1975) had a many-faceted career in many media. After graduating from George Washington University in his hometown of Washington, D.C., he worked during the 1930s writing about sports, drama, and other features for the Washington Post *and* Washington Herald. *During World War II he was a war correspondent for the International News Service. Postwar, as a trial reporter he was one of three witnesses to the Rosenbergs' execution; he was also a radio broadcaster, television commentator, contributor to many national magazines, and author of twenty-five books, including* The Babe Ruth Story *(1948), winner of the first Catholic Writers Guild Golden Book Award. Considine knew everyone, Gehrig and Dempsey, popes and presidents, but retained a becoming modesty, "When the customers write in to accuse me of being a bum, let me consider the possibility that I am. . . ."*

Considine's account of Joe Louis's knockout of Max Schmeling in the 1938 World Heavyweight Championship is first-class sportswriting. He begins as a down-to-earth ("Listen to this, buddy") but knowledgeable eyewitness, quickly detailing the highlights of the event in short, choppy, punchy sentences and paragraphs: the four steps of the knockout, the brilliant onslaught of Lewis, the staggering ineptitude of Schmeling, the audience reaction, the boxers' behavior after the fight. Sports, like the arts, often have political implications that extend far beyond the performing arena. Indeed, Considine emphasizes through his consistent good-guy/bad-guy imagery that this was not just another fight, but a symbolic gladiatorial contest between a Black American and Hitler's representative of the "Aryan race." Considine's appropriately partisan writing lends a moral dimension to Louis's victory.

1   Listen to this, buddy, for it comes from a guy whose palms are still wet, whose throat is still dry, and whose jaw is still agape from the utter shock of watching Joe Louis knock out Max Schmeling.

2   It was a shocking thing, that knockout—short, sharp, merciless, complete. Louis was like this:

3   He was a big lean copper spring, tightened and retightened through weeks of training until he was one pregnant package of coiled venom.

4   Schmeling hit that spring. He hit it with a whistling right-hand punch in the first minute of the fight—and the spring, tormented with tension, suddenly burst with one brazen spang of activity. Hard brown arms, propelling two unerring fists, blurred beneath the hot white candelabra of the ring lights. And Schmeling was in the path of them, a man caught and mangled in the whirring claws of a mad and feverish machine.

5   The mob, biggest and most prosperous ever to see a fight in a ball yard, knew that there was the end before the thing had really started. It knew, so it stood up and howled one long shriek. People who had paid as much as $100

for their chairs didn't use them—except perhaps to stand on, the better to let the sight burn forever in their memories.

There were four steps to Schmeling's knockout. A f.w seconds after he landed his only punch of the fight, Louis caught him with a lethal little left hook that drove him into the ropes so that his right arm was hooked over the top strand, like a drunk hanging to a fence. Louis swarmed over him and hit with everything he had—until Referee Donovan pushed him away and counted one. 6

Schmeling staggered away from the ropes, dazed and sick. He looked drunkenly toward his corner, and before he had turned his head back Louis was on him again, first with a left and then that awe-provoking right that made a crunching sound when it hit the German's jaw. Max fell down, hurt and giddy, for a count of three. 7

He clawed his way up as if the night air were as thick as black water, and Louis—his nostrils like the mouth of a double-barreled shotgun—took a quiet lead and let him have both barrels. 8

Max fell almost lightly, bereft of his senses, his fingers touching the canvas like a comical stew-bum doing his morning exercises, knees bent and the tongue lolling in his head. 9

He got up long enough to be knocked down again, this time with his dark unshaven face pushed in the sharp gravel of the resin. 10

Louis jumped away lightly, a bright and pleased look in his eyes, and as he did the white towel of surrender which Louis' handlers had refused to use two years ago tonight came sailing into the ring in a soggy mess. It was thrown by Max Machon, oblivious to the fact that fights cannot end this way in New York. 11

The referee snatched it off the floor and flung it backwards. It hit the ropes and hung there, limp as Schmeling. Donovan counted up to five over Max, sensed the futility of it all, and stopped the fight. 12

The big crowd began to rustle restlessly toward the exits, many only now accepting Louis as champion of the world. There were no eyes for Schmeling, sprawled on his stool in his corner. 13

He got up eventually, his dirty gray-and-black robe over his shoulders, and wormed through the happy little crowd that hovered around Louis. And he put his arm around the Negro and smiled. They both smiled and could afford to—for Louis had made around $200,000 a minute and Schmeling $100,000 a minute. 14

But once he crawled down in the belly of the big stadium, Schmeling realized the implications of his defeat. He, who won the title on a partly phony foul, and beat Louis two years ago with the aid of a crushing punch after the bell had sounded, now said Louis had fouled him. That would read better in Germany, whence earlier in the day had come a cable from Hitler, calling on him to win. 15

It was a low, sneaking trick, but a rather typical last word from Schmeling. 16

JOHN UPDIKE

Hub Fans Bid Kid Adieu

Updike excels at many forms of writing: short stories, novels, plays, screenplays, poetry, children's fiction, and essays. Although "Hub Fans Bid Kid Adieu" is his only piece of sportswriting, the essay's graceful, classic, writing befits Updike's graceful, classic subject. Updike, born in Shillington, Pennsylvania, in 1932, was encouraged to be a writer by his mother, an unpublished novelist. He attended Harvard on a full scholarship, edited the Lampoon, graduated summa cum laude in 1954, and, after a fellowship year at Oxford, began writing for The New Yorker *at 23. Four years later, after publishing his first novel,* The Poorhouse Fair, *he moved to Ipswich, Massachusetts, where he still lives. He has now published over twenty books, including* Rabbit, Run *(1960) and related novels that present the continuing saga of Harry "Rabbit" Angstrom, a Pennsylvania suburbanite. His most recent books are a novel,* The Witches of Eastwick *(1984),* Facing Nature *(1985), and a collection of essays,* Hugging the Shore *(1983), which won the National Book Critics Circle Award for criticism.*

In this complex and literary eyewitness account of Ted Williams's last game, Updike mythologizes the baseball star, comparing him overtly to the Greek heroes Jason, Achilles, and Nestor and implicitly to Odysseus, a loner. Updike reinforces this mythology with facts, contrasting the predictable analyses of baseball strategy ("the Williams shift") and comparisons of batting averages, seasonal and lifetime records, with anecdotes and graphic description. Updike has said that "Reality is—chemically, atomically, biologically—a fabric of microscopic accuracies." This fabric of accuracy makes "Hub Fans" convincing when combined with Updike's belief that "there will always lurk, around a corner in a pocket of our knowledge of the odds, an indefensible hope." For hope animates the career of the slugger from Boston as it does the lives of Updike's fictional characters. In certain moments such hope can be realized; when this happens, the actuality and the myth sail together out of the park.

1 Fenway Park, in Boston, is a lyric little bandbox of a ballpark. Everything is painted green and seems in curiously sharp focus, like the inside of an old-fashioned peeping-type Easter egg. It was built in 1912 and rebuilt in 1934, and offers, as do most Boston artifacts, a compromise between Man's Euclidean determinations and Nature's beguiling irregularities. Its right field is one of the deepest in the American League, while its left field is the shortest; the high left-field wall, three hundred and fifteen feet from home plate along the foul line, virtually thrusts its surface at right-handed hitters. On the afternoon of Wednesday, September 28th, 1960, as I took a seat behind third base, a uniformed groundkeeper was treading the top of this wall, picking batting-practice home runs out of the screen, like a mushroom gatherer seen in Wordsworthian perspective on the verge of a cliff. The day was overcast, chill, and uninspirational. The Boston team was the worst in twenty-seven seasons. A jangling medley of incompetent youth and aging competence, the Red Sox were finishing in seventh place only because the Kansas City Athletics had locked them out of the cellar. They were scheduled to play the Baltimore Orioles, a much nimbler blend of May and December, who had

been dumped from pennant contention a week before by the insatiable Yankees. I, and 10,453 others, had shown up primarily because this was the Red Sox's last home game of the season, and therefore the last time in all eternity that their regular left fielder, known to the headlines as TED, KID, SPLINTER, THUMPER, TW, and, most cloyingly, MISTER WONDERFUL, would play in Boston. "WHAT WILL WE DO WITHOUT TED? HUB FANS ASK" ran the headline on a newspaper being read by a bulb-nosed cigar smoker a few rows away. Williams' retirement had been announced, doubted (he had been threatening retirement for years), confirmed by Tom Yawkey, the Red Sox owner, and at last widely accepted as the sad but probable truth. He was forty-two and had redeemed his abysmal season of 1959 with a—considering his advanced age—fine one. He had been giving away his gloves and bats and had grudgingly consented to a sentimental ceremony today. This was not necessarily his last game; the Red Sox were scheduled to travel to New York and wind up the season with three games there.

I arrived early. The Orioles were hitting fungos on the field. The day before, they had spitefully smothered the Red Sox, 17–4, and neither their faces nor their drab gray visiting-team uniforms seemed very gracious. I wondered who had invited them to the party. Between our heads and the lowering clouds a frenzied organ was thundering through, with an appositeness perhaps accidental, "You *maaaade* me love you, I didn't wanna do it, I didn't wanna do it. . . ."

The affair between Boston and Ted Williams was no mere summer romance; it was a marriage composed of spats, mutual disappointments, and, toward the end, a mellowing hoard of shared memories. It fell into three stages, which may be termed Youth, Maturity, and Age; or Thesis, Antithesis, and Synthesis; or Jason, Achilles, and Nestor.

First, there was the by now legendary epoch[1] when the young bride-

---

[1] This piece was written with no research materials save an outdated record book and the Boston newspapers of the day; and Williams' early career preceded the dawning of my *Schlagballewusstsein* (Baseball-consciousness). Also for reasons of perspective was my account of his beginnings skimped. Williams first attracted the notice of a major-league scout—Bill Essick of the Yankees—when he was a fifteen-year-old pitcher with the San Diego American Legion Post team. As a pitcher-outfielder for San Diego's Herbert Hoover High School, Williams recorded averages of .586 and .403. Essick balked at signing Williams for the $1,000 his mother asked; he was signed instead, for $150 a month, by the local Pacific Coast League franchise, the newly created San Diego Padres. In his two seasons with this team, Williams hit merely .271 and .291, but his style and slugging (23 home runs the second year) caught the eye of, among others, Casey Stengel, then with the Boston Braves, and Eddie Collins, the Red Sox general manager. Collins bought him from the Padres for $25,000 in cash and $25,000 in players. Williams was then nineteen. Collins' fond confidence in the boy's potential matched Williams' own. Williams reported to the Red Sox training camp in Sarasota in 1938 and, after showing more volubility than skill, was shipped down to the Minneapolis Millers, the top Sox farm team. It should be said, perhaps, that the parent club was equipped with an excellent, if mature, outfield, mostly purchased from Connie Mack's dismantled A's. Upon leaving Sarasota, Williams is supposed to have told the regular outfield of Joe Vosmik, Doc Cramer, and Ben Chapman that he would be

groom came out of the West and announced "All I want out of life is that when I walk down the street folks will say 'There goes the greatest hitter who ever lived.' " The dowagers of local journalism attempted to give elementary deportment lessons to this child who spake as a god, and to their horror were themselves rebuked. Thus began the long exchange of backbiting, bat-flipping, booing, and spitting that has distinguished Williams' public relations.[2] The spitting incidents of 1957 and 1958 and the similar dockside courtesies that Williams has now and then extended to the grandstand should be judged against this background: the left-field stands at Fenway for twenty years have held a large number of customers who have bought their way in primarily for the privilege of showering abuse on Williams. Greatness necessarily attracts debunkers, but in Williams' case the hostility has been systematic and unappeasable. His basic offense against the fans has been to wish that they weren't there. Seeking a perfectionist's vacuum, he has quixotically desired to sever the game from the ground of paid spectatorship and publicity that supports it. Hence his refusal to tip his cap[3] to the crowd or turn the

---

back and would make more money than the three of them put together. At Minneapolis he hit .366, batted in 142 runs, scored 130, and hit 43 home runs. He also loafed in the field, jabbered at the fans, and smashed a water cooler with his fist. In 1939 he came north with the Red Sox. On the way, in Atlanta, he dropped a foul fly, accidentally kicked it away in trying to pick it up, picked it up, and threw it out of the park. It would be nice if, his first time up in Fenway Park, he had hit a home run. Actually, in his first Massachusetts appearance, the first inning of an exhibition game against Holy Cross at Worcester, he *did* hit a home run, a grand slam. The Red Sox season opened in Yankee Stadium. Facing Red Ruffing, Williams struck out and, the next time up, doubled for his first major-league hit. In the Fenway Park opener, against Philadelphia, he had a single in five trips. His first home run came on April 23, in that same series with the A's. Williams was then twenty, and played *right* field. In his rookie season he hit .327; in 1940, .344.

[2] See *Ted Williams*, by Ed Linn (Sport Magazine Library), Chapter 6, "Williams vs. the Press." It is Linn's suggestion that Williams walked into a circulation war among the seven Boston newspapers, who in their competitive zeal headlined incidents that the New York papers, say, would have minimized, just as they minimized the less genial side of the moody and aloof DiMaggio and smoothed Babe Ruth into a folk hero. It is also Linn's thought, and an interesting one, that Williams thrived on even adverse publicity, and needed a hostile press to elicit, contrariwise, his defiant best. The statistics (especially of the 1958 season, when he snapped a slump by spitting in all directions, and inadvertently conked an elderly female fan with a tossed bat) seem to corroborate this. Certainly Williams could have had a truce for the asking, and his industrious perpetuation of the war, down to his last day in uniform, implies its usefulness to him. The actual and intimate anatomy of the matter resides in locker rooms and hotel corridors fading from memory. When my admiring account was printed, I received a letter from a sports reporter who hated Williams with a bitter and explicit immediacy. And even Linn's hagiology permits some glimpses of Williams' locker-room manners that are not pleasant.

[3] But he did tip his cap, high off his head, in at least his first season, as cartoons from that period verify. He also was extravagantly cordial to taxi-drivers and stray children. See Linn, Chapter 4, "The Kid Comes to Boston": "There has never been a ballplayer—anywhere, anytime—more popular than Ted Williams in his first season in Boston." To this epoch belong Williams' prankish use of the Fenway scoreboard lights for rifle practice, his celebrated expressed preference for the life of a fireman, and his determined designation of himself as "The Kid."

other cheek to newsmen. It has been a costly theory—it has probably cost him, among other evidences of good will, two Most Valuable Player awards, which are voted by reporters[4]—but he has held to it. While his critics, oral and literary, remained beyond the reach of his discipline, the opposing pitchers were accessible, and he spanked them to the tune of .406 in 1941.[5] He slumped to .356 in 1942 and went off to war.

In 1946, Williams returned from three years as a Marine pilot to the second of his baseball avatars, that of Achilles, the hero of incomparable prowess and beauty who nevertheless was to be found sulking in his tent while the Trojans (mostly Yankees) fought through to the ships. Yawkey, a timber and mining maharajah, had surrounded his central jewel with many gems of slightly lesser water, such as Bobby Doerr, Dom DiMaggio, Rudy York, Birdie Tebbetts, and Johnny Pesky. Throughout the late forties, the Red Sox were the best paper team in baseball, yet they had little three-dimensional to show for it, and if this was a tragedy, Williams was Hamlet. A succinct review of the indictment—and a fair sample of appreciative sports-page prose—appeared the very day of Williams' valedictory, in a column by Huck Finnegan in the Boston *American* (no sentimentalist, Huck):

> Williams' career, in contrast [to Babe Ruth's], has been a series of failures except for his averages. He flopped in the only World Series he ever played in (1946) when he batted only .200. He flopped in the playoff game with Cleveland in 1948. He flopped in the final game of the 1949 season with the pennant hinging on the outcome (Yanks 5, Sox 3). He flopped in 1950 when he returned to the lineup after a two-month absence and ruined the morale of a club that seemed pennant-bound under Steve O'Neill. It has always been Williams' records first, the team second, and the Sox non-winning record is proof enough of that.

There are answers to all this, of course. The fatal weakness of the great Sox slugging teams was not-quite-good-enough pitching rather than Williams' failure to hit a home run every time he came to bat. Again, Williams'

5

6

[4] In 1947 Joe DiMaggio and in 1957 Mickey Mantle, with seasons inferior to Williams', won the MVP award because sportswriters, who vote on ballots with ten places, had vengefully placed Williams ninth, tenth, or nowhere at all. The 1941 award to Joe DiMaggio, even though this was Williams'. 406 year, is more understandable, since this was also the *annus miraculorum* when DiMaggio hit safely in 56 consecutive games.

[5] The sweet saga of this beautiful decimal must be sung once more. Williams, after hitting above .400 all season, had cooled to .39955 with one doubleheader left to play, in Philadelphia. Joe Cronin, then managing the Red Sox, offered to bench him to safeguard his average, which was exactly .400 when rounded to the third decimal place. Williams said (I forget where I read this) that he did not want to become the .400 hitter with just his toenails over the line. He played the first game and singled, homered, singled, and singled. With less to gain than to lose, he elected to play the second game and got two more hits, including a double that dented a loudspeaker horn on the top of the right-field wall, giving him six-for-eight on the day and a season's average that, in the forty years between Rogers Hornsby's .403 (1925) and the present, stands as unique.

depressing effect on his teammates has never been proved. Despite ample coaching to the contrary, most insisted that they *liked* him. He has been generous with advice to any player who asked for it. In an increasingly combative baseball atmosphere, he continued to duck beanballs docilely. With umpires he was gracious to a fault. This courtesy itself annoyed his critics, whom there was no pleasing. And against the ten crucial games (the seven World Series games with the St. Louis Cardinals, the 1948 playoff with the Cleveland Indians, and the two-game series with the Yankees at the end of the 1949 season, when one victory would have given the Red Sox the pennant) that make up the Achilles' heel of Williams' record, a mass of statistics can be set showing that day in and day out he was no slouch in the clutch.[6] The correspondence columns of the Boston papers now and then suffer a sharp flurry of arithmetic on this score; indeed, for Williams to have distributed all his hits so they did nobody else any good would constitute a feat of placement unparalleled in the annals of selfishness.

7   Whatever residue of truth remains of the Finnegan charge those of us who love Williams must transmute as best we can, in our own personal crucibles. My personal memories of Williams began when I was a boy in Pennsylvania, with two last-place teams in Philadelphia to keep me company. For me, "W'ms, lf" was a figment of the box scores who always seemed to be going 3-for-5. He radiated, from afar, the hard blue glow of high purpose. I remember listening over the radio to the All-Star Game of 1946, in which Williams hit two singles and two home runs, the second one off a Rip Sewell "blooper" pitch; it was like hitting a balloon out of the park. I remember watching one of his home runs from the bleachers of Shibe Park; it went over the first baseman's head and rose methodically along a straight line and was still rising when it cleared the fence. The trajectory seemed qualitatively different from anything anyone else might hit. For me, Williams is the classic ballplayer of the game on a hot August weekday, before a small crowd, when the only thing at stake is the tissue-thin difference between a thing done well and a thing done ill. Baseball is a game of the long season, of relentless and gradual averaging-out. Irrelevance—since the reference point of most individual contests is remote and statistical—always threatens its interest, which can be maintained not by the occasional heroics that sportswriters feed upon but by players who always *care;* who care, that is to say, about themselves and their art. Insofar as the clutch hitter is not a sportswriter's myth, he is a vulgarity, like a writer who writes only for money. It may be that, compared to such managers' dreams as the manifestly classy Joe DiMaggio and the

---

[6] For example: In 1948, the Sox came from behind to tie the Indians by winning three straight; in those games Williams went two for two, two for two; and two for four. In 1949, the Sox overtook the Yankees by winning nine in a row; in that streak, Williams won four games with home runs.

always helpful Stan Musial, Williams was an icy star. But of all team sports, baseball, with its graceful intermittences of action, its immense and tranquil field sparsely settled with poised men in white, its dispassionate mathematics, seems to me best suited to accommodate, and be ornamented by, a loner. It is an essentially lonely game. No other player visible to my generation concentrated within himself so much of the sport's poignance, so assiduously refined his natural skills, so constantly brought to the plate that intensity of competence that crowds the throat with joy.

By the time I went to college, near Boston, the lesser stars Yawkey had assembled around Williams had faded, and his rigorous pride of craftsmanship had become itself a kind of heroism. This brittle and temperamental player developed an unexpected quality of persistence. He was always coming back—back from Korea, back from a broken collarbone, a shattered elbow, a bruised heel, back from drastic bouts of flu and ptomaine poisoning. Hardly a season went by without some enfeebling mishap, yet he always came back, and always looked like himself. The delicate mechanism of timing and power seemed sealed, shockproof, in some case deep within his frame.[7] In addition to injuries, there was a heavily publicized divorce, and the usual storms with the press, and the Williams Shift—the maneuver, custom-built by Lou Boudreau of the Cleveland Indians, whereby three infielders were concentrated on the right side of the infield.[8] Williams could easily have learned to punch singles through the vacancy on his left and fattened his average hugely. This was what Ty Cobb, the Einstein of average, told him to do. But the game had changed since Cobb; Williams believed that his value to the club and to the league was as a slugger, so he went on pulling the ball, trying to blast it through three men, and paid the price of perhaps fifteen points of lifetime average. Like Ruth before him, he bought the occasional home run at the cost of many directed singles—a calculated sacrifice certainly not, in the case of a hitter as average-minded as Williams, entirely selfish.

8

---

[7]Two reasons for his durability may be adduced. A non-smoker, non-drinker, habitual walker, and year-round outdoorsman, Williams spared his body the vicissitudes of the seasonal athlete. And his hitting was in large part a mental process; the amount of cerebration he devoted to such details as pitchers' patterns, prevailing winds, and the muscular mechanics of swinging a bat would seem ridiculous, if it had not paid off. His intellectuality, as it were, perhaps explains the quickness with which he adjusted, after the war, to the changed conditions—the night games, the addition of the slider to the standard pitching repertoire, the new cry for the long ball. His reaction to the Williams Shift, then, cannot be dismissed as unconsidered.

[8]Invented, or perpetrated (as a joke?) by Boudreau on July 14, 1946, between games of a doubleheader. In the first game of the doubleheader, Williams had hit three homers and batted in eight runs. The shift was not used when men were on base and, had Williams bunted or hit late against it immediately, it might not have spread, in all its variations, throughout the league. The Cardinals used it in the lamented World Series of that year. Toward the end, in 1959 and 1960, rather sadly, it had faded from use, or degenerated to the mere clockwise twitching of the infield customary against pull hitters.

9   After a prime so harassed and hobbled, Williams was granted by the relenting fates a golden twilight. He became at the end of his career perhaps the best *old* hitter of the century. The dividing line falls between the 1956 and the 1957 seasons. In September of the first year, he and Mickey Mantle were contending for the batting championship. Both were hitting around .350, and there was no one else near them. The season ended with a three-game series between the Yankees and the Sox, and, living in New York then, I went up to the Stadium. Williams was slightly shy of the four hundred at-bats needed to qualify; the fear was expressed that the Yankee pitchers would walk him to protect Mantle. Instead, they pitched to him. It was wise. He looked terrible at the plate, tired and discouraged and unconvincing. He never looked very good to me in the Stadium.[9] The final outcome in 1956 was Mantle .353, Williams .345.

10   The next year, I moved from New York to New England, and it made all the difference. For in September of 1957, in the same situation, the story was reversed. Mantle finally hit .365; it was the best season of his career. But Williams, though sick and old, had run away from him. A bout of flu had laid him low in September. He emerged from his cave in the Hotel Somerset haggard but irresistible; he hit four successive pinch-hit home runs. "I feel terrible," he confessed, "but every time I take a swing at the ball it goes out of the park." He ended the season with thirty-eight home runs and an average of .388, the highest in either league since his own .406, and, coming from a decrepit man of thirty-nine, an even more supernal figure. With eight or so of the "leg hits" that a younger man would have beaten out, it would have been .400. And the next year, Williams, who in 1949 and 1953 had lost batting championships by decimal whiskers to George Kell and Mickey Vernon, sneaked in behind his teammate Pete Runnels and filched his sixth title, a bargain at .328.

11   In 1959, it seemed all over. The dinosaur thrashed around in the .200 swamp for the first half of the season, and was even benched ("rested," Manager Mike Higgins tactfully said). Old foes like the late Bill Cunningham began to offer batting tips. Cunningham thought Williams was jiggling his elbows;[10] in truth, Williams' neck was so stiff he could hardly turn his head to

[9] Shortly, after his retirement, Williams, in *Life,* wrote gloomily of the Stadium, "There's the bigness of it. There are those high stands and all those people smoking—and, of course, the shadows. . . . It takes at least one series to get accustomed to the Stadium and even then you're not sure." Yet his lifetime batting average there is .340, only four points under his median average.

[10] It was Cunningham who, when Williams first appeared in a Red Sox uniform at the 1938 spring training camp, wrote with melodious prescience: "The Sox seem to think Williams is just cocky enough and gabby enough to make a great and colorful outfielder, possibly the Babe Herman type. Me? I don't like the way he stands at the plate. He bends his front knee inward and moves his foot just before he takes a swing. That's exactly what I do just before I drive a golf ball and knowing what happens to the golf balls I drive, I don't believe this kid will ever hit half a singer midget's weight in a bathing suit."

look at the pitcher. When he swung, it looked like a Calder mobile with one thread cut; it reminded you that since 1954 Williams' shoulders had been wired together. A solicitous pall settled over the sports pages. In the two decades since Williams had come to Boston, his status had imperceptibly shifted from that of a naughty prodigy to that of a municipal monument. As his shadow in the record books lengthened, the Red Sox teams around him declined, and the entire American League seemed to be losing life and color to the National. The inconsistency of the new super-stars—Mantle, Colavito, and Kaline—served to make Williams appear all the more singular. And off the field, his private philanthropy—in particular, his zealous chairmanship of the Jimmy Fund, a charity for children with cancer—gave him a civic presence matched only by that of Richard Cardinal Cushing. In religion, Williams appears to be a humanist, and a selective one at that, but he and the abrasive-voiced Cardinal, when their good works intersect and they appear in the public eye together, make a handsome pair of seraphim.

Humiliated by his '59 season, Williams determined, once more, to come 12 back. I, as a specimen Williams partisan, was both glad and fearful. All baseball fans believe in miracles; the question is, how *many* do you believe in? He looked like a ghost in spring training. Manager Jurges warned us ahead of time that if Williams didn't come through he would be benched, just like anybody else. As it turned out, it was Jurges who was benched. Williams entered the 1960 season needing eight home runs to have a lifetime total of 500; after one time at bat in Washington, he needed seven. For a stretch, he was hitting a home run every second game that he played. He passed Lou Gehrig's lifetime total, and finished with 521, thirteen behind Jimmy Foxx, who alone stands between Williams and Babe Ruth's unapproachable 714. The summer was a statistician's picnic. His two-thousandth walk came and went, his eighteen-hundredth run batted in, his sixteenth All-Star Game. At one point, he hit a home run off a pitcher, Don Lee, off whose father, Thornton Lee, he had hit a home run a generation before. The only comparable season for a forty-two-year-old man was Ty Cobb's in 1928. Cobb batted .323 and hit one homer. Williams batted .316 but hit twenty-nine homers.

In sum, though generally conceded to be the greatest hitter of his era, he 13 did not establish himself as "the greatest hitter who ever lived." Cobb, for average, and Ruth, for power, remain supreme. Cobb, Rogers Hornsby, Joe Jackson, and Lefty O'Doul, among players since 1900, have higher lifetime averages than Williams' .344. Unlike Foxx, Gehrig, Hack Wilson, Hank Greenberg, and Ralph Kiner, Williams never came close to matching Babe Ruth's season home-run total of sixty.[11] In the list of major-league batting records, not one is held by Williams. He is second in walks drawn, third in home runs, fifth in lifetime average, sixth in runs batted in, eighth in runs scored and in total bases, fourteenth in doubles, and thirtieth in hits.[12] But if

---

[11] Written before Roger Maris' fluky, phenomenal sixty-one.

[12] Again, as of 1960. Since then, Musial may have surpassed him in some statistical areas.

we allow him merely average seasons for the four-plus seasons he lost to two wars, and add another season for the months he lost to injuries, we get a man who in all the power totals would be second, and not a very distant second, to Ruth. And if we further allow that these years would have been not merely average but prime years, if we allow for all the months when Williams was playing in sub-par condition, if we permit his early and later years in baseball to be some sort of index of what the middle years could have been, if we give him a right-field fence that is not, like Fenway's, one of the most distant in the league, and if—the least excusable "if"—we imagine him condescending to outsmart the Williams Shift, we can defensibly assemble, like a colossus induced from the sizable fragments that do remain, a statistical figure not incommensurate with his grandiose ambition. From the statistics that are on the books, a good case can be made that in the *combination* of power and average Williams is first; nobody else ranks so high in both categories. Finally, there is the witness of the eyes; men whose memories go back to Shoeless Joe Jackson—another unlucky natural—rank him and Williams together as the best-looking hitters they have seen. It was for our last look that ten thousand of us had come.

14   Two girls, one of them with pert buckteeth and eyes as black as vest buttons, the other with white skin and flesh-colored hair, like an underdeveloped photograph of a redhead, came and sat on my right. On my other side was one of those frowning chestless young-old men who can frequently be seen, often wearing sailor hats, attending ball games alone. He did not once open his program but instead tapped it, rolled up, on his knee as he gave the game his disconsolate attention. A young lady, with freckles and a depressed, dainty nose that by an optical illusion seemed to thrust her lips forward for a kiss, sauntered down into the box seat right behind the roof of the Oriole dugout. She wore a blue coat with a Northeastern University emblem sewed to it. The girls beside me took it into their heads that this was Williams' daughter. She looked too old to me, and why would she be sitting behind the visitors' dugout? On the other hand, from the way she sat there, staring at the sky and French-inhaling, she clearly was *somebody*. Other fans came and eclipsed her from view. The crowd looked less like a weekday ballpark crowd than like the folks you might find in Yellowstone National Park, or emerging from automobiles at the top of scenic Mount Mansfield. There were a lot of competitively well-dressed couples of tourist age, and not a few babes in arms. A row of five seats in front of me was abruptly filled with a woman and four children, the youngest of them two years old, if that. Someday, presumably, he could tell his grandchildren that he saw Williams play. Along with these tots and second-honeymooners, there were Harvard freshmen, giving off that peculiar nervous glow created when a sufficient quantity of insouciance is saturated with enough insecurity; thick-necked Army officers with brass on their shoulders and steel in their stares; pepper-

ings of priests; perfumed bouquets of Roxbury Fabian fans; shiny salesmen from Albany and Fall River; and those gray, hoarse men—taxi drivers, slaughterers, and bartenders—who will continue to click through the turn-stiles long after everyone else has deserted to television and tramporamas. Behind me, two young male voices blossomed, cracking a joke about God's five proofs that Thomas Aquinas exists—typical Boston College levity.

The batting cage was trundled away. The Orioles fluttered to the sidelines. Diagonally across the field, by the Red Sox dugout, a cluster of men in overcoats were festering like maggots. I could see a splinter of white uniform, and Williams' head, held at a self-deprecating and evasive tilt. Williams' conversational stance is that of a six-foot-three-inch man under a six-foot ceiling. He moved away to the patter of flash bulbs, and began playing catch with a young Negro outfielder named Willie Tasby. His arm, never very powerful, had grown lax with the years, and his throwing motion was a kind of muscular drawl. To catch the ball, he flicked his glove hand onto his left shoulder (he batted left but threw right, as every schoolboy ought to know) and let the ball plop into it comically. This catch session with Tasby was the only time all afternoon I saw him grin. [15]

A tight little flock of human sparrows who, from the lambent and pampered pink of their faces, could only have been Boston politicians moved toward the plate. The loudspeakers mammothly coughed as someone huffed on the microphone. The ceremonies began. Curt Gowdy, the Red Sox radio and television announcer, who sounds like everybody's brother-in-law, delivered a brief sermon, taking the two words "pride" and "champion" as his text. It began. "Twenty-one years ago, a skinny kid from San Diego, California . . ." and ended, "I don't think we'll ever see another like him." Robert Tibolt, chairman of the board of the Greater Boston Chamber of Commerce, presented Williams with a big Paul Revere silver bowl. Harry Carlson, a member of the sports committee of the Boston Chamber, gave him a plaque, whose inscription he did not read in its entirety, out of deference to Williams' distaste for this sort of fuss. Mayor Collins, seated in a wheelchair, presented the Jimmy Fund with a thousand-dollar check. [16]

Then the occasion himself stooped to the microphone, and his voice sounded, after the others, very Californian; it seemed to be coming, excellently amplified, from a great distance, adolescently young and as smooth as a butternut. His thanks for the gifts had not died from our ears before he glided, as if helplessly, into "In spite of all the terrible things that have been said about me by the knights of the keyboard up there. . . ." He glanced up at the press rows suspended behind home plate. The crowd tittered, appalled. A frightful vision flashed upon me, of the press gallery pelting Williams with erasers, of Williams clambering up the foul screen to slug journalists, of a riot, of Mayor Collins being crushed. ". . . And they *were* terrible things," Williams insisted, with level melancholy, into the mike. "I'd like to forget them, but I can't." He paused, swallowed his memories, and went on, "I want to say that [17]

479

my years in Boston have been the greatest thing in my life." The crowd, like an immense sail going limp in a change of wind, sighed with relief. Taking all the parts himself, Williams then acted out a vivacious little morality drama in which an imaginary tempter came to him at the beginning of his career and said, "Ted, you can play anywhere you like." Leaping nimbly into the role of his younger self (who in biographical actuality had yearned to be a Yankee), Williams gallantly chose Boston over all the other cities, and told us that Tom Yawkey was the greatest owner in baseball and we were the greatest fans. We applauded ourselves lustily. The umpire came out and dusted the plate. The voice of doom announced over the loudspeakers that after Williams' retirement his uniform number, 9, would be permanently retired—the first time the Red Sox had so honored a player. We cheered. The national anthem was played. We cheered. The game began.

18   Williams was third in the batting order, so he came up in the bottom of the first inning, and Steve Barber, a young pitcher born two months before Williams began playing in the major leagues, offered him four pitches, at all of which he disdained to swing, since none of them were within the strike zone. This demonstrated simultaneously that Williams' eyes were razor-sharp and that Barber's control wasn't. Shortly, the bases were full, with Williams on second. "Oh, I hope he gets held up at third! That would be wonderful," the girl beside me moaned, and, sure enough, the man at bat walked and Williams was delivered into our foreground. He struck the pose of Donatello's David, the third-base bag being Goliath's head. Fiddling with his cap, swapping small talk with the Oriole third baseman (who seemed delighted to have him drop in), swinging his arms with a sort of prancing nervousness, he looked fine—flexible, hard, and not unbecomingly substantial through the middle. The long neck, the small head, the knickers whose cuffs were worn down near his ankles—all these clichés of sports cartoon iconography were rendered in the flesh.

19   With each pitch, Williams danced down the baseline, waving his arms and stirring dust, ponderous but menacing, like an attacking goose. It occurred to about a dozen humorists at once to shout "Steal home! Go, go!" Williams' speed afoot was never legendary. Lou Clinton, a young Sox outfielder, hit a fairly deep fly to center field. Williams tagged up and ran home. As he slid across the plate, the ball, thrown with unusual heft by Jackie Brandt, the Oriole center fielder, hit him on the back.

20   "Boy, he was really loafing, wasn't he?" one of the collegiate voices behind me said.

21   "It's cold," the other voice explained. "He doesn't play well when it's cold. He likes heat. He's a hedonist."

22   The run that Williams scored was the second and last of the inning. Gus Triandos, of the Orioles, quickly evened the score by plunking a home run over the handy left-field wall. Williams, who had had this wall at his back for

twenty years,[13] played the ball flawlessly. He didn't budge. He just stood still, in the center of the little patch of grass that his patient footsteps had worn brown, and, limp with lack of interest, watched the ball pass overhead. It was not a very interesting game. Mike Higgins, the Red Sox manager, with nothing to lose, had restricted his major-league players to the left-field line— along with Williams, Frank Malzone, a first-rate third baseman, played the game—and had peopled the rest of the terrain with unpredictable youngsters fresh, or not so fresh, off the farms. Other than Williams' recurrent appearances at the plate, the *maladresse* of the Sox infield was the sole focus of suspense; the second baseman turned every grounder into a juggling act, while the shortstop did a breathtaking impersonation of an open window. With this sort of assistance, the Orioles wheedled their way into a 4–2 lead. They had early replaced Barber with another young pitcher, Jack Fisher. Fortunately (as it turned out), Fisher is no cutie; he is willing to burn the ball through the strike zone, and inning after inning this tactic punctured Higgins' string of test balloons.

Whenever Williams appeared at the plate—pounding the dirt from his cleats, gouging a pit in the batter's box with his left foot, wringing resin out of the bat handle with his vehement grip, switching the stick at the pitcher with an electric ferocity—it was like having a familiar Leonardo appear in a shuffle of *Saturday Evening Post* covers. This man, you realized—and here, perhaps, was the difference, greater than the difference in gifts—really desired to hit the ball. In the third inning, he hoisted a high fly to deep center. In the fifth, we thought he had it; he smacked the ball hard and high into the heart of his power zone, but the deep right field in Fenway and the heavy air and a casual east wind defeated him. The ball died. Al Pilarcik leaned his back against the big "380" painted on the right-field wall and caught it. On another day, in another park, it would have been gone. (After the game, Williams said, "I didn't think I could hit one any harder than that. The conditions weren't good.")

The afternoon grew so glowering that in the sixth inning the arc lights were turned on—always a wan sight in the daytime, like the burning headlights of a funeral procession. Aided by the gloom, Fisher was slicing through the Sox rookies, and Williams did not come to bat in the seventh. He was second up in the eighth. This was almost certainly his last time to come to the plate in Fenway Park, and instead of merely cheering, as we had at his three previous appearances, we stood, all of us, and applauded. I had never before heard pure applause in a ballpark. No calling, no whistling, just an ocean of handclaps, minute after minute, burst after burst, crowding and running together in continuous succession like the pushes of surf at the edge of the sand. It was a sombre and considered tumult. There was not a boo in it. It

23

24

---

[13] In his second season (1940) he was switched to left field, to protect his eyes from the right-field sun.

seemed to renew itself out of a shifting set of memories as the Kid, the Marine, the veteran of feuds and failures and injuries, the friend of children, and the enduring old pro evolved down the bright tunnel of twenty-two summers toward this moment. At last, the umpire signalled for Fisher to pitch; with the other players, he had been frozen in position. Only Williams had moved during the ovation, switching his bat impatiently, ignoring everything except his cherished task. Fisher wound up, and the applause sank into a hush.

25   Understand that we were a crowd of rational people. We knew that a home run cannot be produced at will; the right pitch must be perfectly met and luck must ride with the ball. Three innings before, we had seen a brave effort fail. The air was soggy, the season was exhausted. Nevertheless, there will always lurk, around the corner in a pocket of our knowledge of the odds, an indefensible hope, and this was one of the times, which you now and then find in sports, when a density of expectation hangs in the air and plucks an event out of the future.

26   Fisher, after his unsettling wait, was low with the first pitch. He put the second one over, and Williams swung mightily and missed. The crowd grunted, seeing that classic swing, so long and smooth and quick, exposed. Fisher threw the third time, Williams swung again, and there it was. The ball climbed on a diagonal line into the vast volume of air over center field. From my angle, behind third base, the ball seemed less an object in flight than the tip of a towering, motionless construct, like the Eiffel Tower or the Tappan Zee Bridge. It was in the books while it was still in the sky. Brandt ran back to the deepest corner of the outfield grass, the ball descended beyond his reach and struck in the crotch where the bullpen met the wall, bounced chunkily, and vanished.

27   Like a feather caught in a vortex, Williams ran around the square of bases at the center of our beseeching screaming. He ran as he always ran out home runs—hurriedly, unsmiling, head down, as if our praise were a storm of rain to get out of. He didn't tip his cap. Though we thumped, wept, and chanted "We want Ted" for minutes after he hid in the dugout, he did not come back. Our noise for some seconds passed beyond excitement into a kind of immense open anguish, a wailing, a cry to be saved. But immortality is nontransferable. The papers said that the other players, and even the umpires on the field, begged him to come out and acknowledge us in some way, but he refused. Gods do not answer letters.

28   Every true story has an anticlimax. The men on the field refused to disappear, as would have seemed decent, in the smoke of Williams' miracle. Fisher continued to pitch, and escaped further harm. At the end of the inning, Higgins sent Williams out to his left-field position, then instantly replaced him with Carrol Hardy, so we had a long last look at Williams as he

ran out there and then back, his uniform jogging, his eyes steadfast on the ground. It was nice, and we were grateful, but it left a funny taste.

One of the scholasticists behind me said, "Let's go. We've seen every- 29 thing. I don't want to spoil it." This seemed a sound aesthetic decision. Williams' last word had been so exquisitely chosen, such a perfect fusion of expectation, intention, and execution, that already it felt a little unreal in my head, and I wanted to get out before the castle collapsed. But the game, though played by clumsy midgets under the feeble glow of the arc lights, began to tug at my attention, and I loitered in the runway until it was over. Williams' homer had, quite incidentally, made the score 4–3. In the bottom of the ninth inning, with one out, Marlin Coughtry, the second-base juggler, singled. Vic Wertz, pinch-hitting, doubled off the left-field wall, Coughtry advancing to third. Pumpsie Green walked, to load the bases. Willie Tasby hit a double-play ball to the third baseman, but in making the pivot throw Billy Klaus, an ex-Red Sox infielder, reverted to form and threw the ball past the first baseman and into the Red Sox dugout. The Sox won, 5–4. On the car radio as I drove home I heard that Williams, his own man to the end, had decided not to accompany the team to New York. He had met the little death that awaits athletes. He had quit.

Questions

1. Updike's essay has two major motifs. He reports the events of Wednesday, September 28, 1960, in Boston's Fenway Park, when Ted Williams played his last game (paragraphs 1–2, and paragraphs 14–29). In between he makes a case for Williams's career ambition, to be "the greatest hitter who ever lived." What is the relationship between Updike's sports reportage and his biographical and character analysis?

2. What is Updike's attitude toward Williams—as a ballplayer and as a man? How does this affect his overall assessment of Williams's career? How does the title of this piece, originally published in the *New Yorker,* with its newspaperlike headline of one-syllable words ("Hub Fans Bid Kid—") followed by the graceful, formal "Adieu" reflect the personality of its subject? his relationship to the spectators?

3. This piece has an extremely lengthy, detailed windup to the pitch—Williams's last time at bat. Is the buildup perceptible? predictable? necessary? Suppose that Williams had struck out rather than hitting a final home run; what writing strategies would that conclusion to a career have dictated?

4. In this unusually long piece of sportswriting, Updike has the latitude to be philosophical. What does he mean by his lead into Williams's last time at bat: "Nevertheless, there will always lurk, around the corner in a pocket of our knowledge of the odds, an indefensible hope, and this was one of the times, which you now and then find in sports, when a density of expectation hangs in the air and plucks an event out of the future" (paragraph 25)? Explain the meaning and comment on the appropriateness of Updike's concise conclusion: "He had met the little death that awaits athletes. He had quit."

RED SMITH

Good Ol' Boy Woody Hayes

The 1978 Gator Bowl contest will be remembered by sports fans not as a victory of Clemson over Ohio State, but as the ultimate defeat of Ohio State's coach of twenty-eight years, Woody Hayes. Although the action that precipitated Hayes's firing was clearly unsportsmanlike (he punched out the Clemson team member who made the decisive victory play), cynics pointed out that for the preceding decade, as Dave Kindred says, "Only Muhammed Ali . . . threw more punches. [Hayes] aimed at . . . a student reporter in the '77 Oklahoma game. He once punched his own fullback and . . . even hit a goal post in the Superdome. . . . Hayes always lashed out when he was losing." These critics suggest that only when Hayes was reaching retirement age did Ohio State fire him for offenses it should have cracked down on long before.

Distinguished sportswriters like Kindred and Red Smith serve a moral function in reaffirming the true goals of sports, to take pride in a good performance played according to the spirit as well as the letter of the rules. This view directly contradicts Hayes's contention, "I don't think it's possible to be too intent on winning. . . . This country is built on winning and on that alone." Smith implies his point in the first paragraph—that unsportsmanlike conduct is never justified—and through irony and sarcasm, he never lets up. He repeatedly refers to the football players as "scholar-athletes," an ironic reminder to readers of the initial aims of collegiate sports, and with sarcasm to the football game as "their pursuit of culture." In taking a moral stance, such sportswriters may defy the values of the sporting world in general (Ohio State players and other college coaches were sympathetic to Hayes), and of their readers. But they force their readers to pay attention to their articulate voices of conscience. As Kindred sums up:

> *At 65, Hayes had run out of time to grow up. Churchill said, "Success is never final, failure is never fatal." Intercollegiate athletics often seems without value. Hypocrisy reigns as surely today as it did 50 years ago when the University of Chicago quit the game in disgust at what it had become: a commercial circus with hired hands posing as students. If the college games have a redeeming value it is that they teach well the truth of Churchill's memorable line. That was Hayes' real transgression. He taught Ohio State to win, but not to lose.*

1   People keep saying that Woody Hayes is a great football coach who overstayed his time. This implies that there was a time when slugging a member of the opposing team was proper coachly deportment.

2   Let's face it, throwing a punch at Charlie Bauman of Clemson was only the last degrading incident in a pattern of behavior that had long distinguished the Ohio State coach. For years, Hayes had been throwing tantrums, screaming abuse and striking out at anyone within reach when his team was losing. His employers shrugged off these embarrassments, his idolators chuckled over them and agreed that there was good ol' Woody for you, and the objects of his spleen turned the other cheek. After he shoved a camera into the face of a *Los Angeles Times* photographer while Southern California was horsewhipping Ohio State in the 1973 Rose Bowl, the photographer

was persuaded to drop charges; when Hayes punched Mike Friedman, a cameraman for ABC, after an Ohio State fumble in a 14–6 defeat by Michigan, that admirable network stood up for its man by saying ABC wasn't going to make trouble because ABC would have to do business with Woody in the future.

Evidently nobody in authority realized that a full-grown man who attached such importance to a game was, at best, immature, not to say a case of arrested development. The saddest part of the whole affair is that nobody at Ohio State saw the denouement approaching and protected Hayes from himself.

The only way to protect him would have been to ease him into retirement, and he would have resisted that. Still, it would have been infinitely preferable to what happened. By procrastinating, the Ohio State brass invited a situation where it became necessary to throw Hayes out on his ear after twenty-eight years of service. The college wound up looking as bad as the coach.

College football began as a recreation for undergraduates, but it outgrew that role many years ago. Not many thoughtful persons, aware of the abuses that accompanied it, would argue that it had been an altogether healthy growth. Indeed, some might wonder how far the cause of higher education was advanced by shipping a consignment of scholar-athletes from Columbus, Ohio, to Jacksonville, Florida, during their Christmas holidays to lose in the Gator Bowl to scholar-athletes from Clemson, South Carolina.

"I don't think it's possible to be too intent on winning," Woody Hayes has said. "If we played for any other reason, we would be totally dishonest. This country is built on winning and on that alone. Winning is still the most honorable thing a man can do."

Woody and his scholar-athletes were trying to win in the closing moments of last Friday night's game, when Charlie Bauman intercepted a pass and went out of bounds right where the Ohio State coach stood. That architect of young manhood laid hold of Bauman and fetched him a roundhouse right to the chops. Fists flailing, he tried to charge onto the field, but his own scholar-athletes, already bruised and bleeding from their pursuit of culture, overpowered him.

Curiously, although all this was visible to a national television audience, it escaped the attention of the ABC broadcasters in Jacksonville. There was neither comment nor replay. For that matter, there was no kickoff in ABC's version of the Sugar Bowl game later in the weekend. When that game between Penn State and Alabama started, a commercial was on the screen.

"No alumni and nobody else, not even you members of the press, fire the coach," Hayes has said. "The players fire the coach and as long as I'm on the same wavelength with them, I can coach as long as I want to."

It didn't work out exactly that way, for the comments of Ohio State players, published after Hayes had been dismissed, indicated that most of them remained loyal to him. Comments from other college coaches were generally sympathetic to Woody, too.

11   "I think you ought to take into consideration the enormous pressure of coaching football today," said Bo Schembechler of Michigan. The authorities at Ohio State had been taking that into consideration for twenty-eight years in Woody's case. They had to take it into consideration before Hayes arrived, for there was pressure on Wes Fesler, Carroll Widdoes, Paul Brown and all their predecessors in Columbus, back to Doc Wilce and beyond.

12   Coaching in Columbus is not quite like coaching in New Haven. When Francis Schmidt had the Ohio State job, he drove his car into a filling station to have the oil changed and stayed behind the wheel, drawing plays in a notebook while the car was raised on a hoist.

13   Oblivious to the world around him, the coach pored over his X's and O's, devising an intricate double reverse, setting up a defense to stop it, trying something else. At length he came up with a play that looked unstoppable. With a small cry of triumph, he slapped the notebook shut, opened the door, stepped out and fell ten feet to the concrete.

Questions

1. In a brief sports column, the writer has to get to the point quickly. How soon are you aware of Smith's attitude toward Woody Hayes, Ohio State's tempestuous football coach for twenty-eight years? To what extent can Smith count on a readership sympathetic to his views?

2. Why does Smith repeatedly refer to the Ohio State and Clemson football players as "scholar-athletes," and to the game of football as "their pursuit of culture"? Can he count on his readers to recognize the irony?

3. To what extent can sportswriters promote and recognize high ideals, a code of good conduct, and standards of good sportsmanship? What kind of a leader and sportsman does Smith imply that an ideal coach should be? How far from that ideal is Woody Hayes at the end of his career?

4. Compare and contrast the last games of Woody Hayes and Ted Williams, described in Updike's "Hub Fans Bid Kid Adieu," as they symbolize the characters of the two men.

DAVE KINDRED

Smile, Rosie, and Give Them a Run for the Money

Kindred's lively sportswriting brings imagination and a fresh point of view to sport after sport, season after season. Born in Lincoln, Illinois in 1941, Kindred has been writing sports columns and feature articles since his graduation from Illinois Wesleyan University in 1963. In Louisville he wrote for the Courier Journal and the Times, and was named Kentucky

Sportswriter of the Year in 1968, and in the successive years 1973 through 1976. Since 1977 he has been a sports columnist, first for The Washington Post, *where he was named Sportswriter of the Year in 1979, and currently for* The Atlanta Constitution. *He has also written two books,* Baseball: The Dream Game in Kentucky *(1976) and* A Year with the Cats: From Breathitt County to the White House *(1977).*

Sports columns, like the events to which they refer, quickly become dated and lose their appeal unless made memorable by either the athletes' performance, the writer's, or both. In "Smile, Rosie, and Give Them a Run for the Money," both the athletic performance and the writing are memorable, but for opposite reasons. Rosie Ruiz, a New York officeworker, had apparently placed twenty-third in the Women's Division of the 1980 New York Marathon, a victory necessary to qualify her for participation in the Boston Marathon, the Olympics of world-class runners. Even as she claimed victory in the Women's Division of the Boston, her New York performance was invalidated by officials who contended that she took a subway and entered the race near the finish line. Her Boston victory was suddenly invalidated for similar reasons; witnesses saw Ruiz enter the course with two miles to go.

Despite a swipe at racing purists (runners "are morally superior to ordinary people"), Kindred is essentially on their side, taking the moral high road against cheaters who take the low road, or no road if they ride the subway. He can count on his readers, who share the ethic of amateur racing, to appreciate each satiric jab at the corrupt racer who deserves what she gets. A sermon on the evils of cheating would have seemed holier than most of us could tolerate, especially on the sports page, but a broad satire entertains even as it makes its point.

Dear Rosie,   1

    Two rich Washington guys want to make a deal with you. Henry Buchanan wrote The Post yesterday to say he'll put up $100,000 that is yours if you beat him in a marathon. Alex Fraser called to say he'll put up $10,000 if you come within five minutes of your time in Boston.   2

    Buchanan's a certified public accountant who's a runner himself. Four marathons, best time 2 hours 58 minutes. He ran Monday in Boston, in 3 hours 2 minutes. He said you can pick the marathon, preferably in May for "Rosie's benefit. I don't want her to think I want 10 or 12 weeks to improve my condition . . . she can pick the time and the date."   3

    He'll put the money in escrow. You beat him, it's yours. Lose, and you must permit "qualified and recognized officials at the (Boston) race to make a binding judgment whether or not she was . . . the women's winner.   4

    "My motivation," Buchanan wrote, "is for other marathoners, both men and women, but especially for the girl who finished second (Jacqueline Gareau of Montreal). That's a disgrace. For these world-class runners, this year's Boston marathon is their Olympics."   5

    Here's what Fraser said: 6

    "I will offer $10,000 to the charity of her choice, the American Cancer Fund, the Heart Fund, whatever—I will put the money on deposit, The Post can hold it—I will give $10,000 if she comes to Washington in the next six months and runs a marathon within five minutes of the time she ostensibly ran at Boston."   7

    Fraser, you should know, is an investor with money in oil. If he says he'll   8 put up $10,000, you can run to the bank with it. What he's interested in is the same thing, Rosie, that you're trying to do. He wants everyone to know the answer.

9   Did you or didn't you?

10   Did Runnin' Rosie run 26 miles 385 yards in the Boston marathon?

11   Or did you take a taxi 24 miles, 385 yards and then slip into the race?

12   "I don't like people who bend the rules as much as she did," Fraser said, adding quickly, ". . . if she did, in fact, bend them. On the other hand, if she really ran the race, she ought to get credit for it.

13   "Otherwise, she'll forever be like the guy who ran the football the wrong way (Roy Riegels) or Wrong Way Corrigan who intended to fly to South Dakota or somewhere and wound up in Ireland."

14   What Alex is saying, Rosie, is that you'll forever be remembered as the Boston Straggler unless you do something to stop it. That is why he is putting up the $10,000. He figures the money will be nice incentive for you.

15   Alex Fraser is serious about this.

16   So are you, Rosie. You insist you ran the whole way, just as you insist you ran every step of the 26 miles 385 yards in New York to qualify for the world's most famous marathon in Boston. You have offered to take a lie-detector test. You have cried in front of television cameras when asked hostile questions such as, "What's the scenery along the Boston route?"

17   There was "beautiful countryside," you said.

18   Wow.

19   "There were roads winding in and out," you said.

20   What a picture.

21   And still people don't believe you.

22   New York invalidated your time of 2 hours 56 minutes yesterday. They said you didn't run the entire route. They said you took the subway to the finish line. And they didn't even ask you about the scenery in Manhattan. You could have told them that there were a lot of tall buildings. They'd have had to believe you then.

23   The Boston people are investigating your finish time of 2:31:56. They have talked to witnesses who said you entered the course with about two miles to go. If they are to maintain the Boston marathon as a religion, well, they can't have people coming to church in the middle of the sermon.

24   Other runners are just as serious about things as you are. These runners are outraged at the thought of a fraud. They see marathons as a symbol of wholesomeness, a tribute to asceticism. They are, you should know, morally superior to ordinary people.

25   That's why they don't like your advisor, Steve Marek. They don't understand why anyone would run a marathon wearing a Superman costume. Steve does that. So when he showed up as your advisor right away other runners said that if Marek had anything to do with it, it was a disgrace for sure.

Everybody is too serious, Rosie. 26

It could have been fun. 27

Think of it, Rosie. 28

Instead of crying on national TV, you could have written a book. 29

"Shortcuts to Fame" would have been a nice title. The book, naturally, 30
would start on Chapter 20.

As Bill Rodgers has done, you could have become rich selling your line 31
of running gear.

Rosie Ruiz shoes—So comfortable that when the marathon is over, your 32
feet feel like they've only gone a mile or two. These shoes leave no tracks.

Rosie Ruiz shirts and shorts—Science brought us Day-Glo so that Ray 33
Charles could see us coming from a mile away, but it took Runnin' Rosie to
invent Day-Fade, the fabric that makes you invisible. Dog's can't bite what
dogs can't see.

Rosie Ruiz deodorant—Splash it on and you smell like someone who 34
has just run a marathon.

Rosie Ruiz doll—Wind it up and it takes the subway. 35

Soon enough all of America would be on the Rosie Ruiz diet. You get so 36
thin you disappear. We would see you, Rosie, on an American Express
commercial, saying, "Don't go to Boston without it." And your card has no
name on it.

You might be interested, Rosie, in one man's theory about what really 37
happened in New York and Boston. He thinks you were just out having fun
and got carried away. His name is Wayne Welch and he's a 40-ish marathoner
from Washington who dropped out of Boston after 18 miles because the day
was too hot.

"I suspect Rosie didn't intend to win Boston," said Welch, who based his 38
suspicions on the story in which a woman photographer said she had ridden
with you on the subway to the New York finish line.

"It was probably innocent. Rosie took the subway to the finish line and 39
walked up behind the chutes for the finishers. She had a bad ankle. She
probably said, 'Can you give me some help?' And someone else said, 'Injured
runner here.'"

Runners in New York wore computer-coded labels on their racing num- 40
bers. Racing officials took those labels as runners crossed the finish line.
Welch theorizes that someone simply took Rosie's label by mistake and she
wound up with that 2:56:29 clocking even though she'd spent most of the
time riding underground, not running on the ground.

"People around her office must have been congratulating her for weeks," 41
Welch said, "and she probably liked it, so she figured she'd do it again at
Boston. She was 23rd in New York and maybe she wanted to be fifth or sixth
in Boston.

"But being so ignorant of running—she just doesn't have the skin tone 42
or the muscle tone of a runner—she didn't know what a good time would be

and she jumped into the race too soon. She came flopping in like a wounded duck. You could see she wasn't a runner."

43   What you ought to do, Rosie, if you can smile about all this, is put on your own marathon for Buchanan's $100,000 and Fraser's $10,000. The winner's trophy should be a subway token.

Writing About Performance

Strategies

1. Do I know well what I'm reviewing—either the general area (modern drama, rock music, soccer, for instance) or the particular performer or group (Ibsen, Springsteen, the Hometown Hornets)? Do I like—preferably, love—the subject under consideration, if not the particular performance? If the answer to either question is *no,* then should I be writing this review or sports article?

2. Do I know enough about the subject to explain its background, technical points, controversies, standards (within the field, and by which it is judged), alternate ways of performing, to readers who don't know much about it? to readers who do? Who will read this? What will they be looking for?

3. How long can the review be? What information, background or current, is essential? What is less essential? On what grounds will I decide what to emphasize, subordinate, and omit? How will I organize this review or sports article? In what ways will the organization reinforce my major points and interpretation of the subject?

4. How general, technical, or otherwise specialized will my language be? How colorful? What will my prevailing tone be? How can I avoid excessive jargon or clichés common to reviewers in my subject area?

5. Is my review convincing? enjoyable to read? If not, what can I do to make it more compelling or engaging?

Suggestions

1. Write a review of a book, play, film, or lecture with which your readers are unfamiliar. Be sure to tell them enough about the main points of the content or plot so they can decide whether or not they want to read or see it. Will you have space to discuss other aspects of the work in detail, such as its style, accuracy, quality of writing, symbolism, or recurrent motifs? (See D. H. Lawrence, "Benjamin Franklin," 443–51; Paul Fussell, "The Boy Scout Handbook," 451–55; Eudora Welty, *Charlotte's Web,* 456–58.

2. Write a review of a play or film you can be certain your readers are familiar with, and concentrate instead on the quality of the performance. Consider such aspects as how well the principals and supporting cast played their parts, and what was notable (either positive or negative) about such aspects as the sets, costumes, lighting and sound effects, and timing and pace of the performance. How little or how much of your own values, taste, or personality will you make apparent in the review; i.e., will you tell your readers what you liked best—and least—about the production, and why? (See George Bernard Shaw and John Simon on "Hamlet," 429–37.)

3. Write a review of a musical performance (any kind), art show, or stand-up comic. Consider the selections performed or displayed in terms of their variety, balance, traditionalism or innovation; the interpretation(s) of the subject; the artist's or performers' technical mastery, style, and relation to past performances or showings; and the audience reaction. (See Harold Schonberg, "Why a Critic Follows the Score," 397–99, and Jennifer M. Young, "The Rock Fantasy," 400–403.)

4. Write a review of a restaurant, bar, or nightclub, in which you comment on the physical setting and ambience, and identify the intended patrons (families, business people, tourists, singles); provide a sampling of representative food and beverages; note the quality of the food and service, and the price range; and comment on any special features, such as the kind and quality of music or entertainment. (See Phyllis C. Richman, "Hunan Dynasty," 459–61; Gwyneth Cravens, "The M & J Sanitary Tortilla Factory," 461–67; Calvin Trillin, "Eating in Cincinnati," 282–87.)

5. Write an interpretive commentary on a sports event or individual athletic performance, in which you discuss either the nightlights of an individual game, season, or other segment of a team or individual performance. You may wish to identify the low points as well as the high, the opponents' performance, and any colorful sidelights. Relate this event/performance to the player's or team's characteristic performance. Is this one better or worse? typical or atypical? Why? (See Bob Considine, "Louis Knocks Out Schmeling," 468–69; Red Smith, "Good Ol' Boy Woody Hayes," 484–86; and John Updike, "Hub Fans Bid Kid Adieu," 470–83.)

6. Write a review in which you take issue with the premises of the performance (or content, if it's a book or play). Be sure to justify your negative opinion in terms of either the standards of the medium, or your own critical, ethical, or other principles. This may be a satire rather than a straightforward essay. (See D. H. Lawrence, "Benjamin Franklin," 443–51; Dorothy Parker, "The Grandmother of the Aunt of the Gardener," 562–65; and Dave Kindred, "Smile, Rosie, and Give Them a Run for the Money," 486–90.)

7. Write an interpretive essay identifying and explaining the major features of a particular medium, such as Restoration comedy, science fiction, Dixieland jazz, women's gymnastics, New Orleans cooking. (See James Agee, "Comedy's Greatest Era," 404–19; Gerald Mast, "Comic Plots and Comic Climate," 420–28; Jennifer M. Young, "The Rock Fantasy," 400–403.)

8. Write a review of an amateur performance, such as a local theater or sports team, or a children's play, concert, or sports event. Do you need to establish special criteria for this review, to avoid judging the performance by professional standards? Will any others besides a local audience read your review—and care about it? (See Michael Kernan, "Bard Times at the Folger Theater," 437–39.)

9. Compare and contrast two performances or productions in the same medium, along the same dimensions and according to comparable criteria.

10. Use your review to parody either the medium, the subject, an author, or a particular performance. (See Kindred, "Smile, Rosie . . . ," 486–90; Ken Wunderlich, "Playing the Sax," 565–68. For suggestions on writing parody, see 495–99.)

CHAPTER SIX

Humorous Writing

S ome types of humor exist mostly for fun—puns, jokes, parodies, and tall tales; other types of humor, benign and gentle, celebrate the pleasures of life; still other types of humor—laughter as the alternative to tears—help us cope with anger and outrage, disorder, disruption, defeat, and disaster.

Humorous writing can celebrate joy, through savoring the pleasant aspects of life, through recapturing good times past, a simpler world, an innocence unspoiled by the cynicism of age or the disappointments of experience. Such writing, though benign in spirit, is often gentle and low key, rather than raucous and rowdy. This is epitomized by E. B. White's "Once More to the Lake" (232–37). Because such writing is often a narrative of personal experience or reminiscence, it's a favorite of student and professional writers alike. In "Uncle John's Farm" (237–42), Mark Twain's succulent description of the joys of picking watermelon, cooling it, anticipating the outcome, and finally eating the delectable fruit not only recreates a blissful—perhaps idealized—childhood, but suspends adult morality in favor of juvenile pranks: "I know the taste of the watermelon which has been honestly come by, and I know the taste of the watermelon which has been acquired by art. Both taste good, but the experienced know which tastes best."

Other writings of joyous good humor in this volume include two essays that combine descriptions of favorite places with the gusto of enjoying good food: Calvin Trillin's "Eating in Cincinnati" (282–87), and Gwyneth Cravens's "The M & J Sanitary Tortilla Factory" (461–67). These are but a few of life's favorite things, all suitable for writing that is good natured and good humored.

Humorous writing can depict memorable characters. Particularly engaging, amusing, eccentric, or otherwise unusual people make good subjects for comic portraits. You (and your readers) can either laugh *with* such characters or *at* them, depending on how you treat your subject's personality, tastes, and behavior. Thus in "Mr. L. G. Broadmoore and the Way It Was" (546–

50), Eugene Meyer sympathetically portrays this twenty-three-year-old "authentic obsolete man" who earns a living by "repairing player pianos, gramophones and other outdated machinery":

> Though short of stature, he cuts an imposing figure in his pince-nez spectacles, waxed moustache . . . high-neck starched collar. He looks like a yellowing photograph in an ancient family album, the young man on the make, the rugged individualist of Main Street.

Broadmoore's intentionally anachronistic, highly principled, often difficult way of life has evoked Meyer's respect and admiration, which he expects his readers to share.

Humorous writing can provide comic relief. Humor can take the sting out of an astringent, humiliating, or otherwise miserable experience. The very act of writing about the humorous aspects of a painful subject can help the writer to gain distance from it, and thereby to understand, interpret, and cope with it. If irony is life's joke on life ("Cheer up," they told him, "It could be worse." So he cheered up and it got worse.), the humorist can have the last laugh. In "Death of a Pig" (533–39), seeking a comic respite from the untimely death of a pig he has been raising, E. B. White transforms death into art. The sick pig, which White nursed, "had evidently become precious to me," and when it died "the loss we felt was not the loss of ham but the loss of pig." Endowing the incident with mock-epic grace, White transforms the pig into an Agamemnon, whose "suffering soon became the embodiment of all earthly wretchedness," and his busybody dog, Fred, into a "dishonorable pallbearer."

Humorous writing can call attention to the paradoxical, quixotic, bizarre, and unpredictable aspects of human behavior. In simply laughing at unusual behavior, humorists authenticate the incongruous by encouraging readers to laugh, too. In "The Night the Bed Fell" (540–43), James Thurber recalls the chaos that allegedly ensued in his household one night when the army cot on which he was sleeping collapsed on top of him, causing panic among the other members of his bizarre household: "a nervous first cousin . . . named Briggs Beall, who believed that he was likely to cease breathing when he was asleep"; Thurber's mother, who mistakenly believed that her husband's bed had fallen: "She therefore screamed, 'Let's go to your poor father' "; her son Herman, who countershouted, " 'You're all right, Mamma!' "; and Thurber's father, who "decided that the house was on fire. 'I'm coming, I'm coming!' he wailed in a slow, sleepy voice . . ." Whether this incident really happened that way or not (we allow humorists a certain license), we can laugh at this volatile family, nudged into hysterics by a trivial incident, now immortalized.

Such humorous writing can vent the author's anger with the subject. In "It's the Only Video Game My Mom Lets Me Chew" (527–28)—the title signals the humor—student Craig Swanson presents himself as a character addicted to the very activity he burlesques, as we realize from his opening response to the "beeps, twoozers, fanfares, and fugues" of the video games, competing "for dominance" in a video parlor that bears a striking resemblance to a men's room. Although Swanson, who "simply stares mindlessly into the video screen as long as his twenty-five cent pieces last," regrets his compulsion ("My vision is distorted and I am devoid of all intelligent thought"), he expects his readers primarily to laugh at his mindless activity, and perhaps to recognize in his account a cautionary tale.

Humorous writing can also provide an opportunity for acts of daring, defiance, even revenge. The lowly humorist can attack the privileged and the powerful, the oppressors and the overbearing, and can thereby find a socially appropriate expression of his own hostility or desire for change. Many of Russell Baker's political satires are critical of public institutions, politicians (presidents, senators, congressmen, lesser functionaries), public policy, and agencies and agents of the bureaucracy. These writings implicitly defend the views of the average voters, in opposition to the powerful establishment. "Universal Military Motion" (525–26), a critique of the MX missile system, burlesques the mobile silo system by projecting "250 fake Pentagons constantly cruising the roads," supplemented by "1,500 Pentagon-shaped fast-food restaurants along the nation's highways," and complemented by "850 United States Capitols," also in motion—daringly fanciful symbols of defiance.

Humorous writing can be a form of social commentary or social criticism, designed to promote change and reform. Some social commentary exists just to poke fun at its subject. Ironic writers often assume that they're intellectually, morally, or culturally superior to their subject. Deadpan, they present specific details of clothing, behavior, conversations, mannerisms, anything intended to devastate their subject. In "The Yellow Bus" (500–14), Lillian Ross presents a stock situation of comedy: the hayseeds (the senior class from Bean Blossom [Indiana] Township High School) on a visit to the big city. She counts on her readers to enjoy her ironic ridicule, as the victims fall short of the critic's allegedly superior standards. Not knowing where to stay, the Bean Blossomites take the advice of their bus driver (also from Bean Blossom), and check in at the Hotel Woodstock. Not knowing where to eat, they follow the driver's recommendation of Hector's Cafeteria. Not knowing how to dress, all the boys wear matching outfits, "white beachcomber pants" and white sneakers, for a tour of the Statute of Liberty. Not knowing what to buy, they take home such souvenirs as "a George Washington Bridge teapot." Ross, of course, implies that she and her readers know better, and that the tourists' behavior and values are simply laughable.

Satirists are idealists; as social critics, they write from a desire to point out flaws in the subject and to promote reform, whether their corrective laughter is gently sympathetic, or bitter with the anger of moral outrage. The "Modest Proposal" (518–24) was a cry from the heart of Jonathan Swift, a prominent Anglican clergyman in Dublin. Published in 1729, when many Irish tenant farmers and their families were not only starving because of poor crops, but were ignored by the English absentee landlords, it is an implicit call for reform of "man's inhumanity to man." Swift, in the guise of a public-spirited gentleman, proposes that poor mothers fatten up and sell their year-old children for food:

> I have been assured by a very knowing American [in Swift's opinion, a savage member of a barbarous nation] . . . that a young healthy child well nursed is at a year old a most delicious, nourishing, and wholesome food, whether stewed, roasted, baked, or boiled . . . . [especially] proper for landlords, who, as they have already devoured most of the parents, seem to have the best title to the children.

This proposal, claims Swift, would help to rid the country of its large number of paupers and beggars, and would promote the public good "by advancing of trade, providing for infants, relieving the poor, and giving some pleasure to the rich."

The "proposal," of course, is not modest but monstrous, as is its nominally disinterested narrator. For the author to have really meant people to practice infanticide and cannibalism, especially of their own children, is thoroughly depraved. Swift's ironic, detached tone reinforces the readers' common-sense conclusion that he must have meant the opposite of what he said; their moral outrage should rally them to his cause.

Comic Techniques

Here we'll examine some of the most fundamental and versatile techniques of humorous writing, recognizing that many of these may also be used in serious contexts with very different effects.

Comic Personae

You may want to present your subject from the point of view of a comic persona, a created character who is likely to be a caricature or stock figure in the story he or she is telling. Or you can identify or create an unusual comic character to write about. A common comic persona is *the helpless victim of circumstances*—someone who functions as an incompetent in an otherwise competent world, where everyone else knows what to do and how to do it except this antihero—the klutz, the sap, the fool, the fall guy, the harried housewife, the innocent. Many of Thurber's characters are ineffectual people, such as the browbeaten, henpecked husband and universal wimp who sees "The Unicorn in the Garden" (561–62), but who ultimately has the last laugh on his domineering wife.

Another familiar comic figure is the *neurotic,* a character, like the victim of circumstances, harassed by phenomena he can't afford, but much more distressed and depressed by his failures. Woody Allen portrays in "Selections from the Allen Notebooks" (60–63) the same well-meaning, neurotic, ineffectual, self-conscious character that he portrays in his films, influenced by and dependent on psychoanalysis, which never cures him: "Getting through the night is becoming harder and harder. Last evening, I had the uneasy feeling that some men were trying to break into my room to shampoo me. But why? . . ."

Other comic types include *egotists,* such as the narrator in Ken Wunderlich's "Playing the Sax," who erroneously believes he can "become a virtuoso overnight" through mastery of a single note on the saxophone. And, among others, *morally naive or innocent characters*—children, country bumpkins, or pseudo-innocents, such as the narrator of "A Modest Proposal," allegedly unaware of the comic or moral implications of their behavior or values.

Comic Language

Irony

Verbal ironists say the opposite of what they mean; the music undermines the words, which may involve understatement, overstatement, sarcasm, or the juxtaposition of incongruous images or concepts to comment ironically on one another.

Understatement

By representing the subject as less important or less significant than it really is, you depend on your readers to use their outside knowledge to identify its true meaning and to appreciate the implied contrast between things as they *seem* and things as they *are.* Swift's "proposal" is the antithesis of "modest," despite its humble name. Lillian Ross writes deadpan about the trip of "The Yellow Bus," as does Joan Didion about Las Vegas weddings, yet in each essay the restrained expression and tight stylistic control reinforce the authors' implied criticism and disapproval of their subject.

Overstatement

You can create humor through overstatement by exaggerating your subject's emotions, physical characteristics, behavior, clothing, or manner of speaking. You can complicate simple actions, inflate their cost (in time, money, or effort), or dramatize their negative or positive effects. Your readers can be counted on to measure the extent of the overstatement against the normal or predictable; recognizing the discrepancy between the two will make them laugh. John Leonard says of "My Son, the Roman" (544–46):

> In a month or so, he will be fifteen, which is absurd. . . . He was supposed to stay eight, or maybe twelve. . . . His feet are huge; I have ordered seven-league boots.

By recognizing the literal truth, that Leonard's son is fifteen and has huge feet, readers can also recognize that the rest of these statements are metaphors for Leonard's ambivalent attitude toward his son's maturation—regret and pride.

Overstatement is a common technique of satire. Indeed, Russell Baker's critique of the MX missile system depends on inflated numbers, such as "250 fake Pentagons." *Burlesque,* a type of overstatement characterized by ridiculous exaggeration, distorts the real point in order to call attention to it. Burlesque can elevate a trivial subject, diminish an important subject, dignify the ridiculous, or make the bad worse; there is always a conspicuous, critical discrepancy between subject and style. Frank Sullivan's Cliché Expert (557–61) invariably testifies in a string of clichés: a book being reviewed is "original in conception, devoid of sentimentality, highly informative, consistently witty, and rich in color." Their excess makes them even more ridiculous, if not reprehensible, than a single cliché would have been.

Comic Dialogue and Language

Many humorists play with language, paying attention to the sounds and letting the sense take care of itself. You can re-create or exaggerate the intonation, emphasis, dialect, clichés, and jargon of ordinary or specialized language. Ironists like Ross and Didion let ordinary people speak for themselves; simple quotation calls attention to its banality, as when the underage pregnant Las Vegas bride sobs at her wedding, " 'It was just as nice as I hoped and dreamed it would be.' " In "The Whore of Mensa" (552–56) Woody Allen parodies detective stories through exaggerating the dialect and internal thoughts of a stereotypical, hard-boiled detective:

> "Kaiser?" [the "quivering pat of butter named Word Babcock"] said, "Kaiser Lupowitz?"
> "That's what it says on my license," I owned up.
> "You've got to help me. I'm being blackmailed. Please!"
> He was shaking like the lead singer in a rumba band. I pushed a glass across the desk top and a bottle of rye I keep handy for nonmedicinal purposes. "Suppose you relax and tell me about it."

Humorists also use funny proper names, invented or real ("Bean Blossom, Indiana"), and mottoes and advertising appeals, often as ironic commentaries on the situations to which they pertain, as Didion does with the slogans advertising wedding services in Las Vegas: "Your Wedding on a Phonograph Record, Candlelight with Your Ceremony . . . Free Transportation from Your Motel to Courthouse to Chapel and Return to Motel."

Non Sequitur

You can follow a logical premise with an illogical, unexpected, or ridiculous conclusion. Dorothy Parker's entire book review, "The Grandmother of the Aunt of the Gardener" (562–65), is based on the incongruity between the premise of *Just the French One Wants to Know* and the ridiculously useless phrases the book tries to teach: "I admire the large black eyes of this orphan" and "Obey, or I will not show you the beautiful gold chain."

Humorous writing often combines a number of these purposes and techniques. Try out your humorous writing on one or two typical members of your audience. If they laugh in the right places, you've succeeded; if not, you can fine-tune your work so that even apparently innocuous words, phrases, characters have humorous connotations in context, whether the subject be a sick pig, eating watermelon, Las Vegas weddings, the MX missile, you have but to name it. . . .

Social Criticism

LILLIAN ROSS

The Yellow Bus

Ross begins Reporting *with a statement of her own philosophy as a writer: "Write about people, situations, events that attract you, for whatever reason. You may be attracted to an event that you do not approve of, but you must, for one reason or another, like being there." She has evidently liked being at* The New Yorker, *where she began her career in 1948 at age 21 and has remained ever since, writing profiles, fiction, casual pieces, and longer articles investigating events and phenomena that intrigue her even when they do not please. Her articles, including her controversial "Portrait of Hemingway," are collected in* Reporting *(1964, 1981) and* Reporting Two *(1969), her short stories in* Vertical and Horizontal *(1963), and her "Talk of the Town" pieces in* Talk Stories *(1966).*

    Ross asserts that the writer's focus "at all times should be on your subject, not on you. . . . Do not, in effect, say, 'Look at me. See what a great [writer] I am!' " Indeed, Ross pioneered the New Journalistic approach of writing from an omniscient third-person perspective in which the reporter seems to disappear completely, presenting the story with directness and seeming objectivity. However, Ross is far from objective in "The Yellow Bus." Deadpan, she takes a stock situation of comedy, the yokels come to the big city, and satirizes this Bean Blossom contingent through a detailed depiction of scenes (Arriving in the Big Apple, Eating a First Meal at Hector's Cafeteria), characters ("the valedictorian, a heavyset, firm-mouthed girl"), dialogue (" 'It was there, and it was free, so we did it.' "), costumes ("white beachcomber pants reaching to below the knee . . . white socks . . . and white sneakers"), souvenirs purchased ("a Statue of Liberty thermometer, large-size"). Throughout, Ross regards her subject with ironic amusement, which she expects her readers (even those who like small towns) to share.

I   A few Sundays ago, in the late, still afternoon, a bright-yellow school bus, bearing the white-on-blue license plate of the State of Indiana and with the words "BEAN BLOSSOM TWP MONROE COUNTY" painted in black letters under the windows on each side, emerged into New York City from the Holland Tunnel. Inside the bus were eighteen members of the senior class of the Bean Blossom Township High School, who were coming to the city for their first visit. The windows of the bus, as it rolled out into Canal Street, were open, and a few of the passengers leaned out, deadpan and silent, for a look at Manhattan. The rest sat, deadpan and silent, looking at each other. In all, there were twenty-two people in the bus: eleven girls and seven boys of the senior class; their English teacher and her husband; and the driver (one of the regular bus drivers employed by the township for the school) and his wife. When they arrived, hundreds of thousands of the city's eight million inhabitants were out of town. Those who were here were apparently minding their own business; certainly they were not handing out any big hellos to the visitors. The little Bean Blossom group, soon to be lost in the shuffle of New York's resident and transient summer population, had no idea of how to elicit any hellos—or, for that matter, any goodbyes or how-are-yous. Their plan for visiting New York City was divided into three parts: one, arriving; two, staying two days and three nights; three, departing.

Well, they had arrived. To get here, they had driven eight hundred and 2 forty miles in thirty-nine and a half hours, bringing with them, in addition to spending money of about fifty dollars apiece, a fund of $957.41, which the class had saved up collectively over the past six years. The money represented the profits from such enterprises as candy and ice-cream concessions at school basketball games, amusement booths at the class (junior) carnival, and ticket sales for the class (senior) play, "Mumbo-Jumbo." For six years, the members of the class had talked about how they would spend the money to celebrate their graduation. Early this year, they voted on it. Some of the boys voted for a trip to New Orleans, but they were outvoted by the girls, all of whom wanted the class to visit New York. The class figured that the cost of motels and hotels—three rooms for the boys, three rooms for the girls, one room for each of the couples—would come to about four hundred dollars. The bus driver was to be paid three hundred and fifty dollars for driving and given thirty for road, bridge, and tunnel tolls. Six members of the class, who were unable to participate in the trip, stayed home. If there should be any money left over, it would be divided up among all the class members when the travellers returned to Bean Blossom Township. The names of the eighteen touring class members were: R. Jay Bowman, Sheida Bowman (cousin of R. Jay), Robert Britton, Mary Jane Carter, Lynn Dillon, Ina Hough, Thelma Keller, Wilma Keller (sister of Thelma), Becky Kiser, Jeanne Molnar, Nancy Prather, Mike Richardson, Dennis Smith, Donna Thacker, Albert Warthan, Connie Williams, Larry Williams (not related to Connie), and Lela Young.

It was also a first visit to New York for the English teacher, a lively young 3 lady of twenty-eight named Polly Watts, and for her husband, Thomas, thirty-two, a graduate student in political science at Indiana University, in Bloomington, which is about twelve miles from the Bean Blossom Township school. The only people on the bus who had been to New York before were the driver, a husky uncommunicative man of forty-nine named Ralph Walls, and his wife, Margaret, thirty-nine and the mother of his seven children, aged twenty-one to two, all of whom were left at home. Walls was the only adviser the others had on what to do in New York. His advice consisted of where to stay (the Hotel Woodstock, on West Forty-third Street, near Times Square) and where to eat (Hector's Cafeteria, around the corner from the hotel).

The Bean Blossom Township school is in the village of Stinesville, which 4 has three hundred and fifty-five inhabitants and a town pump. A couple of the seniors who made the trip live in Stinesville; the others live within a radius of fifteen miles or so, on farms or in isolated houses with vegetable gardens and perhaps a cow or two. At the start of the trip, the travellers gathered in front of their school shortly after midnight, and by one in the morning, with every passenger occupying a double seat in the bus (fifty-four-passenger, 1959 model), and with luggage under the seats, and suits and dresses hung on a homemade clothes rack in the back of the bus, they were on their way.

5   The senior-class president, R. (for Reginald) Jay Bowman, was in charge of all the voting on the trip. A wiry, energetic eighteen-year-old with a crew haircut, he had been president of the class for the past five years, and is one of two members of the class who intend to go to college. He wants to work, eventually, for the United States Civil Service, because a job with the government is a steady job. Or, in a very vague way, he thinks he may go into politics. With the help of a hundred-and-two-dollar-a-year scholarship, he plans to pay all his own expenses at Indiana University. The other student who is going to college has also chosen Indiana University. She is Nancy Prather, an outdoorsy, freckle-faced girl whose father raises dairy and beef cattle on a two-hundred-and-fifty-acre farm and who is the class salutatorian. As for the valedictorian, a heavyset, firm-mouthed girl named Connie Williams, she was planning to get married a week after returning home from New York. The other class members expected, for the most part, to get to work at secretarial or clerical jobs, or in automobile or electronic-parts factories in Bloomington. The New York trip was in the nature of a first and last fling.

6   Ralph Walls dropped the passengers and their luggage at the Woodstock and then took the bus to a parking lot on Tenth Avenue, where he was going to leave it for the duration of the visit. His job, he told his passengers, was to drive *to* New York, not *in* it. He had also told them that when he got back to the Woodstock he was going to sleep, but had explained how to get around the corner to Hector's Cafeteria. The boys and girls signed the register and went to their rooms to get cleaned up. They all felt let down. They had asked Walls whether the tall buildings they saw as they came uptown from the Holland Tunnel made up the skyline, and Walls had said he didn't know. Then they had asked him which was the Empire State Building, and he had said they would have to take a tour to find out. Thus put off, they more or less resigned themselves to saving any further questions for a tour. Jay Bowman said that he would see about tours before the following morning.

7   Mrs. Watts and her husband washed up quickly and then, notwithstanding the bus driver's advice, walked around the Times Square area to see if they could find a reasonably priced and attractive place to have supper. They checked Toffenetti's, across the street from the hotel, but they decided that it was too expensive (hamburger dinners at two dollars and ten cents, watermelon at forty cents) and too formidable. When they reconvened with the senior class in the lobby of the Woodstock, they recommended that everybody have his first meal at Hector's. The party set out—for some rea-

son, in Indian file—for Hector's, and the first one inside was Mike Richardson, a husky, red-haired boy with large swollen-looking hands and sunburned forearms. A stern-voiced manager near the door, shouting "Take your check! Take your check!" at all incomers, gave the Indiana group the same sightless once-over he gave everybody else. The Bean Blossom faces, which had been puzzled, fearful, and disheartened since Canal Street, now took on a look of resentment. Mike Richardson led the line to the counter. Under a sign reading "BAKED WHITEFISH," a white-aproned counterman looked at Mike and said, "Come on, fella!" Mike glumly took a plate of fish and then filled the rest of his tray with baked beans, a roll, iced tea, and strawberry shortcake (check—$1.58). The others quickly and shakily filled their trays with fish, baked beans, a roll, iced tea, and strawberry shortcake. Sweating, bumping their trays and their elbows against other trays and other elbows, they found seats in twos and threes with strangers, at tables that still had other people's dirty dishes on them. Then, in a nervous clatter of desperate and noisy eating, they stuffed their food down.

"My ma cooks better than this," said Albert Warthan, who was sitting 8 with Mike Richardson and Larry Williams. Albert, the eldest of seven children of a limestone-quarry worker, plans to join the Army and become a radar technician.

"I took this filet de sole? When I wanted somethin' else, I don't know 9 what?" Mike said.

"I like the kind of place you just set there and decide what you want," 10 said Larry, who is going to work on his grandfather's farm.

"My ma and pa told me to come home when it was time to come home, 11 and not to mess around," Albert said. "I'm ready to chuck it and go home right now."

"The whole idea of it is just to see it and get it over with," Mike said. 12

"You got your money divided up in two places?" Albert asked. "So's 13 you'll have some in one place if it gets stolen in t'other?"

The others nodded. 14

"Man, you can keep this New York," said Larry. "This place is too hustly, 15 with everybody pushin' and no privacy. Man, I'll take the Big Boy any old day."

Frisch's Big Boy is the name of an Indiana drive-in chain, where a ham- 16 burger costs thirty cents. The general effect of Hector's Cafeteria was to give the Bean Blossom Class of 1960 a feeling of unhappiness about eating in New York and to strengthen its faith in the superiority of the Big Boys back home.

Jay Bowman went from table to table, polling his classmates on what 17 they wanted to do that evening. At first, nobody wanted to do anything special. Then they decided that the only special thing they wanted to do was go to Coney Island, but they wanted to save Coney Island for the wind-up night, their last night in New York. However, nobody could think of anything to do that first night, so Jay took a re-vote, and it turned out that almost all of them wanted to go to Coney Island right away. Everybody but three girls voted to go to Coney Island straight from Hector's. Mrs. Watts was mildly apprehensive about this project, but Mike Richardson assured her it was easy; somebody at the hotel had told him that all they had to do was go to the subway and ask the cashier in the booth which train to take, and that would be that. Mrs. Watts said she was going to walk around a bit with her husband. The three girls who didn't want to go to Coney Island explained that they firmly believed the class should "have fun" on its last night in the city, and not before. The three were Ina Hough, whose father works in an R.C.A.-television manufacturing plant in Indianapolis (about fifty miles from Stinesville); Lela Young, whose foster father works in a Chevrolet-parts warehouse in Indianapolis; and Jeanne Molnar, whose father is a draftsman at the Indiana Limestone Company, in Bloomington. All three already knew that they disliked New York. People in New York, they said, were all for themselves.

18   At nine o'clock, while most of their classmates were on the Brighton B.M.T. express bound for Coney Island, the three girls walked to Sixth Avenue and Fiftieth Street with Mr. and Mrs. Watts, who left them at that point to take a walk along Fifth Avenue. The girls stood in a long line of people waiting to get into the Radio City Music Hall. After twenty minutes, they got out of the line and walked over to Rockefeller Plaza, where they admired the fountain, and to St. Patrick's Cathedral, which looked bigger to them than any church they had ever seen. The main church attended by the Bean Blossom group is the Nazarene Church. No one in the senior class had ever talked to a Jew or to more than one Catholic, or—with the exception of Mary Jane Carter, daughter of the Nazarene minister in Stinesville—had ever heard of an Episcopalian. At ten o'clock, the three girls returned to the Music Hall line, which had dwindled, but when they got to the box office they were told that they had missed the stage show, so they decided to skip the Music Hall and take a subway ride. They took an Independent subway train to the West Fourth Street station, which a subway guard told them was where to go for Greenwich Village. They decided against getting out and looking, and in favor of going uptown on the same fare and returning to their hotel. Back at the Woodstock, where they shared a room, they locked themselves in and started putting up their hair, telling each other that everybody in New York was rude and all for himself.

19   At Coney Island, the Indiana travellers talked about how they could not get over the experience of riding for forty-five minutes, in a shaking, noisy train, to get there.

20   "The long ride was a shock to what I expected," said Albert Warthan.

21   Nancy Prather said she didn't like the looks of the subway or the people on it. "You see so many different people," she said, "Dark-complected ones one minute, light-complected ones the next."

"I hate New York, actually," Connie Williams said. "I'm satisfied with what we got back home." 22

"Back home, you can do anything you please in your own backyard any time you feel like it, like hootin' and hollerin' or anything," said Larry Williams. "You don't ever get to feel all cooped up." 23

"I sort of like it here in Coney Island," said Dennis Smith. "I don't feel cooped up." 24

Dennis's buddies looked at him without saying anything. His "sort of liking" Coney Island was the first sign of defection from Indiana, and the others did not seem to know what to make of it. Dennis is a broad-shouldered boy with large, beautiful, wistful blue eyes and a gold front tooth. 25

"I hate it," Connie said. 26

Jay Bowman organized as many of the group as he could to take a couple of rides on the Cyclone. Most of the boys followed these up with a ride on the parachute jump, and then complained that it wasn't what they had expected at all. Some of the boys and girls went into the Spookerama. They all rode the bobsled, and to top the evening off they rode the bumper cars. "The Spookerama was too imitation to be frightening," Albert said. Before leaving Coney Island, Jay got to work among his classmates, polling them on how much money they were prepared to spend on a tour of the city the next day. They stayed in Coney Island about an hour. Nobody went up to the boardwalk to take a look at the ocean, which none of the class had ever seen. They didn't feel that they had to look at the ocean. "We knew the ocean was there, and anyway we aim to see the ocean on the tour tomorrow," Jay said later. 27

When Ina, Lela, and Jeanne got in line for the Music Hall, the Wattses took their stroll along Fifth Avenue and then joined a couple of friends, Mike and Ardis Cavin. Mike Cavin plays clarinet with the United States Navy Band, in Washington, D.C., and is studying clarinet—as a commuter—at the Juilliard School of Music. At Madison Avenue and Forty-second Street, the two couples boarded a bus heading downtown, and while talking about where to get off they were taken in hand by an elderly gentleman sitting near them, who got off the bus when they did and walked two blocks with them, escorting them to their destination—the Jazz Gallery, on St. Mark's Place. Mike Cavin wanted to hear the tenor-saxophone player John Coltrane. The Wattses stayed at the Jazz Gallery with the Cavins for three hours, listening, with patient interest, to modern jazz. They decided that they liked modern jazz, and especially Coltrane. Leaving the Jazz Gallery after one o'clock, the two couples took buses to Times Square, walked around for twenty minutes looking for a place where they could get a snack, and finally, because every other place seemed to be closed, went to Toffenetti's. Back at the hotel, the Wattses ran into one of the Coney Island adventurers, who told them that Ina, Lela, and Jeanne were missing, or at least were not answering their telephone or knocks on their door. Mr. Watts got the room clerk, unlocked the girls' door, and found them sitting on their beds, still putting up their 28 hair. Everybody was, more or less unaccountably, angry—the three girls who hadn't gone to Coney Island, the girls who had, the boys who had, the Wattses, and the room clerk. The Wattses got to bed at 3:30 a.m.

29   At 6:30 a.m., Mrs. Watts was called on the telephone. Message: One of the anti-Coney Island trio was lying on the floor of the room weeping and hysterical. Mrs. Watts called the room clerk, who called a doctor practicing in the Times Square area, who rushed over to the hotel, talked with the weeping girl for twenty minutes, and left her with a tranquillizing pill, which she refused to take.

30   By the time everybody had settled down enough to eat breakfast in drugstores and get ready to start out, it was after nine in the morning, half an hour behind time for the scheduled (by unanimous vote) all-day tour of the city by chartered sightseeing bus, at six dollars per person. The tour was held up further while Mrs. Watts persuaded the weeper to take a shower, in an effort to encourage her to join the tour. After the shower, the unhappy girl stopped crying and declared that she would go along. By the time the group reached the Bowery, she felt fine, and in Chinatown, like the other boys and girls, she bought a pair of chopsticks, for thirty-five cents. The Cathedral of St. John the Divine was the highlight of the tour for many of the students, who were delighted to hear that some of the limestone used in the cathedral interior had very likely come from quarries near Stinesville. Mrs. Watts, on the other hand, who had studied art, had taught art for five years at Huntington College, in Huntington, Indiana, and had taken an accredited art tour of Europe before her marriage, indignantly considered the cathedral "an imitation of European marvels."

31   Mrs. Watts took the Bean Blossom teaching job, at thirty-six hundred dollars a year, last fall, when her husband decided to abandon a concrete-building-block business in Huntington in order to study for a Ph.D. in political science, a subject he wants to teach. Since he had decided that Indiana University was the place to do this, they moved from Huntington—where Mr. Watts had won the distinction of being the youngest man ever to hold the job of chairman of the Republican Party of Huntington County—to Bloomington. Mrs. Watts drives the twelve miles from Bloomington to Stinesville every day. She teaches English to the tenth, eleventh, and twelfth grades, and, because the school had no Spanish teacher when she signed up for the job, she teaches Spanish, too. She considers the Bean Blossom Township school the most democratic school she has ever seen. "They vote on everything," she says. "We have an average of two votes on something or other every day." Having thus been conditioned to voting as a way of life, Mrs. Watts left the voting on day-to-day plans for the group visit in the capable hands of Jay Bowman. He solved the problem of the tour's late start that morning by taking a vote on whether or not to leave out the Empire State Building. It was promptly voted out of the tour, and voted in for some later time as a separate undertaking.

The tour included a boat trip to the Statue of Liberty, where the group 32
fell in with crushing mobs of people walking to the top of the torch. Mrs.
Watts found the experience nightmarish, and quit at the base of the torch.
Most of the boys and girls made it to the top. "There are a hundred and sixty-
eight steps up the torch, and there were forty thousand people ahead of me,
but I was determined to climb up it," Jay Bowman reported to Mrs. Watts.
"It took me twenty minutes, and it was worthwhile. The thing of it was I had
to do it."

For the tour, Jay, like the other boys, had put on dress-up clothes bought 33
specially, at a cost of about twenty-five dollars an outfit, for the trip to New
York—white beachcomber pants reaching to below the knee, white cotton-
knit shirt with red and blue stripes and a pocket in one sleeve, white socks
with red and blue stripes, and white sneakers. The girls wore cotton skirts,
various kinds of blouses, white cardigan sweaters, and low-heeled shoes. Mrs.
Watts wore high-heeled pumps, even for sightseeing. Everyone else on the
tour was astonished at the way New York City people dressed. "They look
peculiar," Nancy Prather said. "Girls wearing high heels in the daytime, and
the boys here always got a regular suit on, even to go to work in."

"I wouldn't trade the girls back home for any of the girls here," Jay 34
Bowman says. "New York girls wear too much makeup. Not that my interests are centered on Nancy Glidden. She's in the junior class. I take her to
shows in Bloomington. We eat pizzas, listen to Elvis Presley—things of that
nature—and I always get her home by twelve. Even though my interests are
centered on the junior class, I'm proud to say my classmates are the finest
bunch of people in the world."

Jay lives with his parents and two brothers in an old nine-room house on 35
thirty acres of land owned by Jay's father, who works in the maintenance
department of the Bridgeport Brass Company, in Indianapolis. His mother
works in Bloomington, on the R.C.A. color-television-set assembly line. Jay's
grandfather, who has worked in limestone quarries all his life, lives across the
road, on five acres of his own land, where he has a couple of cows and raises
beans and corn for the use of the family. The Bowman family had no plumbing in their house while Jay was a child, and took baths in a tub in the kitchen
with water from a well, but a few years ago, with their own hands, they
installed a bathroom and a plumbing system, and did other work on the
house, including putting in a furnace. Jay's parents get up at four in the
morning to go to work. Jay, who hasn't been sick one day since he had
the mumps at the age of twelve, never sleeps later than seven. He is not in the
least distressed at having to work his way through college. He plans to get to
school in his own car. This is a 1950 Chevrolet four-door sedan, which he
hopes to trade in, by paying an additional four hundred dollars, for a slightly
younger model before the end of the year.

"The thing of it is I feel proud of myself," Jay says. "Not to be braggin' or 36
anything. But I saved up better than a thousand dollars to send myself to

college. That's the way it is. I scrubbed floors, put up hay, carried groceries, and this last winter I worked Saturdays and Sundays in a country store on the state highway and got paid a dollar an hour for runnin' it."

37   The Bowman family has, in addition to a kind of basic economic ambition, two main interests—basketball and politics. Jay, like most of the other boys on the trip, played basketball on the school basketball team, which won the first round in its section of the Wabash Valley tournament last season. Jay talks about basketball to his classmates, but never about politics. Talk about the latter he saves for his family. His grandfather is a Democrat. "If it was up to my grandpa, he'd never want a single Republican in the whole country," he says. "And my Dad agrees with him. I agree with my Dad. My Dad thinks if Franklin D. Roosevelt was still President, this country wouldn't be in the trouble it finds itself in."

38   At 5 p.m. of this second day in the City of New York, the members of the Bean Blossom senior class returned to their hotel and stood in the lobby for a while, looking from some distance at a souvenir-and-gift stand across from the registration desk. The stand was stocked with thermometers in the form of the Statue of Liberty, in two sizes, priced at seventy-nine cents and ninety-eight cents; with silver-plated charm bracelets; with pins and compacts carrying representations of the Empire State Building; with scarves showing the R.C.A. Building and the U.N. Building; and with ashtrays showing the New York City skyline. Mike Richardson edged over to the stand and picked up a wooden plaque, costing ninety-eight cents, with the Statue of Liberty shown at the top, American flags at the sides, and, in the middle, a poem, inscribed "Mother" which read:

> To one who bears the sweetest name
> And adds a luster to the same
> Who shares my joys
> Who cheers when sad
> The greatest friend I ever had
> Long life to her, for there's no other
> Can take the place of my dear mother.

39   After reading the poem, Mike smiled.

40   "Where you from?" the man behind the stand asked him.

41   "Indiana," Mike said, looking as though he were warming up. "We've been on this tour? The whole day?"

42   "Ya see everything?" the man asked.

43   "Everything except the Empire State Building," said Mike.

44   "Yeah," said the man, and looked away.

45   Mike was still holding the plaque. Carefully, he replaced it on the stand. "I'll come back for this later," he said.

46   Without looking at Mike, the man nodded.

47   Mike joined Dennis Smith and Larry Williams, who were standing with

a tall, big-boned handsome girl named Becky Kiser. Becky used to be a cheerleader for the Bean Blossom Township basketball team.

"We was talkin' about the way this place has people layin' in the streets on that Bowery sleepin'," Larry said. "You don't see people layin' in the streets back home."

48

"I seen that in Chicago," Dennis said. "I seen *women* layin' in the streets in Chicago. That's worse."

49

The others nodded. No argument.

50

Mike took a cigarette from his sleeve pocket and lit it with a match from the same pocket. He blew out a stream of smoke with strength and confidence. "I'll be glad when we light out of here," he said. "Nothin' here feels like the farm."

51

Becky Kiser, with an expression of terrible guilt on her attractive, wide-mouthed face, said, "I bet you'd never get bored here in New York. Back home, it's the same thing all the time. You go to the skating rink. You go to the Big Boy. In the winter, there's basketball. And that's all."

52

"When I was in Chicago, I seen a man who shot a man in a bar," Dennis said. "I stood right across the street while the man who was shot the people drug him out." He looked at Becky Kiser. The other boys were also looking at her, but with condemnation and contempt. Dennis gave Becky support. "In Stinesville, they see you on the streets after eleven, they run you home," he said. "Seems like here the city never closes."

53

"Man, you're just not lookin' ahead," Mike said to Dennis, ignoring Becky.

54

"You like it here?" Larry asked, in amazement. "Taxes on candy and on everything?"

55

The Nazarene minister's daughter, Mary Jane Carter, came over with Ina Hough.

56

"Dennis, here, likes New York," Mike announced.

57

"I don't," said Ina. "I like the sights, but I think they're almost ruined by the people."

58

"The food here is expensive, but I guess that's life," said Mary Jane, in a mood of forbearance.

59

"Oh, man!" said Mike.

60

"Oh, man!" said Larry. "Cooped up in New York."

61

Ina said stiffly, "Like the guide said today, you could always tell a New Yorker from a tourist because a New Yorker never smiles, and I agree with him."

62

"After a while, you'd kinda fit in," Dennis said mildly.

63

Before dinner that night, Mr. Watts walked through the Times Square area checking prices and menus at likely restaurants. He made tentative arrangements at The Californian for a five-course steak or chicken dinner, to cost $1.95 per person, and asked Jay Bowman to go around taking a vote on the proposition. Half an hour later, Jay reported to Mr. Watts that some of

64

the boys didn't want to go to The Californian, because they thought they'd have to do their own ordering. So Mr. Watts talked to the boys in their rooms and explained that the ordering was taken care of; all they had to say was whether they wanted steak or chicken. On the next ballot, everybody was in favor of The Californian. The class walked over. When the fifth course was finished, it was agreed that the dinner was all right, but several of the boys said they thought the restaurant was too high-class.

65   After dinner, it started to rain, and it rained hard. The Wattses and seven of the girls decided that they wanted to see "The Music Man." The four other girls wanted to see "My Fair Lady." None of the boys wanted to see a musical show. In the driving rain, the Wattses and the girls ran to the theatres of their choice, all arriving soaked to the skin. By good luck, each group was able to buy seats. At "The Music Man," the Wattses and the seven girls with them sat in the balcony, in the direct path of an air-conditioning unit [that] blew icy blasts at their legs. The girls liked their shows. The "My Fair Lady" group was transported by the costumes. Ina Hough, who went to "The Music Man," thought that it was just like a movie, except for the way the scenes changed.

66   The boys split up, some of them taking the subway down to Greenwich Village, the others heading for the Empire State Building, where they paid a dollar-thirty for tickets to the observatory and, once up there, found that the fog and rain blotted out the view completely. "We stood there about an hour and a half messin' around, me and my buddies," Jay later told Mrs. Watts. "Wasn't no sense in leavin' at that price." In Greenwich Village, Mike Richardson, Dennis Smith, and Larry Williams walked along the narrow streets in a drizzling rain. All were still wearing their beachcomber outfits. Nobody talked to them. They didn't see anybody they wanted to talk to. They almost went into a small coffeehouse; they changed their minds because the prices looked too high. They went into one shop, a bookstore, and looked at some abstract paintings, which appealed to them. "Sort of inter-estin', the way they don't look like nothin'," Mike said. Then they took the subway back to Times Square, where they walked around for a while in the rain. Toward midnight, Mike and Dennis told each other they were lonesome for the smell of grass and trees, and, the rain having stopped, they walked up to Central Park, where they stayed for about an hour and got lost.

67   The next morning, a meeting of the class was held in the hotel lobby to take a vote on when to leave New York. Jay Bowman reported that they had enough money to cover an extra day in the city, plus a side trip to Niagara Falls on the way home. Or, he said, they could leave New York when they had originally planned to and go to Washington, D. C., for a day before heading home. The bus driver had told Jay that it was all one to him which they chose. The class voted for the extra day in New York and Niagara Falls.

68   "I'm glad," Becky Kiser said, with a large, friendly smile, to Dennis Smith. Several of her classmates overheard her and regarded her with a

uniformly deadpan look. "I like it here," she went on. "I'd like to live here. There's so much to see. There's so much to do."

Her classmates continued to study her impassively until Dennis took   69
their eyes away from her by saying, "You get a feelin' here of goin' wherever you want to. Seems the city never closes. I'd like to live here, I believe. People from everyplace are here."

"Limousines all over the joint," Albert Warthan said.   70

"Seems like you can walk and walk and walk," Dennis went on dreamily.   71
"I like the way the big buildin's crowd you in. You want to walk and walk and never go to sleep."

"I hate it," Connie Williams said, with passion.   72

"Oh, man, you're just not lookin' ahead," Mike Richardson said to Den-   73
nis. "You got a romantic notion. You're not realistic about it."

"This place couldn't hold me," Larry Williams said. "I like the privacy of   74
the farm."

"I want to go to new places," said Becky, who had started it. "I want to   75
go to Europe."

"Only place I want to go is Texas," Larry said. "I got folks in Texas."   76

"There's no place like home," Mike said. "Home's good enough for me."   77

"I believe the reason of this is we've lived all of our lives around Stines-   78
ville," Dennis said. "If you took Stinesville out of the country, you wouldn't be hurt. But if you took New York out of the country, you'd be hurt. The way the guide said, all our clothes and everything comes from New York."

Becky said, "In Coney Island, I saw the most handsome man I ever saw   79
in my whole life. I think he was a Puerto Rican or something, too."

Albert said, "When we get back, my pa will say, 'Well, how was it!' I'll   80
say, 'It was fine.' "

"I'd like to come back, maybe stay a month," Jay Bowman said diplomat-   81
ically. "One thing I'd like to do is come here when I can see a major-league baseball game."

"I'd like to see a major-league baseball game, but I wouldn't come back   82
just to see it," Mike said.

"I hate New York," Connie said.   83

"Back home, everybody says 'Excuse me,' " Nancy Prather said.   84

"I like it here," Dennis said stubbornly.   85

This day was an open one, leaving the boys and girls free to do anything   86
they liked, without prearranged plan or vote. Mike passed close by the souvenir-and-gift stand in the hotel lobby, and the proprietor urged him to take home the Statue of Liberty.

"I'd like to, but it won't fit in my suitcase," Mike said, with a loud laugh.   87

A group formed to visit the zoo in Central Park, got on the subway, had   88
a loud discussion about where to get off, and were taken in hand by a stranger, who told them the zoo was in the Bronx. Only the boy named Lynn Dillon listened to the stranger. The others went to the zoo in Central Park.

Lynn stayed on the subway till it reached the Bronx, and spent the entire day in the Bronx Zoo by himself. The rest of the zoo visitors, walking north after lunch in the cafeteria, ran into the Metropolitan Museum of Art and went in. "It was there, and it was free, so we did it," Nancy Prather said. "There were these suits of armor and stuff. Nothin' I go for myself."

89   That morning, the Wattses had tried to get some of the boys and girls to accompany them to the Guggenheim Museum or the Museum of Modern Art, but nobody had wanted to pay the price of admission. "Why pay fifty cents to see a museum when they got them free?" the class president asked. Mrs. Watts reported afterward that the Guggenheim was the most exciting museum she had ever seen, including all the museums she had seen in Europe on her accredited art tour. "There aren't big crowds in there, for one thing," she said. "And I don't think the building overpowers the paintings at all, as I've heard." From the Guggenheim, the Wattses went to Georg Jensen's to look at silver, but didn't buy anything. Then they went to the Museum of Modern Art and had lunch in the garden. "Lovely lunch, fabulous garden, fabulous sculpture, but I'm disappointed in the museum itself," Mrs. Watts said. "Everything jammed into that small space! Impossible to get a good view of Picasso's 'Girl Before a Mirror.' "

90   By dinnertime, more than half of the Bean Blossomers had, to their relief, discovered the Automat. Jay Bowman had a dinner consisting of a ham sandwich (forty cents), a glass of milk (ten cents), and a dish of fresh straw-berries (twenty cents). Then, with a couple of buddies, he bought some peanuts in their shells and some Cokes, and took them up to his room for the three of them to consume while talking about what to do that night. They decided, because they had not yet had a good view of the city from the Empire State observatory, that they would go back there. They were accompanied by most of the girls and the other boys, and this time the group got a cut rate of sixty-five cents apiece. Dennis went off wandering by himself. He walked up Fifth Avenue to Eighty-fifth Street, over to Park Avenue, down Park to Seventy-second Street, across to the West Side, down Central Park West to Sixty-sixth Street, over behind the Tavern-on-the-Green (where he watched people eating outdoors), and on down Seventh Avenue to Times Square, where he stood around on corners looking at the people who bought papers at newsstands.

91   The Wattses had arranged to meet anybody who was interested under the Washington Arch at around nine-thirty for an evening in Greenwich Village. The boys had decided to take a walk up Broadway after leaving the Empire State Building, but the girls all showed up in Washington Square, along with two soldiers and three sailors they had met in the U.S.O. across the street from the Woodstock. The Wattses led the way to a coffeehouse, where everybody had coffee or lemonade. Then the girls and the service men left the Wattses, saying they were going to take a ride on the ferry to Staten Island. The Wattses went to the Five Spot, which their jazz friend had told them had good music.

After breakfast the following morning, the bus driver, Ralph Walls,   92
showed up in the hotel lobby for the first time since the group's arrival in
New York and told Jay Bowman to have everyone assembled at five-forty-five
the following morning for departure at six o'clock on the dot. The driver said
that he was spending most of his time sleeping, and that before they left he
was going to do some more sleeping. He had taken his wife on a boat trip
around Manhattan, though, he said, and he had taken a few walks on the
streets. After reminding Jay again about the exact time planned for the departure, he went back upstairs to his room.

Mrs. Watts took nine of the girls (two stayed in the hotel to sleep) for a   93
walk through Saks Fifth Avenue, just looking. Mr. Watts took three of the
boys to Abercrombie & Fitch, just looking. Everybody walked every aisle on
every floor in each store, looking at everything on the counters and in the
showcases. Nobody bought anything. The two groups met at noon under the
clock in Grand Central; lunched at an Automat; walked over to the United
Nations Building, where they decided not to take the regular tour, and took a
crosstown bus to the Hudson River and went aboard the liner S.S. Independence, where they visited every deck and every lounge on the boat, and a
good many of the staterooms. Then they took the bus back to Times Square
and scattered to do some shopping.

Mike Richardson bought all his gifts—eleven dollars' worth—at the   94
hotel stand, taking not only the plaque for his mother but a set of salt and
pepper shakers, with the Statue of Liberty on the salt and the Empire State
Building on the pepper, also for his mother; a Statue of Liberty ashtray for
his father; a George Washington Bridge teapot for his sister-in-law; a mechanical dog for his niece; a City Hall teapot-cup-and-saucer set for his
grandparents; and a cigarette lighter stamped with the Great White Way for
himself. At Macy's, Becky Kiser bought a dress, a blouse, and an ankle chain
for herself, and a necklace with matching bracelet and earrings for her
mother, a cuff-link-and-tie-clasp set for her father, and a bracelet for her
younger sister. Albert Wall then bought a miniature camera for himself and a
telephone-pad-and-pencil set stamped with the George Washington Bridge
and a Statue of Liberty thermometer, large-size, as general family gifts, at the
hotel stand. Jay Bowman bought an unset cultured pearl at Macy's for his girl
friend in the junior class, as well as silver-looking earrings for his married
sister and for his mother, and at a store called King of Slims, around the
corner from the hotel, he bought four ties—a red toreador tie (very narrow)
for his older brother, a black toreador tie for his younger brother, a conservative silk foulard for his father, and a white toreador tie for himself. Dennis
Smith bought a Statue of Liberty ashtray for his mother and a Statue of
Liberty cigarette lighter for his father. Connie Williams bought two bracelets
and a Statue of Liberty pen for herself. The bus driver and his wife spent sixty
dollars on clothes for their children, six of whom are girls. Nancy Prather
didn't buy anything. The Wattses spent about a hundred dollars in the course
of the visit, most of it on meals and entertainment.

95　　On their last evening in New York, all the boys and girls, accompanied by the Wattses, went to the Radio City Music Hall, making it in time to see the stage show. Then they packed and went to bed. The bus driver, after an early dinner with his wife at Hector's Cafeteria, brought the yellow school bus over from Tenth Avenue and parked it right in front of the hotel, so that it would be there for the early start.

96　　Next morning at five-forty-five,, the Bean Blossomers assembled in the lobby; for the first time since the trip had started, nobody was late. The bus pulled out at exactly 6 a.m., and twenty minutes after that, heading west over the George Washington Bridge, it disappeared from the city.

Questions

1. Ross uses a stock comedic situation—the yokels come to the big city—and satirizes this Bean Blossom Township High School group of twenty-two, come from the village of "three hundred and fifty-five inhabitants and a town pump" (paragraph 4) for the senior class trip to New York City in 1960. Why would readers of *The New Yorker*, where this essay was first published, find it humorous? In your answer, consider not only the basic situation, but the characters, their actions (including their innumerable votes on how to do things, where they go, what they do, how they spend their money), their reactions to their experiences, and other memorable features.

2. Why does Ross provide so many details, minute as well as large, in her account? Does the accumulation of such details intensify or diminish the humor? Explain.

3. One of Ross's principal comic techniques is her continually ironic perspective, as if she is culturally and intellectually superior to her subject and can measure the Bean Blossomites' naiveté against her superior knowledge. Find some examples of this. Do you find her irony humorous? Why or why not (and to what extent does your response depend on whether or not you like small town living)?

4. Why does Ross quote such unmemorable dialogue so extensively? Through what techniques does she re-create the sounds and cadence of oral speech?

JOAN DIDION

Marrying Absurd

Didion uses the word absurd *in the title of this essay to connote the discrepancy between our exalted expectations of marriage and the reality of this experience in Las Vegas, where "marriage, like craps, is a game to be played when the table seems hot." She continually reminds us of the ironic disparity between a wedding as a solemn symbolization of a lifelong commitment and the speedy, slick commercial package offered in the Strip "wedding chapels." Yet that kind of incongruity can be just plain funny, as well. Didion illustrates both senses of "absurd" in "late-night liaisons between show girls and baby Crosbys" and in the oddly formal weddings of innocents who confuse the accessories (formal clothes and pink champagne) with the essence of a personally significant ceremony.*

In social commentary of this type, the critic expects her audience to ally with her, sharing values in critical opposition to those of the subject.

To be married in Las Vegas, Clark County, Nevada, a bride must swear that 1 she is eighteen or has parental permission and a bridegroom that he is twenty-one or has parental permission. Someone must put up five dollars for the license. (On Sundays and holidays, fifteen dollars. The Clark County Courthouse issues marriage licenses at any time of the day or night except between noon and one in the afternoon, between eight and nine in the evening, and between four and five in the morning.) Nothing else is required. The State of Nevada, alone among these United States, demands neither a premarital blood test nor a waiting period before or after the issuance of a marriage license. Driving in across the Mojave from Los Angeles, one sees the signs way out on the desert, looming up from that moonscape of rattlesnakes and mesquite, even before the Las Vegas lights appear like a mirage on the horizon: "GETTING MARRIED? Free License Information First Strip Exit." Perhaps the Las Vegas wedding industry achieved its peak operational efficiency between 9:00 p.m. and midnight of August 26, 1965, an otherwise unremarkable Thursday which happened to be, by Presidential order, the last day on which anyone could improve his draft status merely by getting married. One hundred and seventy-one couples were pronounced man and wife in the name of Clark County and the State of Nevada that night, sixty-seven of them by a single justice of the peace, Mr. James A. Brennan. Mr. Brennan did one wedding at the Dunes and the other sixty-six in his office, and charged each couple eight dollars. One bride lent her veil to six others. "I got it down from five to three minutes," Mr. Brennan said later of his feat. "I could've married them *en masse,* but they're people, not cattle. People expect more when they get married."

What people who get married in Las Vegas actually do expect—what, in 2 the largest sense, their "expectations" are—strikes one as a curious and self-contradictory business. Las Vegas is the most extreme and allegorical of American settlements, bizarre and beautiful in its venality and in its devotion to immediate gratification, a place the tone of which is set by mobsters and call girls and ladies' room attendants with amyl nitrite poppers in their uniform pockets. Almost everyone notes that there is no "time" in Las Vegas, no night and no day and no past and no future (no Las Vegas casino, however, has taken the obliteration of the ordinary time sense quite so far as Harold's Club in Reno, which for a while issued, at odd intervals in the day and night, mimeographed "bulletins" carrying news from the world outside); neither is there any logical sense of where one is. One is standing on a highway in the middle of a vast hostile desert looking at an eighty-foot sign which blinks

"STARDUST" or "CAESAR'S PALACE." Yes, but what does that explain? This geographical implausibility reinforces the sense that what happens there has no connection with "real" life; Nevada cities like Reno and Carson are ranch towns, Western towns, places behind which there is some historical imperative. But Las Vegas seems to exist only in the eye of the beholder. All of which makes it an extraordinarily stimulating and interesting place, but an odd one in which to want to wear a candlelight satin Priscilla of Boston wedding dress with Chantilly lace insets, tapered sleeves and a detachable modified train.

3   And yet the Las Vegas wedding business seems to appeal to precisely that impulse. "Sincere and Dignified Since 1954," one wedding chapel advertises. There are nineteen such wedding chapels in Las Vegas, intensely competitive, each offering better, faster, and, by implication, more sincere services than the next: Our Photos Best Anywhere, Your Wedding on A Phonograph Record, Candlelight with Your Ceremony, Honeymoon Accommodations, Free Transportation from Your Motel to Courthouse to Chapel and Return to Motel, Religious or Civil Ceremonies, Dressing Rooms, Flowers, Rings, Announcements, Witnesses Available, and Ample Parking. All of these services, like most others in Las Vegas (sauna baths, payroll-check cashing, chinchilla coats for sale or rent) are offered twenty-four hours a day, seven days a week, presumably on the premise that marriage, like craps, is a game to be played when the table seems hot.

4   But what strikes one most about the Strip chapels, with their wishing wells and stained-glass paper windows and their artificial bouvardia, is that so much of their business is by no means a matter of simple convenience, of late-night liaisons between show girls and baby Crosbys. Of course there is some of that. (One night about eleven o'clock in Las Vegas I watched a bride in an orange minidress and masses of flame-colored hair stumble from a Strip chapel on the arm of her bridegroom, who looked the part of the expendable nephew in movies like *Miami Syndicate*. "I gotta get the kids," the bride whimpered. "I gotta pick up the sitter, I gotta get to the midnight show." "What you gotta get," the bridegroom said, opening the door of a Cadillac Coupe de Ville and watching her crumple on the seat, "is sober.") But Las Vegas seems to offer something other than "convenience"; it is merchandising "niceness," the facsimile of proper ritual, to children who do not know how else to find it, how to make the arrangements, how to do it "right." All day and evening long on the Strip, one sees actual wedding parties, waiting under the harsh lights at a crosswalk, standing uneasily in the parking lot of the Frontier while the photographer hired by The Little Church of the West ("Wedding Place of the Stars") certifies the occasion, takes the picture: the bride in a veil and white satin pumps, the bridegroom usually in a white dinner jacket, and even an attendant or two, a sister or a best friend in hot-pink *peau de soie*, a flirtation veil, a carnation nosegay. "When I Fall in Love It Will Be Forever," the organist plays, and then a few bars of Lohengrin. The

mother cries; the stepfather, awkward in his role, invites the chapel hostess to join them for a drink at the Sands. The hostess declines with a professional smile; she has already transferred her interest to the group waiting outside. One bride out, another in, and again the sign goes up on the chapel door: "One moment please—Wedding."

I sat next to one such wedding party in a Strip restaurant the last time I   5
was in Las Vegas. The marriage had just taken place; the bride still wore her dress, the mother her corsage. A bored waiter poured out a few swallows of pink champagne ("on the house") for everyone but the bride, who was too young to be served. "You'll need something with more kick than that," the bride's father said with heavy jocularity to his new son-in-law; the ritual jokes about the wedding night had a certain Panglossian character, since the bride was clearly several months pregnant. Another round of pink champagne, this time not on the house, and the bride began to cry. "It was just as nice," she sobbed, "as I hoped and dreamed it would be."

Questions

1. Comment on the significance of the title "Marrying Absurd." Show how Didion's consistently ironic tone and point of view, use of settings (including the desert, restrooms, casinos, and Strip), and dialogue reveal her disapproval of the Las Vegas assumption that "marriage, like craps, is a game to be played when the table seems hot" (paragraph 3).

2. What are the conventional connotations of weddings? Can Didion count on most readers to share these? How do these differ from the "absurd" weddings performed by Las Vegas justice of the peace James A. Brennan "between 9:00 p.m. and midnight of August 26, 1965" (paragraph 1), and those performed in the Las Vegas Strip chapels?

3. What does the juxtaposition of the "moonscape of rattlesnakes and mesquite" with the "Getting Married?" signs (paragraph 1) indicate about the relation of the environment to a major activity performed there? Can you find other instances of comparable incongruities? Why has Didion included so many advertising and business slogans, even stringing them together to comprise much of paragraph 3?

4. In the last two paragraphs Didion provides three vignettes, like snapshots, of weddings: the drunken showgirl bride in the "orange minidress and masses of flame-colored hair" and her "expendable nephew" bridegroom; "actual wedding parties, waiting under the harsh lights at a crosswalk"; and the wedding group in the restaurant where the pregnant, underage bride sobs with pleasure at the "niceness" of her wedding. What does Didion intend to convey through each of these illustrations, arranged in that particular order?

JONATHAN SWIFT

A Modest Proposal

Swift, author of Gulliver's Travels *(1726) and other satiric essays, poems, and tracts, was well acquainted with irony. Born in Dublin in 1667, the son of impoverished English Anglicans, he obtained a degree from Trinity College, Dublin, in 1685 only by "special grace." Swift, along with many Anglo-Irish, sought fame and fortune in England, was eventually ordained as an Anglican priest, and rose prominently in London literary and political circles until 1713. Although he had hoped for a church appointment in England, his desertion of the Whig Party for the Tories was ironically rewarded with an appointment as Dean of St. Patrick's (Anglican) Cathedral in Dublin, which he regarded as virtual exile. Nevertheless, despite his religious differences with the Irish people, Swift became a beloved leader in the Irish resistance to English oppression, motivated less by partisan emotions than by his own "savage indignation" against injustice. He died in Dublin in 1745.*

Swift wrote "A Modest Proposal" in the summer of 1729, after three years of drought and crop failure had forced over 35,000 peasants to leave their homes and wander the countryside looking for work, food, and shelter for their starving families, ignored by the insensitive absentee landowners. This "proposal" carries the English landowners' treatment of the Irish to its logical but repugnant extreme; if they are going to devour any hope the Irish have of living decently, why don't they literally eat the Irish children? The persona Swift creates is logical, consistent, seemingly rational, and utterly inhumane—an advocate of infanticide and cannibalism. Yet nowhere does the satirist condemn the speaker; he relies on the reader's sense of morality for that. This tactic can be dangerous, for a reader who misses the irony may take the Proposal at face value. But for most readers Swift's satire makes its point, with particular effectiveness because Swift has forced his readers to engage their own moral judgment, their own "savage indignation."

1   It is a melancholy object to those who walk through this great town, or travel in the country, when they see the streets, the roads, and cabin doors, crowded with beggars of the female sex, followed by three, four, or six children, all in rags and importuning every passenger for an alms. These mothers, instead of being able to work for their honest livelihood, are forced to employ all their time in strolling to beg sustenance for their helpless infants: who as they grow up either turn thieves for want of work, or leave their dear native country to fight for the Pretender in Spain, or sell themselves to the Barbadoes.

2   I think it is agreed by all parties that this prodigious number of children in the arms, or on the backs, or at the heels of their mothers, and frequently of their fathers, is in the present deplorable state of the kingdom a very great additional grievance; and, therefore, whoever could find out a fair, cheap, and easy method of making these children sound, useful members of the commonwealth, would deserve so well of the public as to have his statue set up for a preserver of the nation.

3   But my intention is very far from being confined to provide only for the

children of professed beggars; it is of a much greater extent, and shall take in the whole number of infants at a certain age, who are born of parents in effect as little able to support them as those who demand our charity in the streets.

As to my own part, having turned my thoughts for many years upon this important subject, and maturely weighed the several schemes of our projectors, I have always found them grossly mistaken in their computation. It is true, a child just dropped from its dam may be supported by her milk for a solar year, with little other nourishment; at most not above the value of two shillings, which the mother may certainly get, or the value in scraps, by her lawful occupation of begging; and it is exactly at one year old that I propose to provide for them in such a manner as instead of being a charge upon their parents or the parish, or wanting food and raiment for the rest of their lives, they shall on the contrary contribute to the feeding, and partly to the clothing, of many thousands. 4

There is likewise another great advantage in my scheme, that it will prevent those voluntary abortions, and that horrid practice of women murdering their bastard children, alas! too frequent among us! sacrificing the poor innocent babes I doubt more to avoid the expense than the shame, which would move tears and pity in the most savage and inhuman breast. 5

The number of souls in this kingdom being usually reckoned one million and a half, of these I calculate there may be about two hundred thousand couple whose wives are breeders; from which number I subtract thirty thousand couple who are able to maintain their own children (although I apprehend there cannot be so many, under the present distress of the kingdom); but this being granted, there will remain an hundred and seventy thousand breeders. I again subtract fifty thousand for those women who miscarry, or whose children die by accident or disease within the year. There only remain an hundred and twenty thousand children of poor parents annually born. The question therefore is, how this number shall be reared and provided for? which, as I have already said, under the present situation of affairs, is utterly impossible by all the methods hitherto proposed. For we can neither employ them in handicraft or agriculture; we neither build houses (I mean in the country) nor cultivate land; they can very seldom pick up a livelihood by stealing, till they arrive at six years old, except where they are of towardly parts; although I confess they learn the rudiments much earlier; during which time they can, however, be properly looked upon only as probationers; as I have been informed by a principal gentleman in the county of Cavan, who protested to me that he never knew above one or two instances under the age of six, even in a part of the kingdom so renowned for the quickest proficiency in that art. 6

I am assured by our merchants, that a boy or a girl before twelve years old is no saleable commodity; and even when they come to this age they will not yield above three pounds, or three pounds and half a crown at most on the Exchange; which cannot turn to account either to the parents or king- 7 dom, the charge of nutriment and rags having been at least four times that value.

8   I shall now therefore humbly propose my own thoughts, which I hope will not be liable to the least objection.

9   I have been assured by a very knowing American of my acquaintance in London, that a young healthy child well nursed is at a year old a most delicious, nourishing, and wholesome food, whether stewed, roasted, baked, or broiled; and I make no doubt that it will equally serve in a fricassee or a ragout.

10   I do therefore humbly offer it to public consideration that of the hundred and twenty thousand children already computed, twenty thousand may be reserved for breed, whereof only one-fourth part to be males; which is more than we allow to sheep, black cattle, or swine; and my reason is, that these children are seldom the fruits of marriage, a circumstance not much regarded by our savages; therefore one male will be sufficient to serve four females. That the remaining hundred thousand may, at a year old, be offered in sale to the persons of quality and fortune through the kingdom; always advising the mother to let them suck plentifully in the last month, so as to render them plump and fat for a good table. A child will make two dishes at an entertainment for friends; and when the family dines alone, the fore or hind quarter will make a reasonable dish, and seasoned with a little pepper or salt will be very good boiled on the fourth day, especially in winter.

11   I have reckoned upon a medium that a child just born will weigh twelve pounds, and in a solar year, if tolerably nursed, will increase to twenty-eight pounds.

12   I grant this food will be somewhat dear, and therefore very proper for landlords, who, as they have already devoured most of the parents, seem to have the best title to the children.

13   Infant's flesh will be in season throughout the year, but more plentiful in March, and a little before and after: for we are told by a grave author, an eminent French physician, that fish being a prolific diet, there are more children born in Roman Catholic countries about nine months after Lent than at any other season; therefore, reckoning a year after Lent, the markets will be more glutted than usual, because the number of popish infants is at least three to one in this kingdom: and therefore it will have one other collateral advantage, by lessening the number of papists among us.

14   I have already computed the charge of nursing a beggar's child (in which list I reckon all cottagers, laborers, and four-fifths of the farmers) to be about two shillings per annum, rags included; and I believe no gentleman would repine to give ten shillings for the carcass of a good fat child, which, as I have said, will make four dishes of excellent nutritive meat, when he has only some particular friend or his own family to dine with him. Thus the squire will learn to be a good landlord, and grow popular among the tenants; the mother will have eight shillings net profit, and be fit for work till she produces another child.

Those who are more thrifty (as I must confess the times require) may flay 15
the carcass; the skin of which artificially dressed will make admirable gloves
for ladies, and summer boots for fine gentlemen.

As to our city of Dublin, shambles may be appointed for this purpose in 16
the most convenient parts of it, and butchers we may be assured will not be
wanting: although I rather recommend buying the children alive, and dressing them hot from the knife as we do roasting pigs.

A very worthy person, a true lover of his country, and whose virtues I 17
highly esteem, was lately pleased in discoursing on this matter to offer a
refinement upon my scheme. He said that many gentlemen of this kingdom,
having of late destroyed their deer, he conceived that the want of venison
might be well supplied by the bodies of young lads and maidens, not exceed-
ing fourteen years of age nor under twelve; so great a number of both sexes in
every country being now ready to starve for want of work and service; and
these to be disposed of by their parents, if alive, or otherwise by their nearest
relations. But with due deference to so excellent a friend and so deserving a
patriot, I cannot be altogether in his sentiments; for as to the many males, my
American acquaintance assured me from frequent experience that their flesh
was generally tough and lean, like that of our schoolboys by continual exercise, and their taste disagreeable; and to fatten them would not answer the
charge. Then as to the females, it would, I think, with humble submission be
a loss to the public, because they soon would become breeders themselves:
and besides, it is not improbable that some scrupulous people might be apt to
censure such a practice (although indeed very unjustly), as a little bordering
upon cruelty; which, I confess, has always been with me the strongest objection against any project, how well soever intended.

But in order to justify my friend, he confessed that this expedient was put 18
into his head by the famous Psalmanazar, a native of the island Formosa, who
came from thence to London about twenty years ago: and in conversation
told my friend, that in his country when any young person happened to be
put to death, the executioner sold the carcass to persons of quality as a prime
dainty; and that in his time the body of a plump girl of fifteen, who was
crucified for an attempt to poison the emperor, was sold to his imperial
majesty's prime minister of state, and other great mandarins of the court, in
joints from the gibbet, at four hundred crowns. Neither indeed can I deny,
that if the same use were made of several plump young girls in this town, who
without one single groat to their fortunes cannot stir abroad without a chair,
and appear at the playhouse and assemblies in foreign fineries which they
never will pay for, the kingdom would not be the worse.

Some persons of a desponding spirit are in great concern about that vast 19
number of poor people, who are aged, diseased, or maimed, and I have been
desired to employ my thoughts what course may be taken to ease the nation
of so grievous an encumbrance. But I am not in the least pain upon that
matter, because it is very well known that they are every day dying and
rotting by cold and famine, and filth and vermin, as fast as can be reasonably

expected. And as to the young laborers, they are now in as hopeful a condition: they cannot get work, and consequently pine away for want of nourishment, to a degree that if at any time they are accidentally hired to common labor, they have not strength to perform it; and thus the country and themselves are happily delivered from the evils to come.

20 I have too long digressed, and therefore shall return to my subject. I think the advantages by the proposal which I have made are obvious and many, as well as of the highest importance.

21 For first, as I have already observed, it would greatly lessen the number of papists, with whom we are yearly overrun, being the principal breeders of the nation as well as our most dangerous enemies; and who stay at home on purpose to deliver the kingdom to the Pretender, hoping to take their advantage by the absence of so many good Protestants, who have chosen rather to leave their country than stay at home and pay tithes against their conscience to an Episcopal curate.

22 Secondly, The poor tenants will have something valuable of their own, which by law may be made liable to distress and help to pay their landlord's rent, their corn and cattle being already seized, and money a thing unknown.

23 Thirdly, Whereas the maintenance of an hundred thousand children from two years old and upward, cannot be computed at less than ten shillings a piece per annum, the nation's stock will be thereby increased fifty thousand pounds per annum, beside the profit of a new dish introduced to the tables of all gentlemen of fortune in the kingdom who have any refinement in taste. And the money will circulate among ourselves, the goods being entirely of our own growth and manufacture.

24 Fourthly, The constant breeders beside the gain of eight shillings sterling per annum by the sale of their children, will be rid of the charge of maintaining them after the first year.

25 Fifthly, This food would likewise bring great custom to taverns, where the vintners will certainly be so prudent as to procure the best receipts for dressing it to perfection, and consequently have their houses frequented by all the fine gentlemen, who justly value themselves upon their knowledge in good eating; and a skillful cook who understands how to oblige his guests, will contrive to make it as expensive as they please.

26 Sixthly, This would be a great inducement to marriage, which all wise nations have either encouraged by rewards or enforced by laws and penalties. It would increase the care and tenderness of mothers toward their children, when they were sure of a settlement for life to the poor babes, provided in some sort by the public, to their annual profit instead of expense. We should see an honest emulation among the married women, which of them would bring the fattest child to the market. Men would become as fond of their wives during the time of their pregnancy as they are now of their mares in foal, their cows in calf, their sows when they are ready to farrow; nor offer to beat or kick them (as is too frequent a practice) for fear of a miscarriage.

Many other advantages might be enumerated. For instance, the addition 27
of some thousand carcasses in our exportation of barreled beef, the propagation of swine's flesh, and improvement in the art of making good bacon, so
much wanted among us by the great destruction of pigs, too frequent at our
table; which are no way comparable in taste or magnificence to a well-grown,
fat, yearling child, which roasted whole will make a considerable figure at a
lord mayor's feast or any other public entertainment. But this and many
others I omit, being studious of brevity.

Supposing that one thousand families in this city would be constant 28
customers for infants' flesh, besides others who might have it at merry-
meetings, particularly at weddings and christenings, I compute that Dublin
would take off annually about twenty thousand carcasses; and the rest of the
kingdom (where probably they will be sold somewhat cheaper) the remaining eighty thousand.

I can think of no one objection that will possibly be raised against this 29
proposal, unless it should be urged that the number of people will be thereby
much lessened in the kingdom. This I freely own, and it was indeed one
principal design in offering it to the world. I desire the reader will observe,
that I calculate my remedy for this one individual kingdom of Ireland and for
no other that ever was, is, or I think ever can be upon earth. Therefore let no
man talk to me of other expedients; of taxing our absentees at five shillings a
pound: of using neither clothes nor household furniture except what is of our
own growth and manufacture: of utterly rejecting the materials and instruments that promote foreign luxury: of curing the expensiveness of pride,
vanity, idleness, and gaming in our women: of introducing a vein of par-
simony, prudence, and temperance: of learning to love our country, in the
want of which we differ even from Laplanders and the inhabitants of To-
pinamboo: of quitting our animosities and factions, nor acting any longer
like the Jews, who were murdering one another at the very moment their city
was taken: of being a little cautious not to sell our country and conscience for
nothing: of teaching landlords to have at least one degree of mercy toward
their tenants: lastly, of putting a spirit of honesty, industry, and skill into our
shopkeepers; who, if a resolution could now be taken to buy only our native
goods, would immediately unite to cheat and exact upon us in the price, the
measure, and the goodness, nor could ever yet be brought to make one fair
proposal of just dealing, though often and earnestly invited to it.

Therefore I repeat, let no man talk to me of these and the like expedients, 30
till he has at least some glimpse of hope that there will be ever some hearty
and sincere attempts to put them in practice.

But as to myself, having been wearied out for many years with offering 31
vain, idle, visionary thoughts, and at a length utterly despairing of success, I
fortunately fell upon this proposal; which, as it is wholly new, so it has
something solid and real, of no expense and little trouble, full in our own
power, and whereby we can incur no danger in disobliging England. For this

kind of commodity will not bear exportation, the flesh being of too tender a consistence to admit a long continuance in salt, although perhaps I could name a country which would be glad to eat up our whole nation without it.

32   After all, I am not so violently bent upon my own opinion as to reject any offer proposed by wise men, which shall be found equally innocent, cheap, easy, and effectual. But before something of that kind shall be advanced in contradiction to my scheme, and offering a better, I desire the author or authors will be pleased maturely to consider two points. First, as things now stand, how they will be able to find food and raiment for an hundred thousand useless mouths and backs. And secondly, there being a round million of creatures in human figure throughout this kingdom, whose subsistence put into a common stock would leave them in debt two millions of pounds sterling, adding those who are beggars by profession to the bulk of farmers, cottagers, and laborers, with the wives and children who are beggars in effect; I desire those politicians who dislike my overture, and may perhaps be so bold as to attempt an answer, that they will first ask the parents of these mortals, whether they would not at this day think it a great happiness to have been sold for food at a year old in the manner I prescribe, and thereby have avoided such a perpetual scene of misfortunes as they have since gone through by the oppression of landlords, the impossibility of paying rent without money or trade, the want of common sustenance, with neither house nor clothes to cover them from the inclemencies of the weather, and the most inevitable prospect of entailing the like or greater miseries upon their breed for ever.

33   I profess, in the sincerity of my heart, that I have not the least personal interest in endeavoring to promote this necessary work, having no other motive than the public good of my country, by advancing our trade, providing for infants, relieving the poor, and giving some pleasure to the rich. I have no children by which I can propose to get a single penny; the youngest being nine years old, and my wife past child-bearing.

Questions

1. What is the overt thesis of Swift's essay? What is the essay's implied (and real) thesis? How do these theses differ? What is the essay's main purpose?

2. What persona (a created character) does the narrator of Swift's essay have? How are readers to know that this character is not Swift himself? How do the narrator's alleged aims and values, especially as seen through the proposal he offers in paragraphs 9–16, differ from those of Swift as the essay's author?

3. Why did Swift choose to present his argument indirectly rather than overtly? What advantages does this indirect, consistently ironic technique provide? How does the prevailing tone of the essay undermine what the narrator says? How does the tone reinforce Swift's implied meaning?

4. Why does the narrator use so many mathematical computations and words associated with animals ("a child just dropped from its dam"—paragraph 4; "breeders"—paragraph 17)? How do they reinforce his economic argument? How do they enhance the image of his cold-bloodedness?

RUSSELL BAKER
Universal Military Motion

Baker was born in rural Loudon County, Virginia, in 1925, and grew up in New Jersey and Baltimore. As he explains in his Pulitzer Prize–winning autobiography Growing Up *(1982), his mother was determined that he would "make something" of himself; his career in journalism began when she obliged her quavering eight-year-old to sell magazines door-to-door, and encouraged him to become a writer. Baker trained as a navy pilot during World War II, earned a B.A. from Johns Hopkins in 1947, and after working as a reporter on the* Baltimore Sun, *joined* The New York Times *in 1954 as a Congressional reporter. After eight years, "exasperated with the pomposities of official D.C.," he began writing "The Observer," a widely syndicated column of political satire, of which "Universal Military Motion" is a characteristic example. The most recent of the nine collections of Baker's essays is* The Rescue of Miss Yaskell *(1983).*

Exaggeration, carrying to ridiculous extremes a subject that the writer regards as intrinsically ridiculous, is a common technique of satire. Whether or not Baker's audience favors the MX missile, constantly in motion "so enemy bombers will not have a fixed target," it could scarcely take seriously Baker's immodest proposal to supplement these with 250 movable "fake Pentagons," in turn supplemented with "1,500 Pentagon-shaped fast-food restaurants." The analogy is double-edged: the writer makes the projected extremes so ridiculous he forces readers to examine the core subject, in hopes that they will recognize its essential flaws, as well.

The idea behind the MX missile system is sound enough. Place bomb-bearing missiles on wheels and keep them moving constantly through thousands of miles of desert so enemy bombers will not have a fixed target. To confuse things further, move decoy missiles over the same routes so the enemy cannot distinguish between false missiles and the real thing.

As my strategic thinkers immediately pointed out, however, the MX missile system makes very little sense unless matched by an MX Pentagon system. What is the point, they asked, of installing a highly mobile missile system if its command center, the Pentagon, remains anchored like a moose with four broken legs on the bank of the Potomac River?

This is why we propose building 250 moveable structures so precisely like the Pentagon that no one can tell our fake Pentagons from the real thing and to keep all of them, plus the real Pentagon, in constant motion through the country.

Our first plan was to move only the real Pentagon, which would be placed on a large flat-bottom truck bed and driven about the countryside on the existing highway system. We immediately realized, however, that this would not provide sufficient protection against nuclear attack. The Pentagon is very big and easily noticeable. When it is driven along at 55 miles per hour, people can see it coming from miles away. It attracts attention. In short, it is a fat, easily detected target.

5   With 250 fake Pentagons constantly cruising the roads, the problem is solved. Now, trying to distinguish the real Pentagon from the fake Pentagons, enemy attackers will face the maddening problem of finding a needle in a haystack. With 251 Pentagons in circulation, the sight of a Pentagon on the highway will attract no more attention than a politician's indictment. Thus we foil the enemy's spies.

6   Still, to add another margin of security we will confuse matters further by building 1,500 Pentagon-shaped fast-food restaurants along the nation's highways.

7   Each will be an exact replica of the real Pentagon, at least as seen from the outside. Inside, of course, they will be equipped to provide all the necessities for producing acute indigestion, thus providing the wherewithal of highway travel and, in the process, earning the Government a little return on its investment.

8   Occasionally, when generals and admirals tire of touring and yearn for a little stability, the real Pentagon will be parked alongside the road to masquerade as a fast-food Pentagon. The danger of highway travelers wandering in for a quick hot dog and making trouble while the authentic Pentagon is in the "parked" or "fast-food" mode has also been considered.

9   These interlopers will simply be told by receptionists that hot dogs are in the back of the building and directed to walk the long route around the Pentagon's outer ring. As they drop from exhaustion they will be removed by military police, carried to their cars, given free hot dogs and advised that next time they should enter their Pentagon fast-food dispensary through the rear door.

10   There are problems to be ironed out in the MX Pentagon, but we are too busy at the moment perfecting our MX Congress system to trifle with details. With 850 United States Capitols on the highway, we have an extremely touchy problem in deciding whether a Capitol or a Pentagon should have the right of way when they meet at an intersection.

CRAIG SWANSON (Student)

It's the Only Video Game
My Mom Lets Me Chew

Swanson says of his life,

> *I was born in Ridgewood, New Jersey, in the year 1961. Not since 1881 has there been a year that can be read the same upside-down as right side up. And there won't be another until 6009. I grew up in the rural town of Hopewell, New Jersey, strikingly similar to the Lionel Train town, Plasticville. I studied at Rutgers and Syracuse universities before completing my bachelor's of Mathematics/Computer Science at Virginia Commonwealth University in May 1984. Now we arrive at the point of much mental anguish. You asked if I have any writing aspirations. That's tough to face up to. I seem to have nothing but writing aspirations. If I could write all day long—I have convinced myself—I'd be a very happy man. But alas, one cannot write all day, presuming he has financial obligations,*

which Swanson met by working as a data processor at Best Products in Richmond before returning to VCU in 1986 for graduate work in artificial intelligence.

Swanson says, "I wrote 'It's the Only Video Game My Mom Lets Me Chew' in an attempt to make fun of an obsession of mine. If you cannot laugh at the things you do, then you are truly a victim of them." Thus Swanson presents himself as a character addicted to the very activity he criticizes, as we realize from the opening salvo, with its implicit comparison of the video parlor to a men's room. Although he realizes intellectually that video games are programmed to extract money from the hapless player "as long as his twenty-five cent pieces last," he is emotionally ensnared by the mindless possibility of winning "bonus gobblers, shooters, racers, fighters, markers. . . ." The technique of self-satire enables many writers to criticize potentially sensitive subjects; if they show themselves to be personally affected by the problem, their criticisms may seem more valid.

1   Even before I walk into the room I feel the electronic presence sink to my bones. The beeps, twoozers, fanfares, and fugues of the video games compete for dominance. As I enter the game room I notice how much the machines look like urinals. People fill the room, each playing "their" game.

2   My game is Tron. It is the only video game that is also a movie. I do expect, however, to someday see a series of Pacman films—"The Return of the Son of Pacman," Part II. Although I play Tron often, I have never seen the movie. I just don't have the money. I place my two hundredth quarter on the control panel to reserve the next game.

3   Before it's my turn I have some time to watch the other people within the parlor. All video players develop their own ways of playing the games. Inexperienced players handle the controls spasmodically and nervously. To make up for their slow reaction time they slam the joystick much harder than

necessary, under the assumption that if they can't beat the machine through skill, then they'll win out of brute strength. This often includes kicking the coin return or beating upon the screen. Of course this is exactly what the machine wants. The sarcastic whines or droning catcalls that accompany the flashing "game over" sign are designed to antagonize the player. The angrier you get when you play these games, the worse you play. The worse you play the more games you play. Determined to get even, you pop quarter after quarter into the gaping coin slot.

4   A more experienced video player rarely shows emotion. A casual stance, a plop of the coin, a flip of an eyebrow, and he's ready. If he happens to win bonus gobblers, shooters, racers, fighters, markers, flippers, diggers, jugglers, rollers, or air ships, he does not carry on with a high-pitched, glass-shattering scream. When he loses a man, he doesn't get worked up or display fits of violence. He simply stares mindlessly into the video screen as long as his twenty-five cent pieces last.

5   In goes my quarter. The machine sings out its familiar song of thanks, remarkably similar to Bach's Toccata in D-Minor. I am then attacked by spider-like "grid-bugs," an army of tanks, zooming "light cycles," and descending blocks that disintegrate me into a rainbow of dust particles. When my last player is played, Tron tells me the game is over by casting out the celebrated raspberry, then slowly droning out "Taps."

6   I walk out relieved. My pockets are quarterless. My vision is distorted and I am devoid of all intelligent thought. I step out, ready to avoid reality for another day.

S. J. PERELMAN

The Machismo Mystique

Perelman is a humorist's humorist; other comic writers of the twentieth century have considered him "the funniest man alive," and credit him with some of their most outrageous inspirations. Perelman, a Brooklynite, was born in 1904, graduated with a B.A. from Brown in 1925, and worked as a cartoonist and writer for Judge *and* College Humor *magazines. From 1939 until his death forty years later, he was a regular contributor to* The New Yorker, *particularly during its heyday as a humorists' humor magazine that regularly published the works of James Thurber, E. B. White, and Robert Benchley. Indeed, Perelman's twenty books are mostly collections of his* New Yorker *pieces, including* Westward Ha! Or, Around the World in Eighty Clichés *(1947),* The Rising Gorge *(1961),* Baby, It's Cold Inside *(1970), and* Vinegar Puss *(1975). He also wrote the screenplays for two Marx Brothers classics,* Monkey Business *(1931) and* Horse Feathers *(1932), and won an Oscar for* Around the World in Eighty Days *(1956).*

*   "The Machismo Mystique" is a typical Perelman melange of parody, burlesque, incongruity, puns, and free association of truth, myth, and embellishment, with other oddities*

thrown in just for fun. To analyze the nature of Perelman's humor would be to lose most of it in the translation; to imitate it would be equally difficult; better just to laugh at Perelman's hilarious combination of subtlety and grossness, sophistication and bawdiness, wordplay and swordplay.

It was 3 P.M., that climactic midafternoon moment toward which every gallant worthy of the name bends his energies, and I'd done all the preparatory work time and an unencumbered credit card could accomplish. I had stoked my Chilean vis-à-vis with three vodka martinis, half a gallon of Sancerre, and two balloons of Armagnac until her eyes were veritable liquid pools. Under my bold, not to say outrageous, compliments her damask skin and the alabaster column of her throat glowed like a lovely pink pearl; her hair, black as the raven's wing, shimmered in the reflection of the boudoir lamp shading our discreet banquette; and every now and again as my knee nudged hers under the table, my affinity's magnificent bosom heaved uncontrollably. I had glissed through all those earnest confidences that begin, "You know, I've never said this to anyone before," to, "Look, I'm not very articulate, but I feel that in these parlous times, it behooves us all to reach out, to cling to another lonely person—do you know what I mean?" Suddenly I had the feeling that she knew what I meant, all right. In a swift glance, I encompassed the small chic restaurant whence all but we had fled—its idle barman and the maître d'hôtel stifling a yawn—and I struck.

"Listen," I said as if inspired. "This friend of mine, the Marquis de Cad, who has a wonderful collection of African sculpture, was called away to Cleveland, and I promised to stop by his flat and dust it. Why don't we pick up a bottle of lemon oil . . ."

Inamorata threw back her sleek head and shouted with laughter. "Stop, *querido*," she implored. "You're ruining my mascara. Such *machismo*—who would have expected it from a shrimp like you?"

Quicker than any hidalgo of Old Spain to erase an insult, I sprang up prepared to plunge my poniard into her bosom (a striking demonstration of the maxim that man kills that which he most loves). Unfortunately, I had left my poniard at home on the bureau and was wearing only a tie-tack that could never penetrate anyone so thick-skinned. Nonetheless, I made the hussy smart for her insolence. "Let me tell you something, Chubby," I rasped. "Never underestimate the American male. I may not dance the mambo or reek of garlic, but I'm just as feisty as those caballeros of yours below the Rio Grande. Remember that our first colonial flag in Kentucky, the Dark and Bloody Ground, portrayed a coiled rattlesnake over the legend, 'Don't Tread on Me.' "

"Big deal," she scoffed. "Do you want an example of real *machismo*—the kind of masculinity Latin-American men are capable of? Tell them to bring me another Armagnac."

Downcast at the realization that our matinee had blown out the back, I sullenly acceded. The story as she related it dealt with a bar in Guatemala City called *Mi apuesta* (The Wager) after a bet once made there. Two young bloods or *machos,* it appeared, had swaggered in one evening, stiff with conceit and supremely self-confident, arrogant as a pair of fighting cocks. Lounging at the bar over a glass of manzanilla, one of them remarked to the other, "*Te apuesto que no eres bastante macho para matar al primero que entre*" (I wager you're not man enough to kill the first hombre who comes in).

7   The other sneered thinly. "No?" he said. "I bet you fifty *centavos* I will."

8   The bet was covered, whereupon the challenged party extracted a Beretta from his waistband, and a moment later, as a totally inoffensive stranger stepped through the saloon door, a bullet drilled him through the heart.

9   "*Madre de Dios,*" I exclaimed, shocked. "What happened to the assassin?"

10   "*Niente,*" said Inamorata calmly. "The judge gave him a three months' suspended sentence on the ground that the crime was in no way premeditated."

11   Needless to say, whenever Inamorata rang up after our abortive meeting and besought me to lunch her again, I showed her a clean pair of heels. (They were two fellows who dispensed towels at the Luxor Baths; they pursued her madly, and I hope with more success than I had.) At any rate, in pondering the whole business of *machismo,* of male bravado and excessive manliness, it occurred to me that I had met quite a few *machos* in my time, both in the entertainment world and belles-lettres. The one I remember most vividly in the former was a Hollywood screenwriter—big redheaded blowhard I'll call Rick Ferret. A Montanan who claimed to have grown up on the range, Ferret was forever beating his gums about his amatory exploits; by his own blushing admission, he was Casanova reborn, the swordsman supreme, the reincarnation of Don Juan. According to him, women in every walk of life—society leaders and shopgirls, leading ladies and vendeuses—fell in windrows in his path, and though it was obvious to his auditors at the Brown Derby that he dealt in quantity rather than quality, the references he dropped to his nuclear power and durability left us pale with jealousy.

12   One evening, I attended a party at his house in Laurel Canyon. Living with him at the time was a lady named Susie, quite well-endowed and with a rather sharp tongue. So late was the hour when the bash ended that the two insisted I stay over, and the next morning, while I was adjusting my false lashes, Ferret entered the bathroom and proceeded to take a shower. Just as he was snorting and puffing like a grampus, I chanced to observe a quite formidable scar on his *Sitzfleisch.* With an apology for the personal nature of the question, I asked if it was a war wound of some kind.

13   "Yes, in a way," he said carelessly, turning off the taps. "There's quite a story attached to it." He opened the door of the bathroom to disperse the steam, and I glimpsed his Susie breakfasting in bed a few feet distant. "The fact is," he went on, "it happened some years ago down on the south fork of the Brazos while I was rounding up some mavericks. This gang of rustlers

from Durango way cut into the herd, and I took after them hell for leather. Well, the greasers were spoiling for action, and they got it." He chuckled. "Before I could yank out my six-guns, they creased me here, but I managed to rub out the whole dad-blamed lot."

"Oh, for God's sake, Ferret," I heard Susie's voice croak from the bedroom. "You know perfectly well you had a boil lanced on your tail only last Tuesday." 14

The two most celebrated *machos* I ever knew, I suppose, were Ernest 15 Hemingway—unquestionably the holder of the black belt in the Anglo-Saxon world—and Mike Todd, who, to pilfer a phrase from Marcel Proust, might aptly be termed the Sweet Cheat Gone. My go-around with Hemingway took place in the winter of 1954, directly after his two widely publicized plane crashes in East Africa. He was borne into the New Stanley Hotel in Nairobi in a somewhat disoriented state, suffering a double concussion, a smashed kidney, and alarming symptoms of *folie de grandeur*. I turned up there two days later from Uganda with fourteen women comprising the first American all-girl safari (quite another story), and since my room was adjacent to his, saw a good bit of him thereafter. What with his tribulations and frequent infusions of hooch, Papa was inclined to ramble somewhat, and it was not always easy to follow the thread of his discourse. Once in a while, though, the clouds dissipated, and we were able to chat about mutual friends in the Montparnasse of the 'twenties. It was on such an occasion, one night, that he told me an anecdote that stunningly dramatized his *machismo*.

It concerned a period when he used to box at Stillman's Gymnasium in 16 New York, a favorite haunt of enthusiasts of what is termed the manly art. His adversaries, Hemingway blushingly admitted, never matched his own speed and strength, but one of them improved so under his tutelage that occasionally the pair had a tolerable scrimmage. Thinking to intensify it, Hemingway suggested they discard their gloves and fight bareknuckle. This, too, while diverting, soon palled, but at last he had an inspiration.

"The room we boxed in," Hemingway explained, "had these rows of 17 pipes running along the walls—you know, like backstage in a theater? Well, we flooded the place with steam, so thickly that it looked like a peasoup fog in London. Then we started charging each other like a couple of rhinos. Butting our heads together and roaring like crazy. God, it was terrific—you could hear the impact of bone on bone, and we bled like stuck pigs. Of course, that made the footwork a bit more difficult, slipping and sliding all over, but it sure heightened the fun. Man, those were the days. You had to have real *cojones* to stand up to it."

The same hormonal doodads were imperative in order to cope with Mike 18 Todd and his vagaries. Todd's *machismo* was that common form that afflicts all undersized men—megalomania. He freely identified himself with Napoleon, P. T. Barnum, and Carl Laemmle, Junior, not to mention the Roman emperors of the decline. Whereas the latter, however, believed in giving the populace bread and circuses, Todd gave them circuses and kept the bread. Rarely if ever has there been anyone more unwilling to fork over what he owed to those actors, writers, and technicians who aided him in his grandiloquent projects of stage and screen. The little corpuscle, in short, believed in flaunting money where it made the most impression—at Deauville, Monaco, and the gaming tables of Las Vegas. In this respect, he was a true *macho*. My sole souvenir of our frenetic association is a replica of the carpetbag Phileas Fogg carried on his celebrated journey, a thousand of which Todd distributed in lordly fashion to Broadway companions, investors, accountants, dentists, and other sycophants. But surely, his admirers have since queried me, I must have been awed by his tremendous vitality; Only in part, I respond: *Moi-même,* I prefer the anthropoid apes. The gibbon swings farther, the chimpanzee's reflexes are quicker, the orangutan can scratch faster, and the gorilla—my particular love object—has been known to crunch a Stillson wrench in his teeth.

19   Of such literary *machos* was the late Robert Ruark, who of course patterned himself on Hemingway. Their careers afford ample demonstration of my two favorite maxims: a) that the gaudier the patter, the cheaper the scribe, and b) that easy writing makes hard reading. The legend of Ruark's fatal charisma with women still gives one a pain in the posterior when recounted, and his press interviews, studded with reference to the millions of words he merchandised, act as a tourniquet on bleeders like myself who labor over a postcard. Even John O'Hara, somewhat more talented, was not above buttonholing acquaintances and boasting that he had written this or that deathless vignette in three quarters of an hour. It is interesting, by the way, that Scott Fitzgerald, with whom O'Hara was given to comparing himself, never made any claims to his own facility when I knew him in Hollywood. On the contrary, both he and Nathanael West were continually obsessed by delusions of their inadequacy with sex and their small literary output.

20   Looking back over a long and mottled career, I think the best illustration of real *machismo* I ever beheld took place on the terrace of the Café du Dôme in Paris in 1927. I was seated there at dusk one day with a fellow journalist when an enormous yellow Hispano-Suiza landaulet driven by a chauffeur drew up at the curb. From it emerged a tall and beautiful, exquisitely clad lady, followed by another even more photogenic—both clearly high-fashion mannequins. Reaching into the tonneau, they brought forth a wizened homunculus with a yellow face resembling Earl Sande, the celebrated jockey. Hooking their arms through his, they assisted him to a table farther down the terrace. I turned to my *copain* with my eyebrows raised, searching for some explanation of the phenomenon. A slow smile overspread his countenance, and he held his hands apart as does one when asked to steady a skein of wool.

21   That's *machismo,* sweetheart.

Narrative

E. B. WHITE

Death of a Pig

As the narrative begins, White reminds us that stories are told only when the rhythms of life are broken. Love stories are recited only when "the course of true love doesn't run smooth," and tales of dying pigs are told only when the rituals of butchering are broken. Yet, paradoxically, stories must also echo other stories. This story, if you'll pardon the pun, "piggybacks" on all the stories we've ever read of the death of the hero. White, ever the champion of animals, transforms his pig into an Agamemnon, whose "suffering soon became the embodiment of all earthly wretchedness," and his busybody dog Fred into a "dishonorable pallbearer." The comparison of pig and hero is sardonic, of course, which is why White has to admit that the grave scene is "over-written." Nevertheless, although White writes in the mock "penitence and grief of a man who failed to raise his pig," we, too, respond not to "the loss of ham but the loss of pig."

I spent several days and nights in mid-September with an ailing pig and I feel driven to account for this stretch of time, more particularly since the pig died at last, and I lived, and things might easily have gone the other way round and none left to do the accounting. Even now, so close to the event, I cannot recall the hours sharply and am not ready to say whether death came on the third night or the fourth night. This uncertainty afflicts me with a sense of personal deterioration; if I were in decent health I would know how many nights I had sat up with a pig.

The scheme of buying a spring pig in blossomtime, feeding it through summer and fall, and butchering it when the solid cold weather arrives, is a familiar scheme to me and follows an antique pattern. It is a tragedy enacted on most farms with perfect fidelity to the original script. The murder, being premeditated, is in the first degree but is quick and skillful, and the smoked bacon and ham provide a ceremonial ending whose fitness is seldom questioned.

Once in a while something slips—one of the actors goes up in his lines and the whole performance stumbles and halts. My pig simply failed to show up for a meal. The alarm spread rapidly. The classic outline of the tragedy was lost. I found myself cast suddenly in the role of pig's friend and physician—a farcical character with an enema bag for a prop. I had a presentiment, the very first afternoon, that the play would never regain its balance and that my sympathies were now wholly with the pig. This was slapstick—the sort of dramatic treatment that instantly appealed to my old dachshund, Fred, who

1

2

3

joined the vigil, held the bag, and, when all was over, presided at the interment. When we slid the body into the grave, we both were shaken to the core. The loss we felt was not the loss of ham but the loss of pig. He had evidently become precious to me, not that he represented a distant nourishment in a hungry time, but that he had suffered in a suffering world. But I'm running ahead of my story and shall have to go back.

4   My pigpen is at the bottom of an old orchard below the house. The pigs I have raised have lived in a faded building that once was an icehouse. There is a pleasant yard to move about in, shaded by an apple tree that overhangs the low rail fence. A pig couldn't ask for anything better—or none has, at any rate. The sawdust in the icehouse makes a comfortable bottom in which to root, and a warm bed. This sawdust, however, came under suspicion when the pig took sick. One of my neighbors said he thought the pig would have done better on new ground—the same principle that applies in planting potatoes. He said there might be something unhealthy about that sawdust, that he never thought well of sawdust.

5   It was about four o'clock in the afternoon when I first noticed that there was something wrong with the pig. He failed to appear at the trough for his supper, and when a pig (or a child) refuses supper a chill wave of fear runs through any household, or ice-household. After examining my pig, who was stretched out in the sawdust inside the building, I went to the phone and cranked it four times. Mr. Dameron answered. "What's good for a sick pig?" I asked. (There is never any identification needed on a country phone; the person on the other end knows who is talking by the sound of the voice and by the character of the question.)

6   "I don't know, I never had a sick pig," said Mr. Dameron, "but I can find out quick enough. You hang up and I'll call Henry."

7   Mr. Dameron was back on the line again in five minutes. "Henry says roll him over on his back and give him two ounces of castor oil or sweet oil, and if that doesn't do the trick give him an injection of soapy water. He says he's almost sure the pig's plugged up, and even if he's wrong, it can't do any harm."

8   I thanked Mr. Dameron. I didn't go right down to the pig, though. I sank into a chair and sat still for a few minutes to think about my troubles, and then I got up and went to the barn, catching up on some odds and ends that needed tending to. Unconsciously I held off, for an hour, the deed by which I would officially recognize the collapse of the performance of raising a pig; I wanted no interruption in the regularity of feeding, the steadiness of growth, the even succession of days. I wanted no interruption, wanted no oil, no deviation. I just wanted to keep on raising a pig, full meal after full meal, spring into summer into fall. I didn't even know whether there were two ounces of castor oil on the place.

9   Shortly after five o'clock I remembered that we had been invited out to dinner that night and realized that if I were to dose a pig there was no time to

lose. The dinner date seemed a familiar conflict: I move in a desultory society and often a week or two will roll by without my going to anybody's house to dinner or anyone's coming to mine, but when an occasion does arise, and I am summoned, something usually turns up (an hour or two in advance) to make all human intercourse seem vastly inappropriate. I have come to believe that there is in hostesses a special power of divination, and that they deliberately arrange dinners to coincide with pig failure or some other sort of failure. At any rate, it was after five o'clock and I knew I could put off no longer the evil hour.

When my son and I arrived at the pigyard, armed with a small bottle of 10 castor oil and a length of clothesline, the pig had emerged from his house and was standing in the middle of his yard, listlessly. He gave us a slim greeting. I could see that he felt uncomfortable and uncertain. I had brought the clothesline thinking I'd have to tie him (the pig weighed more than a hundred pounds) but we never used it. My son reached down, grabbed both front legs, upset him quickly, and when he opened his mouth to scream I turned the oil into his throat—a pink, corrugated area I had never seen before. I had just time to read the label while the neck of the bottle was in his mouth. It said Pure-test. The screams, slightly muffled by oil, were pitched in the hysterically high range of pigsound, as though torture were being carried out, but they didn't last long: it was all over rather suddenly, and, his legs released, the pig righted himself.

In the upset position the corners of his mouth had been turned down, 11 giving him a frowning expression. Back on his feet again, he regained the set smile that a pig wears even in sickness. He stood his ground, sucking slightly at the residue of oil; a few drops leaked out of his lips while his wicked eyes, shaded by their coy little lashes, turned on me in disgust and hatred. I scratched him gently with oily fingers and he remained quiet, as though trying to recall the satisfaction of being scratched when in health, and seeming to rehearse in his mind the indignity to which he had just been subjected. I noticed, as I stood there, four or five small dark spots on his back near the tail end, reddish brown in color, each about the size of a housefly. I could not make out what they were. They did not look troublesome but at the same time they did not look like mere surface bruises or chafe marks. Rather they seemed blemishes of internal origin. His stiff white bristles almost completely hid them and I had to part the bristles with my fingers to get a good look.

Several hours later, a few minutes before midnight, having dined well 12 and at someone else's expense, I returned to the pighouse with a flashlight. The patient was asleep. Kneeling, I felt his ears (as you might put your hand on the forehead of a child) and they seemed cool, and then with the light made a careful examination of the yard and the house for a sign that the oil had worked. I found none and went to bed.

We had been having an unseasonable spell of weather—hot, close days, 13 with the fog shutting in every night, scaling for a few hours in midday, then creeping back again at dark, drifting in first over the trees on the point, then suddenly blowing across the fields, blotting out the world and taking possession of houses, men, and animals. Everyone kept hoping for a break, but the break failed to come. Next day was another hot one. I visited the pig before breakfast and tried to tempt him with a little milk in his trough. He just stared at it, while I made a sucking sound through my teeth to remind him of past pleasures of the feast. With very small, timid pigs, weanlings, this ruse is often quite successful and will encourage them to eat; but with a large, sick pig the ruse is senseless and the sound I made must have made him feel, if anything, more miserable. He not only did not crave food, he felt a positive revulsion to it. I found a place under the apple tree where he had vomited in the night.

14   At this point, although a depression had settled over me, I didn't suppose that I was going to lose my pig. From the lustiness of a healthy pig a man derives a feeling of personal lustiness; the stuff that goes into the trough and is received with such enthusiasm is an earnest of some later feast of his own, and when this suddenly comes to an end and the food lies stale and untouched, souring in the sun, the pig's imbalance becomes the man's vicariously, and life seems insecure, displaced, transitory.

15   As my own spirits declined, along with the pig's, the spirits of my vile old dachshund rose. The frequency of our trips down the footpath through the orchard to the pigyard delighted him, although he suffers greatly from arthritis, moves with difficulty, and would be bedridden if he could find anyone willing to serve him meals on a tray.

16   He never missed a chance to visit the pig with me, and he made many professional calls on his own. You could see him down there at all hours, his white face parting the grass along the fence as he wobbled and stumbled about, his stethoscope dangling—a happy quack, writing his villainous prescriptions and grinning his corrosive grin. When the enema bag appeared, and the bucket of warm suds, his happiness was complete, and he managed to squeeze his enormous body between the two lowest rails of the yard and then assumed full charge of the irrigation. Once, when I lowered the bag to check the flow, he reached in and hurriedly drank a few mouthfuls of the suds to test their potency. I have noticed that Fred will feverishly consume any substance that is associated with trouble—the bitter flavor is to his liking. When the bag was above reach, he concentrated on the pig and was everywhere at once, a tower of strength and inconvenience. The pig, curiously enough, stood rather quietly through this colonic carnival, and the enema, though ineffective, was not as difficult as I had anticipated.

17   I discovered, though, that once having given a pig an enema there is no turning back, no chance of resuming one of life's more stereotyped roles. The pig's lot and mine were inextricably bound now, as though the rubber tube were the silver cord. From then until the time of his death I held the pig

steadily in the bowl of my mind; the task of trying to deliver him from his misery became a strong obsession. His suffering soon became the embodiment of all earthly wretchedness. Along toward the end of the afternoon, defeated in physicking, I phoned the veterinary twenty miles away and placed the case formally in his hands. He was full of questions, and when I casually mentioned the dark spots on the pig's back, his voice changed its tone.

"I don't want to scare you," he said, "but when there are spots, erysipelas has to be considered." 18

Together we considered erysipelas, with frequent interruptions from the telephone operator, who wasn't sure the connection had been established. 19

"If a pig has erysipelas can he give it to a person?" I asked. 20

"Yes, he can," replied the vet. 21

"Have they answered?" asked the operator. 22

"Yes, they have," I said. Then I addressed the vet again. "You better come over here and examine this pig right away." 23

"I can't come myself," said the vet, "but McFarland can come this evening if that's all right. Mac knows more about pigs than I do anyway. You needn't worry too much about the spots. To indicate erysipelas they would have to be deep hemorrhagic infarcts." 24

"Deep hemorrhagic what?" I asked. 25

"Infarcts," said the vet. 26

"Have they answered?" asked the operator. 27

"Well," I said, "I don't know what you'd call these spots, except they're about the size of a housefly. If the pig has erysipelas I guess I have it, too, by this time, because we've been very close lately." 28

"McFarland will be over," said the vet. 29

I hung up. My throat felt dry and I went to the cupboard and got a bottle of whiskey. Deep hemorrhagic infarcts—the phrase began fastening its hooks in my head. I had assumed that there could be nothing much wrong with a pig during the months it was being groomed for murder; my confidence in the essential health and endurance of pigs had been strong and deep, particularly in the health of pigs that belonged to me and that were part of my proud scheme. The awakening had been violent and I minded it all the more because I knew that what could be true of my pig could be true also of the rest of my tidy world. I tried to put this distasteful idea from me, but it kept recurring. I took a short drink of the whiskey and then, although I wanted to go down to the yard and look for fresh signs, I was scared to. I was certain I had erysipelas. 30

It was long after dark and the supper dishes had been put away when a car drove in and McFarland got out. He had a girl with him. I could just make her out in the darkness—she seemed young and pretty. "This is Miss Owen," he said. "We've been having a picnic supper on the shore, that's why I'm late." 31

McFarland stood in the driveway and stripped off his jacket, then his 32 shirt. His stocky arms and capable hands showed up in my flashlight's gleam as I helped him find his coverall and get zipped up. The rear seat of his car contained an astonishing amount of paraphernalia, which he soon over-hauled, selecting a chain, a syringe, a bottle of oil, a rubber tube, and some other things I couldn't identify. Miss Owen said she'd go along with us and see the pig. I led the way down the warm slope of the orchard, my light picking out the path for them, and we all three climbed the fence, entered the pighouse, and squatted by the pig while McFarland took a rectal reading. My flashlight picked up the glitter of an engagement ring on the girl's hand.

33   "No elevation," said McFarland, twisting the thermometer in the light. "You needn't worry about erysipelas." He ran his hand slowly over the pig's stomach and at one point the pig cried out in pain.

34   "Poor piggledy-wiggledy!" said Miss Owen.

35   The treatment I had been giving the pig for two days was then repeated, somewhat more expertly, by the doctor, Miss Owen and I handing him things as he needed them—holding the chain that he had looped around the pig's upper jaw, holding the syringe, holding the bottle stopper, the end of the tube, all of us working in darkness and in comfort, working with the instinctive teamwork induced by emergency conditions, the pig unprotest-ing, the house shadowy, protecting, intimate. I went to bed tired but with a feeling of relief that I had turned over part of the responsibility of the case to a licensed doctor. I was beginning to think, though, that the pig was not going to live.

36   He died twenty-four hours later, or it might have been forty-eight—there is a blur in time here, and I may have lost or picked up a day in the telling and the pig one in the dying. At intervals during the last day I took cool fresh water down to him and at such times as he found the strength to get to his feet he would stand with head in the pail and snuffle his snout around. He drank a few sips but no more; yet it seemed to comfort him to dip his nose in water and bobble it about, sucking in and blowing out through his teeth. Much of the time, now, he lay indoors half buried in sawdust. Once, near the last, while I was attending him I saw him try to make a bed for himself but he lacked the strength, and when he set his snout into the dust he was unable to plow even the little furrow he needed to lie down in.

37   He came out of the house to die. When I went down, before going to bed, he lay stretched in the yard a few feet from the door. I knelt, saw that he was dead, and left him there: his face had a mild look, expressive neither of deep peace nor of deep suffering, although I think he had suffered a good deal. I went back up to the house and to bed, and cried internally—deep hemorrhagic intears. I didn't wake till nearly eight the next morning, and when I looked out the open window the grave was already being dug, down beyond the dump under a wild apple. I could hear the spade strike against the small rocks that blocked the way. Never send to know for whom the grave is

dug, I said to myself, it's dug for thee. Fred, I well knew, was supervising the work of digging, so I ate breakfast slowly.

It was a Saturday morning. The thicket in which I found the gravedig- 38
gers at work was dark and warm, the sky overcast. Here, among alders and young hackmatacks, at the foot of the apple tree, Lennie had dug a beautiful hole, five feet long, three feet wide, three feet deep. He was standing in it, removing the last spadefuls of earth while Fred patrolled the brink in simple but impressive circles, disturbing the loose earth of the mound so that it trickled back in. There had been no rain in weeks and the soil, even three feet down, was dry and powdery. As I stood and stared, an enormous earthworm which had been partially exposed by the spade at the bottom dug itself deeper and made a slow withdrawal, seeking even remoter moistures at even lonelier depths. And just as Lennie stepped out and rested his spade against the tree and lit a cigarette, a small green apple separated itself from a branch overhead and fell into the hole. Everything about this last scene seemed over-written— the dismal sky, the shabby woods, the imminence of rain, the worm (legendary bedfellow of the dead), the apple (conventional garnish of a pig).

But even so, there was a directness and dispatch about animal burial, I 39
thought, that made it a more decent affair than human burial: there was no stopover in the undertaker's foul parlor, no wreath nor spray; and when we hitched a line to the pig's hind legs and dragged him swiftly from his yard, throwing our weight into the harness and leaving a wake of crushed grass and smoothed rubble over the dump, ours was a businesslike procession, with Fred, the dishonorable pallbearer, staggering along in the rear, his perverse bereavement showing in every seam in his face; and the post mortem performed handily and swiftly right at the edge of the grave, so that the innards that had caused the pig's death preceded him into the ground and he lay at last resting squarely on the cause of his own undoing.

I threw in the first shovelful, and then we worked rapidly and without 40
talk, until the job was complete. I picked up the rope, made it fast to Fred's collar (he is a notorious ghoul), and we all three filed back up the path to the house, Fred bringing up the rear and holding back every inch of the way, feigning unusual stiffness. I noticed that although he weighed far less than the pig, he was harder to drag, being possessed of the vital spark.

The news of the death of my pig traveled fast and far, and I received 41
many expressions of sympathy from friends and neighbors, for no one took the event lightly and the premature expiration of a pig is, I soon discovered, a departure which the community marks solemnly on its calendar, a sorrow in which it feels fully involved. I have written this account in penitence and in grief, as a man who failed to raise his pig, and to explain my deviation from the classic course of so many raised pigs. The grave in the woods is unmarked, but Fred can direct the mourner to it unerringly and with immense good will, and I know he and I shall often revisit it, singly and together, in seasons of reflection and despair, on flagless memorial days of our own choosing.

Questions

1. Why is White writing about the death of his "spring pig"? Why would readers of *The New Yorker,* that urbane urban magazine, be interested in this mock-heroic tale of a minor rural woe? Is it possible to generalize from this incident to the deaths of other animals one has known—pets, perhaps?

2. Identify the personalities and explain the functions of the following characters in this narrative: White as narrator; White as pig-raiser; the pig (Are you aware that this helpless adolescent weighs "more than a hundred pounds"?—paragraph 10); McFarland; Miss Owen; the telephone operator; Fred.

3. Why does White furnish so many graphic details of the pig's physical condition? If these are distressing or disgusting to read about, how can the work be considered humorous?

4. The humor of this tale does not come from the pig's suffering, which is real and laden with genuine misery, but from the implied comparison of the death of an epic hero with that of the thoroughly mundane pig, and from the behavior and thoughts of the pig's various attendants (including Fred) during its days of woe. Explain. Why does White say that the grave scene is "over-written" (paragraph 38)? If you have read *Charlotte's Web* (see Eudora Welty's review, 456–58), can you understand how White could have written a classic children's novel with an adolescent pig as a central character?

JAMES THURBER

The Night the Bed Fell

Thurber's sense of the ridiculous is sublime. Some of the funniest of his comic sketches are derived from his childhood in Columbus, Ohio, where he was born in 1894, and from his college days at Ohio State University. After working briefly as a reporter for the Columbus Dispatch, *Thurber migrated to New York via Paris, where he was a reporter for the Paris edition of the* Chicago Tribune. *At The New Yorker he was first hired as managing editor, but within six months he had managed to work himself "down to a more comfortable position." For the next forty years—despite progressive blindness—Thurber contributed articles, stories, fables, and quirky line drawings (Dorothy Parker called them "unbaked cookies") to the magazine, until his death in 1961. He mines the quirky commonplaces of ordinary people in ordinary life in such books as* Is Sex Necessary? *(1929), with E. B. White, and the autobiographical* My Life and Hard Times *(1933). Among his other twenty volumes are a play,* The Male Animal *(1939), with Elliott Nugent; a cartoon book,* Men, Women, and Dogs *(1943); several children's books, among them* The Wonderful O *(1957); and* The Years with Ross *(1959), an account of the magical, symbiotic relationship between* The New Yorker *and its crusty, perfectionist editor, Harold Ross.*

Thurber claimed that English humor "treats the commonplace as if it were remarkable," while American humor "treats the remarkable as if it were commonplace." Thurber illustrates this dictum in "The Night the Bed Fell," matter-of-factly informing us that everyone in the Thurber household borders on insanity. His humor here depends on the deadpan delivery of a scene that, had it been filmed instead of written, would certainly have been played as slapstick comedy.

I suppose that the high-water mark of my youth in Columbus, Ohio, was the 1
night the bed fell on my father. It makes a better recitation (unless, as some
friends of mine have said, one has heard it five or six times) than it does a
piece of writing, for it is almost necessary to throw furniture around, shake
doors, and bark like a dog, to lend the proper atmosphere and verisimilitude
to what is admittedly a somewhat incredible tale. Still, it did take place.

It happened, then, that my father had decided to sleep in the attic one 2
night, to be away where he could think. My mother opposed the notion
strongly because, she said, the old wooden bed up there was unsafe, it was
wobbly and the heavy headboard would crash down on father's head in case
the bed fell, and kill him. There was no dissuading him, however, and at a
quarter past ten he closed the attic door behind him and went up the narrow
twisting stairs. We later heard ominous creakings as he crawled into bed.
Grandfather, who usually slept in the attic bed when he was with us, had
disappeared some days before. (On these occasions he was usually gone six or
eight days and returned growling and out of temper, with the news that the
federal Union was run by a passel of blockheads and that the Army of the
Potomac didn't have any more chance than a fiddler's bitch.)

We had visiting us at this time a nervous first cousin of mine named 3
Briggs Beall, who believed that he was likely to cease breathing when he was
asleep. It was his feeling that if he were not awakened every hour during the
night, he might die of suffocation. He had been accustomed to setting an
alarm clock to ring at intervals until morning, but I persuaded him to abandon this. He slept in my room and I told him that I was such a light sleeper
that if anybody quit breathing in the same room with me, I would wake
instantly. He tested me the first night—which I had suspected he would—by
holding his breath after my regular breathing had convinced him I was
asleep. I was not asleep, however, and called to him. This seemed to allay his
fears a little, but he took the precaution of putting a glass of spirits of
camphor on a little table at the head of his bed. In case I didn't arouse him
until he was almost gone, he said, he would sniff the camphor, a powerful
reviver. Briggs was not the only member of his family who had his crotchets.
Old Aunt Melissa Beall (who could whistle like a man, with two fingers in her
mouth) suffered under the premonition that she was destined to die on South
High Street, because she had been born on South High Street and married
on South High Street. Then there was Aunt Sarah Shoaf, who never went to
bed at night without the fear that a burglar was going to get in and blow
chloroform under her door through a tube. To avert this calamity—for she
was in greater dread of anesthetics than of losing her household goods—she
always piled her money, silverware, and other valuables in a neat stack just

outside her bedroom, with a note reading: "This is all I have. Please take it and do not use your chloroform, as this is all I have." Aunt Gracie Shoaf also had a burglar phobia, but she met it with more fortitude. She was confident that burglars had been getting into her house every night for forty years. The fact that she never missed anything was to her no proof to the contrary. She always claimed that she scared them off before they could take anything, by throwing shoes down the hallway. When she went to bed she piled, where she could get at them handily, all the shoes there were about her house. Five minutes after she had turned off the light, she would sit up in bed and say "Hark!" Her husband, who had learned to ignore the whole situation as long ago as 1903, would either be sound asleep or pretend to be sound asleep. In either case he would not respond to her tugging and pulling, so that presently she would arise, tiptoe to the door, open it slightly and heave a shoe down the hall in one direction, and its mate down the hall in the other direction. Some nights she threw them all, some nights only a couple of pair.

4   But I am straying from the remarkable incidents that took place during the night that the bed fell on father. By midnight we were all in bed. The layout of the rooms and the disposition of their occupants is important to an understanding of what later occurred. In the front room upstairs (just under father's attic bedroom) were my mother and my brother Herman, who sometimes sang in his sleep, usually "Marching Through Georgia" or "Onward, Christian Soldiers." Briggs Beall and myself were in a room adjoining this one. My brother Roy was in a room across the hall from ours. Our bull terrier, Rex, slept in the hall.

5   My bed was an army cot, one of those affairs which are made wide enough to sleep on comfortably only by putting up, flat with the middle section, the two sides which ordinarily hang down like the sideboards of a drop-leaf table. When these sides are up, it is perilous to roll too far toward the edge, for then the cot is likely to tip completely over, bringing the whole bed down on top of one, with a tremendous banging crash. This, in fact, is precisely what happened, about two o'clock in the morning. (It was my mother who, in recalling the scene later, first referred to it as "the night the bed fell on your father.")

6   Always a deep sleeper, slow to arouse (I had lied to Briggs), I was at first unconscious of what had happened when the iron cot rolled me onto the floor and toppled over on me. It left me still warmly bundled up and unhurt, for the bed rested above me like a canopy. Hence I did not wake up, only reached the edge of consciousness and went back. The racket, however, instantly awakened my mother, in the next room, who came to the immediate conclusion that her worst dread was realized: the big wooden bed upstairs had fallen on father. She therefore screamed, "Let's go to your poor father!" It was this shout, rather than the noise of my cot falling, that awakened Herman, in the same room with her. He thought that mother had become, for no apparent reason, hysterical. "You're all right, Mamma!" he shouted, trying to calm her. They exchanged shout for shout for perhaps ten seconds:

"Let's go to your poor father!" and "You're all right!" That woke up Briggs. By this time I was conscious of what was going on, in a vague way, but did not yet realize that I was under my bed instead of on it. Briggs, awakening in the midst of loud shouts of fear and apprehension, came to the quick conclusion that he was suffocating and that we were all trying to "bring him out." With a low moan, he grasped the glass of camphor at the head of his bed and instead of sniffing it poured it over himself. The room reeked of camphor. "Ugf, ahfg," choked Briggs, like a drowning man, for he had almost succeeded in stopping his breath under the deluge of pungent spirits. He leaped out of bed and groped toward the open window, but he came up against one that was closed. With his hand, he beat out the glass, and I could hear it crash and tinkle on the alleyway below. It was at this juncture that I, in trying to get up, had the uncanny sensation of feeling my bed above me! Foggy with sleep, I now suspected, in my turn, that the whole uproar was being made in a frantic endeavor to extricate me from what must be an unheard-of and perilous situation. "Get me out of this!" I bawled. "Get me out!" I think I had the nightmarish belief that I was entombed in a mine. "Gugh," gasped Briggs, floundering in his camphor.

By this time my mother, still shouting, pursued by Herman, still shouting, was trying to open the door to the attic, in order to go up and get my father's body out of the wreckage. The door was stuck, however, and wouldn't yield. Her frantic pulls on it only added to the general banging and confusion. Roy and the dog were now up, the one shouting questions, the other barking.   7

Father, farthest away and soundest sleeper of all, had by this time been awakened by the battering on the attic door. He decided that the house was on fire. "I'm coming, I'm coming!" he wailed in a slow, sleepy voice—it took him many minutes to regain full consciousness. My mother, still believing he was caught under the bed, detected in his "I'm coming!" the mournful, resigned note of one who is preparing to meet his Maker. "He's dying!" she shouted.   8

"I'm all right!" Briggs yelled to reassure her. "I'm all right!" He still believed that it was his own closeness to death that was worrying mother. I found at last the light switch in my room, unlocked the door, and Briggs and I joined the others at the attic door. The dog, who never did like Briggs, jumped for him—assuming that he was the culprit in whatever was going on—and Roy had to throw Rex and hold him. We could hear father crawling out of bed upstairs. Roy pulled the attic door open, with a mighty jerk, and father came down the stairs, sleepy and irritable but safe and sound. My mother began to weep when she saw him. Rex began to howl. "What in the name of God is going on here?" asked father.   9

The situation was finally put together like a gigantic jig-saw puzzle.   10
Father caught a cold from prowling around in his bare feet but there were no other bad results. "I'm glad," said mother, who always looked on the bright side of things, "that your grandfather wasn't here."

Comic Portraits

JOHN LEONARD

My Son, the Roman

Here Leonard continues his concern with family relationships, but in a much lighter vein than in "The Only Child." A perennial technique of humor is to juxtapose differences in perspective on a given subject, such as the clandestine drinking of beer viewed across the generation gap, or to examine the generation gap itself. Leonard, proud father, can poke wistful fun at himself (and by implication, at other parents) for expecting his child never to grow up ("He was supposed to stay eight"), and can enjoy his son's apparently successful survival of his high school, a miserable period in Leonard's own life ("I flunked volleyball and puberty rite."). Another technique of humor is to exploit incongruity; in this essay Leonard finds considerable incongruity—and humor—between a subject (the studying of Latin) and its context (in Florida)—"Is it a language in which peninsulas specialize?" Sometimes, too, allusions can be fun; Leonard's own use of allusions shows that his son isn't the only one who has studied the classics, or the Beach Boys. Knowledge of the classics and serious modern writers, such as Heinrich Heine and Robert Graves, is useful for a writer, but so, too, is knowledge of the contemporary scene in the jumbo-shrimp shacks and taco parlors. If the "barbarians" are here, it's good to know the vernacular.

1   In a month or so, he will be fifteen, which is absurd. I never intended him to be old enough to contemplate driving a car or applying to college. He was supposed to stay eight, or maybe twelve. I examine him for stigmata of sullenness; no, merely the clouded look of afternoons with books, and, where the light collects—at the rims of his aviator glasses, in the braces on his teeth—some fire. His feet are huge; I have ordered seven-league boots.

2   According to a Hungarian proverb, the owl always believes his son is a hawk.

3   He is reporting on the folkways of inscrutable Florida. It seems that the students of Latin are restless. All over Florida the students of Latin in junior and senior high schools have been agitating. Each school competes against the other schools in each city. Winners then advance to a state competition in Miami. There will be a national competition later this summer.

4   What do they compete about? He explains: Roman history, Roman literature, Latin grammar and vocabulary, costumes. They build chariots and stage skits. I quote Heinrich Heine: "The Romans would never have found time to conquer the world if they had been obliged first to learn Latin." But Latin is his favorite subject. I tell him that the Greeks built the Parthenon and the Romans built sewers. But he is checking up on Claudius in Robert Graves.

5   The idea that everybody in Florida is learning Latin for some reason makes me uneasy. Is it a language in which peninsulas specialize?

6   He describes at length his trip to Miami for the state competition. He doesn't much approve of Miami as a town. But they spent the night in a

hotel, and they stayed up late, well past their curfew, and they played poker for real money. He is excited: he won seventy-five cents. What's more—and he lowers his voice, as if Tiberius might be listening—they drank beer.

His father, who once kept Anheuser-Busch in business, wants to know   7
how much beer they drank at night in a hotel room in Miami. A can, says his son. A can apiece? No, a can period. An eighteen-year-old girl bought a sixteen-ounce can of beer and they all had sips while playing poker for real money after curfew. And on the bus ride back from Miami they sang songs, making up verses that poked fun at Roman history.

Remember when sin was fun? I once said in this space that not only   8
wouldn't I want to be sixteen years old again, but that I hadn't wanted to be sixteen years old the first time. Other people, however, are entitled. Now if only it were possible to skip the terrors of sexuality, to buy nostalgia like a golden oldie without having gone through the bruising experience. Authenticity is overrated.

He has more to report. At the end of the school year, the Latin classes   9
have a banquet. The week before the banquet there is an auction. At this auction the advanced students, those in Latin II and Latin III, bid on members of the Latin I class and buy them as slaves. The money spent at the auction helps pay for the banquet. A slave, if he is caught by his master, is obliged to carry books, fetch sodas, walk to class on his knees, run around the quad at lunchtime shouting, "The British are coming" and otherwise make a fool of himself.

I approve of slavery as a pedagogical device somewhat less than my son   10
approves of Miami. But of course it's very Roman, like so many quaint customs that have come down from the Empire to modern statecraft. (Whereas Caesar wouldn't even read Pompey's mail, Tiberius specialized in paid informers and considered almost anything that annoyed him to be high treason.) And the slaves were freed at midnight after the banquet.

This freedom allowed them, the following weekend, to go to the Latin   11
beach party. The beach party marks the end of the busy social season for students of Latin in a Florida public high school. By car caravan, they seek the sea and sand. The cars, I am told, all had CB radios, and the students of Latin monopolized a channel. At the beach they ate and drank and swam and ate and drank. They also gathered for one last rendition of the number in their skit that brought down the house in Miami.

In this number, hooded figures come on stage and lurk. They are ordered   12
to identify themselves. They remove their hoods, are revealed to be wearing sunglasses, and, to the tune of a popular rock approximation of music, burst into song:

> Ba-ba-ba
> Bar-bar-a-barians
> Ba-ba-ba
> Bar-bar-a-barians . . .

And so on.

13   I am unglued. Fatherhood flounders. A wheel fell off my Oedipal cycle. Yes, it's true: when the barbarians arrive, it will be in snowmobiles with CB radios. My son will be reading Lucretius, or playing the clarinet while condominiums burn. I will go for beer. "No poems can please for long or live that were written by water-drinkers," said Horace in a hot epistle.

14   In my youth, in the jumbo-shrimp shacks and taco parlors along the southern California coast, the surfers couldn't speak English, much less Latin. I never went to a beach party where I wasn't humiliated. Grunion always ran the other way. I flunked volleyball and puberty rite. Can it be that my son is going to be happier being young than I was? If so, and even though he deserves it, poker-faced behind my sunglasses, I will never let him know. It would be bad for his character.

EUGENE L. MEYER

Mr. L. G. Broadmoore
and the Way It Was

Meyer was born in New York City (not far from Tivoli, New York) in 1938, and after graduation from Columbia in 1964 began his career in journalism as a reporter on the New York Herald Tribune. *From there he moved to the* Philadelphia Evening Bulletin, *and joined the staff of the* Washington Post *in 1970. He was awarded a Newspaper Guild Front Page Citation for a series of articles on the politics of inner-city redevelopment.*

Eccentric people, the source of eternal fascination, are too often the objects of callous laughter; we have only to think of high school bullies making fun of the class oddball. Yet on closer acquaintance, we may find eccentrics at least as sane—and a lot more interesting—than our more conventional, less colorful friends and neighbors. The wise fool is a comic type worth paying attention to. Meyer's portrait of Broadmoore, a twenty-three-year-old "authentic obsolete man" who earns a living "by repairing player pianos, gramophones and other outdated machinery," is good humored and fundamentally respectful of both the man and his philosophy. Meyer demonstrates Broadmoore's eccentricity by quoting the subject himself ("Balderdash!"), and by naming the obsolete and eccentric paraphernalia with which he surrounds himself in his attempt, perhaps futile but nevertheless admirable, to retain the best of the past.

1   Tivoli, N.Y.—Since time immemorial, mankind has striven to achieve new frontiers of knowledge and experience, consigning old theories, technologies and patterns to the junk heap of history.

2   Not Lawrence Gilbert Broadmoore.

3   At the age of 23, he is, as much as he can be, the authentic obsolete man, frozen inside a protective pre-World War I time capsule. He says things like "Balderdash!" And, with a restless 3½-year-old visitor pounding his parlor piano, "One mustn't bang too loudly."

His present is an eternal past in which the future is but more of the same,   4
"except I hope to become more skillful in every field of endeavor which
requires skill."

In this Hudson River hamlet of 800, he exists by repairing player pianos,   5
gramophones and other outdated machinery, and he lives in an old house
with no plumbing or central heating.

Though short of stature, he cuts an imposing figure in his pince-nez   6
spectacles, waxed moustache, hair parted down the middle and high-neck
starched collar. He looks like a yellowing photograph in an ancient family
album, the young man on the make, the rugged individualist of Main Street.

He learned how to dress from old mail-order catalogs, and how to speak   7
from 19th-century parlor novels. "It sometimes feels as if I'm talking to
myself," he says, frustrated by the unwillingness or inability of others to role
play with him. "Etiquette is a type of play," he concedes. "One can't expect
everyone to play along."

Of course, it is all affected, but it is a sincere affectation, not a put-on,   8
and it goes much deeper than trendy nostalgia. For L. G. Broadmoore has
thoroughly thought through his odd lifestyle and deeply believes in it, even if
nobody else does.

His is a philosophy born of extreme dissatisfaction with a society that   9
tears down its finest old buildings in the name of renewal, that substitutes
quantity for quality, whose science only computers can comprehend. Civilization, he believes, peaked with the Industrial Revolution: Mechanics hold
more to marvel at than megatons and modules in atomic weaponry and
space. World War I, on the other hand, "marks the end of esthetic civilization
in this country, due to new frontiers in immorality opened by the war."

He admits: "I live in a totally insular world, guarded from philosophical   10
relevance by my own vigilance." He is, he knows, eccentric, but not crazy,
really. "I've not permitted myself to lose the grip of reason. I try to make
myself insane in a certain sense, oblivious to the fact there is anything abnormal about this type of life. When I become sensitive to it, it causes me a
certain amount of anxiety."

Anxiety, in a sense, propelled L. G. Broadmoore into the past.   11

Eight years ago, he was "mostly miserable," living a "significantly   12
mediocre" existence in a middle-class Cincinnati suburb. "I never got along
with people my own age," he recalls. But he had two interests to assuage the
loneliness: mechanics and history.

After school, he would ride the buses downtown to marvel at the remain-   13
ing 19th-century buildings. Armed with an 1893 guide, he would look at the
magnificent edifice pictured in the book and the decaying ruin behind him,
and he would become filled with a sense of poignancy, and outrage. "I
refused to accept the idea I had to be a historical pauper."

Suddenly, "this scheme of living in the past struck me—like an inspira-   14 tion." Lawrence G. Broadmoore, unhappy in the present, would find happiness in the past. He began wearing old-fashioned clothes to school and was threatened with suspension. His parents sent him to a Massachusetts private school and then to offbeat Bard College, a few miles from Tivoli. He dropped out after three years to open the Tivoli Player-Piano Shop.

15   He picked Tivoli because "it looked as though everyone forgot about it. I thought no one would meddle with it." Now, he worries about the intrusions of developers and speculators—not immediately apparent to a visitor—and takes consolation from reports that there are other still-forgotten towns elsewhere.

16   "Someday," he says, fatalistically, "I may have to migrate."

17   Meanwhile, his life is complicated by its very simplicity: "It's very expensive to live simply in a way I consider acceptable. What was simple years ago is now considered complicated."

18   Thus, "I have some trouble getting non-safety [eyeglass] lenses. I see that they're ground in the 19th-century manner, smaller and flatter."

19   High-neck collars are also a problem, especially finding anyone to launder them. So he buys them newly starched from Brooks Brothers, at $1.25 each.

20   Then there is ice. Broadmoore keeps all his perishables in an ice box (but requires an electric refrigerator to keep his week's supply of ice from melting). Until his death two years ago, an 88-year-old local iceman who refused to quit made deliveries. Now Broadmoore drives his 1949 Ford pickup ("as old as I can afford") across the Hudson to Kingston, where he buys a 300-pound block for $3.

21   "Fortunately, I can still get coal delivered," he says.

22   His parents, well, they still love him. But they don't understand him. "I'm a total mystery to them," he says. "They feel I'm making trouble for myself. They consider me to have great potential they see better spent in ecology or working in some great laboratory to reduce noise levels."

23   Notwithstanding such parental misgivings, his father, a wine merchant, contributed toward the $2,000 purchase of a green frame shop on Tivoli's main street. It is next to the Hotel Morey, a two-story, turn-of-the-century inn whose rooms have not been let for years; only its first-floor tavern is open for business.

24   On Saturdays, the shop is a gathering place for kids to wonder at mechanics the way children several generations ago must have flocked in fascination to the Wright brothers bicycle shop.

25   For L. G. Broadmoore, it was a rough road to local acceptance, much less stardom: "I've been the subject of ridicule in many cases. Those youngsters in the shop, when I first knew them, were continually nasty to me and manifested impoliteness to me in many ways. But after a while, I'd get an ally, and he would explain to everyone else there was a great deal of value in what I was doing."

Broadmoore feels no affinity in his work or lifestyle with the craftsperson 26
dropout. "They have a society consciousness that I don't have." But he enjoys
talking with "these people." He says it as if it's a cultural exchange program.

"I haven't met anyone with whom I have much in common," he says, a 27
bit sadly. He has one like-minded friend in New York City, "but he has no
mechanical inclination, so he has to be involved with people. It's a hopeless
task."

The player-piano shop is dimly illuminated by clear, non-frosted bulbs, 28
which look like the old Edison lights. The wiring is '20s vintage porcelain
knob and tube. "I've sort of fostered an interest in unsafe wiring over the
years," he says.

A framed picture of his hero, Thomas A. Edison, sits on top of a rolltop 29
desk, whose small reference library includes *The How Book: A Standard Guide
for the Homeworker, Businessman and Mechanic,* published in 1913.

There is an old Remington typewriter and an inoperative two-piece desk 30
phone. He has no working telephone at the shop or his house, only an
answering service number. "I had a phone for a while," he says, "but I found
it really disturbed me too much, so I got rid of it."

The shop is an essential part of his lifestyle, because "everything I use I 31
have to be equipped to service myself. The shop, to a large degree, is a
maintenance shop for the trappings of my existence, since society refuses to
maintain them anymore." And mechanics have made it possible for him to
support his simple-complex way of life.

How well he has been supporting himself has been the subject of recent 32
"extensive self-auditing," he says. "I tried to run the business on a 19th-
century basis, at 19th-century rates. Sometimes I would work six months for
$200. After accumulating a debt over three years, I have had to evaluate time
and raise all prices."

Broadmoore rents a former tenant farmer's two-story house, built 33
around 1915 on a back country road three miles from the shop. He pays $85
a month. The only condition is that he not use kerosene lamps. He uses
candles mostly, "when I can afford them." Two small electric bulbs droop
apologetically from the living room ceiling, flies swarming around them.

He lives alone with a cat. At first, he said, he experienced "a certain 34
amount of trepidation" about living without central heating or indoor
plumbing. The transition, however, proved relatively painless. "At this point,
obstacles are no longer obstacles." That's not true, however, for all guests.
His parents can't deal with the lack of plumbing and stay at motels when
visiting.

He has no electrical appliances, save for the ice storage refrigerator hid- 35
den under the basement steps—the skeleton in his closet—and a 1910
vacuum cleaner. "I used to use a broom, but now that time has become so
valuable, to a certain extent I've had to appease the modern gods of finance,"
he explains. Such concessions to modern times are few and hidden.

36   The living room centerpiece is a wood-coal furnace. Stacks of 78 r.p.m. records—none after 1930, most circa 1915—clutter up two bureaus. There is an upright piano and a Grafanola gramophone, but no radio. "I won't have one," he said. "It wouldn't do me any good because I couldn't get old programs. My grandfather was interested in that kind of modern stuff."

37   Above the piano is an old photograph of a young woman, his great-grandmother. On one wall is a 1900 painted photo portrait of Josephine Cole, now 90 and a neighbor in Tivoli. Hanging on racks are several boaters and stovepipe hats. There is a stereopticon viewer with a set of Yellowstone slides.

38   In the kitchen, the sink is filled by water pump. It provides only rainwater, from a 5,000 gallon cistern in the basement that fills with every cloudburst, "like an eternal spring." The water is drinkable, he says, but there is also an outside pump for well water.

39   He uses a straight-edge razor sharpened on a leather strop. Dishes are dried "in two seconds" on a drying rack placed above the coal stove. There is also a 1904 American Wringer Co. gravity clothes washer. As another recent time-money concession, he has his shop apprentice take his wash to a laundromat.

40   In the dining room, there is a china closet containing a youthful picture of his grandparents. Upstairs, there are three bedrooms, two with big brass beds. His room contains an upright Edison diamond disc phonograph and a dresser. There is a guest room. Old suits are strewn across the bed in "the library," whose books include several Tom Swifts and *Who's Who in America, 1920–1921*.

41   In back of the house, in what was once a barn, is the world's most pristine privy and an engineless 1921 Ford.

42   L. G. Broadmoore is concerned with style, not events, for events mark the passage of time and that is unthinkable in his world. Thus, his walls contain no pictures of the martyred William McKinley or the hero of Manila Bay, Admiral Dewey; his tables hold no souvenir paperweights from the 1904 St. Louis World's Fair.

43   Such items were common in many middle-class homes in those turn-of-the-century days of innocence. But then, Lawrence G. Broadmoore is not average, nor common, nor even innocent. He is a wax-museum figure come to life and living on his own terms with the past.

Questions

1. Writers can laugh with or at comic characters, and can thereby establish how their readers will respond. What does Meyer do throughout the essay to make sure that his readers will react to Broadmoore with appreciation, if not downright affection, rather than with derision or contempt? At what point in the essay is Meyer's approval of his subject apparent?

2. Highly original people, such as Broadmoore, make good subjects for comic portraits. Why? What idiosyncrasies of Broadmoore's does Meyer emphasize? How does Meyer manage to point out such features as Broadmoore's high-neck collars, non-safety eyeglass lenses, and a pickup truck " 'as old as I can afford'," without making his subject appear foolish?

3. Broadmoore's speech, like his way of living, is intentionally anachronistic. Illustrate this, and explain how the numerous quotations contribute to the portrait's engaging good humor.

4. Meyer describes Broadmoore's house, his workshop, his clothing, his income, even his manner of shaving (with "a straight-edge razor sharpened on a leather strop," paragraph 39), and his barn, which contains "the world's most pristine privy" (paragraph 41). How does all of this information contribute to the portrait of Broadmoore? How does it increase our admiration for this eccentric man?

Parody/Burlesque

WOODY ALLEN

The Whore of Mensa

"The Whore of Mensa" is a double parody. Allen takes one of the most anti-intellectual forms of literature—tough-guy, private-eye, detective fiction—and parodies it through burlesquing its conventions and its language. The situation is typical: the distressed victim comes to the detective for help, and through a superabundance of exaggerated clichés—of thoughts, actions, and language—translates a minor into a major key. Lupowitz, the "private investigator," thinks in cliché terms: " 'you've got to go with your hunches.' " He has the instincts of a stereotyped hardboiled dick: "I should have trusted the cold chill that shot up my spine." He acts like one, keeping a "bottle of rye handy for nonmedicinal purposes." But especially he talks like one, using exaggerated metaphors (his client is a "quivering pat of butter . . . shaking like a lead singer in a rumba band") coupled with super-terse, no-nonsense language: " 'Kaiser Lupowitz?' 'That's what it says on my license.' "

Allen replaces the expected prostitutes in Flossie's "pleasure palace" with educated call girls with "Long straight hair, leather bag . . . no makeup," who provide a "quick intellectual experience"—the more sophisticated, the higher the price—and then leave. No commitments. These women sound very much like the people who constitute Allen's real-life audience, people who might fake an intellectual response, or pencil " 'Yes, very true' into the margin of some book on Kant." And Allen parodies these, too, the pseudo-intellectuals who rattle off their "ideas glibly" but mechanically in jargon they don't understand ("the substructure of pessimism") before having anxiety attacks or faking suicide. Funny, n'est-ce pas?

1   One thing about being a private investigator, you've got to learn to go with your hunches. That's why when a quivering pat of butter named Word Babcock walked into my office and laid his cards on the table, I should have trusted the cold chill that shot up my spine.

2   "Kaiser?" he said, "Kaiser Lupowitz?"

3   "That's what it says on my license," I owned up.

4   "You've got to help me. I'm being blackmailed. Please!"

5   He was shaking like the lead singer in a rumba band. I pushed a glass across the desk top and a bottle of rye I keep handy for nonmedicinal purposes. "Suppose you relax and tell me all about it."

6   "You . . . you won't tell my wife?"

7   "Level with me, Word. I can't make any promises."

8   He tried pouring a drink, but you could hear the clicking sound across the street, and most of the stuff wound up in his shoes.

9   "I'm a working guy," he said. "Mechanical maintenance. I build and service joy buzzers. You know—those little fun gimmicks that give people a shock when they shake hands?"

"So?" 10

"A lot of your executives like 'em. Particularly down on Wall Street." 11

"Get to the point." 12

"I'm on the road a lot. You know how it is—lonely. Oh, not what you're 13
thinking. See, Kaiser, I'm basically an intellectual. Sure, a guy can meet all the
bimbos he wants. But the really brainy women—they're not so easy to find
on short notice."

"Keep talking." 14

"Well, I heard of this young girl. Eighteen years old. A Yassar student. 15
For a price, she'll come over and discuss any subject—Proust, Yeats, anthropology. Exchange of ideas. You see what I'm driving at?"

"Not exactly." 16

"I mean, my wife is great, don't get me wrong. But she won't discuss 17
Pound with me. Or Eliot. I didn't know that when I married her. See, I need
a woman who's mentally stimulating, Kaiser. And I'm willing to pay for it. I
don't want an involvement—I want a quick intellectual experience, then I
want the girl to leave. Christ, Kaiser, I'm a happily married man."

"How long has this been going on?" 18

"Six months. Whenever I have that craving, I call Flossie. She's a madam, 19
with a master's in comparative lit. She sends me over an intellectual, see?"

So he was one of those guys whose weakness was really bright women. I 20
felt sorry for the poor sap. I figured there must be a lot of jokers in his
position, who were starved for a little intellectual communication with the
opposite sex and would pay through the nose for it.

"Now she's threatening to tell my wife," he said. 21

"Who is?" 22

"Flossie. They bugged the motel room. They got tapes of me discussing 23
The Waste Land and *Styles of Radical Will,* and, well, really getting into some
issues. They want ten grand or they go to Carla. Kaiser, you've got to help
me! Carla would die if she knew she didn't turn me on up here."

The old call-girl racket. I had heard rumors that the boys at headquarters 24
were on to something involving a group of educated women, but so far they
were stymied.

"Get Flossie on the phone for me." 25

"What?" 26

"I'll take your case, Word. But I get fifty dollars a day, plus expenses. 27
You'll have to repair a lot of joy buzzers."

"It won't be ten Gs' worth, I'm sure of that," he said with a grin, and 28
picked up the phone and dialed a number. I took it from him and winked. I
was beginning to like him.

Seconds later, a silky voice answered, and I told her what was on my 29
mind. "I understand you can help me set up an hour of good chat," I said.

"Sure, honey. What do you have in mind?" 30

"I'd like to discuss Melville." 31

32   "*Moby Dick* or the shorter novels?"

33   "What's the difference?"

34   "The price. That's all. Symbolism's extra."

35   "What'll it run me?"

36   "Fifty, maybe a hundred for *Moby Dick*. You want a comparative discussion—Melville and Hawthorne? That could be arranged for a hundred."

37   "The dough's fine," I told her and gave her the number of a room at the Plaza.

38   "You want a blonde or a brunette?"

39   "Surprise me," I said, and hung up.

40   I shaved and grabbed some black coffee while I checked over the Monarch College Outline series. Hardly an hour had passed before there was a knock on my door. I opened it, and standing there was a young redhead who was packed into her slacks like two big scoops of vanilla ice cream.

41   "Hi, I'm Sherry."

42   They really knew how to appeal to your fantasies. Long straight hair, leather bag, silver earrings, no make-up.

43   "I'm surprised you weren't stopped, walking into the hotel dressed like that," I said. "The house dick can usually spot an intellectual."

44   "A five-spot cools him."

45   "Shall we begin?" I said, motioning her to the couch.

46   She lit a cigarette and got right to it. "I think we could start by approaching *Billy Budd* as Melville's justification of the ways of God to man, *n'est-ce pas?*"

47   "Interestingly, though, not in a Miltonian sense." I was bluffing. I wanted to see if she'd go for it.

48   "No. *Paradise Lost* lacked the substructure of pessimism." She did.

49   "Right, right. God, you're right," I murmured.

50   "I think Melville reaffirmed the virtues of innocence in a naïve yet sophisticated sense—don't you agree?"

51   I let her go on. She was barely nineteen years old, but already she had developed the hardened facility of the pseudo-intellectual. She rattled off her ideas glibly, but it was all mechanical. Whenever I offered an insight, she faked a response: "Oh, yes, Kaiser. Yes, baby, that's deep. A platonic comprehension of Christianity—why didn't I see it before?"

52   We talked for about an hour and then she said she had to go. She stood up and I laid a C-note on her.

53   "Thanks, honey."

54   "There's plenty more where that came from."

55   "What are you trying to say?"

56   I had piqued her curiosity. She sat down again.

57   "Suppose I wanted to—have a party?" I said.

58   "Like, what kind of party?"

59   "Suppose I wanted Noam Chomsky explained to me by two girls?"

"Oh, wow."   60

"If you'd rather forget it . . ."   61

"You'd have to speak with Flossie," she said. "It'd cost you."   62

Now was the time to tighten the screws. I flashed my private-investiga-   63
tor's badge and informed her it was a bust.

"What!"   64

"I'm fuzz, sugar, and discussing Melville for money is an 802. You can   65
do time."

"You louse!"   66

"Better come clean, baby. Unless you want to tell your story down at   67
Alfred Kazin's office, and I don't think he'd be too happy to hear it."

She began to cry. "Don't turn me in, Kaiser," she said. "I needed the   68
money to complete my master's. I've been turned down for a grant. *Twice.*
Oh, Christ."

It all poured out—the whole story. Central Park West upbringing,   69
Socialist summer camps, Brandeis. She was every dame you saw waiting in
line at the Elgin or the Thalia, or penciling the words "Yes, very true" into
the margin of some book on Kant. Only somewhere along the line she had
made a wrong turn.

"I needed cash. A girl friend said she knew a married guy whose wife   70
wasn't very profound. He was into Blake. She couldn't hack it. I said sure, for
a price I'd talk Blake with him. I was nervous at first. I faked a lot of it. He
didn't care. My friend said there were others. Oh, I've been busted before. I
got caught reading *Commentary* in a parked car, and I was once stopped and
frisked at Tanglewood. Once more and I'm a three-time loser."

"Then take me to Flossie."   71

She bit her lip and said, "The Hunter College Book Store is a front."   72

"Yes?"   73

"Like those bookie joints that have barbershops outside for show. You'll   74
see."

I made a quick call to headquarters and then said to her, "Okay, sugar.   75
You're off the hook. But don't leave town."

She tilted her face up toward mine gratefully. "I can get you photographs   76
of Dwight Macdonald reading," she said.

"Some other time."   77

I walked into the Hunter College Book Store. The salesman, a young   78
man with sensitive eyes, came up to me. "Can I help you?" he said.

"I'm looking for a special edition of *Advertisements for Myself.* I under-   79
stand the author had several thousand gold-leaf copies printed up for friends."

"I'll have to check," he said. "We have a WATS line to Mailer's house."   80

I fixed him with a look. "Sherry sent me," I said.   81

"Oh, in that case, go on back," he said. He pressed a button. A wall of   82
books opened, and I walked like a lamb into that bustling pleasure palace
known as Flossie's.

83   Red flocked wallpaper and a Victorian décor set the tone. Pale, nervous girls with black-rimmed glasses and blunt-cut hair lolled around on sofas, riffling Penguin Classics provocatively. A blonde with a big smile winked at me, nodded toward a room upstairs, and said, "Wallace Stevens, eh?" But it wasn't just intellectual experiences—they were peddling emotional ones, too. For fifty bucks, I learned, you could "relate without getting close." For a hundred, a girl would lend you her Bartók records, have dinner, and then let you watch while she had an anxiety attack. For one-fifty, you could listen to FM radio with twins. For three bills, you got the works: A thin Jewish brunette would pretend to pick you up at the Museum of Modern Art, let you read her master's, get you involved in a screaming quarrel at Elaine's over Freud's conception of women, and then fake a suicide of your choosing—the perfect evening, for some guys. Nice racket. Great town, New York.

84   "Like what you see?" a voice said behind me. I turned and suddenly found myself standing face to face with the business end of a .38. I'm a guy with a strong stomach, but this time it did a back flip. It was Flossie, all right. The voice was the same, but Flossie was a man. His face was hidden by a mask.

85   "You'll never believe this," he said, "but I don't even have a college degree. I was thrown out for low grades."

86   "Is that why you wear that mask?"

87   "I devised a complicated scheme to take over *The New York Review of Books,* but it meant I had to pass for Lionel Trilling. I went to Mexico for an operation. There's a doctor in Juarez who gives people Trilling's features— for a price. Something went wrong. I came out looking like Auden, with Mary McCarthy's voice. That's when I started working the other side of the law."

88   Quickly, before he could tighten his finger on the trigger, I went into action. Heaving forward, I snapped my elbow across his jaw and grabbed the gun as he fell back. He hit the ground like a ton of bricks. He was still whimpering when the police showed up.

89   "Nice work, Kaiser," Sergeant Holmes said. "When we're through with this guy, the F.B.I. wants to have a talk with him. A little matter involving some gamblers and an annotated copy of Dante's *Inferno.* Take him away, boys."

90   Later that night, I looked up an old account of mine named Gloria. She was blond. She had graduated *cum laude.* The difference was she majored in physical education. It felt good.

Questions

1. A common kind of parody is a burlesque version of another literary, musical, or artistic form. If you're familiar with conventional detective fiction, show how Allen

has exaggerated its features in "The Whore of Mensa." Would readers unfamiliar with detective fiction be able to enjoy this, if they didn't recognize what was being parodied?

2. By the same token, is it possible to appreciate Allen's parody of the stereotypical brothel and its employees if one has never been in a brothel or encountered a prostitute? Will merely having read about such things be enough? Given the reader's customary expectations of a call girl, what is the impact of our first meeting with Sherry, "Long straight hair, leather bag, silver earrings, no make-up," who gets right to the point by " 'approaching *Billy Budd* as Melville's justification of the ways of God to man, *n'est-ce pas?* " "

3. What dimensions of humor does the dialogue add to the narrative? Is much lost if readers don't recognize the references (paragraphs 65–80) to Melville, Alfred Kazin, the Thalia, Kant, Blake, *Commentary,* Tanglewood, *Advertisements for Myself,* or Mailer? Is it enough simply to recognize these allusions as a spoof on pseudo-intellectuals?

4. The purpose of satire, as in "A Modest Proposal" (518–24), is reform. Parody, like hypocrisy, may merely be the tribute vice pays to virtue; it may or may not imply the need to reform the original after which it is modeled. Does "The Whore of Mensa" imply the need to reform anything, or can it simply be enjoyed for its own sake? Explain your answer.

FRANK SULLIVAN

The Cliché Expert Testifies as a Literary Critic

Francis John Sullivan was born in Saratoga Springs, New York, in 1892. After graduating from Cornell in 1914, he began a career as a straight news reporter on The New York World, *but gave vent to his comic impulse in reporting the 1924 Democratic convention by inventing a woman "who saved her butter and egg money to come to the convention and root for Al Smith. Then to give the item piquancy I added that she was 104 years old." This led, in 1926, to a lifelong career as a humorist on the staff of* The New Yorker, *where wit and bizarre wisdom reigned supreme in the works of Sullivan and such other notable comic writers as Robert Benchley, Dorothy Parker, S. J. Perelman, and James Thurber. Sullivan's jocular irreverence is implied by the titles of his numerous collections of essays, including* In One Ear *(1933),* A Pearl in Every Oyster *(1938),* A Rock in Every Snowball *(1946), and* The Night the Old Nostalgia Burned Down *(1953).*

Sullivan's humorous devices include incongruities, funny names ("Lake Wassamat-tawichez"), and the exaggerated strings of clichés uttered by Mr. Arbuthnot, "The Cliché Expert." Arbuthnot, invariably interviewed by a questioner who sets him up for the predictable bon mot, utters firm opinions on every subject under the sun in the ringing tones of one smug with absolute certainty. Thus the Cliché Expert, in testifying on baseball, says that "Big-league baseball is customarily played by brilliant outfielders, veteran hurlers, powerful sluggers, knuckle-ball artists, towering first basemen, key moundsmen," and a host of others.

In testifying on politics he affirms that he has "undying faith in the principles laid down by the Founding Fathers. And I shall exercise eternal vigilance that our priceless heritage may be safeguarded." Here, in an essay reprinted from Sullivan at Bay *(1929), Sullivan wrings every conceivable ounce of humor out of the tired clichés of long-suffering and overbearing book reviewers.*

1   Q: *Mr. Arbuthnot, you are an expert in the use of the cliché as applied to literary criticism?*

2   A: I am told that I am, Mr. Sullivan.

3   Q: *We shall soon find out. What is this object, marked Exhibit A?*

4   A: That is a book.

5   Q: *Good. What kind of book is it?*

6   A: It is a minor classic.

7   Q: *And what kind of document is it?*

8   A: It is a valuable document.

9   Q: *Very good, Mr. Arbuthnot. Please continue.*

10   A: It is a book in which the results of painstaking—or scholarly—research are embodied, and it should appeal to a wide public. This reviewer could not put it down.

11   Q: *Why not?*

12   A: Because of its penetrating insight. It is a sincere and moving study of family life against the background of a small cathedral town. It is also a vivid and faithful portrayal.

13   Q: *How written?*

14   A: Written with sympathy, pathos, and kindly humor. It throws a clear light on a little understood subject and is well worth reading.

15   Q: *How is it illustrated?*

16   A: Profusely. It is original in conception, devoid of sentimentality, highly informative, consistently witty, and rich in color. You should place it on your library list.

17   Q: *Why?*

18   A: Because it strikes a new note in fiction. Mystery and suspense crowd its pages. The author has blended fact and fiction and the result is an authentic drama of social revolution, a definite contribution to proletarian literature.

19   Q: *Told with a wealth of what?*

20   A: Told with a wealth of detail.

21   Q: *And how portrayed?*

22   A: Realistically portrayed, in staccato prose. For sheer brilliance of style there has been nothing like it since *Moby Dick*. Rarely does a narrative move at such a fast pace.

23   Q: *What is it a shrewd comment on?*

24   A: The contemporary scene. It marks a red-letter day in current literature. It is capital entertainment.

25   Q: *What pervades it?*

A: A faint tinge of irony. 26

Q: *And how is it translated?* 27

A: Ably. It is a penetrating study in abnormal psychology, and unlike most 28
scientific works it is written in language understandable to the layman. It
belongs in the front rank of modern picaresque literature. Ideology.

Q: *I beg your pardon?* 29

A: I said ideology. Also catharsis. 30

Q: *What about them?* 31

A: Well, they have to come in somewhere. 32

Q: *I see. Now, to return to the minor classic, Mr. Arbuthnot. Would you call it a* 33
subtle and arresting piece of work?

A: Certainly I would. Why do you suppose I'm an expert in the use of the 34
cliché? I'd also call it an honest attempt to depict, a remarkable first novel, a
veritable triumph, a genuine contribution, a thrilling saga of life in frontier
days, and the most impressive study of degeneration since Zola. It bids fair to
go down as one of the great biographies of all time, including *Moby Dick*. In
short, it has unusual merit.

Q: *How does it augur?* 35

A: It augurs well for the future of the author. 36

Q: *And how does it bid?* 37

A: It bids fair to become a best-seller. 38

Q: *And how does it end?* 39

A. It ends upon a distinct note of despair. It is a work of art. 40

Q: *I'm glad you liked it, Mr. Arbuthnot.* 41

A: Who said I liked it? 42

Q: *Didn't you?* 43

A: Certainly not. 44

Q: *Why not?* 45

A: Because it is, one fears, mawkishly sentimental and, one regrets, faintly 46
pretentious. Curiously enough, it does not carry conviction. Strangely
enough, it lacks depth. Oddly enough, the denouement is weak. It is to be
regretted that the title is rather misleading and it need hardly be pointed out
that the book as a whole lacks cohesion and form. I am very much afraid, one
regrets, that it falls definitely into the escapist school of fiction. And of course,
like all first novels, it is autobiographical.

Q: *I'm glad you told me. I won't buy it.* 47

A: Ah, but in spite of its faults it contains much of real value. It kept me 48
awake till three. In the opinion of the present reviewer it would be the long-
awaited great American novel except for one serious defect.

Q: *What is that?* 49

A: It lacks an index. 50

Q: *Mr. Arbuthnot, it is easy to see that you have earned your spurs in the field of* 51
literary criticism. So much for the book. Now, observe this object I hold here in my
hand, marked Exhibit B. What is it?

52   A: That. *That* is an *author*.

53   Q: *Whose are those italics, Mr. Arbuthnot?*

54   A: The italics are mine.

55   Q: *What kind of author is this?*

56   A: A promising young author who should be watched.

57   Q: *What does he write?*

58   A: Powerful first novels.

59   Q: *What kind of storyteller is he?*

60   A: He's a born storyteller.

61   Q: *What kind of satirist is he?*

62   A: A satirist of the first order.

63   Q: *Tell us more about this interesting creature.*

64   A: Well, he cannot be lightly dismissed. He is undoubtedly to be reckoned with, one feels, as a definite force. He is in the front rank of the younger writers.

65   Q: *Why?*

66   A: Because his work plainly shows the influence of Joyce, Hemingway, Huxley, Proust, Gertrude Stein, Auden, Eliot, and Virginia Woolf. Here is an authentic talent from which we may expect great things.

67   Q: *So what do you do?*

68   A: So I hail him. And I acclaim him. He has a keen ear for the spoken word. He also has a flair. He sets out to tell. He deals with themes, or handles them. He recaptures moods. His execution is brilliant, his insight is poetic, his restraint is admirable, and he has a sense of values. There is something almost uncanny in his ability to look into men's souls. And he paints a vivid word picture and works on a vast canvas.

69   Q: *How?*

70   A: With consummate artistry. He writes with commendable frankness.

71   Q: *Using what kind of style?*

72   A: Using a limpid prose style. He has a real freshness of approach that stamps him as an artist in the true sense of the word. He culls his material and his niche in the hall of literary fame seems secure.

73   Q: *I'm glad you like him, Mr. Arbuthnot.*

74   A: But I don't.

75   Q: *No? Why not?*

76   A: Because his talent is plainly superficial and ephemeral. He has an unfortunate habit of allowing his personality to obtrude. His book is badly documented and not the least of his many irritating mannerisms is his addiction to inexcusable typographical errors. His book is full of clichés and he does not make his characters live and feel and breathe. And he writes with one eye on Hollywood.

77   Q: *You mean to tell me that a cad like that has the audacity to call himself an author?*

78   A: Well now, don't be too hard on him. Although he decidedly does not

justify his early promise it is as yet too early to evaluate his work. Want to know about the plot?

Q: *Yes, indeed. What about the plot?* 79

A: It is well rounded and fully developed. But it is marred by structural 80
weaknesses.

Q: *What kind of structural weaknesses?* 81

A: Inherent structural weaknesses. It is motivated, of course. And its threads 82
are cunningly woven into a harmonious texture by the deft hand of a skilled
literary craftsman.

Q: *Just one thing more, Mr. Arbuthnot. How many kinds of readers are there?* 83

A. Three—casual, general, and gentle. 84

Q: *Mr. Arbuthnot, I think that is all. I can't thank you enough for having come* 85
here today to help us out.

A: It has been a pleasure—a vivid, fascinating, significant, vigorous, timely, 86
gracious, breath-taking, mature, adequate, nostalgic, unforgettable, gripping,
articulate, engrossing, poignant, and adult pleasure to be of service to you,
Mr. Sullivan. Good day, sir.

JAMES THURBER

The Unicorn in the Garden

This classic from Thurber's Fables for Our Time and Famous Poems Illustrated *(1940)*
contains a number of the components of classic comedy: the nagging, domineering wife
(Xanthippe, echoed in Blondie); the modest, henpecked, secretly resentful husband (Andy
Capp, and Thurber's own immortal Walter Mitty); an incredible but purportedly true
situation (the unicorn in the garden); and the reversal. In Thurber's Fables, *the reversal of*
the expected situation is invariably summarized in the moral, a punch line packing a
surprising and hilarious double whammy.

Once upon a sunny morning a man who sat in a breakfast nook looked up 1
from his scrambled eggs to see a white unicorn with a gold horn quietly
cropping the roses in the garden. The man went up to the bedroom where his
wife was still asleep and woke her. "There's a unicorn in the garden," he said.
"Eating roses." She opened one unfriendly eye and looked at him. "The
unicorn is a mythical beast," she said, and turned her back on him. The man
walked slowly downstairs and out into the garden. The unicorn was still
there; he was now browsing among the tulips. "Here, unicorn," said the
man, and he pulled up a lily and gave it to him. The unicorn ate it gravely.
With a high heart, because there was a unicorn in his garden, the man went
upstairs and roused his wife again. "The unicorn," he said, "ate a lily." His
wife sat up in bed and looked at him, coldly. "You are a booby," she said,

"and I am going to have you put in the booby-hatch." The man, who had never liked the words "booby" and "booby-hatch," and who liked them even less on a shining morning when there was a unicorn in the garden, thought for a moment. "We'll see about that," he said. He walked over to the door. "He has a golden horn in the middle of his forehead," he told her. Then he went back to the garden to watch the unicorn; but the unicorn had gone away. The man sat down among the roses and went to sleep.

2   As soon as the husband had gone out of the house, the wife got up and dressed as fast as she could. She was very excited and there was a gloat in her eye. She telephoned the police and she telephoned a psychiatrist; she told them to hurry to her house and bring a strait-jacket. When the police and the psychiatrist arrived they sat down in chairs and looked at her, with great interest. "My husband," she said, "saw a unicorn this morning." The police looked at the psychiatrist and the psychiatrist looked at the police. "He told me it ate a lily," she said. The psychiatrist looked at the police and the police looked at the psychiatrist. "He told me it had a golden horn in the middle of its forehead," she said. At a solemn signal from the psychiatrist, the police leaped from their chairs and seized the wife. They had a hard time subduing her, for she put up a terrific struggle, but they finally subdued her. Just as they got her into the strait-jacket, the husband came back into the house.

3   "Did you tell your wife you saw a unicorn?" asked the police. "Of course not," said the husband. "The unicorn is a mythical beast." "That's all I wanted to know," said the psychiatrist. "Take her away. I'm sorry, sir, but your wife is as crazy as a jay bird." So they took her away, cursing and screaming, and shut her up in an institution. The husband lived happily ever after.

Moral: Don't count your boobies until they are hatched.

DOROTHY PARKER

The Grandmother of the Aunt
of the Gardener

Parker, among the sharpest New York wits of the Jazz Age and the Depression, was credited with such bons mots as, "You can lead a horticulture but you can't make her think." Born Dorothy Rothschild in 1893 in West End, New Jersey, she was educated at Miss Dana's School in Morristown, New Jersey, and at the Blessed Sacrament Convent in New York. She had the good fortune to begin her career as a writer for magazines themselves in their experimental infancy: Vogue in 1916; Vanity Fair, 1916–1920; and The New Yorker, 1925–1957, to which she contributed stories, verse (not serious enough to be "poetry," she said), and reviews. Although she wrote under the name of her first husband, she married actor Alan Campbell twice (1934–47, 1950–63), and with him—despite nearly paralyzing writer's block—wrote over twenty screenplays, the most famous being A Star Is Born (1937). Parker's legacy to modern literature is several volumes of short stories and verse, all of it wry, witty, and latently feminist; some of it sentimental, much of it currently available in The Portable Dorothy Parker *(1944, 1973).*

The purpose of most book reviews is to provide an interpretive overview of the work in question. Parker's review, however, calls attention more to the reviewer's wit than to the book at hand. Indeed, Just the French One Wants to Know *is a generically familiar volume, guaranteed by its very nature to be full of locutions never appropriate to any situation in any country. Here Parker presents the persona of a woman of a certain age, struggling to learn a language that forever escapes her, in hopes of capturing a romantic culture also beyond her grasp. She becomes progressively more frustrated and enraged by the ridiculous sentences the book proposes, such as "It was to punish your foster-brother" and "I am afraid he will not arrive in time to accompany me on the harp." Representative of a nation of maladroit language learners, Parker easily proves "that bitchiness [is] the soul of wit"—and of some memorable reviews.*

Once I went through Spain, like a bat out of hell, with a party that in-   1
cluded—nay, grew to center upon—a distinguished American of letters. He spoke French as a Frenchman, rather than like one; his German was flawless; he was persuasive in Italian, and read Magyar for easy amusement; but, at the hour of our start, he did not have a stitch of Spanish to his name. Yet, when the train clacked out of Hendaye, he began trading droll anecdotes with the guard, and by the time we were set in Zaragoza, he was helping the natives along with their subjunctives. It was enough to make me, in a word, sick.

For so lavish a gift of ear and of tongue has, to one forever denied any   2
part of it, something of the repellent quality of black magic. How am I not to be bitter, who have stumbled solo round about Europe, equipped only with *"Non, non et non!"* and *"Où est le lavabo des dames?"* How shall I leash my envy, who have lived so placed that there were weeks at a stretch when I heard or saw no word of English; who was committed entirely and eagerly to French manners, customs, and abbreviations, yet could never get it through the head that the letter "c" on a water-faucet does not stand for "cold"?

It isn't that I have not been given every opportunity; it is simply and   3
dismally that I am incapable of acquiring an extramural language. It is true that I can read French at glacier speed, muffing only the key-word of every sentence. It is true that I can understand it as spoken, provided the speaker is reasonably adept at pantomime. It is also, I am afraid, true that, deep in New York, there are certain spells during certain evenings—cognac is best for a starter—when my English slips from me like the shucked skin of a snake, and I converse only in the elegant French tongue. But what French! O God, O Montreal, what French! It must be faced. Struggle though I have and I do and I will, I am no darned use as a linguist. And to think that there are those, like that man of letters, to whom other languages than their own come as sweetly and as naturally as so many Springtimes is to acquire a pain in the neck for which there is no relief.

But I don't give up; I forget why not. Annually I drag out the conversa-   4
tion books and begin that process called brushing up. It always happens

about this time, when the *Wanderlust* is as overpowering as the humidity, and I develop my yearly case of the get-away-from-it-alls. And it seems to me only the part of wisdom to dust off the Continental tongues, because you can't tell—maybe any time now one of the steamship lines will listen to reason and accept teeth instead of money, and I will be on my way back to the Old Country.

5   And annually I am licked right at the start. It is happening to me even now. I have here before me a small green book called *The Ideal System for Acquiring a Practical Knowledge of French* by Mlle. V. D. Gaudel (who, in case you're going over and you don't know anyone in Paris, lives at 346 Rue Saint-Honoré). Well, everything might have been all right if Mlle. Gaudel—now why do I picture her as fond of dancing and light wines, with a way of flipping up her skirts at the back, to the cry of "Oh-la-la"?—had not subtitled her work *Just the French One Wants to Know*. Somehow, those words antagonized me, by their very blandness, so that I forgot the thirst for knowledge and searched the tome only for concrete examples of just the French one will never need. Oh-la-la, yourself, Mademoiselle, and go on and get the hell back into *La Vie Parisienne!*

6   Now you know perfectly well that at my time of life it would be just a dissipation of energy for me to learn the French equivalent of "Either now, or this afternoon at five." It is, at best, a matter of dark doubt that I shall ever be in any position in which it will be necessary for me to cry: "Although the captain is far from here, I always think of him." It is possible, of course, but it's a nasty wrench to the arm of coincidence that I shall find occasion for the showing-off of the phrase "Her marriage took place (*eut lieu*) on the 2nd of April, 1905"; or that it will be given me to slide gently into a conversation with "I admire the large black eyes of this orphan." Better rest I silent forever than that I pronounce: "In this case, it is just that you should not like riding and swimming"; or that I inquire: "Are you pleased that they will bring the cricket set?"; or that I swing into autobiography with the confession: "I do not like to play blindman's buff"; or that I so seriously compromise myself as to suggest: "I propose that you breakfast with me and afterwards look for our friends."

7   The future is veiled, perhaps mercifully, and so I cannot say that never, while I live, shall I have occasion to announce in French: "It was to punish your foster-brother"; but I know which way I would bet. It may be that some day I shall be in such straits that I shall have to remark: "The friend of my uncle who took the quill feather bought a round black rice-straw hat trimmed with two long ostrich feathers and a jet buckle." Possibly circumstances will so weave themselves that it will be just the moment for me to put in: "Mr. Fouchet would have received some eel." It might occur that I must thunder: "Obey, or I will not show you the beautiful gold chain." But I will be damned if it is ever going to be of any good to me to have at hand Mlle. Gaudel's masterpiece: "I am afraid he will not arrive in time to accompany me on the harp."

Oh, "Just the French One Wants to Know" *mon oeil*, Mademoiselle. And 8
you know what you can do, far better than I could tell you.

There is a little more comfort in a booklet called *The American in Europe*, 9
where neat sentences are listed for use in almost every contingency. Yet,
somehow there sneaked in under the curious heading of "The Theatre, the
Music" this monologue: "I love you; Don't forget me; The beautiful blue
eyes; Let us love one another; I play all my pieces by heart without any
music." Doubtless they order those things rather better in France, but I feel
that, according to our New York ideas, that last phrase is all wrong. It should
run, for its place in the sequence: "Come on down to my apartment—I want
to show you some remarkably fine etchings I just bought."

To turn to Spanish proves small good. Here I have a stamp-sized work, 10
sent out by Hugo's Simplified System, entitled *How to Get All You Want
While Travelling in Spain* (and a pretty sweeping statement, too, Mr. Hugo,
if I may say so). Mr. Hugo has captured the Iberian spirit so cleverly as to
enable his pupils phonetically to learn "I don't like this table—this waiter—
this wine," and to go on from there into truly idiomatic crabbing.

Mr. Hugo is good, but his book can never touch that manual of Spanish 11
conversation that it was once my fortune to pick up in Madrid; though I
curse myself for leaving it there, one scene in it is forever branded on my
brain and engraved upon my heart. The premise is that a mother and her
engaged daughter visit a furniture shop to select the double bed (*matrimonio*)
for the future bride's home. (The work was titled, as I recall it, *Easy Conversations for Everyday Occasions*.) The mother sees a bed that she approves—the
daughter, in the Latin manner, never opens her trap. Mom asks the salesman
the price of the piece of furniture, and he tells her, with respect, "Thirteen pesetas." To which the dear little grayhaired lady replies, very simply,
"Jesu!" . . .

Well. I got a long way from the place I started. All I meant to do was 12
moan over my trouble in working on foreign languages. And it took me all
these words to do it. The thing to do, surely, is to give the French and the
Spanish books to some deserving family, and get to work on that English.

KEN WUNDERLICH (Student)

Playing the Sax

*After graduating from the College of William and Mary in 1982 with a B.A. in economics,
Wunderlich earned an M.B.A. from the University of Chicago. He now works as a financial
analyst for Hewlett-Packard in Boise, Idaho.*

   *As Wunderlich discovered in writing this, self-parody can be an engaging sort of
humor. As the butt of his or her own jokes, the writer can evoke an audience's sympathy along*

with their laughter at the innocent, the klutz, the self-deluded, the vain or pompous or prideful or other comic character type he represents. This technique works especially well if the writer clues the readers in early that he's actually aware of his shortcomings, so that both writer and audience know they're laughing at the same flaws and foibles. Thus in "Playing the Sax" Wunderlich presents himself as an egotistical character who believes he can "become a virtuoso overnight" through mastery of a single note or two, whereas both the author and his audience know very well that the sax player's great expectations ("Those record companies . . . you just can't keep them away.") are the height of folly. This is the theme; the author exploits variations on this as the listeners consistently regard the character's playing as horrible while the saxophonist blindly misinterprets their anguished reactions as approval. Indeed, the author duly reports Wunderlich's view, "Kevin [my roommate] sat sick with envy at my musical proficiency" and its comic translation, " 'Do you know what I wish,' [Kevin said] 'I wish I had gone to school in Boston like my parents wanted me to.' " Comic writers can take this again from the top, and again, as long as the joke holds up.

1   Friday afternoon rolled around once again and, as usual, I made my weekly pilgrimage to Roger's to get clobbered at backgammon. During one of the many times in which I was unable to move, I thoughtfully examined the almost ritualistic lack of excitement I associate with each weekend. The time had come, I decided, to do something crafty and bizarre. After all, you can only play backgammon for so many Friday afternoons before people begin wondering what in the world is wrong with you. Roger woke me out of my trance.

2   "Hey, are you going to move, or what?"

3   "Roger, would you let me borrow your saxophone just for this weekend," I asked. The sax couldn't be hard to play. So what if I didn't even know how to hold one, let alone makes notes come out of it. I figured I would at least be able to say I had done something different and who knows, perhaps I might have a little fun for a change.

4   Roger lent me the saxophone contingent upon my being elsewhere when I played it. Roger knew I played the piano well, but he must have had some sixth sense about my ability to play sax. I was counting heavily upon the fact that I once read a book about Charlie Parker, the legendary jazz saxophonist, to provide all the background I would need to become a virtuoso overnight. I went back home with the sax lovingly wedged into the front seat of my car, and I slept that night giddy with anticipation about my fate.

5   The next day, I ran into some problems just setting up. For one thing, a tenor sax is too big to sit properly in your lap, so if you sit down and try to play it the mouthpiece ends up in your eyes. Also, all the reeds were either the wrong size or broken. I used one of the wrong-sized reeds, thus denying myself the sheer pleasure of splinters in my mouth. My final difficulty was the fact that my hands did not know where to go by themselves, as I had hoped they would. A piano is different: since a piano has eighty-eight keys, no one can begin to try to cover them all. But the way they put the sax together, it looks as if you ought to be able to push all the buttons down at once. It was a frustrating experience trying to seat my hands comfortably yet cover the necessary holes. Once I arrived at something feasible, I squatted on the floor

to keep the oversized reed out of my eyes and got ready to play my first note. But my debut was delayed by a knock on the door.

Those record companies, I thought. You just can't keep them away. The minute they hear about new and rising talent, they hound you no end. But it was only Kevin. Kevin made a few ill-mannered queries about what in the world I thought I was doing, but I silenced him with my first note. 6

That first note came out sounding a lot more like a herd of wild animals that I had anticipated. Kevin was rolling on the floor with laughter. Doors opened all up and down the hall, and heads bobbed in and out looking for the source of the confusion. Obviously, they wanted more. I pranced up and down the hall playing note after note, all of which sounded pretty much the same, since I didn't know how to change notes just yet. Then I went back into my room and practiced my note for fifteen or twenty minutes, while Kevin sat sick with envy at my musical proficiency. 7

"Do you know what I wish," he said, after a particularly impressive blast, "I wish I had gone to school in Boston like my parents wanted me to." 8

By mid-afternoon I had developed quite a following. Several of my excited hallmates asked if I intended to keep it up much longer. Not all of the reactions were favorable, though, as is to be expected of the early reviews. Some of the girls on the second floor who think they know so much about music sent an anonymous sympathy card to "whoever is dying down there." The police stopped by under the assumption that someone was being murdered and shrieking hideously. I shrugged off my critics as being obvious neophytes to the world of art-saxophone. 9

I was overcoming the problems of exposure in leaps and bounds. The telephone turned out to be my best broadcasting source. Kevin dialed the numbers of some of my friends and I gave them free samples of my newfound talent without having to leave my own hall, which had become mysteriously deserted. By the time I had learned to play two different notes in succession, I was famous all over campus. 10

At the height of my glory, I realized the transience of my situation. Monday morning I would have to give this all up, for Roger demanded that I give his horn back by the end of the weekend. I didn't want to become another Cinderella, with only a pumpkin to show for all my skill. Then I became stricken with another wonderful idea. I would record this music for posterity, so that none of this incredible experience would be lost. After some coercion and threats, Kevin agreed to meet at the piano lounge in my dorm after dinner. 11

I had to hunt for Kevin, for he apparently forgot about our recording date. I found him cowering in the library. We got back to the dorm only to discover that the piano room was in use by someone playing conventional music. By now I knew how to use the power of the saxophone effectively. A couple quick blasts on my favorite note right outside the door produced a vacant lounge within seconds. We moved in the recording apparatus and proceeded to create music. 12

13   The session was uneventful. We were left to ourselves the entire evening, and Kevin and I took turns playing both the piano and sax as best we could. After listening to the finished product, Kevin suggested that we call ourselves the Crim Dell Ducks, a tribute to our feathered quackers on the campus pond. The only regret I have is that many of the songs sound the same, most likely due to a slight lack of sophistication. But we did, after all, produce an hour's worth of sheer musical joy that no one would ever be able to deny us. I went to bed feeling secure in my newly discovered love.

14   My hallmates ruined Sunday for me, because it turned out that every single one of them had three tests on Monday and regretfully had to ask me not to play. Not wanting to be selfish, I packed up the sax and took it back to Roger.

15   Roger met me at the door and disarmed me instantly. I related the activities of the previous day to him as he hid the instrument well out of my sight. He was especially surprised when I produced the tape we had made.

16   "I thought I told you I didn't want to hear any of it," he jested. I laughed and popped the cassette into the player as Roger sat in dumbfounded amazement. Roger's roommates unfortunately had to go to the library, so they postponed listening to the Ducks until some later date. Roger didn't move the whole time the album was playing, except to make some offhand remarks about my technical expertise or to go to the bathroom. When it was all over, Roger looked at me and said, "You did this, huh?" He paused. "And with my saxophone," he added. Roger just shook his head as I beamed with the proud countenance of an innovator in a brave new world.

17   Most of my friends were too busy all the next week to listen to the tape, and I began to wonder whether my overnight sensation was to go unnoticed by the masses. Friday rolled around again and as usual I found myself at Roger's losing at backgammon. My mind wandered with all sorts of schemes to market my tape and to go on tour. Roger coaxed me back into reality.

18   "Hey, are you going to move, or what?"

19   "Roger, I was just thinking . . ."

20   "Would you just shut up and move?"

Questions

1. Writers, like storytellers, can be the butt of their own jokes if they are sufficiently aware of the humor of the situation or their own inadequacies, previous or current. Whether or not they can control their own lives, they can nevertheless control how they handle their narrative material. Is this the case in "Playing the Sax"?

2. What kind of a character is Wunderlich in this essay? Have we any clues that Wunderlich as author is not as egotistical and obtuse as his character of the same name appears to be? Are readers expected to laugh at or with Wunderlich the character?

3. What features of college life in general and dormitory living in particular does Wunderlich the author draw on in his self-parody? Can he count on his readers to be familiar with the generic scene, if not the setting at his particular college?

4. A joke such as this, essentially on one theme, will falter or get boring or otherwise uninteresting if it is prolonged beyond its "natural" length. Does Wunderlich stop in time? Why or why not?

Writing Humor

Strategies

1. Is this subject suitable for humor? What makes it funny? Is it particularly enjoyable? foolish? frivolous? odd? paradoxical? an actual or potential problem? downright evil?

2. Why am I writing this? Do I want to move my readers to appreciation, enjoyment, laughter, ridicule, or social reform? Do I want also to dazzle them with my wit?

3. How are my readers likely to regard my subject initially? Are they likely to find the subject itself—or my treatment of it—taboo or potentially offensive? If so, how (if at all) can I overcome their objections? Should I try?

4. Will benign or more biting humor best accomplish my purpose? What type of writing will work best—narrative, portrait, social criticism, satire, parody, or something else?

5. Am I letting the humor speak for itself, without trying to explain the jokes or interpret the subtle wit? Is my humorous writing funny to other people? (Have I tried it out on sample readers to determine their reaction?) If the humor falls flat, what should I alter to affect my readers' reaction? Or should I leave the writing unchanged?

Suggestions

1. Write a good-humored narrative recollecting a wonderful, delightful, or otherwise thoroughly enjoyable experience you've had, as a child, adolescent, or adult. As you re-create this, try to convey its magic through precise details of setting, characters (including dialogue), their interaction and activities, atmosphere, and the tone of your words. You may want to use lots of sensory details, of sight, sound, taste, smell and touch, as Mark Twain does in "Uncle John's Farm" (237–42). (See also E. B. White, "Once More to the Lake," 232–37.)

2. Initiations—into the mysteries of driving, dating, drinking, cooking, team sports, dormitory (or other group) living, or other phenomena—can often be funny. As a writer, you have to be sufficiently removed from the phenomenon (often, by having survived the initiation and learned the skill) to see the humor in it in order to exploit its humorous potential. Write a humorous essay re-creating your initiation in an area you've subsequently mastered, from the point of view of someone who's sadder (or more relieved) but wiser. (See Ken Wunderlich, "Playing the Sax," 565–68.)

3. Write a portrait of an unusual, eccentric, or otherwise bizarre person whom you like, admire, or in other ways approve of, as Eugene Mayer does in "Mr. L. G. Broadmoore and the Way It Was" (546–50). See "Writing About People," writing suggestions 2–4 (193–94), for details.

4. Write a seemingly objective account of a phenomenon or some aspect of human behavior of which you actually disapprove, either because the form and context seem at variance (for instance, in Las Vegas weddings, as interpreted by Joan Didion in

"Marrying Absurd," 514–17), or because the phenomenon itself seems to you wrong, or causing problems, or otherwise inappropriate. Justify your opinion (and convince your readers) through your choice of details and selection of a revealing incident or several vignettes (brief glimpses of scenes or actions). Social and cultural phenomena are subjects particularly suitable for such an essay—preppie or Yuppie behavior, habits of television watching, ways of spending money (and foolish, trivial, or wasteful things to spend it on), styles of giving or going to parties. . . . (See Lillian Ross, "The Yellow Bus," 500–14.)

5. Write a variation on #4 in which a created character, a narrative persona, speaks ironically (as Swift's narrator does in "A Modest Proposal," 518–24) about your subject. The character's values should be at variance with the values you (and at least some of your audience) share. For instance, if you want to propose stiff penalties for drunk driving, your narrator—demonstrably unreliable—could be a firm advocate of drinking, and of driving without restraint, and could be shown driving unsafely while under the influence of alcohol, indifferent to the dangers. (See Craig Swanson, "It's the Only Video Game My Mom Lets Me Chew," 527–28.)

6. Write a humorous essay in which you divide a larger category (such as students, parents, Southerners, Californians, renters) into subcategories, and then characterize each subcategory through comparing and contrasting its parts (working students, athletes, grinds, preps, partygoers. . . .). Or write an analysis of the comic characteristics of an individual or group, either with benign intent (as John Leonard does in "My Son, the Roman," 544–46) or for satiric purposes (as S. J. Perelman does in "The Machismo Mystique," 528–32).

7. Write a modest proposal of your own, in the manner of Swift's "Modest Proposal" (518–24). Pick some significant problem that you think needs to be solved, and propose a radical (and patently outrageous) solution—perhaps a dramatic way to bring about world peace, to preserve endangered species, to dispose of chemical or nuclear waste. (In addition to Swift, see Russell Baker, "Universal Military Motion," 525–26.)

8. Write a parody of a literary style or literary mode, imitating and exaggerating its major features of structure, characters, language, dialogue, symbolism, allusions. Or pick a particular work of literature, a fairy tale or something serious, and parody that. (See Woody Allen's "Selections from the Allen Notebooks," 60–63, and "The Whore of Mensa," 552–56; Frank Sullivan's "The Cliché Expert Testifies as a Literary Critic," 557–61.) Or parody writings of other types exemplified in this book, such as a review, interview, sports article, how-to writing, travel directions, or other form.

9. Write a self-parody, either of yourself at a time in your life when you were bratty, irritating, or otherwise obnoxious; or when you held values that you now repudiate; or when in connection with your family or some other group, you were doing something foolish or regrettable (see Ken Wunderlich, "Playing the Sax," and James Thurber, "The Night the Bed Fell," 540–43). Or simply write an exaggerated account of an embarrassing incident, a day when everything went wrong, or a series of events that seemed calamitous at the time. This implies that you now have some distance from the values or behavior you exhibited then, and have sufficient perspective now to enable others to laugh, either at you or with you.

10. Write a fable or a more contemporary story with a comic twist. (See James Thurber, "The Unicorn in the Garden," 561–62.)

CHAPTER SEVEN

How-To-Do-It Writing

Writers of how-to-do-it essays or books have two main tasks: to help readers to understand, clearly and unambiguously, how to perform a particular process themselves, and to convince the readers that they have enough knowledge and skill to do so. How-to writings usually find a receptive audience, so congenial is the concept to the American dream. For we not only believe that if we work hard enough and long enough we will succeed, but that we can learn to do almost anything ourselves. All we need are the right instructions.

Subjects of How-To Writing

Almost anything that people can learn to do, grow, make, or aspire to can be the subject of a how-to writing. How to choose and use equipment: "Buying a Pickup Truck" (577–84). How to develop a skill: "A Personal Note on Tone" (how to play the French horn, 593–96). How to produce an object or product: "The Turning Point" (how to make pottery, 597–98) and "Brownies and Bar Cookies" (656–59). How to save, manage, or make money: "Rules for Writing and Endorsing Checks" (638–42). How to attain a state of mind or body: "Poor Richard's Rules for Success" (635–37) and "Exercising the Psyche" (622–28). How to accomplish personal or professional goals: "How to Submit Writing for Publication" (602–609) and "Coming Out on Top in the Job Interview" (642–50). Many of the subjects of how-to writings are of perennial interest: health, wealth, beauty, love, independence, power and status, long life. You can write on anything you want, whether it's a brand-new subject or an old but flourishing chestnut, as long as you can tell your readers how to do it.

Assumptions of How-To Writers and Readers

All how-to writings assume that it is good, useful, pleasurable, or otherwise desirable to achieve the aims promised by the how-to process, for any subject at all. Most writings promise satisfaction, if not joy, in either the performance of the process or the completion of it, or both. Thus in "Exercising the Psyche," Dianne and Robert Hales write carefully but optimistically about evidence that "the body can really help to heal the psyche," for "exercise can shift the focus from drugs and doctors to the individual, who can use it as a practical tool for improving the quality of life"—as a way to cope with stress, depression, anxiety, Type A behavior, alcoholism, and hyperactivity.

A second assumption is that readers can not only learn how to perform the process explained in the how-to writing, but that they can learn to do it well enough to be considered successful. Even the titles of some works imply success: *How to Get Happily Published, The Robert Half Way to Get Hired in Today's Job Market, Sylvia Porter's Money Book—How to Earn It, Spend It, Invest It, Borrow It, and Use It to Better Your Life*. Implicit in such titles is the promise that as readers gain control over the process described—in the book or in the chapters of the book reprinted in this section—they will gain control over that segment of their lives to which the process pertains. Voila!

In his advice on "Coming Out on Top in the Job Interview," Half exudes the optimism characteristic of how-to authors, successful practitioners of the subject, when writing for readers who probably lack the skills they're trying to impart. Half contends that "Knowing how to *get* a job is as important as knowing how to *do* a job"; that "it isn't necessarily the most 'qualified' person who gets a particular job but the most convincing applicant interviewed—it could be you." Although he does not dismiss the importance of innate talent, relevant training, and willingness to learn or improve one's professional performance, Half does downplay these qualities in focusing on successful job-seeking tactics: "Our surveys show that the single most influential factor in the job-interview situation is not your experience or your qualification but your personality—*how you present yourself during the interview*. How you look, how you communicate your ideas, how well you listen, how much enthusiasm you generate." So Half, typical of pragmatic how-to writers, offers advice for every contingency; if one method or plan doesn't work, there are alternative routes to the pot of gold at the end of the rainbow.

The How-To Writer's Qualifications

A third assumption of how-to writings is that the writer is an expert on the subject, either because of formal training (Robert Half) or personal experience (Benjamin Franklin), or else that the writer is accurately reporting the process an expert recommends, as you might in an essay for a newspaper or a course.

To decide whether you can do something well enough to give advice to others on how to do it, consider the following:

1. Can I perform well or very well the process I want to write about?
2. How well can I perform this process in comparison with other people whose skill I respect, whether they're amateurs or professionals?

3. Has my performance been validated by other experts? employers? peers? awards or other forms of recognition?
4. How up-to-date is my knowledge? How comprehensive? If you're just learning to touch type, you'll lose your credibility with an audience of computer buffs; how-to writers need to know the state of the art.

If your answers to these questions are satisfying, you probably know enough about the subject to start writing. If they're not, you may decide to write a more derivative how-to piece. If you need to depend on outside authorities for some information, you can still supplement this with your own firsthand experience and common sense. (Even experts do this. Although Robert Hales is a psychiatrist, he supplements his medical advice in "Exercising the Psyche" with reference to other medical research.) Many "how-to" works, including those in this section by Perrin ("Buying a Pickup Truck"), Payne ("A Personal Note on Tone"), and McWilliams ("Word Processing for Writers"), are written by nonspecialists—journalists, hobbyists, students, and others who can present information clearly and engagingly. Indeed, sometimes they can reach a general audience better than specialists can. Not insulated from their audience by the baffle of experience, these less-than-experts can easily understand what their readers don't know and need to know, and can thereby accommodate the unsophisticated.

For instance, "A Personal Note on Tone" was written when Tim Payne was a senior English major studying the French horn for fun. His advice on tone production comes not from expertise (though he was good enough to play in the college orchestra) but from "my own struggles with the horn and my in-practice adaptations of the words and models of several instructors." He has learned enough as a student to provide an explanation that is clear and comprehensive, elegant and interesting to anyone who knows the rudiments of music, horn or otherwise. After explaining the disagreement over "bright" and "dark" tones, and indicating his own bias (paragraphs 1 and 2), Payne begins his discussion of tone production with an analogy ("The process is much like walking in a dense fog: as you take a step forward into what little distance you can see, you are able to see that much further . . . the vision always just beyond the present location"), followed by eight paragraphs of step-by-step instructions.

How much your intended readers know about the subject is especially critical in how-to writing because you have to mesh your explanation so closely with their level of knowledge. You'll be insufferable if you're condescending, as in the chef's advice to the novice cook, "First, stand and face the stove." And if you're over their heads, either because of highly complex instructions full of nuances and alternatives they can't cope with, or if you talk in technical jargon they can't understand, you'll have lost them before you start. Most of the writers in this section avoid these problems; the authors are clearly addressing an unspecialized readership, and only Sylvia

Porter writes with a magisterial air, paragraphs full of prescriptive "do's" and "don'ts," and the assumption that her readers know nothing at all about her subject—in this case, writing and endorsing checks (638–41). At the other extreme is M. F. K. Fisher, whose narratives about food, "Bar Cookies" (658–59) in this instance, are lyrical appreciations of good eating rather than specific instructions on how to do it. Readers will already need to know how to make bar cookies in order to try out her suggested variations on the—unstated—basic recipe, for which she refers them to "Mrs. Rombauer" (see "Brownies Cockaigne," 656–57).

How thorough or casual the how-to directions are may be both a function of the writer's personality and an indication of what's at stake. The writers of medical essays (Jane Brody, Dianne and Robert Hales) and financial advice (Sylvia Porter) can assume that there's a lot at stake for their readers (in these cases, health and financial survival), and that their directions should be explicit, precise, and detailed. More casual discussions of food preparation, as in Euell Gibbons's various recipes for dandelions as well as M. F. K. Fisher's variations on bar cookies, reflect processes that are more an art than a science, and that consequently allow for greater variation.

How-To Form and Variations

Most how-to writings that require precise explanations proceed in some logical sequence from the beginning of the process to the end, divided into steps according to what has to be done first, second, and so on. There may be variations in how to perform a process, simple or complex, or a particular aspect of a process (how to build a fire, for example; see Colin Fletcher, 629–34). Whether you want to discuss any or all of them depends on how important you think they are, and how many variations your readers can cope with. One way is enough for most beginners; experts find alternatives challenging.

A recipe—for instance Maida Heatter's "Brownies" (657–58)—provides a prototypical format for short how-to writings:

1. A descriptive title states the *subject* at the outset; the *objective,* how to make the particular food, is understood. The *outcome,* in this case "24 or 32 brownies," is stated at the beginning; it's useful to know what the end result of a process will be in quantity, as well as in kind.
2. If any *special equipment* or *unusual conditions* must be met before beginning the cooking, they are identified first. None exist in this case.
3. The *list of ingredients* comes next, arranged in the order that they'll be used (with the sub-order usually proceeding from largest quantity to smallest quantity used in a given step). Heatter violates this convention by identifying a smaller quantity of chocolate (5 oz.) before the larger quantity of sweet butter (5⅓ oz.).
4. Then the *steps* in preparing the recipe are detailed, in the sequence in

which they must occur, from start to finish. Usually these are numbered, or paragraphed by stages in the preparation, unless several simple steps, in sequence, can be grouped together in a single paragraph.

Even the simplest set of directions is likely to involve subprocesses, but where they should be explained is often a problem. If they come where they would ordinarily be performed in the overall procedure, the inserted directions may appear to be digressions, and prove distracting. Often they are explained at the end, as either alternative methods, or variations on a basic formula or recipe. In a longer work—say, a book—basic processes (whip, fold, sauté, purée) may be explained separately, in an appendix or glossary.

Many how-to writings begin by putting the subject into context (historical, philosophical, theoretical, personal, or some other relevant perspective) before tackling the practical aspects. Euell Gibbons does this in "The Official Remedy for Disorders" (652–55), explaining the versatility of dandelions, lamenting their debased status as weeds, and showing what fun they are to play with, before providing a number of dandelion recipes. The student author of "The Turning Point" establishes the human context in which his father, recently fired from his job, turns to potting. Only then does the author explain the process of throwing a pot—which in itself, in this narrative, becomes a device to show how the father has mastered this skill—and how much his son loves him.

Additional Suggestions on Form

1. In how-to writings, define each new term and concept when you first use it, in language your readers can understand. Use consistent terminology and measurements to avoid confusing your readers.
2. Be as specific as possible on measurements (lengths, weights, quantities, times) so the end product will approximate the ideal. Experienced performers will know when they can allow variations, and novices won't go astray.
3. Cite specific prices and other figures subject to change if your writing is intended for short-term reading, say a class paper or a newspaper article. Omit such figures in long-range works, for they'll go out of date quickly and will date your writing.
4. Use illustrations and diagrams, where necessary. They can show what a part looks like, where it goes, how big it is, how it relates to a larger mechanism. They can illustrate design and proportion, steps in a process, right and wrong, before and after, simple and complicated alternatives. Pictures, diagrams, charts, and lists can often compress, organize, and simplify complicated information to make it manageable. When in doubt about whether or not to illustrate, do. (See the chart in "Exercising the Psyche," 626).
5. Some how-to writings may be organized more clearly around issues or

goals than around steps in a process. This is particularly true in works dealing with human relationships and emotions. Thus Raymond Williams's essay on "Farming" (590–93) is a narrative account of a typical day of haying; the rhythm of the day and the cooperation among the farm laborers are the major motifs; the process of getting the work done is secondary. Barry Lopez's "My Horse" (584–90) is organized according to points of comparison in an extended analogy between his truck and a horse.

6. Make sure your instructions are not only precise but unambiguous—a virtue of the essays in this section. If there is more than one equally good way to perform a process, and you have space to deal with more than the bare essentials, specify the alternatives and identify which one is preferable under what conditions. Thus Perrin helps prospective truck buyers decide between half-ton, three-quarter-ton, and one-ton pickups; narrow-bed and wide-bed trucks; Japanese or American makes; conventional drive and four-wheel drive; six or eight cylinders; four-speed shift or automatic transmission, and many other features (577–84). Everything you needed to know but didn't know enough to ask. That's the motto of the how-to writer.

The Right Stuff:
Choosing and Using Equipment

NOEL PERRIN
Buying a Pickup Truck

Although the titles of some of Perrin's books reflect rural life, including Amateur Sugar Maker *(1972),* Vermont in All Weathers *(1973), and* First Person Rural *(1978), in which "Buying a Pickup Truck" appears, Perrin was born in New York City, in 1927. He earned a B.A. from Williams College in 1949, an M.A. from Duke, and then served in the Korean War, receiving a Bronze Star, before earning an M.Lit. from Cambridge in 1958. Since 1959 he has taught English at Dartmouth College, but he lives and writes on a farm near Thetford Center, Vermont. His philosophical reflections on country living, often spiced with wry good humor, appear in publications as diverse as* Vermont Life *and* The New Yorker, Country Journal *and* The New York Times. *His essays, he says, "range from intensely practical to mildly literary."*

Although "Buying a Pickup Truck" first appeared in Country Journal, *Perrin's intended readers are not full-time, fifth-generation farmers but transplanted city folk who hold other jobs and do some farming on the side, as he does, including people so green they don't even know they need a truck, let alone which kind to buy. After he's established that his readers need the information he's about to provide (by justifying the utility of a truck), Perrin proceeds systematically, clearing up popular misconceptions (driving a truck doesn't mean you have to give up Beethoven), explaining alternatives truck buyers have (used or new, American or Japanese, narrow or wide bed), and options (number of cylinders, types of tires and bumpers). By the end, Perrin has provided all the basic information a novice would need to make a wise choice—that is, a choice favoring the author's preferences. How-to-do-it writings do not have to be objective, as long as readers can see why the writer's preferences are justified.*

One of the ways a newcomer to the country knows he's getting acclimated is when he begins to notice trucks. (I say 'he' strictly through obedience to grammar. The phenomenon happens to women almost as much as to men. Under age 25, I'd say just as much.) 1

Back in his other life, back when he was urban or suburban, it may have been sports cars that caught the newcomer's eye. Or maybe a showroom full of compacts, fresh and glittering from the factory. Now he finds himself eyeing some neighbor's sturdy green pickup with a big load of brush in the back and wondering how much one like it would cost. Welcome to the club. 2

Pickups aren't necessary in the country, but they are certainly handy. Any rural family that can afford two vehicles should probably make one of them a truck. And it is quite possible to have a truck as a family's sole transportation. It is also quite economical, since pickups begin almost as cheap as the cheap- 3 est cars, and go up in price, size, and quality at the same rate cars do—except that about halfway up the car price range, you have reached the most expensive pickups there are.

4   What's handiest about pickups is their versatility. First, obviously, in load. Because of that big open space in back, you can carry almost anything. Two beef cattle. Two full-length sofas that you're donating to the rummage. All the apples in a small orchard. With the tailgate down, a load of sixteen-foot boards. About 40 bales of hay. A full cord of firewood (provided its dry). All your fence posts, your wire, and your tools, when you're building a fence. It's possible to get a little drunk with power, just thinking what a pickup can do.

5   Second, in range. Even without four-wheel drive, a pickup is a great deal freer than most cars to leave roads and drive over fields. Picking up hay bales, for example. Or to squeeze along homemade woods roads. This freedom comes partly because pickups are designed to have fairly high road clearance, even when loaded. Partly because they can take tires that will walk you right through a wet spot or over a (not-too-big) rock. Most pickup owners in rural New England keep a pair of oversize snow tires mounted on the rear wheels all year round. And partly because you can shift weight around in a truck to get maximum traction in a way that would cause the average car to collapse on its fat Detroit springs.

6   Third, a pickup is versatile in function. Besides its truck role, a pickup can do anything a car can do, with one exception—about which, more later. It can drive you to work, for example, using no more gas than a car, and when you arrive, it will not only park in the regular lot, it will do so in a smaller space than a Cadillac or an Oldsmobile.

7   Nor are you going to complain on the way that it drives like a truck, because it doesn't. It drives like a car. The ride is reasonably smooth, the surreptitious U-turn reasonably easy. Drivers of big highway trucks have ten gears to shift, and air brakes to worry about. Drivers of pickups have a standard shift and regular car brakes. And if they hate shifting, most pickups can be had with automatic transmission. For that matter, most can be equipped with a stereo tape deck, so that you barrel out to the woods playing Beethoven. I admit that a fully loaded pickup—say, a Chevrolet c-10 with a ton of rocks in the back or a six-barrel gathering tank full of maple sap—doesn't corner quite so neatly as an M G, but it still drives essentially like a car.

8   The one exception is that a pickup is not much good for carrying a big load of people. At least, not in the winter or in wet weather. On a sunny summer day, its capacity is something else. Giving hayrides at our local fair, I once had fifteen children and two mothers back there in the hay, plus myself and a friend in the cab. I make that eighteen passengers.

9   Even if two couples are going out to dinner, a pickup is not handy. Four adults will fit not too uncomfortably in the cab of an American (though not a Japanese) pickup—but the law says three. The other husband may or may

not want to crouch in back. Furthermore, it doesn't take many bags of groceries to produce a sense of claustrophobia in a pickup cab. A mother taking two children shopping on a rainy day in a pickup generally wishes she had a car.

There *is* a solution, to be sure. People who go out to dinner a lot, or mothers with four children, can get a crew-cab pickup. This is not what you'd call a glamour vehicle. It has two cabs, one behind the other, and looks something like a centipede dragging a large box. But it does seat six people. The only problem is that you now have a truck not only so ugly but so big that it is no longer versatile in the woods. I do not recommend it.

One last advantage of pickups should be mentioned. They never make hideous noises or refuse to start because you haven't fastened the seat belt. Like other trucks, they are exempt from that law. You can use the belts when you're roaring down the highway and skip them when you're going one mile an hour if the woods. Handy.

So much for pickups and their virtues. The time has now come to discuss the art of buying one. It *is* an art, incidentally, unlike car buying. A few wrong decisions on options can cut a farm pickup's usefulness by 50%.

The first decision, of course, is new or used. A really old pickup, small and square and no-nonsense, is about the most charming vehicle there is. Also one of the cheapest. You can get one for $200. Any children you know will adore the running boards and—if you have an old enough one—the windshield that pushes open for ventilation.

On the other hand, old pickups tend to have unreliable brakes and not notably reliable anything else. The 1947 Dodge I once owned—from its nineteenth to its twenty-first years—couldn't be counted on to start at any temperature much below freezing. That meant a long period of parking on hills and losing my temper, each October and November, until I finally gave up and put it in the barn until spring. One year I waited a week too late and had it frozen in the barnyard, in the way of practically everything, for three and a half months.

Even much newer pickups have generally led hard lives. (Little old ladies seldom own pickups.) Furthermore, it's difficult and expensive to have heavy-duty springs and other desirable country equipment installed in an existing truck. Probably only people with real mechanical ability should consider getting one.

But one last word. If you do get one, take a nice winter vacation and get it in some place like South Carolina. South Carolina pickups have never experienced road salt. At least the body won't rust out on you in a few years.

Now let's turn to new pickups. They come, basically, in three sizes and three styles. The sizes are called half-ton, three-quarter-ton, and one ton. Not one of these names means what it says. Which is a good thing, because a bunch of trucks that could carry only 1,000 to 2,000 pounds wouldn't be worth much.

18   Let me define the three. A half-ton is the basic pickup: what you find at a car dealer, what people mean when they speak of a pickup. At the moment it comes in two avatars. It is a small Japanese-made truck that can carry almost a ton of cargo. Or it is a somewhat larger American-made truck that, with proper springs and tires, can manage a ton and a half.

19   A three-quarter ton looks much the same, but has a much larger, truck-type rear axle. It costs more, gives a rougher ride, and carries loads of up to about three tons. People with campers put them on three-quarter-ton pickups—and then usually get about six miles to the gallon.

20   A one-ton has an even bigger rear axle. With dual rear wheels, it can carry up to near five tons. Neither it nor a three-quarter is what most people need for use on a country place. Not unless they plan to get into the lumber-delivery business, or maybe have always wanted, since they were kids, to have their own personal dump truck. (No fooling. There are truck shops in every New England state that will put a dump body on a three-quarter or a one-ton. The cost runs around $1,200. I have sometimes played with the notion.) But for general country use a half-ton is right; and for the rest of this article I shall talk about half-tons only.

21   Of the three styles, one can be dismissed right off. This is the tarted-up and chromed-up half-ton which attempts to pass itself off as a car. Chevrolet calls its El Camino; other makes have equally foolish names.

22   For families that are sincerely embarrassed at having to own a truck and that really think it would be preferable to drive something that looks like a scooped-out car, spending the extra money for an El Camino may make sense. Especially in those flat and treeless parts of the country where taking your truck out to the back forty must be something like driving across a very large football field. But to get one as a working truck on a rocky, hilly, wooded New England farm would be an act of insanity.

23   The other two styles are narrow-bed and wide-bed. Just as the half-ton is the classic American pickup, the narrow-bed is the classic half-ton. The design has been stable for 50 years now. Behind the cab you have—in most makes—a wooden-floored metal box four feet wide and six or eight feet long. (You get to pick.) This sits inside the rear wheels. Because it doesn't rust, and because it gives surer footing to any livestock you happen to be transporting, the wooden floor is a considerable advantage.

24   Until a few years ago, the narrow-bed was the cheapest of all pickups; now it costs exactly the same as a wide-bed. It retains two other advantages. Since the rear wheels don't stick up into the bed, you can slide slidable cargo in and out with great ease. And because this is the classic model, the tailgate in most makes is still the traditional kind that you hook with a chain on each side. That matters. You are able either to put such a tailgate down level, as an extension of the bed, if you are carrying a load of long boards, or to let it drop all the way down for ease in loading. Now that I no longer have one, I miss it.

All the Japanese-made pickups and most of the current American ones 25
are wide-bed. These have a cargo space five and a half feet wide (American) or
four and a half feet (Japanese). Obviously you can carry a lot more cargo. On
the other hand, the rear wheel housings stick in on each side, which is
sometimes inconvenient. (I will say they are handy for children to sit on.)
And on many wide-beds you get a fancy one-handled tailgate, like a station
wagon's, which won't drop down unless you disconnect the hinges. It's not
difficult, it's just tedious. And when you want to close the tailgate, you have
to reconnect them.

Which style is better? Myself, I used to have a narrow-bed and now have 26
a wide-bed. I think the advantages and disadvantages of the two models just
about balance. So on my current truck, I made the choice on esthetic
grounds. The narrow-bed lost. Properly designed, it is the truest of trucks,
the very platonic essence of a truck. But in the last five years Ford, Dodge,
Chevrolet, Jeep, and International Harvester (a G M C pickup is just a
relabeled Chevrolet)—all have moved to such enormously wide cabs that a
new narrow-bed looks hydrocephalic. Wide-bed is now the handsomer truck.

As to whether Toyota, Datsun, L U V, or an American make, the decision 27
really rests on how much highway driving you're going to do. The Japanese
trucks, with their four-cylinder engines, get far better gas mileage. According
to *Consumer Reports,* they average about twenty mpg, while American half-
tons average fifteen. My own experience suggests that Japanese pickups do a
little better than twenty, and American pickups a little worse than fifteen. For
a vehicle that I was going to commute to work in, and just use as a truck on
the occasional weekend, I would probably choose to save gas (plus about
$300 in purchase price) and get a Japanese.

But for a truck that was to be mainly or even considerably a working 28
farm vehicle, I still prefer the larger and more versatile American pickup. It's
not just that you can carry more weight, it's that you can get a specially
adapted country model. The Japanese trucks tend to be unadaptable, the
same for an appliance dealer in New York City as for a family with 60 acres of
woods in Colebrook, Connecticut.

The man delivering refrigerators in the Bronx doesn't need any special 29
traction. He never leaves the pavement. But the family in Colebrook does.
And one of the most humiliating things that can happen is to get stuck in
your own truck on your own place. Especially since you're so unlikely to be
able to jack, or rock, or bull your way out.

The trick is not to get stuck. Which means that you may want the four- 30
wheel drive available as an option (a very expensive one) on all the American
but none of the little Japanese trucks. Otherwise, you will certainly want
limited-slip differential. This inexpensive ($75 to $100) option means a special rear axle designed so that when one rear wheel starts to spin, all the
power goes to the other wheel. Normally when one wheel starts to spin, all

the power goes to *it,* and that's why you get stuck. Limited-slip differential is said to have its dangers, especially in very fast highway driving, where you may fishtail in a skid, but it is highly desirable in a farm pickup. I would rate it, quite impressionistically, as making about a third of the difference between regular two-wheel drive and four-wheel drive. You can get it on American pickups, but not Japanese. It's only fair to add that I know farmers with Datsun pickups who say they have no trouble at all zipping up and down their rolling fields, even on dewy mornings, but I still commend limited-slip differential.

31   If you decide on a Japanese truck anyway, about all you have to do is go get it. Maybe settle whether or not you want a radio. But if you opt for an American truck, you still have to pick your engine, with at least six more country options to consider.

32   The engine is easy. Get a six-cylinder. Almost all pickups—including three-quarter and one-tons—can be had either six or eight cylinders. A six has all the power you will ever need, and wastes less gas. As to options, the first and most important is to specify heavy-duty springs in the rear, and heavy-duty shock absorbers front and rear. All this costs about $40; its value in increased usefulness must be about 50 times that much.

33   Second, for any pickup that's going to leave roads, either a four-speed shift or automatic transmission is a great asset. Why? Because going through a field with long grass (and hidden rocks), or up into the woods, you need to be able to creep along, almost literally feeling your way, and still not lose momentum. Low speed in a three-speed shift will not let you go slowly enough.

34   Here the Japanese trucks have an advantage, since all of them come with a four-speed shift. It costs an extra $125 on an American pickup. But even better than four-speed is an automatic transmission. You can creep with astonishing slowness, and still have power. I have never owned a car with automatic transmission and never plan to, but on my sturdy green pickup I find it marvelous. It does, of course, use too much gas, and my next truck will be four-speed manual.

35   Third, you ought to get a step-and-tow bumper. Unlike cars, trucks are sold with no rear bumper at all. (How much rear bumper have you ever seen on a tractor-trailer or on a gasoline truck?) But a step-and-tow—which is a broad bumper covered with sheet steel—really is handy for pulling, and as a rear step. The ones you get factory installed, for about $50, are not nearly as sturdy as they look, but are still worth having. The ideal is to have one made by a local welder. Rodney Palmer, the man who owns the garage in Thetford Center, is a superb welder; and for $101.50 I have a rear bumper that will fend off anything short of a Centurion tank, that is heavy enough to give me good traction with no load in the truck, and that will last for a hundred years. (Rodney designed it so that I can move it from pickup to pickup for the rest

of my life. Then I'll will it to my daughters.) Incidentally, if you don't get a bumper like that, you should plan to keep a couple of large flat rocks or about four cement blocks in the back each winter. Way back. Otherwise you'll find yourself spinning to a halt halfway up icy hills. Better anchor them too, so that if you have to slam the brakes on hard they won't come hurtling through the back of the cab and kill you.

Fourth, for a family truck it is worth getting extra padding in the seat. A pickup has a reasonably smooth ride, but not so smooth that additional cushioning won't be pleasing to visiting grandparents, people with bad backs, and so on. If you're going to get stereo tapes, you might even want to pad the whole cab, so as to reduce road noise.   36

Fifth, if you can talk the dealer into it, get him to remove the four automobile tires the truck comes equipped with, and have him put on four truck tires. They should be not merely heavier ply, but if possible an inch larger in diameter. And as I said earlier, the rear ones should probably be snow tires, even if you get the truck in May. (Come winter, put snow tires on the front, too. They won't improve traction unless you have four-wheel drive, but they will help astonishingly in preventing sideslipping.)   37

If you can't talk the dealer into it, you're no horsetrader. In that case, resign yourself to your helpless condition, and pay extra for big tires. Or go to another dealer. Or hurry home and read Faulkner's *The Hamlet*. Then you will learn—from a master—how to trade.   38

Sixth, get the truck undercoated. Presumably any New Englander knows about undercoating anyway—but it's even more important on pickups than cars, since people usually keep pickups longer. The process called Ziebarting is probably the best and certainly the most expensive. If you can stand having your truck smell like fish oil for a month or so, I recommend it. If not, a grease undercoating is said to be adequate. But the full mysteries of Duracoat (acrylic resin), asphalt, and all the other undercoatings, I do not pretend to be a master of.   39

There are all sorts of other machismo things one can get with a pickup. You can have a snowplow mounted—in which case be sure to get four-wheel drive. Plan also to have the front end realigned frequently, because plowing will spoil the wheel alignment with surprising speed. You can have an electric winch put on the front, and thus be sure of freeing yourself 99% of the time when you get stuck. (Though a two-ton manual winch of the kind called a come-along will do nearly as well. You can get one for about $45, and keep it under the seat.) You can have a power take-off on most larger pickups, and run your own sawmill. You can merely buy a logging chain, keep that under the seat, too, and then when you find eight-foot poplars growing in the corners of your best field, you hook the chain on your step-and-tow bumper and pull them out by the roots. They don't grow back next year *that* way.   40

But just a basic pickup is machismo (or feminismo) enough. In fact, I can   41 think of just one problem. Someday when you're going past the post office with a big load of brush, you'll glance up and see a whole row of summer people staring at you. With naked envy in their eyes.

Questions

1. What gives Perrin, a writer and English professor, the authority to tell other people what to look for in buying a pickup truck? What features of his essay are likely to give his readers, themselves new to rural life, the confidence that Perrin knows what he's talking about? Would you want this man to sell you a used truck?

2. Perrin's approach to his subject is very systematic. What, therefore, is the logic of his organization? Why does he spend the first quarter of the essay (paragraphs 3–11) justifying the purchase of a pickup truck? And the last quarter discussing (30–40) options, such as four-wheel drive, a step-and-tow bumper, and other features? What comes in the essay's central portion?

3. Perrin's illustrations are practical and homespun. Instead of citing dimensions in terms of figures, he will refer to, for instance, "that big open space in back [of the truck where] you can carry almost anything. Two beef cattle. Two full-length sofas that you're donating to the rummage" (paragraph 4). Cite other examples. Are such illustrations preferable to figures? Or would you want both, if you were contemplating the purchase of a pickup truck, especially your first one?

4. Does Perrin's style—conversational, slightly slangy, breezy, using occasional sentence fragments, beginning sentences with conjunctions or prepositions—suit his subject? Explain why or why not.

BARRY LOPEZ

My Horse

Barry Lopez, like Noel Perrin, is a native New Yorker (born 1945) who has chosen to live closer to nature than Manhattan permits. He received a B.A. from Notre Dame in 1966 and an M.A. in teaching in 1968, after which he studied at the University of Oregon (1969–70). He now lives in Finn Rock, Oregon, where he is a professional writer of fiction and nonfiction. Much of his writing presents sympathetic, sometimes poetic, interpretations of animal behavior in relation to other animals or humans. Among his books are Desert Notes: Reflections in the Eye of a Raven *(1976);* River Notes: The Dance of Herons *(1979);* Of Wolves and Men *(1979); and* Arctic Dreams: Imagination and Desire in a Northern Landscape *(1986).*

Lopez, like Perrin, is writing about trucks and their uses, but from a very different perspective. Perrin's essay is an example of Yankee pragmatism: here's what you need to know in order to be able to do what you have to do. Lopez's essay is a cowboy's song about a man and—well, his "horse," which happens to be a truck. In Lopez's interpretation a truck is a companion, with a mind and character all its own, rather than the mechanical implement of Perrin's essay. Lopez begins with a romantic picture of the Indian West; makes elaborate comparisons between his truck and his horse; and demonstrates how his relationship with his truck is analogous to the Indians' relationships with their horses. Lopez reminds us that not all the uses of a truck are economic or even utilitarian; they can build "heart." How-to-do-it writing usually emphasizes practicality, utility, value—but what is ultimately more valuable than showing readers how to build heart?

It is curious that Indian warriors on the northern plains in the nineteenth century, who were almost entirely dependent on the horse for mobility and status, never gave their horses names. If you borrowed a man's horse and went off raiding for other horses, however, or if you lost your mount in battle and then jumped on mine and counted coup on an enemy—well, those horses would have to be shared with the man whose horse you borrowed, and that coup would be mine, not yours. Because even if I gave him no name, he was my horse. 1

If you were a Crow warrior and I a young Teton Sioux out after a warrior's identity and we came over a small hill somewhere in the Montana prairie and surprised each other, I could tell a lot about you by looking at your horse. 2

Your horse might have feathers tied in his mane, or in his tail, or a medicine bag tied around his neck. If I knew enough about the Crow, and had looked at you closely, I might make some sense of the decoration, even guess who you were if you were well-known. If you had painted your horse I could tell even more, because we both decorated our horses with signs that meant the same things. Your white handprints high on his flanks would tell me you had killed an enemy in a hand-to-hand fight. Small horizontal lines stacked on your horse's foreleg, or across his nose, would tell me how many times you had counted coup. Horse hoof marks on your horse's rump, or three-sided boxes, would tell me how many times you had stolen horses. If there was a bright red square on your horse's neck I would know you were leading a war party and that there were probably others out there in the coulees behind you. 3

You might be painted all over as blue as the sky and covered with white dots, with your horse painted the same way. Maybe hailstorms were your power—or if I chased you a hailstorm might come down and hide you. There might be lightning bolts on the horse's legs and flanks, and I would wonder if you had lightning power, or a slow horse. There might be white circles around your horse's eyes to help him see better. 4

Or you might be like Crazy Horse, with no decoration, no marks on your horse to tell me anything, only a small lightning bolt on your cheek, a piece of turquoise tied behind your ear. 5

You might have scalps dangling from your rein. 6

I could tell something about you by your horse. All this would come to me in a few seconds. I might decide this was my moment and shout my war cry—*Hoka hey!* Or I might decide you were like the grizzly bear: I would 7 raise my weapon to you in salute and go my way, to see you again when I was older.

8   I do not own a horse. I am attached to a truck, however, and I have come to think of it in a similar way. It has no name; it never occurred to me to give it a name. It has little decoration; neither of us is partial to decoration. I have a piece of turquoise in the truck because I had heard once that some of the southwestern tribes tied a small piece of turquoise in a horse's hock to keep him from stumbling. I like the idea. I also hang sage in the truck when I go on a long trip. But inside, the truck doesn't look much different from others that look just like it on the outside. I like it that way. Because I like my privacy.

9   For two years in Wyoming I worked on a ranch wrangling horses. The horse I rode when I had to have a good horse was a quarter horse and his name was Coke High. The name came with him. At first I thought he'd been named for the soft drink. I'd known stranger names given to horses by whites. Years later I wondered if some deviate Wyoming cowboy wise to cocaine had not named him. Now I think he was probably named after a rancher, an historical figure of the region. I never asked the people who owned him for fear of spoiling the spirit of my inquiry.

10   We were running over a hundred horses on this ranch. They all had names. After a few weeks I knew all the horses and the names too. You had to. No one knew how to talk about animals or put them in order or tell the wranglers what to do unless they were using the names—Princess, Big Red, Shoshone, Clay.

11   My truck is named Dodge. The name came with it. I don't know if it was named after the town or the verb or the man who invented it. I like it for a name. Perfectly anonymous, like Rex for a dog, or Old Paint. You can't tell anything with a name like that.

12   The truck is a van. I call it a truck because it's not a car and because "van" is a suburban sort of consumer word, like "oxford loafer," and I don't like the sound of it. On the outside it looks like any other Dodge Sportsman 300. It's a dirty tan color. There are a few body dents, but it's never been in a wreck. I tore the antenna off against a tree on a pinched mountain road. A boy in Midland, Texas, rocked one of my rear view mirrors off. A logging truck in Oregon squeeze-fired a piece of debris off the road and shattered my windshield. The oil pan and gas tank are pug-faced from high-centering on bad roads. (I remember a horse I rode for a while named Targhee whose hocks were scarred from tangles in barbed wire when he was a colt and who spooked a lot in high grass, but these were not like "dents." They were more like bad tires.)

13   I like to travel. I go mostly in the winter and mostly on two-lane roads. I've driven the truck from Key West to Vancouver, British Columbia, and from Yuma to Long Island over the past four years. I used to ride Coke High

only about five miles every morning when we were rounding up horses. Hard miles of twisting and turning. About six hundred miles a year. Then I'd turn him out and ride another horse for the rest of the day. That's what was nice about having a remuda. You could do all you had to do and not take it all out on your best horse. Three car family.

My truck came with a lot of seats in it and I've never really known what 14 to do with them. Sometimes I put the seats in and go somewhere with a lot of people, but most of the time I leave them out. I like riding around with that empty cavern of space behind my head. I know it's something with a history to it, that there's truth in it, because I always rode a horse the same way— with empty saddle bags. In case I found something. The possibility of finding something is half the reason for being on the road.

The value of anything comes to me in its use. If I am not using some- 15 thing it is of no value to me and I give it away. I wasn't always that way. I used to keep everything I owned—just in case. I feel good about the truck because it gets used. A lot. To haul hay and firewood and lumber and rocks and garbage and animals. Other people have used it to haul furniture and freezers and dirt and recycled newspapers. And to move from one house to another. When I lend it for things like that I don't look to get anything back but some gas (if we're going to be friends). But if you go way out in the country to a dump and pick up the things you can still find out there (once a load of cedar shingles we sold for $175 to an architect) I expect you to leave some of those things around my place when you come back—if I need them.

When I think back, maybe the nicest thing I ever put in that truck was 16 timber wolves. It was a long night's drive from Oregon up into British Columbia. We were all very quiet about it; it was like moving clouds across the desert.

Sometimes something won't fit in the truck and I think about improving 17 it—building a different door system, for example. I am forever going to add better gauges on the dash and a pair of driving lamps and a sunroof, but I never get around to doing any of it. I remember I wanted to improve Coke High once too, especially the way he bolted like a greyhound through patches of cottonwood on a river flat. But all I could do with him was to try to rein him out of it. Or hug his back.

Sometimes, road-stoned in a blur of country like southwestern Wyoming 18 or North Dakota, I talk to the truck. It's like wandering on the high plains under a summer sun, on plains where, George Catlin wrote, you were "out of sight of land." I say what I am thinking out loud, or point at things along the road. It's a crazy, sun-stroked sort of activity, a sure sign it's time to pull over, to go for a walk, to make a fire and have some tea, to lie in the shade of the truck.

I've always wanted to pat the truck. It's basic to the relationship. But it 19 never works.

20   I remember when I was on the ranch, just at sunrise, after I'd saddled Coke High, I'd be huddled down in my jacket smoking a cigarette and looking down into the valley, along the river where the other horses had spent the night. I'd turn to Coke and run my hand down his neck and slap-pat him on the shoulder to say I was coming up. It made a bond, an agreement we started the day with.

21   I've thought about that a lot with the truck, because we've gone out together at sunrise on so many mornings. I've even fumbled around trying to do it. But metal won't give.

22   The truck's personality is mostly an expression of two ideas: "with-you" and "alone." When Coke High was "with-you" he and I were the same animal. We could have cut a rooster out of a flock of chickens, we were so in tune. It's the same with the truck: rolling through Kentucky on a hilly two-lane road, three in the morning under a full moon and no traffic. Picture it. You roll like water.

23   There are other times when you are with each other but there's no connection at all. Coke got that way when he was bored and we'd fight each other about which way to go around a tree. When the truck gets like that— "alone"—it's because it feels its Detroit fat-ass design dragging at its heart and making a fool out of it.

24   I can think back over more than a hundred nights I've slept in the truck, sat in it with a lamp burning, bundled up in a parka, reading a book. It was always comfortable. A good place to wait out a storm. Like sleeping inside a buffalo.

25   The truck will go past 100,000 miles soon. I'll rebuild the engine and put a different transmission in it. I can tell from magazine advertisements that I'll never get another one like it. Because every year they take more of the heart out of them. One thing that makes a farmer or a rancher go sour is a truck that isn't worth a shit. The reason you see so many old pickups in ranch country is because these are the only ones with any heart. You can count on them. The weekend rancher runs around in a new pickup with too much engine and not enough transmission and with the wrong sort of tires because he can afford anything, even the worst. A lot of them have names for their pickups too.

26   My truck has broken down, in out of the way places at the worst of times. I've walked away and screamed the foulness out of my system and gotten the tools out. I had to fix a water pump in a blizzard in the Panamint Mountains in California once. It took all day with the Coleman stove burning under the engine block to keep my hands from freezing. We drifted into Beatty, Nevada, that night with it jury-rigged together with—I swear—baling wire, and we were melting snow as we went and pouring it in to compensate for the leaks.

27   There is a dent next to the door on the driver's side I put there one

sweltering night in Miami. I had gone to the airport to meet my wife, whom I hadn't seen in a month. My hands were so swollen with poison ivy blisters I had to drive with my wrists. I had shut the door and was locking it when the window fell off its runners and slid down inside the door. I couldn't leave the truck unlocked because I had too much inside I didn't want to lose. So I just kicked the truck a blow in the side and went to work on the window. I hate to admit kicking the truck. It's like kicking a dog, which I've never done.

Coke High and I had an accident once. We hit a badger hole at a full 28 gallop. I landed on my back and blacked out. When I came to, Coke High was about a hundred yards away. He stayed a hundred yards away for six miles, all the way back to the ranch.

I want to tell you about carrying those wolves, because it was a fine 29 thing. There were ten of them. We had four in the truck with us in crates and six in a trailer. It was a five hundred mile trip. We went at night for the cool air and because there wouldn't be as much traffic. I could feel from the way the truck rolled along that its heart was in the trip. It liked the wolves inside it, the sweet odor that came from the crates. I could feel that same tireless wolf-lope developing in its wheels; it was like you might never have to stop for gas, ever again.

The truck gets very self-focused when it works like this; its heart is strong 30 and it's good to be around it. It's good to be *with* it. You get the same feeling when you pull someone out of a ditch. Coke High and I pulled a Volkswagen out of the mud once, but Coke didn't like doing it very much. Speed, not strength, was his center. When the guy who owned the car thanked us and tried to pat Coke, the horse snorted and swung away, trying to preserve his distance, which is something a horse spends a lot of time on.

So does the truck. 31

Being distant lets the truck get its heart up. The truck has been cold and 32 alone in Montana at 38 below zero. It's climbed horrible, eroded roads in Idaho. It's been burdened beyond overloading, and made it anyway. I've asked it to do these things because they build heart, and without heart all you have is a machine. You have nothing. I don't think people in Detroit know anything at all about heart. That's why everything they build dies so young.

One time in Arizona the truck and I came through one of the worst 33 storms I've ever been in, an outrageous, angry blizzard. But we went down the road, right through it. You couldn't explain our getting through by the sort of tires I had on the truck, or the fact that I had chains on, or was a good driver, or had a lot of weight over my drive wheels or a good engine, because it was more than this. It was a contest between the truck and the blizzard— and the truck wouldn't quit. I could have gone to sleep and the truck would have just torn a road down Interstate 40 on its own. It scared the hell out of me; but it gave me heart, too.

We came off the Mogollon Rim that night and out of the storm and 34 headed south for Phoenix. I pulled off the road to sleep for a few hours, but before I did I got out of the truck. It was raining. Warm rain. I tied a short piece of red avalanche cord into the grill. I left it there for a long time, like an eagle feather on a horse's tail. It flapped and spun in the wind. I could hear it ticking against the grill when I drove.

35   When I have to leave that truck I will just raise up my left arm—*Hoka hey!*—and walk away.

Questions

1. What is the main subject of Lopez's essay, his truck or his horse? Why does he title the essay "My Horse," and what does he mean by the title?

2. In what ways does Lopez's truck resemble a horse—in functions, relationship with its owner, appearance, and other features? Which comparisons does Lopez make explicit? Which does he imply?

3. In what respects are the horse and the truck different (paragraphs 15 and 19, for instance)? Is it wise, in an extended comparison, to acknowledge differences as well as similarities? What is the effect of discussing, as Lopez does in paragraphs 26–28, the problems he has had with his truck and with his horse?

4. Lopez uses a number of symbols in this essay. Most conspicuous, of course, is the continuous equation of the truck and the horse. What symbolic overtones are there to transporting the timber wolves (paragraphs 16 and 29)? What does Lopez intend Detroit to symbolize (paragraph 32)? Given Lopez's sophisticated use of symbols, why does he merely refer to his truck by its anonymous brand name, *Dodge*, rather than giving it a more individual name, as many people give their special cars and trucks?

RAYMOND WILLIAMS (Student)

Farming

Williams was born in rural Rocky Mount, Virginia, in 1959. An English major, he graduated, Phi Beta Kappa, from the College of William and Mary in 1980. As "Farming" reveals, he punctuated his academic years with summers of farm work, which satisfied both body and spirit in a cooperative atmosphere unlike the competition of college. After five years of teaching high school English in rural Virginia, Williams is considering the pursuit of a doctorate in teaching writing, and becoming a professional writer. To further these aims, he attended the Bread Loaf School in the summer of 1985.

The description of a job, any job, often tells how to do it, or at least, how the writer does it. Williams's "typical-day-in-the-life-of . . ." a farmer in the summer provides a comprehensive explanation, in a chronological framework. Yet explaining how to farm is secondary to Williams's primary purpose, to clarify for himself (and his readers) why he does it. His interpretation provides an articulate analysis of what a farmer's life is like—body, mind, and soul. As with many well-written accounts of a process, to read is to want to participate; Williams is so thoughtfully appreciative of the many benefits of farming, while candidly acknowledging its limitations, that he makes us want to experience farming for ourselves.

Six A.M. and my mother arises to cook breakfast. Twenty minutes later, she comes to my room and tells me breakfast is ready; I ignore her, but ten minutes later when she calls from the kitchen I force myself out of bed. I shuffle into the kitchen, pour a cup of coffee, and eat my cold scrambled eggs and toast. After eating and dressing, I start the '67 pickup truck and begin a fifteen-mile drive to Windswept Farm, Holstein. 1

A week ago, at this time, I was at William and Mary and had another hour to sleep. At school, my classes began at nine o'clock and ended at noon. For the rest of the day I was free to play, to study, or to socialize. 2

But at the farm, by nine o'clock, I have already bottle-fed three calves, poured milk into buckets for six more, given grain and water to ten, and carried six bales and three fifty pound bags of feed to twenty young heifers. At noon all work stops, and I eat with the other workers; unlike at college, our day has just begun. 3

After lunch we drive to the hay field where the alfalfa lies in windrows waiting for the balers to rake it up and compact it into tight seventy-pound bales. One person can handle the baling; it takes four to load and unload the hay efficiently. Chris, by virtue of being the youngest and of being allergic to hay, drives the truck. Fred, the herdsman, and Vern, the farmer's oldest son, load the bales onto the truck, and I stack. 4

Stacking involves more than just setting one bale on top of another, for each layer must cross-tie the layer below, or when the truck hits a bump or goes uphill, the stack comes apart and spills hay to the ground. The first few layers are easy, but once the stack becomes taller than chest high, the job becomes more difficult. I heave two or three bales on top of the stack before climbing up to arrange them; once on top of the hay, I maintain a precarious balance as the truck jerks along, travelling up and down the slopes of the field. Once I arrange the bales, I jump down to the truck bed, throw more bales to the top and begin the cycle again. This process continues until I have stacked one hundred and twenty-five bales in six layers. 5

Then Fred and Vern climb on the truck, and we take the hay to the barn to unload it. There is perhaps only one job which farmers hate worse than loading hay, and that is unloading it. The temperature in the barn is at least one hundred degrees, and dust fills the air; loud sneezes echo through the barn along with our grunts as we hurl each bale from one level to the next, until finally it is placed at the top of the stack, some thirty feet high. When Fred shoves the final bale into place, we all collapse for a short break; Chris hands us the water jug, and after the last person gulps his share, we reluctantly climb into the truck, and return to the field. 6

7   One trip takes an hour and fifteen minutes, and today we make six trips. After four trips, we stop for supper, and I am ready to quit. My shirt drenched with sweat, my arms green from the hay which has stuck to them, and my pants filled with scratchy hay particles, I desire a shower and sleep. But two hundred bales remain in the field, and the weather threatens rain, so sleep must wait. We gather the fifth load in twilight, and we finish the final load by moonlight.

8   I return home, shower, and eat the two pieces of cold chicken my mother saved for me. Although tired, I read the paper before going to bed at ten-thirty. As I drift asleep, I think about what my friends are doing on this Friday night, and I wonder why I choose to spend my summers working on a farm.

9   Other jobs pay more and require fewer hours. By working on a farm, I miss the "experiences" which counselors advise students to seek during their summers, such as travel or working in a field related to possible career interests. Nor does listing farmhand in the category "previous employment" look impressive on a résumé.

10   However, in spite of these disadvantages, farming offers numerous advantages, and the physical nature of the work ranks high as a positive characteristic. Carrying feed bags, throwing hay bales, hammering nails, and halter-breaking heifers increases my muscle tone and the efficiency of my cardio-vascular system by one hundred percent of what they are during the school year. I enjoy the exertion, the sweat, and the sense of tiredness which a day of work brings; it differs from the drowsiness of studying, and this tiredness makes sleep welcome. "The sleep of a laborer is sweet," declares a proverb; as a farmhand, I know the truth of that statement.

11   The variety of tasks appeals to me; with the exception of milking and feeding and getting up hay when it is cut, the chores differ from day to day. I start each day by feeding the calves and young heifers and usually end each day with the same task, but in-between I rarely work at the same chore. One day, I cut weeds, do carpentry, and unload feed off the truck. The next, I build fences, and clean stalls.

12   But the value and the appeal of farm work goes beyond the physical benefits and the variety of tasks, for farming is conducive to reflection, and it offers experiences which college often fails to provide. Much of college centers around competition; competition for grades, for honors, and for admission to graduate schools influence much of the students' activities. On the farm, cooperation replaces competition: the farmers help each other pick up hay, loan each other equipment, and help host a 4-H Dairy Judging contest. This cooperation extends beyond the sphere of farmer helping farmer; the farmer must learn to cooperate with nature. Unlike the student of science who creates an artificial environment in which to conduct carefully controlled experiments, the farmer works in the natural environment which, even with numerous technological mechanisms, can be only partially controlled at best.

The farmer may possess advanced techniques of soil sampling, better fertilizers and seeds, and more sophisticated tractors, but he still depends on getting a good rainfall.

Although veterinary medicine has improved greatly, animals still die with regularity. In one week I hauled away two calves which failed to respond to treatment; the treatment followed the prescribed steps perfectly. But on the farm prescribed steps do not always lead to their designated end. Man's knowledge and efforts may accomplish much, but they are not always sufficient. Science may prolong life and increase the individual's chance of living, but death remains part of this world. Yes, everyone in our society realizes that death is part of the cycle of life, but most persons are removed from death and illness. On the farm, however, I witnessed the drama of birth and death many times, and it increased my appreciation of the natural cycle of existence. In helping deliver two breech birth calves and watching one live and one die, I felt a part of the cycle, and my affirmation of life's sacredness became more than a concept, more than a belief I held; that affirmation became a part of my experience. 13

Working on a farm is valuable, because it allows me to feel and to experience rather than to think and to discuss. Although farming offers much time to think (one of the advantages of picking up hay is that it engages the muscles but not the mind), thought is tempered by experience in a way which college does not offer. This valuable function more than compensates for the long hours of hard work and the moderate pay of farm life; my true reward comes from my increased sense of the richness of life and of my place within that life. 14

TIM PAYNE (Student)

A Personal Note on Tone

Typical of many how-to-do-it essays, the author shows how to do it (in this case, how to play the French horn) his particular way to achieve a particular, though debatable, result. Thus "A Personal Note on Tone" becomes as much an argument for "do it my way" as an explanation of how to perform the process. Many process essays, like this one, begin by explaining the theory and predicting the intended result before proceeding to a step-by-step account of the actual process. Just as a picture of the completed garment tells the tailor what to aim for, such an explanation at the outset lets the novice horn player know what sort of tone to try to produce.

There is disagreement among horn players and other appreciators of the French horn as to whether the ideal sound for horn is bright or dark—what I like to call the difference between the hunting horn and the "haunting" horn. 1

The bright-siders often say the dark tone sounds too much like a tuba, and the dark-siders respond that the bright tone sounds too much like a trombone. It can be argued that the bright sound is ideal for some settings and the dark sound for others: for instance, the bright sound is generally more fitting for a brass ensemble and the dark sound for a woodwind quintet, bright for a sparkling allegro, dark for a death march. I feel, however, that players and tastes—even in accommodating different styles of music and different instrumentations—fall basically on one side or the other: a dark-side player will take on, say, the soaring, heroic passages of "Jupiter" from Holst's *The Planets* with a *brighter* darkness in his tone, but it's still a darkness at heart.

2   My point here is one of forewarning and perhaps of self-introduction—but also, I hope, of clarification: I am a dark-sider, a "haunter"; therefore, because the comments I wish to make about tone-production are relatively specific and are based entirely on both what I've gained from my own struggles with the horn and my in-practice adaptations of the words and models of several instructors, I must admit that what I have to say refers to and hopes (if fully applied) to facilitate the production of a dark tone. But (before you bright-siders throw this essay to the ground to vent your spit-valve on) not *merely* a dark tone, but a dark good tone—emphasis on the *good*. Beyond the bright/dark debate there are several elements of good tone on which there is general agreement: openness, resonant or ringing quality, consistency throughout the register, consistency over the duration of individual notes and phrases (including attacks, releases, and slurs), consistency (or control) throughout the volume spectrum, and focus. Since the concept of sound to which I aspire contains these widely accepted elements of good tone, I hope that anyone, bright or dark, can find something of interest and of use in the following practical suggestions based on my experience.

3   My first directive recalls perhaps the first instruction you ever received on horn-playing: take the horn and find the open note which comes most naturally and easily to you. This will probably be the written *e* or *g* above middle *c* and perhaps even third-space *c*. Using this note, along with your ears, your mind's eye, your concentration, and what I will call your response adaptation, you will develop your concept of tone and your model or reference point for this concept. Response adaptation is your physical adjustment, largely by trial and error, *toward* the realization of what your ear and mind are continuously envisioning as better tone. This process is much like walking in a dense fog: as you take a step forward into what little distance you can see, you are able to see that much further, and so it is with the next step and the next, the vision always just beyond the present location, so that you can continue forward until you reach your destination or goal.

4   Play the note you have selected with medium loudness, listening carefully for the openness, purity, consistency in support, and resonance of the tone. Continuing to listen, especially for *changes* in the tone, press your lips in toward the center from both sides with the surrounding facial muscles, as if

594

you were puckering, but restrain them from protruding in the center at the mouthpiece. At the same time pull your lower jaw down and your upper lip up, without allowing the position of the mouthpiece on your lips to slip. Do not, however, allow the lips to press more tightly against the mouthpiece. This is very difficult to do, because in effect you are pulling away from two borders at once and in opposite directions: outward at the very center, enlarging the aperture, and inward from the inner rim of the mouthpiece, relieving the pressure of the lips on the rim. The only way this can be done is to compress the tissue of the lips, which causes you to feel the lips more fully, giving you more awareness of, and thus eventually more control over, them. Cease to think of your lips as two clumsy slabs that you must squeeze together or tug apart or squish against the metal of the mouthpiece if you are to get any use out of them.

The effect of these lip motions is to make the aperture rounder and to   5
make its perimeter taut and well-defined. These adjustments in the embouchure should be made slowly for two reasons: first, so that you don't slip down to the next lower open note; and, second, so that you can hear at which point the sound is clearest and most open, and hold that position.

Now, think round. Picture in your mind a circular target with a bull's   6
eye. Let the target be the point of your lips enclosed by the mouthpiece rim and the bull's eye be the aperture. Now, picture a cylinder with a solid core created by some medium or motion passing through and beyond the target, embracing the full circle and focusing on the bull's eye. Let the air flow be this cylinder, a solid column proceeding up from the bottom of your lungs, aligning its focus with the aperture but with a sense also of it filling up your whole mouth and passing through your whole embouchure. Sense the solid continuation of this column through the horn so that the sound you perceive seems to be the direct realization of the column you control.

Think fullness: fill up the sound by filling up the air column. Adjust the   7
air and embouchure toward the greater fullness and greater focus of the sound you hear. You will find it a natural result of your response adaptation toward the biggest, most-focused sound that much of the burden of intensity and pressure is transferred to the air stream, allowing the lips to further relax their pressure against the mouthpiece. This will allow your lips to vibrate more freely and more consistently, which will increase the resonance of your tone. Resonance involves, technically, the positive reinforcement of sound waves: it is what can give a live, bell-like quality to your sound. And you can literally *feel* it as well, in your inner ear and filling your head and sometimes even setting the atmosphere of the whole room in vibrant motion. Adjust toward it! Producing or hearing a really resonant, focused tone is quite an experience in itself.

But there is more work to do. After achieving a good tone on the initial   8
open note, repeat the note several times to establish the concept of the tone more firmly in your mind and the position involved more securely in your

lips. When you have done this, play the note again, and then, maintaining the flow of air and basically the same lip position, slur down one-half step. Adjust to this new note. This adjustment should involve increasing the diameter of the aperture slightly, both horizontally and vertically, and adjusting the focus of the air stream accordingly. By response adaptation try to establish the same quality of tone for this note as you did for the first one. If it helps, you can slur slowly back and forth between the notes until the tone quality seems even. This practice also helps to familiarize you with the relationship between the proper positions and focuses of the two notes.

9   Continue in this manner chromatically downward, achieving a solid good tone on each note before proceeding to the next one. Maintain a tautness and compression in the embouchure, rather than relaxing it, which is a more natural tendency in playing lower notes. When you get to a note for which you cannot maintain the lip position, return to the note above it and try to slur down several times, making [an] effort to hold the embouchure. Diligent work at the border regions will extend these outer limits in the next practice session or within the next few. Also, anytime you feel you are losing the tone concept, return to the initial, model note to refresh your memory.

10   Follow basically the same process going up chromatically from the initial note as you followed going down. There is something you should keep in mind about positioning as you go up, however. Many players achieve higher notes by pressing harder against the mouthpiece; others shrink the aperture by pulling the corners of the mouth outward and closing vertically at the center. For me, neither of these methods has proved conducive to good tone production. I suggest maintaining the rounded firm-edged aperture, decreasing its diameter by continuing to press *toward* the middle from the sides and distending toward the center the compressed upper and lower lips. In other words, while keeping the position of the lips on the mouthpiece firmly anchored and actually pulling downward on the lower jaw to balance its natural tendency to close upward, stretch the tissue of the lips in toward the aperture from the top and the bottom.

11   Also practice slurs on larger intervals, because these will help to establish the feel of instantaneous position changes and of melodic, rather than just note-wise or scale-wise continuity of tone. All your practice on these exercises should be slow for several days in order for you to develop the necessary muscle structure, to listen carefully and critically to yourself, and to make a habit of thinking about and recognizing good tone.

12   Because these practices require more complex control of the embouchure than many players are used to, intonation, attacks, accuracy, and consistency will probably all be worse than usual at first. But precisely because this greater complexity leads to a greater awareness and a greater control of the embouchure and of the relationship between the embouchure and the air flow, the development of a better tone, in the long run, enhances each of these other aspects of horn-playing as well.

ANONYMOUS (Student)

The Turning Point

[Because the problem presented in this essay still continues, I've decided, as editor, not to provide information that might embarrass the author's father. Consequently, until that matter is resolved, I can't provide any information about the student, either. L.Z.B.]

Ostensibly, "The Turning Point" is an essay about making a pot, and directions for the process occupy two-thirds of the text. With the addition of a few more specific details, such as what was used for the slip in paragraph 6, and what the "finishing touches" were in paragraph 8, the process is fairly complete. Moreover, the author has defined unfamiliar terms as he uses them, such as wedge and slip, to make sure novice readers will understand.

But the paper is about much more than potting. Sometimes writers describe a process in great detail as a way of focusing on the person performing it, or on the people affected by either the process or the performance. Here, the activity of making the pot is the catalyst that draws the son and his father together. The first two paragraphs place the father's potting in its painful context; the potter's wheel is the consolation for the loss of his job, and he can engage in the potting itself because he has no formal claim on his time. Through the author's appreciation of his father's skill as a potter we recognize his respect, love, and concern for the man who performs this process so well. And so we come to appreciate the pain and the pleasure, as well as the process, in this essay with a wonderfully ambiguous title.

Dad lost his job last summer. They say that it was due to political reasons. After twenty years in the government it was a shock to us all. Dad never talked much about what he did at work, although it took up enough of his time. All I really know was his position: Deputy Assistant Commissioner of the State Department of Education. I was impressed by his title, though he rarely seemed to enjoy himself. Just the same, it was a job. These days it's hard enough to support a family without being out of work.

Apparently his co-workers felt so badly about the situation that they held a large testimonial dinner in his honor. People came from all over the east coast. I wish I could have gone. Everyone who went said it was really nice. It's a good feeling to know that your Dad means a lot to so many people. As a farewell present they gave Dad a potter's wheel. Dad says it's the best wheel he's ever seen, and to come from someone who's done pottery for as long as he has, that's saying a lot. Over the years Dad used to borrow potter's wheels from friends. That's when I learned how to "throw" a pot.

When I came home for Thanksgiving vacation the first thing I did was rush down to the basement to check it out. I was quite surprised. Dad had fixed the whole corner of the basement with a big table top for playing with the clay; an area set up for preparing the clay, including a plaster bat and a wedging board; the kiln Walt built for Dad one Christmas; one hundred and fifty pounds of clay; nine different glazes; hand tools for sculpting, and the brand new potter's wheel. It had a tractor seat from which you work the clay.

It could be turned manually or by motor, and it offered lots of surface area, which always comes in handy. Dad was right, it was beautiful. He had already made a couple dozen pots. I couldn't wait to try it.

4   The next day I came down into the basement to find Dad in his old gray smock preparing the clay. I love to watch Dad do art, whether it's drawing, painting, lettering, or pottery. I stood next to him as he wedged a ball of clay the size of a small canteloupe. He'd slice it in half on the wire and slam one half onto the wedging board, a canvas-covered slab of plaster; then he'd slam the other half on top of the first. He did this to get all the air bubbles out of the clay. You put a pot with air bubbles in the kiln, the pot'll explode in the heat and you've got yourself one heck of a mess to clean up. Dad wedged the clay, over and over.

5   When he was finished he sat down, wet the wheelhead, and pressed the clay right in the center of the wheel. Dad hit the accelerator and the clay started turning. He wet his hands and leaned over the clay. Bracing his elbows on his knees he began centering the clay. Steady right hand on the sides of the clay. Steady left hand pushing down on the clay. Centering the clay is the toughest part for me. The clay spins around and around and you have to shape it into a perfectly symmetric form in the center by letting the wheel do all the moving. Your hands stay motionless until the clay is centered. It takes me ten or fifteen minutes to do this. It takes Dad two. I shake my head and smile in amazement.

6   Dad's hands cup the clay, thumbs together on top. He wets his hands again and pushes down with his thumbs. Slowly, steadily. Once he's as far down as he wants to go he makes the bottom of the pot by spreading his thumbs. His hands relax and he pulls them out of the pot. Every motion is deliberate. If you move your hands quickly or carelessly you can be sure you will have to start again. Dad wipes the slip, very watery clay, off his hands with a sponge. It is extremely messy.

7   To make the walls Dad hooks his thumbs and curls all of his fingers except for his index fingers. Holding them like forceps, he reaches into the pot to mold the walls to just the right thickness. He starts at the bottom and brings them up slowly, making the walls of the pot thin and even all the way up, about twelve inches.

8   Dad sponges off his hands, wets them, and then cups his hands around the belly of the pot. Slowly, as the pot spins around, he squeezes his hands together, causing it to bevel slightly. Dad spends five minutes on the finishing touches. He's got himself a real nice skill.

9   It is a rare treat to watch Dad do something that he enjoys so much.

Questions

1. What are the meanings of the title "The Turning Point"? How do they reinforce one another? What is the essay's main subject? its secondary subject?

2. Could one learn to make a pot from the process described in this essay? What other information, if any, would the author need to provide to complete the explanation? Given the essay's main subject, does it matter whether the process of making a pot is explained as fully as it could be?

3. What is the son's attitude toward his father? How can you tell? How does this attitude function as a catalyst to integrate the main and secondary subjects?

4. What are the personalities of father and son? How are these conveyed? Are these of relevance to the main subject? to the secondary subject? Explain.

Preparing a Manuscript
and Publishing One's Writing

PETER A McWILLIAMS
Word Processing for Writers

McWilliams was born in Detroit in 1949, and with characteristically fey wit identifies himself as "The best selling poet in America under thirty"—without identifying the nine volumes of a poetry series that he brags has sold over 2,500,000 copies. He has co-authored The TM Book *(1975) and* Surviving the Loss of a Love *(1976), but in recent years has been concentrating on explaining personal computers to amateurs, in various updated versions of* The Personal Computer Book *(first edition, 1982) and* The Word Processing Book *(first edition, 1982).*

"Word Processing for Writers," typical of how-to writings, identifies the advantages of the process at hand in a numbered list of ten items. (How-to writers like tidy—and usually short—lists with even numbers.) McWilliams's list essentially identifies the reasons why a writer should use a word processor rather than a typewriter; he does not spend space here explaining how to use a word processor to add, delete, revise, or move text—its essential functions. His breezy tone is more flippant than that of most how-to writers; how readers react may depend on whether they feel such levity undermines the writer's authority. Can an advice-giver who cracks jokes be trusted? Especially one who proclaims that he himself is new to the field, as McWilliams does at the outset: "This book is written for the absolute novice, which is precisely what I was less than two years ago."

[A few] of the ways in which word processors can enhance and assist the writing process [are]:

1. Change is effortless. Adding to, taking from, and moving around of text is simple. The changes are displayed at once, neatly "typed" on the video screen, with no cross-outs, " ∧ " marks or scribbles in the margin.

2. Retyping is unnecessary. Even after a manuscript is printed and an error or area of improvement is discovered, all one needs to do is bring up the original on the video screen, make the change, and print a new page. Simple changes take but a few minutes, and most of that time is spent waiting for the printer. Only the changes need be typed. No more agonizing over whether the replacement of one word is worth retyping a whole page. Manuscripts are neat and free from penciled-in changes.

3. Spelling is perfect. Spelling and typing errors are detected by the computer. My mother feels that she must clean house before she can call a cleaning lady. Many writers feel that way about proofreaders: They're there to verify the perfection of the piece, not to correct it. Spell-check programs will let you know that every word in your text is a genuine, properly spelled word. Whether those words are used correctly or creatively is another story. There is, however, a program that will help with grammar and punctuation.

4. *Word processors are quiet.* I remember advertisements for Exercycle from the 1960s. There was a photograph of a man exercycling away next to a bed, and on the bed was a woman smilingly asleep. (Back in the 1960s one automatically assumed this was his wife.) Under the photograph was written: "Exercycle: So Quiet He Can Exercise While She Sleeps."

I think the same approach can be used to sell word processors. At the word processor sits a Barbara Cartland type, smilingly writing away, and in bed lies a 19-year-old hunk, smilingly asleep. The caption would read, "Word Processors: So Quiet She Can Write While He Sleeps."

I think, too, it would be interesting to record a version of LeRoy Anderson's "The Typewriter Song" entitled "The Word Processor Song." The portions of the song devoted to typewriter clicking would be silent.

Until it comes time to print something, word processors are blessedly quiet. If neighbors, roommates, lovers, or spouses have narrowed your hours of typewriter writing, word processing will provide you with a lengthened creative day. In a pinch you can even write in the dark. Just to see if that last sentence were true, I turned off the lights and am writing this in total darkness, the keyboard being illuminated only by the light of the video screen. If you can watch TV with earphones and not disturb the slumber of another, then you could write with a word processor as well.

5. *You are not chained to a typewriter table.* The detachable keyboard, available on many personal computers, is wonderful. As I write this the keyboard is on my lap. With an extension, I could lie down and write, take the keyboard out on the patio (if I had a patio), or even use it in the bathroom. The long hours of sitting in the one position necessary to operate a stationary typewriter with the cramps and tensions caused by that position are no more.

6. *No more carriage returns.* Most word processing programs automatically place the next word on the next line when the right hand margin is reached. In this way the words can flow, and you need only hit the carriage-return button when you want to start a new paragraph. No more little bells telling you that in eight more keystrokes your typewriter will stop dead.

7. *Correspondence is easy.* How often have you wanted to write essentially the same thing to five friends? In circulating this information you might get off a letter or two before boredom ("I have to type that *again*") or guilt ("I should be writing my book and not these letters") encourage you to abandon the project. With a word processor all you have to write is one letter and print out five copies, changing only the recipient's name each time. *I* know this is a form letter, and *you* know this is a form letter, but *they* won't know it's a form letter, unless, of course, they too have a word processor, in which case they are probably sending you form letters already.

There are other form letters you may want to send out. In selling your works, it will no doubt be necessary to circulate a series of letters each saying the same thing, to a variety of people: editors, publishers, agents, mothers. These must be individually typed and personalized to the recipient; a Xerox copy simply wouldn't do. In the same way that personalized form letters can help a businessman make a sale, personalized form letters can help you make a sale, too.

Some writers maintain their correspondence but feel that they should be keeping a journal as well; others keep a journal but fall behind in their correspondence. With a word processor you can do both. If you enjoy correspondence, you can write about your life in letters to your friends, then choose the best paragraphs and copy them into your electronic journal. If journal-keeping is your preference, write your journal on the word processor, then send excerpts in the form of letters to your friends. In this way, both literary traditions are maintained.

8. Research is easier. Using . . . data banks, . . . researching a project that might have required many trips to the library and much correspondence can often take place in the comfort of your own computer terminal.

9. Other programs are available. Writers seldom have one-track minds; their interests are broad, passionate, and varied. The many programs that can be run on personal computers when they're not being used for word processing might prove invaluable in satisfying a writer's greatest passion: curiosity. (All right, a writer's second greatest passion.)

10. They're fun. Computers are great, expensive, fascinating toys. As a [professional] writer you can justify the purchase of such a toy to just about anyone, including the taxman. (In most cases. See your accountant or the Tax People at H & R Block for full details. Located at larger Sears, J.C. Penney and Montgomery Ward stores coast to coast. Offer void where prohibited by law. Subject to cancellation without notice.)

LYNN Z. BLOOM

How to Submit Writing
for Publication

Bloom, born in Ann Arbor, Michigan, in 1934, returned there after growing up in New Hampshire to earn a B.A., M.A., and Ph. D. in English from the University of Michigan. Currently a professor of English at Virginia Commonwealth University, she has taught and directed writing programs at Butler University, the University of New Mexico, and the

College of William and Mary. Her dozen books include Doctor Spock: Biography of a Conservative Radical *(1972), written while her own small children were playing in the same room;* The New Assertive Woman *(1975); and several books on writing, including* Strategic Writing *(1983),* The Essay Connection *(1984), and* Fact and Artifact: Writing Nonfiction *(1985), from which the following essay was taken. She has received grants and fellowships from the National Endowment for the Humanities for research on American autobiography.*

"How to Submit Writing for Publication" conveys two messages. The explicit message consists of step-by-step directions on how to do it, each step set off by boldface type, italics, or white space for emphasis and clarity. The implicit message is the reassuring one that it's possible for student writers (the assumed audience of Fact and Artifact*) to publish their own writing even if they've never done so before. Consequently, the tone is friendly (typical of many how-to writings) but not condescending, even though basic information (type in black ink, proofread, include return postage) is being presented. Knowledge is power, assume how-to writers, who provide information that they hope will give their readers enough power to do what they want to do—and to succeed. How-to writers—and readers—are incurable optimists.*

Polishing the appearance of a manuscript may be like polishing a car; it may not run any better, but it certainly looks more impressive. You can increase the chances that your manuscript will be treated with respect if you make it look professional by following the conventions identified below.

First Contact with Editor

It's usually advisable to query an editor of a publication to which you wish to submit your writing, to find out whether your subject, general ideas, and approach are suitable. Sending a brief letter of inquiry rather than the whole manuscript will enable you to submit your manuscript where it's most likely to be received with interest. Advance queries will save you potential rejections, and postage, and your manuscript won't be tied up in an editorial office where it isn't wanted.

Editors Judith Appelbaum and Nancy Evans explain that while "on the surface a query is simply a letter that asks an editor whether he'd be interested in a work you're planning or have already produced," actually "It's an introductory move, used to pave the way for submitting articles to periodicals and proposals or finished manuscripts to book publishing houses. . . . With magazines, queries may also function as proposals, in the sense that they can earn you an assignment. . . . But the query's most important function is . . . [as] a tool for steering your manuscript clear of the slush pile" (75–76) (where unsolicited manuscripts are placed, and often given cursory or less careful attention than solicited manuscripts). A query gains solicited status for a

The citations to Appelbaum and Evans are from *How to Get Happily Published* (New York: Harper & Row, 1978).

manuscript because it allows you to submit a manuscript in which an editor has expressed prior interest, and this guarantees that it will be read.

4   The following format, say Appelbaum and Evans (78–79), epitomizes the advice most editors offer for drafting a one or two page query letter for a nonfiction article:

State your specific idea (as opposed to your general subject). A title that conveys the essence of your article is also useful here.

Explain your approach. Will it be a first person narrative, a how-to article, a summary of opinions. . . . What will your style be?

Cite your sources—interviews, case histories, personal experience, published sources (if so, which ones?).

Estimate the length. Depending on your typewriter or word processor, you can get between 220–300 words to a typed page. Your estimate should reflect the importance of the subject and the magazine's format.

Identify a realistic completion date for the manuscript.

Briefly identify your qualifications, both to write on the subject and as a writer. If you've ever worked for a newspaper or won any awards for writing, in high school, college, or elsewhere, specify these. Include no more than two clippings of your previously published work, and only if they're relevant to your proposed article or if they're extraordinarily good.

Convey your enthusiasm for the project. A sample query letter might look like this:

```
Mr. Keith K. Howell, Editor-in-Chief
Oceans
315 Fort Mason
San Francisco, CA 94123

Dear Mr. Howell:

I have recently completed a 5000-word article on "Our
Vanishing Beaches: Citizens and Survival." The arti-
cle's thesis is that the natural ecology and recre-
ational potential of many of America's best beaches
are being destroyed by overuse; private citizens must
act now to preserve these natural treasures for cur-
rent and future generations. Would you be interested
in considering this for possible publication in
Oceans?

Although the problem addressed is perennial, my arti-
cle takes a new slant on the subject--that of the in-
volvement of private citizens in public policy specif-
ically aimed at beach preservation. It begins with
some horror stories documented with evidence obtained
```

by the Sierra Club (I'm president of the U.C.L.A. student branch) and the Wilderness Society on the effects on the ecology of oil spills, dumping of toxic wastes, and beachfront condominium complexes. Then, using projections derived from information provided by the Environmental Protection Agency, the article demonstrates the potential destructiveness on the beaches and on marine life in 1995 and 2005. The potential consequences are horrifying, even by conservative estimates; they imply the destruction of 50% of the existing usable beachfront and a comparable destruction of marine life.

The article will conclude with a threefold plan for action by concerned citizens: 1) Organized lobbying—an intensification of what environmental groups are currently doing. 2) Citizen action, based on the experiences of myself, fellow students, and citizens in our community, to inform and educate not only industrial polluters and land developers, but schoolchildren. This sometimes includes boycotts of the polluters' products. 3) Individual action, based on my own experiences and on interviews with surfers, beachcombers, and others who spend considerable time at the beach. This ranges from simply picking up litter along the beach, to personal lobbying of elected officials, to aiding in the rescue of birds afflicted by oil slicks. In general, the focus is on action and on prevention of future problems.

Although the manuscript is completed, if you like the idea but have suggestions for changes, I can try to incorporate these and have the article to you within two weeks of receipt of your letter. I write a weekly ecology column for the Daily Bruin, which is also reprinted in my hometown paper, The Orange County Weekly. Considering the paper's conservative slant, I have been gratified by the readers' responses to my articles, two of which I enclose because of their relevance to "Our Vanishing Beaches."

Thank you for considering my proposal. I look forward to hearing from you.

Sincerely,

Boyd Bradley

Boyd Bradley

This query letter follows the format suggested above. It is straightforward, sufficiently specific to convey the argument of the article, the research methodology, and supporting evidence. Bradley has had experience both with the subject and as a writer; his own writing style is apparent from the query letter and from the clippings of articles he encloses.

5   But will this letter, however well-written and authoritative, be sufficiently intriguing for the editor of *Oceans* to want to see "Our Vanishing Beaches: Citizens and Survival"? Without knowing what other submissions on the subject Howell has received lately, this is impossible for either Bradley or other outsiders to predict. If the article strikes Howell as original, imaginative, and he hasn't seen others like it in recent months, he's likely to be interested. If it's repetitive of earlier submissions, published, waiting in the wings, or rejected, Howell is less likely to be attracted, but at least Bradley should get a quick answer—in a stamped, self-addressed envelope—at minimum cost of time and expense to himself.

Submitting Work for Consideration

6   If the editor says, "Yes, send along the article," follow the suggestions under "Responsibilities," above, to make the manuscript as accurate and elegantly written as you can, and use the suggestions that follow to prepare your manuscript for reading by an editor who has expressed interest in your work.

Use plain white, heavy weight (20-pound) standard size paper, 8-½" × 11", unless computer software discs or printouts on computer paper are acceptable. Avoid erasable paper; one swipe of the editor's elbow and you've lost half a page.

The manuscript should be typed or printed out in black ink (distinct, not faint), double spaced, on one side of the paper only.

Identify your article by title and author (and by institutional affiliation, if relevant) on the first page, or on a separate sheet if the article will be read blind (editor or manuscript reader is not shown author's name). Leave a four-inch top margin on the first page only. Triple space between the last line of the title/author identification and the first line of the text of the article.

Use standard margins: 1-½" at the left and top, 1" at the right and bottom. The left-hand margin should be even; the right-hand margin should be ragged. It's better not to justify (align text) the right-hand margin because you will want the spacing within your text to be reproduced in type exactly as you have it in the manuscript. Justification defeats this aim by altering the internal spacing to make the right-hand margin even. Indent each new paragraph about an inch.

Number each page in Arabic numerals (1, 2, 3) in the upper right-hand corner. Indicate on the first page, above the pagination, the total of the number of words in the article, rounded to the nearest fifty or hundred.

Unless your article will be read blind, it's a good idea to put your name on each page, as well, to avoid mix-ups: Perry Katz, 4. Or, Perry Katz, p. 4 of 8 [or whatever the total number] pages.

Try not to end lines with hyphens; i.e. try to end the line with an entire word rather than breaking the word across two lines. If you're writing on a word processor, this can be programmed automatically. Because your manuscript will guide the typesetter, the hyphens are likely to get reproduced by mistake even when the word isn't divided.

Proofread for typing errors. Check also for misspellings, missing words or lines, and misquotations (compare your version with the original source). White correction liquid or tape, self-correcting typewriters, or computers (which can't make strikeovers) make it easy to produce a clean copy. If your page looks messy or unclear, redo it.

Clip the pages together. Don't staple or otherwise bind them.

Make a copy of the final, corrected version to keep for yourself in case the original goes astray in the mails or in the editor's office. If the original is returned with editorial comments, incorporate these (if you agree with them) in your subsequent rewriting. If the original is returned in pristine condition, you can send it out again as is.

Always enclose a self-addressed stamped envelope (SASE) for your own protection, to get the manuscript back in case it's rejected. If you're likely to move within six months, indicate an alternative address and the date after which it should be used; manuscripts sometimes sit around in editorial offices longer than you'd like them to. It's advisable to use first-class postage (clipped, not stuck, to the return envelope) and to supply a return envelope big enough to hold your manuscript without folding, so it will look crisp when you send it out again. If your manuscript returns from the rounds of several editors' offices limp and smudged, retype it before mailing it out again; editors are far more receptive to professional-looking manuscripts than to waifs that exude authorial weariness or naiveté.

Enclose a short, simple cover letter. If you've sent the manuscript in response to a favorable query letter, you should refer to the editor's invitation, to try to ensure a thoughtful reading of your article. At this point, however, you won't need to say much about the article itself; the manuscript should be self-evident, and should not require additional explanation. Some professional journals request a one-paragraph abstract to be submitted with the article; you can determine this in advance. To refresh the editor's mind, you may wish to include a sentence or two of biographical information as it bears on your authorial expertise. A sample cover letter might read [like the one on p. 608].

Mr. Keith K. Howell, Editor-in-Chief
<u>Oceans</u>
315 Fort Mason
San Francisco, CA 94123

Dear Mr. Howell:

At your invitation, in response to my initial query
about "Our Vanishing Beaches: Citizens and Survival,"
I enclose the article for possible publication in
<u>Oceans</u>. In accord with your suggestions, I revised the
manuscript to include more first-hand information
about the ecological activities of student groups in
the Los Angeles area, and have included quotations
from interviews with several student leaders to reinforce this material.

As you may recall, I have been active in student ecology groups for some years; the article grew out of my
experience and my convictions on the subject. I write
an ecology column for the U.C.L.A. <u>Daily Bruin</u>, which
is reprinted in <u>The Orange County Weekly</u>. Thank you
for considering the article. I look forward to hearing
from you soon.

Sincerely,

Boyd Bradley

Boyd Bradley

Keep track of where you've sent the manuscript, and when. The safest way is
to keep a copy of your cover letter to the editor. As a routine matter, keep
copies of all business correspondence for later reference. If you keep a
separate manila file folder for each manuscript, you can file the related
correspondence in the same place. If you haven't heard from the editor
after three months (six months for scholarly journals), write a brief letter
inquiring whether your manuscript is still under consideration. Enclose a
self-addressed, stamped envelope for this reply, also.

***Generally do not submit the same article simultaneously to more than one
publication,*** unless you ask for and receive prior permission from the
editor. Little magazines, low-budget magazines, and scholarly journals
often have volunteer readers of manuscripts; multiple submissions abuse
editorial time and good will. And if your manuscript should be accepted
simultaneously by more than one editor, you'll have to reject one offer of
publication—an embarrassment if you wish to maintain cordial relations
with the editor.

After Work Is Accepted

If your work is accepted for publication you will need to get permission to   7
reprint direct quotations totalling 300 words of prose from any single copy-
righted published source, and for even a single line of poetry or a song lyric.
You can usually obtain permission to quote by writing to the publishers of
the works in question. If this seems like too much effort (and often it will be),
transform enough of your direct quotations into paraphrases to come under
the word limit, and then you'll save yourself the bother and expense of
obtaining permission. Current popular song lyrics are often prohibitively
expensive, if they're available at all.

Whether or not permissions fees are charged depends on the editorial   8
policies of different publishers. Whether you will be charged a fee to quote
from other sources depends on the author, the publisher's general policy, the
context in which the work appeared originally, and the context in which it
will be reprinted. The rule of thumb is, if reprinting portions of someone
else's writing will help the reprinter make money, then the original author or
author's publisher usually requests a fee. If the reprinting is not for profit,
then the fee may be waived.

Writers who have submitted manuscripts have to fight the natural incli-   9
nation to linger by the mailbox, waiting with moist palms and palpitating
heart for an answer. There are two good antidotes for this. One is to keep
several manuscripts in circulation at a time, as a way to avoid putting all your
emotional investment into one editor's basket. The other is to continue to
write new manuscripts, which may require such concentration that those out
in the mail will occupy only your peripheral vision.

Writing that hides in a cozy desk drawer or file folder is safe—snug and   10
securely tucked away. And it remains in the dark—where no one can read it.
Writing needs exposure to the light of public scrutiny, however revealing,
however risky this may be. Such illumination is necessary for you to gain
your place in the sun, as a real writer.

JUDITH APPELBAUM AND NANCY EVANS

Procedures, or How to Submit
Your Manuscript

Appelbaum, a New Yorker born in 1939, joined the editorial staff of Harper's *immediately
after her graduation from Vassar in 1960, and worked there for fourteen years before
serving as an editor and columnist for various other publications. Her advice on publishing
stems, in part, from a three-year stint at* Publisher's Weekly. *Evans, a Philadelphian born
in 1950, earned a B.A. from Skidmore in 1972 and an M.A. from Columbia in 1974.*

After a two-year editorial stint at Harper's 1974–76, she embarked on a career as a free-lance writer, and contributes to numerous popular magazines, including Ms. and Esquire.

Appelbaum and Evans offer advice here on how writers can make the best match between their work and a prospective publisher or editor. They begin by identifying the broad range of publishers by type—large and small, mainstream and offbeat. They then suggest step-by-step strategies for learning the tastes of individual editors, contending that editors publish and promote works they're enthusiastic about. They identify resources, such as Literary Market Place, to consult in determining various publisher's current lists and needs, and the importance of timing in placing a manuscript—to coincide with current interest or notoriety, for instance. They end with a list of "the most hospitable" places for unknown writers to start submitting their work. Although Appelbaum and Evans, as experienced editors, acknowledge the possibility of rejection and even cite some negative examples, on the whole their advice, like that of other how-to writers, is essentially positive—if aspiring writers try hard enough, and send their works out to the right places, they're eventually bound to find a publisher. It's up to readers of such books to factor in the negative possibilities and decide how much weight to give them; most aspiring contributors to the arts (any art) need all the encouragement they can get.

1   Choosing markets for your manuscripts is a two-step process. First, you must become aware of the tens of thousands of outlets that exist; and second, having learned how enormous your range of options is, you must figure out how to narrow it sensibly, so that you end up sending your work to the particular publishers and editors who are most apt to be receptive to it and enthusiastic about it.

2   We're about to describe a variety of selection tools that will help you locate the best markets for your writing. As you wield them, however, you ought to keep one question very much in mind: Would you, generally speaking, be happier with a large publishing firm or a small one?

3   Large publishing operations offer certain obvious advantages: everybody's heard of them, so their imprint on your writing tends to confer prestige; they pay better than small firms; they have more clout with reviewers and talk-show hosts, as well as with bookstore managers and newsstand distributors; and they employ professional designers, copy editors, and other skilled specialists to process the raw copy they buy.

4   On the other hand, most big firms are more likely than most small ones to reject serious fiction and poetry and anything else that's noncommercial, and they're quite apt to offer you little or nothing in the way of promotion unless you're a celebrity or about to become one. Furthermore, large companies are often—although by no means always—impersonal, and they have an irritating habit of getting tangled up in red tape.

5   Small firms have roughly opposite strengths, weaknesses, and special interests. Until recently, the terms "alternative press," "small press," and "little magazine" sufficed to describe their output, which consisted mainly of avant-garde literature from the small presses and little magazines, and leftist political prose from the alternative publishing concerns, and which had nothing to do with the goal of commercial success. . . .

In some cases, it will make sense to aim straight at Doubleday or *The New*   6
Yorker; in others, the best targets may be distinguished small presses like
Black Sparrow or the *Hudson Review;* under a third set of circumstances you
might decide to submit to both large and little houses—Harcourt Brace
Jovanovich, say, along with John Muir—and under still a fourth you could
consider trying a special-interest quarterly first and then using a clip of your
piece as it appeared there to boost your chances at a slick mass-market magazine.

Because the paths to publication are so numerous, you can probably   7
discover a variety of promising markets for every manuscript you have to
place. If you maintain your awareness of the distinctions that result from size
as you confront placement puzzles, you should be able to use the strategies
outlined below and the "Foot in the Door Resources" to concoct a thoroughly workable (if not an entirely watertight) solution to any problem you
face.

The Affection Approach

"I judge mostly by an editor's enthusiasm," said Richard Marek, explaining   8
how he decided whether to buy a book manuscript when he was editor in
chief of the Dial Press. It's a popular criterion; in fact, with the possible
exception of those responsible for mass-market paperbacks, most book and
magazine editors see excitement as more important than sales forecasts in
determining publishability. Herman Gollob, Atheneum's editor in chief,
goes so far as to predict "an unending chain of disasters—financial as well
as psychological—for houses that publish books no editor feels strongly
about."

The emphasis is undeniably attractive. Unlike the outdoor grill manufac-   9
turer or the automobile designer or the orthodontist, an editor can—and
should and frequently does—allow passion to rule, at least where acquiring
manuscripts is concerned, with the result that publishing doesn't suffer as
much from homogenization as most other industries.

Unfortunately, the reverse side of this coin shows a less pleasant picture   10
. . . because it's extraordinarily difficult for a writer to figure out which editor,
among hundreds, is going to respond passionately to him. "Love" is a word
even the gruffest editors like to use in high praise—"I loved this story," they'll
scribble on the back of its envelope without embarrassment—but, as when
boy meets girl, the chemistry is hard to predict and impossible to manufacture.

Fixing yourself up with a promising editorial partner—which is the best   11
possible way to ensure a happy publishing future—is largely a matter of
learning a lot about individual editorial tastes; try one or more of the following tactics.

1. Compile a data bank, using a separate index card for each editor's   12
name and filling each card with as much information about that editor as you
can glean; perhaps eventually you'll be able to sell a piece about nonsmokers'

rights because your files led you to somebody who'd run two pieces on minority power.

13   One good way to get to know an editor without actually meeting her is by reading about her in a publishing memoir. You'll find dozens of lively portraits in books like Hiram Haydn's *Names and Faces* or William Targ's *Indecent Pleasures* (consult the *Subject Guide to Books in Print* for other current titles), and once you've made allowances for bias and for that striving after color which afflicts editors as diarists no less than other people, you can use acquaintanceship through print to facilitate acquaintanceship in person.

14   Publishing memoirs get published a lot (for obvious reasons), but they're by no means the only things that editors write. Poems, novels, and nonfiction by editors appear often, and should prove revealing, so that skimming reviews and ads and biographical notes to find writing by working editors may be worthwhile.

15   Other good data for your files can come from comments about particular editors that you collect at writers' conferences or from friends; from *PW* items about which editor is responsible for which new title; from dedications and prefatory notes that express gratitude for an editor's work; and from the assorted across-the-editor's-desk jottings you'll find sprinkled through magazines.

16   2. Break through editorial anonymity by investigating personal publishing, which is flourishing today on two fronts. Within the large commercial houses, it's becoming more and more common for an editor to arrange to put out a line of books chosen and supervised solely by her and issued under her own personal imprint. Pioneers in this system, like Joan Kahn and Seymour Lawrence, have been joined recently by a host of new recruits. Moreover, the number of independent, one-person publishing operations is growing outside the establishment too.

17   Brief descriptions of one-man publishing outfits appear in the "Book Publishers" listings in *Literary Market Place* and in the *International Directory of Little Magazines and Small Presses*. (Naturally, publishers are not formally categorized as one- [or two- or 112-] man operations, but you can tell which houses are an individual's property by checking staff rosters for number of employees and similarity of surnames.) When a company's description attracts you, write to the head of the firm and ask for a catalog; from the catalog you'll be able to infer a great deal about the personality in charge and about your own potential relationship to him.

18   3. Discover an editor through a book you feel passionate about. One young writer who greatly admired Robert Pirsig's *Zen and the Art of Motorcycle Maintenance* figured there might be an emotional affinity between him and Pirsig's editor. He therefore placed a call to the publicity department of *Zen's* publisher, William Morrow, and asked who had edited Pirsig's book. They told him—no questions asked; he got in touch with the editor, and his book proposal was subsequently accepted at Morrow.

Though it takes considerable nerve, this approach will undoubtedly put you on a good footing with the editor at the receiving end. He'll be impressed by your effort to find out something about him, and perhaps his pleasure in learning that you enjoyed a book he helped create will lead him to greet your submission with a small prejudice in its favor. [19]

4. Advertise. The Committee of Small Magazine Editors and Publishers, known as COSMEP, has a regional newsletter which is experimenting with a "Publishers Wanted" section where writers can summarize their available work. COSMEP hopes it will be a good resource for small-press publishers, and it's just possible that a similarly direct approach—perhaps through a *PW* ad—might strike the fancy of an editor at a large house. [20]

Indirect advertising is worth thinking about too, especially since it can be obtained easily and without cost through biographical notes on current published work. If you ask the editor who's printing your study of utopian theory to run a line saying, "The author is halfway through a novel called *Bravest New World*," you may hear from far-flung editors who want a chance at the book. [21]

Matching Exercises

For a straightforward approach to manuscript placement nothing beats matching the subject matter of your work with the subject matter that appeals to a particular publisher. [22]

Perhaps, without fully realizing it, you've already formed a mental image of what attracts the editors of magazines you read regularly, in which case you'll know almost instinctively whether your work belongs there. Though your sense of a book publisher's range of interests is likely to be hazier, you can bring it into equally sharp focus by studying the *Publishers Trade List Annual,* where current catalogs from firms that issue three or more titles a year are gathered. Lists from small houses and from subsidiaries of large houses and regional or special-interest presses are easiest to categorize, but even a general-interest publishing giant has a personality of its own, and whatever you can conclude about the likes and dislikes of any size firm will help you with placement. [23]

To supplement impressions formed through study, you can turn to descriptions in a writer's single most valuable reference book, *Literary Market Place* (which is commonly referred to as *LMP;* see "Resources" for a full description), or to the subject indexes in *Writer's Market* and the small-press directories. Moreover, you can get hold of COSMEP's newsletter to see whether anything in the "Manuscripts Wanted" column matches up with anything you're working on or would like to tackle. (Have you, for instance, written an article about practical alternatives for humanizing city life; an essay on fear; or a poem that deals with the laundromat experience? Not long ago, publishers were looking for just such material.) [24]

Furthermore, you can try the *Subject Guide to Books in Print*. When you [25] look up your topic you're apt to discover that several related titles have been published by a single house, and you may be tempted to conclude that the editors there are now surfeited with the subject. That's possible. It's at least as likely, however, that they're still hungry for more. They wouldn't have done a second book on solar energy, after all, if the first hadn't sold well, and the fact that they issued a third or a fourth indicates that they've tapped a lucrative market they'll be reluctant to abandon.

26   If an abundance is good for placement purposes, an absence may be still better; instead of matching your subject to a company's demonstrated strength, you can match it to an obvious weakness. Is one national magazine you read short on profiles, when the form is clearly fashionable? Are there no gardening books in the publisher's catalog you've been studying, even though *PW* has just announced an unprecedented boom in their sales? If so—like a high school student we know who accused the editor of the local paper of ignoring the kids' point of view and got himself hired to write a column—you've found a gap in need of filling.

Timing

27   Consider "A Day in the Life of a Peanut Farmer." Before Jimmy Carter began his ascent to the White House, only farming journals or local peanut-country weeklies would have bought such a story. As the presidential campaign got under way, however, big-city dailies and national magazines might have gotten interested. And after Carter's election it's probable that no ready market existed for still another peanut piece.

28   The point, clearly, is that each moment creates and destroys publishing potential, so that sensitivity about timing is an enormous aid in placement.

29   If you are alert to passing events you can sometimes hang an already completed manuscript on a newspeg to attract editors. A much-rejected book about Big Foot, for example, might suddenly become salable the instant that new evidence of the monster's existence turned up. Similarly, if an article about man's unquenchable desire for war has been repeatedly turned down on the grounds of familiarity, a timely new lead might help. Perhaps, for instance, the piece could be sold to a newspaper for the June 25 issue if it began by pointing out that June 25 marks not only the anniversary of Custer's Last Stand and of the invasion that began the Korean War, but also the occasion of the National Skillet Throw Championship (this celebration, along with hordes of others that delight and inform, is listed in *Chase's Calendar of Annual Events*; see "Resources").

30   People unprepared with manuscripts can also take advantage of propitious moments for getting published. Was it your town the tornado hit? Your aunt who gave the governor a ticket for jaywalking when he came to speak at a medical convention? Your college that voted overwhelmingly to reinstitute curfews? When you're involved in any way in a newsworthy event, it makes sense to offer an eyewitness report to interested publications that have no

representative on the scene. If you can plan ahead for the story, query selected editors about it beforehand (see "Procedures"); otherwise make a few phone calls to see if you can get an expression of interest.

Either way, you might consider parlaying the temporary position of on-the-spot reporter into an ongoing job as a stringer for one of the national newsmagazines or large metropolitan papers that like to keep up with news breaking locally around the country; get in touch with the nearest bureau chiefs (you'll find their names on mastheads) if the prospect appeals to you. Stringers' assignments are sporadic; their copy is generally rewritten beyond recognition; both their by-lines and their pay may be virtually invisible. But think of it this way: magazines like *Time* and *Newsweek* make nice additions to anyone's list of credits, and being even partly responsible for what millions of people get to read has its charms.

Not every story needs, or should have, explicit links with current events, but no manuscript can be sensibly submitted unless targets are selected with timing very much in mind, because every publishing enterprise has a definite position on a temporal spectrum. As we noted in "Subject Matter Matters," the small and the specialized tend to congregate near the leading edge, getting to the future way ahead of most mass-market, general-interest publications. Thus a piece that the *Berkeley Barb* might like this month probably won't be suitable for the *Saturday Review* until sometime next year and might not be welcomed at the *Reader's Digest* until long after that (for tips on making several sales with the same story, see "Spinoffs").

Art Harris, a prep-school teacher turned freelance writer, learned his lesson about timing the hard way: "In 1968, having three sons and a wife who was reading all these articles on 'How Safe Are Birth Control Pills?' I had a sterilization operation—the vasectomy. What a great idea for an article, I thought. It even tied in with another subject—zero population growth. 'You're a nice fellow,' the editors said, 'but frankly nobody wants to hear about your operation. Forget it. It's too personal a subject.' So I put the idea aside only to see a whole crop of articles on the subject a year or two later. If I were to approach an editor today with 'My Male Sterilization,' I would get laughed out of the office; the subject has been well covered, thank you."

However painful Harris's education, he learned enough in the end to write a piece called "Timing the Submission" that he sold to *The Writer*. The advantages you'll derive from developing timing skills may not be quite as direct, but they're sure to aid your progress nonetheless.

Easy Access

"We regret that we are unable to consider unsolicited manuscripts" is a sentence that causes a lot of needless anguish. It's true, as enraged would-be authors are quick to point out, that many publishers make it a rule to return unsolicited material unread. But that policy can't debar anybody's work as long as editors respond to queries and proposals with invitations to submit

615

the manuscripts described. And besides, no matter what rejection slips may say, the periodical press is increasingly open to contributions from unknowns, as witness the following rundown.

36   1. *Reader-participation departments*. Magazines and newspapers of all sizes and sorts are now actively soliciting material from the general public. Like the physicists and politicians of the mid-twentieth century, publishers have recently discerned that our deepest sense of reality demands some confluence of subject and object, of actor and acted upon. The results of this realization—which is especially powerful because it's not entirely conscious—vary among disciplines, but in publishing it has led editors to try making writers of readers. "The magazine game has tended to look on readers as spectators," editor Tony Jones explained when he sparked the trend. "We think they should be players, and we're looking for ingenious ways around the limitations on how many can play."

37   Not long ago, the only place open to readers as players was the "Letters to the Editor" column, but today ordinary folk are cordially urged to contribute to "Viewpoint" in *Glamour*, "Second Thoughts" in *Human Behavior*, the "Living" section of *The New York Times*, the Op Ed pages of innumerable newspapers, "Opinion" in *Mademoiselle*, and the gazette pages of *McCall's* and *Ms.*—to name a few items on the steadily expanding list of reader participation departments.

38   In all these columns, and in the letters column too (which remains a good launching pad for an idea and/or a writing career), short pieces that emphasize specific, significant experience rather than abstract theory are most likely to succeed. Editors can use writers with reputations when they want opinion and analysis; it's for the small wisdoms of everyday life, the personal stories that will resonate in readers' minds and lives, that they have to turn to you.

39   2. *Book review columns*. In addition to sections that solicit contributions from readers, there are a good many periodical departments that are entirely open to the public, though they seldom proclaim that fact. One of these, as Robert Cassidy discovered seven years ago, is the book review section. Cassidy, who got his start with a review, is the author of *What Every Man Should Know About Divorce* and editor of *Planning* magazine. You can follow his example by checking publishers' catalogs and *PW* for forthcoming titles you'd be able and eager to write about, and then querying an editor to see if he'd either let you cover a book you'd like to discuss (mention title, author, publisher, and publication date) or try you out on one he has up for grabs. Book review editors' names are listed in *Literary Market Place*, and their preferences as to style and substance can be inferred from the reviews they ordinarily run; try your library for copies. Book reviewing doesn't usually pay much (in fact, the book itself may be your only payment), but the rewards in terms of exposure and contacts and credits and pride of performance can be considerable.

Other editors who are especially receptive to newcomers include those who work on: 40

3. *Community newspapers*. Applying to a neighborhood weekly for a particular beat is a fine way to begin a career as a published writer; once you've regularly covered dance, say, or home repairs for a small periodical, you've got credentials to present to a big one. And if you've written anything with a local focus, you should find a ready market among community weeklies. 41

4. *Company magazines and newsletters*. Both profit and nonprofit organizations need people to discern and relay ideas relevant to their concerns. Here again, the pay may be low or nonexistent, but the audience will consist of anything from a couple of hundred employees to thousands of sympathetic members of the general public, so that you can expect high dividends in the form of exposure. 42

5. *Campus publications* (including alumni magazines). The connection between you—or your subject—and the school will give you an edge here, and though the pay scale varies widely, most editors in this field—like their counterparts on other small publications—are generous with assistance. "We have to scratch harder for good stuff," Elise Hancock, editor of *Johns Hopkins Magazine*, says. "So if something has possibilities we'll work on it rather than turn it down because the possibilities weren't quite realized. I once published a piece called 'Bald Is Beautiful,' a magnificent parody on radical manifestoes that maintained (quite rightly) that bald people *are* discriminated against. The author was urging the *Ten Commandments* be refilmed starring Woody Allen. It was a great piece, but *Esquire* had turned it down. I think they just weren't willing to spend the hour required to cut it by two-thirds, which was all it needed. So that's a plus of working with alumni magazines if you're starting out." 43

6. *Contents*. Both book and periodical publishers use assorted competitions to attract new talent and, not incidentally, to generate publicity. Announcements about them appear from time to time in trade journals, in a firm's own publications, and in the directories listed in "Resources." 44

It would be misguided to treat the easy-access openings with less respect than any others; what you've written must be right for the specific publisher you send it to in terms of subject matter, style, tone, and timing. But if you submit to the most hospitable editors with the same care you'd use for the most forbidding, you can anticipate better results. 45

Health and Safety

JANE BRODY

Stress: Some Good, Some Bad

Brody, born in Brooklyn in 1941, earned a B.S. from Cornell in 1963, an M.A. in journalism from the University of Wisconsin in 1963, and began writing the New York Times *personal health column in 1965. Among her numerous honors for writing is the 1978 Science Writer's Award. All of Brody's books, including* You Can Fight Cancer and Win *(with Arthur Holleb, 1977) and* Jane Brody's Nutrition Book *(1981), some of them compilations of her* Times *columns, focus positively on how ordinary people can attain or maintain good health—in cooperation with doctors, nutritionists, psychiatrists, and other specialists, to be sure, but in large measure through their own common sense. The following essay is from* Jane Brody's The New York Times Guide to Personal Health *(1982).*

Typical of writings on scientific or technical subjects for general readers, Brody begins by defining stress and explaining that stress itself is not the problem, "it's how you react to the different stresses in your life that matters." She then explains mostly the negative effects of stress, humanizing her analysis by using her own history of headaches as a case in point. Like all careful science writers, she enhances her own authority by citing experts (three psychologists and a cardiologist, among others, supplemented by a bibliography) as she offers suggestions on ways to react to stress (avoid spending " '10 dollars worth of energy on a 10-cent problem' ") and appropriate stress-reducing techniques (as opposed to "wrong solutions"— "tranquilizers, sleeping pills, alcohol, and cigarettes"), which she lists in summary form ("set priorities," "organize your time"). Her short column doesn't provide space for elaboration, but again, Brody is careful not to make excessive claims or to recommend solutions that will get her readers—or herself as a writer—into trouble. Indeed Brody, like her fellow advice-givers, offers the classic suggestion, "If things are really bad, don't hesitate to seek professional counseling."

1   Stress is a factor in every life, and without some stress life would be drab and unstimulating. Too little stress can produce boredom, feelings of isolation, stagnation, and purposelessness. Stress in and of itself is not bad; rather, it's how you react to the different stresses in your life that matters.

2   Many people thrive on stress. They find working under pressure or against deadlines highly stimulating, providing the motivation to do their best. And they rarely succumb to adverse stress reactions. To slow such "racehorses" down to the pace of a turtle would be as stressful as trying to make the turtle keep up with the horse. Yet others crumble when the crunch is on or the overload light flashes. Some take life's large and small obstacles in stride, regarding them as a challenge to succeed in spite of everything. Others are thwarted by every unexpected turn of events, from a traffic delay to a serious illness in the family.

What Stress Does

All stress, positive or negative, stimulates a basic biological reaction called   3
fight or flight. This is a hormonally stimulated state of arousal that prepares
you to face whatever challenge is at hand, be it your daughter's wedding, a
job interview, an argument with your spouse, or the assault of a would-be
mugger. The chemical reaction influences your heart, nervous system, muscles, and other organs, preparing them for action.

Problems arise when the stress reaction is frequently called into play for   4
inappropriate circumstances, such as a missed bus, long line, or reservation
mix-up, or when the circumstances of your life result in more stress than you
can handle at any one time.

When most people talk about stress, they mean the negative reactions: a   5
churning gut, aching back, tight throat, rapid heartbeat, elevated blood pressure, mental depression, short temper, crying jags, insomnia, impotence, viral
infections, asthma attacks, ulcers, heart disease, or cancer.

My stress reaction was headaches. I got them often: when I was writing   6
on deadline, doing a lot of sewing, preparing for a dinner party, driving in
heavy traffic. For years I had attributed them to a variety of causes, including
eyestrain and allergic reactions to my colleagues' tobacco smoke and to the
fumes from my gas stove. But not until I awoke one morning from a bad
dream with my teeth tightly clenched did I get a hint of the real reason—a
reaction to stress.

Over the next several weeks I realized that whenever I was concentrating   7
hard on something (even opening a stubborn package or chopping an onion)
or feeling tense or anxious, I clenched my teeth. After a while the strain on
the supporting muscles would result in a headache.

It was an unconscious reaction, a habit that I was finally able to break—   8
with the aid of my dentist—by becoming acutely aware of it and making a
conscious effort to relax my jaw when formerly I would have tightened it.
Now tension headaches, which account for 80 percent of the head pains that
afflict Americans, rarely sneak through my surveillance.

Dr. Donald A. Tubesing, psychologist from Duluth, Minnesota, and   9
author of *Kicking Your Stress Habits,* likens stress to the tension on a violin
string—you need "enough tension to make music but not so much that it
snaps."

Whereas some stress reduction programs offer only techniques to induce   10
relaxation, Dr. Tubesing's simply written self-help guide helps you get to the
roots of your stress reactions and modify them. He points out that most
stress is not the result of great tragedies, but rather an accumulation of minor
irritations that "grind us down over the years." He tells you how to recognize
the sources of those irritations and what to do about them.

For example, he points out, stress is inherent not in an event but rather in   11
how you *perceive* that event; by modifying your perceptions, you can reduce
your stress. Let's say you just missed your bus. You could focus on the fact

that you'll be late for work (stressful) or on the fact that you'll now have time to read the paper (not stressful).

12   He cautions against spending "10 dollars worth of energy on a 10-cent problem." Before you gear up for a battle, stop and think: is the threat real? Is the issue really important? Can you make a difference? Dr. Tubesing's guide helps you to identify your beliefs, values, and goals, which in turn will enable you to focus on what really counts and stop worrying about irrelevant events or concerns.

13   "There are millions of 'want to's' and 'have to's' in life," he notes. "Ultimately, these pressures create stress only when your time-and-energy spending decisions aren't consistent with your goals, beliefs, and values."

14   There are many ways to cope with excess stress, and some methods are better than others. Too often people turn to the wrong solutions for stress relief, such as tranquilizers, sleeping pills, alcohol, and cigarettes, and end up further impairing their health while doing nothing to gain an upper hand on the causes of their stress reactions. Others resort to short-term solutions—shouting, crying, taking a hot bath—that help for a while. More lasting, "low-cost" relief could be obtained through regular exercise or talking with friends, Dr. Tubesing says.

How to Cope with Stress

15   Everyone should have a repertoire of stress-reducing techniques. Here are some that Dr. Tubesing and others have found helpful.

16   *Set priorities.* Divide your tasks into three categories—essential, important, and trivial—and forget about the trivial. Hire others, including your own children, to do the tasks that can be farmed out. Learn to say no when you're asked to do something that overloads your time or stress budget or diverts you from what you really consider most important. Be satisfied with a less than perfect job if the alternative is not getting a job done at all. Identify the activities you find satisfying in and of themselves, and focus on enjoying them, rather than on your performance or what rewards the activities might bring.

17   *Organize your time.* Identify the time wasters. Figure out when in the day you are most productive, and do your essential and important tasks then. Pace yourself by scheduling your tasks, allowing time for unexpected emergencies. If at all possible, leave your work at the office to reduce conflicts with the demands at home and give yourself time to recharge your batteries.

18   *Budget your stress.* The Metropolitan Life Insurance Company recommends taking a periodic glance at your schedule for the next three months to see what events may be coming up that may cause you to overdraw your stress account. Try to avoid clusters of stressful events by spreading them out.

19   *Try "clean living."* Be more consistent in your living habits by trying to eat, sleep, and exercise at about the same time every day. Don't overindulge in

alcohol or rely on pills to induce sleep (they're counter-productive). Be sure to get enough sleep and rest because fatigue can reduce your ability to cope with stress. Eat regular, well-balanced meals with enough variety to assure good nutrition and enough complex carbohydrates (starchy foods) to guarantee a ready energy reserve. Reverse the typical American meal pattern, and instead, eat like a king for breakfast, a prince for lunch, and a pauper for supper; you'll have more daytime energy and sleep better at night.

Listen to your body. It will let you know when you are pushing too hard. 20
When your back or head aches or your stomach sours, slow down, have some fun, take time to enjoy the world around you. Set aside some time each day for self-indulgence. Focus on life's little pleasures.

Choose fight or flight. Don't be afraid to express anger (hiding it is even more 21
stressful than letting it out), but choose your fights; don't hassle over every little thing. When fighting is inappropriate, try fleeing—learn to fantasize or take a short break (do a puzzle, take a walk, go to a concert, or away for the weekend) to reenergize yourself. You can also give in once in a while, instead of always insisting you are right and others are wrong.

Learn relaxation techniques. These include deep breathing exercises, tran- 22
scendental meditation, the relaxation response (a demystified form of meditation formulated by Dr. Herbert Benson, a Harvard cardiologist), religious experiences, yoga, progressive relaxation of muscle groups, imagery, biofeedback, and behavior modification. The last four may require professional help. On a tightly scheduled day, take a minute or two between appointments or activities for a relaxation break—stretching, breathing, walking around.

Revitalize through exercise. A body lacking in physical stamina is in no 23
shape to handle stress. An exercise tune-up can increase your emotional as well as your physical strength. Exercise enhances, rather than saps, your energy; it also has a distinct relaxing effect.

Talk it out. Problems often seem much worse when you alone carry their 24
burden. Talking to a trusted friend or relative or to a professional counselor can help you sort things out and unload some of the burden. If things are really bad, don't hesitate to seek professional counseling or psychotherapy.

Get outside yourself. Stress causes people to turn into themselves and focus 25
too much on their own problems. Try doing something for someone else. Or find something other than yourself and your accomplishments to care about. Be more tolerant and forgiving of yourself and others.

Finally, Drs. Robert L. Woolfolk and Frank C. Richardson, psycholo- 26
gists and authors of *Stress, Sanity and Survival* (see "For Further Reading" below), caution against "waiting for the day when 'you can relax' or when 'your problems will be over.' The struggles of life never end. Most good things in life are fleeting and transitory. Enjoy them; savor them. Don't waste time looking forward to the 'happy ending' to all your troubles."

For Further Reading

Benson, Herbert, M.D. *The Relaxation Response.* New York: William Morrow, 1975; Avon, 1976.

Carrington, Patricia. *Freedom in Meditation.* New York: Anchor/Doubleday, 1977.

Madders, Jane. *Stress and Relaxation.* New York: Arco, 1979.

McQuade, Walter, and Ann Aikman. *Stress: What It Is, What It Can Do to Your Health, How to Fight Back.* New York: Bantam, 1975.

Norfolk, Donald. *The Stress Factor.* New York: Simon & Schuster, 1977.

Selye, Hans, M.D. *The Stress of Life.* New York: McGraw-Hill, 1956; rev. ed., 1976.

———. *Stress Without Distress.* New York: Lippincott, 1974.

Steinmetz, Jenny; Jon Blankenship; Linda Brown; Deborah Hall; and Grace Miller. *Managing Stress.* Palo Alto, Calif.: Bull, 1980.

Tubesing, Donald A. *Kicking Your Stress Habits.* Duluth: Whole Person Associates, 1981. Available for $10 plus $1 for postage and handling from Whole Person Associates, Inc., P.O. Box 3151, Duluth, Minn. 55803.

Woolfolk, Robert L., and Frank G. Richardson. *Stress, Sanity and Survival.* New York: Sovereign Books (Simon & Schuster), 1978.

DIANNE HALES AND ROBERT HALES
Exercising the Psyche

Robert Hales, M.D., a psychiatrist, and his wife, Dianne Hales, are the authors of The U.S. Army Total Fitness Program. *"Exercising the Psyche," originally published in* American Health Magazine, *illustrates the thesis that "aerobic exercise—the kind that strengthens the heart and lungs—is a practical way to treat the emotional problems of daily living." After defining the biochemical basis for the beneficial effects of exercise, the authors present evidence from research to show the effects of exercise on depression, stress, anxiety, Type A behavior, alcoholism, and hyperactivity. The accompanying chart, a feature of many how-to writings, provides additional information to enable the reader to "match your exercise program to your psychological needs," and the material in the box (another how-to feature) explains how to meditate on the run—a combination of the physical and the spiritual that makes the most of these seemingly contradictory activities.*

1   Imagine a drug so powerful it can alter brain chemistry, so versatile it can help prevent or treat many common psychological problems, so safe that moderate doses cause few, if any, side effects and so inexpensive anyone can afford it. For the last few years, doctors and psychotherapists have been experimenting with just such a potential wonder drug—exercise.

Studies are showing that aerobic exercise—the kind that strengthens the heart and lungs—is a practical way to treat the emotional problems of daily living. From depressed men and women in Madison, Wis., to driven Type A's in California and anxious students at Harvard, exercise is proving its healing power. For patients recovering from heart surgery, for example, exercise is "the single most effective way to lift . . . spirits and to restore feelings of potency about all aspects of life," says Harvard psychiatrist Thomas Hackett.

There's nothing revolutionary in the notion that mental and physical fitness are linked. But in thinking about the mind-body connection, most of us have put the mind first. Psychosomatic medicine, for example, has focused on how the mind can heal the body. Now psychiatrists and psychologists are asking the opposite question: How can working out the body soothe the mind?

They're finding that the body really can help to heal the psyche. And they're finding ways to tailor exercise programs, prescribing different types of activity, duration and frequency for different psychological problems (see chart).

Like psychoactive drugs, regular doses of aerobic exercise produce chemical and physiological changes in the body and brain. Exactly how these changes cause mood shifts is still unclear. Increased blood flow and oxygenation may play an important role. Much research is also focusing on how exercise affects catecholamines, a group of neurotransmitters produced by the brain. Of particular interest is norepinephrine, a catecholamine that increases blood pressure, heart rate and cardiac output. (Norepinephrine is closely related to adrenaline, the "fight-or-flight" hormone produced in the adrenal gland.)

An imbalance in catecholamines has been linked to certain psychiatric problems, especially depression and anxiety. Now studies of runners suggest that intense, sustained exercise can cause a rise in catecholamines that may somehow help to stabilize mood.

Like traditional psychotherapies, exercise may produce gradual psychological changes as well. Physical activity distracts the mind from its troubles and also serves as a healthy release for anger and anxiety. And meeting the challenge of losing weight or firming up muscles can increase confidence and boost mood.

Although exercise can help people cope with the problems of everyday living, it's no substitute for professional treatment of serious psychiatric disorders. It's also true that the data on exercise and the mind are still preliminary. Most of the research studies have been small, have not compared aerobic exercisers with a sedentary control group and have focused almost exclusively on running. It's still not clear whether nonaerobic exercise such as stretching or flexibility might also help mood.

Still, the growing evidence is promising. For people who suffer from psychological troubles, exercise can shift the focus from drugs and doctors to the individual, who can use it as a practical tool for improving the quality of life. The chart summarizes the basic guidelines for using the body to treat the mind. Here are the reasons behind the exercise prescriptions from psychiatrists and psychologists.

Depression

10 In one study, psychiatrist John H. Greist of the University of Wisconsin in Madison attempted to discover whether running could be as effective as psychotherapy in alleviating depression. So he randomly divided 28 mildly to moderately depressed men and women into three groups. One group ran slowly and steadily for 10 weeks. The other two underwent psychotherapy— either short-term or time unlimited. Within a week, most of Greist's running patients began to feel better, and within three weeks they were "virtually well." Greist concluded that running was not only as good as brief psychotherapy in lifting their mild depression, but more effective than long-term, time-unlimited therapy. In a two-year follow-up, most of his patients were still running.

11 Greist's findings were not unusual. Study after study of both normal people experiencing a slump and patients with mild clinical depression has found that regular aerobic exercise tends to improve mood. Many depressed people, though, need more than aerobics to work through their problems. For them, the combination of psychotherapy and physical activity may be most effective.

12 How does exercise do it? Scientists know that levels of norepinephrine tend to be low in depressed people. Like antidepressant drugs, exercise may bring the level up to normal. One study has shown that running five times a week helps depressed people more than just three workouts a week. But more isn't always better. In another study, six-mile runs reduced mild feelings of depression more than a 26-mile marathon in well-conditioned men and women.

Coping With Stress

13 Your car breaks down in the middle of the highway, you're on deadline at work, you're giving a speech before a packed auditorium. Such stressful situations can sound a sudden alarm in the body. Preparing to fight or flee, the heart speeds up, blood pressure rises, muscles tense, levels of catecholamines (especially norepinephrine) soar.

14 Regular workouts can help your body cope with such sudden stress. The reason is paradoxical: Aerobic exercise can cause physical symptoms similar to a stressful situation, though not as intense—the racing heart, higher blood pressure, etc. In this way, intense workouts "condition" your body to cope with stress when you're in a sudden jam. Psychologist Richard Dienstbier of the University of Nebraska notes that athletes typically react more calmly when they're in stressful situations than healthy but untrained people do.

Once again, the key may be catecholamines, especially norepinephrine.   15
Many scientists believe regular exercise increases your body's reserves of the
hormones, so you need to produce less when stress hits.

Be warned, though. Competitive thinking during workouts may raise   16
norepinephrine levels excessively—to heart-harming highs. In a study by
psychologist Kenneth France at Shippensburg University in Pennsylvania,
when exercisers focused on competitive words such as "push," "harder,"
"faster," they more than doubled their norepinephrine levels over days when
they concentrated on words such as "steady" or "smooth."

Anxiety

Exercise can also help you cope with a feeling of dread over an impending   17
disaster, real or imagined—what's called situational anxiety. When your
nerves are frayed, a bout of exercise provides a positive channel for the body's
excess energy. Even a single moderate "dose" of exercise can have what
exercise physiologist Herbert deVries calls a "tranquilizer effect" on muscular
tension.

But though exercise can help calm the anxious body, other procedures   18
like meditation can better deal with symptoms of a worried mind—
brooding, insomnia, nervousness, etc.—that come with this kind of anxiety.
In a comparative study of exercisers and meditators at Harvard University,
the exercisers had fewer physical complaints; the meditators, fewer mental
symptoms. The best therapy for anxiety may be a combination of exercise and
cognitive, or mental, techniques. For the best effect, you might combine
exercise and meditation following the guidelines [in the box on p. 627].

Type A Behavior

Type A's, according to one definition, are those who go through life with   19
stopwatches clenched in their fists. Exercise can help them unwind, but only
if they become less competitive.

At Stanford University, Dr. William Haskell and his team of behavioral   20
researchers showed the impact of jogging on sedentary faculty and staff. Half
of the 80 subjects participated in a supervised jogging program, the other
half remained sedentary. Type A's who ran more than eight miles a week
adopted more Type-B behaviors than those who stayed on the sidelines.

"The time-out aspect of exercise, the physical separation from work, may   21
explain the benefits," says Haskell. "Obviously, some Type A's might take on
exercise in the same obsessive, goal-oriented way they approach everything
else, which would defeat its purpose. But a moderate, relaxed exercise program can help Type A's become like Type B's."

Alcoholism

Alcoholism takes a toll on both body and psyche. Exercise can help repair the   22
damage. In one study, recovering alcoholics who jogged at least a mile a day

625

What Kind of Exercise Do You Need?

This chart gives some general guidelines for matching your exercise program to your psychological needs. These guidelines, based on data from many different studies, are intended as goals to work toward. You should start any exercise program gradually, and check with your doctor if you have any doubts about whether you should work out.

Remember that exercise is not meant to replace appropriate psychiatric treatment, especially for people who are having serious problems. But it can be a useful addition to treatment. Also remember that the goals in this chart are based on studies of runners: if you do another type of activity, you may want to change the goals to fit your needs.

Problem	Intensity	Duration	Frequency	Time of Day	Setting/Condition	For Maximum Benefits
Depression	Brisk	40–60 minutes	5 days a week	When depressed or when convenient	Scenic; with running group or aerobically equal partner	Combine with psychotherapy
Stress or Situational Anxiety	Moderate	20–30 minutes	3–5 days a week	Midday, late afternoon or when tense	Quiet, scenic	Combine with meditation or relaxation exercises. Don't push to exhaustion; don't think competitively
Type-A Behavior	Moderate	30–60 minutes	3 days a week	Afternoon, early evening	Scenic	Don't record time or distance; focus on enjoyment
Alcoholism	Mild	20 minutes	4 days a week	Morning	In a group	Combine with Alcoholics Anonymous or group therapy
Hyperactive Children	Mild	30–45 minutes	4 days a week	Personal choice	Supervised group	Monitor medication doses
Goal						
Enhanced Psychological Well-being	Moderate to brisk	20–60 minutes	3–5 days a week	To fit schedule	Personal choice	Don't overdo; seek help for serious psychological problems
Running Meditation Response	Mild	60 minutes	3–5 days a week	Morning or when convenient	Quiet	Coordinate pace and breathing as described in box on page 627

The 'Om' Advantage: Meditation on the Run

Running and meditation seem like completely opposite states: one strenuous, the other serene; one physical, the other spiritual. Yet both are paths to altered states of consciousness. And together they profoundly affect both body and mind.

Dr. Herbert Benson, the Harvard cardiologist who demystified transcendental meditation in developing the "relaxation response," found that exercisers who meditated as they worked out literally changed the way their hearts and lungs worked. They burned less oxygen and used energy more efficiently.

Tibetan Monks, using a similar approach and concentrating on a mantra, or repetitive phrase, have run distances of 300 miles over mountain trails in less than 30 hours.

Dr. Earl Solomon, a psychiatrist at Harvard Medical School, and research assistant Ann Bumpus have adapted Benson's meditation technique so runners can elicit the "relaxation response" with eyes open and feet moving.
- Run at a gentle, regular pace, effortlessly, almost mechanically.
- Deeply relax all your muscles, starting with your feet and working up to your face.
- Breathe in long, through your nose if you can, breathe out short and sharp through your mouth.
- Repeat the mantra "om" or a meditative word of your choice silently to yourself as you exhale.
- Don't worry about your state of relaxation; let it come at its own pace.
- Overcome distracting thoughts by focusing on a mantra.
- Remain vigilant to any external danger, such as approaching buses, bicycles or automobiles.

---

for 20 days showed greater improvement in self-esteem, sleep patterns and physical fitness than nonexercisers. Among 18 men hospitalized for psychiatric problems, including alcoholism, daily jogging for three weeks increased fitness, decreased hypochondria and shortened some of their hospital stays.

Exercise helps recovering alcoholics physically by improving metabolism and speeding detoxification, and psychologically by improving self-concept and sense of mastery. As part of treatment, patients run in groups at moderate pace for two or more miles, four or more times a week; Alcoholics Anonymous or group therapy meetings follow. Morning runs allow ex-alcoholics to launch the day with positive activity that provides a sense of achievement and reinforces their commitment to abstinence.

Hyperactivity

Children and running go together naturally. But for hyperactive children, long-distance running can be more than play. Dr. W. Mark Shipman, medical director of the San Diego Center for Children, had 56 children between 6 and 13 run at a slow pace for an average of 30 minutes, four times a week. After 12 weeks they needed much less medication to control their symptoms. The improvements were greatest for the most over-aggressive, impulse-ridden, hyperkinetic children. And the more the children ran, the less medication they needed.

25 "Slow long-distance running seems to provide an option for a significant percentage of children who would otherwise be rendered tolerable in the classroom and at home only through medication," concludes Shipman. Exercise enhances their self-esteem, reduces stress, works off excess energy and sublimates aggression, he says.

Enhanced Psychological Well-Being

26 Working out can also help psychologically healthy people improve their moods. In fact, it may be necessary for psychological well-being.

At the University of Wisconsin and Purdue University, people who were not under psychiatric care were tested for general mood. The least physically fit had more psychological distress and dysfunction. And the less fit they were, the less they resembled psychologically normal people. But when they started exercising, they improved more dramatically—in body and mind—than those who started off in better shape.

27 Whether you're generally happy with life, or dealing with ongoing emotional problems, exercise lets you use all your resources to work through your troubles. Psychiatrists and psychologists are starting to realize that and are breaking through the old barriers that separated mental from physical fitness. In a similar way, they're starting to combine talking therapy with a new understanding of brain chemistry to develop more powerful forms of treatment. The message is clear. A sound mind and a sound body really go together.

Questions

1. The thesis of this how-to article, the third sentence, appears very early in the text—at the beginning of the second paragraph. Why is it important for how-to articles to get to the point quickly?

2. The authors claim that exercise can relieve depression, stress, anxiety, Type A behavior, alcoholism, and hyperactivity, and can enhance one's sense of well-being. Do the authors claim more than they can justify? Brief though the evidence has to be in such a short article, is it convincing? Why or why not?

3. How-to articles are often accompanied by charts, which can convey a great deal of information in a format much more concise than it would be in a written text. Is that true in this case? What does the chart tell readers that the article doesn't? How are the chart and the article complementary?

4. Likewise, how-to articles often contain or are accompanied by lists or boxes of steps of a process—in this case, advice on how to meditate while running. What is the advantage of putting this in a box rather than incorporating it into the text of the article? How essential is it to the rest of the article?

COLIN FLETCHER

Fires

Fletcher's how-to books on walking derive from his passionate involvement with hiking and his commitment to share with others the sensitivity and skill that make this not just an enjoyable activity but a spiritual communion with the wilderness. Fletcher has lived and hiked all over the world. Born in Cardiff, Wales, in 1922, he attended the West Buckland School in North Devonshire, England, before serving in the British Royal Marine Commandos 1940–1947. He then emigrated to Kenya; in the 1950s he spent summers in Canada, and finally settled in San Francisco in 1957. During his roaming over three continents he worked the wanderer's proverbial assorted odd jobs—janitor, road builder, farmer, miner, hotel manager—before becoming a successful free-lance writer.

Fletcher's books include The Thousand Mile Summer *(1964),* The Man Who Walked Through Time *(1968),* The Winds of Mara *(1973),* The Man from the Cave *(1981), and his classic,* The Complete Walker *(1968, revised 1971 and 1974), from which his observations on "Fires" are taken. Typical of many how-to works, Fletcher organizes his material topically in short, self-contained sections, but he is much more philosophical than many how-to-writers. He combines appreciation of the natural world and sound ecological principles with practicality—how to find dry wood, how to keep wood dry, how to keep wanted fires ablaze and extinguish unwanted fires. He is tolerant of greenhorns and intolerant of "woodsy fanatics" who try to start fires the hard way, without the civilized comfort of matches.*

Cooking Fire

Except when stove fuel runs low or I brew tea on sidetrips away from my pack, the only time I cook on an open fire nowadays is for frying—and that generally means frying fish. A stove is not really satisfactory for this job: its concentrated heat makes fish stick to the pan. So I resign myself to having a blackened frying pan, and before putting it in the pack I wrap it carefully in two large plastic bags.   1

For frying, I find that the best hearth is a two- or three-stone affair with a shallow trough for the fire. The stones must be flat enough to form a stable rest for the pan, and deep enough to leave space for a sizable fire. Wind direction and strength dictate the angle of the trough. A light breeze blowing down its length keeps flame and glow healthy; a high wind is best blocked off by the side stones, perhaps with an assist from others.   2

On the rare occasions I use an open fire with my cooking pots, I usually make a two- or three-stone hearth. A useful alternative that makes it easier to   3

build and replenish a sizable fire and to control its heat is a double-Y-stick-with-crossbar rig [as shown in the drawing above].

4   The two forked (or, more often, branched) sticks must be planted firmly, and far enough apart to be safe from burning. As a precaution, I may splash them from time to time with water. The crossbar must be tolerably straight and either green or wet enough not to burn too readily.

5   If there is any hint of fire hazard, I carefully seal off my fire, no matter which kind, with a circle of stones.

6   The hottest fire comes from small sticks; the best are those that burn fairly slowly and/or remain glowing for a long time.

7   Another satisfactory cooking method that I occasionally use, especially for frying, is to build a small extension to the stone ring around a big campfire. It's simple, then, to transfer a few glowing embers from the main fire, and to keep replenishing them.

Campfires: To Have or Not to Have

8   A campfire is one of the long-standing traditions of outdoor life. Understandably so. For cheer and warmth—not to mention drying out wet clothes—there is nothing quite like it. The warmth is not very efficient—you tend to be toasted on one side, iceberged on the other—but there's no doubt about the cheer. Beside your fire, you live in a private, glowing little world. All around you, fire-shapes dance across rocks and bushes and tree trunks. A grasshopper that you have been watching as it basks on one verge, motionless, leaps without warning clear over the flames and out into the darkness. But most of the time you just sit and gaze into the caverns that form and crumble and then form again between the incandescent logs. You build fantastic worlds among those pulsating walls and arches and colonnades. No, not quite "build," for that is too active and definite a word. Rather, you let

your mind slip away, free and unrestricted, roaming wide yet completely at rest, unconnected with your conscious self yet reporting back quite clearly at some low, quiet, strangely decisive level. You sit, in other words, and dream. The East African has an almost limitless capacity for this masterly and delightful form of inactivity, and when his friends see him squatting there, lost, they understand and say in Swahili, poetically, that he is "dreaming the fire."

Yet as often as not I do without a campfire. Perhaps laziness has a lot to do with it. But I am very aware that a fire cuts you off from the night. Within the fire's domain you exist in a special, private, personal, isolated world. It is only when you walk away and stand for a while as a part of the silence and immensity beyond that you understand the restriction. And then you find that the silent, infinite, mysterious world that exists beyond the campfire is truer than the restricted world that exists around it—and that in the end it is more rewarding. I walk out into wilderness primarily, I think, to re-establish a sense of unity with the rest of the world—with the rock and the trees and the animals and the sky and its stars. Or perhaps I mean only that when I return to the city a renewed sense of this affinity is, above all, what I bring back with me. A campfire, by its very charms, disrupts my sense of inclusion.

But if I do not build a fire I build no lasting barriers. After I have cooked the evening meal and switched off the hissing stove and registered the unfailing astonishment I experience at the noisiness of that hissing, I am alone in and with the night. I can hear, now, the magnified sounds of its silence: a field mouse thinly complaining; a dry leaf rustling; a wedge of wind sliding down the far slope of the valley. And I can look deep into the shadowy blackness or the starlit dimness or the moonlit clarity. Or, best of all, I can watch the moon lever itself up and flood the starlit dimness into landscape.

Always, over each of these separate mysteries, spreads the sky, total. And I, at the center—my center of it—am small and insignificant; but at the same time a part of it and therefore significant.

Lighting a Fire

An outdoorsman's ability to start a fire—anywhere, anytime—is the traditional criterion for judging his competence, and I suppose I have always accepted the criterion in an unthinking, uncritical sort of way. But now that I try to assess my own competence I find it surprisingly difficult to award a grade. Perhaps it is just because I am not a prolific lighter of fires. But I suspect that the traditional criterion has outlived its validity.

Every modern outdoorsman should be able to light a fire, but the act is not, it seems to me, a particularly important or testing part of his life. There are exceptions, of course. In cold, wet country where you are always needing a fire for warmth or for drying out clothes, getting one alight quickly is both a testing and an important business. And doubly so in an emergency, without matches. But the generalization stands.

I certainly seem to have survived without undue discomfort on a meager and rather incoherent grab bag of fire-lighting rules that I've made up as I went along: Carry plenty of matches, and *keep them dry*. The kindling is what matters; once you've got a small but healthy fire going, almost anything will burn on it. Unless your kindling is very dry indeed and very small, use paper as a starter. If the whole place is dripping wet, look for big stuff that will be dry in the center and from which you can cut out slivers that are easily split and shaved into serviceable kindling (the dry side of a dead cedar is a good bet, and so are the dead and sheltered twigs at the foot of many conifers), but don't overlook sheltered rock crevices and hollow trees (mice or other small animals will often store small sticks there, and you can rob them with remarkably little guilt). If you anticipate real trouble in starting a fire (if, for example, you had just one hell of a time doing so last night), carry along some kindling from wood that you dried out on last night's hard-won fire; and don't just stuff it into your pack; wrap it in a plastic bag and keep out the damp air. If necessary, do the same with some fire-dried paper too; in really wet weather, even paper can be hard to light. Some people, when they expect bad conditions, take along some kind of starter: candles (which are dual purpose tools), heat tablets, or tubes of barbecue igniter paste.

15   The rules for lighting a fire are simple and fairly obvious: Have plenty of wood ready in small, graduated sizes. Arrange the sticks of kindling more or less upright, wigwamwise, so that the flame will creep up them, preheating as it climbs. Keep the wigwam small. Apply your match at the bottom. In the first critical moments, carefully shield the flame from wind.

16   With these simple rules I seem to have got by without serious trouble. Oddly enough, the only real difficulties I can recall have been in the desert. Lighting a fire there is normally simple: you just break off a few twigs of almost any growth, dead or alive, and it lights. But desert plant life must, to survive, be adapted to absorb every drop of moisture. And it does so alive or dead. One sharp shower of rain, and every plant or fragment of plant you break off will feel like damp blotting paper. I vividly remember one cold and windy evening in Grand Canyon when a day of intermittent rain had ended with a snowstorm. At dusk I found a shallow rock overhang that offered shelter from both wind and snow but fell distinctly short of total coziness. Tired and damp and cold after a long day, I wanted a fire more than anything else. But every piece of wood I could find under the thin blanket of snow was soggy, clean through. I made a few abortive attempts at starting a fire with the driest wood, but even the scraps of paper from my pocket did little more than smolder. I was running desperately short of white gas too, and could not afford to use the stove as wood drier. Eventually I found the fairly thick stem of a cactus-like century plant or agave and managed to whittle some shreds of dry kindling from its center. It lit first time, and I spent a cheerful and almost luxuriously warm evening.

17   It is only common sense to site a fire so that the smoke from it will blow away from your campsite—but it is also common sense to expect that the

moment you light the fire the wind will reverse itself. Impartial research would probably confirm the existence of something more statistically verifiable behind this expectation than the orneriness of inanimate objects: campfires tend to be lit around dusk, and winds tend to change direction at that time, particularly in mountain country.

Some men speak learnedly about the virtues of different firewoods. Frankly, I know almost none by name. But it does not seem to matter too much. It is no doubt more efficient to know at a glance the burning properties of each kind of wood you find; but you have only to heft a piece of dead wood to get a good idea of how it will burn. Generally speaking, light wood tends to catch easily and burn fast. Heavy wood will last well, though the heaviest may be the devil to get started, even in a roaring blaze. 18

I have never, thank God, had to produce a flame without matches. I have not even given the matter the thought it deserved. The magnifying glass that I carry primarily for other purposes is always there as an emergency concentrator of sunlight onto paper or tinder, but I have never, in spite of intermittent good resolves, actually tried it out. In any case, the day on which you need a fire most desperately is likely to be wet and cold, and a magnifying glass would be about as useful as a station wagon in outer space. A flint-stick might be just the answer. 19

In an emergency, it is theoretically possible to do the trick with a piece of string or bootlace that you wrap around a rotator of a stick whose end is held in a depression in a slab of wood. The idea is to twirl the stick fast enough and long enough to create by friction enough heat to ignite some scraps of tinder dropped into the depression. Simple, primitive men certainly started fires this way; but I have an idea that we clever bastards might find it quite difficult. 20

To be honest, I'm singularly unimpressed by the woodsy fanatic who's rich in this kind of caveman lore, especially if he'll pass it all on at the drop of a snowflake. I always suspect that he'll turn out to be the sort of man who under actual field conditions can stop almost anywhere, any time, and have a pot of water on the very brink of boiling within two hours and thirty-five minutes—provided it isn't actually raining, and he has plenty of matches. But maybe you'd be right to chalk my cynicism up to plain jealousy. 21

Fire Hazards

These days, the way a man guards and leaves his fire may well be a more valid criterion for judging his outdoor competence than the way he starts one. A deliberately apprehensive common sense is your best guide; but the Forest Service lays down some useful rules: 22

Never build a fire on deep litter, such as pine needles. It can smolder for days, then erupt into a catastrophic forest blaze.

Clear all inflammable organic material from an area appreciably bigger than your fire, scraping right down to bare earth.

Generally speaking, and where possible, build a ring of stones around your fire. It will contain the ash and considerably reduce the chances of spread.

Never leave a fire unattended.

Where a fire hazard exists, do not build a fire on a windy day.

Avoid wood that generates a lot of sparks. The sparks can start fires in surrounding vegetation—and your sleeping bag.

Above all, *don't just put your fire out—kill it, dead.* Stir the ashes, deep and thoroughly, even though the fire seems to have been out for hours. Then douse it with dirt and water. You can safely stop when it's so doused you could take a swim in it.

23   Oddly enough, you can forgo such precautions in most kinds of desert. The place is curiously immune to arson. I have only once seen an extensive "burn" in treeless desert. Individual bushes may catch fire rather easily, but vegetation is so widely spaced (a necessary adaptation to acute moisture shortage) that the fire rarely spreads. The heat and dryness of deserts would seem sure to cause fires in mass-inflammable vegetation, so susceptible species have no doubt been selected out by the natural process of destruction by fire.

General Fire Precautions

24   Cultivate the habit of breaking all matches in two before you throw them away. The idea is not that half a match is much less dangerous than a whole one, but that the breaking makes you aware of the match and conscious of any lingering flame or heat. Book matches are rather difficult to break, but as I use mine only for fires or the stove, I always put used matches into the former or under the latter.

25   The big match danger comes from smokers (with a seven-year nonsmoking halo now tilted rakishly over my bald patch I feel comfortably smug). In some critical fire areas you are forbidden to carry cigarettes at certain times of year. In many forests you are not allowed to smoke while on the move, and can do so only on a site with at least three-foot clearance all around—such as a bare rock or a broad trail. Make absolutely sure you put your cigarette stub OUT. Soak it in water; or pull it to shreds. If you doubt the necessity of following such irritating rules to the letter, make yourself go and see the corpse of a recently burned forest.

Business

BENJAMIN FRANKLIN

Poor Richard's Rules for Perfection

Franklin (1706–90), America's Renaissance man, not only epitomizes the spirit of its citizens, but creates in his Autobiography *(written 1771–1789) an exemplary model for them to follow in their quest of the American dream. Of perennial interest, as is Franklin himself, the* Autobiography *shows how to succeed in business by working hard (or at least, appearing to), and trying to attain the moral perfection represented by the thirteen rules below— "humility," he says, was an afterthought. He wrote and published the popular* Poor Richard's Almanack *annually from 1732 on, dispensing useful information and good advice ("Early to bed and early to rise . . .).*

Franklin retired from business at 42, and devoted the remainder of his life to science, public service, politics, and international diplomacy. One of the foremost scientists of the time, he made numerous discoveries in physics, navigation, and astronomy, and applied his discoveries to practical inventions, as well. Thus in addition to proving that lightning and electricity are identical, Franklin also invented the lightning rod. Franklin's contributions to American culture are equally numerous and wide-ranging, including the founding of a public lending library, a municipal fire fighting company, the American Philosophical Society, and the University of Pennsylvania. An active patriot, he served in the Continental Congress and as Minister to France in the critical period during and after the Revolutionary War—an American for all seasons.

1 It was about this time I conceived the bold and arduous project of arriving at moral perfection. I wished to live without committing any fault at any time; I would conquer all that either natural inclination, custom, or company might lead me into. As I knew, or thought I knew, what was right and wrong, I did not see why I might not *always* do the one and avoid the other. But I soon found I had undertaken a task of more difficulty than I had imagined. While my attention was taken up and care employed in guarding against one fault, I was often surprized by another. Habit took the advantage of inattention. Inclination was sometimes too strong for reason. I concluded at length that the mere speculative conviction that it was our interest to be completely virtuous was not sufficient to prevent our slipping, and that the contrary habits must be broken and good ones acquired and established before we can have any dependence on a steady, uniform rectitude of conduct. For this purpose I therefore contrived the following method.

2 In the various enumerations of the moral virtues I had met with in my reading, I found the catalogue more or less numerous, as different writers included more or fewer ideas under the same name. Temperance, for example, was by some confined to eating and drinking, while by others it was

extended to mean the moderating every other pleasure, appetite, inclination, or passion—bodily or mental, even to our avarice and ambition. I proposed to myself, for the sake of clearness, to use rather more names with fewer ideas annexed to each than a few names with more ideas; and I included under thirteen names of virtues all that at that time occurred to me as necessary or desirable, and annexed to each a short precept which fully expressed the extent I gave to its meaning.

3   These names of virtues with their precepts were

1. *Temperance.* Eat not to dulness. Drink not to elevation.
2. *Silence*. Speak not but what may benefit others or yourself. Avoid trifling conversation.
3. *Order*. Let all your things have their places. Let each part of your business have its time.
4. *Resolution*. Resolve to perform what you ought. Perform without fail what you resolve.
5. *Frugality*. Make no expence but to do good to others or yourself; i.e., waste nothing.
6. *Industry*. Lose no time. Be always employed in something useful. Cut off all unnecessary actions.
7. *Sincerity*. Use no hurtful deceit. Think innocently and justly; and, if you speak, speak accordingly.
8. *Justice*. Wrong none by doing injuries or omitting the benefits that are your duty.
9. *Moderation*. Avoid extremes. Forbear resenting injuries so much as you think they deserve.
10. *Cleanliness*. Tolerate no uncleanness in body, clothes or habitation.
11. *Tranquillity*. Be not disturbed at trifles or at accidents common or unavoidable.
12. *Chastity*. Rarely use venery but for health or offspring—never to dulness, weakness, or the injury of your own or another's peace or reputation.
13. *Humility*. Imitate Jesus and Socrates.

4   My intention being to acquire the *habitude* of all these virtues, I judged it would be well not to distract my attention by attempting the whole at once but to fix it on one of them at a time, and when I should be master of that, then to proceed to another, and so on till I should have gone thro' the thirteen. And as the previous acquisition of some might facilitate the acquisition of certain others, I arranged them with that view as they stand above. *Temperance* first, as it tends to procure that coolness and clearness of head which is so necessary where constant vigilance was to be kept up, and guard maintained, against the unremitting attraction of ancient habits, and the force of perpetual temptations. This being acquired and established, *Silence* would be more easy, and my desire being to gain knowledge at the same time that I improved in virtue, and considering that in conversation it was obtained

rather by the use of the ear than of the tongue, and therefore wishing to break a habit I was getting into of prattling, punning, and joking, which only made me acceptable to trifling company, I gave *Silence* the second place. This and the next, *Order,* I expected would allow me more time for attending to my project and my studies. *Resolution,* once become habitual, would keep me firm in my endeavours to obtain all the subsequent virtues; *Frugality* and *Industry,* freeing me from my remaining debt and, producing affluence and independence, would make more easy the practice of *Sincerity* and *Justice,* etc., etc. Conceiving then that agreeable to the advice of Pythagoras in his golden verses, daily examination would be necessary, I contrived the following method for conducting that examination.

I made a little book in which I allotted a page for each of the virtues. I   5
ruled each page with red ink so as to have seven columns, one for each day of the week, marking each column with a letter for the day. I crossed these columns with thirteen red lines, marking the beginning of each line with the first letter of one of the virtues, on which line and in its proper column I might mark by a little black spot every fault I found upon examination to have been committed respecting that virtue upon that day.

I determined to give a week's strict attention to each of the virtues   6
successively. Thus in the first week my great guard was to avoid even the least offence against temperance, leaving the other virtues to their ordinary chance, only marking every evening the faults of the day. Thus if in the first week I could keep my first line marked "T." clear of spots, I supposed the habit of that virtue so much strengthened and its opposite weakened that I might venture extending my attention to include the next, and for the following week keep both lines clear of spots. Proceeding thus to the last, I could go thro' a course complete in thirteen weeks, and four courses in a year. And like him who, having a garden to weed, does not attempt to eradicate all the bad herbs at once, which would exceed his reach and his strength, but works on one of the beds at a time, and having accomplished the first, proceeds to a second; so I should have, (I hoped) the encouraging pleasure of seeing on my pages the progress I made in virtue by clearing successively my lines of their spots, till in the end by a number of courses, I should be happy in viewing a clean book after a thirteen weeks' daily examination. . . .

I entered upon the execution of this plan for self-examination and con-   7
tinued it with occasional intermissions for some time. I was surprized to find myself so much fuller of faults than I had imagined, but I had the satisfaction of seeing them diminish.

Questions

1. Franklin's definitions of the thirteen virtues are extremely brief. Is this brevity in itself a virtue, or should the definitions be elaborated on? Explain your answer.

2. What determines the order of Franklin's list?

3. Is "paying strict attention to each of the virtues successively" for a week (paragraph 6) a feasible way to become virtuous? Franklin is accountable only to himself for adhering to his plan of promoting virtue. Do people succeed better in personal reform if they have a confidante or a helper, as in Alcoholics Anonymous and Weight Watchers, than if they try to make major changes all by themselves?

4. Franklin began this accounting of his life as a memorandum to his son (illegitimate but publicly acknowledged) at a time in his own life when he was America's elder statesman, respected genius, and folk hero. How might he have expected his son (also the father of an illegitimate son) to react to this advice? Would this response be the same or different from the reaction that could be expected from the American public, for whom the *Autobiography* quickly became a perennial best-seller?

SYLVIA PORTER

Rules for Writing and Endorsing Checks

Sylvia Porter (b. 1913) is the Ann Landers of money. After graduating Phi Beta Kappa from Hunter College in 1932, she took graduate courses in business administration. Her career as a financial columnist has spanned three decades, the first two for the New York Post, *the last for the* New York Daily News; *her syndicated column appears nationwide.* Sylvia Porter's Income Tax Guide *has been published annually since 1960. The title of one of Porter's many books of fiscal advice for general readers explains her characteristically comprehensive treatment of the subject:* Sylvia Porter's Money Book—How to Earn It, Spend It, Invest It, Borrow It, and Use It to Better Your Life.

*   "Rules for Writing and Endorsing Checks" is typical of Porter's advice. She presents the distillation of banking customs and conventional wisdom as a set of clear, terse, logically organized, no-nonsense rules that she didn't invent but will surely enforce for the reader's own good. The "do's" and "don'ts" that abound in Porter's writing reinforce her magisterial air. She assumes, rightly or wrongly, that her readers don't know even the fundamentals of what she's discussing; she is determined to keep them out of trouble at all costs.*

1   Millions of Americans do not know the basic rules for writing, endorsing, and depositing a check. Do not permit yourself to be among them—for you may be unwittingly courting the bank's refusal to honor your checks—or even inviting costly check-doctoring by a professional earning a living in this craft.

2   Heed these main do's and don'ts on writing checks:

3   *Do* date each check properly. A bank may refuse to accept a check which is dated ahead or hold it until its date is reached. The bank's reasoning is that if the check were charged to your account before you expected it to be, it might cause other checks you wrote to bounce.

Don't leave any spaces between the dollar sign and the amount of the check   4
you are writing, or between the amount you spell out in the middle line
and the word "dollars" at the end of that line. Or, if you do leave such
spaces, draw lines across them.

Do make sure each check is numbered properly—for your own bookkeeping   5
purposes.

Don't alter the way you sign your checks (e.g., by adding your middle initial)   6
once you have decided on a standard signature.

Do, if you are a married woman, sign checks with your own first name, plus   7
your married name—"Mary Dowd," *not* Mrs. Jack Dowd."

Don't use "Mr.," "Miss," or "Mrs." as part of your signature.   8

Do fill out the middle line ending with the word "dollars" in this format: 9
"Five and 50/100," or "One hundred and fifty and no/100." If you write
a check for less than $1.00, be sure to put a decimal point between the
printed dollar sign and the amount of the check—followed by the word
"cents." On the line where you write out the amount of the check, write,
for example, "Only 95 cents," and cross out the word "dollars."

Don't use somebody else's check unless you punch a hole in at least one   10
number of the special magnetic code which usually appears at the lower
left-hand corner of the check. Inking it out won't do the trick with
today's electronic check-"reading" devices; if you don't actually cut out
this account number, you risk having the check charged against your
friend's account. (Technically, you can write a check on any surface from
a paper bag to an eggshell, but banks shudder at this sort of eccentricity.)

For the identical reasons, don't lend anyone one of your checks. Because of   11
the indelible symbols, your pre-imprinted check will be sorted according
to its magnetic coding and charged to your account even if someone else,
with no dishonest intentions at all, has crossed out your identifying
number and name and written in his own.

Do endorse a check only on the back of the left-hand side (the perforated side,   12
in one type of checkbook), *exactly* as your name appears on the front of
the check. If this is not your usual signature, add the correct signature
below your first endorsement. Of course, if your address is on the check
too, you need not include this—or the "Miss," "Mrs.," or "Mr." which
may also be included.

Don't ever underestimate the importance of your endorsement or forget that   13
your endorsement on someone else's check means you would be willing
to cover the check yourself should the bank for any reason refuse to
honor it.

A blank endorsement—your signature only—means you transfer the own-   14
ership of the check to the person holding it at the time. This person may
then cash it.

15   An endorsement in full—or special endorsement—means you sign a check over to someone else by writing on the back of a check "Pay to the order of" this person or organization.

16   A *restrictive endorsement* should be used on checks you wish to deposit by mail. You write "For deposit only" over your signature. Or, if you give someone a check which has been made out to you or cash, you write "Pay to the order of _____" and sign your name beneath this.

17   *Do* deposit all checks you receive as soon as you get them. Not only is it a big bookkeeping nuisance for the person who has issued the check if you keep it for a month or more, but many banks refuse to honor checks which are two or three months old—unless they are "reauthorized" to do so by the payer.

18   *Don't* write checks out to "cash" unless you yourself are cashing them at a bank, supermarket, or elsewhere. Such checks are negotiable by any bearer and leave you with no record of how the money was spent.

19   *Do* record on your check stub the key facts about every check you write. This includes the date, check number, payee, amount, and the purpose of the check if the "payee" notation doesn't make that evident. The best way to make sure you don't forget to record this information is to do so *before* you write the check itself.

20   And *don't* ever, ever give signed blank checks to anybody whom you do not trust completely; blank checks are as good as cash—unlimited amounts of it, for that matter. As a matter of fact, it's risky ever to sign a blank check!

Key Questions about Writing Checks

21   Now here are additional questions you almost surely would like to have answered—leading logically from the rules covered in the preceding pages.

22   Q: *When you deposit a check from another bank, how long should you wait for it to be cleared before you can safely draw checks against your deposit?*

23   A: If the other bank is in the same city, allow at least three days for the check to be collected. If the bank is out of town, allow five to fifteen days depending on its location. When it's important for you to know exactly when a check will actually be credited to your own account—so you won't risk having any of your own checks returned—ask one of your bank's officers about the particular check.

24   Q: *Is it legal to write a check in pencil?*

25   A: Yes. But it's obviously dangerous since anyone could erase the amount and substitute a larger one. Write all checks in ink.

26   Q: *May a check be dated on Saturday, Sunday, or a holiday?*

27   A: Yes. The folklore to the contrary is wrong. However, since some people

who believe the folklore may refuse to accept the check, it's generally safer to date it on a previous day.

Q: *What happens when you make the mistake of writing one amount in words and another amount in figures?*   28

A: Some banks pay the amount which is spelled out, but many more return the check.   29

Q: *Should you ever erase or cross out anything on a check?*   30

A: No. Even if you initial the change, the bank often will not honor an altered check. And knowing this, you should never accept or cash an altered check yourself.   31

Q: *How long does a check remain valid?*   32

A: Technically, a check is good for six years. In actual practice, though, most banks consult with the payer before honoring a check which is more than six months old and many, I repeat, do this after only two or three months.   33

Q: *Will your bank give you a new check if you spoil one for which you've already paid?*   34

A: Yes.   35

Q: *How do you stop payment on a check?*   36

A: You can, for a fee of $4.00 to $9.00, stop payment on any check you have written simply by *telephoning* your bank's stop payment department and giving the details, including: the date, amount, name of payee, check number, and the reason for stopping the payment. Then immediately confirm the order in writing. The bank will issue a stop payment form which you must complete and which the bank will keep on file—to be sure your intention *not* to have the bank honor your check is properly carried out.   37

When you stop payment, be sure you notify the payee—the person or company or organization who was to have received the amount of money you specified on the check.   38

As a general rule, *don't* send a check in payment unless you are willing to have it honored. Stopping payment itself won't damage your credit rating but not paying your bill—unless it's in dispute—will.   39

Questions

1. Many how-to writings consist of lists of "do's" and "don'ts," as is the case with Porter's rules. By their very nature, these have the effect of prescriptive, non-negotiable commands. What is the tone of such advice? Does it admit of alternatives or arguments? Why or why not?

2. Does the writer have to be an expert to issue lists of "do's" and "don'ts"? Explain your answer. Is it possible for a student, or someone who has not fully mastered the subject at hand (such as Franklin on virtue) to give compelling advice?

3. Porter's advice is extremely concentrated—twenty-five rules in thirty-nine paragraphs—and this is only one segment of a book with over eight hundred comparable pages. How intense a dose of advice can readers be expected to cope with in a single reading? Or is such advice intended to be dipped into as needed, rather than to be read straight through?

4. Does the visual format of this advice, with a new paragraph (usually labeled *Do* or *Don't*, or a question-and-answer form to set off each separate item, enable readers to quickly find what they want? Does such a broken-up format encourage readers to stop reading after they've found the single answer they're looking for? Why or why not? What is the effect of such a format on the style?

ROBERT HALF

Coming Out on Top in the Job Interview

Half (born in New York City in 1918) writes about business for Forbes *and other magazines and papers from the multiple perspectives of money, management, and manpower. He has worked as an accountant (with a B.S. from New York University, 1940), as an office and personnel manager of Kayser-Roth, and since 1948 as chairman of the board of his own personnel agency, Robert Half of New York. He is also president of Robert Half International, and an executive officer of Accountemps Inc. "Coming Out on Top in the Job Interview" is a chapter in* The Robert Half Way to Get Hired in Today's Job Market *(1981).*

Half explains that the strategy of a job interview is "very much a game—a game, moreover, in which the rules are constantly changing." The interviewer is playing a role, and is paying attention to how well the job candidate plays the game by delivering a particular quality of performance during the interview. Like many how-to writers, Half boils down the essence of the subject at hand (in this case, the "typical interview situation") into three questions:

1. *Can you do the job?*
2. *Will you do the job?*
3. *Do you fit in with the company's style?*

He then offers specific suggestions on how candidates can prepare themselves for the interview: through finding out as much as possible about the company offering the job, through rehearsing "the role of job candidate" (including taping practice interview answers), and through anticipating key questions. Half's voice as a writer does not sound like that of an intimidating international executive, but rather like a human being who's at ease and genuinely wants to be helpful. Half's own writing style suggests that his advice for people facing interviews is equally good for people facing a blank sheet of paper: "Be yourself—just a more convincing, confident, and articulate version of yourself."

1 The job interview is the moment of truth in job hunting—so crucial and organic an aspect of getting hired that entire books have been devoted to the

subject. Yet interviews are probably the trickiest aspect of job hunting in which to dispense advice.

The problem is that the interview is very much a game—a game, moreover, in which the rules are constantly changing. Ostensibly, you and the interviewer (sometimes other people are involved, too) are having a civilized conversation. You greet one another. There's some small talk. The interviewer asks you some questions. You answer them. The interviewer asks you if *you* have any questions. The questions get answered. And so forth.

But while all of this is going on, the interviewer is playing out his or her role in the game: paying attention not only to what you're saying but to how you're responding. The interviewer is making an evaluation, computing nearly everything you say and do, the better to judge whether your ability, experience, education, and personality fit the job and the company. The interviewer *knows* you're doing your best to create a positive impression. The interviewer *knows* that as hard as the two of you may try to make the interview seem natural and unforced, the interview is, by nature, an unnatural and forced situation. Much of how the interviewer evaluates you will be determined not so much by the qualifications you enumerate and the personal qualities you exhibit during the interview, but by your *interview performance in general*. How you play the game!

So what we're going to be talking about throughout this chapter is the job interview as a performance in itself. You already know—or should know—the qualities that make you special. You already know—or should know—the skills and the attributes it takes to do the job being offered. Your task in the interview is to make a sale: to sell the person (or persons) who interviews you on the idea you already know ahead of time: that you're the best person for the job.

Taking Control

There are two ways to approach a job interview. One is to be passive: to sit there and answer whatever questions you're given to the best of your ability. The other is to be active: to take control of the interview, to give the interviewer what *you* want to give, not necessarily what the interviewer is trying to find out. One of the most successful insurance salesman I know had an interesting theory that applies as much to getting hired as it does to selling insurance. "Other insurance salesmen," he said, "present facts and answer questions. I inspire confidence."

The way you inspire confidence in an interview is to give the interviewer every reason to believe that you can handle the job for which you're being considered, and little reason to believe that you *can't*. You supply these reasons (one way or the other) with much more than the answers you give to questions. You supply reasons with the way you look, with the enthusiasm you show or don't show, with the personality you show or don't show, with the energy, the confidence, and the ambition you show or don't show.

You are in control. The interviewer is asking the questions, but if you know what to expect and how to sell yourself, you can take control of the interview in a way that will give the interviewer reasons to hire you.

8   So let's put ourselves for the moment in the chair of the person—or persons—sitting across the desk or table from you at a typical interview.

9   I can tell you from more than thirty years of experience that virtually everything an interviewer is concerned about in a typical interview situation boils down, in the end, to one of three questions:

1. Can you do the job?
2. Will you do the job?
3. Do you fit in with the company's style?

Underlying these three questions is a fourth factor: what the interviewer has to gain or lose by hiring you or by recommending you to be hired. I know some interviewers who need very strong positive answers to all three questions before they'll hire you or recommend you for hiring. Other interviewers will take a chance if you're particularly strong in one or two of the areas covered by the three questions above and not necessarily all of them. You never know until you get to the interview which type of interviewer you're going to encounter.

10   But now you know what the interviewer is looking for. Regardless of the questions you are asked—and you may be asked any one of three hundred different questions—the answers you give must be plugged into one of these three areas: *your ability to do the job, your willingness to do the job, your suitability for the job and the company.* Every answer you give should, one way or another, say one of the following three things:

1. I am able to do this job.
2. I am willing to do this job.
3. I can fit in.

The more your answers and actions in a job interview express these three statements, the more control you are exercising in the interview and the better your chances of winning the ultimate prize of an interview—a job offer.

Sizing Up the Situation

11   The main reason why most job candidates fall short in the job interview is that they don't inspire confidence. They give the interviewer more reasons to say no than to say yes.

12   In most cases, the reason is a simple matter of fear—the fear of failing. I've seen it happen hundreds of times in my career. Candidates with marvelous qualifications lose out not because they couldn't do the job or even lacked the confidence that they could do the job. They lose out because their confidence didn't come through in the interview situation. They didn't "sell" themselves convincingly enough. They didn't inspire confidence.

Let's tackle the root of the problem: the nervousness most people feel 13
any time there is pressure on them to perform. There is a job opening and
you want the job, maybe need it very badly. The interview is an obstacle. Can
you be blamed for being anxious?

Not at all. In fact, a little anxiety is good for you. Ask any championship 14
athlete, and they'll tell you that what *really* worries them before an important
match or tournament is not feeling any nerves.

The challenge, of course, is to *control* this anxiety: to make it work for 15
you, not defeat you. One thing that might help is to keep in mind that you
have nothing to lose in a job interview. *Nothing.* Even if you don't get the
job, you won't be much worse off than you were a short while before you
heard about it.

If you get turned down—and, remember, most people who get inter- 16
viewed get turned down—there will be other interviews, other chances to do
what you may not have done as well as you wanted to do in this last interview.

As hard as it may seem to do, it's possible to divorce the significance of 17
the interview—what is at stake—from the interview itself. Athletes do it all
the time. "I'm not competing for the Wimbledon championship," tennis
great Fred Perry used to say. "I'm just going out to play a game of
tennis."

Do the same thing in a job interview. Forget about whether or not you're 18
going to get the job. Concentrate on the interview itself. *Get good at the skill.*
Learn from past mistakes. See every interview you go on as a chance to put
into practice what you learned at your last interview. If you handle the
interview well, the job offer will take care of itself. Don't even think about the
outcome: it will only interfere.

Develop confidence in yourself as a job interviewee. I'm serious! I've known 19
dozens and dozens of people whose employment record had little to recommend them. Yet, get these people in a one-to-one interview situation, and
they were world-beaters. They were offered jobs. They didn't always keep
these jobs, unfortunately, but that's another story. "I *know* I don't have the
qualifications," I remember one young woman telling me years ago, "but it's
never been a problem in the past. Set up the interview."

Confident job candidates know that in spite of what a lot of the books 20
and articles about job interviewing might lead you to believe, the person
doing the interviewing, much of the time, is *not* a professional interviewer
schooled in "secret" techniques. He or she is simply a person with a problem:
hiring somebody to fill a job. Confident job candidates know that far from
fighting your attempts to take control over the interview situation, most
interviewers will *welcome* it: you're making their job easier. Confident job
candidates know that they, the candidates, know more about interviewing,
about the job, and about themselves than the interviewer knows. They know
that as long as the subject of discussion is one of the areas the candidate

knows more about than the interviewer, the candidate (not the interviewer) holds the upper hand.

21 Make it *your* business to develop the same confidence: it's not nearly as hard as you might think.

Being Prepared

22 Confidence is rooted in knowledge, knowledge, in turn, is rooted in preparation. If you've been following the guidelines I've set down throughout this book, you know the qualities and attributes that set you apart from other candidates. You know the qualities and attributes needed in the kind of job you're looking for. The job interview introduces a new element: the company offering the job.

23 Never go into any interview unless you've thoroughly researched the company offering the job. You should know its products, its size, its top executives, its growth pattern, its recent financial performance, its strengths, and its weaknesses.

24 For large companies, this kind of information is easy to come by: a morning in the library, going through various business directories like Dun & Bradstreet's, Standard & Poor's and Moody's Manuals, should give you basic information. Check through the *Reader's Guide to Periodical Literature* for a list of recent articles that may have appeared on the company in publications like *Time, Newsweek, Business Week, Dun's Review,* or *Financial World*. Get hold of the trade publications that deal with the industry in which the company is involved; you might discover some interesting data. At the very least, get your hands on the company's annual report and on any brochures or internal publications (newsletters, company papers, etc.) you can latch onto. The simplest way to get an annual report is to call a stockbroker you know, the secretary of the company, or the company's public relations department.

25 Another source of information is the company's 10-K form. A 10-K form is a form that every public company has to file with the Securities and Exchange Commission. In some cases, it's little more than a financial statement; in other cases, you'll find such information as the salary the company pays to its top officers—useful information to have. You could probably get one of these forms from the Securities and Exchange Commission, but it may take time. If you're in a hurry, there's a company in New York that will send you the 10-K on any company in one day for a modest fee. The company is called National Investment, Inc., and its address is 80 Wall St., New York, N.Y. 10005.

26 Read the material you gather with an inquiring eye. Look for trends. See if you can discern a company philosophy. Is the company adopting a new marketing philosophy, changing its product lines, experiencing certain kinds of problems you might be able to help solve? Find out about the president and other officers. Jot down whatever information you get on note cards, or, better still, in a notebook bought for this purpose only.

See if you can locate somebody who knows the company well. It might   27
be an employee or an ex-employee, or a professional person who does work
for them. See what you can dig out of these people. Many firms, although
they won't admit it, have a preconceived idea of who "their" kind of people
are. The "style" usually filters down from the chief executive. You may not fit
the mold, but it doesn't hurt to find out what the mold is.

Discovering somebody who knows the company pretty well is especially   28
important if it's a smaller company that hasn't generated much publicity. You
may find when you go to the library and consult the various indexes that
there is virtually no material about this particular company. This being the
case, you are pretty much forced to go directly to the source. Talk to the
person who has either set up the interview for you or is, in fact, going to
conduct the interview. Explain the problem. Tell him—or her—you'd like
some information that isn't confidential about the company before the interview and would they be kind enough to send you whatever they can. Most
executives will oblige you.

Don't overlook, or take for granted, this research aspect of the interview.   29
*Our surveys show that not being familiar with the company with whom you're
interviewing will hurt your chances with as many as 75 percent of the interviewers
you may encounter.*

Getting Yourself Ready for the Game

At the beginning of this chapter, I said that the key to doing well in a job   30
interview is the ability to give a performance. At the same time, however, you
have to be yourself. What I'm talking about here is not as paradoxical as it
may seem.

Think about the last time you took part in a sport, whether it was golf or   31
tennis or bowling. Or played bridge. You were performing there, too, and
yet you were being yourself. You were playing a role, whether of golfer,
tennis player, bowler, or bridge player.

A job interview is a game because it represents a reality within a reality. It   32
has rules. It asks the people involved with it to play certain roles. The person
who interviews you is a person, not an interviewer: he or she is playing the
role of interviewer. And you are not a job candidate: you are a person who, in
this particular situation, is *playing the role of job candidate.*

Appreciate the job interview situation in these role-playing terms, and it   33
will help you immeasurably when it comes to presenting the best side of
yourself in an interview. Understand the game. Understand the role you
must play in it. You're not faking or being insincere when you play this role
the way it should be played. The game, after all, is *real*—and so must the role
you play in it be.

The best way to play this role is to *be* the person the role calls for. Who   34
gets the job? Our surveys show that the single most influential factor in the
job interview situation is not your experience or your qualification, but your

personality—*how you present yourself during the interview*. How you look, how you communicate your ideas, how well you listen, how much enthusiasm you generate.

35   You have a personality, for better or worse, and it's not a *fixed* personality. I know boisterous people who are often subdued, and I know painfully shy people who, under the right set of circumstances, can become outlandishly outgoing. You have a great deal of range within your own personality. Chances are you don't have to *change* anything about yourself when you go into a job interview: you simply have to present the best and most saleable side of that personality.

How Role Playing Can Work for You

36   If you don't already have one, buy or get hold of a cassette tape recorder. You can probably get one for $25 or even less. Don't worry too much about the sound quality; you're not going to be recording any piano concertos on it. (If you own or have access to a video camera and playback machine, that's even better.)

37   Once you get it, conduct this little experiment. Find a quiet spot in your house and pretend for a moment that you're on a job interview and you are asked, as often happens at such interviews, to "tell us something about yourself." Turn the tape recorder on and talk into it for three or four minutes, free associating as you go.

38   Now play it back and listen. Really listen. What if you didn't know the person whose voice you're listening to? What conclusions would you draw about this person, based on the comments alone? Would you consider the person sure of himself or herself, perceptive, articulate? If your answer is definitely yes, you probably have no problem presenting yourself. My guess, though, is that you'll be a little disappointed by what you hear.

39   Don't be. Unless you have special training or are in a field that requires you to be "on" a lot of the time, there's no reason why you should be especially impressive or effective at "selling yourself." Don't be dismayed. You have time to get better at it.

40   Now I'd like you to try the same exercise again, but this time, I want you to play a role. I want you to play the role of a confident person. It doesn't matter whether you are or aren't a confident person. You know what confidence is and what a confident person sounds like: behave like one into the tape recorder. *Overdo* it.

41   When you play the tape back a second time, you're going to be surprised. You will *sound* confident. What's more, you should be able to recognize a difference between the confidence level of certain things you say and the confidence level of other things.

42   Do one more thing. Think for a moment about all the points that, in your judgment, make you the best candidate to be hired. Write them down. In fact, go back to the notes you used in drafting your résumé. Once you have

a half-dozen or so of these qualities, talk them into the tape recorder, mentioning the quality first—i.e., "I'm a very hard worker."—and then saying a few words to back the statement up.

Now play it back and evaluate it. How believable did you sound? If you   43
were an interviewer and this tape were all you had to judge by, how would you evaluate the person you're listening to? Just as important, what might you do to make that person *more* believable?

Working with a tape recorder in this way does wonders. I know because   44
I've used one myself in preparing for television and radio appearances. I don't memorize anything. I simply interview myself. I ask questions; I give answers. Then I listen and evaluate myself.

Rehearse your part in the job interview. When you're alone in your car,   45
answer questions aloud—with or without a tape recorder. Take your time, be as articulate as you can.

The beauty of this approach is that *you* are making the changes consistent   46
with your personality and consistent with what you're comfortable with. But don't force it. Be yourself—just a more convincing, confident, and articulate version of yourself.

Fielding the Key Questions

Most of the conversation that takes place in a job interview will revolve   47
around questions you get asked by the interviewer. The nature—and the intensity—of these questions will vary according to the type of interview. The questions that get asked during interviews with personnel executives will be more general than the questions that get asked when you're across from somebody who is making the hiring decision. Your answers to decision making executives, moreover, won't have to be as detailed, and there won't be as much give and take in the general pattern of questions and answers. In personnel interviews, where the purpose is either to screen you out or send you ahead for future interviews, questions will be asked in a more or less one-at-a-time fashion. Later on, you can expect questions keyed to the kind of answers you give.

Should You Tell the Truth? I've known job placement specialists who've   48
encouraged their clients to lie when confronted with a potentially damaging question. I've known other specialists who advocate complete candor. I myself have never and would never come out and tell any job candidate to lie deliberately but neither do I recommend that you *volunteer* irrelevant information about yourself that may hurt your chances, or to dwell on your negative features simply because they happen to be true. Never forget, your "negatives" hurt you more than your "positives" help.

There is the principle to keep in mind when you're answering tough   49
questions: steering the information away from a possibly negative picture of yourself to a positive aspect of yourself.

50   Here's another example. The interviewer asks if you've ever worked directly in a particular field: "Have you ever worked with people in the food industry?" The truth here is that you haven't. I say, answer the question truthfully, but don't just leave the answer lying there. Build on it. "No, I haven't," you might say. "But I've worked with a lot of people in the liquor industry, and I know a good deal about the food industry . . ." Do you see the principle? Here, you've given a truthful answer but defused truth if the truth doesn't work to your advantage.

51   ### The Most Frequently Asked Questions and How to Answer Them

     1. Tell me about yourself . . .

This is a typical ice-breaker in many interview situations. Interviewers like it because it gives them a good initial "feeling" about you. They figure if you can't be articulate when you're talking about yourself, you're not going to be very articulate about anything.

52   Generally, it isn't so much what you say when you answer this question that's important, it's *how* you say it. Don't fumble with it. A good way to start an answer might be to come right out and say that you're darn good at what you do. "Well," you could say, "people tell me I'm a very good administrator." Having made this statement, however, you now have an obligation to back it up. How well you back up your general statements is another thing many interviewers are going to be looking for. "I'm organized," you might say. "I know how to delegate. I work well under pressure."

53   As long as you stay within reasonable bounds, don't worry about tooting your own horn. The interviewer knows you're not going to emphasize your negative points. But concentrate on those things about yourself that *relate to the job you're being interviewed for,* remembering (again) to back up your general statements with specific details. Instead of merely saying, "I get along well with others," and letting it go at that, give a couple of specific examples that illustrate how well you get along with others. "I've always had a good rapport with the people I work for and the people I supervise. In fact, I'm very close friends with one of my former bosses."

54   So, the main things to bear in mind when you're answering this question are:

Stress only positive features.

Back up general statements with proof—specific examples that illustrate the statements. Stress accomplishments.

Try to key most of what you say to the qualifications needed for the job that's open.

Keep it brief—no more than two or three minutes.

When you've finished, ask the interviewer if he or she needs to know any more.

Questions

1. One of Half's major premises is that *"You,"* the person being interviewed for the job, "are in control. The interviewer is asking the questions, but if you know what to expect and how to sell yourself, you can take control of the interview in a way that will give the interviewer reasons to hire you" (paragraph 7). Show how Half's advice is calculated to give the interviewee that desired control.

2. Suppose one has had an unsatisfactory employment record—and has been fired from several jobs, or has worked only a short time at a variety of jobs. Would Half's advice apply equally well to such a person, who might justifiably lack confidence on going into a job interview, as to a job candidate with a better track record?

3. Half analyzes the interview situation in terms of game strategy: "It has rules. It asks the people involved with it to play certain roles. The person who interviews you . . . is playing the role of interviewer. And you are . . . *playing the role of job candidate"* (paragraph 32). What are the advantages to the job candidate to think of the interview as a game? If one thinks of playing a game, does this imply playing to win? playing by a prior set of agreed-upon rules? deceptiveness or manipulation? not taking the situation with sufficient seriousness? Has game-playing any other connotations relevant to job interviews?

4. How effective is Half's advice to practice for an interview by tape recording yourself responding to an interviewer's imaginary questions and then revising your responses to sound more confident (paragraphs 36–46)? Proof is in the practice; if you have access to a tape recorder, try out Half's suggestions before you answer this question—or before you go to an interview.

Food/Cooking

EUELL GIBBONS

Dandelions,
The Official Remedy for Disorders

Gibbons (1911–1975), a naturalist, is the Julia Child of wild foods. He grew up in New Mexico and on the Pacific Coast, and graduated from the University of Hawaii, living the beachcomber's life while studying biology, anthropology, and creative writing. He then taught at a Quaker school, Pendle Hill, in Pennsylvania, before writing full-time. His elegant, popular books on wild food gathering were inspired by "a saving streak of the primitive," and reinforced by the author's belief in the importance of living off the land to reinforce individual independence. Gibbons had "strange roots, bulbs, stems, fruits, seeds and leaves" all over the house in the course of gathering, testing, and preparing various wild dishes and remedies for Stalking the Blue-Eyed Scallop *(1964),* Stalking the Healthful Herbs *(1966),* The Beachcomber's Handbook *(1967), and* Stalking the Wild Asparagus *(1962), in which "Dandelions" appeared.*

After justifying the life-saving qualities of "this vitamin-filled . . . herbal hero," Gibbons tries to rehabilitate its reputation. He sees it not as a weed but as a thoroughly delicious plant, from root to leaf tip, in season. Incorporating a wealth of knowledge about this versatile plant, Gibbons offers directions on how to find, harvest, and peel dandelions before providing recipes for dandelion coffee, dandelion salads, even dandelion wine. As with some (not all) other cookbook authors, Gibbons's instructions alternate between the highly specific and the vague—he doesn't identify specific amounts of dandelion greens in salad or cooked vegetable recipes, for instance—or the temperature at which to roast dandelion coffee, leaving his readers to rely on their common sense or past experience.

1   The chapter heading above is the approximate translation of *Taraxacum officinale,* the botanical name of the common dandelion. Until quite recently, thousands of people about the earth died each winter and early spring from diseases now known to have been caused by vitamin deficiencies. Ancient herb doctors dug up the perennial roots of the dandelion, which could be obtained even in midwinter. These were washed, then the juice was expressed from them and given to the sufferers. When this was done, the patient always improved. Then, in early spring he was advised to eat raw as many of the first young dandelion leaves as he could consume. This healthful salad soon restored him to health and vigor. I do not think it is an exaggeration to say that this vitamin-filled wild plant has, over the centuries, probably saved a good many lives.

2   But how the mighty have fallen! This herbal hero, one of the most healthful and genuinely useful plants in the materia medica of the past, is now a despised lawn weed. Now that supermarkets sell green vegetables through-

out the winter and the druggists are vending tons of synthetic vitamins, we no longer need to depend on the roots and leaves of this humble plant to ward off sickness and death, so we have turned on the dandelion. Every garden-supply house offers for sale a veritable arsenal of diggers, devices and deadly poisons, all designed to exterminate this useful and essentially beautiful little plant which has so immensely benefited the human race.

I learned to love dandelions when I was a small child. Not only did I enjoy the delicious dandelion greens my mother gathered and prepared, but the bright yellow flower, with its wonderful composite construction, fascinated me. I never believed that spring had really come until I saw the first dandelion in bloom.

Did you ever see a child who did not enjoy blowing the fuzz-winged seeds from the hoary seed balls of the dandelion? This always tells the child something, though what he learns from it seems to vary from place to place. We used to blow three times, then the number of seeds left indicated how many children we would have. It was sometimes an alarming number. Other children have told me that if one blows three times on a dandelion head, the number of seeds left would tell the time of day, thus making it unnecessary to carry a watch. I sometimes think my own children must use some such system to determine when it is time to stop playing and come in for dinner. Once in southern California a little girl ran up to me and said, "Look. I blew on a dandelion head and there's four seeds left. That means I'll get married four times."

Fortunately the dandelion still has important uses other than as a dispenser of somewhat unreliable information. I believe we would be better off, both financially and nutritionally, if we still procured as many of our vitamins and minerals as possible from wild green plants rather than depending on the synthetic products dispensed by the druggist. This is especially true when the vitamins come in as palatable a form as dandelion greens in early spring.

Nearly everyone has heard that dandelion greens are edible, but the actual gathering and preparation of them seems to be an almost forgotten art. How many people have told me that they have tried dandelion greens and didn't like them? On questioning, it always turns out that these trials consisted of boiling some leaves from old flowering plants. Would you decide that you disliked asparagus because the old stalks and foliage of midsummer are inedible? Our most prized vegetables are only good when gathered at just the right stage, and dandelions are no exception. Don't judge this most wholesome and delicious of all boiling greens until you have tasted them at their best.

The best dandelions are never found in closely mowed lawns but in some place where they and the grass have been allowed to grow freely. Long before the last frost of spring, a slightly reddish tangle of leaves appear at the top of the well-developed perennial roots. At this time the dandelion is a three-storied food plant. Using a narrow spade or bar, dig out the dandelions, roots and all. Occasionally one sees a dandelion root that is single, like a thin parsnip, but most of them have several forks as large as your little finger. In my opinion, these white roots furnish a better vegetable than either parsnips or salsify, although it tastes very little like either of them. The newly grown roots are tender and peel readily with an ordinary potato peeler. Slice them thinly crosswise, boil in two waters, with a pinch of soda added to the first water, then season with salt, pepper and butter.

8   These roots also furnish what I consider to be the finest coffee substitute to be found in the wild. For this purpose, the roots are roasted slowly in an oven until they will break with a snap and appear very dark brown inside. This roasting will take about four hours. These roots are then ground and used just as one uses coffee, except that you need slightly less of the dandelion root to make a brew of the same strength. Drink it with or without sugar and cream, just as you take your coffee.

9   On top of the dandelion root, which is usually down two or three inches, there is a crown of blanched leaf stems reaching to the surface. This tender white crown is one of the finest vegetables furnished by the dandelion and can be eaten raw in salads or cooked. Slice the crowns off the roots just low enough so they will stay together and slice again just where the leaves start getting green. Wash them thoroughly to dislodge all grit. Soak in cold salted water until they are ready to be cooked or made into salads.

10   To make a tasty Dandelion Crown Salad, cut the crowns finely crosswise, add a little salt, a pinch of sugar and 1 small onion chopped fine. Fry 2 or 3 slices of bacon cut in small pieces. When the bacon is crisp, remove it and add 2 tablespoons of cider vinegar to the hot bacon fat; then, as it boils up, pour it over the chopped dandelion crowns and stir. Garnish with the pieces of crisp bacon and slices of hard-boiled egg and serve immediately.

11   To prepare dandelion crowns as a cooked vegetable simply boil in considerable water for about 5 minutes, then drain and season with butter and salt. Return to the fire just long enough to dry out slightly and allow the seasoning to permeate it throughout. Many people consider this the finest way of all to eat dandelions.

12   The only food product of the dandelion that is known to most people is furnished by the tangled rosette of leaves above the surface. These are the justly famous Dandelion Greens, and, if gathered early enough, they are really fine and require very little cooking. After the plant blooms they are too bitter and tough to eat. Wash the young, tender greens well, place them in a kettle and pour boiling water over them. Let them boil 5 minutes, then drain and season with salt and butter or bacon fat.

13   One of the secrets of the dandelion's ability to bloom very early is that it starts producing the beginnings of the blossoms down atop the root in the center of the protecting crown, then only shoves them up on stems when the weather is favorable. The developing blossom material is found inside the crown as a yellowish, closely packed mass. This material, when cut out and

cooked, furnishes still another dandelion vegetable. Just covered with boiling water and cooked only about 3 minutes, then drained and seasoned with butter and salt, these little chunks of embryonic blossoms are delicious, with something of the flavor and texture of the finest artichokes. Until this blossom material is fairly well developed, the crowns and greens are still edible, although it would be advisable to cook them in two or more waters toward the end of the season. As soon as the plant starts sending up bloom stalks, the dandelion season is over as far as vegetables are concerned. I have tried cooking the unopened buds of the flowers later, and they make a passable vegetable but are not nearly so delicious as the developing buds that are still hidden inside the crown. Dandelion Coffee can be made of the roots at any time of the year, although I prefer that made in early spring while the roots are still filled with foodstuff intended for the developing plant.

A better-known and more ardent beverage made from this versatile plant is Dandelion Wine. I used to think that this wine was just another of the clever concoctions invented by Americans in the twenties to evade prohibition, but now I find that Dandelion Wine has been made and appreciated in England for many generations. 14

Gather 1 gallon of dandelion flowers on a dry day. Put these in a 2-gallon crock and pour 1 gallon of boiling water over them. Cover the jar and allow the flowers to steep for 3 days. Strain through a jelly cloth so you can squeeze all the liquid from the flowers. Put the liquid in a kettle, add 1 small ginger root, the thinly pared peels and the juice of 3 oranges and 1 lemon. Stir in 3 pounds of sugar and boil gently for 20 minutes. Return the liquid to the crock and allow it to cool until barely lukewarm. Spread ½ cake of yeast on a piece of toasted rye bread and float it on top. Cover the crock with a cloth and keep in a warm room for 6 days. Then strain off the wine into a gallon jug, corking it loosely with a wad of cotton. Keep in a dark place for 3 weeks, then carefully decant into a bottle and cap or cork tightly. Don't touch it until Christmas or later. My "drinking uncle" says that, even during the worst blizzard in January, a glass of Dandelion Wine will bring summer right into the house. 15

Once I called the attention of some friends to a report that some of the inhabitants of the Island of Minorca had, during a famine, been forced to subsist on dandelions. This was in March, so we decided to see how much of a meal we could prepare using only dandelion products and added seasonings. We had Dandelion Roots, boiled and buttered, Dandelion Crowns, both cooked and in a salad, Dandelion Greens, and the tender developing blossom material cut from the crowns, cooked and seasoned. All this was washed down with glasses of Dandelion Wine left over from the former season, and we finished with steaming cups of Dandelion Coffee. That meal was so delicious that it completely cured any anguish we were feeling over the plight of the Minorcans. 16

IRMA S. ROMBAUER AND MARION ROMBAUER BECKER, MAIDA HEATTER, AND M. F. K. FISHER

Brownies and Bar Cookies

Each of these expert cooks is the author of classic cookbooks renowned for the high quality of the recipes therein, the thoughtful and imaginative instructions on how to prepare diverse dishes, and the well-written contexts, literary as well as culinary, in which this good advice is embedded. It is interesting to compare the variations in the directions on the relatively simple process of how to make brownies, as provided by Rombauer and Becker in The Joy of Cooking *(revised 1975), Heatter in* Maida Heatter's Book of Great Chocolate Desserts *(1978), and M. F. K. Fisher in* With Bold Knife and Fork *(1968). Indeed, in her autobiographical account of how her family made and ate* biscuit au chocolat, *Fisher simply refers to Rombauer's recipe for the specific ingredients and details; her book focuses mostly on the contexts, physical and psychological, in which the cooking takes place. Yet one reason for the popularity of* The Joy of Cooking *and Heatter's books is the humanity of the writers; Rombauer and Becker admit that they love "this classic American confection," and Heatter carries a few individually wrapped brownies in her purse to give away. How can we resist?*

Irma S. Rombauer and Marion Rombauer Becker:
Brownies Cockaigne

About 30 brownies.

Almost everyone wants to make this classic American confection. Brownies may vary greatly in richness and contain anywhere from 1½ cups of butter and 5 ounces of chocolate to 2 tablespoons of butter and 2 ounces of chocolate for every cup of flour. If you want them chewy and moist, use a 9 × 13-inch pan. We love the following.

Preheat the oven to 350.
   Melt in a double boiler:

½ cup butter
4 oz. unsweetened chocolate

▶ Cool this mixture. If you don't, your brownies will be heavy and dry.
   Beat until light in color and foamy in texture:

4 eggs at 70°
¼ teaspoon salt

Add gradually and continue beating until well creamed:

2 cups sugar
1 teaspoon vanilla

With a few swift strokes, combine the cooled chocolate mixture and the eggs and sugar. ▶ Even if you normally use an electric mixer, do this manually. Before the mixture becomes uniformly colored, fold in, again by hand:

1 cup sifted all-purpose flour

And before the flour is uniformly colored, stir in gently:

1 cup pecan meats

Bake in a greased 9 × 13-inch pan about 25 minutes. Cut when cool, as interiors are still moist when fresh from the oven.

Good ways to serve Brownies are to garnish with whipped cream, ice cream or an icing.

Maida Heatter: ### Brownies

24 or 32 brownies

This is from my dessert book. These are the Brownies with which I started my reputation as a pastry chef when I was about ten years old. People who barely knew me, knew my Brownies. Since I always wrapped them individually I usually carried a few to give out. I occasionally meet people I never knew well and haven't seen in many years, and the first thing they say is, "I remember your Brownies." Sometimes they have forgotten my name—but they always remember my Brownies.

5 ounces (5 squares) unsweetened chocolate
5⅓ ounces (10⅔ tablespoons) sweet butter
1 tablespoon powdered (not granular) dry instant coffee
½ teaspoon salt
4 eggs (graded large or extra-large)
2 cups granulated sugar
1 teaspoon vanilla extract
¼ teaspoon almond extract
1 cup sifted all-purpose flour
10 ounces (2½ generous cups) walnut halves or large pieces

Adjust rack one-third up from the bottom of the oven and preheat oven to 450 degrees. Butter a 10½ × 15½ × 1-inch jelly-roll pan. Line the bottom and sides with one long piece of wax paper, butter the paper lightly, dust it with flour, and invert over a piece of paper to tap lightly and shake out excess flour.

Place the chocolate and the butter in the top of a small double boiler over hot water on moderate heat. Cover until melted, stirring occasionally with a small wire whisk. Add the powdered dry instant coffee and stir to dissolve. Remove the top of the double boiler and set aside, uncovered, to cool slightly.

Meanwhile, in the small bowl of an electric mixer, add the salt to the eggs and beat until slightly fluffy. Gradually add the sugar and beat at medium-high speed for 15 minutes. Transfer to the large bowl of the mixer.

Stir the vanilla and almond extracts into the chocolate mixture. On lowest speed add the chocolate to the eggs, scraping the bowl with a rubber spatula and beating *only enough to blend*. Still using lowest speed and the rubber spatula, add the flour, beating *only enough to blend*. Fold in the nuts, handling the mixture as little as possible.

Turn into the prepared pan and spread very evenly.

Place in the oven and *immediately* reduce the oven temperature to 400 degrees. Bake 21 to 22 minutes or until a toothpick gently inserted in the middle just barely comes out clean. Do not overbake. These should be slightly moist.

Remove from the oven and immediately cover with a large rack or cookie sheet and invert. Remove the pan and wax paper. Cover with a large rack and invert again. After 10 or 15 minutes cover with a rack or cookie sheet and invert only for a moment to be sure that the Brownies are not sticking to the rack.

Cool completely. The cake will cut more neatly if it is chilled first—it is even best if it is partially frozen. (It may be cut in half and partially frozen one piece at a time if you don't have room in your freezer for the whole thing.)

Transfer to a cutting board. To mark portions evenly, measure with a ruler and mark with toothpicks. Use a long, thin, very sharp knife or one with a finely serrated edge. Use a sawing motion when you cut in order not to squash the cake.

Wrap the Brownies individually in clear cellophane or wax paper (not plastic wrap, which is too hard to handle) or package them any way that is airtight—do not let them stand around and dry out.

M. F. K. Fisher:
Bar Cookies

1   Such small baked cakes must have evolved from the cooking of the early Scots, and then further back, but they seem very American in their gastronomical importance. Cookies are made commercially, and sold in uncountable shapes, flavors and sizes, usually packed in cellophane envelopes, in California supermarkets and Missouri crossroads stores, and whereas a French schoolchild would snatch a slice of bread with some jam on it, our children prefer the convenient and more varied (and perhaps richer and sweeter) little pastries. Truck drivers munch them for hoped-for nourishment on long hauls. Schoolteachers and stenographers nibble low-calorie Vanilla Gems and high-calorie fig bars during Free Period. Dutiful daughters-in-law placate Gramps with a honeyed soft confection tactfully free of seeds, nuts, roughage, and other geriatric hazards. And I am told that Chocolate Brownies are "a universal favorite," although I would hesitate to serve one to a Jordanian or even a Marseillais.

The nearest I ever came in another country to what I suspect is our own 2
national invention was when my landlady in Aix gave tea parties for two
Swedish aristocrats who added luster to her circle and loved pastries of all
kinds as long as they were rich and sweet. The cook always made, among
other dainties, a *biscuit au chocolat,* which I never would have tasted otherwise, just as I never would have been invited with the other more socially
acceptable guests if the Swedes had not liked me and the cake too. It was a
large flat round dusted with confectioner's sugar, and of an almost chewy
texture which reminded me of our cruder Brownies. I think it would have
been much better at the end of a light meal, perhaps served with *crème
Chantilly:* it called for coffee and not tea, or better yet a cool merciful glass of
wine. But we all tucked into it, no matter how awkwardly on our tiny
balanced plates, as we sat in a large circle in the drawing room, and when it
had vanished there was a great bowing and hand kissing and the Swedes and
I ran up to the Cours Mirabeau for a quick beer. . . .

A noted home economist once wrote asking me the origin of our Brown- 3
ies, and I had to plead real ignorance, except for their possibly elegant beginnings in a chocolate biscuit. She said, "I have made them all my life and since
friends old and young like them so much I have become curious." I looked in
many books, with no luck except for the dependable Mrs. Rombauer, who
gives several recipes for them, starting out #1 flatly by stating, in a rare burst
of prose, "Than which there are no others." She reneges a little with #2,
saying of it, "A lighter Bar than Brownies #1, and even better." I always
believe this lady without cavil, if not always with full obedience, and I am
sure her recipes are the best for what I described to the home economist as
having to be "rich, chewy, sticky, full of walnut or pecan meats, indigestible,
and generally delicious."

I should perhaps have added, "to them as likes them," for by now in my 4
progress toward the pap and pabulum of senility I would rather do several
other unpleasant things than eat one. We seldom had them at home: Mother
was liverish, and rightfully ascribed dangers to chocolate which she managed
to ignore in the huge amounts of butter we downed at the Ranch. (I know,
because for several years I did the Saturday churning. It was a strangely
satisfying but irksome job, and when I showed signs of rebellion I was easily
conned back to the chore by crass flattery for my knack of turning out much
better butter than could, or would, any other available slavey.)

On the cookie baking days now, usually when young people will be 5
around, I pour the dough into pans to make squares, or drop it bit by bit on
cookie sheets. I admire the thinly rolled kinds, but am lazy about them,
perhaps because of my innate lack of interest in the national nibble. I have
found that rather moist dark spicy cookies are generally pleasing, to eat
with a glass of milk if one is growing fast or is in other ways needful of
soothing.

How-To-Do-It Writing

Strategies

1. Do I understand the process or phenomenon I'm writing about well enough to explain it to others? Is my knowledge firsthand? derivative? up to date?

2. Are my intended readers familiar or unfamiliar with the general subject area? with the specific process I'm discussing? Are they laypeople, or specialists in this area? How simple must the instructions and language be for my readers to understand the process?

3. Have I stated the purpose or objective of the process clearly, at the outset? Have I included all the essential steps in the process in the sequence in which they occur? Have I explained them unambiguously, in clear and consistent terminology?

4. Have I explained all the crucial terms, special equipment, concepts, and/or sub-processes at appropriate places in the overall organization? If not, should I have done so? Or would to do so complicate instructions that should be simpler?

5. Can I follow my own directions? Will a typical reader be able to follow my directions successfully? with reasonable ease and efficiency? Is there anything I need to change to enhance these?

Suggestions

1. Write an essay in which you provide directions on how to perform a process—how to do or make something at which you are particularly skilled. In addition to the essential steps, you may wish to explain your own special technique or strategy that makes your method unique or better than other existing ways to do this. Some possible subjects, which may be narrowed or adapted as you wish are:

(a) How to play a particular game—chess, bridge, Trivial Pursuit, a computer game.

(b) How to perform a particular athletic activity—scuba dive, hang glide, rappel, bicycle long distances, figure skate.

(c) How to perform a given task requiring physical skill—rope a calf, drive a tractor, ride a horse, cut hair.

(d) How to perfom a task requiring specialized knowledge of a field—build a basic library of books, tapes, records, videocassettes; design and build a piece of laboratory equipment, a sailboat, a dress, or a house.

(e) How to administer first aid—for choking, drowning, burns, bleeding, shock, or other medical emergency.

(f) How to succeed in business—prepare for a particular job or career, get a job in a particular field, perform particular aspects of that job, attain fame and/or wealth.

(g) How to survive in college—write papers, do original research in a particular field, schedule your time, study, have a satisfying social life.

(h) How to attain personal happiness—through satisfying relationships with one's parents, friends, spouse, children, employer; through a pet or hobby; through healthful living—proper diet, exercise, stress reduction.

(i) How to be a skillful consumer—how to shop for a particular good (say, a used car) or service (say, a good doctor), how to return or exchange unsatisfactory merchandise, how to hunt bargains at a yard sale or secondhand store, how to buy a first (or second) house, how to invest in the stock market.

2. Write a humorous paper parodying a process, either of the kind identified below, or suggested above, or, for that matter, anything else that strikes your fancy or your funnybone.

(a) How to survive—in college, or on a particular job, or on vacation, or on a blind date, or one's own adolescence (or that of one's children).

(b) How to be a model babysitter/son/daughter/student/employee/lover/spouse/parent/neighbor/citizen/public servant.

(c) A parody of the step-by-step directions for making or doing anything.

(d) How to arrange a social event—a candlelight dinner for two, a cocktail party, a fraternity or sorority party, a children's birthday party, a wedding, a fundraiser.

(e) How to overcome inertia and do something good for yourself—lose weight, stop smoking, start exercising, etc.

(f) How to operate a mechanical device that is utterly foreign to you—a pasta maker, a computer, a lawnmower, etc.

CHAPTER EIGHT

Writing About the Social and Physical Sciences

Writers in the physical, natural, and social sciences are often called on to explain phenomena, concepts, processes, or techniques to an audience that needs to understand the subject, clearly and unambiguously. Of course you will interpret it, as well, to enable your readers to see it your way. These two statements capture the essence of the transaction between science writers and their readers.

Americans as a nation are curious about what things are, how things work, and why, but most people don't know much about the concepts and phenomena of the sciences and technology, even the very basic ones. As a simple test, ask a few of your college graduate friends to explain some of the subjects discussed in this section—the origin of language, one or two fundamental paradigms of biology (or physics or economics or mathematics or a subdivision thereof), or the concept and consequences of the nuclear winter. Do they understand these things? Do you—or can you, after you've read the essays?

As a consequence of our general insecurity (if not ignorance), most Americans rely on experts or interpreters to explain and analyze these unfamiliar scientific subjects. As a researcher, a writer, a student, or an employee, you may need to provide scientific or technical writing for general readers or for specialists that addresses some or all of these questions: What is the scientific or technical phenomenon under consideration? How was it formed, created, discovered? How does it work? Why is one version or variation (mine or another's) better than other versions?

You'll need also to identify some essential characteristics of your audience. How much do they already know about the subject? If they're innocents who, like James Thurber's grandmother, imagine that electricity is "dripping invisibly all over the house" from the wall sockets, you'll need to treat the subject at a far more elementary level than if your readers are highly specialized researchers in the field of your writing. Do you know enough to address your intended readers at their level of knowledge? (If not, either shift to a subject you know better, or to a less knowledgeable audience.) You will also want to ask why your readers want to know what you're telling them. because of sheer interest in the subject? because of its current significance? to be able to apply the knowledge to their professional work, hobby, or to their everyday life? to satisfy the curiosity that your writing or your work has aroused?

In order to understand the processes of science and the way scientists think, it is useful to examine the ways they look at their own fields, and how they do research in them. In his landmark book, *The Structure of Scientific Revolution,* in which "The Route to Normal Science" (669–77) appears, philosopher and historian of science Thomas S. Kuhn explains how scientists use paradigms—structures or patterns that allow them to share a common set of assumptions, theories, laws, applications as they do work in their respective fields:

> Men whose research is based on shared paradigms are committed to the same rules and standards for scientific practice. That commitment and the apparent consensus it produces are prerequisites for normal science, i.e., for the genesis and continuation of a particular research tradition.

Workable paradigms emerge in every scientific field, compete for dominance, and can shift as the state of knowledge—and the state of the art—changes.

Paradigms notwithstanding, scientists—individually and collectively—have their own styles of investigation, and much debate in scientific circles centers on methodology. The excerpt from Evelyn Fox Keller's biography of Nobel Prize–winning geneticist Barbara McClintock, *A Feeling for the Organism* (678–81), explains McClintock's "style" as a scientist, a modern amalgamation of the "naturalist" and experimental traditions in biological research. For McClintock, years of painstaking, solitary observation led to an intuitive understanding of complex phenomena, a "Eureka!" experience that validated her theoretical knowledge. As a consequence of that experience, she could provide the scientific proof of what she already "knew" to be true because of her "feeling for the organism."

In contrast to McClintock's solitary style, "A Contemporary Touch" (681–92), an essay from Berton Roueché's Annals of Medicine series, explains complicated investigative teamwork. In the fashion of a Sherlock Holmes story the painstaking investigative process unfolds, involving as "medical detectives" pathologists, public health doctors and nurses, lab technicians, and others, who collaborate to find the villain, in this case, the cause of a mysterious outbreak of food poisoning. After establishing the context in which the investigation will be conducted and identifying the operative hunches or hypotheses, Roueché details the step-by-step process of checking clues (including false leads and frustrations), analyzing evidence, and rejecting alternative interpretations. Ultimately, he presents the triumphant solution, but briefly because he has already interpreted the clues leading up to it.

The social sciences essays in this section approach the nature of language from multiple perspectives—that of the anthropologist (Edward T. Hall, Thomas and Jean Sebeok), linguist (Charles Barber), philosopher (Susanne Langer), and interpreter of culture and literature (Alison Lurie). In "Time Talks" (694–706), through an analysis of time in various cultures, Hall defines, explains, and illustrates different concepts of time: formal (day, night, morning, afternoon, hours, minutes); informal (the perceived duration of situations, ranging on a continuum from "instantaneous event" to "forever"); and technical (solar, sidereal, and anomalistic). In "The Origin of Language" (707–17), Barber systematically examines various theories about the origin of spoken language some half million years ago. Typical of many science writers, he labels and categorizes each theory ("The Bow-wow Theory," "The Yo-he-ho Theory"), identifies the characteristics of each, and then demonstrates its inadequacy to explain all the phenomena that a suitably comprehensive theory would have to cover to be truly workable. With characteristic scientific conservatism, and despite his personal preference, Barber refuses to assert the superiority of one theory over another, for all have limitations.

In "Signs and Symbols" (717–22), Langer uses anthropological and linguistic evidence to support the philosophical distinction she makes between man and beast. As she searches for the characteristics that discriminate between humans and other species, she concludes that:

> Language is the highest and most amazing achievement of the symbolistic human mind. . . . without it anything properly called "thought" is impossible. The birth of language is the dawn of humanity. The line between man and beast—between the highest ape and the lowest savage—is the language line.

Langer furnishes extended definitions that distinguish signs (which animals use and respond to) from symbols (which are uniquely human) and, adopting the method of cultural anthropologists, she illustrates these with comparative examples of human and animal behavior.

Langer's work provides philosophical reinforcement for the Sebeoks' skeptical, negative analysis of the alleged linguistic ability of "Performing Animals" (733–39), notably Clever Hans, the "talking" circus horse cued in by his trainer, and Washoe, a chimpanzee whose ability to use sign language the Sebeoks also attribute to her trainers' "inadvertent cues." Yet Darwin's "Reasoning in Animals" (745–48), which distinguishes between instinctive and reasoned animal behavior (sled dogs spread out on thin ice "so that their weight might be more evenly distributed"), might provide contradictory evidence. Darwin carefully demonstrates that no alternative explanations fit the evidence as well as his does, and one could ask (though Darwin does not do so here) whether such animals need language in order to reason. More recent experiments have also challenged the views of Langer and the Sebeoks, especially when "talking" chimps teach other chimps the same symbol system. And so the controversy continues.

Lurie's article "Clothing as a Sign System" (723–32) is a logical working out of the metaphor that clothing is language, and that various attributes of clothing are analogous to various parts of speech and types of usage. For example, in Lurie's view accessories, such as gloves and hats, are "modifiers." Proper language is the equivalent of clean and tidy clothing; the alternatives are antisocial: "to wear dirty, rumpled or torn clothing is to invite scorn and condescension."

All of the essays here representing "The Natural and Physical Sciences" are written by scientists for general, nonspecialized readers except for two essays by biology students—Laird Bloom explaining "Methods of Pest Control Using Insect Pheromones" (760–73) for his biology teacher, and Kelly Shea explaining "Acid Rain" for a general audience. These essays have a number of features in common. All are written in clear language that is not overly technical or full of specialized jargon. When the authors introduce a term or concept new to their intended readers, they explain it on the spot. For instance, in "What Is Matter?" (740–44), Bertrand Russell identifies the atomists as people "who thought that matter consisted of tiny lumps which could never be divided; these were supposed to hit each other and then bounce off in various ways."

All deal with a combination of theory, general principles, and practical application or illustration. Thus in "On Being the Right Size" (748–52), geneticist J. B. S. Haldane presents at the outset his general principle: "For every type of animal there is a most convenient size, and a large change in size inevitably carries with it a change of form"—as evidenced in the illustration of the gazelle, rhinoceros, and giraffe, all members of the same zoological order, all exhibiting "mechanically successful" body structures that reflect comparable ratios of weight to supporting area of bone. Haldane adduces other laws of physics to explain related phenomena: why gravity presents few dangers to very small animals, who can fall long distances without harm, but is fatal to larger ones; why "comparative anatomy is largely the story of the struggle to increase surface in proportion to volume."

The professional scientists who are writing (but not the less experienced student writers) are also willing to engage in controversy—to present conflicting and contradictory theories and information, and to interpret evidence so that it supports their point of view—as in Darwin's controversial claim in "Reasoning in Animals" that "animals possess the power of reasoning." Yet these writers are not dogmatic; they are willing to admit when they don't know something for certain, when they are speculating. The most controversial of these essays, probably because it is the most threatening, is cancer researcher Lewis Thomas's "The Long Habit" (753–57), in which he contends that death—and a timely death—is inevitable. This is true, he asserts, despite the belief, common to scientists and laypersons alike, that "If we can rid ourselves of some of our chronic, degenerative diseases, and cancer, strokes, and coronaries, we might go on and on." Eternal life is unnatural, says Thomas, and supports his view with multiple examples, from the natural and civilized worlds. Yet Thomas himself acknowledges that neither he nor anyone else knows where consciousness goes when it vanishes: "This is for another science, another day."

The papers of the student writers illustrate two different ways that people just learning a discipline can write about it. Shea picks a phenomenon, "Acid Rain" (773–75), and drawing on information in her biology textbook and her own experience, explains it for readers unfamiliar with the subject. She does not claim or intend to be original or innovative; to do so would exceed her level of knowledge. But she does try to be clear, accurate, and to present the information in a logical order. So does Bloom, though the information in "Methods of Pest Control Using Pheromones" is derived from an extensive array of scientific journals, and is conveyed in more technical language than Shea's, with the sources cited in scholarly, academic fashion. Bloom's paper is appropriately cautious; as a student, rather than a specialist, he must rely on the research and interpretations of experts to inform his own views of the subject, and to stimulate and reinforce his recommendations. Both students were relative novices when they wrote these papers; as they learned more, they would be better able to depart from their sources and even to take issue with them.

The essays in this chapter, particularly those concerned with "Ethical and Social Issues," by Stephen Jay Gould, Norbert Wiener, William Warner, and Carl Sagan, should dispel any lingering opinions that scientific writing is obliged to be objective, dispassionate, balanced, and free of values. Even though many of the essays in this chapter are derived from objectively measured or gathered data, they are written by humans bringing their personal values, beliefs, biases, hopes and fears to bear on their interpretations of that information. Warner, in "The Islands [of Chesapeake Bay]: Looking Ahead" (788–97), which comes near the end of his book-length study *Beautiful Swimmers: Watermen, Crabs, and the Chesapeake Bay,* analyzes the effects of environmental pollution on the Bay's whole, complex ecosystem and makes a plea for cleaning up the Bay before "general eutrophication" destroys its extensive, valuable, and beautiful marine life. In "Racism and Recapitulation" (776–80), Gould, a geologist and historian of science whom we may infer does not believe that either blacks or women are inferior to whites or males, adduces a mixture of scientific evidence and logical argument to point out the flaws in two contradictory but equally racist arguments that "Blacks are inferior, Brinton tells us, because they retain juvenile traits. Blacks are inferior, claims Bolk, because they develop beyond the juvenile traits that whites retain."

In "Moral Problems of a Scientist" (780–88), mathematician Wiener analyzes the various self-serving and political reasons that scientists working on the Manhattan Project to develop the atomic bomb during World War II gave for using this thoroughly devastating weapon to bomb Japan in 1945. His ethical reprehension is apparent as he emphasizes the conflict between disinterested scientific research ("true science") and science used (or perverted) for military and political ends—which in fact could have been accomplished by means of conventional and far less destructive weapons. Carl Sagan, an astronomer who can count on popular recognition and respect because of his popular television series *Cosmos,* presents an updated extension of the implications of Wiener's argument. Put simply, the world is now capable of waging global thermonuclear war. If such a war were to occur, Sagan speculates (but asserts as fact):

> Many species of plants and animals would become extinct. Vast numbers of surviving humans would starve to death. The delicate ecological relations that bind together organisms on Earth in a fabric of mutual dependency would be torn, perhaps irreparably. There is little question that our global civilization would be destroyed. The human population would be reduced to prehistoric levels, or less. . . . And there seems to be a real possibility of the extinction of the human species.

These essays demonstrate that scientists care deeply not only about the discipline of their research but also about the uses to which it is put. The ultimate purpose of their writing is to maintain not just life but the quality of life that science has the power to create—or to destroy.

Scientific Frameworks

THOMAS S. KUHN

The Route to Normal Science

Kuhn's writings as a professor of philosophy and history of science approach the ways scientists think and work from a philosophical and humanistic perspective. He was born in Cincinnati, Ohio, in 1922, educated as a physicist at Harvard (B.A., 1943; M.A., 1946; Ph.D., 1949), and since then has taught at Harvard (1948–56), the University of California, Berkeley (1958–64), Princeton (1964–79), and since 1979 at the Massachusetts Institute of Technology. His illuminating books, profoundly influential on the ways scientists and humanists alike understand their own and each other's work, include The Copernican Revolution: Planetary Astronomy in the Development of Western Thought *(1957)* and The Essential Tension *(1977). Particularly significant is* The Structure of Scientific Revolutions *(1962), from which the following essay is taken; its discussion of paradigms has in itself proven paradigmatic.*

Nothing is as practical as a good theory, or in this case, a good definition of a theory. Kuhn begins by defining paradigms—structures or patterns that allow scientists to share a common set of assumptions, theories, laws, applications as they look at their fields. Scientists whose research is based on shared paradigms, who "learned the bases of their field from the same concrete models . . . are committed to the same rules and standards for scientific practice" and do not disagree over the fundamentals. The rest of this essay explains how and why this is so, and shows the random state of any scientific field before the emergence of a workable paradigm, the effects of competing paradigms on the discipline, and the consequences to the field of shifting from one paradigm to another.

In this essay, "normal science" means research firmly based upon one or more past scientific achievements, achievements that some particular scientific community acknowledges for a time as supplying the foundation for its further practice. Today such achievements are recounted, though seldom in their original form, by science textbooks, elementary and advanced. These textbooks expound the body of accepted theory, illustrate many or all of its successful applications, and compare these applications with exemplary observations and experiments. Before such books became popular early in the nineteenth century (and until even more recently in the newly matured sciences), many of the famous classics of science fulfilled a similar function. Aristotle's *Physica,* Ptolemy's *Almagest,* Newton's *Principia* and *Opticks,* Franklin's *Electricity,* Lavoisier's *Chemistry,* and Lyell's *Geology*—these and many other works served for a time implicitly to define the legitimate problems and methods of a research field for succeeding generations of practitioners. They were able to do so because they shared two essential characteristics. Their achievement was sufficiently unprecedented to attract an enduring

1

group of adherents away from competing modes of scientific activity. Simultaneously, it was sufficiently open-ended to leave all sorts of problems for the redefined group of practitioners to resolve.

2   Achievements that share these two characteristics I shall henceforth refer to as "paradigms," a term that relates closely to "normal science." By choosing it, I mean to suggest that some accepted examples of actual scientific practice—examples which include law, theory, application, and instrumentation together—provide models from which spring particular coherent traditions of scientific research. These are the traditions which the historian describes under such rubrics as "Ptolemaic astronomy" (or "Copernican"), "Aristotelian dynamics" (or "Newtonian"), "corpuscular optics" (or "wave optics"), and so on. The study of paradigms, including many that are far more specialized than those named illustratively above, is what mainly prepares the student for membership in the particular scientific community with which he will later practice. Because he there joins men who learned the bases of their field from the same concrete models, his subsequent practice will seldom evoke overt disagreement over fundamentals. Men whose research is based on shared paradigms are committed to the same rules and standards for scientific practice. That commitment and the apparent consensus it produces are prerequisites for normal science, i.e., for the genesis and continuation of a particular research tradition.

3   Because in this essay the concept of a paradigm will often substitute for a variety of familiar notions, more will need to be said about the reasons for its introduction. Why is the concrete scientific achievement, as a locus of professional commitment, prior to the various concepts, laws, theories, and points of view that may be abstracted from it? In what sense is the shared paradigm a fundamental unit for the student of scientific development, a unit that cannot be fully reduced to logically atomic components which might function in its stead? There can be a sort of scientific research without paradigms, or at least without any so unequivocal and so binding as the ones named above. Acquisition of a paradigm and of the more esoteric type of research it permits is a sign of maturity in the development of any given scientific field.

4   If the historian traces the scientific knowledge of any selected group of related phenomena backward in time, he is likely to encounter some minor variant of a pattern here illustrated from the history of physical optics. Today's physics textbooks tell the student that light is photons, i.e., quantum-mechanical entities that exhibit some characteristics of waves and some of particles. Research proceeds accordingly, or rather according to the more elaborate and mathematical characterization from which this usual verbalization is derived. That characterization of light is, however, scarcely half a century old. Before it was developed by Planck, Einstein, and others early in this century, physics texts taught that light was transverse wave motion, a conception rooted in a paradigm that derived ultimately from the optical writings of Young and Fresnel in the early nineteenth century. Nor was the

wave theory the first to be embraced by almost all practitioners of optical science. During the eighteenth century the paradigm for this field was provided by Newton's *Opticks*, which taught that light was material corpuscles. At that time physicists sought evidence, as the early wave theorists had not, of the pressure exerted by light particles impinging on solid bodies.

These transformations of the paradigms of physical optics are scientific revolutions, and the successive transition from one paradigm to another via revolution is the usual developmental pattern of mature science. It is not, however, the pattern characteristic of the period before Newton's work, and that is the contrast that concerns us here. No period between remote antiquity and the end of the seventeenth century exhibited a single generally accepted view about the nature of light. Instead there were a number of competing schools and sub-schools, most of them espousing one variant or another of Epicurean, Aristotelian, or Platonic theory. One group took light to be particles emanating from material bodies; for another it was a modification of the medium that intervened between the body and the eye; still another explained light in terms of an interaction of the medium with an emanation from the eye; and there were other combinations and modifications besides. Each of the corresponding schools derived strength from its relation to some particular metaphysic, and each emphasized, as paradigmatic observations, the particular cluster of optical phenomena that its own theory could do most to explain. Other observations were dealt with by *ad hoc* elaborations, or they remained as outstanding problems for further research.

At various times all these schools made significant contributions to the body of concepts, phenomena, and techniques from which Newton drew the first nearly uniformly accepted paradigm for physical optics. Any definition of the scientist that excludes at least the more creative members of these various schools will exclude their modern successors as well. Those men were scientists. Yet anyone examining a survey of physical optics before Newton may well conclude that, though the field's practitioners were scientists, the net result of their activity was something less than science. Being able to take no common body of belief for granted, each writer on physical optics felt forced to build his field anew from its foundations. In doing so, his choice of supporting observation and experiment was relatively free, for there was no standard set of methods or of phenomena that every optical writer felt forced to employ and explain. Under these circumstances, the dialogue of the resulting books was often directed as much to the members of other schools as it was to nature. That pattern is not unfamiliar in a number of creative fields today, nor is it incompatible with significant discovery and invention. It is not, however, the pattern of development that physical optics acquired after Newton and that other natural sciences make familiar today.

The history of electrical research in the first half of the eighteenth century provides a more concrete and better known example of the way a science develops before it acquires its first universally received paradigm. During that period there were almost as many views about the nature of electricity as there were important electrician experimenters, men like Haukshee, Gray, Desaguliers, Du Fay, Nollett, Watson, Franklin, and others. All their numerous concepts of electricity had something in common—they were partially derived from one or another version of the mechanico-corpuscular philosophy that guided all scientific research of the day. In addition, all were components of real scientific theories, of theories that had been drawn in part from experiment and observation that partially determined the choice and interpretation of additional problems undertaken in research. Yet though all the experiments were electrical and though most of the experimenters read each other's works, their theories had no more than a family resemblance.

8   One early group of theories, following seventeenth-century practice, regarded attraction and frictional generation as the fundamental electrical phenomena. This group tended to treat repulsion as a secondary effect due to some sort of mechanical rebounding and also to postpone for as long as possible both discussion and systematic research on Gray's newly discovered effect, electrical conduction. Other "electricians" (the term is their own) took attraction and repulsion to be equally elementary manifestations of electricity and modified their theories and research accordingly. (Actually, this group is remarkably small—even Franklin's theory never quite accounted for the mutual repulsion of two negatively charged bodies.) But they had as much difficulty as the first group in accounting simultaneously for any but the simplest conduction effects. Those effects, however, provided the starting point for still a third group, one which tended to speak of electricity as a "fluid" that could run through conductors rather than as an "effluvium" that emanated from non-conductors. This group, in its turn, had difficulty reconciling its theory with a number of attractive and repulsive effects. Only through the work of Franklin and his immediate successors did a theory arise that could account with something like equal facility for very nearly all these effects and that therefore could and did provide a subsequent generation of "electricians" with a common paradigm for its research.

9   Excluding those fields, like mathematics and astronomy, in which the first firm paradigms date from prehistory and also those, like biochemistry, that arose by division and recombination of specialties already matured, the situations outlined above are historically typical. Though it involves my continuing to employ the unfortunate simplification that tags an extended historical episode with a single and somewhat arbitrarily chosen name (e.g., Newton or Franklin), I suggest that similar fundamental disagreements characterized, for example, the study of motion before Aristotle and of statics before Archimedes, the study of heat before Black, of chemistry before Boyle and Boerhaave, and of historical geology before Hutton. In parts of biology—the study of heredity, for example—the first universally received paradigms are still more recent; and it remains an open question what parts of social science have yet acquired such paradigms at all. History suggests that the road to a firm research consensus is extraordinarily arduous.

History also suggests, however, some reasons for the difficulties encoun-   10
tered on the road. In the absence of a paradigm or some candidate for
paradigm, all of the facts that could possibly pertain to the development of a
given science are likely to seem equally relevant. As a result, early fact-
gathering is a far more nearly random activity than the one that subsequent
scientific development makes familiar. Furthermore, in the absence of a reason for seeking some particular form of more recondite information, early
fact-gathering is usually restricted to the wealth of data that lie ready to hand.
The resulting pool of facts contains those accessible to casual observation and
experiment together with some of the more esoteric data retrievable from
established crafts medicine, calendar making, and metallurgy. Because the
crafts are one readily accessible source of facts that could not have been
casually discovered, technology has often played a vital role in the emergence
of new sciences.

But though this sort of fact-collecting has been essential to the origin of   11
many significant sciences, anyone who examines, for example, Pliny's ency-
clopedic writings or the Baconian natural histories of the seventeenth century
will discover that it produces a morass. One somehow hesitates to call the
literature that results scientific. The Baconian "histories" of heat, color, wind,
mining, and so on, are filled with information, some of it recondite. But they
juxtapose facts that will later prove revealing (e.g., heating by mixture) with
others (e.g., the warmth of dung heaps) that will for some time remain too
complex to be integrated with theory at all. In addition, since any description
must be partial, the typical natural history often omits from its immensely
circumstantial accounts just those details that later scientists will find sources
of important illumination. Almost none of the early "histories" of electricity,
for example, mention that chaff, attracted to a rubbed glass rod, bounces off
again. That effect seemed mechanical, not electrical. Moreover, since the
casual fact-gatherer seldom possesses the time or the tools to be critical, the
natural histories often juxtapose descriptions like the above with others, say,
heating by antiperistasis (or by cooling), that we are now quite unable to
confirm.[1] Only very occasionally, as in the cases of ancient statics, dynamics,
and geometrical optics, do facts collected with so little guidance from pre-
established theory speak with sufficient clarity to permit the emergence of a
first paradigm.

This is the situation that creates the schools characteristic of the early   12
stages of a science's development. No natural history can be interpreted in the
absence of at least some implicit body of intertwined theoretical and methodological belief that permits selection, evaluation, and criticism. If that body of
belief is not already implicit in the collection of facts—in which case more
than "mere facts" are at hand—it must be externally supplied, perhaps by a

[1] Bacon [in the *Novum Organum*] says, "Water slightly warm is more easily frozen than quite
cold"; *antiperistasis:* an old word meaning a reaction caused by the action of an opposite quality
or principle—here, heating through cooling.

current metaphysic, by another science, or by personal and historical accident. No wonder, then, that in the early stages of the development of any science different men confronting the same range of phenomena, but not usually all the same particular phenomena, describe and interpret them in different ways. What is surprising, and perhaps also unique in its degree to the fields we call science, is that such initial divergences should ever largely disappear.

13 For they do disappear to a very considerable extent and then apparently once and for all. Furthermore, their disappearance is usually caused by the triumph of one of the pre-paradigm schools, which, because of its own characteristic beliefs and pre-conceptions, emphasized only some special part of the too sizable and inchoate pool of information. Those electricians who thought electricity a fluid and therefore gave particular emphasis to conduction provide an excellent case in point. Led by this belief, which could scarcely cope with the known multiplicity of attractive and repulsive effects, several of them conceived the idea of bottling the electrical fluid. The immediate fruit of their efforts was the Leyden jar, a device which might never have been discovered by a man exploring nature casually or at random, but which was in fact independently developed by at least two investigators in the early 1740's. Almost from the start of his electrical researches, Franklin was particularly concerned to explain that strange and, in the event, particularly revealing piece of special apparatus. His success in doing so provided the most effective of the arguments that made his theory a paradigm, though one that was still unable to account for quite all the known cases of electrical repulsion.[2] To be accepted as a paradigm, a theory must seem better than its competitors, but it need not, and in fact never does, explain all the facts with which it can be confronted.

14 What the fluid theory of electricity did for the subgroup that held it, the Franklinian paradigm later did for the entire group of electricians. It suggested which experiments would be worth performing and which, because directed to secondary or to overly complex manifestations of electricity, would not. Only the paradigm did the job far more effectively, partly because the end of interschool debate ended the constant reiteration of fundamentals and partly because the confidence that they were on the right track encouraged scientists to undertake more precise, esoteric, and consuming sorts of work.[3] Freed from the concern with any and all electrical phenomena, the

---

[2] The troublesome case was the mutual repulsion of negatively charged bodies.

[3] It should be noted that the acceptance of Franklin's theory did not end quite all debate. In 1759 Robert Symmer proposed a two-fluid version of that theory, and for many years thereafter electricians were divided about whether electricity was a single fluid or two. But the debates on this subject only confirm what has been said above about the manner in which a universally recognized achievement unites the profession. Electricians, though they continued divided on this point, rapidly concluded that no experimental tests could distinguish the two versions of the theory and that they were therefore equivalent. After that, both schools could and did exploit all the benefits that the Franklinian theory provided.

united group of electricians could pursue selected phenomena in far more detail, designing much special equipment for the task and employing it more stubbornly and systematically than electricians had ever done before. Both fact collection and theory articulation became highly directed activities. The effectiveness and efficiency of electrical research increased accordingly, providing evidence for a societal version of Francis Bacon's acute methodological dictum: "Truth emerges more readily from error than from confusion."

We shall be examining the nature of this highly directed or paradigm-based research in the next section, but must first note briefly how the emergence of a paradigm affects the structure of the group that practices the field. When, in the development of a natural science, an individual or group first produces a synthesis able to attract most of the next generation's practitioners, the older schools gradually disappear. In part their disappearance is caused by their members' conversion to the new paradigm. But there are always some men who cling to one or another of the older views, and they are simply read out of the profession, which thereafter ignores their work. The new paradigm implies a new and more rigid definition of the field. Those unwilling or unable to accommodate their work to it must proceed in isolation or attach themselves to some other group.[4] Historically, they have often simply stayed in the departments of philosophy from which so many of the special sciences have been spawned. As these indications hint, it is sometimes just its reception of a paradigm that transforms a group previously interested merely in the study of nature into a profession or, at least, a discipline. In the sciences (though not in fields like medicine, technology, and law, of which the principal *raison d'être* is an external social need), the formation of specialized journals, the foundation of specialists' societies, and the claim for a special place in the curriculum have usually been associated with a group's first reception of a single paradigm. At least this was the case between the time, a century and a half ago, when the institutional pattern of scientific specialization first developed and the very recent time when the paraphernalia of specialization acquired a prestige of their own.

The more rigid definition of the scientific group has other consequences. When the individual scientist can take a paradigm for granted, he need no longer, in his major works, attempt to build his field anew, starting from first principles and justifying the use of each concept introduced. That can be left to the writer of textbooks. Given a textbook, however, the creative scientist can begin his research where it leaves off and thus concentrate exclusively

15

16

---

[4]The history of electricity provides an excellent example which could be duplicated from the careers of Priestley, Kelvin, and others. Franklin reports that Nollet, who at mid-century was the most influential of the Continental electricians, "lived to see himself the last of his Sect, except Mr. B.—his *Eleve* [pupil] and immediate Disciple." More interesting, however, is the endurance of whole schools in increasing isolation from professional science. Consider, for example, the case of astrology, which was once an integral part of astronomy. Or consider the continuation in the late eighteenth, and early nineteenth centuries of a previously respected tradition of "romantic" chemistry.

upon the subtlest and most esoteric aspects of the natural phenomena that concern his group. And as he does this, his research communiqués will begin to change in ways whose evolution has been too little studied but whose modern end products are obvious to all and oppressive to many. No longer will his researches usually be embodied in books addressed, like Franklin's *Experiments . . . on Electricity* or Darwin's *Origin of Species,* to anyone who might be interested in the subject matter of the field. Instead they will usually appear as brief articles addressed only to professional colleagues, the men whose knowledge of a shared paradigm can be assumed and who prove to be the only ones able to read the papers addressed to them.

17   Today in the sciences, books are usually either texts or retrospective reflections upon one aspect or another of the scientific life. The scientist who writes one is more likely to find his professional reputation impaired than enhanced. Only in the earlier, pre-paradigm, stages of the development of the various sciences did the book ordinarily possess the same relation to professional achievement that it still retains in other creative fields. And only in those fields that still retain the book, with or without the article, as a vehicle for research communication are the lines of professionalization still so loosely drawn that the layman may hope to follow progress by reading the practitioners' original reports. Both in mathematics and astronomy, research reports had ceased already in antiquity to be intelligible to a generally educated audience. In dynamics, research became similarly esoteric in the latter Middle Ages, and it recaptured general intelligibility only briefly during the early seventeenth century when a new paradigm replaced the one that had guided medieval research. Electrical research began to require translation for the layman before the end of the eighteenth century, and most other fields of physical science ceased to be generally accessible in the nineteenth. During the same two centuries similar transitions can be isolated in the various parts of the biological sciences. In parts of the social sciences they may well be occurring today. Although it has become customary, and is surely proper, to deplore the widening gulf that separates the professional scientist from his colleagues in other fields, too little attention is paid to the essential relationship between that gulf and the mechanisms intrinsic to scientific advance.

18   Ever since prehistoric antiquity one field of study after another has crossed the divide between what the historian might call its prehistory as a science and its history proper. These transitions to maturity have seldom been so sudden or so unequivocal as my necessarily schematic discussion may have implied. But neither have they been historically gradual, coextensive, that is to say, with the entire development of the fields within which they occurred. Writers on electricity during the first four decades of the eighteenth century possessed far more information about electrical phenomena than had their sixteenth-century predecessors. During the half-century after 1740, few new sorts of electrical phenomena were added to their lists. Nevertheless, in important respects, the electrical writings of Cavendish, Coulomb, and Volta in

the last third of the eighteenth century seem further removed from those of Gray, Du Fay, and even Franklin than are the writings of these early eighteenth-century electrical discoverers from those of the sixteenth century.[5] Sometime between 1740 and 1780, electricians were for the first time enabled to take the foundations of their field for granted. From that point they pushed on to more concrete and recondite problems, and increasingly they then reported their results in articles addressed to other electricians rather than in books addressed to the learned world at large. As a group they achieved what had been gained by astronomers in antiquity and by students of motion in the Middle Ages, of physical optics in the late seventeenth century, and of historical geology in the early nineteenth. They had, that is, achieved a paradigm that proved able to guide the whole group's research. Except with the advantage of hindsight, it is hard to find another criterion that so clearly proclaims a field a science.

Questions

1. What does Kuhn mean by "normal science" (paragraph 1 and elsewhere)? What is "the route to normal science," as he explains it in this essay?

2. What does Kuhn mean by a "paradigm" in science (paragraph 2 and elsewhere)? What is the relation of "paradigm" to "normal science" (paragraph 2 and elsewhere)?

3. Explain in your own words the prevailing paradigm in one of the sciences Kuhn uses for illustrative purposes in this essay: physics, chemistry, biology, psychology. What is the prevailing paradigm in another science you know about? How does the search for or finding of paradigms in the sciences help you (or people new to the field) understand the field? What are some of the paradigms of other fields you know, such as business, education, engineering, the arts, and the humanities?

4. Explain what Kuhn means by the following: "When the individual scientist can take a paradigm for granted, he need no longer, in his major works, attempt to build his field anew, starting from first principles and justifying the use of each concept introduced. That can be left to the writer of textbooks" (paragraph 16). What paradigms do your natural science, social science, or other textbooks exemplify?

---

[5] The post-Franklinian developments include an immense increase in the sensitivity of charge detectors, the first reliable and generally diffused techniques for measuring charge, the evolution of the concept of capacity and its relation to a newly refined notion of electric tension, and the quantification of electrostatic force.

Styles of Scientific Investigation

EVELYN FOX KELLER

Barbara McClintock:
A Feeling for the Organism

That biographers have a particular affinity for their subjects has been no secret ever since James Boswell recorded every word of his adored mentor, Samuel Johnson—whom he ulti- mately portrayed, "warts and all," larger than life for eternity. The career of Barbara McClintock (b. 1907), a research biologist who won the 1983 Nobel Prize for her discovery of "jumping genes" and attained eminence late in life after some forty years of professional neglect and sex discrimination, evoked Keller's immediate sympathy. Keller, born in New York City in 1936, has written on her profoundly demoralizing experience as a woman graduate student in theoretical physics at Harvard in the late 1950s in the ironically titled "The Anomaly of a Woman in Physics"; her constructive response was an active commitment to equality for women scientists, which included the writing of McClintock's biography. Despite consistent discrimination, Keller earned her Ph.D. in physics from Harvard in 1963 and worked in New York as a research scientist in molecular biology for a decade before becoming a professor of mathematics at the State University of New York at Purchase in 1972. She is currently Professor of Mathematics and Humanities at Northeastern Univer- sity, and a Visiting Scholar in Science, Technology, and Society at M.I.T.

Keller's most recent major publications, in addition to many scientific papers, are Reflections on Gender and Science *(1985) and* A Feeling for the Organism: The Life and work of Barbara McClintock *(1984); the section of the latter reprinted here explains McClintock's "style" as a scientist—an insightful, intuitive understanding of complex phe- nomena that resulted from years of painstaking, solitary observation. After the "Eureka!" experience, McClintock's vast scientific knowledge and sensitivity enabled her to analytically work out the scientific proof of what she already "knew" to be true because of her "feeling for the organism."*

1   In her mid-thirties, Barbara McClintock's particular scientific style was al- ready well defined and emerging in ever-sharper relief. Its distinctive features were polar in character: its ultimate strength derived from a dialectic between two opposing tendencies. The reader may recall from the previous chapter a characterization of her work by Morgan as "highly specialized." And, al- though few would accept Morgan's description of the cytology of maize genetics as any more narrow a category than the cytology of *Drosophila* genet- ics, one aspect of McClintock's scientific preoccupations may easily have led him to such a description: her focus on the minutest of details. The tenacity with which she hunted down every observable chromosomal modification, the thoroughness and rigor that accompanied her virtuoso technique—all

678

these might lead one to think of the focus of her search as narrow. In fact, what she consistently pursued was nothing less than an understanding of the entire organism.

The word "understanding," and the particular meaning she attributed to it, is the cornerstone of Barbara McClintock's entire approach to science. For her, the smallest details provided the keys to the larger whole. It was her conviction that the closer her focus, the greater her attention to individual detail, to the unique characteristics of a single plant, of a single kernel, of a single chromosome, the more she could learn about the general principles by which the maize plant as a whole was organized, the better her "feeling for the organism."

To some extent the stories she tells to illustrate the meaning of "understanding" recall what might be called the "naturalist" tradition—a tradition that in most parts of biology had long been replaced by the experimental tradition, but traces of which nevertheless still survived in the mid-1930s. McClintock was able to incorporate and integrate these traces into an otherwise thoroughly experimental stance. No scientist ever develops in a vacuum, but it is difficult to find any direct intellectual influences that can be held responsible for this element in her thought. Rather, it would seem that she came to this amalgam in her own highly individualistic way, dictated more by internal forces than by external ones. The stories themselves reflect this.

She describes, for example, an experience from her early days at Missouri when she was pursuing some elaborations of the ring chromosome motif. "Most of the time, ring chromosomes undergo semiconservative replication, but there are occasional sister strand exchanges which will produce a double-size ring, having two centromeres," she says. "At anaphase, [the two centromeres] start to go to opposite poles, but [since] it's a double-size ring, it breaks. It breaks in different places, and the broken ends fuse to form new rings—different from the old. If they are small, they will frequently get lost—they will not make the telophase. Among the plants that were growing in the culture I was dealing with, there were those that could have one, two, or three of these rings, in any combination. One ring might be small; the other two could be a bit larger. In these plants, the ring chromosomes carried the dominant genes, and in order to get the recessive expression, the ring carrying the gene would have to get lost."

So adept did she become at recognizing the outward signs of those structural alterations in chromosomal composition that she could simply look at the plants themselves and know what the microscopic inspection of the cells' nuclei would later reveal. "Before examining the chromosomes, I went through the field and made my guess for every plant as to what kind of rings it would have—would it have one, two, or three, small or large, which combination? And *I never made a mistake,* except once. When I examined that one plant I was in agony. I raced right down to the field. It was wrong; it didn't say what the notebook said it should be! I found that . . . I had written the number from the plant adjacent, which I had not cut open. And then everything was all right."

6   Her belief is that the mind functions "like a computer"—processing and integrating data far more complex than we can possibly be conscious of. And finding the cause of her mistake—a misfiling error, as it were—was reassuring. "That made me feel perfect, because it showed me that whatever this computer was doing, it was doing it right." All she was conscious of doing was "looking at these fine stripes of recessive tissue"; she says the computer did the rest. "And I never made a mistake." The crucial point of this story, to her, is the state of mind required in making such judgments. "It is done with complete confidence, complete understanding. I understood every plant. Without being able to know what it was I was integrating, I *understood* the phenotype." What does understanding mean here? "It means that I was using a computer that was working very rapidly and very perfectly. I couldn't train anyone to do that."

7   Since her days as a young graduate student, she had always carried out the most laborious parts of her investigations herself, leaving none of the labor, however onerous or routine, to others. In this she did as almost all beginning scientists do. But most scientists, as they mature, learn to delegate more and more of the routine work to others. There are, of course, exceptions, and Emerson, who, according to Harriet Creighton, "didn't regard anything as routine," was one. He prided himself on doing his own work. For McClintock, more than pride was involved. Her virtuosity resided in her capacity to observe, and to process and interpret what she observed. As she grew older, it became less and less possible to delegate any part of her work; she was developing skills that she could hardly identify herself, much less impart to others.

8   The nature of insight in science, as elsewhere, is notoriously elusive. And almost all great scientists—those who learn to cultivate insight—learn also to respect its mysterious workings. It is here that their rationality finds its own limits. In defying rational explanation, the process of creative insight inspires awe in those who experience it. They come to know, trust, and value it.

9   "When you suddenly see the problem, something happens that you have the answer—before you are able to put it into words. It is all done subconsciously. This has happened too many times to me, and I know when to take it seriously. I'm so absolutely sure. I don't talk about it, I don't have to tell anybody about it, I'm just *sure* this is it."

10   This confidence was not new. She tells of an occasion from her early days at Cornell—another instance in which "understanding" seemed to bypass any conscious awareness: "A particular plant was heterozygous with respect to a translocation; that is, one chromosome carried the translocation, while the homologous chromosome was normal. According to meiotic segregation, it would normally give pollen grains which would be 50 percent defective

[hence sterile] and 50 percent normal. We had at that time a post doc who had just started working with translocations. He was examining pollen from these plants, expecting them to be either perfect [having no translocations] or to be heterozygous [where 50 percent of the pollen would be sterile]. He came to me and said, 'There are some plants that are 25 to 30 percent sterile, *not* 50 percent sterile.' He told me this in the field and he was disturbed." McClintock was disturbed too—so much so that she left the field, down in the hollow, and walked up to her laboratory. There she sat for about thirty minutes, "just thinking about it, and suddenly I jumped up and ran down to the field. At the top of the field (everyone else was down at the bottom) I shouted, 'Eureka, I have it! I have the answer! I know what this 30 percent sterility is.' " When she got to the bottom of the hollow, the group of corn geneticists working there gathered around her, and she realized she couldn't provide the reasoning behind her insight. "Prove it," they said. "I sat down with a paper bag and a pencil and I started from scratch, which I had not done at all in my laboratory. It had all been done fast; the answer came, and I'd run. Now I worked it out step by step—it was an intricate series of steps—and I came out with what it was. [The post doc] looked at the material and it was exactly as I'd said it was, and it worked exactly as I'd diagrammed it. Now, why did I know, without having done a thing on paper? Why was I so sure that I could tell them with such excitement and just say, 'Eureka, I solved it!'?"

Perhaps the answer, once again, depends on the intimate and total knowledge she sought about each and every plant. A colleague once remarked that she could write the "autobiography" of each plant she worked with. Her respect for the unfathomable workings of the mind was matched by her regard for the complex workings of the plant, but she was confident that, with due attentiveness, she could trust the intuitions the one produced of the other. In the years to come, that confidence would become a source of vital sustenance.

BERTON ROUECHÉ
Annals of Medicine:
A Contemporary Touch

Roueché's distinguished medical writing derives from his journalistic background, a fund of medical knowledge, and a sense of the drama of medical research and scientific investigation. Roueché was born in Kansas City, Missouri, in 1911, earned a degree in journalism from the University of Missouri in 1933, and worked for the next decade as a reporter on Missouri's major newspapers. Since 1944 he has been a staff writer for The New Yorker; *many of his sixteen books are collections of his* New Yorker *articles and other writings, including* Eleven Blue Men, and Other Narratives of Medical Detection *(1953);* The Neutral Spirit: A Portrait of Alcohol *(1960); and* The Medical Detectives *(1980, vol. II, 1984). Roueché's many awards for medical writing include honors from the Lasker Foundation, the American Medical Association, and the American Academy of Arts and Letters.*

"A Contemporary Touch" is one of Roueché's characteristic medical detective stories, in which a team of dedicated—but never stereotyped—pathologists, lab technicians, nurses, and other public health officials collaborate to find the villain causing a mysterious outbreak of food poisoning in Steubenville, Ohio. With the drama of a detective story, Roueché recreates step by painstaking step of the investigation, and in the process of uncovering who done it tells readers a great deal about the nature of salmonella; the principles and practices of medical detection; and the social and economic as well as medical consequences of the epidemic.

1   Dr. Taylor—David N. Taylor, an Epidemic Intelligence Service officer attached to the Enteric Diseases Branch, Bacterial Diseases Division, of the national Centers for Disease Control, in Atlanta—pushed the telephone away and sat for a moment glancing over his notes. Then he gathered them up and walked down the long hall, the fifth-floor hall, to the office of his superior, Dr. Roger A. Feldman, the director of the Bacterial Diseases Division. That was around three o'clock in the afternoon of Wednesday, January 28, 1981. Dr. Feldman, a tall man with a pepper-and-salt beard, a wide smile, and a riveting eye, was at his desk, and he smiled Dr. Taylor into a chair. Dr. Taylor—slim, straight, neatly parted sandy hair, small sandy mustache, steel-rimmed glasses—is thirty-three years old and a product of Kenyon College, Harvard Medical School, and the London School of Hygiene and Tropical Medicine. He took out his notes and made his report. He had, he said, just received a call from an epidemiologist named Frank Holtzhauer, at the Ohio State Department of Health, in Columbus. Holtzhauer was calling for Dr. Thomas Halpin, the State Epidemiologist, and his call was a call for federal help in investigating a perplexing outbreak of gastroenteritis in the town of Steubenville. The outbreak had begun on December 10th with the illness and subsequent hospitalization of a five-month-old girl. Since then, in the course of the past six weeks, twelve more cases, both adults and children, had been reported to the local authorities, and it was expected that there were more to come. The nature of the outbreak had been established. The enteritis was bacterial in origin. Laboratory analysis of stool samples of the victims had shown the microorganism involved to be a member of the genus Salmonella and of the species known as *S. muenchen.* But that was all. There was no other apparent link between the several victims.

2   "Roger listened and smiled and nodded," Dr. Taylor says. "He asked a couple of questions. I knew he would be calling Dr. Halpin for a formal confirmation and for a formal invitation to intervene. But the handwriting was already on the wall. I was going to Steubenville."

Salmonellosis, as the disease caused by the Salmonella organism is properly   3
called, is the most frequent single cause of what is commonly called food
poisoning. It accounts for at least twenty-five per cent of the numberless
outbreaks of mingled nausea and vomiting, abdominal cramps, diarrhea, and
fever that occur in this and every other country every year. Its name com-
memorates the nineteenth-century American pathologist Daniel Elmer
Salmon, who first identified the genus, and it is a commemoration of international reach. "Bacteria of the genus Salmonella," Robert H. Rubin and Louis
Weinstein, both of the Harvard Medical School, noted in a 1977 mono-
graph, "are perhaps the most ubiquitous pathogens in nature, affecting, in a
worldwide distribution, not only man and his domestic animals but also
reptiles, wild mammals, birds, and even insects." The usual cause of human
salmonellosis is contaminated (and insufficiently cooked) beef, lamb, pork,
duck, turkey, chicken, or, particularly, eggs. Other causes include food or
drink contaminated by the excreta of infected animals or by tainted equipment. An outbreak in Boston's Massachusetts General Hospital in 1966 was
traced to contaminated carmine dye, a diagnostic staining material. The salmonellae are almost as various as they are abundant. Since 1941, when the
Danish bacteriologist Fritz Kauffmann perfected a serotyping technique by
which the different salmonellae could be specifically identified, the number of
species that make up the genus has grown from a handful to the hundreds.
Some twenty-two hundred distinct serotypes are now known. The names of
these (with two or three exceptions) indicate where they were first isolated—
S. moscow, for example, and S. panama, S. miami, S. senegal. Some of these are
still found only in their place of discovery, but most have long since achieved
a cosmopolitan prevalence. The ten most frequently reported serotypes in the
United States (as of 1979) are S. typhimurium/copenhagen, S. enteritidis, S.
heidelberg, S. newport, S. infantis, S. agona, S. saintpaul, S. typhi, S. montevideo,
and S. oranienburg. S. javiana is No. 11. No. 12 is S. muenchen.

"S. muenchen wasn't much of a clue," Dr. Taylor says. "A really uncommon—a   4
relatively localized—serotype can make things somewhat easier. At least conceivably, it can tell you where to look, and even what to look for as the source
of contamination. But S. muenchen turns up everywhere—all over the country, all over the world. Around three hundred and fifty cases are reported to
the C.D.C. every year. So I was prepared for some hard work, for plenty of
old-fashioned shoe-leather epidemiology. I should say we were prepared. I
had an assistant—a fourth-year medical student at Duke who was assigned to
the C.D.C. for a term as a sort of interne. A very bright guy named Emmett
Schmidt. Emmett and I left the next morning—Thursday morning—by
plane for Pittsburgh. We rented a car there and drove on down to Steubenville. Steubenville is in the eastern part of the state, across the Ohio River
from West Virginia. I come from Ohio. I was raised in Columbus. But

Steubenville was an Ohio I had never seen before. It's a mill town—a steel town, down in a deep valley, very old and very run-down. I don't know—maybe it was the time of year, the dead of winter, or because most of the mills were barely running and everybody was out of work, but I've never seen a more depressing place. It took the heart out of me.

5   "There was a Holiday Inn. We registered there and then drove around to the city Health Department and met some of the people we would be working with. We met Maurice Pizzoferrato, the Steubenville Commissioner of Health, and two state epidemiologists—Charlene Steris and Robert Campbell—and Janice Schrader, a microbiologist. It was Janice who had determined that the cause of the outbreak was Salmonella, later serotyped in Columbus as *S. muenchen*. The first thing we learned was that the outbreak was still going on. I've forgotten just how many new cases there were—I didn't keep a daily report card. But I can tell you the total. By the time the outbreak had finally run its course, we had thirty-six confirmed cases. Janice Schrader was a remarkable person. She was doing *all* the laboratory work for the whole area, and she was still able to find time to help us every way she could. She was a big help in working out our game plan and getting it into action. She seemed to know just about everybody in town. She was involved, she cared about what had happened. Charlene briefed us on the cases—age, sex, date of onset. The incubation period for salmonellosis is about three days. The date of the appearance of symptoms indicates the approximate time of exposure and can often indicate its place and nature. We learned that the outbreak was, on the whole, pretty severe. There is no treatment for salmonellosis. Antibiotics tend to do more harm than good. But eighty per cent of the affected children here were sick enough to be hospitalized, and about sixty-five per cent of the adult cases. The age range was enormous. It stretched from a one-month-old boy to a woman of seventy-three. It was hard to know what that signified. The cases were scattered all over town, and only a few of them even knew each other. In such outbreaks, there is always a common denominator—an eating place, a wedding reception, a picnic, a dinner party, a church social. Something in which everybody was involved. This one was a total mystery.

6   "We formed two teams. I joined up with Charlene, and Emmett worked with Bob Campbell. There was nothing to do but start almost from scratch—to start visiting households of the patients. I was especially interested in the first two cases reported—the five-month-old girl and a twenty-five-year-old man. That was because the baby's father—a man I'll call Frank Lowell—was bosom buddies with the second case, whom I'll call Gene Russell. And then there was Case No. 3, a close friend of both Lowell and Russell. He was a twenty-seven-year-old man I'll call Paul James. Russell was out of work, but Lowell and James both had jobs on a municipal garbage truck. The three of them had been friends since high school. My thinking was this: Young guys, young couples, do things together, so let's see what the Lowells, the Russells,

and the Jameses do for recreation. They all lived in the same neighborhood, down by the river. We decided to start with Mrs. Lowell. It's easier to talk to the mother of a sick infant than to a sick adult. The mother cares, the adult tends to shrug it off. Mrs. Lowell was sort of typical—twenty-seven years old, pretty face, overweight. And very nervous. Her house was old and rundown, but it was scrubbed clean. Not a speck of dust. The baby's illness seemed to embarrass her, as though it reflected on her as a mother and a housekeeper. She didn't see how a thing like food poisoning could have happened in *her* house. I asked about formulas, about Christmas or holiday foods. There was a famous outbreak of *S. eastbourne* that involved contaminated chocolate Christmas candy. I asked about deli meats—a notorious vehicle. About restaurant meals. All dead ends. The Lowells couldn't afford to eat in restaurants or patronize delis. During the holidays, they had eaten turkey, ham, and some venison. Gene Russell had shot a deer, and dressed it himself at home. They rarely went out. They sometimes played cards with the Jameses and the Russells, or just hung out together.

"So Charlene and I moved on down the street to the Russells," Dr. Taylor went on. "Same kind of household—father, mother, two-month-old boy. Russell was out of work and at home. But this wasn't like the Lowell house. These people were relaxed. Mrs. Russell said that she hadn't been sick, and neither had the baby, even though later tests showed that both had been infected. And Russell himself was the picture of unconcern: 'Gee, Doc, I don't know what happened. I got sick, but I feel O.K. now. What do you think it was, Doc? Could it have been that deer? I shot it out near an old abandoned dump. But, what the hell, it's all over now.' Another dead end. It was the same with the Jameses, around the corner. James was at work and his wife was at home with two children—a boy of five and a daughter of six. James and the boy had been sick, and were treated at the Ohio Valley Hospital. The Jameses hung out with the Lowells and the Russells, played cards, drank a little beer. Had a ham for Christmas. That was interesting. I had never thought of ham as a holiday food, but everybody around here seemed to eat it at Christmastime. I filed the thought away. And on we went, from house to house, still fishing, still getting nowhere. But two things did take shape—three, including those Christmas-ham dinners. The first thing was that the cases seemed to fall into three groups. There were the blue-collar cases down in the valley. There were a couple of middle-class cases up on the hill, in a neighboring village called Wintersville. And there were some cases in a middle-class neighborhood of a suburb called Mingo Junction. Which, of course, was the reverse of helpful. It simply made things more mysterious.

"The other finding was a little more positive. It was only a statistic, but it had the feel of something solid. This was the age breakdown. The largest single age group in the outbreak was the one between twenty and twenty-nine. That group accounted for twenty-eight per cent of the cases. But the national average of salmonella outbreaks in that group is just twelve per cent.

This suggested that something a little different was happening here. Why the prevalence of young adults? Was there a preponderance of families of young adults in Steubenville? We decided to find out. So we picked out a set of controls. We selected at random thirty-two households in the neighborhoods of our established cases and called them up. What was the makeup of the household? And—aha! It was *not* usual in Steubenville to find a young adult in every family. All our case households included persons aged from fifteen to thirty-five, but only forty-one per cent of the randomly selected households included persons in that age range. Well, now we had a common denominator. Maybe not *the* common denominator but *a* common denominator. The next question was: What do young adults do? Where do they go? Bars. Fast-food places. We went back to shoe leather, walking the streets. Nothing came of it. These people still didn't have any haunts in common.

9   "There were two cases up in Wintersville. Both were students—a seventeen-year-old boy and an eighteen-year-old girl—at the local Catholic high school. The boy was in the hospital. The girl had been treated in the emergency room and sent home. We talked to the boy, and he gave us the story of his life. Video games. Pizza parlors. A few private parties. We talked to the girl's parents. The mother had a theory: her daughter had been poisoned by frozen king crab. I thought of the Lowells and the Russells and the Jameses. They had probably never even heard of king crab. And then the girl's mother seemed to finish things off. She said that her daughter and the boy in the hospital moved in entirely different circles and hardly knew each other.

10   "I'm going to go back a few days now," Dr. Taylor continued. "The morning that Emmett and I left Atlanta, I had had a few words with Roger Feldman, in the Bacterial Diseases Division, and he showed me a yellow office-memo slip. It said, 'S. *muenchen,* Michigan.' It was dated about a week earlier. Roger told me what it meant: Michigan had reported an outbreak of S. *muenchen* and wanted to know if the C.D.C. had had any similar reports. Roger said he had told them about Steubenville. He would pass my reports along to them. O.K. So on the way back down the hill to the Holiday Inn after that wasted day in Wintersville, I got to thinking about that Michigan outbreak. S. *muenchen* is common enough, but still . . . Back at the motel, I called a man I knew in the Michigan State Department of Health named Harry McGee. Harry told me they had twenty-odd cases, all with onset dates much like ours here, and all were in Lansing. Not in East Lansing, the university town, but in Lansing, the blue-collar auto town. They hadn't a clue to the source. Eight of the cases were young adults, and nine or ten were babies—infants—which meant that they were in households that included young adults. I began to get a little excited. I thanked Harry and called Roger Feldman. I told him the situation here, that we were stymied. The people were getting tired of us. The Health Commissioner wanted the case solved and cleared up and ended—he had all the eating places in town on his back. I suggested that a trip to

Lansing and a look at those very similar cases might give us a new perspective. Or something. Roger said no. He said to stay where we were. He said that the answer was there and that we'd find it. And to let him know when we did. That was on Thursday, February 5th. It was snowing. The charm of motel life fades very quickly. Emmett and I were homesick for our wives, who kept asking when we were ever coming home. We went out in the snow and found a new place to eat and had another awful dinner. Then we went back to the motel. We stared at our data, turning it this way and that, until about 2 A.M. And the only item that meant a thing was all those young adults.

"We started out the next morning on a new tack. I still had ham on my mind—those holiday ham dinners. So we decided to settle the question one way or another. Commissioner Pizzoferrato lent us one of his department's sanitarians, and with him as our guide we undertook a tour of the city's meat markets. We picked up samples of different kinds of ham at each place, and Janice Schrader would culture them for possible salmonellae. Most of the markets were ethnic—Polish, Italian, Greek. Steubenville is that kind of town. The proprietors were a little suspicious. They didn't want to get involved in food poisoning. But we got what we wanted. And, all in all, it was a pretty dull tour. There was one incident. It was at the third place we visited. As we were leaving, a young woman came in. Pretty but bedraggled. She was crying, her eye makeup was smeared, and she was acting strange. Stoned. Spaced out. Something. The proprietor went over to her and soothed her, and she left. It was sort of sad, and we talked about it on the way to the next market. Was she drunk? Or was she on drugs? The sanitarian said something about a relationship between unemployment and drugs and alcohol. Looking around Steubenville—those crippled mills, all that depression—I could believe him. Anyway, we finished up and took our samples to Janice. And that, as it turned out, was the end of the ham idea. The cultures all were negative.

"Emmett and I had dinner that night with Janice. We ate at an Italian place she knew about, and for once it wasn't bad, and we sat there afterward, drinking coffee and shooting the breeze about what the heck was going on. We got to talking about those first three families—the Lowells and the Russells and the Jameses. In case you've forgotten, the outbreak was still not over. We were still getting new cases, and all the cases, new and old, were being monitored once a week. Their stool samples came to Janice, and she cultured them. Well, Janice said we might be interested to know that one of the cases had just been cleared. That was Mrs. Russell. For the first time, her weekly sample was negative. The rest of her family was still positive, and so were the Jameses and the Lowells. It *was* interesting. We wondered why her. Janice said that Mrs. Russell was also pregnant. Maybe that had something to do with it. Then we broke up, and Emmett and I went back to the motel. I remember that Emmett called his wife and they talked and talked, and he mentioned the woman in the meat market and they talked about drugs.

When he hung up, we started talking about drugs. I was thinking of tranquil-lizers and Quaaludes and things like that—drugs in capsules that could get contaminated in processing or packaging. It was a thought.

13   "It still seemed like a good idea in the morning. Janice had mentioned Mrs. Russell, and she seemed as good a place as any to start. We went around to the Russell place right after breakfast, at about nine o'clock. Mrs. Russell received us. Russell was still in bed—and why not? He was out of work and it was a dismal morning. We asked Mrs. Russell once again about food, about mixes, about condiments. We did a thorough kitchen inventory, and it was the kind of kitchen you wouldn't be surprised to find any kind of contamina-tion in. These were real easygoing people—not like Mrs. Lowell. But that was all just thrashing around. Finally, I got down to business and asked her if she or anybody in the family was taking any kind of drugs. She said, 'You mean like medicine? Oh, no.' What about the other kind—illicit drugs? Like, say, 'ludes? 'Oh, *no*—certainly not.' Then there was a funny kind of silence. Then she said, 'Well, Gene and I and most of our friends, we do smoke a little pot when we're hanging out together. But I stopped last week. I mean, I'm pregnant, so I thought I'd better.' Pot? Marijuana? I was thinking capsules—swallowing something contaminated. Pot was smoking. I didn't know what to think. And then Russell came strolling into the living room. I guess he'd waked up and heard us talking. He was very cool, very relaxed. He said, 'Sure, we smoke a little pot. What else is there to do in this town?' I was still trying to think, to adjust. I asked him very carefully if he happened to have any marijuana on hand—if I could have a sample for laboratory analysis. He looked at me for a moment. Then he said, 'Sure.' He said, 'Man, I'll roll you a joint.' I told him just a sample for the lab would do. But I was aware of what he was doing. To him and his wife, Emmett and I were some kind of Feds. He wanted to get me involved. He wanted to get me neutralized. Anyway, he just shrugged and laughed, and went off somewhere and came back with a couple of grams in an envelope—about enough for one joint. Emmett and I exchanged a look. We finally, at last, had something concrete. It was a weird idea. I had never heard of marijuana as a vehicle for salmonella. Nobody had. But it was an idea. It was concrete, and I had it in my hand.

14   "Our next move was going to be a little more difficult. Russell had nothing much to lose—he was unemployed, and who cared if he smoked a little pot? But that wasn't true of most of the other cases. The Lowells and the Jameses were city employees. It was going to be hard to get anything out of them. I decided that our best move was through Russell. I explained to him that our interest in marijuana had nothing to do with the law. Emmett and I weren't any kind of police. We had no intention of getting him or anybody else in trouble. We were only trying to get at the source of the outbreak. We rapped like that for a little while, and then I said that we would need to talk to the other cases, including his friends the Lowells and the Jameses. I won-

dered if he would try to sort of pave the way for us. Would he mind calling Mrs. Lowell? Be glad to. He went to the phone and called her. He was very good, very persuasive. You remember that she was a very nervous, worrying kind of woman. But she agreed to see us. We went right over. She was very stiff and strained. I guess this was as close as she had ever come to a drug bust. But she was making an effort to be calm and sophisticated. She said, well, yes, they did smoke pot. She said, well, yes, they did have some in the house. She went off and came back with about two grams in a plastic bag. She said it came from the same guy that the Jameses and the Russells bought their pot from. She asked me if I really thought that the outbreak was caused by pot. I said it seemed to be a possibility. 'Well,' she said, 'I'm not really surprised. I thought this batch had a kind of funny smell.' That made me smile. But I really wanted to shout. A possibility, of course, was all it was. But it was a possibility that seemed to fit in very nicely with that preponderance of young adults. We were cooking. We were really cooking.

"But down here in this blue-collar valley, down here by the river—this was only one neighborhood, only one part of the outbreak. There was Mingo Junction, and there was Wintersville, up on the hill. When we made our first round of house calls, we had talked to a young woman at Mingo Junction— Linda Something-or-Other. She was the one confirmed case there, but her brother and her boyfriend were both subclinical cases—positive but asymptomatic. Linda was twenty-one, a salesgirl in a nut shop by day and a dancing teacher evenings. She never had any reason to go down to the valley. She took sick on December 28th. She lived at home but very seldom ate there. She told us she lived on tacos, submarine sandwiches, and such. When we finished up with Mrs. Lowell, we went out to Mingo and ran Linda down again and had a talk. Pot? She said she never used it. Her brother did, though, and so did her friend. She thought she could get us a sample from her friend. We arranged to meet that evening. Then we went on to Wintersville. We got nowhere with the two high-school kids. We had to be careful, and they weren't telling: getting caught using pot meant expulsion from school. But I talked with a counsellor at the school, and he told me that while our two kids moved in different circles, the circles they moved in were very far from the best. We met Linda and her friend that evening, and they had a nice sample for us. I don't know how Emmett and I got through Saturday night. We were really keyed up. I called Janice on Sunday morning and told her what we had, and she agreed to meet us at her lab. Very quietly. This was ticklish business at this point—we didn't know how the Health Department would react. On Monday afternoon, Janice told us that preliminary results showed evidence of contaminated pot—all three samples. By Tuesday, it was definite. She had cultured salmonellae from the samples, and they were salmonellae of a group of eighty-odd serotypes called C/2. C/2 includes *S. muenchen*. On Wednesday, Janice went on to make it certain: our marijuana samples were definitely contaminated with *S. muenchen*. But on Tuesday morning the C/2 finding was enough. I called Roger Feldman, and he said, 'Well, well! I'll be damned!'

16 "Maurice Pizzoferrato had very much the same reaction. Only more so. Roger was naturally pleased that we had solved the problem, and as a professional he was very much interested that we had found a new vehicle for salmonellae. But Maurice! Maurice was euphoric. He had been getting very edgy, very impatient. His lab was tied up, his people were on call to us, and all the eating places in town were on his phone every day and afraid of hearing the worst. And, of course, the press was pressing. Marijuana was an absolutely perfect answer. It took him entirely off the hook. Illicit drugs were no responsibility of his. He wanted the world to know what we had found. He wanted me to call an immediate press conference. And Roger, when I asked him for instructions, agreed. Emmett and I worked up a statement, and the conference was set for ten o'clock on Wednesday morning, February 11th, in Maurice's office at the Health Department. They even had me sitting in Maurice's own big chair, at his own big desk.

17 "It was my début in this sort of thing. All the media were there—the local newspaper, the local radio, the local television, and the stringers for the wire services. I read our statement. I told them that the source of the outbreak wasn't water, it wasn't any eating place, it wasn't any food. I told them—and this is from our prepared statement—'Our most important lead suggests that a noncommercial product with an unknown distribution is the source of this salmonella. We have tested samples of marijuana associated with three different cases, and we have found the identical salmonella which has been isolated from the ill persons. This finding suggests that the marijuana currently in use in Jefferson County has become contaminated with salmonella and represents the primary vehicle of transmission for the illness.' I told them that having diarrhea caused by salmonella didn't necessarily mean that the person was a *user* of marijuana. Many of our cases, I said, were infected indirectly from a person who was a silent carrier, or from environmental sources. The salmonella was in the marijuana. When a marijuana smoker rolled a cigarette, his hands became contaminated, and when he put the cigarette in his mouth his lips became contaminated. Then a touch or a kiss or any sort of contact could spread the infection. I said we didn't know yet just how heavily contaminated the marijuana was—actually, it turned out to be *very* heavily contaminated—but even a light contamination would be enough to make a susceptible person sick. And not only that. Pot decreases the gastric acid, and gastric acid is an important defense against infections of all kinds. Regular pot smokers are especially susceptible to infection. Then came the tricky part. Here's what I said in our statement: 'To substantiate our theory that marijuana is the culprit, it is most important that we continue to

test marijuana samples from the area. If it were a commercial product, we could just pull it off the shelves and test it—but that is not possible with marijuana. We therefore need the community to help us by allowing us to test additional marijuana samples. People may drop off their samples either at the Jefferson County Center for Alcoholism and Drug Abuse . . . or the samples may be brought directly to Steubenville City Health Department. Because we think this is a major health risk, we are testing marijuana free and anonymously. Your sample will be given a number . . .' And so on. The police had agreed to look the other way for a day or two. Then came the questions. I did the best I could. It was really very exciting. A big story. And not only locally. Both the wire services carried it. It wasn't so much that we had solved the mystery. It was the marijuana. That gave it a contemporary touch.

"That was our last day in Steubenville. There was no reason for Emmett and me to stay on for the windup of the investigation. We flew back to Atlanta that afternoon. I had a day at home—Thursday, February 12th—and then on Friday Roger sent me off to Michigan. I wasn't exactly eager to leave, and yet, of course, I wanted to go. I felt that Steubenville was only one side of the coin. I didn't feel that we had absolutely proved our case. What I wanted was what I had wanted before—to do a good case-control study. Our studies in Steubenville weren't really precise. The supreme court for an epidemiological problem is a case-control study, and I wanted that supreme-court verdict. As I said, my contact in Michigan was Harry McGee, of the Michigan State Department of Health. Nothing had really changed in Lansing since Harry and I last talked. There was a total of seventeen confirmed cases. The source of the outbreak was still unknown. But now, after Steubenville, we had a lead to work with. The study went like this: We selected thirty-four households to serve as controls. These households matched the case households in neighborhood and in general social and economic status, and they had much the same prevalence of young children and young adults. The one crucial difference was that the controls were households in which there had been no diarrheal illness for at least two months. We did our interviews in person. People respond to a personal visit with trust. We asked a comprehensive set of questions. We asked about restaurant meals. About deli foods. About alcohol. And then about marijuana. The results were very satisfactory. The case households used marijuana more than three times as often as the control households. We also collected eight samples of marijuana from six households. Only one of them was positive for salmonella—for *S. muenchen*. But that was enough.

"I went back to Atlanta feeling very pleased. The news there made me feel even better. The final reports from Steubenville were in. The public appeal has brought in fifty-four new samples of marijuana, and five of them were positive for *S. muenchen*. Then came some totally unexpected news:

18

19

There had been two outbreaks of *S. muenchen* gastroenteritis that were more or less coincident with Steubenville and Lansing—one in Alabama, involving two cases, and another in Georgia, in and around Atlanta, involving twenty-one cases. When the health people there saw our first Steubenville report, they sat up in a hurry. They went back to their cases and interviewed them all over again and collected some samples of marijuana and analyzed them, and the results were positive for *S. muenchen* contamination. The contamination in every instance was very considerable. It was almost incredible—four million organisms to a gram of marijuana. That was so high that it enabled us to make a very reasonable assumption. This was that the contamination could not have occurred by accident—by contamination on the hands of the processors. It must have occurred either in the field—from untreated animal manure used as fertilizer, or by contamination during drying or storage—or by direct adulteration of the marijuana with dried manure, to increase the weight and therefore increase the profits. We generally favor the last hypothesis. A good reason for this theory was that *S. muenchen* was not the only contaminating pathogen found in the marijuana. All the samples also showed the presence of such organisms as *Staphylococcus epidermidis, E. coli, K. pneumoniae, Ps. aeruginosa,* and Group D *Streptococci,* which would also be present in manure. Our only disappointment was that we were never able to determine where the stuff came from. The Drug Enforcement Administration of the Department of Justice estimated that in 1980 about seventy-five per cent of the marijuana consumed in the United States came from Colombia, about ten per cent from Jamaica, and about eight per cent from Mexico, and that the rest is grown locally. Locally grown marijuana is consumed locally, and Mexican marijuana is consumed largely in the Southwest. So we can assume that our marijuana came from either Colombia or Jamaica.

20   "There was one last piece of news. Samples of the marijuana collected in Ohio, in Michigan, in Alabama, and in Georgia were passed along to the C.D.C. They were then turned over to a research microbiologist in the microbiology laboratory in the Enterobacteriology Branch. She was Dr. Kaye Wachsmuth. She examined the samples by a very delicate technique developed in 1975 as a research tool by Stanley Falkow and his associates at the University of Washington, in Seattle. What Kaye did was to apply this technique for the first time to an epidemic situation. To put it very simply, the cultured *S. muenchen* is broken down and its DNA is extracted and the molecular weights of its parts are measured. These weights are distinguished by a pattern of plasmid banding. Different strains of *S. muenchen*—and every other serotype—have different banding patterns: different, as we say, plasmid fingerprints. Kaye examined all our samples and compared the results with the fingerprints of other—non-marijuana—*S. muenchen* strains. All the marijuana *S. muenchen* were identical, and distinctly different from the non-marijuana strains. That was the ultimate confirmation. That was the final touch. That put the icing on the cake."

Questions

1. Summarize the extensive process of medical detection that RouEché presents here. Why does he describe it in such detail?

2. Why does the detection of a public health menace require a team of investigators of diverse specialties, as well as the cooperation of the victims? What is the point of pursuing such an investigation after the outbreak of disease has apparently died down?

3. Why would *New Yorker* readers (or anyone else) want to read about this detective process? How does Rouéché manage to combine a great deal of scientific information with the format and pace of a detective story? Do the two blend well together? Explain.

4. Compare the investigative style of "the medical detectives" described here with Barbara McClintock's painstaking research over forty years in "a feeling for the organism" (678–81). How much and what kind of information does one need to know before one can have an "aha"—intuitive—understanding of the overt evidence that leads to theory, or to an understanding of the fundamentals, or to some creative synthesis of evidence that goes beyond just the facts at hand? How comparable is the "aha" experience to creative insight in art, literature, music, or some other humanistic area—either in interpretation or performance?

The Social Sciences

EDWARD T. HALL

Time Talks

Hall, an anthropologist, professor, and author, has done field work among the Hopi, the Navajo, Hispanic-Americans, Europeans, and Micronesians, but he nevertheless maintains, "The ultimate reason for such study is to learn more about how one's own system works." Hall was born in Webster Groves, Missouri, in 1914; earned a B.A. from the University of Denver in 1936, an M.A. from the University of Arizona in 1938, and a Ph.D. from Columbia in 1942. After directing various anthropological field studies, and State Department training programs, Hall became president of Overseas Training and Research (1955– 60), and then taught at Illinois Institute of Technology (1963–67) and at Northwestern (1967–77). His cross-cultural research has resulted in perceptive analyses of how people use space, time, gestures, posture, and other features of nonverbal communication to say a great deal—and how the cultural context dictates the interpretation. His books include The Hidden Dimension *(1966),* Handbook for Proxemic Research *(1975),* The Fourth Dimension in Architecture *(1975),* Beyond Culture *(1976), and* The Silent Language *(1959), the classic from which the chapter on "Time Talks" is reprinted below.*

The entire essay is an extended definition of different concepts of time—formal, informal, and technical—each with its own vocabulary, concepts, and meanings that make sense in particular contexts, especially when contrasted or compared with examples from other cultures, whether diverse areas or populations (such as Mormons or Hopi Indians) of the United States or abroad. "Informal time," for instance, is vague "because it is situational in character"; "eternity" may be "the time it takes to hit the water" when first jumping from a high diving board, or a month spent away from one's family. Without being condescending or overly technical, Hall conveys very sophisticated concepts with clarity, grace, and wit.

1   At the beginning of this book I offered a cursory analysis of time as an element of culture which communicates as powerfully as language. Since my conceptual scheme had not yet been developed in detail at that point my survey was of necessity rather sketchy. Now that I have presented the technical tools for probing the secrets of culture, I return to time again. Here I shall consider the way Americans use time and communicate by it, stressing the details and the subtleties which close analysis turns up. Some of the points I make may arouse a shock of recognition, a feeling that here is something which the reader knew all along. This is the way it should be. The analysis of one's own culture simply makes explicit the many things we take for granted in our everyday lives. Talking about them, however, changes our relation with them. We move into an active and understanding correspondence with those aspects of our existence which are all too frequently taken for granted or which sometimes weigh heavily on us. Talking about them frees us from their restraint.

A well-known authority on children in the United States once stated that 2
it took the average child a little more than twelve years to master time. This
estimate is probably somewhat conservative. Young people of this age know
how our basic time system works but do not yet seem to have fully inter-
nalized either the details or the emotional overtones of the formal time
system.

Why does it take a child so long to learn time? The answer is not simple. 3
In fact, when one begins to discover how many complications are involved he
may wonder whether the full subtleties of time can be mastered at all.

The three systems I have discussed—formal, informal, technical—often 4
use identical items of vocabulary. This does not make it any easier for the
child, or the foreigner, to learn them. The year, for instance, is a *formal* or
traditional part of our time system. It means three hundred sixty-five days
plus one fourth day which is accounted for by inserting leap year. It can also
mean twelve months, as well as fifty-two weeks.

Informally, we may say, "Oh, it takes years to get that done." You have to 5
be there and know the person and the background of the remark before you
know exactly what his word "years" means. It may be a matter of minutes,
weeks, or actual years. *Technically,* the year is quite another thing again. Not
only is it counted in days, hours, minutes, seconds, but there are different
types of years of different lengths. Minutes, hours, months, and weeks are
also used in all three contexts. It is only the total context that tells which type
of time is being referred to.

Almost anyone can recapture that moment of his childhood when the 6
day was almost spent and Mother was asked, "Mommy, how long will it be
before we get home? I'm tired." And Mother replies, "Just a little while, dear.
Now you just be good and before you know it we'll be home."

"How long is a while?" "It's hard to say, dear." "Is a while five minutes, 7
Mommy?" "Sometimes, dear, but not always. In this case it will be a little
longer than five minutes." "Oh."

At this point the child gives up—for the time being at least. 8

Not only are there three different categories of time, but each has its own 9
subdivisions; its sets, its isolates, and its patterns, which make nine different
types of time found for our culture. Fortunately, to simplify matters, the
layman need not know the whole technical system in order to get along. Yet
he depends upon others to know it.

The layman, for example, thinking he is getting technical, may ask an 10
astronomer exactly how long a year is. At which point he discovers his own
ignorance by being asked what kind of year he has in mind—the tropical or
solar year (365 days, 5 hours, 48 minutes, 45.51 seconds plus a fraction); the
sidereal year (365 days, 6 hours, 9 minutes, 9.54 seconds); or the anomalistic
year (365 days, 6 hours, 13 minutes, 53.1 seconds).

Our formal time system is that part of the over-all system which we 11
would not change and don't want others tampering with. Yet this formal

system we take so much for granted was once a technical system known only to a few priests along the Nile who had perfected it in response to a need to forecast annual floods more accurately.

Formal Time: Sets, Isolates, and Patterns

12 A quick way to discover how our European time sets operate is to teach them to children. The day is a formal set deeply rooted in the past. It has two primary isolates, day and night, and is further broken down into morning and afternoon, punctuated by meals and naps, and other recurrent occasions. There are seven different categories of days: Monday, Tuesday, Wednesday, etc. They are valued differently, Sunday being set apart. The child is usually in control of these notions by the age of six. At eight most children learn to tell time by the clock. This process can be simplified for them if it is explained that there are two types of time (two categories of sets): hours and minutes. The hours—one to twelve—have to be learned so well that recognition is instantaneous. Before learning the minutes the child learns that the quarter hour is the isolate most useful to him. He can grasp these quite quickly: five-fifteen, five-thirty, and five forty-five begin to make sense. Minutes should not be taught as isolates first but as sets, of which there are sixty. However, to make life a little simpler since the child can't perceive a minute, these cluster together in five-minute periods; five, ten, and fifteen after the hour, right on up to five fifty-five. Finally, the two sets of sets are blended into one system.

13 In America any Easterner or urban Middle Westerner conversant with the way his own culture values time can perceive that five minutes is different from ten minutes. That is, the five-minute period is the smallest formal set. It has only recently crossed the boundary from isolate to set. Twenty years ago the five-minute period was an isolate of a particular type that went to make up the quarter hour. Now people are aware of whether they are five minutes late or not and will apologize.

14 In Utah the Mormons have developed promptness to a degree that is unknown in the rest of the country. In their system the minutes would seem to be an inviolate set. On the northwest coast the traditional feelings about time are altered and are not experienced in as pressing a manner as they are elsewhere. The Northwest uses the same time structure as the rest of the country, but nobody seems particularly driven by it. The main difference is that they lack the informal isolate of urgency.

15 Above the five-minute period there is the *ten*-minute period, the quarter hour, the half hour, and the hour. Then there is the morning divided into early, middle, and late; the noon hour; early, mid- and late afternoon; and evening, as well as similar divisions for the nighttime.

16 Formally, our day starts at midnight. The periods set off by meals and by sleeping and waking are probably the earliest of the perceived temporal sets for children. Television is speeding up the process of helping children to notice the difference between, say, five o'clock and six o'clock, since these are the times when their pet programs come on.

The week is also a set, introduced as a part of the Egyptian's technical   17
time system. It is not, however, universally grasped. The term fortnight, like
many other Anglo-Saxon survivals, remains present in the system, a reminder
of earlier times. It is still used as the pay period in the government and as a
publication period for certain periodicals. It is, however, a bit archaic and is
slowly falling into disuse. The month, like the day, is a set that has been
established as a component in our time system for a long time. It is used for
payments and rendering of accounts, reports of almost every type, and jail
sentences.

The season is both a formal set and an informal one. It is probably one of   18
the oldest of our sets. It used to mark plowing, planting, cultivating and
harvesting time, as well as the time when the soil could rest. Now, of course,
there are hunting, fishing, skiing, tourist, or Christmas seasons, as well as the
traditional summer, fall, winter, spring class of sets. The season and the
quarter are probably related, although the quarter is tied to the calendar while
the season, being older, is rooted in climatic changes and activities associated
with agriculture.

Formal isolates are difficult to pin down. Like all isolates, they are ab-   19
stractions, yet because they are formal abstractions which seem right and
proper little attention has been paid to them. They are often overlooked
because they seem so "natural."

The list of true isolates which follows is undoubtedly incomplete. It   20
includes what I call ordering, cyclicity, synthesisity, valuation, tangibility,
duration, and depth.

The week is the week not only because it has seven days but because they   21
are in a fixed *order*. Ordering as a formal isolate would seem to be an expression of *order* as in the laws of order, selection, and congruence. The Western
world has elaborated this to some extent. That is, we keep constant track of
all sorts of things which are otherwise identical and *only distinguish between
them because of their order*. The six millionth Ford built becomes a milestone,
as does the fifty millionth passenger-mile flown by an airplane. The first-born,
first president, first position, the number-two man, the tenth in a class of one
thousand assume meaning because of their order. The seventh day is different
from the first day; the middle of the week is different from the end, and so on.

For most temporal events the *cyclic* element is taken for granted. One day   22
follows the next, as does the week, month, year, and century. The common
cycles are limited in number. The sixty-cycle series (minutes and seconds) the
seven-day week, and the twelve-month year.

Valuation is expressed in our attitude that time itself is valuable and   23
should not be wasted.

Tangibility is expressed in the fact that we consider time is a commodity.   24
It can be bought, sold, saved, spent, wasted, lost, made up, and measured.

For people raised in the European tradition time is something that oc-   25
curs between two points. *Duration* is the most widely shared implicit assumption concerning the nature of time in the Western world. It seems inconceiv-

able to those of us who have learned to take this one isolate so much for granted that it would be possible to organize life in any other way. Yet one of the miracles of human existence is the tremendous variety that occurs in such basic matters as this. For instance, the Hopi are separated from us by a tremendous cultural gulf. Time, for example, is not duration but many different things for them. It is not fixed or measurable as we think of it, nor is it a quantity. It is what happens when the corn matures or a sheep grows up—a characteristic sequence of events. It is the natural process that takes place while living substance acts out its life drama. Therefore, there is a different time for everything which can be altered by circumstances. One used to see Hopi houses that were in the process of being built for years and years. Apparently the Indians had no idea that a house could or should be built in a given length of time since they could not attribute to it its own inherent time system such as the corn and the sheep had. This way of looking at time cost the government untold thousands of dollars on construction projects because the Hopi could not conceive of there being a fixed time in which a dam or a road was supposed to be built. Attempts to get them to meet a schedule were interpreted as browbeating and only made things worse.

26   It was mentioned earlier that in contrast to some of the African systems, the components of American time—the minutes, the hours—have to add up. Americans start with the assumption that they are working with a *synthesized* system. Basically the reason why time has to add up is that we start with the assumption that we are dealing with a system and that there is order in the universe. We feel it is a man's job to discover the order and to create intellectual models that reflect it. We are driven by our own way of looking at things to synthesize almost everything. Whenever we have to deal with people whose time systems lack this isolate of synthesisity we experience great difficulty. To us it's almost as if they were missing one of their senses and were therefore unaware of part of nature. The synthesisity isolate is basic to most if not all of our appraisal of life around us.

27   Americans consider *depth* as a necessary component of time; that is, there is a past on which the present rests. Yet we have not elaborated the depth isolate to the extent that this has been done in the Middle East and South Asia. The Arab looks back two to six thousand years for his own origins. History is used as the basis for almost any modern action. The chances are that an Arab won't start a talk or a speech or analyze a problem without first developing the historical aspects of his subject. The American assumes that time has depth but he takes this for granted.

28   Most of the formal patterns of time in the United States will seem immediately obvious to the American reader though he may not have taken the trouble to think about them. They would not be formal patterns if they were not so easily recognized. But for the benefit of the foreign reader I will summarize briefly the American formal pattern.

29   The American never questions the fact that time should be planned and

future events fitted into a schedule. He thinks that people should look forward to the future and not dwell too much on the past. His future is not very far ahead of him. Results must be obtained in the foreseeable future—one or two years or, at the most, five or ten. Promises to meet deadlines and appointments are taken very seriously. There are real penalties for being late and for not keeping commitments in time. From this it can be surmised that the American thinks it is natural to quantify time. To fail to do so is unthinkable. The American specifies how much time it requires to do everything. "I'll be there in ten minutes." "It will take six months to finish that job." "I was in the Army for four and a half years."

The Americans, like so many other people, also use time as a link that chains events together. *Post hoc, ergo propter hoc* (after the fact, therefore because of the fact) is still an integral part of the traditional structure of our culture. The occurrence of one event on the heels of another results inevitably in attempts on our part to attribute the second to the first and to find a causal relationship between them. If A is seen in the vicinity of B's murder shortly after the crime has been committed we automatically form a connection between A and B. Conversely, events which are separated by too much time are difficult for us to connect in our minds. This makes it almost impossible for us as a nation to engage in long-range planning.

Informal Time: Sets, Isolates, and Patterns

To complicate matters for the young who are trying to learn the culture and the scientist who is trying to analyze it, the vocabulary of informal time is often identical with that of technical and formal time. Words such as minute, second, year are common to all three. The context usually tells the hearer which level of discourse is being used. There are, of course, words which are typically informal and are recognized as such (a while, later, a long time, etc.). In describing informal time we begin with the sets, because it is the set that is most easily perceived.

When a person says, "It'll take a while," you have to know him personally and also a good deal about the total context of the remark before you can say what the term "a while" means. Actually, it is not as vague as it seems at first, and people who have this information can usually tell what is meant. What is more, if a man whose normal "while" is thirty to forty-five minutes returns to his office after an hour, having said he would only be gone for "a while" he will usually apologize or make some remark about having been gone longer than he expected. This is proof that he himself realized that there was a limit to the degree to which you stretch "a while."

The basic vocabulary of informal time is simple. There are only eight or nine different distinctions made by Americans. It is as if we measured informal time with a rubber ruler which could be infinitely expanded or compressed but which would still maintain the integrity of the basic relationships. The shortest time on the informal scale is the "instantaneous event." The following additional distinctions are interposed between the "instantaneous event" and "forever": very short duration, short duration, neutral duration (neither noticeably short nor long), long duration, very long duration, and impossibly long duration. The last is sometimes indistinguishable from "forever."

34   In general, informal time is quite vague because it is situational in character. The circumstances vary, hence the measured time varies: The "longest time," "forever," and "an eternity" are all words or expressions which are used to describe any time which is experienced as being excessively drawn out. Depending on circumstances, "eternity" may be the time it takes to hit the water when one jumps from a high diving board for the first time, or it may be a month or two spent overseas away from one's family.

35   Informally, for important daytime business appointments in the eastern United States between equals, there are eight time sets in regard to punctuality and length of appointments: on time, five, ten, fifteen, twenty, thirty, forty-five minutes, and one hour early or late. Keeping in mind that situations vary, there is a slightly different behavior pattern for each point, and each point on the scale has a different meaning. As for the length of appointments an hour with an important person is different from thirty minutes with that same person. Ponder the significance of the remark, "He spent over an hour closeted with the President." Everyone knows the business must have been important. Or consider, "He could only spare ten minutes, so we didn't get much accomplished." Time then becomes a message as eloquently direct as if words were used. As for punctuality no right-minded American would think of keeping a business associate waiting for an hour; it would be too insulting. No matter what is said in apology, there is little that can remove the impact of an hour's heel-cooling in an outer office.

36   Even the five-minute period has its significant subdivisions. When equals meet, one will generally be aware of being two minutes early or late but will say nothing, since the time in this case is not significant. At three minutes a person will still not apologize or feel that it is necessary to say anything (three is the first significant number in the one-to-five series); at five minutes there is usually a short apology; and at four minutes before or after the hour the person will mutter something, although he will seldom complete the muttered sentence. The importance of making detailed observations on these aspects of informal culture is driven home if one pictures an actual situation. An American ambassador in an unnamed country interpreted incorrectly the significance of time as it was used in visits by local diplomats. An hour's tardiness in their system is equivalent to five minutes by ours, fifty to fifty-five minutes to four minutes, forty-five minutes to three minutes, and so on for daytime official visits. By their standards the local diplomats felt they couldn't arrive exactly on time; this punctuality might be interpreted locally as an act relinquishing their freedom of action to the United States. But they didn't want to be insulting—an hour late would be too late—so they arrived fifty

minutes late. As a consequence the ambassador said, "How can you depend on these people when they arrive an hour late for an appointment and then just mutter something? They don't even give you a full sentence of apology!" He couldn't help feeling this way, because in American time fifty to fifty-five minutes late is the insult period, at the extreme end of the duration scale; yet in the country we are speaking of it's just right.

For another way of apportioning informal time consider the eastern Mediterranean Arab. He makes fewer distinctions than we do. His scale has only three discernible points to our eight. His sets seem to be: no time at all; now (or present), which is of varying duration; and forever (too long). In the Arab world it is almost impossible to get someone to experience the difference between waiting a long time and a very long time. Arabs simply do not make this temporal distinction. 37

Informal time isolates will be more significant to the reader if he will sit back for a minute and think in some detail about times when he was aware that time was either passing very rapidly or else dragging. It may even be helpful if he will note what it was in the situation that made time behave the way it did. If he goes even further and thinks at length about how he was able to distinguish between a very short time and a long time regardless of the clock time, he will be well on the road to understanding how the American system works. What follows below merely attempts to simply put into words things that people know but have not formulated precisely. 38

Four isolates enable people to distinguish between the duration sets mentioned above. The most difficult of all to characterize, they are: urgency, monochronism, activity, and variety. 39

The impression of time as passing rapidly or slowly is related to *urgency*. The more urgent the need, the more time appears to drag. This applies to everything from basic physiological needs to culturally derived needs. A man who has an urgent need to succeed and reach the top will experience the passage of time on the way up with more anguish than will another man who is more relaxed about success. The parent with a sick child desperately in need of medical attention feels time moving very slowly; so does the farmer whose crops are withering for lack of rain. One could list many more examples. However, more to the point is what is not included when we consider urgency as an informal temporal isolate: First, urgency on different levels of analysis is both a set and a pattern. Second, our own variety of urgency distinguishes us from the rest of western European culture. A lack of a sense of urgency has been very apparent to Americans traveling abroad. 40

Even physiological urgency is handled quite differently by people around the world. In many countries people need less of what Americans would call urgency in order to discharge a tension. In the United States the need must be highly critical before people act. 41

The distribution of public toilets in America reflects our tendency to deny the existence of urgency even with normal physiological needs. I know 42 of no other place in the world where anyone leaving home or office is put to periodic torture because great pains have been taken to hide the location of rest rooms. Yet Americans are the people who judge the advancement of others by their plumbing. You can almost hear the architect and owner discussing a new store's rest room. Owner: "Say, this is nice! But why did you hide it? You'd need a map to find it." Architect: "I'm glad you like it. We went all out on this washroom, had a lot of trouble getting that tile to match. Did you notice the anti-splash aerated faucets on the wash basins? Yes, it would be a little hard to find, but we figure people wouldn't use it unless they had to, and then they could ask a clerk or something."

43   *Monochronism* means doing one thing at a time. American culture is characteristically *monochronic*. As Americans we find it disconcerting to enter an office overseas with an appointment only to discover that other matters require the attention of the man we are to meet. Our ideal is to center the attention first on one thing and then move on to something else.

44   North Europeans and those of us who share in this culture make a distinction between whether or not a person is engaged in an *activity*. In fact, we distinguish between the "active" and "dormant" phases of everything. I therefore refer to this isolate, in terms of its Latin root, as an *ageric* isolate (from *agere,* to act). Just plain sitting, trying to capture a sense of self, is not considered to be *doing anything*. Hence, such remarks as, "You didn't seem to be doing anything, so I thought I would stop in and talk to you for a while." The exception is, of course, prayer, which has special and easily identified postures associated with it.

45   In a number of other cultures, including the Navajo, Trukese, eastern Mediterranean Arab cultures, Japanese, and many of those of India, just plain sitting is doing something. The distinction between being active or not is not made. Thus there are ageric cultures and non-ageric ones. A culture is non-ageric if, in the process of handling the matter of "becoming later," it makes no difference whether you do something or not. With us, we have to work to get ahead. We do not get ahead automatically. In the cultures mentioned above, this is not nearly so important.

46   *Variety* enables us to distinguish between intervals such as short duration and long duration, or long duration and very long duration. Variety is a factor in boredom, while the degree of boredom experienced depends on how rapidly time passes.

47   We look for variety in occupations, careers, and hobbies. Our public "demands" a variety of material objects, food, clothing, and so forth. Consider for a moment the fact that few of us can say what we are going to have for lunch or dinner three days from now, let alone next year. Yet there are millions of people in the world who know exactly what they are going to have, if they are to have anything at all. They will eat the same thing they had today, yesterday, and the day before.

48   For us it is a matter of importance whether or not there is variety in life.

Take the teen-age girl who complains to her mother that there weren't any boys at the dance, meaning that there weren't any new boys. Our demand for variety and for something new would seem to exceed that of almost any other culture in the world today. It is necessary to an economy like ours. Without constant innovation we could never keep our industrial plant expanding.

On the informal level of time the basic distinction is between sameness   49
and variety. With variety, time moves more rapidly. People who are imprisoned away from light where they cannot tell whether it is day or not apparently lose practically all sense of the passage of time. They become disoriented and if kept away long enough they may "lose their minds."

As was the case with activity, we associate variety with external events.   50
Maturing and aging—just getting old—are not considered by us to constitute variety except in someone else, so that we will say, "My, he certainly has aged a lot since I last saw him." To the Pueblo of New Mexico, however, aging is something to be experienced. It means increased stature in the community and a greater part in decision making. Variety, from this point of view, is a natural part of living, and an inherent aspect of the self, providing a basically different view of life from our own.

To summarize this discussion of informal time isolates we can say that   51
Americans determine relative duration by four means: degree of urgency, whether they are trying to do more than one thing at a time, whether they are busy or not, and the degree of variety that enters into the situation. In the informal isolates of a culture, one finds the building blocks of time that go to make up the values and driving forces which characterize a culture.

The informal patterning of time is one of the most consistently over-   52
looked aspects of culture. This is not because men are blind or stupid or pigheaded, although their capacity to hold on to informal patterns in the face of weighty evidence sometimes makes them appear to be so.

It seems that it is impossible to participate in two different patterns at the   53
same time. As I will illustrate below, a person has to stop using one in order to take up another. Furthermore, patterns are anchored, when they are being learned and forever after, in the behavior of groups and institutions. They are the ways of doing things that one learns early in life and for which one is rewarded or punished. Hence, it is no wonder that people hold on to them so tenaciously and look askance at all other patterns.

Informal patterns are seldom, if ever, made explicit. They exist like the air   54
around us. They are either familiar and comfortable, or unfamiliar and wrong. Deviations from the pattern are usually greeted with highly charged emotion because people are not doing things our way. "Our way" is, of course, almost invariably supported or reinforced by a technical rationalization such as the following: "If you are five minutes late for a meeting and have kept ten people waiting, you have therefore wasted almost an hour of their time."

In the United States the nature of the points on a time scale is a matter of   55 patterning, as is the handling of the interval between them. By and large, the space between the points is inviolate. That is, compared to some other systems, there is only a limited amount of stretching or distortion of the interval that is permissible. Conditioning for this way of conceiving time begins very early for us. A mother says, "I thought I told you you could play with Susan until five o'clock. What do you mean by staying over there until almost suppertime?" Later in life we hear Father saying to a friend, "I promised to spend an hour with Johnny working on his tree house, and I can't very well get off with much less." And in adult life, "But Mr. Jones, this is the third time Mr. Brown has tried to see you, and you promised to spend at least thirty minutes going over those specifications with him."

56   Our pattern allows very little switching of the position of "intervals" once they are set in a schedule, nor does it allow for much tampering with either the content or the position of the points on the time scale. An appointment to talk about a contract scheduled to begin at ten o'clock and end at eleven o'clock is not easily moved, nor can you talk about anything but the contract without offending people. Once set, the schedule is almost sacred, so that not only is it wrong, according to the formal dictates of our culture, to be late, but it is a violation of the informal patterns to keep changing schedules or appointments or to deviate from the agenda.

57   How much this is a factor in other cultures has not been determined precisely. There are cases, however, where the content or "agenda" of a given period of time is handled quite differently. In the Middle East, again, refusal of one party to come to the point and discuss the topic of a meeting often means he cannot agree to your terms but doesn't want to turn you down, or simply that he cannot discuss the matters under consideration because the time is not yet ripe. He will not, moreover, feel it is improper to meet without ever touching on the topic of the meeting.

58   Our pattern calls for the fixing of the agenda informally beforehand. We do not, as a whole, feel too comfortable trying to operate in a semi-public situation, hammering out an agenda, the way the Russians do. We prefer to assume that both parties want to talk about the subject, otherwise they wouldn't be there; and that they are sufficiently involved in the topic to make it worth their while. With the Russians there is some indication that, while this is true, negotiation over the separate points of the agenda signals to the other side how the opponent is going to react during the actual conference. Softness on our part in early negotiation, because we do not technically fix the agenda but agree informally about what should be taken up, is often interpreted as weakness. Or it may give the impression that we are going to give in on certain points when we aren't at all.

59   Earlier it was mentioned that the content and limits of a period of time were sacrosanct. If, however, the topic for discussion is completed satisfactorily, or it is apparent that no progress can be made, then the meeting or visit may be cut short. This often leaves people feeling a little funny. By and large,

the overriding pattern with us is that once you have scheduled the time, you have to use it as designated, even when it turns out that this is not necessary or advantageous.

All of which seems very strange to the Arab. He starts at one point and goes until he is finished or until something intervenes. Time is what occurs before or after a given point. The thing to remember in contrasting the two systems is that Americans cannot shift the partitions of schedules without violating a norm; Arabs can. With us the compartments are sacred. If we have allocated so much time to a certain activity, we can change it once, or maybe twice, when we are trying to discover the proper amount of time for the activity. We cannot continually move the walls of our time compartments back and forth, even though an activity may actually call for such flexibility. The pattern of the immovable time wall applies in most situations, even long periods of time, such as how long it takes to complete a college career.

It is not necessary to leave the country to encounter significantly different time patterns. There are differences between families and differences between men and women; occupational differences, status differences, and regional differences. In addition there are two basic American patterns that often conflict. I have termed these the "diffused point pattern" and the "displaced point pattern." The difference between them has to do with whether the leeway is on one side of the point or is diffused around it.

Contrasting the behavior of two groups of people participating in the two patterns, one observes the following: Taking 8:30 A.M. as the point, participants in the "displaced point" pattern will arrive ahead of time anywhere from 8 A.M. to 8:27 A.M. (cutting it fine), with the majority arriving around 8:25 A.M. Diffused point people will arrive anywhere from 8:25 A.M. to 8:45 A.M. As can be seen, there is practically no overlap between these two groups.

The reader can recall his own behavior during evening engagements. A person asked to spend the evening and arrive about "nineish," wouldn't think of using the daytime "diffused point" pattern. The "displaced point" pattern is mandatory, usually at least ten or fifteen minutes after the hour but not more than thirty-five or forty minutes. If asked for dinner, with cocktails before, the leeway is much less. It is permissible to arrive for a seven o'clock engagement at 7:05 but not much later than 7:15. The "mutter something" period starts at 7:20 and by 7:30, people are looking around and saying, "I wonder what's happened to the Smiths!" The hostess may have a roast in the oven. In New York City there is a big difference between a "5 to 8" cocktail party, when people arrive between 6 and 7:30 to stay for hours, and dinner-party time when ten minutes late is the most allowed.

In these terms, the actual displacement of the point is a function of three things: (a) the type of social occasion and what is being served; (b) the status of the individual who is being met or visited; (c) the individual's own way of handling time.

65   When a shift occurs in an office from diffused point to displaced point, people feel strongly about it. The diffused point people never really feel comfortable with the other pattern. Such shifts are often interpreted as robbing professional people of status. That is, they *feel* they have been lowered in the esteem of the boss. This is because of the use of this same pattern when meeting dignitaries and when great social distance exists between individuals. The displaced pointers, on the other hand, regard everyone else as very unbusinesslike, sloppy, and as having poor organizational morale. They feel the lack of control and are distrustful of the academic types who are so cavalier about being "on time." Persistent efforts to restrict scientists to the displaced point pattern by enforcing rigid schedules is one of the many things that helped drive many scientists from government work in the last few years.

66   Regionally in the United States there are seemingly endless variations in the way time is handled. These variations, however, are comparable to the variations in the details of speech associated with the different parts of the country. Everybody participates in the over-all pattern which makes it possible for us to be mutually understood wherever we go.

67   In Utah, where the Mormons at first got somewhat technical about time and later developed strong formal systems emphasizing promptness, you find the displaced point pattern with very little leeway. That is, the attempt is made to arrive "on time," which means a little before the hour and no more than one minute late. Since, according to their system, it's worse to be late than early, they arrive on the early side of the point, just as military personnel do. What this communicates to other Americans is that Mormons are more serious about their work than the average American.

68   The northwest coastal region of the United States does some very strange things with time, when looked at in terms of the rest of the country. They will ask a person for 6 P.M. if they want him to arrive by 6:30 P.M., and then hope that he gets there. The detail of muttering an apology after four minutes is quite uncommon and is decried by many.

69   The more traditional part of the South, on the other hand, seems to behave pretty much as predicted; people slow things down by allowing leeway in both patterns. One finds a greater permissible spread, or a wider range of deviation from the point, than in the urban Northeast. The same could be said for the Old West.

Questions

1. How does Hall define "formal," "informal," and "technical" time? If American culture is time-bound, as commentators have charged, is it bound equally to all three kinds of time, or does one or the other predominate? Explain.

2. How do definitions of these three kinds of time structure Hall's essay? How much space (equivalent to time!) does he devote to discussing each? What determines the proportioning?

3. One can't escape membership in the cultural subgroup determined by geography—where one lives or where one grew up. How does this orientation (as well as membership, perhaps, in other cultural subgroups) determine how one treats informal time? Why is it useful to compare one's own understanding or treatment of a phenomenon with the way other cultures regard the same thing—as Hall does throughout his essay?

4. Hall says, "The analysis of one's own culture simply makes explicit the many things we take for granted in our everyday lives. Talking about them, however . . . frees us from their restraint" (paragraph 1). Explain what Hall means with reference to what you have learned about time from reading this essay.

CHARLES BARBER
The Origin of Language

After earning a B.A. from Cambridge in 1937 and an M.A. in 1941, Barber (born in England in 1915) began his career as a professor of language and linguistics at the University of Gothenburg, Sweden, 1947–1956, from which he also received his doctorate. Since 1959 he has taught English at the University of Leeds. Although his first book was The Idea of Honour in the English Drama: 1591–1700 *(1957), Barber's later works have focused on the history of language and include* Early Modern English *(1976) and* The Story of Speech and Language *(1964), from which "The Origin of Language" is reprinted.*

Claiming that language is "the most remarkable tool that man has invented," Barber systematically examines "more or less plausible speculations" about its origin, prefaced by appropriate cautions about the disparity between the oldest written records ("only a few thousand years") and the probable origin of spoken language some half a million years before that. Typical of many science writers, he labels and categorizes each theory ("the bow-wow theory," "the pooh-pooh theory" . . .), identifies the characteristics of each, and then—often on the basis of evidence from many languages—demonstrates its inadequacy to explain all the phenomena that an appropriately comprehensive theory would have to cover to be truly workable. Barber, a conservative scientist, is not willing to go beyond the evidence to claim certainty where some doubt exists, or to proclaim one theory superior to the others when all have their limitations.

We are profoundly ignorant about the origins of language, and have to content ourselves with more or less plausible speculations. We do not even know for certain when language arose, but it seems likely that it goes back to the earliest history of man, perhaps half a million years. We have no direct evidence, but it seems probable that speech arose at the same time as tool making and the earliest forms of specifically human cooperation. In the great Ice Ages of the Pleistocene period, our earliest human ancestors established the Old Stone Age culture: they made flint tools, and later tools of bone, ivory, and antler; they made fire and cooked their food; they hunted big game, often by methods that called for considerable cooperation and coordination. As their material culture gradually improved, they became artists, and made carvings and engravings on bones and pebbles, and wonderful paintings of animals on the walls of caves. It is difficult to believe that the makers of these Palaeolithic cultures lacked the power of speech. It is a long step, admittedly, from the earliest flint weapons to the splendid art of the late Old Stone Age: the first crude flints date back perhaps to 500,000 BC, while the finest achievements of Old Stone Age man are later than 100,000 BC; and in this period we can envisage a corresponding development of language, from the most primitive and limited language of the earliest human groups to a fully developed language in the flowering time of Old Stone Age culture.

Evidence about the Origins of Language

2 How did language arise in the first place? There are many theories about this, based on various types of indirect evidence, such as the language of children, the language of primitive societies, the kinds of changes that have taken place in languages in the course of recorded history, the behavior of higher animals like chimpanzees, and the behavior of people suffering from speech defects. These types of evidence may provide us with useful pointers, but they all suffer from limitations, and must be treated with caution.

3 When we consider the language of children we have to remember that their situation is quite different from that of our earliest human ancestors, because the child is growing up in an environment where there is already a fully developed language, and is surrounded by adults who use that language and are teaching it to him. For example, it has been shown that the earliest words used by children are mainly the names of things and people ("Doll," "Spoon," "Mummy"): but this does not prove that the earliest words of primitive man were also the names of things and people. When the child learns the name of an object, he may then use it to express his wishes or demands: "Doll!" often means "Give me my doll!" or "I've dropped my doll: pick it up for me!"; the child is using language to get things done, and it is almost an accident of adult teaching that the words used to formulate the child's demands are mainly nouns, instead of words like "Bring!"; "Pick up!"; and so on.

4 One thing that we can perhaps learn from the small child is the kind of articulated utterance that comes easiest to a human being before he has learned the sound system of one particular language. The first articulate word pronounced by a child is often something like *da, ma, na, ba, ga,* or *wa*. The vowel is most commonly a short *ah* sound, and the consonant a nasal or a plosive. Nearly always, these early "words" consist of a consonant followed by a vowel or of a sequence of syllables of this type (*dadada,* etc.). When the child attempts to copy words used by adults, he at first tends to produce words of this form, so that "grandfather" may be rendered as *gaga,* "thank you" as *tata,* and "water" as *wawa*. This explains why, in so many languages,

the nursery words for mother and father are *mama* or *dada* or *baba* or something similar: there is no magic inner connection between the idea of parenthood and words of this form: these just happen to be the first articulated sounds that the child makes, and the proud parent attributes a suitable meaning to them. Such words may also have been the first utterances of primitive man, though hardly with this meaning.

The languages of primitive peoples, and the history of languages in literate times, may throw some light on the origin of language by suggesting what elements in it are the most archaic. But again we have to be careful, because the language of the most primitive people living today is still a very ancient and sophisticated one, with half a million years of history behind it; and the earliest written records can take us back only a few thousand years. It is probable, of course, that in early times language changed more slowly than in historical times. The whole history of human culture has been one of an accelerating rate of change: it took man about half a million years to develop through the Old Stone Age to the higher material culture of the Middle and New Stone ages, but a mere 5,000 years or so for these to give way to the Bronze Age, and perhaps 1,000 for the Bronze Age to develop into the Iron Age; and since the Industrial Revolution, the pace has become dizzying. It is perhaps arguable that the rate of change in language has been parallel to that in material culture, and in that case the gap of half a million years between the origin of language and the first written records becomes a little less daunting. It remains daunting enough, however, and we must obviously be careful in theorizing about the remote past.

Still, we may be able to pick up some hints. For example, it is noticeable among primitive peoples how closely their languages are adapted to their material needs: in Eskimo, there is no single word for "snow," but a whole series of words for "new fallen snow," "hard snow," and so on; and in general a primitive people tends to have words for the specific things that are materially important to it (like the particular birds or plants that it eats), and to lump together other things (like birds or plants that it does not eat) under some generic expression. We may also find some evidence about the types of word and the types of expression which are oldest: there is a good deal to suggest that words of command (like "Give!"; "Strike!") are very archaic, since in the earliest known forms of many languages these imperative forms are identical with the simple stem of the verb, without any special ending added. Compare, for example, Latin *dic* ("say!") with *dicit* ("he says"), *dicunt* ("they say"), or *dicere* ("to say"): the form used for giving a command is the shortest, the most elementary. Some of the personal pronouns, like *me,* also seem to be very archaic, and so do vocatives (the forms of words used in addressing people).

A study of the higher animals can help us by suggesting what man was like in the prelinguistic stage, immediately before he became man. The expressive noises, signals, and gestures of the higher apes show us what man

5

6

7

started from in his creation of language; but they cannot show us how he created language, for it is man alone who has broken through to the use of symbols: the apes, however expressive their signals may be, remain on the other side of language. Apes, of course, have smaller brains than men; and man's development, as part of his adaptive evolution, of a larger and more complex brain than any other creature was undoubtedly a prerequisite for the emergence of language.

8   The last source of evidence, the behavior of people suffering from speech defects, is probably the least helpful. The condition which has especially been referred to is *aphasia,* in which the power of speech is wholly or partially lost, often as a result of a brain injury. In recovering from aphasia, the patient to some extent repeats the process gone through by a child in learning to speak for the first time, and some psychologists have suggested that he also repeats the history of the human race in inventing language. It is difficult, however, to see the grounds for this belief, since language, though it uses inherited biological skills and aptitudes, is not itself a biological inheritance but a cultural one; and the kind of prehistory of language which has been constructed on evidence of this kind is not a very convincing one.

9   Emphasis on one type of evidence or another has led to rather different theories of the origin of language. Different authors, too, seem to mean different things when they talk about the origin of language: some are thinking especially of the prelanguage situation, and of the basic human skills and equipment that were a prerequisite for the invention of language; others are thinking more of the actual situations in which the first truly linguistic utterances took place; others again are thinking of the very early stages of language after its invention, and the ways in which it expanded its resources.

The Bow-wow Theory

10   One theory is that primitive language was an imitation of natural sounds, such as the cries of animals. This has been called the bow-wow theory. Supporters of the theory point to the large number of words in any language which are, it seems, directly imitative of natural sounds—words like *quack, cuckoo, peewit.* They add that many other words show a kind of "sound symbolism," enacting in sound whatever it is that they denote; examples of such words in English would be *splash, sludge, slush, grumble, grunt, bump,* and *sneeze.* It is certainly plausible to believe that a primitive hunter, wishing to tell his companions what kind of game he had found, may have imitated in gesture and sound whatever kind of animal it was—horse, or elephant, or quail; and this may well have played a part in the development of vocal symbols.

11   This theory, however, does not explain how language obtained its articulated structure. When we invent an imitative word like *whizzbang* or *crump,* we use an already existing language system, with its vowels and consonants, its laws of word structure, and so on, and we make our imitative

word conform to this pattern. But man in the prelinguistic stage had no such language system, and his imitation of a horse or an elephant would simply be a whinnying or trumpeting sound, without the articulation characteristic of speech. Imitation of this kind may explain part of the primitive vocabulary, and it may have played a part in the transition from expressive cry to vocal symbol, but it cannot by itself account satisfactorily for the rise of language.

Moreover, we probably deceive ourselves about the extent and impor- 12 tance of sound symbolism in language. Because of our intimate knowledge of our language since our early years, and the way it is bound up with our whole emotional and intellectual life, the words that we use inevitably *seem* appropriate to what they mean, simply by constant association. It may be retorted that some groups of sounds really are appropriate to certain meanings, and this is shown by their occurrence in a number of words of similar meaning: for example, in English we find initial *fl-* in a number of words connected with fire and light (e.g., *flame, flare, flash*) and in an even larger number of words connected with a flying or waving kind of motion (e.g., *flail, flap, flaunt, flay, flicker, flog, fluctuate, flurry, flutter*). But it is difficult to see any *inherent* appropriateness in the *fl-* sound for expressing ideas of flame or flickering motion: the sense of appropriateness surely arises from the fact that it occurs in all these words, not vice versa. And once a group of words like this exists in the language, new words may be coined on the same model (as perhaps happened with *flash* and *flap*), and words of similar form may develop new meanings on analogy with the members of the group (as has perhaps happened with *flourish*). But there are many other words in English which begin with *fl-*, which have nothing to do with flames or flickering, and yet which by long familiarity sound equally appropriate to their meanings, like *flange, flank, flannel, flask, flat, flesh, flimsy, flinch, flock*, and so on. It is noticeable that, when you learn a foreign language, the words that strike you as particularly appropriate in sound (or, sometimes, as grotesquely inappropriate) are very often ones that do not strike a native speaker in this way.

The Pooh-pooh Theory

A second theory of the origins of language has been called the pooh-pooh 13 theory. This argues that language arose from instinctive emotional cries, expressive for example of pain or joy. On this view, the earliest linguistic utterances were interjections, simple exclamations expressive of some emotional state. This theory, it seems to me, suggests some of the material which language may have used, rather than the process by which it arose. The theory does nothing to explain the articulated nature of language, and it does little to bridge the gap between expressive cry and symbol. We can, indeed, imagine how, by association, an emotional cry may have become a signal: a cry of fear or of pain, for example, could easily become a signal which warned the group of danger; but this level has already been reached by the higher animals, which react to signals of this kind; the further step from trigger stimulus to symbol must also be explained. And the theory does not suggest any motivation for this development; a tremendous task like the creation of language would surely have been undertaken only under the pressure of man's needs.

The Ding-dong Theory

14 A third theory is the so-called nativistic theory, nicknamed the ding-dong theory. This begins from a fact we have already noticed, namely, that there is an apparently mysterious harmony between sound and sense in a language. On this basis, the theory argues that primitive man had a peculiar instinctive faculty, by which every external impression that he received was given vocal expression. Every sensory impression was like the striking of a bell, producing a corresponding utterance. The trouble with this theory is that it explains nothing: it merely describes the facts in a different terminology, and so is only a pseudotheory.

The Yo-he-ho Theory

15 A fourth theory, put forward by the nineteenth-century scholar Noiré, has been called the yo-he-ho theory. This envisages language arising from the noises made by a group of men engaged in joint labor or effort—moving a tree trunk, lifting a rock. We all know from experience that, while performing work of this kind, we make involuntary vocal noises. While exerting powerful muscular effort we trap the breath in our lungs by tightly closing the glottis (the vocal cords); in the intervals of relaxation between the bursts of effort, we open the glottis and release the air, making various grunting and groaning noises in the process; since a stop is released, these noises often contain a consonantal sound as well as a vowel. Vocal noises of this kind might then develop into words meaning such things as "heave!"; "rest!"; "lift!" This theory has two great virtues: it gives a plausible explanation for the origin of the consonant-vowel structure of language, and it envisages the origin of language in a situation involving human cooperation, with adequate motivation. It also envisages the earliest speech utterances as commands, and we have already seen that there is some linguistic evidence for the antiquity of such imperative forms. Against the theory, it has been argued that it postulates too advanced a form of social cooperation: language, it is argued, would be necessary *before* men could embark on the kind of complex communal labor that the theory demands. I am not sure that this objection is very compelling: we must surely envisage language and cooperative human labor arising *simultaneously,* each making the other possible; they would continually react on one another, so that there would be a progressive development from the simplest utterances and acts of cooperation to the most complex speech and division of labor.

16 A variant of the theory has recently been elaborated by A. S. Diamond. He agrees that the first articulated words were commands, uttered simulta-

neously with the execution of violent arm movements, but argues that all the evidence shows that the most primitive words did not mean such things as "Haul!" but rather such things as "Strike!"; "Cut!"; "Break!"; he therefore envisages the rise of language in requests for assistance from one man to another in situations where maximum bodily effort was required. He does not speculate on the exact nature of these situations, but presumably they might be such things as tool making, the breaking off of tree branches, and the killing of animals during hunting. Such things might occur at a more primitive stage of human society than the communal heaving suggested by Noiré.

The Gesture Theory

A fifth theory of the origins of language takes the view that gesture language preceded speech. Supporters of this theory point to the extensive use of gestures by animals of many different kinds, and the highly developed systems of gesture used by some primitive peoples. One of the popular examples is the sign language formerly used by the Indians of North America; this was an elaborate system of gestures which was used for negotiations between tribes that spoke different languages. It is certainly true that speech and gesture are closely intertwined; the centers in the brain which control hand movements are closely linked with those that control the vocal organs, and it seems highly probable that speech and gesture grew up together. This does not prove, however, that gesture came *first*. And, while it is true that animals use gestures, it is also true that they use cries: the chimpanzee makes signals and expresses its feelings both by bodily movements and by vocal noises, and the same was probably true of early man. 17

An extreme form of the gesture theory argues that speech arose very late (round about 3500 B.C.) and was derived from early pictorial writing; this writing itself, it is argued, was derived from gesture language. I must say that I find this incredible. We are asked to believe that man lacked speech right through the Old and New Stone ages, and did not develop it until the time of the city civilizations of the early Bronze Age. But it is difficult to believe that man could have built up the elaborate cultural apparatus of the New Stone Age (agriculture, pottery, weaving, house building, religious burial) without the aid of speech; for a gesture language, however highly developed, has grave disadvantages compared with a spoken language. To use a gesture language you have to have your hands free; but as soon as man becomes a tool maker and a craftsman his hands cease to be free; and the times when primitive man needed to communicate most urgently must have been precisely the times when he had a tool or a weapon in his hand. It is in fact arguable that it was just this preoccupation of man's hands with tools and weapons that led to the increased importance of vocal language compared with gestures; and this would support the view that spoken language goes right back to the beginning of man's career as tool maker. Gesture, too, has 18 the disadvantage that it cannot be used in the dark, or when the users are separated by obstructions like trees—a serious disadvantage for a hunting band, which would surely develop hunting calls and similar cries. Nor can a gesture be used to attract the attention of somebody who is looking in another direction, and so it has very limited value as a warning of the approach of danger. None of these disadvantages of gesture can *prove* that early man had a spoken language, but they do suggest that he had very powerful motives for creating one.

19   A more attractive version of the gesture theory is the *mouth gesture* theory, which was strongly argued by Sir Richard Paget and has recently been supported by an Icelandic professor, Alexander Jóhannesson. Paget argues that primitive man at first communicated by gestures; as his intelligence and technique developed he needed more exact gestures, but at the same time found that his eyes and hands were more occupied by his arts and crafts. But the gestures of the hands were unconsciously copied by movements of the tongue, lips, and mouth; and when the man was unable to go on gesturing with his hands because of their other uses, the mouth gestures continued without them, and he discovered that if air was blown through the mouth or nose the gesture became audible as whispered speech; if he simultaneously sang or roared or grunted, he produced voiced speech. To support his theory of the sympathetic movements of the speech organs, Paget quotes a passage from Darwin's book *The Expression of the Emotions*:

> There are other actions which are commonly performed under certain circumstances independently of habit, and which seem to be due to imitation or some kind of sympathy. Thus, persons cutting anything with a pair of scissors may be seen to move their jaws simultaneously with the blades of the scissors. Children learning to write often twist about their tongue as their fingers move, in a ridiculous fashion!

Language was thus produced by a sort of pantomime, the tongue and lips mimicking the movements of the hands in a gesture. As an elementary example, Paget takes the movement of the mouth, tongue, and jaws as in eating, as a gesture sign meaning "eat." If, while making this sign, we blow air through the vocal cavities and switch on voice, we produce the sounds *mnyum mnyum* or *mnya mnya*, which, Paget says, would be universally understood. Similarly, the action of sucking a liquid in small quantities into the mouth produces words like *sip* or *sup*. Paget goes on to analyze large numbers of words in terms of mouth gestures of this kind, and this work has been continued by Jóhannesson, who has examined large numbers of the basic words of the earliest known languages. Some of these analyses strike me as fanciful, and there are times when one feels that, with sufficient ingenuity, any movement of the tongue could be construed as a gesture representing anything one liked. Nevertheless, the theory has considerable plausibility, and must be taken seriously. It has the merit of accounting for the articulated nature of speech, and of giving an explanation for the way the linkage was effected between sound and meaning.

The Musical Theory

A sixth theory sees the origin of language in song, or at any rate sees speech [20] and music as emerging from something earlier that included both. This theory was put forward by the great Danish linguist Otto Jespersen. He thought that the bow-wow, pooh-pooh, and yo-he-ho theories could all explain the origins of parts of language, but that none of them could explain the whole of it. His own method was to trace the history of language backwards, to see what the long-term trends were, and then to assume that these same trends had existed since the beginning of language. By this means he arrived at the view that primitive language consisted of very long words, full of difficult jaw-breaking sounds; that it used tone and pitch more than later languages, and a wider range of musical intervals; and that it was more passionate and more musical than later languages. Earlier still, language was a kind of song without words; it was not communicative, but merely expressive; the earliest language was not matter-of-fact or practical, but poetic and emotional, and love in particular was the most powerful emotion for eliciting outbursts of music and song. "Language," he writes, "was born in the courting days of mankind; the first utterances of speech I fancy to myself like something between the nightly love-lyrics of puss upon the tiles and the melodious love-songs of the nightingale." A romantic picture.

It may be doubted, however, whether the trends in language are as [21] constant and universal as Jespersen thinks. His theory assumes that the same kinds of general change have taken place in all languages throughout their history. But we know nothing of languages before the Bronze Age; even if there has been a universal trend in language since the beginnings of Bronze Age civilization (which is by no means certain), it does not follow that the same trend occurred in the Old Stone Age, when man's circumstances were entirely different. Moreover, we have a historical knowledge of relatively few of the world's languages: of the two thousand languages spoken today, only a handful have records going back to the pre-Christian era.

The Contact Theory

Finally, mention may be made of the contact theory, which has recently been [22] advanced by G. Révész, a former professor of psychology at Amsterdam. He sees language as arising through man's instinctive need for contact with his fellows, and he works out a series of stages by which language may have developed. First comes the contact sound, which is not communicative, but merely expresses the individual's need for contact with his fellows; such as the noises made by gregarious animals. Next comes the cry, which is communicative, but which is directed to the environment generally, not to an individual; examples are mating calls and the cries of young nestlings in danger. Then there is the call, which differs from the cry in being directed to an individual; it is the demand for the satisfaction of some desire, and is found in domestic animals (begging) and speechless infants (crying for their mother); the call is seen as the starting point for both music and language. Finally comes the word, which has symbolic function and is found only in man. Révész thinks that the earliest speech was an "imperative language," consisting only of commands; this later developed into mature human language, which contains also statements and questions. Révész's sequence of stages is carefully worked out, and is made very plausible. He does not, however, explain how human language came to be articulated; and he places undue emphasis on the instinctive need for contact as a motive for the invention of language, while rather neglecting the urgent practical motives in cooperative labor which must surely have impelled early man.

The Probabilities

23 What are we to make of this welter of theories? It is plain that no finality is possible at present, and that it is merely a matter of weighing the probabilities. It seems to me that we should attach great weight to the question of motivation in the origin of language, since such a great intellectual achievement would hardly have been possible except under the pressure of definite needs. Since the basic function of language is to influence the behavior of our fellow men, this would favor theories that emphasize the origins of language in situations of social cooperation: such for example are the yo-he-ho theory and Diamond's variant of it. However, other theories, such as the bow-wow theory and the mouth gesture theory, can also be adapted to views of this kind. In the second place, I think we should attach great importance to the articulatedness of language, as seen for example in its vowel and consonant structure; and it seems to me the weakness of many theories that they do nothing to explain this structure; the theories that come off best on this count are the yo-he-ho theory and the mouth gesture theory. But at present we cannot reach absolute certainty.

24 We must also remain in doubt about the nature of the earliest language, and we do not even know if there was one original language or whether language was invented independently at several different times and places. Jespersen, we have seen, postulates a primitive language that was musical and passionate; he believes that it was very irregular; that it dealt with the concrete and particular rather than the abstract and general; that it contained very long words full of difficult combinations of sounds; and indeed that the earliest utterances consisted of whole sentences rather than single words. Somewhat similar views have been advanced by investigators who have attached great significance to the babbling stages of child speech. But Révész thinks that the earliest language consisted solely of commands; so does Diamond, who argues that these were single words and had the structure consonant-vowel-consonant-vowel (like *bada* or *taka*). The bow-wow theory, on

the other hand, demands a primitive language full of imitative sounds like the howling of wolves or the trumpeting of elephants. In the absence of certainty about the origins of language, we must obviously lack certainty about the form which that language took (though the kind of language envisaged by Révész or Diamond seems more plausible than that envisaged by Jespersen).

Inevitably we remain in the realm of more or less plausible speculation as long as we are dealing with a period which has left us no record of its language. [Only when] we reach periods in which writing was practiced [are we] on much firmer ground.

25

SUSANNE K. LANGER

Signs and Symbols

Langer, a philosopher, was born in New York City in 1895. She earned three degrees from Radcliffe (Ph.D. in 1926), taught at Columbia University 1945–1950, and thereafter at Connecticut College until her retirement in 1962. Her concern with the ability of humans to symbolize integrates her research on topics as seemingly different as aesthetics, examined in Feeling and Form: A Theory of Art *(1953); the nature of the human mind, explored in* Mind: An Essay on Human Feeling *(2 vols., 1967–72); and symbolic logic, analyzed in the landmark* Philosophy in a New Key: A Study in the Symbols of Reason, Rite, and Art *(1942), which includes the essay reprinted here.* Mind *focuses on "the nature and origin of the veritable gulf that divides human from animal mentality" and makes human nature unique in the animal kingdom.*

"Signs and Symbols" epitomizes this view: "Language is the most amazing achievement of the symbolistic human mind . . . . Without it anything properly called 'thought' is impossible. . . . The line between man and beast—between the highest ape and the lowest savage—is the language line." Langer offers extended definitions that distinguish signs (which animals use and respond to) from symbols (a uniquely human phenomenon), and illustrates these with numerous examples of human and animal behavior. Her views, though controversial, provide philosophical reinforcement for Lurie's sociological and cultural study of clothing as a sign system and the Sebeoks' anthropological analysis of performing animals that follow.

The trait that sets human mentality apart from every other is its preoccupation with symbols, with images and names that *mean* things, rather than with things themselves. This trait may have been a mere sport of nature once upon a time. Certain creatures do develop tricks and interests that seem biologically unimportant. Pack rats, for instance, and some birds of the crow family take a capricious pleasure in bright objects and carry away such things for which they have, presumably, no earthly use. Perhaps man's tendency to see certain forms as *images,* to hear certain sounds not only as signals but as expressive tones, and to be excited by sunset colors or starlight, was originally just a

1

peculiar sensitivity in a rather highly developed brain. But whatever its cause, the ultimate destiny of this trait was momentous; for all human activity is based on the appreciation and use of symbols. Language, religion, mathematics, all learning, all science and superstition, even right and wrong, are products of symbolic expression rather than direct experience. Our commonest words, such as "house" and "red" and "walking," are symbols; the pyramids of Egypt and the mysterious circles of Stonehenge are symbols; so are dominions and empires and astronomical universes. We live in a mind-made world, where the things of prime importance are images or words that embody ideas and feelings and attitudes.

2   The animal mind is like a telephone exchange; it receives stimuli from outside through the sense organs and sends out appropriate responses through the nerves that govern muscles, glands, and other parts of the body. The organism is constantly interacting with its surroundings, receiving messages and acting on the new state of affairs that the messages signify.

3   But the human mind is not a simple transmitter like a telephone exchange. It is more like a great projector; for instead of merely mediating between an event in the outer world and a creature's responsive action, it transforms or, if you will, distorts the event into an image to be looked at, retained, and contemplated. For the images of things that we remember are not exact and faithful transcriptions even of our actual sense impressions. They are made as much by what we think as by what we see. It is a well-known fact that if you ask several people the size of the moon's disk as they look at it, their estimates will vary from the area of a dime to that of a barrel top. Like a magic lantern, the mind projects its ideas of things on the screen of what we call "memory"; but like all projections, these ideas are transformations of actual things. They are, in fact, *symbols* of reality, not pieces of it.

4   A symbol is not the same thing as a sign; that is a fact that psychologists and philosophers often overlook. All intelligent animals use signs; so do we. To them as well as to us sounds and smells and motions are signs of food, danger, the presence of other beings, or of rain or storm. Furthermore, some animals not only attend to signs but produce them for the benefit of others. Dogs bark at the door to be let in; rabbits thump to call each other; the cooing of doves and the growl of a wolf defending his kill are unequivocal signs of feelings and intentions to be reckoned with by other creatures.

5   We use signs just as animals do, though with considerably more elaboration. We stop at red lights and go on green; we answer calls and bells, watch the sky for coming storms, read trouble or promise or anger in each other's eyes. That is animal intelligence raised to the human level. Those of us who are dog lovers can probably all tell wonderful stories of how high our dogs have sometimes risen in the scale of clever sign interpretation and sign using.

6   A sign is anything that announces the existence or the imminence of some event, the presence of a thing or a person, or a change in a state of affairs. There are signs of the weather, signs of danger, signs of future good

or evil, signs of what the past has been. In every case a sign is closely bound up with something to be noted or expected in experience. It is always a part of the situation to which it refers, though the reference may be remote in space and time. In so far as we are led to note or expect the signified event we are making correct use of a sign. This is the essence of rational behavior, which animals show in varying degrees. It is entirely realistic, being closely bound up with the actual objective course of history—learned by experience, and cashed in or voided by further experience.

If man had kept to the straight and narrow path of sign using, he would be like the other animals, though perhaps a little brighter. He would not talk, but grunt and gesticulate and point. He would make his wishes known, give warnings, perhaps develop a social system like that of bees and ants, with such a wonderful efficiency of communal enterprise that all men would have plenty to eat, warm apartments—all exactly alike and perfectly convenient— to live in, and everybody could and would sit in the sun or by the fire, as the climate demanded, not talking but just basking, with every want satisfied, most of his life. The young would romp and make love, the old would sleep, the middle-aged would do the routine work almost unconsciously and eat a great deal. But that would be the life of a social, superintelligent, purely sign-using animal.

To us who are human, it does not sound very glorious. We want to go places and do things, own all sorts of gadgets that we do not absolutely need, and when we sit down to take it easy we want to talk. Rights and property, social position, special talents and virtues, and above all our ideas, are what we live for. We have gone off on a tangent that takes us far away from the mere biological cycle that animal generations accomplish; and that is because we can use not only signs but symbols.

A symbol differs from a sign in that it does not announce the presence of the object, the being, condition, or whatnot, which is its meaning, but merely *brings this thing to mind*. It is not a mere "substitute sign" to which we react as though it were the object itself. The fact is that our reaction to hearing a person's name is quite different from our reaction to the person himself. There are certain rare cases where a symbol stands directly for its meaning: in religious experience, for instance, the Host is not only a symbol but a Presence. But symbols in the ordinary sense are not mystic. They are the same sort of thing that ordinary signs are; only they do not call our attention to something necessarily present or to be physically dealt with—they call up merely a conception of the thing they "mean."

The difference between a sign and a symbol is, in brief, that a sign causes us to think or act in *face* of the thing signified, whereas a symbol causes us to think *about* the thing symbolized. Therein lies the greatest importance of symbolism for human life, its power to make this life so different from any other animal biography that generations of men have found it incredible to suppose that they were of purely zoological origin. A sign is always embedded in reality, in a present that emerges from the actual past and stretches to the future; but a symbol may be divorced from reality altogether. It may refer to what is *not* the case, to a mere idea, a figment, a dream. It serves, therefore, to liberate thought from the immediate stimuli of a physically present world; and that liberation marks the essential difference between human and nonhuman mentality. Animals think, but they think *of* and *at* things; men think primarily *about* things. Words, pictures, and memory images are symbols that may be combined and varied in a thousand ways. The result is a symbolic structure whose meaning is a complex of all their respective meanings, and this kaleidoscope of *ideas* is the typical product of the human brain that we call the "stream of thought."

11   The process of transforming all direct experience into imagery or into that supreme mode of symbolic expression, language, has so completely taken possession of the human mind that it is not only a special talent but a dominant, organic need. All our sense impressions leave their traces in our memory not only as signs disposing our practical reactions in the future but also as symbols, images representing our *ideas* of things; and the tendency to manipulate ideas, to combine and abstract, mix and extend them by playing with symbols, is man's outstanding characteristic. It seems to be what his brain most naturally and spontaneously does. Therefore his primitive mental function is not judging reality, but *dreaming his desires.*

12   Dreaming is apparently a basic function of human brains, for it is free and unexhausting like our metabolism, heartbeat, and breath. It is easier to dream than not to dream, as it is easier to breathe than to refrain from breathing. The symbolic character of dreams is fairly well established. Symbol mongering, on this ineffectual, uncritical level, seems to be instinctive, the fulfillment of an elementary need rather than the purposeful exercise of a high and difficult talent.

13   The special power of man's mind rests on the evolution of this special activity, not on any transcendently high development of animal intelligence. We are not immeasurably higher than other animals; we are different. We have a biological need and with it a biological gift that they do not share.

14   Because man has not only the ability but the constant need of *conceiving* what has happened to him, what surrounds him, what is demanded of him— in short, of symbolizing nature, himself, and his hopes and fears—he has a constant and crying need of *expression.* What he cannot express, he cannot conceive; what he cannot conceive is chaos, and fills him with terror.

15   If we bear in mind this all-important craving for expression we get a new picture of man's behavior; for from this trait spring his powers and his weaknesses. The process of symbolic transformation that all our experiences undergo is nothing more nor less than the process of *conception,* which underlies the human faculties of abstraction and imagination.

16   When we are faced with a strange or difficult situation, we cannot react directly, as other creatures do, with flight, aggression, or any such simple instinctive pattern. Our whole reaction depends on how we manage to con-

ceive the situation—whether we cast it in a definite dramatic form, whether we see it as a disaster, a challenge, a fulfillment of doom, or a fiat of the Divine Will. In words or dreamlike images, in artistic or religious or even in cynical form, we must *construe* the events of life. There is great virtue in the figure of speech, "I can *make* nothing of it," to express a failure to understand something. Thought and memory are processes of *making* the thought content and the memory image; the pattern of our ideas is given by the symbols through which we express them. And in the course of manipulating those symbols we inevitably distort the original experience, as we abstract certain features of it, embroider and reinforce those features with other ideas, until the conception we project on the screen of memory is quite different from anything in our real history.

Conception is a necessary and elementary process; what we do with our conceptions is another story. That is the entire history of human culture—of intelligence and mortality, folly and superstition, ritual, language, and the arts—all the phenomena that set man apart from, and above, the rest of the animal kingdom. As the religious mind has to make all human history a drama of sin and salvation in order to define its own moral attitudes, so a scientist wrestles with the mere presentation of "the facts" before he can reason about them. The process of *envisaging* facts, values, hopes, and fears underlies our whole behavior pattern; and this process is reflected in the evolution of an extraordinary phenomenon found always, and only, in human societies—the phenomenon of language. 17

Language is the highest and most amazing achievement of the symbolistic human mind. The power it bestows is almost inestimable, for without it anything properly called "thought" is impossible. The birth of language is the dawn of humanity. The line between man and beast—between the highest ape and the lowest savage—is the language line. Whether the primitive Neanderthal man was anthropoid or human depends less on his cranial capacity, his upright posture, or even his use of tools and fire, than on one issue we shall probably never be able to settle—whether or not he spoke. 18

In all physical traits and practical responses, such as skills and visual judgments, we can find a certain continuity between animal and human mentality. Sign using is an ever evolving, ever improving function throughout the whole animal kingdom, from the lowly worm that shrinks into his hole at the sound of an approaching foot, to the dog obeying his master's command, and even to the learned scientist who watches the movements of an index needle. 19

This continuity of the sign-using talent has led psychologists to the belief that language is evolved from the vocal expressions, grunts and coos and cries, whereby animals vent their feelings or signal their fellows; that man has elaborated this sort of communion to the point where it makes a perfect exchange of ideas possible. 20

I do not believe that this doctrine of the origin of language is correct. The essence of language is symbolic, not signific; we use it first and most 21 vitally to formulate and hold ideas in our own minds. Conception, not social control, is its first and foremost benefit.

22   Watch a young child that is just learning to speak play with a toy; he says the name of the object, e.g.: "Horsey! horsey! horsey!" over and over again, looks at the object, moves it, always saying the name to himself or to the world at large. It is quite a time before he talks to anyone in particular; he talks first of all to himself. This is his way of forming and fixing the *conception* of the object in his mind, and around this conception all his knowledge of it grows. *Names* are the essence of language; for the *name* is what abstracts the conception of the horse from the horse itself, and lets the mere idea recur at the speaking of the name. This permits the conception gathered from one horse experience to be exemplified again by another instance of a horse, so that the notion embodied in the name is a general notion.

23   To this end, the baby uses a word long before he *asks for* the object; when he wants his horsey he is likely to cry and fret, because he is reacting to an actual environment, not forming ideas. He uses the animal language of *signs* for his wants; talking is still a purely symbolic process—its practical value has not really impressed him yet.

24   Language need not be vocal; it may be purely visual, like written language, or even tactual, like the deaf-mute system of speech; but it *must be denotative*. The sounds, intended or unintended, whereby animals communicate do not constitute a language, because they are signs, not names. They never fall into an organic pattern, a meaningful syntax of even the most rudimentary sort, as all language seems to do with a sort of driving necessity. That is because signs refer to actual situations, in which things have obvious relations to each other that require only to be noted; but symbols refer to ideas, which are not physically there for inspection, so their connections and features have to be represented. This gives all true language a natural tendency toward growth and development, which seems almost like a life of its own. Languages are not invented; they grow with our need for expression.

25   In contrast, animal "speech" never has a structure. It is merely an emotional response. Apes may greet their ration of yams with a shout of "Nga!" But they do not say "Nga" between meals. If they could *talk about* their yams instead of just saluting them, they would be the most primitive men instead of the most anthropoid of beasts. They would have ideas, and tell each other things true or false, rational or irrational; they would make plans and invent laws and sing their own praises, as men do.

Questions

1. How does Langer define signs and symbols? Why are these definitions, and the distinctions between them, important to an understanding of human mentality?

2. Definitions use some or all of the following techniques: illustration; comparison and contrast; negation (saying what something is not); analysis; examination of etymological origins; simile, metaphor, and/or analogy; reference to authority, experi-

ence, or personal observation. Which of these techniques does Langer use in her extended definitions of sign and symbol? Does she use any other techniques, as well?

3. What right does Langer, a philosopher, have to draw so extensively on anthropology and biology in gaining evidence for her assertions about the nature of the human mind?

4. This essay was originally published in *Fortune*, a business magazine, in 1944. Why would it be of interest to business executives? What other types of readers could benefit from a knowledge of these definitions? Do the recent experiments in which chimpanzees and gorillas "talk" in American Sign Language or by pressing word or symbol keys on special typewriters, and even teach what they've learned to others of their species, threaten the definition of mankind as the exclusively symbol-using species?

ALISON LURIE

Clothing as a Sign System

Lurie's experience as a wry, witty author of satirical novels of social fashions—she has been called "the Queen Herod of Modern Fiction"—enhances her acute analysis of fashions in clothing. She was born in 1926, grew up in New York City, and graduated from Radcliffe in 1947. At one point she was ready to give up writing—she had married, had borne two of her three sons, and had written two novels that she couldn't get published—before publishers became interested in her essay about a friend who died young. Her third novel was published, and her career as a novelist began in earnest. Lurie's seven published novels include The War Between the Tates *(1974),* Only Children *(1979), and* Foreign Affairs *(1984). Lurie, a professor of English at Cornell, also writes ironically humorous nonfiction—essays for such publications as the* New York Review of Books, *and* The Language of Clothes *(1981), of which "Clothing as a Sign System," abridged here, is the opening chapter.*

Despite the novelist's keen powers of observation, Lurie lacks the formal credentials of a social scientist that would enhance the authority of the social analysis of clothing that she presents here. However, her profession and observations as a writer lend credibility to her logical working out of the metaphor that clothing is language, and that various attributes of clothing are analogous to various parts of speech (accessories, such as gloves and hats, are "modifiers") and types of usage (casual dress, such as jeans and sneakers, is the sartorial equivalent of casual speech). As with other signs and symbols, "the meaning of any costume depends on circumstances"—including the time, place, and wearer. Lurie reinforces her analysis with continual reference to other minders of manners in different fields, including novelists (Balzac, Barthes), etiquette experts (Emily Post), fashion arbiters (Worth, Mary Quant), art historians (Kenneth Clark), and sociologists (Erving Goffman). When writing about a field in which one might not be recognized as an expert, reinforcements help.

For thousands of years human beings have communicated with one another 1 first in the language of dress. Long before I am near enough to talk to you on the street, in a meeting, or at a party, you announce your sex, age and class to me through what you are wearing—and very possibly give me important information (or misinformation) as to your occupation, origin, personality, opinions, tastes, sexual desires and current mood. I may not be able to put what I observe into words, but I register the information unconsciously; and you simultaneously do the same for me. By the time we meet and converse we have already spoken to each other in an older and more universal tongue.

2   The statement that clothing is a language, though occasionally made with the air of a man finding a flying saucer in his backyard, is not new. Balzac, in *Daughter of Eve* (1839), observed that for a woman dress is "a continual manifestation of intimate thoughts, a language, a symbol." Today, as semiotics becomes fashionable, sociologists tell us that fashion too is a language of signs, a nonverbal system of communication. The French structuralist Roland Barthes, for instance, in "The Diseases of Costume," speaks of theatrical dress as a kind of writing, of which the basic element is the sign.

3   None of these theorists, however, have gone on to remark what seems obvious: that if clothing is a language, it must have a vocabulary and a grammar like other languages. Of course, as with human speech, there is not a single language of dress, but many: some (like Dutch and German) closely related and others (like Basque) almost unique. And within every language of clothes there are many different dialects and accents, some almost unintelligible to members of the mainstream culture. Moreover, as with speech, each individual has his own stock of words and employs personal variations of tone and meaning.

4   The vocabulary of dress includes not only items of clothing, but also hair styles, accessories, jewelry, make-up and body decoration. Theoretically at least this vocabulary is as large as or larger than that of any spoken tongue, since it includes every garment, hair style, and type of body decoration ever invented. In practice, of course, the sartorial resources of an individual may be very restricted. Those of a sharecropper, for instance, may be limited to five or ten "words" from which it is possible to create only a few "sentences" almost bare of decoration and expressing only the most basic concepts. A so-called fashion leader, on the other hand, may have several hundred "words" at his or her disposal, and thus be able to form thousands of different "sentences" that will express a wide range of meanings. Just as the average English-speaking person knows many more words than he or she will ever use in conversation, so all of us are able to understand the meaning of styles we will never wear.

5   To choose clothes, either in a store or at home, is to define and describe ourselves. Occasionally, of course, practical considerations enter into these choices: considerations of comfort, durability, availability and price. Especially in the case of persons of limited wardrobe, an article may be worn because it is warm or rainproof or handy to cover up a wet bathing suit—in the same way that persons of limited vocabulary use the phrase "you know" or adjectives such as "great" or "fantastic." Yet, just as with spoken language, such choices usually give us some information, even if it is only equivalent to the statement "I don't give a damn what I look like today." And there are limits even here. In this culture, like many others, certain garments are taboo

for certain persons. Most men, however cold or wet they might be, would not put on a woman's dress, just as they would not use words and phrases such as "simply marvelous," which in this culture are considered specifically feminine.

Besides containing "words" that are taboo, the language of clothes, like   6
speech, also includes modern and ancient words, words of native and foreign origin, dialect words, colloquialisms, slang and vulgarities. Genuine articles of clothing from the past (or skillful imitations) are used in the same way a writer or speaker might use archaisms: to give an air of culture, erudition or wit. Just as in educated discourse, such "words" are usually employed sparingly, most often one at a time—a single Victorian cameo or a pair of 1940s platform shoes or an Edwardian velvet waistcoat, never a complete costume. A whole outfit composed of archaic items from a single period, rather than projecting elegance and sophistication, will imply that one is on one's way to a masquerade, acting in a play or film or putting oneself on display for advertising purposes. Mixing garments from several different periods of the past, on the other hand, suggests a confused but intriguingly "original" theatrical personality. It is therefore often fashionable in those sections of the art and entertainment industry in which instant celebrities are manufactured and sold.

When using archaic words, it is essential to choose ones that are decently   7
old. The sight of a white plastic Courrèges miniraincoat and boots (in 1963 the height of fashion) at a gallery opening or theater today would produce the same shiver of ridicule and revulsion as the use of words such as "groovy," "Negro," or "self-actualizing."

In *Taste and Fashion,* one of the best books ever written on costume, the   8
late James Laver proposed a timetable to explain such reactions; this has come to be known as Laver's Law. According to him, the same costume will be

Indecent	10 years before its time
Shameless	5 years before its time
Daring	1 year before its time
Smart	
Dowdy	1 year after its time
Hideous	10 years after its time
Ridiculous	20 years after its time
Amusing	30 years after its time
Quaint	50 years after its time
Charming	70 years after its time
Romantic	100 years after its time
Beautiful	150 years after its time

Laver possibly overemphasizes the shock value of incoming fashion, which today may be seen merely as weird or ugly. And of course he is speaking of the complete outfit, or "sentence." The speed with which a single "word" passes in and out of fashion can vary, just as in spoken and written languages.

9   The appearance of foreign garments in an otherwise indigenous costume is similar in function to the use of foreign words or phrases in standard English speech. This phenomenon, which is common in certain circles, may have several different meanings.

10   First, of course, it can be a deliberate sign of national origin in someone who otherwise, sartorially or linguistically speaking, has no accent. Often this message is expressed through headgear. The Japanese-American lady in Western dress but with an elaborate Oriental hairdo, or the Oxford-educated Arab who tops his Savile Row suit with a turban, are telling us graphically that they have not been psychologically assimilated; that their ideas and opinions remain those of an Asian. As a result we tend to see the non-European in Western dress with native headgear or hairdo as dignified, even formidable; while the reverse outfit—the Oriental lady in a kimono and a plastic rain hat, or the sheik in native robes and a black bowler—appears comic. Such costumes seem to announce that their wearers, though not physically at ease in our country, have their heads full of half-baked Western ideas. It would perhaps be well for Anglo-American tourists to keep this principle in mind when traveling to exotic places. Very possibly the members of a package tour in Mexican sombreros or Russian bearskin hats look equally ridiculous and weak-minded to the natives of the countries they are visiting.

11   More often the wearing of a single foreign garment, like the dropping of a foreign word or phrase in conversation, is meant not to advertise foreign origin or allegiance but to indicate sophistication. It can also be a means of advertising wealth. When we see a fancy Swiss watch, we know that its owner either bought it at home for three times the price of a good English or American watch, or else he or she spent even more money traveling to Switzerland.

12   Casual dress, like casual speech, tends to be loose, relaxed and colorful. It often contains what might be called "slang words": blue jeans, sneakers, baseball caps, aprons, flowered cotton housedresses and the like. These garments could not be worn on a formal occasion without causing disapproval, but in ordinary circumstances they pass without remark. "Vulgar words" in dress, on the other hand, give emphasis and get immediate attention in almost any circumstances, just as they do in speech. Only the skillful can employ them without some loss of face, and even then they must be used in the right way. A torn, unbuttoned shirt, or wildly uncombed hair, can signify strong emotions: passion, grief, rage, despair. They are most effective if people already think of you as being neatly dressed, just as the curses of well-spoken persons count for more than those of the customarily foul-mouthed.

13   Items of dress that are the sartorial equivalent of forbidden words have

more impact when they appear seldom and as if by accident. The Edwardian lady, lifting her heavy floor-length skirt to board a tram, appeared unaware that she was revealing a froth of lacy petticoats and embroidered black stockings. Similarly, today's braless executive woman, leaning over her desk at a conference, may affect not to know that her nipples show through her silk blouse. Perhaps she does not know it consciously; we are here in the ambiguous region of intention vs. interpretation which has given so much trouble to linguists.

In speech, slang terms and vulgarities may eventually become respectable dictionary words; the same thing is true of colloquial and vulgar fashions. Garments or styles that enter the fashionable vocabulary from a colloquial source usually have a longer life span than those that begin as vulgarities. Thigh-high patent leather boots, first worn by the obvious variety of rentable female as a sign that she was willing to help act out certain male fantasies, shot with relative speed into and out of high fashion; while blue jeans made their way upward much more gradually from work clothes to casual to business and formal wear, and are still engaged in a slow descent. 14

Though the idea is attractive, it does not seem possible to equate different articles of clothing with the different parts of speech. A case can be made, however, for considering trimmings and accessories as adjectives or adverbs—modifiers in the sentence that is the total outfit— but it must be remembered that one era's trimmings and accessories are another's essential parts of the costume. At one time shoes were actually fastened with buckles, and the buttons on the sleeves of a suit jacket were used to secure turned-up cuffs. Today such buttons, or the linked brass rods on a pair of Gucci shoes, are purely vestigial and have no useful function. If they are missing, however, the jacket or the shoes are felt to be damaged and unfit for wear. 15

Accessories, too, may be considered essential to an outfit. In the 1940s and 1950s, for instance, a woman was not properly dressed unless she wore gloves. Emily Post, among many others, made this clear: 16

> Always wear gloves, of course, in church, and also on the street. A really smart woman wears them outdoors always, even in the country. Always wear gloves in a restaurant, in a theatre, when you go to lunch, or to a formal dinner, or to a dance. . . . A lady never takes off her gloves to shake hands, no matter when or where. . . . On formal occasions she should *put gloves on* to shake hands with a hostess or with her own guests.

If we consider only those accessories and trimmings that are currently optional, however, we may reasonably speak of them as modifiers. It then becomes possible to distinguish an elaborately decorated style of dress from a simple and plain one, whatever the period. As in speech, it is harder to communicate well in a highly decorated style, though when this is done successfully the result may be very impressive. A costume loaded with acces- 17 sories and trimmings can easily appear cluttered, pretentious or confusing. Very rarely the whole becomes greater than its many parts, and the total effect is luxurious, elegant and often highly sensual.

18   As writers on costume have often pointed out, the average individual above the poverty line has many more clothes than he needs to cover his body, even allowing for washing and changes of weather. Moreover, we often discard garments that show little or no wear and purchase new ones. What is the reason for this? Some have claimed that it is all the result of brainwashing by commercial interests. But the conspiracy theory of fashion change—the idea that the adoption of new styles is simply the result of a plot by greedy designers and manufacturers and fashion editors—has, I think, less foundation than is generally believed. Certainly the fashion industry might like us to throw away all our clothes each year and buy a whole new wardrobe, but it has never been able to achieve this goal. For one thing, it is not [true] that the public will wear anything suggested to it, nor has it ever been true. Ever since fashion became big business, designers have proposed a bewildering array of styles every season. A few of these have been selected or adapted by manufacturers for mass production, but only a certain proportion of them have caught on.

19   As James Laver has remarked, modes are but the reflection of the manners of the time; they are the mirror, not the original. Within the limits imposed by economics, clothes are acquired, used and discarded just as words are, because they meet our needs and express our ideas and emotions. All the exhortations of experts on language cannot save outmoded terms of speech or persuade people to use new ones "correctly." In the same way, those garments that reflect what we are or want to be at the moment will be purchased and worn, and those that do not will not, however frantically they may be ballyhooed.

20   In the past, gifted artists of fashion from Worth to Mary Quant have been able to make inspired guesses about what people will want their clothes to say each year. Today a few designers seem to have retained this ability, but many others have proved to be as hopelessly out of touch as designers in the American auto industry. The classic case is that of the maxiskirt, a style which made women look older and heavier and impeded their movements at a time (1969) when youth, slimness and energy were at the height of their vogue. The maxiskirt was introduced with tremendous fanfare and not a little deception. Magazines and newspapers printed (sometimes perhaps unknowingly) photos of New York and London street scenes populated with hired models in long skirts disguised as passers-by, to give readers in Podunk and Lesser Puddleton the impression that the capitals had capitulated. But these strenuous efforts were in vain: the maxiskirt failed miserably, producing well-deserved financial disaster for its backers.

21   The fashion industry is no more able to preserve a style that men and

women have decided to abandon than to introduce one they do not choose to accept. In America, for instance, huge advertising budgets and the whole-hearted cooperation of magazines such as *Vogue* and *Esquire* have not been able to save the hat, which for centuries was an essential part of everyone's outdoor (and often of their indoor) costume. It survives now mainly as a utilitarian protection against weather, as part of ritual dress (at formal wed-dings, for example) or as a sign of age or individual eccentricity.

As with speech, the meaning of any costume depends on circumstances. 22 It is not "spoken" in a vacuum, but at a specific place and time, any change in which may alter its meaning. Like the remark "Let's get on with this damn business," the two-piece tan business suit and boldly striped shirt and tie that signify energy and determination in the office will have quite another reso-nance at a funeral or picnic.

According to Erving Goffman, the concept of "proper dress" is totally 23 dependent on situation. To wear the costume considered "proper" for a situation acts as a sign of involvement in it, and the person whose clothes do not conform to these standards is likely to be more or less subtly excluded from participation. When other signs of deep involvement are present, rules about proper dress may be waived. Persons who have just escaped from a fire or flood are not censured for wearing pajamas or having uncombed hair; someone bursting into a formal social occasion to announce important news is excused for being in jeans and T-shirt.

In language we distinguish between someone who speaks a sentence 24 well—clearly, and with confidence and dignity—and someone who speaks it badly. In dress too, manner is as important as matter, and in judging the meaning of any garment we will automatically consider whether it fits well or is too large or too small; whether it is old or new; and especially whether it is in good condition, slightly rumpled and soiled or crushed and filthy. Clean-liness may not always be next to godliness, but it is usually regarded as a sign of respectability or at least of self-respect. It is also a sign of status, since to be clean and neat always involves the expense of time and money.

In a few circles, of course, disregard for cleanliness has been considered a 25 virtue. Saint Jerome's remark that "the purity of the body and its garments means the impurity of the soul" inspired generations of unwashed and smelly hermits. In the sixties some hippies and mystics scorned overly clean and tidy dress as a sign of compromise with the Establishment and too great an attachment to the things of this world. There is also a more widespread rural and small-town dislike of the person whose clothes are too clean, slick and smooth. He—or, less often, she—is suspected of being untrustworthy, a smoothie or a city slicker.

In general, however, to wear dirty, rumpled or torn clothing is to invite 26 scorn and condescension. This reaction is ancient; indeed it goes back beyond the dawn of humanity. In most species, a strange animal in poor condition—

mangy, or with matted and muddy fur—is more likely to be attacked by other animals. In the same way, shabbily dressed people are more apt to be treated shabbily. A man in a clean, well-pressed suit who falls down in a central London or Manhattan street is likely to be helped up sooner than one in filthy tatters.

27   At certain times and places—a dark night, a deserted alley—dirt and rags, like mumbled or growled speech, may be alarming. In Dickens's *Great Expectations* they are part of the terror the boy Pip feels when he first sees the convict Magwitch in the graveyard: "A fearful man, all in coarse grey, with a great iron on his leg. A man with no hat, and with broken shoes, and with an old rag tied round his head."

28   A costume not only appears at a specific place and time, it must be "spoken"—that is, worn—by a specific person. Even a simple statement like "I want a drink," or a simple costume—shorts and T-shirt, for example—will have a very different aspect in association with a sixty-year-old man, a sixteen-year-old girl and a six-year-old child. But age and sex are not the only variables to be considered. In judging a costume we will also take into account the physical attributes of the person who is wearing it, assessing him or her in terms of height, weight, posture, racial or ethnic type and facial features and expression. The same outfit will look different on a person whose face and body we consider attractive and on one whom we think ugly. Of course, the idea of "attractiveness" itself is not only subjective, but subject to the historical and geographical vagaries of fashion, as Sir Kenneth Clark has demonstrated in *The Nude*. In twentieth-century Britain and America, for instance, weight above the norm has been considered unattractive and felt to detract from dignity and status; as Emily Post put it in 1922, "The tendency of fat is to take away from one's gentility; therefore, any one inclined to be fat must be ultra conservative—in order to counteract the effect." The overweight person who does not follow this rule is in danger of appearing vulgar or even revolting. In Conrad's *Lord Jim* the shame of the corrupt Dutch captain is underlined by the fact that, though grossly fat, he wears orange-and-green-striped pajamas in public.

29   In dress as in language there is a possible range of expression from the most eccentric statement to the most conventional. At one end of the spectrum is the outfit of which the individual parts or "words" are highly incongruent, marking its wearer (if not on stage or involved in some natural disaster) as very peculiar or possibly deranged. Imagine for instance a transparent sequined evening blouse over a dirty Victorian cotton petticoat and black rubber galoshes. (I have observed this getup in real life; it was worn to a lunch party at a famous Irish country house.) If the same costume were worn by a man, or if the usual grammatical order of the sentence were altered—one of the galoshes placed upside down on the head, for example—the effect of insanity would be even greater.

At the opposite end of the spectrum is the costume that is the equivalent   30
of a cliché; it follows some established style in every particular and instantly
establishes its wearer as a doctor, a debutante, a hippie or a whore. Such
outfits are not uncommon, for as two British sociologists have remarked,
"Identification with and active participation in a social group always involves
the human body and its adornment and clothing." The more significant any
social role is for an individual, the more likely he or she is to dress for it.
When two roles conflict, the costume will either reflect the more important
one or it will combine them, sometimes with incongruous effects, as in the
case of the secretary whose sober, efficient-looking dark suit only partly
conceals a tight, bright, low-cut blouse.

The cliché outfit may in some cases become so standardized that it is   31
spoken of as a "uniform": the pin-striped suit, bowler and black umbrella of
the London City man, for instance, or the blue jeans and T-shirts of high-
school students. Usually, however, these costumes only look like uniforms to
outsiders; peers will be aware of significant differences. The London businessman's tie will tell his associates where he went to school; the cut and
fabric of his suit will allow them to guess at his income. High-school students, in a single glance, can distinguish new jeans from those that are fashionably worn, functionally or decoratively patched or carelessly ragged; they
grasp the fine distinctions of meaning conveyed by straight-leg, flared, boot-
cut and peg-top. When two pairs of jeans are identical to the naked eye a label
handily affixed to the back pocket gives useful information, identifying the
garment as expensive (so-called designer jeans) or discount-department-
store. And even within the latter category there are distinctions: in our local
junior high school, according to a native informant, "freaks always wear Lees,
greasers wear Wranglers, and everyone else wears Levis."

Of course, to the careful observer all these students are only identical   32
below the waist; above it they may wear anything from a lumberjack shirt to a
lace blouse. Grammatically, this costume seems to be a sign that in their
lower or physical natures these persons are alike, however dissimilar they may
be socially, intellectually or aesthetically. If this is so, the opposite statement
can be imagined—and was actually made by my own college classmates thirty
years ago. During the daytime we wore identical baggy sweaters over a wide
variety of slacks, plaid kilts, full cotton or straight tweed or slinky jersey
skirts, ski pants and Bermuda shorts. "We're all nice coeds from the waist up;
we think and talk alike," this costume proclaimed, "but as women we are
infinitely various.". . .

Dress is an aspect of human life that arouses strong feelings, some in-   33
tensely pleasant and others very disagreeable. It is no accident that many of
our daydreams involve fine raiment; nor that one of the most common and
disturbing human nightmares is of finding ourselves in public inappropriately
and/or incompletely clothed.

34   For some people the daily task of choosing a costume is tedious, oppressive or even frightening. Occasionally such people tell us that fashion is unnecessary; that in the ideal world of the future we will all wear some sort of identical jump suit—washable, waterproof, stretchable, temperature-controlled; timeless, ageless and sexless. What a convenience, what a relief it will be, they say, never to worry about how to dress for a job interview, a romantic tryst or a funeral!

35   Convenient perhaps, but not exactly a relief. Such a utopia would give most of us the same kind of chill we feel when a stadium full of Communist-bloc athletes in identical sports outfits, shouting slogans in unison, appears on TV. Most people do not want to be told what to wear any more than they want to be told what to say. In Belfast recently four hundred Irish Republican prisoners "refused to wear any clothes at all, draping themselves day and night in blankets," rather than put on prison uniforms. Even the offer of civilian-style dress did not satisfy them; they insisted on wearing their own clothes brought from home, or nothing. Fashion is free speech, and one of the privileges, if not always one of the pleasures, of a free world.

Questions

1. Lurie uses an extended analogy between clothing and language as a way of explaining the "sign system" of clothing. Show how she does this throughout the essay as she regards various types of clothing as analogous to various parts of speech (accessories are "modifiers") and types of usage ("Casual dress, like casual speech, tends to be loose, relaxed and colorful." [paragraph 12]).

2. Lurie often interprets the nuances of clothing in terms applicable to language. Explain, for instance, what she means by "Besides containing 'words' that are taboo, the language of clothes, like speech, also includes modern and ancient words, words of native and foreign origin, dialect words, colloquialisms, slang and vulgarities" (paragraph 6).

3. Lurie interprets clothing not only in the grammar of a single language but as a mingling of languages. Explain how she illustrates her observation that "The appearance of foreign garments in an otherwise indigenous costume is similar in function to the use of foreign words or phrases in standard English speech" (paragraph 9).

4. It is rare to find an analogy carried throughout an entire chapter, let alone through an entire book, as Lurie has done in *The Language of Clothes,* because at some point the differences between the two phenomena being compared will surface and are likely to overcome the similarities. Has that occurred in this chapter, "Clothing as a Sign System"? Can you think of any significant differences between clothing and language that would undermine Lurie's extensive and complicated analogy?

THOMAS SEBEOK AND JEAN UMIKER-SEBEOK

Performing Animals:
Secrets of the Trade

Thomas Sebeok was born in Budapest, Hungary, in 1920, emigrated to the United States in 1937, and soon earned a B.A. from the University of Chicago (1941), and a Master's and doctorate from Princeton (1943, 1945). His entire career has been spent at Indiana University, where he is currently Distinguished Professor of Linguistics and Semiotics and Professor of Anthropology. He serves on the editorial boards of several linguistics and semiotics (the study of signs and symbols) journals, and is a co-editor of Approaches to Animal Communication *(1969). Sebeok and his wife, Jean Umiker-Sebeok, an anthropologist and research associate at Indiana University, have also edited* Speaking of Apes: A Critical Anthology of Two-Way Communication with Man *(1980), considered "the most complete single volume on the subject."*

This article, written for the popular press, examines critically a number of recent attempts to teach chimpanzees sign language. The Sebeoks, skeptical even at the outset, detect actual or presumed flaws in every experiment designed to study whether animals can use language, and so reinforce their claim that human investigators are "unwittingly entering into a subtle nonverbal communication with [their animal subjects] while convincing themselves . . . that the apes' reactions are more humanlike than direct evidence warrants." By associating Washoe, the chimpanzee using sign language, with Clever Hans, the "talking" circus horse cued in by his trainer, the Sebeoks also employ the ancient and venerated rhetorical strategy of guilt by association and comparison, and thereby reinforce our willingness to believe that "real breakthroughs in man-ape communication are still the stuff of fiction." Here rhetorical skill supports scientific expertise.

So-called talking animals are nothing new. They have appeared in European circuses for centuries and on American television for as long as the medium has been popular. Roy Rogers' horse, Trigger, could count; he answered with his hooves just about any question requiring a yes or no response. Except for the fact that there is no intended deception, the linguistic apes of recent fame are part of the same tradition of animal-human communication as four-legged performers and talking horses.

Thirteen years ago, Beatrice and Allen Gardner of the University of Nevada began their now famous effort to teach Washoe, a chimpanzee, American Sign Language (ASL), the gestural language used by the deaf in the United States. Other experiments to teach chimpanzees to speak had failed, the Gardners reasoned, because chimpanzees lacked the apparatus to vocalize. Within a year, they were able to report that Washoe had command of about 10 signs and was beginning to invent combinations of them, such as *gimme tickle*. Washoe was capable of language. It seemed that humans were not the only species in the universe capable of language. Other researchers, some using ASL and some using artificial languages of various forms, found

733

evidence that appeared to support the Gardners' results. Now Herbert Terrace, through careful linguistic analysis of chimpanzee-human conversations, has concluded that we may indeed still be the only talking animals. But Terrace's approach is only half the critique. The other half is to be found in unconscious bias, self-deception, magic, and circus performance.

3   Man trains animals in one of two distinct ways: *apprentissage,* or scientific training, and *dressage,* or performance training. In *apprentissage,* the animal's behavior is, in theory, guided not by its relationship with a trainer, but by a fixed set of rewards and punishments consciously applied according to the classic rules of behavioral psychology. Rats are taught to run a maze and pigeons to peck at different shapes and colors by *apprentissage.* In *dressage,* the emotional interaction between man and animal is a crucial part of the training, since the animal must learn to read the verbal and nonverbal cues of its trainer. Horses taught to perform for the purpose of exhibition and porpoises taught to play basketball are trained by *dressage.*

4   The most thorough examination of *dressage* to date is Oskar Pfungst's study of the circus horse Clever Hans early in this century. The stallion, it was claimed, could spell, read, and solve problems in math and musical harmony. But Pfungst, a psychologist at the celebrated Berlin Psychological Institute, noticed that as the distance between Hans and his questioners increased, the animal's accuracy decreased, and that if the questioners did not know the correct answer, Hans's performance suffered. Pfungst then began a series of experiments in which a number of elements of the question-and-answer procedure were systematically altered. He was able to uncover several types of visual and auditory cues that were unwittingly being given Hans by his questioners. The feats of Clever Hans amounted to nothing more, Pfungst concluded, than *go* and *no-go* responses to minimal cues provided by the people around him.

5   One way to distinguish *apprentissage* from *dressage* is to examine the variation in an animal's performance with different experimenters. People vary in the amount of nonverbal cuing they do, so that a *dressage*-trained animal will do better with some people than with others. Pfungst noted that certain questioners were more successful than others at eliciting correct responses from Hans. Hans preferred, and performed best for, people who exhibited an "air of quiet authority," "intense concentration," a "facility for motor discharge," and the power to "distribute tension economically." In other words, after giving the animal the cue to begin, the successful examiner would tense and lean forward slightly to focus intently on the horse's tapping response or on other correct movement. When the horse had completed the correct response, the questioner would relax with a barely perceptible movement that would signal Hans to stop performing. Whenever the questioner was inattentive, tired, unaware of the correct answer, or for some other reason incapable of producing the necessary muscular signal, and Hans was

left to his own, somewhat limited, horse sense, he produced the wrong answer.

A similar dependence on human guidance seems to arise in training apes 6 to use language. David Premack once attempted to test his chimpanzee Sarah with a "dumb" trainer, one who was unfamiliar with Sarah's language of word tokens. The trainer was to present Sarah with a problem on a display board and to report the token she selected by microphone to another trainer in an adjacent room. Under these conditions, Sarah's accuracy decreased sharply and, to Premack's surprise, she reverted to an earlier form of sentence production. "Early in [her] training," writes Premack, "she had not produced sentences in their final order: she put correct words on the board in incorrect order and then made one or two changes before settling on a final order. Although she had abandoned this mode of production at least 10 months earlier, she reverted to it with the 'dumb' trainer." This is precisely the sort of behavior one might expect from an animal searching for clues from the experimenter. She would display the word tokens and then move them around, waiting for some unintentional sign from the trainer that one particular arrangement was considered acceptable.

Aware of the Clever Hans phenomenon, researchers sometimes go to 7 great lengths to eliminate possible cuing in their experiments. Some experimenters have attempted to limit the social interaction between the animal and trainers in order to create conditions appropriate to *apprentissage,* but in every case that has proved to be a major impediment to learning. Sarah's trainers first worked inside her cage so that they could guide her hands, turn her head in the proper direction when her attention began to wane, and even pat her back and encourage her with words of affection. After many months of training in these intimate conditions, Sarah became sexually mature and sometimes dangerous (the project started when Sarah was already six years old). Thereafter, training had to be carried on through a small door in her cage, and Premack noted that under these conditions she rejected far more lessons than before.

Sarah's trainers recognized the potential for inadvertent cuing, but assert 8 that they took precautions against it. They realized, for instance, that when she did not know an answer, she would look into the trainer's face for clues. The trainers supposedly controlled this by "refusing" to give clues and by redirecting the chimpanzee's attention to the task. But the use of self-control as a protection against unintentional cuing is of dubious value. Pfungst, after having decoded the system of minimal cues being given Clever Hans, admits that he was himself unable to keep from cuing the horse, even though he made an effort not to.

Washoe's training by the Gardners involved even more socializing with 9 people than did Sarah's. Unlike Sarah, Washoe was not caged, but lived in a homelike, enriched environment. All those in contact with her communicated by ASL. Yet, in the absence of consistently neutral controls, the team of dedicated psychologists and graduate students who surrounded Washoe, like those on similar projects with other apes, appear to have been unaware of the possibility of overinterpreting the animal's moves to fit their own expectations about her language capability.

10   Washoe's signing *water* and *bird* on seeing a swan is a case in point, as H. S. Terrace has noted. . . . Her trainer, Roger Fouts, provides no evidence that Washoe actually characterized the swan as "bird that inhabits water" by making up a compound word, only that the chimp communicated the two words in sequence.

11   This is similar to the clever interpretations made by gullible observers of the "telepathically communicated images" drawn by allegedly psychic persons, such as Uri Geller. Wishing to believe in his extraordinary powers, they eagerly project their own concept onto the crude but suggestive scribbles of the performer. Time and again, researchers read anomalous chimpanzee and gorilla signs as jokes, insults, metaphors, and the like. In one case, an animal was reported to be deliberately joking when, in response to persistent attempts to get it to sign "drink" (by tilting its hand at its mouth), it made the sign perfectly, but at its ear rather than its mouth.

12   In general, there appears to be a tendency on the part of many researchers to consider any answer from a test animal correct if the answer is in the proper category. In response to the question *what color*, for example, the Gardners accepted as correct Washoe's answer of *blue*, even though the object was a red ball.

13   The Gardners' response to claims that Washoe was being cued has been to invite outside experts to witness conversations and to use so-called double-blind tests. But the experts invited were expert only in *apprentissage*. What is needed is an expert in *dressage*, performance-oriented activities involving subtle deception, such as conjury or nonverbal cuing communication. These are the people who are best able to detect nearly imperceptible affective cues. The situation somewhat parallels the investigation by the magician Amazing Randi of Uri Geller's claims of the ability to teleport objects and people and to read minds. Randi reports that Geller had no objection to working in front of an audience of scientists, whom Randi characterizes as some of the easiest people to deceive. But he refused to perform before expert magicians who were skilled in deception themselves and could spot anyone else's quickly.

14   The double-blind experiments are a more complex matter. The strategy, borrowed from pharmacology, is one in which neither the experimenter nor the subject knows which responses are considered correct (or appropriate), and which incorrect (or inappropriate). The ideal experimenter in a double-blind test is one who knows the least about the research. But Washoe, like most other apes in such experiments, essentially refused to cooperate with experimenters she did not know, and known researchers had to be used. As

occurs in some parapsychological research, the subject was being permitted to choose his own tester, which makes the test suspect.

Nevertheless, the Gardners' double-blind experimental procedure was well constructed. Washoe was seated in front of a booth, before a sliding door that she could open or close. Behind the door was a screen on which slides were projected. One "blind" observer (called o-1) sat to one side of the box, where he could not view the screened image but could see the chimp. When Washoe opened the sliding door as she was accustomed to do in such situations, she would see a picture projected on the screen inside. Observer o-1 then asked her in ASL what she had seen, recorded her sign-language response on a slip of paper, and deposited it in a message slot a short distance away. Meanwhile, a second "blind" observer (o-2) was located behind the booth facing Washoe, observing the chimp (but not the slides) through a one-way glass set above the picture screen. He also recorded his interpretation of the chimp's signed responses. The two observers' notations were collected and compared by the experimenter, who was seated behind the message slot in a separate compartment from Washoe's viewing screen. The experimenter also projected the slides, which were prearranged in random order.

Since Observer o-1—the only person visible to the chimp—did not know which slides had been projected on the screen, he presumably could not help Washoe come up with the proper signal by providing cues. If the chimp's responses to the slides were accurate, the theory goes, they would demonstrate her language capability.

In one version of the test, all three participants were project assistants; in a control situation, o-2 was a deaf person without any particular association with the Washoe project, but o-1 and the experimenter were members of the Gardners' staff. Despite the added precaution of two "blind" observers, there were thus holes in the experiment. It is conceivable that the research assistants could, through their familiarity with Washoe's relatively small vocabulary, guess which object was being shown on the screen, even though the ones exhibited were not precisely those used in training and were presented in random order.

Observers experienced in the ways of Washoe could also inadvertently pick up familiar nonverbal clues given off by the chimpanzee in response to certain objects—if, for instance, she commonly smacked her lips at the sign for a favorite food. This "extralingual" understanding could affect an observer's interpretation of Washoe's signs. That the two observers agreed with each other more and more on their reading of Washoe's signs with each subsequent session suggests that they may have been learning both the kinds of objects being used in the tests and Washoe's nonlinguistic cues.

There was another possibility of "leakage," too. After o-1 wrote down Washoe's response, he passed in front of the sliding door in order to reach the

15

16

17

18

19

message slot. If, to take one example, the door was open as he passed by, he could have seen into the booth, and if the experimenter left a slide on the screen until o-1 had actually delivered the message, the observer may have had a chance to learn whether or not Washoe had given the correct answer; he could also have assessed the accuracy of his own reading of the chimp's signing. Although we assume that o-1 was not permitted to change his reading of a given sign en route to the message slot, this type of feedback would greatly enhance his ability to interpret the chimp's signs, and to register unconsciously which objects had not yet appeared on the screen and guess which might be shown subsequently.

20   The possibilities for illicit communication in double-blind experiments are numerous, involving unwitting signals in several modalities. Harvard social psychologist Robert Rosenthal cites an example of auditory cuing in which the experimenter, using a scratchy pen, unintentionally cued a subject by the recording system he was using (long versus short scratches). Without careful on-site scrutiny of the actual trials or conversations in progress, it is difficult to discover the precise nature of the unintended signaling. Oskar Pfungst spent several years studying Clever Hans, who was no doubt clever, but probably not as clever as a chimpanzee. Whenever photographs or films of the apes are examined, as we and Terrace have both done, cuing appears to be present. The similarities between the performances of Hans and the chimpanzees are too strong to be ignored. We believe that when a careful analysis is permitted by the researchers, much of the human-ape communication will be shown to be a product of inadvertent cues.

21   The latest attempts to avoid the Clever Hans effect by reducing human involvement in testing leave us as much in doubt about apes' linguistic capacity as did the earlier research. E. Sue Savage-Rumbaugh, Duane Rumbaugh, and their colleagues at the Yerkes Regional Primate Research Center in Atlanta, for example, have devised experiments in which two chimps try to communicate by means of a computer console—without human intervention or interpretation. In the first test, one chimp must inform the other what food is in a closed container, and in the second, one chimp must tell the other which tool is necessary to open a container (also holding food).

22   In neither experiment was a human explicitly required for the communication to take place. Yet without the presence of a human, the investigators report, the chimps "tended to play and to become easily distracted, like preschool children." Thus, in the first test, an experimenter was present during all the different trials, holding the animals' leashes to keep them focused on the task. By learning from the informer chimp's signal what was in the box, this experimenter could unwittingly have cued the second "observer" chimp—by touch, sound, leash pressure, or other body movement. In the second set of tests, an experimenter was also present and aware of the correct answer during most of the trials. Although the Rumbaughs report a high rate of success in trials with the experimenter "blind or absent," they do not

specify how often the experimenter was actually absent, and they have not ruled out the possibility that the animals were acting according to behaviors that they had learned while the experimenters were still present.

The problem may be insoluble. Apes simply do not take part in such   23
man-made laboratory tests without a great deal of coaxing. The world's leading authority on human-animal communication, Heini Hediger, former director of the Zurich zoo, in fact deems the task of eliminating the Clever Hans effect analogous to squaring the circle—"if only for the reason that every experimental method is necessarily a human method and must thus, per se, constitute a human influence on the animal." Hediger adds: "The concept of an experiment with animals—be it psychological, physiological, or pharmacological—without some direct or indirect contact between human being and animal is basically untenable."

That apes can be taught fairly large vocabularies of symbols has been well   24
established. Time and again, however, reports indicate that there is only a faint resemblance between a chimpanzee's or gorilla's application of these newly acquired tools and that of humans. What we have at the moment, in the ape-language projects, is both accommodation and conflict between worlds as experienced by different species. The chimpanzees and gorillas placed in a totally man-made environment—whether a private home, experimental laboratory, or primate-research colony—adapt themselves, somewhat reluctantly, by learning a number of arbitrary associations between signifier and signified, symbol and object. They learn to utilize those symbols in situations in which trainers will accept no alternative type of response. In other words, the animals will follow certain elementary prescribed rules of play, but there is no indication that they are playing the same "game."

Investigators and experimenters, in turn, accommodate themselves to the   25
expectations of their animal subjects, unwittingly entering into a subtle nonverbal communication with them while convincing themselves, on the basis of their own human rules of interpretation, that the apes' reactions are more humanlike than direct evidence warrants. Real breakthroughs in man-ape communication are still the stuff of fiction.

The Natural and Physical Sciences

BERTRAND RUSSELL

What Is Matter?

Russell's significant works on mathematical logic, Principles of Mathematics (1903), Principia Mathematica (three volumes, with Alfred North Whitehead, 1910–1913), and Introduction to Mathematical Philosophy (1919) helped to shape both mathematical thought and analytic philosophy in the twentieth century. Born in South Wales in 1872, Russell was imprisoned for six months and fired from a lectureship in Philosophy at Cambridge, his alma mater, in 1916, because of his pacifistic opposition to World War I. Many of Russell's major books reflect not only his philosophical brilliance but his philosophical and social radicalism, including Marriage and Morals *(1929),* Education and the Social Order *(1932), and* Why I Am Not a Christian *(1957). Russell's unconventional views on sex (including a proposal of temporary marriage for undergraduates!) led in 1940 to the cancellation of his appointments at Harvard and the City College of New York; his appointment at Cambridge was reinstated in 1944. His* History of Western Philosophy *(1945) remains the quintessential work on the subject. In 1950 he was awarded a Nobel Prize for Literature; later in the decade the septuagenarian was jailed again for antinuclear protests. In his eighties and nineties he wrote on the impact of science on society, and completed a three-volume autobiography, characteristically outspoken, the year before he died in 1970.*

"What Is Matter?" is from The ABC of Relativity *(1925), written to explain abstract scientific concepts to a popular audience. Russell begins by challenging the two "traditional conceptions of matter," "tiny lumps which could never be divided," and undulating waves of the "aether." Having dissociated "matter" from "substance," he proceeds, introducing new concepts, such as "space-time" and "event-particles," to explain the physical properties of atoms and to account for their configurations. All the while he acknowledges that "it is absolutely impossible to know" through physical means what occurs within the atom; "an atom is known by its effects."*

1   The question "What is matter?" is of the kind that is asked by metaphysicians, and answered in vast books of incredible obscurity. But I am not asking the question as a metaphysician: I am asking it as a person who wants to find out what is the moral of modern physics, and more especially of the theory of relativity. It is obvious from what we have learned of that theory that matter cannot be conceived quite as it used to be. I think we can now say more or less what the new conception must be.

2   There were two traditional conceptions of matter, both of which have had advocates ever since scientific speculation began. There were the atomists, who thought that matter consisted of tiny lumps which could never be divided; these were supposed to hit each other and then bounce off in various ways. After Newton, they were no longer supposed actually to come into

contact with each other, but to attract and repel each other, and move in orbits round each other. Then there were those who thought that there is matter of some kind everywhere, and that a true vacuum is impossible. Descartes held this view, and attributed the motions of the planets to vortices in the aether. The Newtonian theory of gravitation caused the view that there is matter everywhere to fall into discredit, the more so as light was thought by Newton and his disciples to be due to actual particles travelling from the source of the light. But when this view of light was disproved, and it was shown that light consisted of waves, the aether was revived so that there should be something to undulate. The aether became still more respectable when it was found to play the same part in electromagnetic phenomena as in the propagation of light. It was even hoped that atoms might turn out to be a mode of motion of the aether. At this stage, the atomic view of matter was, on the whole, getting the worst of it.

Leaving relativity aside for the moment, modern physics has provided proof of the atomic structure of ordinary matter, while not disproving the arguments in favour of the aether, to which no such structure is attributed. The result was a sort of compromise between the two views, the one applying to what was called "gross" matter, the other to the aether. There can be no doubt about electrons and protons, though, as we shall see shortly, they need not be conceived as atoms were conceived traditionally. The truth is, I think, that relativity demands the abandonment of the old conception of "matter," which is infected by the metaphysics associated with "substance," and represents a point of view not really necessary in dealing with phenomena. This is what we must now investigate.   3

In the old view, a piece of matter was something which survived all through time, while never being at more than one place at a given time. This way of looking at things is obviously connected with the complete separation of space and time in which people formerly believed. When we substitute space-time for space and time, we shall naturally expect to derive the physical world from constituents which are as limited in time as in space. Such constituents are what we call "events." An event does not persist and move, like the traditional piece of matter; it merely exists for its little moment and then ceases. A piece of matter will thus be resolved into a series of events. Just as, in the old view, an extended body was composed of a number of particles, so, now, each particle, being extended in time, must be regarded as composed of what we may call "event-particles." The whole series of these events makes up the whole history of the particle, and the particle is regarded as *being* its history, not some metaphysical entity to which the events happen. This view is rendered necessary by the fact that relativity compels us to place time and space more on a level than they were in the older physics.   4

This abstract requirement must be brought into relation with the known facts of the physical world. Now what are the known facts? Let us take it as conceded that light consists of waves travelling with the received velocity. We   5 then know a great deal about what goes on in the parts of space-time where there is no matter; we know, that is to say, that there are periodic occurrences (light-waves) obeying certain laws. These light-waves start from atoms, and the modern theory of the structure of the atom enables us to know a great deal about the circumstances under which they start, and the reasons which determine their wave-lengths. We can find out not only how one light-wave travels, but how its source moves relatively to ourselves. But when I say this I am assuming that we can recognize a source of light as the same at two slightly different times. This is, however, the very thing which had to be investigated.

6   ... A group of connected events can be formed, all related to each other by a law, and all ranged about a centre in space-time. Such a group of events will be the arrival, at various places, of the light-waves emitted by a brief flash of light. We do not need to suppose that anything particular is happening at the centre; certainly we do not need to suppose that we know *what* is happening there. What we know is that, as a matter of geometry, the group of events in question are ranged about a centre, like widening ripples on a pool when a fly has touched it. We can hypothetically invent an occurrence which is to have happened at the centre, and set forth laws by which the consequent disturbance is transmitted. This hypothetical occurrence will then appear to common sense as the "cause" of the disturbance. It will also count as one event in the biography of the particle of matter which is supposed to occupy the centre of the disturbance.

7   Now we find not only that one light-wave travels outward from a centre according to a certain law, but also that, in general, it is followed by other closely similar light-waves. The sun, for example, does not change its appearance suddenly; even if a cloud passes across it during a high wind, the transition is gradual, though swift. In this way a group of occurrences connected with a centre at one point of space-time is brought into relation with other very similar groups whose centres are at neighbouring points of space-time. For each of these other groups common sense invents similar hypothetical occurrences to occupy their centres, and says that all these hypothetical occurrences are part of one history; that is to say, it invents a hypothetical "particle" to which the hypothetical occurrences are to have occurred. It is only by this double use of hypothesis, perfectly unnecessary in each case, that we arrive at anything that can be called "matter" in the old sense of the word.

8   If we are to avoid unnecessary hypotheses, we shall say that an atom at a given moment *is* the various disturbances in the surrounding medium which, in ordinary language, would be said to be "caused" by it. But we shall not take these disturbances at what is, for us, the moment in question, since that would make them depend upon the observer; we shall instead travel outward from the atom with the velocity of light, and take the disturbance we find in each place as we reach it. The closely similar set of disturbances, with very

nearly the same centre, which is found existing slightly earlier or slightly later, will be defined as *being* the atom at a slightly earlier or slightly later moment. In this way, we preserve all the laws of physics, without having recourse to unnecessary hypotheses, or inferred entities, and we remain in harmony with the general principle of economy which has enabled the theory of relativity to clear away so much useless lumber.

Common sense imagines that when it sees a table it sees a table. This is a gross delusion. When common sense sees a table, certain light-waves reach its eyes, and these are of a sort which, in its previous experience, has been associated with certain sensations of touch, as well as with other people's testimony that they also saw the table. But none of this ever brought us to the table itself. The light-waves caused occurrences in our eyes, and these caused occurrences in the optic nerve, and these in turn caused occurrences in the brain. Any one of these, happening without the usual preliminaries, would have caused us to have the sensations we call "seeing the table," even if there had been no table. (Of course, if matter in general is to be interpreted as a group of occurrences, this must apply also to the eye, the optic nerve and the brain.) As to the sense of touch when we press the table with our fingers, that is an electric disturbance on the electrons and protons of our fingertips, produced, according to modern physics, by the proximity of the electrons and protons in the table. If the same disturbance in our finger-tips arose in any other way, we should have the sensations, in spite of their being no table. The testimony of others is obviously a second-hand affair. A witness in a law court, if asked whether he had seen some occurrence, would not be allowed to reply that he believed so because of the testimony of others to that effect. In any case, testimony consists of sound-waves and demands psychological as well as physical interpretation; its connection with the object is therefore very indirect. For all these reasons, when we say that a man "sees a table," we use a highly abbreviated form of expression, concealing complicated and difficult inferences, the validity of which may well be open to question. 9

But we are in danger of becoming entangled in psychological questions, which we must avoid if we can. Let us therefore return to the purely physical point of view. 10

What I wish to suggest may be put as follows. Everything that occurs elsewhere, owing to the existence of an atom, can be explored experimentally, at least in theory, unless it occurs in certain concealed ways. But what occurs within the atom (if anything occurs there) it is absolutely impossible to know: there is no conceivable apparatus by which we could obtain even a glimpse of it. An atom is known by its "effects." But the word "effects" belongs to a view of causation which will not fit modern physics, and in particular will not fit relativity. All that we have a right to say is that certain groups of occurrences happen together, that is to say, in neighbouring parts of space-time. A given observer will regard one member of the group as earlier than the other, but 11 another observer may judge the time-order differently. And even when the time-order is the same for all observers, all that we really have is a connection between the two events, which works equally backwards and forwards. It is not true that the past determines the future in some sense other than that in which the future determines the past: the apparent difference is only due to our ignorance, because we know less about the future than about the past. This is a mere accident: there might be beings who would remember the future and have to infer the past. The feelings of such beings in these matters would be the exact opposite of our own, but no more fallacious.

12   It seems fairly clear that all the facts and laws of physics can be interpreted without assuming that "matter" is anything more than groups of events, each event being of the sort which we should naturally regard as "caused" by the matter in question. This does not involve any change in the symbols or formulae of physics: it is merely a question of interpretation of the symbols.

13   This latitude in interpretation is a characteristic of mathematical physics. What we know is certain very abstract logical relations, which we express in mathematical formulae; we know also that, at certain points, we arrive at results which are capable of being tested experimentally. Take, for example, the eclipse observations by which Einstein's theory as to the bending of light was established. The actual observation consisted in the careful measurement of certain distances on certain photographic plates. The formulae which were to be verified were concerned with the course of light in passing near the sun. Although the part of these formulae which gives the observed result must always be interpreted in the same way, the other part of them may be capable of a great variety of interpretations. The formulae giving the motions of the planets are almost exactly the same in Einstein's theory as in Newton's, but the meaning of the formulae is quite different. It may be said generally that, in the mathematical treatment of nature, we can be far more certain that our formulae are approximately correct than we can be as to the correctness of this or that interpretation of them. And so in the case with which this chapter is concerned; the question as to the nature of an electron or a proton is by no means answered when we know all that mathematical physics has to say as to the laws of its motion and the laws of its interaction with the environment. A definite and conclusive answer to our question is not possible, just because a variety of answers are compatible with the truth of mathematical physics. Nevertheless some answers are preferable to others, because some have a greater probability in their favour. We have been seeking, in this chapter, to define matter so that there *must* be such a thing, if the formulae of physics are true. If we had made our definition such as to secure that a particle of matter should be what one thinks of as substantial, a hard, definite lump, we should not have been *sure* that any such thing exists. That is why our definition, though it may seem complicated, is preferable from the point of view of logical economy and scientific caution.

CHARLES DARWIN
Reasoning in Animals

Darwin (1809–1882) descended from a distinguished British scientific family; his father was a physician, and his grandfather was the renowned Erasmus Darwin, amateur naturalist, physician, and poet who wrote in rhymed couplets on such subjects as The Botanic Garden. *As a youth Darwin was repelled by the study of medicine because of his horror at operations performed on children without the use of anesthesia. Instead, after graduating from Cambridge he shipped aboard the H.M.S.* Beagle *on a scientific expedition around South America, 1831–36. As the ship's naturalist, he recorded careful observations of plants, animals, and human behavior that were published in* The Voyage of the Beagle *(1839) and eventually led to his theories of natural selection (roughly translated as "the survival of the fittest") and evolution. The publication of the revolutionary* The Origin of Species *(1859), which proposed the theory of evolution—the natural and gradual change of species—did not apply this theory to man. Its complement,* The Descent of Man *(1871) did, and provoked enormous controversy between theologians and scientists, which even now is reflected in the debate between creationists and evolutionists.*

"Reasoning in Animals" (title supplied), from Chapter 3 of The Descent of Man, *illustrates Darwin's lucid and engaging literary style as well as his inductive scientific method. After observing natural phenomena, Darwin establishes a hypothesis, and then seeks more evidence—which he presents in careful, colorful anecdotes—that will confirm or deny his original speculation. Thus he convinces himself (and his readers) that dogs have sufficient reasoning ability to spread out on thin ice, rather than clustering and falling through; that monkeys learn from a single painful experience to avoid sharp objects; and so on. Always aware that he must convince skeptics, Darwin takes pains to demonstrate that no alternative explanations fit the facts as well as his does.*

Of all the faculties of the human mind, it will, I presume, be admitted that *Reason* stands at the summit. Only a few persons now dispute that animals possess some power of reasoning. Animals may constantly be seen to pause, deliberate, and resolve. It is a significant fact, that the more the habits of any particular animal are studied by a naturalist, the more he attributes to reason and the less to unlearnt instincts. In future chapters we shall see that some animals extremely low in the scale apparently display a certain amount of reason. No doubt it is often difficult to distinguish between the power of reason and that of instinct. For instance, Dr. Hayes, in his work on "The Open Polar Sea," repeatedly remarks that his dogs, instead of continuing to draw the sledges in a compact body, diverged and separated when they came to thin ice, so that their weight might be more evenly distributed. This was often the first warning which the travellers received that the ice was becoming thin and dangerous. Now, did the dogs act thus from the experience of each individual, or from the example of the older and wiser dogs, or from an inherited habit, that is from instinct? This instinct, may possibly have arisen since the time, long ago, when dogs were first employed by the natives in drawing their sledges; or the Arctic wolves, the parent-stock of the Esquimaux dog, may have acquired an instinct impelling them not to attack their prey in a close pack, when on thin ice.

2 We can only judge by the circumstances under which actions are performed, whether they are due to instinct, or to reason, or to the mere association of ideas: this latter principle, however, is intimately connected with reason. A curious case has been given by Prof. Möbius, of a pike, separated by a plate of glass from an adjoining aquarium stocked with fish, and who often dashed himself with such violence against the glass in trying to catch the other fishes, that he was sometimes completely stunned. The pike went on thus for three months, but at last learnt caution, and ceased to do so. The plate of glass was then removed, but the pike would not attack these particular fishes, though he would devour others which were afterwards introduced; so strongly was the idea of a violent shock associated in his feeble mind with the attempt on his former neighbours. If a savage, who had never seen a large plate-glass window, were to dash himself even once against it, he would for a long time afterwards associate a shock with a window-frame; but very differently from the pike, he would probably reflect on the nature of the impediment, and be cautious under analogous circumstances. Now with monkeys, as we shall presently see, a painful or merely a disagreeable impression, from an action once performed, is sometimes sufficient to prevent the animal from repeating it. If we attribute this difference between the monkey and the pike solely to the association of ideas being so much stronger and more persistent in the one than the other, though the pike often received much the more severe injury, can we maintain in the case of man that a similar difference implies the possession of a fundamentally different mind?

3 Houzeau relates that, whilst crossing a wide and arid plain in Texas, his two dogs suffered greatly from thirst, and that between thirty and forty times they rushed down the hollows to search for water. These hollows were not valleys, and there were no trees in them, or any other difference in the vegetation, and as they were absolutely dry there could have been no smell of damp earth. The dogs behaved as if they knew that a dip in the ground offered them the best chance of finding water, and Houzeau has often witnessed the same behaviour in other animals.

4 I have seen, as I daresay have others, that when a small object is thrown on the ground beyond the reach of one of the elephants in the Zoological Gardens, he blows through his trunk on the ground beyond the object, so that the current reflected on all sides may drive the object within his reach. Again a well-known ethnologist, Mr. Westropp, informs me that he observed in Vienna a bear deliberately making with his paw a current in some water, which was close to the bars of his cage, so as to draw a piece of floating bread within his reach. These actions of the elephant and bear can hardly be attributed to instinct or inherited habit, as they would be of little use to an animal in a state of nature. Now, what is the difference between such actions, when performed by an uncultivated man, and by one of the higher animals?

The savage and the dog have often found water at a low level, and the 5 coincidence under such circumstances has become associated in their minds. A cultivated man would perhaps make some general proposition on the subject; but from all that we know of savages it is extremely doubtful whether they would do so, and a dog certainly would not. But a savage, as well as a dog, would search in the same way, though frequently disappointed; and in both it seems to be equally an act of reason, whether or not any general proposition on the subject is consciously placed before the mind. The same would apply to the elephant and the bear making currents in the air or water. The savage would certainly neither know nor care by what law the desired movements were effected; yet his act would be guided by a rude process of reasoning, as surely as would a philosopher in his longest chain of deductions. There would no doubt be this difference between him and one of the higher animals, that he would take notice of much slighter circumstances and conditions, and would observe any connection between them after much less experience, and this would be of paramount importance. I kept a daily record of the actions of one of my infants, and when he was about eleven months old, and before he could speak a single word, I was continually struck with the greater quickness, with which all sorts of objects and sounds were associated together in his mind, compared with that of the most intelligent dogs I ever knew. But the higher animals differ in exactly the same way in this power of association from those low in the scale, such as the pike, as well as in that of drawing inferences and of observation.

The promptings of reason, after very short experience, are well shewn by 6 the following actions of American monkeys, which stand low in their order. Rengger, a most careful observer, states that when he first gave eggs to his monkeys in Paraguay, they smashed them, and thus lost much of their contents; afterwards they gently hit one end against some hard body, and picked off the bits of shell with their fingers. After cutting themselves only *once* with any sharp tool, they would not touch it again, or would handle it with the greatest caution. Lumps of sugar were often given them wrapped up in paper; and Rengger sometimes put a live wasp in the paper, so that in hastily unfolding it they got stung; after this had *once* happened, they always first held the packet to their ears to detect any movement within.

The following cases relate to dogs. Mr. Colquhoun winged two wild- 7 ducks, which fell on the further side of a stream; his retriever tried to bring over both at once, but could not succeed; she then, though never before known to ruffle a feather, deliberately killed one, brought over the other, and returned for the dead bird. Col. Hutchinson relates that two partridges were shot at once, one being killed, the other wounded; the latter ran away, and was caught by the retriever, who on her return came across the dead bird; "she stopped, evidently greatly puzzled, and after one or two trials, finding she could not take it up without permitting the escape of the winged bird, she considered a moment, then deliberately murdered it by giving it a severe crunch, and afterwards brought away both together. This was the only known instance of her ever having wilfully injured any game." Here we have reason though not quite perfect, for the retriever might have brought the wounded bird first and then returned for the dead one, as in the case of the two wild-ducks. I give the above cases, as resting on the evidence of two independent witnesses, and because in both instances the retrievers, after deliberation, broke through a habit which is inherited by them (that of not killing the game retrieved), and because they shew how strong their reasoning faculty must have been to overcome a fixed habit.

8 I will conclude by quoting a remark by the illustrious Humboldt. "The muleteers in S. America say, 'I will not give you the mule whose step is easiest, but *la mas racional,*—the one that reasons best;' " and as he adds, "this popular expression, dictated by long experience, combats the system of animated machines, better perhaps than all the arguments of speculative philosophy." Nevertheless some writers even yet deny that the higher animals possess a trace of reason; and they endeavour to explain away, by what appears to be mere verbiage, all such facts as those above given.

J. B. S. HALDANE
On Being the Right Size

The reputation of Haldane, a geneticist, rests on his application of mathematical analyses to genetic phenomena, and in particular on his "study of the evolution of living populations." Born in Oxford, England, in 1892, he was educated at Eton, earned an M.A. from Oxford, taught biochemistry at Cambridge 1922–37, and ultimately became a professor of genetics at the University of London, 1937–57. He wrote numerous biology books, including Animal Biology *(with J. S. Huxley, 1929) and* Possible Worlds *(1929), which includes "On Being the Right Size," reprinted below. Like many other intellectuals, he became a Communist in the 1930s;* The Marxist Philosophy and the Sciences *(1938) and* Why Professional Workers Should Be Communists *(1945) manifest his beliefs. In 1957, dissatisfied with British politics, he went into self-exile in India and was appointed a research professor at the Indian Statistical Institute, Calcutta. His last book,* Science and Indian Culture *(1965), was published the year after his death.*

 Many of Haldane's popular essays were written from the conviction that "the public has a right to know what is going on inside the laboratories." This essay on the concept of scale in biology is typical of Haldane's ability to present complicated concepts through clear, precise, easily understood examples, in witty, sometimes fanciful terms, as in his comparison of the flight potential of airplanes, pigeons, eagles—and angels. This essay is often commended as "an example of the way in which science can change how we look at things."

1 The most obvious differences between different animals are differences of size, but for some reason the zoologists have paid singularly little attention to them. In a large textbook of zoology before me I find no indication that the

eagle is larger than the sparrow, or the hippopotamus bigger than the hare, though some grudging admissions are made in the case of the mouse and the whale. But yet it is easy to show that a hare could not be as large as a hippopotamus, or a whale as small as a herring. For every type of animal there is a most convenient size, and a large change in size inevitably carries with it a change of form.

Let us take the most obvious of possible cases, and consider a giant man sixty feet high—about the height of Giant Pope and Giant Pagan in the illustrated *Pilgrim's Progress* of my childhood. These monsters were not only ten times as high as Christian, but ten times as wide and ten times as thick, so that the total weight was a thousand times his, or about eighty to ninety tons. Unfortunately the cross sections of their bones were only a hundred times those of Christian, so that every square inch of giant bone had to support ten times the weight borne by a square inch of human bone. As the human thighbone breaks under about ten times the human weight, Pope and Pagan would have broken their thighs every time they took a step. This was doubtless why they were sitting down in the picture I remember. But it lessens one's respect for Christian and Jack the Giant Killer. 2

To turn to zoology, suppose that a gazelle, a graceful little creature with long thin legs, is to become large, it will break its bones unless it does one of two things. It may make its legs short and thick, like the rhinoceros, so that every pound of weight has still about the same area of bone to support it. Or it can compress its body and stretch out its legs obliquely to gain stability, like the giraffe. I mention those two beasts because they happen to belong to the same order as the gazelle, and both are quite successful mechanically, being remarkably fast runners. 3

Gravity, a mere nuisance to Christian, was a terror to Pope, Pagan, and Despair. To the mouse and any smaller animal it presents practically no dangers. You can drop a mouse down a thousand-yard mine shaft; and, on arriving at the bottom, it gets a slight shock and walks away, provided that the ground is fairly soft. A rat is killed, a man is broken, a horse splashes. For the resistance presented to movement by the air is proportional to the surface of the moving object. Divide an animal's length, breadth, and height each by ten; its weight is reduced to a thousandth, but its surface only to a hundredth. So the resistance to falling in the case of the small animal is relatively ten times greater than the driving force. 4

An insect, therefore, is not afraid of gravity; it can fall without danger, and can cling to the ceiling with remarkably little trouble. It can go in for elegant and fantastic forms of support like that of the daddy-longlegs. But there is a force which is as formidable to an insect as gravitation to a mammal. This is surface tension. A man coming out of a bath carries with him a film of water of about one-fiftieth of an inch in thickness. This weighs roughly a pound. A wet mouse has to carry about its own weight of water. A wet fly has to lift many times its own weight and, as everyone knows, a fly once wetted 5 by water or any other liquid is in a very serious position indeed. An insect going for a drink is in as great danger as a man leaning out over a precipice in search of food. If it once falls into the grip of the surface tension of the water—that is to say, gets wet—it is likely to remain so until it drowns. A few insects, such as water-beetles, contrive to be unwettable; the majority keep well away from their drink by means of a long proboscis.

6   Of course tall land animals have other difficulties. They have to pump their blood to greater heights than a man, and, therefore, require a larger blood pressure and tougher blood-vessels. A great many men die from burst arteries, especially in the brain, and this danger is presumably still greater for an elephant or a giraffe. But animals of all kinds find difficulties in size for the following reason. A typical small animal, say a microscopic worm or rotifer, has a smooth skin through which all the oxygen it requires can soak in, a straight gut with sufficient surface to absorb its food, and a single kidney. Increase its dimensions tenfold in every direction, and its weight is increased a thousand times, so that if it is to use its muscles as efficiently as its miniature counterpart, it will need a thousand times as much food and oxygen per day and will excrete a thousand times as much of waste products.

7   Now if its shape is unaltered its surface will be increased only a hundredfold, and ten times as much oxygen must enter per minute through each square millimetre of skin, ten times as much food through each square millimetre of intestine. When a limit is reached to their absorptive powers their surface has to be increased by some special device. For example, a part of the skin may be drawn out into tufts to make gills or pushed in to make lungs, thus increasing the oxygen-absorbing surface in proportion to the animal's bulk. A man, for example, has a hundred square yards of lung. Similarly, the gut, instead of being smooth and straight, becomes coiled and develops a velvety surface, and other organs increase in complication. The higher animals are not larger than the lower because they are more complicated. They are more complicated because they are larger. Just the same is true of plants. The simplest plants, such as the green algae growing in stagnant water or on the bark of trees, are mere round cells. The higher plants increase their surface by putting out leaves and roots. Comparative anatomy is largely the story of the struggle to increase surface in proportion to volume.

8   Some of the methods of increasing the surface are useful up to a point, but not capable of a very wide adaptation. For example, while vertebrates carry the oxygen from the gills or lungs all over the body in the blood, insects take air directly to every part of their body by tiny blind tubes called tracheae which open to the surface at many different points. Now, although by their breathing movements they can renew the air in the outer part of the tracheal system, the oxygen has to penetrate the finer branches by means of diffusion. Gases can diffuse easily through very small distances, not many times larger than the average length travelled by a gas molecule between collisions with other molecules. But when such vast journeys—from the point of view of a

molecule—as a quarter of an inch have to be made, the process becomes slow. So the portions of an insect's body more than a quarter of an inch from the air would always be short of oxygen. In consequence hardly any insects are much more than half an inch thick. Land crabs are built on the same general plan as insects, but are much clumsier. Yet like ourselves they carry oxygen around in their blood, and are therefore able to grow far larger than any insects. If the insects had hit on a plan for driving air through their tissues instead of letting it soak in, they might well have become as large as lobsters, though other considerations would have prevented them from becoming as large as man.

Exactly the same difficulties attach to flying. It is an elementary principle of aeronautics that the minimum speed needed to keep an aeroplane of a given shape in the air varies as the square root of its length. If its linear dimensions are increased four times, it must fly twice as fast. Now the power needed for the minimum speed increases more rapidly than the weight of the machine. So the larger aeroplane, which weighs sixty-four times as much as the smaller, needs one hundred and twenty-eight times its horsepower to keep up. Applying the same principle to the birds, we find that the limit to their size is soon reached. An angel whose muscles developed no more power weight for weight than those of an eagle or a pigeon would require a breast projecting for about four feet to house the muscles engaged in working its wings, while to economize in weight, its legs would have to be reduced to mere stilts. Actually a large bird such as an eagle or kite does not keep in the air mainly by moving its wings. It is generally to be seen soaring, that is to say balanced on a rising column of air. And even soaring becomes more and more difficult with increasing size. Were this not the case eagles might be as large as tigers and as formidable to man as hostile aeroplanes.

But it is time that we pass to some of the advantages of size. One of the most obvious is that it enables one to keep warm. All warm-blooded animals at rest lose the same amount of heat from a unit area of skin, for which purpose they need a food-supply proportional to their surface and not to their weight. Five thousand mice weigh as much as a man. Their combined surface and food or oxygen consumption are about seventeen times a man's. In fact a mouse eats about one quarter its own weight of food every day, which is mainly used in keeping it warm. For the same reason small animals cannot live in cold countries. In the arctic regions there are no reptiles or amphibians, and no small mammals. The smallest mammal in Spitzbergen is the fox. The small birds fly away in winter, while the insects die, though their eggs can survive six months or more of frost. The most successful mammals are bears, seals, and walruses.

Similarly, the eye is a rather inefficient organ until it reaches a large size. The back of the human eye on which an image of the outside world is thrown, and which corresponds to the film of a camera, is composed of a mosaic of "rods and cones" whose diameter is little more than a length of an average light wave. Each eye has about a half a million, and for two objects to be distinguishable their images must fall on separate rods or cones. It is obvious that with fewer but larger rods and cones we should see less distinctly. If they were twice as broad two points would have to be twice as far apart before we could distinguish them at a given distance. But if their size were diminished and their number increased we should see no better. For it is impossible to form a definite image smaller than a wave-length of light. Hence a mouse's eye is not a small-scale model of a human eye. Its rods and cones are not much smaller than ours, and therefore there are far fewer of them. A mouse could not distinguish one human face from another six feet away. In order that they should be of any use at all the eyes of small animals have to be much larger in proportion to their bodies than our own. Large animals on the other hand only require relatively small eyes, and those of the whale and elephant are little larger than our own.

12   For rather more recondite reasons the same general principle holds true of the brain. If we compare the brain-weights of a set of very similar animals such as the cat, cheetah, leopard, and tiger, we find that as we quadruple the body-weight the brain-weight is only doubled. The larger animal with proportionately larger bones can economize on brain, eyes, and certain other organs.

13   Such are a very few of the considerations which show that for every type of animal there is an optimum size. Yet although Galileo demonstrated the contrary more than three hundred years ago, people still believe that if a flea were as large as a man it could jump a thousand feet into the air. As a matter of fact the height to which an animal can jump is more nearly independent of its size than proportional to it. A flea can jump about two feet, a man about five. To jump a given height, if we neglect the resistance of air, requires an expenditure of energy proportional to the jumper's weight. But if the jumping muscles form a constant fraction of the animal's body, the energy developed per ounce of muscle is independent of the size, provided it can be developed quickly enough in the small animal. As a matter of fact an insect's muscles, although they can contract more quickly than our own, appear to be less efficient; as otherwise a flea or grasshopper could rise six feet into the air.

Questions

1. In "On Being the Right Size," is Haldane proving or merely illustrating his thesis that "For every type of animal there is a most convenient size, and a large change in size inevitably carries with it a change of form" (paragraph 1)? Is Haldane's conception of size or magnitude relative (as in a "big dog" or a "small whale") or absolute? Why is the nature of this conception important to his analysis of the subject?

2. How does Haldane explain the relation of gravity to optimum body size (see paragraphs 4–5)? How does he explain the relation of optimum body surface to body size (paragraphs 7–9)?

3. Is Haldane writing for an audience of lay persons or of zoologists? How can you tell—in terms of choice of examples, amount of technical language, extent of technical analysis, and other features?

4. This essay has been praised as "an example of the way in which science can change how we look at things." Has this essay changed the way you look at human or animal size? Why or why not? Could you extend the reasoning here to other objects in the universe that possess absolute magnitudes, whether they are atoms, plants, planets, galaxies, or other phenomena?

LEWIS THOMAS

The Long Habit

As a distinguished medical researcher and administrator, Thomas (b. 1913) is the author of some two hundred research papers on immunology and pathology. He is better known to the public, however, for his witty, luminous reflections on biology and on life in general that began as monthly columns in the New England Journal of Medicine *and have been collected in* The Lives of a Cell: Notes of a Biology Watcher *(1974), winner of a 1974 National Book Award;* The Medusa and the Snail: More Notes of a Biology Watcher *(1979); and* Late Night Thoughts on Listening to Mahler's Ninth Symphony *(1983). As a biology major at Princeton (B.S., 1933) he published poetry in the college literary magazine, then earned an M.D. from Harvard Medical School (1937). After naval service in the South Pacific during World War II, Thomas taught at Johns Hopkins and other medical schools before becoming Dean of the School of Medicine at New York University. In 1969 he moved to the Yale Medical School, where he became Dean in 1972; he was president of the Memorial Sloan-Kettering Cancer Center 1973–1980, where he is now president emeritus.*

"The Long Habit" is, as Thomas explains early in this essay, the habit of living, which "has become an addiction." We find the prospect of death "unmentionable, unthinkable"— even though it is, says Thomas, perfectly natural and an "absolute certainty." Having taken a position calculated to be unpopular with his readers, medical and laypersons alike, Thomas then proceeds to justify his view, calmly and rationally. He cites analogous examples from other species—flies dying "like flies"—and from humans to demonstrate that a normal death is "a coordinated, integrated physiologic process," gradual and without agony. He further implies that life should not be prolonged artificially, unnaturally. But he ends with an unanswered question pertaining to the final threat—what happens during the loss of consciousness? "Where on earth does it go?" True scientists don't claim to have all the answers; only mythmakers can explain everything.

We continue to share with our remotest ancestors the most tangled and   1
evasive attitudes about death, despite the great distance we have come in
understanding some of the profound aspects of biology. We have as much
distaste for talking about personal death as for thinking about it; it is an
indelicacy, like talking in mixed company about venereal disease or abortion

in the old days. Death on a grand scale does not bother us in the same special way: we can sit around a dinner table and discuss war, involving 60 million volatilized human deaths, as though we were talking about bad weather; we can watch abrupt bloody death every day, in color, on films and television, without blinking back a tear. It is when the numbers of dead are very small, and very close, that we begin to think in scurrying circles. At the very center of the problem is the naked cold deadness of one's own self, the only reality in nature of which we can have absolute certainty, and it is unmentionable, unthinkable. We may be even less willing to face the issue at first hand than our predecessors because of a secret new hope that maybe it will go away. We like to think, hiding the thought, that with all the marvelous ways in which we seem now to lead nature around by the nose, perhaps we can avoid the central problem if we just become, next year, say, a bit smarter.

2   "The long habit of living," said Thomas Browne, "indisposeth us to dying." These days, the habit has become an addiction: we are hooked on living; the tenacity of its grip on us, and ours on it, grows in intensity. We cannot think of giving it up, even when living loses its zest—even when we have lost the zest for zest.

3   We have come a long way in our technologic capacity to put death off, and it is imaginable that we might learn to stall it for even longer periods, perhaps matching the life-spans of the Abkhasian Russians, who are said to go on, springily, for a century and a half. If we can rid ourselves of some of our chronic, degenerative diseases, and cancer, strokes, and coronaries, we might go on and on. It sounds attractive and reasonable, but it is no certainty. If we became free of disease, we would make a much better run of it for the last decade or so, but might still terminate on about the same schedule as now. We may be like the genetically different lines of mice, or like Hayflick's different tissue-culture lines, programmed to die after a predetermined number of days, clocked by their genomes. If this is the way it is, some of us will continue to wear out and come unhinged in the sixth decade, and some much later, depending on genetic timetables.

4   If we ever do achieve freedom from most of today's diseases, or even complete freedom from disease, we will perhaps terminate by drying out and blowing away on a light breeze, but we will still die.

5   Most of my friends do not like this way of looking at it. They prefer to take it for granted that we only die because we get sick, with one lethal ailment or another, and if we did not have our diseases we might go on indefinitely. Even biologists choose to think this about themselves, despite the evidences of the absolute inevitability of death that surround their professional lives. Everything dies, all around, trees, plankton, lichens, mice, whales, flies, mitochondria. In the simplest creatures it is sometimes difficult to see it as death, since the strands of replicating DNA they leave behind are more conspicuously the living parts of themselves than with us (not that it is fundamentally any different, but it seems so). Flies do not develop a ward

round of diseases that carry them off, one by one. They simply age, and die, like flies.

We hanker to go on, even in the face of plain evidence that long, long   6
lives are not necessarily pleasurable in the kind of society we have arranged
thus far. We will be lucky if we can postpone the search for new technologies
for a while, until we have discovered some satisfactory things to do with the
extra time. Something will surely have to be found to take the place of sitting
on the porch re-examining one's watch.

Perhaps we would not be so anxious to prolong life if we did not detest   7
so much the sickness of withdrawal. It is astonishing how little information
we have about this universal process, with all the other dazzling advances in
biology. It is almost as though we wanted not to know about it. Even if we
could imagine the act of death in isolation, without any preliminary stage of
being struck down by disease, we would be fearful of it.

There are signs that medicine may be taking a new interest in the process,   8
partly from curiosity, partly from an embarrassed realization that we have not
been handling this aspect of disease with as much skill as physicians once
displayed, back in the days before they became convinced that disease was
their solitary and sometimes defeatable enemy. It used to be the hardest and
most important of all the services of a good doctor to be on hand at the time
of death and to provide comfort, usually in the home. Now it is done in
hospitals, in secrecy (one of the reasons for the increased fear of death these
days may be that so many people are totally unfamiliar with it; they never
actually see it happen in real life). Some of our technology permits us to deny
its existence, and we maintain flickers of life for long stretches in one community of cells or another, as though we were keeping a flag flying. Death is not
a sudden-all-at-once affair; cells go down in sequence, one by one. You can, if
you like, recover great numbers of them many hours after the lights have
gone out, and grow them out in cultures. It takes hours, even days, before the
irreversible word finally gets around to all the provinces.

We may be about to rediscover that dying is not such a bad thing to do   9
after all. Sir William Osler took this view: he disapproved of people who
spoke of the agony of death, maintaining that there was no such thing.

In a nineteenth-century memoir on an expedition in Africa, there is a   10
story by David Livingston about his own experience of near-death. He was
caught by a lion, crushed across the chest in the animal's great jaws, and saved
in the instant by a lucky shot from a friend. Later, he remembered the episode
in clear detail. He was so amazed by the extraordinary sense of peace, calm,
and total painlessness associated with being killed that he constructed a theory that all creatures are provided with a protective physiologic mechanism,
switched on at the verge of death, carrying them through in a haze of tranquillity.

I have seen agony in death only once, in a patient with rabies; he re-   11
mained acutely aware of every stage in the process of his own disintegration

over a twenty-four-hour period, right up to his final moment. It was as though, in the special neuropathology of rabies, the switch had been prevented from turning.

12   We will be having new opportunities to learn more about the physiology of death at first hand, from the increasing numbers of cardiac patients who have been through the whole process and then back again. Judging from what has been found out thus far, from the first generation of people resuscitated from cardiac standstill (already termed the Lazarus syndrome), Osler seems to have been right. Those who remember parts or all of their episodes do not recall any fear, or anguish. Several people who remained conscious throughout, while appearing to have been quite dead, could only describe a remarkable sensation of detachment. One man underwent coronary occlusion with cessation of the heart and dropped for all practical purposes dead, in front of a hospital; within a few minutes his heart had been restarted by electrodes and he breathed his way back into life. According to his account, the strangest thing was that there were so many people around him, moving so urgently, handling his body with such excitement, while all his awareness was of quietude.

13   In a recent study of the reaction to dying in patients with obstructive disease of the lungs, it was concluded that the process was considerably more shattering for the professional observers than the observed. Most of the patients appeared to be preparing themselves with equanimity for death, as though intuitively familiar with the business. One elderly woman reported that the only painful and distressing part of the process was in being interrupted; on several occasions she was provided with conventional therapeutic measures to maintain oxygenation or restore fluids and electrolytes, and each time she found the experience of coming back harrowing; she deeply resented the interference with her dying.

14   I find myself surprised by the thought that dying is an all-right thing to do, but perhaps it should not surprise. It is, after all, the most ancient and fundamental of biologic functions, with its mechanisms worked out with the same attention to detail, the same provision for the advantage of the organism, the same abundance of genetic information for guidance through the stages, that we have long since become accustomed to finding in all the crucial acts of living.

15   Very well. But even so, if the transformation is a coordinated, integrated physiologic process in its initial, local stages, there is still that permanent vanishing of consciousness to be accounted for. Are we to be stuck forever with this problem? Where on earth does it go? Is it simply stopped dead in its tracks, lost in humus, wasted? Considering the tendency of nature to find uses for complex and intricate mechanisms, this seems to me unnatural. I prefer to think of it as somehow separated off at the filaments of its attachment, and then drawn like an easy breath back into the membrane of its origin, a fresh memory for a biospherical nervous system, but I have no data on the matter.

This is for another science, another day. It may turn out, as some scientists suggest, that we are forever precluded from investigating consciousness by a sort of indeterminacy principle that stipulates that the very act of looking will make it twitch and blur out of sight. If this is true, we will never learn. I envy some of my friends who are convinced about telepathy; oddly enough, it is my European scientist acquaintances who believe it most freely and take it most lightly. All their aunts have received Communications, and there they sit, with proof of the motility of consciousness at their fingertips, and the making of a new science. It is discouraging to have had the wrong aunts, and never the ghost of a message.

Questions

1. What is Thomas's thesis? At what point in the essay does it become apparent?

2. Is Thomas accurate in saying that "death on a grand scale does not bother us in the same special way . . . . [that] the naked cold deadness of one's own self" does (paragraph 1)? Alden Whitman, *New York Times* obituary writer par excellence (175–84) says that "Only the young fear death," and that as people get older they realistically come to terms with the inevitable. Can the views of Thomas and Whitman be reconciled? How would Thomas and Whitman react to Cousins's "The Right to Die" (332–34)?

3. Thomas's argument in paragraph 5 can be explained as a syllogism: (1) All living things inevitably die. (2) Human beings are living things. (3) Therefore, human beings must inevitably die. What is the effect of reducing this phenomenon to a syllogism? Why do "even biologists" choose, despite their knowledge of this inevitability, to think that "if we did not have our diseases we might go on indefinitely" (paragraph 5)?

4. Isn't this a very short essay in which to argue a very controversial subject? What sorts of evidence does Thomas adduce, in this limited space, to try to convince readers that "dying is not such a bad thing to do after all" (paragraph 9)? Has he convinced you? Has Thomas completely convinced himself? Why does he end with the unanswered question, "Where does consciousness go after it has vanished" (paragraph 15)? Why can't scientists claim to know all the answers?

LEWIS THOMAS

A Fear of Pheromones

In this definition of pheromones for an audience of medical and lay readers who may never have heard of the term, Thomas takes risks unusual for science writers. There's always a danger in asking rhetorical questions—some smart aleck may retort with completely unexpected and irreverent answers. Nevertheless, Thomas begins with not one but a series of rhetorical questions; the third ("Why would we want to release odors into the air to convey information?") and fourth ("Why a gas, or droplets of moisture?") imply a definition.

Danger also lurks in personifying animals, as in sentimental verses about cute doggies and cuddly kitties. Why, then, would Thomas take that risk and refer to microbes that "eke out a living, like eighteenth-century musicians, producing chemical signals by ornamenting the products of their hosts"? Why would this scientific researcher anthropomorphize an essentially involuntary, biological process? Yet Thomas does, through the characters of a female moth who, "in a fragrance of ambiguity," sends a message in the manner of Mae West, "At home, 4 p.m. today," and her male consorts, racing toward the target, "all in a good mood," rejoicing in their good luck, " 'Bless my soul, what have we here!' " Scientific writers usually define unfamiliar technical terms or processes immediately when they're introduced into the essay; yet when referring to "short-chain aliphatic compounds" and "estradiol," Thomas does not follow this convention.

Yet somehow this risky writing works, borne aloft by Thomas's wit and ability to clarify complex concepts in a memorably concise way. Would you care to try this?

1   What are we going to do if it turns out that we have pheromones? What on earth would we be doing with such things? With the richness of speech, and all our new devices for communication, why would we want to release odors into the air to convey information about anything? We can send notes, telephone, whisper cryptic invitations, announce the giving of parties, even bounce words off the moon and make them carom around the planets. Why a gas, or droplets of moisture made to be deposited on fence posts?

2   Comfort has recently reviewed the reasons for believing that we are, in fact, in possession of anatomic structures for which there is no rational explanation except as sources of pheromones—tufts of hair, strategically located apocrine glands, unaccountable areas of moisture. We even have folds of skin here and there designed for the controlled nurture of bacteria, and it is known that certain microbes eke out a living, like eighteenth-century musicians, producing chemical signals by ornamenting the products of their hosts.

3   Most of the known pheromones are small, simple molecules, active in extremely small concentrations. Eight or ten carbon atoms in a chain are all that are needed to generate precise, unequivocal directions about all kinds of matters—when and where to cluster in crowds, when to disperse, how to behave to the opposite sex, how to ascertain what *is* the opposite sex, how to organize members of a society in the proper ranking orders of dominance, how to mark out exact boundaries of real estate, and how to establish that one is, beyond argument, one's self. Trails can be laid and followed, antagonists frightened and confused, friends attracted and enchanted.

4   The messages are urgent, but they may arrive, for all we know, in a fragrance of ambiguity. "At home, 4 p.m. today," says the female moth, and releases a brief explosion of bombykol, a single molecule of which will tremble the hairs of any male within miles and send him driving upwind in a confusion of ardor. But it is doubtful if he has an awareness of being caught in an aerosol of chemical attractant. On the contrary, he probably finds suddenly that it has become an excellent day, the weather remarkably bracing,

the time appropriate for a bit of exercise of the old wings, a brisk turn upwind. En route, traveling the gradient of bombykol, he notes the presence of other males, heading in the same direction, all in a good mood, inclined to race for the sheer sport of it. Then, when he reaches his destination, it may seem to him the most extraordinary of coincidences, the greatest piece of luck: "Bless my soul, what have we here!"

It has been soberly calculated that if a single female moth were to release   5
all the bombykol in her sac in a single spray, all at once, she could theoretically attract a trillion males in the instant. This is, of course, not done.

Fish make use of chemical signals for the identification of individual   6
members of a species, and also for the announcement of changes in the status of certain individuals. A catfish that has had a career as a local leader smells one way, but as soon as he is displaced in an administrative reorganization, he smells differently, and everyone recognizes the loss of standing. A bullhead can immediately identify the water in which a recent adversary has been swimming, and he can distinguish between this fish and all others in the school.

There is some preliminary, still fragmentary evidence for important pher-   7
omones in primates. Short-chain aliphatic compounds are elaborated by fe- male monkeys in response to estradiol, and these are of consuming interest to the males. Whether there are other sorts of social communication by phero- mones among primates is not known.

The possibility that human beings are involved in this sort of thing has   8
not attracted much attention until recently. It is still too early to say how it will come out. Perhaps we have inherited only vestiges of the organs needed, only antique and archaic traces of the fragrance, and the memory may be forever gone. We may remain safe from this new challenge to our technology, and, while the twentieth century continues to run out in concentric circles down the drain, we may be able to keep our attention concentrated on how to get energy straight from the sun.

But there are just the slightest suggestions, hints of what may be ahead.   9
Last year it was observed that young women living at close quarters in dormitories tended to undergo spontaneous synchronization of their men- strual cycles. A paper in *Nature* reported the personal experience of an anony- mous, quantitatively minded British scientist who lived for long stretches in isolation on an offshore island, and discovered, by taking the dry weight of the hairs trapped by his electric razor every day, that his beard grew much more rapidly each time he returned to the mainland and encountered girls. Schizophrenic patients are reported to have a special odor to their sweat, traced to trans-3-methylhexanoic acid.

The mind, already jelled by the advances in modern communication so   10
that further boggling is impossible, twitches. One can imagine whole new industries springing up to create new perfumes ("A Scientific Combination of Primer and Releaser"), and other, larger corporations raising new turrets

with flames alight at their tops on the Jersey flats, for the production of phenolic, anesthetic, possibly bright green sprays to cover, mask, or suppress all pheromones ("Don't Let On"). Gas chromatography of air samples might reveal blips of difference between substances released over a Glasgow football match, a committee meeting on academic promotions, and a summer beach on Saturday afternoon, all highly important. One can even imagine agitated conferences in the Pentagon, new agreements in Geneva.

II   It is claimed that a well-trained tracking hound can follow with accuracy the trail of a man in shoes, across open ground marked by the footsteps of any number of other people, provided the dog is given an item of the man's clothing to smell beforehand. If one had to think up an R&D program for a National Institute of Human Fragrance (to be created by combining the budgets of the FDA and FCC), this would be a good problem to start with. It might also provide the kind of secondary, spin-off items of science that we like to see in federally supported research. If it is true, as the novels say, that an intelligent dog can tell the difference between one human being and any other by detecting differences in their scents, an explanation might be geometric differences in 10-carbon molecules, or perhaps differences in the relative concentrations of several pheromones in a medley. If this is a fact, it should be of interest to the immunologic community, which has long since staked out claims on the mechanisms involved in the discrimination between self and nonself. Perhaps the fantastically sensitive and precise immunologic mechanisms for the detection of small molecules such as haptenes represent another way of sensing the same markers. Man's best friend might be used to sniff out histocompatible donors. And so forth. If we could just succeed in maintaining the research activity at this level, perhaps diverting everyone's attention from all other aspects by releasing large quantities of money, we might be able to stay out of trouble.

LAIRD BLOOM (Student)

Methods of Pest Control
Using Insect Pheromones

Bloom (yes, he is the editor's son!) was born in Cleveland in 1964, and attended high school in Clayton, Missouri, and Williamsburg, Virginia, where he edited the student newspaper and wrote a weekly sports column for the Virginia Gazette. *He graduated from the University of Michigan, Phi Beta Kappa, with a B.S. in cellular and molecular biology, which he also studied at Cambridge University on a Churchill Fellowship, 1985–86, before pursuing doctoral work in the same field at the Massachusetts Institute of Technology.*

"Methods of Pest Control Using Insect Pheromones," excerpted below, is a careful term paper written by a beginning science student. Typical of many such students, Bloom wrote the

paper to learn more about the subject, essentially for an instructor far more knowledgeable than himself. In such cases, as demonstrated here, the writer cannot go beyond his depth, and must document everything he says that is derived from outside sources. Yet such a paper cannot be merely a catalog of others' investigations; the writer has to demonstrate an understanding of the material through his ability to discern essential issues in the subject matter, to interpret these—highlighting trends, problems, and points of agreement and dissension among researchers.

. . . Pheromones are chemicals an insect secretes to send signals to members of its own species. They may serve as a silent mating call, mark a trail to a food source, cause grouping, or bring about one of several other highly predictable responses in insects, and as the biological and environmental drawbacks to the use of chemical pesticides become more apparent, the possibilities of using pheromones to control the behavior of specific pest species become increasingly attractive. According to some scientists, it may soon become imperative for new substances such as pheromones to replace insecticides in pest control, as they find that conventional chemicals may cause unwanted changes in both the target insects and their environments (Birch *et al.*, 1974). "To an agricultural system now heavily dependent on chemicals," wrote entomologist Martin C. Birch in 1974, "the prospects of insect resistance, diminishing returns on investments and loss of environmental quality are portents of imminent disaster." Current pheromone research is an attempt to prevent this "disaster," or at least to forestall it.

The object of agricultural pest control is to minimize crop damage caused by insects, and this is usually achieved by reducing the insect population to a level where the damage is "economically acceptable"—less than 1 percent of the total crop (Siddall and Olsen, 1976). The two strategies employed to do this with pheromones alone are the direct elimination of the insect, through killing or physically removing it, and the prevention of reproduction (Shorey, 1977); other systems which combine pheromones and conventional control methods are also being investigated.

The advantages of using pheromones are manifold. First, they are selective for one or a few closely related species and presumably do not affect other species sharing the same range. Second, they are biodegradable. Third, they appear to be nontoxic. Finally, and most importantly, they prompt *specific* patterns of behavior, and so calculated use of pheromones can in theory be used to manipulate species to man's advantage (Wood, 1977).

The greatest potential for development lies in manipulating the mating and aggregation (grouping) responses, according to H. H. Shorey (1977). The two most widely used strategies in field tests in the past 15 years, he writes, are use of the normal response to one of these pheromones to remove the insect from the crop (in traps, for the most part) and the use of abnormally large amounts of the substance to disrupt the normal response to "confuse" the insect. The pheromones of over 100 moths (Lepidoptera) and 20 beetles (Coleoptera) were chemically identified as of 1977 (Minks, 1977), and the U.S. Department of Agriculture has listed 185 chemicals, including these known pheromones, which have been demonstrated to be active in field tests (Inscoe and Beroza, 1976). Many of the compounds which stimulate responses in economically important pests have been field tested as the "active ingredient" in normal-response and response-disruption programs, but the experiments have met with varying degrees of success.

I. Pheromone Identification

4   The first step in developing a pheromone pest-control program is determining the chemical structure of the insect's natural pheromones. In the early days of pheromone research it was thought that a given species had a single, unique chemical that elicited a given response, but analyses of the pheromones of many Lepidoptera and Coleoptera have shown that single-component pheromones are more the exception than the rule (Koehler *et al.*, 1977). Many species have pheromones that are made up of several chemicals, some of which have little or no potency by themselves; and furthermore, some closely related species have certain of these components in common. The degree to which a pheromone is unique for a species depends on the insect and the ratios in which the components are combined (Koehler *et al.*, 1977).

5   To determine the composition of a pheromone, researchers generally employ chromatography to break the chemical down into "fractions" (Hedin *et al.*, 1979). These fractions are further fractionated until their chemical structure can be determined, and then laboratory tests are conducted to pinpoint the components that stimulate insect response. In the case of sex attractants and aggregation pheromones, air containing the chemical in question is drawn through a container of live insects, and the degree to which insects orient themselves toward the source of the chemical determines the chemical's biological activity (Hedin *et al.*, 1979). Field tests serve a similar purpose, with activity being measured on the basis of the number of insects caught in traps baited with potential pheromones (Kraemer *et al.*, 1979; Bierl and Beroza, 1970).

6   Problems, however, have arisen because of the complex compounds involved. Gyplure, identified as the sex attractant of gypsy moths, was later found to be biologically inactive in its pure form (Bierl and Beroza, 1970), and the reason for the mistake was that small amounts of a geometrical isomer of gyplure had been mixed into the original formulation. It was this isomer, and not gyplure, which stimulated the insects. By the same token, impurities can also reduce the effectiveness of pheromone compounds (Tette, 1974). In some cases, one isomer can effectively block out another (Roelofs and Comereau, 1968; Roelofs *et al.*, 1972), thereby reducing or eliminating its attractiveness. . . .

II. Methods of Pest Control Using Pheromones

Once the composition of a pheromone is determined and a method for synthesizing it is found, it is ready to be tested for its practicality in pest control. There are two methods which have received the most attention in recent years, both of which are aimed at lowering insect populations by preventing reproduction rather than by direct killing or removal. One involves the use of sex attractants to trap most of the members of one sex—the male, usually—to the point where the number of fertilized eggs deposited is substantially reduced. The other involves the prevention of mating through disruption of normal pheromone communication. Comparatively large quantities of pheromone are released in infested areas so that insects will not be able to locate individual sources of pheromone, including other insects, and mating is prevented unless insects meet by chance.

A. Trapping. Traps can either kill males directly, keep them alive so that they can be collected, sterilized, and released, or simply hold them so that their natural aggregation pheromone augments the female sex pheromone bait and attracts more insects (Shorey, 1977). The principle is simple: males cannot distinguish the trap bait from live females, and sufficiently high numbers of traps will catch most of the males before they have a chance to mate. H. H. Shorey (1970) calculated that over 99 percent of the males in a population must be removed before the population can be significantly reduced. Male Lepidoptera live an average of 14 days and are able to copulate once a night on an average of 10 nights, meaning that every male can inseminate up to 10 females during its lifetime (Shorey, 1966). A sex ratio of 10 males : 90 females would still result in the insemination of most of the females. A 1 : 99 ratio should eliminate 90 percent of mating, but Shorey (1966) maintains that this is not economically acceptable. Nearly 100 percent of the males must be removed for trapping to be considered an effective control mechanism.

This requirement is complicated by characteristics of the target pest. Some moths are found only in one vegetative habitat, and trapping will normally not be affected by immigration of insects from other infestations if the plot being controlled is fairly well isolated (Shorey, 1977). Other pests, such as the cabbage looper (Saario et al., 1971), are relatively independent, making immigration a problem in testing, and some insects' egg masses easily become airborne and can be carried into uninfested areas (Beroza and Knipling, 1972—gypsy moths).

In addition, the attractiveness of any one trap cannot be too much greater than the attractiveness of a virgin female, Shorey (1977) has found, since males are sensitive to the concentration of the pheromone as well as its presence or absence. When a male moth senses that the pheromone concentration has reached the level of a virgin female, he may stop and begin visual searching, and so traps with extremely high concentrations of pheromone are often less effective than traps with more moderate amounts because they effectively repel some males. Still, Shorey (1970) found, a trap must release the equivalent of 1000 female pheromone gland contents a week to compete with one live female; while both release pheromones in the same concentration at a given time, a live female can produce up to 100 times the capacity of her pheromone gland in a week and will only release the attractant at certain times during the day, while traps are releasing pheromones constantly.

11   Other variables affecting traps' effectiveness are the weather, which may influence insect activity; stage in growing season; the density of the population; the design and placement of traps; and the sex being trapped—trapping females is more successful in limiting egg deposition (Minks, 1977; Shorey, 1977). Trap design has been of particular concern recently, with many researchers attempting to find a pheromone dispenser that gives an even, slow release of the highly volatile chemicals (Flint *et al.*, 1979; Nakagawa *et al.*, 1979). Even the color of the trap has an effect on the number of insects it catches, one group found (Childers *et al.*, 1979), with a trap resembling the coloration of a female lesser peachtree borer being one of the most effective attractants of males of that species.

12   The results of field tests are on the whole not encouraging. In most experiments, trapping alone has had little or no success in areas of high infestation, but in a few areas with small pest populations, researchers report that trapping has potential. In one case, an experiment involving the redbanded leafroller (Glass *et al.*, 1970), two seasons of trapping in a heavily infested orchard could only reduce damage to 32 percent of the fruit. In another orchard, with a very low level of infestation, trapping reduced damage to 0.1 percent in one season. Tests on other orchards with low infestations yielded similar results (Kenneth Trammel in Birch *et al.*, 1974). An analysis of the costs of these experiments also pointed to the use of traps to control only low-level infestations; while only 25 traps per hectare were required to control the low population, an impractical 5000 traps/ha (50 per tree) were needed to achieve 95 percent control in a highly infested orchard. Trammel (in Birch, *et al.*, 1974) suggested that the codling moth, an apple pest, might be a good target for trapping programs because past spraying programs had made the moths relatively scarce. Later experiments, however (MacLellan, 1976; Hagley, 1978; Madsden and Carty, 1979), showed that even the codling moth could not be controlled economically without extremely low populations and an impractically high degree of orchard isolation. . . .

13   **B. Disruption.** The disruption of normal pheromone communication by releasing large quantities of pheromone into the air was first suggested in 1960 (Beroza, 1960) and was first tested in 1967 (Gaston *et al.*, 1967). It is based on the assumption that insects exposed to high concentrations of pheromone from multiple sources will not "home in" on any one source, will not find each other, and thus will not mate. Although little is known about the

behavior mechanisms involved, evidence suggests that this will occur for four possible reasons (E. A. Cameron in Birch *et al.*, 1974; Shorey, 1977):

males' olfactory receptors soon stop registering the presence of the pheromone and males stop trying to locate the pheromone source;
males may find little success in responding to pheromone stimuli—they find
no females—and stop searching;
males may become "confused" and unable to locate the pheromone source;
and females may be inhibited from releasing pheromone if they sense a certain threshold background concentration of the attractant.

In addition, simple probability is on man's side: since more synthetic pheromone is released than pheromone from wild females, the likelihood of a male
finding a female if it does orient toward a pheromone source is very small
(Shorey and Gaston in Birch *et al.*, 1974). In large populations, however,
probability also helps the pest, since the likelihood of an accidental encounter
between male and female is much higher (E. J. Sanders in Birch *et al.*,
1974). . . .

In 1971, an experiment using small pieces of paper treated with the [14]
gypsy moth pheromone, disparlure, succeeded in reducing the ability of
males to find females by two-thirds of what it was in nearby untreated plots
(Beroza and Knipling, 1972). For several days after the paper was scattered,
no males released were captured by virgin female or disparlure traps, and the
researchers attribute the fact that males were later able to find females to the
decline in the papers' potency over time and the degradation of disparlure by
the acid forest floor. 1972 tests using microcapsules (E. A. Cameron in Birch
et al., 1974) showed "no evidence that even one female in a treated plot was
mated." Tests of different types of aerial applications conducted in 1979
(Schwalbe *et al.*, 1979) revealed that microcapsules containing disparlure
could disrupt 83 percent of gypsy moth mating in areas of high infestation
and up to 97 percent in low-density populations. . . .

Better results have been achieved using evaporators placed in fields. [15]
Shorey and Gaston (in Birch *et al.*, 1974) cite experiments with the cabbage
looper between 1966 and 1972 which have reduced mating by 90 to nearly
100 percent (Shorey *et al.*, 1967, 1971, 1972; Gaston *et al.*, 1967; Kaae *et al.*,
1972, 1973). Disruption of 90 percent was obtained by using 10 milligrams
of looplure per hectare per day, while almost 100 percent was achieved
with 100 mg/ha/day. With the cost of looplure projected at $1.00 per
gram (1974 price), they foresee a feasible program costing $.10 per hectare
per day. . . .

Mitchell *et al.* (1975) and Shorey and Gaston (in Birch *et al.*, 1974) note [16]
that some pheromones or combinations of pheromones and related chemicals
have succeeded in disrupting mating in up to seven species in the same plot.

Shorey and Gaston further speculate that a few key chemicals may be found that can effectively disrupt a wide variety of species that attack the same crop.

17   In spite of the comparative success enjoyed by disruption programs, this method still has several drawbacks. It is still inefficient, because entomologists know little about the optimum place for evaporation of pheromone for most species (Shorey, 1977) and because current spray technology is wasteful of the costly pheromone/microcapsule formulations (Sower *et al.*, 1979; Schwalbe *et al.*, 1979). W. E. Burkholder (1977) suggests that disruption techniques will apply great selection pressure that favors the development of new methods of insect communication. With the rapid rate of insect species change, such adaptation could make pheromone pest control programs obsolete relatively quickly.

18   **C. Other Methods of Control.** While male trapping and communication disruption have attracted the most attention, there are several other methods of pheromone pest control being explored. One of the most effective uses of traps is in detecting pests and monitoring pest population levels (Martin Birch in Birch *et al.*, 1974), which has been used successfully in conjunction with conventional pesticides. As of 1977, studies were underway to correlate trap catches with population size, taking into account such factors as weather and crop development (Minks, 1977), so that insecticide applications could be timed for maximum effectiveness. Studies with codling moth trapping have shown that one spray application a season might be eliminated with this prediction method (Hagley, 1978).

19   In some areas, particularly warehouses, in which any infestation is not tolerable, pheromone traps have potential as early detection systems (W. E. Burkholder in Birch *et al.*, 1974; Burkholder, 1977). They allow estimation of population size and assist in pinpointing the location of insects in much the same way population levels are determined from field trap catches. Burkholder mentions that pheromone traps can also be used with conventional insecticides or biological control methods—harmful insect diseases—in that insects can be attracted to traps where they are either killed or infected and released. The diseased insects then return to transmit the disease to others, and the population is controlled without damage to the stored product. Both sex and aggregation pheromones have been tested, with a high rate of success (Burkholder in Birch *et al.*, 1974; Burkholder, 1977; Borden *et al.*, 1979).

20   Morton Beroza and E. F. Knipling (1972) list one additional use of mass-trapping: prevention of insect population spread. Particularly with gypsy moths, which are devastating to timber, buffer zones containing aggregation pheromone traps are likely to stop most insect movement, with the added benefit of costing only one-tenth of insecticide treatments which are "doubtful" at best, according to Beroza and Knipling. . . .

21   A different type of pheromone is used by females in egg-laying. Some insects mark the spot where they have deposited eggs so as to warn other

members of the species against laying their eggs in the same place (Katsoyan-nos, 1975; Zimmerman, 1979), and Martin C. Birch (in Birch *et al.*, 1974) suggests that these may be used in larger quantities to inhibit female pests from depositing eggs at all. Other chemicals found in some plants encourage insect feeding and oviposition, Birch writes, and these might be used to encourage females to lay their eggs on a surface laden with pesticides. Larvae of Lepidoptera generally are not selective in what they eat, and the new generation could be killed quickly if it hatches on a poisoned surface.

III. The Cost of Pheromone Programs

In the 20 years that pheromone-based systems of pest control have been considered, only research on the western pine beetle and the gypsy moth has reached the stage of large-scale field experiments (Wood, 1977). The reasons are largely economic, and they explain why even the most promising programs are not yet used widely in commercial agriculture. Research has been slowed, according to Wood, because of the enormous expenses involved in isolating chemicals and synthesizing large quantities, the lack of grant money, the low market potential due to the high species-specificity of pheromones, and the costs involved in meeting Environmental Protection Agency standards. And yet the western pine beetle causes between $280 million and $600 million in damage each year (Bedard and Wood, in Birch *et al.*, 1974), and the gypsy moth considerably more than that, killing a peak of 1.9 million acres of timber in 1971 (Beroza and Knipling, 1972). According to preliminary estimates by Beroza and Knipling in 1972, both disruption and trapping of gypsy moths are no higher in cost than spray applications. Why, then, have these methods not been adopted on a larger scale, which would reduce their costs even further?

The answer, according to J. B. Siddall and C. M. Olsen (1976), lies in the cost involved in developing a pheromone for commercial use. They estimate that to introduce a single pheromone for disruption programs would cost $960,000 over four years. This is broken down as follows:

1. Chemical process development $250,000
2. Formulation research and development $ 60,000
   (testing of processes)
3. Toxicology and registration $330,000
4. Administrative overhead $320,000
                                                     ─────────
                                                     $960,000

In the development stage, special costs stem from the large numbers of insects needed to produce natural pheromone for analysis—78,000 gypsy moth females in one experiment (Beroza and Knipling, 1972). The need for extremely pure compounds, to prevent inhibitory impurities, means that additional money must be spent equipping the laboratory (Tette, 1974).

These extra costs need not show up in the cost of developing the pheromone if the government underwrites the project, say Siddall and Olsen (1976), but private industry has historically been responsible for footing the bill.

25   The government further adds cost to pheromone programs by classifying them as pesticides for EPA registration purposes (Birch, in Birch *et al.*, 1974). The EPA requires tests to prove that pheromones work, demonstrations of their physical and chemical properties, studies on how long they stay in the environment before being biodegraded and on the buildup of residues in nontarget populations, and reviews of hazards to soil, water, air, plants, and animals in both the short and the long run. Such thorough testing, according to Siddall and Olsen (1976), accounts for nearly one-third of the development cost.

26   . . . Siddall and Olsen (1976) estimate that the user cost of a pheromone program must be $25 per acre per season to compete with the average of $30 per acre cost of pesticides. In the case of the codling moth pheromone, they have calculated the maximum acceptable cost at $.44 per gram; at the time of their study it listed at $12 per gram, or $7.50 per gram in bulk orders. The difference is typical of most pheromones that have potential use in pest control. Disparlure, the gypsy moth pheromone used in both disruption and trapping, is an exception to this, costing approximately $.22 per gram as formulated by the U.S. Department of Agriculture.

27   The reason why pheromones are not in widespread commercial use, say Siddall and Olsen (1976), is that their cost is prohibitive. "Based on the assumptions made in this analysis," they write, "the investment of almost $1 million for development of codling moth control by disruption of pheromonal communication could not be justified on a commercial basis."

IV. The Future of Pheromone Programs

28   From an economic standpoint, the use of pheromone programs is impractical without large-scale industrial or governmental support. From a biological standpoint, certain programs are practical and deserve further investigation, but careful study and caution are needed before they can see widespread use. Authorities in the field stress this need for thorough research, citing entomologists' ignorance of many facets of insect behavior and physiology as one of the major impediments to widespread success (Birch in Birch *et al.*, 1974; Shorey, 1977; Koehler *et al.*, 1977). What is needed, they agree, are the following:

1. Studies of insect behavior.
2. Physiologic studies of how stimulatory and inhibitory chemicals work.
3. Population studies to determine the effects of pheromone programs on pest populations and nontarget plants and animals.
4. Studies of dispersion of the target species.
5. Studies of the pheromones and their effects on the atmosphere.

6. Commercial cooperation in the development of pheromone deployment technology.
7. Large-scale financial support for research on the most economically important pests; financial encouragement of research on other pests.
8. Government support, both legal and financial.

The most likely use of pheromones in the near future is in integrated pest-control programs, which combine pheromonal and conventional methods to maintain pest population below economic threshold levels (Birch, in Birch *et al.*, 1974). The ecological benefits of using pheromones have become apparent over the past 20 years, as have their limitations and dangers. The word for the future is caution. As Koehler *et al.* (1977) put it, "Pheromones are extremely potent biologic agents. . . . They are not panaceas." 29

References

Beroza, M. 1960. *Agricultural Chemistry*. Vol. 57, No. 7. Cited in Beroza, M., and E. F. Knipling. 1972.

Beroza, Morton, and E. F. Knipling. 1972. Gypsy moth control with the sex attractant pheromone. *Science*. Vol. 177, No. 4043, pp. 19–27.

Bierl, Barbara A., Morton Beroza, and C. W. Collier. 1970. Potent sex attractant of the gypsy moth: its isolation, identification and synthesis. *Science*. Vol. 170, No. 3953, pp. 87–89.

Birch, M., K. Trammer, H. H. Shorey, L. K. Gaston, D. D. Hardee, E. A. Cameron, C. J. Sanders, W. D. Bedard, D. L. Wood, W. E. Burkholder, and D. Muller-Schwarze. 1974. Programs utilizing pheromones in survey or control. In *Pheromones,* ed. Martin C. Birch, (North-Holland Publishing Company, Amsterdam/London), pp. 411–461.*

Borden, J. H., M. G. Dolinski, L. Chang, V. Verigin, H. D. Pierce, Jr., and A. C. Oelschlager. 1979. Aggregation pheromone in the rusty grain beetle, *Cryptolestes ferrucineus* (Coleoptera: Cucujidae). *Canadian Entomologist*. Vol. III, No. 6.

Burkholder, W. E. 1977. Manipulation of insect pests of stored products. In *Chemical control of insect behavior: theory and application*, eds. H. H. Shorey and John J. McKelvey, Jr., (John Wiley & Sons, New York), pp. 345–351.

Childers, Stanley H., Rodney L. Holloway, and Dale K. Pollet. 1979. Influence of pheromone trap color in capturing lesser peachtree borer and peachtree borer males. *Journal of Economic Entomology*. Vol. 72, pp. 506–508.

*Articles cited in this chapter have been noted by "Cited in Birch, *et al.*, 1974" following the citations, for the sake of brevity.

Flint, H. M., L. M. McDonough, S. S. Salter, and S. Walker. 1979. Rubber septa; a long lasting substrate for (Z)-11-hexadecenal and (Z)-9-tetradecenal, the primary components of the sex pheromone of the tobacco budworm. *Journal of Economic Entomology*. Vol. 72, pp. 798–800.

Garmon, Linda. 1981. Chemistry: ant-agonize. *Science News*. Vol. 119, No. 16, p. 248.

Gaston, L. K., H. H. Shorey, and S. A. Saario. 1967. Insect population control by the use of sex pheromones to inhibit orientation between the sexes. *Nature*. Vol. 213, No. 1155. Cited in Shorey, H. H. 1977. Manipulation of insect pests of agricultural crops. In *Chemical control of insect behavior: theory and application,* eds. H. H. Shorey and John J. McKelvey, Jr., (John Wiley & Sons, New York), pp. 353–367.

Glass, E. H., W. L. Roelofs, H. Arn, and A. Comeau. 1970. Sex pheromone trapping and red-banded leaf roller moths and development of a long-lasting polyethylene wick. *Journal of Economic Entomology*. Vol. 63, pp. 370–373. Cited in Birch et al., 1974.

Hagley, E. A. C. 1978. Sex pheromones and suppression of the codling moth (Lepidoptera: Olethreutidae). *Canadian Entomologist*. Vol. 110, pp. 781–783.

Hedin, Paul A., Jerry A. Payne, Terry L. Carpenter, and W. Nee. 1979. Sex pheromones of the male and female pecan weevil (*Curcutio dayae*): behavioral and chemical studies. *Environmental Entomology*. Vol. 8, No. 3.

Huber, Roger T., Leon Moore, and Michael P. Hoffman. 1979. Feasibility studies of area-wide pheromone trapping of male pink bollworm moths in a cotton insect pest management program. *Journal of Economic Entomology*. Vol. 72, pp. 222–227.

Inscoe, Mary N., and Morton Beroza. 1976. Insect-behavior chemicals active in field trials. In *Pest management with insect sex attractants,* ed. Morton Beroza, (American Chemical Society, Washington), pp. 145–181.

Kaae, R. S., H. H. Shorey, and L. K. Gaston. 1973. Pheromone concentration as a mechanism for reproductive isolation between two lepidopterous species. *Science*. Vol. 179, pp. 487–488. Cited in Birch *et al.,* 1974.

Kaae, R. S., J. R. McLaughlin, H. H. Shorey, and L. K. Gaston. 1972. Sex pheromones of Lepidoptera. XXXII. Disruption of intraspecific pheromone communication in various species of Lepidoptera by permeation of the air with looplure or hexalure. *Environmental Entomology*. Vol. 1, pp. 651–653. Cited in Birch *et al.,* 1974.

Katsoyannos, Byron I. 1975. Oviposition-deterring, male-arresting, fruit-marking pheromone in *Rhaooletis cerasi. Environmental Entomology*. Vol. 4, No. 5.

Koehler, C. S., J. J. McKelvey, Jr., W. L. Roelofs, H. H. Shorey, R. M. Silverstein, and D. L. Wood. 1977. Advancing toward operational behavior-modifying chemicals. In *Chemical control of insect behavior: theory and application,* eds. H. H. Shorey and John J. McKelvey, Jr., (John Wiley & Sons, New York), pp. 395–400.

Kraemer, M., H. C. Coppel, F. Matsumira, T. Kikukawa, and K. Mori. 1979. Field responses of the white pine sawfly, *Nendiprion pinetum,* to optical isomers of sawfly sex pheromones. *Environmental Entomology.* Vol. 8, No. 3.

Maclellan, C. R. 1976. Suppression of codling moth (Lepidoptera: Olethreutidae) by sex pheromone trapping of males. *Canadian Entomologist.* Vol. 108, pp. 1037–1040.

Madsden, H. F., and B. E. Carty. 1979. Codling moth (Lepidoptera: Olethreutidae): Suppression by male removal with sex pheromone traps in three British Columbia, Canada, orchards. *Canadian Entomologist.* Vol. III, pp. 627–630.

Minks, A. K. 1977. Trapping with behavior-modifying chemicals: feasibility and limitations. In *Chemical control of insect behavior: theory and application,* eds. H. H. Shorey and John J. McKelvey, Jr., (John Wiley & Sons, New York), pp. 385–394.

Mitchell, E. R., M. Jacobson, and A. H. Baumhover. 1975. Environmental Entomology. Vol. 4, pp. 577–579. Cited in Tumlinson, J. H., E. R. Mitchell, and D. K. Chambers. 1976. Manipulating complexes of insect pests with various combinations of behavior-modifying chemicals. In *Pest management with insect sex attractants,* ed. Morton Beroza, (American Chemical Society, Washington), pp. 53–66.

Nakagawa, S., E. J. Harris, and T. Orago. 1979. Controlled release of trimedlure from a three-layer laminated plastic dispenser. *Journal of Economic Entomology.* Vol. 72, pp. 625–627.

Roelofs, W. L. and A. Comeau. 1968. Sex pheromone perception. *Nature* (London), Vol. 220, pp. 600–601. Cited in Tette, James P. 1974. Pheromones in insect population management. In *Pheromones,* ed. Martin C. Birch, (North-Holland Publishing Company, Amsterdam/London) pp. 399–410.

Roelofs, W. L., R. J. Bartell, A. S. Hill, R. T. Carde, and L. H. Waters. 1972. Codling moth sex attractant—field trials with geometrical isomers. *Journal of Economic Entomology.* Vol. 65, pp. 1276–1277. Cited in Tette, James P. 1974. Pheromones in insect population management. In *Pheromones,* ed. Martin C. Birch, (North-Holland Publishing Company, Amsterdam/London), pp. 399–410.

Saario, C. A., H. H. Shorey, and L. K. Gaston. 1971. Sex pheromones of nocturnid moths. XXVIII. Rate of evaporation of a model compound of *Trichoplusia ni. Journal of Economic Entomology.* Vol. 64, pp. 361–364. Cited in Shorey, H. H. 1977. Manipulation of insect pests of agricultural crops. In *Chemical control of insect behavior: theory and application,* eds. H. H. Shorey and John J. McKelvey, Jr., (John Wiley & Sons, New York), pp. 353–367.

Schwalbe, C. P., E. C. Paszek, R. E. Webb, B. A. Bierl-Leonhardt, J. R. Plimmer, C. W. McComb, and C. W. Dull. 1979. Field evaluation of controlled release formulations of disparlure for gypsy moth mating disruption. *Journal of Economic Entomology.* Vol. 72, pp. 322–326.

Shorey, H. H. 1966. *Annals of the Entomological Society of America.* Vol. 50, p. 371. Cited in Shorey, H. H. 1970. Sex pheromones of Lepidoptera. In *Control of insect behavior by natural products,* eds. David L. Wood, Robert M. Silverstein, and Minoru Nakajima, (Academic Press, New York), pp. 249–284.

Shorey, H. H. 1970. Sex pheromones of Lepidoptera. In *Control of insect behavior by natural products,* eds. David L. Wood, Robert M. Silverstein, and Minoru Nakajima, (Academic Press, New York), pp. 249–284.

Shorey, H. H. 1977. Manipulation of insect pests of agricultural crops. In *Chemical control of insect behavior: theory and application,* eds. H. H. Shorey and John J. McKelvey, Jr., (John Wiley & Sons, New York), pp. 353–367.

Shorey, H. H., L. K. Gaston, and C. A. Saario. 1967. Sex pheromones of nocturnid moths. XIV. Feasibility of behavioral control by disrupting pheromone communication in cabbage loopers. *Journal of Economic Entomology.* Vol. 60, pp. 1541–1545. Cited in Birch *et. al.,* 1974.

Shorey, H. H., L. K. Gaston, and L. L. Sower. 1971. The male inhibition technique—cabbage looper control by confusing sex pheromone communication. *California Agriculture.* Vol. 25, No. 5. Cited in Birch *et al.,* 1974.

Shorey, H. H., R. S. Kaae, L. K. Gaston, and J. R. McLaughlin. 1972. Sex pheromones of Lepidoptera. XXX. Disruption of sex pheromone communication in *Trichoplusia ni* as a possible means of mating control. *Environmental Entomology.* Vol. 1, pp. 641–645. Cited in Birch *et al.,* 1974.

Siddall, J. B., and C. M. Olsen. 1976. Pheromones in agriculture—from chemical synthesis to commercial use. In *Pest management with insect sex attractants,* ed. Morton Beroza, (American Chemical Society, Washington), pp. 30–52.

Sower, L. L., G. E. Dalemar, R. D. Orchard, and C. Sartwell. 1979. Reduction of Douglas-fir tussock moth reproduction with synthetic sex pheromone. *Journal of Economic Entomology.* Vol. 72, pp. 739–742.

Tette, James P. 1974. Pheromones in insect population management. In *Pheromones,* ed. Martin C. Birch, (North-Holland Publishing Company, Amsterdam/London), pp. 399–410.

Wood, David L. 1977. Manipulation of forest insect pests. In *Chemical control of insect behavior: theory and application,* eds. H. H. Shorey and John J. McKelvey, Jr., (John Wiley & Sons, New York), pp. 369–384.

Zimmerman, Michael. 1979. Oviposition behavior and the existence of an oviposition-deterring pheromone in *Hylemya.* 1979. *Environmental Entomology.* Vol. 8, pp. 277–279.

KELLY SHEA (Student)

Acid Rain

Shea (b. 1961), a 1982 graduate of the College of William and Mary, worked for two seasons as a national park ranger and is currently a copy editor at Computerworld *magazine. Her expertise in both disciplines of her double major, English and biology, is evident in "Acid Rain," an example of a common type of scientific writing, in which the author explains a natural phenomenon for a general audience. First, she defines the central term, "acid rain," using a general chemistry textbook as her source of information, and devotes the first third of her paper to explaining that phenomenon in clear, nontechnical language. This explanation becomes the basis for the next third of the paper, a comparison between the buffering that occurs with rain of "normal" acidity, and the more devastating effects of acid rain. The last third of the paper analyzes the causes of acid rain, projects even more devastating long-term consequences, examines possible solutions, and ends with a brief argument advocating cleaner air.*

The structure and strategy of Shea's essay are typical of some science writing: beginning with an extended definition; using that definition as the basis for the paper's next section; and concluding with an examination of the consequences of the phenomenon—in this case, negative and potentially even worse—and an appeal for responsible social action and reform. Indeed, William Warner's entire book, Beautiful Swimmers *(788–97) is structured according to this plan.*

We live in an era that has ostensibly become concerned with the natural environment, conservation, and pollution. Every day there is something new to be worried about in the resources we use, including the air we breathe, the food we eat, the water we drink. If we destroy what we have, use it up, or pollute it, we will inevitably lose these valuable natural resources. Among the many possible victims of environmental exploitation are lakes, streams, soils, buildings, monuments, statues, and ancient ruins. All of these static, vulnerable treasures are in danger of being eaten away by a recently recognized phenomenon called acid precipitation.

Although acid precipitation includes snow, hail, sleet, water vapor, mist and even dew, it is often termed simply, "acid rain." Describing the "acid" portion of the phrase is more complicated. A general chemistry textbook defines an acid as a substance dissolved in water producing a solution of pH less than seven. So what does pH mean? The pH scale is one which describes the concentration of hydrogen ions in substances. The more the ions, the more "acid"; the less the ions the more "basic." A lower pH value indicates high acidity, while a higher pH indicates high alkalinity (basicity). The pH scale goes from one to fourteen. One is highly acidic, fourteen is highly basic, and seven is neutral (neither acidic nor basic)—the ions are in balance.

3   Normal precipitation has an average pH of 5.6, already on the acidic side of the scale, but not dangerously so. The various "rained on" substrates can handle this slight acidity, mainly because they possess a "buffering capacity." That is, they contain enough of certain materials which can, in effect, combine with the acids to produce harmless substances, and thus decrease the acidity. They "buffer" the medium (lake, soil, even a statue) against the acid by neutralizing the effects it can have.

4   What are these effects? What do acids do to lakes, streams, and other substances? Acids have different effects on different materials. In the case of statues, monuments, and stone buildings, acids simply break down the composition of minerals—slowly, for certain, but there is a definite breakdown. If you pour soda onto a hard crust of bread, the crust will hold up for awhile, but soon it will start to melt away and will eventually fall apart. Of course the presence of buffers combats the destruction but if, somehow, the acids become stronger (or the buffers weaker), the defense will be less powerful. More immediately noticeable effects can be seen in aquatic and terrestrial environments. Acids can leach essential nutrients from lakes, streams and soils. They can also increase the ability of toxic metals (lead and mercury, for example) to dissolve into a medium. When these metals are released into water, for example, they can cause pipes to corrode faster, fish to become contaminated and die, and plants to be destroyed. Whole habitats can be wiped out and have been: There are lakes in the Adirondacks which have become completely barren of all life due to the devastation of acid rain.

5   How, then, do acids get into the atmospheric precipitation? Now we come to the core of the problem—the source of the acids. There are certain substances which, when added to rain, dew, and mist, can decrease the pH to 4.5 through 4, and lower, which means increased acidity. This precipitation falls from the sky into lakes, onto soil, and pelts monuments such as the Lincoln Memorial, wreaking its havoc.

6   The "certain substances" added are pollutants, namely sulfur and nitrogen oxides, formed from smelting and the burning of coal, oil, and gas. When these fossil fuels are burned, the oxides are evolved. When combined with water in *any* form, the oxides produce—surprise!—sulfuric and nitric acids. So when the oxides are emitted into the atmosphere, and then precipitation comes down through them, the acids are formed, causing acid rain.

7   So, how are lakes and streams affected, when most industrial smelting factories and comparable industries are located in and around cities? How can the Parthenon be endangered when there are obviously no factories in the immediate area? First, don't forget automobiles, crafty culprits contributing

to the emission of the dangerous oxides. But the four-wheeled demons represent only a small part of the whole picture. The major instigator, ironically, is one which evolved to protect human beings from air pollution. The Clean Air Act of 1977 set up standards by which many industries had to somehow decrease the pollution released at ground level where air is breathed by humans. In response to these mandates, incredibly tall (typically 1000 feet) smokestacks were developed to remove the offensive oxides from the local area. So, the oxides are emitted higher in the sky and are easily carried away by winds from the cities to the air high above the typically endangered areas. Winds can carry oxides for five days over thousands of miles, causing acid rain to be deposited anywhere and everywhere.

Thus an initially local problem (air pollution) has become a devastating phenomenon of global significance. Reports of ever-decreasing pH levels of rain come from all over the world. For example, a 1974 Scotland storm produced rain of pH 2.4, the same pH as vinegar. And as the pH decreases, the deleterious effects increase. 8

The most urgent question now is: What can we do about the problem? Devices called scrubbers have been installed in some smokestacks. These are units which can trap most of the sulfur oxides and prevent their atmospheric getaway. But not all factories are required to install them, and they don't eliminate the other major group of pollutants, the nitrogen oxides. The burning of low-sulfur coal and oil is another alternative solution, but that still doesn't eliminate all the emissions. The real solution lies in controlled technology, the conservation of fuel, and an increased awareness by the general public. Yes, these common solutions used to combat most types of pollution reveal that they can be consistently and accurately applied to any environmental nuisance. The only way our society is ever going to solve the problems of pollution is for us to wake up and examine the world around us. It is slowly and silently falling apart and one day, when we do notice its deterioration and wish we tried to prevent it sooner, it will be too late. We'll have lost much of the beauty, history, and integrity of nature, as well as of man's creativity. 9

Ethical and Social Issues in Science

STEPHEN JAY GOULD

Racism and Recapitulation

Gould (born in New York in 1941) graduated from Antioch in 1963, earned a Ph.D. from Columbia in 1967, and since then has been a geology professor at Harvard, where he teaches paleontology, biology, and history of science. His major books are Ontogeny and Phylogeny *(1977) and* The Mismeasure of Man *(1981), an analysis and ultimately a harsh criticism of quantitative measures and tests of intelligence. The three collections of his columns for* Natural History *include* Ever Since Darwin *(1977), from which "Racism and Recapitulation" (below) is reprinted;* The Panda's Thumb *(1980); and* Hen's Teeth and Horse's Toes *(1983). Gould's numerous awards include the National Magazine Award for Essays and Criticism (1980), the American Book Award in Science (1981), and a MacArthur Prize.*

Gould's list of the qualities of great scientific essayists (T. S. Huxley, J. B. S. Haldane, P. B. Medawar) applies equally well to his own writings, including "Racism and Recapitulation":

> *All write about the simplest things and draw from them a universe of implications. . . . All maintain an unflinching commitment to rationality amid the soft attractions of an uncritical mysticism. . . . All demonstrate a deep commitment to the demystification of science by cutting through jargon; they show by example rather than exhortation that the most complex concepts can be rendered intelligibile to everyone.*

"Racism and Recapitulation," which demonstrates these philosophical perspectives and techniques, is Gould's critical analysis of the contradictory racial (and racist) theories of Brinton and Bolk, showing that they are equally flawed.

1   Blacks are inferior, Brinton tells us, because they retain juvenile traits. Blacks are inferior, claims Bolk, because they develop beyond the juvenile traits that whites retain. I doubt that anyone could construct two more contradictory arguments to support the same opinion.

2   The arguments arise from different readings of a fairly technical subject in evolutionary theory: the relationship between ontogeny (the growth of individuals) and phylogeny (the evolutionary history of lineages). My aim here is not to explicate this subject but rather to make a point about pseudoscientific racism. We like to think that scientific progress drives out superstition and prejudice. Brinton linked his racism to the theory of recapitulation, the belief that individuals, in their own embryonic and juvenile growth, repeat the adult stages of their ancestors—that each individual, in its own development, climbs up its family tree. (To supporters of recapitulation,

the embryonic gill slits of human fetuses represent the adult fish from which we descended. And, in the racist reading, white children will pass through and beyond the intellectual stages that characterize adults of "lower" races.) During the late nineteenth century, recapitulation provided one of the two or three leading "scientific" arguments in the racist arsenal.

By the end of the 1920s, however, the theory of recapitulation had utterly collapsed. In fact, . . . anthropologists began to interpret human evolution in precisely the opposite manner. Bolk led the movement, arguing that humans evolved by retaining the juvenile stages of our ancestors and losing previously adult structures—a process called neoteny. With this reversal, we might have expected a rout of white racism: at least, a quiet putting aside of previous claims; at best, an honest admission that the old evidence, interpreted under the new theory of neoteny, affirmed the superiority of blacks (since the retention of juvenile features now becomes a progressive trait). No such thing happened. The old evidence was quietly forgotten, and Bolk sought new data to contradict the old information and support once again the inferiority of blacks. With neoteny, "higher" races must retain more juvenile traits as adults; so Bolk discarded all the embarrassing "facts" once used by recapitulationists and enlisted the few juvenile features of adult whites in his support.

Clearly, science did not influence racial attitudes in this case. Quite the reverse: an a priori belief in black inferiority determined the biased selection of "evidence." From a rich body of data that could support almost any racial assertion, scientists selected facts that would yield their favored conclusion according to theories currently in vogue. There is, I believe, a general message in this sad tale. There is not now and there never has been any unambiguous evidence for genetic determination of traits that tempt us to make racist distinctions (differences between races in average values for brain size, intelligence, moral discernment, and so on). Yet this lack of evidence has not forestalled the expression of scientific opinion. We must therefore conclude that this expression is a political rather than a scientific act—and that scientists tend to behave in a conservative way by providing "objectivity" for what society at large wants to hear.

To return to my story: Ernst Haeckel, Darwin's greatest popularizer, saw great promise for evolutionary theory as a social weapon. He wrote:

> Evolution and progress stand on the one side, marshaled under the bright banner of science; on the other side, marshaled under the black flag of hierarchy, stand spiritual servitude and falsehood, want of reason and barbarism, superstition and retrogression. . . . Evolution is the heavy artillery in the struggle for truth; whole ranks of dualistic sophisms fall before [it] . . . as before the chain shot of artillery.

Recapitulation was Haeckel's favorite argument (he named it the "biogenetic law" and coined the phrase "ontogeny recapitulates phylogeny"). He used it to attack nobility's claim to special status—are we not all fish as embryos?—and to ridicule the soul's immortality—for where could the soul be in our embryonic, wormlike condition?

7   Haeckel and his colleagues also invoked recapitulation to affirm the racial superiority of northern European whites. They scoured the evidence of human anatomy and behavior, using everything they could find from brains to belly buttons. Herbert Spencer wrote that "the intellectual traits of the uncivilized . . . are traits recurring in the children of the civilized." Carl Vogt said it more strongly in 1864: "The grown up Negro partakes, as regards his intellectual faculties, of the nature of the child. . . . Some tribes have founded states, possessing a peculiar organization, but, as to the rest, we may boldly assert that the whole race has, neither in the past nor in the present, performed anything tending to the progress of humanity or worthy of preservation." And the French medical anatomist Etienne Serres really did argue that black males are primitive because the distance between their navel and penis remains small (relative to body height) throughout life, while white children begin with a small separation but increase it during growth—the rising belly button as a mark of progress.

8   The general argument found many social uses. Edward Drinker Cope, best known for his "fossil feud" with Othniel Charles Marsh, compared the cave art of Stone Age man with that of white children and "primitive" adults living today: "We find that the efforts of the earliest races of which we have any knowledge were similar to those which the untaught hand of infancy traces on its slate or the savage depicts on the rocky faces of hills." A whole school of "criminal anthropology". . . branded white wrongdoers as genetically retarded and compared them again with children and adult Africans or Indians: "Some of them [white criminals]," wrote one zealous supporter, "would have been the ornament and moral aristocracy of a tribe of Red Indians." Havelock Ellis noted that white criminals, white children, and South American Indians generally do not blush.

9   Recapitulation had its greatest political impact as an argument to justify imperialism. Kipling, in his poem on the "white man's burden," referred to vanquished natives as "half devil and half child." If the conquest of distant lands upset some Christian beliefs, science could always relieve a bothered conscience by pointing out that primitive people, like white children, were incapable of self-government in a modern world. During the Spanish-American War, a major debate arose in the United States over whether we had a right to annex the Philippines. When antiimperialists cited Henry Clay's contention that the Lord would not have created a race incapable of self-government, Rev. Josiah Strong replied: "Clay's conception was formed before modern science had shown that races develop in the course of centuries as individuals do in years, and that an underdeveloped race, which is incapable of self-government, is no more of a reflection on the Almighty than is an undeveloped child who is incapable of self-government." Others took

the "liberal" viewpoint and cast their racism in the paternalist mode: "Without primitive peoples, the world at large would be much what in small it is without the blessing of children. . . . We ought to be as fair to the 'naughty race' abroad as we are to the 'naughty boy' at home."

But the theory of recapitulation contained a fatal flaw. If the adult traits of ancestors become juvenile features of descendants, then their development must be speeded up to make room for the addition of new adult characters onto the end of a descendant's ontogeny. With the rediscovery of Mendelian genetics in 1900, this "law of acceleration" collapsed, carrying with it the whole theory of recapitulation—for if genes make enzymes and enzymes control the rates of processes, then evolution may act either by speeding up or slowing down the rate of development. Recapitulation requires a universal speeding up, but genetics proclaims that slowing down is just as likely. When scientists began to look for evidences of slowing down, our own species took the limelight. . . . [h]umans have, in many respects, evolved by retaining juvenile features common to primates and even to mammals in general—for example, our bulbous cranium and relatively large brain, the ventral position of our foramen magnum (permitting upright posture), small jaws, and relative hairlessness.

For a half century the proponents of recapitulation had collected racial "evidence"; all of it argued that adults of "lower" races were like white children. When the theory of recapitulation collapsed, supporters of human neoteny still had these data. An objective reinterpretation should have led to an admission that "lower" races are superior; for as Havelock Ellis (an early supporter of neoteny) wrote: "The progress of our race has been a progress in youthfulness." Indeed, the new criterion was accepted—the more childlike race would henceforward wear the mantle of superiority. But the old evidence was simply discarded, and Bolk scurried about for some opposing information to prove that adult whites are like black children. He found it, of course (you always can if you want to badly enough): adult blacks have long skulls, dark skins, strongly prognathous jaws, and an "ancestral dentition"; while adult whites and black babies have short skulls, light (or at least lighter) skins, and small, nonjutting jaws (we'll pass on the teeth). "The white race appears to be the most progressive, as being the most retarded," said Bolk. Havelock Ellis had said much the same in 1894: "The child of many African races is scarcely if at all less intelligent than the European child, but while the African as he grows up becomes stupid and obtuse, and his whole social life falls into a state of hidebound routine, the European retains much of his childlike vivacity."

Lest we dismiss these statements as lapses of a bygone age, I note that the neotenic argument was invoked in 1971 by a leading genetic determinist in the IQ debate. H. Eysenck claims that African and black American babies display faster sensorimotor development than whites. He also argues that rapid sensorimotor development in the first year of life correlates with lower

IQ later. This is a classic example of a potentially meaningless, noncausal correlation: suppose that differences in IQ are completely determined by environment; then, rapid motor development does not cause low IQ—it is merely another measure of racial identification (and a poorer one than skin color). Nonetheless, Eysenck invokes neoteny to support his genetic interpretation: "These findings are important because of a very general view in biology according to which the more prolonged the infancy the greater in general are the cognitive or intellectual abilities of the species."

13   But there is a hooker in the neotenic argument, one that white racists have generally chosen to ignore. It can scarcely be denied that the most juvenilized of human races are not white, but mongoloid (something the American military never understood when it claimed that the Vietcong were manning their armies with "teen-agers"—many of whom turned out to be in their thirties or forties). Bolk darted around it; Havelock Ellis met it squarely and admitted defeat (if not inferiority).

14   If the racist recapitulationists lost their theory, perhaps the racist neotenists will lose on facts (even though history suggests that facts are simply selected to fit prior theories). For there is another embarrassing point in the data of neoteny—namely, the status of women. All was well under recapitulation. Women are more childlike in their anatomy than men—a sure sign of inferiority, as Cope argued so vociferously in the 1880s. Yet, in the neotenic hypothesis, women should be superior by the same evidence. Again, Bolk chose to ignore the issue. And again, Havelock Ellis met it honestly to admit the position that Ashley Montagu later championed in his treatise on "the natural superiority of women." Ellis wrote in 1894: "She bears the special characteristics of humanity in a higher degree than man. . . . This is true of physical characters: the largeheaded, delicate-faced, small-boned man of urban civilization is much nearer to the typical woman than is the savage. Not only by his large brain, but by his large pelvis, the modern man is following a path first marked out by woman." Ellis even suggested that we might seek our salvation in the closing lines of Faust:

> Eternal womanhood
> Lead us on high.

NORBERT WIENER
Moral Problems of a Scientist

The philosophical and ethical concerns of Wiener, a mathematician, are paramount throughout his life and work. Wiener was born in Columbia, Missouri, in 1894, graduated from high school when he was only 12, and at 15 received a B.A. from Tufts, with majors in mathematics and classics. He then studied philosophy at Cornell, earned an M.A. in math-

ematics from Harvard in 1912, and a year later, a Ph.D. and a Bowdoin Prize for his dissertation, which combined mathematics and philosophy. In 1919 he began a lifetime career at the Massachusetts Institute of Technology, a "well-loved and increasingly legendary" professor of mathematics. Wiener's research in information processing led him to discern similarities between computers and the human brain explained in Cybernetics *(1949) and other works and resulted in his reputation as "the father of automation." During World War II he worked for the government in research on guided missiles; his profound understanding of the interrelationship between science, ethics, and politics during wartime is demonstrated in the excerpt from his autobiography,* I Am a Mathematician *(1956) reprinted here.*

Autobiographers interpret for public record the events of their lives and the motives for their actions; in the process they fight old battles over again and re-argue the underlying issues, even though there is no guarantee that they'll have the last word. Wiener does this here in analyzing the various self-serving and political reasons that scientists working on the Manhattan Project to develop the atomic bomb during World War II had for using it to bomb Japan in 1945. In so doing, he emphasizes the conflict between pure, disinterested scientific research ("true science") and science used (or perverted) for military and political ends. The ethical dilemmas for science and the implications for world peace and for the survival of civilization are perennial, as Carl Sagan's "Nuclear Winter" (797–803) also makes clear.

One day during the Second World War I was called down to Washington to see Vannevar Bush. He told me that Harold Urey, of Columbia, wanted to see me in connection with a diffusion problem that had to do with the separation of uranium isotopes. We were already aware that uranium isotopes might play an important part in the transmutation of elements and even in the possible construction of an atomic bomb, for the earlier stages of this work had come before the war and had not been made in the United States.

I went to New York and had a talk with Urey, but I could not find that I had any particular qualification for solving the special problem on which he requested help. I was also very busy with my own work on predictors. I felt that there I had found my niche for the duration of the war. It was a place where my own ideas were particularly useful, and where I did not feel that anyone else could do quite so good a job without my help.

I therefore showed no particular enthusiasm for Urey's problem, although I did not say in so many words that I would not work on it. Perhaps I was not cleared for the problem, or perhaps my lack of enthusiasm itself was considered as a sufficient reason for not using me, but that was the last I heard of the matter. This work was a part of the Manhattan Project and the development of the atomic bomb.

Later on, various young people associated with me were put on the Manhattan Project. They talked to me and to everyone else with a rather disconcerting freedom. At any rate, I gathered that it was their job to solve long chains of differential equations and thereby handle the problem of repeated diffusions. The problem of separating uranium isotopes was reduced to a long chain of diffusions of liquids containing uranium, each stage of which did a minute amount of separation of the two isotopes, ultimately leading in the sum to a fairly complete separation. Such repeated diffusions were necessary to separate two substances as similar in their physical and chemical properties as the uranium isotopes. I then had a suspicion (which I still have, though I know nothing of the detail of the work) that the greater part of this computation was an expensive waste of money. It was explained to me that the effects on which one was working were so vanishingly small that without the greatest possible precision in computation they might have been missed altogether.

5   This however did not look reasonable to me, because it is exactly under these circumstances of the cumulative use of processes which accomplish very little each time that the standard approximation to a system of differential equations by a single partial differential equation works best. In other words, I had and have the greatest doubts, to the effect that in this very slow and often repeated diffusion process those phenomena which may not be justifiably treated as continuous are of very slight real importance.

6   Be that as it may, while I did not have any detailed knowledge of what was being done on Manhattan Project, the time came when neither I nor any other active scientist in America could fail to be aware that such a project was under way. Even then we did not have any clear idea of how it was to be used. We were afraid that the main use to be made of radioactive isotopes was as poisons. We feared that here we might well find ourselves in the position of having developed a weapon which international morality and policy would not permit us to use, even as they had held the Germans back from the use of poison gas against cities. Even were the work to result in an explosive, we were not at all clear as to the possibilities of the bomb nor as to the moral problems which its use would involve. I was very certain of at least one thing: that I was most happy to have had no share in the responsibility for its development and its later use. . . .

7   At the time of the bombing of Hiroshima [my emotional experiences were devastating]. At first I was of course startled, but not surprised, as I had been aware of the possibility of the use of the new Manhattan Project weapons against an enemy. Frankly, however, I had been clinging to the hope that at the last minute something in the atomic bomb would fail to work, for I had already reflected considerably on the significance of the bomb and on the meaning to society of being compelled to live from that time on under the shadow of the threat of limitless destruction.

8   Of course I was gratified when the Japanese war ended without the heavy casualties on our part that a frontal attack on the mainland would have involved. Yet even this gratifying news left me in a state of profound disquiet. I knew very well the tendency (which is not confined to America, though it is extremely strong here) to regard a war in the light of a glorified football game, at which at some period the final score is in, and which we have to

count as either a definite victory or a definite defeat. I knew that this attitude of dividing history into separate blocks, each contained within itself, is by no means weakest in the Army and Navy.

But to me this episodic view of history seemed completely superficial. 9 The most important thing about the atomic bomb was, in my opinion, not the termination of a specific war without undue casualties on our part, but the fact that we were now confronted with a new world and new possibilities with which we should have to live ever after. To me the most important fact about the wars of the past was that, serious as they had been, and completely destructive for those involved in them, they had been more or less local affairs. One country and one civilization might go under, but the malignant process of destruction had so far been localized, and new races and peoples might take up the torch which the others had put down.

I did not in the least underrate the will to destructiveness, which was as 10 much a part of war with a flint ax and of war with a bow and arrow as it is of war with a musket and of war with a machine gun. What came most strongly to my attention was that in previous wars the power of destruction was not commensurate with the will for destruction. Thus, while I realized that as far as the people killed or wounded are concerned, there is very little difference between a cannonade or an aerial bombardment with explosive bombs of the type already familiar and the use of the atomic bomb, there seemed to me to be most important practical differences in the consequences to humanity at large.

Up to now no great war, and this includes World War II, had been 11 possible except by the concerted and prolonged will of the people fighting, and consequently no such war could be undertaken without a profoundly real share in it by millions of people. Now the new modes of mass destruction, expensive as they must be in the bulk, have become so inexpensive per person killed that they no longer take up an overwhelming share of a national budget.

For the first time in history, it has become possible for a limited group of 12 a few thousand people to threaten the absolute destruction of millions, and this without any highly specific immediate risk to themselves.

War had made the transition between an overwhelming assertion of 13 national effort and the push-button declaration of the will of a small minority of people. Fundamentally this is true, even if one includes in the military effort all the absolutely vast but relatively small sums which have been put into the whole body of nuclear research. It is even more devastatingly true if one considers the relatively minimal effort required on the part of a few generals and a few aviators to place on a target an atomic bomb already made.

Thus, war has been transported, at least as a possibility, from the field of 14 national effort to the field of private conspiracy. In view of the fact that the great struggle to come threatens to be one between the United States and the Soviet Government, and in view of the additional fact that the whole atmosphere and administration of the Soviet Government shares with that of the Nazis an extremely strong conspiratorial nature, we have taken a step which is intrinsically most dangerous for us.

15   I did not regard with much seriousness the assertions which some of the great administrators of science were making, to the effect that the know-how needed for the construction of the atomic bomb was a purely American thing and could not be duplicated by a possible enemy for many years at least, during which we could be counted upon to develop a new and even more devastating know-how. In the first place, I was acquainted with more than one of these popes and cardinals of applied science, and I knew very well how they underrated aliens of all sorts, in particular those not of the European race. With my wide acquaintance among scholars of many races and many countries, I had not been able to discern that scientific ability and moral discipline were the peculiar property of those of blanched skin and English speech.

16   But this was not all. The moment that we had declared both our possession of the bomb and its efficiency by using it against an enemy, we had served notice on every country that its continued existence and independence of policy were conditioned on its prompt possession of a similar weapon. This meant two things: that any country which was our rival or potential rival was bound to push nuclear research for the sake of its own continued independent existence, with the greatly stimulating knowledge that this research was not intrinsically in vain; and that any such country would inevitably set up an espionage system to get hold of our secrets.

17   This is not to say that we Americans would not be bound in self-defense to oppose such leaks and such espionage with our full effort for the sake of our very national existence; but it does mean that such considerations of legality and such demands on the moral responsibility of loyal American citizens could not be expected to have the least force beyond our frontiers. If the roles of Russia and the United States had been reversed, we should have been compelled to do exactly what they did in attempting to discover and develop such a vital secret of the other side; and we should regard as a national hero any person attached to our interests who performed an act of espionage exactly like that of Fuchs or the Rosenbergs.

18   I then began to evolve in my mind the general problem of secrets; not so much as a moral issue, but as a practical issue and a policy which we might hope to maintain effectively in the long run. Here I could not help considering how soldiers themselves regard secrets in the field. It is well recognized that every cipher can be broken if there is sufficient inducement to do it and if it is worthwhile to work long enough; and an army in the field has one-hour ciphers, twenty-four-hour ciphers, one-week ciphers, perhaps one-year ciphers, but never ciphers which are expected to last an eternity.

19   Under the ordinary circumstances of life, we have not been accustomed to think in terms of espionage, cheating, and the like. In particular, such ideas

are foreign to the nature of the true scientist, who, as Einstein has pointed out, has as his antagonist a world which is hard to understand and interpret, but which does not maliciously and malignantly resist this interpretation. "The Lord is subtle, but he isn't plain mean."

With ordinary secrets of limited value, we do not have to live under a 20 perpetual fear that somebody is trying to break them. If, however, we establish a secret of the supreme value and danger of the atomic bomb, it is not realistic to suppose that it will never be broken, nor that the general good will among scientists will exclude the existence of one or two who, either because of their opinions or their slight resistance to moral pressure, may give our secrets over to those who will endanger us.

If we are to play with the edged tools of modern warfare, we are running 21 not merely the danger of being cut by accident and carelessness but the practical certainty that other people will follow where we have already gone and that we shall be exposed to the same perils to which we have exposed others. Secrecy is thus at once very necessary and, in the long run, quite impossible. It is unrealistic to give over our main protection to such a fragile defense.

There were other reasons, moreover, which, on much more specific 22 grounds, made me feel skeptical of the wisdom of the course we had been pursuing. It is true that the atomic bomb had been perfected only after Germany had been eliminated from the war, and that Japan was the only possible proving ground for the bomb as an actual deadly weapon. Nevertheless, there were many both in Japan and elsewhere in the Orient who would think that we had been willing to use a weapon of this terribleness against Japan when we might not have been willing to use it against a white enemy. I myself could not help wondering whether there might not be a certain degree of truth in this charge. In a world in which European colonialism in the Orient was rapidly coming to an end, and in which every oriental country had much reason to be aware of the moral difference which certain elements in the West were in the habit of making between white people and colored people, this weapon was pure dynamite (an obsolete metaphor now that the atomic bomb is here) as far as our future diplomatic policy was concerned. What made the situation ten times worse was that this was the sort of dynamite which Russia, our greatest potential antagonist if not our greatest actual enemy, was in a position to use, and would have no hesitation whatever in using.

It is the plainest history that our atomic bomb effort was international in 23 the last degree and was made possible by a group of people who could not have been got together had it not been for the fact that the threat of Nazi Germany was so strongly felt over the world, and particularly by that very scholarly group who contributed the most to Nuclear theory. I refer to such men as Einstein, Szilard, Fermi, and Niels Bohr. To expect in the future that a similar group could be got together from all the corners of the world to defend our national policy involved the continued expectation that we should always have the same moral prestige. It was therefore doubly unfortunate that we should have used the bomb on an occasion on which it might have been thought that we would not have used it against white men.

24   There was another matter which aroused grave suspicion in the minds of many of us. While the nuclear program did not itself involve any overwhelming part of the national military effort, it was still in and for itself an extremely expensive business. The people in charge of it had in their hands the expenditure of billions of dollars, and sooner or later, after the war, a day of reckoning was bound to come, when Congress would ask for a strict accounting and for a justification of these enormous expenditures. Under these circumstances, the position of the high administrators of nuclear research would be much stronger if they could make a legitimate or plausible claim that this research had served a major purpose in terminating the war. On the other hand, if they had come back empty-handed—with the bomb still on the docket for future wars, or even with the purely symbolic use of the bomb to declare to the Japanese our willingness to use it in actual fact if the war were to go on—their position would have been much weaker, and they would have been in serious danger of being broken by a new administration coming into power on the rebound after the war and desirous of showing up the graft and ineptitude of its predecessor.

25   Thus, the pressure to use the bomb, with its full killing power, was not merely great from a patriotic point of view but was quite as great from the point of view of the personal fortunes of people involved in its development. This pressure might have been unavoidable, but the possibility of this pressure, and of our being forced by personal interests into a policy that might not be to our best interest, should have been considered more seriously from the very beginning.

26   Of the splendid technical work that was done in the construction of the bomb there can be no question. Frankly, I can see no evidence of a similar high quality of work in the policy-making which should have accompanied this. The period between the experimental explosion at Los Alamos and the use of the bomb in deadly earnest was so short as to preclude the possibility of clear thinking. The qualms of the scientists who knew the most about what the bomb could do, and who had the clearest basis to estimate the possibilities of future bombs, were utterly ignored, and the suggestion to invite Japanese authorities to an experimental exhibition of the bomb somewhere in the South Pacific was flatly rejected.

27   Behind all this I sensed the desires of the gadgeteer to see the wheels go round. Moreover, the whole idea of push-button warfare has an enormous temptation for those who are confident of their power of invention and have a deep distrust of human beings. I have seen such people and have a very good idea of what makes them tick. It is unfortunate in more than one way that the war and the subsequent uneasy peace have brought them to the front.

All these and yet other ideas passed through my mind on the very day of   28
Hiroshima. One of the strong points and at the same time one of the burdens
of the creative scholar is that he must stand alone. I wished—oh how I
wished!—that I could be in a position to take what was happening passively,
with a sincere acceptance of the wisdom of the policy makers and with an
abdication of all personal judgment. The fact is, however, that I had no
reason to believe that the judgment of these men on the larger issues of the
situation was superior to my own, whatever their technical information
might be. I knew that more than one of the high officials of science had not
one tenth my contact with the scientists of other countries and of other
standpoints and was in nowhere nearly as good a position to assess the world
reaction to the bomb. I knew, moreover, that I had been in the habit of
considering the history of science and of invention from a more or less
philosophic point of view, and I did not believe that those who made the
decisions could do this any better than I might. The sincere scientist must
back his bets and guesses, even when he is a Cassandra and no one believes
him. I had behind me many years of lonely work in science where I had finally
proved to be in the right. This inability to trust the Powers That Be was a
source of no particular satisfaction to me, but there it was, and it had to be
faced.

One of my greatest worries was the reaction of the bomb on science and   29
on the public's attitude to the scientist. We had voluntarily accepted a measure of secrecy and had given up much of our liberty of action for the sake of
the war, even though—for that very purpose, as many of us thought—more
secrecy than the optimum was imposed, and this at times had hampered our
internal communications more than the information-gathering service of the
enemy. We had hoped that this unfamiliar self-discipline would be a temporary thing, and we had expected that after this war—as, after all, before—we
should return to the free spirit of communication, intranational and international, which is the very life of science. Now we found that, whether we
wished it or not, we were to be the custodians of secrets on which the whole
national life might depend. At no time in the forseeable future could we again
do our research as free men. Those who had gained rank and power over us
during the war were most loath to relinquish any part of the prestige they had
obtained. Since many of us possessed secrets which could be captured by the
enemy and could be used to our national disadvantage, we were obviously
doomed to live in an atmosphere of suspicion forever after, and the police
scrutiny on our political opinions which began in the war showed no signs of
future remission.

The public liked the atomic bomb as little as we did, and there were many   30
who were quick to see the signs of future danger and to develop a profound
consciousness of guilt. Such a consciousness looks for a scapegoat. Who
could constitute a better scapegoat than the scientists themselves? They had
unquestionably developed the potentialities which had led to the bomb. The
man in the street, who knew little of scientists and found them a strange and

self-contained race, was quick to accuse them of a desire for the power of destruction manifested by the bomb. What made this both more plausible and more dangerous was the fact that, while the working scientists felt very little personal power and had very little desire for it, there was a group of administrative gadget workers who were quite sensible of the fact that they now had a new ace in the hole in the struggle for power.

31   At any rate, it was perfectly clear to me at the very beginning that we scientists were from now on to be faced by an ambivalent attitude. For the public, who regarded us as medicine men and magicians, was likely to consider us an acceptable sacrifice to the gods as other, more primitive publics do. In that very day of the atomic bomb the whole pattern of the witch hunt of the last eight years became clear, and what we are living through is nothing but the transfer into action of what was then written in the heavens. . . .

WILLIAM W. WARNER

The Islands [of Chesapeake Bay]: Looking Ahead

Warner, currently a writer and research associate at the Smithsonian Institution, has a worldwide perspective. He was born in New York City in 1920 and graduated from Princeton in 1943. After a career in the foreign service, and in the Peace Corps as program Coordinator for Latin America, he joined the Smithsonian Institution in 1964. There his fascination with the life and lore of the Chesapeake Bay led ultimately to the Pulitzer Prize–winning study, Beautiful Swimmers: Watermen, Crabs and the Chesapeake Bay *(1976), which also won the Phi Beta Kappa Book Award. His second book,* Distant Water *(1984) continues his study of the subject, again from the combined perspectives of the natural scientist and humanist.*

This chapter, abridged from Beautiful Swimmers, *reflects Warner's emphasis on the quality of life—human, plant, and animal—in the Chesapeake Bay region. He characterizes the two main crabbing islands, Smith and Tangier, showing how their inhabitants, history, and economy are intimately intertwined with the health of the crustacean population—which in turn is affected by state fishing regulations.[1] Warner moves gradually but inexorably to a discussion of the effects of environmental pollution on the whole, complex ecosystem, concluding that "General eutrophication is Lake Erie. Simple as that." And as deadly.*

1   Around noon every day of the week except Sunday, Crisfield goes through a well-practiced ritual. Down at the County Dock at this hour lies the gateway

---

[1] Since *Beautiful Swimmers* was written, a number of changes have been written into the fishing regulations, largely as a result of the book's influence in increasing public and official awareness of the delicacy of the Bay's ecosystem.

to "another world, a unique world where time holds still and where Elizabethan speech may yet be heard," as legions of hyperbolic travel writers have expressed it. The preparations for journeying to this other world, at any rate, are certainly unique. Most noticeably, they are attended by great commotion, out of which there eventually comes a reassuring sense of order and regularity. Cluttering the waterfront are cases of soft drinks, cartons of wholesale groceries and, in summer, towering stacks of soft crab boxes. Taxis race down to the foot of Main Street to deposit breathless housewives loaded down with the rewards of two hours of hurried shopping. People come and go with last-minute messages, exchanges of money, or diligences performed for third parties. At half past twelve—not precisely, but thereabouts—the passenger ferries that are the lifelines of the Chesapeake's two inhabited offshore islands will cast off. The *Dorolena*, Captain Rudy Thomas, goes to Virginia's Tangier; the *Island Belle*, Captain Frankie Dize, to Maryland's Smith.

Smith and Tangier Islands are both very important to the Chesapeake's blue crab fishery. The statement is reversible; it works either way. The islands could not exist economically without crabs, and the fishery would be much impoverished without the islanders' skill and industry in catching them. Earlier in this century finfish and oysters were the mainstays of Tangier's economy. "Don't say we didn't have fish traps!" says Tangier's ninety-one-year-old Captain Johnny Parks. "Whole Bay shore was full of them. Use to be one hundred and fifty between here and Tangier Light alone."

"But nary no more," he adds.

As happened with other Eastern Shore communities, Tangier's pound fishery was done in during the years between the Great Depression and World War II. Tumbling wholesale fish prices and the rising costs of maintaining and working the big nets, as compared to gill netting[2] or trawling,[3] put an impossible squeeze on Tangier's fishermen. Only on the western shore, with its greater runs of river herring, could the pound netters hold out. But coincidental with the demise of Tangier's pound fishery was the introduction of the modern crab pot.[4] There is not a Tangierman who does not hail the latter event as the island's salvation. "Best thing that ever happened here" or "God's hand" are the expressions most frequently heard. Armed with this new device, the island's fishermen quickly became extraordinarily successful crabbers and have remained so ever since. Year round, one must also remember, since Tangier contributes some twenty-two ships to Virginia's winter crab dredging fleet down at the mouth of the Bay. Thanks to this advantage Tangier is responsible for more crabs than any other single locality

[2] *gill netting:* using a net, set upright in the water, which entangles the catch in its mesh

[3] *trawling:* using a boat to drag a large, baglike net along the bottom of the fishing bank

[4] *modern crab pot:* a cubical cage, 2 feet square top and bottom and 21 inches high, made of wire mesh, which is placed with bait under water to catch crabs

in the Chesapeake Bay region, Crisfield and other larger communities included. Since the Chesapeake has long been and remains today the world's most intensive crab fishery, it is therefore quite accurate to say that Tangiermen catch more crabs than anyone else under the sun. One does not speak disparagingly, therefore, of *Callinectes sapidus* on Tangier Island.

5   Next in rank to the Tangiermen are the watermen of neighboring Smith Island. There would be little difference in the crab catch of the two islands—indeed, Smith might easily surpass Tangier—except for the fact that the Smith Islanders (and all other Maryland watermen) are not allowed to cross the state water boundary and join Virginia's dredging fleet.[5] Winter on Smith Island thus means the oyster, and nothing else. But the disadvantage is balanced out in another season. Summer and the soft crab are Smith's glory. The island is surrounded by the best crab bottoms in the Bay, has a larger scraping fleet[6] than Tangier and, as suggested elsewhere, goes all-out twelve hours a day every day of the season for the capture of peelers[7] and softs.[8] Although neither Maryland nor Virginia keeps accurate catch records by point of origin, there is little doubt that Smith Island is the champion of the Chesapeake in soft crab production. The packing plant managers know it and will tell you so. As far away as Fulton Market, too, you will hear the same opinion. If you want to know how the crop of big jumbos and whales is shaping up, the stand owners say, you get in touch with Smith Island. . . .

6   Smith Island may not be to everyone's liking, as I have ruefully discovered from recommending visits to friends. But for those who want to see the water trades at their traditional best, Smith will never disappoint. Nor the naturalist, poking around the creeks and guts in the broad marshland north of the Big Thorofare, all of which has recently been set aside by the Department of Interior as the Glenn W. Martin National Wildlife Refuge. Those wishing to visit the refuge must simply bear in mind that it is not universally popular with the islanders, many of whom fondly recall the lethal punt guns and multicannoned batteries used when market gunning for waterfowl was a way of life and an important source of winter income. (Stanley Marshall, a native of Ewell, is the refuge manager; his brother has not spoken to him since he accepted the position.) But provided you can disavow any close association with conservation organizations or the federal government, a boat and friendly guide service can easily be secured from among the islanders. Late fall or winter is the time for waterfowl; spring and summer, for the heron rookeries. Hurry, too. Although Smith has not yet been discovered by tourists, at least on the Tangier scale, there is every sign that it may soon be.

[5] This is no longer so. *Beautiful Swimmers* was introduced in a Maryland court case; the court ruled in favor of Maryland watermen, declaring that state boundaries do not hold for migrating species.

[6] *scraping fleet:* boats using long net bags to crop eelgrass where peelers and softs hide

[7] *peelers:* crabs showing signs of readiness to moult

[8] *softs:* crabs that have just moulted and whose new shells are still soft

For still others Smith Island's greatest fascination lies with the memory 7
of its older citizens, who enjoy telling how it was only thirty years ago living
without electricity and working the water mainly by sail. To be sure, with the
sole exception of Deal Island, there is no better place on the Bay to learn of
forgotten craft and the skills required to take crabs and oysters under a full
press of canvas. The older watermen like to talk most about the sporty little
Smith Island crab skiffs—"dinkies" they were called locally—that went in
flotillas to spend the week trotlining[9] or dipping for peelers up around
Bloodsworth or South Marsh. Not much more than eighteen feet in length,
the dinkies had a single large sprit-sail and carried one hundred pound sand-
bags as movable ballast, the dexterous placement of which was essential to
maintaining an upright position. "Breeze up strong and didn't we go!" says
William Wilson Sneade, seventy-three, who now occupies himself making
fine buster floats[10] of cedar and spruce. "Just wicker [luff] the sail a little, move
your bags around and you made out all right. But come squalls, you could
capsize easy enough! Thing to do was head for the shallers, where you could
get your feet on the bottom, unstep the mast and right your boat. Then step
her up, set your spreet pole and off you go again!"

"That's right," laughs Omar Evans, the proprietor of Smith Island's lone 8
crab house. "Capsizing, it made you so mad you scooped out like half of the
water and then drank the balance for cussedness."

Both men remember how bad the bugs were when they spent the week 9
in little shanties on the uninhabited islands up north. "You walked in the
high grass," Evans recalls. "And the green flies carried you off." (They still
do.) Sneade's memory of trotlining techniques is especially clear. "Tide up
and a smart breeze, we put out our lines," he explains. "You set them fair with
the wind, hoisted a little pink of sail, sailed downwind running the lines—
you couldn't reach, that made the line too shaky for the crabs—and then you
tacked back up and did it all over again. Tide down and slick pretty ca'm, we
poled and dipped for peelers, standing right on the bow. Sometimes we took
along a sharp-ended gunning skiff, also good for poling."[11]

Evans is an expert on the larger boats used in crab scraping. There were 10
the Jenkins Creek catboats, "one-sail bateaux," he calls them, and the bigger
jib-headed sloops, out of which the skipjacks[12] probably evolved, that could
pull three crab scrapes in a good breeze. "We built them good here," he says
with pride. "Over in Crisfield they was boxy-stern and messy; they don't do
anything right over there." Both recall that it was hard work hauling in the
scrapes. "No winches, like they got later," Sneade reminds you. "You slacked
off on the sail a bit and just pulled in your scrapes through main strength and
awkwardness."

[9] *trotlining:* using long, bottom-resting pieces of line with multiple baits to catch crabs
[10] *buster floats:* containers built to rest in the water and hold female crabs ready to moult
[11] *poling:* using poles to maneuver small boats through eelgrass to catch peelers and softs
[12] *skipjacks:* sailboats used for crab and oyster dredging

11   "Couldn't do that no more," he adds. "I'm all stove in. Ailing more this year than the last ten. Age is coming to me, that's the thing."

12   Age is coming. To the islands as a whole, many observers believe. Whether Tangier and Smith can in fact hold out is a question that is now sometimes raised. "Oh, no, the islands will never fail," an experienced picking plant owner in Crisfield recently reassured me. "Not as long as there are crabs in the Bay." He went on to explain very patiently that nobody in the Bay country caught more crabs, knew more about them, or went at it harder than the island people. "Why, they *study* crabs," he finished in tones of awe. "And the thing is they pass on all what they know to the young ones."

13   I think the Crisfield packer is right, at least on the subject of generational succession. The blue crab holds great fascination for watermen of all ages. You've got to study him, the older ones say, because he's mean and ornery, very clever and always out to fool you. This is especially true during the long summer when there are erratic day-to-day shifts of the best thick of crabs which do not seem to correspond to the weather or other rational factors. The men talk of them continually, at home over the dinner table or in the general stores as they play checkers.

14   And the young listen and follow. True, many seem tempted to go other ways. You see them around every crab house or shanty standing defiantly in the cockpit of their boats, alternately taciturn or shrill with complaint about the hard times of their profession. To reach them at all one must show some knowledge and appreciation of their work. It is almost as though they had a constant need for outsiders, for the strange persons, paradoxically, to remind them it is all right to be a waterman. I remember particularly a young scraper from Ewell . . . with whom I went to the Fox Islands on a beautiful September morning. As we crossed the Sound in the dark he railed bitterly against the water trades and all those who control them. The authorities in Annapolis were all politicians and crooks, he said. They had not done one single thing to help the watermen and never would. And the Baltimore newspapers print up a pack of lies, like it was the watermen who were the sole cause of everything that is wrong with the Bay. If he could only get those newspaper people out in the freeze of winter, he added, and then see what they say! But as dawn broke and the Foxes came in sight, he quietly bowed his head in prayer and said grace before eating a sandwich and drinking a last cup of coffee. Then, once on the crab grounds, he was a new man. Look here, he told me as we worked the scrapes, here were some egg cases[13] glued to the underside of a big Jimmy.[14] They are called blisters, he explained, and some watermen think they hold the eggs of the oyster toadfish. There was a shark fin cutting the water, right over there! Oh, yes, you often saw sharks around the Foxes. We

[13] *egg cases:* protective structures that surround eggs until the larvae inside them are ready to hatch

[14] *big Jimmy:* a large male crab

should look over all the baby rockfish very carefully, too, he continued. They were tagging the little rocks and you could get a dollar for each recovered tag. He had found one from New Jersey, in fact, just a month ago. "Oh, I like this good enough," he said finally.

There are many like him in the younger generation. They may complain and they seem to want to carry a heavy chip on their shoulder. But the challenges and the independence of working on the water, trying to get the smart of it, continue to attract. If the price is fair, that is. And as long as there are crabs in the Bay.

Crisfield, Tangier, Smith, or most anywhere else in the Bay where men live from the water. As long as there are crabs to catch. The view presently is that there will be. And oysters and finfish, too, but only as long as people in other places do the necessary. The watermen know where the real danger lies. Regulation by Richmond or Annapolis is not going to avert it. All those laws, the watermen scoff. Half of them seem downright foolish. There is for example the matter of the width of the crab scrapes. Everyone knows that if you used a six-foot scrape instead of the prescribed three-and-a-half, it would take you twice as long to haul in and work over each lick and so the day's results would be pretty much the same. Or the much discussed history of the skipjacks. The Maryland law of 1865 requiring oysters to be dredged— taken in motion, that is, as opposed to at anchor—only by sailing craft is still in force. But in 1967 it was amended to allow the little engine-powered yawl or "push" boats carried in davits over skipjack sterns to provide powered dredging on Mondays and Tuesdays, with a daily catch limit of one hundred and fifty bushels. (On "sailing days" during the rest of the week there have as yet been no limits, although the state has the authority to impose them whenever and to what degree it sees fit; tonging boats in recent years have generally been limited to twenty-five bushels per day per licensed tonger aboard.) This concession was made because of increasing costs in maintaining and operating the aging vessels, which have had a hard time competing with the highly efficient and less costly patent tonging boats. So, much as one hates to see the end of the celebrated skipjack fleet, now down to thirty-odd boats, the argument that powered dredging cleans off the oyster rocks too quickly has been broached and there are the daily catch limits in any case. "Let us all drudge," Maryland's three thousand tongers say. "All it means is that we get our limit quicker, so what is the sense in a man staying out in the cold any longer than he has to?" The proposition that all-out power dredging would create too many deep furrows in the bottom and smother too many oysters is not supported by the watermen. They could tow their dredges more smoothly and gently with power, they claim, and still make their jags in a shorter time. Besides, they have been doing it in Virginia for as long as anyone can remember.

But there is no argument the crabs have to be watched. Everyone agrees that if ever the crab stocks bottom out at bad year levels and stay there, that

15

16

17

will be the day to start worrying. The winter dredging must be closely reviewed—the season of 1974–75 was one of the poorest on record—and legislation barring this form of capture may soon be necessary. Similarly, although Virginia has established a 130-square-mile sanctuary for egg-bearing sponge crabs at the mouth of the Bay, it may some day be advisable for the state to prohibit the taking of sponges in all her waters, as Maryland has already done.

18   But none of these measures need be, the watermen insist, if the Bay waters are kept healthy. They know precisely what is wrong. It is not so much the enormous Calvert Cliffs atomic energy plant sucking in bottom dwelling plankton, eggs and larvae at three million gallons per minute. Or the Army Corps of Engineers with its constant proposals to dredge new or deeper ship channels, the effects of which bury bottom dwelling organisms and reduce plankton photosynthesis. Or the proposed oil refinery at Norfolk, which will be dangerously close to the Bay's blue crab nursery. These things are bad enough. The public sees them and protests accordingly. The watermen on the other hand think the real problem is something harder to pinpoint. As they go out year after year, the water seems to be changing. It may be, they think, that it is everywhere getting a little tired. Each summer there are more fish kills and in winter you can sometimes see strange little red dots suspended in the water. Old, tired, and a little messy, you could even say. Age is coming to the Bay, too, perhaps. Simple as that.

19   "I sometime have the feeling we're going to be another Lake Erie," says Vernon Bradshaw. Vernon should know. He has spent a long time watching the water, since the days his father was the keeper of Tangier Light and he and his sister went to live with him summers. "Oh, the Bay was pretty then," he says. "We fished or flew our kites, and all the boats sailed close by to speak us."

20   Some among the Chesapeake's marine biologists could not agree more strongly. The Bay is changing in ways that are very subtle. The agents of destruction take their toll stealthily, and in diffuse and complex patterns that are hard for the public to grasp. Scientists most commonly speak of them as "the doubling rate" and "oxygen deprivation." The doubling rate concerns human populations. In 1960 the population of the Chesapeake Bay drainage area was estimated at eleven million. This figure is expected to triple by the turn of the century. The average annual increase is 1.7 percent, or twice the national average. Significantly, the increase is not merely confined to the Baltimore, Washington and Norfolk metropolitan complexes, but is widely scattered and runs even higher around the Bay's immediate shoreline, where frenzied waterfront real estate development for leisure homes has almost reached Florida proportions in the last two decades. Down from cities large and small, then, come enormous quantities of sewage, some of it still raw and none of it fully processed for the removal of nitrogen and phosphorous. The great and noble rivers of the western shore—the Potomac and the James,

especially—are in effect left to serve as the final treatment stages, natural sewers, in other words. And from the burgeoning waterfront resort developments comes more raw waste, how much no one exactly knows, since low water tables and shoddy planning in these communities frequently cause a high incidence of septic tank failure. To these must be added the 6,000 ocean-going ships that annually wind up the channel to Baltimore, dumping raw sewage equivalent to a town of 25,000. Even greater may be the waste that comes from the Bay's growing armada of pleasure craft, which now numbers over 175,000 licensed vessels.

As a result the Bay is receiving continually heavier loads of disease- 21 producing bacteria, which cause frequent closings of shellfish beds, and of nitrogen and phosphorous, which have a far more devastating effect on water quality and marine resources in general. Again, accurate knowledge of how heavy the load may be in the Bay at large is lacking. But it is easy enough to sample and measure in certain of the tributaries. The District of Columbia offers one clear example. Washington annually discharges into the Potomac River twenty-five million pounds of nitrogen and eight million pounds of phosphorous, the latter being a relative newcomer thanks to the increasing use of miracle-white detergents. These nitrates and phosphates are called "nutrients" by scientists. But the term may strike anyone hearing it for the first time as somewhat misleading, because what these nutrients principally nourish are harmful quantities of blue and green algae. The algae "blooms" or "explodes" in population by catastrophic quantum leaps, thanks to the abundance of the sewage-waste fertilizers. Then, enter oxygen deprivation. As the algae die and decompose, they take from the surrounding water nearly all of its oxygen. All forms of life around these blooms—fish, plants, mollusks and crustaceans—smother and die. You may see the process, if you wish, on the Potomac. Summer after summer, a few miles below Mount Vernon, there is a strange sea. It is slimy and pea-green in color, a horrid soup of a sea that affronts all the senses. To go through it in a small boat is a shocking experience. The same phenomenon, of course, occurs in many of the smaller tributaries, although less dramatically.

"The Patuxent River now receives sewage wastes from 78,000 people and 22 some portions above the estuary show persistent low oxygen content, high fecal coliform bacteria counts and loss of as many as ten species of fish."

"Baltimore's Black River has in effect been sacrificed as a waste treatment 23 lagoon."

So read the technical reports. One tributary after another is checked off 24 as sacrificed or soon to be.

Down on the James River is the historic plantation of Shirley, home of 25 the Carters of Virginia since 1630. It has a simple utilitarian charm, not at all elegant like the bigger plantations near Williamsburg, and a ninth-generation Carter still works it as a farm. Looking out through Shirley's back windows you see a large and beautiful lawn, shaded by tall oak and elm, that extends to a bend in the river. But those who choose to walk the grounds must be prepared for certain shocks. Just around the bend on the other side of the river is a power plant, squat, monolithic and with tall stacks. It happens to be steam-powered, but down the river below Jamestown are two more plants. Nuclear-powered giants, they are, known locally as "Surry Number One" and "Surry Number Two." These three plants and the fact that the James receives the sewage of Richmond (and a host of lesser cities, much of it raw), is constantly being widened or rechannelized, and supports much heavy industry, have combined to alter very seriously the quality of the Chesapeake's most historic river. Walk down to the water's edge. There are no algal blooms, to be sure, but one senses that something is very much wrong. The water is highly turbid, almost opaque. Even in a bright sun the waves of the James are leaden and gray. The river seems to have lost some indefinable life force, its sparkle, if you prefer. Engineers assure us it is not yet sacrificed. But how long it will remain off the dead and dying list is a more troubling question.

26   "I can feel it, I can see it," says Dr. Willard Van Engel. "It's a great blanket of pollution—oil, detritus and just plain filth—slowly rolling down the Bay." Other biologists agree and go on to point out that this blanket has what they call a parallel doubling rate. As population doubles, they explain, so too does the nutrient load of nitrogen and phosphorous, inexorably and exactly, or on a one-to-one ratio. Meanwhile nothing new has been built in the way of tertiary sewage treatment or complete phosphate and nitrate removal in the Chesapeake drainage basin since 1960. Expensive as three-stage disposal may be, many scientists and administrators feel there is no other way. They argue that if the federal government can contribute over $926 million in a Great Lakes compact, no less attention is due what has been accurately called the nation's "most valuable and vulnerable large estuary" or "a spawning and juvenile growth area for marine organisms affecting all the Atlantic seaboard states."

27   "Yes, we discuss these matters forcefully with the federal and state agencies, and I am hopeful of some result," says Loren Sterling, president of the Milbourne Oyster Company, which is Crisfield's largest oyster and crab packing plant. Sterling is an experienced industry spokesman who, like many other Crisfielders, has been instrumental in extending the blue crab fishery to the southern states, as far as Florida, in fact, where he once ran a plant in Cedar Key. He finds the question of human population growth is at last being considered in the smaller towns and communities all around the Bay. "People are beginning to talk now of just how big they want to grow," he says. Sterling also places great faith in the Environmental Protection Agency, although he thinks the E.P.A. and other federal or state conservation agencies frequently put too much attention on small or easy targets. "If only they would work on the big people the way they work on the small," he reasons. "Then I think we'd be all right."

Others are less sanguine. Scientists at Johns Hopkins University's 28
Chesapeake Bay Institute, the University of Maryland's Chesapeake Biological Laboratory and other centers of estuarine research have estimated that
the Bay's nutrient load will double by 1995, unless extraordinary measures
are taken, and that such ". . . doubling of present nitrogen and phosphorous
loading would probably produce general eutrophication of the Upper Bay."

Eutrophication is defined as a body of water in which an increase of 29
mineral and organic nutrients has reduced dissolved oxygen to the point of
causing imbalances among the various organisms inhabiting it. One is
tempted to improve on the dictionary definition. A very one-sided imbalance,
we could say, that produces a suffocating pea-green plant organism at the
expense of nearly all others.

General eutrophication is Lake Erie. Simple as that. 30

CARL SAGAN

The Nuclear Winter

Sagan is a professor of astronomy and space sciences at Cornell, where he also directs the
Laboratory for Planetary Studies. Born in New York City in 1934, Sagan earned four
degrees from the University of Chicago, including a Ph.D. in astronomy in 1960. He taught
at Harvard 1962–68 before moving to Cornell, where he has worked on several space
missions, including Mariner and Viking; he received the NASA Medal for Exceptional
Scientific Achievement and the Joseph Priestly Prize "for distinguished contributions to the
welfare of mankind." His numerous books include the popular Broca's Brain *(1979) and*
The Dragons of Eden: Speculations on the Evolution of Human Intelligence *(1977),*
which won a Pulitzer Prize.

His writings and the series Cosmos, *on public television since 1980, have made Sagan*
a popular scientific spokesman. Typical of many scientists with a following among the general
public, Sagan is criticized by some of his peers for not exhibiting sufficient scientific rigor in
his research and for too "fanciful" scientific speculations in his books on extraterrestrial
intelligence and UFOs, especially. Nevertheless, Sagan has recently become a major spokes-
man for nuclear disarmament, and his speculative essay below, distributed by the antinuclear
Council for a Livable World, shows logically and with scientific evidence the hypothetical and
catastrophic consequences of a nuclear war. Through generating "an epoch of cold and dark,"
such a war would destroy our global civilization, and reduce the human population "to
prehistoric levels or less," if not to extinction—a long and cold nuclear winter indeed.

"Into the eternal darkness, into fire, into ice."

—Dante, *The Inferno*

Except for fools and madmen, everyone knows that nuclear war would be an 1
unprecedented human catastrophe. A more or less typical strategic warhead
has a yield of 2 megatons, the explosive equivalent of 2 million tons of TNT.

But 2 million tons of TNT is about the same as all the bombs exploded in World War II—a single bomb with the explosive power of the entire Second World War but compressed into a few seconds of time and an area 30 or 40 miles across. . . .

2   In a 2-megaton explosion over a fairly large city, buildings would be vaporized, people reduced to atoms and shadows, outlying structures blown down like matchsticks and raging fires ignited. And if the bomb were exploded on the ground, an enormous crater, like those that can be seen through a telescope on the surface of the Moon, would be all that remained where midtown once had been. There are now more than 50,000 nuclear weapons, more than 13,000 megatons of yield, deployed in the arsenals of the United States and the Soviet Union—enough to obliterate a million Hiroshimas.

3   But there are fewer than 3000 cities on the Earth with populations of 100,000 or more. You cannot find anything like a million Hiroshimas to obliterate. Prime military and industrial targets that are far from cities are comparatively rare. Thus, there are vastly more nuclear weapons than are needed for any plausible deterrence of a potential adversary.

4   Nobody knows, of course, how many megatons would be exploded in a real nuclear war. There are some who think that a nuclear war can be "contained," bottled up before it runs away to involve much of the world's arsenals. But a number of detailed analyses, war games run by the U.S. Department of Defense, and official Soviet pronouncements all indicate that this containment may be too much to hope for: Once the bombs begin exploding, communications failures, disorganization, fear, the necessity of making in minutes decisions affecting the fates of millions, and the immense psychological burden of knowing that your own loved ones may already have been destroyed are likely to result in a nuclear paroxysm. Many investigations, including a number of studies for the U.S. government, envision the explosion of 5000 to 10,000 megatons—the detonation of tens of thousands of nuclear weapons that now sit quietly, inconspicuously, in missile silos, submarines and long-range bombers, faithful servants awaiting orders.

5   The World Health Organization, in a recent detailed study chaired by Sune K. Bergstrom (the 1982 Nobel laureate in physiology and medicine), concludes that 1.1 billion people would be killed outright in such a nuclear war, mainly in the United States, the Soviet Union, Europe, China and Japan. An additional 1.1 billion people would suffer serious injuries and radiation sickness, for which medical help would be unavailable. It thus seems possible that more than 2 billion people—almost half of all the humans on Earth—would be destroyed in the immediate aftermath of a global thermonuclear war. This would represent by far the greatest disaster in the history of the human species and, with no other adverse effects, would probably be enough to reduce at least the Northern Hemisphere to a state of prolonged agony and barbarism. Unfortunately, the real situation would be much worse.

In technical studies of the consequences of nuclear weapons explosions, there has been a dangerous tendency to underestimate the results. This is partly due to a tradition of conservatism which generally works well in science but which is of more dubious applicability when the lives of billions of people are at stake. In the Bravo test of March 1, 1954, a 15-megaton thermonuclear bomb was exploded on Bikini Atoll. It had about double the yield expected, and there was an unanticipated last-minute shift in the wind direction. As a result, deadly radioactive fallout came down on Rongelap in the Marshall Islands, more than 200 kilometers away. Almost all the children on Rongelap subsequently developed thyroid nodules and lesions, and other long-term medical problems, due to the radioactive fallout.

Likewise, in 1973, it was discovered that high-yield airbursts will chemically burn the nitrogen in the upper air, converting it into oxides of nitrogen; these, in turn, combine with and destroy the protective ozone in the Earth's atmosphere. The surface of the Earth is shielded from deadly solar ultraviolet radiation by a layer of ozone so tenuous that, were it brought down to sea level, it would be only 3 millimeters thick. Partial destruction of this ozone layer can have serious consequences for the biology of the entire planet.

These discoveries, and others like them, were made by chance. They were largely unexpected. And now another consequence—by far the most dire—has been uncovered, again more or less by accident.

The U.S. Mariner 9 spacecraft, the first vehicle to oribt another planet, arrived at Mars in late 1971. The planet was enveloped in a global dust storm. As the fine particles slowly fell out, we were able to measure temperature changes in the atmosphere and on the surface. Soon it became clear what had happened:

The dust, lofted by high winds off the desert into the upper Martian atmosphere, had absorbed the incoming sunlight and prevented much of it from reaching the ground. Heated by the sunlight, the dust warmed the adjacent air. But the surface, enveloped in partial darkness, became much chillier than usual. Months later, after the dust fell out of the atmosphere, the upper air cooled and the surface warmed, both returning to their normal conditions. We were able to calculate accurately, from how much dust there was in the atmosphere, how cool the Martian surface ought to have been.

Afterwards, I and my colleagues, James B. Pollack and Brian Toon of NASA's Ames Research Center, were eager to apply these insights to Earth. In a volcanic explosion, dust aerosols are lofted into the high atmosphere. We calculated by how much the Earth's global temperature should decline after a major volcanic explosion and found that our results (generally a fraction of a degree) were in good accord with actual measurements. Joining forces with Richard Turco, who has studied the effects of nuclear weapons for many years, we then began to turn our attention to the climatic implications of nuclear war. [The scientific paper, "Global Atmospheric Consequences of Nuclear War," is written by R. P. Turco, O. B. Toon, T. P. Ackerman, J. B.

6

7

8

9

10

11

Pollack and Carl Sagan. From the last names of the authors, this work is generally referred to as "TTAPS."]

12 We knew that nuclear explosions, particularly ground-bursts, would lift an enormous quantity of fine soil particles into the atmosphere (more than 100,000 tons of fine dust for every megaton exploded in a surface burst). Our work was further spurred by Paul Crutzen of the Max Planck Institute for Chemistry in Mainz, West Germany, and by John Birks of the University of Colorado, who pointed out that huge quantities of smoke would be generated in the burning of cities and forests following a nuclear war.

13 Groundbursts—at hardened missile silos, for example—generate fine dust. Airbursts—over cities and unhardened military installations—make fires and therefore smoke. The amount of dust and soot generated depends on the conduct of the war, the yields of the weapons employed and the ratio of groundbursts to airbursts. So we ran computer models for several dozen different nuclear war scenarios. Our baseline case, as in many other studies, was a 5000-megaton war with only a modest fraction of the yield (20 percent) expended on urban or industrial targets. Our job, for each case, was to follow the dust and smoke generated, see how much sunlight was absorbed and by how much the temperatures changed, figure out how the particles spread in longitude and latitude, and calculate how long before it all fell out of the air back onto the surface. Since the radioactivity would be attached to these same fine particles, our calculations also revealed the extent and timing of the subsequent radioactive fallout.

14 Some of what I am about to describe is horrifying. I know, because it horrifies me. There is a tendency—psychiatrists call it "denial"—to put it out of our minds, not to think about it. But if we are to deal intelligently, wisely, with the nuclear arms race, then we must steel ourselves to contemplate the horrors of nuclear war.

15 The results of our calculations astonished us. In the baseline case, the amount of sunlight at the ground was reduced to a few percent of normal—much darker, in daylight, than in a heavy overcast and too dark for plants to make a living from photosynthesis. At least in the Northern Hemisphere, where the great preponderance of strategic targets lies, a deadly gloom would persist for months.

16 Even more unexpected were the temperatures calculated. In the baseline case, land temperatures, except for narrow strips of coastline, dropped to minus 25° Celsius (minus 13° Fahrenheit) and stayed below freezing for months—even for a summer war. (Because the atmospheric structure becomes much more stable as the upper atmosphere is heated and the lower air is cooled, we may have severely *under*estimated how long the cold and the dark would last.) The oceans, a significant heat reservoir, would not freeze, however, and a major ice age would probably not be triggered. But because the temperatures would drop so catastrophically, virtually all crops and farm animals, at least in the Northern Hemisphere, would be destroyed, as would

most varieties of uncultivated or undomesticated food supplies. Most of the human survivors would starve.

In addition, the amount of radioactive fallout is much more than expected. Many previous calculations simply ignored the intermediate time-scale fallout. That is, calculations were made for the prompt fallout—the plumes of radioactive debris blown downwind from each target—and for the long-term fallout, the fine radioactive particles lofted into the stratosphere that would descend about a year later, after most of the radioactivity had decayed. However, the radioactivity carried into the upper atmosphere (but not as high as the stratosphere) seems to have been largely forgotten. We found for the baseline case that roughly 30 percent of the land at northern midlatitudes could receive a radioactive dose greater than 250 rads, and that about 50 percent of northern midlatitudes could receive a dose greater than 100 rads. A 100-rad dose is the equivalent of about 1000 medical X-rays. A 400-rad dose will, more likely than not, kill you.

The cold, the dark and the intense radioactivity, together lasting for months, represent a severe assault on our civilization and our species. Civil and sanitary services would be wiped out. Medical facilities, drugs, the most rudimentary means for relieving the vast human suffering, would be unavailable. Any but the most elaborate shelters would be useless, quite apart from the question of what good it might be to emerge a few months later. Synthetics burned in the destruction of the cities would produce a wide variety of toxic gases, including carbon monoxide, cyanides, dioxins and furans. After the dust and soot settled out, the solar ultraviolet flux would be much larger than its present value. Immunity to disease would decline. Epidemics and pandemics would be rampant, especially after the billion or so unburied bodies began to thaw. Moreover, the combined influence of these severe and simultaneous stresses on life are likely to produce even more adverse consequences—biologists call them synergisms—that we are not yet wise enough to foresee.

So far, we have talked only of the Northern Hemisphere. But it now seems—unlike the case of a single nuclear weapons test—that in a real nuclear war, the heating of the vast quantities of atmospheric dust and soot in northern midlatitudes will transport these fine particles toward and across the Equator. We see just this happening in Martian dust storms. The Southern Hemisphere would experience effects that, while less severe than in the Northern Hemisphere, are nevertheless extremely ominous. The illusion with which some people in the Northern Hemisphere reassure themselves—catching an Air New Zealand flight in a time of serious international crisis, or the like—is now much less tenable, even on the narrow issue of personal survival for those with the price of a ticket.

But what if nuclear wars *can* be contained, and much less than 5000 megatons is detonated? Perhaps the greatest surprise in our work was that even small nuclear wars can have devastating climatic effects. We considered a war in which a mere 100 megatons were exploded, less than one percent of the world arsenals, and only in low-yield airbursts over cities. This scenario, we found, would ignite thousands of fires, and the smoke from these fires alone would be enough to generate an epoch of cold and dark almost as severe as in the 5000-megaton case. The threshold for what Richard Turco has called The Nuclear Winter is very low.

21   Could we have overlooked some important effect? The carrying of dust and soot from the Northern to the Southern Hemisphere (as well as more local atmospheric circulation) will certainly thin the clouds out over the Northern Hemisphere. But, in many cases, this thinning would be insufficient to render the climatic consequences tolerable—and every time it got better in the Northern Hemisphere, it would get worse in the Southern.

22   Our results have been carefully scrutinized by more than 100 scientists in the United States, Europe and the Soviet Union. There are still arguments on points of detail. But the overall conclusion seems to be agreed upon: There are severe and previously unanticipated global consequences of nuclear war— subfreezing temperatures in a twilit radioactive gloom lasting for months or longer.

23   Scientists initially underestimated the effects of fallout, were amazed that nuclear explosions in space disabled distant satellites, had no idea that the fireballs from high-yield thermonuclear explosions could deplete the ozone layer and missed altogether the possible climatic effects of nuclear dust and smoke. What else have we overlooked?

24   Nuclear war is a problem that can be treated only theoretically. It is not amenable to experimentation. Conceivably, we have left something important out of our analysis, and the effects are more modest than we calculate. On the other hand, it is also possible—and, from previous experience, even likely—that there are further adverse effects that no one has yet been wise enough to recognize. With billions of lives at stake, where does conservatism lie—in assuming that the results will be better than we calculate, or worse?

25   Many biologists, considering the nuclear winter that these calculations describe, believe they carry somber implications for life on Earth. Many species of plants and animals would become extinct. Vast numbers of surviving humans would starve to death. The delicate ecological relations that bind together organisms on Earth in a fabric of mutual dependency would be torn, perhaps irreparably. There is little question that our global civilization would be destroyed. The human population would be reduced to prehistoric levels, or less. Life for any survivors would be extremely hard. And there seems to be a real possibility of the extinction of the human species.

26   It is now almost 40 years since the invention of nuclear weapons. We have not yet experienced a global thermonuclear war—although on more than one occasion we have come tremulously close. I do not think our luck can hold forever. Men and machines are fallible, as recent events remind us. Fools and madmen do exist, and sometimes rise to power. Concentrating

always on the near future, we have ignored the long-term consequences of our actions. We have placed our civilization and our species in jeopardy.

Fortunately, it is not yet too late. We can safeguard the planetary civilization and the human family if we so choose. There is no more important or more urgent issue. 27

Questions

1. All of these scientists—Gould, a geologist; Wiener, a mathematician; Warner, a biologist; and Sagan, an astronomer—use their knowledge of science to point out extremely serious problems resulting from what they see as the abuse of either scientific knowledge or the natural environment. What are these problems?

2. What are the solutions, if any, to the problems? Is the function of these essays to elaborate on solutions, or essentially to point with alarm to the problems? Once the problems are understood, what are readers supposed to do with their new understanding?

3. Each of these essays is written to a general audience. Can general readers understand not only the language but the implications of the message of each? Why or why not?

4. In what ways does each of these writers personally dispel, through his eloquent writing and his humane scientific perspective, the stereotypical image of the mad scientist, bent on destroying the human race through unrestrained exercise of scientific power? Which of these essays speculate on that very possibility, however, in the hands of other "mad scientists" or others? How convincing are these speculations on the end of civilization? Does their very familiarity make us take them less seriously than we should?

Writing About the Social and Physical Sciences

Strategies

1. What, precisely, is my topic? Although my writing will probably involve some explanation, will the essay be primarily expository? an extended definition? a narrative, like Roueché's Medical Detectives? a research report? an argument, in favor of my interpretation of the subject and in opposition to others' views? some combination of the above?

2. Do I know enough to write on this topic? from firsthand experience or research? from the research or writings of others? Is my information up to date? Does it represent the state of the art in research design and method; in gathering, analyzing, and interpreting data and other evidence? In what ways, if any, are my sources biased? with what effects?

3. What are my own biases on this topic? How have they influenced my selection and interpretation of data, illustrations, case histories, statistics, and other evidence? Are there other appropriate ways of looking at the material that I have ignored or downplayed? Should I acknowledge or accommodate these?

4. How general or specialized is my intended audience? How will their level of knowledge affect the terminology and background of my presentation? Do I need to define each unfamiliar term when I first use it, or is its meaning clear from the context? Have I explained significant processes and subprocesses essential to the understanding of my subject?

5. Should I use supporting illustrations (facts, figures, graphs, statistics, diagrams, maps) to enhance my presentation? Explain why, and identify the illustrations you would use.

Suggestions

1. Write an essay of extended definition on one of the following topics:

 (a) A key term, concept, or phenomenon in a field of science or social science. (See Susanne Langer, "Signs and Symbols," 717–22; Bertrand Russell, "What Is Matter?" 740–44; Lewis Thomas and Laird Bloom on "Pheromones," 757–73; Kelly Shea, "Acid Rain," 773–75.)

 (b) A field or subfield of science or social science that particularly interests you (for example, molecular biology, sociolinguistics, primate anthropology, particle physics).

 (c) A paradigm in a field of science or social science that particularly interests you. (See Thomas S. Kuhn, "The Route to Normal Science," 669–77, and also essays by Russell, Darwin, Haldane, and Thomas, 740–57.)

2. Write a brief biography of a noted scientist or social scientist, highlighting either the researcher's style of conducting investigations or one or two of the person's major theories, discoveries, or research projects. Be sure to assess the significance of the scientist's work.

3. Write an informative essay in which you explain how one of the following occurs or works. Although you should pick a subject you know something about, you may need to supplement your information by consulting outside sources.

 (a) How a machine (such as a computer, amplifier, piano, microwave oven, or another of your choice) works.

 (b) How a person develops professional competence in his or her chosen field—that is, how one becomes a skilled electrical engineer, petroleum geologist, social psychologist, or American Indian historian. Pick a field or subspecialty you're interested in.

 (c) How the research or investigative process in a particular aspect of science or social science functions—what its assumptions, norms, and typical procedures are. (See Evelyn Fox Keller, "Barbara McClintock: 'A Feeling for the Organism'," 678–81; Berton Roueché, "Annals of Medicine: A Contemporary Touch," 681–92.)

 (d) How a crucial concept or great idea found acceptance—for instance, on the nature of language, the heliocentric theory of the universe, or the concept of right-brain and left-brain intelligence. (See essays on language by Hall, Barber, Langer, Lurie, and Sebeok, 694–739.)

 (e) How a particular drug or other medicine, or medical treatment or cure was developed, tested, refined—and either accepted or rejected, and why. Is it still in use today, or has it become superseded by another medicine or treatment? You may consider bona fide drugs, medicines, or treatments (aspirin, penicillin); or treatments of dubious or unproven value (Laetrile, an alleged cure for cancer made from apricot pits; leeching); or debatable treatments (electroshock therapy or prefrontal labotomy for depressives). You may wish to investigate a medicine or treatment that you've been using or contemplating. (See Sissela Bok, "Placebos," 319–24.)

(f) How a particular culture (ethnic, regional, tribal) or subculture (preppies, pacifists, punks, Yuppies) developed, and what its influence is, or has been. (See Robert Coles, "The Old Ones of New Mexico," 162–66; Joan Didion, "Marrying Absurd," 514–17; Robert Christgau, "Beth Ann and Macrobioticism," 353–60; Alison Lurie, "Clothing as a Sign System," 723–32.)

(g) How individuals or societies invent and refine values, laws, codes of behavior. (See Norbert Wiener, "Moral Problems of a Scientist," 780–88; Lewis Thomas, "The Long Habit," 753–57; Philippe Aries, "The Reversal of Death," 324–31; Norman Cousins, "The Right to Die," 332–34.)

(h) How birds learn to fly, or animals learn to respond to signs, or some other process in the natural world. (See essays on language, 694–739.)

4. Write an essay identifying a particular moral, ethical, or other issue of responsibility or accountability in a scientific or social science field, such as disposal of toxic wastes, use and regulation of nuclear power plants, the ethical responsibilities of researchers to their human subjects. Explain the issue, interpret its significance and any controversy that may exist around it, and suggest a solution. (See essays by Gould, Wiener, Warner, and Sagan, 776–803.)

APPENDIX

"Reading" Photographs and Writing About Them

What Picasso says of painting applies equally well to the eleven news photographs at the beginning of *The Lexington Reader* by Pulitzer Prize–winning photographer Stan Grossfeld: "Painting isn't an aesthetic operation; it's a form of magic designed as a mediator between this strange hostile world and us, a way of seizing the power by giving form to our terrors as well as our desires." Indeed, expert photographs, like expert paintings, do "seize the power." They make visible our feelings, thoughts, experiences; they make permanent the fleeting, transient, temporary flux of life. Paintings capture forever what would otherwise be lost, forgotten, or misremembered; and they make it retrievable. We can look again and again and again at an evocative photograph.

And when we do, chances are that the fifth or the tenth or the hundredth time we scrutinize a by-now-familiar photograph, we'll discover things we hadn't seen earlier; new angles of meaning come from new angles of vision. Some angles of vision depend more on the visual aspects of the photograph than on its subject; in other instances, the emphasis is reversed.

The following questions are reasonable ones to ask when analyzing photographs. The first group primarily considers a photograph's visual aspects; the second group examines its subject matter.

Visual Aspects Dominant

1. Does the photograph contain a dominant figure that occupies a large part of the space, and perhaps the light? Or do the figures—objects, people, features of a landscape, others—share the space? equally, or otherwise?
2. What is in the foreground? in the background? How can you tell—by their relative size? position? lighting? What is the effect of this relationship?
3. Are the dominant lines and planes in this photograph horizontal? vertical? diagonal? What are the relationships among these lines and planes?

807

Do they appear balanced, harmonious? unbalanced? and consequently unstable or antagonistic?

4. Is the photograph in sharp or soft focus? How does this affect your perception of the subject as representational? impressionistic?
5. How is light used in this photograph? Are there sharp contrasts between light and dark areas? What is illuminated, and what is subdued or obscured—and with what effect? Or is the picture more evenly lighted?
6. If the photograph is in color, what colors are dominant? Does the color seem natural? artificial? expressive of a mood or emotion?
7. Where is the photographer in relation to the subject? Are you as the viewer supposed to share this angle of vision?

Subject Matter Dominant

1. What is the subject of the photograph? Is it active or static? What does it "mean"? How do you know?
2. If the photograph focuses on people, what are they doing? What is the relation of the main (probably larger or more brightly lit) figure to the others?
3. Can you "read" the expression (or lack of expression) on the face and in the "body language" (posture, gestures, closeness to or distance from other people) of the main subject? How does this relate to the expressions of others in the photograph? Which people, if any, have their backs to the camera? Why?
4. How do objects in the setting or background reinforce the actions and emotions of the people depicted?
5. If the photograph focuses on one or more objects or scenes, what are they? Why are they of interest to the photographer? to you? Has the photographer emphasized the familiar? the novel?
6. What is the mood of the photograph? serious? comic? active? passive? tense? relaxed?
7. In examining more than one work by the same photographer, can you discern his or her main interests, emphases, "style"?
8. Does pairing or grouping these photographs affect their impact? their meaning?

Suppose, for instance, that you were going to write about the first of Grossfeld's pictures:

In the foreground, a worker in a hardhat pounding on a girder; in the background, looming larger than the worker, a billboard with a giant cowboy on horseback chasing another horse and about to lasso it. The picture throbs with energy. The worker stands bent above the beam, instead of sitting on it. His upraised right arm, ready to bring the hammer down hard, mirrors the cowboy's upraised right arm, lasso twirling, ready to catch the free-running horse. The horse's mane and tail blow in the wind, from the chase. The light strikes the live figure from the same angle that illuminates the billboard figures; both men are wearing light hats, dark shirts and jeans. Because their faces are mostly in shadow, we can't see their features, and must concentrate instead on where the action is, on their bodies.

Yet there is a significant contrast. The billboard is tattered; the fact that we can see pieces of it peeling off reminds us that we're looking at a photograph of a photograph. The billboard scene—the free, romantic Wild West, the harmony of the cowboy forever astride a galloping horse—are, after all, an advertiser's construct, designed as a backdrop to sell a product. The real, workaday world is represented by the man in the foreground, whose back is to the billboard, and whose energies are devoted to the task at hand. *He* rides the girder, so high up that we cannot see the ground beneath; *he* takes the risk—no net, no visible scaffolding. In real life, he will ultimately finish his task, get down off the beam, and be off to new endeavors.

But to the extent that the photographer has frozen the moment, the worker, the cowboy, and the horses are captured in time. Like the figures in Keats's "Ode on a Grecian Urn," they will remain forever in motion but forever static, never aging but ultimately susceptible to the passage of "slow time" that will continue to wear away the billboard and eventually to erode the photograph itself.

One of Wallace Stevens's poems is concerned with "Thirteen Ways of Looking at a Blackbird." There are as many ways of looking at a billboard—or any other photograph—as there are viewers. The preceding analysis is only one among the many that are possible; it moves from a literal examination of physical details, to an interpretation of the context of both billboard and construction worker, to an abstract consideration of art and time. Look again at this picture. What do *you* see?

GLOSSARY

abstract   refers to qualities, ideas, or states of being that exist but that our senses cannot perceive. What we perceive are the concrete by-products of abstract ideas. No single object or action can be labeled *love,* but a warm embrace or a passionate kiss is a visible, concrete token of the abstraction we call "love." In many instances abstract words such as *beauty, hatred, stupidity,* or *kindness* are more clearly understood if illustrated with **concrete** examples (*see* **concrete** *and* **general/specific**).

allusion   is a writer's reference to a person, place, thing, literary character, or quotation that the reader is expected to recognize. Because the reader supplies the meaning and the original context, such references are economical; writers don't have to explain them. By alluding to a young man as a *Romeo, Don Juan,* or *Casanova,* a writer can present the subject's amorous nature without needing to say more. To make sure that references will be understood, writers have to choose what their readers can reasonably be expected to recognize.

analogy   is a comparison made between two things, qualities, or ideas that have certain similarities although the items themselves may be very different. For example, Barry Lopez makes an analogy between his horse Coke High and his Dodge van in the essay "My Horse" (584–90) that shows the similarities between animal and machine. Despite their obvious differences, Lopez stresses their likeness in function, response, and importance to him. The emphasis is on the objects' similarities; dissimilarities significant in number and kind would have weakened the analogy. Metaphors and similes are two figures of speech that are based on analogies, and such comparisons are often used in argumentation (*see* **figures of speech** *and* **argumentation**).

appeal to emotion   is one of several ways writers can move their readers to accept what they say. As a means of persuasion, the writer's appeal to emotion allows words and examples to affect readers in ways that advertisements sometimes affect consumers. Orwell's powerful essay "Marrakech" (341–46) engages the reader's emotions as he describes the deplorable life and death circumstances of the natives. As momentary eyewitnesses, we are moved by the descriptions and convinced of Orwell's truthfulness. When a writer presents himself as a person of integrity, intelligence, and good will, he appeals to the reader's sense of ethics, as Martin Luther King, Jr. does in "Letter from Birmingham Jail" (304–18). Although one approach touches the heart and the other the mind, these appeals are not mutually exclusive and, indeed, are often intertwined.

argument,   in a specialized literary sense, is a prose summary of the plot, main idea, or subject of a prose or poetic work.

argumentation   is one of the four modes of discourse, as commonly identified (*see* **description, exposition,** *and* **narration**). It seeks to convince the reader of the truth or falseness of an idea. Writers sometimes accomplish this by appealing to readers' emotions, as Orwell does in "Marrakech" (341–46) or by appealing to readers' ethics, as is the case in "None of This Is Fair" by Richard Rodriguez (*see* 361–65). Others, such as Philippe Aries in "The Reversal of Death" (324–31), can argue for or against a volatile issue by appealing to the readers' sense of reason, though often in an argument these appeals are interrelated. An argument can be *overt,* when its real point is explicitly stated, or *implied,* when its point is made more obliquely. Common techniques of implied argument include using illustrative case (*see* George Orwell, "Shooting an Elephant," 335–40), satire (*see* Jonathan Swift, "A Modest Proposal," 518–24), ridicule (*see* Russell Baker, "Universal Military Motion," 525–26) or an ironic tone (*see* Joan Didion, "Marrying Absurd," 514–17).

audience   consists of the readers of a given writing. Writers may write some pieces solely for themselves; others for their peers, teachers, or supervisors; others for people with special interest in and knowledge of the subject. Writers aware of some of the following dimensions can adapt the level of their language and the details of their presentation to different sorts of readers. What is the age range of the intended readers? The educational level? Their national, regional, or local background? Have they relevant biases, beliefs? How much do they know about the subject? Why should they be interested in it or in the writer's views? Gertrude Stein once observed, "I write for myself and strangers." By answering some of the questions above, the writer can perhaps convert strangers into friends.

burlesque   is overstatement characterized by ridiculous exaggeration that distorts the subject or the real point in order to call attention to it. Like a distinguished building altered by age and neglect, the original shape shows through the changes, in recognizable and ironic contrast to the original. Burlesque can elevate the trivial, diminish the significant, dignify the ridiculous, ridicule the dignified, or make the bad worse. In burlesque there is always a crucial and conspicuous disparity between subject and style. In S. J. Perelman's "The Machismo Mystique" (528–32) the narrator, in trying to exhibit machismo, exposes the concept of exaggerated masculinity to ridicule and trivialization: "Quicker than any hidalgo of Old Spain to erase an insult, I sprang up prepared to plunge my poinard into her bosom. . . . Unfortunately, I had left my poinard at home on the bureau and was wearing only a tie-tack that could never penetrate anyone so thick-skinned."

cause and effect   writing examines in detail the relationship between the *why* (cause) and *what* (effect) of an incident, phenomenon, or event. A writer could focus on the causes of a particular social, medical, or fictional occurrence (the Depression, psychotic depression in general, or Hamlet's depression in particular), or she might emphasize the effects of one or a combination of causes, such as the consequences of excessive indulgence in drugs, alcohol, or video games. In "A Room of One's Own: Shakespeare's Sister" (50–60) Virginia Woolf explains the cultural causes for the small number of women writers, and their unfortunate effects. As the poet William Butler Yeats observed, "How can we know the dancer from the dance?"

classification   groups items or concepts to emphasize their similarities, and then, through division, breaks down the larger category into its separate components or subgroups to show their distinguishing features. For example, in "Time Talks" (694–706) Edward T. Hall classifies time as formal, informal, and technical, and illustrates the characteristics of each category. The writer who classifies information first determines the overall features of the forest and then identifies the specific trees it contains.

cliché is a commonplace expression that reveals the writer's lack of imagination to use fresher, more vivid language. If a person finds himself *between a rock and a hard place,* he might decide to use a cliché, *come hell or high water,* in hopes that it will hit his reader *like a ton of bricks.* Such expressions, though, *fall on deaf ears* and roll off the reader *like water off a duck's back.* A cliché is *as dead as a mackerel;* its excessive familiarity dulls the reader's responses, as Frank Sullivan's "The Cliché Expert Testifies as a Literary Critic" (557–61) reveals.

coherence indicates an orderly relationship among the parts in a whole essay or other literary work. Writing is coherent when the interconnections among clauses, sentences, and paragraphs are clearly and logically related to the main subject under discussion. The writer may establish and maintain coherence through the use of transitional words or phrases (however; likewise), a consistent point of view, an ordered chronological or spatial presentation of information, appropriate pronoun references for nouns, or strategic repetition of important words or sentence structures.

colloquial expressions (*see* **diction**)

colloquialism (*see* **diction**)

comparison and contrast aims to show the reader similarities and differences that exist between two or more things or ideas. Items that are alike (all apples) are compared, while those that are dissimilar are contrasted (cherries, kumquats, passion fruit). *See* Raymond Williams's "Farming" (590–93).

conclusion refers to sentences, paragraphs, or longer sections of an essay that bring the work to a logical or psychologically satisfying end. Although a conclusion may (**a**) summarize or restate the essay's main point, and thereby refresh the reader's memory, it may also end with (**b**) the most important point, or (**c**) a memorable example, anecdote, or quotation, or (**d**) identify the broader implications or ultimate development of the subject. Stylistically, it's best to end with a bang, not a whimper; Lincoln's "Gettysburg Address" concludes with the impressive ". . . and that government of the people, by the people, and for the people, shall not perish from the earth." A vigorous conclusion grows organically from the material that precedes it and is not simply tacked on to get the essay over with.

concrete terms give readers something specific to see, hear, touch, smell, or feel, while abstract terms are more general and intangible. Writers employ concrete words to show their subject or characters in action, rather than merely to tell about them. Yet a concrete word does not have to be hard, like cement; anything directly perceived by the senses is considered concrete, including an ostrich plume, the sound of a harp, a smile, or a cone of cotton candy (*see* **abstract** *and* **general/specific**).

connotation and denotation refer to two levels of interpreting the meanings of words. Denotation is the literal, explicit "core" meaning—the "dictionary" definition. Connotation refers to additional meanings implied or suggested by the word, or associated with it, depending on the user's or reader's personal experience, attitudes, and cultural conditioning. For example, the word *athlete* denotes a skilled participant in a sport. But to a sports enthusiast, *athlete* is likely to connote not just the phenomenon of one's participation in sports, but positive physical and moral qualities, such as robust physical condition, well-coordinated movements, a wholesome character, a love of the outdoors, and a concern with fair play. Those disenchanted with sports might regard an *athlete* as a marketable commodity for unscrupulous businessmen, an overpaid exploiter of the public, or someone who has developed every part of his anatomy but his brain—a "dumb jock." Note Red Smith's ironic use of "scholar-athletes" in "Good Ol' Boy Woody Hayes" (484–86).

contrast (*see* **comparison/contrast**)

deduction (*see* **induction/deduction**)

deductive (*see* **induction/deduction**)

definition explains the meaning of a word, identifying the essential properties of a thing or idea. Dictionaries furnish the various literal interpretations of individual words (*see* **connotation/denotation**), but a writer may provide extended or altered definitions, sometimes of essay length, to expand or supplement "core" meanings. "My Dog, Phydeaux" might be an extended personal definition of *dog*. Whether short or long, definitions may employ other strategies of exposition, such as classification ("Phydeaux, a collie"), comparison and contrast ("is better natured than Milo, my brother's bassett . . ."), description ("and has an unusual star-shaped marking on his forehead"). *See* Henry Beston's "The Headlong Wave" (202–204) and Bertrand Russell's "What Is Matter?" (740–44).

denotation (*see* **connotation/denotation**)

description is a mode of discourse (*see* **argumentation, exposition,** *and* **narration**) aimed at bringing something to life by telling how it looks, sounds, tastes, smells, feels, or acts. The writer tries to convey a sense impression, depict a mood, or both. Thus, the writer who conveys the heat of an August sidewalk; the sound, sight, and smell of the Atlantic breaking on the jagged coastline of Maine; or the bittersweetness of an abandoned love affair, enables readers to experience the situations. Description is a writer's spice; a little goes a long way. Except in extensively descriptive travel pieces, description is primarily used to enhance the other modes of discourse and is seldom an end in itself (*see* Mark Twain's "Uncle John's Farm," 237–42).

diction is word choice. Hemingway was talking about diction when he explained that the reason he allegedly rewrote the last page of *A Farewell to Arms* thirty-nine times was because of problems in "getting the words right." Getting the words right means choosing, arranging, and using words appropriate to the purpose, audience, and sometimes the form of a particular piece of writing. Puns are fine in limericks and shaggy-dog stories ("I wouldn't send a knight out on a dog like this"), but they're out of place in technical reports and obituaries. Diction ranges on a continuum from highly formal (a *repast*) to informal writing and conversation (a *meal*) to slang (*eats*):

formal English words and grammatical constructions used by educated native speakers of English in sermons, oratory, and in many serious books, scientific reports, and lectures.

informal (conversational or colloquial) *English* ranges from the more relaxed but still standard usage in polite (but not stuffy) conversation or writing, as in much newspaper writing and in many of the essays in this book. In informal writing it's all right to use contractions ("I'll go to the wedding, but I won't wear tails") and some abbreviations, but not all (As Angela attached the IV bottle to the holder, she wondered whether the patient had OD'd on carbohydrates).

O.K. is generally acceptable in conversation, but it's not O.K. in most formal or informal writing.

slang highly informal (often figurative) word choice in speech or writing. It may be used by specialized groups (*pot, grass, uppers*) or more general speakers to add vividness and humor (often derogatory) to their language ("Bluto, zoned out on brews, found booking for a rocks for jocks final really awesome."). Although some slang is old and sometimes even becomes respectable (cab), it often erupts quickly into the language and just as quickly disappears (*twenty-three skidoo*); it's better to avoid all slang than to use outmoded slang.

regionalisms expressions used by people of a certain region of the country, often derived from the native languages of earlier settlers, such as *arroyo* for *deep ditch* used in the Southwest.

dialect the spoken (and sometimes written) language of a group of people that reflects their social, educational, economic, and geographic status ("My mama done tole me . . ."). Dialect may include regionalisms. In parts of the Northeast, *youse* is a dialect form of *you*, while its counterpart in the South is *y'all*. Even some educated Southerners say *ain't*, but they don't usually write it, except to be humorous.

technical terms (jargon) words used by those in a particular trade, occupation, business, or specialized activity. For example, medical personnel use *stat* (immediately) and *NPO* (nothing by mouth); surfers' vocabularies include *shooting the curl, hot-dogging,* and *hang ten; hardware* has different meanings for carpenters and users of computers.

division (*see* **classification**)
effect (*see* **cause/effect**)
emphasis makes the most important ideas, characters, themes, or other elements stand out. The principal ways of achieving emphasis are through the use of:

proportion saying more about the major issues and less about the minor ones.
position placing important material in the key spots, the beginning or ends of paragraphs or larger units. Arrangement in climactic order, with the main point of an argument or the funniest joke last, can be particularly effective.
repetition of essential words, phrases, and ideas (Jacques adored expensive women and fast cars—or was it fast women and expensive cars?).
focus pruning of verbal underbrush and unnecessary detail to accentuate the main features.
mechanical devices such as capitalization, underlining (italics), and exclamation points, conveying enthusiasm, excitement, and emphasis, as advertisers and new journalists well know. Tom Wolfe's title, *Las Vegas (What ?) Las Vegas (Can't Hear You! Too Noisy) Las Vegas!!!!,* illustrates this practice, as well as the fact that nothing exceeds like excess.

essay refers to a nonfiction composition on a central theme or subject, usually brief and written in prose. As the contents of this book reveal, essays come in varied modes—among them descriptive, narrative, analytic, argumentative—and moods, ranging from humorous to grim, whimsical to bitterly satiric. Essays are sometimes categorized as *formal* or *informal,* depending on the author's content, style, and organization. Formal essays, written in formal language, tend to focus on a single significant idea supported with evidence carefully chosen and arranged, such as the Carl Sagan essay "The Nuclear Winter" (797–803). Informal essays sometimes have a less obvious structure than formal essays; the subject may seem less significant, even ordinary; the manner of presentation casual, personal, or humorous. Yet these distinctions blur. Although E. B. White's "Once More to the Lake" (232–37) discusses a personal experience in conversation and humorous language, its apparently trivial subject, the vacation of a boy and his father in the Maine woods, takes on universal, existential significance.

etymology   is information about the origin and history of words. Most dictionaries provide the etymologies of words in brackets or parentheses located before or after the definitions. In addition to furnishing clues about the current meanings of words, etymologies can show how the definitions have changed over time. Some words flaunt their origin: *denim* from its place of manufacture (Serge de Nîmes), *guy* from Guy Fawkes, who tried to blow up the British Parliament. Some have become more general (*Kleenex* for any facial tissue), and others more specific (*corn* used to mean any grain). Some have taken a turn for the better and others for the worse: *housewife* and *hussy,* no longer sisters under the skin, have the same etymology. Consequently, etymologies give hints to the wondrous workings—logical, psychological, quirky—of the human mind.

evidence   is supporting information that explains or proves a point. General comments or personal opinions that are not substantiated with evidence leave the reader wanting some proof of accuracy. Writers establish credibility by backing general statements with examples, facts, and figures that make evident their knowledge of the subject. We believe what Joan Didion says about Las Vegas weddings in "Marrying Absurd" (514–17) because her specific examples show that she's been there and has understood the context.

example   (*see* **illustration**)

exposition   is a mode of discourse that, as its name indicates, exposes information, through explaining, defining, or interpreting its subject. Expository prose is to the realm of writing what the Ford automobile has been historically to the auto industry—useful, versatile, accessible to the average person, and heavy duty, for it is the mode of most research reports, critical analyses, examination answers, case histories, reviews, and term papers. In exposition, writers employ a variety of techniques, such as definition, illustration, classification, comparison and contrast, analogy, and cause-and-effect reasoning. Exposition is not an exclusive mode; it is often blended with the other three (*see* **argumentation, description,** *and* **narration**) to provide a more complete or convincing discussion of a subject.

fable   is a brief tale, leading up to or epitomized by a moral statement at the end. The characters are often animals, as in Joel Chandler Harris's *Uncle Remus* stories, but they may be inanimate objects or people, as in James Thurber's "The Unicorn in the Garden" (561–62), the moral of which is a parody on the moral of a conventional fable: "Don't count your boobies until they are hatched."

figures of speech   are used by writers who want to make their subject unique or memorable through vivid language. Literal language often lacks the connotations of figurative language. Instead of merely conveying information (The car was messy), a writer might use a figure of speech to attract attention (The car was a dumpster on wheels). Figures of speech enable the writer to play with words and with the reader's imagination. Some of the most frequently used figures of speech include the following:

metaphor   an implied comparison that equates two things or qualities without an explicit connecting word. "Manhattan . . . the greatest of all the zoos, whose inhabitants prowl up and down . . ." (Jan Morris, "Manhattan," 222–30).

simile   a direct comparison, usually with the connecting word *like* or *as*. "On a gray lowering day [Manhattan] is like some darkling forest. The tops of the buildings are lost in fog, and only their massive bases, like the trunks of so many gigantic oaks, are to be seen beneath the cloud base" (Morris, "Manhattan," 224).

personification   the giving of human qualities to inanimate or nonhuman objects. "I prefer Manhattan . . . reticent and heavy-eyed" (Morris, "Manhattan," 224).

hyperbole   an elaborate exaggeration, often intended to be humorous or ironic. "When I was younger I could remember anything, whether it had happened or not; but my faculties are decaying now, and soon I shall be so I cannot remember any but the things that never happened" (Mark Twain, "Uncle John's Farm," 237–42).

understatement   a deliberate downplaying of the seriousness of something. As with the *hyperbole,* the antithesis of understatement, this is often done for the sake of humor or irony. My mother "was not a suspicious person, but full of trust and confidence; and when I said, 'There's something in my coat pocket for you,' she would put her hand in [and feel a live bat]. But she always took it out again, herself; I didn't have to tell her. It was remarkable, the way she couldn't learn to like private bats" (Mark Twain, "Uncle John's Farm," 237–42).

paradox   a contradiction that upon closer inspection is actually truthful. (You never know what you've got until you lose it.)

rhetorical question   a question that demands no answer, asked for dramatic impact. "What are we going to do if it turns out that we have pheromones? What on earth would we be doing with such things? With the richness of speech, and all our new devices for communication, why would we want to release odors into the air to convey information about anything?" (Lewis Thomas, "A Fear of Pheromones," 757–60).

metonomy   the representation of an object, public office, or concept by something associated with it. Watergate brought down the White House, as Woodward and Bernstein explain in *All The President's Men.*

dead metaphor   a word or phrase, originally a figure of speech, that through constant use is treated literally (the *arm* of a chair, the *leg* of a table, the *head* of a bed).

focus   represents the writer's control and limitation of a subject to a specific aspect or set of features, determined in part by the subject under discussion (*what* the writer is writing about), the audience (to *whom* the writer is writing), and the purpose (*why* the writer is writing). Thus, instead of writing about food in general, someone writing for college students on limited budgets might focus on imaginative but economical meals.

general and specific   are the ends of a continuum that designates the relative degree of abstractness or concreteness of a word. General terms identify the class (*house*); specific terms restrict the class by naming its members (a *Georgian mansion,* a *Dutch colonial,* a *brick ranch*). To clarify relationships, words may be arranged in a series from general to specific: writers, twentieth-century authors, Southern novelists, William Faulkner (*see* **abstract** *and* **concrete**).

generalization   (*see* **induction/deduction** *and* **logical fallacies**)

hyperbole   (*see* **figures of speech**)

illustration   refers to providing an example, sometimes of essay length, that clarifies a broad statement or concept for the reader. This technique takes the reader from a general to a specific level of interpretation (*see* **general/specific**).

induction and deduction   refer to two different methods of arriving at a conclusion. Inductive reasoning relies on examining specific instances, examples, or facts in an effort to arrive at a general conclusion. If you were to sample several cakes—chocolate, walnut, mocha, and pineapple upside-down—you might reach the general conclusion that all cakes are sweet. Conversely, deductive reasoning involves examining general principles in order to arrive at a specific conclusion. If you believe that all cakes are sweet, you would expect the next cake you encounter, say, lemon chiffon, to be sweet. Yet both of these types of reasoning can lead to erroneous generalizations if the reasoner or writer has not examined all of the relevant aspects of the issue. For instance, not all cakes are sweet—consider the biscuit cake in strawberry shortcake. Likewise, even if a writer cited five separate instances in which members of a particular ethnic group displayed criminal behavior, it would be incorrect to conclude that all members of this group are criminal. Beware, therefore, of using absolute words such as *always, never, everyone, no one, only,* and *none.*

inductive   (*see* **induction/deduction**)

introduction   is the beginning of a written work that is likely to present the author's subject, focus (perhaps including the thesis), attitude toward it, and possibly the plan for organizing supporting materials. The length of the introduction is usually proportionate to the length of what follows; short essays may be introduced by a sentence or two; a book may require an entire introductory chapter. In any case, an introduction should be sufficiently forceful and interesting to let readers know what is to be discussed and entice them to continue reading. An effective introduction might do one or more of the following:

1. state the thesis or topic emphatically;
2. present a controversial or startling focus on the topic;
3. offer a witty or dramatic quotation, statement, metaphor, or analogy;
4. provide background information to help readers understand the subject, its history, or significance;
5. give a compelling anecdote or illustration from real life;
6. refer to an authority on the subject.

irony   is a technique that enables the writer to say one thing while meaning another, often with critical intention. Three types of irony are frequently used by writers: *verbal, dramatic,* and *situational.* Verbal irony is expressed with tongue in cheek, often implying the opposite of what is overtly stated. Thus, when said in the right tone, "That's baaad" means "That's extra good." The verbal ironist maintains tight control over tone, counting on the alert reader (or listener) to recognize the discrepancy between words and meaning, as did Jonathan Swift in "A Modest Proposal" (518–24), where deadpan advocacy of cannibalism is really a monstrous proposal. Dramatic irony, found in plays, novels, and other forms of fiction, allows readers to see the wisdom or folly of characters' actions in light of information they have—the ace up their sleeve—that the characters lack. For example, readers know Desdemona is innocent of cheating on her husband, Othello, but his ignorance of the truth leads him to murder her in a jealous rage. Situational irony, life's joke on life, entails opposition between what would ordinarily occur and what actually happens in a particular instance. In O. Henry's "The Gift of the Magi," the husband sells his watch to buy his wife combs for her hair, only to find out she has sold her hair to buy him a watch chain.

jargon (*see* **diction**)

logical fallacies are errors in reasoning and often occur in arguments:

> *ad hominem* attacking a person's ideas or opinions by discrediting him as a person (Napoleon was too short to be a distinguished general).
>
> *arguing from analogy* comparing only similarities between things, concepts, or situations while overlooking significant differences that might weaken the argument (Having a standing army is just like having a loaded gun in the house. If it's around, people will want to use it).
>
> *begging the question* assuming that what is to be proven is already true without further proof, often through circular reasoning ("Rapists and murderers awaiting trial shouldn't be let out on bail" assumes that the suspects have already been proven guilty, which is the point of the impending trial).
>
> *either/or reasoning* restricting the complex aspects of a difficult problem to only one of two solutions (Marry me or you'll end up single forever).
>
> *non sequitur* making a conclusion that doesn't logically come from a cited instance (The Senator must be in cahoots with that shyster developer, Landphill. After all, they were fraternity brothers).
>
> *hasty generalization* erroneously applying information or knowledge of one or a limited number of representative instances to an entire, much larger category (Poor people on welfare cheat. Why, just yesterday I saw a Cadillac parked in front of the tenement at 9th and Main).
>
> *oversimplification* providing simplistic answers to complex problems (Ban handguns and stop organized crime).
>
> *post hoc ergo propter hoc* erroneously citing a cause as an effect and vice versa (It always rains after I wash the car. Since I want to go to the beach, I won't wash it).

metaphor (*see* **figures of speech**)

metonomy (*see* **figures of speech**)

modes of discourse are traditionally identified as narration, description, argumentation, and exposition. In writing they are often intermingled. The *narration* of Orwell's "Marrakech" (341–46), for instance, involves *description of characters* and settings, an explanation (*exposition*) of their motives, while the expression of its theme serves as an *argument,* direct and indirect. "Marrakech" argues, through its characters, actions, and situations, that for a white society to treat blacks as invisible is to violate their humanity.

narration is one of four modes of discourse (*see* **argumentation, description,** *and* **exposition**) that recounts an event or series of interrelated events. Jokes, fables, fairy tales, short stories, plays, novels, and other forms of literature are narrative if they tell a story. Although some narrations provide only the basic *who, what, when, where,* and *why* of an occurrence in an essentially chronological arrangement, as in a newspaper account of a murder, others contain such features as plot, conflict, suspense, characterization, and description to intensify readers' interest. Whether as pared down as a nursery rhyme ("Lizzie Borden took an axe/Gave her father forty whacks . . ."), of intermediate length such as Lillian Ross's "The Yellow Bus" (500–14), or as full-blown as Melville's *Moby Dick,* the relaying of what happened to someone or something is a form of narration.

nonfiction is writing based on fact but shaped by the writer's interpretations, point of view, style, and other literary techniques. Nonfiction writings in essay or book form include interviews, portraits, biographies and autobiographies, travel writings, direct arguments, implied arguments in the form of narratives or satires, investigative reporting, reviews, literary criticism, sports articles, historical accounts, how-to instructions, and scientific and technical reports, among other types. These vary greatly in purpose (to inform, argue, entertain . . .), form, length (from a paragraph to multiple volumes), intended audience (from general readers to specialists), and mood (somber to joyous, straightforward to parody). *The Lexington Reader* contains examples of most of these types of writing.

non sequitur a conclusion that does not follow logically from the premises. In humorous writing, the *non sequitur* conclusion is illogical, unexpected, and perhaps ridiculous; the resulting surprise startles readers into laughter. In Woody Allen's "Selections from the Allen Notebooks" (60–63), many of the parodistic notebook entries consist of false leads and surprising conclusions, such as: "Thought: Why does man kill? He kills for food. And not only food: frequently there must be a beverage."

objective refers to the writer's presentation of material in a personally detached, unemotional way that emphasizes the topic, rather than the author's attitudes or feelings about it. Some process analyses, such as Sylvia Porter's "Rules for Writing and Endorsing Checks" (638–41), are written objectively. Many other process writings, including most of the how-to instructions in *The Lexington Reader,* combine objective information with the author's personal (and somewhat subjective views) on how to do it.

oxymoron a contradiction in terms, as Red Smith implies in his ironic use of "scholar-athletes" (484–86).

paradox (*see* **figures of speech**)

paragraph has a number of functions. Newspaper paragraphs, which are usually short and consist of a sentence or two, serve as punctuation—visual units to break up columns for ease of reading. A paragraph in most other prose is usually a single unified group of sentences that explain or illustrate a central idea, whether expressed overtly in a topic sentence, or merely implied. Paragraphs emphasize ideas; each new topic (or sometimes each important subtopic) demands a new paragraph. Short (sometimes even one-sentence) paragraphs can provide transitions from one major area of discussion to another, or indicate a change of speakers in dialogue.

parallelism   is the arrangement of two or more equally important ideas in similar grammatical form ("I came, I saw, I conquered"). Not only is it an effective method of presenting more than one thought at a time, it also makes reading more understandable and memorable for the reader because of the almost rhythmic quality it produces. Within a sentence parallel structure can exist between nouns that are paired (All work and no play made Jack a candidate for cardiac arrest), items in a series (His world revolved around debits, credits, cash flows, and profits), phrases (Reading books, preparing reports, and dictating interoffice memos—these were a few of his favorite things), and clauses (Most people work only to live; Jack lived only to work). Parallelism can also be established between sentences in a paragraph and between paragraphs in a longer composition, often through the repetition of key words and phrases, as Martin Luther King, Jr. did in his famous speech in which eight paragraphs in a row begin, "I have a dream . . ."

parallel structure   (*see* **parallelism**)

paraphrase   is putting someone else's ideas into your own words. Not to be confused with a summary, which condenses the original material, a paraphrase is a restatement that may be as long as the original or longer. For example, someone reading the following from Pope's *Essay on Criticism,* "True ease in writing comes from art, not chance, /As those move easiest who have learned to dance," might summarize the author's idea by saying: *Practice makes perfect.* A paraphrase of the same passage would demand further elaboration: *Writing is a skill acquired through training and practice, and luck has no part in successful composition.* Students writing research papers frequently find that paraphrasing information from their sources eliminates successive, lengthy quotations, and may clarify the originals. Be sure to acknowledge the source of either quoted or paraphrased material to avoid plagiarism (*see* **summary**).

parody   exaggerates the subject matter, philosophy, characters, language, style, or other features of a given author or particular work. Such imitation calls attention to both versions; such scrutiny may show the original to be a masterpiece—or to be in need of improvement. Parody derives much of its humor from the double vision of the subject that writer and readers share; Woody Allen's "The Whore of Mensa" (552–56) gains in comic effect when readers recognize that Allen is burlesquing the conventions of stereotypical hardboiled detective fiction.

person   is a grammatical distinction made between the speaker (first person—I, we), the one spoken to (second person—you), and the one spoken about (third person—he, she, it, they). In an essay or fictional work the point of view is often identified by person. Joan Didion's "Why I Write" (29–34) is written in the first person, while Paul Fussell's "The Boy Scout Handbook" (451–55) is a third-person work (*see* **point of view**).

persona,   literally a "mask," is a fictitious mouthpiece devised by a writer for the purpose of telling a story or making comments that may or may not reflect the author's feelings and attitudes. The persona may be a narrator, as in Swift's "A Modest Proposal" (518–24), whose ostensibly humanitarian perspective advocates cannibalism and regards the poor as objects to be exploited. Swift as author emphatically rejects these views. In such cases the persona functions as a disguise for the highly critical author.

personification (*see* **figures of speech**)

persuasion, like argumentation, seeks to convince the reader or listener of an idea's truth or falseness. A persuasive argument can not only convince, but also arouse, or even move a reader to action, as in Martin Luther King, Jr.'s "Letter from Birmingham Jail," 304–18 (*see* **argumentation** *and* **appeal to emotion**).

plot is the cause-and-effect relationship between events that tell a story. Unlike narration, which is an ordering of events as they occur, a plot is a writer's plan for showing how the occurrence of these events actually brings about a certain effect. The plot lets the reader see how actions and events are integral parts of something much larger than themselves.

point of view refers to the position—physical, mental, numerical—a writer takes when presenting information (*point*), and his attitude toward the subject (*view*). A writer sometimes adopts a point of view described as "limited," which restricts the inclusion of thoughts other than the narrator's, as Ken Wunderlich does in "Playing the Sax" (565–68). Conversely, the "omniscient" point of view allows the writer to know, see, and tell everything, not only about himself, but about others as well, as Robert Christgau does in "Beth Ann and Macrobioticism," 353–60 (*see* **person**).

prewriting is a writer's term for thinking about and planning what to say before the pen hits the legal pad. Reading, observing, reminiscing, and fantasizing can all be prewriting activities if they lead to writing something down. The most flexible stage in the writing process, prewriting enables writers to mentally formulate, compose, edit, and discard before they begin the physical act of putting words on paper. Joan Didion discusses this in "Why I Write" (29–34).

process analysis is an expository explanation of how to do something or how something is done. Sometimes the writer provides directions that the reader can follow to achieve the desired results, as in John Trimble's "Write to Be Read" (67–71). Other discussions of a process explain how something was made or how it works; thus Thomas S. Kuhn helps us understand "The Route to Normal Science" (669–77). As the three discussions on how to make "Brownies and Bar Cookies" (656–59) indicate, there is often more than one good way to perform any process, and the directions reflect the writers' preferences, philosophy, and experience.

purpose identifies the author's reasons for writing. The purposes of a writing are many and varied. One can write to *clarify an issue for oneself,* or to *obtain self-understanding* ("Why I Like to Eat"). One can write to *tell a story, to narrate* ("My 1000-Pound Weight Loss"), or to *analyze a process* ("How to Make Quadruple Chocolate Cake"). Writing can explain *cause and effect* ("Obesity and Heart Attacks: The Fatal Connection"); it can *describe* ("The Perfect Meal"), *define* ("Calories"), *divide and classify* ("Fast Food, Slow Food, and Food that Just Sits There"). Writing can *illustrate* through examples ("McDonald's as a Symbol of American Culture"), and it can *compare and contrast* people, things, or ideas. Writing can *argue, deductively or inductively* ("Processed Foods Are Packaged Problems"), sometimes appealing more to emotions than to reason ("Anorexia! Beware!"). Writing can also provide *entertainment,* sometimes through parody or satire (*Real Men Don't Eat Quiche*).

revise to revise is to make changes in focus, accommodation of audience, structure or organization, emphasis, development, style, mechanics, and spelling in order to bring the written work closer to one's ideal. For many writers, revising is the essence of writing. Donald Murray discusses the revising process in "The Maker's Eye" (89–93); Chapter 1 also includes original drafts and revisions of writing by Richard Wright and student Teresa Whitlock.

rhetoric, the art of using language effectively to serve the writer's purpose, originally referred to speech-making. Rhetoric now encompasses composition; the information in this book is divided into rhetorical modes, such as exposition, narration, description, and argumentation.

rhetorical question (*see* **figures of speech**)

satire is humorous, witty criticism of people's foolish, thoughtless, or evil behavior. The satirist ridicules some aspect of human nature—or life in general—that should be changed. Depending on the subject and the severity of the author's attack, a satire can be mildly abrasive, as in Craig Swanson's "It's the Only Video Game My Mom Lets Me Chew" (527–28), or viciously scathing, as is Swift in "A Modest Proposal" (518–24). Usually (although not always), the satirist seeks to bring about reform through criticism.

sentence, grammatically defined, is an independent clause containing a subject and verb, and may also include modifiers and related words. *Sentence structure* is another name for *syntax,* the arrangement of individual words in a sentence that shows their relationship to each other. Besides word choice (*diction*), writers pay special attention to the way their chosen words are arranged to form clauses, phrases, entire sentences. A *thesis sentence* (or *statement*) is the main idea in a written work that reflects the author's purpose. Some writings, notably parodies and satires, only imply a thesis; direct arguments frequently provide an explicitly stated thesis, usually near the beginning, and organize subsequent paragraphs around this central thought. A *topic sentence* clearly reflects the major idea and unifying thought of a given paragraph. When it is placed near the beginning of a paragraph, a topic sentence provides the basis for other sentences in the paragraph. When the topic sentence comes at the end of a paragraph or essay, it may function as the conclusion of a logical argument, or the climax of an escalating emotional progression.

simile (*see* **figures of speech**)

slang (*see* **diction**)

specific (*see* **general/specific**)

style, the manner in which a writer says what he wants to say, is the result of the author's *diction* (word choice) and *syntax* (sentence structure), *arrangement of ideas, emphasis,* and *focus.* It is also a reflection of the author's *voice* (personality). Although both Twain's "Uncle John's Farm" (237–42) and McPhee's "The Pine Barrens" (205–10) affectionately describe particular rural locations, the writers' styles differ considerably.

subjective refers to writing that expresses the author's beliefs in and attitudes toward a particular subject. Although Charles Darwin makes a case for "Reasoning in Animals" (745–48) based on his personal interpretation of zoological evidence, he is less subjective and emotional than Barry Lopez, who reveals the deep attachment he has for an old Dodge van in "My Horse" (584–90). Darwin is not at all sarcastic, in contrast to Jessica Mitford's subjectively scathing "Let Us Now Appraise Famous Writers" (377–88).

summary is a condensation of main ideas from a given work that is usually much shorter than the original. Unlike a *paraphrase,* a summary seeks to reveal only the major points an author has made in a piece of writing (*see* **paraphrase**).

symbol   refers to a person, place, thing, idea, or action that represents something other than itself. In "Signs and Symbols" (717–22), Susanne Langer distinguishes between a sign, whose meaning is related to "the situation to which it refers" (such as "signs of the weather, signs of danger") and a symbol, whose meaning is arbitrary. Humans and animals alike can respond to signs, but only humans can create and interpret symbols, which are dependent on language—such as the knowledge of what "house," or "red," or "walking" means. In "A Room of One's Own: Shakespeare's Sister" (50–60), Woolf's created character—Shakespeare's imaginary sister—symbolizes all women whose potential for creativity has been stifled by cultural expectations that would keep women essentially barefoot, pregnant, and uneducated.

syntax   (*see* **sentence**)

thesis sentence   (*see* **sentence**)

tone,   the author's attitude toward a subject being discussed, can be serious (*see* William Warner, "The Islands [of Chesapeake Bay]: Looking Ahead," 788–97), critical (*see* John Simon, "Hamlet," 435–37), laudatory (*see* James Agee, "Comedy's Greatest Era," 404–19), nostalgic (*see* E. B. White, "Once More to the Lake," 232–37), loving (*see* Mary Ruffin, "Mama's Smoke," 145–47), among many possibilities. Tone lets readers know how they are expected to react to what the writer is saying.

topic sentence   (*see* **sentence**)

transition   is the writer's ability to move the reader smoothly along the course of ideas. Abrupt changes in topics confuse the reader, but transitional words and phrases help tie ideas together. Stylistically, transition serves another purpose by adding fullness and body to otherwise short, choppy sentences and paragraphs. Writers use transition to show how ideas, things, and events are arranged chronologically (*first, next, after, finally*), spatially (*here, there, next to, behind*), comparatively (*like, just as, similar to*), causally (*thus, because, therefore*), and in opposition to each other (*unlike, but, contrary to*). Pronouns, connectives, repetition, and parallel sentence structure are other transitional vehicles that move the reader along.

understatement   (*see* **figures of speech**)

voice   refers to the extent to which the writer's personality is expressed in his or her work. In *personal voice,* the writer is on fairly intimate terms with the audience, referring to herself as "I" and the readers as "you." In *impersonal voice* the writer may refer to himself as "one" or "we," or try to eliminate personal pronouns when possible. Formal writings, such as speeches, research papers, and sermons, are more likely to use an impersonal voice than are more informal writings, such as personal essays. In grammar, *voice* refers to the *active* ("I *mastered* the word processor") or *passive* ("The word processor *was mastered* by me") form of a verb.

INDEX OF
AUTHORS

Index of Authors

Index of Authors

1 2 3 4 5 6 7 8 9 0

828